Literature Criticism from 1400 to 1800

Guide to Gale Literary Criticism Series

For criticism on	Consult these Gale series
Authors now living or who died after December 31, 1999	*CONTEMPORARY LITERARY CRITICISM (CLC)*
Authors who died between 1900 and 1999	*TWENTIETH-CENTURY LITERARY CRITICISM (TCLC)*
Authors who died between 1800 and 1899	*NINETEENTH-CENTURY LITERATURE CRITICISM (NCLC)*
Authors who died between 1400 and 1799	*LITERATURE CRITICISM FROM 1400 TO 1800 (LC)* *SHAKESPEAREAN CRITICISM (SC)*
Authors who died before 1400	*CLASSICAL AND MEDIEVAL LITERATURE CRITICISM (CMLC)*
Authors of books for children and young adults	*CHILDREN'S LITERATURE REVIEW (CLR)*
Dramatists	*DRAMA CRITICISM (DC)*
Poets	*POETRY CRITICISM (PC)*
Short story writers	*SHORT STORY CRITICISM (SSC)*
Black writers of the past two hundred years	*BLACK LITERATURE CRITICISM (BLC)* *BLACK LITERATURE CRITICISM SUPPLEMENT (BLCS)*
Hispanic writers of the late nineteenth and twentieth centuries	*HISPANIC LITERATURE CRITICISM (HLC)* *HISPANIC LITERATURE CRITICISM SUPPLEMENT (HLCS)*
Native North American writers and orators of the eighteenth, nineteenth, and twentieth centuries	*NATIVE NORTH AMERICAN LITERATURE (NNAL)*
Major authors from the Renaissance to the present	*WORLD LITERATURE CRITICISM, 1500 TO THE PRESENT (WLC)* *WORLD LITERATURE CRITICISM SUPPLEMENT (WLCS)*

ISSN 0740-2880

Volume 75

Literature Criticism from 1400 to 1800

Critical Discussion of the Works
of Fifteenth-, Sixteenth-, Seventeenth-, and
Eighteenth-Century Novelists, Poets, Playwrights,
Philosophers, and Other Creative Writers

Lynn M. Zott
Project Editor

GALE®

THOMSON

GALE

Detroit • New York • San Diego • San Francisco • Cleveland • New Haven, Conn. • Waterville, Maine • London • Munich

THOMSON
GALE

Literature Criticism from 1400 to 1800, Vol. 75

Project Editor
Lynn M. Zott

Editorial
Jenny Cromie, Kathy D. Darrow, Elisabeth Gellert, Madeline S. Harris, Edna M. Hedblad, Jelena O. Krstović, Marie Lazzari, Michelle Lee, Jessica Menzo, Thomas J. Schoenberg, Lawrence J. Trudeau, Russel Whitaker

Research
Nicodemus Ford, Sarah Genik, Tamara C. Nott, Tracie A. Richardson

Permissions
Debra Freitas

Imaging and Multimedia
Dean Dauphinais, Robert Duncan, Leitha

Etheridge-Sims, Mary K. Grimes, Lezlie Light, Michael Logusz, Dan Newell, David G. Oblender, Christine O'Bryan, Kelly A. Quin, Luke Rademacher

Composition and Electronic Capture
Gary Leach

Manufacturing
Stacy L. Melson

LIBRARY OF CONGRESS CATALOG CARD NUMBER 94-29718

ISBN 0-7876-5812-X
ISSN 0740-2880

Printed in the United States of America
10 9 8 7 6 5 4 3 2 1

Contents

Preface

*L*iterature Criticism from 1400 to 1800 (*LC*) presents critical discussion of world literature from the fifteenth through the eighteenth centuries. The literature of this period is especially vital: the years 1400 to 1800 saw the rise of modern European drama, the birth of the novel and personal essay forms, the emergence of newspapers and periodicals, and major achievements in poetry and philosophy. *LC* provides valuable insight into the art, life, thought, and cultural transformations that took place during these centuries.

Scope of the Series

LC provides an introduction to the great poets, dramatists, novelists, essayists, and philosophers of the fifteenth through eighteenth centuries, and to the most significant interpretations of these authors' works. Because criticism of this literature spans nearly six hundred years, an overwhelming amount of scholarship confronts the student. *LC* organizes this material concisely and logically. Every attempt is made to reprint the most noteworthy, relevant, and educationally valuable essays available.

A separate Gale reference series, *Shakespearean Criticism,* is devoted exclusively to Shakespearean studies. Although properly belonging to the period covered in *LC,* William Shakespeare has inspired such a tremendous and ever-growing body of secondary material that a separate series was deemed essential.

Each entry in *LC* presents a representative selection of critical response to an author, a literary topic, or to a single important work of literature. Early commentary is offered to indicate initial responses, later selections document changes in literary reputations, and retrospective analyses provide the reader with modern views. The size of each author entry is a relative reflection of the scope of the criticism available in English. Every attempt has been made to identify and include the seminal essays on each author's work and to include recent commentary providing modern perspectives.

Volumes 1 through 12 of the series feature author entries arranged alphabetically by author. Volumes 13-47 of the series feature a thematic arrangement. Each volume includes an entry devoted to the general study of a specific literary or philosophical movement, writings surrounding important political and historical events, the philosophy and art associated with eras of cultural transformation, or the literature of specific social or ethnic groups. Each of these volumes also includes several author entries devoted to major representatives of the featured period, genre, or national literature. With volume 48, the series returns to a standard author approach, with some entries devoted to a single important work of world literature and others devoted to literary topics.

Organization of the Book

An *LC* entry consists of the following elements:

- The **Author Heading** cites the name under which the author most commonly wrote, followed by birth and death dates. Also located here are any name variations under which an author wrote, including transliterated forms for authors whose native languages use nonroman alphabets. If the author wrote consistently under a pseudonym, the pseudonym will be listed in the author heading and the author's actual name given in parenthesis on the first line of the biographical and critical information. Uncertain birth or death dates are indicated by question marks. Topic entries are preceded by a **Thematic Heading,** which simply states the subject of the entry. Single-work entries are preceded by the title of the work and its date of publication.

- The **Introduction** contains background information that introduces the reader to the author, work, or topic that is the subject of the entry.

- A **Portrait of the Author** is included when available.

- The list of **Principal Works** is ordered chronologically by date of first publication and lists the most important works by the author. The genre and publication date of each work is given. In the case of foreign authors whose works have been translated into English, the title and date (if available) of the first English-language edition is given in brackets following the original title. Unless otherwise indicated, dramas are dated by first performance, not first publication. Lists of **Representative Works** by different authors appear with topic entries.

- Reprinted **Criticism** is arranged chronologically in each entry to provide a useful perspective on changes in critical evaluation over time. The critic's name and the date of composition or publication of the critical work are given at the beginning of each piece of criticism. Unsigned criticism is preceded by the title of the source in which it appeared. All titles by the author featured in the text are printed in boldface type. Footnotes are reprinted at the end of each essay or excerpt. In the case of excerpted criticism, only those footnotes that pertain to the excerpted texts are included. Criticism in topic entries is arranged chronologically under a variety of subheadings to facilitate the study of different aspects of the topic.

- Critical essays are prefaced by brief **Annotations** explicating each piece.

- A complete **Bibliographical Citation** of the original essay or book precedes each piece of criticism.

- An annotated bibliography of **Further Reading** appears at the end of each entry and suggests resources for additional study. In some cases, significant essays for which the editors could not obtain reprint rights are included here. Boxed material following the further reading list provides references to other biographical and critical sources on the author in series published by Gale.

Cumulative Indexes

A **Cumulative Author Index** lists all of the authors that appear in a wide variety of reference sources published by the Gale Group, including *LC*. A complete list of these sources is found facing the first page of the Author Index. The index also includes birth and death dates and cross references between pseudonyms and actual names.

A **Cumulative Nationality Index** lists all authors featured in *LC* by nationality, followed by the number of the *LC* volume in which their entry appears.

A **Cumulative Topic Index** lists the literary themes and topics treated in the series as well as in *Nineteenth-Century Literature Criticism, Twentieth-Century Literary Criticism,* and the *Contemporary Literature Criticism* Yearbook, which was discontinued in 1998.

An alphabetical **Title Index** accompanies each volume of *LC*. Listings of titles by authors covered in the given volume are followed by the author's name and the corresponding page numbers on which the titles are discussed. English translations of foreign titles and variations of titles are cross-referenced to the title under which a work was originally published. Titles of novels, dramas, nonfiction books, and poetry, short story, or essay collections are printed in italics, while individual poems, short stories, and essays are printed in roman type within quotation marks.

Citing *Literature Criticism from 1400 to 1800*

When writing papers, students who quote directly from any volume in the Literary Criticism Series may use the following general format to footnote reprinted criticism. The first example pertains to material drawn from periodicals, the second to material reprinted from books.

Eileen Reeves, "Daniel 5 and the *Assayer*: Galileo Reads the Handwriting on the Wall, " *The Journal of Medieval and Renaissance Studies,* 21, no. 1 (Spring 1991): 1-27; reprinted in *Literature Criticism from 1400 to 1800,* vol. 45, ed. Jelena Krstović and Marie Lazzari (Farmington Hills, Mich.: The Gale Group, 1999), 297-310.

Margaret Anne Doody, *A Natural Passion: A Study of the Novels of Samuel Richardson* (Oxford University Press, 1974), 17-22, 132-35; excerpted and reprinted in *Literature Criticism from 1400 to 1800,* vol. 46, ed. Jelena Krstović and Marie Lazzari (Farmington Hills, Mich.: The Gale Group, 1999), 20-2.

Suggestions are Welcome

Readers who wish to suggest new features, topics, or authors to appear in future volumes, or who have other suggestions or comments are cordially invited to call, write, or fax the Managing Editor:

Managing Editor, Literary Criticism Series
The Gale Group
27500 Drake Road
Farmington Hills, MI 48331-3535
1-800-347-4253 (GALE)
Fax: 248-699-8054

Acknowledgments

The editors wish to thank the copyright holders of the excerpted criticism included in this volume and the permissions managers of many book and magazine publishing companies for assisting us in securing reproduction rights. We are also grateful to the staffs of the Detroit Public Library, the Library of Congress, the University of Detroit Mercy Library, Wayne State University Purdy/Kresge Library Complex, and the University of Michigan Libraries for making their resources available to us. Following is a list of the copyright holders who have granted us permission to reproduce material in this volume of *LC*. Every effort has been made to trace copyright, but if omissions have been made, please let us know.

PHOTOGRAPHS AND ILLUSTRATIONS APPEARING IN *LC*, VOLUME 75, WERE RECEIVED FROM THE FOLLOWING SOURCES:

Literary Criticism Series Advisory Board

The members of the Gale Group Literary Criticism Series Advisory Board—reference librarians and subject specialists from public, academic, and school library systems—represent a cross-section of our customer base and offer a variety of informed perspectives on both the presentation and content of our literature criticism products. Advisory board members assess and define such quality issues as the relevance, currency, and usefulness of the author coverage, critical content, and literary topics included in our series; evaluate the layout, presentation, and general quality of our printed volumes; provide feedback on the criteria used for selecting authors and topics covered in our series; provide suggestions for potential enhancements to our series; identify any gaps in our coverage of authors or literary topics, recommending authors or topics for inclusion; analyze the appropriateness of our content and presentation for various user audiences, such as high school students, undergraduates, graduate students, librarians, and educators; and offer feedback on any proposed changes/ enhancements to our series. We wish to thank the following advisors for their advice throughout the year.

Thomas Hoccleve
c. 1367-c. 1426

English poet.

INTRODUCTION

The medieval English poet Thomas Hoccleve is often grouped together with John Lydgate and others as one of the "English Chaucerians," followers of the first major English poet, Geoffrey Chaucer. Hoccleve was best known by early critics for his association with authors of greater renown, such as the more widely read poet Lydgate. However, the passage of time has improved Hoccleve's reputation. His penchant for autobiographical detail and his political verse—both of which distinguish him from Chaucer—have won him the interest of modern scholars. Some critics consider Hoccleve to be the earliest English autobiographer, and he is also noted for producing the first English version of the *Fürstenspiegel,* or advice to monarchs, in verse.

BIOGRAPHICAL INFORMATION

Despite Hoccleve's autobiographical inclination, not much is known of his early years. Based on his name, some biographers believe his family may have come from the village of Hockliffe, in Bedfordshire. Scholars place his birth year as somewhere between 1366 and 1369; leading Hoccleve scholar J. A. Burrow proposes 1367 as the most likely date, with later dates only a remote possibility. The facts of Hoccleve's education are unknown; it assumed that he was not a university graduate. However, in 1387 Hoccleve began working as a clerk in the office of the Privy Seal in Westminster, a position that would have required a knowledge of French and Latin, indicating some degree of formal education. In a career in the office of the Privy Seal that lasted for nearly forty years, he was responsible for issuing authenticated royal documents and correspondence, and for authorizing the activities of the Chancery and Exchequer in matters ranging from minor purchases to the issuance of pardons. In 1394 King Richard II granted Hoccleve a corrody, a type of pension, giving him the right to free room and board at the Priory of Hayling on the Isle of Wight; Burrow suggests that Hoccleve likely accepted a cash payment in lieu of the accommodations, as was common. At some time in the late fourteenth century Hoccleve met Chaucer; the means of their acquaintance is unknown, and in fact the acquaintance itself has at times been disputed. Most of the evidence for Hoccleve's relationship with Chaucer, whom he considered his poetic mentor, comes from Hoccleve's own poems.

Hoccleve also describes himself as poor in his poetry, reflecting the financial struggles of the court during the reign of King Henry IV, who took the crown from Richard II in 1399. Hoccleve's first work for which a date is known with certainty is "Letter of Cupid," which was published in 1402. A translation and adaptation of the popular French poet Christine de Pisan's 1399 *Epistre au Dieu d'Amours,* the poem was one of Hoccleve's most popular works. His next major poem is the strongly autobiographical "La Male Regle" ("The Ill-Regulated Youth," 1406), in which Hoccleve complains of the hardships of his life, many of which, he confesses, he brought on himself. Despite the exaggerations of the poem, scholars have generally agreed that Hoccleve likely did describe his physical ailments, financial strains, and moral failings accurately. Hoccleve married around 1410 or 1411, indicating that he had changed his mind about former plans to enter the priesthood. Nothing at all is known of his wife, although Hoccleve asserts in his poetry that he loved her. Following his marriage he began work on *De Regimine Principum* (*Regement of Princes,* 1411-12), which he presented to the future Henry V, then Prince Hal, with the hope of winning the favor of the heir to the throne. Consisting of advice to the prince on the proper conduct of a monarch, the poem was Hoccleve's most successful and widely read work. The prologue includes a lengthy dialogue between Hoccleve and a beggar, and an address to Chaucer. Several surviving copies of the poem include a portrait of Chaucer that Hoccleve commissioned to be included in the work. Hoccleve continued to write poems for Henry V, but there is no indication that his financial status improved, although he continued to draw a small annuity. At some point following the publication of the *Regement,* Hoccleve suffered from a period of mental illness, perhaps depression. The illness probably began sometime around 1414; Burrow and others have noted that between 1414 and 1417 Hoccleve did not go to the Exchequer to collect his annuity, suggesting the period of his malady. Hoccleve mentions his illness in his "Complaint," one of the works that makes up his *Series,* a collection of works written primarily between 1419 and 1422. Henry VI ascended to the throne in 1422, and Hoccleve's annuity was continued, although by 1423 he was probably no longer working in the Privy Seal office. Nonetheless, at that time he was likely working on the comprehensive *Formulary,* a painstakingly detailed guide to the workings of the office, written to assist his successors. He was also granted another corrody in 1424, having petitioned Henry V's younger brother, Humphrey of Gloucester. Records relating to this corrody in Southwick, Hampshire, provide evidence of the date of Hoccleve's death. The documents indicate that a payment was made to Hoccleve in March 1426 but by May of that year the pension was granted to someone else, suggesting that Hoccleve had died in the interim.

MAJOR WORKS

Hoccleve wrote in a number of genres popular in his day. His first major work, the "Letter of Cupid," is an example of courtly poetry in the manner of the lines of the *Roman de la Rose.* It contains a dream vision, complex allegory, and wit typical of the courtly style. The original poem by Christine de Pisan was a defense of women, often considered an early example of proto-feminist literature. In Hoccleve's translation, however, the humor becomes ambiguous; scholars have long been uncertain whether Hoccleve was faithfully delivering Pisan's message to an English audience or slyly mocking her. Hoccleve's most important work, the *Regement of Princes,* was also written for a courtly audience. Effectively an instruction manual for a prince, the *Regement* was one of the earliest English examples of the genre, which increased in popularity during the medieval era and the early Renaissance. The work follows the pattern of the well-known *Secreta Secretorum,* an eighth-century work often incorrectly attributed to Aristotle. The *Regement* lists the virtues important to a monarch, exemplified in legends and historical events. Hoccleve instructed Prince Henry in dignity, justice, mercy, generosity, peace, and similar topics; he used the sections on liberality and prudence to remind the prince to pay his

annuity. The *Regement* is preceded by a prologue considered by many scholars to be at least as interesting as the *Regement* itself. Like the earlier "La Male Regle," the prologue is highly autobiographical, offering the poet a forum for voicing his grievances and for repeating his debt to Chaucer. In fact, the very form of the poem is Chaucerian, consisting mainly of rhyme royal stanzas (*ababbcc*), which had been popularized by the earlier poet. Several of Hoccleve's poems were at one time attributed to Chaucer, including the "Letter of Cupid" and such short religious poems as "Mother of God" (before 1426) and "Prologue and a Miracle of the Blessed Virgin" (before 1426). Another of his religious poems, "Learn to Die," which is included in the *Series,* is the first poetic treatment of the so-called *ars moriendi* (art of dying) theme in English. Hoccleve also addressed more explicitly political subjects in his shorter verse, most often ballads praising the king, written for a court audience. An exception is the "Address to Sir John Oldcastle" (1415), in which he accused the Lollard knight of heresy and urged him to return to the Church. He also wrote works in the minor genre of the "begging" poem, which, like Chaucer's *Complaint to His Purse,* were designed to solicit money from his benefactors. Hoccleve wrote little of the narrative poetry at which his mentor had excelled, apart from the anecdotes included in the *Regement.* The *Series,* however, does include two poetic narratives drawn from a highly popular collection of stories entitled *Gesta Romanorum*: "The Tale of Jerelaus' Wife" and "The Tale of Jonathas and Fellicula." Later scholars have also considered Hoccleve's highly personal work in the context of autobiography, a genre that did not exist in the Middle Ages but one whose conventions Hoccleve nonetheless sometimes observed.

CRITICAL RECEPTION

Hoccleve was widely read in his day, but the larger lights of Medieval literature quickly relegated him to the status of a minor poet in later centuries. Early criticism of Hoccleve tended to focus on his relationships with other poets, both personal and literary. He claimed Chaucer among his acquaintances, referring often to him in his poetry and relying on Chaucerian forms and themes for his own writing; thus scholarship has often grouped Hoccleve among the minor "sons of Chaucer." In this context, Hoccleve is frequently paired with John Lydgate, who wrote successfully in many of the genres attempted by Hoccleve. Lydgate, a cleric, was better educated than Hoccleve and much more influential. Because both were deeply influenced by Chaucer, comparisons between the two often serve to demonstrate their different understanding of their mentor. As Derek Pearsall has noted, when placed next to Lydgate, the Chaucerian vernacular style of Hoccleve stands out all the more, as does Hoccleve's adoption of a Chaucerian narrative persona and sense of irony. Jerome Mitchell has also suggested that Hoccleve's rhetorical style and diction owe a great deal to Chaucer's influence. More recent criticism, however, has attempted to bring Hoccleve out from under Chaucer's shadow, arguing that Hoccleve typically wrote in forms Chaucer showed little interest in. In particular, as J. A. Burrow has suggested, Chaucer did not often address political themes explicitly, nor did he revel in autobiographical detail in the manner of Hoccleve. Hoccleve's unusual level of self-disclosure has been of particular interest to scholars, such as Malcolm Richardson, who has emphasized the accuracy with which Hoccleve described the life of a clerk in the office of the Privy Seal. However, some critics have questioned the extent to which Hoccleve truly revealed the details of his life. D. C. Greetham has contended that the persona Hoccleve presented served mainly as a literary device. Hoccleve's uncertain view of women has also continued to interest critics. While earlier critics tended to view Hoccleve's "Letter of Cupid" as a straightforward rendering of Christine de Pisan's feminist view, later scholars such as Karen A. Winstead have held that the tone and style of Hoccleve's work suggest that he was satirizing rather than merely translating the French original. The historical turn in literary studies has also brought increased attention to Hoccleve, particularly his *Regement of Princes*. Larry Scanlon, for instance, has stressed the role of poems such as the *Regement* in shaping contemporary beliefs about kingship and authority.

PRINCIPAL WORKS

"Letter of Cupid" (poetry) 1402

"La Male Regle" ["The Ill-Regulated Youth"] (poetry) 1406

De Regimine Principum [*Regement of Princes*] (poetry) 1411-12

"Address to Sir John Oldcastle" (poetry) 1415

Series (collected poetry) 1419-22

"Mother of God" (poetry) before 1426

"Prologue and a Miracle of the Blessed Virgin" (poetry) before 1426

Poems by Thomas Hoccleve, Never Before Printed (poetry) 1796

The Regement of Princes [edited by Thomas Wright] (poetry) 1860

*The Minor Poems in the Phillipps MS. 1851 (Cheltenham) and the Durham MS. III 9 (poetry) 1892

*The Regement of Princes A.D. 1411-12, from the Harleian MS. 4866, and Fourteen of Hoccleve's Minor Poems from the Egerton MS. 615 (poetry) 1897

*The Minor Poems in the Ashburnham MS. Addit. 133 (poetry) 1925

The Formulary of Thomas Hoccleve (manual) 1965

Thomas Hoccleve's Series: An Edition of MS Durham Cosin V iii 9 (poetry) 1968

†*Hoccleve's Works: The Minor Poems* (poetry) 1970

Selections from Hoccleve (poetry) 1981

Thomas Hoccleve: Selected Poems (poetry) 1982

The Regement of Princes [edited by Charles R. Blyth] (poetry) 1999

Thomas Hoccleve's Complaint and Dialogue (poetry) 1999

*These works comprise the three-volume *Hoccleve's Works*, edited by F. J. Furnivall and Israel Gollancz.

†This work is Jerome Mitchell and A. I. Doyle's revision in one volume of Furnivall and Gollancz's three-volume edition of *Hoccleve's Works*.

CRITICISM

Jerome Mitchell (essay date 1967)

SOURCE: Mitchell, Jerome. "The Autobiographical Element in Hoccleve." *Modern Language Quarterly* 28, no. 3 (1967): 269-84.

[*In the essay that follows, Mitchell attempts to distinguish convention from fact in the self-referential passages of Hoccleve's works. While Mitchell suggests that elements such as Hoccleve's extreme poverty and his bout with mental illness may be fictional or exaggerated, he contends that they are convincing and sincere. Also, Hoccleve's detail, loose organization, and conversational style suggest a greater degree of self-revelation than was typical in medieval English poetry.*]

Many scholars have felt that the autobiographical element is the most interesting feature of Thomas Hoccleve's poetry.[1] This paper re-examines Hoccleve's autobiographical passages in relation to the work of his contemporaries and immediate predecessors and suggests that they reveal a degree of individuality unparalleled in Middle English poetry.

Details presumably relating to the poet's life crop up in many of his works, the most important and extensive of the autobiographical passages being found in **"La Male Regle"** (1406), the **"Prologue"** to the *Regement of Princes* (1412), the **"Complaint"** (1422), and the **"Dialogue with a Friend"** (1422).[2] The dates, fairly accurate, have been arrived at through calculations based on references Hoccleve makes to his own age in the poems themselves. He wrote **"La Male Regle"** when he was a relatively young man and still a novice in the art of poetry; he wrote the **"Prologue"** to the *Regement* in middle age; and he wrote the **"Complaint"** and the **"Dialogue"** some five years after his bout with an emotional disorder which bordered on insanity. Thus the poems span Hoccleve's entire productive period.

Just how much of what Hoccleve says in his first-person narratives is really true, how much is pseudoautobiographical, and how much is pure convention are questions not easily answered. Much ink has been spilt on the same problem as it is found in Chaucer's dream-poems. Fortunately, the question of Hoccleve's persona is not so complex as that of Chaucer's, since in this case matters are not further complicated by the machinery of the dream-poem. Yet the basic problem remains. To what extent can the "I" of the so-called autobiographical poems be identified with Hoccleve himself? To what extent can the autobiographical passages be regarded as genuine, individualized self-revelation? Most of Hoccleve's critics have accepted these passages at their face value. In some instances the poet's entire life has been reconstructed from them. Indeed, the only writer to question Hoccleve's veracity was G. Gregory Smith, who believed that the so-called personal element in Hoccleve (and in Lydgate) was "more conventional and rhetorical, and of a pattern, than individual."[3]

Smith's observations cannot be dismissed lightly. Much of what Hoccleve tells us about himself cannot be substantiated with any existing official records.[4] In the **"Prologue"** to the *Regement of Princes* (lines 1447 ff.), he tells the Beggar that he intended to be a priest and waited long for a benefice. When it seemed clear that none was forthcoming, he married, even though he had some second thoughts about losing his freedom as a bachelor. In the **"Dialogue with a Friend"** he refers again to his wife. Yet there are no official records to support his remarks regarding either his marriage or his thwarted intention of becoming a priest. What Hoccleve has said may be true, but we do not know for certain. In addition to passages that cannot be verified with other sources of information, there are several "autobiographical" passages that have a decidedly conventional ring. Smith cites the **"Complaint"** and the **"Dialogue"** as examples. Possibly the conventional element is even more pronounced in the opening stanzas of the **"Prologue"** to the *Regement,* in which Hoccleve broods on the misery in the world, the capriciousness of Fortune, and his own emotional turmoil. There is one personal touch—Hoccleve's reference to his dwelling "at Chestre ynne"—but there is certainly nothing individual either in the ideas presented or in the general situation. Similar passages can be found in other Middle English poems. Chaucer's *Book of the Duchess,* for instance, begins in much the same fashion.

Some of the details in the "autobiographical" poems are seemingly contradicted by known facts. For one thing, Hoccleve incessantly complains about his straitened financial circumstances both in these poems and in the short poems of solicitation, such as the **"Balade to My Lord the Chancellor,"** the **"Balade and Roundel . . . to Mr. Henry Somer,"** the **"Balade to King Henry V for Money,"** and the **"Balade to My Maister Carpenter."** Yet the records show that Hoccleve was not so hard up as he would have us believe. In November, 1399, he was granted an annuity of £10 for life, and this was increased in May, 1409, to 20 marks (£13 6*s.* 8*d.*)—no mean sum for a scrivener in the early fifteenth century ("Appendix," pp. li and lvii). Hoccleve was paid semiannually and, apparently, with some degree of regularity. In addition, he derived money from sources other than his regular income. On one occasion he and three of his fellow clerks divided £40 worth of goods confiscated from outlaws (Bennett, p. 82). It seems, then, that there is a certain amount of conventional poverty in Hoccleve's frequent complaints to his empty purse. Similar poems can be found among the works of Chaucer and Lydgate.

In the **"Complaint"** and the **"Dialogue,"** probably written in 1422, Hoccleve discusses at some length the emotional disorder which he experienced five years previously. Exactly how long the sickness lasted he does not say, but he implies a substantial period of time. When, as he puts it, the substance of his memory finally returned from play, he had great difficulty in being admitted again into the fellowship of his former friends, who were mistakenly convinced that his madness would return. But the poet's own words are the only record we have of his sickness; the official government documents make no mention of it. Moreover, during the time of his supposed madness and the period immediately following it, he drew his annuity regularly, sometimes "by his own hands" ("Appendix," pp. lxiii-lxiv). It seems odd that there should be no other record of his illness if it was really as severe and as noticeable to others as he would have us believe.

So much for the questionable autobiographical details. On the other hand, Hoccleve relates many personal details that are verifiable. He refers several times to his work in the office of the Privy Seal. In **"La Male Regle"** he tells us that none of his colleagues "in al the priuee seel" ever drank so much as he (lines 307-308). In the **"Prologue"** to the *Regement of Princes* he alludes to the length of time he has served as a scrivener (801-805). He also tells the Beggar the amount of his annuity—20 marks—the figure agreeing perfectly with the official records (820-22). A few lines later he expatiates on the many inconveniences a professional scribe is apt to encounter (988 ff.). In the **"Complaint"** he writes that his former friends would often ask his "fellawes / of the prive seale" about the state of his health (295-98). Finally, in a few of the autobiographical passages, Hoccleve refers to himself by name. At first glance this would seem a trivial point, but in some of the most celebrated medieval "autobiographical" poems (such as *The Kingis Quair*) the "I" never identifies himself.

Thus we cannot dismiss Hoccleve's work as pure convention, Gregory Smith notwithstanding. Smith's remarks are also open to debate because he equates Hoccleve's autobiographical passages with what he believes to be similar passages in Lydgate's *Testament.* What the two poets have done, however, is not so similar as might appear at first glance. Finally, although Smith implies that no complete study of fifteenth-century "anticipations" of the personal quality characteristic of later times has ever been made, he gives the impression that Hoccleve's type of work, especially **"La Male Regle,"** was common in medieval times. This, it seems to me, is another questionable point.

In earlier English poetry genuinely autobiographical passages are exceptional. We know, for example, really nothing about the life of the *Pearl*-poet from his works. Langland refers vaguely to himself in a few places, notably in the sixth passus of the C-text of *Piers Plowman.*[5] At one point he tells Conscience that in past years he had his "tyme mysspended" (line 93); but, unlike Hoccleve, he gives no specific details. Gower also has very little to say about himself that could not be labeled pure convention. There is perhaps no reason to doubt his account, in the first version of the Prologue to the *Confessio Amantis*[6] of his meeting Richard II on the Thames and his receiving the king's suggestions for a new book (34-53). But one learns almost nothing about the man John Gower from these lines; the personal touch is lacking. Even in Chaucer's poetry there are few clearly autobiographical passages, and most of these occur in the *House of Fame.* Yet Chaucer's work in this vein, though slight, may have had some influence on Hoccleve.

The poets of Hoccleve's own day do not talk about themselves except in general terms. In the second stanza of his *Moral Balade,* Henry Scogan appears to be much concerned about his misspent youth, but he is unwilling to reveal what his vices were.[7] The poem lacks specific detail, as do most of the other fifteenth-century "autobiographical" poems. *The Kingis Quair,* for example, has often been admired as an early specimen of autobiographical poetry.[8] But even if one accepts the tradition that King James I of Scotland was the author, the celebrated passages of self-revelation are neither numerous nor explicit. In one well-known section (sts. 22-25), the poet writes that when he was three years past the state of innocence, his guardians, for reasons unmentioned, advised him to leave the country. During the journey by sea, he and his party were captured by enemies and taken by force to a strange country. There he was put into a "strong prisoun," where he was to remain for twice nine years. This passage perhaps refers to an episode in the life of King James, but whoever wrote it obviously intended it to be vague. We do not know who the "I" is. Nor do we know what country he is from, or what land he is bound for, or who his enemies are, or where he is imprisoned.

Autobiographical passages cannot be found in John Walton's verse translation of Boethius' *Consolation of Philosophy* or in the poetical works of John Capgrave.[9] But in the poetry of Osbern Bokenham[10] and George Ashby,[11] both of whom flourished in the years immediately following Hoccleve's death, occasional autobiographical passages can be pointed out. In the General Prologue to his *Legendys of Hooly Wummen,* Bokenham alludes briefly to the last time he was in Italy (lines 107 ff.). He notes that the relics of St. Margaret are kept at a priory near the place where he was born, and he comments on some of the miracles performed by means of them (133 ff.). Once, while he was in Venice, he managed to avoid misfortune and possible death through a miracle involving these relics. Several wicked men had thrown him from his barge into a fen and were about to leave him to his fate. They allowed him to come back on board when he promised to bring them a ring with which he had touched St. Margaret's bare foot (157-72). Bokenham's account of this incident is memorable mainly because of his use of specific detail. His passages of self-revelation comprise a relatively small segment of his nearly 11,000 verses. They can certainly be compared with the autobiographical material in Hoccleve, but Hoccleve's work in this vein is much more extensive

and, as I shall attempt to show, more convincing and more minutely detailed. As for Ashby, the opening stanzas of *A Prisoner's Reflections* are apparently autobiographical. Ashby has been thrown into the Fleet "By a gret commaundment of a lord" (9); he gives us his name; he laments that he has been forsaken by his old friends; he is unable to get out of debt. He spent his best years in the service of Henry VI, Margaret of Anjou, and their uncle, the Duke of Gloucester; now, in his old age, Fortune has turned against him. Ashby's account of his troubles is sincere enough, but most of what he says could be said by many a prisoner. That is, his stanzas of self-revelation lack individuality; they convey almost nothing of their author's personality. Ashby has not managed (or perhaps not even attempted) to characterize himself.

Essentially the same thing can be said about the autobiographical passages in Lydgate's *Testament.*[12] Even in Part IV, which contains many autobiographical details, Lydgate has not given his work the personal touch he might have. One reason for the lack of individuality is that he chooses to give many short allusions to his childhood days, one after another, instead of limiting himself to a few points and elaborating on these. One stanza will illustrate my point:

> I had in custome to come to skole late,
>   Nat for to lerne but for a contenaunce,
> With my felawes redy to debate,
>   To Iangle or Iape was sett all my pleasaunce;
>   Wherof rebuked this was my chevesaunce,
> To forge a lesyng, and thervpon to muse,
> Whanne I trespaced, my-selven to excuse.
>
> (628-34)

The details summarily presented here could have been developed much more fully. Lydgate might have described, for example, a specific occasion on which he arrived at school late. He might have given the exact words that passed between himself and his comrades during their arguments. He might have told us some of the lies he concocted, and he might have described a specific incident in which he tried to lie his way out of some wrong he had committed. But because he has not developed the autobiographical material by describing specific incidents, his confessions apply to almost any childhood.

None of the writers discussed so far wrote autobiographical passages similar to those of Hoccleve. Before examining Hoccleve's work, however, we must return to Chaucer, especially his *House of Fame.*[13] It is sometimes difficult to draw a line between what are autobiographical allusions and what are not, but three or four passages almost certainly reflect Chaucer's own life. Near the beginning of Book II, for instance, the poet makes what is probably a humorous allusion to his wife Philippa. When the eagle says to him, "Awak!" he is reminded of one whom he could name, one who often awakened him with the same word, but not so gently (lines 554-66). Several lines later Chaucer refers to his own physical appearance. The eagle says,

"Seynte Marye!
Thou art noyous for to carye,
And nothyng nedeth it, pardee!"

(573-75)

From the pictures of Chaucer that have come down to us—including Hoccleve's famous portrait—we know that he was short in stature, but rather thickset. The most interesting autobiographical allusion appears in the well-known lines wherein we catch a glimpse of Chaucer's life when he was Controller of the Customs (641-60). Finally, in line 729 the eagle calls Chaucer by his given name, *Geffrey.* The direct discourse Chaucer uses in all four instances makes the autobiographical allusions livelier in tone, more realistic and lifelike in their impact upon an audience or a reader—in a word, more convincing. Another prominent aspect of Chaucer's autobiographical material is its humor—something totally lacking in the work of Bokenham, Ashby, Lydgate, and the others. Finally, Chaucer has managed to convey something of his own personality in these brief passages. Somehow the lines bear his individual stamp. There is no question of the allusions being couched in general terms that would apply to almost anyone. The autobiographical element in Chaucer is very scanty, but Hoccleve apparently took a hint from Chaucer and developed his own autobiographical technique along the lines suggested in the *House of Fame.*

Although **"La Male Regle,"** the **"Prologue"** to the *Regement of Princes,* the **"Complaint,"** and the **"Dialogue with a Friend"** differ from each other in subject matter, presentation of material, and tone, the autobiographical element is prominent in all four works. Indeed, it is the most striking feature. **"La Male Regle,"** perhaps Hoccleve's best-known poem, consists of fifty-six eight-line stanzas of pentameter with a rhyme scheme of *ababbcbc.* Interestingly, Hoccleve wrote **"La Male Regle"** at approximately the same time that Scogan wrote *A Moral Balade.* Both poems are didactic; both are in eight-line stanzas. But instead of merely alluding, like Scogan, to his misspent youth, Hoccleve relates his youthful follies in detail.

The poem opens with an invocation to the god Health (sts. 1-8), wherein Hoccleve contrasts the health that he took for granted in his youth with his present bodily infirmities. The invocation is followed by a thoroughly conventional digression on Youth and Reason (sts. 9-11)—Youth representing unrestraint, nonconformity, and folly, and Reason the opposite qualities. The next division (sts. 12-26) is apparently autobiographical. If some of the details are not actually true, one would never know the difference, for Hoccleve has a knack of making all his autobiographical allusions seem genuine. He begins by talking in general terms about his misspent youth, but he gradually becomes more specific. The series of intimate confessions gets under way in stanza 16 with a brief description of the "signe of Bachus," which lures the poet into a London tavern. In each stanza thereafter, Hoccleve has painted a miniature self-portrait. He has made these stanzas memorable by means of specific, descriptive details and through intimate, unabashed remarks about his own rather effeminate personality. He chases after girls at "Poules heed" (st. 18); he treats them to wine and wafers (st. 19); he likes them to kiss him (line 155); and he is as content with a kiss as he would have been "with the deede" (156). "Of loues aart," he writes, "yit touchid I no deel" (153). When men speak of sexual matters in his presence, he waxes "as reed as is the gleede" (159). Afraid of fighting, he either keeps his mouth shut or whispers bad things about a person behind his back (st. 22). He pays the taverners and the cooks at Westminster gate so well that they think he is "a verray gentil man" (st. 23). After a visit to the tavern, he often takes a boat ride, tipping the boatmen lavishly and being highly pleased when they call him "maistir" (sts. 24-26). On this personal note the first autobiographical section ends.

The next division consists of a conventional didactic discourse on the troubles that befall men when they listen to flatterers. Then, at stanza 39, Hoccleve returns to an account of his misspent youth. He describes amusingly his unwillingness to get out of bed on the morning after a night of debauchery. Only his two fellow clerks, Prentys and Arondel, are worse offenders than he. Sometimes they sleep until "it drawith ny the pryme" (see lines 317-26). Next, in an apostrophe to himself (351 ff.), Hoccleve alludes to his want of money. In the last part of the poem, he implores the god Health to see to it that Lord Fourneval, the treasurer, pay his overdue annuity of £10. (The figure is correct, according to the official government records.) By asking the god Health to intercede for him, Hoccleve is able to beg for his annuity in a manner that does not seem offensively overt.

"La Male Regle" obviously contains some conventional subject matter, such as the discourse on Youth and Reason, the sermon on flattery, and the plea for money. Even the idea of a wasted youth is nothing unusual. But the foregoing summary suggests that Hoccleve's handling of autobiographical material is quite different from that of the writers discussed earlier. He makes a point of telling us exactly how he dissipated his youth by describing certain aspects of his personal life instead of simply mentioning or listing them. The humorous tone of some of the passages is also a factor not to be overlooked. Like Chaucer, Hoccleve has managed to give his passages of self-revelation an individual stamp. A real personality emerges from the pages of **"La Male Regle"**—a personality which we can watch develop and can observe in different circumstances in the **"Prologue"** to the *Regement,* the **"Complaint,"** and the **"Dialogue."**

The opening stanzas of the **"Prologue"** to the *Regement* are, as I have remarked earlier, quite conventional. The persona finds himself in a typical medieval intellectual dilemma. Unable to sleep, he meditates on the capriciousness of Fortune—so well exemplified in the recent case of Richard II—and concludes pessimistically that inconstancy rules the world. Only a person who has nothing is safe from the wiles of Fortune, but such a person is already miserable. The narrator sees no purpose in striving and begins to look forward to death. In this frame of mind, he goes out the next morning into the fields, where he encounters an old beggar. Again the situation is conventional. Sometimes such old men are symbolic of Reason or Wisdom (like Vergil in the *Divine Comedy*) and sometimes of Death (like the old man in Chaucer's *Pardoner's Tale*). Indeed, the conflict between Youth and Age is a leitmotiv in medieval literature. Many writers seem to have felt that old men had somehow solved the riddle of human existence, that they had discovered the meaningful life.

With all these ideas in the background, the scene is suddenly brought to life as the Beggar awakens Hoccleve from his reverie:

> He sterte vp to me, & seyde, "scleepys þou, man?
>   Awake!" & gan me schake wonder faste,
>   And with a sigh I answerde atte laste.
> "A! who is þer?" "I," quod þis olde greye,
>   "Am heer," & he me tolde the manere
> How he spak to me, as ye herd me seye;
>   "O man," quoþ I, "for cristes loue dere,
> If þat þou wolt aght done at my preyere,
>   As go þi way, talke to me no more,
>   Þi wordes al annoyen me ful sore;
> "Voyde fro me; me list no compaignye;
>   Encresse noght my grife; I haue I-now."
>
>   (131-42)

But the talkative old man has no intention of leaving and, humorously enough, imposes himself on the melancholy poet when he is in no mood to be disturbed. The lively, realistic dialogue is typical of many portions of the **"Prologue."** Indeed, Hoccleve has made it a consistent practice to interrupt the Beggar's long didactic sermons either with lively repartee or with passages of self-revelation.

The material of the **"Prologue"** to the *Regement* has no well-defined organization. The conversation rambles on from one topic to another. The first passage of self-revelation comes not from Hoccleve but from the Beggar, whose account of his misspent youth (610 ff.) resembles in many respects Hoccleve's account of himself in **"La Male Regle."** In his youth the Beggar, like Hoccleve, spent too much of his time in taverns. He shied away from all physical violence; but, unlike Hoccleve, he seems often to have "done the deed" with females, whether they were maids, wives, or even nuns. Eventually, he ran out of money and was forsaken by his friends.

At line 750 Hoccleve begins a long passage of self-revelation in which he tells the Beggar the cause of his melancholy. He is in straitened financial circumstances and fears that he will be destitute in his old age. During the course of his long-winded complaint, he digresses on the English soldiers who once fought gloriously in France but who were now back home—old, penniless, and friendless (869 ff.). He fears that his plight will be the same as theirs unless his annuity is paid. Probably, as I suggested earlier,

Hoccleve was never so destitute as he pretends in this "autobiographical" passage. On the other hand, his references to his work in the Privy Seal (802), the length of his service (804-805), and the exact amount of his annuity (822) *are* true and can be substantiated with the official records. His complaint contains just enough truth to seem plausible as a whole.

In stanzas 142-47, Hoccleve comments vividly on the troubles and tribulations encountered by scribes. The entire section owes its effectiveness to specific detail and is reminiscent of the passage, not so minutely detailed, in the *House of Fame* in which the eagle refers to Chaucer's bookwork. Other passages of self-revelation include the poet's allusions to his wife (1226, 1453-56, 1560-61) and his discussion of the mistreatment which the clerks of the Privy Seal experience in their dealings with servants of important lords (1499-1547). After a lengthy didactic section on marriage, the conversation returns to Hoccleve's fear that his annuity will not be paid (1779 ff.), and a few lines later the Beggar suggests that the poet appeal to Prince Henry for help (1842 ff.). The last passage of self-revelation contains the much-quoted lines in which Hoccleve laments the death of Chaucer (1958-74). He refers briefly to Gower at line 1975 and then apologizes for his own limitations as a poet in a short passage of conventional self-deprecation (1982-86). Suddenly the Beggar announces to Hoccleve that he must go. He and the poet quickly take leave of each other, and the long, rambling **"Prologue"** to the *Regement of Princes* ends.

As an autobiographical poem, the **"Prologue"** differs from the work of other medieval poets. Hoccleve has written passages of self-revelation which are much longer than those of other writers; he mixes known facts with conventional material in such a way that the whole seems true; he uses lively, realistic dialogue throughout; he makes a point of giving concrete details; he describes fully various aspects of his life; and, finally, he has the knack of revealing his own feelings convincingly. The personality that emerges from the **"Prologue"** to the *Regement* is that of a weak, timorous, self-centered, but very human individual.

Hoccleve's **"Complaint"** and the **"Dialogue with a Friend"** have received less attention than they deserve and have been printed in their entirety only once—in Furnivall's edition of the *Minor Poems*. The prologue to the **"Complaint"** is reminiscent of the opening stanzas of the **"Prologue"** to the *Regement of Princes*; but in the **"Complaint"** Hoccleve is more successful in giving the impression of sincerity, despite the conventional element. The first stanza is remarkable as one of the few examples of nature description in Hoccleve's works. The poet sees in the dying year a reflection of his own depressed spirits. He cannot sleep; he has found himself out of favor since his last sickness; and he longs for death. Hoccleve's sickness is the subject of the **"Complaint."** He analyzes the symptoms of the severe emotional disorder he experienced, discusses his difficulty in readjusting himself to normal life, and comments on the reactions of his friends both during the illness and after his recovery.

Like the **"Prologue"** to the *Regement,* the **"Complaint"** has no well-defined organization. Hoccleve rambles from one point to another, apparently simply putting down his thoughts as they come to him. Unlike the earlier work, however, the **"Complaint"** does contain one unifying element—the subject of the poet's illness—and everything relates to this one central theme. Hoccleve looks back on his illness as a time when, as he puts it, the substance of his memory went to play (50-51). After he had recovered, five years prior to the time when he actually wrote the **"Complaint,"** his friends would not readmit him into their company. They even made a conscious practice of avoiding him, and they believed that his recovery was only temporary. Hoccleve records some of their remarks verbatim:

> "all-thowghe from hym / his siknesse savage
> with-drawne and passyd / as for a tyme be,
> Resorte it wole / namely in suche age
> as he is of". . . .
>
> "whane passinge hete is," quod they, "trustyth this,
> assaile hym wole agayne that maladie."
>
> (86-93)

He then observes that men should not pretend to be wiser than they really are. Only God knows what the future holds. It was God who visited him and afflicted him with "that wildenesse" (107) when he least expected it.

At this point Hoccleve recalls a few of the incidents that occurred during the time of his illness. He writes that his friends observed him closely and discussed among themselves the outward manifestations of his disorder:

> Men seyden, I loked / as a wilde steer,
> and so my loke abowt I gan to throwe;
> myne heed to hie / a-nother seide I beer,
> ful bukkyshe is his brayne / well may I trowe;
> and seyde the thirde / and apt is in the rowe
> to site of them / that a resounles reed
> Can geve / no sadnesse is in his heed.
>
> Chaungid had I my pas / some seiden eke,
> for here and there / forthe stirte I as a Roo,
> none abode / none arrest, but all brain-seke.
> A-nother spake / and of me seide also,
> my feete weren aye / wavynge to and fro
> whane that I stonde shulde / and withe men talke,
> and that myne eyne / sowghten every halke.
>
> (120-33)

Because of a speech difficulty that accompanied his illness—"I hadd lost my tonges key" (144)—Hoccleve was unable to answer the allegations of his friends. In the privacy of his home, he often looked at his face in a mirror but could find no change in his physical appearance. He did not know whether to be seen on the streets when he was out of favor or to stay at home and run the risk of

being held more seriously ill than he really was (183 ff.). Finally his memory returned. In the remaining part of the poem, he discusses his feelings about the present state of his mind, his difficulty in being accepted once again by his friends, his near surrender of himself to utter despair, and his final religious solution to his problems.

How much of Hoccleve's rambling discourse is true, one cannot say for certain, since there is nothing in any of the existing government documents to indicate that the poet ever suffered from a mental breakdown. But Hoccleve's account of his illness, whether entirely true or not, is certainly most convincing. The detail with which he describes various aspects of his malady and the apparent sincerity with which he relates certain incidents and his feelings toward them make the **"Complaint"** seem very real, while the subject matter alone makes it a unique Middle English poem of self-revelation.

The **"Dialogue with a Friend"** immediately follows the **"Complaint"** in Durham MS. Cosin V. III. 9 (the holograph on which Furnivall's text is based). The first two stanzas exemplify the colloquial, natural, unadorned style that Hoccleve uses in most of the poem's direct discourse:

> And, endyd my "complaynt" / in this manere,
> one knocked / at my chambre dore sore,
> and cryed a-lowde / "howe, hoccleve! arte thow here?
> open thy dore / me thinkethe it full yore
> sythen I the se / what, man, for goddes ore
> come out / for this quartar I not the sy,
> by owght I wot" / and out to hym cam I.
>
> This man was my good frynde / of farn a-gon,
> that I speke of / and thus he to me seyde:
> "Thomas / as thow me lovest, tell a-non
> what dydist thow / when I knocked and leyde
> so fast upon thy dore" / And I obeyde
> vnto his will / "come in," quod I, "and se."
> and so he dyd / he streyght went in with me.
>
> (1-14)

There are fewer long speeches in the **"Dialogue with a Friend"** than in the **"Prologue"** to the *Regement of Princes,* and the dialogue frequently moves back and forth within a single stanza—sometimes even within a single line. The casual, freely moving discourse gives a realistic touch to the autobiographical material presented.

Because of the great diversity of its subject matter, the **"Dialogue with a Friend"** cannot be summarized easily. It can best be described as a pleasant metrical hodgepodge of varying moods and ideas. Between the half-serious, half-affected melancholy that is prevalent as Hoccleve broods on the world's perennial sorrows (246-87) and the good-humored fun to be found in the section on women (715-826)—a section that reveals the poet's feminist sympathies—there is a middle ground where Hoccleve and his friend bandy ideas on various subjects. Hoccleve inveighs against coin-clippers in a passage that reveals his interest in a serious social and political problem of the times (99-196); he digresses on friendship, having nothing original to add to the time-worn subject (323-64); and he sings the praises of Humphrey, Duke of Gloucester, in a *topos* involving the eulogy of a great man (554-623). The last two items are largely conventional; the others reveal something of the poet's personality. The most important theme of the dialogue, however, reveals much of Hoccleve's own personality. As in the **"Complaint,"** the predominant theme is autobiographical, namely, the question of Hoccleve's sanity. Hoccleve wants to translate a Latin treatise on the art of dying, but his friend objects. He is afraid that the poet has not recovered sufficiently from his nervous disorder to engage in work that would require much mental exertion. Many arguments for and against Hoccleve's resumption of his efforts in verse are amicably exchanged, until the friend is thoroughly convinced that the poet is in control of his mental faculties. If the **"Dialogue"** has a *raison d'être*, it may be simply that Hoccleve felt a need to prove to himself that his mind was stable and that he was capable of writing poetry once again.

Whether or not the passages of self-revelation in the **"Dialogue"** should be taken at face value, they are convincing. Much of Hoccleve's personality is revealed in the pleasant, chatty direct discourse. The **"Dialogue"** is a mellow poem. There are no unpleasant emotional outbursts, no passages of impassioned rhetoric, no woeful appeals for money. It gives the appearance of having been written by an older man—or at least by a man who has come to terms with the world. In its rambling movement from one mood and idea to another, the poem has the flavor of an informal essay.

A clear, individualized portrait of Thomas Hoccleve emerges from the pages of **"La Male Regle,"** the **"Prologue"** to the ***Regement of Princes,*** the **"Complaint,"** and the **"Dialogue with a Friend."** If the portrait is not flattering in all instances, it is certainly very human. Hoccleve's passages of self-revelation are longer and more numerous than those of any other medieval English poet. In a complex self-portrait, sheer bulk is an important factor, but it is not the only one. Hoccleve succeeds mainly through his willingness to describe fully various aspects of his life and his feelings toward them. His use of lively, colloquial, good-humored direct discourse gives his work a decidedly realistic touch. Few Middle English poems contain autobiographical passages comparable to those of Hoccleve in realism, individuality, and apparent sincerity.

Notes

1. Hoccleve's literary reputation is discussed at length in the first chapter of my doctoral dissertation, "Thomas Hoccleve: His Traditionalism and His Individuality: A Study in Fifteenth-Century English Poetic" (Duke University, 1965).

2. "La Male Regle," the "Complaint," and the "Dialogue" are included in Frederick J. Furnivall's edition of Hoccleve's *Minor Poems*, EETS, E.S., No. 61

(London, 1892). The *Regement of Princes,* also edited by Furnivall, is a separate issue: EETS, E.S., No. 72 (London, 1897). All quotations from Hoccleve follow these texts.

3. *The Transition Period* (Edinburgh and London, 1900), pp. 19-20.

4. The best source of biographical information on Hoccleve other than his poems is Furnivall's "Appendix of Entries about Grants and Payments to Hoccleve, from the Privy-Council Proceedings, the Patent- and Issue-Rolls, and the Record Office," included in the prefatory material to his edition of the *Minor Poems*; hereafter cited in text as "Appendix." A few additional items, most of which have been pointed out before in scattered places, comprise the second appendix to my doctoral dissertation. See also H. S. Bennett's chapter on Hoccleve in *Six Medieval Men and Women* (Cambridge, Eng., 1955), pp. 66-99. For the date of Hoccleve's death, see H. C. Schulz, "Thomas Hoccleve, Scribe," *Speculum*, XII (1937), 76-81.

5. Ed. Walter W. Skeat (Oxford, 1886).

6. *Complete Works of John Gower*, ed. G. C. Macaulay, II (Oxford, 1901).

7. Included in *Chaucerian and Other Pieces*, ed. Walter W. Skeat (Oxford, 1897), pp. 237-44.

8. Ed. Walter W. Skeat, Scottish Text Society, N.S., No. 1, 2nd ed. (Edinburgh and London, 1911).

9. In Capgrave's prose histories, however, a few personal allusions do occur. See Francis Charles Hingeston's introduction to the *Chronicle of England* (London, 1858), pp. xi-xii.

10. *Legendys of Hooly Wummen*, ed. Mary S. Serjeantson, EETS, O.S., No. 206 (London, 1938 [for 1936]).

11. *George Ashby's Poems*, ed. Mary Bateson, EETS, E.S., No. 76 (London, 1899).

12. Included in *Minor Poems of John Lydgate*, ed. Henry Noble MacCracken, Pt. 1, EETS, E.S., No. 107 (London, 1911 [for 1910]), pp. 329-62.

13. *Works of Geoffrey Chaucer*, ed. F. N. Robinson, 2nd ed. (Boston, 1957).

John V. Fleming (essay date 1971)

SOURCE: Fleming, John V. "Hoccleve's *Letter of Cupid* and the 'Quarrel' over the *Roman de la Rose*." *Medium Aevum* 40, no. 1 (1971): 21-40.

[*In this essay, Fleming examines the "Letter of Cupid," Hoccleve's translation of Christine de Pisan's* L'Epistre au Dieu d'Amours. *Instead of seeing the work as a critique of de Pisan's defense of women, Fleming proposes that the "Letter of Cupid" obliquely attacks de Pisan's criticisms of the* Roman de la Rose.]

It is not in the spirit of launching a Hoccleve 'revival' that I would invite a re-examination of Hoccleve's **'Letter of Cupid.'** But poems are historical as well as literary documents, and while no amount of 're-examination' is likely to transform Hoccleve into a major poet on the basis of the **'Letter,'** a close look at that piece can perhaps reveal him as a clever and articulate witness to the literary fortunes of a greater poet and a greater poem, and give some valuable indications of English court taste at the beginning of the fifteenth century. For it seems to me very probable that Hoccleve's **'Letter of Cupid'** is a scholarly Chaucerian's response to the so-called 'Quarrel' over the *Roman de la Rose.*

The **'Letter of Cupid'** is conspicuous among Hoccleve's poems both for its early date and for its subject matter. Written in 1402, when Hoccleve was still a youngish man of about thirty-five, it is by several years the earliest of his dated poems; it was probably his first public work. In fact, it is also one of the best written of his shorter pieces—largely, doubtless, because it seldom departs from its elegant French source, which (as has long been known) was Christine de Pisan's *L'Epistre au dieu d'Amours.* 'In 1402, Hoccleve wrote his **"Letter of Cupid,"**' says Furnivall. 'He based it mainly on Christine de Pisan's *L'Epistre au Dieu d'Amours . . .* needless to say that he never alludes to her.'[1] Skeat similarly drew attention to the French original when he edited the **'Letter'** for his supplementary volume to Chaucer's *Works*: 'This poem is imitated, rather than translated, from the French poem entitled *L'Epistre au Dieu d'Amours,* written by Christine de Pisan in May, 1399. . . . Hoccleve even rearranges some of the material.'[2] Furnivall went so far as to provide a somewhat perfunctory collation of the English and French texts, and Skeat drew attention to a number of passages wholly original with Hoccleve. There the matter has rested, with Hoccleve's poem accurately enough characterized as at once a translation, an imitation, a *précis,* and a rearrangement of Christine's.

So far as its subject matter is concerned, Christine's *Epistre* is a difficult piece to classify. It is usually called a 'defence of women', and so it is; but much of its charm and effectiveness lies in the temperance and judiciousness of its claims on behalf of ladies. Christine avoids countering the absurd generalizations of the clerical misogyny she sets out to refute with unsupportable counter-exaggerations of her own. Thus the *Epistre* is not so much a 'feminist' polemic as an essay in anti-antifeminism, which is not the same thing. Cupid does not deplore the *seigneurie* of men, but the harsh, ungenerous, and unrealistic generalizations of professional misogynist literature, the caricature illustrations to the 'book of wikked wyves'. On the face of it, it seems an odd poem to capture Hoccleve's attention. His muse's interests were narrow: praising and counselling famous men, adoring the Blessed Virgin, scolding heretics,

and trying to get people to pay him his money. The **'Letter'** does not entirely avoid these concerns—it is ostensibly didactic, and it includes a passage, original with Hoccleve, in praise of the Virgin, who 'hath swich excellence þat al to weyk is mannes facultee to declare it'—but it is Hoccleve's only poem dealing with themes usually associated with 'courtly love'. He never translated or composed anything remotely like it again.

In order to talk about Hoccleve's 'artistry' in this poem, a work far from uncommon in an age innocent of the laws of plagiarism, one would be required to do a certain amount of tedious spade work, to sort out the elements of the poem which have been translated, those imitated, those added, and so on; then to attempt some explanation for Hoccleve's strategy in his rearrangements and interpolations. Apart from some useful hints tossed off by Furnivall and Skeat, this has not been done—which may be one of the reasons that nothing noticeably illuminating has ever been said on the subject of the poem's construction and meaning. In so far as the **'Letter of Cupid'** can be said to have a reputation at all, it is a reputation for antifeminism. Thus Derek Pearsall has recently written that: '**"The Letter of Cupid"** (A.D. 1402), a translation of Christine de Pisan's defence of women against detraction, shows that Hoccleve could laugh at women as well as himself.'[3] This remark strikes me as somewhat cryptic, to say the least, since it is not clear on the face of it why a defence of women against detraction should laugh at women; but as a judgment on Hoccleve's poem it is, as we must presently see, part of the thin trickle which is the mainstream of the poem's criticism. The immediate question, however, is not whether a charge of antifeminism against the **'Letter of Cupid'** jibes with scholarly tradition, but whether it jibes with the poem. So far as I can see, it does not. If Hoccleve really turned a defence of women into a joke against women *en translant,* how could he have gone about it? We have already seen that the operations of translation and adaptation which Hoccleve performed on Christine's *Epistre* were complex, and each offered him opportunities significantly to alter its spirit. The technical transformation of Christine's rhyming couplets into rhyme royal stanzas was for Hoccleve only a beginning. He also rearranged the poem substantially, shortened it, and made several additions of his own.

The best copy of the **'Letter,'** in the Ashburnham MS., reorganizes the French text in a curious way. Hoccleve has taken Christine's poem apart as though it were made of so many building blocks, then discarded half the blocks and put the rest back together without paying much attention to their original positions. Another manuscript of the English text (Fairfax MS.), differing very markedly from the Ashburnham MS., is somewhat closer to the French but still by no means very close.[4] So far as I can tell, heresy though it may be against theories of the organic unity of poetry, this rearrangement makes little difference. The ordering of the elements in Christine's poem hardly displays the rigour of a syllogism in any case. Her arguments are gently repetitive and, while not exactly thrown together at random, loosely organized; so far as I can tell Hoccleve has distorted neither the tone nor the thrust of her poem.

The matter of Hoccleve's omissions is a thornier bush. His translation leaves out altogether a number of Christine's arguments, including some amusing and effective ones; but since the whole of her poem is a chain of cognate arguments, it would have been virtually impossible for Hoccleve to have shortened the poem by half (as in effect he did) without disposing of some of them entirely. If this amounts to a kind of editorial special pleading on his part, it is nowhere blatant. The first lengthy passage in the *Epistre* largely dispensed with in the English text argued that men should not generalize about women from a few unfortunate examples, that they should hate not the sinner but the sin (197-258)—a point made sufficiently elsewhere in the text.[5] Hoccleve further neglects Cupid's opinion that antifeminist books, Latin and French, 'plus dient de mençonges qu'uns yvres' (281); he is likewise silent on the good examples of Penelope and others (461 ff.). Only one of the best passages in Christine's poem is lost—a delightful section in which she parodies the ingeniousness of clerical arguments against women, neatly reversing against the clerks one of their own exegetical arguments. Women, says Christine

> ne fu pas (faitte) du lymon de la terre
> Mais seulement de la coste de l'omme,
> Lequel corps ja estoit, c'en est la somme,
> Le plus noble des choses terriennes.
>
> (601-3)

Furnivall thought that at least one of Hoccleve's suppressions (Cupid's statement that books about women would be different had they been written by women) was disingenuous, but this is by no means clear. The fact is that Hoccleve reduced Christine's poem to half its original size without totally neglecting more than a few of her disparate lines of attack. The final test here would seem to be the test of tone. Taken as a whole, Hoccleve's **'Letter'** captures and preserves the tone of Christine's *Epistre*. The editorial excisions needed to compress the French poem to fit the dimensions of the English **'Letter'** inevitably involved some violence, but they did not, so far as I can see, conceal an attack on the spirit, intent, or effectiveness of the original. There is no evidence of antifeminism here either. What of Hoccleve's additions to Christine's text?

Skeat gives a list of the stanzas in the **'Letter'** which seem to be wholly original with Hoccleve, so that it is possible to make a quick and rough-and-ready survey of the translator's interpolations. Stanza 11 says that a man who boasts of his seduction of a woman is worse than the woman; 14 says that men often use a two-faced friend to help their progress. Other men (19), whose dishonourable advances have been rejected by ladies, revenge themselves through lying slanders. 'A foul vice is of tonge to be light' (21). Stanza 24 draws an analogy between the band of the Disciples and womankind: one in twelve was untrue, but

that should not condemn the rest. Men should honour their mothers (26) and not defile their own nests (27). If men were constant, women would love them (39). The final two additions contain the real meat of Hoccleve's own implied arguments, and they must be examined separately and in some detail; but it must be obvious from the gist of Hoccleve's original stanzas so far summarized that his additions can by no stretch of the imagination be said to 'laugh at women'. On the contrary, his original moral commentary is sober if not solemn criticism of some typical vices of men; it points out, without spoiling the case by making extravagantly 'courteous' claims on women's behalf, that a number of the conventional antifeminist arguments are double-edged.

To summarize briefly, we may say that Hoccleve's reorganization of the *Epistre au dieu d'Amours* does not violate its spirit of anti-anti-feminism, that his editorial excisions do not seriously blunt its arguments, and that his own additions do not distort its principal intent. Accordingly, if we wish to agree with Derek Pearsall that 'the **'Letter of Cupid'** . . . shows that Hoccleve could laugh at women' we shall require some other evidence than the text of that poem; for what the text shows is that Hoccleve could fairly represent Christine's best arguments against the conventional extravagances of mediæval literary antifeminism and add a few more of his own. What other evidence is there?

Stowe published the **'Letter of Cupid'** in his edition of Chaucer in 1561, together with the gossipy speculation that Hoccleve had originally called the poem *A Treatise of the conuersation of men and women in the little Island of Albion: which gate hime such hatred among the gentlewomen of the Court, that he was inforced to recant in that book of his, called Planctus proprius.* In a manner not uncommon with Stowe, this is half fiction and half simple error. The preciousness of the title is presumably a Renaissance affectation of the antique: certainly it has no manuscript basis, least of all in the Durham MS. which Stowe annotated; and the poem in which Hoccleve was 'inforced to recant' was not the **'Complaint'** but the **'Dialogue'** [**'Dialogue with a Friend'**]. More to the point, Hoccleve does not 'recant' antifeminism in the **'Dialogue,'** he denies it.

The context of Hoccleve's discussion of the **'Letter'** in his **'Dialogue'** is revealing. In a general discussion of some literary and moral questions with a 'friend', Hoccleve mentions that he has long owed a book to his patron Duke Humphrey, but that illness and depression have kept him from the task. He has considered translating for him the *Epitoma Rei Militaris* of Vegetius, but rejected the plan since Duke Humphrey's proved martial valour shows he has small need of primers of military tactics. The friend then offers a suggestion: why not write something praising women? That will please Duke Humphrey, who enjoys innocent companionship with the ladies, and at the same time placate women offended by his earlier poems:

> 'Euene as thow by scripture hem haast offendid,
> Right so let it be by wrytynge amendid.'[6]

Hoccleve is nonplussed by this report that he has written against women, but the friend is insistent:

> 'Yis, Thomas, yis in thepistle of Cupyde
> Thow haast of hem so largeliche said,
> That they been swartwrooth & ful euele apaid.'
>
> (754-6)

Hoccleve responds by saying that although there may be some things in the **'Letter'** which 'sowneth but right smal to hir honour', he has merely followed his 'Auctour' (which is true) and that it is a gross misrepresentation to say that he has attacked women:

> 'Who-so þat seith I am hir Aduersarie,
> And dispreise hir condicions and port,
> ffor þat I made of hem swich a report,
> He mis-auysed is and eek to blame.
> Whan I it spak I spak conpleynyngly;
> I to hem thoghte no repreef ne shame.
> What world is this how vndirstande am I?
> Looke in the same book what stikith by?
> Who so lookith aright ther-in may see
> Þat they me oghten haue in greet cheertee.'
>
> (768-77)

It is true that taken as a whole, the passages in the **'Dialogue'** which discuss Hoccleve's alleged mysoginism are light-heafted, and even comical: but the gentle laughter is directed not against women, but against those who cannot understand the meaning of a text. That the **'Dialogue'** bears historical testimony to any substantial criticism of antifeminism against the **'Letter of Cupid,'** whether 'among the gentlewomen of the Court' or anywhere else, may be seriously doubted. Rather, the passages in question seem to be Hoccleve's adaptation of the elegant fiction spun by Chaucer in the Prologue to the *Legend of Good Women* which introduces that poem much in the way Hoccleve's **'Dialogue'** introduces his translation of the story of Jereslaus's wife from the *Gesta Romanorum*. In any case, it is possible to sustain a charge of antifeminism against the **'Letter of Cupid'** only if, like Hoccleve's friend, one is irrelevantly impressed by the opinions of the Wife of Bath (694 ff.), or if, again like the friend, one has not actually read the poem (781).

Both the poem and the poet, then, emphatically deny the charge of laughing at women. How is it that the charge could ever have been made, even if only as a part of a playful fiction? I think the answer must be this: while the **'Letter of Cupid'** does not laugh at women in general, it does laugh a little at *one* woman, Christine de Pisan, and this motive in the translation was apprehended by many readers. Hoccleve pokes fun at Christine not for advancing anti-antifeminist arguments with which he himself seems totally in sympathy, let alone for being a woman, but for being a bad literary critic. While he does not go so far as Jean de Montreuil, the 'father of French humanism', who said that Christine was behaving like 'the Greek whore who dared to write against Theophrastus', Hoccleve clearly does imply—at least to those *au courant* of literary and scholarly affairs—that she was making a public fool of herself.

Furnivall thought that Hoccleve could have spared himself trouble if he had but owned up that the **'Letter of Cupid'** was really a translation of Christine's *Epistre*; but it is almost certain that the courtly audience for whom his poem was intended would have already known this. So far as I know, the most relevant fact about the historical importance of the *Epistre*, the circumstance which probably explains why Hoccleve would have known the poem and been interested in it in the first place, has never been brought to bear on the question of his treatment of it. It is true, as Maurice Roy says, that the *Epistre* begins the major phase of Christine's career as a public poet, and that 'nous sommes autorisés à penser que *L'Epistre au dieu d'Amours* eut un retentissement considérable et dût certainement placer Christine au rang des écrivains les plus remarqués';[7] but a chief reason for its wide circulation, quite apart from its intrinsic merit, was its intentionally public and polemic character. It was the first blast of Christine's trumpet against the monstrous regiment of women-haters. And, whatever the circumstances surrounding its actual composition by Christine in 1399, by the time Hoccleve came to translate it in 1402 it had become part of a public *dossier* documenting a *cause célèbre*; for it was the first manifesto of the so-called 'Quarrel' over the *Roman de la Rose*. The 'Quarrel' is usually said to have had its origins in conversations between Christine and Jean de Montreuil in 1400; Jean then wrote a letter or treatise, now lost, defending the *Roman*; Christine replied, Gontier Col joined battle against her, and the 'Quarrel' was well under way.[8] But such an account of the origins of the 'Quarrel', like the accounts given of the immediate causes of most wars, is somewhat arbitrary; in fact, Christine's slur on the *Roman* in her *Epistre* was as good a *causa belli* as another. Her poem was not, it is true, a schematic attack on the *Roman*; Jean de Meun is mentioned only once, in passing, and he receives but a glancing blow. The connection of the poem with the development of the 'Quarrel' is nonetheless likely, it was an 'incident' which presaged a larger attack, and for all we know it may have been the immediate stimulus for Montreuil's supposed lost letter. Certainly, when the *Epistre* was published in the Renaissance it was entitled *Le Contre Rommant de la Rose nomme le Gratia dei*.[9] There is good reason to follow Alfred Coville in viewing the piece as the first document of the 'Quarrel'.[10]

The *Epistre* is ostensibly Cupid's reply to all detractors of women, but the only two misogynists he attacks by name are Ovid and Jean de Meun; the only books, Ovid's and the *Roman de la Rose*. A lady poet who had, as yet, produced no more than a number of polite pieces of promising conventional verse, had attacked the greatest French poet who had ever lived principally on the grounds of alleged antifeminism. My argument in this article is that one of Hoccleve's motives in translating the *Epistre*, as evidenced by two skilful additions to the French text, is to engage himself on the side of Christine's opponents in the controversy over the *Roman de la Rose* which her poem had initiated and her further attacks had protracted.

The intrepid explorer of the intellectual history of Europe in the late fourteenth century frequently must hesitate by the banks of swift streams of uncertain depth; for often he will find no serviceable bridges built for his amenity by the scholarly giants of old, or only rickety and treacherous ones. Such a stream is the so-called 'Quarrel' about the *Roman de la Rose,* a unique episode in the history of mediæval vernacular literature. For a period of several years, beginning in 1399 with the publication of the French original of the **'Letter'** which is the subject of this article, a number of the top people of France publicly and energetically argued about France's top poem. Epistles were penned, dispatched, copied, and circulated; there followed more letters, defence and counter-attack, and a couple of sermons. The Chancellor of the University of Paris experienced a literary vision. The 'Quarrel' was, in short, a notable affair, remarkable for its distinguished participants no less than for its subject matter, and charged with extraordinary suggestion for the student of literary allegory in the age of Chaucer. The documents in the debate have, for the most part, long since been edited, and the episode has been the subject of a certain amount of serious historical analysis. The 'Quarrel' is well known, but badly understood. 'Nous le verrons de mieux en mieux . . .' wrote André Combes some years ago, 'l'histoire du débat relatif au Roman de la Rose est à peine ébauchée.'[11]

Combes's strictures are directed against serious scholarly confusion concerning various *minutiae* of the 'Quarrel', well illustrated by the many infelicities of C. F. Ward's edition of the documents in the debate.[12] But such philological deficiencies were venial sins; what has chiefly impeded a fruitful understanding of the 'Quarrel' is not the imperfection of accessible texts of the polemical documents so much as the faulty historical perspective from which they have been viewed.[13] The trouble is that the two censors of the *Roman,* Christine de Pisan and Jean Gerson, are much more famous than their opponents in the debate, Jean de Montreuil and the brothers Col. They have had, for the most part, a 'good press'; and the chief discussions of the 'Quarrel' have been in the context of approving assessments of the work of one or other of them. The most extensive discussion of the 'Quarrel' is in a biography of Christine de Pisan, where the actual issues in the debate, and the positions taken, fight a losing battle against the author's hero (or rather heroine) worship.[14] Gerson's admirers are likely to maintain that the 'Quarrel' was 'the old conflict, so often repeated when the spirit of Art for Art's Sake runs afoul of sober judgement';[15] Gerson is supposed to have taken up Christine's cause out of 'concern for the spiritual welfare of the ordinary Christian faithful. . . . Though more than a century old, the *Romance,* with its contempt for the Christian ideals of chastity and its frank encouragement to uncurbed indulgence of natural pleasures, as well as its philosophic determinism, was judged by Gerson to contain both moral and intellectual dangers.'[16] So far as these particular judgments are concerned, the chief objection is simple historical implausibility. The 'spirit of *Art for Art's Sake*' was a most unfamiliar spirit in Parisian clerical circles; and 'the ordinary Christian

faithful', who were illiterate, were unlikely either to read the *Roman* or to be rescued from its intellectual dangers by Latin sermons preached at the University. But a more serious objection is that no account of the 'Quarrel' which assumes the unquestionable rightness of the case for censorship is likely to yield an illuminating analysis, since the entirely indisputable fact is that the points of view taken by Christine and Gerson were, so far as the poem's reputation can bear witness, novel and eccentric.[17]

Fortunately, there is now a brief account of the 'Quarrel' which neglects neither the relevant primary materials in the debate nor the relevant historical background, and which can serve as a safe introduction to the principal intellectual problems raised by the episode.[18] Christine and Gerson attacked the *Roman de la Rose* from quite different points of view. Of the two critics, Gerson is unquestionably the more interesting mind; and, for the broader cultural implications raised by the 'Quarrel', his impressive *Traité* is perhaps the most important of all the documents in the dossier. But he cannot be considered here since the *Traité* comes too late (it is dated 18 May, 1402) to have had a bearing on Hoccleve's translation of the *Epistre.* So far as Christine is concerned—and it is of course her attitude to the *Roman* which is relevant to the discussion of Hoccleve's **'Letter'**—the objections to the *Roman de la Rose* are two: it is antifeminist, and it is filthy. With regard to the first point she cites the long speeches of La Vieille and 'Jalousie' (she means, of course, the Jaloux); and as evidence of smut she refers to the end of the poem, and to the fact that Dame Reason openly refers to Saturn's testicles by their quite proper French name of *coilles.*

Taken at face value, neither of Christine's principal arguments seems very telling, or even very intelligent; and her squeamishness about calling *coilles coilles* borders on the ludicrous in light of the passage in the *Roman,* one of Jean de Meun's greatest comic *coups,* where the lecherous Lover registers similar sensitivity to the obscenities of 'God's daughter' Lady Reason. It is probably worth mentioning that the late Rosamond Tuve, who yielded to none in her admiration of Christine, found this line of argument so extraordinary that she concluded that Christine's posture in the 'Quarrel' had been largely whimsical. There is no real evidence that Christine's opponents thought she was joking, though it must be said that throughout the 'Quarrel' the attitude of the brothers Col remained good-natured if not light-hearted, and even the Ciceronian epistles of Jean de Montreuil sparkle with laughter. Gerson's *Traité* changed all that: no guffaws from him, or even smiles. But when Hoccleve responded to the 'Quarrel' in 1402 with his **'Letter,'** the affair was by no means mirthless.

That the **'Letter'** *is* a response to the 'Quarrel' is strongly suggested both by the date of its appearance and (more importantly) by Hoccleve's final editorial interpolations into Christine's text. The *Epistre* is dated May 1399, and the next document in the debate is the supposed 'lost treatise' of Montreuil, which it had perhaps provoked, hypothetically assigned by Piaget to late 1400 or early 1401. The year 1401 saw a flurry of letters—Christine's response to the 'lost treatise', Gontier Col's quite remarkable piece of 15 September, and Christine's spirited and unrepentant response. It is clear from references in the correspondence that, all along, the affair was considered public, but Christine took steps to ensure not only that it was public, but that it would become a *cause célèbre*. In late 1401 or early 1402 she gathered together the correspondence to date into *dossiers* and sent them, apparently for chivalric adjudication, to Isabeau de Bavière, the French queen, and Guillaume de Tignonville, Provost of Paris.[19] Hoccleve's '**Letter**' is of course dated May 1402; but both Furnivall and Skeat were of the opinion that while Christine's *Epistre* actually *was* written in May as suggested in the text, the date in Hoccleve's translation is mere imitation. Neither assumption is absolutely safe since (1) May is Cupid's month, but (2) people *do* sometimes actually write things in May—witness Gerson's *Traité*; hence it is possible that Christine is being imitative, and Hoccleve literal. We are perhaps justified in saying no more than that the '**Letter**' was written in 1402, and that it shows no evidence that Hoccleve was aware of Gerson's entry into the 'Quarrel'. The likelihood, then, is that Hoccleve had seen a copy of one of Christine's *dossiers*, which clearly must have circulated widely outside the immediate circle of the contending parties to judge from surviving copies.[20] While it cannot be positively established that there was a copy in London in 1402, the suggestion is reasonable. The unfortunate nature of Anglo-French relations at the time did not keep a copy of Christine's *Epistre*, at any rate, out of Westminster Palace at a time when that poem was chiefly famous as a document in the 'Quarrel'.

H. S. Bennett maintains that 'on the whole Hoccleve had not a sensitive alert mind'.[21] But if we accept this judgment at all, it appears that the '**Letter of Cupid**' shows him at his exceptional best, where, indeed, mental agility is his conspicuous virtue. For what Hoccleve really 'does' to Christine's poem, without for a moment vitiating its effectiveness as a piece of anti-antifeminism, is very cleverly, by means of two skilful additions to her text, to render it harmless as an attack on the *Roman*. In the first place he calls to the witness box in defence of Jean de Meun the greatest English poet of the Middle Ages, Geoffrey Chaucer; and, secondly, he forcefully draws attention to the blunder in literary criticism on which the attacks on the *Roman de la Rose* had been founded.

Christine mentions in the *Epistre* (437 ff.) the examples of Medea and Dido, two faithful women cruelly deceived by men, and Hoccleve translates the passage without comment (st. 44 and 45). But Hoccleve knew, as Christine perhaps did not know, that the histories of those two noble ladies had already been incorporated in the canon of Love's martyrology, so that he makes Cupid go on to say (st. 46):

> In our legende of martirs may men fynde,
>   who-so þat lykith ther-in for to rede,

> That ooth noon ne byheeste may men bynde:
>   Of repreef ne of shame han they no drede;
>   In herte of man conceites trewe arn dede;
>   The soile is naght ther may no trouthe growe:
>   To womman is hir vice nat vnknowe.

The reference to the *Legend of Good Women* here is entirely apt for a brief against male fickleness since there are indeed a number of men mentioned in that poem who behaved very badly toward their women. But the allusion is also relevant as regards the *Roman de la Rose,* since according to the light-hearted fiction of its Prologue, the *Legend of Good Women* was written as a penance for literary offences against the god of Love Chaucer had anticipated Christine in presenting Cupid as a literary critic presiding over a Star Chamber for the suppression of naughty books. In the Prologue of the *Legend of Good Women* the two works of Chaucer's singled out for proscription are the translation of the *Roman de la Rose* and *Troilus and Criseyde*. Speaking rather loosely, one may say that Cupid's complaint against *Troilus* is 'antifeminism'; it is the story of a bad woman for which a collection of stories about good women might be an appropriate reparation. But the god's charge against the *Roman* is not antifeminism but 'heresye'; for in that poem Jean de Meun portrays sexual passion as a kind of folly, and counsels wise readers to flee Cupid:

> Thou hast translated the Romauns of the Rose,
> That is an heresye ageyns my lawe,
> And makest wyse folk fro me withdrawe.
> And thinkest in thy wit, that is ful cool,
> That he nis but a verray propre fool
> That loveth paramours, to harde and hote.

> (A255-60)

Needless to say, such a characterization of the *Roman* has little in common with currently fashionable scholarly opinion about that poem, which derives largely from the schools of 'courtly love' on the one hand (C. S. Lewis) and 'scolastique courtoise' on the other (Gérard Paré); but it does have the advantage of corresponding very closely indeed with the view of the *Roman* put forward by the defenders of Jean de Meun at the time of the 'Quarrel', particularly in the fine essay of Pierre Col. D. W. Robertson, whose brief but brilliant analysis of the *Roman* has brushed away some of the cobwebs spun around Jean's poem since the time of the 'Quarrel', has rightly drawn attention to this evidence of Chaucer's attitude toward the great work of his old 'auctor'.[22] Hoccleve's quiet insertion of Cupid's *Legende of Martirs* does the same thing.

Chaucer's defence of himself in the Prologue of the *Legend of Good Women* is entirely adequate. Alceste attempts to get him off the hook by pleading, on his behalf, diminished responsibility: 'he wroot the Rose and eek Crisseyde / Of innocence, and niste what he seyde' (A344-5). Chaucer, however, not disposed to acquiesce in a plea of imbecility, maintains that he *did* know what he was doing:

> Ne a trewe lover oghte me nat blame,
> Thogh that I speke a fals lover som shame,

They oghte rather with me for to holde,
For that I of Cresseyde wroot or tolde,
Or of the Rose; what-so myn auctour mente,
Algate, god wot, hit was myn entente
To forthren trouthe in love and hit cheryce;
And to be war fro falsnesse and fro vyce
By swich ensample; this was my meninge.

(A456-65)

Whatever truth there may be in this argument about the *Roman* and *Troilus,* or in any other arguments he might put forward, is not likely to launch any boats in Cupid's ocean since 'Love ne wol nat countrepleted be / In right ne wrong' (A466-7). Such a policy of dictatorial whim well befits a polite personification of *cupido,* or irrational passion; but Hoccleve himself seems to have found Chaucer's argument more compelling. We have already seen that Chaucer's Prologue provided Hoccleve with the inspiration for the discussion of antifeminism in the **'Dialogue,'** and elsewhere he appropriates Chaucer's arguments, and his words, to defend himself against charges such as those reported by his friend:

To goode wommen shal it be no shame
Al thogh þat thow vnhonest wommen blame.[23]

In the **Regement of Princes** Hoccleve calls Chaucer 'the mirour of fructuous entendement'; whatever precisely he may have meant by this, he presumably cannot have considered Chaucer a pornographer and a bully. Yet Christine's attack on the *Roman,* a poem which Chaucer had translated and which had left its mark on practically every page he ever wrote, insisted on Jean de Meun's misogynism and his lubricity. If Jean had undertaken a 'lewede occupaccioun' in writing the *Roman,* what of 'virtuous' Chaucer, *grant translateur*? If we knew no more than Chaucer's reverence for the *Roman,* and Hoccleve's for Chaucer, there would be a strong *a priori* case for believing that Hoccleve would be much more likely to associate himself with Jean de Montreuil and the brothers Col in the 'Quarrel' than with Christine de Pisan. His adroit use of allusion to the *Legend of Good Women* in his translation of Christine's *Epistre* removes the matter entirely from doubt. Cupid claims by lawful right the poem written especially for him by a penitent English poet; but in, appropriating the *exempla* of Chaucer's 'good women', Cupid cannot but revive, in the minds of English readers, his own quarrel with the poet about the *Roman de la Rose,* the playful debate which strikingly anticipates the quite serious exchange of letters and invective taking place in Paris in 1402. Chaucer had maintained against the god of Love, whose only argument was wilful *fiat,* that his aim in translating the *Roman* had been 'to forthren trouthe in love' (cf. Eph. iv:15), and 'to be war fro falsnesse and fro vyce'. Similarly for Pierre Col the *Roman* was rich in teachings 'to follow all virtues and flee all vices'. The forty-sixth stanza of Hoccleve's **'Letter of Cupid'** raises the ghost of Geoffrey Chaucer to defend the French poet at whose feet he had learned the major skills of his craft against unprecedented and intemperate attack.

Hoccleve realizes a satiric and ironic end within the **'Letter of Cupid'** without marring its glossy enamel finish with open parody or brash intrusion. The poem remains the elegant essay in anti-antifeminism it was for Christine, but for readers who held the memory of Chaucer dear, its force as a polemic against Jean de Meun must have been spent in gentle laughter. This is a most skilful poetic achievement, and one important to appreciate. Hoccleve applauds Christine's canons of courtesy, but suggests that Christine has misapplied them to Jean de Meun's poem. If his translating really 'gate him such hatred among the gentlewomen of the Court, that he was inforced to recant' it cannot be because the **'Letter of Cupid'** sullies the good name of women which Christine had set out to defend, but because it amusingly suggests the irrelevance of a charge of antifeminism in a public debate about the *Roman de la Rose.*

A word must be said about the alleged misogynism of Jean de Meun's part of the *Roman de la Rose* itself, since it is at the heart of Christine's attitude in the *Epistre* and since it nicely exemplifies the larger problem of literary criticism at the heart of the entire 'Quarrel'. It has become a cherished *cliché* of literary history that Jean de Meun 'hated women', and that he turned Guillaume de Lorris's allegory of courtly idealism into a bourgeois-realistic satire 'against many aspects of mediæval life, but especially women'. As is often the case, the fiction of the critics is here greater than the fiction of poets. Claude Fauchet (Jean de Meun's Stowe, as it were) puts the matter into perspective. The ladies of the court—perennially in arms against the poets so far as Renaissance antiquaries can be believed—are supposed to have once captured Jean de Meun to thrash him soundly for the way he had treated them. Jean agreed to the punishment, provided that it be administered by 'la plus forte putain de toutes celles que i'ay blasmees'.[24] There is more in the story than just a good laugh. It is true that Jean *used* some of the materials of traditional mediæval antifeminism—just as he used materials from virtually every major literary tradition, and it is also true that antifeminist comedians of the fourteenth and fifteenth centuries cited the *Roman* as an 'authority'.[25] On the other hand, readers used the *Roman* on a great many subjects including philosophy, theology, and ethics. But this was, in effect, to treat the *Roman* as an encyclopedia, and some readers, alert to its dramatic integrity, insisted on treating it as a poem instead. For example, there is a fourteenth-century French *débat* poem in which a married and an unmarried man argue the excellences of their respective states. One of the arguments marshalled by the bachelor, on the authority of the *Roman,* is that women are notoriously unfaithful. The married man counters in a surprising way:

Quant est du livre de la Rose
Il n'en parle que bien a point
Et, qui bien entend la glose,
Des femmes il ne mesdit point.[26]

Chaucer knew the 'glose'; so, apparently, did Hoccleve. It involves none of the 'glorious' and mysterious hermeneutics of Friar John in the 'Summoner's Tale', merely the common sense of literary decorum.

The principal 'antifeminist' episode in the *Roman* is to be found in Amis's discourse to Amant (beginning at l. 8425 in the new Lecoy edition); Amis first describes the grotesque plight of the Jealous Husband and then actually brings the Jaloux onto the stage, so to speak, to dramatize his attitudes. The Jaloux, of course, speaks in the manner of the absurd buffoon he is and, in this context, delivers the antifeminist monologue for which the *Roman* is famous. Now it was pointed out five and a half centuries ago by Pierre Col, and more recently by Lionel Friedman, that to accuse Jean de Meun of antifeminism on the basis of this text is to fall somewhat short of sound literary criticism. Friedman points out that both Amis and the Jaloux are stock characters of academic comedy, and he concludes that there is no justifiable critical basis for confusing opinions expressed by them with Jean de Meun's own opinions.[27]

As the unpublished commentary to the Old French *Echecs Amoureux* puts it, the *Roman de la Rose* is that kind of allegory in which 'several characters appear in turn and speak according to their natures'.[28] That is to say, the *Roman de la Rose* is dramatic. It might at first appear that the dramatic integrity and autonomy of the *personae* in a poem of this sort would be taken for granted as a matter of common sense. We do not often hear it said that beginning in 1595 Shakespeare was determined to be a villain, or that after 1604 evil had become his good. But we do hear that for Jean de Meun 'love is simply an expression of the reproductive instinct, and this he regards as wholly and necessarily good . . . something to be followed at all times and in all circumstances, something that ought not to be confined by any regulations or institutions'.[29] The question of dramatic decorum in the *Roman* has been, historically, a crucial one for the poem's interpretation; it has proved to be a *pons asinorum* for critics from the time of the 'Quarrel' down to our own day. One of Jean de Montreuil's letters recently made accessible in the splendid edition of his *Epistolario* states the issue with admirable clarity. Of those who attack the *Roman* he justly says: 'Qui de personatuum varietate non discernunt, seu notant quibus passionibus moreantur aut induantur affectibus et quem ad finem quave dependentia aut quamobrem sint loquuti, nec quod demum satirici is instructor fungitur officio, quo respectu plura licent, que aliis actoribus prohibentur.'[30] Some few of the objects of Jean de Meun's satire have been allowed by the critics to live in their own 'variety'; so far as I know the long Faussemblant 'chapter' has escaped autobiographical interpretation. But in order to make Jean an antifeminist it is necessary to equate him with an absurdly jealous fool or an old whore, and to make him the sex mystic described by Professor Cohn, Jean's own views must be identical with those of his character Genius, a personification of natural concupiscence.

The last major addition Hoccleve made to the text of Christine's *Epistre* exposes this very serious confusion which lies behind her attack on Jean de Meun. As he approaches the end of his reorganization of her poem, Hoccleve expands Christine's lines in praise of the Virgin (st. 59 and 60). Somewhat unexpectedly, Cupid then moves on to praise the martyr St. Margaret: 'Thow precious gemme . . . O constant womman . . . holy virgyne.' But even more unexpected, in light of the tone established by Christine's poem, is the following stanza, 62, in which Cupid qualifies his praise:

> But vndirstondith We commende hir noght
> By encheson of hir virginitee:
> Trustith right wel it cam nat in our thought,
> For ay We werreie ageyn chastitee,
> And euere shal but this leeueth wel yee:
> Hir louyng herte and constant to hir lay,
> Dryue out of remembrance we nat may.

This passage, wholly original with Hoccleve, is in its context in the **'Letter of Cupid'** very startling. 'This stanza is spoken by Cupid in his own character,' says Skeat in his editorial notes. 'It is, moreover, obvious that this stanza would hardly have been approved of by Christine.' Of course not; but the speaker in the poem is *supposed* to be Cupid, god of Love, son of Venus Citherea. It is his letter, not Christine's. The ostensible form of the *Epistre au dieu d'Amours* is that of a 'dramatic monologue'. There is on the face of it no more reason that Christine should approve its sentiments than that Browning should approve the sentiments expressed in 'My Last Duchess'—or that Jean de Meun should in his own person agree with everything that *his* fictional creations say. But the fact of the matter is that Christine's poem does not work this way, as Hoccleve rather brilliantly demonstrates. Whatever else may be said of Christine's allegorical poetry, it cannot be given high marks for clever indirection or iconographic sophistication. Her allegorical veil is spun of fine transparent silk; it richly adorns, but barely conceals. When Cupido speaks in the *Epistre*, the voice is Christine's. There is no great distance between the poet and the fictive speaker in the poem, who is in a quite limited sense a mouthpiece. Indeed, what is startling about st. 62 is that for a moment Cupid stops talking like Christine and talks like himself. Hoccleve teaches Christine how to read the *Roman* by shock treatment.

What one makes of the *Roman* depends in large measure upon what one makes of its *dramatis personae,* since as Jean de Montreuil remarks the satirist operates through the manipulation of *personae*. For Christine the god Cupid seems a proper arbiter of French chivalry. So he did to Thomas Bradwardine who in his victory sermon after Crecy listed among the execrable vices of the French knights which had sapped their manliness and offended God the stinking sin of lechery. 'Errorem septimum amplexantes,' he says, 'simulari videntur antiquis gentilibus colentibus Hymeneum sive Cupidinem, deum carnalis amoris.'[31] Christine's canons of sexual seemliness, as is well known, were severe: she was scandalized by the very mention of the word *coilles,* even when it came from the mouth of the daughter of God. It is accordingly unlikely that she revered the memory of Hutin de Vermeilles or Odo de Grandson because they had been famous fornicators; yet there they are in her poem, Cupid's unofficial saints. Obviously, Bradwardine and Christine are not talking about the same dainty god. The bishop had in mind the *dieu d'Amours* of the *Roman de la Rose,* whose poetic function is left in doubt neither by his inconographic attributes nor by the explicit mythographic tradition of such poems as Alain de Lille's *De planctu Naturae,* Jean de Meun's richest quarry. The god of Love in the *Roman* is the son of Venus and brother to Jocus, called Deduit in French, into whose garden Amant is admitted by Oiseuse (Idleness).[32] Amant's subjection to Cupid involves the formal abjuration of Reason, clearly associated with the sapiential Christ by both Guillaume de Lorris and Jean. And so it goes on: the god of Love has a firm mythographic identity *in malo* which crucially qualifies the *Roman's* religion of love and activates the ironies of its principal action. In Christine's *Epistre,* on the other hand, Cupido is merely a vaguely benign force, made elegant and slightly exotic with handbook mythology, who represents a chivalrous attitude towards women. Hoccleve draws the reader up short by giving him a glimpse of Jean's Cupid momentarily superimposed on Christine's. 'For ay We werreie ageyn chastitee.' With its obvious Chaucerian echo of passionate Palamon's oath to Venus to become her 'trewe servant' and 'holden werre alwey with chastitee', Hoccleve's line must remind us of those techniques of dramatic allegory of which Christine herself is innocent but which his master Chaucer had found so brilliantly exploited by Jean de Meun.

A common critical view of the *Roman* has it that its two authors reflect contrasting poetic visions—that of the one (Guillaume de Lorris) 'courtly' or 'chivalric idealism'; that of the other (Jean de Meun) 'bourgeois realism'. And Huizinga, among others, would see the 'Quarrel' in terms of a clash of such attitudes as they focus on the subject of love. This line of attack has been manifestly fruitless in terms of tenable criticism of the *Roman de la Rose,* and its usefulness for discussing the 'Quarrel' is extremely questionable. Thomas Bradwardine was not a 'bourgeois realist'. Neither was Jacques Legrand, who told Isabeau de Bavière to her face that Venus ruled her court—a remark neither offered nor received as a compliment, but nonetheless a remark motivated by 'courtly idealism'.[33] Both men were courtiers, and the differences between their treatments of amorous mythology and Christine's cannot be explained by reference to fictitious social distinctions. Similarly, the 'Quarrel' was a debate between a group of literary critics (all of whom were 'courtly'), not an obscure early episode in the Class War. The questions raised by the 'Quarrel' have little to do with sociology, but a good deal to do with the theory of allegory, principles of literary criticism and literary taste.

The formal arguments advanced by Christine and Gerson against the *Roman* have this much in common: from the point of view of both mediæval literary theory and literary practice, they are obtuse and naïve. Their shared argument seems to be a smokescreen for saying that some ideas are so nasty or so horrible that it is disgraceful to broach them under any circumstances. One must never say 'coilles', just as one must never say (no matter with what tone of irony) that all good fornicators will go to Heaven. Perhaps it is no longer possible to talk about Jean de Meun's Cupid at all, and still be courteous. But if we choose to call this kind of squeamish inhibition 'courtly' or 'chivalric', surely there is some obligation to justify the adjectives by reference to actual courtly and chivalric institutions. What might be called the chivalric scene in France at the end of the fourteenth century was complex. While the widespread disillusion about the Schism and the disastrous war with England clearly bred despair in some circles, it also stimulated a new wave of chivalric idealism. Some of the manifestations of the 'courtesy' of the period are, from the point of view of stylistic history, altogether fascinating; and their possible connections with changing styles in 'courtly' literature is an intriguing question crying out for close and careful study, though only a word or two can be said about it here.

After the death of Odo de Grandson in a trial by combat which sadly reflects some of the ambiguities of 'courtesy', the two most vocal chivalric figures in France were probably the saintly Philippe de Mézières and the *maréchal* Boucicault; both men founded new chivalric orders. Philippe's, the Order of the Passion of Jesus Christ, had as its grandiose and visionary aim the permanent security of the Holy Land and the safeguard of the pilgrimage routes, while Boucicault's Order of the Green Shield was dedicated to the protection of women: God and the ladies, indeed! It must be admitted that both these new orders, seen from one point of view, were rather like the military band organized by Tom Sawyer. They formulated an impressive protocol of dragon-slaying, but produced few dead dragons. Still, the kind of spiritual and literary attitudes represented by Mézières, who was among other things a fluent allegorist, are most suggestive for an analysis of the 'Quarrel'. Philippe's holiness insulated him totally from bourgeois realism, yet his attitude toward Jean de Meun's *Roman* is indicated by his approving citation of it in the *Songe du viel pelerin.*[34]

A connection between the 'Quarrel' and the order founded by Boucicault and a dozen friends for the defence of persecuted women was taken for granted by Maurice Roy, partly because of the date of the order's foundation (April 1400) and partly because he believed Christine to be the author of the anonymous *Livre des faicts,* Boucicault's biography.[35] The case is not compelling, and the *maréchal's* order remains largely obscure. The knights wore as an emblem 'vne targe d'or esmaillee de verd, a tout vne Dame blanche dedans'[36]—but whether they ever actually did anything we are not told. It seems evident from their rule, at any rate, that their conception of chivalric *Frauendienst* is better reflected by Duke Theseus' championing of the Theban widows than by the Wife of Bath's burning her husband's copy of *Wikked Wyves.* Christine's tactics in the 'Quarrel' reveal her as both clever and resilient, whatever capital she might try to make out of being a defenceless woman; it is difficult to see her playing Dulcinea to Bouci-cault's Quixote.

Christine is supposed to have been greatly encouraged, once again according to M. Roy, by the foundation of the *Cour amoureuse* by Philip the Bold and Charles VI on St. Valentine's day, 1401.[37] This 'whimsical academy' (to use Richard Vaughan's nice phrase) is for the literary scholar perhaps the most promising of the chivalric foundations of the period, and seems at first glance particularly promising in its suggestions about the 'Quarrel'. Of the two known recipients of Christine's *dossiers,* one was Isabeau de Bavière, wife of Charles VI, and the other was Guillaume de Tignonville, Provost of Paris and one of the twenty-four *ministres* of the *Cour amoureuse*. The trouble with this line of argument is that Gontier Col was also a *minis-tre,* a fact which 'astonished' M. Roy.[38] Since Charles VI was mad much of the time, and Isabeau de Bavière shared her throne with Venus, one might hope that the *Cour amoureuse* would reveal the exotic naughtiness of 'courtly love' come true at last. Instead, it seems to have been no more than an elaborate *puy* and dining club, organized to take people's minds off the plague.[39] In addition to writing suitable love poems and courteous praises of ladies, its 'amorous' members (practically all of whom were either married or professional celibates) were expected, on one of her five great feast days, to write in honour of the most noble Lady of all, 'dame des angeles et mere de nostre tres doulz createur, advocatte de tous amoureux cueurs'.[40] Charles VI owned at least three copies of the *Roman de la Rose,* so that any of the *ministres* who wished to examine Christine's charges against the primary text would not have had far to go.[41] Yet there is no record that the *Cour amoureuse* as a body ever examined Cupid's brief against Jean de Meun. The only official ministerial opinion which has survived, Gontier Col's, claims Jean was a 'vray catholique, solennel maistre, et docteur en son temps en sainct theologie, philosophe tresperfont et excellent, sa-chant tout ce qui a entendement humain est scible'.[42]

Robertson has characterized the 'Quarrel' as an invaluable 'indication of a change in taste which took place in certain quarters after the death of Chaucer'.[43] In this respect, at least, the *Cour amoureuse* and other manifestations of the moist chivalry of the Middle Ages in decline are relevant to the study of the controversy. Clearly enough, the 'amorous' deeds performed by the civil servants and rank-ing prelates gathered at banquet in the Hôtel de Bourgogne differed from the amorous deeds of the young hero of the *Roman de la Rose*. The gentile god who, according to Bradwardine, could be nothing but the 'incentor luxuriae et nutritor' presides with Victorian propriety over Christine de Pisan's Order of the Rose, now a fumigated flower, and wanders innocently at will through the lyrics of Charles d'Orleans and a dozen other poets. All this is not simply a matter of iconographic nuance; it testifies to marked shifts in taste, and a softening of the Gothic conventions of 'humanistic' allegory, of which Jean de Meun's *Roman de la Rose* was the greatest monument.

From this point of view, Hoccleve's attitude as indicated by his clever handling of Christine's *Epistre* may perhaps be considered old-fashioned. Certainly he was champion-ing a poem which had had its day, and which would never again father a Machaut, or a Deschamps, or a Chaucer. Perhaps to be unstylish was also to be impolite, and to invite the groundless charge of antifeminism which sup-posedly links the 'Quarrel' with courtly attitudes. Here one would like to know what is fact and what fiction in the passage in Hoccleve's **'Dialogue'** dealing with the public reputation of the **'Letter of Cupid,'** since aside from the **'Letter'** itself the jocular exchange between poet and friend represents the only indication we have of what the attitude of English court circles toward the 'Quarrel' was likely to have been. As for Hoccleve, both the occasion of his translation and the motives behind his subtle but tell-ing interpolations seem certain; and when a complete and accurate edition of the documents in the debate of the *Ro-man de la Rose* is put together, the relevant passages from the **'Letter of Cupid'** should claim a place.

Notes

1. EETS, ES 61 p. xi.

2. *Chaucerian and Other Pieces* (Oxford 1897) p. 499.

3. 'The English Chaucerians' in *Chaucer and Chaucerians* ed. D. S. Brewer (London 1966) p. 225.

4. The Ashburnham MS. was published by Israel Gol-lancz in *Hoccleve's Works* II (EETS, ES 73) pp. 20-34, and my references are to this text. The differ-ences in the ordering of the stanzas in the Ashburnham and Fairfax MSS. are noted by Furni-vall, EETS, ES 61 p. 92.

5. References are to *L'Epistre au dieu d'Amours* in *Œuvres poétiques de Christine de Pisan* ed. Maurice Roy (Paris 1891) II 1-27.

6. Ll. 699-700; references to the 'Dialogue' in *Hoc-cleve's Works* I ed. Furnivall pp. 110-39.

7. *Œuvres de Christine* II vii.

8. A. Piaget 'Chronologie des *Epistres sur le Roman de la Rose*' in *Etudes romanes dédiées à Gaston Paris* (Paris 1891) pp. 113-20.

9. *Œuvres de Christine* II ix.

10. *Gontier et Pierre Col et l'humanisme en France au temps de Charles VI* (Paris 1934) p. 194.

11. *Jean de Montreuil et le Chancelier Gerson* (Paris 1942) p. 39.

12. *The Epistles on the Romance of the Rose and Other Documents in the Debate* ed. C. F. Ward (Chicago 1911); see the review by E. Langlois in *Kritischer Jahresbericht über die Fortschritte der romanischen Philologie* XIII (1913/14) ii 61-3.

13. E.g., the discussion of the 'Quarrel' by J. Huizinga *The Waning of the Middle Ages* (London 1924) pp. 102 ff., despite some brilliant suggestions, is funda-

mentally misleading both in its account of the *Roman* and its analysis of the documents in the debate. Important views on the 'Quarrel' are summarized by Franco Simone *Il Rinascimento Francese* (2nd ed., Turin 1965) p. 245.

14. M. J. Pinet *Christine de Pisan* (Paris 1927) pp. 64-87.

15. James L. Connolly *John Gerson Reformer and Mystic* (Louvain 1927) p. 124.

16. John B. Morrall *Gerson and the Great Schism* (Manchester 1960) p. 12.

17. For the evidence see 'The Moral Reputation of the *Roman de la Rose* Before 1400' *Romance Philology* XVIII (1965) 430-5.

18. D. W. Robertson *A Preface to Chaucer* (Princeton 1962) pp. 361 ff.

19. Piaget 'Chronologie des *Espistres*' p. 118.

20. There are at least four copies in the Bibliothèque Nationale alone: MSS. fr. 835, 604, 1563, 12779. See Léopold Delisle *Recherches sur la librairie de Charles V* (Paris 1907) II 270* no. 292 *bis*.

21. *Chaucer and the Fifteenth Century* (Oxford 1947) p. 149.

22. *Preface to Chaucer* p. 104.

23. *Hoccleve's Works* I 218.

24. *Les Œuvres de feu M. Claude Fauchet* (Paris 1610) p. 590ᵛ. Hoccleve may have known this joke, or a similar one, since he has his 'friend' say with regard to his own supposed antifeminism: 'No womman wole to thee ward maligne, / But swich oon as hath trode hir shoo amis', *Hoccleve's Works* I 218.

25. *Recueil de farces françaises inédites du XVᵉ siècle* ed. G. Cohen (Cambridge, Mass. 1949) p. 55.

26. *Recueil de poésie françoise* ed. Anatole de Montaiglon (Paris 1865) IX 161.

27. '"Jean de Meung", Antifeminism, and "Bourgeois Realism"' *Modern Philology* LVII (1959) 13-23.

28. Bibliothèque nationale MS. fr. 9197 f. 14ʳ.

29. Norman Cohn *The World-View of a Thirteenth-Century Parisian Intellectual* (Durham 1961) p. 16.

30. Jean de Montreuil *Opera* ed. E. Ornato I (Turin 1963) 220-1. Gerson was cognizant of the principle of dramatic decorum; it is the affirmative proposition which 'Theological Eloquence' sets out to refute (but fails to) in his *Traité* ed. E. Langlois *Romania* XLV (1918/19) 33-4.

31. 'The *Sermo Epinicius* Ascribed to Thomas Bradwardine (1346)' ed. H. A. Oberman & J. A. Weisheipl *Archives d'histoire doctrinale et littéraire du Moyen Age* XXV (1958) 323.

32. Such is the mythographic analysis of the exegete of the *Echecs Amoureux* in Bibliothèque nationale MS. fr. 9197 f. 197ʳ.

33. 'In tua curia domina Venus solium occupans, ipsi eciam obsequntur ebrietas et commessacio, que noctes vertunt in diem, continuantes choreas dissolutas.' *Chronique du religieux de Saint-Denys* ed. L. Bellaguet (Paris 1839-52) III 268.

34. *Le Songe du Vieil Pelerin* ed. G. W. Coopland (Cambridge 1969) I 625.

35. *Œuvres poétiques de Christine* II ii-iv.

36. *Histoire de Mre Iean de Bovcicavlt* ed. Theodore Godefroy (Paris 1620) p. 145.

37. *Œuvres poétiques de Christine* II pp. x-xi; see also A. Piaget 'La Cour Amoureuse dite de Charles VI' *Romania* XX (1891) 446-7.

38. 'La Cour Amoureuse' pp. 427, 429; *Œuvres de Christine* II xi*n*.

39. A. Piaget 'Un manuscrit de la *Cour Amoureuse de Charles VI*' *Romania* XXXI (1902) 599.

40. C. Potvin 'La Charte de la Cour d'Amour de l'année 1401' *Bulletin de l'Académie Royale de Belgique* 3me série XII (1886) 211-12.

41. *Inventaire de la bibliothèque du roi Charles VI* (Paris 1867) nos. 109, 319, 321.

42. Ward *Epistles on the Romance of the Rose* p. 29.

43. *Preface to Chaucer* p. 364.

J. A. Burrow (essay date 1982)

SOURCE: Burrow, J. A. "Autobiographical Poetry in the Middle Ages: The Case of Thomas Hoccleve." *Proceedings of the British Academy* 68 (1982): 389-412.

[*In this essay, Burrow responds to critics who interpret Hoccleve's persona as mere convention with no basis in reality, and suggests that ignoring the autobiographical aspects of Hoccleve's poetry denies the reader a useful basis for understanding his works.*]

Thomas Hoccleve earned his living as a clerk in the office of the Privy Seal, but he also employed his pen in the copying of poetry, his own included. Three autograph copies of his work survive, in fact; and one of these (now Huntington MS HM 744) formerly belonged to Sir Israel Gollancz, the scholar commemorated in this series of lectures. Gollancz edited poems from this manuscript as part of the edition of Hoccleve's works published by the Early English Text Society.[1] I therefore imagine that he would have sympathised with one purpose of the present lecture, which is to contribute to a revaluation of Hoccleve's poetry. The poet's own confession that he was 'dull' and learned 'little or nothing' from his master Chaucer is still commonly accepted as a fair summary of his achievement; but such self-depreciation is itself eminently Chaucerian, and I want to suggest that the disciple's poetry in fact displays, at its best, a lively intelligence and a command of English verse which give the lie to his talk of incompetence and stupidity. At the same time I shall take up some of the problems presented by those autobiographical passages which are so characteristic (and unChaucerian) in Hoccleve. Gollancz's fellow editor, F. J. Furnivall, made much of these passages, freely deriving from them conclusions about the poet's life and character; but modern critics are uneasy with such naïvely literalistic interpretation. They stress rather, as we shall see, the conventional and non-factual elements in Hoccleve's self-revelations. But in this as in some other areas of medieval literary studies, the reaction against autobiographical readings has begun to overreach itself, so that it now seems necessary to argue that not *all* autobiographical passages in medieval writings are simply 'conventional', and also that there are some cases, Hoccleve's included, where interest in the poetry is actually inseparable from interest in the man.

Gollancz and Furnivall would simply have taken this for granted; but modern scholars and critics have generally reacted to such declarations of biographical interest with increasing disapproval. Three distinct schools of thought, otherwise often at variance, have converged to make this anti-biographical position overpoweringly strong in recent times. Historical criticism has stressed the conventional character of authorial self-reference in medieval times (the use of traditional topics, the influence of St. Augustine, and so on); the New Criticism has discouraged biographical interest as a distraction from the words on the page; and formalist or structuralist criticism treats first-person discourse as part of the fictive world of 'le texte'. All these developments, in their different ways, have helped to make the frank man-to-man response of Furnivall to his author seem very old-fashioned indeed. Writing, as he tells us, in the British Museum on Monday, 29 February 1892, at 7.30 p.m. 'under the electric light', the Victorian editor characterised Hoccleve as a 'weak, sensitive, look-on-the-worst kind of man': 'But he has the merit of recognizing his weakness, his folly, and his cowardice. He makes up for these by his sentimental love of the Virgin Mary, his genuine admiration for Chaucer, his denunciation of the extravagant fashions in dress, the neglect of old soldiers, &c. We wish he had been a better poet and a manlier fellow; but all of those who've made fools of themselves, more or less, in their youth, will feel for the poor old versifier'.[2]

The directness of Furnivall's response to his 'poor old versifier' is delightful, but it is no longer possible today after studies such as those by Curtius on the topos of affected modesty, Spitzer and Zumthor on the 'non-empirical I', Donaldson on the Chaucerian narrator, and Kane on the autobiographical fallacy.[3] If autobiographical interpretation is to become respectable again, and if the term 'autobiographical' itself is ever to escape from that guard

of inverted commas which regularly now accompanies it, the whole matter needs to be thought out afresh, so that there may be some new understanding of the proper criteria for valid and useful work in this area. Full recognition of the part played by literary tradition and free-ranging invention in first-person utterances need not deprive criticism, as it tends to do at present, of the capacity to recognize equally fully those cases where such utterances are *not* fictional or conventional.

Literary critics commonly apply the epithet 'autobiographical' quite generally to all passages where an author says things about himself which are judged to be true, at least in part. This terminology involves some awkwardness, to which I shall return later; but first let me offer a few observations on the judgement of truth. It will be clearly understood, to begin with, that in some first-person discourse the question of autobiographical truth simply does not arise, because the writer is not referring to himself at all. Thus no competent reader, knowing the relevant facts, could fail to see that the following little poem, despite its direct first-person form, is to be understood dramatically as spoken *in persona alterius*:

> I have labored sore and suffered deth,
> And now I rest and draw my breth;
> But I shall come and call right sone
> Heven and erth and hell to dome;
> And then shall know both devil and man
> What I was and what I am.[4]

The same prior question, that of reference, can be settled equally decisively in the opposite direction—in favour, that is, of formally *non*-dramatic utterance—where the first-person speaker bears the author's own proper name. This happens once in Chaucer's poetry, when the eagle calls the dreamer in the *House of Fame* 'Geoffrey', and much more frequently in Hoccleve, where the first person is many times identified as either 'Thomas' or 'Hoccleve'.[5] Such naming is important because it establishes clearly that the first-person pronoun does at least refer to the author, not to some other person, real or imaginary. Hence it will always be in order to raise the question of autobiographical truth in such cases. But the substantial question of truth is nearly always more difficult than the formal question of reference, because there are so many things besides the truth that one can speak about oneself (not all of which one would want to call lies).

The question can be easily and decisively settled only in those cases where an author's statement about himself can be checked in a reliable independent source. Such cases do not occur very often in medieval literature, but Hoccleve's poetry provides some instances. Like his master Chaucer, Hoccleve was a civil servant, and his career can therefore be documented, like Chaucer's, from the official archives. In Chaucer's poetry there is nothing for such documents to confirm except a passing and dismissive reference, again in the *House of Fame* (653), to his 'rekenynges' in the Customs House; but Hoccleve's writings refer quite freely to his life at the Privy Seal. He mentions, for instance, the name of the Privy Seal hostel at which he lodged (Chester's Inn, on the south side of the modern Aldwych), the amount of his annuity (£10 in 1406), and the names of fellow clerks (Baillay, Hethe, Offorde).[6] The researches in the Public Record Office of Furnivall's collaborator, R. E. G. Kirk, and of the administrative historians T. F. Tout and A. L. Brown have provided documentary confirmation of these details. Tout and Brown, both good, hard-headed historians, find nothing, it should be noted, in Hoccleve's poetry to deter them from using it as a trustworthy source of information on the workings of the Privy Seal.[7]

The fact that in these matters, where it is possible to check, Hoccleve's poetry nowhere departs from the actual circumstances of his life must be borne in mind when approaching those other more contentious matters where documentary checks are not available. In his lecture entitled 'The Autobiographical Fallacy in Chaucer and Langland Studies', Professor George Kane has rightly insisted on the dangers and difficulties of making 'inferences from texts about . . . undocumented matters respecting the life and personality of an author'.[8] One may therefore be tempted to set the whole insoluble problem aside; but in practice this proves difficult to do. Many modern critics who profess complete agnosticism in the matter go on to talk like unblushing atheists. They slip easily, for instance, from declaring that we cannot tell whether Chaucer's poetry does or does not represent his ordinary personality into taking it for granted that it does not. This is because the reaction against the speculative excesses of older criticism has left a distinct, though unacknowledged, bias against any recognition of autobiographical reference at all in medieval literature. This bias appears in a number of ways, and most notably in the handling of the tricky and vital question of conventionality.

I want in particular to question the belief, to be traced in much recent polemic, that convention and autobiographical truth are in general to be taken as incompatible alternatives. Here again one needs to distinguish, as I did earlier, between the question of reference and the question of truth. The former tends to be a straight either/or problem: either the first-person pronoun refers to the writer or it does not. So here recognition of conventionality can indeed exclude autobiographical interpretation altogether, simply by establishing that the 'I' of the poem is not the author at all. In the *pastourelle,* for instance, one of the rules of the genre makes writers speak of themselves, in the first person, as walking out one May morning. For a competent reader the question of truth will not arise in this case. Here the conventional and the autobiographical can indeed be treated as mutually exclusive. But in those other cases where the writer does refer to himself and where the question of truth consequently arises, matters are more complex. Questions of truth rarely allow of a single either/or answer; and where they are concerned, the customary modern opposition between the conventional and the autobiographical, insofar as it claims to distinguish fact from fiction, often simplifies and distorts the issues.

Let me give an example, taken from the excellent lecture by Kane already referred to. Kane remarks that Chaucer 'repeatedly professes inexperience, or lack of aptitude, or lack of success as a lover'; and he goes on to ask the following question: 'Do we accept this as autobiography, or call it a conventional pose, or take the position that we cannot possibly know?'[9] This is indeed a difficult case, but I am concerned here only with Kane's statement of the alternatives: 'autobiography' or 'conventional pose'. The main objection to this formulation is simply that people strike 'poses' (conventional or otherwise) in life as well as in literature. Furthermore, we do not always find it easy to distinguish such attitudes, especially where they come to be assumed as a matter of habit, from the truth or reality of a person's life and opinions. How could such a distinction be made, for instance, in the well-documented case of William Butler Yeats? In such a case, the 'poses' will be of no less interest to the biographer than to the critic.

Kane warns of an 'autobiographical fallacy', and he is right to do so. But there is also an opposite error, which must be called the 'conventional fallacy'. Victims of the latter combine a learned and sophisticated awareness of literary convention with an apparently naïve and reductive notion of what real life is like—naïve and reductive, because they talk as if non-literary experience were not itself shaped by conventions. Of course, everyone knows that it *is*; but the knowledge seems to desert medievalists when they argue that the conventional character of a text *proves* that it has no autobiographical content. In reply to this objection, it might be argued that, insofar as life and literature do indeed share the same conventional character, the distinction between them ceases to be of any interest to criticism and can be ignored. From this point of view it would be a matter of indifference whether Chaucer did or did not in real life adopt that 'pose' of the unsuccessful lover which he strikes in his poems. Even if he could be shown to have done so, it might be said, the passages in question would still not count as significantly autobiographical—not, that is, unless one could prove that Chaucer actually *was* an unsuccessful lover. But when modern critics deny the autobiographical character of a medieval poem, they are not concerned only with the hard facts which might be deduced from it. Their stress on the conventional character of authorial self-reference usually leads them to state, or suggest, that such reference has no bearing whatsoever on the life and experience of the author. We are offered instead, in and out of season, the purely literary, dramatic, or fictive utterances of the authorial persona, the 'I of the poem', the narrator, and so on.

Instances of the 'conventional fallacy' are not hard to find in modern discussions of Hoccleve. Let me give three examples. These concern Hoccleve's three most interesting and memorable poems: **'La Male Regle de T. Hoccleve,'** written in 1405 or 1406 when the poet was in his later thirties; *The Regement of Princes,* written for Prince Hal in the last years of Henry IV (1411-12); and the so-called *Series,* Hoccleve's last datable work, put together a few years before his death in 1426.[10]

'La Male Regle' is a highly characteristic, indeed an inimitable, literary creation. In it Hoccleve laments the present sad state both of his health and of his finances. He is suffering, he says, from a double sickness in purse and in body (337-8, 409), caused by the excesses of his riotous and unbridled youth. This is the *male regle* or misrule of the title, which Hoccleve describes with a good deal of lively detail concerning his irregular life as a young man in London and Westminster taverns and eating-houses. Furnivall treated these descriptions as direct transcripts of reality, unmediated by any literary convention; but in 1967 Eva Thornley pointed out the influence of the Middle English penitential lyrics on Hoccleve's poem.[11] Hoccleve's account of his wild youth, she observed, owes something to the traditional scheme of the seven deadly sins, commonly employed in the penitential lyrics. Thornley herself did not draw any anti-autobiographical conclusions from her evidence, but later scholars have not hesitated to do so. Thus Penelope Doob, in an important discussion of Hoccleve to which I shall have occasion to return, notes approvingly that Thornley 'finds the poem more conventional than autobiographical'. Elsewhere she writes as follows: 'Hoccleve's **Male Regle** is, as Thornley demonstrates, an exceptionally good example of the conventional informal penitential lyric; and its colourfulness and realism may relate it more closely to such works of fiction as the *Wife of Bath's Prologue* or the lively confessions of the seven deadly sins and of Haukyn in *Piers Plowman* . . . than to a true confession from the heart.'[12] The weakness of this argument lies in its tacit identification of conventionality with fictionality. This is particularly shaky where a scheme such as that of the seven deadly sins is concerned. That conventional scheme did indeed figure in literary fictions such as *Piers Plowman*; but it also provided the moral grid-system most commonly used by men of the period whenever they attempted to map their inner lives. That was how people thought about themselves. Hence if Hoccleve had wanted, for whatever reason, to describe his own experiences as a wild young man, he would most naturally have sorted them out into sin-categories. Even if this sorting were more systematic than it in fact is in the **Male Regle,** there would still be no reason to conclude that the poet's confession must be a 'work of fiction'. We would still be left free to make what we could of its 'colourfulness and realism':

> Wher was a gretter maister eek than y,
> Or bet aqweyntid at Westmynstre yate,
> Among the tauerneres namely,
> And Cookes / whan I cam / eerly or late?
> I pynchid nat at hem in myn acate,
> But paied hem / as þat they axe wolde;
> Wherfore I was the welcomere algate,
> And for 'a verray gentil man' y-holde.

> (177-84)

One must agree with Doob that such a passage does not read like a 'true confession from the heart'. The self-depreciation has a humorous, slightly weary note. We all know, it implies, what motives might prompt a cook or an innkeeper to welcome such a big spender, flattering him with titles such as 'master' and 'a real gentleman'. But the 'true confession from the heart' is only one form—and that the most vulgarly romantic—which autobiographical writing can take. When Hoccleve chooses to write about himself, as I believe he does in the **'Male Regle'** and elsewhere, he does so for reasons quite different from those suggested by Dr Doob's teasingly inappropriate phrase.

I shall return to this point later. For the present let us turn to a second instance of the conventional fallacy. In his most widely read work, ***The Regement of Princes,*** Hoccleve refers on four occasions to Geoffrey Chaucer, who had died some twelve years earlier. Hoccleve himself is sometimes referred to as an English Chaucerian, and there can be no doubt that he learned much from his predecessor's work. He imitated it quite closely on occasion, as when, at the request of a London stationer, he wrote a Miracle of the Virgin, in rhyme royal and with a Marian prologue, which derives so directly from Chaucer's *Prioress's Prologue and Tale* that it found a place in one copy of the *Canterbury Tales.*[13] Although direct echoes of Chaucer occur less frequently than one might expect in Hoccleve's verse, his metrical art and especially his mastery of the syntax of the rhyme royal stanza would have been almost impossible without Chaucer's example. Such dependence upon Chaucer is, of course, common in fifteenth-century poetry; but two of the passages in ***The Regement of Princes*** have been generally accepted, until quite recently, as evidence that Hoccleve actually knew Chaucer and was personally instructed by him in the art of English poetry. In the long and interesting encounter with the poor almsman which forms the prologue to the ***Regement,*** the old man responds to Hoccleve's disclosure of his name with these words:

> 'Sone, I haue herd, or this, men speke of þe;
> Þou were aqueynted with Caucher, pardee'

> (1866-7)

Later, in dedicating his poem to the future Henry V, the poet apologizes for his lack of learning and skill:

> Mi dere maistir—god his soule quyte!—
> And fadir, Chaucer, fayn wolde han me taght;
> But I was dul, and lerned lite or naght.

> (2077-9)

The meaning of this passage seems plain enough; but Jerome Mitchell, in a discussion entitled 'Hoccleve's Supposed Friendship with Chaucer', has suggested that 'this so-called autobiographical allusion is nothing more than a conventional expression of self-deprecation'.[14] Here again, the proposed alternative between autobiography and convention proves misleading. Certainly there does exist a convention of self-depreciation in polite letters, as in polite society; and no doubt Hoccleve's modest protestations, like those of Chaucer himself, owe something to the literary topic of affected modesty, studied by Curtius. Also, when Hoccleve goes on to his threnody for Chaucer, lamenting the loss of one who was a Cicero in rhetoric, an Aristotle in philosophy, and a Virgil in poetry, he is following a literary tradition already established in the vernaculars: the lament for a dead master.[15] Such considerations should certainly make one hesitate to derive from Hoccleve's words either a just estimate of his own merits or a discriminating account of his master's; but they do nothing to explain why he claimed Chaucer as an acquaintance. When John Lydgate in his *Troy Book* describes how Chaucer treated the verses of other poets, he does so from hearsay ('I have herde telle'); but Hoccleve claims direct personal knowledge.[16] Mitchell remarks that there is no indication of any friendship in the life-records of either man; but one has only to recall the character of those documents to see the absurdity of this argument. The Public Record Office is not rich in records of literary friendships.

The question of Hoccleve's friendship with Chaucer is not in itself very important; but Mitchell's discussion of the matter may be taken as representative of a general approach which can be seriously disabling. Many readers today are only too ready to accept the historical critic's pronouncement that such and such an 'autobiographical' passage is no more than conventional or fictional. Whether they belong to the older school of the New Criticism or to the newer schools of formalism, these readers will be glad enough to be relieved of biographical considerations which both schools regard as in any case *hors de discours*. But even in medieval literature there are occasions when exclusive concentration on 'le texte' or 'the words on the page' leads to an impoverished and dehumanized reading of works whose true force and character can only be appreciated if their particular extratextual reference is duly recognized and acknowledged. Hoccleve's **'Complaint'** and his **'Dialogue with a Friend'** are cases in point.

The **'Complaint'** and **'Dialogue'** are the first two items in Hoccleve's last and most original major work: what Hammond, for want of a better title, called the **Series**. This consists of a sequence of linked writings, dedicated to Humphrey duke of Gloucester in the last years of Henry V. In the opening **'Complaint,'** Hoccleve represents himself at the age of 53 musing on the uncertainty of worldly fortunes. In particular, he recalls a 'wild infirmity' which changed his own fortunes some years before, causing him to lose his wits. He recovered from this breakdown—five years ago, he says, on All Hallows' Day—but ever since his friends and acquaintances have persisted in doubting his mental stability; and it is of this that he chiefly complains. People cannot believe that he is really better. They watch for signs of his former brain-sickness in his present ways of walking and standing and looking:

> Chaungid had I my pas / some seiden eke,
> For here and there / forthe stirte I as a Roo,
> None abode / none arrest, but all brain-seke.
> Another spake / and of me seide also,
> My feete weren aye / wavynge to and fro

Whane that I stonde shulde / and withe men talke,
And that myne eyne / sowghten every halke.

(127-33)

In her study of 'conventions of madness in Middle English literature' entitled *Nebuchadnezzar's Children,* Penelope Doob cites a medieval parallel to show that these are among the 'standard symptoms of the madman'.[17] She also stresses the conventional character of Hoccleve's view of the aetiology of madness: like most medieval men, he sees it as a visitation of God. These are valuable observations; but they do not, as Doob appears to believe, show that Hoccleve's account is to be understood as a conventional fiction. It is precisely those 'standard symptoms of the madman' that nervous friends would look for; and there is no reason to think that Hoccleve himself, musing on his traumatic experience, would have attempted to understand it otherwise than in the religious terms of his age, just as we today would use psychoanalytic terms.[18] Doob herself is aware of this complication, and at one point opines that 'it does not matter very much' whether one takes the account as autobiographical or not; but she reveals herself as an atheist rather than an agnostic in this matter when, for instance, she observes that the 'fairly extensive records' of Hoccleve's life contain no reference to his madness.[19] I have already objected to this kind of argument *a silentio*.

Doob offers her own interpretation of the **'Complaint'** and **'Dialogue,'** as an alternative to autobiographical readings. Hoccleve's subject, she writes, is 'the sinful madness of mankind'.[20] But is it? The poet does indeed speak of his madness as a visitation from God, and in one place he interprets it as divine punishment for his 'sinful governance' in times of prosperity (**'Complaint'** 393-406); but there is nothing in the text, so far as I can see, to justify Doob's conclusion that the wild infirmity is simply a 'traditional metaphor for the crippling state of sin which is the subject of the poem'.[21] On the contrary, Hoccleve clearly treats it as an actual illness, from which he recovered at a specified time, five years ago on All Hallows' Day. But if this is indeed the true subject of Hoccleve's poem, what were his reasons for writing it? Medievalists will appreciate that this is a more difficult question than it seems. It is only too easy to see why a medieval poet might write about 'the sinful madness of mankind'; but why should he choose to write about his own mental breakdown and its aftermath? Here as elsewhere the autobiographical interpretation will be in danger of seeming merely anachronistic unless it can be supported by some historically plausible account of the poet's reasons for writing about himself. Indeed, this question of the purpose or function of autobiographical writing is, as I shall try to suggest, crucial for a proper understanding of poems such as the **'Complaint'** or the **'Male Regle.'**

This is a question which the term 'autobiographical' itself most unfortunately begs. As was remarked earlier, critics commonly treat this epithet as if it were appropriate to any occasion when an author says things about himself which the reader has reason to believe are true; but in fact the word carries further implications, unwanted in most medieval contexts and generally unacknowledged there. These concern the presumed purpose of the self-referring utterance. In modern usage the term 'autobiography' denotes a genre of non-fictional narrative—a species of biography and (theoretically at least) a sub-species of history. There are, of course, many possible reasons for writing such a book; but those most commonly avowed—the official reasons, as it were—are rather grand and disinterested: to record the events of one's life for posterity, to explain how one came to be how one is, and the like.[22] Autobiographical discourse, in fact, has come to the distinguished as a literary and formal kind of talk about oneself; and as such it is not directly or primarily concerned with the ordinary practical businesses of such talk—excusing, confessing, complaining, and all those other everyday speech-acts which involve reference to one's own actions or experiences.

Did any medieval author write such an autobiography? Some scholars, notably Georg Misch, have found it possible to devote many hundreds of pages to medieval examples of the genre; but others, notably Philippe Lejeune, have argued that these so-called medieval 'autobiographies' are better called something else.[23] I think that Lejeune's judgement is correct, although the reasons which he gives are suspect. Following Zumthor, he speaks of 'absence de la notion d'auteur' and of 'absence d'emploi littéraire autoréférentiel de la première personne'; but the Middle Ages, at least from the thirteenth century onwards, had a very clear 'notion d'auteur', and their writers were perfectly capable on occasion of using the first-person pronoun 'autoreferentially'. The true difference is to be looked for rather in the realm of authorial purpose. Unlike the modern autobiography, the corresponding medieval texts will present themselves as written versions, albeit elaborated and formalized, of an everyday self-referring speech-act. They are addressed to particular recipients, and they serve explicitly stated practical ends. The greatest of them, St. Augustine's *Confessions,* addresses itself to God with a persistence which many modern readers find disappointing; and the saint's account of his life is shaped throughout by the confessional purpose of this address. Another text frequently cited in this connection, the *Monodiae* of Gilbert of Nogent (1115), also addresses itself as a confession to God. Peter Abelard's so-called *Historia Calamitatum* takes the form of a letter to a friend offering consolation and encouragement 'based upon the experience of my misfortunes'. These works contain many facts about their authors' lives; but even they—medieval autobiographies, if ever there was such a thing—cannot be so described on any functional definition of the genre. Functionally considered, the *Confessions* and the *Monodiae* are confessions, and the *Historia Calamitatum* is a consolation.[24]

The same questions of address and function arise in the consideration of Hoccleve's autobiographical passages. To whom is he speaking? And for what purpose? Most of his works are occasional pieces, and of himself he certainly never speaks without occasion. These occasions often fall outside the province of literature as we now understand it; but they hold the key to the understanding of Hoccleve's own particular brand of autobiographical writing.

Hoccleve entirely lacked his master Chaucer's ability to speak in voices other than his own. In his **'Dialogue,'** the exchanges between himself and his friend display a real skill in rendering general conversational effects; but the friend never establishes himself with a distinct individual idiom, as Chaucer's Pandarus does in his talks with Troilus. The same must be said of Cupid, the speaker in **'The Letter of Cupid,'** of the Virgin Mary in **'The Compleynte of the Virgin before the Cross,'** and of the eminently forgettable characters in Hoccleve's two most ambitious verse narratives, the *Gesta Romanorum* stories in the *Series.* Even the old almsman in the prologue to the *Regement of Princes,* Hoccleve's equivalent to Wordsworth's leech-gatherer and perhaps his least insubstantial dramatic creation, is no more than a pale shadow by comparison with the old man in Chaucer's *Pardoner's Tale.* This poet's skills lay elsewhere, in the articulation of his own voice. Hoccleve speaks best when he speaks *in propria persona,* either in soliloquy, as in the **'Complaint,'** or when he speaks to another person, as he most often does. His is above all a poetry of address; and the list of persons to whom he addresses himself at one time or another is long and varied. It includes: the members of the Trinity, Health (personified), Lady Money (personified), the Virgin Mary, King Henry V and his two brothers Humphrey of Gloucester and Edward of York, John duke of Bedford, the Chancellor of the Exchequer Henry Somer, Treasurer Fourneval, the Town Clerk of London John Carpenter, and the Lollard knight John Oldcastle. Such varying occasions and purposes call for varying roles (by which I do *not* mean fictional roles); and as Hoccleve presents his self differently, to the King or to the heretic, so the character of his autobiographical writing changes accordingly. I distinguish here three main roles: the good citizen, the friend or colleague, and (most important) the dependant or petitioner.

From the present point of view (and from most others) Hoccleve the good citizen is the least interesting of the three. This is the Hoccleve who, like John Gower in the previous generation, took upon himself the role of upholding standards by giving moral counsel to the great and deploring the abuses of modern times. Examples of this kind of writing are: the poem to Oldcastle attacking the Lollard heresy, the passage on the evils of flattery in the **'Male Regle'** (209-88), the passage in the **'Dialogue'** (99-196) deploring the clipping, washing, and adulterating of coins, the story of Jonathas and Fellicula told in the *Series* as a warning to young men against the wiles of women, and above all the *Regement of Princes.* Apart from its lengthy prologue, the *Regement* devotes itself entirely to instructing Prince Hal in the proper virtues of a ruler. Such treatises 'de regimine principum' were very popular in the fifteenth century, and the *Regement* was by far and away the most successful of Hoccleve's works. It survives in more than forty manuscripts.[25] Although here as elsewhere he can command a sinewy, plain, and expressive English, it must be confessed that Hoccleve is not at his best in the role of the good citizen, loyal to country and crown, orthodox in religion, and honest in all his personal dealings. However, even Hoccleve the good citizen has his complexities, for in the *Series* especially, in the '**Male Regle,**' and to a much lesser degree in the *Regement,* Hoccleve's various confessions of personal inadequacy cast fitful shadows across the adjacent passages of moral and prudential counsel. For how, after all, could a writer whose own standing was so avowedly insecure, financially, morally, and medically, take it upon himself to speak on behalf of his society, as a solid citizen, to the coiners and heretics at its margins and to the kings and lords at its centre? Readers who credit Hoccleve with no awareness of this contradiction commonly react to his orthodoxies with something of that mixture of embarrassment and derision which society reserves for those of its members who try too hard to be one of the boys; but the poet who described how he practised sane faces in front of the mirror in his room was self-aware as well as self-conscious; and that self-awareness certainly embraced some knowledge of his own weakness in seeking to be accepted as a 'verray gentil man'. I have argued elsewhere that this awareness is particularly strong in the *Series.*[26] This sequence of poems enacts, I believe, the progress of that rehabilitation in society which Hoccleve, after his wild infirmity and its unhappy aftermath, so longs for. It begins in solitude and alienation, with the '**Complaint**'; progresses with the ministrations of the friend; and ends with the poet comfortably ensconced in the orthodox role of *père de famille,* responding to the friend's anxious request for help with his own wild and uncontrollable son. Here at least a touch of moralizing complacency may be forgiven in a good citizen who has himself so recently suffered the miseries of alienation.

Hoccleve's 'rehabilitation' in the *Series* comes about largely through the agency of that unnamed friend who visits him, comforts and advises him, lends him books, and finally sets the seal on his recovery by asking for his help. The familiar exchanges between the two men are well rendered. Indeed, in the role of friend and companion Hoccleve generally commands a voice of notable ease and conviction, anticipating later English literary voices even more, perhaps, than Chaucer does in the *Envoy to Scogan.* He is a poet of *urban* companionship, evoking already something of that distinctive, almost cosy, sense of familiarity which unites those living in the busy 'press' of a great town who actually happen to know each other, either socially or at the office. Hoccleve's London was not big by modern standards; but, as he portrays it in such poems as the '**Male Regle**' or the *Series,* it is already recognisably the tense, gossipy London of the satires of Donne and Pope.[27] Indeed, as Stephen Medcalf has well observed, Hoccleve can even put one in mind of a later metropolitan writer, Charles Lamb—another 'impecunious but clubbable London clerk of literary leanings'.[28] There were already clubs in Hoccleve's London. The poet belonged to one, called the 'Court de bone conpaignie',

which met periodically for convivial dinners at the Temple. On behalf of this club he wrote a double ballade to one of its distinguished members, the Chancellor of the Exchequer Henry Somer.

But the most important club in Hoccleve's London life was the office of the Privy Seal, in which he served as clerk for nearly forty years. The clerks of the Privy Seal were more than simply colleagues at the office.[29] They lived communally at the *hospicium privati sigilli,* or Privy Seal hostel; and in the '**Male Regle**' Hoccleve uses an expressive phrase when he speaks of going 'hoom to the priuee seel' (l. 188). All the poet's 'fellawes of the prive seale', as he calls them ('**Complaint**' 296), shared his chronic difficulty in getting paid, and sometimes in his petitionary poems he pleads for them as well as for himself:

> We, your seruantes, Hoccleue & Baillay,
> Hethe & Offorde, yow beseeche & preye,
> 'Haastith our heruest / as soone as yee may!'[30]

He also complains feelingly of their other troubles. In a well-known passage in the *Regement of Princes,* he compares their demanding work at the writing-desk with the simpler and more companionable tasks of common craftsmen:

> This artificers se I day be day,
> In þe hotteste of al hir bysynesse
> Talken and syng, and make game and play,
> And forth hir labour passith with gladnesse;
> But we labour in trauaillous stilnesse;
> We stowpe and stare vpon þe shepes skyn,
> And keepe muste our song and wordes in.

> (1009-15)

This stanza shows how especially well Hoccleve can write when he is dealing with the particulars of his own experience. The contrast between the talking, singing, and joking in a craftsman's shop and the 'trauaillous stilnesse' of the Privy Seal office is drawn with great precision and economy of language. Notice, for instance, how in the line, 'We stowpe and stare vpon þe shepes skyn', the word *stare,* neat enough already in its alliterative coupling with *stowpe,* gathers extra force from the ensuing 'shepes skyn'—a phrase which defamiliarizes the parchment and so converts the writer's fixed gaze into a real weary, hypnotized 'stare'. A tanner would at least have whistled.

A little later in the *Regement,* Hoccleve has another less well-known passage where he speaks with similar force and precision on behalf of the 'fellows of the Privy Seal', describing one of the tricks by which they were deprived of the legitimate rewards of their labours. A stranger comes to Westminster to get some necessary document issued from the office of the Privy Seal. He encounters one of those unscrupulous hangers-on so familiar from later satirical writings—in this case, a 'lord's man' who promises to use his influence to get the document without delay. Pocketing the stranger's fee, he persuades the Privy Seal clerks to expedite the business by promising them that his own influential master, who has (he claims) the interests of the stranger at heart, will do them a favour in return at some later date. But the lord, of course, does not know the petitioner from Adam, and the hanger-on will later claim to have given the clerks their fee. The clerks know what is going on; but what can they do? 'His tale schal be leeued, but nat ourys.' Let me quote the first part of this striking passage, which takes the law-abiding modern reader deep into an unfamiliar world of chicanery and influence:

> But if a wyght haue any cause to sue
> To vs, som lordes man schal vndertake
> To sue it out; & þat þat is vs due
> For oure labour, hym deyneþ vs nat take;
> He seiþ, his lord to þanke vs wole he make;
> It touchiþ hym, it is a man of his;
> Where þe reuers of þat, god wot, sooþ is.
> His letter he takiþ, and forþ goþ his way,
> And byddeþ vs to dowten vs no thyng,
> His lord schal þanken vs an oþer day;
> And if we han to sue to þe kyng,
> His lord may þere haue al his askyng;
> We schal be sped, as fer as þat oure bille
> Wole specifie þe effecte of oure wylle.
> What schol we do? we dar non argument
> Make ageyn him, but fayre & wel hym trete,
> Leste he roporte amys, & make vs schent . . .

(*Regement* 1499-515)

And so on. These stanzas end less well than they begin; but the specious assurances of the lord's man are very well caught in lines such as 'It touchiþ hym, it is a man of his' and 'His lord schal þanken vs an oþer day'; and the complex workings of power and influence about the king's court are displayed with authority. This is a world where documents are 'sued out' in return for a promise that some future 'bill' will itself be favourably received higher up, and where petitioners depend for their success upon the sponsorship of some great lord or else upon the good offices of some lesser intermediary who may, for his own reasons, agree to undertake their cause. Even established civil servants such as Hoccleve and his colleagues could easily come to grief on what Thomas Wyatt a century later called 'the slipper top of court's estates'. The payment of their supposedly regular annuities was far from being a matter of course; and the extra fees 'due for their labour', upon which they depended to make ends meet, could finish up in other hands, as we have seen. They had to look after themselves as best they could, in accordance with the harsh dictum of Arcite in Chaucer's *Knight's Tale*:

> And therefore, at the kynges court, my brother,
> Ech man for hymself, ther is noon oother.

(*Canterbury Tales* I 1181-82)

It is within this social context that the modern reader should try to understand and sympathize with Hoccleve in his third and most significant role: that of petitioner. For the image of himself which he projects in his poetry is determined most of all by the harsh requirements of

survival in the treacherous world of the court. Furnival wished he had been a manlier fellow and not complained so much; but the conduct of an independent nineteenth-century gentleman would have soon led to destitution in any medieval man dependent upon the favours of the great. When Hoccleve speaks of himself, as he often does, 'conpleynyngly', he does so for a purpose, and with the technique of an expert. Most of the business with which his office dealt concerned petitions submitted to the King or his Council and handed on, if they were granted, to the Privy Seal clerks for the drafting of the appropriate warrant.[31] In the formulary which he compiled in the last years of his life for the benefit of his colleagues, Hoccleve included five model 'supplications' or 'petitions ensellez du prive seel'.[32] He himself was well acquainted with the uncertainty of reward and the misery of hope deferred. One of the *sententiae* recorded in his formulary is *Expectantes excrucial dilatio promissorum* ('the putting-off of promised benefits torments those that await them').[33] It is therefore easy to understand why so much of his poetic output should take the form of a complaint about hardships or wrongs suffered, coupled with a petition for the remedy addressed either to the potential benefactor himself or else to some other person who could act as mediator on his behalf.[34] Thus Huntington MS 111 contains a group of petitionary balades addressed to the Lord Chancellor, the Subtreasurer, the King, and the Town Clerk of London; the **'Male Regle'** culminates in an appeal to the Treasurer for payment of his annuity; and the **Regement of Princes** makes a similar appeal for relief to Prince Hal himself.[35] Hoccleve's religious poems, too, often take the form of complaints and petitions, appealing to Christ or the Virgin Mary as mediators who can use their influence to win him favour with God the Father. The pattern of complaint and supplication, as these examples show, was deeply impressed upon Hoccleve's consciousness.

He evidently gave the matter of petitioning a good deal of thought. Seneca's *De Beneficiis* taught him what he no doubt already knew, that even successful begging exacts its own high price:

> Senek seith, he haþ nat þat þing for noght
> That byeth it by speche and by prayere.
> There is no thyng þat is in eerthe wroght,
> As þat he seith, þat is y-bought so deere.[36]

But what is the alternative? As he says in the **'Male Regle,'** the 'shameless craver' gets what he wants by sheer importunity, while the 'poor shamefast man' stays poor. So he must learn to crave. But nagging repetition is, in fact, not the best way. Variety and inventiveness help:

> Whoso him shapith mercy for to craue,
> His lesson moot recorde in sundry wyse.

(**'Male Regle'** 397-8)

There are more 'sundry wises' of petitionary approach in Hoccleve's writings than can be illustrated in this lecture; but, in view of the poet's reputation as a monotonous whiner, one should emphasize that there *is* variety, and that this variety includes a good deal of wit and comic byplay. Playing the fool, if stylishly done, can save a little face; and it also serves to keep potential benefactors entertained. Hoccleve describes one of his poems as an 'owter of my nycetee', displaying his folly to amuse, in this case, the Duke of York.[37] The phrase draws attention to an aspect of his autobiographical writing which neither Doob nor Furnivall recognizes.

An extreme example of the light petitionary touch is the group of three roundels in which the poet complains to Lady Money and receives her unfavourable reply, a *jeu d'esprit* worthy to be compared with Chaucer's *Complaint to his Purse*. But let me end by returning briefly to that more substantial piece of 'shameless craving', the **'Male Regle.'** In this poem the complaint, as I remarked earlier, concerns two kinds of sickness, physical and financial, both caused by the poet's excesses in his riotous youth. Thornley and Doob interpreted the piece as a penitential lyric; and certainly Hoccleve does express regret for the past, as well as a resolution to live a better-regulated life in the future. But these confessional sentiments serve an overriding petitionary purpose, from which the poem derives its form and its tone. Corresponding to the two sicknesses of purse and body we find here two subtly intertwined requests for relief, one addressed to the personified god of health, the other to Fourneval, the King's Treasurer. The practical point of the poem emerges clearly enough in its last four stanzas, where Hoccleve appeals to Fourneval for payment of his annuity, which is overdue; but this unavoidable act of importunity is approached in the most amusingly roundabout fashion. The poem opens with a lofty and fanciful appeal to Health, addressing that personification as if he were the great lord who could bring Hoccleve the 'socour and releef' that he needs. It then goes on to speak of the poet's youthful misrule, referring first to the excessive and irregular eating and drinking which have helped to ruin his constitution:

> twenti wyntir past continuelly
> Excesse at borde hath leyd his knyf with me.

> (111-12)

It is in this context that Hoccleve first mentions money, when he refers at l. 130 to the 'penylees maladie' which sometimes kept him out of his favourite taverns. From this point on, references to his youthful extravagance and its financial consequences occur with more than accidental frequency. Thus immediately after the account, quoted earlier, of his reputation with cooks and inn-keepers as a big spender, he describes how instead of walking 'hoom to the priuee seel' he took a boat (evidently an extravagance, like a taxi in modern London). His explanations of this self-indulgence bear all the hallmarks of his best manner: fullness of detail specified in precise, unlaboured English. How economically, for instance, the muted personifications of the line 'Heete & vnlust and superfluitee' express his three reasons for taking a boat in summer: he was hot, he had had too much to eat and drink, and he didn't feel like walking.

> And if it happid on the Someres day
> Þat I thus at the tauerne hadde be,
> Whan I departe sholde / & go my way
> Hoom to the priuee seel / so wowed me
> Heete & vnlust and superfluitee
> To walke vnto the brigge / & take a boot /
> Þat nat durste I contrarie hem all three,
> But dide as þat they stired me / god woot.
> And in the wyntir / for the way was deep,
> Vnto the brigge I dressid me also,
> And ther the bootmen took vpon me keep,
> For they my riot kneewen fern ago:
> With hem I was I-tugged to and fro,
> So wel was him / þat I with wolde fare;
> For riot paieth largely / eueremo;
> He styntith neuere / til his purs be bare.

> (185-200)

It may seem strange to claim of a passage such as this that it is shaped by a petitionary intention. Fourneval, one might suppose, would hardly be inclined to help replenish a purse which had been made bare by such extravagances. But the Privy Seal clerk knew what he was at:

> Whoso him shapith mercy for to craue,
> His lesson moot recorde in sundry wyse.

Hoccleve would have every reason to know that the Lord Treasurer received quite enough straight hard-luck stories in the ordinary way of business; so he could be trusted to appreciate the amusing alternative which the poet offered him—something very different from the customary 'wife and three children to support'. There is, it must be admitted, something slavish in the readiness with which Hoccleve makes a fool of himself to amuse the great man, as when he shamingly confesses that he was too shy and sheepish to do more than kiss the girls who attracted him to the Paul's Head Tavern; but he makes sure to recover his dignity in the closing pages of the poem. Here his mastery of the 'sundry wises' of petitionary address can be most clearly seen. First he addresses himself, with the warning that his modest annuity and uncertain fees make it essential for him to live a life of reason and moderation in future: 'Be waar, Hoccleue' (351). Then, in a loftier style, he addresses Health, confessing his past irregularities and renewing his pleas for relief. And finally he names Fourneval, and plainly asks him for the money that can heal all his sicknesses. It comes down to coin in the end:

> By coyn, I gete may swich medecyne
> As may myn hurtes alle, þat me greeue,
> Exyle cleene / & voide me of pyne.

> (446-8)

It will be evident from this discussion that one should not look in Hoccleve's poetry for the simple truth about him, whatever that may have been. Traditional moral psychology helped to shape the account he gives in the **'Male Regle'** of his youthful behaviour, just as traditional morbid psychology helped to shape the account of his breakdown in the **'Complaint.'** Both these accounts, furthermore, owe much of their distinctive tone and emphasis to their original occasion and purpose; and the unhappy Hoccleve of these bills of complaint is not the same as the orthodox Hoccleve who reproaches Oldcastle or the gregarious Hoccleve who invites Somer to dinner at the Temple. But to put the matter in this way implies, not only that Hoccleve really does talk about himself in his poetry, but also that his departures from the imaginary norm of simple autobiographical truth are themselves best understood by reflecting upon his particular circumstances. Here, for once, we are not reduced to generalization or speculation in considering the life and the social context of a medieval poet. The details are available, in the poems themselves and in the work of historians; and it is readers least embarrassed by these details who are most likely, I think, to appreciate the character of this remarkable, though uneven, writer.

Notes

1. All quotations are from this three-volume edition: *The Minor Poems in the Phillipps MS. 8151 (Cheltenham)* [now Huntington MS HM 111] *and the Durham MS. III. 9,* ed. F. J. Furnivall, ES 61 (1892); *The Regement of Princes,* ed. F. J. Furnivall, ES 72 (1897); *Minor Poems from the Ashburnham MS. Addit. 133* [now Huntington MS HM 744], ed. Sir I. Gollancz, ES 73 (1925). In 1970 the two volumes of minor poems were reissued in one volume revised by J. Mitchell and A. I. Doyle, from which I cite. Selections are edited by E. P. Hammond, *English Verse between Chaucer and Surrey* (Durham, NC, 1927) and by M. C. Seymour, *Selections from Hoccleve* (Oxford, 1981). There is an admirable edition of the *Series* by M. R. Pryor (Ph.D. thesis, University of California, Los Angeles, 1968).

2. *Minor Poems,* p. xxxviii.

3. E. R. Curtius, *European Literature and the Latin Middle Ages,* trans. W. R. Trask (London, 1953), pp. 83-5; L. Spitzer, 'Note on the Poetic and the Empirical "I" in Medieval Authors', *Traditio* iv (1946), 414-22; P. Zumthor, *Essai de poétique médiévale* (Paris, 1972), and 'Autobiography in the Middle Ages?', *Genre* 6 (1973), 29-48; E. T. Donaldson, 'Chaucer the Pilgrim', *Speaking of Chaucer* (London, 1970), pp. 1-12; G. Kane, 'The Autobiographical Fallacy in Chaucer and Langland Studies' (Chambers Memorial Lecture, London, 1965).

4. From *English Verse 1300-1500,* ed. J. A. Burrow (London, 1977), p. 309. This anthology also contains an edition of Hoccleve's *Complaint,* ll. 1-308.

5. 'Thomas': throughout the *Series,* especially in the 'Dialogue' (10, 20, 25, 199, 203, etc.). 'Hoccleve': 'Dialogue' 3, *Roundel II* (*Minor Poems,* p. 310) 1 etc., 'Male Regle' 351, *Regement of Princes* 1864-5, 4360, *Balade to Maister Somer* (*Minor Poems,* p. 59) 25. Philippe Lejeune stresses the importance of identity of proper name between author and narrator in establishing the autobiographical character of a work: *Le Pacte autobiographique* (Paris, 1975). This

valuable book provides an up-to-date bibliography of modern studies.

6. Chester's Inn, *Regement of Princes* 5; annuity, 'Male Regle' 421; Baillay etc., *Balade to Maister Somer* 25-6.

7. R. E. G. Kirk, Appendix of Hoccleve Documents, *Minor Poems,* pp. li-lxx; T. F. Tout, *Chapters in the Administrative History of Mediaeval England,* vol. v (Manchester, 1930), ch. xvi; A. L. Brown, 'The Privy Seal in the Early Fifteenth Century' (D.Phil. thesis, Oxford, 1954), and 'The Privy Seal Clerks of the Early Fifteenth Century', *The Study of Medieval Records,* ed. D. A. Bullough and R. L. Storey (Oxford, 1971), pp. 260-81. Brown writes in his essay (p. 271): 'What he [Hoccleve] wrote was apparently in essence true. His service in the Privy Seal, his annuity, his hostel, even to some extent his breakdown, can be substantiated from the records.' (I am grateful to my colleague John Guy for help with Privy Seal matters.)

8. Kane, p. 5.

9. Kane, p. 5.

10. The date of Hoccleve's death was established by A. L. Brown: see *The Study of Medieval Records,* p. 270. On the date of the 'Male Regle,' see J. H. Kern, 'Een en ander over Thomas Hoccleve en zijne werken', *Verslagen en Mededeelingen der Koninklijke Akademie van Wetenschappen,* 5th series, i (1915), 344-47 (I am grateful to Hanneke Wirtjes for excerpting this article from the Dutch). Kern's dating, late 1405 or early 1406, is followed by Seymour, *Selections,* pp. 109-10. On the date of the *Regement,* see Kern, art. cit., 351-58. On the date of the *Series,* see Kern, art. cit., 362-71, and 'Die Datierung von Hoccleve's Dialog', *Anglia* xl (1916), 370-3. Kern dates the 'Dialogue' (the second part of the *Series,* and the only part that can be dated) in 1422; but he fails to notice that the wording of the reference to a coinage statute of the Parliament of May 1421 ('Dialogue' 134-40) clearly shows that it is a later insertion in a passage written before the statute was passed. The 'Dialogue' was therefore presumably first composed during Humphrey of Gloucester's first, not his second, spell as 'lieutenant' ('Dialogue' 533): between 30 December 1419 and 1 February 1421. The allusion in 'Dialogue' 542-3 to Humphrey's *secundo reditu* from France must refer to his return late in 1419 from his second campaign in France, not to his return in 1422 from his third, as Seymour supposes (*Selections,* p. 136). Since Hoccleve says that he was 53 years old at the time of writing the 'Dialogue' (l. 246), he was most likely born in 1366 or 1367.

11. E. A. Thornley, 'The Middle English Penitential Lyric and Hoccleve's Autobiographical Poetry', *Neuphilologische Mitteilungen* 68 (1967), 295-321. Thornley refers especially to the lyric beginning 'In my youth

full wild I was', No. 6 in F. A. Patterson, *The Middle English Penitential Lyric* (New York, 1911).

12. P. B. R. Doob, *Nebuchadnezzar's Children: Conventions of Madness in Middle English Literature* (New Haven, Conn., 1974), pp. 213, 226.

13. *Minor Poems,* pp. 289-93. For the identity of Thomas Marleburgh, Hoccleve's patron, see *Minor Poems,* p. 272. The poem appears as the 'Ploughman's Tale' in the copy of the *Canterbury Tales* in Christ Church, Oxford. On the relation of Hoccleve's poetry to Chaucer's, see generally the remarks of M. R. Pryor in her edition of the *Series* (p. 389 n. 1 above), pp. 30-54.

14. J. Mitchell, *Thomas Hoccleve: A Study in Early Fifteenth-Century Poetic* (Urbana, Ill., 1968), p. 117.

15. *Regement* 2080-107, cf. 1958-74. The French poet Deschamps wrote in similar terms about his master Machaut: ballades nos. 123 and 124 in Deschamps, *Œuvres,* ed. le marquis de Queux de Saint-Hilaire and G. Raynaud (Paris, 1878-1903).

16. *Troy Book,* ed. H. Bergen, EETS, ES 97, 103, 106, 126 (1906-20), V 3519-26.

17. Doob, p. 221.

18. In his illuminating discussion of Hoccleve, S. Medcalf cites a modern psychoanalyst's judgement on the case: *The Later Middle Ages,* ed. Medcalf (London, 1981), pp. 129-30.

19. Op. cit., p. 226. Note, however, Brown's opinion: 'In his "Complaint" . . . written about 1420-1, perhaps during Lent 1421, Hoccleve states that he regained his sanity on 1 Nov., five years previously. This may be one reason why he did not come to the Exchequer personally between May 1414 and Mar. 1417 to collect payments due to him,' *The Study of Medieval Records,* p. 271.

20. Op. cit., p. 230.

21. Op. cit., p. 228.

22. Philippe Lejeune defines autobiography as follows: 'Récit rétrospectif en prose qu'une personne réelle fait de sa propre existence, lorsqu'elle met l'accent sur sa vie individuelle, en particulier sur l'histoire de sa personnalité', *Le Pacte autobiographique,* p. 14.

23. *Pacte autobiographique,* p. 315, citing Georg Misch, *Geschichte der Autobiographie,* 8 vols (Frankfurt, 1949-69) and Zumthor, *Essai de poétique médiévale,* pp. 68-9, 172-4.

24. For a discussion of autobiography laying emphasis on functional considerations and employing the Austin/Searle concept of speech-acts, see E. W. Bruss, 'L'autobiographie considérée comme acte littéraire', *Poétique* xvii (1974), 14-26.

25. The editors of the proposed new critical edition of the *Regement* count 43 MSS. The Robbins-Cutler *Supplement to the Index of Middle English Verse* counts 45 (including two MSS with short extracts), putting the poem ninth in their list of Middle English works preserved in the most MSS. On the popularity of such works in the fifteenth century, see R. F. Green, *Poets and Princepleasers: Literature and the English Court in the Late Middle Ages* (Toronto, 1980), ch. 5.

26. 'Hoccleve's *Series*: Experience and Books', forthcoming in a volume of essays on fifteenth-century literature edited by R. F. Yeager. Hoccleve describes his antics in front of the mirror in *Complaint* 155-68.

27. See for example *Complaint* 70-98 and 183 ff., describing the poet's nervous reactions to the 'press' in Westminster Hall and on the London pavements. Unlike Donne and Pope, Hoccleve does not appear to have known the satires of Horace or Juvenal.

28. *The Later Middle Ages,* p. 127.

29. On the life of the Privy Seal clerks, see the studies by Tout and Brown cited at p. 392 n. 3 above, especially ch. 7 of Brown's thesis.

30. *Balade to Maister Somer* (*Minor Poems,* p. 59) 25-7; also *Balade to Henry V* (*Minor Poems,* p. 62).

31. Brown's thesis describes the function of the Privy Seal clerks in dealing with many of the several thousand petitions presented to the King each year (ch. 2) and discusses the general importance of petitions as 'the key to all administrative action' (pp. 340-5). See also Green, *Poets and Princepleasers,* pp. 42-3, and J. A. Tuck, 'Richard II's System of Patronage', in *The Reign of Richard II,* ed. F. R. H. Du Boulay and C. M. Barron (London, 1971), pp. 1-20. Tuck writes: 'The importance of the petition in medieval government can hardly be over-emphasized: patronage as much as justice was founded upon it' (p. 4). For a collection of petitions from Hoccleve's time, see *Anglo-Norman Letters and Petitions from All Souls MS. 182,* ed. M. D. Legge, Anglo-Norman Text Society 3 (Oxford, 1941), pp. 1-41. See also J. A. Burrow, 'The Poet as Petitioner', *Studies in the Age of Chaucer* 3 (1981), 61-75.

32. The formulary is BL MS Add. 24062. See 'The Formulary of Thomas Hoccleve', ed. E.-J. Y. Bentley (Ph.D. thesis, Emory University, 1965), item 175, p. 166. Brown discusses the formulary in his thesis, Appendix B.

33. Ed. Bentley, item 892, p. 1030.

34. The importance for a petitioner of having a sponsor willing to use influence on his behalf at court is stressed by Brown (thesis, pp. 30 and 345), Green (*Poets and Princepleasers,* pp. 49-52), and Tuck (*Reign of Richard II,* pp. 15-17). Hoccleve's petitionary poetry, both secular and religious, frequently refers to such intermediaries or 'menes': e.g. *Regement* 302, 3187; *Minor Poems* p. 46 l. 89, p. 53 l. 44, p. 54 l. 83, p. 63 l. 23, p. 71 l. 125, p. 135 l. 709, p. 277 l. 64.

35. *Minor Poems,* pp. 58-64; 'Male Regle' 417-48; *Regement* 4360-403. The *Regement* appeal is neatly worked into a discussion of Prodigality (to which Hoccleve confesses, as in 'Male Regle') and Largesse (for which he hopes).

36. *Regement* 4705-8. Cf. Seneca, *De Beneficiis,* ed. J. W. Basore (Loeb, 1935), II. i. 4: 'Non tulit gratis, qui, cum rogasset, accepit, quoniam quidem, ut maioribus nostris gravissimis viris visum est, nulla res carius constat, quam quae precibus empta est.'

37. *Balade to My Gracious Lord of York (Minor Poems,* p. 49) 17-18.

John Burrow (essay date 1984)

SOURCE: Burrow, John. "Hoccleve's *Series*: Experience and Books." In *Fifteenth-Century Studies: Recent Essays,* pp. 259-273. Hamden, Conn.: Archon Books, 1984.

[*In the following essay, Burrow reviews the structure of Hoccleve's collection of writings titled the* Series. *Burrow emphasizes similarities to Chaucerian works, especially the* Canterbury Tales, *and examines Hoccleve's tendency toward self-reference.*]

Criticism has hardly begun to do justice to the poetry of Thomas Hoccleve. The names of Hoccleve and Lydgate are often coupled together, like Gray and Collins, or Moody and Sankey; but the two poets are different in many ways. Lydgate is, in my judgment, distinctly inferior to his contemporary as a writer—in his command, that is, of English idiom, syntax, and meter. Yet ever since the fifteenth century the massive bulk of Lydgate's work has overshadowed Hoccleve and obscured the qualities and merits of his work. To define his qualities and merits is not easy, for Hoccleve is in some ways an eccentric and peculiar writer—not at all the Chaucer clone of some literary histories—and he is also very uneven in the quality of his work. One moment the reader is startled by a sinewy felicity of phrase or a bold originality of conception; the next moment he is yawning over the "bore of the Privy Seal." But all Hoccleve's works—the shorter poems, the **Regement of Princes,** and the *Series*—merit more attention than they have so far received from editors, critics, and readers.[1] The present essay is devoted to the boldest and most interesting of them: the so-called *Series.*

The title *Series* was given by E. P. Hammond to a linked sequence of writings, mostly verse but including three short pieces of prose, composed by Hoccleve in the last years of his life (he died in 1426) and preserved complete or nearly so in six manuscripts.[2] It consists of the following parts: a prologue, the **"Complaint,"** the **"Dialogue with a Friend"**; an envoy, the **"Tale of Jereslaus's Wife,"** four linking stanzas, a prose **"Moralization"** of the preceding **"Tale," "Learn to Die,"** three linking stanzas, a prose version of the ninth lesson for All Hallows' Day, a linking prologue, the **"Tale of Jonathas,"** a prose **"Moralisation"** of the tale, and (in one manuscript only) a single-stanza envoy.

Derek Pearsall draws attention to the chief peculiarity of the *Series* when he describes it, somewhat tartly, as "an attempt to make a longish poem out of nothing."[3] At the core of the work, in the **"Dialogue with a Friend,"** Hoccleve does indeed represent himself as wishing to write but uncertain what to write about; and when after long discussion with his friendly advisor he finally settles on a story from the *Gesta Romanorum* (the story of Jereslaus's wife) and a moral discourse on holy dying, these decisions, though not random, are frankly advertised as secondary to that initial desire to "make a longish poem." Indeed, the *Series* as a whole is to an unusual degree preoccupied with the business of its own composition. It is a measure of the general neglect of Hoccleve that the current fashion for reading texts as "self-referential" or "reflexive" has not yet caught up with the *Series,* which is far and away the most reflexive of all medieval English writings.

Hoccleve, as I hope to show, understood quite well the tricks which could be played with self-reference. His conventional sections of narrative and moral discourse (the two tales, their moralisations, **"Learn to Die,"** and the version of the All Hallows lesson) are all "framed" by passages which purport to describe how they came to be written; and these passages of explanation, since they themselves form part of the work whose production they describe, enjoy a special double status, which Hoccleve from time to time exploits to produce that effect described by André Gide as "mise en abyme." The work turns in upon itself, as in the Escher drawing of a hand drawing itself. However, such reflexive tricks are neither so difficult of execution nor so profound in implication as some contemporary writers, artists, and film-makers seem to suppose; and if Hoccleve's *Series* were chiefly a book concerned with its own production, it would indeed deserve to be dismissed as a longish poem "made out of nothing." A profoundly bookish work it certainly is— aware of its own existence as a book, of its derivation from other books, and of its destination in the hands of patrons and readers. But books are themselves a part of life, not least in the case of an author who was himself a professional scribe; and Hoccleve takes pains to represent the production of this particular book as an event of great importance in his own life.[4] He has, he confesses, suffered a breakdown; and his friends and acquaintances still regard him with anxiety and suspicion, even though he has long since recovered. The *Series* is therefore designed both to affirm his recovery and also, by its very existence, to prove it by showing that he can indeed talk sense again. Both ways the book marks a stage in that social rehabilitation which has, he complains, been so slow to follow his medical recovery. The reflexiveness of the work is accordingly as far as could be from mere mandarin cleverness. With all its faults, the *Series* has deep roots in painful human experience.[5]

The prologue opens with an elaborate *chronographia* which invites comparison with Chaucer's *Canterbury Tales:*

After that hervest Inned had his sheves
And that the broune season of myhelmesse
Was come and gan the trees robbe of ther leves
That grene had bene / and in lusty fresshnesse
And them into colowre / of yelownesse
Hadd dyen / and doune throwne undar foote
That chaunge sanke / into myne herte roote.

("Complaint," lines 1-7)

The plangent description of the "brown season of Michael-mas" seems designed, as Pryor suggests, to contrast point-edly with Chaucer's April opening; and this contrast is sustained in what follows. Whereas in the *Canterbury Tales* April inspires the poet to go out and join a company of pilgrims, November drives Hoccleve in upon himself in solitary meditation. He passes a sleepless night at the end of November, brooding on the unhappy aftermath of his illness:

I see well sythen I with sycknes last
Was scourged / clowdy hath bene the favoure
That shone on me / full bright in tymes past
The sonne abatid / and the derke showre
Hildyd downe right on me.

(lines 22-26)

Hoccleve here develops Chaucer's image of Fortune "covering her bright face with a cloud" (*Monk's Tale, Canterbury Tales* VII 2766). The violent dark shower which pours straight down upon him represents the extreme distress which leads Hoccleve, next morning, to burst out in his complaint:

I thowght I nolde it kepe cloos no more
Ne lett it in me / for to olde and hore
And for to pryve / I cam of a woman
I braste oute on the morowe / and thus began.

(lines 32-35)

The rubric which follows these lines, "here endythe my prologe and folowythe my complaynt," may remind the reader that he is reading a book, in which a "**Prologue**" is followed by a "**Complaint**"; but the ensuing pages dispel this awareness for the time being. Hoccleve does indeed "braste oute" in his distress; and, apart from one Chaucerian reference to "my mater" (line 119), the 378 lines of the "**Complaint**" create an uninterrupted impression of direct and impassioned utterance. Hoccleve recalls his breakdown, the "wyld infirmytie" from which he claims to have recovered fully five years before on All Hallows' Day, and regrets that people do not even now believe that he is fully better:

Chaungid had I my pas / some seiden eke
For here and there / forthe stirte I as a Roo
None abode / none arrest but all brain seke.

(lines 127-29)

The more or less well-intentioned doubts of his acquaintances, so sharply etched in lines such as these (the choppy movement of 129 is particularly good), both depress and exasperate Hoccleve; and the exasperation and depression find convincing utterance in the rambling, repetitive progress of his complaint. At one point he reports "words of consolation" found recently in a book; but here, as in Chaucer's *Parliament of Fowls,* the record of reading serves only to confirm the actual reader's tendency to forget that what *he* is reading is also, in fact, a book.[6]

The opening of the "**Dialogue with a Friend,**" however, disturbs the illusion created by the preceding "**Complaint.**" With something of the impetuosity of Chaucer's Pandarus, a friend beats on the poet's door:

And ended my complaynt / in this manere
One knocked / at my chambre dore sore
And cryed a lowde / howe hoccleve arte thow here.

("Dialogue," lines 1-3)

Is "complaynt" in line 1 the title of a text, or does it simply refer to the utterance? The indecisive punctuation in Furni-vall's edition, with inverted commas but no capital *C,* reflects a real uncertainty; but this is resolved once Hoc-cleve, in response to the friend's question "What dydist thow when I knocked?", reads the "**Complaint**" out to him (line 17; see also lines 39-42, 317). Hoccleve, in fact, has been writing. This is a new discovery, not prepared for in the previous section: indeed, the expression "braste out" distinctly suggested a spontaneous utterance, not a composition. If the "**Complaint**" can now be accepted as a piece of writing, this can only be because we have in fact been reading it. The logic of this response, it may be noted, would have been stronger in an age of manuscript that it is in the age of print. When the record of an act of writing is itself printed (in epistolary novels, for instance), no reader will ever be tempted actually to identify the two texts; but the reader of manuscript is in a rather different position. Hoccleve was himself a clerk and scribe; and Durham University Library still possesses a copy of the *Series* itself written in his own hand. It is not that any reader of the Durham *Series,* even if he had known the hand to be Hoccleve's, would have believed that the formal copy which lay before him, with its capital letters il-luminated in red, blue, and gold, contained the actual leaves from which the poet read to his friend. The ques-tion is not one of real belief, but of suspended disbelief or literary illusion: the particular illusion which Hoccleve is here aiming at would have been easier for the author and stronger for the reader at a time when books were handwritten. It is surprising, in fact, that medieval writers did not more often employ this kind of reflexive device.[7]

After Hoccleve had read out his "**Complaint**" and discussed it with his friend (up to line 198 of the "**Dialogue**"), they go on to consider what he should write next. The "**Dialogue,**" in fact, acts as an extended "link" (in Canterbury terminology) between the "**Complaint**" and the two next parts of the *Series*: the "**Tale of Jere-slaus's Wife**" and "**Learn to Die.**" This manner of construction implies that the "**Dialogue**" is itself not a composition, just as the Canterbury links are not tales; and Hoccleve sustains this pretense successfully, on the whole,

31

with lively conversational effects. The main blemish—and it is a serious one—is the passage in which the poet harangues his friend on the evils of tampering with coin of the realm (**"Dialogue,"** lines 99-196). The impression of a written set-piece here is confirmed by an untimely reminder of its textual character in the shape of a clumsy postscript announcing that, since the passage was written, Parliament has made a new law to deal with the abuse (lines 134-40). In general, the **"Dialogue"** is certainly too long (826 lines); but it derives considerable interest from its relationship to the preceding and succeeding compositions.

The discussion of the **"Complaint"** turns on the question of whether this composition should be published ("made forthe to goo amonge the people," lines 23-24). The friend advises against, on the principle of letting sleeping dogs lie:

> How it stode with the / leyde is all a slepe
> Men have forget it / it is owt of mynd.
>
> (**"Dialogue,"** lines 29-30)

He counsels a prudent silence, like the well-intentioned Arbuthnot in Pope's *Prologue to the Satires*: "Good friend, forbear! you deal in dangerous things."[8] But the friend's reasons for this advice exasperate Hoccleve, for he is displaying just that failure to understand which has been making life so difficult for the poet. How can he say that Hoccleve's history of mental illness is "owt of mynd"? Wasn't he listening when the poet, so very recently, read him his **"Complaint"**? The tragic theme of human isolation and misunderstanding is here given a comic twist, for the reader knows that the publication of the **"Complaint"** is a foregone conclusion. Also, Hoccleve seems to recognize in his own response something of that touchiness for which authors have always been notorious.

Discussion of the **"Complaint"** comes to an end with Hoccleve's harangue about the coinage. This display of public spirit evidently reassures the friend for the time being, and the conversation turns to future works. Now that the **"Complaint"** is finished, Hoccleve declares his intention of composing one last English piece: a translation of a little treatise in Latin called **"Learn to Die"** (lines 205-06). It seems an appropriate task for a poet who, at fifty-three years of age, realizes the vanity of life and the inevitability of death:

> Shee is the rogh besom / which shal us alle
> Sweepe out of this world / whan god list it falle.
>
> (lines 286-87)

At this, Hoccleve's friend begins to worry again. The poet's breakdown, he says, was caused by excessive study (musing, staring, and poring upon books, lines 404-05), and further bookwork may cause a relapse. With an effect of repetition which certainly does not lack point, the friend again gives expression to that mistrust from which Hoccleve seems unable to escape, in an image of great beauty and simplicity:

> Thogh a strong fyr / that was in an herth late
> Withdrawen be / and swept away ful cleene
> Yit aftirwarde / bothe the herth ande plate
> Been of the fyr warm / thogh no fyr be seene.
>
> (lines 309-12)

Hoccleve responds with appeals to friendship and protestations that his breakdown was caused not by study but by a physical illness, from which he is now fully recovered; and after he has promised not to overexert himself, the friend professes himself satisfied (lines 512-25).

The reader expects **"Learn to Die"** to follow on the next leaf, but it does not. Instead, three hundred more lines of the **"Dialogue"** serve as introduction to a composition which, in the event, precedes the moral discourse in the order of the *Series*: the **"Tale of Jereslaus's Wife."** Courthope may have had this section in mind when he spoke of Hoccleve's "crude and inartistic conception";[9] but the unexpected developments in this last part of the **"Dialogue"** in fact confirm just the impression which the *Series* as a whole is seeking to create—the impression of a book whose contents are being inscribed, as it were, before the reader's very eyes. Despite all the thought and calculation of which we see so much, such a work will be a prey to present contingencies. On this occasion, the friend calls to mind that last September Hoccleve said he had promised a book to Humphrey, Duke of Gloucester. Is "this book" then meant for him (line 539)? Hoccleve answers this eminently reflexive question in the affirmative, but goes on to confess that he is not sure what will best please the Duke—a translation of Vegetius on the art of chivalry, perhaps, or a chronicle of Humphrey's own chivalrous deeds. The friend acknowledges the difficulty, and cites a well-known passage from Geoffrey of Vinsauf about the importance of planning or "avisament" in literary composition.[10] He proposes that Hoccleve should write something in praise of women, as an act of penance for the offense he gave them in an earlier work, the **"Letter of Cupid."** The Duke himself will enjoy such a book, and also no doubt, being given to polite "daliance" with ladies, will show it to them and so restore Hoccleve to their favor. The friend leaves, and Hoccleve addresses a formal envoy of three stanzas to his female readers ("My ladyes alle . . . ," line 806). He will translate a story of a good woman from the *Gesta Romanorum*:

> and that shal pourge I hope
> My guilt / as cleene / as keverchiefs dooth sope.
>
> (lines 825-26)

With this spirited, even faintly rebellious couplet Hoccleve concludes the **"Dialogue"** and introduces the **"Tale of Jereslaus's Wife."**

The story of the virtuous wife of the Emperor of Rome is extravagant both in plot and character, much in the manner of Chaucer's *Man of Law's Tale*; but this very extravagance serves to mark the story off as existing on a different plane of reality from what has preceded it. In this case it seems entirely appropriate that Hoccleve should read it out to his friend, and that the friend should criticize it as a composition for lacking the *moralisatio*:

> Where is the moralizynge / y yow preye
> Bycome heere of / was ther noon in the booke
> Out of the which / that thow this tale tooke.

(lines 12-14)

When the friend goes off home to get his own more complete copy, from which Hoccleve then obediently translates the allegorical moralization, the realism of these comings and goings is such that the reader is surprised when the prose text is followed immediately by the promised **"Learn to Die,"** with no link other than a rubric: "Explicit moralizatio & incipit ars utillissima sciendi mori."[11] In the *Canterbury Tales* the absence of a prologue or epilogue tears a hole in the fabric of the fiction; but the effect here is rather different, since the reader must by now understand the double nature of the book he is reading. It not only describes the making of a book, but also *is* that book—in which a simple rubric would be enough to link the most diverse items.

After translating part of the Latin **"Learn to Die,"** Hoccleve confesses that he has had enough and substitutes for the remainder his version of the ninth lesson for All Hallows' Day (the day on which, five years earlier, he had recovered from his breakdown, **"Complaint,"** lines 55-56). This describes the joys of the celestial Jerusalem, and its conclusion brings with it a strong sense of an ending: "to grete foles been we / but if we cheese the bettre part / which part god of his infynyt goodnesse graunte us alle to cheese / Amen." Hoccleve has produced the two works promised in the **"Dialogue"**; and the words just quoted suggest that, like Chaucer at the end of the *Canterbury Tales,* "the maker of this book here taketh his leave." But Hoccleve has one more surprise in store. The word *Amen* is followed immediately by another rubric: "Hic additur alia fabula ad instanciam amici mei predilecti assiduam." Hoccleve had indeed intended to end with the lesson ("This booke thus to han endid had y thoght," **"Jonathas,"** line 1); but his friend requests one more item: another *Gesta Romanorum* story to warn his unruly fifteen-year-old son against the wiles of women. He promises to let the poet use his own copy again; and Hoccleve, although afraid that such a tale may undo all his previous good work with women readers, agrees to make a version:

> He glad was ther withal / and wel content
> The copie on the morwe sente he me
> And thus y wroot as yee may heere see.

(**"Jonathas,"** lines 82-84)

With that last characteristic direction to the reader, Hoccleve vanishes from the scene, leaving us, for what remains of the *Series,* face-to-face with a conventional book—first, the fantastic *Gesta* story of Jonathas and his unscrupulous mistress, then (without a link) a prose *moralisatio,* and finally, in the Durham copy, a single eight-line stanza directing the whole "smal booke" to the Countess of Westmorland.[12] The author's conjuring tricks are over.

As we have seen, Hoccleve presents himself throughout the *Series* as a reader of books engaged in producing, by translation from Isidore, Suso, and the *Gesta Romanorum,* a book of his own, and concerned that this book should meet a favorable reception from its readers. To appreciate the *Series* it is above all necessary to understand, and if possible sympathize with, the nature of this concern about the work's reception. From the start, Hoccleve displays an acute, even morbid, sensitivity to the possibilities of unfavorable response. First there is the question, discussed at length in the **"Dialogue,"** of whether his **"Complaint"** should be published at all. Hoccleve himself in the poem insists that it should, to set the record straight; but the friend's profound doubts and anxieties create a distinctly uneasy impression, preserved as they are in the text which Hoccleve in fact did publish. Then there is the question of what the poet should write for Humphrey of Gloucester. **"Learn to Die"** may please the "devout man" who first suggested it (**"Dialogue,"** lines 234-35), but is it not rather too heavy for the duke? And what about those ladies whom Hoccleve has unwittingly offended by an earlier act of translation? In the event, the friend persuades him to kill two birds with one stone by telling the story of Jereslaus's wife; but Hoccleve's worries are not over yet. The friend's innocent request for something to give his wayward son raises further problems, for a thoroughgoing exposure of female wiles, suitable for the boy, may once again alienate respectable lady readers. Even the conventional closing words of the *Series,* in the Durham autograph manuscript, seem to be tinged with anxiety. Hoccleve commands his "smal booke" to present itself to Joan, Countess of Westmorland (daughter of John of Gaunt and aunt of Humphrey of Gloucester):

> And byseeche hire / on my behalve and preye
> Thee to receyve / for hire owne right
> And looke thow / in al manere weye
> To plese hir wommanhede / do thy might
>   Humble servant
>   to your gracious
>   noblesse

: T: Hoccleve

Authors frequently express eagerness to please readers, not least wealthy and powerful patrons; but there is much more than mere convention or normal self-interest in Hoccleve's persistent expressions of concern about how his book will be received by his acquaintances, the Duke of Gloucester, the ladies, and the Countess of Westmorland. They are to be understood, in part, as manifestations of that "thowghtfull dissease and woo" (**"Complaint,"** line 388) of which he speaks at length in the **"Complaint"** and **"Dialogue"**—the same state of anxiety which drove him to practice sane faces in the mirror at home (**"Complaint,"** lines 155-68). His recovery from his breakdown (allowing him to have indeed recovered) has left him morbidly concerned about what people think of him and his work.

Hoccleve may have taken some hints for this self-portrait from Chaucer's dream poems; but no English writer had attempted such a full representation of anxiety before his time. He is our first chronicler of private worries—an ancestor, perhaps, of Charles Lamb and Philip Larkin. In his lowest moments, he seems simply to indulge his gloom: "This troubly lyfe / hathe all to longe enduryd // Not have I wyst / how in my skynne to turne." (**"Complaint,"** 302-03). But in the *Series* as a whole, he tries hard to "turn in his skin," and the work benefits morally and artistically from the effort. Hoccleve sees the writing and publication of his latest book as an important stage in the process by which he may finally be rehabilitated after his illness and its long aftermath. Furthermore, the book itself seems to trace the steps of such a rehabilitation. It is not tightly constructed, but the order of its parts is more significant than may at first appear. It begins in solitary alienation, and it ends with the reassumption (albeit hesitant) of a social role proper to a man of fifty-three. The structure of the work, though imperfect, does something to articulate the author's deepest concern.

The opening complaint is at first presented simply as a solitary outburst of unbearable misery; but, like Boethius's *planctus* at the beginning of *De Consolatione Philosophiae*, Hoccleve's marks the starting-point for a process of consolation.[13] In both works this process begins with the arrival of a second person: Lady Philosophy in the Latin, a friend in the English. The progress from one to two is itself significant; and in Hoccleve's discussion with his friend, as noted earlier, we for the first time see his complaint not as a mere solitary outburst but as a publishable writing.[14] Hoccleve's determination to publish it, against the advice of the friend (not, like Lady Philosophy, infallible), represents the first and decisive step in his rehabilitation. He is, he says, not ashamed of his affliction: it was "the stroke of god" (**"Dialogue,"** line 79). He is therefore ready to "make an open shryfte" (line 83) by publishing the **"Complaint,"** which both confesses his mental illness and affirms his recovery from it.

However, such a publication is itself too abnormal to mark a return to normality, and discussion of the three remaining publications (**"Learn to Die"** and the two *Gesta* stories) is colored by Hoccleve's still unsatisfied yearning for completely normal relations with his fellow men. **"Learn to Die"** is an entirely conventional moral treatise undertaken at the urging of a devout man, and there is nothing abnormal in the poet's desire to cleanse his soul by this act of translation (**"Dialogue,"** line 214-17); yet it is made clear in Hoccleve's discussion with his friend that the composition also has a private significance. It is the first true literary labor he has undertaken since his breakdown. He has waited for five years "al to preeve my selfe" (line 444); and now he is ready for the work which he has pondered so long. To perform it successfully will prove both to himself and to others that his mind really is, as he claims, "as sad and stable / As evere it was at any tyme or this" (lines 366-67).

Despite its impersonal and conventional nature, then, **"Learn to Die"** still plays a part in the private drama of Hoccleve's recovery. One might also see in Suso's description of the dying man deserted by his friends (following lines 424 and 709) a reflection of the poet's own sense of isolation. By contrast, the two *Gesta* stories, of the virtuous wife of Jereslaus and the wicked Fellicula, have no direct bearing on Hoccleve's personal circumstances; and his account of their composition claims for them no diagnostic or therapeutic significance. Hoccleve, it seems, now takes for granted his ability to fulfill literary commissions. Yet there remains the question of how his writings will be received. Perhaps the discussion of Humphrey's literary tastes displays no more than a customary concern for the satisfaction of a patron; but when the friend speaks of Hoccleve's offense to women, we recognize the familiar, nagging personal note. The idea of making amends to women readers for an earlier literary offense is presumably borrowed from Hoccleve's master, Chaucer: the tale of Jereslaus's wife is a latter-day *Legend of Good Women*. Yet Hoccleve's tone is, in a very characteristic way, different from Chaucer's. When Chaucer has Alceste plead that he wrote about Criseyde "of innocence, and nyste what he seyde" (Prologue to the *Legend*, G 345), the unlikely claim coolly outstares the facts, with an effect of teasing comedy. By contrast, Hoccleve's defense of the **"Letter of Cupid,"** although conducted along similar lines, leaves an impression of real anxiety:

> Considereth / ther of / was I noon Auctour
> I nas in that cas / but a reportour
> Of folkes tales / as they seide I wroot
> I nat affermed it on hem / god woot . . .
> Who so that seith I am hire Adversarie
> And dispreise hir condicions and port
> For that I made of hem swich a report /
> He mis avysed is / and eek to blame.
>
> (**"Dialogue,"** lines 760-63, 768-71)

Such misunderstandings and mistaken gossip are no laughing matter, in the context of the *Series,* and the poet's attempt to set the record straight quite lacks Chaucer's *sang froid*. A note of pleading in Hoccleve's voice serves as a reminder that women formed an influential part of that society from which his illness alienated him.

Although Hoccleve's last conversation with his friend, in the prologue to **"Jonathas,"** still expresses some fear of being misunderstood, the main impression which he creates, in this final appearance, is one of confidence restored and status regained. To produce a moral tale for the benefit of his friend's erring son is a comfortable sort of commission. The poet, at last, has the advantage of his worried friend, and it is now Hoccleve who speaks for society, uttering the common wisdom of the elders of the tribe. It is a very different sort of utterance from the solitary grieving with which the *Series* began; and it seems intended to mark a happy ending to the poet's struggle to rehabilitate himself.

In the world of Hoccleve's *Series,* books are part of life—patrons commission them, readers borrow them, authors worry about them—and the *Series* itself strikes many readers as an almost painfully "real" book. One mark of this reality is the curious irritation which it seems to provoke. Like Lydgate, Hoccleve can be rambling and wordy; but his artistic defects do not fully account for the common response, which seems to have in it something of the herd's reaction to a wounded animal. Hoccleve's anxiety to be once more accepted puts backs up; and when he takes it upon himself to speak of the common good, as in the harangue on the coinage, readers are quick to detect a false note. We understand only too well, in short, why even his friend found it so hard to believe in him. But it is time that criticism began to do justice to a writer who had, besides his terrible frankness, a real literary talent.

Notes

1. The Early English Text Society edition is still standard: *Minor Poems* I, ed. F. J. Furnivall, ES 61 (London, 1892); *Regement of Princes,* ed. Furnivall, ES 72 (London, 1897); *Minor Poems* II, ed. Israel Gollancz, ES 73 (London, 1897). See also *Selections from Hoccleve,* ed. M. C. Seymour (Oxford: Clarendon Press, 1981). Further bibliography in the only book-length study, Jerome Mitchell, *Thomas Hoccleve: A Study in Early Fifteenth-Century English Poetic* (Urbana: University of Illinois Press, 1968) and in his essay in this present volume. The discussion of Hoccleve's metrical art in Ian Robinson, *Chaucer's Prosody* (Cambridge: Cambridge University Press, 1971), pp. 190-99, is a valuable recent addition.

2. Durham University Library Cosin MS. V.iii.9; Bodleian Library MS. Bodley 221; Bodleian Library MS. Laud Misc. 735; Bodleian Library MS. Arch. Selden Supra 53; Coventry City Record Office MS. Accession 325/1; Yale University Library MS. 493. The Durham copy is in the hand of Hoccleve himself from "Dialogue" line 253 to the end, and provides the basis of the text in *Minor Poems* I, and also in M. R. Pryor's doctoral thesis, "Thomas Hoccleve's *Series*: An Edition of MS. Durham Cosin V.iii.9," (University of California, Los Angeles, 1968), from which all quotations in this essay are taken. "Complaint" lines 1-308, is edited in J. A. Burrow's *English Verse 1300-1500* (London: Longman, 1977), "Dialogue," lines 498-826, in E. P. Hammond's *English Verse between Chaucer and Surrey* (Durham, N.C.: Duke University Press, 1927). For the date of Hoccleve's death and other biographical matters, see A. L. Brown, "The Privy Seal Clerks in the Early Fifteenth Century," in *The Study of Medieval Records: Essays in Honour of Kathleen Major,* ed. D. A. Bullough and R. L. Storey (Oxford: Oxford University Press, 1971), pp. 260-81.

3. *Old English and Middle English Poetry* (London: Routledge and Kegan Paul, 1977), p. 237.

4. See H. C. Schulz, "Thomas Hoccleve, Scribe," *Speculum* 12 (1937): 71-81. Also A. I. Doyle and M. B. Parkes, "The Production of MSS. of the *Canterbury Tales* and the *Confessio Amantis* in the Early Fifteenth Century," in *Medieval Scribes, Manuscripts and Libraries: Essays Presented to N. R. Ker,* ed. M. B. Parkes and A. G. Watson (London: Scolar Press, 1978), pp. 164-210.

5. Penelope Doob, *Nebuchadnezzar's Children: Conventions of Madness in Middle English Literature* (New Haven, Conn.: Yale University Press, 1974), remarks that "many 'autobiographical' details in all [Hoccleve's] poems could easily be conventional or borrowed" (p. 228), stressing traditional elements in the poet's account of his breakdown in the *Series.* But it is not safe to assume that a real experience will not be described (or indeed experienced) in conventional terms; and A. L. Brown, "Privy Seal Clerks," gives grounds for supposing that Hoccleve was indeed ill at about the time indicated ("Complaint," line 56): "He did not come to the Exchequer personally between May 1414 and March 1417 to collect payments due to him" (p. 271). Pryor observes: "Comparing the records with events and personalities mentioned in the poems, there seems to be a remarkable coincidence between the autobiographical 'fictions' and the established facts" ("Hoccleve's *Series,*" p. 28). See also J. A. Burrow, "Autobiographical Poetry in the Middle Ages: The Case of Thomas Hoccleve," *Proceedings of the British Academy* 68 (1982): 389-412.

6. The book has been identified by A. G. Rigg as Isidore of Seville's *Synonyma,* subtitled *De Lamentatione Animae Dolentis*: "Hoccleve's *Complaint* and Isidore of Seville," see *Speculum* 45 (1970): 564-74. The sudden intrusion of the owner, who takes the Isidore back before Hoccleve can finish it, ingeniously marks the distinction, in the poem's fictive space, between Hoccleve's primary, foreground world and the secondary, recessed world in the books he reads. The commonplace critical term "three-dimensional" applies here with special force, since it is only in three dimensions that the edge of one thing can interrupt our view of another.

7. In his *Livre du Voir-Dit,* Guillaume de Machaut describes himself as compiling a book and invites the reader to identify the result with the volume in his hands ("ce livre"). He records the love poems and letters exchanged with Peronne d'Armentières, as they were written and received by him, in his "true-story book": see the edition of Paulin Paris (Paris: Société des Bibliophiles François, 1875; reprint, Geneva: Slatkine Reprints, pp. 17, 66, 76, 84-85, 134, 191, 202-03, 259, 261, 262, 263, 363. Hoccleve's younger contemporary, James I of Scotland, in his *Kingis Quair,* provides another example: "I set me doun, / And furthwithall my pen in hand I tuke / And maid a [cros], and thus begouth my buke" (ed. J. Norton-Smith [Oxford: Clarendon Press, 1971] lines 89-91). Where the editor's text reads "[cros]," the sole remaining manuscript has an actual cross.

8. A comparison suggested by W. J. Courthope in his interesting discussion of Hoccleve, *A History of English Poetry,* 6 vols. (London and New York: Macmillan, 1895), 1:333-40.

9. Ibid., p. 337.

10. *Poetria Nova,* ed. Edmond Faral, in *Les arts poetiques du XIIe et du XIIIe siècle* (Paris: Champion, 1924), pp 43-45. In the Durham MS. Hoccleve writes in the margin opposite "Dialogue," lines 638ff., Geoffrey's words: "Si quis habet fundare domum non currit ad actum Impetuosa manus & c." The same sidenote appears in the three Bodleian MSS. I have not examined the Conventry or Yale MSS.

11. The source is Heinrich Suso's *Horologium Sapientiae.* See Benjamin P. Kurtz, "The Source of Occleve's *Lerne to Dye.*" *Modern Language Notes 38* (1923): 337-40, and his "The Relation of Occleve's *Lerne to Dye* to Its Source," *PMLA* 40 (1925): 252-75.

12. The Westmorland envoy and final signature can be seen in Hoccleve's own hand in Furnivall's facsimile opposite page 242 of his edition. Neither envoy nor signature is present in the other five MSS., in all of which the "Jonathas" moralisation is followed immediately by a separate item, Lydgate's *Dance Macabre.* Lydgate's poem is introduced by the peculiar rubric "Verba translatoris" in three of the MSS. (Conventry, Selden, and Laud; not so in Bodley 221; I have not seen Yale). Readers of these MSS. might well have taken the *Dance* to be part of the *Series.* I cannot explain the rubric.

13. Rigg, "Hoccleve's *Complaint,*" assigns the *Series* to the genre *consolatio* or *Trostbuch,* comparing Boethius.

14. In the *De Consolatione,* similarly, the reader discovers that Boethius has been writing his *planctus* (book I, meter 1) only in retrospect, when Lady Philosophy enters: "Haec dum mecum tacitus ipse reputarem querimoniamque lacrimabilem stili officio signarem" ("In the mene while that I, stille, recordede these thynges with myself, and merkid my weply compleynte with office of poyntel, I saw, stondynge aboven the heghte of myn heved, a womman"; Chaucer's translation.)

Malcolm Richardson (essay date 1986)

SOURCE: Richardson, Malcolm. "Hoccleve in His Social Context." *Chaucer Review* 20, no. 4 (1986): 313-22.

[*In this essay, Richardson reconstructs the life Hoccleve likely led as a king's clerk in the fourteenth century. Richardson finds that the pathetic persona Hoccleve created in his poetry was not merely a generic convention, but rather an accurate picture of Hoccleve's circumstances and social status.*]

Among other things, the unfortunate poet Thomas Hoccleve is that most characteristic modern literary figure, the little man who tries unsuccessfully to maneuver in a bureaucracy designed to crush him. This Hoccleve *persona* is one of the most meticulously constructed, endearing, and human in Middle English literature. While Hoccleve's poetry is almost certainly not as feeble as F. J. Furnivall led several generations to believe, we assuredly read Hoccleve chiefly for the autobiographical details he so carefully includes. As Jerome Mitchell notes in our solitary book-length study of the poet, Hoccleve's sole attraction for compilers of Middle English anthologies rests in the autobiographical elements embedded in a handful of his poems.[1]

Given the importance of this autobiographical element, understanding Hoccleve the Privy Seal clerk is essential to understanding Hoccleve the poet. Hoccleve implicitly urges his readers to judge him by fifteenth-century standards of a successful public career, for his alleged failure as a bureaucrat and churchman is one of the basic ingredients in his *persona.* Despite Hoccleve's own emphasis on his financial and career problems, among the several excellent literary biographies of the poet none gives more than a passing glance at Hoccleve's place in the royal bureaucracy. H. S. Bennett's popular account in *Six Medieval Men and Women* presents more hard facts than others, but it is largely an intelligent if selective summary of the description of the Privy Seal office in Thomas Frederick Tout's classic *Chapters in the Administrative History of Mediaeval England.*[2] The emphasis in many recent Hoccleve studies has been to suggest that much of the supposed autobiographical element about Hoccleve's *persona* is either metaphorical or a mixture of literary conventions. This essay suggests just the opposite. Seen in his social context, Hoccleve was exactly what he claimed to be, a conspicuous underachiever, a man who did not or could not avail himself of the opportunities open to him.

His poems, for instance, make his life in London sound as isolated and solitary as that of a modern New York apartment dweller. Hoccleve is nearly always seen alone, haunting taverns and wandering the streets. Yet certainly he is relying on his reader's presumed knowledge of what London life for a king's clerk was like in the 1390's. He tells without further comment, for example, that he lived at Chester's Inn in the Strand, one of the Inns of Chancery attached to the Middle Temple.[3] In all likelihood he had lived either at Chester's Inn or at one of the many other inns around the London district of Farringdon since he became a king's clerk in the 1380's.[4] In bachelor days he commuted daily by boat between his inn and his workplace at Westminster, doubtless in the company of clerks of the Privy Seal, Chancery, Signet, Wardrobe, and Exchequer, many complaining about the drudgery of their upcoming day's work and shaking off hangovers. Although Hoccleve's begging poems contain so much name-dropping that the unwary might be led to believe that he supped nightly with Lord Furnival or the Keeper of the Privy Seal himself, in reality he must have talked, dined, and roistered almost exclusively with other clerks from the inns of Far-ringdon, at least after working hours. Contemporary evidence suggests that Hoccleve lived there among a rich and varied assortment of other young men. The earliest record books from the old Inns of Chancery are lost or never existed, so the exact names and positions of the occupants is not clear. We know, however, that they were filled not only with various levels of king's clerks, but also with attorneys, apprentices to the law, and scriveners, all young men who hoped to make their way in life through the use of the written word. They were united, whatever their grades, by the study of the English writ system and the medieval *dictamen* or art of letter-writing. A list of Chancery regulations and prohibitions issued between the late 1380's and 1415, the *Ordinaciones cancellarie,* attempts to stop the various grades of Chancery clerks from living with non-Chancery personnel.[5] The inferential evidence seems to indicate, however, that a collegiate system grew up around Farringdon whereby king's clerks taught the mysteries of the writ system to young clerks, fledgling attorneys, and scriveners, probably in exchange for pay, room and board, or the copying of routine writs and letters.[6] Clerks and law apprentices played games together in Fickett's Field just up the Strand from Chester's Inn, apparently with such exuberance that in 1375 a man was convicted of setting an iron trap for them there.[7] It was almost certainly a more varied and stimulating world than either Hoccleve or his biographers have led us to believe, and certainly a less solitary one. We can therefore assume that Hoccleve's subtle insistence on his isolation reveals a psychological and poetic truth, not a literal one.

Living under these conditions, Hoccleve could scarcely have avoided gauging the non-progress of his career against the successes of the people who lived and worked around him. Hoccleve, as we know, was the type of man who sees his own glass half empty and his companion's glass half full. It must have been particularly grating to him to see some of his former colleagues and peers far surpass him in worldly success. But what options were open to young clerks who had no strong connections with the men in power?

Hoccleve was unfortunate in his choice—if choice it was—of the Privy Seal as his place of employment. Of all the major officers of the royal administration, the Privy Seal was the one, in Tout's words, least "attractive to the abler and more ambitious aspirants after government service."[8] Despite the name, the privy seal of the king had long since ceased to be the king's private seal. By Hoccleve's time the Privy Seal office had become the theoretical clearing house for dozens of classes of writs and documents on their way to and from and among the king, Council, chancery, Signet office, and Exchequer. In theory, the king's wishes expressed in a letter sent out under his true "private" seal, the signet seal, had first to be reissued under the more authoritative privy seal. Then it passed on to the chancery, where the king's wishes would receive their final form as a writ under yet a third seal, the Great Seal.[9] In practice, a number of significant writs and orders

could come directly from the Privy Seal office, especially writs of *Liberate* and *Allocate,* which authorized payment from the Exchequer.[10] From the point of view of a clerk like Hoccleve, however, the Privy Seal office's main attraction was that it was lax but secure: after years of investigation, Tout found no instance of a clerk being dismissed for carelessness, poor performance, or any other reason.[11] In addition, Privy Seal clerks were housed at the expense of the Keeper of the Privy Seal at hostels like Chester's Inn. Whatever income they received could be spent on investments or on their own amusements. However, Privy Seal clerks also faced several drawbacks in comparison to other royal clerks, particularly chancery clerks.

For example, Privy Seal clerks were denied access to the law courts except as private citizens. Unlike their chancery colleagues, they could not practice as attorneys and consequently could not receive attorney's fees or represent clients in the chancellor's court. Chancery clerks could be retained by prominent men and women and frequently appeared in their own court as both plaintiff and defense attorneys. The printed calendars are full of instances where chancery clerks are on opposing sides in the same case.

A second drawback was that Privy Seal clerks had no access to the vast royal legal and administrative records. Chancery and Exchequer clerks worked daily with an immense body of carefully preserved if poorly indexed information. Then as now, information was power. A chancery clerk, reading a colleague's report of an Inquisition *Post Mortem,* could easily search among the chancery rolls for the status of the lands described in the Inquisition. If the land was open for leasing or sale, he could snap it up himself and expect to make a nice profit later. Chancery clerks could inspect incoming documents and watch out for one another's interests, too. In one case, when a problem arose in an Inquisition concerning some land near Swineshead, a sharp-eyed chancery clerk noticed that one of the landholders was his chancery colleague John Mapilton. He simply wrote in his own hand across the top of the Inquisition, "Let no delivery be made because Mapilton is tenant; let him be warned to answer the king."[12] The Privy Seal files, by contrast, were poorly developed and even more poorly maintained, so that similar opportunities were infrequent for Hoccleve and his associates.

A third drawback to Privy Seal clerkship was the chronic understaffing of the office. The number of clerks was supposed to be set at four, but this number proved to be only a guideline. Sometimes clerks were conscripted for other tasks and had to be replaced by inexperienced outsiders. The number of clerks during Hoccleve's tenure seems to have varied between four and twelve. The important fact, nevertheless, was that the scope of work at the Privy Seal was expanding faster than the office could absorb it.[13] Considering the rough-and-ready management of the office and the poor record-keeping, Hoccleve's complaints about his long hours must have had some justification. Hoccleve's formulary, for example, which includes almost nine hundred sample writs and letters, would have been unnecessary in a well-regulated office like the chancery, which had its own long-standing exemplars.

We can safely say, therefore, that Hoccleve was laboring under severe constraints, most of them beyond his control. Can these disadvantages explain entirely his bleak opinion of a clerk's career? Hoccleve, of course, is even more concerned about the financial hardships of his job than about the tedious work. Evidence outside his poems suggests that he had at least five options open to him which should have relieved his chronic financial ills.

One position of considerable prestige and salary open only to Privy Seal clerks was the clerkship of the King's Council, where, if nothing else, Hoccleve could have thrust his poems into the unwilling hands of great magnates. More important, his salary would have doubled or even quadrupled, with little chance of missed payments. Besides his salary, Hoccleve could have collected gifts and bribes from people whose cases he had brought to the Council's attention, as was the accepted custom of the time. In Hoccleve's earlier years the position had belonged to John Prophete, a well-connected clerk whom Hoccleve could not hope to usurp. After Prophete, however, the position went to Hoccleve's more vigorous peer Robert Frye (see below).

A second and easier option was to serve as a bailbondsman or *mainpernor* in medieval terms. Chancery records are filled with instances of king's clerks and attorneys who served as mainpernors, often in informal corporations determined by the clerks' home counties. Several clerks from, say, Yorkshire would come together and give their pledge for the good character or the court appearance of another individual, and naturally would collect a fee for their services. The astonishing number of surviving writs involving mainpernors is a guide to the prevalence of this normally painless way of collecting fees. Hoccleve's name is mentioned only twice in these records, however, and in one of those instances he was merely helping out a fellow Privy Seal clerk.[14]

A third option was influence-peddling. Anyone who expected to get anything out of the government also expected to pay at every step of the way. Many of the more prosperous men and women simply paid clerks in the various offices regular salaries just to assure that their paperwork would make it through with ease, or come to the attention of the right official. Although Privy Seal clerks had influence over less important business than clerks in the chancery or Exchequer, they could still act as agents or factors for anyone willing to pay. Hoccleve's associate Frye, for example, "collected the annuities and watched over the interests of John Spertgrave and John Fairhood, two merchants trading overseas."[15] Frye's letters show him to have been a man willing to do anyone a favor, for a price. Hoccleve's name is predictably absent from any record of such dealings.

The chief source for additional income for all king's clerks during this period, however, was moneylending. Records of moneylending are often difficult to interpret, but even a cursory glance at the printed rolls calendars makes it clear that king's clerks were lending money on a vast scale in sums ranging from a few shillings to thousands of pounds, with Chancellor (later Cardinal) Henry Beaufort eventually setting the pace. The usual procedure was for the lender to go to court before actually handing over the money and to get a judgment for debt against the borrower for the amount of loan. The judgment was then entered on the chancery rolls as if it were a genuine debt case in the modern sense. Then and only then was the money handed over. If the debt was not paid on time, the borrower already had a judgment against him and the lender could send him straight to prison. If the debt was paid, it was then "forgiven" in the records.[16] With their easy access to the records, the chancery clerks were the greatest moneylenders among the king's clerks. Since they entered the debts on their own rolls, sent out their own writs in the case of non-payment, and finally tried the debtor in their own court with their friends and colleagues as judges, few debtors were likely to try to escape payment. The Privy Seal clerks were in a less powerful position, but the opportunity for moneylending was present, particularly for clerks who had a little ready cash and whose bed and board was at the state's expense. One of Hoccleve's immediate predecessors, Henry Ingelby, enjoyed a thirty-year career as a money-lender and real estate investor. Ingelby took the prudent step of forming a syndicate with several chancery clerks, including David Wooler, Keeper of the chancery rolls, so that not only were his resources expanded, but his loans would be carefully recorded by his partners. Other Privy Seal clerks were likewise involved.[17] Hoccleve, however, was not among them. Had he ever appeared in court for a debt action, is there any doubt that he would be the defendant rather than the plaintiff?

As a final, if extreme, option, Hoccleve could have transferred out of the Privy Seal office as opportunities arose. Although Tout emphasizes the stability of the office, the records show plainly that clerks transferred in and out of the Privy Seal regularly. Robert Frye, for example, began as a Signet clerk before transferring to the Privy Seal in the early 1390's.[18] John Offord transferred in about 1406. The general movement for more ambitious clerks was probably out, however. John Stone and John Hethe were two who moved to the Signet and accompanied Henry V in his second invasion of France in 1417. The able Stone became the king's personal secretary for a time.[19]

With these options open to him, Hoccleve characteristically chose instead to rely exclusively on three other options in which his chance of failure was almost certain: his clerk's salary, an ecclesiastical benefice, and poetry. Of poetry, the record speaks fairly clearly. Hoccleve received no identifiable benefit from his poetry, certainly none of any lasting value. Perhaps misled by the success of the aristocratically connected and more able Geoffrey Chaucer,

Hoccleve worked hard at poetic achievement but at most succeeded in getting annuities and emoluments which were his by right anyway. Although biographers have sometimes claimed powerful patrons for the poet, his long apostrophes to the rich and powerful of the land show no growing intimacy with them over the passing years.

Hoccleve's frequent complaint that he received no benefice is perhaps more justified. If we assume that he joined the Privy Seal about 1388, he waited a long time indeed. But as Tout points out, the Privy Seal was an office in which only hardworking clerks could expect a significant benefice. Hoccleve's faith in the System was slightly misplaced considering his own bad habits and the experiences of his peers, few of whom received benefices of the value that Hoccleve was apparently contemplating. At the same time, careers of chancery clerks of the 1380's and '90's suggest that good benefices normally came slowly, and that they were given to clerks who had already shown industry in other ways. And the chancery, we should remember, had more and better benefices to hand out. At the same time, at least three of Hoccleve's Privy Seal associates (Lawrence Bailay, William Donne, and John Wellingborough the elder) received small benefices,[20] while two others (Offorde and Stone) received numerous and large ones.[21] This may only prove that Hoccleve was, as he says, a slacker, but it also shows that he should have realized from what he saw around him that waiting idly for a benefice to materialize was a certain way to assure that it would not.

As for his clerk's salary, most writers since Furnivall have claimed that not only was his salary perfectly adequate, but that Hoccleve appears from the records to have drawn it regularly, even when he claims to have been mentally disturbed. Tout, however, believed that the standard £10 annual salary drawn by Privy Seal clerks was not really enough to live on, even for a single man. We should recall also that medieval salaries were nearly always in arrears. One of his predecessors in the Privy Seal, for example, was not paid for six years running.[22] We can never be sure, given the notorious level of creative accounting in many medieval financial records, that he actually received payment when the record says he did. Nor should we discount Furnivall's suggestion that at least some of his salary was being both received and absorbed by creditors. Whatever the case, Hoccleve should never have counted on his clerk's salary as a reliable source of income.

Given his lack of interest in business, his spendthrift habits, and the uncertain financial sources that he depended on, there was little Hoccleve could do to worsen his position. He found something, however: he got married. This step, as he himself admits, destroyed any hope of ecclesiastical preferment. It also meant that he had to abandon the comforts of the Privy Seal Keeper's inn and sleep with Mrs. Hoccleve on his "poor cot" in less-than-genteel poverty. Hoccleve's marriage came at a bad time, when the puritanical Henry V was on his way to the throne and there was already a general if ultimately unsuccessful

movement to keep married clerks out of government service. The *Ordinaciones cancellarie* contain several prohibitions agains married clerks in the chancery, for example, and in the rolls we find occasional stern notes about married officials. When at about the time of Hoccleve's marriage Ralph Grenehurst, a married man, was appointed notary of the chancery, an addition to his appointment noted that "the king is unwilling, however, that by color of this present grant to Ralph, who is bound by the conjugal bond, others of this conjugal position shall be raised to this estate and grade."[23]

In short, Hoccleve had laid firm foundations for his poverty and misery after his marriage. In the less prestigious Privy Seal, he might have got away with being a *clericus uxoratus*. Had he attended to business affairs, his marriage would have been an inconvenience rather than a catastrophe. Even among the chancery clerks, a married clerk had some hope of success. The careers of Richard Colman and Thomas Smith in that office are long and apparently prosperous, even though both were married.[24] But Colman and Smith were businessmen and moneylenders, and Hoccleve had done nothing to prepare himself financially for marriage. Consequently, his laments resemble those of modern students who complain bitterly that they cannot have at the same time a university education, two children, and a new automobile.

Finally, having confirmed thus far a fairly bleak picture of life at the Privy Seal, we should look briefly at the careers of Hoccleve's peers to assure ourselves that the poet was not the victim of a malignant fate, but of himself. Of Prentys and Arundel, whom Hoccleve disapprovingly shows lying in bed until after nine, no significant record remains, appropriately. Other clerks, however, left extensive records which form an instructive contrast to Hoccleve's.

Hoccleve's best remembered colleague is Robert Frye, mentioned above. Frye's tenuous immortality is based on a number of accidentally preserved letters he wrote in three languages which have found their way into several historical and linguistic studies.[25] As we have seen, Frye was clerk of the Council from the late 1390's until after 1420, and a successful businessman. Besides his £10 annuity and (after 1406) 40 mark salary, he enjoyed what must have been a large income as factor or agent for people from all walks of life, anyone who could pay, in fact. He received appeals for help from prisoners in Newgate and from prominent churchmen. We even have letters to his mother which indicate that he was running a family business. Most startling to us, at the very time when Hoccleve's career and mental health were deteriorating, Frye was elected M.P. for Wilton for at least three parliaments. One might think from the numerous records of his business affairs that he neglected his Privy Seal duties, but in fact he seems to have been responsible for improving the record-keeping procedures of both the Privy Seal and the Council.

John Offorde, mentioned in Hoccleve's ballade to Henry Somer,[26] was less of a businessman but successful in quieter ways.[27] He was the illegitimate son of Sir Laurence

Pabenham of Offord in Bedfordshire, Hoccleve's home county. Offorde came to the Privy Seal from the Signet in 1406 after having received several grants from the king. In 1409 he was granted two shops in the Shambles of London with an annual value of 10 marks, and also several other pensions from Henry V. Late in life he seems to have received several church livings, but in any case his income must have been four times that of Hoccleve. A letter of his printed in Rymer's *Foedera* shows an easy familiarity with several active businessman-clerks of the time, including the busy chancery clerk John Brokholes.[28]

John Stone's career was more traditional than Frye's and more successful than Offorde's. During his career he served both in the Privy Seal and as Henry V's secretary.[29] Between 1404 and his death in 1419 he received numerous important benefices, including the deanery of St. Martin le Grand in London in 1414. At various times he was a prebendary at Lichfield and two other places, archdeacon of Northampton, principal of Hart Hall, Oxford, and warden of King's Hall, Cambridge. Stone seems to have moved about incessantly, taking careful advantage of each move.

These Privy Seal clerks, each successful in his own way, indicate that an industrious clerk could carve out a secure position for himself despite the other disadvantages of the Privy Seal office. Many of Hoccleve's less successful fellow clerks have been lost to history, it is true, but three such successful men out of such a small office is a significant percentage.

In summary, while this examination of Hoccleve's position in the official world of his time proves little about his autobiographical accuracy, it indicates strongly that Hoccleve's image of himself as a failed bureaucrat was based on fact. It is clear, however, that Hoccleve had opportunities and threw them away. As a professional bureaucrat, Hoccleve was exactly what he tells us he was, a bungler, misfit, and perpetual also-ran.

Notes

1. Jerome Mitchell, *Thomas Hoccleve: A Study in Early Fifteenth-Century English Poetic* (Urbana: Univ. of Illinois Press, 1968), p. 2.

2. H. S. Bennett, "Thomas Hoccleve," in *Six Medieval Men and Women* (Cambridge, Engl.: University Press, 1955), pp. 69-99; T. F. Tout, *Chapters in the Administrative History of Mediaeval England,* 6 vols. (1920-33; rpt. New York: Barnes and Noble, 1967). The most pertinent section is V, 1-112. Unless otherwise indicated, all further references to Tout are to this work and volume.

3. *The Regement of Princes,* ed. F. J. Furnivall, EETS, ES 72 (1897; rpt. Millwood, N.Y.: Kraus Reprints, 1978), line 5.

4. For an overview of the history of these inns, see Robert Megarry, *Inns Ancient and Modern* (London: Selden Society, 1972). Specialized studies are listed in Desmond Bland, *A Bibliography of the Inns of Court and Chancery,* Selden Society, Supp. Ser., no. 3 (London: Selden Society, 1965).

5. Printed in B. Wilkinson, *The Chancery Under Edward III* (Manchester: University Press, 1929), pp. 214-23; and George William Sanders, *Orders of the High Court of Chancery* (London, 1845), I, 1-7d.

6. Hermann Cohen, *A History of the English Bar and "Attornatus" to 1450* (London: Sweet and Maxwell, 1929), pp. 446ff.

7. *Calendar of Patent Rolls,* 1374-77, p. 108.

8. Tout, p. 105.

9. A. L. Brown, "The Privy Seal Clerks in the Early Fifteenth Century," in *The Study of Medieval Records: Essays in Honour of Kathleen Major,* ed. D. A. Bullough and R. L. Storey (Oxford: Clarendon Press, 1971), pp. 260-81. This article is omitted from Mitchell's bibliography. V. H. Galbraith, *An Introduction to the Use of Public Records* (Oxford: University Press, 1934), pp. 15-34.

10. Tout, p. 58.

11. Tout, p. 76.

12. *Calendar of Inquisitions Miscellaneous,* 1399-1422, p. 68.

13. Tout, pp. 81-83.

14. *Hoccleve's Works: The Minor Poems,* ed. F. J. Furnivall and Israel Gollancz, rev. Jerome Mitchell and A. I. Doyle, EETS, ES 61, 73 (Oxford: University Press, 1970), pp. lxxi-lxxii. Evidence for corporations of mainpernors is found especially in Public Record Office classification C.237.

15. Brown, p. 273.

16. Frederick Pollock and F. W. Maitland, *The History of English Law Before the Time of Edward I,* 2nd ed. (1898; rpt. Cambridge, Engl.: University Press, 1968), II, 203-04. For money-lending in earlier times, see Richard H. Bowers, "From Rolls to Riches: King's Clerks and Moneylending in Thirteenth-Century England," *Speculum,* 58 (1983), 60-71.

17. Tout, pp. 99-100.

18. Brown, p. 272.

19. Joyce Otway-Ruthven, *The King's Secretary and the Signet Office in the XV Century* (Cambridge, Engl.: University Press, 1939), pp. 168-69.

20. Tout, p. 98.

21. Otway-Ruthven, pp. 168-69, 180-81.

22. Tout, pp. 84-86.

23. *Calendar of Patent Rolls,* 1408-13, p. 272.

24. Malcolm Richardson, "The Influence of Henry V on the Development of Chancery English," Ph.D. diss., University of Tennessee, 1968, pp. 124-25, 157-58.

25. John H. Fisher, Malcolm Richardson, and Jane Fisher, *An Anthology of Chancery English* (Knoxville: Univ. of Tennessee Press, 1984); Brown, pp. 273-75, especially p. 273, n. 4 and 275, n. 4; since Brown's article was published, Frye's letters have been collected in PRO classification E.28/29/44-77.

26. *Minor Poems,* p. 60, line 126.

27. Otway-Ruthven, pp. 180-81.

28. J. H. Kern, "Der Schreiber Offorde," *Anglia,* 40 (1916), 374.

29. Brown, p. 262, n. 2; Otway-Ruthven, pp. 168-69.

D. C. Greetham (essay date 1989)

SOURCE: Greetham, D. C. "Self-Referential Artifacts: Hoccleve's Persona as a Literary Device." *Modern Philology* 86, no. 3 (1989): 242-51.

[*In the essay below, Greetham places Hoccleve between Chaucer and Robert Burton (author of* Anatomy of Melancholy*) on a continuum extending from medieval writers to post-modern authors like John Fowles and Woody Allen. Comparing Hoccleve to both earlier and later authors, Greetham argues that Hoccleve could be fruitfully considered a Menippean satirist in the tradition of Boethius.*]

Until very recently, we took Thomas Hoccleve at his word. When he claimed to have "lewde speche" and "yonge konynge,"[1] C. S. Lewis agreed.[2] When he accused himself of "meetrynge amis" on account of his poor eyesight,[3] H. C. Schulz readily concurred.[4] When he insisted that he was "but a repertour / of folkes tales,"[5] and greatly indebted to his sources, H. S. Bennett merely nodded without further investigation.[6] And when he characterized himself as an inferior disciple of his master Chaucer, all critics accepted the justice of the self-denigration, the only argument being whether the teacher-pupil relationship was to be seen literally or figuratively—that is, whether the pupil had learned his craft at his master's knee or from his books.[7] Criticism of Hoccleve was, in other words, a perfect confirmation of Lounsbury's dictum, in judging Hoccleve's reputation, that "the world is apt to rate a man at his own valuation."[8]

But there was a problem. The "disciple" role (and especially the unlearned, unoriginal, derivative, unwitty dullard following in the footsteps of a great predecessor) was, of course, one of the favorite games played by medieval authors,[9] and particularly by Hoccleve's own "worthi maister honorable" (***De Regimine Principum*** 2080), Chaucer himself. While it is true that there was a time when the ingenuous, naif Chaucerian narrator was accepted almost at face value, criticism had, by the early twentieth century, long since seen the Chaucerian pose as a rhetorical and narrative technique, not an autobiographical (or self-descriptive) statement. This persuasion avoided having to believe that a customs officer could be as innocently gullible as a Canterbury pilgrim. Thus, Chaucer's claim that he followed his sources religiously in *Troilus and Criseyde* (indeed, that he could do no other), that he lacked fine discrimination as an observer of mankind's follies in *The Canterbury Tales,* that he failed to understand the story of the Man in Black in *The Book of the Duchess*—all these devices were rescued from historical (or psychological) necessity and debated as critical or literary problems. But Hoccleve's inferior status remained a donnée of the criticism of late Middle English poetry. While there were occasional mumblings that Hoccleve's methods might be more parodic and ironic than autobiographically accurate, even such comparatively recent studies of Hoccleve as Jerome Mitchell's and Penelope Doob's tended to concern themselves with (and in general to accept) the historical rather than the literary validity of Hoccleve's self-characterization.[10] To borrow the critical vocabulary of a nonmedievalist for a moment, it was as if Hoccleve had been arrested before the *clinamen* stage of Harold Bloom's anxiety of influence, and had failed to achieve *tessera, kenosis, daemonization, askesis,* or *apophrades* in his wrestling with his forerunner.[11] My purpose here is to deny this arrested development and to suggest instead that Hoccleve not only extended the reach and competence of his inherited narrator (Bloom's daemonization, if you will) but also anticipated much of the subsequent development of narrative method in the literature of later centuries—thus pushing him off Bloom's chart at the other end.

To begin with the rhetorical problem. The "discipleship" topos (with its inevitable acceptance of *humilitas* before the master) is very common, and is supported by such ancillary topoi as the "Golden Age" and the "dwarves on the shoulders of giants."[12] But the evidence of such perennial debates as the *moderni* versus *antiqui* demonstrates that the topos can in fact be used as an ironic stick with which to beat one's predecessors (Bloom's tessera perhaps). The pose is all, for it provides the poet's invention with a respectable heredity, gives scurrility, obscenity, libel, or aesthetic deficiency a decent cover, and yet allows the work great freedom and independence through the apparent artlessness and objectivity of the narrator. But it is a device, with a rhetorical name (*diminutio*), and only one of many such literary devices available to "belated" poets. Mitchell calculates that Hoccleve uses over half of the "figures of thought" endorsed by Vinsauf[13]—from *confirmatio* to *expolitio* to *notatio*—and yet only *diminutio* is taken seriously by modern critics and not given its full rhetorical status in discussion of his work. Why? One of the obvious answers can be given simply by pointing to the content of Hoccleve's work—he does, admittedly, make so much of his own life in his poetry that critics are inevitably tempted to allow such ostensibly autobiographical statements more value and credit than they might otherwise receive in a more reticent author. And like Wordsworth in his unease about the autobiographical nature of his oeuvre (especially the unpublished "Prelude"), Hoccleve is equally conscious of the dangers of such self-exposure.

Ay, what is me, that to my self, thus longe,
Clappid have I, I trowe that I raue.

["La Male Regle," 393-94]

And while the beggar's advice in the **"Prologue"** to the ***De Regimine Principum [DRP]—Regiment of Princes***— might be to overcome melancholy by writing, "Sharpe thi penne, and write on lustily" (***DRP*** 1905), Hoccleve is forever aware that such self-conceit might become tiresome to the reader. But the sheer pervasiveness of the autobiographical elements might therefore suggest that they are not merely rhetorical colors in the manner of Vinsauf but show a genuine concern with the role, abilities, and self-awareness of the author's narrator. I would agree with this explanation, but with a difference: where others see the deference, humility, and self-castigation as betraying a lack of confidence in the composer, I would see it as an early comment on the problems of composition—indeed, on the art of narration itself, which now becomes not just a device for getting the story moving or for unifying the disparate sections of a text (as it had largely been in Chaucer) but the proper, and perhaps the only, subject for the artist—his own work. One can see easily where this early burgeoning of self-referential art and artifacts goes: via Burton and *Hamlet* in the seventeenth century and Sterne and Fielding in the eighteenth, to Wordsworth and Browning in the nineteenth century and a general ubiquitousness in the twentieth. Mann's *Dr. Faustus,* Calvino's *If on a Winter's Night a Traveller,* Mailer's *Armies of the Night,* Hemingway's *A Movable Feast,* Nabokov's *Pale Fire,* Fowles's *The French Lieutenant's Woman,* Martin Hansen's *The Liar,* Truffaut's *Day for Night,* Woody Allen's *Annie Hall,* Strauss's *Heldenleben, Intermezzo,* and *Capriccio*—the list is endless, and simply demonstrates that modern literature, film, opera, and so on have quite accepted the ironic standing of artist and artifact. Self-referentiality (not merely of the work to the artist but of the work to itself) has become such a decidedly modern conceit—part of the legacy of Formalist defamiliarisation of the fictiveness of art—that its presence in the fifteenth century may come as a surprise.

Consider now two examples drawn from Hoccleve (in *The Regement of Princes* and the *Series* poems) of this early transformation of the narrator and the medium from a method of relating a fiction to the very subject of that fiction.

1. I first became conscious of the peculiar qualities of Hoccleve's narrative technique when beginning work as general editor of an edition of his ***Regement of Princes.***[14] This is a strangely schizophrenic work, even to a bibliographer or codicologist. The 3,000-line poem proper has a 2,000-line so-called **"Prologue,"** which deals exclusively with the psychological, professional, aesthetic, financial, and marital problems of the narrator, one "Thomas Hoccleve" (just as "Mailer" is a character in *Armies of the Night* and "Stross"—i.e., Strauss—a character in *Intermezzo,* and, of course, "Geoffrey Chaucer" in *The Canter-*

bury Tales and elsewhere). I say co-called **"Prologue,"** for the scribes of the forty-four extant manuscripts appear to have been as puzzled as modern critics by the imbalance of the work: sometimes the entire 5,000 lines occur under the rubric **"De Regimine Principum"** (but sometimes in a later—or different—hand), sometimes only the last 3,000, sometimes the **"Prologue"** and the body of the poem separately. But the **"Prologue"**—if such it be—is clearly intended to be there, and there is no bibliographical evidence for its having been added to the 3,000-line didactic poem at another date (as one might write the introduction to a book after having written the book itself, with this introduction then printed as front matter subsequent to the rest of the volume). If the apparent self-indulgence of this **"Prologue"** was intended as a genuine part of the work at large, how can the *Regement*'s unity be defended?

There are two answers to this question. The first I can deal with only briefly here. I believe that the poem does have an internal coherence, a coherence which is created by a deft cross-referencing of a number of points in the personal (**"Prologue"**) and didactic (*Regement*) sections. Thus, such terms as *muk, conceyt, melancholye,* and *thoght* (of which more later) act as devices for fulfilling the first part of the poem in the second—almost as an exercise in poetic typology—whereby there is a consistent reflection of the self in the world and the world in the self. This motivation for the work is suggested at the very beginning, where,

Musyng vpon the restless bisynesse
Which that this troubly world hath ay on honde

[*DRP* "Prologue," 1-2]

Thomas the narrator notes that

not long ago
Fortunes strok doun threst estaat royal
Into myscheef

[*DRP* "Prologue," 22-24]

a "fall of princes" exemplum which acts both centripetally upon the narrator (in mirroring his own personal anxiety) and ultimately centrifugally upon the specific prince— Henry, Prince of Wales—for whom the *Regement* is written, as a moral sermon on how to avoid such falls. This is all a conventional enough structure for a medieval poem (although in Hoccleve's case the cross-referencing is worked out with remarkable clarity and balance)—but it has not, to my knowledge, been much noticed by critics of Hoccleve.

The second answer to the problem of unity in the *Regement* is more complex and, in a sense, might appear to contradict the first answer. For I also believe that while the *Regement* has an internal unity of sorts, it is finally to be seen as only a part of Hoccleve's concern with the narrative persona. The "Thomas Hoccleve" of the *Regement* **"Prologue"** finds his ultimate fulfilment not in the 3,000-line didactic poem but in the occasional pieces written as scribe at the Privy Seal, and most particularly, in the so-called *Series* poems.[15]

Consider, for example, the term *thoght*. In the **"Prologue,"** Hoccleve begins to use this not just in the common Middle English sense of "the act of thinking" but as an intellectual illness, approximating the Burtonian use of the term "melancholy." In fact, since Hoccleve's oeuvre is so much concerned with the problems of melancholy (under that term or another), his narrator is faced with, and advances the same cure for, the disease which engendered Burton's *Anatomy* (i.e., to write about madness in order to avoid going mad). What this encourages is a consistent involvement with the act of writing, for that becomes both the problem itself (i.e., too much *studie*, as Hoccleve's Friend is to point out in the **"Complaint"**) but, paradoxically, its only cure. Without implying that all writers are inevitably neurotic, I would suggest there is little doubt that in the examples of Burton and Hoccleve, the genre of the "hodgepodge" or *lanx satura* anatomy of satire is a discursive and prolix self-conceit on the problems of both psychological self-analysis and literary creation. It is both criticism (of the self) and invention (of the work) at the same time, and is ironically both the unfortunate cause and the fortunate result of this faculty of *thoght*. *Thoght* is, therefore, anxiety:

> Man, at a word, it is encumbrous thoght
> That causeth me this sorowe & fare amyss.

> [*DRP* **"Prologue,"** 185-86]

It is illness:

> Thoght is wastyng seed,
> Swich in the, and that in gret foysoun,
> An thou, redeles, nat canst voyde his poysoun

> [*DRP* **"Prologue,"** 201-3]

and a danger to the intellectual man: "Be war of thoght, for it is perillous" (*DRP* **"Prologue"** 267). Indeed, the condition of this "Thomas Hoccleve" of the **"Prologue"** is rather close to that of Hamlet—inactivity because of too much thought, where a concentration similar to Hamlet's "thinking too precisely on th'event" leads, in Hoccleve's case, to a 2,000-line poem bemoaning the fact that he can no longer write poetry.

2. In the *Series* poems, this "thoghtful dissease" becomes a primary subject for narrative as well as psychological analysis. Here, Hoccleve's exploitation of a previously created persona is given full license to dominate the work. The self-contained poems—**"Jereslaus Wife," "Lerne to Die,"** and so forth—which are supposedly the motivation for the **"Complaint"** as frame become in fact really digressions in the portrayal of the poet's psyche. They react to, and are the product of, emotional and psychological disturbances to a far greater degree than are the individual stories in *The Canterbury Tales,* over which the Chaucerian narrator has little apparent control. Now, admittedly, *The Canterbury Tales* is a much more complex work in terms of narrative structure, if only because it uses so many different narrators, each interacting with another. But what Hoccleve seems to have done is to have taken the inherited Chaucerian persona, the dreamer of the early works, the naif translator of the *Troilus,* the penitent of *The Legend of Good Women,* and the pilgrim of *The Canterbury Tales,* and to have brought this frame device into the center of the poem, placing the stories on the periphery of the work. The *Series* is, structurally, *The Canterbury Tales* inside out.

The *Series* poems are full of moments when Hoccleve displays his narrative skill in the continuous dramatic re-enactment of stress, suffering, and self-analysis through fine observation. One example will have to suffice—the famous "mirror scene."

> Many a sawte made I to this myrrowre,
> Thinkynge, "yf that I loke in this manere
> Amonge folke as I now do, none errowr
> Of suspecte loke may in my face appere,
> This countinance, I am svre, and this chere,
> If I forthe vse is no thinge repreuable
> To them that have conseytes resonable."

> And therewithall I thowghte thus anon:
> "Men in theyr owne case bene blynd alday,
> As I haue hard say many a day agon,
> And in that same pliyght I stonde may;
> How shall I doo which is the beste way,
> My trowbled spirit for to bringe at reste
> Yf i wist howe, fyne wolde I do the beste."

> [**"Complaint,"** 162-75]

In looking at the mirror to adjust his appearance (an "image" which obviously acquires particular sensitivity for the Lacanian psychological critic), Hoccleve realizes that because of his emotional and mental state, he may not be able to see "reality" as observed by friends, but only the "illusion" caused by his own illness, so that he lacks an objective standard for judging any potential improvement. This concern with reality and illusion as a psychological and critical problem is another of Hoccleve's anticipations of the issues taken up in later literature (one thinks of Robbe-Grillet's *The Voyeur,* Gardner's *Grendel,* Beckett's *Molloy,* and perhaps particularly, in this discussion of the uncertain effects of madness upon perception, of Roth's *The Breast,* where, as in the **"Complaint,"** the narrator realizes that he will never know illusion from reality— whether he is still a breast or no—since he will never be sure that even when he seems normal it is not his madness deceiving his judgment). For narrators in both Roth and Hoccleve, the testimony of others' judgment—that, for example, one is indeed cured—must be similarly suspect, for the narrator will never be sure that they are to be trusted or that he has heard them aright. The to-and-fro pull of such argument (to go back to work or not, to go out in public or not, to express grief or not) is exemplified in the internal debate between Reason (a personification) and Man (Thomas), growing out of a similar debate between Self and Wit—a schizophrenic division recalling, with its split pronouns, I and Thou, the aesthetic theories of Joyce (based on personal pronouns) in *Portrait of the Artist as a Young Man,*[16] and the alienation of the author from lyric to fiction to drama (all of which genres are incorporated within the general narrative method of the *Series*). The function of Reason here is very similar to that of Philosophy in Boethius's *Consolation.* Indeed, much of Hoccleve's work in the *Regement,* the *Series,* and elsewhere is derived from, and in imitation of, Boethius, the generic archetype for the medieval Menippean anatomy.

I would go further and suggest that this formal similarity confirms Hoccleve as a conscious Menippean, or "anatomic" satirist, especially since Frye's definition of the anatomy[17] depends very largely upon the archetype of Boethius, with its dialogue form, interludic disposition, and contemplative, ironic, tone. Furthermore, M. C. Randolph's analysis of the structural design of formal verse satire[18] recognizes that the dichotomous frame of Bionean diatribe, connected with Scholastic formal dialectic, inevitably leads to a dialogue conducted in the "middle" style (i.e., discursive and colloquial, incorporating miniature dramas, apostrophes to abstractions, *sententiae* and other proverbial wisdom, homilies, and fictional experiences, culminating in the necessary auctorial apologia). Randolph specifically cites the medieval morality play, with its dramatic reenactment of Reason versus Unreason, and the conventional debate of the Body and Soul as early vernacular paradigms for the satiric mode. Since all these rhetorical elements are present in Hoccleve, it seems very likely that the combination of Boethius and the Scholastic debate might have produced a tendency toward a formalization of the Menippean mode in a poet who linked this technique to a predisposition for self-dramatization, through an artfully created fictive persona inherited from Chaucer. Pope does no more than this in, for example, the *Epistle to Doctor Arbuthnot,* and Anne Payne has already demonstrated the prevalence of the Menippean method in Chaucer himself.[19]

The longstanding debate over the function of such satiric literature appears in Hoccleve's intention to use the **"Complaint"** as a means of chastizing false friends for their inconstancy. The traditional *adversarius* / Friend,[20] however (like Dr. Arbuthnot), sees writing as a very dangerous enterprise since Hoccleve has apparently recovered his good name and his sanity and should not run the risk of exposing himself again.

> Of studie was engendred thy seeknesse,
> And that was hard / woldest thou now agayn
> Entre into that laborious bisynesse,
> Syn it thy mynde and eek thy wit had slayn?
> Thy conceit is nat worth a payndemayn:
> Let be, let be, bisye thee so no more,
> Lest thee repente and rewe it ouersore.

> ["**Dialogue**," 379-85]

The **"Complaint"** and the **"Dialogue"** are, therefore, forms of the expected apologia (the "Why did I write?" topos present in, e.g., Horace and Pope).[21]

The **"Dialogue"** is thus already firmly concerned with the problems of authorship, in both a psychological and social sense. What follows is a series of discussions on books

planned or already written (some to appear as part of the *Series*), on the ill effects of writing and studying too much, on misreading and misinterpretation by inadequate critics (specifically of the **"Letter of Cupid"**), plus the expected satirical disgressions prompted by certain inevitable foci in the conversation—these include clipped money and the evils it causes society at large, corruption in high places, and the domination of women in the household.

Throughout the discussion, Hoccleve retains the naif defense of his position as a mere translator or reporter (especially in dealing with the offending *Letter*) with the same ironic disavowal of complicity that Chaucer used in the "General Prologue" to *The Canterbury Tales.* Hoccleve says:

> Considereth thereof was I noon Auctour;
> I nas in that cas but a reportour
> Of folkes tales / as they seide I wroot:
> Who so that shal reherce a mannes sawe,
> As that he seith moot he seyn and nat varie,
> For, and he do, he dooth ageyn the lawe
> Of trouwthe, he may tho wordes nat contrarie.

> [**"Dialogue,"** 760-67]

The parallel with the passage in Chaucer—both of them in prologues to a series of linked tales with at least some satiric bent—can hardly be missed.

> Whoso shal telle a tale after a man
> He moot reherce as ny as euere he kan
> Euerich a word, if it be in his charge,
> Al speke he never so rudeliche and large,
> Or ellis he moot telle his tale untrewe,
> Or fynde thyng, or fynde wordes newe.

> [*CT.* Gen. Prol., 731-36]

Each of the stories (potential or realized) in the *Series* is made dependent on the discussion of the author's ability or inability to compose satisfactorily, usually with ironic effect. For example, after the passage dealing with the inadvisability of publishing the **"Complaint,"** the Friend warns Hoccleve of the dangers of study (as *thoght* is now called) and a too-great love of literary scholarship, reminding the narrator of the social duties of the poet, such as the promised book for the Duke of Gloucester. Here begins a peculiar section, for, over several hundred lines, Hoccleve's narrator proclaims his inability to write a poem about the duke's deeds at this moment—because of his own illness. The irony, of course, is that in discussing why he cannot deal now with the bravery and knightly reputation of Gloucester, Hoccleve actually does compose the very poem he claims that he cannot write. It is an extremely artful extension of the rhetorical trope of *occupatio* to encompass an entire work—in the same fashion that the **"Prologue"** to the *Regement* was produced.

Thus, we are faced with a poem (the **"Dialogue"**) which begins by discussing the writing of poem A (the **"Complaint,"** which we have already seen), proceeds to claim that the poet will not write poem B (**"Lerne to Die"**), promptly ignores poem B in favor of a negative evaluation of poem C (on Gloucester), which is composed almost in spite of its narrator, and concludes by introducing not, as expected, poems A, B, or C, but a fourth poem (**"Jereslaus Wife"**), about which there had been no hint at the opening of the dialogue. Hoccleve's satire seems to be extending not only to social conditions but to the very genres in which he is writing, a suspicion which is confirmed when, at the conclusion of **"Jereslaus Wife,"** the dialogue continues with the Friend's complaint that any poem without a moral is no poem at all, and the Friend proceeds to accuse Hoccleve of using an inferior text for his translation, going home to get his own copy of the story which he then presents to Hoccleve as a model for an appended moral allegorical interpretation. However, the irony is that the *explicatio* which Hoccleve adds to the tale renders totally inappropriate the supposed feminist rationale for writing the story in the first place,[22] the model here probably being Chaucer's ironic "Envoy" to the *Clerk's Tale*.

This is not the occasion for a complete account of Hoccleve's Menippean development of the inherited Chaucerian narrator. What we can see in this overall view, however, is that this narrator with his inability to compose (because of his *thoght* and *studie*) has moved from a Chaucerian norm (the structural or rhetorical device) to a Burtonian obsession with the unbalanced psyche of the narrator and the problem of madness. If the *Anatomy of Melancholy* was, with all the Menippean associations of its title, the first book on madness written to avoid going mad, then perhaps Hoccleve's "booke" (as he calls the *Series* as a whole) was the first written about madness as paradoxically both a restraint upon, and a stimulus for, composition. That the **"Prologue"** to the *Regement* and the *Series* poems exist at all is testimony to this movement, and to the subsequent directions it will take.

Notes

1. Thomas Hoccleve, *The Regement of Princes* (lines 1982, 1984) in *Hoccleve's Works*, ed. Frederick J. Furnivall, EETS E.S. 72 (1897), hereafter cited as *DRP (De Regimine Principum)*.

2. C. S. Lewis, *The Discarded Image* (Cambridge, 1964), p. 204.

3. Hoccleve, *Balade to the Duke of York* (line 48) in *Hoccleve's Works: The Minor Poems*, ed. Frederick J. Furnivall and I. Gollancz, EETS E.S. 61, 73 (1892; reprint, 1937; 1925 for 1897), rev. Jerome Mitchell and A. I. Doyle (1970). Similar complaints occur elsewhere in the *Balade* and in other poems, e.g., *DRP* 985-86, "Balade to the Duke of Bedford" 8-9, 12-14, "Dialogue with a Friend" 246-52.

4. H. C. Schulz, "Thomas Hoccleve, Scribe," *Speculum* 12 (1937): 76.

5. "Dialogue with a Friend," 761-62.

6. H. S. Bennett, *Chaucer and the Fifteenth Century* (Oxford, 1947), pp. 148-49. Bennett typically accepts Hoccleve's word (*DRP* 2052-53) that the *Regement*

is simply a "translation" of Aegidius Romanus's *De Regimine Principum*—apparently missing Hoccleve's later references to his other sources—an omission repeated in the same author's *Six Medieval Men and Women* (Cambridge, 1955; reprint, New York, 1962), p. 85. However, Jerome Mitchell (*Thomas Hoccleve: A Study in Early Fifteenth-Century Poetic* [Urbana, Ill., 1968] pp. 84-86), following the work of Friedrich Aster ("Das Verhältnis des altenglischen Gedichtes 'De Regimine Principum' von Thomas Hoccleve zu seinen Quellen nebst einer Einleitung über Leben und Werke des Dichters" [Ph.D. diss., Leipzig, 1888]), has established that *DRP* is in fact a very liberal compilation rather than a translation, making use of much original material (especially in the "Prologue") in addition to the three major sources: Aegidius, the *Secreta Secretorum,* and Jacobus de Cessolis's *Liber de Ludo Scacchorum*. Mitchell's judgment is that Hoccleve "comes up with a work quite different from any of his sources" (p. 86).

7. See *DRP* 1866-67, where the Beggar says, "Sone, I haue herd, or this, men speke of þe; / þou were aqueynted with Chaucer, pardee"; and *DRP* 2078-79, "And fadir Chaucer, fayn wolde han me taght; / But I was dul, and lerned lite or naght." See also *DRP* 1958-74, 4978-98, and Mitchell (pp. 115-18) for an account of Hoccleve's supposed friendship with Chaucer.

8. T. R. Lounsbury, *Studies in Chaucer* 3 (New York, 1962): 24.

9. See Mitchell, pp. 62-63. See also Ernst Robert Curtius, *European Literature and the Latin Middle Ages,* trans. Willard R. Trask (New York, 1953), pp. 83-85, on the topos of self-deprecation in classical and medieval literature.

10. See Mitchell, pp. 1-19, on the "autobiographical element" in Hoccleve. Mitchell does express some doubt whether the "passages of self-revelation . . . should be taken at face value" (p. 18), as does Penelope B. R. Doob (*Nebuchadnezzar's Children* [New Haven, Conn., 1974], pp. 208-31), where, in her analysis of Hoccleve's madness, Doob admits that her account would not be materially changed if Hoccleve had not in fact been mad but had simply been describing common beliefs about the origins and symptoms of madness. A more comprehensive view, seeing Hoccleve's madness as a part of the long Western tradition of the literary representation of mental disturbance, occurs in Lillian Feder's *Madness in Literature* (Princeton, N.J., 1980), pp. 101-9. But very few recent critical studies of Hoccleve as poet (and particularly as "Chaucerian") have explored the potential literary or rhetorical value of Hoccleve's autobiographical verse. See, however, Eva M. Thornley, "The Middle English Lyric and Hoccleve's Autobiographical Poetry," *Neuphilologische Mitteilungen* 68 (1967): 295-321; and A. G. Rigg, "Hoccleve's *Complaint* and Isidore of Seville," *Speculum*

45 (1970): 564-74. Charles R. Blyth encouraged the serious critical estimation of Hoccleve as poet with a paper on Hoccleve at the 1980 MLA convention, and John Burrow has recently dealt with Hoccleve's self-referential poetry as a process of "rehabilitation" through writing ("Hoccleve's *Series:* Experience and Books," in *Fifteenth-Century Studies,* ed. R. F. Yeager [Hamden, Conn., 1984, pp. 259-73]). In 1982 Burrow gave the Gollancz British Academy lecture ("Autobiographical Poetry in the Middle Ages: The Case of Thomas Hoccleve," *Proceedings of the British Academy* 63 [1982]: 389-412) on Hoccleve's persona in relation to both literary tradition and Hoccleve's dependent circumstances, seen as the source of his constant "petitionary role." These "dependent circumstances" (real or imaginary) clearly have a bearing on our evaluation of Hoccleve's literary use of known or invented biographical detail. They have been argued over by such historians as A. Compton Reeves ("Thomas Hoccleve, Bureaucrat," *Medievalia et Humanistica* N.S. 5 [1974]: 201-14, claiming that "evidence for the financial rewards of [Hoccleve's] career suggests that he had an adequate and comfortable income, quite enough to satisfy his needs," p. 209) and, from the opposing viewpoint, Malcolm Richardson ("Hoccleve in His Social Context," a paper delivered at the 1983 MLA convention), who maintains that "Hoccleve's image of himself as a failed bureaucrat was based on fact." At this same MLA session ("Hoccleve's Complaints: Truth and Tradition"—the first ever devoted entirely to Hoccleve), Rita Copeland suggested in her paper, "Hoccleve and the Tradition of the Dramatic Monologue in Middle English Religious Verse," that a study of the tradition of the dramatic monologue in medieval verse might provide a model for Hoccleve's supposed "autobiographical" techniques, and I have pressed the claims of Menippean satire (to which I advert in this article) at the City University of New York Medieval Institute and in a separate forthcoming study. Mitchell surveys much of the recent literature on Hoccleve in the Yeager volume cited above (pp. 49-63).

11. Harold Bloom (*Anxiety of Influence* [New York, 1973] and subsequent works) uses these so-called revisionary ratios as a means of charting the process through which an author will gradually move from emulation and awe of the "precursor" to a deliberate "swerving" from him and finally to a conscious "misprision," whereby a "strong reading" of the precursor will endow the "belated" poet with an apparent "priority," thus overcoming the constraining influence of the clearly Freudian "father-figure."

12. See, e.g., Curtius, pp. 83-85, 252-55, 407-13.

13. Mitchell, pp. 62-63.

14. On the peculiar documentary circumstances of Hoccleve's *Regement* and the editorial method employed, see D. C. Greetham, "Normalisation of Accidentals in Middle English Texts: The Paradox of Thomas Hoccleve," *Studies in Bibliography* 38 (1985): 121-50, and "Challenges of Theory and Practice in the Editing of Hoccleve's *Regement of Princes,*" in *Manuscripts and Texts: Editorial Problems in Later Middle English Literature,* ed. Derek Pearsall (Woodbridge, Suffolk, 1987), pp. 60-86.

15. That there was a perceived unity to the Hoccleve corpus can be seen by the several attempts at manuscripts of "collected works" (e.g., British Library MS Royal 17. D. vi; Bodley Laud Misc. 735; Selden Supra 53; Bodley 221; and the Coventry Record office MS).

16. That is, chap. 5 of James Joyce, *A Portrait of the Artist as a Young Man* (New York: 1968), pp. 214-15, where the first person pronoun is seen as generically characteristic for lyric, the second person for fiction, and the third person for drama. As noted, Hoccleve uses all three genres in the *Series* and its links (and therefore all three characteristic pronouns), but there is a peculiar irony in his indecision—in the account of his identity crisis—over the holograph spelling of the first person pronoun (I or Y), for Hoccleve's orthography in the holographs is remarkably, even obsessively, consistent otherwise (see Greetham, "Normalisation," for a preliminary account of this consistency).

17. Northrop Frye, *Anatomy of Criticism: Four Essays* (Princeton, N.J., 1957), esp. pp. 308-12.

18. Mary Claire Randolph, "The Structural Design of Formal Verse Satire," *Philological Quarterly* 21 (1942): 368-84.

19. F. Anne Payne, *Chaucer and Menippean Satire* (Madison, Wis., 1981). It is, of course, quite appropriate that Payne's earlier book should have been on the Old English version of Boethius's *Consolation* (Madison, Wis., 1968) and perhaps equally appropriate that nowhere in the Chaucer book does she mention Hoccleve's use of the Menippean satire.

20. See, e.g., the same device used in Horace (Trebatius, in *Satire* 2.1), Juvenal (*Satire* 1, esp. lines 150-68), and Persius (*Satire* 1).

21. See Pope, *Epistle to Dr. Arbuthnot,* esp. lines 125 ff.; and the references in n. 16. Parallel passages in Hoccleve include "Dialogue" 22 ff., on the dangers of publishing (e.g., "reherse thow it not, ne it a-wake; / kepe all that cloos for thyn honours sake" 27-28); "Dialogue" 64-67, 99 ff., on the need to publish open satires on vice—especially, in Hoccleve's case, coin-clippers; *Complaint* 386 ff., on the act of writing as a means of unburdening the satirist's woes. As in the *Arbuthnot* satire, all the *Series* poems by Hoccleve can be seen as a meditation on the "Why did I write?" topos.

22. Like the "Envoy" to the *Clerk's Tale,* the *moralizacio* of "Jereslaus Wife," by allegorizing the story (with the Emperor as Christ, his brother as man's body, his

wife as the soul), undermines the apparently "real" narrative of the perfect long-suffering woman in the tale, just as "patient Griselda" is removed from history to theology in Chaucer's story. Hoccleve's supposed "penitence" for having merely translated the "Letter of Cupid" and thereby having unintentionally offended women begins to look as suspect as Chaucer's *Legend of Good Women* does as an act of penitence for the *Troilus*—although Hoccleve did at least finish his act of contrition. See John V. Fleming, "Hoccleve's *Letter of Cupid* and the 'Quarrel' over the *Roman de la Rose*," *Medium Aevum* 40 (1971): 21-40, for a discussion of the multiple ironies in the composition of the "Letter of Cupid," on which the later ironies of the "Dialogue" and other works depend.

J. A. Burrow (essay date 1990)

SOURCE: Burrow, J. A. "Hoccleve and Chaucer." In *Chaucer Traditions: Studies in Honor of Derek Brewer,* 54-61. Cambridge: Cambridge University Press, 1990.

[*In the essay that follows, Burrow briefly outlines Hoccleve's debt to Chaucer as well as the ways in which Hoccleve might be appreciated more favorably on his own terms. Although Hoccleve's literary art owes much to his mentor, his best work is in the explicit political themes and autobiographical details that Chaucer himself eschewed.*]

Some twelve years after Chaucer's death, Thomas Hoccleve paid tribute to the eloquence, wisdom, and piety of his predecessor in three passages of *The Regement of Princes*.[1] Hoccleve's admiration, he claims, is based upon personal acquaintance; for when, in the *Regement* prologue, he first reveals his name to the old almsman, the latter's immediate reaction is to identify him as one of those people who knew Chaucer:

> 'Hoccleve, some?' 'Iwis, fadir, þat same.'
> 'Sone, I have herd or this men speke of þe;
> Þou were aqueynted with Caucher, pardee—
> God have his soule best of any wyght!'
>
> (1865-8)

Later, Hoccleve recalls how Chaucer was accustomed to help him with 'consail and reed':

> 'Mi dere maistir—God his soule quyte!—
> And fadir Chaucer fayn wolde han me taght;
> But I was dul, and lerned lite or naght.'
>
> (2077-9)

The apology for dullness is conventional enough; but there are no good reasons to doubt that Hoccleve had, towards the end of the previous century, sat at Chaucer's feet and received from him some kind of instruction in the art of English poetry.[2]

Given this association, it is not surprising that certain of Hoccleve's own poems should have been attracted into the Chaucerian orbit during the fifteenth and sixteenth centuries. Like Chaucer, Hoccleve 'wroot ful many a lyne' in praise of the Virgin Mary (*Regement,* 4987), and two of his eight Marian poems proved capable of being mistaken for the master's. The Miracle of the Virgin which he wrote in imitation of the *Prioress's Tale* found a place in one manuscript of the *Canterbury Tales,* introduced there in a spurious prologue as the *Plowman's Tale;*[3] and one of his Marian lyrics, having been attributed to Chaucer by two Scottish scribes, was accepted as his by Victorian editors—even, to begin with, by Furnivall and the Chaucer Society.[4] One of Chaucer's other voices is to be heard in the '**Letter of Cupid,**' for here Hoccleve followed his master in adapting the courtly matter of Cupid from the French: the god Cupid writes a letter to his loyal servants offering a defence of women against false lovers and slanderers of the sex (he mentions Ovid and Jean de Meun). It is clear that Hoccleve had Chaucer's *Legend of Good Women* in mind here, for Cupid refers to 'our legende of martirs'.[5] In later life, Hoccleve was to report that some ladies took offence at the '**Letter,**' presumably because it quoted the opposition anti-feminist case at too great length; but the poem won a secure place in that select group of courtly pieces, many of them by Chaucer himself (including the *Legend*), which circulated in fifteenth- and sixteenth-century copies. It appears in three manuscripts of the so-called Oxford group, in one of Shirley's manuscripts, in a Scottish 'Chaucerian' collection, in the Findern anthology, and in two major sixteenth-century volumes, the Bannatyne and Devonshire manuscripts.[6] The poem was printed by Thynne in his 1532 Chaucer, and it continued to appear in later 'Chaucers' up to and including Urry's in 1721.[7]

If all Hoccleve's poems were like his Marian pieces or the '**Letter of Cupid,**' he might be remembered only as a technically proficient Chaucer clone; but his actual body of work creates a very different impression. Hoccleve's claim to attention in his own right rests mainly upon *The Regement of Princes,* the so-called *Series,* and the '**Male Regle**'; and these works, taken together with some of the epistolary ballades, witness to a mind quite unlike that of his master. The essential, and undoubtedly damaging, difference is that Hoccleve had very little imagination—if by that one understands a capacity and desire to dwell in imaginary worlds, or at least to transgress the limits of one's own immediate experience:

> He had as much imagination
>   As a pint-pot;—he never could
> Fancy another situation
> From which to dart his contemplation,
>   Than that wherein he stood.[8]

Chaucer is supreme among English poets in his ability to 'fancy another situation': even in such a short piece as the *Prioress's Tale* he manages to conjure up a whole little world of people and places—the school, the street, the Jewish quarter, the boy and his schoolmate, the mother—

and also to persuade many readers that it is seen from that other situation which the fancied Prioress occupies. By contrast, Hoccleve's Miracle of the Virgin lacks imaginative body. His story of the miraculous origin of Our Lady's Psalter is competently told; but it leaves (if my own experience is to be trusted) only the faintest imprint of its outlines upon the memory. Hoccleve's best imagined narratives concern encounters between himself and another—the old almsman in the **Regement** prologue and the friend in the **Series**. These scenes display the poet's undoubted skill at rendering dialogue in verse; but he can hardly be said here to get outside the 'situation wherein he stood', for the energy of the scenes is drawn most from precisely that situation, which is the chief subject of the conversation in both. The friend has opinions but no character; and the almsman is a far fainter presence than Wordsworth's corresponding creation, the old leechgatherer, let alone the old man in the *Pardoner's Tale*.[9] Both the **Regement** and the **Series,** it is true, also incorporate a variety of subsidiary narratives set in imagined worlds (fictive or not) quite remote from the real worlds, private and public, of Hoccleve's own experience—the two *Gesta Romanorum* stories in the **Series** and the numerous moral *exempla* in the **Regement**—but even the best of these 'goodly tales', the story of John of Canace (**Regement,** 4180-354), remains firmly subordinated to its non-imaginary context and occasion.

Yet if Hoccleve cannot hold a candle to his master as a poet of imaginary worlds, he has his own distinctive strength as a poet of the non-imaginary worlds of public and private life. He does best, in fact, what Chaucer hardly does at all. Chaucer rarely addresses himself to the public affairs of the day, either in general or in particular (witness his passing reference to the Peasants' Revolt), and he only once permits more than a glimpse of his private circumstances—and that in a fantastically imaginary context.[10] The private and public worlds displayed in the *Chaucer Life-Records* bear little or no relation to the worlds we inhabit as readers of his poems. By contrast, the 'Appendix of Hoccleve Documents, copied from the Record Office by Mr R. E. G. Kirk' in Furnivall's edition of the Minor Poems takes one directly into the world of the poems themselves.[11] 'Thomas Hoccleve, unus clericorum nostrorum de officio privati sigilli nostri', is recognizably the author of the **Series,** the **'Male Regle,'** and the **Regement,** living in a state of anxious dependency upon the favour of the great and the uncertain grant of his annuity.

The Hoccleve who writes on public themes has attracted rather little attention recently: the righteous indignation of his attack on Lollardy in the **'Address to Sir John Oldcastle'** has repelled most readers, and Furnivall's 1897 edition of the **Regement** has yet to be replaced by a critical and annotated edition in modern times.[12] Yet the **Regement,** which survives in no less than forty-three manuscripts, was far and away Hoccleve's most successful poem in its day, and it must presumably again occupy a central place in any future account of his achievement. Recent studies have shown more interest in that other unChauce-

rian Hoccleve, the poet of the home and the office, the pub and the club. This is the Hoccleve whom Derek Brewer justly characterizes as 'amusing but undignified'.[13] If Chaucer may be considered an example of the 'negative capability' of which Keats spoke, this Hoccleve can only represent, by contrast, the egotistical ridiculous. Like Pandarus, Hoccleve 'japes at himself', and his japes expose him to ridicule in a way that Chaucer's more guarded self-depreciations rarely if ever do.[14] Yet this peculiar mixture of clowning and complaint is neither pointless nor artless: Hoccleve is at once bringing himself to the attention of those upon whom his livelihood depended and at the same time discovering his own distinctive way of writing poems. Both the **'Male Regle'** and also, in its much more ambitious fashion, the **Series** represent something new in English poetry—nothing less, in the latter case, than a long poem in which the poet himself plays the leading role.[15]

Hoccleve and Chaucer hardly resembled each other in temperament, and most of Hoccleve's poems, as I have suggested, are of a kind quite different from his predecessor's. Yet it remains evident that he could not have written them in the way he does—not even the least Chaucerian of them—had Chaucer not lived. The example of *Troilus,* the *Conterbury Tales,* and the shorter poems might well have been enough, even if Hoccleve had not been 'aqueynted with Caucher'; but it is tempting to suppose that the master's 'consail and reed' played a significant part in forming the younger poet's awareness of the disciplines of English verse. Lydgate (who does not claim to have known Chaucer) records that Chaucer 'said alway the best' when called upon to comment on other people's poems:

> My maister Chaucer, þat founde ful many spot,
> Hym liste nat pinche nor gruche at every blot,
> Nor meve hym silf to parturbe his rest
> (I have herde telle) but seide alweie þe best.[16]

This interesting piece of anecdotal evidence confirms the impression given by his poems, that Chaucer was not one to speak of the innermost secrets of his art. Perhaps, like some more recent poets, he preferred to confine discussion to technical matters and so minimize any perturbation of his rest. Yet the poet who in the *House of Fame* feared for the error of a single syllable in his verses (line 1098) and who in *Troilus* prayed that they should not be 'mismetred' by scribes (v, 1796) was not one to speak lightly about technical matters; and it may be conjectured that his discussions with Hoccleve were quite earnestly concerned with the duty of composing lines and stanzas of verse according to the dictates of the 'art poetical'.

Hoccleve's sense of responsibility to that art as it was practised by his master finds its clearest expression, characteristically, in an apologetic request for correction:

> If þat I in my wrytynge foleye,
> As I do ofte, I can it nat withseye,
> Meetrynge amis, or speke unfittyngly,
> Or nat by iust peys my sentences weye,

And nat to the ordre of endytyng obeye,
And my colours sette ofte sythe awry,
With al myn herte wole I buxumly
It to amende and to correcte him preye;
For undir his correccioun stande y.[17]

Like Chaucer's coinage 'mysmetre', Hoccleve's 'meet-rynge amis' must refer (though not exclusively) to the matter of syllable count. In a recent essay, Judith Jefferson has demonstrated the scrupulosity of Hoccleve's attention to this matter, as displayed in his own autograph copies. These copies show, for instance, that Hoccleve consistently employed variant forms of words in order to ensure that his lines should not 'fayle in a sillable'. Chaucer would certainly have approved.[18] After referring to this matter, in the stanza quoted, Hoccleve goes on to invoke the standard rhetorical doctrines of *decorum* ('speke unfittyngly'), *dispositio* ('the ordre of endytyng'), and *colores* ('my colours'). Like Chaucer's similar apologies, Hoccleve's imply a claim—a claim to be at least aspiring to meet the high standards of premeditated art set by the Latin *artes poetriae*. The ideal was expressed by Geoffrey of Vinsauf in a passage which both Hoccleve and Chaucer rendered into English. Here is Hoccleve's version:

'Thow woost wel, who shal an hous edifie
Gooth nat therto withoute avisament
If he be wys, for with his mental ye
First is it seen, pourposid, cast and ment,
How it shal wroght been, elles al is shent.'[19]

But the most interesting of Hoccleve's apologies concerns the possibility that he may on occasion 'nat by iust peys my sentences weye'. The ideal of artistic premeditation or 'avisament' evidently requires that a poet's thoughts or ideas should be weighed out 'by just measure'.[20] I guess that Hoccleve had in mind here, among other things, his experience in writing the kind of stanzaic verse that he learned from Chaucer. In the majority of his works, Hoccleve employs long ballade stanzas, most often rhyme royal but sometimes eight- or nine-line stanzas.[21] The composition of these requires that the mind or 'mental ye' should see in advance how they are to turn out—the shape of the syntax of cach, and the development of its thought. In particular, the principle of 'iust peys' requires that the thought should be weighed out so prudently that the stanza does not, as it were, run out of matter in its closing lines. One of the pleasures of reading Hoccleve is to see how well, on the whole, he succeeded in mastering this art—controlling the syntax and sense of the whole stanza with a firm hand. Here, for instance, is his stanzaic amplification of an ancient commonplace:

'How fair thyng or how precious it be
Þat in the world is, it is lyk a flour,
To whom nature yeven hath beautee
Of fressh heewe and of ful plesant colour,
With soote smellynge also and odour;
But as soone as it is bicomen drye,
Farwel colour, and the smel gynneth dye.'

(**'Dialogue,'** 267-73)

In this rhyme-royal stanza, the first five lines are devoted to comparing the beauty and value of earthly things to the colour and scent of a flower. The fourth and fifth lines depart from the concise manner of the first three to indulge in what may seem merely slack synonymy: 'heewe . . . colour', 'smellynge . . . odour'; but the final couplet, which concerns the dying flower, makes this expansiveness meaningful by setting against it the bald manner, without variation or epithet, in which the last line recapitulates the flower's colour and smell:

But as soone as it is bicomen drye,
Farwel colour, and the smel gynneth dye.

Hoccleve's style of writing is in some ways unlike Chaucer's. Although he is just as careful about the syllable count, his rhythms seem more uncertain; and his English tends more to the plain and to the colloquial than Chaucer's does. There are, as several critics have noticed, far fewer verbal echoes of Chaucer than one would expect to find in the work of an immediate follower.[22] Yet Hoccleve's debt to Chaucer, and especially to rhyme-royal Chaucer, was immense. One way of measuring it is to compare his version of the miracle of Our Lady's Psalter with the version in the Auchinleck Manuscript—taking the latter (perhaps a little unfairly) to represent the state of English verse as Chaucer found it. Here are the two opening of the story:

AUCHINLECK:

A riche man was while
Þat loved no gile;
He loved holi chirche.
Bisiden him a mile
An abbay of Seyn Gile
His eldren dede wirche.

HOCCLEVE:

Ther was whilom, as þat seith the scripture,
In France a ryche man and a worthy,
That God and holy chirche to honure
And plese enforced he him bisily;
And unto Crystes modir specially
Þat noble lady, þat blissid virgyne,
For to worsshipe he dide his might and payne.[23]

Hoccleve's stanza of rhyme royal is by no means one of his best; but it does represent, by contrast with his predecessor's tail rhyme, that enhanced awareness of the ample potentialities of English verse which Hoccleve was among the first to learn from Chaucer.

Notes

1. *The Regement of Princes,* ed. F. J. Furnivall, *EETS,* e.s. 72 (1897), 1958-74, 2077-107, 4978-5012. Citations throughout are from the *EETS* editions of Hoccleve's works, but with some altered punctuation.

2. Doubts are expressed by Jerome Mitchell, *Thomas Hoccleve: A Study in Early Fifteenth-Century English Poetic* (Urbana, Ill., 1968), 115-18, and in his essay,

'Hoccleve's Tribute to Chaucer', in A. Esch (ed.), *Chaucer und Seine Zeit: Symposion für Walter F. Schirmer* (Tübingen, 1968), 275-83. For arguments to the contrary, see J. A. Burrow, 'Autobiographical Poetry in the Middle Ages: The Case of Thomas Hoccleve', *Proceedings of the British Academy*, 68 (1982), 397-8.

3. Christ Church, Oxford, MS 152. Like Chaucer, Hoccleve prefaces the miracle narrative with a Marian prologue: items VI and VII in *The Minor Poems II*, ed. I. Gollancz, *EETS*, e.s. 73 (1897), reissued with *The Minor Poems I*, ed. F. J. Furnivall, *EETS*, e.s. 61 (1892), in one volume revised by J. Mitchell and A. I. Doyle (1970).

4. *Minor Poems I*, item x. The two manuscripts are Bodleian MS Arch. Selden B. 24 and National Library of Scotland MS Adv. 18, 2, 8. On the career of this poem as 'Chaucer's "Mother of God"' in the nineteenth century, see E. P. Hammond, *Chaucer: A Bibliographical Manual* (New York, 1908), 438-9, and *Minor Poems I*, xxxix-xl. It may be noted that both Chaucer and Hoccleve translated Marian poems of Deguileville: Chaucer from *Le Pelerinage de la Vie Humaine* ('An ABC'), Hoccleve from *Le Pelerinage de l'Ame* (*Regement*, xxxvii-xlv).

5. Line 316, not in the French of Christine de Pisan. The best discussion of the *Letter* is by John V. Fleming, 'Hoccleve's "Letter of Cupid" and the "Quarrel" over the *Roman de la Rose*', *Medium Aevum*, 40 (1971), 21-40. Fleming notes that Hoccleve's later defence of the poem ('Dialogue,' 745-84) may be seen as his 'adaptation of that elegant fiction spun by Chaucer in the "Prologue" to the *Legend of Good Women*'.

6. Bodleian MSS Fairfax 16, Tanner 346, and Bodley 638; Trinity College, Cambridge, MS R. 3, 20; Bodleian MS Arch. Selden B, 24; Cambridge University Library MS Ff. 1, 6; National Library of Scotland MS Adv. 1, 1, 6 and British Library MS Add. 17492. The 'Letter' is also found with Chaucer's *Troilus* in Durham University Library MS Cosin V, ii, 13. There are two other MS copies: Huntington Library MS HM. 744 (Hoccleve's holograph) and Bodleian MS Digby 181.

7. Hammond, *Chaucer*, pp. 434-6.

8. Shelley on Wordsworth, *Peter Bell the Third*, 298-302.

9. Comparison between the *Regement* prologue and the *Pardoner's Tale* is suggested by M. C. Seymour (ed.), *Selections from Hoccleve* (Oxford, 1981), xxiii.

10. *Nun's Priest's Tale*, VII, 3396; *House of Fame*, 614-60. Even in *Melibee* Chaucer addresses public affairs obliquely within a fictional context. It is Hoccleve, not Chaucer, who refers to Edward III and John of Gaunt by name (*Regement*, 2556, 512). Yet Hoccleve defers to Chaucer on a matter of public policy (the holding of council meetings on holy days): Chaucer, he says, makes this kind of point better than I can (*Regement*, 4978-81). Chaucer's surviving works offer no obvious 'caas semblable'.

11. *Minor Poems I*, li-lxx, with additions on pp. lxxi-lxxii.

12. A new edition is in preparation by David Greetham and others.

13. D. S. Brewer (ed.), *Chaucer and Chaucerians: Critical Studies in Middle English Literature* (London, 1966), 28.

14. Pandarus 'gan at hymself to jape faste' (*Troilus*, II, 1164). Chaucer's own style of japing is best sampled in the *Envoy to Scogan*.

15. J. A. Burrow, 'Hoccleve's *Series*: Experience and Books', in R. F. Yeager (ed.), *Fifteenth-Century Studies: Recent Essays* (Hamden, Conn., 1984), 259-73.

16. Lydgate, *Troy Book*, ed. H. Bergen, *EETS*, e.s. 97, 103, 106, 126 (1906-20), V, 3521-4.

17. 'Balade to my gracious Lord of York', *Minor Poems I*, item IX, lines 46-54.

18. Judith A. Jefferson, 'The Hoccleve Holographs and Hoccleve's Metrical Practice', in Derek Pearsall (ed.), *Manuscripts and Texts* (Cambridge, 1987), 95-109. Jefferson's discussion of final *-e* in the Hoccleve holographs incidentally throws light on the still sometimes disputed question of final *-e* in Chaucer, for she shows beyond doubt that *-e* is syllabic in the disciple. Can it have been otherwise in the master?

19. 'Dialogue,' 638-42. The holograph adds parts of Geoffrey's Latin in the margin: 'Si quis habet fundare domum, non currit ad actum' and 'Impetuosa manus, &c' (*Poetria Nova*, 43-4). Compare *Troilus*, I, 1065-9. J. Mitchell, *Thomas Hoccleve*, 119-20, rightly notes that Hoccleve's version is independent of Chaucer's.

20. 'Peyse' (glossed 'id est pondus') appears in a similar context in Lydgate's *Reson and Sensuallyte*, ed. E. Sieper, *EETS*, e.s. 84 (1901), line 1666.

21. See the excellent discussion of Hoccleve's relation to Chaucer in M. R. Pryor, 'Thomas Hoccleve's Series: An Edition of MS Durham Cosin V, iii, 9' (unpublished Ph.D. thesis, University of California, Los Angeles, 1968), pp. 52-3. Hoccleve uses the term 'balade' for what we would now call a rhyme-royal stanza in 'Dialogue,' 551.

22. Thus Pryor, 'Thomas Hoccleve's Series', 38-44, Mitchell, *Thomas Hoccleve*, 118-22, Seymour, *Selections*, xxi-xxvii. Echoes do occur, of course. Thus, the *Regement* occasionally echoes Chaucer's shorter poems: 'þis olde dotyd Grisel' (401, cf. *Scogan*, 35); 'Pyte, I trowe, is beried' (882, cf. *Pity*, 14); 'it sore me agaste / To bynde me, where I was at my large'

(1454-5, cf. *Bukton,* 11-12); 'Suffiseth to your good' (5375, cf. *Truth,* 2). See also A. C. Spearing, *Medieval to Renaissance in English Poetry* (Cambridge, 1985), 114-17.

23. Auchinleck MS f. 259[rb], corresponding to lines 19-24 in the Digby text edited by C. Horstmann, *Altenglische Legenden: Neue Folge* (Heilbronn, 1881), p. 220; *Minor Poems II,* item VII, lines 1-7.

Larry Scanlon (essay date 1990)

SOURCE: Scanlon, Larry. "The King's Two Voices: Narrative and Power in Hoccleve's *Regement of Princes.*" In *Literary Practice and Social Change in Britain, 1380-1530,* edited by Lee Patterson, pp. 216-47. Berkeley: University of California Press, 1990.

[*In this essay, Scanlon considers Hoccleve's* Regement of Princes *in terms of medieval English thought on kingship and authority. Drawing from Ernst Kantorowicz's work on political theology,* The King's Two Bodies, *Scanlon looks at how Hoccleve's poem constructs and critiques the voice of the king. For Scanlon, the* Regement *reflects the increasing power of vernacular literature to influence and disseminate political ideology.*]

PROLOGUE: THE DEPOSITION OF RICHARD II

Thomas Hoccleve's **Regement of Princes,** written between 1410 and 1412 for the future Henry V, is something of a forgotten masterpiece.[1] A witty, subtle, and relentlessly self-conscious poem, its language is magisterial, modulating effortlessly between the philosophical and colloquial with a Chaucerian fluency. Its numerous exempla and extended autobiographical petitions to the prince make it predominantly narrative, but it draws on nonnarrative philosophical genres as well—the complaint, the dialogue, and chiefly, the *Fürstenspiegel,* or Mirror of Princes. Indeed, it takes its title, as well as some of its content, from Aegidius Romanus's widely influential *De Regimine Principum.* The poem situates these philosophical genres narratively, producing both a coherent moral vision of kingship and an examination of the rhetorical means by which that vision has been itself produced.

The work has been forgotten because the ideology of kingship is not a problem modern scholarship has considered very interesting. Literary scholars have been particularly remiss in this respect, despite the constant preoccupation of medieval poets with the subject.[2] Dante, Petrarch, and Boccaccio all wrote major works dealing with kingship, which modern scholars routinely ignore: respectively, *De Monarchia, De Viris Illustribus,* and *De Casibus Virorum Illustrium.* In addition, Petrarch also wrote a short *Fürstenspiegel, De Re Publica Optime Administranda.*[3] The last major treatment of Chaucer and kingship appeared in 1945.[4] It is generally acknowledged that the three major poets following Chaucer in the Chaucerian tradition,

Gower, Hoccleve, and Lydgate, remain underexamined, and it seems hardly accidental that the *chef d'oeuvre* of each, the *Confessio Amantis,* the **Regement of Princes,** and the *Fall of Princes,* centrally concerns kingship.

Why was kingship such a dominant concern in later medieval literature? At first glance, the answer to this question seems straightforward and not particularly interesting. Secular literature needed to differentiate itself from the discourse of the Church without directly challenging ecclesiastical authority. In the figure of the king, secular writers found a single, central source of authority analogous to the figure of God in ecclesiastical discourse and yet fully secular.

There is, however, much more to say about the matter than this. Secular authority, political or literary, was an extremely fluid category at this time, dependent on the very ecclesiastical traditions from which both secular rulers and secular writers were attempting to wrest it. Throughout this process of secularization the political and the literary interpenetrated—kings were as ideologically dependent on their writers as the writers were politically dependent on kings. For as poets like Hoccleve staked out the claims of a new vernacular tradition, what they encountered in kingship was not some fully formed and uncontested institution. Rather, they encountered a dynamic political structure in the midst of defining itself ideologically in order to maintain and extend its power politically.[5] The representation of kingship in works like the **Regement of Princes** was part of this larger ideological project. For this reason consideration of the formal integrity of such works will continue to be impossible until it is grounded in an understanding of kingship as an ideological structure. We cannot hope to understand the discursive strategies whereby kingship was represented in literature until we understand the ideological strategies whereby its power relations were reproduced within the social structure.

On this point historians have been as remiss as literary scholars. While they have hardly ignored kingship, they have generally kept its ideology separate from its practice. Perhaps as a reaction to the teleological excesses of constitutional history, regnal biographers and administrative historians have tended to view the administrative growth of medieval kingship in preponderantly local terms (a series of practical solutions to immediate problems) while resisting any appeal to larger theoretical conceptions. On the other hand, comprehensive accounts of medieval theory, such as the classic works of Ernst Kantorowicz and Michael Wilks, treat their subject as an intellectual drama in which the only actors are ideas, and in which the primary motivation is the purely ratiocinative desire for ever clearer solutions to logical dilemmas. The agency that is always missing is power. Because these scholars are interested in ideas rather than ideology, they have little to say about the way medieval ideas about kingship functioned culturally, how they maintained the power structure they conceptualized.

A particularly striking illustration of this point can be found in one of the central political documents of Hoccleve's time: the Articles of Deposition of Richard II. One of the most famous articles defines the problem of royal power as precisely a problem of representation.

> 33. ITEM, the same King, did not wish to preserve or protect the just Laws and Customs of his Reign, but to make whatever decision occurred to him according to the judgment of his own will. Whenever the Laws of his Reign were explained and declared to him by the Justices and others of his Council, and according to these Laws justice for the suitors exhibited, he would say expressly with a stern and shameless countenance, that his Laws were in his mouth, and several times, in his heart, and that he himself alone was able to change or institute the Laws of his Reign . . .[6]

This story is usually read as a simple denunciation of tyranny, consistent with the standard constitutionalist view of the Deposition as "one more step in the transference of the centre of political gravity from ruler to people."[7] Indeed, more recent historians, who have been suspicious of this Whig teleology, also treat Article 33 as an essentially accurate depiction of Richard, even though, as Anthony Tuck concedes, there is no proof of its truth.[8] But the crucial point about this article is not its accuracy but its rhetorical debt to medieval conceptions of kingship and the practical power they lend to its ideological mission.

Before the article is a constitutional claim it is a narrative, and as a narrative it convinces fictively rather than referentially. For it recapitulates the complex of corporate and organological fictions that Kantorowicz's classic study has shown ultimately issue in the notion of the "King's Two Bodies." "The Prince (or Pope) has the laws in the shrine of his breast" was a maxim the canonists adopted from Roman law.[9] But in its earlier instances, the intent of the fiction seems to have been, at least in part, to constrain the royal *voluntas* by counsel. Thus, the jurist Cynus of Pistoia interpreted "shrine of his breast" to mean "Doctors of Law through whose mouths the most law-abiding Prince himself speaks."[10] Similar formulations occur in French jurists, and Bracton exchanges the terms of the trope so that the Prince becomes the "mouth of the council," making laws "as he pleased" after hearing their advice.[11] In Article 33, however, this intent seems to have been reversed. Richard is depicted as claiming the law is in his breast or mouth precisely in order to free himself from counsel. This apparent inconsistency can be resolved by reconsidering the intent of the earlier instances and reinserting the missing term "power." A product of Roman thought, the fiction's first major instance occurs in Livy, where the patrician Menenius Agrippa uses it to quell a plebeian revolt.[12] Though it passed into the Middle Ages via the Pauline concept of the Church as *corpus Christi*, it was not actively applied to medieval institutions until the later growth of the papacy, when papalists began casting the pope as *caput* of the *ecclesia*.[13] It was soon taken up by royal apologists, as a way of both resisting the claims of the papacy and defining their own. In both cases its

political value was the same: to reduce an aggregate of individuals to a single entity, imagined in one way or another as a single person, or a single body. It reinforced the unity and the preeminence of a central institution undergoing a massive administrative expansion. Accordingly, the point of the fiction is not to democratize a unitary form of power, but to enable that power to maintain its ideological unity as it is being institutionally diffused. And even as the fiction occurs in Bracton and earlier writers its point is not so much to neutralize the prince as it is to empower his council. In other words, the point of the metaphor is not to disperse power but to solidify it, not to hedge it about with constraints but to reinforce its stability and dominance. And the crucial line of demarcation is thus not between prince and his council but between the governing class and everyone else.

In more complex fashion, the same sort of empowerment is at work in Article 33. Appealing to the expanded notion of the king's council as embodied in Parliament, the narrative employs an expanded version of the corporate fiction.[14] It retains the ideal of a unified royal voice, even in disavowing Richard's right to it. For at the very moment Richard voices his ostensibly discredited claim, the narrative focuses not on the specific legal results of the claim, but on his body, on what his face looked like as he spoke: "with a stern and shameless countenance." The narrative returns to his merely physical body in order to dissociate him from the institutional royal body. Ironically, then, for the story to make its case against Richard it must concede to him the very power to embody the law it accuses him of illicitly claiming. In those cases so vaguely cited here, where Richard made this claim, his voice *did* have the force of law. He was able effectively to void precedent and nullify counsel simply by announcing, according to his own *voluntas,* that he wished to do so. If the story makes Richard out as a tyrant it is not because he violated some explicitly established constitutional principle. It is because he declined to live up to the ideal of the corporate fiction. He refused to embody counsel and legal precedent in a single unifying voice: he literalized the body politic and thus revealed monarchical theory to be a metaphor—that is, a fiction.

The story is also vague about the constitutional issues it raises. Which were the cases where Richard claimed his prerogative? What specific legal issues were at stake? How specifically should he have been limited by precedent and counsel? Should any prerogatives have been open to him at all? The article does not begin to address these questions. Instead it is entirely focused on the power of the king's voice. The article does not wish to do away with royal *voluntas,* but rather desires a *voluntas* at one with the law. If the law is imagined as the property of the realm as opposed to the king (which is what the phrase *Leges & Consuetidines Regni* implies), then what the article desires is a royal voice that is spoken by the realm, a king whose voice unifies the nobility's interests. The article resorts to narrative because any attempt to define this ideal juridically or constitutionally—that is, to conceptualize it—would destroy it. If the king is to be a living embodiment of the law, a *lex animata,* he must be so naturally and spontaneously. A *lex animata* produced entirely by prior external constraint is by definition not a *lex animata.* By presenting its case narratively, the article can dispose of Richard and yet retain the ideal it would have had him embody. And Richard *must* be disposed of, because his literalization of the metaphor has rendered it unavailable to the nobility as a whole.

In the first instance, the ideal was crucial to Bolingbroke and the other architects of the deposition. A usurper rather than a revolutionary, Bolingbroke wanted to replace Richard but not alter the structure of kingship. Indeed, he rejected out of hand the one tentative suggestion that he accept a parliamentary title.[15] But the practical value the ideal of a spontaneously lawful *voluntas* had for Henry was matched by its ideological value to the rest of the ruling class. In respect to those below him, the legislative and juridical prerogative of a nobleman was not essentially different from the royal prerogative to which Richard here lays claim.[16] In the main, medieval justice was indeed what the nobility said it was. It was instituted by them, interpreted by them, and administered by them as, in Maitland's phrase, "a proprietary right."[17] In the Middle Ages, justice was something the nobility *owned.* While one may not wish to go as far as Perry Anderson when he claims that medieval justice "was the ordinary name of power," it is hard to argue with Alan Harding's observation that medieval courts served a double function: "first, the maintenance of social peace by the settlement of disputes between individuals, and second, the maintenance of the social dominance of the king and noble who held the court. Practically, the two are inseparable."[18] While seigneurial justice was, by the end of the fourteenth century, being gradually displaced by royal justice, the manner of this displacement was such that it made the unity of the royal *voluntas* that much more attractive.[19] For the decline of seigneurial courts coincided with the advent of the justices of the peace. Though nominally an officer of the king, the justice of the peace was invariably a local landowner who would follow the local interests of his class. So what the nobility gave up in direct juridical control it regained through its alliance with the bureaucracy of the crown. As Harding has said, "the sessions of the Justices of the Peace replaced the manorial courts as a means of social control as the relationship of peasant to landlord changed from a legal subjection to a purely economic subjection."[20]

The juridical power the nobility once exercised purely in its own name it now exercised in the name of the king. Though the form had changed, the fundamental ideological presumption had not. Legal authority was still the property of a single class, and the immediate effect of the change of form was to bring the prerogative of the nobility even closer to that of the king. When a justice of the peace spoke, he spoke with the king's voice. The result of this institutional diffusion of the king's voice was a more efficient concentration of the legal power of the ruling class as a whole. It also meant that the ruling class as a whole

had a greater stake in defining how royal power was to be exercised. While this condition certainly does not explain Richard's deposition by itself, it does help explain the particular form the deposition took. The nobility was not likely to call for structural changes in the status quo, because the status quo was precisely the prize they were gaming for. By giving them control of Richard's voice the narrative of Article 33 helped them take control of the power structure without having to change it.

The power of this narrative thus inheres neither in its referential fidelity to some actual statement of Richard's, a correspondence that seems vague at best and an outright fabrication at worst, nor in its articulation of some constitutional principle. Its power inheres instead in a formal capacity that modern criticism has identified as one of narrative's central features: the capacity to speak convincingly in the voice of another. Older Anglo-American accounts of narrative treat this capacity, also identified as narrative's shifting point of view, as their primary object of study.[21]

More recently, under the influence of Continental narratology, Anglo-American criticism has moved from considerations of narrative voice to more theoretically rigorous considerations of the various forms of narrative discourse. I retain the older term here for two reasons. First, as Jonathan Culler has pointed out, the modes of inquiry are not that dissimilar.[22] To begin, as narratology does, with the distinction between the way a story is told ("discourse," or *sjuzhte*) and the sequence of events it records ("story," or *fabula*) is in fact to study the problem of point of view. Indeed, narrative's capacity to speak convincingly in the voice of another is simply the most extreme instance of the more general capacity narratologists identify as narrative's power to make events "seem to tell themselves."[23] When a narrative shifts into the voice of one of its characters it is presenting that voice as pure event, as if an entirely distinct entity were now speaking. Narrative thus has the ideological power not only to present events neutrally, as if they were actually unfolding, but also to present equally neutrally other ways of viewing these events, as if the other viewpoints were speaking directly for themselves.

This is my second reason for retaining the term "voice": to foreground precisely this power to coopt other points of view. Despite its theoretical rigor, narratology's emphasis on event threatens to conceal narrative's ideological power rather than expose it. Unfortunately, it is a short step between observing with Roland Barthes that narrative "is simply there, like life itself," to assuming (as he later does in the same essay) that in its purest form, narrative is ideologically neutral.[24] On the contrary, narrative's ideological power inheres precisely in its illusion of neutrality, an illusion narrative produces as assiduously as a Petrarchan sonnet produces the illusion of artifice. Analyzing narrative as a matrix of voices penetrates the illusion at its most mystifying moment, the moment when it turns a point of view into an event.

In Article 33, the voice that the narrative constructs for Richard becomes *his* voice, which is how Article 33 makes moot the issue of its referential accuracy. The Lancastrian narrator can reproduce Richard's voice without needing Richard actually to have spoken the words assigned him. Were the issue sheer referential accuracy, then the question who is speaking here, Richard or his Lancastrian accusers, would have to be settled before the story could be of any use. But as the reaction of Tuck and other modern historians illustrates, whether Richard actually spoke these words is not finally the crucial question. What is more important is that the article gives Richard a voice that plausibly explains what the article perceives to be the basis of his actions, a plausibility that depends upon, and reproduces, the dominant ideology of kingship.

The plausibility thus produced is itself a fictional effect. The voice assigned to Richard is plausible because it recapitulates previous fictions of the royal voice. It is the very essence of these fictions to present a voice at once itself and the voice of others. The royal voice is thus incipiently narratorial in that it defines itself by its capacity to speak for others without losing its own specificity. The king both speaks the communal voice and is spoken by it. This broad structural similarity between the medieval ideology of kingship and narrative may well explain medieval political theory's preponderant dependence on fictions. This dependence has usually been viewed in teleological terms as a weakness. Medieval theorists are seen to have resorted to fictions and metaphors as stopgaps because they had not yet arrived at adequate conceptualizations. It may be, however, that the opposite is true, that medieval theorists preferred fiction because it was better suited to the ideological task at hand, a positive means of empowerment, rather than a stopgap.

Such certainly seems the case with the narrative of Article 33. To be able to tell this story of the royal voice was quite literally to usurp its authority. Narrative becomes a species of political power. Yet despite this convergence, the two categories are not completely interchangeable. Within medieval ideologies of kingship, narrative was precisely that species of power that could never know itself as such. The ideological fictions of kingship had always to be subordinated to the form of power they maintained. Article 33's story of Richard's voice, though primarily the product of previous traditional fictions, works precisely by suppressing its fictionality and presenting itself as the truth.

At the same time, this fiction was public in a way that its predecessors hadn't needed to be. The quasi-parliamentary status of the Articles of Deposition testify to the increased dispersion of the ruling class they were attempting to unify. For the Lancastrians this dispersion meant that kingship's dependence on public modes of legitimation was greater than ever before. They could not be satisfied simply to commission works in Latin; they needed legitimation in the vernacular. Here the needs of political authority and the needs of the newly emergent Chaucerian tradition converged, and royal patronage of vernacular poetry was an important item on the Lancastrian ideological agenda, particularly for Henry V.[25]

As an early example of this trend, the *Regement of Princes* emerges as a remarkable meditation on the relation between the literary and the political. Narrative, the rhetorical form common to both, provides the meeting ground. Like many *Fürstenspiegel,* the work consists of a series of moral discussions interspersed with exempla. But if these moral discussions constitute kingship's other voice—that is, the voice of counsel—they are framed by the larger narrative of Hoccleve's autobiography. The autobiography exposes Hoccleve's material dependence on Henry, subjugating the voice of counsel he embodies to the very power it would constrain. The effect of the narrative, then, is to present the Prince as at once constrained by the voice of counsel and independent of it.

The autobiography further complicates matters by introducing Chaucer into the poem as Hoccleve's "maister deere," an independent source of literary authority.[26] This complication is necessary to the legitimation of Henry even as it seems to transcend it. The vernacular legitimation of Henry requires a vernacular moral authority, and this is what the canonization of Chaucer provides. In effect, the very thoroughness with which Hoccleve pursues the celebration of Henry leads him to canonize Chaucer. Both aims are offered to an expanding ruling-class audience as complementary aspects of the same general project of cultural empowerment. I have already sketched this project's largest ideological outlines. It is now time to examine Hoccleve's text, and the specific models of authority with which it grapples, to see how he works out the project in detail.

THE VOICES OF TRADITION: CHAUCER AND THE *FÜRSTENSPIEGEL*

The *Regement* brings together the primarily Latin tradition of the *Fürstenspiegel* with the vernacular tradition presided over by Chaucer. Hoccleve's interest in kingship was anticipated by both Chaucer and Gower as well as by poets in the alliterative tradition. *Wynnere and Wastoure,* the early passus of *Piers Plowman,* and *Mum and the Sothsegger* all treat the king as society's moral center.[27] Gower returns to the problem of kingship throughout the *Confessio Amantis,* and he presents the seventh book of that work as a recapitulation of the *Secretum Secretorum,* perhaps the most popular *Fürstenspiegel* in fourteenth- and fifteenth-century England. The issue surfaces in the *Canterbury Tales* as well. Like Lydgate's *Fall of Princes,* the *Monk's Tale* is a *De Casibus* collection, a genre related to the *Fürstenspiegel.* And the tale Chaucer presents in his own voice, the *Tale of Melibee,* while not explicitly concerned with kingship, is a "serious and thoughtful address to the powerful on how to save their power."[28]

Many scholars still view the political concerns of these writers as regrettable concessions to public taste. What this view fails to recognize is that the audience that supported the tradition's explicitly political work, though perhaps larger, was basically the same audience that supported the putatively apolitical Chaucerian tales modern scholarship has found more to its liking. This audience came from the newly empowered strata of the ruling class, the gentry and the richest of the urban bourgeoisie, who looked to the royal court as the source of cultural as well as political authority.[29] For this audience, the growing consumption of vernacular literature was no less an exercise in cultural entitlement than the growing participation in political discourse.

Chaucer's participation in this project was not restricted to *Melibee* and the *Monk's Tale*. The entire Canterbury collection is built around the dialectic between narrative voice and social position. As Jill Mann has shown, the General Prologue is an estates satire.[30] As the frame tale, it thus locates each of the many narrative voices of the *Tales* within a social totality, a solidarity within which the apparently inexhaustible capacity of Chaucerian narrative for shifting voices is played out. This fact alone would seem to call into question the formalist assumption that Chaucer's shifting perspectives signal his desire to transcend the communal demands of his audience.

Mann herself reserves judgment on this point, preferring to see the Prologue as a detached exercise in ethnography, rather than the reinforcement of the moral values associated with estates satire. As the narrative voice shifts from one character to the next, demonstrating that each character's point of view is conditioned by his social position, within which it is perfectly coherent, the reader recognizes the impossibility of any totalizing judgment.[31] But this view will produce an apolitical reading of the *Tales* only if one assumes a complete separation between the discursive and the political. If not, then to the extent that the shifts in voice are rendered intelligible by the social categories the frame tale imposes, the categories are themselves validated. It may be impossible to judge the value of the Knight's point of view in relation to the Miller's, but the very fact that the estates frame enables one viewpoint to be recognized as a "noble" tale and the other as a "cherles" tale gives the frame a heuristic validity that depends ultimately on its social content. For this reason, Chaucer's ethnography is not ultimately any more detached from estates ideology than the more explicitly evaluative claims of earlier estates satires.[32]

This is particularly true when one considers the function Chaucer's ethnography would have had for his original audience. To an audience of the lesser nobility, the frame tale presents figures who are mostly inferior in social status. The estates frame is precisely what enables this audience to have access to these less privileged voices. It is politically empowering in that it assigns these voices their social meanings. As Article 33 gave the same audience access to the voice of the king, the *Canterbury Tales* gives it access to the voices of the socially excluded.

I am not suggesting that the contemporary political value of the *Tales* exhausts their meaning. But I am suggesting that this political value underlies the Chaucerian tradition's

reading of Chaucer, and that it makes that reading of Chaucer as valid as any other. The modern cliché that the fifteenth-century's version of Chaucer was narrow or distorted is a purely ideological preference presented as an indisputable poetic law. That version of Chaucer is certainly no narrower than the modern view that celebrates Chaucer's romances and fabliaux and discards the *Melibee,* the *Monk's Tale,* and the devotional works. Modern commentators are as entitled to their ideological preferences as the fifteenth century was to its, but when they make those preferences the basis of their literary history, they have failed as historians. The fifteenth century was not a period of cultural decline. It was a period that carried on the cultural expansion that had begun in the last half of the fourteenth, an expansion about which texts like the **Regement of Princes** were entirely self-conscious.

The dialectic between narrative voice and social position that Chaucer achieved through estates satire, Hoccleve achieves through a generic mutation of another sort. In a **"Prologue"** that accounts for almost half the work's total length, he presents an extended dialogue with a beggar, whom he clearly intends as a surrogate (at one point the Beggar offers an autobiography reminiscent of the one Hoccleve himself offers in **"La Male Regle"** [596-742]). At the end of the **"Prologue"** the Beggar suggests Hoccleve write the **Regement** as a way of petitioning for an annuity. The next day Hoccleve sits down to write and places in the middle of the work the request for an annuity the Beggar suggested he make (1842-2016).

Framing his *Fürstenspiegel* in this way counters the discursive authority Hoccleve assumes within the text with his social subordination to the prince outside of it. In fact, this framing breaks down the distinction between inside and outside, self-reflexively bringing into the text the projected exchange of the text itself for an annuity. This narrative in turn suggests Henry's actual presence, an impression Hoccleve reinforces throughout the poem by continually presenting his moral instruction in the second person. At least one of the manuscripts takes the fiction a step further still, inserting between the text of the **"Prologue"** and the text of the **"Proem,"** at the very point where Hoccleve begins to address Henry directly, an illustration in which a small, kneeling poet presents his book to a larger standing figure wearing a crown.[33]

The begging poem was a comparatively late genre, emerging in France in the fourteenth century.[34] It presupposes a court in transition from the personal to the bureaucratic, one sufficiently bureaucratized that petitions for small sums of money have become routine, but still sufficiently invested in the personal to want to see the granting of such petitions as the whimsical response to a *jeu d'esprit*. The begging poem postulates a royal *voluntas* that acts entirely at its own pleasure, and thus stands as a striking counterpoise to the didactic presumptions of the *Fürstenspiegel,* which posits a king who relies on counsel.

Nevertheless, yoking the two genres together simply underlines a tension already long established within the *Fürstenspiegel* itself. The compilers of *Fürstenspiegel* almost invariably display their dependence on a particular ruler. These works were customarily dedicated to a prince or ecclesiastical magnate on whom the compiler was dependent or from whom he wished preferment. Often, as in the **Regement of Princes,** the second-person address would continue within the body of the work. *Fürstenspiegel* also served as public celebrations of their dedicatees, appearing at moments of opportunity or dispute. For example, John of Salisbury's *Policraticus,* which commences the high medieval tradition, was dedicated to Becket while he was still chancellor to Henry II. The work is strenuously theocratic, arguing the king should be subject to the pope and should heed clerical counselors.[35] Similarly, the equally relentlessly royalist *De Regimine Principum,* one of the three sources Hoccleve names in his opening address to the prince (2038-2128), was compiled by Aegidius Romanus for Philip the Fair, whose later arrest of Boniface VIII would mark the beginning of the end for papal absolution.[36] And the source that Hoccleve names first and seems to take as the model of the genre is the *Secretum Secretorum*: presented as if authored by Aristotle for Alexander, it opens with Aristotle's lavish praise of Alexander and frames the philosophical instruction to come as a means of inducing his subjects to obedience and lawful activity.[37] Widely circulated and translated in fourteenth- and fifteenth-century England, both these works stage the paradox of an omnipotent ruler who nonetheless requires advice, a royal *voluntas* from which proceeds reward and yet a royal ear eager to listen and so acknowledging its own insufficiency.

The *Fürstenspiegel* was a discrete generic expression of the larger medieval discourse of sovereignty. This discourse is generally seen as moving from theocratic absolutism to secular and constitutional monarchism, a movement through which, in the words of Wilks, "the Ages of Faith become transmuted into an Age of Reason."[38] As I have suggested, this Whig teleology ignores the deep attraction absolutist arguments had for both secular monarchs and their noble cohorts, the very attraction that in fact made the transition from the theocratic to the secular possible in the first place. The theocratic argument for papal sovereignty was not simply an argument for faith against reason, or the eternal against the temporal. It was an argument that wanted, on the basis of mutual consent (that is, shared belief in Christ), to center all communal authority in a single figure.

As medieval monarchy became increasingly institutionalized, this conception of authority became increasingly attractive, because it provided a way of intellectually concentrating the power that was being institutionally dispersed. The *Fürstenspiegel* enacted this concentration by its rhetorical celebration of its dedicatee. But it also acknowledged the fact of dispersion by its performance of public instruction. This may explain the popularity of the genre among an English ruling class continually seeking a greater share in royal power. It may also explain both the *Regement*'s specific political motivation and its ostentatious exploitation of the tradition's paradoxes.

For all of its ideological shrewdness, Bolinbroke's accession to the crown left him in a precarious position. The basis for his title was not and could not be made entirely clear. He faced revolts in 1400 and 1402, and by 1410 his ailments had forced him to leave the overseeing of the kingdom to councillors who were openly feuding with the prince.[39] Against this background the **Regement of Princes** can be seen as a direct attempt to secure the continuity of Lancastrian rule. By addressing a *Fürstenspiegel* to the future Henry V, Hoccleve effectively settles the question of dynastic rights by treating it as if it were already settled. He reinforces the point by scattering through the poem favorable invocations of the prince's patrimony: his father, the king (816-26, 1835, 3347-67), his grandfather, John of Gaunt (3347-67), and his great-grandfather, Henry of Lancaster (2647-53). This rhetorical representation of Henry as dynastically legitimate with a long, honorable patrimony and about to receive a *Fürstenspiegel* can appropriately be described as a narrative positioning. It is narrative because it historicizes: it not only locates the *persona* it produces within a preexistent social totality, indeed, but produces the *persona* precisely by so locating it.

The projected dynastic succession is thus implicit in the projected acceptance of a *Fürstenspiegel,* and both are framed by the projected exchange of begging poem for royal grant. These evocations of Henry concretize the abstract set of moral lessons the text contains as the property of a specific, already established figure of supreme social authority. This narrative entails both idealization and coercion. There is the ideal of royal *voluntas* in general and Henry in particular as the personal embodiment of the text's commonly held moral principles. But there is also the coercion inherent in precisely this capacity of narrative to concretize: to present the ideal as if it were already embodied. In the equivocation between idealization and coercion lie both the risk and the aim of the **Regement of Princes.**

Hoccleve uses narrative's capacity for continually shifting point of view to resolve or bypass (to resolve by bypassing) the constitutional tensions surrounding the Lancastrian monarchy. Because of the severity of these tensions, he exploits his shifting point of view to the fullest, and thereby continually risks exposing its arbitrary, propagandistic aim. Yet he takes the risk precisely to convert it to his goal, which is to make his rhetorical construction of Prince Henry not simply a construction but the truth.

THE VOICES OF AUTHORITY: CHAUCER AND THE PRINCE

One measure of the risk Hoccleve takes is the care he devotes to the frame tale that makes the **Regement** a begging poem. The **"Prologue"** is 2016 lines long, accounting, as I said before, for almost half the poem. It opens with an autobiographical detail that ties Hoccleve's fate to the prince's. "Musyng upon the restles bisynesse / Which that this troubly world hath ay on honde" (1-2) the poet spends a sleepless night at the Chester Inn. His reflections on the "brotlynesse" of Fortune (15-21) quickly become generalized:

Me fel to mynde how that, not long ago,
ffortunes strok doun threst estaat royal
Into myscheef; and I took heed also
Of many anothir lord that had a falle.

(22-25)

Obviously this allusion to Richard is risky. Besides the more general presumption involved in comparing his situation to a king's, the allusion raises other awkward questions as well. Is he sympathizing with Richard? Is he presenting Richard as an unwitting victim of Fortune, when the logic of deposition assumes that Richard brought his fate entirely upon himself? Doesn't this recollection of the uncertainty of Richard's position call attention to the fragility of Henry's? All of these implicit questions give the passage an indefinite charge that stops just short of indecorous confrontation. For the topicality of the allusions is quickly absorbed into the conventional status of its context. This opening is similar to the moment of psychic disturbance that often opened dream visions. It is particularly close to the insomnia that opens the *Book of the Duchess*: what Chaucer finds in the Book of Ceyx and Alcyone, Hoccleve will find in the addition of another voice, the Beggar's.

In the place of a vision, the Beggar will provide the solution to Hoccleve's dilemma that addresses both its personal and its global dimensions. The appeal to Henry through the composition of a *Fürstenspiegel* will solve Hoccleve's financial problem at the same time it strengthens a threatened "estaat royal." The **"Prologue"** comes to this solution indirectly yet deliberately. After a long dialogue on Fortune and the many ways to protect oneself against it, and after several other suggestions, the Beggar finally broaches the appeal to Henry:

"O my good sone, wolt þou yit algate
Despeired be? nay, sone, lat be þat!
Þou schalt as blyue entre into þe yate
Of þi comfort. now telle on pleyn and plat:
My lord þe prince, knowyth he þe nat?
If þat þou stonde in his benevolence,
He may be salue vnto þin indigence.

No man bet, next his fadir, our lord lige."
"Yis fadir, he is my good gracious lord."
"Wel sone, þan wole I me oblige,—
And god of heuen vouch I to record,—
Þat if þou wolt be ful of myn accord,
Thow schalt no cause haue more þus to muse,
But heuynesse voide, and it refuse.

"Syn he þi good lord is, I am ful seur
His grace to þe schal nat be denyed;
Þou wost wele, he benying is and demeur
To sue vnto; naght is his goost maistried
With daunger, but his hert is ful applied
To graunte, and nat þe needy werne his grace;
To hym pursue, and þi releef purchace."

(1828-48)

This suggestion comes much more easily via the Beggar than it would have had it been made in Hoccleve's own voice. The Beggar's praise of Prince Henry would have

had the appearance of crass flattery had it been addressed to Henry directly by Hoccleve. But because it arises in the course of a conversation where the prince is not present, it acquires the givenness of an objective truth. When the Beggar offhandedly concludes, "No man bet, next his fadir," his very offhandedness increases the impression that Henry's virtue is a matter of both lineage and simple common knowledge, both now standing beyond any possible dispute.

Hoccleve links this assertion of Henry's virtue to the granting of his suit, leaving the onus of proof deftly and almost imperceptibly on Henry, but making such proof, by the very imperceptibility of the link, a matter of course. The suit is at once a test of Henry's generosity and a ratification of his future. For as Hoccleve's projected redeemer, Henry becomes a moral force standing outside the cycle of Fortune, impervious to the instabilities that undid Richard.

The Beggar enforces this impression with the specific suggestion that the appeal take the form of a *Fürstenspiegel*:

"looke if þou fynde canst any tretice
Groundid on his estates holsumnesse;
Swych thing translate, and unto his hynesse
As humbely as þat þou canst, present."

(1949-52)

Hoccleve will appeal not simply to Henry's grace, but to his presumed enthusiasm for moral instruction. The Beggar precedes this final suggestion with a warning against flattery: "But of a thyng be wel waar in al wise, / On flaterie þat þou þe nat founde," adding that advisors are afraid to tell their lords the truth, and instead "thei stryuen who best rynge shal þe bell / Of fals plesance" (1912-13, 29-30). Lords are so continually surrounded by such flattery that it is impossible for them to learn their true condition, and therefore the greatest service Hoccleve can perform for Henry is to tell him the truth (1933-46).

The Beggar so firmly associates pleasant news with flattery that the measure of the truth becomes virtually its unpleasantness to princely ears. At this point the narrative frame for Hoccleve's authority has been fully articulated, providing the prince with moral grounds for granting his suit. By accepting the *Fürstenspiegel* Hoccleve offers, the prince will demonstrate that he is a ruler who prefers the truth to flattery—a virtue with which, of course, the Beggar has already endowed him. The Beggar's intervention transforms a self-interested petition into a fully moral exchange between a model ruler and a loyal subject. In return for moral instruction, Henry will award an annuity, not as mere compensation, but as a sign of his devotion to morality. The **"Prologue"** has transformed its terms of address, pretending all the while to have changed nothing.

Both the pretense and the transformation are specifically narrative products; both result from the addition of the Beggar's voice. Like the voice of any narrative figure, the Beggar's is at once his author's and his own, but Hoccleve intensifies the effect of this resemblance in difference precisely by identifying this voice as a Beggar's. This diffuses the begging position from which he himself speaks, making it more general and thus enabling him to present it favorably. The Beggar resembles Hoccleve in that both are beggars; he differs from Hoccleve in that Hoccleve is his social superior. This difference means that when he speaks to Hoccleve, and through Hoccleve to Prince Henry, both Hoccleve and the prince are now in the same position: social superiors being addressed by a subordinate.

Also, of course, Hoccleve uses this social positioning to affirm the Beggar's moral authority. When the Beggar first offers his assistance Hoccleve scoffs at his infirmity and meager appearance, concluding that "it moste be a greter man of myght / þan þat þou art, þat scholde me releue" (176-77). In the long dialogue that follows, as the Beggar breaks down Hoccleve's resistance he implicitly breaks down the prince's as well. When he suggests the appeal to the prince at the end of the dialogue, the suggestion comes as if it were completely external. The considerable presumption involved in both begging poems and *Fürstenspiegel* is diffused, for the suggestion that the two are in fact one is made by a figure who has just demonstrated the independent moral authority beggars can possess.[40] And this independent authority has been produced by Hoccleve himself through his narrative, an act of production that has also, by means of the manipulation of narrative voice, been disguised.

This elaborate representational strategy is an extension of the begging poem's central ploy, the construction of a conceit whose intricacy will distract attention from the crassness of the request. The implication is that what the prince pays for is the elegance of the poetic structure: a begging poem always pays its patron the compliment of making him the arbiter of poetic value. In the *Regement of Princes,* the poetic structure is also a moral one. By being a *Fürstenspiegel* and begging poem at once, it defines Henry as the repository of moral as well as poetic value. This combination allows Henry to have it both ways. Accepting the *Regement* as a begging poem will certify his moral rectitude; acceding to it as a *Fürstenspiegel* will not diminish his social authority.

The tension this combination produces is one to which Hoccleve can return again and again. When after the **"Prologue"** ends Hoccleve finally addresses Henry directly, he can do so in the language of compliment, for that language now carries moral weight.

> Hye and noble prince excellent,
> My lord the prince, o my lord gracious,
> I, humble servant and obedient
> Vnto your estate hye & glorious,
> Of whiche I am full tendir & full ielous,
> Me recomaunde unto your worthynesse,
> With hert entier, and spirite of mekenesse.
>
> Right humbly axyng of you the license,
> That with my penne I may to you declare

> (So as that kan my wittes innocence,)
> Myne inward wille that thursteth the welefare
> Of your persone; and elles be I bare
> Of blisse, whan þat the cold stroke of deth
> My lyfe hath quenched, & me byraft my breth.

> (2017-30)

The tension between producing an effect and disguising it recurs here in the abandonment of will Hoccleve wants his writing to signify. As the very ornateness of these introductory lines make clear, direct address does not merely locate a *persona* but constitutes it as well. Hoccleve is not simply addressing a prince all of whose attributes are immediately available outside the text, but a prince whom he makes high, noble, and excellent by so addressing. To the extent this *persona* is perceived as simply Hoccleve's invention, the project fails. Asking for "license" from the very *persona* being produced at once acknowledges and disclaims the inventiveness, which is effaced under the sign of the real Henry. The textual *persona* of the model prince becomes an unnecessary recreation of virtues already embodied in Henry's actual personality.

As I have already noted, Hoccleve keeps his moral instruction in the second person, maintaining the fiction of Henry's personal presence throughout the poem. Hoccleve cannot assert his own independent moral authority without simultaneously reiterating his status as a dependent addressing a prince. His authority is always dependent on the central fiction of Henry's presence. This frame intensifies the personal component in the already heavily personalized conceptions of royal authority that Hoccleve inherits from the *Fürstenspiegel* tradition.

The poem proper is divided into fifteen sections with an envoy. The first four deal with the royal *voluntas*: royal dignity, the coronation oath, justice, and the observance of the laws. Next are five personal virtues: piety, mercy, patience, chastity, and magnanimity. After three on the management of wealth and two on counsel, there is a concluding section on peace. The emphasis throughout is on the power of the royal example, the social order that Henry will produce by assuming these virtues. Upon occasion Hoccleve explicitly invokes Henry's absolute freedom, making his acceptance of moral constraint an act of grace:

> Who-so þat in hye dignite is sette,
> And may do grevous wrong & cruelte,
> If he for-bere hem, to commend is bette,
> And gretter shal his mede and meryte be.

> (2843-48)

But even where this freedom is not made explicit, the aspect of Henry's personal moral restraint Hoccleve stresses most is the awe and respect it will arouse in his subjects. When moral restraint meets royal power, the result is social control, and the moral shades into the ideological.

The transaction is most evident where the personal and political are hardest to distinguish: royal speech. The discussion of coronation oaths returns this issue to a *locus classicus* of medieval tradition. The coronation oath was a symbolic instrument for finessing the ambiguities surrounding the problem of royal prerogative. In taking the oath, a monarch voluntarily constrains his own prerogative to the laws of his predecessors. Thus the oath was a ceremonial recognition of the practical constraint on royal prerogative that nonetheless left it theoretically absolute. Hoccleve trades on this ambiguity by stressing the performative aspect of oath-keeping, its prescription of internal consistency rather than its assertion of simple conformity to an external standard.

> And syn a kyng, by wey of his office,
> To god I-likned is, as in manere,
> And god is trouthe itself, þan may the vice
> Of vntrouthe, naght in a kyng appeere,
> If his office schal to god referre.
> A besy tonge bringeth in swiche wit,
> He þat by word naght gilteþ is perfit.
>
> A! lord, what is fair and honurable,
> A kyng from mochil speche him refreyne;
> It sitte him ben of wordes mesurable,
> ffor mochil clap wole his estate desteyne.
> If he his tonge with mesures reyne
> Governe, than his honur it conserveth.

(2409-21)

To what extent is the God-like king "trouthe itself"? Obviously royal speech is not absolutely performative in the way of divine speech; it cannot call truth into being simply by articulating it. And yet Hoccleve strongly implies that so long as "untrouthe" is avoided, royal speech may become God-like.

In this paradoxical formulation royal speech is performative within certain bounds, bounds that become clearer as the passage proceeds. The advice against speaking too often follows directly the warning against "untrouthe," as if the two were equivalent. To view royal speech as capable of excess is to assume that royal prerogative is safest when least evident, as if ultimately it were incapable of justifying itself in purely linguistic terms. It is to assume a status quo that operates best when least observed. "For mochil clap wole his estate desteyne": a king who speaks too much is likely to expose himself as no more in control of language than its other users.

A king can control his estate by controlling his tongue; the status quo provides the reference point against which "untrouthe" is to be judged. Royal speech becomes performative precisely by not seeking to be, by always seeking to submerge its effects in its preservation of royal power. It is as if the ideal of royal speech were silence. This is the reason kingship always needs another voice, like Hoccleve's. Justification spoken in another voice will always make royal authority seem to be a power beyond language, which it must always be in order to be justified at all.

This view of political authority is both profoundly conservative and yet self-consciously constructive at the same time. Contradictory as the combination may seem to

a modern consciousness, the two tendencies are actually mutually reinforcing. Hoccleve's often spectacularly self-conscious poetic mastery continually serves his political conservatism, but just as significantly the conservatism is also what motivates the poetry. The Shelleyan view of poetry as politically redemptive runs extraordinarily deep in twentieth-century literary studies. It persists *mutatis mutandis* in the deconstructive tenet that a text's representational strategies will always subvert its explicit ideology. The **Regement** presents a strong counterexample to this view, demonstrating instead the capacity that Terry Eagleton has called "the cunning of the ideological"—the capacity of an ideological position to strengthen itself precisely by exposing its assumptions.[41]

Hoccleve's conservatism is so intertwined with his poetry that it motivates his most poetic of moments: his canonization of Chaucer. This canonization is another way in which Hoccleve makes authority narrative. Chaucer's is an authorizing voice more historically and linguistically continuous with Hoccleve's than those of classical or ecclesiastical authors. And Hoccleve consistently locates Chaucer's authority biographically. There are three discussions of Chaucer, which all follow essentially the same pattern. After a celebration of Chaucer's authority there is a lament for his death. In the last two discussions, there is also a prayer that he rest in peace. In several of the manuscripts this final invocation is accompanied by a portrait. The portrait in British Museum Harleian Manuscript 4866 (leaf 91) is the earliest known of Chaucer and is probably the source of most later portraits, including the equestrian portrait of the Ellesmere manuscript.[42] This fact, though it may seem no more than a charming bit of antiquarianism, signals a crucial change. It signals an increasing historicization of discursive authority, an increasing desire to locate authority within a personage historically and linguistically immediate.

The literary canonization of historically proximate, vernacular authors has traditionally been taken as the hallmark of Renaissance humanism. Though the trend predates Hoccleve, beginning in Italy with Boccaccio and Petrarch, Hoccleve is the first to articulate it fully in English. If, as A. C. Spearing argues, Chaucer invents "the possibility of a history of English poetry," Hoccleve makes that possibility actual by establishing Chaucer as the source of such a history.[43] Of course, this canonization is not so much a break with older notions of authority as an attempt to recuperate them in a more usable way.

Hoccleve clearly presents Chaucer as the most immediate source of his own authority. The first invocation occurs in the **"Prologue"** directly after he agrees to write the **Regement** (1954-81) and begins with the regret that Chaucer is not available to lend "consail and reed" (1960). The second occurs in the discussion of his sources, where he makes it clear his access to these authorities, meager though it is ("Simple is my goost, and scars my letterure" [2073]), comes through Chaucer, who "fayn wolde han me taght" (2078). In both passages he is the center of traditional authority, like Cicero in rhetoric, like Aristotle (whom Hoccleve has just named as author of the *Secretum Secretorum*) in philosophy, and like Virgil in poetry (2085-90). This displacement of Latin authority into the vernacular authority of Chaucer is obviously meant to make the authority of tradition more accessible to Hoccleve's audience. But this broadening of textual authority has as its larger goal the solidification of royal authority.

For to the extent that the textual is historicized, immediate political authority is strengthened. As Hoccleve elevates Chaucer to the status of an *auctor,* his insistence on the biographical makes the textual even more dependent on the actualities of historical existence. Chaucer's authority inheres most fully in his person; it does not survive complete in his texts alone. Though he is "universel fadir of science" (1964) and "first fyndere of our fair langage" (4978), what Hoccleve learned from him he learned personally. The implication of the lament that Chaucer is no longer available for "consail and reed" is that once Chaucer is no longer alive and producing, the power of his texts to put the cultural world in order begins to fade. The final portrait, which abandons language altogether in favor of pictorial representation, takes this idea to its logical limit.

Vernacular authority is thus tied more directly to historical actuality than either the classical or the sacred. If authorizing the vernacular means a greater freedom from the past, it may also mean a greater subordination to the immediate status quo. These two tendencies are not necessarily opposed, for freedom from the past may be enabled by an increase in political empowerment. This was the case for Hoccleve's audience, and his canonization gave them a new, vernacular authority in the guise of the old. As the "Mirour of fructuous entendement," the "universal fadir in science" (1963-64), Chaucer becomes the Aristotle to Henry's Alexander, the source of the communally held moral values to be embodied in the ideal prince.

The legitimacy of Henry is the cost of this new, vernacular access to discursive authority. Without an immediately available embodiment of moral order, Hoccleve cannot grant any moral privilege to the historically immediate. And if historical immediacy is without moral value, then so too is the vernacular. Hoccleve's celebration of the nascent English tradition embodied in Chaucer and the political authority embodied in Henry are the twin faces of the same moral vision. As this vision empowers itself by exposing the assumptions of the Latin traditions it inherits, it also solidifies its empowerment in the figure of Henry. Henry must become the guarantor of moral order because it is he who will become king. This is perhaps the one assumption of which the *Regement* can never become fully self-conscious. Like any *Fürstenspiegel*, it must assume that there is moral value in the very structure of kingship, regardless of the moral status of the individual who occupies it. Without this assumption, the *Fürstenspiegel* has lost its raison d'être.

NARRATIVE POWER

I have already discussed many of the ways in which the **Regement** expresses this central tenet of the ideology of monarchy. Perhaps its most extreme expression occurs in the one aspect of the work I have not yet discussed: the exempla. In the exemplum medieval thought explicitly recognized the persuasive power of narrative. Early discussions of preaching recommended the use of exempla on the grounds that narrative was more immediately persuasive than doctrine. The first medieval exemplum collection was Gregory's *Dialogues;* Gregory remarks on several occasions that exempla touch the heart more directly than doctrine or rational argument.[44] Not surprisingly, the form was viewed as particularly suited to persuading the uninstructed or the unconverted. The sermon exemplum achieved its zenith during the great preaching campaigns of the twelfth and thirteenth centuries, when the urban lower classes were being proselytized for the first time.[45]

The exemplum had a similar rhetorical profile in the *Fürstenspiegel,* though obviously its audience was different. John of Salisbury, whose *Policraticus* became a dominant repository of exempla both within and without the tradition, comments extensively on the form. In book 4, he buttresses the claim that the prince is an inferior minister of the priests with classical exempla, then justifies his appeal to the classical by asserting Paul used such exempla to preach to the Athenians.[46] This characterization of the form achieves a double purpose. It places John's royalist opposition in the position of uninstructed pagans, and then suggests that like Paul, John can convert them by his superior handling of their own forms. In a more general discussion elsewhere, he describes exempla as *strategemma* and *strategemmatica,* sites of polemical conflict.[47]

The exemplum thus came to secular writers like Hoccleve as a form charged with ecclesiastical authority, but also as a form suited to polemic. The latter capacity enabled these writers to turn the form against the Church and put it to the service of secular authority. Many of Hoccleve's exempla turn on a ruler's voluntary restraint of some power or prerogative otherwise freely avaialbe to him. While occasionally these are stories of self-sacrifice, such as that of Regulus, the Roman commander who convinced the senate to return him to execution in Carthage rather than complete an unfavorable exchange of prisoners (2248-96), more typically the restraint redounds to the ruler's advantage. For instance, there are two similar stories of Roman generals Camillus (2584-2646) and Scipio Africanus (3676-3710). A schoolmaster in a city Camillus is besieging kidnaps the children of the wealthy citizens who employ him and offers them to Camillus to use as a bargaining chip. Camillus refuses, and when the citizens discover this, they decide to surrender in recognition of his great virtue. In the other story, Scipio is offered a virgin betrothed to a lord in Carthage, and his refusal brings about the same result, the surrender of the city. In both cases moral restraint effects a significant gain in political power, producing a sovereignty that has not existed before.

Camillus and Scipio bend a hitherto refractory population to their will through the ideological power of example, through their personal enactment of a public moral narrative, acts of virtue that cannot be separated from the political positions they reinforce.

An even greater interdependence of the moral and the political occurs in two successive exempla, Lycurgus and his Laws (2948-89) and the Phalarean Bull (3004-38), which end the section on Justice and begin the section on Piety. Both of these exempla were widely circulated in the later Middle Ages, both within the *Fürstenspiegel* and outside it. Both occur in the seventh book of the *Confessio Amantis,* which was probably Hoccleve's most immediate source.[48] He does all that he can to intensify the representation of kingship as the source of moral value already implicit in both exempla. He juxtaposes them, and adds dialogue to what had been primarily plot summary. He makes their protagonists anonymous, as if to focus attention on their political position. Private personal virtue is either moot, in the case of Lycurgus, or nonexistent, in the case of Phalaris. Moral order is something they produce simply through their manipulation of political authority.

In Hoccleve's version, Lycurgus becomes an anonymous knight who devises a new code of law. After his "sharp lawes" are read to the "froward peple," they are "wondir wroth," and "wold han artyd [compelled] þis knyght hem repele, / Makyng ageyn hym an haynous querele" (2950-61). The knight assigns the authorship of the laws to Apollo: "I mad hem naght, it was god appollo; / And on my bak . . . þe charge he leyde / To kepe hem; sires, what sey ye here-to?" (2963-65). But the people are unimpressed and still demand their repeal. He promises to ask Apollo about the matter, on the condition that no changes be made until he returns. Going off to Greece but not to Apollo, he stays there until his death, thus insuring that the code will remain unchanged.

While the story never calls into question the independent existence of Apollo, his introduction into political life as moral authority is purely the invention of the knight. The knight's position as the sole voice of law puts divine authority entirely at his disposal, and makes him the source of moral truth. He produces this truth through the narrative about Apollo, a narrative that is wholly fictitious. Moral truth is thus produced not merely *through* but *as* narrative fiction, with the single constraint that the fiction can never acknowledge itself as such. The knight must always keep the referential accuracy of his story an open question. He must leave his state never to return. In exchange for this sacrifice of day-to-day control he gains an ideological control that is absolute. In effect, he replaces his person with his story, and controls the state not simply through the imposition of the story, but by having constructed a story that will always maintain the distance between the story and the reality it claims to represent—a story, that is, that will always maintain its fiction. The referential accuracy of the story is neither affirmed nor denied; it is always held in reserve. This holding in reserve enables the

status quo, also the product of the knight (through his new laws), to remain in force. Indeed, the truth the story holds in reserve is precisely the truth of the status quo, and the story maintains the status quo precisely by holding it in reserve.

The same power is depicted in the next exemplum in a manner that corresponds even more closely to the ideological structure of medieval kingship. The exemplum of the Phalarean Bull presents an attempt to construct kingship's other voice. The wicked counselor of a cruel tyrant makes a brass bull as an instrument of torture. Victims are placed within it and roasted alive. Moreover, the device is so constructed that their cries of pain always sound like the lowing of a bull. The cruelty of this machine so offends God that he causes the counselor to be the first to use it:

> ffor whan þe kyng, his cruel werk had seyne,
> Þe craft of it commendith he ful wele;
> But þe entent he fully held a-gayne,
> And seyde, "þou þat art more cruel
> Than I, þe maydenhede of this Iuel
> Shalt preve anone; þis is my Iugement."
> And so as blyue he was þer-in I-brent.

(3032-38)

While the counselor's cruelty is punished, the tyrant's is simply accepted as a given, providing the ground that gives the counselor's crime meaning. The building of the bull is an attempt, however misguided, to satisfy the tyrant's appetite for cruelty; the bull is a response to the prevailing standard of cruelty the tyrant has already established. The bull monumentalizes this standard precisely by depriving resistance to tyranny of its own voice. It destroys the tyrant's enemies by forcing them to speak their resistance in the voice he has ordained for them. The logic of this machine is so remorseless in its perfection that it can bring benefit to the tyrant alone, and accordingly destroys its maker. If the counselor is punished for his cruelty, he is also punished for his presumption, that is, for attempting to become more cruel than the tyrant. The structure of kingship makes it impossible for the tyrant to be surpassed in cruelty. The voice of evil counsel concretized in the bull is always subject to the modification of the tyrant's own voice. In this case the absolute privilege of the tyrannical voice has a restraining effect, producing moral order even as it aims at tyranny.

With this exemplum we are a far cry from modern platitudes about the bland morality of medieval *Fürstenspiegel.* The story defines a wholly arbitrary yet inevitable balance between ideology and power. The monarch's unconstrained political power gives him an unlimited control over ideological forms, yet the ideological and the political are still mutually constraining. Ideology's prior dependence on royal power will always give it a predetermined shape; monarchy's need to maintain the integrity of its ideology will influence its mode of action. The tyrant's need to be recognized as the cruelest restrains the cruelty of his ministers.

A society where tyranny is possible is by definition also a society where the politically empowered can impose ideological forms by fiat. In return for acquiescence to the authority of Henry's *voluntas,* Hoccleve's audience gets their own ideological empowerment. This exchange of royal prerogative for ideological control is not so much a logical unity as it is two divergent tendencies the narrative holds together. Like all the other reconciliations Hoccleve offers between royal interests and the common interests of the ruling class, it must remain implicit, half hidden within the manipulations of his narrative.

Yet implication does not lessen the power of ideological reconciliations; rather it enhances them. The exempla of Lycurgus and the Phalarean Bull are narrative expositions of the ideological power of narrative. To a lesser extent so are the other exempla, with their continual emphasis on the monarch's exemplary status. Like the larger narratives that frame them—the genealogy of Henry, the canonization of Chaucer, the placement of Hoccleve's *Fürstenspiegel* within his own autobiography—the knowledge they convey must remain within its narrative form. To this narrative knowledge the **Regement**'s moral teaching is always tied. Indeed, the work's most practical lesson may well have been its continual narrative framing of the moral. With this framing it showed its audience how moral authority could be submitted to ideological control.

For modern scholars, the **Regement** may still hold a similar lesson. Works like the **Regement** present a challenge both to our view of the past and to our sense of our own present. First there is the challenge to the sense that the past lacked the critical sophistication of the present. Where one expects piety, Hoccleve offers a shrewd meditation on the political value of moral authority. Where one expects bland didacticism, Hoccleve offers a complex set of narratives that make the ideological and the moral interdependent, producing the very authority by which they claim to be governed. And here Hoccleve indirectly challenges our view of ourselves. For his example shows that literary self-consciousness is itself historically variable, and that far from being proof against an ideological status quo, a self-consciously critical stance may often be its most powerful instrument. This is a particularly chastening lesson at a time when critical self-consciousness is next to Godliness—not that such self-consciousness should be abandoned, just that it should never be complacent about the power of the status quo.[49]

Notes

1. Since the work is addressed to Henry as the Prince of Wales, it would have to have been written before 21 March 1413, the date of his coronation. Its allusion in the "Prologue" to the 1 March 1410 execution of the Lollard John Badby places it after that date. Furnivall settles on 1412 because the Court Rolls seem to indicate an interruption in Hoccleve's annuity in that year (*Hoccleve's Works: I. The Minor Works* [London: pub. for the Early English Text Society by Kegan Paul, Trench Trübner & Co., 1892],

xiii). This date, however, depends on a strictly literal reading of the poem's begging stance.

2. One recent exception to this trend is David Lawton's excellent article, "Dullness and the Fifteenth Century," *ELH* 54 (1987): 761-99.

3. Wilhelm Berges, *Die Fürstenspiegel des hohen und späten Mittelalters* (Stuttgart: Hiersemann Verlag, 1938), 352-53.

4. Margaret Schlauch, "Chaucer's Doctrine of Kings and Tyrants," *Speculum* 20 (1945): 133-56.

5. That ideology reproduces relations of power is a Marxist truism. Cf. Karl Marx and Friedrich Engels, *The German Ideology,* ed. C. J. Arthur (New York: International Publishers, 1970), esp. 42-68; Gyorgy Lukács, "What is Orthodox Marxism?" in *History and Class Consciousness,* trans. Rodney Livingstone (Cambridge, Mass.: MIT Press, 1971), esp. 15-18; and Louis Althusser, "Ideology and Ideological State Apparatuses," in *Lenin and Philosophy,* trans. Ben Brewster (New York and London: Monthly Review Press, 1971), 127-86. For a succinct, incisive history of the term "ideology," see Stuart Hall, "The Hinterland of Science: Ideology and the 'Sociology of Knowledge,'" in *On Ideology* (Birmingham: Centre of Contemporary Cultural Studies, 1977; London: Hutchinson, 1978), 9-33. The concept of ideology I use throughout this essay is drawn mainly from Althusser.

6. *Rotuli Parliamentorum,* ed. J. Strachey (London, 1767-83), 3:419: "33. ITEM, idem Rex nolens justas Leges & Consuetudines Regni sui servare se protegere, set secundum sue arbitrium Voluntatis facere quicquid desideriis ijus occurrerrit, quandoque & frequentius quando sibi expositi & declarati fuerant Leges Regni sui per Justic' & alios de Consilio suo, & secundum Leges illas petentibus justiciam exhiberet; Dixit expresse, voltu austero & protervo, quod Leges sue erant in ore suo, & aliquotiens in pectore suo: Et qd ipse solus posset mutare & condere Leges Regni sui . . ." (the translation is mine).

7. B. Wilkinson, *Politics and the Constitution 1307-1399,* vol. 2 of *Constitutional History of Medieval England 1216-1399* (London: Longmans & Green, 1952), 298. In fairness I should say that as constitutional history has become less fashionable, more recent accounts have become less explicitly teleological. Nevertheless they still treat Richard's deposition as primarily a matter of resisting tyranny and to this extent are guilty of a similar form of anachronism. By modern standards, all of the medieval nobility were tyrants in the sense that most of the populace lacked adequate redress against them. In this context to single out Richard's tyranny is to ignore the larger issue of class relations within which his relation to the rest of the nobility was played out. Even recent accounts do not address the issue of class and tend to reduce Richard's "tyranny" to personal traits: accord-

ing to Anthony Tuck, he was arrogant and petulant (*Crown and Nobility 1272-1461* [Oxford: Basil Blackwell, 1986], 222); to May McKisack, vindictive and possibly insane (*The Fourteenth Century* [Oxford: Clarendon Press, 1959], 496-98); to A. B. Steel, definitely on the verge of insanity (*Richard II* [Cambridge, Eng.: Cambridge University Press, 1941], 278-79).

8. Anthony Tuck, *Richard II and the English Nobility* (London: Edward Arnold, 1973), 204.

9. Ernst H. Kantorowicz, *The King's Two Bodies: A Study in Medieval Political Theology* (Princeton: Princeton University Press, 1957), 153.

10. Cynus de Pistoia, *Commentarium in Codicem et Digestum vetus* (Frankfurt, 1578), 6, 23, 19. Cited in Kantorowicz, *King's Two Bodies,* 154.

11. See Kantorowicz, *King's Two Bodies,* 152-55.

12. Livy, *Ad Urbe Condita,* 2.32, 8-33, 2.

13. M. J. Wilks, *The Problem of Sovereignty in the Later Middle Ages* (Cambridge, Eng.: Cambridge University Press, 1963), 15-64, 455-78.

14. Parliament was originally conceived as an extension of the royal council. For a brief discussion and additional bibliography see Bryce Lyon, *A Constitutional and Legal History of Medieval England* (New York: Harper & Row, 1960), 408-30.

15. The suggestion was made by Archbishop Arundel. See McKisack, *Fourteenth Century,* 494-96; K. B. McFarlane, *Lancastrian Kings and Lollard Knights* (Oxford: Clarendon, 1972), 54-58.

16. Record remains of at least one case in which the prerogatives of a lord were denounced in the same terms that the Articles of Deposition used to denounce Richard. In the 1320s Hugh Despenser was accused of *voluntrif seigneurie* by the English community of Glamorgan. See Alan Harding, "Political Liberty in the Middle Ages," *Speculum* 55 (1980): 441, and William Rees, *Calendar of Ancient Petitions Relating to Wales* (Cardiff: University of Wales Press, 1975), 279.

17. Sir Frederick Pollock and Frederick William Maitland, *The History of English Law Before the Time of Edward I,* 2nd ed., reissued with a new introduction and bibliography by S. F. C. Milsom (Cambridge, Eng.: Cambridge University Press, 1968), 527.

18. Perry Anderson, *Passages from Antiquity to Feudalism* (London: Verso, 1974), 153; Alan Harding, *The Law Courts of Medieval England* (London: Allen & Unwin, 1973), 13. I might add that when Harding claims in the next sentence that "kings, princes, and also priests, come onto the scene as the chosen arbiters of society," he comes perilously close to the kind of anachronism I noted above. For the vast majority of those who faced medieval justice, the judge was in no way chosen.

19. See Alan Harding, "The Revolt Against the Justices," in *The English Rising of 1381,* ed. R. H. Hilton and T. H. Aston (Cambridge, Eng.: Cambridge University Press, 1984), 167-68, for a brief discussion and additional bibliography.

20. *Law Courts,* 116. Harding observes somewhat earlier on that "a striking feature of English social history from the fourteenth century to the seventeenth century is the combined use of civil and criminal law by the members of the gentry class in order to gain local advantage" (93-94).

21. See Wayne Booth, "The Author's Many Voices," in *The Rhetoric of Fiction,* 2nd ed. (Chicago: University of Chicago Press, 1983), 16-20.

22. "Story and Discourse in the Analysis of Narrative," in *The Pursuit of Signs* (Ithaca: Cornell University Press, 1981), 170-71.

23. The phrase is Benveniste's. For a brief discussion, see Hayden White, "The Value of Narrativity in the Representation of Reality," in *The Content of the Form: Narrative Discourse and Historical Representation* (Baltimore: Johns Hopkins University Press, 1987), 3-4.

24. "Introduction to the Structural Analysis of Narratives," in *A Barthes Reader,* ed. Susan Sontag (New York: Hill and Wang, 1982), 252. For example, Barthes declares that "'what happens'" in narrative "is language alone, the unceasing adventure of its coming" (295).

25. G. L. Harriss, "Introduction: The Exemplar of Kingship," in *Henry V: The Practice of Kingship* (Oxford: Oxford University Press, 1985), 1-29.

26. Thomas Hoccleve, *Regement of Princes,* ed. Frederick J. Furnivall (London: 1897), 1961. All subsequent citations are from this edition and will hereafter be given in the text.

27. Indeed, discussions of kingship are so prevalent in fourteenth-century poetry of complaint that Janet Coleman has suggested such works "be classified *thematically* as mirrors for princes" ("English Culture in the Fourteenth Century," in *Chaucer and the Italian Trecento,* ed. Piero Boitani [Cambridge, Eng.: Cambridge University Press, 1983], 60).

28. Stephen Knight, *Geoffrey Chaucer* (Oxford: Basil Blackwell, 1986), 139.

29. For a general overview of the reading public in late medieval England, see Janet Coleman, *Medieval Readers and Writers 1350-1400* (New York: Columbia University Press, 1981); Richard Firth Green, *Poets and Princepleasers* (Toronto: University of Toronto Press, 1980); and Anne Middleton, "The Idea of Public Poetry in the Reign of Richard II," *Speculum* 53 (1978): 94-114. For Chaucer's audience, see Paul Strohm, "Chaucer's Audience," *Litera-*

ture and History 5 (1977): 26-41, and "Chaucer's Fifteenth-Century Audience and the Narrowing of the Chaucer Tradition," *Studies in the Age of Chaucer* 4 (1982): 3-32.

30. *Chaucer and Medieval Estates Satire* (Cambridge, Eng.: Cambridge University Press, 1973).

31. Ibid., esp. 187-202.

32. Mann as much as concedes this when she characterizes Chaucer's ethnography in the following way: "This is how the world operates, and as the world, it can operate no other way. The contrast with heavenly values is made at the end of the *Canterbury Tales,* but it is made in such a way that it cannot affect the validity of the initial statement—the world can only operate by the world's values" (201). The very force with which this apparent tautology (the world operates as the world operates) asserts the indisputability of the status quo conceals the validation of a particular status quo. So far as the General Prologue is concerned the claim "the world can operate no other way" always assumes "no other way" means "no other way than according to these categories, the categories of medieval estates satire." There are in fact lots of other ways to understand the way the world operates—as the teacher of Chaucer rediscovers each time he or she attempts to explain what a manciple is to a survey class of college sophomores.

33. Furnivall, ed., *Regement,* 73.

34. A. C. Spearing, *Medieval to Renaissance in English Poetry* (Cambridge, Eng.: Cambridge University Press, 1985), III.

35. For the position of the *Policraticus* within the tradition, see Berges, *Die Fürstenspiegel,* 3-8. For John's relation to Becket, see Beryl Smalley, *The Becket Conflict and the Schools: A Study of Intellectuals in Politics* (Totowa, N.J.: Rowman and Littlefield, 1973), 87-108.

36. For a good, brief discussion and additional bibliography, see Richard Jones, *The Royal Policy of Richard II* (New York: Barnes and Noble, 1973), 154-59.

37. *Secretum Secretorum* as edited and glossed by Roger Bacon, ed. Robert Steele, fasc. 5 of *Opera hactenus inedita Rogeri Baconi* (Oxford: Clarendon, 1920), 40-42. The third source Hoccleve names, Jacob de Cessolis's *Libellus super Ludo Schachorum,* is the most important of the three for sheer bulk of material borrowed. (See William Mathews, "Thomas Hoccleve," in *A Manual of the Writings in Middle English 1050-1500,* ed. Albert E. Hartung, vol. 3 (New Haven: Connecticut Academy of Arts and Sciences, 1972), 749-50.) Though not dedicated to an actual monarch, it begins with a fictionalized scene of public instruction. The game of chess, it claims, was devised by a philosopher who needed an indirect stratagem to correct a tyrannical king. This work is generally considered an estates satire. However, Ray-

mond D. Di Lorenzo, on the basis of this scene, argues it should be considered a *Fürstenspiegel* ("The Collection Form and the Art of Memory in the *Libellus super Ludo Schachorum* of Jacobus de Cessolis," *Medieval Studies* 34 [1973]: 206-9).

38. *Sovereignty,* 529.

39. McFarlane, *Lancastrian Kings,* 106-12. See also Lawton, "Dullness," who reads the situation somewhat differently (776-77).

40. Of course there was a powerful cultural precedent for this position in Langland's begging *persona* in *Piers Plowman.*

41. Terry Eagleton, "Text, Ideology, Realism," in *Literature and Society: Selected Papers from the English Institute, 1978,* ed. Edward Said (Baltimore: Johns Hopkins University Press, 1980), 153.

42. Jerome Mitchell, *Thomas Hoccleve: A Study in Early Fifteenth-Century English Poetic* (Urbana: University of Illinois Press, 1968), 110-15.

43. Spearing, *Medieval to Renaissance,* 34.

44. See J.-Th. Welter, *L'exemplum dans la littérature religieuse et didactique du Moyen Age* (Paris: Occitania, 1927), 14-15.

45. On the class significance of the preaching campaigns, see Barbara Rosenswein and Lester K. Little, "Social Meaning in the Monastic and Mendicant Spiritualities," *Past and Present* 63 (1974): 18-32.

46. *Policraticus* 4.3.

47. *Policraticus* 8.14, 2. Cited and discussed in Peter von Moos, "The Use of *Exempla* in the *Policraticus* of John of Salisbury," in *The World of John of Salisbury,* ed. Michael Wilks (Oxford: Basil Blackwell, 1984), 227-28.

48. John Gower, *Confessio Amantis* 2917-3021, 3295-3332.

49. This essay grew from an MLA talk to its present length in large part because of the possibilities others saw in it. I would like to thank Winthrop Wetherbee, Charles Blyth, and Seth Lerer both for their helpful comments and for their bibliographical suggestions. I would also particularly like to thank Lee Patterson, whose extensive commentary in the later stages of the essay's preparation greatly strengthened it.

David R. Carlson (essay date 1991)

SOURCE: Carlson, David R. "Thomas Hoccleve and the Chaucer Portrait." *Huntington Library Quarterly* 54, no. 4 (1991): 283-300.

[*In the essay below, Carlson argues for the authenticity of the Chaucer portrait Hoccleve commissioned for his* Regement of Princes. *In Carlson's view, Hoccleve promoted his relationship with Chaucer, an earlier recipient of royal favor, as a part of his petition for patronage, and contends that the portrait would only be effective if it were a true likeness.*]

Of the numerous images proposed as representations of Chaucer in early manuscript illuminations, one portrait type has some claim to be a "true portraiture of Geffrey Chaucer":[1] the Ellesmere-Hoccleve type. It occurs earliest in the miniature of Chaucer as one of the Canterbury pilgrims in the Ellesmere manuscript of the *Canterbury Tales,* now in the Huntington Library and probably made c. 1400-1410;[2] and it recurs soon thereafter as an illustration to a passage about Chaucer in a number of copies of Thomas Hoccleve's *Regiment of Princes* (figs. 1-2). Some reason for believing this Ellesmere-Hoccleve portrait type to be a true-to-life image of Chaucer may lie in the relations between the Ellesmere miniature and the miniature that recurs in the Hoccleve manuscripts; the best reason, however, resides in the peculiarities of the material and literary context in which the type occurs with Hoccleve's writing.

The issue of the truth of the Ellesmere-Hoccleve portrait type is bound up with the issue of Hoccleve's relations with Chaucer, specifically, the nature of Hoccleve's interest in Chaucer's likeness. Briefly, it was to Hoccleve's advantage to see to it that any portrait he put about with his *Regiment of Princes* really looked like Chaucer. Hoccleve's poem is a versified *Fürstenspiegel,* written in 1411 for Prince Henry of Monmouth, later Henry V, and published by Hoccleve in a series of presentation copies, the production of which he supervised;[3] the publication's purpose was to elicit patronage. Along with other claims to familiarity with Chaucer put forward in the poem, to circulate a portrait of Chaucer with it would serve Hoccleve's purpose of linking himself with a poet who stood high in the esteem of his targeted audience; but the effectiveness of this device depended on its being recognizably a *true* portrait of Chaucer. In other words, Hoccleve's celebration of Chaucer in the *Regiment of Princes,* including his incorporation of Chaucer's portrait into authorized presentation copies of the poem, was not disinterested; it was not simply praise due a praiseworthy fellow-poet. Like others, Hoccleve was trying to use an image of Chaucer to advance his own interests; in light of the context in which Hoccleve's Chaucer portrait has been transmitted, this effort to use Chaucer's reputation serves to confirm the truth of the portrait type.

If the miniature in the Ellesmere manuscript is a true image of Chaucer, evidence of its veracity must come from elsewhere. As with the miniatures of the other pilgrims,[4] the Chaucer miniature may do a good job of showing what Chaucer the pilgrim should have looked like; but its success in capturing the notorious persona is not by itself evidence that it does a similarly good job of capturing the appearance of Chaucer the bureaucrat cum poet.[5] It may or it may not do so; the occurrence of the image as a representation of a fictional character, however, precludes

resolution of the question of verisimilitude on the basis of the Ellesmere miniature alone. The Ellesmere miniature is disproportionate: the figure's upper body is too large for the legs associated with it and the horse which it surmounts (i.e., too large for those parts of the illustration unique to it); and this disproportion has been taken as evidence that the Ellesmere miniature's depiction of Chaucer, or at least its depiction of Chaucer from the waist up, was copied, not altogether satisfactorily, from something else. This evidence for copying, however, is not in itself necessarily evidence that the image is verisimilar, since the nature of the hypothetical model from which the Ellesmere miniature could have been copied remains a matter for conjecture. The model probably cannot have been one of the occurrences of the Hoccleve portrait, all of which apparently postdate the Ellesmere manuscript's production. A panel portrait, for which Chaucer sat while alive, has been hypothesized but, in the absence of access to this hypothetical model and of an understanding of how and why it came to be made, speculation about its implications for the nature of the Ellesmere miniature remains speculation. Most importantly, the motive for the copying which produced the Ellesmere miniature also remains a matter for conjecture. The hypothetical model may have been copied because it was believed or known to show a Chaucer recognizable to persons who had been his familiars; on the other hand, it may have been copied simply because it was available.[6]

Evidence for the truth of the Ellesmere miniature could come from the Hoccleve portrait. If the Hoccleve portrait is verisimilar, the Ellesmere must also be; for the best— and crucial—occurrence of the Hoccleve portrait, that in the British Library manuscript Harley 4866, is too like the Ellesmere miniature for the two of them to be altogether unrelated.[7] Three occurrences of the Hoccleve portrait survive, in a pair of British Library manuscripts, Harley 4866 and Royal 17.D.vi, and in a former Phillips manuscript, now in Philadelphia at the Rosenbach Foundation, MS. 1083/30.[8] In addition, two other manuscripts at the British Library, Arundel 38 and Harley 4826, probably once incorporated instances of the portrait, but from them it appears to have been subsequently excised. Whereas Harley 4826 is a late miscellany, incorporating writings of Lydgate as well as Hoccleve's *Regiment,* and probably made after 1450, this Arundel manuscript is an important, early copy, evidently one of the original presentation copies.[9] Of the extant miniatures, that in the Rosenbach manuscript is either a very late (possibly eighteenth-century) forgery or a derivative, very close copy of the Harley 4866 miniature, still less interesting because occurring in a second-, or subsequent, generation copy of Hoccleve's poem, probably made sometime after his death or at least significantly later than the copies the production of which Hoccleve supervised; and the miniature in the Royal manuscript is evidently a late, degenerate derivative from an earlier instance, likewise occurring in a second-, or subsequent, generation copy of the poem.[10] The miniature in Harley 4866 is therefore the only one of the extant miniatures that matters for my purpose here, but less because of its artistic qualities—though in this regard it far excels the Royal miniature—than because of the pedigree and affiliations of the manuscript in which it occurs.

The manuscript Harley 4866 is one of the presentation copies, probably executed to Hoccleve's orders, for Edward, Duke of York, a cousin of Henry IV, or for John, Duke of Bedford, a younger brother of Prince Henry.[11] In addition, the *mis-en-page* and program of decoration of Harley 4866 are so like those of Arundel 38, another of the first-generation presentation copies of the poem that Hoccleve had made, as to indicate that the two manuscripts were manufactured by the same group or interrelated groups of workers to the same orders;[12] and the Arundel manuscript is either the presentation copy for the poem's dedicatee Prince Henry or a close copy, for some other highly placed benefactor, of the manuscript made for Henry.[13] The miniature showing Hoccleve presenting his work to the prince, which is found in the Arundel manuscript, has been excised from the Harley manuscript, and the portrait of Chaucer, which is found in the Harley manuscript, has been excised from the Arundel manuscript; otherwise, where they can be compared, the manuscripts are so like one another as to suggest that the Chaucer miniature formerly in the Arundel manuscript was indifferent from that still extant in the Harley manuscript, and may have been the work of the same artist. In other words, the Harley miniature can be believed to be practically the same as the miniature that would have been seen by the dedicatee of Hoccleve's poem, Prince Henry; and Prince Henry, not to mention other potential benefactors who would have seen presentation copies of the poem, was in a position to judge the veracity of an image of Chaucer.[14]

None of the early images of Chaucer circulated in manuscript is a free-standing, independent portrait. Their significance as portraits depends entirely on the literary contexts in which they occur. The early images show individuals or groups, making typical legible gestures or interacting in typical legible ways. The miniature in the *Canterbury Tales* manuscript Lansdowne 851, for example, shows a man reading a book; the better-known frontispiece to the Corpus Christi, Cambridge, copy of the *Troilus and Criseyde* shows a speaker speaking and an audience attending; the Ellesmere miniature shows a Canterbury pilgrim pointing; and so on.[15] It is only by reference to the bibliographic and textual situations in which these early, dependent images occur that the figures depicted in them can be read as representing Chaucer at all. The images accompany his writings; the gestures that the figures make are ones Chaucer might have made, and the relations are ones he could be imagined to have entered; therefore, the figures are Chaucer, but only in a special, limited sense. The representations of him in the early, dependent images are limited strictly to representing Chaucer in terms of what he purportedly did—read books, spoke to assembled companies, went on pilgrimage to Canterbury, and so on; but not in terms of a characteristic, distinctive physiognomy. Because of their dependence on their textual situations, the early images need not have been ambitious to

show, and in most cases almost certainly did not attempt to show, how Chaucer had really looked.

If the Hoccleve miniature were a free-standing, independent portrait, or were like an independent portrait, in the sense that it had as its only reason for being "the depiction of the individual in his own character,"[16] it would be reasonable to suppose—on the basis of such a hypothetical portrait's participation in a vivid tradition of verisimilar portraiture—that it was a true image. There was no such tradition circa 1400, and so to imagine the Hoccleve miniature to be, or to be like, an independent portrait is to imagine it beyond what was artistically plausible at the moment.[17] The Hoccleve miniature is dependent, however, like the other early images of Chaucer. It is largely without the sort of iconographic marking that in other instances helps identify figures; the man shown in the Hoccleve miniature has a pen case around his neck, a sign of literacy, and beads in one hand, a sign of piety; and he is fat, a characteristic of the Chaucerian persona that may be no more than a sign of the persona's companionable worldliness.[18] What indicates that the figure is Chaucer is the passage adjacent to it, asserting that it is Chaucer's likeness:

> Although his lyfe be queynt, the resemblaunce
> Of him hath in me so fressh lyflynesse,
> That, to putte othir men in remembraunce
> Of his persone, I have heere his lyknesse
> Do make, to this ende in sothfastnesse,
> That they that have of him lest thought and mynde,
> By this peynture may ageyn him fynde.
>
> (4992-98)[19]

The claim that the image and these words make together— that the author of these lines knew what Chaucer looked like—figures in Hoccleve's work, a work of which the picture itself thus becomes part, as one element, perhaps the crucial element, in an effort to solicit royal patronage. Hoccleve was evidently concerned, intermittently if not constantly in the *Regiment of Princes,* to establish himself in the perception of Prince Henry and other highly placed potential benefactors as a poetic follower of Chaucer, and as an especially privileged one, by virtue of an ostensive intimacy between himself and the dead poet, because Hoccleve seems to have imagined that he could benefit himself materially by causing Henry and others to see him in light of such a connection. Hoccleve's *Regiment of Princes* is fundamentally a petition:[20] an entreaty for patronage, both explicit and implicit in the poem's autobiographical prologue and the envoys that circulated with it, as well as within the body of the poem, its ostensibly disinterested collocation of counsels for Prince Henry.

In the prologue, Hoccleve voices a number of distinct complaints—the physical damage his nearly twenty-four years' service in the Office of the Privy Seal has caused him (988-1029; cf. 801-5); his failure to gain a benefice from his service (1401-2, 1447-53, 1485-91); being constantly cheated of his fees (1492-1550); the negligence of lords he has served (1793-95)—but the prologue is chiefly a lamentation on his poverty, focused on two kinds of problems, repeatedly averred. His present income is inadequate, Hoccleve asserts, because the six marks he has beyond his annuity is too little (932ff., 974-75, 1214-18, 1224-25) and his annuity of twenty marks is paid him too irregularly (820-31). Second, his future seems to him likely to be even more impoverished because of an increased difficulty about collecting his dues that he expects will come once he is compelled by age to retire from court to his "pore cote" (831-40, 948-53).[21] Hoccleve's interlocutor, a sapient Old Man he chances to meet after a night of sleepless agonizing over his financial situation, summarizes for him these points of worry:

> In schort, this is of thi grief enchesoun:
> Of thin annuitee, the paiement,
> Whiche for thi long servyse is thi guerdoun,
> Thou dredest, whan thou art from court absent,
> Schal be restreyned, syn thou now present
> Unnethes mayst it gete, it is so streit;
> Thus understode I, sone, thi conceit;
> For of thi liflode is it the substaunce.
>
> (1779-86)

Hoccleve is uncommonly frank about the motives of his work; faced with such circumstances, he would even bribe the Old Man in exchange for a solution to his problems: "Wisseth me how to gete a golden salve; / And what I have, I wele it with yow halve" (1245-46). The Old Man proposes that Hoccleve petition his prince, simply and straightforwardly, for the "golden salve" he needs:

> . . . now, syn thou me toldist
> My lord the prince is good lord the to,
> No maistri is it for the, if thou woldist
> To be releeved; wost thou what to do?
> Writte to hym a goodly tale or two,
> On which he may desporten hym by nyghte,
> And his fre grace schal upon the lighte
>
> (1898-1904)

Adjacent passages amplifying the Old Man's proposal render the flatteringly nebulous "fre grace" of this one less ambiguous: Prince Henry, whom Hoccleve claims "is my good gracious lord" (1836), "may be salve unto thin indigence," says the Old Man (1834); "To hym pursue, and thi releef purchace" (1848):

> Compleyne unto his excellent noblesse,
> As I have herd the unto me compleyne;
> And but he qwenche thi grete hevynesse,
> My tonge take, and slitte in peeces tweyne.
>
> (1849-52)[22]

By its prologue, the **Regiment of Princes** represents itself to Prince Henry as the execution of this plan for Hoccleve's material betterment; and the body of the poem reiterates the petition of the prologue in various ways. The tenth through the thirteenth of the poem's fifteen didactic sections, comprising various injunctions against niggardliness and suasions to "largesse," recall Hoccleve's particular needs constantly, by means of generalities about annuities, for example, as well as direct reference:[23]

> Now, if that ye graunten by your patente
> To your servauntes a yeerly guerdoun,
> Crist scheelde that your wil or your entente
> Be sette to maken a restriccioun
> Of paiement; for that condicioun
> Exileth the peples benevolence,
> And kyndeleth hate undir prive scilence.
>
> (4789-95)

> My yeerly guerdoun, myn annuite,
> That was me graunted for my long labour,
> Is al behynde, I may naght payed be,
> Whiche causeth me to lyven in langour.
> O liberal prince! ensample of honour!
> Unto your grace lyke it to promoote
> Mi poore estat, and to my woo beth boote!
>
> (4383-89)

Elsewhere, for example, justice is defined as offering "to the nedy . . . releve in hevynesse" (2472-76); and charity is lauded, *inter alia,* as what proves "that we disciples ben of God almyghty" (3607). A recurrent theme is the prince's obligation to "help him that wel doth" (2940): "as the men disserven, so be fre" (4128); or, in a passage that recalls the descriptions in the prologue of Hoccleve's long, debilitating service, he equates neglect of him with murder and threatens the prince with retribution for it:

> He that his flesche dispendith, and his blood,
> Mi lorde, in your service, him yiftes bede;
> There is largesse mesurable good;
> A kyng so bounde is, he moot doo so nede;
> Service unquyt and murdre, it is no drede,
> As clerkes writen, and disheritaunce,
> Bifore almighty God auxen vengeaunce.
>
> (4173-79)[24]

The **Regiment** also, if less directly, puts some of its case for Hoccleve's preferment on the grounds that he is a good, potentially useful poet, and in this it may have been successful. M. C. Seymour has suggested, on the evidence of Hoccleve's subsequent poetic output, that the poem's publication at court resulted in his becoming for a time "an acknowledged quasi-official writer of verse on political occasions."[25] In its prologue and envoys, the **Regiment** is often affectedly modest about Hoccleve's accomplishments: the poem's envoy to Prince Henry describes it as "all naked . . . of eloquence" (5443), for example; Hoccleve has only "smal konyng," "withal so treewe an herte" (2066-67);

> . . . I am no thyng fourmeel;
> My yonge konyng may no hyer reche,
> Mi wit is also slipir as an eel;
> But how I speke, algate I mene weel.
>
> (1983-86)[26]

Such remarks need be seen for the typical *captationes benevolentiae* they are, to be read here, as in other occurrences of the topos, as attempts to elicit a sympathetic, positive response to the writing, while also asserting an intention to do good.[27]

Notwithstanding his protestations to the contrary (and in fact complemented by them) Hoccleve's implicit claim in the *Regiment* that he is a good and useful poet rests in large measure on the more specific claims the poem puts forward to being Chaucerian, to being like the work of a poet who had previously enjoyed royal support. It is not now possible to document a connection between Chaucer's literary labors and the extensive preferments that came to him from his various noble and royal benefactors, in the form of the several annuities and remunerative (if still demanding) offices, with their associated emoluments and perquisites, that he acquired in the course of his forty-year career of dedicated, competent service. The life-records that make clear the extent of Chaucer's success at attracting such preferment to himself omit to make mention of his poetry writing.[28] Nevertheless, the facts were that Chaucer had risen high in the favor of England's most rich and powerful, and that he had written poetry addressed to them, at times poetry that could be believed to have been commissioned, in effect, by the likes of John of Gaunt.[29] That Chaucer had both accomplished much as a poet and stood high in noble and royal esteem provides grounds for the inference that his writing had in fact brought him material returns, if not immediately and directly then at least indirectly, by way of a generally enhanced standing in court circles that was later translated into preferment.

As a consequence of his literary and material successes, Chaucer should have seemed an especially useful forebear to those later English writers who were ambitious for their own preferment; and the evidence of the first fifty (at least) of Caroline Spurgeon's five hundred years of Chaucer criticism and allusion is that English-language poets of the early fifteenth century did find it expedient to hitch their own work to the wagon of Chaucer's success.[30] Among late fourteenth-century English poets, William Langland was one of Chaucer's nearest rivals for the esteem of the reading public, as measured, albeit imprecisely, in terms of surviving manuscripts.[31] But while the earliest allusions to Langland's writings occur in the revolutionary propaganda of the 1381 Peasants' Revolt,[32] the earliest allusions to Chaucer's writings occur in the works of poets who, like him, already enjoyed standing at court or who, like Hoccleve, were hoping for advancement. Langland—a writer rather different from Chaucer, one who, for example, represented himself as living in penury—had no literary afterlife to speak of, until he was reinvented as a proto-reformer by Robert Crowley in the middle of the sixteenth century;[33] on the other hand, Chaucer's name and work were celebrated persistently, throughout the fifteenth century. As John Burrow remarked, long since, this "rapid spread of Chaucer's reputation cannot be ascribed simply to the force of his genius."[34]

Hoccleve did not invent the topic of praise for Chaucer that was to recur so frequently in writings of the Chaucerian strand of fifteenth-century English literary achievement. Hoccleve may have known Chaucer, as he claims; and his situation was sufficiently like that of Chaucer—another government servant given to writing poetry—to

suggest the topic to him. In any case, Hoccleve, like others, seems to have imagined that his chances of coming to enjoy a Chaucer-like material success would be increased if he could produce Chaucerian writing, writing that his audience might be persuaded to see as descended from and like that of Geoffrey Chaucer; he seems to have imagined that establishing links between himself and Chaucer, the nearer the better, could benefit him.[35]

In the *Regiment of Princes,* Hoccleve repeatedly puts forward the claim that Chaucer had been his "master" in matters poetical. The claim is not only that a knowledge of Chaucer's work informed his own writing, though this point Hoccleve does establish by the broadly Chaucerian qualities of his verse[36] and by the appreciations of Chaucer's particular excellences built into the poem's three substantial eulogies of the dead poet (1958-74, 2077-2107, 4978-5012): Hoccleve perceives in Chaucer a "flour of eloquence," a "mirour of fructuous entendement" . . . "universel . . . in science," and "excellent prudence" (1962-65); he compares him to Tully in "swetnesse of rethorik," Aristotle "in philosophie," and Vergil "in poesie" (2084-89); he was "the firste fyndere of our faire langage" (4978); and so on. Most to the point, Hoccleve also claims that he had known Chaucer; and, furthermore, in no doubt purposefully ambiguous passages, he suggests that Chaucer had personally taken in hand his instruction in poetry. A remark of the Old Man implies that Hoccleve already enjoys a reputation for a personal association with Chaucer: hearing Hoccleve's name, he responds, "Sone, I have herd, or this, men speke of the: / Thou were aqueynted with Caucher, pardee" (1866-67). Hoccleve will admit to him, as if apologetically, that "I wont was han consail and reed" of "the honour of englyssh tonge" (1959-60):

> Mi dere maistir—God his soule quyte!—
> And fadir, Chaucer, fayn wolde han me taght;
> But I was dul, and lerned lite or naght.

> (2077-79)[37]

The Hoccleve portrait of Chaucer is put forward in this context, of Hoccleve's efforts to insinuate into the minds of his royal and noble audience an idea of his intimacy with Chaucer, as part of his effort to elicit benefaction. Hoccleve's tactical need to establish the idea of such a relationship between himself and Chaucer should confirm the truth of the image of Chaucer he put in circulation with the poem. Hoccleve was petitioning for patronage, in some measure on the basis of the quality of the poetic service he had provided and could provide; he sought to base his claim for the quality of his poetic service in some measure on the claim that his work was Chaucerian; this claim that his poetry was Chaucerian was in turn based in some measure on his claim to have known Chaucer, not only through his writing but also personally; and he bases his claim to have known Chaucer personally in some measure on a claim to know what Chaucer had looked like. In the end, Hoccleve's petition for patronage comes to rest in part on the demonstration of a knowledge of Chaucer's appearance that his lines about it and the portrait miniature adjacent to them must make. Henry and the others with whom Hoccleve needed to establish the claim that Chaucer was his master were in a position to verify the knowledge of Chaucer's appearance to which Hoccleve pretends, since Chaucer would have been known by sight among them; consequently, it would have cost Hoccleve if the image of Chaucer he offered his prospective patrons failed to show Chaucer as he had been known to them.

No doubt some measure of wishful thinking—of a naive sort, or of the cynical variety characteristic, for example, of the various sixteenth-century printer-publishers who sought to market editions of Chaucer by claiming to offer ever more accurate pictures of his life and work[38]—has been and is invested in any belief that the Ellesmere-Hoccleve type shows the poet's true image. On the other hand, another sort of wishful thinking—the romantic notion that poetry's place is some realm of the imagination rather than the material world[39]—may have tended to occlude Hoccleve's interest in the veracity of the portrait he caused to be circulated. The evidence of the material world—specifically, that Hoccleve had reason to believe he could profit from promulgating a true image of Chaucer with his poem—suggests that the Ellesmere-Hoccleve type may be Chaucer's "true portraiture" after all, wishful thinking or no.

Notes

1. The phrase is used in a 1598 portrait engraving of Chaucer, in the first Speght edition of the works (STC 5077-79), to describe an image derived from the Ellesmere-Hoccleve type; see Arthur M. Hind, *Engraving in England in the Sixteenth and Seventeenth Centuries,* pt. 1, The Tudor Period (Cambridge, 1952), 286-89 and pl. 121. The best comprehensive treatment of Chaucer portraiture remains that of M. H. Spielman, *The Portraits of Geoffrey Chaucer,* Chaucer Society, 2d ser., 31 (London, 1900); see also Aage Brusendorff, *The Chaucer Tradition* (1925; rpt., New York, 1965), 13-27; Roger Sherman Loomis, *A Mirror of Chaucer's World* (Princeton, 1965), figs. 1-6 and 68; and Roy Strong, *Tudor and Jacobean Portraits* (London, 1969), 1:46-48; and, on particular portraits, Margaret Rickert, "Illuminations," in John M. Manly and Edith Rickert, *The Text of the Canterbury Tales* (Chicago, 1940), 1:583-90; George M. Lam and Warren H. Smith, "George Vertue's Contributions to Chaucerian Iconography," *Modern Language Quarterly,* 5 (1944): 303-22; Reginald Call, "The Plimpton Chaucer and Other Problems of Chaucer Portraiture," *Speculum,* 22 (1947): 135-44; Hilton Kelliher, "The Historiated Initial in the Devonshire Chaucer," *Notes and Queries,* 222 (1977): 197; David Piper, "The Chesterfield House Library Portraits," in *Evidence in Literary Scholarship: Essays in Memory of James Marshall Osborn,* ed. René Wellek and Alvaro Ribeiro (Oxford, 1979), 186; Michael Seymour, "Manuscript Portraits of Chaucer and Hoccleve," *Burlington Magazine,* 124, no. 955 (October 1982): 618-23; and R. F. Yeager, "British Library Additional MS. 5141: An Unnoticed Chaucer Vita," *Journal of Medieval and Renaissance Studies,* 14 (1984): 261-81.

2. On the Ellesmere manuscript, see Manly and Rickert, *Text of the Canterbury Tales,* 1:148-59; Margaret Rickert, "Illuminations," 587-90; and Herbert C. Schulz, *The Ellesmere Manuscript of Chaucer's Canterbury Tales* (San Marino, 1966).

3. For the 1411 date of the *Regiment of Princes,* see Seymour, *Selections from Hoccleve* (Oxford, 1981), 114-15; and for Hoccleve's role in the production of presentation copies of the poem, see Seymour, "The Manuscripts of Hoccleve's Regiment of Princes," *Edinburgh Bibliographical Society Transactions,* 4 (1974): 255-56, and *Selections,* 114.

4. See Edwin Ford Piper, "The Miniatures of the Ellesmere Chaucer," *Philological Quarterly,* 3 (1924): 241-56; Loomis, *Mirror,* figs. 80-101; or Schulz, *The Ellesmere Manuscript,* 3-4.

5. The distinction between the person and the persona is commonly credited to E. Talbot Donaldson, "Chaucer the Pilgrim," *PMLA,* 69 (1954): 928-36.

6. The disproportion and the conclusion to be drawn from it are remarked by Margaret Rickert, "Illuminations," 587-88; Schulz, *The Ellesmere Manuscript,* 3; Seymour, "Manuscript Portraits," 618 and 621; and Jeanne E. Krochalis, "Hoccleve's Chaucer Portrait," *Chaucer Review,* 21 (1986): 244 n. 15. The panel-portrait hypothesis is tendered by Seymour, *Selections,* 124, and "Manuscript Portraits," 618; cf. Krochalis, "Hoccleve's Chaucer Portrait," 244 n. 15. If Thomas Chaucer had something to do with the production of the Ellesmere manuscript, his involvement would seem to improve the odds that the Ellesmere miniature is a true portrait. Nothing beyond the speculations of Manly and Rickert (see *Text of the Canterbury Tales,* 1:159) has been advanced in support of this theory, however, except the remarks of John M. Bowers, "Chaucer & Son: The Business of Lancastrian Poetry" (Southeastern Medieval Association Conference, Raleigh, N. C., USA, 28 September 1990).

7. Cf. Margaret Rickert, "Illuminations," 588-90; and Seymour, *Selections,* 124. In "Manuscript Portraits," Seymour suggests that the Ellesmere manuscript and the two Hoccleve manuscripts Arundel 38 and Harley 4866 "were illuminated in one atelier in London or Westminster" (618); cf. Seymour, *Selections,* 124, and A. I. Doyle and M. B. Parkes, "The Production of Copies of the Canterbury Tales and the Confessio Amantis in the Early Fifteenth Century," in *Medieval Scribes, Manuscripts and Libraries: Essays Presented to N. R. Ker,* ed. M. B. Parkes and Andrew G. Watson (London, 1978), 203 and n. 106. The likelihood of this sort of relation among the three manuscripts is increased by the evidence, adduced by Doyle and Parkes, that Hoccleve and the copyist of the Elles-

mere manuscript both contributed to the manufacture of a manuscript of Gower's *Confessio Amantis,* now Cambridge, Trinity College, R.III.2 ("The Production of Copies," esp. 170-74, 182-85, and 198-203); Hoccleve is linked, professionally, by the mediation of this copyist, to those who produced the Ellesmere manuscript's illumination. Cf. John M. Bowers, "Hoccleve's Huntington Holographs: The First 'Collected Poems' in English," *Fifteenth-Century Studies,* 15 (1989): 29-30. Charles L. Kuhn, in "Herman Scheere and English Illumination of the Early Fifteenth Century," *Art Bulletin,* 22 (1940): 155; and Gereth M. Spriggs, in "Unnoticed Bodleian Manuscripts Illuminated by Herman Scheere and his School," *Bodleian Library Record,* 7 (1964): 195, would associate the artist of Arundel 38 with the workshop of Herman Scheere.

8. See esp. Seymour, "Manuscripts of Hoccleve's Regiment," 258, and his descriptions of the three manuscripts, 269, 272-73, and 292; and cf. Jerome Mitchell, *Thomas Hoccleve: A Study in Early Fifteenth-Century English Poetic* (Urbana, 1968), 110-15.

9. On these manuscripts and their relations with the others, see Seymour, "Manuscripts of Hoccleve's Regiment," 263-64 and 268-69; D. C. Greetham, "Normalisation of Accidentals in Middle English Texts: The Paradox of Thomas Hoccleve," *Studies in Bibliography,* 38 (1985): 123 n. 5; Marcia Smith Marzec, "Scribal Emendation in Some Later Manuscripts of Hoccleve's Regiment of Princes," *Analytical and Enumerative Bibliography,* n.s., 1 (1987): esp. 41-42; and Greetham, "Challenges of Theory and Practice in the Editing of Hoccleve's Regement of Princes," in *Manuscripts and Texts: Editorial Problems in Later Middle English Literature,* ed. Derek Pearsall (Cambridge, 1987), 65-67, where a stemma representing the textual tradition of the *Regiment* is printed.

10. See esp. Seymour, "Manuscript Portraits," 621 and n. 8; and on the Rosenbach portrait, see also Krochalis, "Hoccleve's Chaucer Portrait," 642 n. 2.

11. Envoys by Hoccleve addressing copies of the *Regiment* to each of these persons, though not transmitted by any extant manuscripts of the *Regiment,* are preserved in the holograph miscellany of Hoccleve's shorter poems, San Marino, Huntington Library, HM 111 (ed. Seymour, *Selections,* 55-57); the missing first and final leaves of Harley 4866 probably contained one or the other of these envoys and perhaps some armorial indication of the identity of the manuscript's intended recipient; see Seymour, "Manuscripts of Hoccleve's Regiment," 269. The nature of these two envoys has been the subject of some controversy. Thorlac Turville-Petre, in "'Maistir Massy'," *Review of English Studies,* n.s., 26 (1975): 129-33, identifies the "Massy" named in the Bedford envoy and the "Picard" named in the York envoy as financial officers in the households of the respective

lords, and characterizes the Bedford envoy as a begging poem. David Farley-Hills, in a letter in *Review of English Studies,* n.s., 26 (1975): 451, and Clifford Peterson, in "Hoccleve, the Old Hall Manuscript, Cotton Nero A.x., and the Pearl-Poet," *Review of English Studies,* n.s., 28 (1977): 48-55, demur. Albeit that they are not as direct as the other poems of Hoccleve characterized by Mitchell as "begging poems" (*Thomas Hoccleve,* 33-34), no doubt these envoys, like the *Regiment*'s envoy to Prince Henry, are, at least by virtue of their circulation with presentation copies of the *Regiment,* as Mitchell says, "poems of indirect solicitation" (33).

12. See Seymour, "Manuscripts of Hoccleve's Regiment,", where he describes Harley 4866 as "an almost exact replica of MS. Arundel 38 (269)."

13. See esp. Kate Harris, "The Patron of British Library MS. Arundel 38," *Notes and Queries,* 229 (1984): 462-63.

14. Cf. Krochalis, "Hoccleve's Chaucer Portrait," 240; Prince Henry himself would have been thirteen at the time of Chaucer's death, if Chaucer in fact died in 1400.

15. On the Lansdowne miniature, see Margaret Rickert, "Illuminations," 584-85, Seymour, "Manuscript Portraits," 621, and Krochalis, "Hoccleve's Chaucer Portrait," 637; it is reproduced in Seymour, "Manuscript Portraits," fig. 42, and in Strong, *Tudor and Jacobean Portraits,* vol. 2, fig. 82. On the Troilus frontispiece, see esp. Elizabeth Salter, "The 'Troilus Frontispiece'," in *Troilus and Criseyde: A Facsimile of Corpus Christi College Cambridge MS. 61* (Cambridge, 1978), 15-23, a volume which includes a color reproduction of the painting; Derek Pearsall, "The Troilus Frontispiece and Chaucer's Audience," *Yearbook of English Studies,* 7 (1977): 68-74; and Seymour, "Manuscript Portraits," 622, and his review of the facsimile volume, in *The Library,* 6th ser., 4 (1982): 190-91.

16. John Pope-Hennessy's definition of "portraiture," in *The Portrait in the Renaissance* (New York, 1966), xi.

17. But cf. Janet Backhouse, "Illuminated Manuscripts and the Early Development of the Portrait Miniature," in *Early Tudor England: Proceedings of the 1987 Harlaxton Symposium,* ed. Daniel Williams (Woodbridge, Conn., 1989), where she remarks: "realistic portraits from the life were increasingly favoured in manuscript contexts from the late fourteenth century onwards, in parallel with the development of the true portrait on a larger scale. Illuminators in England at the beginning of the fifteenth century seem to have been very much attracted by the challenge of representing human features, and lifelike but anonymous faces appear in the initials and margins of several of the finest manuscripts of the period, including the Bedford

Psalter and Hours, the Hours of Elizabeth the Queen, and the Sherborne Missal" (2).

18. Chaucer, or "Chaucer," alludes to his corpulence in the *House of Fame,* 574 and 660; the prologue to *Sir Thopas, Canterbury Tales,* 7:700-702; the envoy to Scogan, 27-31; and "Merciles Beaute," 27.

19. Quotations from and references to the *Regiment,* most often made only within the body of the paper, are taken from *Hoccleve's Works,* vol. 3, ed. F. J. Furnivall, *The Regement of Princes,* EETS es 72 (London, 1897). In quoting this edition, I replace thorn with *th,* yogh with *y,* modernize the distributions of *u* and *v,* and modernize word divisions.

20. By use of this term, I mean to refer to J. A. Burrow's papers "The Poet as Petitioner," *Studies in the Age of Chaucer,* 3 (1981): 61-75, and "Autobiographical Poetry in the Middle Ages: The Case of Thomas Hoccleve," *Proceedings of the British Academy,* 68 (1982): 389-412, esp. 407-11, where he argues: "The image of himself that [Hoccleve] projects in his poetry is determined most of all by the harsh requirements of survival in the treacherous world of the court" (407). See also Larry Scanlon, "The King's Two Voices: Narrative and Power in Hoccleve's *Regement of Princes,*" in *Literary Practice and Social Change in Britain, 1380-1530,* ed. Lee Patterson (Berkeley, 1990), 227-42, esp. 230-33, on the consequences of Hoccleve's amalgamation of the begging poem and the *Fürstenspiegel* in a single work: "The begging poem postulates a royal *voluntas* that acts entirely at its own pleasure, and thus stands as a striking counterpoise to the didactic presumptions of the *Fürstenspiegel,* which posits a king who relies on counsel" (230).

21. The substantive basis of these complaints is established by Malcom Richardson in "Hoccleve in his Social Context," *Chaucer Review,* 20 (1986): 313-22. Essentially the same evidence was reviewed by A. Compton Reeves in "Thomas Hoccleve, Bureaucrat," *Medievalia et Humanistica,* n.s., 5 (1974): 201-14; but Reeves came to a rather less charitable conclusion: "The evidence for the financial rewards of [Hoccleve's] career suggests that he had an adequate and comfortable income, quite enough to satisfy his needs. If he were truly poor, it was because of his own prodigality, not meager earnings. There can, however, be no denial of the worry and insecurity that came from the unsure and irregular payments of the poet's annuity" (209). In other words, although Hoccleve's annuities were not paid at all for long periods and, when they were paid, were frequently less than they should have been (as Reeves himself shows), still, according to Reeves, Hoccleve's problem was not poverty or material insecurity but only his own feckless malcontent.

22. Cf. 1874-76: "Thi penne take, and write / As thou canst, and thi sorowe tourne schal / Into gladnesse."

23. Cf. Burrow, "Autobiographical Poetry," 408 and n. 5.

24. Cf. 4670-76: "liberalitee" and "largesse" "bothe moot in hir conseytes chue / Where is good yeve, and where to eschue, / The persone, and the somme, and cause why: / What they yeven, yeve it vertuously."

25. Seymour, *Selections,* xiii; cf. xvi-xvii.

26. Cf. 2152-55: "Yit, for to putte in prees my conceyte small, / Goode wille me arteth take on me the peyne; / But sore in me quappeth every veyne, / So dredefull am I of myne ignoraunce."

27. Cf. E. R. Curtius, *European Literature and the Latin Middle Ages,* trans. Willard R. Trask (Princeton, 1952), 83-85; and D. C. Greetham, "Self-Referential Artifacts: Hoccleve's Persona as a Literary Device," *Modern Philology,* 86 (1989): 242-44. For the ramifications of this pose of "dullness" that Hoccleve adopts, see David Lawton, "Dullness and the Fifteenth Century," *ELH,* 54 (1987): 762-71.

28. James Root Hulbert, in his 1912 study *Chaucer's Official Life* (rpt., New York, 1970), puts much weight on this sequestration of the official's activities from the poet's in the evidence (77-91, esp. 79 and 85); cf. the balanced remarks of V. J. Scattergood, "Literary Culture at the Court of Richard II," in *English Court Culture in the Later Middle Ages,* ed. Scattergood and J. W. Sherborne (London, 1983), esp. 30-32.

29. For examples: "Lak of Stedfastnesse" addresses Richard II; "The complaint of Chaucer to his Purse" addresses Henry IV; and "Fortune" addresses some unnamed "princes," most likely the Dukes of Lancaster, York, and Gloucester; the *Book of the Duchess* was certainly written for John of Gaunt; and the *Legend of Good Women* appears to have been written for Richard II's Queen Anne, by the suggestion of one of its prologues (F 496-97). On Chaucer's relations with his royal and noble audience, see Elizabeth Salter, "Chaucer and Internationalism," *Studies in the Age of Chaucer,* 2 (1980): 71-79, esp. 78-79; and Scattergood, "Literary Culture at the Court of Richard II," 37-41. The persistence and proliferation, well into the sixteenth century, of rumors that other Chaucerian writings were similarly addressed or occasioned—John Shirley's claim, for example, that the "Complaint of Mars" was made "at the commandement of the renommed and excellent prince my lord the duke John of Lancastre," or the 1602 Speight edition's claim that "An ABC" was made "at the request of Blanche Duchess of Lancaster"—suggest that Chaucer's esteem continued to rest, in some measure, on his putative royal and aristocratic connections.

30. Caroline F. E. Spurgeon, *Five Hundred Years of Chaucer Criticism and Allusion, 1357-1900* (Cambridge, 1925), 1:15ff. The earliest clear attempts to trade on Chaucer's reputation, in the way that

Hoccleve does in the *Regiment,* which happen also to be by persons probably acquainted with Chaucer, seem to me to be those of Thomas Usk, in his *Testament of Love* (c. 1387), and Henry Scogan, in his "Moral Ballad" (c. 1407), both cited by Spurgeon in *Five Hundred Years of Chaucer Criticism,* 8 and 18-19.

31. Carleton Brown and Rossell Hope Robbins, in *Index of Middle English Verse* (New York, 1943), list sixty-four known surviving manuscripts of the *Canterbury Tales,* fifty of *Piers Plowman,* and forty-nine of the *Confessio Amantis* (737). Such a comparison probably favors Chaucer and Gower over Langland, to the extent that the work of Chaucer and Gower—comparatively "up-market" poets—seems likely to have been copied into deluxe versions, which, by their nature, tend to be better preserved, with greater frequency than the work of Langland.

32. Ann Hudson, "The Legacy of *Piers Plowman,*" in *A Companion to Piers Plowman,* ed. John A. Alford (Berkeley, 1988), 251-52.

33. For Langland's representation of himself as poor, see, e.g., *Piers Plowman* C VI.1-104. The suggestion that Langland's literary afterlife is of no account is an exaggeration; the fifteenth-century offspring of *Piers Plowman* include *Pierce the Ploughman's Crede, Richard the Redeless, Mum and Sothsegger,* and a few less eminent writings. The topic is surveyed by Hudson in "The Legacy of *Piers Plowman,*" 251-66. Nonetheless, it remains true that, as Ann Middleton has said in her introduction to *A Companion to Piers Plowman,* "the reception and influence of these two contemporaries," Chaucer and Langland, "contrasted strikingly from the beginning" (2). On Crowley's role in the reinvention of Langland in the sixteenth century, see John N. King, "Robert Crowley's Editions of *Piers Plowman*: A Tudor Apocalpyse," *Modern Philology,* 73 (1976): 342-52.

34. Burrow, "The Audience of Piers Plowman," *Anglia,* 75 (1957): 377.

35. Cf. Richardson, "Hoccleve in his Social Context," 318; and Paul Strohm, "Chaucer's Fifteenth-Century Audience and the Narrowing of the 'Chaucer Tradition,'" *Studies in the Age of Chaucer,* 4 (1982): 14.

36. Cf. Seymour, *Selections,* xxi-xxvii; and Mitchell, *Thomas Hoccleve,* 118-22, esp. 121.

37. Mitchell, in *Thomas Hoccleve,* casts doubt on this "supposed friendship" between Hoccleve and Chaucer (115-18); Seymour (*Selections,* 119) and Burrow ("Autobiographical Poetry," 397-98) are less skeptical. Whatever the substance underlying Hoccleve's claims in the *Regiment,* it was in his interest to emphasize and exaggerate the relation. Krochalis, in "Hoccleve's Chaucer Portrait," in light of *Regiment* 4999-5012, characterizes Hoccleve's representation

of Chaucer as a sort of literary hagiolotry (239-41), his attempt "to secure and sanctify the place of Chaucer and of English poetry itself" (241).

38. Alice Miskimin's discussion of the sixteenth-century Chaucer makes something of the printer-publishers' venality as a motive for their efforts to augment and improve the Chaucer canon; see *The Renaissance Chaucer* (New Haven, 1975), 226-61, esp. 239.

39. The influence of this notion is described by Jerome McGann in *The Romantic Ideology* (Chicago, 1983).

Anna Torti (essay date 1991)

SOURCE: Torti, Anna. "Specular Narrative: Hoccleve's *Regement of Princes.*" In *Glass of Form: Mirroring Structures from Chaucer to Skelton,* pp. 87-106. Cambridge: D.S. Brewer, 1991.

[*In the following essay, from her study of mirror metaphors in medieval English literature, Torti discusses Hoccleve's* Regement of Princes *in terms of its function as autobiography. Torti argues that in his construction of a "mirror" in which Prince Henry can see examples of statesmanship, Hoccleve often reflects an image of himself.*]

Critical evaluation of Thomas Hoccleve as a mere imitator of Chaucer has had too long a currency,[1] and Hoccleve himself is partly to blame for this. His references to Chaucer are numerous. In the ***Regement of Princes*** he apostrophizes his 'maister' as 'flour of eloquence, / Mirour of fructuous entendement, / O, vniuersel fadir in science' (1962-4), and, using the *diminutio* technique, contrasts Chaucer's excellence with his own inability to express himself correctly: 'My yonge konyng may no hyer reche, / Mi wit is also slipir as an eel' (1984-5).

In recent years, however, critics like S. Medcalf and J. Burrow have stressed the autobiographical substratum—which thrusts itself to the surface in the **'Prologue'** and in the so-called *Series*[2]—that makes Hoccleve's narrative uniquely his notwithstanding his observance of medieval conventions. His use of different literary genres, such as the petition that parodies the penitential lyric[3] in **'La Male Regle'** and the *consolatio*[4] in the **'Prologue'** and in the *Series* cannot prevent his readers from receiving an impression of 'modernity' from Hoccleve's poetry, especially when he offers them a minutely-detailed description of his deeply depressive state.[5]

Hoccleve's ***Regement of Princes*** is divided into two parts: the **'Prologue'** and the ***Regement*** proper. The **'Prologue'** has a quasi-typical dream setting. The poet cannot sleep: he is too worried about the world's problems and his own misfortunes. The next morning he goes out and meets an old beggar. They start a conversation, with Hoccleve showing moments of self-revelation and the Beggar trying to comfort the poet with long didactic sermons and by talking about his past life. At line 750 Hoccleve tells the Beggar about his melancholy. Being poor he fears for his old age. He then gives a detailed account of his work in the Privy Seal and of his annuity and complains about the troubles to which scribes are subject. After other allusions to his life, he laments the death of Chaucer, the flower of eloquence. Then the Beggar goes away and the poet announces that he will write a poem for Prince Henry.

At the beginning of the **Regement** proper, Hoccleve indicates his sources and refers again to Chaucer, whom he praises greatly. The **Regement** was divided by the editor into fifteen sections named after the virtues that Hoccleve considers necessary for a king. The sections vary in length and in the number of the examples introduced to describe the various subjects. Personal allusions are also present, as in section 11 where he presses the prince for his annuity. The concluding section is on peace. To restore peace Hoccleve suggests the marriage of Prince Hal and the Princess of France.

The **Regement of Princes** is the work in which Hoccleve's personal history is allowed to merge most transparently with a theme of public importance, in this case the timeless history of princes. He achieves this blending by means of the mirror metaphor:[6] it is the way in which he juxtaposes two *specula* that constitutes the particular interest of the **Regement.** The 'Prologue' is the mirror of Hoccleve's life for Prince Henry, and the **Regement** is the mirror of the good ruler,[7] i.e. Henry, for Hoccleve as subject and poet. By his own admission Hoccleve used three *auctoritates* ('Aristotle', Jacobus and Aegidius)[8] for his *speculum principis,* but he prefaces his treatise with the story of his life at the time of composing the **Regement.**

Hoccleve's attempt to put micro-history—his own life history—and macro-history—*exempla* for the prince—on the same plane becomes apparent when the structure and language of the two parts that make up the work are carefully examined. As Medcalf points out,[9] Hoccleve is firmly attached to the principles of order and planning set out by Geoffrey of Vinsauf in the *Poetria Nova* and celebrated by the narrator in Chaucer's *Troilus* (I, 1065-9). In the **'Dialog'** he asserts:

> Thow woost wel / who shal an hous edifie,
> Gooth nat ther-to withoute auisament,
> If he be wys, for with his mental ye
> ffirst is it seen / pourposid / cast & ment,
> How it shal wroght been / elles al is shent.
> Certes, for the deffaute of good forsighte,
> Mis-tyden thynges / þat wel tyde mighte.
>
> (638-44)

It is to satisfy these principles of order and architectonic construction that Hoccleve juxtaposes the two parts in a play of reflected images, of analogies and dissimilarities. The length of the **'Prologue'** is in itself an indication of the importance Hoccleve wishes to give the dialogue between the first-person narrator and the Beggar, the wise old man who has learned life's lessons.

The opening of the poem is constructed according to the canons of the dream vision tradition.[10] The poet is worried, 'Mvsyng vpon the restles bisynesse / Which that this troubly world hath ay on honde' (1-2), and cannot sleep, because 'Thought' (7) keeps him awake. He adds that he has many a time suffered the same anguish and felt the need to flee the world to remain alone with himself, 'To sorwe soule, me thought it dide me good' (91).

Constance Hieatt[11] holds that the structure of the dream-vision admits of a subdivision into four parts: Prologue, Break in Consciousness, Guidance and Epilogue. If this subdivision is applied to the **Regement,** Hoccleve's second part can be seen as a substantial modification. After the 'stormy nyght' (113) the poet wakes and, while walking through the fields, meets the Beggar—who is a character from real life. That he does not belong to the dream is made clear from his first words, 'Awake! & gan me schake wonder faste' (132), and '"I," quod þis olde greye, / "Am heer"' (134-5), almost as if to point out the necessity of distinguishing between the imaginary world created by the poet's oppressed mind and the everyday real world. Moreover, as we will see, Hoccleve is so taken up with his financial problems that he makes everything turn towards his own personal advantage, and here outer motives and inner reasons merge and mingle.

In his deeply depressive state Hoccleve shows from the very beginning that he is certain of at least one thing: that his poetry is a possible stepping-stone to personal and social success. Unlike Skelton in the *Garlande of Laurell,* Hoccleve does not exalt his poetic craft, but, from the moment he meets the Beggar, he speculates on the value of writing and the possibility of exploiting it for his own ends. According to the Beggar, men of letters have 'gretter descrecioun' (155) and put their faith in 'resoun' (157), thus distancing themselves much more rapidly from 'folye' (158) than ignorant men who have no 'maner of lettrure' (160). Hoccleve gives weight to his role as a writer by quoting Chaucer as his master on many occasions: he declares that Chaucer is too exalted a model for others to imitate, but he nonetheless makes a direct association between his writings and Chaucer. Hoccleve goes even further: he passes over Lydgate and inserts himself after Chaucer and Gower as the third element in the literary triad, even though he does so to the accompaniment of yet another declaration of his inferiority. The **'Prologue'** ends on his expressed intention to write the Poem for Prince Henry.

Two characteristics, which are common to the two parts, emerge from a careful analysis of the structure of the **'Prologue'** both by itself and in connection with the actual **Regement.** These characteristics are, firstly, the close similarity between the *ordo* of the treatment of the subjects and, secondly, the affinity between Hoccleve's position and that of the future king. As regards the first element held in common, the **'Prologue'** is subdivided into: (1) Indication of the causes of the deeply depressive state; (2) Meeting with the guide, (2a) *Exempla* from the Bible and from contemporary society for didactic purposes (to fit Hoccleve's circumstances), (2b) Beggar's confession and repentance; (3) Hoccleve's life history with *exempla* from the Bible and from contemporary society, with no repentance but with a petition to Prince Henry. The **Regement** instead is subdivided into: (1) Proem with acknowledgment of the three authorities, 'Aristotle', Jacobus and Aegidius, whose words the author intends to transcribe into the vernacular for the future king's benefit; (2) Fifteen Sections given over to the virtues to practise and the vices to shun; (3) An Envoy with the customary reference to the inadequacy of the 'litell booke'.

The structural links between the **Regement** and the **'Prologue'** can be recognized in the content of the single sections. Section 11, entitled **'De Virtute Largitatis & De Vicio Prodigalitatis,'** is a case in point. The first part refers to 'Aristotil, of largesse' (4124), thus establishing the *auctoritas*. The second part consists of the *exemplum* of John of Canace, a very popular story in the Middle Ages, intended as a warning to Henry about when and how to distribute benefices. The novelty of the work, however, lies in the fact that it also connects the a-temporal nature of exemplification to Hoccleve's temporal condition. He admits he has been too prodigal with his money, yet, on this occasion just as in the **'Prologue,'** he fails to repent and immediately goes on to his petition to the prince. He admits 'I me repent of my mysrewly lyfe' (4376), but adds 'My yeerly guerdoun, myn annuite, / That was me graunted for my long labour, / Is al behynde, I may naght payed be' (4383-5). The originality of Hoccleve's *speculum* lies, then, in his going on from his own impoverished condition to the likelihood of the king's own destruction if he allows himself to be pressed into distributing benefices by the bad advice of his flatterers. Hoccleve is aware of the irony of his position as a petitioner[12] presenting a book to obtain money. He asserts, however, that his sole purpose in writing is to add to the 'renoun' of the prince, seeing that his words are dictated by good faith.[13] Hoccleve hits out at flatterers in an attempt to persuade the king to loosen his purse-strings for the poor scribe's benefit.

The short section 13, **'De regis prudencia,'** where Hoccleve deals with the customary commonplace of the moral virtues to be cultivated, is another example of structural likeness. Hoccleve addresses the prince directly, urging him 'Be prudent, as þat þe scripture vs lereth' (4752) and thus quoting his *auctoritas*. Of moral virtues the sovereign must possess above all prudence, by the light of which he will be enabled to observe 'in euery herne / Of þynges past, and ben, & þat schul be' (4765-6).[14] The poet continues talking about the necessity for prudence and then falls at once into the usual pattern of associating the king's conduct with his own condition, although this time the allusion is indirect. In reality, Hoccleve implores the future king to keep the agreements he has put his seal to, taking the pensions granted to subjects as an example: 'Now, if þat ye graunten by your patente / To your seruauntes a yeerly guerdoun, / Crist scheelde þat your wil or

your entente / Be sette to maken a restriccioun / Of paiement' (4789-93). In this case too the obsessive reference to the failure to pay his stipend appears.

In the last section, entitled **'Of Peace,'** which is the most 'public' part of the **Regement** in that Hoccleve here declares himself in favour of the fusion of the royal houses of England and France through Henry and Catherine's marriage,[15] the motif of the two evils the sovereign must avoid, Avarice and Flattery, is introduced. These evils lead back inevitably to Hoccleve's situation. On one hand Avarice (embodied in the Roman *populus*) puts 'profyte singuler' (5249) before 'profyt commun' (5250)—the implication here is that the sovereign thinks neither of the people's welfare nor of Hoccleve's tranquillity; on the other, Flattery rules over the country to the extent that the livings and the various ecclesiastical benefices go to the flatterers rather than to the Oxford and Cambridge 'worthi clerk famouse' (5272), i.e., the intellectuals do not receive privileges worthy of their reputation, and Hoccleve too is damaged by this situation. Hoccleve's intention to relate the various issues to himself is therefore evident. Hoccleve introduces commonplaces familiar to the public into the **Regement** and these allow him to locate his poem within a well-defined tradition that can be traced through Boethius, the *psychomachia* and the *specula principum*. He modifies this tradition, however, in terms of his own self, by setting his own story and that of the prince side by side.

As we have already seen, the structure of the dream vision poem has been maintained almost intact,[16] even if the basic premise, the dream itself, is lacking. The subject on which it is centred is a commonplace handed down from Boethius—how to parry Fortune's blows—but this is paradoxically whittled down to a single opposition that was vital for Hoccleve: poverty/material well-being. Hoccleve endeavours to camouflage this obsession of his—the fruit, certainly, of an objective situation—by using the genres with the widest circulation for the purposes of his petition. In this operation Hoccleve shows himself to be very skilful. Just as a figure of consolation appeared to Boethius, so the Old Beggar appears to Hoccleve. This Beggar, while he allows him to put all the available commonplaces on show, neither consoles him nor induces him to repent. Like the Beggar, Hoccleve has sinned, but the central problem, the cause of all the ills that beset him, is not sin alone but above all lack of money:

> It goht ful streite and scharp or I it haue;
> If I seur were of it be satisfied
> ffro yeer to yeer, than, so god me saue,
> My deepe rootid grief were remedied
> Souffissantly; but how I schal be gyed
> Heer-after, whan þat I no lenger serue,
> This heuyeth me, so þat I wel ny sterue.

(827-33)

In the two parts of the **Regement,** the motif of the need for material well-being recurs again and again, and in this way traditionally allegorical themes and motifs are subjected to a *de facto* secularization. The poem reveals the considerable influence of morality-play subject matter. One might even say that Hoccleve anticipates what Skelton was to do in *Magnyfycence,* where he combines precepts for the prince with an attack on his sworn enemy, Wolsey. Here Hoccleve keeps a thematic and structural distinction between the two parts, the **'Prologue'** and the *speculum,* even though this distinction is more apparent than real. Unlike Skelton, he does not hurl invective. However, what I have said in the foregoing pages gives an idea of how the poet endeavours to exploit for his own individual purposes the Boethian theory of opposites,[17] and together with this the tradition of allegorical personifications of evil which were already in the process of dramatic transformation towards more realistic presentation in the morality play.[18]

According to Diane Bornstein,[19] the main interest of the **Regement** lies in the fact that Hoccleve deals with the problems that the men of his times felt most keenly, such as absenteeism, adultery, injustice and corruption, but this is no more than standard practice, seeing that he is writing an *exemplum* for the prince's benefit. Instead, the real focus of interest is in the emphasis given to the role of the poet and his ability to manipulate literary tradition in favour of his petition. Boethius is certainly the authority the **'Prologue'** refers to and *De Consolatione Philosophiae* the work taken by Hoccleve as his model, to judge from the opening to the poem:

> And how in bookes thus I wryten fynde,
> 'The werste kynde of wrecchednesse is,
> A man to have been weelful or this.'

> (54-6)

Immediately prior to these lines, however, Hoccleve establishes the opposition that will be the referent for the two parts:

> I seey weel povert was exclusion
> Of all weelfare regnyng in mankynde.

> (52-3)

This opposition, which is formally of a moral nature but was in fact realistically present in Hoccleve's life, is connected with the structure of the morality play. Here the opposition is fall/salvation, the fall caused by the vices (especially certain vices) and salvation due to the grace of God, by means of the help the virtues confer on man.[20]

At this point it is interesting to see what vices Hoccleve intends taking as his target, and what virtues are to be practised. Just as the slow process of secularization of the drama was reducing the figures of evil and centring their role in a particular vice,[21] so in Hoccleve's poem the two evils considered to be worst with reference to the prince and to his people are Flattery and Avarice. On the other hand the virtues that the common people (in the **'Prologue'**) and the prince (in the **Regement**) must cultivate are Chastity, Humility, Prudence, etc., all of which tend towards the well-being of the sovereign but also of his subjects.

Both formally and thematically the poem has a circular structure, as the play of symmetries and variations shows. In the **'Prologue'** Hoccleve is consumed by anxiety and cannot rest; he then meets the Beggar, whose tale relates to the poet's past life and indicates the vices to shun and the virtues to practise; and finally there is the announcement that he will write a poem for Henry. In the **Regement** Hoccleve proposes to put together the stories he has found in his three authorities, and hopes that

> Yf þat you liste of stories to take hede,
> Somwhat it may profite, by your leve:
> At hardest, when þat ye ben in Chambre at eve,
> They ben goode to drive forth the nyght;
> They shull not harme, yf þey be herd a-right.

> (2138-42)

He makes didactic use of the stories that refer to real or imaginary happenings involving sovereigns of past ages, and finally there is the Envoy to the book that has been completed, and which begins with the sleepless night. The circular structure of both the **'Prologue'** and the **Regement** can be described in synthesis as follows:

'Prologue'

Hoccleve's sleeplessness and the uselessness of his tale. Beggar's *exempla* (need for virtue). Usefulness of the poet's writing (Chaucer's help).

Regement

Prince's sleeplessness and the usefulness of Hoccleve's tale. *Exempla* for the prince (need for wealth, for himself and his subjects; need for virtue). Chaucer's sanctification. Appeal both for internal pacification and external pacification with France. The book ends with a section dedicated to peace.

The complexity and symmetry of the structure show how deeply aware Hoccleve is, even when he denies it, of his role as poet. As such he is able to imitate the great authors of the past—and he adds quite openly that he may be able to make practical use of his writing. Hoccleve then uses the most traditional of genres and themes, but what he is really stressing is that certain values from the past, valid though they may still be, are less impelling than they once were. In the final analysis the *psychomachia* is reduced to the struggle between poverty and riches, these riches being individual and social welfare. Like the **Regement**, *Piers Plowman* suggested equality and social justice as the starting point for spiritual salvation, but Hoccleve seems to attach a different importance to the two poles. There are many episodes in the **Regement**—like the story of John of Canace—that urge the sovereign not to place his trust in transient riches. However, John of Canace's story relates to Hoccleve's poverty if the prince does not pay him his annuity, even though the poet hints at his folly and repentance: 'I me repent of my mysrewly lyfe; / Wherfor, in þe wey of sauacioun / I hope I be' (4376-8); and it is the conclusion to this story that reveals how material well-being is considered as important as spiritual well-being, and that the intellectual, like the rest of the king's servants, has a right to a just reward. The identification and denunciation of the social ills of his time serve Hoccleve's purpose, which is to show the need to eliminate poverty, and so attain to a more acceptable standard of living. This does not mean that Hoccleve is a kind of Everyman, an emblem of humanity as a whole, but rather that he, like all men, has a right to survive. As a poet his right is to have patrons that protect him by holding his work in due esteem and saving him from ruining his eyesight as a scribe.[22] In order to explain the reasons for a lack of social justice he uses what were destined to become the worst sins a century later, in the full reawakening of humanism—Flattery and Avarice in close connection. That the account of the ills that threaten his subjects, and Hoccleve in particular, anticipates and is then incorporated into the description of the ills that the sovereign must avoid inflicting on his subjects and on Hoccleve himself, is a demonstration of the specular nature of the two parts of the poem.

Both in the **'Prologue'** and in the *Regement* Flattery and Avarice join forces to lead man to wretchedness. In those who embody these sins this wretchedness will be of a moral kind; in those who are subjected to the effects of these sins, it will be material. In the **'Prologue'** the Flatterer is described by the Beggar as a man dressed in costly, sumptuous clothes; only by eliminating the squandering of money induced by Pride will there be more for the people: 'Than myghte siluer walke more thikke / Among þe peple þan þat it doþ now' (526-7). Hoccleve is alluding to the fact that the Lords are lavish with money for their own interests, but not equally so for the benefit of their subjects. Towards the end of the **'Prologue,'** after Hoccleve's insistence on the need for a regular stipend, the Beggar reintroduces the theme of the flattery the Lords, unaware of their unpopularity, are subject to. In the **'Prologue,'** therefore, the Lords' flattery towards the king and the king's avarice towards the people combine to bring about the ruin, that is, the material poverty of the people and of the poet in particular. While the **'Prologue'** is characterized by the emphasis on the poet's personal situation, the *Regement* stresses above all the vices to be shunned, and this is the case even in the sections dedicated to a single virtue. It is here that Flattery and Avarice assume a principal role. As early as the fourth section, **'On Observing of the Laws,'** there is the description of the Flatterers who have already made a place for themselves at court and prevent the Lords from acting justly:

> But certes, fauel hath caght so sad foote
> In lordes courtes, he may naght þens slyde;
> Who com or go, algate abyde he moote;
> His craft is to susteyne ay þe wrong syde;
> And fro vertu his lorde to devide.
>
> (2941-5)

There is also here an insistence on the division, in this case inner division, which adulation effects; this will lead to social division and hence to civil war. Further on, in **'De Pietate'** (section 5), Hoccleve hurls wrathful invective at the Flatterers:

> ffor þu hast neuer þi lordys estate
> To herte chere, but al þi bysynesse
> Is for þi lucre, and þi cofres warmnesse.
>
> (3057-9)

In language taken from the world of commerce he compares them to blind merchants:

> O ffauel! a blynde marchant art þou oone,
> That, for wordly goode, & grace and fauoure.
>
> (3074-5)

From the ninth to the fifteenth section Hoccleve exploits the examples taken from the *auctores* to show the connection between Flattery and Avarice. Given that for Avarice there is no remedy (section 12) and that it is 'Roote of al harmes, fo to conscience' (4734), it is against this evil that the king must take precautions. He must practise the opposite virtue, that is, generosity, liberality, if he has his people's good at heart:

> . . . a kyng moot algates flee
> A chynches herte, for his honeste
> And for þe profyte, as I seide aboue,
> Of his peple, if he þynke wynne here loue.
>
> (4659-62)

Section 11, dedicated to liberality (and also to its abuse, prodigality) lays stress on the king's not giving heed to the Flatterers: he must follow the advice of his true counsellors and know how to make a correct choice of men to give to and the amounts to give them. Seeing that Hoccleve is asking the king for the payment of his annuity, his way of relating the general question of the liberality of the king to his personal problem as an individual and as a poet is evident. The fact is that he intends to be paid not only for his 'long labour' (4384), but also for the book he is writing (and for other works he has already written). The book in hand will serve to increase the king's 'renoun' (4400) and is dictated by good faith. In section 13, headed **'De regis prudencia,'** he returns to the subject of the payment of pensions, which a king must keep up if he wishes to retain his people's confidence. He deals with this subject indirectly, but he uses the same terms 'yeerly guerdoun' (4790). The close connection between Flattery and Avarice is repeated in section 14, and here Hoccleve advises the prince to avoid both these most dangerous evils:

> In auxenge eeke of reed, ware of fauel;
> Also ware of þe auariciouse;
> ffor none of þo two can conseile wel;
> Hir reed & conseil is envenymouse;
> Þei bothe ben of golde so desirous,
> Þei rekke naght what bryge her lorde be Inne,
> So þat þei mowen golde & siluyr wynne.
>
> (4915-21)

The conclusion to be drawn from the foregoing is that the attack on Flattery and Avarice is no mere expression of a traditional attitude to two allegorical personifications whose negative role had already been brought out in the morality plays; it is above all an attack that Hoccleve makes on the inordinately powerful members of the *camera regis*:[23] these give the sovereign bad counsel, and he makes no objection. Hoccleve does not stop at a simple description of the ills of his time but suggests an alternative: in time of peace as in time of war the king must be counselled by elderly men and not young ones, who often prove to be fool-hardy. At this point he introduces the 'sanctification' of Chaucer,[24] who is invoked as 'The firste fyndere of our faire langage' (4978), 'my fadir' (4982), 'My worthi maister Chaucer' (4983).[25] The terms used are connected with the terms in which Hoccleve's previous recommendation of elderly, expert counsellors was couched. The question raised here is what Chaucer's presence, iconographic though it may be, signifies in this part of the work.

In the first place, Chaucer is recalled as an author of sacred texts, in particular of prayers to the Virgin Mary. Then there is his portrayal in colours, as a permanent reminder for those who have perhaps forgotten him and in opposition to those who argue that images are false. Hoccleve stresses the positive value of holy images, because

> . . . whan a þing depeynt is,
> Or entailed, if men take of it heede,
> Thoght of þe lyknesse, it will in hem brede.
>
> (5003-5)

In this way he creates an association between the picture of Chaucer and likenesses of the saints, thus making of Chaucer's image an object of adoration. Just as the Beggar recalled Hoccleve's friendship with the great Chaucer in the '**Prologue**'—to the accompaniment of professions of modesty on the poet's part—so the figure of Chaucer, father and master, stands out, iconographically, at the end of the *Regement.* Chaucer's 'sanctification' is placed directly after the admonition to the king to take heed of older counsellors and before the reference to the limitations of his book:

> More othir þing, wolde I fayne speke & touche
> Heere in þis booke; but such is my dulnesse—
> ffor þat al voyde and empty is my pouche,—
> Þat al my lust is queynt with heuynesse,
> And heuy spirit comaundith stilnesse.
>
> (5013-17)

In this way Hoccleve justifies his own writing, putting his work, inadequate though it may be, in relation to the master, who is also the symbol of the type of counsellor a king should give heed to.[26] Thus the reference to those who have perhaps forgotten the master may be read as a specular allusion, which relates to the reality under Hoccleve's eyes: he is an honest labourer who, unlike the farmer, uses a pen; he deserves to be paid for what he does, because his work as an intellectual is performed in good faith, for the prince's honour, with as guide and mentor the poet who was the first to join the tradition of the classical writers. 'Aristotle', Jacobus and Aegidius are his *auctoritates,* and he can benefit by their example

because he has been a disciple in direct contact (as he asserts) or in indirect contact with the teachings of Chaucer.

This is not the end of the *Regement,* however, even though Hoccleve considers the following section (15, '**Of Peace**') as a corollary and a hoped-for condition of moral and material tranquillity that would favour writing:

> And haue I spoke of pees, I schal be stille;
> God sende vs pees, if þat it be his wille.
>
> (5018-19)

In this concluding section Hoccleve indicates on the one hand the causes of civil and foreign wars, and on the other expresses his hope for peace as the fruit of man's spiritual life, from which material peace may ensue. Stanza 723 is highly autobiographical, contrasting as it does the state of tranquillity of men at peace with themselves with the terrible state of a man without peace of mind, a man identifiable with the poet himself:

> The thrid is eke tranquillite of þought,
> Þat gydeth man to pees; for as a wight
> May in a bedde of þornes reste noght,
> Riȝt so, who is with greuous þoughtes twight,
> May with himself nor othir folk a-riȝt
> Haue no pees; a man mot nedys smert
> When irous þoughtes occupye his hert.
>
> (5055-61)

Here 'tranquillite of þought' is in contrast with 'greuous þoughtes' and 'irous þoughtes', which refer back to the beginning of the '**Prologue**,' when the poet tossed and turned in bed, a prey to disquietude. The image of the bed returns as a synecdoche in the following stanza:

> And euene as vppon a pillow softe,
> Man may him reste wele, and take his ese,
> Riȝt so þat lorde þat sittith in heuen a-lofte,
> Herte peisible can so like and plese.
>
> (5062-5)

In the '**Prologue**' the poet's sleeplessness, which has his spiritual and material insecurity at its root, is described with sea metaphors expressing instability, such as 'And when I hadde rolled vp and doun / This worldes stormy wawes in my mynde' (50-1), 'þe þoghtful wight is vessel of turment' (81), and 'Passe ouer whanne þis stormy nyght was gon' (113). Here instead the state of tranquillity that his inner peace has created suggests images of stability associated with the house: 'To crist ordeyneþ he a mancioun, / Which in his hertes habitacioun' (5023-4) and 'In place of pees, resteth our saviour' (5068).

Heart's ease and civil peace are however a hardly attainable Utopia while Flattery and Avarice still reign, and Hoccleve is obliged to admit:

> Þis is no doute, þat ambicioun
> And couetyse fyre al þis debate;
> Tho two be of wikked condicioun.
>
> (5223-5)

By-hold how auarice crepith inne,
And kyndlith werre, and quenchiþ vnite!
O fauel! þou myghtest ben of hir kynne,

(5251-3)

The two vices are the cause of inner division ('This fauel is of pees a destourbour; / Twix god and mannes soule he werre reisith;'—5258-9) and war between Christian nations ('Alase! Also, þe greet dissencioun, / The pitous harme, þe hateful discorde, / þat hath endured twix þis regioun / And othir landes cristen!'—5314-17). It is the insatiable hungering after wealth that is the cause of war, and war's effects are devastating for society as a whole:

What cornes wast, and doune trode & schent!
How many a wif and maide haþ be by layn!
Castels doun bette, and tymbred houses brent,
And drawen downe, and al to-torne and rent!

(5336-9)

Certain categories, like the 'worthi clerk famouse' (5272) and 'The knyght or sqwier, on þat other syde, / Or Ieman' (5279-80) are particularly hard hit by the injustices to which Avarice and Flattery give rise.

The poet has no need to refer to famous examples from the past to illustrate the ills of division and warfare. The disasters are there for everyone to see:

Now vnto my mateere of werre inwarde
Resort I; but to seke stories olde
Non nede is, syn þis day sharp werre & harde
Is at þe dore here, as men may be-holde.

(5286-9)

In the **'Prologue'** Hoccleve establishes the space-time co-ordinates with particular accuracy, giving his location 'At Chestre ynne, right fast be the stronde' (5), insisting on the sequence of sleepless nights, and then specifying the events of *one particular night* and *the day* of his meeting with the Beggar. Similarly, at the end of the **Regement,** in the Epilogue, he makes use of the Hundred Years' War between France and England and of the state of civil strife by way of exemplification.

Like most dream poems, this work too has a circular structure,[27] in that the epilogue refers back to the prologue: if social peace is an impossibility, there is no hope of individual peace. Assuming unity to be a basic element of peace, then the marriage of the king with Catherine of France (which was indeed celebrated in 1420) would open the way to a fusion of the two nations, France and England, and might ensure lasting peace and the people's welfare as its consequence:

Purchaseth pees by wey of mariage,
And ye þerinne schul fynden auauntage.

(5403-4)

With these lines Hoccleve's obsession comes to the surface again: he considers the attainment of material well-being as the solution to all his problems.

The structural circularity of the **Regement** is made clear by the repetition, at the end, of subject-matter expressed in the same terms as are to be found at the beginning of the **'Prologue.'** In the meditation that foreshadows the meeting with the Beggar the most frequently used terms are 'poverte', 'povert', 'thoght' ('Who so þat thoghty is, is wo-be-gon'—80), as well as terms alluding to inner division—'þe place eschewit he where as ioye is, / ffor ioye & he not mowe accorde a-ryght; / As discordant as day is vn-to nyught'; 94-6. In the last section the three components of peace, 'Conformyng in god', 'in our self humblesse' and 'And with our neigheboures tranquillite' (5035-6) are described in terms of 'concorde' (5032) and 'vnite' (5054), which may be read on both the individual and social plane.

In this way Hoccleve very skilfully induces the reader to connect the question of civil peace with man's inner peace. But the individual man who is the direct and indirect subject of the speeches of the two *personae* in the **'Prologue,'** the poet and the Beggar, is Thomas Hoccleve, product of a sinful life that has reduced him to penury, but victim also of the unjust workings of the court, which often reward the unworthy and disregard the efforts and usefulness of the intellectual. If society is divided, this division and the resulting lack of security have their repercussions on the intellectual, who cannot write because

A writer mot thre thynges to hym knytte,
And in tho may be no disseuerance;
Mynde, ee, and hand, non may fro othir flitte,
But in hem mot be ioynt continuance.

(995-8)

If a man's thoughts are taken up with economic worries, he cannot concentrate on his writing.

The mirror of Hoccleve's life (which is also reflected in the tale of the Beggar's life) is joined to the mirror of the prince's life (for which the histories of the powerful are the image). Both mirrors function positively and negatively, with vices to shun and virtues to practise. The term 'mirour' is used by Hoccleve twice only in this structural sense:[28] the first instance is at the end of the **'Prologue'** and the reference is to Chaucer, 'Mirour of fructuous entendement' (1963); the second is a reference to the governments of France and England at the end of the **Regement,** 'Yeue hem ensamplen! ye ben hir mirrours' (5328). The peoples of France and England must see themselves reflected in their rulers, as Hoccleve, because he is a poet, must see himself reflected in his master, Chaucer. The correlation Hoccleve → Chaucer and people → sovereign can also be read as Hoccleve ↔ people and Chaucer ↔ sovereign, for Hoccleve, as we have seen, seems to imply an allusion to the need to place intellectual and ruler on the same plane.

The mainspring of the poet's writing is his concern about ways and means to solve his pressing everyday financial problems. He goes beyond this aim, however, to the point of asserting that the welfare of the nation depends on a state of peace, and that the sovereign must preserve this peace with the support of able counsellors fulfilling their purpose of constant moral admonition.[29] As the 45 extant manuscripts of the **Regement** itself attest, the literary genre of the *speculum* was very popular in Hoccleve's time, and he exploits it to these ends.[30]

In conclusion, the interest of Hoccleve's work lies in the close connection between the first and second parts, the **'Prologue'** and the **Regement,** and in the 'new' use of literary genres and traditional commonplaces. On the one hand the poet uses the **'Prologue,'** the more personal part, to exalt his role as writer in its most laborious and painful aspects, and the **Regement** to show his skill in putting his literary ability to good account in a work designed to suit the widespread taste for tradition. On the other hand, as I have attempted to show, his use of the conventions is very different. There are all the most fashionable literary genres from the dream vision to the *speculum principis,* but these are copied in different ways and to a greater or lesser degree to tie in with Hoccleve's personal history. Thus there are descriptions of illness and social satire both in the **'Prologue'** and the **Regement** together with moral reflections on Hoccleve's own life and on the events of contemporary history, from the Lollard movement[31] to the greed and injustice of men at court. All these elements, however, bear the hallmark of the author's strong personality. Thus not even the sections of exemplification in the **Regement** can be considered a catalogue of more or less famous stories drawn out with the *amplificatio* technique that Lydgate was to master both in the *Troy Book* and in the *Fall of Princes;* on the contrary, there *are* these exemplary stories, but their purpose is continually to draw the future king's attention to the present—often Hoccleve's own present.

The aim of every *speculum* is certainly to advise the prince, or ruler in general, against falling into the errors of past rulers, errors which could lead ultimately to the ruin of the prince himself and of his people. The novelty of the **Regement** lies in the close connection between the prince's education and the poet's personal situation. The ills of early fifteenth-century English society are brought continually under the future king's eyes with their devastating effects: the concentration of benefices in the hands of the ecclesiastics, the greed of the gentry, the prevailing injustice that caused the old soldiers of the French wars to be forgotten, just like the 'clerkes' of Oxford and Cambridge. Both Lydgate and Hoccleve are authors of long poems, but if one may complain of the lack of invention and structure in the former,[32] the situation is different with the latter. He can be credited with considerable skill in knitting the two parts of the work together with parallels and dissimilarities so as to allow a mirror reading.

Specularity normally permits the presence of reality in a literary text[33] only by means of allusion, but in the **Regement,** Hoccleve's tales, mirroring each other, finally return the reader to the reality of the poet's own life—or at least the fictional account of it. Thus the poet's wretched situation in the present is reflected retrospectively in the past life of the old man, and the parallel 'complaints' for the soldiers and intellectuals at the beginning and end of the work respectively relate to the double role that Hoccleve is trying to assume at court, that of professional writer[34] and therefore worker, and that of poet whose originality can achieve the fusion of his personal anxieties with the traditional presentation of *exempla* for the future sovereign. And Hoccleve's achievement is all the more to be commended in that he has succeeded, not without some stylistic weaknesses and certainly with obsessive references to his lack of means, in communicating the effort needed to write, and in addition to this, the essential role of the intellectual, in a court given over to corruption, by the side of a sovereign who must abandon his policy of warfare and ensure lasting peace. Peace will bring in its train social and individual tranquillity, which is the first essential for economic prosperity and for the inner harmony Hoccleve needs to be able to write.

Notes

1. Beginning with E. P. Hammond, *English Verse between Chaucer and Surrey* (Durham, North Carolina, 1927), pp. 53-6, who observes, however, that 'his constant tendency to the autobiographical is the most interesting of his qualities', p. 54, and up to J. Mitchell, *Thomas Hoccleve: A Study in Early Fifteenth-Century English Poetic* (Urbana, Illinois, 1968). On Chaucer's influence, see D. Pearsall, 'The English Chaucerians', in D. S. Brewer, ed., *Chaucer and Chaucerians* (London, 1966), pp. 222-5, and on his metrical debt to Chaucer, cf. I. Robinson, *Chaucer's Prosody* (Cambridge, 1971), pp. 190-9. Robinson points out that it is not technique but temperament that distances Hoccleve from Chaucer, p. 197. For a brief but fact-filled history of Hoccleve criticism, see the introduction in B. O'Donoghue, ed., *Thomas Hoccleve. Selected Poems* (Manchester, 1982), pp. 7-17.

   The edition used throughout is F. J. Furnivall, ed., *Hoccleve's Works: III. The Regement of Princes and Fourteen of Hoccleve's Minor Poems,* EETS, ES 72 (London, 1897); for the other minor poems the edition used is F. J. Furnivall and I. Gollancz, eds., *Hoccleve's Works: The Minor Poems,* EETS, ES 61 and 73, 1892 and 1925, revised and reprinted as one volume by J. Mitchell and A. I. Doyle (London, 1970).

2. Medcalf in S. Medcalf, ed., *The Later Middle Ages* (London, 1981), pp. 124-40, quotes the impressions of a psychoanalyst as backing for his assertion of the autobiographical interest of Hoccleve's works, which may be considered as an account of the various phases of his depressive illness. J. Burrow examines Hoccleve criticism and analyses various meanings of the term 'autobiography' as applied to medieval and late medieval literature. He concludes that a careful examination of all Hoccleve's works 'implies, not

only that Hoccleve really does talk about himself in his poetry, but also that his departures from the imaginary norm of simple autobiographical truth are themselves best understood by reflecting upon his particular circumstances' (J. A. Burrow, 'Autobiographical Poetry in the Middle Ages: The Case of Thomas Hoccleve', *Proceedings of the British Academy* 68 (1982) 389-412, p. 412. On recent bibliography and the *Series* see the two articles of respectively J. Mitchell, 'Hoccleve Studies, 1965-1981', pp. 49-63, and J. A. Burrow, 'Hoccleve's *Series*: Experience and Books', pp. 259-73, in R. F. Yeager, ed., *Fifteenth Century Studies: Recent Essays* (Hamden, Conn., 1984).

3. The analogy between themes present in the tradition of the penitential lyric and Hoccleve's poetry is shown in E. M. Thornley, 'The Middle English Penitential Lyric and Hoccleve's Autobiographical Poetry', *Neuphilologische Mitteilungen* 68 (1967) 295-321.

4. On the influence of Boethius, see, among others, P. B. R. Doob, *Nebuchadnezzar's Children: Conventions of Madness in Middle English Literature* (New Haven, Conn., 1974), pp. 216-19, where Hoccleve's obsessive preoccupation with physical and mental illness as a consequence of sin is particularly stressed (pp. 208-31).

5. Lewis, while he devotes very few lines to Hoccleve, yet associates him with Aeschylus for his skill in describing the anxiety of a man who is the prey to his own preoccupations, personified in Thought—C. S. Lewis, *The Allegory of Love* (Oxford, 1936), pp. 238-9.

6. On metaphor frequency in general, cf. Mitchell, *T. Hoccleve,* p. 60.

7. On the mirror for the prince as a popular genre in fifteenth-century English literature, see D. Bornstein, 'Reflections of Political Theory and Political Fact in Fifteenth-Century Mirrors for the Prince', in J. B. Bessinger, Jr. and R. R. Raymo, eds., *Medieval Studies. In Honor of Lillian Herlands Hornstein* (New York, 1976), pp. 77-85. See also A. M. Kinghorn, *The Chorus of History. Literary-historical relations in Renaissance Britain* (London, 1971), ch. 11.

8. The texts used by Hoccleve are in fact the *Secreta Secretorum,* considered as a collection of Aristotle's admonitions to the young Alexander, Aegidius Romanus' *de Regimine Principum* and Jacobus de Cessolis' *Liber de Ludo Scaccorum.* On these sources of Hoccleve's see W. Matthews, 'Thomas Hoccleve', in A. E. Hartung, *A Manual of the Writings in Middle English 1050-1500,* iii (1972), pp. 903-8; A. H. Gilbert, 'Notes on the Influence of the *Secretum Secretorum*', *Speculum* 3 (1928) 84-98, especially pp. 93-8, and the introduction to the facsimile edition in N. F. Blake, ed., *Jacobus de Cessolis, The Game of Chess. Translated and printed by W. Caxton, c.1483* (London, 1976).

9. Medcalf, *The Later Middle Ages,* p. 131.

10. See P. Boitani, *English Medieval Narrative in the 13th & 14th Centuries* (Cambridge, 1982), ch. 4.

11. C. B. Hieatt, '*Un Autre Fourme*: Guillaume de Machaut and the Dream Vision Form', *Chaucer Review* 14 (1979) 97-115, especially pp. 105-8.

12. On the circulation and the importance of petitions in Hoccleve's time see A. L. Brown, *The Privy Seal in the Early Fifteenth Century* (D.Phil. thesis, Oxford, 1954), ch. II. See also R. F. Green, *Poets and Princepleasers: Literature and the English Court in the Late Middle Ages* (Toronto, 1980), pp. 42-3 and J. A. Burrow, 'The Poet as Petitioner', *Studies in the Age of Chaucer* 3 (1981) 61-75.

13. *Regement*: ll. 4399-403.

14. On the portrayal of Prudence as triple-faced as well as double-faced in the iconography of the fourteenth and fifteenth centuries, see H. Schwarz, 'The Mirror in Art', *The Art Quarterly* 15 (1952) 97-118, especially pp. 104-5.

15. On the question of peace through union of the two kingdoms of France and England, cf. R. P. Adams, 'Pre-Renaissance Courtly Propaganda for Peace in English Literature', *Papers of the Michigan Academy* 32 (1946) 431-46, especially pp. 440-3; Bornstein, 'Reflections of Political Theory', pp. 81-2. On dual monarchy in the reign of Henry VI, see J. W. McKenna, 'Henry VI of England and the Dual Monarchy: Aspects of Royal Political Propaganda, 1422-1432', *Journal of the Warburg and Courtauld Institutes* 28 (1965) 145-63, especially pp. 145-53.

16. On the popularity of dream poetry among middle-class readers, cf. W. F. Schirmer, *John Lydgate. A Study in the Culture of the XVth Century,* trans. A. E. Keep (Westport, Conn., 1961), pp. 36-7. In addition see P. Strohm's interesting article, 'Chaucer's Audience', *Literature and History* 5 (1977) 26-41, which, although it deals with the public reached by Chaucer, can also be partly applied to Hoccleve.

17. *De Consolatione Philosophiae* IV, pr. 2.

18. Cf. A. Torti, 'La funzione dei "Vizi" nella struttura del *Morality Play* del Primo Periodo Tudor', *Annali della Facoltà di Lettere e Filosofia dell' Università di Perugia* 14 (1976-1977) 177-217.

19. Bornstein, 'Reflections of Political Theory', p. 81.

20. On the structure of the morality play, see the excellent, still valid introduction to the edition of *Magnyfycence* in R. L. Ramsay, ed., *Magnyfycence, by J. Skelton,* EETS, ES 98 (London, 1908); see also E. N. S. Thompson, 'The English Moral Play', *Transactions of the Connecticut Academy of Arts and Sciences* 14 (1910) 291-414.

21. In *The Castle of Perseverance,* the oldest morality play in English that has come down to us with an

unmutilated text and the whole range of vices and virtues, one among the Seven Deadly Sins, Covetousness, dominates all the others on stage.

22. On the complex relationship between poets and court in the late Middle Ages, see Green, *Poets and Princepleasers*. In his capacity as clerk of the Privy Seal, Hoccleve was not in a very high social position, as R. F. Green shows in his essay 'The *Familia Regis* and the *Familia Cupidinis*', in V. J. Scattergood and J. W. Sherborne, eds., *English Court Culture in the Later Middle Ages* (London, 1983), 87-108, p. 106. On Hoccleve's work as scribe, cf. H. C. Schulz, 'Thomas Hoccleve, Scribe', *Speculum* 12 (1937) 71-81 and A. Compton Reeves, 'Thomas Hoccleve, Bureaucrat', *Medievalia et Humanistica* 5 (1974) 201-14.

23. On the role of the king's chamber in the late Middle Ages, see Green, *Poets and Princepleasers*, especially ch. 2.

24. On the importance of the iconographic representation of Chaucer in the *Regement* and on Chaucer's role as a sort of prototype counsellor of princes, see J. H. McGregor's interesting article, 'The Iconography of Chaucer in Hoccleve's *De Regimine Principum* and in the *Troilus* frontispiece', *Chaucer Review* 11 (1976-77) 338-50.

25. On the difficult Chaucerian heritage received by his fifteenth-century followers, see the enlightening essay by A. C. Spearing, 'Chaucerian Authority and Inheritance', in P. Boitani and A. Torti, eds., *Literature in Fourteenth-Century England* (Tübingen and Cambridge, 1983), pp. 185-202, especially pp. 199-202.

26. Cf. McGregor, 'The Iconography of Chaucer', pp. 342-5.

27. On the circular structure of *Pearl,* for example, see '*Pearl*: the circle as figural space', in C. Nelson, *The Incarnate Word. Literature as Verbal Space* (Urbana, Chicago and London, 1973), pp. 25-49.

28. If exception is made for verse 1441: 'Hem hoghte to be mirours of sadnesse', referring to Parsons who give themselves up to lustful living instead of cultivating humilty and moral virtue.

29. Cf. McGregor, 'The Iconography of Chaucer', p. 342.

30. See Green, *Poets and Princepleasers*, especially ch. 5.

31. On Hoccleve's attacks on the Lollards, also in the 'Address to Sir John Oldcastle', cf. Green, *Poets and Princepleasers,* pp. 183-6.

32. D. Pearsall, *Gower and Lydgate* (London, 1969), p. 27.

33. On textual specularity, from Homer to modern literature, see Françoise Létoublon's article, 'Le miroir et la boucle', *Poétique* 53 (1983) 19-36, especially pp. 21-4.

34. On the possibility of Henry V's having commissioned Hoccleve to write the Address to Oldcastle as a form of propaganda against the Lollards, see Green, *Poets and Princepleasers,* pp. 185-6.

Karen A. Winstead (essay date 1993)

SOURCE: Winstead, Karen A. "'I am al othir to yow than yee weene': Hoccleve, Women, and the *Series*." *Philological Quarterly* 72, no. 2 (1993): 143-55.

[*In this essay, Winstead addresses the question of whether Hoccleve's praise of women is genuine or satiric, focusing on two poems from the* Series, *"Jereslaus's Wife" and "Jonathas and Fellicula." Winstead considers the role of the bumbling narrator, whose "praise" of women may effectively function as criticism.*]

In 1399, Christine de Pisan began her assault on the misogynistic writings that were so popular in late medieval Europe with her *Epistre au dieu d'amours,* a poem in which Cupid defends women against what Christine considered the defamation of their sex by Jean de Meun and other male authors.[1] Only three years later, the English Chaucerian Thomas Hoccleve produced an adaptation of the *Epistre,* the **"Letter of Cupid."**[2] Unlike Christine's poem, which scholars regard as a straightforward defense of women, Hoccleve's work has been the subject of dispute. Critics concur that the English adaptation parodies Christine's original, but they have differed as to the degree and the intent of the parody. Jerome Mitchell argued that, although passages in Hoccleve's work are humorous, "the **"Letter of Cupid,"** viewed as a whole, is at least as feminist in outlook as its French source."[3] In much the same vein, Derek Pearsall remarked that the **"Cupid"** "shows that Hoccleve could laugh at women as well as himself."[4] Going further than Pearsall, John V. Fleming not only found "no evidence of antifeminism," but denied that Hoccleve is in fact laughing at women in the **"Cupid."**[5] Rather, Fleming maintained, Hoccleve is poking fun at Christine de Pisan's misreading of Jean de Meun's *Roman de la Rose* as an antifeminist diatribe. More recently, Diane Bornstein has described Hoccleve's God of Love as a "jester" whose maladroit defense of women is frankly satirical.[6] According to Bornstein, "The exaggerated defense that Cupid offers in support of women, the proverbial language used to comment on their behavior, the omission of actual and literary examples of the good deeds of women, and the omission or softening of Christine's criticism of disrespectful men and anti-feminist clerks all combine to undermine Christine's argument and make the work more of a parody of feminism rather than a judicious, courtly defense of women."[7]

Though modern readers debate whether to classify Hoccleve's **"Letter of Cupid"** as feminist or antifeminist, they agree that some women in Hoccleve's audience may not have appreciated his sense of humor. In fact, Hoccleve himself admits as much in a later work, his framed fiction now known as the *Series*.[8] The *Series* consists of four texts—**"The Complaint," "The Tale of Jereslaus's Wife," "Learn to Die,"** and **"The Tale of Jonathas and Fellicula"**—linked by a **"Dialogue"** [**"Dialogues with a Friend"**] between the author of those texts, "Thomas Hoccleve," and an unnamed Friend. In the course of that **"Dialogue,"** the Friend chides Thomas for having offended women "in thepistle of Cupyde," claiming, "Thow haast of hem so largeliche said, / That they been swart wrooth & ful euele apaid" (137/754-56). Thomas responds to this charge with befuddled indignation. He first concedes that some portions of the **"Letter of Cupid"** "sowneth but right smal to hir honour" (758), but protests that women should not blame him for merely translating an offensive text (759-67). Having said that, he reverses himself and accuses his critics of misreading his work: Cupid was *defending* women, not impugning them (137-38/768-80). Finally, he concedes that "it may wel sitte / To axe pardoun thogh I nat trespace" (139/815-16), and he proposes to translate a tale about a virtuous woman, the **"Tale of Jereslaus's Wife,"** to atone for his earlier work.

The **"Dialogue"** I have just described has not attracted as much critical scrutiny as the **"Letter of Cupid,"** yet it, too, has been subject to disparate interpretations. Jerome Mitchell accepted the sincerity of Hoccleve's apology, John Fleming and Jill Mann argued that the **"Dialogue"** is merely a reworking of Chaucer's Prologue to the *Legend of Good Women*, while John Burrow claimed that, despite the obvious debt to Chaucer, "Hoccleve's defense of the **"Letter of Cupid"** . . . leaves an impression of real anxiety" that attests to women's influence as readers.[9]

In this essay, I propose that we can best understand Hoccleve's intentions in the *Series* by considering his two embedded tales, **"Jereslaus's Wife"** and **"Jonathas."** Though written to illustrate the virtue or villainy of women, these stories have been peripheral to most discussions of Hoccleve's feminism or antifeminism.[10] I will argue that when we examine Hoccleve's **"Dialogue"** about women in conjunction with his two inscribed tales, we find that the *Series* is in fact an antifeminist continuation of the **"Letter of Cupid."** As such, it targets "feminist" readers, like Christine de Pisan, who resent all criticism of their sex. Hoccleve resumes his baiting of fractious women by promising an apology for his literary misdeeds but delivering a work that reproduces the principal themes and strategies of the **"Cupid."** In Thomas, for example, he creates a narrator whose admiration for women is as dubious as Cupid's, and whose tales, like Cupid's epistle, provide a platform for the misogynistic rhetoric he purports to reject. Though **"Jereslaus's Wife"** may seem to be "an unexceptionable example of wifely virtue . . . quite untinged by irony,"[11] Thomas repeatedly interrupts the story with clumsy tributes to women that vitiate its effectiveness as a pro-woman exemplum. Adding injury to insult, Hoccleve concludes the *Series* with a tale of feminine perfidy, **"Jonathas and Fellicula,"** that was bound to offend "overly sensitive" women. Taken together,

"Jereslaus's Wife" and **"Jonathas and Fellicula"** form an artfully constructed antifeminist joke, which mocks disorderly women in general and "feminist" readers in particular.

Hoccleve begins making fun of contentious female readers in the portion of the **"Dialogue"** that introduces the **"Tale of Jereslaus's Wife."** Invoking Chaucer's *archewyf*, Alison of Bath, as his "auctrice," the Friend warns Thomas that "wommen han no ioie ne deyntee / þat men sholde vp-on hem putte any vice" (135/695-96). Driven by their craving for "rule and gouernance" (135/718), women have already wrested "maistrie" from their husbands; "Though holy writ witnesse and testifie / Men sholde of hem han dominacioun" (136/732-34). Thomas cannot afford such enemies: "Humble thy goost be nat sturdy of herte; / Bettre than thow art han they maad to smerte" (134/692-93). Swayed by the Friend's arguments, Thomas resolves to regain women's favor, though he grumbles that he still cannot fathom why they are upset with him (138-39/799-826).

However ungraciously Thomas undertakes his penance, he appears to deliver exactly what the Friend insists his critics want, namely, a paean to feminine virtue. The **"Tale of Jereslaus's Wife,"** which Hoccleve adapted from a popular collection of moralized tales, the *Gesta Romanorum,* is one of many romances of long-suffering wives whose goodness is described in quasihagiographical terms.[12] At first, this tale seems especially suited to Thomas's critics, for its protagonist is a Roman empress whose husband gives her absolute sovereignty over the realm during his pilgrimage to the Holy Land. Despite this auspicious beginning, the **"Tale of Jereslaus's Wife"** develops in a way that could only irritate proponents of feminine *maistrie*. Though the heroine is undeniably virtuous, she proves to be an ineffectual regent, unwilling or unable to restrain her brother-in-law, the steward, who takes advantage of the emperor's absence by robbing the rich and oppressing the poor. When he attempts to seduce her, she finally has him imprisoned, but he eventually persuades her to release him only to betray her. This time, his perfidy consigns her to years of exile.

The poor judgment Jereslaus's wife displays both in her dealings with the steward and in her willingness during her exile to trust one scurrilous man after another does not say much for women's capacity for "rule and gouernance." Furthermore, though the tale begins by emphasizing the heroine's power, most of it deals with her victimization at the hands of men. Passive in the face of misfortune, Jereslaus's wife never attempts to remedy her situation or to recover her lost status. Only when her chastity is threatened does she assert herself. She repulses would-be lovers with the zeal of a saint, swearing that she would rather die than betray her wedding vows. The story of this "humble lamb" (161/610), this "treewe wyf" (143/92), with her Griselda-like patience and devotion to her husband, is in fact a slap in the face to the unruly wives in Thomas's audience, who have forgotten their place in the divinely-ordained gender hierarchy.

Not only does Thomas flout his critics with the kind of story he tells, but his commentary repeatedly undercuts the tale's flattering portrayal of women. His praise of women often seems exaggerated and insincere, reminiscent, as I mentioned earlier, of the **"Letter of Cupid."** The introduction of Jereslaus's wife, for example, suggests that Thomas is not simply praising a good woman but that he is consciously constructing a heroine to whom no one could object. Having described the empress's beauty, he adds, "And *for þat* beautee in womman, allone / Withouten bontee, is nat commendable, / Shee was *ther-to* a vertuous persone" (140/8-10, my emphasis). Later in the tale, he offers this left-handed tribute to women:

> In [al] the world so louynge tendrenesse
> Is noon as is the loue of a womman
> To hir chyld namely & as I gesse,
> To hire housbonde also where-of witnesse
> We weddid men may bere if þat vs lyke
>
> (154/393-98)

Thomas's blanket commendation of wives and mothers sounds suspiciously like the facetious tribute to husbands in the Chaucer's "Man of Law's Tale": "Housbondes been alle goode, and han ben yoore; / That knowen wyves; I dar sey na moore."[13] Our understanding of Thomas's assertion that "We weddid men" may bear witness to the solicitude of wives for their husbands ("if þat vs lyke") is strongly colored by his earlier indication that his own wife is something of a shrew (136/739-42). Readers might well conclude that Thomas's experience of women is at odds with the supposed authority of the text he is translating as well as with the message he has undertaken to transmit.

Thomas is no more convincing when he tries to use the empress's good example to exonerate women as a class. He begins by making the politic claim that his heroine's faithfulness proves that women, contrary to popular opinion, are never fickle, that "Constance is vn-to wommanhode entaillid," and that "Swich hir nature is" (157/484-90). His stout defense of women soon wavers, however: "They stidefast been *as fer as y woot*" (491, my emphasis)—unless, indeed, they need to cover up a mistake in order to preserve their reputation:

> But it be wher they take han a purpos
> Þat naght is which, be it neuere so hoot,
> They change lest it hurte mighte hir loos,
> And keepen it secree couert & cloos
>
> (157/492-5)

His greatest blunder, however, occurs at the end of the narrative, when, after describing the empress's joyful reunion with her husband, he observes that many men would prefer a long-lost wife to remain lost:

> O many a wrecche is in this lond, y weene
> Þat thogh his wyf lengere had been him fro,
> No kus but if it had been of the spleene,
> Shee sholde han had & forthermore also,
> ffyndynge of hire had been to him but wo,

> ffor him wolde han thoght þat swich a fyndynge,
> To los sholde han him torned, and harmynge.
>
> (173/939-45)

Hoccleve then deprives his tale of its force as a testimony to women's goodness by appending a prose "moralizacio" informing readers that **"Jereslaus's Wife"** is not about a virtuous woman at all; rather, it is an allegory of the inter-relationship of Christ, the soul, and the body. As if anticipating the objection that he has therefore failed to fulfill his promise to write a tale about feminine virtue, Thomas insists that the "moralizacio" was the Friend's idea, not his. He explains that, on reading **"Jereslaus's Wife,"** the Friend complained that Thomas had left out the moral. When Thomas protested that his source did not include a moral, the Friend supplied one, and Thomas dutifully translated it. This disclaimer should not, however, mislead us. The allegorization of **"Jereslaus's Wife"** fits in beautifully with the other acts of sabotage that Thomas has committed against his assignment of praising women. Thomas the narrator may not be able to control the direction of his work, but Hoccleve the author is adhering to his design of mocking troublesome women.

Although Thomas offers the **"Tale of Jereslaus's Wife"** as an apology for the **"Letter of Cupid,"** the tale is in many respects a restatement of that earlier work. In effect, **"Jereslaus's Wife"** recasts in narrative form Cupid's complaint about how easy it is for "a sely symple and Innocent woman" to be betrayed through the "sleyght and sotilte" of men.[14] Thomas even echoes Cupid's language. Just as Cupid had exclaimed, "O feythful woman ful of Innocence, / thou arte deceyved be fals apparence!"[15] Thomas laments, "O noble lady symple and Innocent, / Trustynge vp-on [man's] ooth and his promesse" (146/169-70). For all his protestations of sympathy for women, Thomas, like Cupid, is something of a buffoon, and he proves no better than Cupid at defending women.

The similarities between **"Jereslaus's Wife"** and the **"Letter of Cupid"** are not the only instances of mischievous parallelism, for Thomas's situation *vis à vis* his female readers is inscribed in various ways within the text. Most obviously, the tale features a protagonist who, like Thomas's readers, is repeatedly betrayed by men. Yet the recurrence of motifs from the **"Letter of Cupid"** in this tale suggests that Thomas himself is a bit like his protagonist, for he, too, fails to learn from old mistakes. Or were they mistakes? After all, "Jereslaus's Wife" is also about a character, the steward, who twice makes an insincere confession, a "lewde shrifte" (168/792). As Hoccleve's apology to women, is the **"Tale of Jereslaus's Wife"** merely a blunder—or is it a "lewde shrifte"?

Hoccleve's second inscribed narrative, the **"Tale of Jonathas and Fellicula,"** answers this question. As he did in introducing **"Jereslaus's Wife,"** Thomas insists that he never intended to produce **"Jonathas"** and that it does not fit into the overall design of his work. He claims that, having just completed **"Learn to Die,"** he intended to bring the *Series* to a close when his Friend again intervened: "This booke thus to han endid had y thoght, / But my freend made me change my cast; / Cleene out of þat purpos hath he me broght" (215/1-3). The Friend, Thomas explains, asked him to translate yet another story from the *Gesta Romanorum*—this one about a perfidious woman, whose example, the Friend hopes, will both warn young men about the dangers of consorting with loose women and also serve to "rebuke . . . the wantonnesse / Of lyf of many a womman þat is nakid / Of honestee and with deshonour blakid" (218/73-75). Thomas protests that translating such a story flies in the face of the Friend's earlier advice to propitiate women:

> This þat yee me now reede is al contrarie
> Vn-to þat yee me red han heer-before;
> Yee seiden syn y many an aduersarie
> Had of wommen for y mis had me bore
> To hem or this; yee redden me therfore
> Humble me to hem and of grace hem preye;
> But this reed haldith al an othir weye.
>
> (217/50-56)

The Friend, however, dusting off one of Cupid's old arguments, claims that a writer does not impugn the virtue of good women simply by castigating bad ones (218/60-70).[16] Thomas reluctantly acquiesces.

Despite Thomas's claim that **"Jonathas"** does not belong in the *Series* and that it undermines the themes he had cultivated in the **"Tale of Jereslaus's Wife,"** the two tales have much in common. In fact, their plots are virtually identical. Jonathas, like Jereslaus's wife, repeatedly gets into trouble by trusting the opposite sex. He inherits three magical "iewelles" from his father, the emperor, and takes each in turn with him to the university. Each time, his mistress, Fellicula, tricks him into revealing his treasure's powers and entrusting it to her care. Like Jereslaus's wife, Jonathas at length takes steps to deal with his adversary: suspecting that Fellicula has stolen rather than lost his magic ring and brooch, he flies her to the end of the world on his magic carpet, intending to leave her there. Fellicula, however, displays the same cunning as the imprisoned steward. She promises to mend her ways, then promptly betrays Jonathas by escaping on his carpet and stranding him at the world's end. Stripped of wealth and status, Jonathas, like Jereslaus's wife, endures a long exile.

The conclusions of the two tales are also remarkably similar. After years of wandering, Jereslaus's wife takes refuge in a convent, where she becomes famous for her healing powers. When the men who have wronged her arrive at the convent stricken with disease, the disguised empress demands that they confess their sins (and in so doing their roles in her misfortunes) before she will cure them. In the course of his exile, Jonathas likewise acquires healing skills, and upon returning home, he sets up a medical practice. When Fellicula asks him to treat her for an illness, he, like Jereslaus's wife, insists that she first confess her misdeeds. Here the exact parallel between the tales ends. Jereslaus's wife forgives her enemies and cures them, displaying the same mercy that she has shown all along. Jonathas, however, has learned from his experience. Once Fellicula has revealed the whereabouts of his stolen treasures, he treats her with magical water that sears flesh and magical fruit that causes leprosy; together, they bring Fellicula to an appropriately gruesome end.

It might seem that, by retelling **"The Tale of Jereslaus's Wife"** with a male protagonist and a female villain, Thomas is simply producing stories with contradictory views of women—one praising them, the other censuring them. Indeed, as I noted earlier, this is Thomas's own criticism. However, the tales are complementary. **"Jereslaus's Wife"** recounts the adventures of a chaste wife whose example challenges misogynistic stereotypes of women, yet the narrator's concluding remarks suggest that many, if not most, women are unlike the protagonist (173/939-45). Whereas that tale fails to disprove antifeminist stereotypes, **"Jonathas"** explicitly confirms them. At the beginning of the tale, Jonathas knows that, since women are inherently duplicitous, he should not trust Fellicula:

> Swich is wommannes inconstant nature,
> They can nat keepe conseil worth a risshe;
> Bettre is, my tonge keepe than to wisshe
> Þat y had kept cloos þat is goon at large,
> And repentance is thyng þat y moot charge.
>
> (222/192-96)

However, he is willing to believe that his mistress is an exception to the rule. When he finally realizes his error, he does not decry the woman who deceived him but his own stupidity in ignoring the conventional wisdom about women in general:

> . . . al this wel disserued y haue.
> What eilid me to be so euel auysid,
> That my Con`seil kowde I nat keepe & saue?
> Who can fool pleye who can madde or raue,
> But he þat to a womman his secree
> Deskeuereth the smert cleueth now on me.
>
> (232/450-55)

Whereas Thomas's comments often subvert the favorable portrayal of women in **"Jereslaus's Wife,"** in **"Jonathas"** his remarks consistently reinforce the tale's warning against women's duplicity. For example, he points out that Fellicula, in feigning distress at losing her lover's ring, is simply employing a standard feminine wile, behaving "As sum womman othir whyle atte beste / Can lye and weepe whan is hir lykyng" (224/248-49). Even his attitude towards Jonathas's mother seems ambiguous, as we see in this passage "praising" widows like the empress for accepting their husbands' deaths with composure:

> In þat cas wommen han swich heuynesse,
> Þat it nat lyth in my konnynge aright
> Yow telle of so greet sorwe the excesse,
> But wyse wommen konne take it light,
> And in short whyle putte vn-to the flight
> Al sorwe and wo and cacche ageyn confort.
>
> (220-21/141-46)

Phrases such as "take it light," "in short whyle," and "al sorwe" hint that "wyse wommen" may display a little too much equanimity in their bereavement to suit Thomas.

Taken together, the two inscribed tales present a consistent view not only of women's "real" nature but of their "proper" role: the first story praises and rewards a chaste wife who is willing to overlook even the grossest transgressions on the part of men; the second tale punishes a thief who, significantly, steals not merely Jonathas's wealth but the very *sources* of his wealth and power that he had inherited from his father. Symbolically, Fellicula is as much a threat to social order as Thomas's disruptive critics, who have seized the authority God conferred upon their husbands and now seek to arrogate his prerogative as an author by dictating what he should write. In Jonathas's destruction of Fellicula, Hoccleve delivers a final blow to the disorderly woman, as wife, reader, and literary character alike.

Though there is much in the *Series* that might offend women—especially women who were already unhappy with the **"Letter of Cupid"**—Hoccleve surely did not intend to antagonize all of his female readers. Indeed, he dedicated an autograph manuscript of the *Series*, Durham University MS Cosin V.III.9, to Joan Beaufort, Countess of Westmorland, the daughter of John of Gaunt and Catherine Swynford.[17] Perhaps he assumed that Joan Beaufort (and most other women, for that matter) would not regard herself as a "disorderly" woman and hence would not take his jibes personally. Yet there may be more in Hoccleve's dedication of the Durham manuscript to Lady Westmorland than meets the eye. After all, Lady Westmorland's name was linked to that of an actual "disorderly woman," Margery Kempe. Kempe was exactly the type of woman Hoccleve had in mind when, in his 1415 **"Address to Sir John Oldcastle,"** he railed against "lewde calates" who, forgetting their proper roles in society, "wole argumentes make in holy writ."[18] We learn from Kempe's *Book* that she had visited Lady Westmorland between 1415 and 1417, and that the countess was "wel plesyd" with her and "lykyd wel [her] wordys."[19] It was also rumored—a charge Kempe denied—that she had encouraged Lady Westmorland's daughter to leave her husband.[20] Though we do not know the details of Kempe's association with Joan Beaufort—or of Hoccleve's knowledge of their association—we cannot dismiss the possibility that, in dedicating the Durham manuscript to Lady Westmorland, Hoccleve intended an oblique criticism of the countess.

The highly personal tone of the *Series* has led many critics to identify the author, Hoccleve, with his narrator, Thomas.[21] That association, however, is misleading. Though Thomas, as presented by Hoccleve, is a bumbler whose authorial agenda is set by the caprice of his Friend, the *Series* reveals substantial unity of design and purpose. Hoccleve's self-parody is a strategic device in his literary war of the sexes. On the one hand, having a mock Hoccleve apologize to mock women for the **"Letter of Cupid"** underscores the insincerity of Hoccleve's "repentance." At

the same time, Hoccleve's caricature of himself blunts the antifeminism of the **"Dialogue"** and the tales, for it allows readers to interpret his mockery of women as nothing more than good-natured fun. Before beginning **"Jereslaus's Wife,"** Thomas assures women, "I am al othir to yow than yee weene; / By my wrytynge hath it, & shal be, seene" (139/811-12). By the end of the *Series,* some women, at least, must have concluded that Thomas is exactly what his fictional critics accused him of being, and that Hoccleve himself is a dubious "freend" (139/810). Hoccleve's playfulness, however, neatly deflects criticism, for the woman who complains risks being classed among the disorderly wives and bad readers of the **"Dialogue,"** who insist on making *ernest* of *game.*

I have argued that far from repudiating the **"Letter of Cupid,"** the *Series* reaffirms Hoccleve's earlier work. Thomas is in many respects a reincarnation of Cupid, a buffoon who insults women even as he "tries" to praise them. The *Series* continues the project Hoccleve began in the **"Cupid"** of twitting "feminist" readers who share Christine de Pisan's sensitivity to criticism of their sex. As they are portrayed in the **"Dialogue,"** such readers exemplify the misogynistic stereotypes that **"Jereslaus's Wife"** supposedly refutes and that **"Jonathas"** confirms. Though the **"Dialogue"** introducing **"Jereslaus's Wife"** cautions that an author can ill afford to rile female readers and that men who cross women may expect a violent response (134-36/680-749), the *Series* concludes with a tale warning women that feminine unruliness ultimately has its price. Through his treatment of disorderly women in the *Series,* Hoccleve demonstrates to his readers—both male and female—that authors as well as women can be dangerous to offend.

Notes

1. *Oeuvres poètiques de Christine de Pisan,* ed. Maurice Roy (Paris: Didot, 1891), 2:1-27.

2. *Hoccleve's Works: The Minor Poems,* ed. Frederick J. Furnivall and I. Gollancz, EETS, ES 61, 73 (1892, 1925; reprint, London: Oxford U. Press, 1970), 72-91.

3. *Thomas Hoccleve: A Study in Early Fifteenth-Century English Poetic* (U. of Illinois Press, 1968), 53.

4. "The English Chaucerians," *Chaucer and Chaucerians: Critical Studies in Middle English Literature* (U. of Alabama Press, 1966), 225.

5. "Hoccleve's '*Letter of Cupid*' and the '*Quarrel*' over the *Roman de la Rose*," *Medium Aevum* 40 (1971): 23.

6. "Anti-feminism in Thomas Hoccleve's Translation of Christine de Pizan's *Epistre au dieu d'amours*," *ELN* 19 (1981): 7-14. William A. Quinn has also described Hoccleve's Cupid as a "buffoon" in "Hoccleve's *Epistle of Cupid*," *Explicator* 45 (1986): 9.

7. Bornstein, 14.

8. *Hoccleve's Works: The Minor Poems*, 95-242. I will use this edition for all page/line references.

9. Mitchell, 53; Fleming, 25; Mann, "Apologies to Women," Inaugural lecture delivered at the University of Cambridge, 20th November 1990 (Cambridge U. Press, 1991), 21-22; Burrow, "Hoccleve's *Series*: Experience and Books," *Fifteenth-Century Studies: Recent Essays,* ed. Robert F. Yeager (Hamden, Ct.: Archon Books, 1984), 269-70. John M. Bowers, accepting the sincerity of Hoccleve's apology, has used the renunciation of the "Cupid" in the *Series* as evidence in dating Hoccleve's autograph manuscripts. See "Hoccleve's Huntington Holographs: The First 'Collected Poems' in English," *Fifteenth-Century Studies* 15 (1989): 40.

10. Exceptions are Mann, who briefly discussed "Jereslaus's Wife" (21-22) but did not consider "Jonathas," and Mitchell, who described "Jereslaus's Wife" as Hoccleve's "supreme contribution to medieval feminist literature" (55). To my knowledge there have been no extended discussions of Hoccleve's two inscribed tales except in Mitchell's book (43-47, 86-96).

11. Janet Cowen, "Women as Exempla in Fifteenth-Century Verse of the Chaucerian Tradition," *Chaucer and Fifteenth-Century Poetry,* ed. Julia Boffey and Janet Cowen (London: King's College Centre for Late Antique and Medieval Studies, 1991), 62.

12. Dieter Mehl discusses three other such romances (*The King of Tars, Emaré,* and *Le Bone Florence of Rome*) in his chapter on "homiletic romances" in *The Middle English Romances of the Thirteenth and Fourteenth Centuries* (London: Routledge & Kegan Paul, 1968), 120-158. See also K. A. Winstead, "Saints, Wives, and Other 'Hooly Thyngers': Pious Laywomen in Middle English Romance," *Chaucer Yearbook* 2 (1993): forthcoming.

13. *The Riverside Chaucer,* ed. Larry D. Benson [based on F. N. Robinson, ed., *The Works of Geoffrey Chaucer* 2nd ed.] (Boston: Houghton Mifflin, 1987), MLT 272-73.

14. "Letter of Cupid," 78-80.

15. "Letter of Cupid," 41-42.

16. "Letter of Cupid," 148-54.

17. *Hoccleve's Works,* 242.

18. *Hoccleve's Works,* 13/146-47.

19. *The Book of Margery Kempe,* ed. Sanford Brown Meech, EETS.OS 212 (Oxford U. Press, 1940), 133-34.

20. *The Book of Margery Kempe,* 133.

21. D. C. Greetham has criticized the longstanding tendency of scholars to take Hoccleve "at his word," insisting that we must distinguish the author from his persona. Yet even Greetham continues the confusing practice of using "Hoccleve" to refer to both author and narrator. See "Self-Referential Artifacts: Hoccleve's Persona as Literary Device," *MP* 86 (1989): 242-51.

Charity Scott Stokes (essay date 1995)

SOURCE: Stokes, Charity Scott. "Thomas Hoccleve's *Mother of God* and *Balade to the Virgin and Christ*: Latin and Anglo-Normal Sources." *Medium Aevum* 64, no. 1 (1995): 74-84.

[*In the essay below, Stokes examines Hoccleve's sources in order to better appreciate his art and rehabilitate his reputation as a poet. Stokes looks at the influence of the Latin Prayer* O intemerata et in aeternum benedicta, specialis et incomparabilis virgo *on Hoccleve's "Mother of God." She also discusses various Anglo-Norman sources for his "Balade to the Virgin and Christ," including several on women and courtly love.*]

The tide of critical appreciation has been turning in favour of Thomas Hoccleve's poetry in recent decades. One of the first scholars to write more positively of Hoccleve's work than had been customary was Jerome Mitchell, whose major re-evaluation was published in 1968.[1] Two selections of Hoccleve's verse are now available in paperback editions.[2] Acknowledgement of his achievements is extending beyond the areas of interest conceded even by disparaging critics: beyond the successful expression of his indebtedness to his master, Chaucer; beyond the vivid detailing of the malady that afflicted him in 1416 when the substance of his memory 'went to pleie as for a certein space';[3] beyond his skilful use of apostrophe and dialogue. Hoccleve was a Privy Seal clerk, so that much of his time was spent writing official letters and documents, which may have given rise in the past to a feeling that his writing is likely to be dreary, but attention has now been drawn to the interesting professional 'bookishness' or 'bookness' of Hoccleve's texts, as well as to the sophisticated creation of the 'book-making' persona in his final sequence of poems.[4] The holograph manuscripts are carefully and clearly written.[5] The introduction to a recent edition of his **'Letter of Cupid,'** which is an abridged translation, or adaptation, of Christine de Pizan's *Epistre,* comments on the 'lively, oddly whimsical, accomplished' aspects of Hoccleve's writing, and to the 'slipperiness' of his apparent anxious sympathy towards women, which has perhaps mistakenly been interpreted as naive and lacking in complexity.[6] Even his metres and versification are receiving neutral, if not positive, appraisal.[7]

The case for a positive re-assessment of the poems is put by M. C. Seymour in the introduction to his *Selections from Hoccleve,* where it is affirmed that future individual studies will make possible a fuller understanding and a more exact recognition of the poet's value: 'Further work of this kind, especially a detailed examination of his sources and analogues, will undoubtedly enhance this understanding.'[8] In the present article, previously unrecognized or incompletely identified source materials for two of Hoccleve's poems are presented. The first of these is the composite Latin prayer *O intemerata et in aeternum benedicta, specialis et incomparabilis virgo, Dei genitrix Maria,* the latter part of which yielded some of the material for the **'Mother of God'** attributed for several centuries to Chaucer, but recognized for the last hundred years as Hoccleve's work. The second is the concluding section of the Anglo-Norman text on which his **'Balade to the Virgin and Christ'** was based.[9]

Most of Hoccleve's religious poetry was probably written during his youth, and much of it is devotional poetry in honour of the Virgin Mary. It follows orthodox patterns of belief and expression, but conveys at the same time a strong sense of personal conviction and faith. The focus is often on suffering: on the suffering and Passion of Christ; on the sorrows of the Virgin; on the suffering and penitence of mankind. The flesh is a recurring theme, and the Devil often features more prominently and more grimly in Hoccleve's texts than in his source materials. Yet the poems are trusting and hopeful. The poems to the Virgin are often based on texts which originated as prayers of private devotion, of the type commonly found in a psalter or Book of Hours. Although liturgical and biblical motifs abound, the emphasis is devotional and contemplative.

There is a marked difference between Hoccleve's religious style and the style of his fifteenth-century contemporaries. As Mitchell observes:

> Because some poets reveled in aureate diction, rhetoric, and bombastic repetition, many of the Marian lyrics, especially those of Lydgate, are highly affected in style and completely devoid of any genuine, personal religious feeling . . . Hoccleve's religious verse, however, is quite different . . . Hoccleve did not adopt the new religious style of the fifteenth century.[10]

Hoccleve does not employ 'aureate diction, rhetoric, and bombastic repetition' in this sense, though his versatility in traditional rhetoric may well have been underestimated.

The expression of orthodox religious beliefs is not confined to the devotional and contemplative poetry. It is found also in Hoccleve's didactic and polemical writing, as for instance in the **'Remonstrance against Oldcastle,'** in which Oldcastle, later to be executed, is indicted for his Lollard beliefs and involvement. The prevailing sentiment in post-Reformation England having favoured Oldcastle rather than his accusers, Hoccleve's failure to find favour with later generations may perhaps be attributed in part to his role in the persecution of perceived heretics, and to an assumed time-serving ingredient in his position. For late twentieth-century readers there may nevertheless be some interest in Hoccleve's distinctive view of the holy images of the saints that he sets out to defend against the Lollards,

however remote his beliefs may be, however mixed his motives. In a notable passage, perhaps more forceful rhetorically than logically, he offers an early association of icons and spectacles in his defence of images as an aid to vision:

> Right as a spectacle helpith feeble sighte
> Whan a man on the book redith or writ
> And causith him to see bet than he mighte
> In which spectacle his sighte nat abit,
> But gooth thurgh and on the book restith it;
> The same may men of ymages seye.
> Though the ymage nat the seint be, yit
> The sighte vs myngith to the seint to preye.[11]

Hoccleve's viewer knows that the image is not the saint, and does not revere the image as such, yet it can enhance true vision. For Hoccleve, as for Chaucer, iconic representations help the viewer to see the truth.[12]

'MOTHER OF GOD'

The latter section of Hoccleve's **'Mother of God'** is addressed to two figures, the Virgin and St John, the disciple whom Christ loved. The close relationship between **'Mother of God'** and the composite Latin prayer *O intemerata et in aeternum benedicta, specialis et incomparabilis virgo* is evident when one compares the concluding sections of the texts as set out below.

The Latin prayer was one of the most widespread of all medieval prayers to the Virgin. It is frequently found in psalters, Books of Hours and books of private devotion, from the twelfth century onwards. St Edmund of Canterbury (1180-1240) is said to have recited it daily. From the fourteenth century onwards it was often attributed, mistakenly, to St Anselm.[13]

The prayer falls into three parts: the first appeals to the Virgin alone, the second appeals to St John, while the third appeals to both. A. Wilmart suggested that the composite prayer originated in a twelfth-century Cistercian house in France. H. Barré subsequently discovered an earlier version of the first part of the prayer, to the Virgin alone, in the eleventh-century psalter which was written at Arras and taken during the second half of the century to Citeaux.[14] This discovery raises the possibility of 'patchwork composition': it is possible that three originally separate prayers were fused together, perhaps in the twelfth century, to form the composite tripartite prayer; it is possible that any two of the three parts were written together, and later fused with the third; it is possible that the second and third parts were written as a single continuation, or as accretive continuations, of the first part. Manuscript tradition, as well as the associations with St Edmund and Anselm, show that the composite prayer was particularly popular in England, where it was expanded further in different ways at different times. Usually the expansions involved elaboration of the first part of the prayer, to the Virgin alone. At various stages of composition, vernacular translations and adaptations were made. Where the vernacular renderings include material not demonstrably derived from the Latin, as is the case with Hoccleve's poem, it is not always possible to determine whether such additional material was originally composed in an unidentified Latin source or in the vernacular.

The first 98 lines of Hoccleve's **'Mother of God'** form an elaborate appeal to the Virgin, interwoven with praise, and these lines may well go back to a Latin, or possibly French, source which further research will identify. About lines 99-140 there can be no doubt: they are derived from the second and third parts of *O intemerata*.

Working here from a prose exemplar, Hoccleve used the verse form most common in his more ambitious poems, namely the rhyme royal stanza which Chaucer had established to such effect. The balancing of verse structure and sentence structure—at times matching, at times with counterpoint effect and enjambment between lines and stanzas—adds emphasis to the drama in the central image of Christ hanging on the cross, and to the words addressed to the 'heuenely gemmes tweyne':

> Be yee oure help and our proteccioun
> Syn for meryt of your virginitee,
> The priuilege of his dileccioun
> In yow confermed God vpon a tree
> Hangynge / and vnto oon of yow seide he
> Right in this wyse / as I reherce can,
> 'Beholde heere / lo thy sone, womman'.
>
> And to þat othir / 'Heer thy modir, lo.'
>
> (120-7)

Hoccleve intensifies and individualizes the central images of the famous prayer. However fervently the prayer was spoken, it will have retained as a prayer a certain formality and impersonality, as a condition of its general validity. There are several phrases in Hoccleve's poem which seem to have a colloquial and poetic immediacy necessarily lacking in the exemplar, such as 'now do your bysy peyne / To wasshe away our cloudeful offense' for 'uestris radiis scelerum meorum effugate nubila', in which formal metaphor is rendered by inventive transferred epithet.[15] In the early part of the poem, for which no direct source has as yet been identified, there are images of the temple, the palace and the womb, interwoven with images of sickness and health and with appeals to the Virgin as mother of mercy and as mediator—'mene'. The theme of building, house and habitation, is continued in the later section, in each case with more individuality and specificity than in the source. The Latin 'Vos estis illi duo in quibus Deus pater per filium suum specialiter aedificauit sibi domum' becomes

> Yee been the two, I knowe verraily,
> In which the fadir God gan edifie,
> By his sone oonly geten specially,
> To him an hows.
>
> (113-16)

Again there is emphatic 'dislocation' between line and sentence structure. Where the Latin prayer focuses on the

Spirit that is to inhabit the heart—'ut cor meum inuisere et inhabitare dignetur Spiritus almus'—Hoccleve focuses more emphatically and specifically on the dwelling-place within the human heart, his heart, means of our 're-creation':

> Helpith now / þat the habitacioun
> Of the holy goost, our recreacioun,
> Be in myn herte now and eueremore.
>
> (137-9)

The concluding section of Hoccleve's text is reproduced here from the holograph manuscript, San Marino, Henry E. Huntington Library, MS HM 111 [fols 36ᵛ-37ʳ]. Modern punctuation has been introduced, except that the holograph indications of breaks in the line—diagonal slashes—are retained. Line and stanza numbering are introduced. The relevant sections of the Latin prayer are reproduced from Wilmart's version [pp. 488-9].

MS HM 111, fols 36ᵛ-37ʳ

XV

> Apostle and freend familier of Cryst
> And his ychosen virgyne, seint Ion, (100)
> Shynynge apostle & euangelyst,
> And best beloued among hem echon,
> With our lady preye I thee to been oon
> Þat vnto Cryst shal for vs alle preye.
> Do this for vs, Crystes derlyng, I seye. (105)

Wilmart, pp. 488-9

O Iohannes beatissime, Christi familiaris amice, qui ab eodem domino nostro Iesu Christo uirgo es electus et inter ceteros magis dilectus atque mysteriis caelestibus ultra omnes imbutus, apostolus eius et euangelista factus es praeclarissimus, te inuoco etiam cum matre eiusdem saluatoris, ut mihi opem tuam cum ipsa ferre digneris.

MS HM 111, fols 36ᵛ-37ʳ

XVI

> Marie and Ion, heuenely gemmes tweyne,
> O lightes two shynynge in the presence
> Of our lord God / now do your bysy peyne
> To wasshe away our cloudeful offense,
> So þat we mowen make resistence (110)
> Ageyn the feend and make him to bewaille
> Þat your preyere may so moche auaille.

Wilmart, pp. 488-9

O duae gemmae caelestes, Maria et Iohannes, o duo luminaria diuinitus ante Deum lucentia, uestris radiis scelerum meorum effugate nubila.

MS HM 111, fols 36ᵛ-37ʳ

XVII

> Yee been the two, I knowe verraily,
> In which the fadir God gan edifie,
> By his sone oonly geten specially, (115)

To him an hows / wherfore I to yow crye,
Beeth leches of our synful maladie.
Preyeth to God / lord of misericorde,
Oure olde giltes / þat he nat recorde.

Wilmart, pp. 488-9

Vos estis illi duo in quibus Deus pater per filium suum
specialiter aedificauit sibi domum

MS HM 111, fols 36ᵛ-37ʳ

XVIII

Be yee oure help and our proteccioun (120)
Syn for meryt of your virginitee,
The priuilege of his dileccioun
In you confermed God vpon a tree
Hangynge / and vnto oon of yow seide he
Right in this wyse / as I reherce can, (125)
'Beholde heere, lo / thy sone, womman'.

Wilmart, pp. 488-9

et in quibus ipse filius Dei patris unigenitus ob sinceris-
simae uirginitatis meritum dilectionis suae confirmavit
privilegium in cruce pendens, uni vestrum ita dicens:
Mulier ecce filius tuus

MS HM 111, fols 36ᵛ-37ʳ

XIX

And to þat othir / 'Heer thy modir, lo.'
Than preye I thee / þat for the greet swetnesse
Of the hy loue þat God twixt yow two
(130) With his mowth made / and of his noblesse
(130)
Conioyned hath yow / thurgh his blisfulnesse,
As modir and sone, helpe vs in our neede
And for our giltes make oure hertes bleede.

Wilmart, pp. 488-9

deinde ad alium: Ecce mater tua. In huius ergo sacratis-
simi amoris dulcedine qua ita tunc ore dominico uelut
mater et filius inuicem coniuncti estis,

MS HM 111, fols 36ᵛ-37ʳ

XX

Vnto yow tweyne / I my soule commende,
Marie and Iohan, for my sauuacioun. (135)
Helpith now / þat the habitacioun
Of the holy goost, our recreacioun,
Be in myn herte now and eueremore,
And of my soule / wasshe away the sore. Amen. (140)

Wilmart, pp. 488-9

uobis duobus ego peccator corpus et animam meam
commendo, ut omnibus horis atque momentis intus et
existere dignemini . . . Agite queso, agite uestris glo-
riosis precibus ut cor meum inuisere et inhabitare
dignetur Spiritus almus, qui me a cuntis uitiorum sordi-
bus expurget.

'BALADE TO THE VIRGIN AND CHRIST'

It has long been known that the **'Balade to the Virgin and Christ,'** commissioned by Robert Chichele, master of the Grocers' Company, mayor of London and brother of Archbishop Chichele, was derived from a French source. The manuscript rubric runs: 'Ceste balade ensuyante feust translatee au commandement de mon Meistre Robert Chichele'. H. E. Sandison identified an Anglo-Norman text with the heading *Pastourelle,* which has survived in a manuscript of the *Roman de la Rose* belonging to St John's College, Cambridge,[16] as the original of the first part of Hoccleve's poem. Sandison printed the Cambridge version of the Anglo-Norman text and the Middle English text for comparison, but since the last forty lines of the Anglo-Norman text are missing in the Cambridge manuscript the comparison remained incomplete. The *Pastourelle* is writ-ten in a fifteenth-century hand on a sheet originally left blank at the end of the manuscript. It is the second short text added, the first being a version of the Anglo-Norman *Bonté de femmes,* a light-hearted equivocal piece in defence of women which draws on several of the well-known 'biblical' and apocryphal arguments for the superiority of women, beginning with the manner of woman's creation from bone rather than mud. These argu-ments were used by Christine de Pizan, and by Hoccleve in his rendering of Christine's *Epistre* and in other poems, though not in the two under discussion here. With the two additional poems at the end, the Cambridge manuscript becomes something of a compendium of late medieval at-titudes to women, ranging from the courtly love and mysti-cal devotion of the *Roman de la Rose,* through the semi-serious *Bonté de femmes,* to the devotional and penitential stanzas of the **'Balade.'**

Two more manuscripts containing the Anglo-Norman text are housed in the British Library: one of these is a fourteenth-century miscellany, which lacks four stanzas in the earlier section; the other is a fifteenth-century miscel-lany which contains the entire text. The fourteenth-century manuscript, MS Add. 44949, is known as the Tywardreath Psalter.[17] It was written in the north of England during the reign of Edward III, and found its way to Tywardreath in Cornwall, whence the name; by the nineteenth century at the latest it was in the possession of the Clifford family of south Devon. Psalter and calendar are preceded by devotional prayers and verses in Latin and French, includ-ing the *Pastourelle*. The fifteenth-century manuscript, MS Royal 20 B.iii, contains an Anglo-Norman treatise on the love of God, *Miroir pour bien vivre,* and at the end some devotional prayers and verses, including the *Pastourelle*. Collation of the three Anglo-Norman manuscripts shows that the two British Library versions are closely related to each other, and often share a reading which is substantially different from that of the Cambridge version. Although it is possible that the British Library versions are closer to the text known to Hoccleve than is the Cambridge version, this cannot be demonstrated with any certainty.

It will be noted that Hoccleve made significant alterations to his source material in the sequence of stanzas and arrangement of material, in content, in style and imagery, and in versification. He was, like many of his predecessors and successors, a responsive reader and 'renewer' of received material.

His starting-point in this instance was an Anglo-Norman text in the medieval mainstream tradition of courtly devotional and penitential poetry, fitting as an 'afterthought' in a manuscript of the *Roman de la Rose*. The Cambridge manuscript title, *Pastourelle,* retained here for convenience of reference, is in keeping with the opening stanza only, and may perhaps have been provided by association with the *Roman de la Rose*. The first stanza of the Anglo-Norman poem describes a garden in the month of May, with beautiful flowers and birdsong, but the thoughts of the narrative persona are drawn from idyllic description to contemplation of the scene at the cross, and death. From stanza iv, the stanzas appeal alternately to the Virgin and to Christ, and narration is interspersed with confession of sins, dwelling on the frailty of the flesh. Christ is the chivalric champion, the king who conquered death, God incarnate who suffered death on the cross for the redemption of mankind, sovereign lord, just judge, the merchant who has paid the price for mortal merchandise, to whom the sinner appeals for help in the battle against sin, the flesh and the Devil. Mary is maiden, noble lady, consort and virgin, worker of miracles, precious jewel, healer, full of grace, solace in time of sorrow, port after perilous sea, peerless flower of womanhood, refuge for the penitent sinner, and queen. These epithets are the common currency of medieval Marian verse, and Hoccleve works most of them into his text; but as a cleric employed in the fifteenth-century equivalent of the civil service, he was at several removes from medieval chivalry, and some of the distinctively feudal imagery of the Anglo-Norman text is replaced in his version by other familiar images of the Christian pilgrimage, wayfaring and seafaring. In the Anglo-Norman text, the Virgin is asked to become the poet's shield and to help him in his hour of need, whereas the English text has the pilgrim's image of the Virgin as the 'soules ship'. The traditional figure of Christ the physician is replaced in Hoccleve's rendering by an appeal to the redemptive power of Christ's blood. The thematic linking of imagery in the Anglo-Norman text, with the image of Christ the merchant, entreated to 'redeem' his merchandise, preceding the appeal for grace in granting of the *besaunt,* is absent from Hoccleve's less specific ending. Hoccleve's re-ordering of the sequence of the final stanzas would in any case have broken the close link between merchant and 'coin', *besaunt.*

The Anglo-Norman text is composed in paired eight-line stanzas, with octosyllabic lines rhyming *a b a b a b a b.* Hoccleve uses instead the 'balade' form, the eight-line stanza with rhyme scheme *a b a b b c b c,* and does not structure the stanzas in pairs. Whereas the Anglo-Norman stanza tends to fall into two halves of equal length, Hoccleve's stanza tends to fall into one five-line + one three-line unit. This involves some expansion and some compression of the Anglo-Norman material, and the

balancing of asymmetrical metrical structures and sentence structures again gives scope for variety and flexibility.

The Anglo-Norman text relies rather heavily on alliterative emphasis, particularly in the repetitive penitential formulas, as for instance in the second stanza reproduced below, with 'Peche puant . . . Grant peril porte . . . Qar ci penaunce ou paine dure', or in the last two stanzas 'Mercy mellez, fesaunt favour / A l'alme qi feistez a ta figure' and 'Raine, refu a repentaunt / Medicine mettez a ma greuance'. This device, though still evident in Hoccleve's version, is used by him more lightly.

The last forty lines of Hoccleve's poem (that is, those for which Sandison failed to find a parallel) are given here from MS HM 111 [fols 46^r-47^r]. The corresponding stanzas from the Anglo-Norman text are reproduced from BL MS Royal 20.B.iii, fols 97^v-98^r, with substantial variants from BL MS Add. 44949, fols 9^v-10^r. Modern punctuation has been introduced, except that the holograph divisions within the line—diagonal slashes—are retained. The Anglo-Norman stanzas are presented in the sequence in which Hoccleve used them, not as they are in the British Library manuscripts, but the manuscript sequence of stanzas is indicated in brackets.

MS HM 111, fols 46^r-47^r

XVI

Blessid virgyne, ensample of al vertu,
Þat peere hast noon / of wommanhode flour,
For the loue of thy sone, our Lord Ihesu,
Strengthe vs to doon him seruice & honour.
Lady, be mene vnto our Sauueour, (125)
Þat our soules þat the feend waytith ay
To hente / & wolde of hem be possessour,
Ne sese hem nat in the vengeable day.

MS Royal 20 B.iii, fols 97^v-98^r

[XVIII]

Plaine de grace, virgine pure,
Sule sanz pere, de femes flour,
Afforsez ma frele nature
De Dieu seruere a soun honour;
Per ta requeste mettez cure,
A mon meschif moustrez socour,
Qi m'alme soit nette, qite & sure
De trouer ioie a mon derain iour.

MS HM 111, fols 46^r-47^r

XVII

The flesshe / the world / & eeke the feend my fo
My wittes alle han at hir retenance: (130)
They to my soule doon annoy & wo,
For why, Lord, dreede I me of thy vengeance.
With mercy, my soule into blisse enhance.
Worthy marchant, saue thy marchandie,
Which þat thow boghtest with dethes penance; (135)
Lat nat the feend haue of vs the maistrie.

MS Royal 20 B.iii, fols 97^v-98^r

[XIX]

Ma char, le munde, le ueuz tiraunt,
Mes senz unt prise en retenaunce,
Contre ma foi, faus recreaunt,

Dount ieo me dout de gref vengeaunce.
Merci, merci, Seignour veillaunt,
Pete prengnes de ta semblaunce;
Sauuez le mercez, trecher marchaunt,
Qe rechatastes a gref penaunce.

MS HM 111, fols 46ʳ-47ʳ

XVIII

Excellent lady, in thy thoght impresse
How & why thy chyld souffrid his tormente;
Preye him to haue on vs swich tendrenesse,
þat in the feendes net we be nat hent. (140)
At the day of his sterne iugement,
Lat nat him leese þat he by deeth boghte.
I woot wel / therto hath he no talent:
Mynge him theron / for thee so to doon / oghte.

MS Royal 20 B.iii, fols 97ᵛ-98ʳ

[XVI]

Ma Dame, pensez pur qoi, coment
Ihesu soun cors suffri pener;
Per taunt li priez mout tendrement
Qi mez defautez deyngne staunger.
E estre propiez au iugement
& m'alme de payne deliuer,
Q'il ne perde par mautalent
Qi par sa mort gayna si cher.

MS HM 111, fols 46ʳ-47ʳ

XIX

Whan in a man, synne growith & rypith,
The fruyt of it is ful of bittirnesse;
But penitence cleene away it wypith,
And to the soule yeueth greet swetnesse.
O steerne Iuge / with thy rightwisnesse,
Medle thy mercy / and shewe vs fauour. (150)
Vnto our soules, maad to thy liknesse,
Graunte pardoun of our stynkyng errour.

MS Royal 20 B.iii, fols 97ᵛ-98ʳ

[XVII]

Peche puant, quaunt crest & mure,
Grant peril porte au bref iour,
Qar ci penaunce ou paine dure
Aillours quert a chief de tour.
Sire, gentiel iuge, oue ta droiture
Mercy mellez, fesaunt fauour
A l'alme qi feistez a ta figure,
& pardoun grauntez a moi pechour.

MS HM 111, fols 46ʳ-47ʳ

XX

O glorious qweene / to the repentaunt
Þat art refuyt / socour and medecyne,
Lat nat the foule feend make his auaunt, (155)
Þat he hath thee byreft any of thyne.
Thurgh thy preyere, thow thy sone enclyne
His merciable grace / on vs to reyne.
Be tendre of vs / o thow blissid virgyne,
For if thee list / we shuln to blisse atteyne. (160)

C'est tout

S Royal 20 B.iii, fols 97ᵛ-98ʳ

[XX]

Raine, refu a repentaunt,
Medicine mettez a ma greuance,
Pur moi soiez toun fitz priaunt
Qe de sa merci eie allegaunce
Et grace de apaier soun besaunt
En dit, en fet a sa plesaunce,
E en pes uiure deesore auaunt
Saunz peche, doloure e encombraunce.

MS Add. 44949, fols 9ᵛ-10ʳ

122	des femmes
126	me mettre s
129	m. si vielz
132	de grant v.
136	Qe rechatez a
138	Ihesu soeffri s.c.
139	Pur taunt li priez tendrement
140	Mes defautes deigne excuser
142	M'alme d.p. deliuerer
143	Ke ne
146	Peril port & brief douzour
147	Kar penaunce
148	Ailours est
151	ta feture
152	grantez mon salueour
156	de merci
157	deprouer s.b.
159	En p.v. desore en auaunt
160	saunz peyne dolour

Notes

1. J. Mitchell, *Thomas Hoccleve* (Urbana, Chicago and London, 1968).

2. *Selections from Hoccleve,* ed. M. C. Seymour (Oxford, 1981); *Thomas Hoccleve: Selected Poems,* ed. B. O'Donoghue (Manchester, 1982).

3. *The Complaint of Hoccleve,* line 51.

4. J. Burrow, 'The poet and the book', in *Genres, Themes and Images in English Literature: The J. A. W. Bennett Memorial Lectures, Perugia, 1986,* ed. P. Boitani and A. Torti (Tübingen, 1988), pp. 230-45. Professor Burrow's *Hoccleve* (Variorum Series, 1994) had unfortunately not appeared when this article was in preparation.

5. The help given by the Huntington Library, San Marino, in providing copies of the holograph manuscripts and in giving permission for extracts from the texts to be reproduced, is gratefully acknowledged.

6. T. S. Fenster and M. C. Erler, *Poems of Cupid, God of Love* (Leiden, 1990), p. 159.

7. See, e.g., E. G. Stanley, 'Chaucer's metre after Chaucer, I: Chaucer to Hoccleve', *Notes and Queries,* 234 (1989), 11-23. Professor Burrow has also drawn my attention to J. A. Jefferson, 'The Hoccleve holographs and Hoccleve's metrical practice', in *Manuscripts*

and Texts: Editorial Problems in Later Middle English Literature, ed. Derek Pearsall (Cambridge, 1987), pp. 95-109.

8. *Selections,* ed. Seymour, p. xxxiii.

9. For early editions, see *Hoccleve's Works: The Minor Poems,* vol. I, ed. F. J. Furnivall, rev. A. I. Doyle and J. Mitchell, EETS, ES 61 (1892; rev. edn London, 1970); vol. II, ed. I. Gollancz, rev. A. I. Doyle and J. Mitchell, EETS, ES 73 (1892; rev. edn London, 1970).

10. Mitchell, *Thomas Hoccleve,* pp. 34-5.

11. *Remonstrance against Oldcastle,* lines 417-24 (*Selections,* ed. Seymour, p. 71).

12. *OED*'s earliest citations for 'spectacle(s)' sg. and pl. meaning 'a device for assisting defective eyesight', used figuratively and literally, are drawn from Chaucer and from this Hoccleve passage.

13. See A. Wilmart, *Les Auteurs spirituels du moyen âge latin* (Paris, 1932), pp. 474-504, for a full discussion of the prayer, and for the text.

14. H. Barré, 'Le Psautier de Robert de Molesme', in *Prières anciennes de l'occident à la mère du Sauveur* (Paris, 1963), p. 195.

15. The inventiveness may of course be derivative. For the possibility that 'bysy peyne' is derived from Chaucer's 'Balade to Truth,' line 108, see *Selections,* ed. Seymour, p. 105.

16. Cambridge, St John's College, MS G 5. See H. E. Sandison, 'En mon deduit a moys de may', in *Vassar Mediaeval Studies,* ed. C. F. Fiske (New Haven, Conn., 1923), pp. 235-44.

17. The manuscript was described by A. Långfors, 'Notice et extraits du manuscrit Additional 44949 du Musée Britannique', *Neuphilologische Mitteilungen,* 40 (1948), 97-123. Assistance from the staff of the British Library Manuscripts Collection and permission to reproduce the text from MS Royal 20 B.iii, with variants from MS Add. 44949, are gratefully acknowledged.

FURTHER READING

Bibliography

Matthews, William. "Thomas Hoccleve." In *A Manual of the Writings in Middle English, 1050-1500,* edited by Albert E. Hartung, pp. 746-56. Hamden, Conn.: Archon, 1972.

Briefly outlines Hoccleve's life and achievements and gives descriptions (including sources) and a brief summary of each of Hoccleve's works.

Biography

Bennett, Henry S. "Thomas Hoccleve." In *Six Medieval Men and Women,* pp. 69-99. New York: Atheneum, 1972.

Offers Hoccleve's biography as one example of the medieval writer's life, emphasizing Hoccleve's work in the Privy Seal office and its influence on his poetry.

Burrow, J. A. *Thomas Hoccleve.* Aldershot, U.K.: Variorum, 1994, 60 p.

Brief biography focusing on Hoccleve's writings and his work in the Privy Seal office. Contains an appendix detailing the official documents substantiating Hoccleve's biography, and a detailed bibliography listing manuscripts, editions, and secondary sources.

Criticism

Burrow, J. A. Introduction to *Thomas Hoccleve's Complaint and Dialogue,* pp. ix-lxv. Oxford: Oxford University Press, 1999.

Provides a brief history of the making of the *Series,* and reviews the text, meter, language, and manuscript variations of two of the poems included in the work. Also comments on Hoccleve's mental breakdown and his relationship to Humphrey Duke of Gloucester.

Burrow, J. A. "Thomas Hoccleve: Some Redatings." *The Review of English Studies* 46 (1995): 366-73.

Argues for earlier dating than previously proposed for Hoccleve's "Dialogue with a Friend," and, by extension, the whole of the *Series* and the significant events in Hoccleve's life.

McMillan, Douglas J. "The Single Most Popular of Thomas Hoccleve's Poems: *The Regement of Princes.*" *Neuphilolgische Mitteilungen* 89 (1988): 63-71.

Reviews the early criticism of the *Regement,* focusing on the various personas and autobiographical elements the poem.

Mitchell, Jerome. *Thomas Hoccleve: A Study in Early Fifteenth-Century English Poetic.* Urbana: University of Illinois Press, 1968. 151 p.

In-depth study of Hoccleve's life and works by a noted Hoccleve scholar.

Pearsall, Derek. "The English Chaucerians." In *Chaucer and Chaucerians: Critical Studies in Middle English Literature,* edited by D. S. Brewer, pp. 201-39. London: Thomas Nelson and Sons, 1966.

Compares Hoccleve to both Lydgate and Chaucer, and discusses other minor poets including Hawes, Skelton, and Barclay.

Quinn, William A. "Hoccleve's *Epistle of Cupid.*" *Explicator* 45, no. 1 (1986): 7-10.

Argues that the frequent narrative blunders and the awkwardness of portions of Hoccleve's translation of Christine de Pisan's *Epistre* undercut Hoccleve's sincerity.

Rigg, A. G. "Hoccleve's *Complaint* and Isidore of Seville." *Speculum* 45, no. 4 (1970): 564-74.

> Proposes Isidore of Seville's *Synonyma* as a source for Hoccleve's "Complaint," and suggests that the extent of autobiographical accuracy does not affect the function of the poem.

Ross, Charles H. "Chaucer and 'The Mother of God.'" *Modern Language Notes* 6, no. 7 (1891): 193-95.

> Analyzes the evidence for both Chaucer and Hoccleve as potential authors of "The Mother of God," concluding that the evidence strongly favors Hoccleve.

Additional coverage of Hoccleve's life and career is contained in the following source published by the Gale Group: *Dictionary of Literary Biography,* **Vol. 146.**

John Wilmot, Earl of Rochester
1647-1680

English poet and playwright.

INTRODUCTION

One of the most gifted writers of the Restoration period and a pioneer of English verse satire, Wilmot—more commonly referred to as Rochester—was as famous among his contemporaries for his atheism and the pornographic tone of his poetry as he was for his skilled verse technique. His work was praised by many, even as it was condemned for its lewd content—the poet Andrew Marvell claimed that Rochester "was the only man in England that had the true veine of satyre." One of the youngest and most handsome of Charles II's courtiers, Rochester was a favorite of the king; nevertheless, his propensity for drinking, brawling, and lasciviousness led to several banishments from court. So infamous was his behavior that it is believed that Rochester was the inspiration for the archetypal rake of the Restoration comedy of manners, Dorimant in George Etherege's 1676 comedy *The Man of Mode*. Rochester's reported deathbed conversion from atheism at age thirty-three also became the subject of legend, and for many years Rochester was celebrated in religious literature as an example of a reformed libertine. At the same time, his works were long neglected by critics due to their unorthodox views and sexual themes. In the twentieth century, however, Rochester's works began to receive more attention from scholars, and today they are widely praised for their wit, imagination, liveliness, and readability. No longer is his poetry dismissed because of its supposed obscenity, anti-rationalism, and nihilism; rather, these aspects are seen as centrally important to his unique brand of satire.

BIOGRAPHICAL INFORMATION

Rochester was born John Wilmot in Oxfordshire on 1 April, 1647. His mother, Anne, was a parliamentarian, and his father, Henry, was a royalist who in 1652 was named the first Earl of Rochester for his military service to Charles II during the king's exile. Henry Wilmot died while serving in Holland in 1658, two years before the restoration of the monarchy in England. His son succeeded to his earldom, becoming the second Earl of Rochester. Rochester's early education took place at home, and he was subsequently sent to Burford Grammar school, where he studied the Latin authors. At the age of twelve he began studies at Oxford—where he is said to have begun drinking heavily and writing poetry—and at fourteen he earned his Master of Arts degree. He then began touring the

Continent, and upon his return entered the court of Charles II. In 1665, recognizing that her son's career as a courtier would require more money than the family possessed, Rochester's mother attempted to arrange a marriage with the wealthy heiress Elizabeth Malet. When negotiations for the match were not progressing quickly enough, Rochester had Malet abducted, an act for which he was imprisoned in the Tower of London for a month. After his release he was sent to Holland on a military exercise, and upon his return the king named him Gentleman of the Bedchamber, a position that carried with it a small stipend. In 1666 Rochester went abroad again in service of the king, and this time his courage in a sea-battle against the Dutch made him a hero.

After his marriage to Malet in 1667, Rochester's career at court gained momentum, although he was involved in a number of scandals, which earned him a reputation for drunkenness, vivacious conversation, and "extravagant frolics." One story that circulated at court told of an incident in which his clothes were stolen by a prostitute; another held that he had assaulted someone in the presence of the king (but was not reprimanded by the monarch). Reportedly, he was also involved in a number of fights and was challenged to several duels. In 1668 Rochester's wife gave birth to a daughter, after which she moved to her own house at Enmore. The couple eventually had three more children together. Elizabeth's family had been careful not to entrust her money to him, and for the rest of his life Rochester was continually in debt due to his lavish spending and gambling.

In 1671 Rochester was banished from the court for composing a lampoon of the king's mistress. By this time Rochester's poems had appeared in a number of publications, in some cases without his knowledge. After a year in disgrace—some weeks of which he spent disguised as an Italian doctor, Dr. Bendo, and maintained a successful, if spurious, medical practice—he was returned to the king's favor, although by all accounts he did not curb his behavior. Around 1675 Rochester began an affair with the actress Elizabeth Barry, whom it is said he coached to become the greatest actress of the Restoration stage. In addition to composing poetry that appeared in various collections and broadsides, Rochester was also writing for the stage, constructing original works as well as scenes for plays by other dramatists, including Elkanah Settle and Francis Fane. His health steadily declined—it is assumed he was suffering from syphilis—and in June of 1680, at age thirty-three, he was confined to bed, where he was to die a month later. His mother had him attended by her religious associates, notably the Anglican rationalist divine Gilbert Burnet, to whom Rochester renounced his atheism. This deathbed confession and conversion became legendary, and was promulgated in religious tracts over the next two centuries.

MAJOR WORKS

During Rochester's lifetime, his songs and poems were circulated mainly in anonymous broadsides and collections of miscellaneous poems; most of his work was not published under his name until after his death. Almost immediately after his death in 1680 there appeared a collection of Rochester's works entitled *Poems on Several Occasions By the Right Honourable The E. of R———*. Other similar editions were released throughout the 1680s and into the 1690s, some stripped of their more sexually explicit content. Rochester's adaptation of John Fletcher's play *Valentinian,* about the power of a monarch who rapes a young woman, was also published shortly after his death. Printings of the play *Sodom, or the Quintessence of Debauchery* (published in 1957), which is sometimes attributed to him, gave rise to charges of obscenity, and were destroyed. Collections of Rochester's works continued to be produced in the eighteenth century, but by the nineteenth century interest in his work had diminished.

Modern critics generally agree that Rochester's most important works are his verse satires, notably *A Satire Against Mankind* (1679; sometimes referred to as *Satire*

Against Reason and Mankind), *Letter from Artemisia in the Towne to Chloe in the Country,* (1679; commonly referred to as *Artemisia to Chloe*), "Tunbridge Wells," "Timon," and "An Allusion to Horace." In *Satire Against Mankind,* Rochester's commentary on the human condition, the speaker attacks the pride, vanity, folly, and treachery of human beings. *Artemisia and Chloe,* regarded by many critics as Rochester's masterpiece, is an epistolary poem; addressed from one woman to another, it presents a satirical look at social attitudes and the nature of love. Another masterwork is *Upon Nothing* (1679), a mock-philosophical poem that conducts an ironic encomium on nothingness to explore the Christian creation, the power of the human intellect, and Rochester's own philosophy of nihilism. Rochester also wrote many shorter poems, the best of which are thought to be "The Maimed Debauchee," "The Fall," "Absent From Thee," "The Mistress," "Love and Life," "Song of a Young Lady to Her Ancient Lover," "A Ramble in St. James's Park," and "The Imperfect Enjoyment." Ostensibly, many of these are love poems, but they typically focus more on sexual matters than the traditional concerns of romantic verse. Critics have noted that while satirizing social mores in many of these poems Rochester also presents unusually favorable portraits of women, depicts sexual frustration, and sometimes makes allusions to homoerotic desire. Because of their explicit nature, readers over the centuries have often judged them pornographic. Most critics today, however, maintain that Rochester's obscenity in these works is integral to his satire, as he violates social convention and forces readers to look at the basest aspects of themselves. Of his prose works, critics have examined with interest Rochester's hundred or so surviving letters and the advertising pamphlet he produced while posing as Dr. Bendo, which include elements of his trademark satire.

CRITICAL RECEPTION

Throughout the years, Rochester's work has been widely praised for its skillful satire while at the same time condemned for its lewd and pornographic imagery. His contemporaries were divided in their opinion of his works—Marvell is said to have admired his work, but the poet John Dryden was critical of Rochester's lack of discipline. Although when his poems were first collected and published in 1680 they attracted a wide readership, many commentators dismissed his work, assuming that no one of Rochester's low morals could write great poetry. In the eighteenth century he was admired by Daniel Defoe but considered a dilettante by Alexander Pope; others, including Samuel Johnson, admired his skill while condemning his obscenity. The famed book collector and author Samuel Pepys reportedly kept his copy of *Poems on Several Occasions* hidden in a locked desk drawer, considering it "unfit to mix with [his] other books" and said of Rochester: "he is past writing any more so bad in one sense, so I despair of any man surviving him to write so good in another." By the nineteenth century Rochester's work had fallen almost completely out of critical discourse and public readership, although he was admired by Alfred Tennyson, Voltaire, and William Hazlitt. Since the twentieth century Rochester criticism has come into its own, and scholars have begun to reassess his poetry, especially his satirical work. Critics such as Thomas H. Fujimura and C. F. Main have focused on the satirical method of *A Satire Against Mankind.* Fujimura has seen the satire as divided into two parts, the first dealing with reason and the second concerning the human condition. Main has argued that it is a classical verse satire. Brean Hammond and Paulina Kewes have examined the work's influence on Restoration drama, especially focusing on libertine debates played out on the Restoration stage. David Sheehan has examined *Artemisia to Chloe,* noting especially the protagonist's ironic worldview, while Gillian Manning has noted Rochester's favorable portrayal of the female condition. Howard D. Weinbrot has maintained that while *Artemisia to Chloe* is an example of Rochester's great satiric talent, "An Allusion to Horace" shows a lack of depth. Pat Rogers, however, has asserted that contextual differences between the latter work and its Horatian model require that it be evaluated on its own merits rather than in comparison to Horace. Critics such as K. E. Robinson, Tony Barley, and David Quentin have focused closely on the ironic nature of *Upon Nothing,* often noting the religious implications of the work. Many critics, such as Howard Erskine-Hill, Anne Righter, and Barbara Everett have explored how Rochester's works reflect his cultural background, while Ronald Paulson, Reba Wilcoxon, and Helen Wilcox have considered the questions of Rochester's use of obscenity and sexual imagery. Modern critics are drawn to Rochester's work for its accessibility, its wittiness, its pioneering use of satire, its sympathetic portrayal of women, its allusions to classical sources, and its use of diverse and interesting voices. The current view of Rochester is that of a gifted satirist and libertine, and his writing now overshadows his reputation as the most notable pornographer and heretic of his day.

PRINCIPAL WORKS

"The Second Prologue at Court," [in *The Empress of Morocco* by Elkanah Settle] (poetry) 1673

"The Epilogue" [in *Love in the Dark, or The Man of Bus'ness* by Francis Fane] (poetry) 1675

Letter from Artemisia in the Towne to Chloe in the Country (poetry) 1679

A Satyr Against Mankind [also known as *A Satire Against Reason and Mankind*] (poetry) 1679

Upon Nothing, a Poem (poetry) 1679

A Very Heroical Epistle from My Lord All-Pride to Dol-Common (poetry) 1679

A Letter To Dr. Burnet, From the right Honourable the Earl of Rochester, As he lay on His Death-Bed, At His Honours Lodge In Woodstock-Park (letter) 1680

Poems on Several Occasions By the Right Honourable The E. of R——— (poetry) 1680

Poems on Several Occasions. Written by a late Person of Honour (poetry) 1680

Valentinian: A Tragedy. As 'tis Alter'd by the late Earl of Rochester, And Acted at the Theatre-Royal [adaptator; from a play by John Fletcher] (play) 1680

The Works of John Earl of Rochester. Containing Poems, On Several Occasions: His Lordship's Letters To Mr. Savil and Mrs. ** with Valentinian, a Tragedy. Never before Publish'd together (collected works) 1680

The Miscellaneous Works of the Right Honourable the Late Earls of Rochester And Roscommon. With The Memoirs of the Life and Character of the late Earl of Rochester, in a Letter to the Dutchess of Mazarine. By Mons. St. Evremont (collected works) 1707

Remains of the Right Honourable John, Earl of Rochester. Being Satyrs, Songs, and Poems; Never before Published. From a Manuscript found in a Gentleman's Library that was Contemporary with him (poetry) 1718

Collected Works of John Wilmot, Earl of Rochester [edited by John Hayward] (poetry) 1761

The Poetical Works Of that Witty Lord John Earl of Rochester: Left in Ranger's Lodge in Woodstock Park, where his Lordship died, and never before Printed; with Some Account of the Life of that ingenious Nobleman. Extracted from Bishop Burnet, and other Eminent Writers (poetry) 1761

John Wilmot Earl of Rochester: His Life and Writings [edited by Johannes Prinz] (poetry) 1927

Rochester's Poems on Several Occasions [edited by James Thorpe] (poetry) 1950

Poems by John Wilmot, Earl of Rochester [edited by Vivian de Sola Pinto] (poetry) 1953

Sodom, or the Quintessence of Debauchery. Written for the Royall Company of Whoremasters, possibly by Rochester (poetry) 1957

The Complete Poems of John Wilmot, Earl of Rochester [edited by David M. Vieth] (poetry) 1968

The Letters of John Wilmot, Earl of Rochester [edited by Jeremy Treglown] (letters) 1980

Lyrics and Satires of John Wilmot, Earl of Rochester [edited by David Brooks] (poetry) 1980

The Rochester-Savile Letters 1671-1680 [edited by John Harold Wilson] (letters) 1980

John Wilmot, Earl of Rochester: Selected Poems [edited by Paul Hammond] (poetry) 1982

The Poems of John Wilmot, Earl of Rochester [edited by Keith Walker] (poetry) 1984

Rochester: Complete Poems and Plays [edited by Paddy Lyons] (collected works) 1993

John Wilmot, Earl of Rochester: The Complete Works [edited by Frank H. Ellis] (collected works) 1994

CRITICISM

Thomas H. Fujimura (essay date 1958)

SOURCE: Fujimura, Thomas H. "Rochester's 'Satyr Against Mankind': An Analysis." *Studies in Philology* 55 (October, 1958): 576-90.

[*In the essay below, Fujimura argues that* A Satire Against Mankind *is divided into two parts, that the first, which deals with epistemology, favors sensory-based "right reason" over speculation, and that the second part, which deals with moral satire, emphasizes the baseness and fear-driven nature of human conduct.*]

The Earl of Rochester's **Satyr Against Mankind** is generally regarded as a powerful satire and an intimate revelation of a striking personality; but beyond this, there is little unanimity of opinion—either as to its originality or its meaning. Probably as a result of this disagreement, the poem has not received the attention it deserves.[1]

One obstacle to the appreciation of the poem has been the question of its originality: here the opinions range from the verdict that everything in the poem is borrowed to the conclusion that the satire is quite original. One may read the opinion of Kenneth B. Murdock, for example, that the poem is a "skilful adaptation of Boileau's verses," that is, of the eighth satire.[2] John F. Moore concludes, after comparing the ideas and structure of Rochester's poem with those of Boileau, that the **Satyr Against Mankind** is assuredly an original work.[3] Again, we read a dogmatic assertion like S. F. Crocker's: "There is scarcely an idea of major or minor importance in Rochester that is not present in Montaigne, and to some extent in La Rochefoucauld.[4] W.J. Courthope, in 1903, expressed the commonly held notion that Rochester is heavily indebted to Thomas Hobbes for the bulk of the ideas in the poem: "He puts forward his principles, moral and religious, such as they are, with living force and pungency, showing in every line how eagerly he has imbibed the opinions of Hobbes."[5] But this has been refuted in part by Vivian de Sola Pinto: "They [the opening lines] are an attack on Man, but still more an attack on Reason, the idol of Hobbes and the freethinkers of the age.[6]

More serious than this disagreement about the originality and sources of Rochester's poem is the disagreement over its meaning. One reads, in Pinto, that the satire is an attack on man's "much-vaunted reason," and in Crocker that it "is a terrible indictment of human reason."[7] Again, Pinto discovers a rich biographical significance in the poem and describes it as "a reasoned statement of the causes of that misery [Rochester's own] and an announcement of the discovery that reason divorced from morality was the chief cause.[8] Elsewhere, Pinto speaks of the "nihilism" of the poem.[9] Moore finds in the poem an attack "against the conception, whenever and by whomever held, that man is by nature intelligent and noble."[10] Less adequately, Harry Levin describes the poem as a "critique of pure wit"; and in an anthology of 17th century writings, the poem is said to express a "general, cold, if somewhat turgid, contempt of life as he had found and made it."[11] Excerpted remarks of this sort are indubitably unfair to the critics concerned, but they do suggest the confusion about the intent of Rochester's satire.

Such differences of opinion point up the need for a precise analysis of the poem to determine what exactly Rochester does say. While the question of what sources he used is more difficult to answer, it might still be rewarding to consider his ideas in relation to those of Hobbes, since Rochester appears to have accepted the philosophy of Hobbes, according to the testimony of contemporaries like Robert Parsons, chaplain to Lady Rochester. Whether the indebtedness to Hobbes be proved or not, a comparison of their ideas may at least put the **Satyr Against Mankind** into clearer focus.

For an understanding of any satirical work, the first step is establishing the criteria on which the poet bases his criticism of human follies and vices. In Rochester's **Satyr Against Mankind,**[12] there is implicit, in the opening attack on man ("Who is so proud of being rational"), a rejection of a certain kind of reason, that is, speculative (or discursive) reason as distinguished from practical reason. This is not an attack on human reason in its totality, nor is it an attempt to base life on a voluntaristic or instinctual basis: Rochester is himself too rationalistic to deny reason completely. The kind of reason he approves is clearly set forth in the satire in the answer to the "formal Band, and Beard":

> Thus, whilst 'gainst false reas'ning I inveigh,
> I own right *Reason,* which I wou'd obey:
> That *Reason* that distingushes by sense,
> And gives us *Rules,* of good, and ill from thence:
> That bounds desires, with a reforming Will,
> To keep 'em more in vigour, not to kill.
> Your *Reason* hinders, mine helps t'enjoy,
> Renewing Appetites, yours wou'd destroy.
> My Reason is my *Friend,* yours is a *Cheat,*
> Hunger call's out, my Reason bids me eat;
> Perversely yours, your Appetite does mock,
> This asks for food, that answers what's a Clock?
> This plain distinction Sir your doubt secures,
> 'Tis not true Reason I despise but yours.
> Thus I think Reason righted.

(99-112)

The notion of *right reason,* and the hierarchy of Reason, Will, and Desires, is common enough in the 17th century, particularly in the writings of Christian humanists like Richard Hooker. But in Rochester, the familiar terminology is used in a different sense: the morally suasive reason of the Christian humanist has been replaced by the purely pragmatic faculty of the naturalistic thinker. In thus diminishing the scope of reason, Rochester obviously strips it of any real moral potency.[13]

Further, in reducing the scope of reason and in emphasizing the role of sense, the poet opens the door to misinterpretation. Murdock, for example, concludes that, in the passage quoted above, Rochester speaks as a complete sensualist: "To trust the senses was reasonable, and to satisfy them. To sharpen desires, by brief restraint if need be, in order to make the pleasure of gratifying them more intense, was better than to be deluded by an airy moral principle."[14] "The senses were all; in them was the only 'light of nature'—in them and in 'Instinct' the only certainty."[15] Crocker likewise suggests that Rochester erected a whole system of morality on the senses: "rules of conduct should be derived from the senses."[16] But this is to confuse with moral rules of conduct the merely pragmatic sanctions of the senses; this is, in fact, Rochester turned inside out.

Actually, in avowing his belief in right reason, Rochester is not at the moment concerned with questions of morality, he is concerned with the question of knowledge—though keenly aware at the same time of the evil consequences of confusion about what is true or false. In the first portion of the poem (to about line 112), Rochester is concerned primarily with epistemology, and not with ethics; the poet's criticism is directed to man's folly in placing so much faith in speculative reason to the neglect of right reason. The epistemological ideas in the poem are paralleled by those in Hobbes, and the similarity in ideas here must lead one to conclude, in disagreement with Pinto,[17] that Rochester was probably influenced by Hobbes.

In *The Leviathan*, Hobbes bases knowledge on sensory experience; the result is a purely empirical epistemology which allows no validity to speculative ideas having no firm basis in the five senses. (This is pretty much the nominalism of the general semanticists today, as set forth in rather crude form in books like Stuart Chase's *The Tyranny of Words*.) Hobbes explains that all thoughts are "a *representation* or *appearance*, of some quality, or other accident of a body without us, which is commonly called an *object*." Further, "the original of them all, is that which we call SENSE, for there is no conception in a man's mind, which hath not at first, totally, or by parts, been begotten upon the organs of sense."[18] "Also because, whatsoever . . . we conceive, has been perceived first by sense, either all at once, or by parts; a man can have no thought, representing any thing, not subject to sense." Anything beyond this is nonsense, "absurd speeches, taken upon credit, without any signification at all, from deceiving schoolmen."[19]

Nature can never err (and knowledge based on sense cannot be erroneous), but man is prone to error because of his ability to verbalize (that is, to give names to objects).[20] Among man's foolish activities in verbalizing is ascribing names to non-existent things, names which are learned by rote in schools, such as "hypostatical, transubstantiate, consubstantiate, eternal-now, and the like canting of schoolmen."[21] Clear terms that have their ultimate basis in sense-experience are a blessing, and contribute to science and the benefit of mankind. "And, on the contrary, metaphors, and senseless and ambiguous words, are like *ignes fatui*; and reasoning upon them is wandering amongst innumerable absurdities; and their end, contention and sedition, or contempt."[22] "And this is incident to none but those, that converse in questions of matters imcomprehensible, as the School-men; or in questions of abstruse philosophy," among which are questions involving terms like Trinity, Deity, and free will.[23]

The nominalistic and materialistic bias of Hobbes's epistemology is found in much the same form in Rochester's attack on man, who prides himself on his speculative reason:

> that vain *Animal,*
> Who is so proud of being rational.
> The senses are too gross, and he'll contrive
> A Sixth, to contradict the other Five;
> And before certain instinct, will preferr
> *Reason,* which Fifty times for one does err.
> *Reason,* an *Ignis fatuus,* in the *Mind,*
> Which leaving light of Nature, sense behind;
> Pathless and dang'rous wandring ways it takes,
> Through errors, Fenny-*Boggs,* and Thorny *Brakes*;
> Whilst the misguided follower, climbs with pain,
> *Mountains* of Whimseys, heap'd in his own *Brain*:
> Stumbling from thought to thought, falls head-long
>   down,
> Into doubts boundless Sea, where like to drown,
> Books bear him up awhile, and makes him try,
> To swim with Bladders of *Philosophy.*

(6-21)

The precise nature of this speculative activity is further indicated in the defense of speculative reason by the "formal Band, and Beard":

> *Reason,* by whose aspiring influence,
> We take a flight beyond material sense,
> Dive into Mysteries, then soaring pierce,
> The flaming limits of the Universe.
> Search Heav'n and Hell, find out what's acted there,
> And give the World true grounds of hope and fear.

(66-71)

Like Hobbes, Rochester has nothing but contempt for vain speculations about matters that transcend sense; the works of such divines as Sibbs and Patrick only confound the mind with mere words. Like Hobbes, too, Rochester is impatient with Schoolmen and their speculations:

> This busie, puzling, stirrer up of doubt,
> That frames deep *Mysteries,* then finds 'em out;
> Filling with Frantick Crowds of thinking *Fools,*
> Those Reverend *Bedlams, Colledges,* and *Schools*
> Borne on whose Wings, each heavy *Sot* can pierce,
> The limits of the boundless Universe.

(80-85)

This contempt for speculative reason does not imply a complete rejection of reason by Rochester. And failure to distinguish between *speculative* reason and *right* reason in the poem has led to untenable generalizations like Pinto's about the opening lines of the satire and about Rochester himself: they "sum up his own realization that 'the life of reason' as conceived by his class and generation was an illusion. They make us feel what it was like, after the intoxication of youth had passed to face the fact that you were living in the soulless 'universe of death' of the new 'scientific' philosophy." Further, that Rochester's use of the phrase "reas'ning Engine" (line 29) "is a bitterly ironic commentary on the mechanistic conception of humanity which was the logical outcome of the new science."[24] Now, I can find no repudiation of materialism or of the "new, scientific philosophy" in the first part of the poem. Actually, Rochester's right reason is the conception accepted by "his class and generation," such as the Duke of Buckingham, King Charles, and Sir Charles Sedley.

In attacking speculative reason but subscribing to right reason, Rochester is more or less in accord with Hobbes. In *The Leviathan,* Hobbes states that reason is intended for utilitarian purposes, and that reason is abused only when it is used for purely speculative thought which does not lead to benefits for mankind.[25] Rochester, in like manner, conceives of right reason as a faculty which leads to the attainment of ends that will produce happiness. Reason cooperates with sense, and "gives us *Rules,* of good, and ill from thence." From the context of the poem, we can assume that these rules concern the proper indulgence of our appetites, but with that degree of moderation that neither satiety nor frustration will result. This wise tempering of the appetites, as of hunger, is necessary if we are to achieve happiness. As Hobbes says, "Nor can a man any more live, whose desires are at an end, than he, whose sense and imaginations are at a stand."[26] This is a variant of Aristotle's view that happiness lies in action, whether physical or intellectual. The acceptance by Rochester of right reason

> That bounds desires, with a reforming Will,
> To keep 'em more in vigour, not to kill
>
> (102-103)

is no more a sanctioning of gross sensuality than Aristotle's views.[27] This activity of right reason is properly confined to pragmatic ends such as the satisfaction of our appetites:

> But thoughts, are giv'n for Actions government,
> Where Action ceases, thoughts impertinent:
> Our *Sphere* of Action, is lifes happiness,
> And he who thinks Beyond, thinks like as *Ass.*
>
> (94-97)

If we decry these ideas as hedonistic, we might remember that they are no more sensual than the views of Epicurus or of Hobbes.

This support of right reason (limited to practical concerns) and the attack on speculative reason (dealing with nonsense) constitute the first section of the poem. The main concern is epistemological, and the basic ideas are largely paralleled by those in Hobbes's *Leviathan.* Though vividly phrased and vigorous in tone, this section of the **Satyr Against Mankind** is hardly original in its strictures nor does it sound the passionately cynical and savage note that we associate with Rochester's satires. It is only when the satirical interest shifts from epistemology to ethics that the voice of the poet is clearly heard.

The section condemning man's moral depravity is prefaced by a denial of man's wisdom (114-123), and this short coda might properly be considered along with the first sec-

tion of the poem. In a more contemptuous tone than earlier, Rochester declares that beasts, following instinct, achieve their goals more surely than man, and Jowler, who can find and kill his hares, is superior to a statesman:

> Those *Creatures,* are the wisest who attain,
> By surest means, the ends at which they aim.
>
> (117-118)

This should not be interpreted as a repudiation of right reason, which the poet has just finished defending; and there is no real ground for believing that Rochester would set up instinct (as Murdock states[28]) in place of reason. Rochester would distinguish between instinct and right reason, and accord the latter a higher place. His criticism is directed against man with "all his Pride, and his Philosophy" (114), that is, once again, the creature of speculative reason. There are simply degrees of wisdom. At one extreme is Jowler, who lives by instinct; at the other extreme is the man, or statesman, who lives by speculative reason. There are also the "Men of sense" (referred to in line 196), who live by right reason. From the point of view of attaining immediate ends, instinct may be swifter than even right reason; but in the attainment of ends that conduce to happiness ("Our *Sphere* of Action"), right reason is equally, or probably more, important. Hobbes, too, makes some distinctions in the kinds of wisdom that men possess: men who have no science (that is, a system of rules to govern the attainment of ends) "are in better, and nobler condition, with their natural prudence; than men, that by mis-reasoning, or by trusting them that reason wrong, fall upon false and absurd general rules."[29] But wisest of all are those that govern their conduct by right reason.

Rochester follows his disparagement of man's wisdom with a savage indictment of man's moral baseness:

> Look next, if humane Nature makes amends;
> Whose Principles, most gen'rous are, and just,
> And to whose *Moralls,* you wou'd sooner trust.
> Be Judge your self, I'le bring it to the test,
> Which is the basest *Creature Man,* or *Beast?*
>
> (124-128)

Whereas beasts kill out of necessity, and live according to nature, man destroys out of sheer wantonness and fear and under the guise of friendship:

> For hunger, or for Love, they fight, or tear,
> Whilst wretched *Man,* is still in Arms for fear;
> For fear he armes, and is of Armes afraid,
> By fear, to fear, successively betray'd.
>
> (139-142)

> The good he acts, the ill he does endure,
> 'Tis all for fear, to make himself secure.
> Meerly for safety, after Fame we thirst,
> For all Men, wou'd be *Cowards* if they durst.
>
> (155-158)

Now, both beasts and man are motivated by passion (as Hobbes states in *The Leviathan*), and in some instances by the same passions, such as hunger or love. The distinction, for Rochester, lies in the difference in the dominant passion: beasts are motivated by positive and aggressive and natural passions like love and hunger; man by a negative and defensive passion like fear. The baseness of human conduct stems, then, from the baseness of his original motivation.

Further, what appears best and noblest in man is founded upon this base passion of fear; so the whole structure of civilization is false and hollow. For man, a debased creature enslaved by fear, every seeming virtue is a cheap and artificial bauble put on to impress one's equally wretched fellows:

> Base fear, the source whence his best passion[s] came,
> His boasted Honor, and his dear bought Fame.
> That lust of Pow'r, to which he's such a *Slave*,
> And for the which alone he dares be brave:
> To which his various Projects are design'd,
> Which makes him gen'rous, affable, and kind.
> For which he takes such pains to be thought wise,
> And screws his actions, in a forc'd disguise:
>
> (143-150)

> Look to the bottom, of his vast design,
> Wherein *Mans* Wisdom, Pow'r, and Glory joyn;
> The good he acts, the ill he does endure,
> 'Tis all for fear, to make himself secure.
>
> (153-156)

W J. Courthope attributes this emphasis on fear to Rochester's reading of *The Leviathan*.[30] Moore likewise speaks of the "highly rhetorical presentation of the Hobbesian conception of the role of fear in human existence. . . ."[31] The emphasis on fear in the poem is, however, a basic departure from Hobbes, and on precisely this fact rests the mordancy of Rochester's satire. Hence, it is necessary to distinguish very clearly between the views of Hobbes and those of the poet.

First of all, man's egoism receives a different emphasis in the two. According to Hobbes, man is motivated by a desire for power: "Competition of riches, honour, command, or other power, inclineth to contention, enmity, and war: because the way of one competitor, to the attaining of his desire, is to kill, subdue, supplant, or repel the other."[32] This "vainglory" is one of the strongest motives in human behavior. In Rochester's satire, by contrast, this motive is considerably de-emphasized, if not denied. As a result, man is depicted, not as an aggressive, predatory creature with strength and will as in Hobbes, but as a wretched, miserable creature eternally on the defensive for fear of other men. The desire for power itself stems from fear. In fact, man is so cowardly that he lacks the courage to be openly a coward.

Second, in Hobbes, fear is a secondary motive. Because of the vaingloriousness of some men and their "hope for precedency and superiority above their fellows," "those men who are moderate, and look for no more but equality of nature, shall be obnoxious to the force of others, that will attempt to subdue them. And from hence shall proceed a general diffidence in mankind, and mutual fear of one another."[33] It is clear, too, that, as Hobbes pictures humanity in its natural state, not all men will be equally motivated by fear, since the most vainglorious must, if they be possessed of power, feel considerable confidence of success in their aggression against their weaker neighbors.

Third, in Hobbes, warfare among men, in which condition fear becomes a strong motive, is a state prior to the establishment of a commonwealth; a second motive, as strong as that for power, leads to the setting up of a civilized society. "The final cause, end, or design of men, who naturally love liberty, and dominion over others, in the introduction of that restraint upon themselves, in which we see them live in commonwealths, is the foresight of their own preservation, and of a more contented life thereby; that is to say, of getting themselves out from that miserable condition of war, which is necessarily consequent . . . to the natural passions of men, when there is no visible power to keep them in awe." So, in accordance with another strong motive, that of self-preservation, men agree by social contract to give over those aggressive actions which will prove mutually destructive, and set up a king who shall, by vested power, preserve peace within the commonwealth. Such desirable ends as justice, mercy, the Golden Rule, are thus established; and security will supplant fear.[34]

In Rochester's satire, by contrast, the commonwealth of men has not achieved the peace and security that Hobbes depicts. Despite the existence of a human society, the state of war is maintained, though now through subterfuge; instead of open acts of aggression, men hypocritically undermine and destroy other men, through "smiles, embraces, Friendship, praise." Man has created a wretched society where "*Men* must be *Knaves,* 'tis in their own defence" (160). In place of Hobbes's more complex analysis of human motivation, Rochester offers just one dominant motive, the base passion of fear. With bitter misanthropy he lashes out at the baseness of man, who, instead of using right reason to achieve happiness within the proper "*Sphere*" of Action," has perverted even right reason to the base motive of fear. Every deed stems from fear of one's kind, and there is no hope of escaping the maze of hypocrisy and treachery:

> Nor can weak truth, your reputation save,
> The *Knaves,* will all agree to call you *Knave.*
> Wrong'd shall he live, insulted o're, opprest,
> Who dares be less a *Villain,* than the rest.
>
> (164-167)

Truth does exist, but it is weak; the only refuge is knavery, for no one is strong or courageous enough to withstand the knaves who dominate society.

The sharp contempt of Rochester cuts deeper than Swift's itself. The ridicule of mankind for his folly, his irrationality, and his baseness in *Gulliver's Travels* is here concentrated into one, fierce indictment of man's pusillanimity. Base coward, Rochester cries in his fury; man is a coward so base that he is trapped by his own cowardice. Here we find no suprahuman Houyhnhnms dedicated to a life of reason; there is not even a common-sensical Gulliver, to learn the lesson that experience and the wise horses teach him. There are only Yahoos, wretched, miserable, and in a state of war. Men are deluded by the will-o'-the-wisp of speculative reason and fancy themselves wiser than beasts; the "formal Band, and Beard" who protests against the poet's paradox is as absurd as the inhabitants of Laputa. The poet himself is a bitter, disillusioned observer of man's baseness. Hence, there is no hope, no escape from a wretched society at war with itself, where men must keep their hearts and doors locked for fear of their neighbors, every man must betray in order to survive, and most men stumble about in a bog of illusion.

The tone of the satire, in its bitterness, also differs sharply from Hobbes's calm, common-sensical approach. For Hobbes, honor and fame are distinct values, and so is power; for these contribute in some ways to the satisfaction of man's basic passions and the attainment of pragmatic ends. For Rochester, man's "boasted Honor, and his dear bought Fame" are hollow mockeries, and merely additional evidence of man's baseness.

Further, in Rochester's satire is implicit a moral standard of some sort. Hypocrisy, treachery, cowardice, and living contrary to nature are condemned. By implication, honesty and truth are absolute values, and desirable, though unattainable in our corrupt society. By contrast, in Hobbes's philosophy, virtues are merely relative: "Every man by nature hath right to all things, that is to say, to do whatsoever he listeth to whom he listeth, to possess, use, and enjoy all things he will and can. For seeing all things he willeth, must therefore be good unto him in his own judgment, because he willeth them, and may tend to his preservation some time or other, or he may judge so, and we have made him judge thereof . . . that all things may rightly also be done by him."[35] For an ethical relativist like Hobbes, good and evil are merely names given by a particular individual to particular things insofar as they affect him favorably or adversely; and virtues are names given to certain pragmatically desirable modes of behavior after the establishment of a commonwealth. On such a shifting basis, one can hardly produce a moral satire like Rochester's on the baseness of mankind.

In the second portion of the poem Rochester departs markedly from Hobbes. Implicit in his criticism is some standard of good and evil; and since no relativistic standard is suggested, the criterion must be more or less absolute (I shall not try to explain why Rochester is not relativistic like Hobbes). As Rochester implicitly rejects Christian supernaturalism and the kind of moral sanction that only speculative reason can supply, the foundation of his moral satire can only be nature, that is, naturalistic. To be sure, the metaphysical background of the poem is never clearly

worked out, so that we may have to infer the relationship between his epistemological first portion and the moral satire of the second part. Rochester apparently believes that man ought to base his conduct on knowledge supplied by the senses; that man should follow right reason, and satisfy his appetites moderately; that man should (though this is impossible in the present state of society) avoid hypocrisy and cowardice. The implicit approval of truth and virtue would be grounded on the belief that truth and virtue have a pragmatic value in contributing to happiness in the daily activities of man—in human intercourse and in the satisfaction of human appetites.[36] If this is only implied and never fully stated, at least there is enough evidence in the poem to suggest a naturalistic creed; and it is on this basis that Rochester lashes man for being foolish and cowardly.

In the light of these assumption, we can also re-interpret the epilogue often found at the end of the poem (174-224). This epilogue can hardly be described, in the way Pinto does, as "a sort of conditional recantation,"[37] nor can we agree with him that "the nihilism of the **Satyr against Mankind** is slightly mitigated in a curious epilogue. . . ."[38] On the contrary, the epilogue is an underlining of Rochester's pessimistic denial that honesty exists anywhere among mankind, and it re-enforces his contemptuous reference to Diogenes, the searcher after an honest man (in lines 90-91).

The epilogue begins with a series of hypothetical suppositions that are impossible and incredible for Rochester: that there might be a just man at Court, an upright statesman, a godly churchman, a truly pious pastor. In proposing the first impossibility, Rochester immediately denies it, to preclude any misundertanding of his position:

> But if in *Court,* so just a Man there be,
> (In *Court,* a just Man, yet unknown to me.)
>
> (179-180)

The irony of this can hardly be lost on the reader familiar with Rochester's career; as a frequenter of the small circle that constituted Whitehall, Rochester was intimately acquainted with everyone from the cynical and dissembling Charles down to the sycophantic servants, and estimate of the Court is etched in the acid lines of a satire like "The History of Insipids."

The hypothetical impossibilities being concluded, Rochester ironically offers his recantation, for which he, of course, sees no likelihood:

> If upon *Earth* there dwell such *God-like Men,*
> I'le here recant my *Paradox* to them.
> Adore those *Shrines* of *Virtue, Homage* pay,
> And with the *Rabble World,* their *Laws* obey.
>
> (219-222)

The promise to recant is hedged around with such reservations that no one is ever likely to hear a recantation from Rochester: such a recantation will be made to the "God-like Men," who, of course, do not exist; he further offers to be so extravagant in his behavior as to obey the conventional "laws" of the "rabble world," an unlikely action from a skeptical aristocrat like the poet. Since there are no such God-like men (but only "some formal Band, and Beard"), there is no likelihood of Rochester ever recanting his paradox, that he would rather be "a *Dog,* a *Monkey,* or a *Bear*" than that vain animal man.

Finally, granting the possibility of a recantation (though this has been illustrated to be quite unlikely), Rochester ironically makes one last reservation:

> If such there are, yet grant me this at least,
> *Man* differs more from *man,* than *Man* from *Beast.*
>
> (223-224)

This is the last impregnable stronghold of Rochester's pessimism: that man is a beast. The furious contempt for mankind is re-enforced by the irony of the epilogue, and to the very end, Rochester remits no portion of his savage satire on man's stupidity and baseness. The unity of the poem is maintained, then, through the epilogue, and there is no recantation.

The analysis of the poem has, I hope, achieved its primary end of clearing up the meaning of the satire. It has not been my intention to argue the perhaps insoluble question of Rochester's indebtedness to Hobbes or anyone else. In considering the poem in three parts, and particularly in distinguishing between the epistemological first portion and the moral satire of the second part, and further, in showing the parallels to Hobbes and the departures from his views in each of these sections, I have tried to clarify the basic ideas in the poem, and the precise objects of satire. Whether this has a bearing on an understanding of Rochester's personal life is a secondary matter. What concerns us chiefly is that an analysis should contribute to our appreciation of the poem: first, by indicating the pattern and the relationship of the parts, and second, by suggesting the ingredients that are Rochester's.

What stands out in the poem is the consistent and biting attack on man's enslavement to speculative reason and fear. For men of sense (among whom one might perhaps number the poet) there may be a faint hope; but for the bulk of mankind, a life of wretchedness worse than a beast's is the only prospect. Whether Rochester considers himself a knave or not, his perspicacious grasp of man's state engenders a furious hate in his heart which finds vent in fierce ridicule. The *saeva indignatio* of the true satirist, but permeated with the irony and bitterness of Rochester, breathes its vitality through the **Satyr Against Mankind.**

Notes

1. Cf. Ian Jack, *Augustan Satire: 1660-1750* (Oxford, 1952), which makes only a passing reference to Rochester and none to the *Satyr Against Mankind.*

2. Kenneth B. Murdock, "A Very Profane Wit," in *The Sun at Noon* (New York, 1939), p. 284.

3. John F. Moore, "The Originality of Rochester's *Satyr Against Mankind," PMLA,* LVIII (June 1943), 393-401.

4. S. F. Crocker, "Rochester's *Satire Against Mankind," West Virginia University Studies*: III. *Philological Papers,* II (May 1937), 73. J.F Moore summarily dismisses Crocker's views (*PMLA*). Crocker's point, however, is taken up by Charles Norman in his slapdash *Rake Rochester* (New York, 1954), p. 136: "[it is a] poem which owes less to Boileau than has been supposed, more to La Rochefoucauld and Montaigne."

In weighing an assertion like Crocker's, one might note the complete difference in tone and purpose between Montaigne's skepticism, in "The Apology of Raimond Sebond," which is but one step to fideism, and the savage cynicism of Rochester's poem; or one might question the verbal parallelisms that Crocker cites: is Rochester's attack on wit (35-45) and his remark that "*Men* of Wit, are dang'rous Tools, / And ever fatal to admiring *Fools*" "paralleled after a fashion in La Rochefoucauld: 'Un homme d'esprit seroit souvent bien embarrassé sans la compagnie des sots.'"?—Crocker, p. 62.

5. W. J. Courthope, *A History of English Poetry,* III (London, 1903), 465.

6. Vivian de Sola Pinto, *Rochester: Portrait of a Restoration Poet* (London, 1935), p. 175.

7. *Poems by John Wilmot, Earl of Rochester,* ed. Vivian de Sola Pinto (London, 1953), p. xxix; Crocker, p. 57.

8. Pinto, *Rochester,* p. 174.

9. Vivian de Sola Pinto, "John Wilmot, Earl of Rochester, and the Right Veine of Satire," *Essays and Studies: 1953,* Vol. VI, n.s., The English Association (London, 1953), p. 69.

10. Moore, p. 399.

11. Earl of Rochester, *A Satire Against Mankind and Other Poems,* ed. Harry Levin (Norfolk, Conn., 1942), p. 5; *Seventeenth-Century Verse and Prose,* Vol. II: 1660-1700, ed. Helen C. White, Ruth C. Wallerstein, Ricardo Quintana (New York, 1952), p. 451.

12. All references to the poem are to the version in *Poems by Rochester,* ed. Pinto, pp. 118-124.

13. Cf. Pinto's remark that the poet regarded the alienation of reason and morality as the chief cause of his own misery—*Rochester,* p. 174. This makes no sense unless the terms "reason" and "morality" are precisely defined, and even then, it is hardly tenable.

14. Murdock, p. 285.

15. *Ibid.,* p. 284.

16. Crocker, p. 57.

17. See Pinto, *Rochester,* p. 175.

18. Thomas Hobbes, *The Leviathan,* Part I, Ch. 1, in *The English Works of Thomas Hobbes,* ed. Sir William Molesworth (London, 1839), III, 1.

19. *Ibid.,* I, 3, in *Works,* III, 17.

20. *Ibid.,* I, 4, in *Works,* III, 25.

21. *Ibid.,* I, 5, in *Works,* III, 35.

22. *Ibid.,* in *Works,* III, 37.

23. *Ibid.,* I, 8, in *Works,* III, 69.

24. Pinto, *Essays and Studies,* p. 68.

25. Hobbes, *Leviathan,* I, 5, in *Works,* III, 36-37.

26. *Ibid.,* I, 11, in *Works,* III, 85.

27. Cf. Murdock, p. 285.

28. *Ibid.,* p. 284.

29. Hobbes, *Leviathan,* I, 5, in *Works,* III, 36.

30. Courthope, p. 466: "ultimately traceable to the *Leviathan.*"

31. Moore, p. 397.

32. Hobbes, *Leviathan,* I, 11, in *Works,* III, 86.

33. Hobbes, *De Corpore Politico, or the Elements of Law,* Part I, Ch. 1, in *Works,* IV, 82.

34. Hobbes, *Leviathan,* II, 17, in *Works,* III, 153.

35. Hobbes, *De Corpore Politico,* I, 1, in *Works,* IV, 84.

36. Cf. Rochester's remarks to Burnet in Gilbert Burnet, *Some Passages of the Life and Death of John Earl of Rochester* (London, 1860), p. 35: "For *Morality,* he confessed, He saw the necessity of it, both for the government of the World, and for the preservation of Health, Life and Friendship."

37. Pinto, *Rochester,* p. 181.

38. Pinto, *Essays and Studies,* p. 69.

C. F. Main (essay date 1960)

SOURCE: Main, C. F. "The Right Vein of Rochester's *Satyr.*" In *Essays in Literary History, Presented to J. Milton French,* edited by Rudolf Kirk and C. F. Main, pp. 93-112. New Brunswick, N.J.: Rutgers University Press, 1960.

[*In the essay which follows, Main seeks to uncover the "true vein" of Rochester's* A Satire Against Mankind *and argues that the work is a formal classical verse satire, as it contains typical elements of such a work, including the arraignment of one vice and commendation of its opposite virtue; a two-part structure; a single theme; the use of an unpleasant, satirical person; and a retraction at the end of the poem.*]

John Aubrey records an interesting contemporary opinion of the Earl of Rochester as a satirist. Andrew Marvell, he tells us, was wont to say that Rochester "was the best English Satyrist and had the right vein."[1] If modern commentators on Rochester never fail to quote Marvell's opinion, they also never fail to leave it unexplained. Clearly Marvell had in mind some sort of contrast between Rochester's satires and other people's, including his own. It is equally clear that at least one of Rochester's satires, **A Satyr against Mankind,** is indeed quite unlike Marvell's political pasquils, Butler's burlesque narratives, or Cleveland's lampoons on the Puritans. When the label *satire* is applied to these representative English works, it refers to a mode or an attitude; when Marvell applies it to Rochester's poem, it refers to a classical genre, the formal verse satire or *satura.* Rochester's *Satyr* breaks with the native tradition. Its closest contemporary affinities are not with English satire but with French, especially with Boileau's *Satire VIII.* In fact, its resemblance to Boileau's *Satire* (1667) and its later date (ca. 1675) have led some critics, including Johnson, to regard it as a mere pendant to the earlier poem. But Rochester's and Boileau's satires are independent works, as John F. Moore has demonstrated; they have only a "broad structural similarity."[2] They are structurally similar, Moore might have added, because they are both in a vein derived from the Roman *satura.* When Marvell calls this vein the right one, he commends as a critic and a classical scholar certain conventions of satire that he ignores as a practicing satirist. His position is like Dryden's, since the *Discourse concerning the Original and Progress of Satire* (1693) describes and praises the kind of formal verse satire that Juvenal, Persius, and Boileau wrote, but that Dryden himself never attempted except in translation. Formal verse satire is so rare in English that Rochester's brilliant and early specimen in the kind deserves a closer study than it has yet received.

A formal verse satire is a quasi-dramatic poem in which a voice is heard arraigning one particular vice and commending its opposite virtue. Though sometimes the first portion of the poem contains the arraignment and the, last the commendation, a formal verse satire never splits into two distinct pieces because the virtue is always present, if not overtly then at least by implication. Thus a formal satire has two main parts in the way that a balance has them: one part will not function without the other. The satirist's "negative" denunciations always imply "positive" standards of some sort, usually a "dominant rationalistic philosophy" of the time.[3] The positive-negative contrast gives the satire its framework, within which a great variety of rhetorical and dramatic devices may be used. At times this "medley" (an etymological meaning of *satura*) of devices may give an impression of disorder and would indeed render the satire quite formless, were it not for the bipartite structure. As a formal satirist Rochester uses several of the conventions: the unpleasant satirical *persona,* the *adversarius* who interrupts him, the partial retraction at the end of the poem. But let us first look at the structure, and first within the structure at the "negative side."

In his *Discourse* Dryden insists that a perfect satire "ought only to treat of one subject; to be confined to one particular theme; or at least, to one principally. If other vices occur in the management of the chief, they should only be transiently lashed."[4] Rochester's practice conforms with the theory that Dryden deduced from the ancient satirists. The *Satyr* lashes one principal vice: pride. Instead of attacking proud individuals, the formal satirist attacks pride itself, the generic pride that mankind assumes from the mere fact of its humanity. The speaker of the satire (a discussion of the nature of this speaker must be postponed until we look at the "positive side") begins by saying that he would rather be a dog, a monkey, or a bear,

> Or any thing but that vain *Animal,*
> Who is so proud of being rational.[5]
>
> (lines 6-7)

The important word here is *proud,* not *rational;* at least the reader who seizes on the latter and ignores the former is bound to ignore the design of the poem. Thomas H. Fujimura, for instance, has recently attempted to define the "precise objects" of Rochester's satire by "distinguishing between the epistemological first portion and the moral satire of the second."[6] This view leaves the poem in two distinct pieces because it overlooks the fact that *all* of a satire must be moral—that is, concerned with judging human attitudes and conduct. Pride, not epistemology, is the error satirized throughout.

At climactic points the satirist arraigns pride by name. After denouncing pride founded on the mistaken notion that man has a rational faculty unique to himself (lines 1-28), the satirist paints this grim picture of man *in extremis*:

> Huddled in dirt, the reas'ning *Engine* lyes,
> Who was so proud, so witty, and so wise.
> *Pride* drew him in, as *Cheats,* their *Bubbles,* catch,
> And made him venture, to be made a *Wre[t]ch.*
>
> (lines 29-32)

Then follows (lines 33-45) an account of a typical figure, the witty man whose pride in his own wit causes his downfall. A couplet (lines 46-47) introduces another speaker in the manner of French satire (in Roman satire the *adversarius* interrupts more abruptly). The other speaker defends all of humanity except wits and justifies human pride by asserting that man is made in God's image (lines 48-71). To silence him, the satirist renews his attack on pride in learning (lines 72-113) and in a triplet clinches his indictment:

> For all his Pride, and his Philosophy,
> 'Tis evident, *Beasts* are in their degree,
> As wise at least, and better far than he.
>
> (lines 114-116)

Having disposed of pride in wisdom, the satirist now demolishes pride in accomplishment (lines 117-173). Man, he says, owes his entire civilization—his moral code, his "Projects," the very government that protects him from his fellows—to his innate fear. Consequently man can no more rightly be proud of what he does than of what he knows. The satire proper ends with these lines:

> All this with indignation I have hurl'd
> At the pretending part of the proud World,
> Who swolne with selfish vanity, devise,
> False freedomes, holy Cheats, and formal Lyes
> Over their fellow *Slaves* to tyrranize.
>
> (lines 174-178)

The poem ends with a partial retraction, a common feature in formal verse satire. This retraction (lines 179-224) was probably not prompted by the writers who answered Rochester's *Satyr,* as Vivian de Sola Pinto suggests;[7] Rochester hardly needed crude rejoinders to remind him of the satirical conventions. The rejoinders to the *Satyr* may help us to discover how the poem was received, but not how it was composed. Despite the versions in which the retraction is labeled "Postscript," it is an integral part of the *Satyr.* It consists, first, of three brief satirical characters. The character of the courtier and that of the clergyman both mention pride, and that of the foppish councilman plainly implies it. In addition, other vices besides pride are, in Dryden's words, "transiently lashed." A succinct commendation of the "meek humble man" follows the characters and ends the poem. Having praised humility, though ever so perfunctorily, the satirist has evaded the charge of complete virulence.

Negatively considered, then, the *Satyr* is an attack on humanity's chief sin. The aristocratic libertine has chosen the most hoary of subjects for his satire, and the most traditional of satirical forms. Yet, or perhaps therefore, he has created an original work. Behind him lies the weight of centuries of sermonizing on pride, sermonizing that he pointedly ignores because his grounds are very different from those of Christian clergymen. The final admonition to be humble is the logical conclusion of an unorthodox view of man that runs through the poem alongside the denunciation of pride.

One must beware of taking the "positive side" of the *Satyr* as Rochester's personal credo, of reading the poem as though it were *The Prelude.* The classical satirist is not "expressing himself." Convention requires him to assume a mask and strike a pose, to be insincere. Nothing, therefore, could be more incorrect than this typical opinion of the *Satyr*: "Browning might have written just such a poem in his *Men and Women,* dramatically; but Rochester is speaking for himself."[8] This comment is incorrect because it implies, among other things, that the darling of Charles's court actually wished to change places with his pet monkey. "That Rochester regarded men as knaves, fools, and animals," another critic remarks, "there can be no doubt; it is the main argument of his satirical masterpiece, *A Satyr Against Mankind*."[9] Although it is always disastrous to re-create the historical poet from the dramatic poem, commentators on Rochester seem irresistibly tempted to do so, perhaps because the poet's life itself was so luridly theatrical. Rochester loved to appear what he was not. "In all his frolicksome Disguises," says the author of the *Memoir* attributed wrongly to Saint-Evremond, "he so truly personated the Thing he would seem, that his most intimate Acquaintance could not discover the Imposture."[10] The man who in real life successfully impersonated a woman on one occasion and a mountebank on another must, surely, be permitted to invent a satirical *persona*. Whatever the positive doctrine of a man contained in the *Satyr* may be, we have no evidence that it is Rochester's private philosophy of life.

Several scholars have canvassed the sources of this doctrine. J.F. Crocker, for instance, traces the *Satyr* to Montaigne's *Apologie de Raimond Sebond*. "There is scarcely an idea of major or minor importance in Rochester," he concludes, with more assurance than proof, "that is not present in Montaigne."[11] Were the parallels that Crocker cites at all close, his conclusion would still be unconvincing because the *Satyr* and the *Apologie* discredit human reason for very different purposes. Montaigne and his fellow skeptics question man's ability to reason in order to stress his need to have faith in divine revelation. The main speaker of Rochester's poem is not skeptical in this sense; he makes no claim for faith. He does not even offer a choice between reason and faith, as Dryden does in *Religio Laici*; instead, he sets up reason and sense as opposites. Man, he says at the beginning of the poem, is inferior to the beasts because he prefers reason to "certain instinct," and because he leaves the "light of Nature, sense, behind" (lines 10-13). The skeptics, in contrast, have no such confidence in the senses. According to Thomas Stanley's *History of Philosophy,* they hold that "the Senses are so far from guiding the Intellect to comprehension, that they contradict one another."[12] Rochester may have known Stanley's *History,* but if he did know it, he drew on its account of epicureanism, as Ronald Crane suggests,[13] rather than on its account of skepticism. Crane also cites some convincing parallels between the theriophilic ideas in the poem and in ancient writers; yet his helpful notes are not intended to be a coherent account of the poem. Moore, who demonstrates Rochester's independence of Boileau, is equally inconclusive: "A single source for the content of the *Satyr* will be difficult to accept,"[14] he says. Finally, and most recently, Fujimura finds in the satire a "naturalistic creed," Hobbist in the main but with significant departures from Hobbes (p. 588). None of these investigators considers the dramatic convention of the satirical genre.

Rochester creates a speaker, who for convenience will be referred to simply as the "satirist," of the sort that will give the maximum amount of offense to godly and conventional people in his audience, the same people whom he affronted when he had the famous portrait painted in which he is elegantly placing a laurel wreath on a monkey. The satirist commits his first offense against conventional morality in the passage denouncing pride in reason. The lines are as interesting for what they leave unsaid as for what they say:

> The senses are too gross, and he'll contrive
> A Sixth, to contradict the other Five;
> And before certain instinct, will preferr
> *Reason,* which Fifty times for one does err.
> *Reason,* an *Ignis fatuus,* in the *Mind,*
> Which leaving light of Nature, sense behind;
> Pathless and dang'rous wandring ways it takes,
> Through errors, Fenny-*Boggs,* and Thorny *Brakes*;
> Whilst the misguided follower, climbs with pain,
> *Mountains* of Whimseys, heap'd in his own *Brain*:
> Stumbling from thought to thought, falls head-long down,
> Into doubts boundless Sea, where like to drown,
> Books bear him up awhile, and makes him try,
> To swim with Bladders of *Philosophy*;
> In hopes still t'oretake the'escaping light,
> The *Vapour* dances in his dazl[ed] sight,
> Till spent, it leaves him to eternal Night.
> Then Old Age, and experience, hand in hand,
> Lead him to death, and make him understand,
> After a search so painful, and so long,
> That all his Life he has been in the wrong;
> Hudled in dirt, the reas'ning *Engine* lyes,
> Who was so proud, so witty, and so wise.
>
> (lines 8-30)

In this bitter attack on intellectual pride the satirist has ignored sin and thus implied a heterodox view of man. With such extremists as Calvin he agrees that man is a worm five feet long, but he fails to give the orthodox reason for that view: man is a fallen creature, worthy only of such merit as God's grace may confer on him. The rejoinders to the *Satyr* call attention to the satirist's failure to mention sin. For instance, Richard Pocock, or whoever wrote *An Answer to the Satyr against Mankind,* agrees that mankind now has little to be proud of, but he argues that original sin deprived the race of merit:

> Must the first draught of Man be vilify'd,
> Scorn'd and contemn'd, 'cause Man himself hath stray'd?
> Or did not *Eve* sufficiently transgress,
> And Bastardise Posterity? unless
> Man, little as he is, be made much less.[15]

The Christian view always leaves man with more than a few rags of pride. Rochester's satirist, in contrast, strips from man even the dignity of having fallen from grace. By indicting the race for stupidity rather than for sinfulness, he commits an outrage against conventional morality.

When the satirist argues that "Sense" should take priority over "Reason," he apparently wishes to appear as a disciple of the most conspicuous contemporary bugbear, Thomas Hobbes. His term *reason,* as Fujimura shows, is synonymous with Hobbes's "abstruse philosophy," the speculations of schoolmen which produce nothing but rigmaroles and verbiage; and his emphasis on sense is reminiscent of the opening chapter of *Leviathan.* Yet the passage in the

Satyr must not be taken as an adequate summary of Hobbes's epistemology. Hobbes obviously lacked the satirist's complete confidence in sense; he relied rather on what he thought of as geometric logic, on reasoning deductively from self-evident axioms in which the terms had been meticulously defined. Sense, after all, can provide data only about the secondary qualities of matter. In *The Questions concerning Liberty, Necessity, and Chance* (1656) Hobbes compared man and beast with results very different from the satirist's:

> There be beasts that see better, others that hear better, and others that exceed mankind in other senses. Man excelleth beasts only in making rules to himself, that is to say, in remembering, and in reasoning aright upon that which he remembereth. They which do, deserve an honor above brute beasts. . . . So that it is not merely the nature of man, that makes him worthier than other living creatures, but the knowledge that he acquires by meditation, and by the right of use of reason in making good rules of his future actions.[16]

The satirist speaks, then, as a quasi Hobbist. By echoing the famous statement about sense in *Leviathan* and by adopting Hobbes's ridicule of inspiration and speculation, he associates himself with the alleged atheism, materialism, and licentiousness of Hobbes.

The satirist takes full advantage of the convention that obliges him to be inconsistent and unfair when he calls the inspired philosopher a "reas'ning *Engine*" (line 29). There is nothing "mechanical" about this philosopher's view of man; on the contrary, "engine" is an epithet more properly applied to the naturalistic satirist himself. Bishop Bramhall accused Hobbes of picturing man as a "wooden top" (V,55), or a "tennis-ball" (V,278), or "a watch which is wound up by God" (V,203)—that is, as a temporary aggregate of material in motion. The satirist, conscious of his audience, forestalls a similar accusation by making it himself. With more boldness than truth, he annoys the supernaturalists by calling them "reasoning engines."

Having made this telling point, the satirist offers some bait to his auditory in the form of what seems to be an attack on wit. His *adversarius,* a "formal Band and Beard," rises to the bait, agrees that wit should be lashed, but finds man in general worthy of more praise than censure:

> *What rage ferments in your degen'rate mind,*
> *To make you rail at Reason, and Mankind?*
> *Blest glorious* Man! *to whom alone kind* Heav'n,
> *An everlasting* Soul *has freely giv'n;*
> *Whom his great* Maker *took such care to make,*
> *That from himself he did the* Image *take;*
> *And this fair frame, in shining* Reason *drest,*
> *To dignifie his* Nature, *above* Beast.
> Reason, *by whose aspiring influence,*
> *We take a flight beyond material sense,*
> *Dive into* Mysteries, *then soaring pierce,*
> *The flaming limits of the Universe.*
> *Search Heav'n and Hell, find out what's acted there,*
> *And give the World true grounds of hope and fear.*
>
> (lines 58-71)

In this utterance the *adversarius* reveals his character. He is a smug prelate, a self-styled idealist of the kind that regards all satirists as degenerates. He believes in the dignity of man, in man's essential difference from beasts, and in man's ability to pierce the infinite and thereby attain ultimate knowledge. These notions are the commonplaces of Renaissance optimism, but never in the Renaissance were they mouthed so complacently and so glibly. The *adversarius* is a proud man defending Pride, a mock Christian who has conveniently forgotten the Fall. Again Rochester has offended the pious by making this facile optimist their spokesman.

It is easy to demolish such a straw man, and the satirist does so by comparing him with three tenth-rate writers: Nathaniel Ingelo, Simon Patrick, and Richard Sibbes. The lines that follow the interruption show that the satirist shares Hobbes's notorious anticlerical bias, his prejudice against "Those Reverend Bedlams, *Colledges* and Schools" (line 83), and his distrust of "reason":

> Borne on whose Wings, each heavy *Sot* can pierce,
> The limits of the boundless Universe.
> So charming Oyntments, make an Old *Witch* flie,
> And bear a Crippled Carcass through the Skie.
>
> (lines 84-87)

The satirist's "heavy Sot" resembles Hobbes's dogmatic man, who takes "*the habitual discourse of the tongue for ratiocination*" (IV,73).

In opposition to this kind of reason, for which a better name would be "revelation," the satirist sets up his own "right reason":

> Thus, whilst 'gainst false reas'ning I inveigh,
> I own right *Reason,* which I wou'd obey:
> That *Reason* that distinguishes by sense,
> And gives us *Rules,* of good, and ill from thence:
> That bounds desires, with a reforming Will,
> To keep 'em more in vigour, not to kill.
> Your *Reason* hinders, mine helps t'enjoy,
> Renewing Appetites, yours wou'd destroy.
> My Reason is my *Friend,* yours is a *Cheat,*
> Hunger call's out, my Reason bids me eat;
> Perversely yours, your Appetite does mock,
> This asks for Food, that answers what's a Clock?
> This plain distinction Sir your doubt secures,
> 'Tis not true Reason I despise but yours.
> Thus I think Reason righted.
>
> (lines 98-112)

This definition of "right reason" is perhaps the most outrageous thing in the poem, for it vastly reduces the meaning that that venerable term had carried for several generations of Christian humanists. Traditionally, right reason signifies the "immutable coalescence of truth and goodness whose source is God and whose formative cosmic role is manifested in all the workings of nature."[17] As the term is used in the *Satyr,* it obviously lacks all its former grandeur. Hobbes might be thought responsible for this particular deflation, since he let the wind out of so many terms, if he had not described right reason as "the natural, moral, and divine law" (II, 166), and if he had not said, "When a man *reasoneth* from *principles* that are found indubitable by experience, all deceptions of sense and equivocation of words avoided, the conclusion he maketh is said to be *according to right reason*" (IV, 24). The satirist and Hobbes clearly use the terms differently.

In fact, to find parallels with the *Satyr* one must descend from the philosophers to the dramatists. Don John, the hero of Shadwell's *The Libertine* (1675), agrees with the satirist that sense is the proper guide of reason:

> Nature gave us our Senses, which we please:
> Nor does our Reason war against our Sense.
> By Natures order, Sense should guide our Reason,
> Since to the mind all objects Sense conveys.
> But Fools for shaddows lose substantial pleasures,
> For idle tales abandon true delight,
> And solid joys of day, for empty dreams at night.[18]

Similarly Deidamia, the lustful queen of Sparta in Otway's *Alcibiades* (1675), speaks of "sense" as man's "God."[19] Finally, in Rochester's own unproduced *Valentinian* the chaste Claudia says:

> Each man I meet I fancy will devour me;
> And sway'd by Rules not natural but affected
> I hate Mankind for fear of being lov'd.

To which Marcellina, a much frailer creature, replies:

> Prithee reform; what Nature prompts us to,
> And Reason seconds, why should we avoid?[20]

In founding reason on sense, or rather in confounding reason with sense, the satirist associates himself with scandalous personages currently being represented on the stage. Like them he overturns the traditional hierarchy in which reason is the master rather than the servant of appetite. No clocks—no external regulators—keep the satirist from satisfying his appetites and thus achieving the ends for which he and the animals were created:

> Those *Creatures,* are the wisest who attain,
> By surest means, the ends at which they aim.
>
>   (lines 118-119)

This couplet leads from the attack on pride in philosophy to the attack on pride in accomplishment. To discredit human accomplishment, the satirist discredits human motivation. Here his "positive" doctrine of man seems entirely derived from Hobbes, whose emphasis on fear as a motive is so well known that it hardly needs rehearsing. Fujimura has recently challenged this traditional view of the *Satyr*; he finds that "the emphasis on fear in the poem is . . . a basic departure from Hobbes" (p. 585). The departure, however, is due to the conventions of satire rather than to divergent philosophies. The satirist does simplify Hobbes's complex analysis of human motivation, as Fujimura indicates, not because he disagrees with it but because

satire must always be simpler than philosophy. Here Rochester has a precedent in Persius, who used only those parts of an elaborate philosophical system that were relevant to his purposes. The very act of attacking only one vice in a satire is a kind of simplification. Again, Fujimura finds "absolute" values in the *Satyr,* "relativistic" ones in Hobbes; and he remarks parenthetically, "I shall not try to explain why Rochester is not relativistic like Hobbes" (p. 588). The question whether Hobbes is a relativist does not concern us here. But we must expect a satirist to assume absolute standards, since satire always measures man against a fixed scale and always finds him short of the mark. In the latter part of the poem the standard is furnished by animals, who, according to Hobbes, live in "good order and government for their common benefit" and are "free from sedition and war amongst themselves." Nor, among animals, is there any "question of precedence in their own species, nor strife about honor, or acknowledgment of one another's wisdom, as there is amongst men" (IV, 120). Animals, in sum, lack pride and fear.

Here, as earlier in the poem, the satirist argues from a naturalistic rather than a Christian bias. After contrasting man with animal, he invites his audience to

> Look to the bottom, of his vast design,
> Wherein *Mans* Wisdom, Pow'r, and Glory joyn;
> The good he acts, the ill he does endure,
> 'Tis all for fear, to make himself secure.
> Meerly for safety, after Fame we thirst,
> For all Men, wou'd be *Cowards* if they durst.
>
>   (lines 153-158)

And again a passage in the *Satyr* is notable for what it omits. Thomas Lessee of Wadham College, who penned some doggerel to reprove the satirist and his mentor, has an explanation of man's fearfulness:

> And first the fear y^t trouble's him within,
> Proceed's not from his nature but his sin.
> Which like pale Ghosts, while they their murderers haunt,
> Doe's cramp his soule, and all his courage daunt.
>   . . . . .
> For lately 'tis evinc't all creatures are
> Noe less y^n man in the wild state of warr,
> Which long agoe, ye weary Emperour knew,
> Who hostile flyes with princely valour slew.
> Is he alone? he startle's when he see's
> His moving shadow, & his shadow flee's,
> For who can evidence but that may bee
> No meere privation, but any Enemy.
> So when alone the tim'rous wretch is scar'd,
> And when hee's not, hee's fearfull of his guard.
> What shall he doe, or whether shall he fly,
> Who durst not live, and yet he dare's not dye.
> Say you, who er'e have felt those painefull stabs,
> Say wretched Nero, or thou more wretched Hobbs.
> Guilt is of all, and always is afraid,
> From fear to fear successively betray'd.
> Ti's guilt alone breeds cowardice & distrust,
> For all men would be valiant, if they durst.[21]

Notwithstanding the *ad hominem* argument, Lessee's ethic is the traditional one.

The satirist's ethic—his "positive" doctrine of man derived from a "dominant rationalistic philosophy of the time"—is a compound of Hobbesean materialism and naturalism with tinctures of epicureanism and libertinism. This doctrine provides a much more effective basis for an attack on pride than either the stoicism of the ancient satirists or the modified stoicism of the Elizabethan, for the stoic himself can always be charged with the vice that he attacks. Hobbism is not a philosophy that glorifies man, either collectively or individually. Hobbes's very exposition of human nature seemed libelous to many of his contemporaries: "If men had sprung up from the earth in a night," complained Bramhall, "like mushrooms or excrescences, without all sense of honour, justice, conscience, or gratitude, he could not have vilified the human nature more than he doth" (IV, 288). And the same doctrine, when calmly set forth in a poem, is more damaging to man's ego than any direct assault.

That Rochester's satirist is calm and self-controlled may be perceived by comparing him with the angry *personae* created by the Elizabethan satirical poets. Unlike the "satyrs" of Hall and Marston, he does not lose his temper, become frenzied, wallow in filth—and thereby discredit everything he says. He is so much in control that he can afford to sneer at misanthropy itself, as he does when he glances at Diogenes, the "Whimsical *Philosopher*" who preferred his tub to "the spacious *World*" (lines 90-91). The satirist, quite at home in the world, is no outraged idealist; he is a sublunary man whose soul is sense. His tone is weary rather than angry, for he does not expect much of the human race except conduct commensurate with the race's limitations. What is unique about the **Satyr,** then, is that the standard it sets is very low, and that man still falls short. The poem derives its extraordinary force from the cooperation between the "positive" doctrine and the "negative" attack. In addition to being a remarkably successful work of art, the **Satyr against Mankind** documents the change in man's view of himself that took place in the seventeenth century. Pride, once a deadly sin, has become a gross absurdity.

I have not tried to document Rochester's own personal views from the **Satyr,** to incorporate the dramatic poem into the morality play that Rochester's biographers make of his life. The numerous ways in which Pope—to mention only one maligned satirist—has been misrepresented stand as a permanent warning against the practice of assuming that the "I" in every poem represents the poet. The analysis has had another purpose: to uncover the true vein of Rochester's masterpiece and to demonstrate that it heads the list of Augustan formal verse satires. With the possible exception of Donne, who escaped the customary Elizabethan confusion between *satyr* and *satura* and thus was able to imitate the spirit of ancient satire more closely than any of his contemporaries,[22] Rochester wrote the first formal verse satire in English.

Notes

1. "John Wilmot: Earl of Rochester," *Brief Lives,* ed. O. L. Dick (London, 1950), p. 321.

2. John F. Moore, "The Originality of Rochester's *Satyr against Mankind*", *PMLA,* LVIII (1943), 401.

3. The terms in quotation marks, as well as the gist of my whole paragraph, are taken from Mary Claire Randolph, "The Structural Design of the Formal Verse Satire," *PQ,* XXI (1942), 368-384.

4. *Essays of John Dryden,* ed. W. P. Ker (Oxford, 1926), II, 102.

5. *Poems by John Wilmot, Earl of Rochester,* ed. Vivian de Sola Pinto (Cambridge, Mass., 1953), p. 118. All quotations from the *Satyr* are taken from this edition.

6. Thomas J. Fujimura, "Rochester's 'Satyr against Mankind': An Analysis," *SP,* LV (1958), 590. Subsequent references will be given in the text.

7. *Poems by John Wilmot,* p. 215.

8. Oliver Elton, *The English Muse* (London, 1933), p. 252.

9. George Williamson, "The Restoration Petronius," *The University of California Chronicle,* XXIX (1927), 275.

10. John Wilmot, *Poetical Works,* ed. Quilter Johns (Halifax, England, 1933), p. xxx.

11. "Rochester's *Satire against Mankind,*" *West Virginia University Studies: III. Philological Papers,* II (1937), 73.

12. Thomas Stanley, *The History of Philosophy* (London, 1660), sig. 4F2^V.

13. Ronald Crane, *A Collection of English Poems, 1660-1800* (New York, 1932), p. 1198.

14. Moore, *op. cit.,* p. 401.

15. (London, *ca.* 1675), p. 2. Wing P2664. I quote from the copy in the Harvard College Library.

16. *The English Works of Thomas Hobbes,* ed. Sir William Molesworth, 5 vols. (London, 1841), V, 186. Subsequent references will be given in the text.

17. Herschel Baker, *The Wars of Truth* (Cambridge, Mass., 1952), p. 92.

18. *The Complete Works of Thomas Shadwell,* ed Montague Summers (London, 1927), III, 26.

19. *The Complete Works of Thomas Otway,* ed. Montague Summers (London, 1926), I, 21.

20. *Collected Works of John Wilmot, Earl of Rochester,* ed. John Hayward (London, 1926), pp. 191-192. With these libertine arguments cf. a "licentious" suppressed stanza of Alexander Pope's "The Universal Prayer" (*Minor Poems,* ed. Norman Ault and John

Butt [London, 1954], p. 147) that Pope quite innocently penned and canceled apparently when his friends showed him its implications:

> Can Sins of Moments claim ye Rod
> Of Everlasting Fires?
> Can those be Sins wth Natures God
> W^ch Natures selfe inspires?

21. "A Satyre, in answer to my Ld Rochesters," British Museum MS. Sloane 1485, fol. 44. Another version of this poem, more than twice as long, is printed among the "Miscellanea" appended to Jane Barker's *Poetical Recreations,* 1688, sigs. 2F2-2G1^v.

22. The ablest discussion of this confusion is chapter three of Alvin Kernan's *The Cankered Muse* (New Haven, 1959).

Howard Erskine-Hill (essay date 1966)

SOURCE: Erskine-Hill, Howard. "Rochester: Augustan or Explorer." In *Renaissance and Modern Essays Presented to Vivian de Sola Pinto in Celebration of his Seventieth Birthday,* edited by G. R. Hibbard, pp. 51-64. London: Routledge and Kegan Paul, 1966.

[*In the following essay, Erskine-Hill considers whether Rochester should be a viewed as an explorer/adventurer— one who lacks a stable pattern of any but the most elementary values—or as an "Augustan," like John Dryden and Alexander Pope, who is confident in a Christian-classical world-view, and concludes he is most clearly the former.*]

I

Rochester, the man and his work, is a major landmark in the terrain of Restoration poetry. That he should come to be recognized as such, in the last fifty years, is due largely to the enthusiasm of the writings and teaching of Vivian de Sola Pinto.[1] But if Rochester's place is assured, the nature of his achievement is in dispute. Pinto, while recognizing Augustan qualities in his work, has also drawn analogies between Rochester and such un-Augustan authors as Marlowe and Blake. David M. Vieth, in an important recent study, considers him fully an Augustan, and finds a strong affinity between his satire and Pope's in respect both of literary techniques and underlying values.[2] The question is whether Rochester's poetry is chiefly that of an explorer through the '*Perplexity* of endless *Thought*', or of a man confident in a stable and ultimately satisfying world-view, by which he can judge the follies of his fellow men.[3]

Without doubt there are interesting and important affinities between Rochester and Pope in respect of qualities which may reasonably be called Augustan. '**An Allusion to Horace**' is the first Augustan imitation in English and is comparable to Pope's *Epistle to Augustus.*[4] '**Tunbridge-Wells**' has resemblances to Pope's *Fourth Satire of Dr* Donne, owing to the common descent from the Ninth Satire of Horace's First Book. ***Artemisa to Cloe,*** in its intimate and delicate modulation of the familiar, Horatian style of formal satire, strikingly anticipates Pope's *Epistle to a Lady.* All these poems of Rochester Pope knew; their relation with Pope's work deserves exploration; but it is not primarily on these that Vieth rests his case.[5] He concentrates rather on the more ironical satires of Rochester: ***Upon Nothing, A Very Heroical Epistle, An Epistolary Essay,*** and deduces from them, in course of a detailed explication of their irony, an underlying attitude towards man and his relation to the cosmos similar to that which he finds explicit in Pope's *Essay on Man.*[6]

There is, however, a poem where Rochester makes explicit his 'general map of man', and which is in this respect the comparable poem to Pope's *Essay.* This is ***A Satyr against Mankind,*** of which it is surprising Vieth takes so little account. For while it resembles *An Essay* in its concern with humankind in general (differing from Satire VIII of Boileau, on which it is partly based, in its exclusion of social satire) it expresses a view of the natural order almost diametrically opposed to Pope's. An investigation of the Augustan nature of Rochester's work must take into account ***A Satyr against Mankind***; I propose to comment on it here, with two other related poems, as a prelude to discussing ***A Very Heroical Epistle*** and ***An Epistolary Essay.***

II

A Satyr against Mankind, like *An Essay on Man,* is a polemic against human pride, proceeding from a consideration of man's place in the universe to his behaviour to his fellow men. Each poem declares man's proper concern to be his immediate 'environment'; Rochester maintains that

> Our *Sphere* of Action, is life's happiness,
> And he who thinks Beyond, thinks like an *Ass*
>
> (ll. 96-7)

while Pope takes as his apparent premise the following lines:

> Say first, of God above, or Man below,
> What can we reason, but from what we know?
> Of Man what see we, but his station here,
> From which to reason, or to which refer?
>
> (I, ll. 17-20)

and at the beginning of Book IV he apostrophizes 'Happiness' as 'our being's end and aim! / Good, Pleasure, Ease, Content! whate'er thy name' (ll. 1-2). But the fundamental conception of Pope's poem is that of the general yet particularly and vividly conceived hierarchy of creation, extending far above man and below, in which the wise, humble and pious person will know the proper place of his kind. It is a paradox from a modern positivist viewpoint that Pope, holding that we can reason only from what we know, should affirm the existence of this partly metaphysical hierarchy with such confident and splendid particularity. In Rochester no such paradox is found. In *A*

Satyr against Mankind, the assertion of the hierarchy, of 'the whole connected creation', is left to the Adversary whose very intervention (and here I would differ from Pinto) Rochester has made subtly ridiculous, and whose views he strongly rebuts in other parts of the poem.[7] The divine is gratified at Rochester's attack on wit, but is sufficiently unmoved by the terrible force of the preceding lines to get in a hint at the irony of it's being *Wilmot* who makes such an attack: '. . . *but you take care, / Upon this point, not to be too severe.*' He then ludicrously displays his own vanity in wit:

> *Perhaps my* Muse, *were fitter for this part,*
> *For I profess, I can be very smart*
> *On* Wit, *which I abhor with all my heart:*

> (ll. 52-4)

following this up with the use of a metaphor (the 'Tide of Ink'—l. 57) both clumsy and rather archaically metaphysical. The divine now proceeds with his counter-assertion of the dignity of man and of his connection with his Creator. There is a bland facility in his expression which speaks for itself.

> *Blest glorious* Man! *to whom alone kind* Heav'n,
> *An everlasting* Soul *has freely giv'n;*
> *Whom his great* Maker *took such care to make,*
> *That from himself he did the* Image *take;*
> *And this fair frame, in shining* Reason *drest,*
> *To dignifie his* Nature, *above* Beast.

> (ll. 60-5)

Next he praises Reason for enabling man to quest beyond material sense for knowledge of the cosmos, and imitates (as Pinto notes) a line from Lucretius's *De Rerum Natura* in praise of Epicurus.[8] This is a subtle passage. The ideas it advances are of so traditional a kind that it seems at first sight possible that Rochester is allowing the divine to put them over to us straight. A closer look reveals a disturbing quality in the language of the divine. A man who can throw together so lightly the two adjectives '*Blest glorious*' does not seem to be weighing his words, but to have a mechanically dutiful sense of the wonder of his theme. The vacuousness of the line: '*Whom his great* Maker *took such care to make*' strengthens this impression and the whole passage, laden as it is with laudatory epithets, seems to be saying something altogether too good to be true. The line from Lucretius is interesting, and is perhaps ironical. If the divine is attempting to argue *ad hominem,* and enlist Rochester's favourite Lucretius in the defence of Reason, he only displays ignorance of his source. As Rochester well knew, Reason operating beyond the guidance of '*material sense*' was precisely what Lucretius distrusted, concepts such as '*Heav'n and Hell*' precisely what he praised Epicurus for exploding.[9] Nearer to what would probably have won the approval of Lucretius is Rochester's own account of 'right *Reason*' in the latter part of this poem. Yet *A Satyr* is not entirely Lucretian; even the value of exploring the material universe, which Lucretius glories in, is doubted by Rochester's scepticism.

Thus the whole intervention of the divine, with its attempt to assert human dignity by reference to a divinely and benevolently ordered cosmic structure relating man to God, has been satirically undermined. What remains is the grim strength with which Rochester had described the human situation, before this ineffectual challenge was made:

> *Reason,* an *Ignis fatuus,* in the *Mind,*
> *Which leaving light of Nature, sense behind;*
> *Pathless and dang'rous wandring ways it takes,*
> *Through errors, Fenny-Boggs, and Thorny Brakes;*
> *Whilst the misguided follower, climbs with pain,*
> *Mountains of Whimseys, heap'd in his own Brain:*
> *Stumbling from thought to thought, falls head-long down,*
> *Into doubts boundless Sea, where like to drown,*
> *Books bear him up awhile, and makes him try,*
> *To swim with Bladders of Philosophy;*
> *In hopes still t'oretake the 'escaping light,*
> *The Vapour dances in his dazled sight,*
> *Till spent, it leaves him to eternal Night.*

> (ll. 12-24)

The verse of this passage enacts the failure to erect structures of knowledge or belief in which human life has a significant place. It justifies Pinto's insistence that Rochester is a poet of exploration; the imagery is almost that of pilgrimage, pilgrimage not towards a goal but in search of one. But the quest fails; man is left confronting 'eternal Night'. This 'Night' is the darkness not of the unknown but of nullity, with which, on the extinction of Reason's deceptive light, human life is seen to be rounded. More specifically, and bearing in mind the possible parallel with Lucretius, 'Night' may express the extinction of the individual soul, and ultimately that of the universe.[10] Yet the poem is not entirely nihilistic. 'Our *Sphere* of Action, is life's happiness'—this still remains; within this sphere moral distinctions are still meaningful. It is here that Rochester's unfavourable comparisons of man to the lower animals, which come from Montaigne's *Apologie de Raimond Sébond* as well as from Boileau, are effectively introduced. Their force is greater than in Montaigne, for while he introduced them experimentally, as a kind of salutary medicine for human pride, within the wider and firm context of orthodox Christian belief, Rochester shows no such wider belief.[11] Thus while *A Satyr against Mankind* and *An Essay on Man* both seek to humble human vanity, they do so in opposite ways. Pope does so by depicting the divinely ordered hierarchy of creation of which man is merely a part; Rochester does so, in perhaps more devastating fashion, by showing the absence of such a hierarchy, the failure of man to fill and systematize the surrounding void. Pope's cosmos teems with life; Rochester's is almost empty. It is clear from this comparison that if D. M. Vieth is correct when he states that Rochester's 'innermost values were as conservative as Pope's and more conservative, perhaps, than Dryden's', conservatism must mean a fundamentally different thing in each case.[12]

The human predicament which Rochester expressed dramatically in *A Satyr against Mankind* he returned to in different ways in two probably later poems: *Upon Nothing* and the imitation from Seneca's *Troades*.[13] The connections between *A Satyr* and *Upon Nothing* are clear; man's '*Sphere* of Action' is surrounded by 'eternal Night' in the earlier poem, as here all things are snatched from Nothing only to be driven back to her 'hungry Womb' like slaves.[14] It is the principle of the 'Great Negative' that Rochester is concerned to express, and it is both logically and poetically appropriate that a poem which enacts the collapse of man's attempt to erect a system or find a faith should be followed up by an ironical encomium upon Nothing. Rochester continues his polemic against the purveyors of religious or philosophical metaphysics:

> Tho' Mysteries are barr'd from Laick Eyes,
> And the Divine alone, with Warrant, pryes
> Into thy Bosom, where the truth in private lies, . . .
>
> Great Negative, how vainly would the Wise,
> Enquire, define, distinguish, teach, devise?
> Didst thou not stand to point their dull Philosophies.[15]

The truth sought after by Divines does not exist; the only significance of philosophy lies in the very void which it seeks to fill and rationalize. These statements are too close to the unambiguous passages of *A Satyr against Mankind* to be regarded as the reverse of what Rochester really means. This poem springs from the experience of scepticism and unbelief. Unless we are prepared to detach it from the rest of Rochester's work, in particular from the preceding *Satyr against Mankind* and the succeeding imitation of Seneca, we must have care how readily we accept it as the 'most nearly archetypal expression' of 'the inverted world of Augustan satire' and 'an ironic eulogy of an Uncreation opposite to God's original act'.[16] That Rochester had the deepest doubts about God's original act should be clear from the foregoing discussion.

Where then is the irony? It pervades the poem, but is of a less thorough-going kind than that, say, of Swift's *Modest Proposal*. It lies in the elevation of nullity to the status of a mock-positive deity, and in the tributes the poet makes to this goddess. Just as in Erasmus's *Encomium Moriae* a claim directly true is often served up in the guise of irony, so here statements in mock-praise of the goddess. Nothing contain a kernel of literal truth. Rochester has changed the manner with which he expresses an unchanged predicament. He has replaced the powerful directness of *A Satyr* by a complex mock-heroic mode, whose humorous ingenuity of wit and word keeps the grim truth at bay. This poem, elevating nothingness into a deity as it does, certainly resembles in method such Augustan mock-heroic poems as *Mac Flecknoe, The Rape of the Lock* and *The Dunciad*; Pinto notes that 'the Triumph of Dullness at the end of The *Dunciad* probably owes a good deal to Rochester's Triumph of Nothing'.[17] That Pope learned much from this poem there can be no doubt; his imitation *On Silence,* of which two early manuscript versions exist, was begun in 1702 and underwent drastic revision before its publication in 1712. These early versions show that over a period of years the young Pope absorbed, understood and reflected on Rochester's poem.[18] We can see that Nothing, Folly and Dullness are connected in the minds of both poets; also that both poems employ a manner at once comic and grand. But most significantly it is the conception of the 'Great Negative'—Dullness or Nothing—that the two poems have in common. In the complexity of literary influences synthesized in Pope's mind to create *The Dunciad,* Rochester's *Upon Nothing,* with Milton's Chaos in the background, was the only one to suggest the mock-philosophical implications with which Dullness might be poetically endowed. At the beginning and end of *Dunciad* IV Dullness assumes an awesome generality; it is addressed as 'eternal Night', 'Uncreating word', 'Universal Darkness', (ll. 2, 654, 656) and in this elevated blend of irony and fear we do indeed, I believe, find Pope close to Rochester. At the same time we must remember that long and complex poem *The Dunciad* as a whole. One of its unifying factors, strong in the earlier books but increasingly submerged as Dullness moves to her triumph, is the mock-parallel to the action of Virgil's *Aeneid*. While it is expressively significant that the parallel should be submerged in this way, its presence in the poem is an assurance that there is a positive standard to which Pope adheres. There is no such factor in *Upon Nothing.* Though Matter, Form and 'Rebel Light', set up like Lucifer in opposition to the original deity, the ultimate victory belongs to Nothing, as in Milton Lucifer must finally submit to God. 'Turn-Coat Time' is on her side; it is in the nature of things that Nothing, which permeates all, should in the end claim all. It is not in the nature of things for Pope that Dullness must *inevitably* triumph. That she does triumph in the poem is a consequence of the actions of men. These inferences are strengthened when we look beyond the two individual poems; Rochester had but recently written *A Satyr against Mankind,* while Pope had not long written *An Essay on Man.* In short, *Upon Nothing* is a sceptical and nihilistic work, lacking the moral assurance we associate with the term Augustan in English literature.

Rochester's outlook emerges even more plainly in his imitation from Seneca's *Troades*. Not only does he follow Seneca in denying the immortality of the soul, but he also totally transforms the calm and quiescent tone of his original; he imputes to the nature of things an energy and violence with which he also animates his poem. He has given it a contemptuous and hostile spirit; Seneca pities those who hope for immortality, Rochester sees through them and despises them. That Rochester should have made this poem so much his own and of his time (Seneca's *avidi* becoming the 'proud' and 'ambitious Zealot', that is the Puritan) shows that the view he expressed in *A Satyr* he continued to hold into the last winter of his life. This is a poem written outside and against the Christian tradition as to the nature of man and the wider context in which the Christian believes mortal life is led. While Pope does not treat specifically of immortality in *An Essay on Man* he is, despite his protests, an unashamed metaphysician, viewing man and his relation to the created order in a way with which Hooker, for example, would have sympathized.[19] The Augustan assurance which Rochester displays in the limited sphere of '**An Allusion to Horace**'—that of a man confident in a stable and satisfying pattern of values—is not found in the poems where Rochester writes of man in general and his relation to the natural order.

III

When we compare Pope's and Rochester's presentation of man in general, we see the stark contrast between a poet of unbelief and a poet of belief.[20] This is even apparent in the relation between **Upon Nothing** and *The Dunciad,* where in satiric conception and procedure Pope had so much to learn from Rochester. This conclusion is relevant to an assessment of **A Very Heroical Epistle** and **An Epistolary Essay.**[21] These poems were once taken as direct expressions of Rochester's egoistic hedonism; Vieth's interpretation, on the other hand, parallels his interpretation of **Upon Nothing** and rests on the detection in each poem of 'a distinctive Augustan poetical technique': the use of systematic irony in a manner generally resembling *The Dunciad,* whose

> structure functions through ironic approval of a spectrum of disvalues . . . diametrically opposed to the traditional Christian-classical standards shared by most of the contemporary audience. Whether the speaker of the poem is a *persona* who is himself satirized—a favorite device with Rochester—or remains anonymously omniscient, the satire operates by ironically replacing traditional norms with their direct contraries. . . .
>
> (op. cit., p. 105)

Let us look at a passage from **A Very Heroical Epistle.** The speaker 'Bajazet' (Mulgrave) grandly absolves himself from any obligation to be constant in love:

> You may as justly at the *Sun,* repine,
> Because alike it does not always shine:
> No glorious thing, was ever made to stay,
> My blazing *Star,* but visits and away.
> As fatal to it shines, as those 'ith' *Skyes,*
> 'Tis never seen but some great *Lady* dyes.
> The boasted favor, you so precious hold,
> To me's no more than changing of my Gold
> What e're you gave, I paid you back in Bliss. . . .
>
> (ll. 18-26)

Clearly these lines express the mentality of egoism and pride; the crucial question, however, concerns Rochester's and our moral relation to the *persona*. If the poem is indeed systematically ironical then he is inviting us to ridicule and condemn. Yet this passage has a certain ambiguity. Though the notion of 'degree' is sufficiently flouted by the speaker to give us the measure of his egoism, and his vanity comically underlined in lines 22-3 particularly, the passage is subtly contrived to invite to some degree the reader's identification and sympathy. The speaker's protestations are not entirely ridiculous: constancy is *not* the rule in nature, glorious things *are* transient, the image of the gold is a compliment as well as an insult, there is a certain justice in the last line. Much of this Vieth ingeniously admits: the 'ironic inversion of

traditional values undergoes a full 360 degrees rotation, so that passages taken out of context may seem to read quite straightforwardly' (op. cit., p. 128). The plain truth is that the irony is not consistent, but weaker at some times than others, and often temporarily absent. Rochester has balanced our critical detachment against a chance to identify with the speaker; this accounts for the quality of exultation in the passage. To find a similar type of satire to this, we shall do better to look back to Rochester's admired Ben Jonson than forward to Pope. Volpone's opening address to his gold has a similar complex effect.[22] Later in Rochester's poem the ironic ridicule grows stronger, and one thinks of Epicure Mammon rather than Volpone, but only at one point (the phrase: 'Secure in solid Sloth'—l. 41) does a comparison with *The Dunciad* seem appropriate. I conclude that this poem is not a work of consistent satirical irony but one which seeks to explore a world of egoism in a less committed way. It is not surprising to find such ambiguity since we know from **A Satyr against Mankind,** written about this time, that the 'Christian-classical' conception of the metaphysical hierarchy of degree, which Rochester does allude to in the present poem, did not command his allegiance.

Rochester's **Epistolary Essay From M.G. to O.B. Upon their mutual Poems** is more ambiguous than **A Very Heroical Epistle.** Vieth is the first critic to read it, not as a kind of confession, but a work systematically deploying an ironical *persona*. It is on this interpretation of the poem itself that he builds his theory that 'M.G.' is *Mul*Grave, 'O.B.' 'Old *B*ays' (i.e. Dryden); that the 'mutual Poem' is Mulgrave's and Dryden's collaborative *Essay upon Satyr*; and that the date of composition must therefore be 1679 rather than 1669 (op. cit., pp. 119-35). Certainly, many lines in this poem resemble the egoistic statements of **A Very Heroical Epistle**; but when read in their context they also have a cogency which does much to modify what might otherwise have been simple irony. Consider the following passage:

> And this is all I'le say in my defence
> T'obtain one Line of your well-worded sense,
> I'le be content t'have writ the *British Prince,*
> I'me none of those who think themselves inspir'd,
> Nor write with the vain hope to be admir'd;
> But from a Rule I have (upon long tryal)
> T'avoid with care all sort of self-denyal.
> Which way soe're, desire and fancy lead,
> (Contemning Fame) that Path I boldly tread;
> And if exposing what I take for wit,
> To my dear self a Pleasure I beget,
> No matter though the cens'ring *Criticks* fret.
> These whom my *Muse* displeases are at strife,
> With equal spleen against my course of life,
> The least Delight of which I'le not forgo,
> For all the flatt'ring praise *Man* can bestow.
>
> (ll. 9-24)

We are struck first by the compliment to Dryden; here at least is a plausible judgement. To disclaim inspiration (l. 12) is not a mark of arrogance, nor is an indifference to admiration (l. 13); in fact 'admiration' probably does not carry the modern sense of well-grounded approval, but the older Horatian sense of uncritical adulation which we find in the Sixth Epistle of Horace's First Book (*Nil admirari*) and which Pope was to use some fifty years later: 'With foolish *Pride* my Heart was never fir'd, / Nor the vain Itch *t'admire*, or *be admir'd*.'[23] M.G.'s contempt for 'Fame', which Vieth sees as a violation of the Augustan norm of deference to educated good taste, is in fact a perhaps equally Augustan scorn of capricious and uninformed public opinion. Such phrases as: 'saucy Censurers', 'dull age', 'cens'ring Criticks', 'flatt'ring praise' seem to confirm this reading. It is not clear that such ordinary sentiments must be ironically intended. But perhaps the challenging and egoistic statements make them so? Yet unlike those in *A Very Heroical Epistle* these lack any kind of comic inflation; in fact they are rather soberly put. Again Rochester is careful to blend the egoistic with the acceptable, so that each modifies the reader's reaction to the other. Having struck this balance in the earlier part of the poem, Rochester can introduce his comparison of writing verse to physical excretion without totally banishing our doubt that there could be some seriousness in its surface-meaning. Any identification with M.G. is reduced to the barest minimum by the sense of revulsion created, yet is there not some truth in the comparison? Is the poet, who in *A Satyr against Mankind* preferred the animals' life of desire and satisfaction to the human life of questing and pretension, incapable of suggesting that self-expression at its lowest may be a sufficient reason for writing verse? As an earlier critic points out, 'his chase had a beast in view, the "happy beast"'.[24] Vieth defends his judgement that this passage is one of undiluted irony by reference to at first sight similar passages in Pope's *Peri Bathous* and *Dunciad* II 'whose irony is beyond question' (op. cit., p. 124). But Augustanism is not a set of absolute attitudes and conventions which all poets of the period use in the same way; that Pope wrote one way in 1728 does not mean that Rochester must have done exactly the same in 1679. *The Epistolary Essay* has now passed its climax; M.G.'s egoism has passed through its most objectionable phase, which is succeeded by a rearguard argument in his own defence. God is hardly generous in providing for man's needs; like a proud but impoverished Lord He keeps more creatures than He can maintain. Only of wit is this not held so, since no man could hold an opinion if he distrusted his own wit. Thus, says M.G., self-esteem is the only 'fame' that is meaningful. Again Vieth finds unmodified irony; these propositions violate the concept of the 'great chain of being' and the principle of plenitude to which, he argues, Rochester as a man of his age must subscribe. But *A Satyr against Mankind* and the imitation from Seneca show that these are precisely the notions to which Rochester did not subscribe; far from directing his irony towards a final condemnation of M.G.'s views, he seems to be following the argument to its conclusion with impartial interest. The speaker now regains a degree of assent from the reader; the quotation from Descartes in line 64, which Pope noted in the margin of his edition of Rochester, seems to clinch this; so does M.G.'s return, at the end of the poem, to the theme of his contempt for 'common Fame' and 'Idle Rumour'.[25] I do not dispute that Rochester is using a *persona* in this poem, nor that M.G. is probably his enemy Mulgrave, and O. B. Dryden. These are valuable and to me convincing suggestions. My contention is rather that the irony of this poem is not a simple '180 degree reversal' of traditional 'norms'; it is spasmodic rather than systematic; the *persona* is made deliberately ambiguous so that Rochester is less attacking a complex of attitudes he already disapproves of than exploring a state of mind through the poem, and prompting approval or disapproval from the reader as each seems appropriate. Fittingly enough for a poet who did not subscribe to the 'Christian-classical' norms implicit *and* explicit in the work of Dryden and Pope, Rochester is less the resolved satirist here, than the satirically inclined explorer. There is thus some truth in the comments of those critics who, in this poem and *A Very Heroical Epistle,* sensed Rochester talking of himself.[26] There is nothing comparable to this effect in the formal satire of Pope whose subtler and more delicate *personae* invariably express different moods of himself *as satirist*. True, *The Dunciad* does explore as well as satirise the world of Folly, and Swift, in a manner closer to Rochester, uses *personae* to this end in *A Tale of a Tub*; to this extent the two poems of Rochester have affinities with these major achievements of Augustan satire.[27] But to find a better pattern for the way Rochester's satire works here we should look back, through the ambiguously satirical oratory of his own Alexander Bendo's Bill, to such protean satirical figures as Erasmus's Folly, Rabelais's Panurge or Cervantes's Quixote; Rochester's mood might sometimes be described as the soul of these satirists in a desolate world of doubt.[28]

I have been led, in this essay, to apply the term 'exploration' to the poems discussed. Exploration should be regarded as one of the characteristic features of Rochester's poetry. Even if we turn to one of the formal satires most resembling Pope, *Artemisa to Cloe,* we notice that the 'Fine Lady' who tells among other things the story of Corinna is twice observed by Artemisa to be 'So very wise, yet so impertinent' (ll. 148-9, 256-7). Rochester thus introduces into the satire a note of ambiguity similar to that more strongly present in *A Very Heroical Epistle* and *An Epistolary Essay*. In the world of Rochester's satire wisdom and folly are often less distinct than in the formal satire of Pope; hence the quality of exploration. We get the same impression from the songs, still more from the biography: the picture of a man caught in a '*Perplexity* of endless *Thought*', pleasing or otherwise; a man who in many respects lacked a stable pattern of any but the most elementary values, yet who was never without an obscure sense that there ought to have been more that he could believe. The contemptuous phrase 'Lumber of the World', in the imitation from Seneca, probably gets its bite from an opinion he confessed to Burnet about this time: 'He said, They were happy that believed: for it was not in every man's power'.[29]

The choice lies between regarding Rochester as a complete Augustan in the sense that Pope is an Augustan, or as a poet who, while Augustan and like Pope in some respects, has more in him of the adventurer through experience than Dryden or Pope. It is the choice between Rochester as a poet who, like Pope and Dryden, subscribed to a complex inheritance of 'Christian-classical' values, or as a poet in very many respects of scepticism and unbelief. The first view is that of D. M. Vieth, the second that of Pinto. The second, I suggest, is the more accurate of the two.

Notes

1. See V. de S. Pinto, *Rochester: Portrait of a Restoration Poet,* 1935, pp. x, 136, for his acknowledgement to earlier critics.

2. Pinto, op. cit., pp. 257-8; *Enthusiast in Wit,* 1962, p. 226; Rochester, *Poems,* ed. V. de S. Pinto, 1953, pp. xxxviii-xl; D. M. Vieth, *Attribution in Restoration Poetry,* 1963, pp. 106, 221, 271-2. Since the Rochester canon is still in some cases in dispute, I propose to confine my references to poems which Pinto and Vieth agree in attributing to him. Quotations from Rochester's poetry are from the above-mentioned edition.

3. *The Works of John Earl of Rochester . . . Printed for Jacob Tonson,* 1714, p. 156.

4. See Harold F. Brooks, 'The "Imitation" in English Poetry', *Review of English Studies,* 25 (1949), pp. 138-9.

5. Pope's knowledge of Rochester: see Joseph Spence, *Anecdotes,* ed. S. W. Singer, 1820, p. 281; *Imitations of Horace, To Mr Murray,* ll. 126-31 (cf. *Artemisa to Cloe,* ll. 44-5); *A New Collection of Poems Relating to State Affairs,* 1705, p. 258 in the British Museum copy, where Pope's manuscript annotation shows he knew 'Tunbridge-Wells' but attributed it to another hand.

6. D. M. Vieth, op. cit., pp. 109-26.

7. Pope, *An Essay on Man,* Argument of the First Epistle. Pinto, *Enthusiast in Wit,* p. 154.

8. Cf. *A Satyr,* l. 69; *De Rerum Natura,* I, ll. 72-4 especially 73; Pinto, *Enthusiast in Wit,* p. 153-4.

9. *De Rerum Natura,* I, ll. 62-79, 102-11. See Rochester, *Poems,* pp. 49-50.

10. Ibid., III, ll. 445-58, 926-30; V, ll. 235-46, 373-5.

11. See especially Montaigne's opening defence of Sébond for seeking to establish religious truths with reason. For specific parallels, see Rochester, *Poems,* pp. 215-19.

12. D. M. Vieth, op. cit., p. 221.

13. *A Satyr against Mankind* seems to have been written between 1674 and early 1676 (*Poems,* p. 214; Vieth, op. cit., p. 293). The earliest date we have for *Upon Nothing* is May 1678 (Vieth, op. cit., p. 399); it is probable though not certain that it post-dates *A Satyr.*

Even were it contemporaneous, however, it would be hard to detach its attitudes from those of the longer, more explicit poem. The imitation from Seneca was probably written early in 1680 (*Poems,* pp. 179-80; Pinto, *Enthusiast in Wit,* pp. 187-90).

14. Thus *Upon Nothing* is not a strictly Lucretian poem; Lucretius rejects the idea that the universe emerged from nothing, as likely to foster theories of divine creation (*De Rerum Natura,* I, ll. 146-58). But from the human viewpoint a disintegration of the universe to its primary particles is as near a return to nothing as makes no matter.

15. Stanzas 8 and 10. The 1680 edition of Rochester's *Poems on Several Occasions* gives 'thy truth' for the last line of stanza 8 (ed. James Thorpe, 1950, p. 52) but the substantial sense remains the same.

16. Vieth, op. cit., p. 106.

17. V. de S. Pinto, 'John Wilmot and the Right Veine of Satire', *Essays and Studies,* 1953, p. 64.

18. The first manuscript version is printed in Pope, *Minor Poems,* ed. Norman Ault and John Butt, 1954, pp. 463-4; the second (almost certainly not in Pope's hand) is to be found in the British Museum, Add. MSS. 28253, ff. 135-6.

19. Cf. *Of the Laws of Ecclesiastical Polity.* I, iii, 2 with *An Essay on Man,* I, ll. 233-58.

20. A distinction applied by Pinto to Rochester and Milton (*Enthusiast in Wit,* p. 114).

21. Vieth dates them respectively late summer 1675, and November or December 1679 (op. cit., pp. 107, 135).

22. Act I, Scene I, ll. 1-27; Rochester 'An Allusion,' l. 81. Though Jonson does subscribe to the metaphysic of 'degree' he lets too much exultation into Volpone's tone for the passage to be termed 'ironical'.

23. *Imitations of Horace, The Fourth Satire of John Donne,* ll. 9-10.

24. Francis Whitfield, *A Beast in View: A Study of the Earl of Rochester's Poetry,* 1936, pp. 56-7. Cf. 'Tunbridge-Wells,' ll. 171-80; *A Satyr against Mankind,* ll. 1-7, 114-44.

25. See Vieth, op. cit., pp. 126-7.

26. See, e.g. Pinto, 'John Wilmot and the Right Veine of Satire', loc. cit., p. 62; *Enthusiast in Wit,* pp. 148-9.

27. On the *exploration* of folly in *The Dunciad,* see my article 'The "New World" of Pope's *Dunciad*', *Essential Articles for the Study of Alexander Pope,* ed. Maynard Mack, 1964, pp. 739-60.

28. See Thomas Alcock and Rochester, *The Famous Pathologist . . . ,* ed. V. de S. Pinto, Nottingham University Miscellany No. 1, 1961, pp. 32-8. It is relevant to note Alcock's description of Bendo '. . .

in an old overgrown Green Gown which he religiously wore in memory of Rabelais his Master . . .', op. cit., p. 29.

29. Gilbert Burnet, *Some Passages of the Life and Death of the Right Honourable John Earl of Rochester . . .* , 1680, p. 71. Rochester's basic values were summed up in what he told Burnet at the end of his life: the 'Two *Maxims* of his *Morality* then were, that he should do nothing to the hurt of any other, or that might prejudice his own health. . . .', ibid., p. 38, to which we should add his contempt for self-importance and pretension.

Anne Righter (essay date 1967)

SOURCE: Righter, Anne. "John Wilmot, Earl of Rochester." *Proceedings of the Royal British Academy* 53 (1967): 42-69.

[*In this essay, Righter interprets Rochester's poetry in terms of the roles he played in real life, nothing that Rochester mythologized himself, used a variety of voices in his poems, and freely imitated other literary styles.*]

In the second act of Jonson's *Volpone,* the Fox disguised as a mountebank harangues a crowd of Venetians beneath Celia's window. His aim is quite straightforward. By pretending to be Scoto of Mantua, the possessor of a marvellous elixir, he hopes to obtain a glimpse of Corvino's young and jealously guarded wife. Volpone's long speech of self-advertisement, cluttered though it is with medieval jargon and false learning, is basically simple. He recognizes that other mountebanks, the charlatans of the profession, may parade accomplishments superficially like his own.

Indeed, very many have assay'd, like apes, in imitation of that, which is really and essentially in me, to make of this oil; bestow'd great cost in furnaces, stills, alembics, continual fires, and preparation of the ingredients (as indeed there goes to it six hundred several simples, besides some quantity of human fat, for the conglutination, which we buy of the anatomists), but when these practitioners come to the last decoction, blow, blow, puff, puff and all flies in fumo: ha, ha, ha! Poor wretches! I rather pity their folly and indiscretion, than their loss of time and money; for those may be recovered by industry: but to be a fool born is a disease incurable.

Here, and throughout his oration, the Fox insists strenuously that he represents truth as opposed to the specious claims of his rivals. Meanwhile, every word he utters reveals him clearly as an impostor. The rational and intelligent members of his stage audience are not deceived for an instant; only the credulous and the foolish—the Sir Politic Would-Be's of the world—could possibly mistake this arrant counterfeit for the true man he pretends to be.

At some point during the winter of 1675-6 John Wilmot, Earl of Rochester, acting not on a stage but in the middle of that Restoration London in which he normally lived, chose to submerge his own extraordinary identity in that of a fictitions Italian mountebank of his devising. Rochester was constitutionally restless and also insatiably curious; he had recently been banished from the court for irreverence; he had a passion for disguise. These are the generalities of the situation. More precise reasons underlying his impersonation of Alexander Bendo, if indeed they existed, remain obscure. Like Volpone in Jonson's play, Rochester in real life addressed a formal peroration to his potential customers.

However Gentlemen in a world like this, where Virtue is so frequently exactly Counterfeited, and hypocrisie so generally taken notice of, that every one armed with Suspicion stands upon his Guard against it, 'twill be very hard, for a Stranger especially, to escape a Censure: All I shall say for myself on this Score is this, if I appear to anyone like a Counterfeit, even for the sake of that chiefly, ought I to be constru'd a true Man, who is the Counterfeit's example, his Original, and that which he imploys his Industry, and Pains to Imitate, & Copy. Is it, therefore my fault, if yᵉ Cheat, by his Witts and Endeavours, makes himself so like me, that consequently I cannot avoid resembling him?[1]

On Volpone's lips, truth and falsehood had remained fixed counters: traditional opposites. He hoped to persuade his listeners to mistake the one for the other, certainly, but he did not doubt the validity of the distinction. In fact, his mock-righteousness played upon it. The movement of mind described by Rochester's prose, by comparison with Jonson's, is positively dizzying. Not even Shakespeare had gone this far when he allowed Imogen, in the third act of *Cymbeline,* to reflect upon the power of hypocrisy to breed a distrust of the honesty it mimics.

True honest men, being heard like false Aeneas,
Were in his time thought false: and Sinon's weeping
Did scandal many a holy tear, took pity
From most true wretchedness: so thou, Posthumus,
Wilt lay the leaven on all proper men;
Goodly and gallant shall be false and perjur'd
From thy great fail.

The reasoning here may seem convoluted; none the less, behind Imogen's speech the values of truth and falsehood stand distanced but inviolate. Honesty may for a time be slandered by its opposite, reality mistaken for appearance, in reversal of the more usual Elizabethan error. Fundamentally, however, these qualities are not interchangeable. Like Jonson, Shakespeare maintained a basic conviction of antithesis, a conviction which Rochester as Bendo overthrows.

It is, Dr. Bendo points out, the principal aim of the counterfeit to be taken for a true man, the thing he imitates. He fulfils his nature only in so far as he can promulgate this confusion. The man who appears false, therefore, is by definition unlikely to be engaged in any duplicity. The one who seems true and honest is the candidate for suspicion. What stance, under these circumstances, can the man who is genuinely honest adopt? How can he distinguish himself from his double, the counterfeit? A pose of deliberate dishonesty would seem to be all that is open to him. To embark upon it, however, would be to contradict his very nature as an honest man. At this point, language breaks down. We are in the country of Epimenides's paradox: the statement that 'All Cretans are liars' made by a man who is himself a Cretan. Truth and falsehood, reason itself, begin to run round in circles. Antipodes touch; extremes and contradictions, bewilderingly, coalesce. This tendency to confound antithesis in identity is not, of course, peculiar to Rochester, though I should wish to claim that both as a person and as a poet he was perhaps its most brilliant seventeenth-century exemplar. The Restoration as a period seems to have been drawn to this activity; its comedy in particular regularly annihilates traditional polarities. 'I know no effectual Difference between continued Affectation and Reality', says Mr. Scandal in Congreve's *Love For Love*. The remark is recognizably part of the world of Dr. Bendo.

To compare Rochester with Byron has become a biographical and critical cliché. The common ground is obvious: aristocracy, exceptional physical beauty, sexual licence, scepticism, immense personal charm, an early death. Both of them minimized and underplayed their own poetry; neither could live without it. Between Rochester's despairing remark in a letter to his wife about the 'disproportion 'twixt our desires and what is ordained to content them'[2] and Byron's description of Cain as a man exasperated by 'the inadequacy of his state to his conceptions'[3] the line runs straight and true. Confirmed empiricists, taking nothing on trust, both Rochester and Byron were committed to a world of fact and sense experience. These were the boundaries of knowledge in which they believed. Unfortunately, because they were the people they were, they persistently asked of sense experience things which were not only in excess of what it could give, but inappropriate to it. They lived intensely; they pushed individual experience as far as it could go, only to find that even in the rarefied air of the extreme it was disappointing. Dedication to a reality which they could not help recognizing as limited, imperfect, and in the proof maddeningly below expectation, left them hankering after intangible absolutes, values fixed beyond sense in a world from which they were debarred by their own rationalism. In the last weeks of his life, Rochester surrendered; he took the leap in the dark into religious faith. Byron, despite his sessions with that earnest Methodist Dr. Kennedy at Missolonghi, did not. On the way to these very different final positions, both men used poetry as a means of coming to terms with a personal quandary that was essentially the same. Neither really believed in poetry in the sense of a man like Keats, yet with both the relationship of life to the art which it generated became so immediate and complex as to call the whole timeworn antithesis into question.

From *Childe Harold* to *Don Juan* Byron systematically mythologized his life in his verse. He came, reluctantly, to depend upon poetry as a means of heightening and transforming a world of objective fact which claimed his allegiance, but which he felt to be basically inadequate. Interestingly enough, Byron was a man who had absolutely no capacity for disguise, either in his life or his verse. No matter where he travelled, no matter how exotic or incongruous his adventures, whether he was sitting at the feet of Ali Pasha in Albania or attempting to seduce the wife of a Venetian baker, he remained Milord Byron. His poetry too is always spoken in his own voice. On those infrequent occasions when he did try to conceal his own identity behind that of a fictitious spokesman—as he did briefly in the first canto of *Don Juan*—the pretence invariably failed and had to be discontinued. All of Byron's heroes, Childe Harold, Lara, the Corsair, the narrators of the satires, are over-life-size versions of himself. It was Byron's characteristic way of overcoming the limitations of things as they are.

The mythologizing of Rochester's life and personality, on the other hand, was for the most part accomplished by people other than himself. Dryden's dedication to *Marriage à la Mode,* in which he claims that 'the best comic writers of our age, will join with me to acknowledge, that they have copied the gallantries of courts, the delicacies of expression, and the decencies of behaviour, from your Lordship' may sound impossibly sycophantic. The fact remains that the drama of the Restoration is filled with Rochester-figures, with (more or less garbled) memories of his conversation, refractions of his wit, attempts to mirror his style. According to John Dennis, all of the town that mattered went away from the first performance of Etherege's *The Man of Mode* in 1676 agreeing that the rake-hero Dorimant was an avatar of Rochester. And Dorimant is the archetype and model for a whole series of later libertines. Nat Lee, baffled by the complexity and contradiction of his former patron's character, introduced him into his strange and brilliant comedy *The Princess of Cleve* (1680) as two separate people: the dead Count Rosidore, whose memory haunts the courtiers who have survived him, and the living Nemours. In the pages of Anthony Hamilton, in a flood of contemporary and posthumous anecdotes, allusions, and lampoons, Rochester achieved semilegendary stature. His spectacular death-bed conversion added a new dimension to the myth. Even Charlotte Brontë, of all people, seems to have had him in mind when she bestowed his name and a number of his personal characteristics, including the penchant for disguise, upon the hero of *Jane Eyre.*

Only once, however, as far as one knows, did Rochester himself make a literary contribution to his own myth. **'The Earl of Rochester's Conference with a Post Boy'** is not a polite poem, but neither is it negligible.

> Son of A whore, God damn you can you tell
> A Peerless Peer the Readyest way to Hell?
> Ive out swilld Baccus sworn of my own make
> Oaths wod fright furies, & make Pluto quake
> Ive swived more whores more ways yⁿ Sodoms walls
> Ere knew or the College of Romes Cardinalls
> Witness Heroick scars, Look here neer go
> sere Cloaths & ulcers from yᵉ top to toe
> frighted at my own mischiefes I have fled
> and bravely left my lifes defender dead
> Broke houses to break chastity & died
> that floor with murder which my lust denyed

Pox on it why do I speak of these poor things
I have blasphemed my god & libelld Kings
the readyest way to Hell come quick!

BOY

                                        Nere stirr
The readyest way my Lords by Rochester

As Mr. David Vieth has pointed out, in his book *Attribution in Restoration Poetry,* this is a better lampoon than any Rochester's enemies were able to compose.[4] As a self-portrait, it is unsparing, worlds away from the kind of romantic self-magnification which Byron practised in his *Oriental Tales.* Rochester's characteristic oaths, the scars and running sores left by the venereal disease which, a few years later, was to kill him, the suggestion not merely of sexual excess but of perversion, the allusion to that gesture of drunken cowardice in the Epsom affair of 1676 which cost the life of his friend Downes, the unlovely propensity to slander: all of these details were based on fact. None are pretty. The efforts of the wretched post boy to escape from the company of this unsavoury and drunken interlocutor are both comic and entirely understandable. Yet, oddly enough, the final effect of the poem is not that of a lampoon, in the sense that it annihilates or even breeds contempt for its subject. The amoral energy, almost daemonism, of the speaker in his deliberate rush to Hell is simply too attractive, and so of course is the intelligence of his self-mockery. The verse employs a hyperbolic style which is persuasive and, at the same time, ironically conscious of its own exaggeration. It manages simultaneously to magnify and deflate *both* its subject and the orthodox values by which that subject is being judged, to invite belief and to undercut it.

In **'The Post Boy'** as a whole, reality and pretence, the counterfeit and the true, take up positions like those they occupy in the vertiginous world of Dr. Bendo. Formally, although not ultimately, the lines belong to the genre of the lampoon. To write a lampoon on oneself is not exactly unique; it is, however, fundamentally paradoxical. The complexity of this situation is only increased by the pretence that the poem represents an actual incident. Professor Pinto prints it in his edition among the other 'Impromptus', alongside the three lines of rueful compliment paid to the Duchess of Cleveland after she had just knocked Rochester down in the street for presuming to steal a kiss. As an immediate response to a real situation, the discomfited epigram addressed to Samuel Pepys's beloved duchess is conceivable: no man, however witty, produces extempore verse like that of **'The Post Boy'**. If a genuine encounter lies behind the poem, it lies a long way behind. The important consideration here is not biographical truth, but the contribution which the anecdotal pose of the dialogue makes to a confusion worked out on a variety of other levels.

Rochester's sins as recorded in **'The Post Boy'** have a particularized reality which must have been even more striking to his contemporaries than to us. They are described, however, in terms which force the reader to question the possibility that a monster like this could exist. He becomes a caricature of vice. Lines 11 and 12 in particular ('Broke houses to break chastity & died / that floor with murder which my lust denyed') suggest an allegorical figure of Lechery invented by some canting and overwrought divine. Here, as in the scurrilous reference to Rome's Cardinals and their sexual predilections, satire glances off to targets other than himself. Those orthodox values by which the wicked Earl of Rochester stands self-condemned are themselves mocked. In the act of invoking traditional verities of good and evil, virtue and sin, **'The Post Boy'** blurs their identity. It is not at all clear in the end how we are meant to feel about this mythologized Earl of Rochester who asks, so peremptorily, for directions to another world. He repels, but he also attracts. The poem is amusing; it is also horrifying. Even more perplexing: what is the point at which one should separate this dramatic character, the subject of the lampoon, from the witty poet of the same name who stage-managed the incident in the first place and who controls in so complex a fashion the tone and language of his self-presentation?

I suggested earlier that **'The Post Boy'** was the only surviving poem of Rochester's in which, like Byron, although with very different results, he mythologized his own life and personality directly. His more characteristic mode was the one which Byron shunned: disguise. Rochester's life is filled with extraordinary impersonations, of which the mountebank Bendo is only one. Hamilton's account of how Rochester exchanged identities with Killigrew in order to deceive two of the Queen's maids of honour reads like a scene from Restoration comedy. He seems also to have transformed himself into a solid merchant, in which role he vanished for a time among the citizens of London, earning their approbation by the vigour with which he railed against the profligacies of the court—particularly those of the wicked Earl of Rochester. (Etherege was perhaps thinking of this particular caper when he had Dorimant charm Harriet's mother Lady Woodvil in *The Man of Mode* by pretending to be the sober and censorious Mr. Courtage.) Even more daringly, Rochester is said to have lost himself among the beggars and the common whores of London in the guise of a porter. The town of Burford retains the tradition of his sudden appearance there as a tinker, in which unglamorous form he collected pots and pans to mend, and then systematically destroyed them. He was released from the stocks upon the arrival of his own coach and four. The kitchen-ware, magnanimously, was replaced.

In much of this, obviously, there is a quality of Haroun-al-Raschid, the caliph of *The Arabian Nights* who liked to walk the streets of Baghdad incognito, in search of the marvellous and the strange. Other members of the court of Charles II, including the King himself, also resorted occasionally to disguise, as Bishop Burnet testifies in his *History of his Own Time.* No one, however, took it as far as Rochester, used it as inventively, or out of as deep a need. By his own admission, he was drunk for five years on end, without an interval of sobriety: excess, as he himself recognized, was another kind of role-playing, permitting him to assume manners and a *persona* heightened and more extravagant than normal. The famous contradiction between his gallantry in the naval action of 1666 and his supposed cowardice in the duel with Mulgrave a few years later probably explains itself in similar terms. 'He thought it necessary', he told Burnet, 'to begin his life with those Demonstrations of his Courage in an Element and way of fighting, which is acknowledged to be the greatest trial of clear and undoubted Valour'.[5] Having done so to his own satisfaction, he discarded the role. In the Mulgrave affair, he was playing another and more wryly exploratory part, as he was presumably when he tried the odd experiment of having his own wife converted to Catholicism by means of an intermediary hired, secretly, by himself. Over and over again in his short life, Rochester seems to have been impelled to alter his perspective on reality, to seek yet another vantage point, by adopting some form of disguise. If (and there seems no reason to doubt the story) he was in fact the architect of Mrs. Barry's genius—rehearsing her over and over again in the parts she had to play until, from being the worst and most incompetent actress on the Restoration stage, she became its acknowledged queen—his success is in no way surprising. This was a man who understood the actor's art.

* * *

Not unexpectedly, therefore, Rochester's own poetry involves a whole series of impersonations, is spoken in a variety of different voices. He invented the cynical old rake counselling his successors in **'The Maim'd Debauchee',** the overblown braggart who addresses his mistress in so insufferable a style in the **'Heroical Epistle in Answer to Ephelia',** and the arrogant but misguided author who pens the **'Epistolary Essay from M.G. to O.B. Upon their Mutual Poems'.** The extremely indecent but impressive **'Ramble in St. James' Park'** represents the point of view of a jaded stallion consumed by sexual hate, a man who speaks out of the ruins of wit and sense. Rochester's **'Dialogue Between Strephon and Daphne'** is much better than the usual Restoration pastoral and one of the reasons is the dramatic credibility of this nymph and shepherd: the individuality of their voices. He was an adept at women's parts as well as men's (there is at least the tradition of a transvestite episode in his own life), as witness that somewhat dismaying young lady who showers dubious endearments upon the ancient person of her heart in the poem **'To Her Ancient Lover'.**

As a study in feminine character alone, the marvellous *Letter from Artemisia in the Town to Cloe in the Country* repays attention. Artemisia herself, the woman composing the letter, is a kind of seventeenth-century Elizabeth Bennett. Witty and self-aware, both amused and exasperated, delighted and saddened by the follies she describes, she is the sister of Jane Austen's heroines. What is astonishing about the poem is the fact that that anonymous knight's lady whose affectations and conversation Artemisia reports

at such length is not, as she so easily might have been, a mere caricature. She too is a fully realized character of some integrity, and her discourse is filled with telling points as well as with absurdity. Artemisia, the detached observer, watches more in sorrow than in anger while the lady cuddles a pet monkey in the house they are both visiting:

> The dirty, chatt'ring Monster she embrac'd;
> And made it this fine Tender Speech at last.
>   Kiss me, thou curious Miniature of Man;
> How odd thou art, how pretty, how japan:
> Oh! I could live and dye with thee; then on
> For half an Hour, in Complements she ran.
> I took this Time to think what Nature meant,
> When this mixt thing into the world she sent,
> So very wise, yet so impertinent.
> One that knows ev'rything, that God thought fit
> Shou'd be an Ass through Choice, not want of wit.
> Whose Foppery, without the help of sense,
> Cou'd ne'er have rose to such an excellence. . . .
> An eminent Fool must be a Fool of parts.
> And such a one was she; who had turn'd o're
> As many Books as Men; lov'd much, read more:
> Had discerning Wit; to her was known
> Ev'ry one's Fault, or Merit, but her own.
> All the good qualities that ever blest
> A Woman so distinguished from the rest,
> Except Discretion only, she possest.

The attitudes which the knight's lady strikes are ridiculous; her mind and endowments are not. A generosity which is both Artemesia's and, ultimately, Rochester's allows her, in what is in effect the play within the play of the letter, to relate with real understanding the scarifying story of Corinna, the girl undone by a Wit, who now

>   unheard of, as a Flie,
> In some dark hole must all the Winter lye;
> And want, and dirt, endure a whole half year,
> That, for one month, she Tawdry may appear.

Disguise, as an aspect of Rochester's verse, governs more than the various *personae* of his poems. There is also the question of literary imitation. In an article published in 1949, 'The Imitation in English Poetry', Dr. Harold Brooks has argued that what was to become with Pope and Johnson the approved method of transmuting a classical or French original appears for the first time in Rochester's satire **'An Allusion to Horace'.**[6] The poet presents, consecutively, his own equivalent of a pre-existing text. If the reader is fully to appreciate the new creation, he must constantly measure it against the original from which it departs. Ideally, he himself will know this original so well that reference back and forth with every line becomes virtually automatic. The imitation is a poem in its own right; it can stand alone, if necessary, but it fulfils itself only in terms of its relationship—a relationship involving both resemblance and contrast—to the work of art it shadows. According to Dr. Brooks, **'An Allusion to Horace'** is the only one of Rochester's poems which exacts this kind of point-by-point comparison with its original. It stands in the true Augustan line, as the more independent arabesques performed against the basic ground-work of Boileau in the *Satyr Against Reason and Mankind* do not.

I do not mean to question Dr. Brooks's general argument. However, I do think that there is one other poem of Rochester's, not a satire and emphatically not in the Augustan line, which asks to be read in the manner of **'An Allusion to Horace'**. On the whole, Rochester's editors have regarded the poem **'To His Mistress'** beginning 'Why do'st thou shade thy lovely face?' with a certain amount of nervousness and suspicion.

> Why do'st thou shade thy lovely face? O why
> Does that Eclipsing hand of thine deny
> The Sun-Shine of the Suns enlivening Eye:
>
> Without thy light, what light remains in me
> Thou art my Life, my way my Light's in Thee,
> I live, I move and by thy beams I see.
>
> Thou art my Life, if thou but turn away
> My Life's a thousand Deaths, thou art my way
> Without thee (Love) I travel not but Stray.

There is not a line here, or in the rest of the poem, which does not derive immediately from Francis Quarles, from either the seventh or the twelfth poem in the second book of his *Emblems*. Whole stanzas are, in some cases, identical.

To accuse Rochester of plagiarism, as some critics have done, is obviously to miss the point. What in Quarles had been a passionate expression of the sinner's abasement before God becomes, in Rochester, the despairing cry of a lover to his mistress. The whole object of the exercise is to change as little as possible of the original while wresting it in a different direction, transforming it into its opposite. The closeness of the Christian language of spiritual adoration to that describing the raptures of physical love is, of course, a well-known psychological phenomenon. This is a place where antinomies cross: body and soul, finite and infinite, sexuality and a world of the spirit. It is a paradox worked out on one level in the occasionally embarrassing language of the great fourteenth-century mystics, agonizing after what comes to seem a physical union with God. On another, it means that the libertine pursuing sense experience to its extremes is precisely the man most susceptible to a dramatic religious conversion. A great deal of the poetry of the seventeenth century—one thinks immediately of Donne and Herbert—deliberately avails itself of the language of transcendence in order to celebrate earthly love, and of a fairly straightforward eroticism in speaking of God. The sacred parody, religious poetry strongly influenced by or even based upon a profane model was by no means an uncommon English form.[7] No one, however, as far as I know, conducted an experiment quite like Rochester's in **'To His Mistress'**. The poem is an analytic inquiry, an attempt to define the exact point at which opposites merge.

Sensuality is inherent in the very rhythms of Quarles's two poems, in the passionate monotony of his reiterated appeals, and Rochester allows it to speak for itself. He is forced to make certain obvious changes: the word 'Lord' becomes 'Love'; 'Great Shepherd' metamorphoses into 'Dear Lover'. On the whole, however, he alters Quarles only where he must, and these alterations, many of them extremely subtle, become a guide to the fragile but genuine distinctions which can be drawn between earthly and heavenly love. Stanza 11 of Quarles's 'Emblem VII' reads as follows:

> If that be all, shine forth and draw thee nigher;
> Let me behold, and die, for my desire
> Is phoenix-like, to perish in that fire.

In Rochester, this becomes:

> If that be all Shine forth and draw thou nigher
> Let me be bold and Dye for my Desire.
> A *Phenix* likes to perish in the Fire.

There are only two verbal substitutions here of any consequence: the witty and almost imperceptible metamorphosis of 'behold' into 'be bold', and the more striking introduction of the word 'likes' in Rochester's version of the third line. Otherwise, the transformation has been effected by means which are not properly linguistic: by end-stopping the second line where Quarles had permitted an enjambment and by a change in punctuation and accentual stress which suddenly throws the erotic connotations of the word 'die' (submerged and unconscious in the original poem) into relief. The lines are the same and not the same; another voice is speaking Quarles's words, from another point of view.

Obviously, **'To His Mistress'** is a far more extreme and idiosyncratic poem than 'An Allusion to Horace'. If Rochester ever subjected another text to this kind of treatment, no record of the experiment survives. Imitation generally, however, was as essential a principle in his verse as in his life. Seneca, Anacreon, Horace, Ovid, Lucretius, Passerat, and Boileau were only a few of the writers upon whose work he built. In his hands, Fletcher's tragedy **Valentinian** became a different and much more interesting play. Nothing, of course, is unique about this method of composition in itself. The idea that an individual style was best achieved through the study and reproduction of (preferably) classical models is a standard part of seventeenth-century aesthetic. As literary archaeologists, Rochester's contemporaries were as assiduous as he. They also tended to imitate one another. Even without considering the whole vexed issue of whether there really was a clear-cut school of Jonson as opposed to the school of Donne, the minor poetry of the Caroline and Restoration periods displays an extremely high and in a certain sense unhealthy mutual awareness. The writers represented in the three volumes of Saintsbury's *Caroline Poets* seem at times to be involved in a kind of never-ending *New Statesman* competition. Fruition (for and against), honour, chastity, the pastoral life: topics like these became an artificial sports ground on which poets consciously vied with one another. Not surprisingly, the exercise tended to become academic, a mere game of rackets played between one poem and its successor.

Elizabethan handling of conventional subject-matter had been different. When Philip Sidney buried timeworn Petrarchan conceits in the structure of his sonnets, he did so because he needed to work by way of their anonymity towards a particularized and felt emotional statement. A poem like Suckling's 'Out upon it, I have lov'd / Three whole days together', on the other hand, invites only one response. And Sir Tobie Matthews provided it: 'Say, but did you love so long? / In troth I needs must blame you.' An already unconvincing because logically imposed stance has been pushed a degree further in a way that is literary in the worst sense of that term. Where can the conversation possibly go beyond Matthews? For most Restoration poets, there was no answer except graceful restatement of what had been said before. With Rochester, something else happens:

> All my past Life is mine no more,
> The flying hours are gone:
> Like transitory dreams giv'n o'er,
> Whose Images are kept in store,
>   By Memory alone.
>
> The Time that is to come is not,
>   How can it then be mine?
> The present Moment's all my Lot,
> And that, as fast as it is got,
>   *Phillis,* is only thine.
>
> Then talk not of Inconstancy,
>   False hearts, and broken Vows;
> If I, by Miracle, can be
> This live-long Minute true to thee,
>   'Tis all that Heav'n allows.

The technique here is not unlike Sidney's: a convention is revealed in the last lines, but it has been arrived at in such a way that it stands transformed. Melodious and elegant, the poem is ultimately terrifying in its denial of the continuum of life, and the consequences of that denial for human relationships. Neither past nor future exists; man is reduced to the needlepoint of the immediate present, and even this reality is in motion. Essentially, this is a Heraclitean poem: it also points forward to Kierkegaard's analysis of Mozart's seducer Don Juan in *Either/Or*: 'he does not have existence at all, but he hurries in a perpetual vanishing, precisely like music, about which it is true that it is over as soon as it has ceased to sound, and only comes into being again, when it again sounds'.[8] The defence of inconstancy, that weariest of Restoration clichés, is revitalized in Rochester's lyric. No one but Donne perhaps could have formulated and placed the phrase 'this live-long Minute' with such sureness. The compression is typical of Rochester; so is the essential seriousness of the wit.

* * *

It is I believe fair to say that at the time Rochester was writing, English verse was facing a double crisis: of language and of subject-matter. The problem was most acute in what had been the glory of the preceding age: the poetry of love. Both Cleveland and Cowley seem to me better poets than they are currently given credit for being, but it would be hard to deny that their work reflects a sense that all the words of love have already been used, and its possible attitudes exhausted. The obvious temptation was to reach out for the extravagant and bizarre, both linguistically and in terms of subject-matter. What has come to be known as 'Clevelandism' is an intelligent dead-end as far as language is concerned, but it is a dead-end all the same. As for subject-matter: not by accident are there so many Caroline and Restoration poems about the love affairs of dwarfs, hermaphrodites, or very young girls married to very old men. It was a way, although a fairly desperate one, of ensuring a certain novelty. The blatant obscenity of much Restoration love poetry can also be explained, in part if not entirely, as a response to this situation. A good deal of Rochester, even after the canon has been purified of the improprieties fathered upon it by other writers, remains extremely obscene. Nor was he above the exploitation of abnormal situations, as witness the **'Young Lady to her Ancient Lover'**, or the song beginning **'Fair Cloris in a Pig-Stye Lay'.** Nevertheless, although the solution he found to the problem was too personal to be of use to other poets, Rochester's love poetry at its best seems to me to cut through the dilemma.

Dr. Johnson thought that Rochester's lyrics had no particular character. 'They tell, like other songs, in smooth and easy language of scorn and kindness, dismission and desertion, absence and inconstancy, with the common places of artificial courtship. They are commonly smooth and easy; but have little nature, and little sentiment.' With all respect to Dr. Johnson, this is one of his 'Lycidas' judgements. Admittedly, there are Rochester lyrics—'My dear Mistress has a heart / Soft as those kind looks she gave me', or ''Twas a dispute 'twixt Heav'n and Earth'—over which one is not tempted to linger, although even here the formal perfection and beauty of sound make one feel churlish in requiring any more of them. At its best, however, Rochester's love poetry achieves individuality and passion by way of an illusory simplicity and coolness of tone.

It is true that the language of these poems is for the most part clear, almost transparent. The vocabulary employed is not wide. Compressed and economical, they make only a sparing use of images and conceits. It has become a commonplace to talk about the gradual shift during the Restoration from the rich, ambiguous, essentially connotative language of Shakespeare and Donne to a kind of Royal Society plain style in which words and images limit themselves to precise and denotative meanings. At first sight, Rochester may appear to belong to the new school in most of his poems. Yet behind the deceptively limpid surface lies a complexity of attitude, an air of strain and doubt, that links him with the metaphysicals. It is worked out, however, by means alien to the school of Donne.

Much of the excitement generated by Rochester's best lyrics springs from their character as tentative and immediate explorations of a particular situation or state of mind. They tend to conclude surprisingly, to arrive at a position in the last lines which seems in some way to be a product of the actual writing of the poem, not a preconceived attitude clothed in verse. If it is often difficult to determine how the poet arrived at this conclusion, it is also obligatory. Yet analysis is made difficult by the fact that so much of what happens in Rochester is a matter of tone. The progression is essentially non-linguistic, one of attitude, and you cannot come to grips with it through the relatively available medium of metaphor and conceit as you can with metaphysical poetry. In the end, of course, this method has a complicating effect of its own upon language. Nothing is more characteristic of Rochester than the way a single word, particularly in the final stanza of a poem, will suddenly move into focus and reveal its possession of a variety of warring meanings. This happens with the word 'severe' in the penultimate line of **'The Fall'**, as it does with the word 'innocent', upon which such a terrible illumination is suddenly cast, in the obscene final stanza of **'Fair Cloris'**.

Fundamentally, however, a discussion of the lyrics must involve itself with somewhat intangible considerations. They are characterized in the first place by the fact that in them the sense tends to flow both forwards and back. A single line, a whole stanza, which had one apparent meaning when first encountered will alter in retrospect: from the vantage point of the end of the poem, or even of the next stanza. This technique can be observed at its most straightforward in Rochester's pastoral **'Dialogue Between Strephon and Daphne'**, at the end of which the forsaken nymph declares abruptly to her inconstant lover that every word she has uttered up to this point was a lie. The volteface of this particular ending is reminiscent of the plays of Fletcher, and indeed it can be defended in terms very like those employed by Professor Philip Edwards in his article, 'The Danger Not the Death: the Art of John Fletcher.'[9] The poem is not summed up and exhausted once the trick conclusion is known, because there is another kind of pleasure to be derived from noticing its effect upon what has gone before, from understanding now the real, below the assumed, meaning of the character's words. With **'Strephon and Daphne'**, a further complexity—characteristic of the creator of Dr. Bendo—is introduced by a certain doubt as to whether Daphne's final assertion that she has been lying is not in itself a face-saving and despairing lie.

'Strephon and Daphne' is anything but a simple poem, but it is more conventional than most of Rochester's lyrics. The brilliant and horrifying **'Fair Cloris'**, for instance, turns not upon a shock ending in itself, but upon the opportunity for misreading or at least misintonation in the second stanza. It is a mistake which it is almost impossible not to make every time, no matter how well you know the poem, so cleverly has Rochester constructed the trap.

> Fair *Cloris* in a Pig-Stye lay,
>   Her tender Herd lay by her:
> She slept, in murmuring gruntlings they,

> Complaining of the scorching Day,
>   Her slumbers thus inspire.

> She dreamt, while she with careful pains
>   Her Snowy Arms employ'd,
> In Ivory Pails, to fill out Grains,
> One of her Love-convicted Swains,
>   Thus hasting to her cry'd.

Verse rhythm, position in the line and sense all persuade the reader to take 'she dreamt' as part of a construction syntactically parallel with that introduced by 'She slept' in the preceding stanza. But the suggestion of symmetry is indeed the trick. Because of it, everything that follows in the poem: the treachery of the swain, the brutal rape of poor Cloris whose honour 'not one God took care to save' looks like a real incident in a waking world clearly distinguished from her interrupted dream of ivory pails. This impression is carefully furthered by the tone of Rochester's description of the rape: deprecating, brutal, matter of fact. Not until the final stanza (unfortunately suppressed in most editions) does the true meaning of the poem become clear: 'Frighted she wakes.' The whole episode was a dream and indeed one inspired appropriately by pigs. Cloris has been the victim, not of an unfeeling rustic, but of her own lustful imagination, and she proceeds to seek sexual gratification in the only way available to her.

Scepticism about the pastoral pretence was not, of course, original with Rochester. Ralegh and Donne before him had cast a mocking eye upon the innocent pleasures of sheepfolds and bowers. **'Fair Cloris'** is in fact part of the whole dialogue initiated by Marlowe's 'Come Live with Me and be my Love' and Ralegh's reply. The poem is not, however, either a simple parody or a hyperbolic extension of a given attitude in the manner of Sir Tobie Matthews's answer to Suckling. Imitation is essential to it; like most Restoration exercises in the pastoral, it presupposes all the pros and cons of earlier poets, speaks largely through a mask. What is remarkable is its ability (admittedly with the assistance of the psychological realism of Hobbes) genuinely to re-create a traditional mode. The ending of **'Fair Cloris'** is not pleasant, but neither is it trivial, pornographic, nor ultimately derivative.

Most important of all, perhaps, the basic technique of this poem could be and was applied by Rochester to subjects of a different nature. Syntactical ambiguity marks many of his lyrics, and it is used for a variety of purposes. In general, he seems to have been fond of words or clauses in apposition:

> Let the Porter and the Groom,
>   Things design'd for dirty Slaves;
> Drudge in fair Aurelia's Womb,
>   To get Supplies for Age and Graves.

Here, the dependence of the second line upon the first is relatively straightforward—although in the context of the third ('Drudge in fair Aurelia's Womb') the seemingly innocent phrase 'design'd for' shifts meaning and direction, attacking Aurelia herself and not simply her ignominious lovers. Far more complex is the situation in the final stanza of **'The Fall'**:

> Then, *Cloris,* while I Duty pay,
>   The Nobler Tribute of my Heart,
> Be not You so severe to say,
>   You love me for a frailer Part.

In this instance, the appositive second line transforms the first from which it apparently derives, underscoring the whole body/soul paradox of the poem. Over and over again in Rochester, constructions of this kind jolt the reader into attention. They force a decision as to the real equivalence of the two halves of a parallel. Does the second part consolidate the meaning of the first, or does it subtly annihilate it?

Syntactical ambiguity of another kind ensures, in the second stanza of that beautiful poem **'An Age in her Embraces Past',** that the conventional dependence of the lover's soul upon the eyes of his mistress should be a grammatical fact, built in to the structure of the lyric, and not simply an imposed conceit:

> But, oh! how slowly Minutes rowl,
>   When absent from her Eyes;
> That feed my Love, which is my Soul,
>   It languishes and dyes.

What seems at first to be the subject of this poem—the relativity of love's time—is a seventeenth-century commonplace. Cowley, one of the English poets Rochester most admired, has two poems on the subject in his collection *The Mistress,* neither of them negligible, both dependent upon metaphysical imagery and style: 'Love and Life' and 'The Long Life'. Rochester begins, apparently, in their manner:

> An Age, in her Embraces past,
>   Would seem a Winters Day;
> Where Life and Light, with envious hast,
>   Are torn and snatch'd away.

This great celebratory opening, a statement in the grand manner, is oddly disturbing, although only the reader already well acquainted with the poem will be able to articulate, at this point, precisely why. In fact, the positive image at the centre is being contradicted by the tone and balance of the stanza as a whole. A sense of deprivation, of violence and negation, threatens to overbear the fragile felicity it is ostensibly there to magnify. The meaning of the words is clear and straightforward: an eternity spent in the lady's arms would seem too short. Cowley had thought so too. The emotional stress of Rochester's stanza, on the other hand, running counter to its intellectual content, falls upon the winter's day and its tragic abridgement. Why it should do so it is the business of the rest of the poem, with its exploration of what Professor George Williamson has rightly called Rochester's 'ethic of pain',[10] to make clear:

> Fantastick Fancies fondly move;
>   And in frail Joys believe;
> Taking false Pleasure for true Love;
>   But Pain can ne're deceive.

> Kind Jealous Doubts, tormenting Fears,
>   And Anxious Cares, when past,
> Prove our Hearts Treasure fixt and dear,
>   And make us blest at last.

The great poem **Upon Nothing** also both invokes and passes beyond the metaphysical style. The basic joke, the paradoxical idea of writing Something in praise of Nothing had been explored by at least two continental poets before Rochester, as he must have known. His own poem is an inversion of the First Chapter of the Book of Genesis and also, in a more limited sense, of Cowley's 'Hymn to Light'. Most immediately of all, it wanders in the country of the pre-Socratic philosopher Parmenides, playing with concepts of Being and non-Being in a way designed to call the structure of language itself into question. After all, how is it possible to articulate an adoration of primal Chaos without sacrilege: without repeating poetically precisely what Rochester castigates as the primal rape of Nothingness by Creation? The poet is a maker, and the act of writing bestows shape and order perforce upon what had previously been formless. Simply by being at all, Rochester's poem perpetuates that contamination of the abstract by the concrete, of Nothing by Something, which it is out to deplore. **Upon Nothing** is an even more dizzying poetic equivalent of Dr. Bendo's bill. This is, with a vengeance, the place where fundamental opposites meet and relinquish their identities, and they do not do so simply in terms of witty images like 'thy fruitful emptiness's hand'. Man's efforts to conceptualize, language itself, is under attack in this poem and verbal analysis can go only so far. Oddly enough, Henry Vaughan can help.

> I saw Eternity the other night
> Like a great *Ring* of pure and endless light,
>   All calm, as it was bright,
> And round beneath it, Time in hours, days, years,
>   Driv'n by the spheres
> Like a vast shadow mov'd, In which the world
>   And all her train were hurl'd;
> The doting Lover in his queintest strain
>   Did their Complain.

After a staggering opening, Vaughan's poem collapses into triviality. The doting lover and his quaint strain are simply not compatible with the ring of endless light, as innumerable critics have pointed out. But this incompatibility is, of course, the whole point. The abrupt downward movement is deliberate, a demonstration of the gap between Heaven and Earth, between great abstractions and a finite world of small fact. Rochester's **Upon Nothing** does something similar, in pursuit of another end. Within fifty-one lines, the poem moves from the noble abstractions of Nothingness, through Creation, to the debased minutiae of a contemporary reality: 'King's Promises, Whores Vows . . . Dutch Prowess, British Policy.' The very form of the poem is a demonstration of its basic premiss, that Nothing is best. Increasingly satirical as it becomes more detailed and concrete, its construction is a silent witness to the ignominy of Being.

Let me end with what seems to me the best of Rochester's lyrics.

> Absent from thee I languish still,
>   Then ask me not, when I return?
> The straying Fool t'will plainly kill,
>   To wish all Day, all Night to Mourn.
>
> *Dear*; from thine Arms then let me flie,
>   That my Fantastick Mind may prove
> The Torments it deserves to try,
>   That tears my fixt Heart from my Love.
>
> When wearied with a world of Woe
>   To thy safe Bosom I retire,
> Where Love, and Peace, and Truth does flow,
>   May I contented there expire.
>
> Lest once more wand'ring from that Heav'n,
>   I fall on some base heart unblest;
> Faithless to thee, False, unforgiv'n,
>   And lose my Everlasting rest.

Here once again is an opening contradicted by what follows. The first line, 'Absent from thee I languish still', seems to introduce a conventional lament in absence. The impression is immediately corrected. This lover has not yet left his lady's arms, nor is he compelled to do so by either the world or time. It is his own fantastic mind which is about to impose a separation which his heart regrets. In the moment of leavetaking, he foresees clearly the pain and loathsomeness of his self-imposed exile; he also foresees his return 'wearied with a world of woe' to a place he should never have left. A man asks leave to be faithless, knowing it will disgust him, predicting his renunciation of what he already recognizes as folly. This would seem a sufficient burden of meaning for any sixteen-line lyric to carry, but Rochester goes further. His narrator can see, beyond this initial separation and return, still another betrayal, a wanton repetition of the whole process. This clear-sightedness is terrifying in itself. Even worse is his recognition that this next absence but one may end in a commitment to 'some base heart unblest', a permanent exile from the true heaven which claims his devotion, but which he can neither live with nor without. Appalled at the possibilities of the future, he asks for death in his lady's arms—not, significantly, now, but at the stage of his first return.

Rochester's conversations with Bishop Burnet provide the real gloss on this poem. It both is and it is not a secular love song. I have not touched in this lecture upon Rochester's *Satyr Against Reason and Mankind.* This is his best-known poem, and it has always been able, unlike the lyrics, to speak for itself. I would, however, remind you of its poise between a firm conviction of the empirical limits of man's mind and an underlying agony that he should in fact be bounded by sense experience. The theme of limitation is everywhere in Rochester and never, not even in poems where it seems most straightforwardly a physical matter: **'The Fall'** or that wry grafting of Donne's 'Extasie' on to Ovid, **'The Imperfect Enjoyment'**, is it without its transcendental shadow. Jeremy Collier once pointed out irately that the association of one's mistress with Heaven had become a blasphemous Restoration commonplace. In **'Absent from Thee'**, it is far more than this. The poem embodies the state of mind in which Burnet found Rochester before his final illness and mystical experience: desirous but at the same time despairing of commitment, haunted by the idea of a position of rest and stasis involving more than mere sexual fidelity, but unable to encompass it.

Rochester's death-bed conversion caused rejoicing among the godly, but also a good deal of perplexity to his old friends. The temptation then, as indeed now, was to regard it as yet another of his roles, the last part assumed. There are certain indications that Rochester himself feared for its permanence. He wished to die before there could be any risk of his mind's alteration. Nat Lee, in *The Princess of Cleve,* could not resist a sneer at the man his play otherwise mourns so movingly Nemours points out acidly in the last lines that

> He well Repents that will not Sin, yet can,
> But Death-bed Sorrow rarely shews the Man.

Rochester's old companion and fellow-reveller Fanshaw fled from the obsessive pieties of the death-bed at Woodstock convinced that his friend had gone mad. He hadn't, but he had effectively ceased to be Rochester. The very anonymity of the last letters, and of the recantation and apology for his past life which he dictated and signed on 19 June 1680 is startling. They could have been written by anyone. A whole personality had collapsed simultaneously with the doubts and contradictions at its centre. Rochester told Robert Parsons, his mother's chaplain, that he intended to turn to the composition of religious poetry if he lived. What it might have been like is an interesting speculation, considering that by his conversion the whole former basis of his art—doubt, rationalism, the confusion of good and evil, sensuality, the assumption of false faces—had been swept away. In a sense, the final scene of his life was inevitable from the beginning. Looking at the poetry, at the letters, the biography, and at that strange portrait in Warwick Castle in which he is depicted crowning an ape with the laurels of poetry, it is hard not to think of Rochester as the archetypal Man of Herbert's 'The Pulley'. Endowed by God with beauty, strength, wisdom, honour, and pleasure, he had everything but peace of mind. And that, in the end, was the point of this sinister compact:

> Yet let him keep the rest,
> But keep them with repining restlessness;
> Let him be rich and wearie, that at least,
> If goodnesse leade him not, yet wearinesse
>   May tosse him to my breast.

Notes

1. Thomas Alcock and John Wilmot, Earl of Rochester, *The Famous Pathologist or The Noble Mountebank,* edited by Vivian de Sola Pinto (Nottingham University Miscellany No. 1), Nottingham, 1961, p. 33.

2. *The Collected Works of John Wilmot, Earl of Rochester,* edited by John Hayward (Nonesuch Press), London, 1926, p. 288 (Letter LXX).

3. *The Works of Lord Byron . . . Letters and Journals,* edited by R. E. Prothero, v. 470 (to Murray, 3 Nov. 1821).

4. David M. Vieth, *Attribution in Restoration Poetry,* New Haven and London, 1963, p. 199. I have used the version of 'The Post Boy' printed by Vieth. Otherwise, all quotations from Rochester's poetry come from the edition of Vivian de Sola Pinto (Muses Library), London, 1953.

5. Gilbert Burnet, *Some Passages of the Life and Death of the Right Hon. John Earl of Rochester,* London (1680), p. 11.

6. H. F. Brooks, 'The Imitation in English Poetry', *Review of English Studies,* xxv (1949), 124-40.

7. Louis L. Martz, *The Poetry of Meditation,* New Haven, 1954, pp. 179-93.

8. Søren Kierkegaard, *Either/Or,* translated by David F. Swenson and Lillian M. Swenson, London, 1944, Part I ('The Immediate Stages of the Erotic'), p. 83.

9. Philip Edwards, 'The Danger Not the Death: the Art of John Fletcher', *Jacobean Theatre* (Stratford-upon-Avon Studies, I), edited by John Russell Brown and Bernard Harris, London, 1960, pp. 159-77.

10. George Williamson, *The Proper Wit of Poetry,* London, 1961, pp. 125-6.

Charles A. Knight (essay date 1970)

SOURCE: Knight, Charles A. "The Paradox of Reason: Argument in Rochester's 'Satyr Against Mankind.'" *Modern Language Review* 65, no.2 (April, 1970): 254–60.

[*In the essay below, Knight argues against previous critics' contentions that* A Satire Against Mankind *should be seen in terms of Rochester's interest in seventeenth-century materialism and his eventual conversion, and maintains that the poem is more complex and playful than previously supposed, which is evident from Rochester's handling of his argumentative method and his paradoxical treatment of reason.*]

One of the most apparently pessimistic elements of Rochester's *Satyr against Mankind* is not his attack on speculative reason but his attack on human nature itself. The forceful lines that open the poem are balanced by Rochester's later distinction between deductive, scholastic reason and 'that reason which distinguishes by sense / And gives us rules of good and ill from thence' (l. 100). Thus the opening picture of man's delusive intellectual journey and of his terrible self-knowledge in death is not a picture of the inevitable human condition. It is a view of man who has strayed, rather than a picture of the road itself. But Rochester's assertion that fear and knavery are at the heart of human nature and human society is left without a redeeming distinction in the original poem. Even in the added 'Epilogue,' Rochester, though dissipating the force of his earlier indictment and speaking in a different tone of voice and from more ostensibly conventional values, does not retract his earlier statements about human nature.[1]

C. F. Main comments (p. 101) that Rochester's initial attack on man's pride in reason is a reflection of the doctrine of original sin. It does seem to share the notion of man's loss of preternatural wisdom and man's disposition to pride. But even more central to the doctrine of original sin is the Augustinian view that man's very nature is deformed and bent towards sinfulness (more than towards illusion and error). In this respect Rochester's attack on human nature seems almost conventionally religious in specifying the workings of original sin in human society. But the context makes it all the more pessimistic, for Rochester, in replying to the theological arguments of the 'formal band and beard', attacks rationalistic theology, especially the tenet that reason distinguishes man from beast and makes man the image of God. Thus man is still the weak victim of original sin without the redeeming likeness to divinity. The story of man's Fall is left without the story of creation. The Pascalian Tension of man with and without grace is removed, for man is seen without grace only.[2]

This dark view of human nature has generally been accepted as Rochester's own, or at least as the view implicit in the poem. Most biographers of the poet see the poem in terms of Rochester's interest in seventeenth-century materialistic philosophy and as an anticipation of his later religious conversion. Thus Vivian de Sola Pinto writes that in the poem 'Rochester had reached the end of the cul-de-sac into which he had been led by materialism. In the epilogue we see the truth beginning to dawn upon him that he must retreat from it'. Later, Pinto, commenting on Rochester's path to religion, claims that 'Hobbes's materialism had appealed to him at first because of its boldness and the justification it offered for the life of pleasure. But the *Satyr against Mankind* shows that by the spring of 1675-6 he was outgrowing that "seducing system", and it was natural that he should turn to the other unorthodox creeds which were current at the time in Western Europe'.[3] Others, like Thomas H. Fujimura, are more cautious about drawing biographical inferences but nonetheless assume that the last lines of the original poem represent a philosophical statement to be taken only at full face value.[4] C. F. Main is careful to couch his reading of the poem in the language of formal verse satire. But though he speaks of 'the satirist' rather than of Rochester, he does not take up the question of tone or see the last half of the

poem as anything but a relatively straightforward philosophical statement. He calls the last section of the poem
almost Hobbesian in its treatment of human fear (p. 107).

Hobbesian the poem may be, but thus far attempts to
consider the poem have done so apart from its tone and
the rhetorical structure of its arguments. My purpose here
is to suggest that in some respects the poem is more playful and more complex than has been previously supposed
and that these qualities derive from Rochester's handling
of his argumentative method and from his paradoxical
treatment of reason in the structure of the poem. Irrelevant
as biography may be to such consideration of the poem,
there is at least some biographical evidence that suggests
suspicion about the poem's straightforwardness, for every
reader of Rochester's antics, even his genuine ones, and
every viewer of Huysmans's famous portrait of him crowning a monkey with bays, can recognize his basic interest
not merely in disguise, but in the put-on, in a deception
that derives from a basic awareness of society and of motive, and in a posing that embodies that awareness in wit.
It is not my purpose here to suggest how deep this
tendency may be in Rochester's basic attitudes or to
speculate on its influence in Rochester's own personal life,
but this public trait in Rochester does suggest that we
ought not to accept too automatically the surface meaning
of the poem without regard for its tone or its wit.

The poem begins by enunciating its primary satiric device,
the preference of beasts to men and the mocking distress
of the speaker that he cannot choose to be other than he is.
This preference dominates most of the poem and is its
formal organizing device. In addition to introducing the
play of stock attitudes concerning the role of reason in
identifying man's position in the cosmic hierarchy, it
presents important aspects of the speaker's cast of thought,
for he sees himself as inextricably caught by his view of
the human situation. But unlike his later adversary, who
indulges in flights of reason to escape human limitations,
the speaker presents alternative choices that he knows are
impossible. Thus he is comically aware that he is trapped
by his situation, and the rest of the poem develops that
awareness.

The speaker quickly focuses on the problem of man's
rationality, and this remains the poem's major concern up
to line 111. The attack on reason is appropriately unreasonable. The speaker makes unargued assertions of his position ('The senses are too gross, and he'll contrive / A
sixth, to contradict the other five', l.8[5]), and on the basis of
these assertions he constructs an elaborate metaphor in
which the reasoner is seen following a will-o'-the-wisp
through various misadventures until 'old age and experience, hand in hand, / Lead him to death, and make him
understand . . .' The force of this passage (ll. 12-30) lies
in the speaker's ability to keep extending his comic
metaphor of the folly of reason until it culminates in a
crashing triplet:

> In hopes still to o'ertake th' escaping light,
> The vapor dances in his dazzling sight
> Till, spent, it leaves him in eternal night.

(l. 22)

The metaphor is serious in its content but it has as well a
playfulness which derives both from its extension and
from the confusion it presupposes between objective and
subjective reality. The searcher's fate, which he has
brought on himself by supposing that the products of his
fancy were objectively real, is dramatized by his final and
absolute realization that 'all his life he has been in the
wrong'.

The poem's initial attack comes, then, not through the
logical argument of an intellectual position but from its
embodiment in metaphor. As the attack is expanded, the
speaker uses analogues from human society to explain his
distinctions: pride is like a gamester, wit like a whore;
pride is directed at dupes and 'bubbles', wit at fops and
fools. Thus the speaker begins to direct his attack, as he
will more fully in the poem's conclusion, towards human
society itself, rather than towards the specific individual
deluded by reason. But this process is interrupted by the
introduction of the adversary.

Rochester's transition to the speech of the adversary seems
at first to be arbitrary, for the adversary does not appear
with surprising and obtrusive anger, nor has his appearance been prepared from the beginning. But his relevance
becomes apparent when he starts his speech itself. The
adversary has a false notion of the speaker's treatment of
wit. Indeed, the speaker's attack was not directed at wit
itself but at its consequences in society. But the adversary
is so defensive in the face of the speaker's attack that he is
glad to glean from his hostile remarks whatever he can
agree with. Howard Erskine-Hill ably corrects Pinto's suggestion tht the adversary represents an argument in which
Rochester wished he could believe, for the lines themselves, as he notes in detail, are weak and unconvincing.[6]

The adversary's remarks represent a break in both the
content and structure of the poem. They give the speaker a
specific position against which to argue and a specific
audience against which to direct his arguments. They also
signal a change in technique. The first forty-five lines of
the poem are organized around rather large, extended, rich
comparisons. In the middle section of the poem the
comparisons are short, more verbal, more immediately
heightened by the structure of the couplets, and more
frequent. The middle section, then, gains force through the
variety and proliferation of its devices.

The speaker's characteristic method of attack in the middle
section is to couple language used by the adversary with
stronger, antithetical terms, making the position of the
adversary seem paradoxical and absurd. Many of these
antitheses are heightened by rhyme: 'mite', with 'infinite',
'void of all rest' with 'ever-blest', or in a couplet like the
following:

Borne on whose wings, each heavy sot can pierce,
The limits of the boundless universe.

(l. 84)

The essential conflict embodied in this method and expressed by it is that the adversary sees reason as a means by which man can achieve the transcendent; but in fact, the speaker implies, such reason is fallacious in the first place and, in the second, more binding on human nature than that which it wishes to transcend:

This made a whimsical philosopher
Before the spacious world, his tub prefer.

(l. 90)

The embodiment of this contradiction in specific antitheses leads, then, to the distinction between proper reason, which begins with the senses and governs rather than restricts them, and reason that is limited by the abstract presuppositions with which it begins. Having undermined the position of his adversary, the speaker now develops his own view contrasting the utility of his reason to the rigidity expressed by his adversary:

My reason is my friend, yours is a cheat;
Hunger calls out, my reason bids me eat;
Perversely, yours your appetite does mock:
This asks for food, that answers, "What's o'clock?"

(l. 106)

The effect of these lines is not to convince us that the speaker's position is philosophically more sound, but primarily to emphasize that his position is more directly conducive to pleasure. Thus here, as earlier in the poem, the speaker carefully avoids a genuinely rationalistic basis for his argument.[7] Rather, he develops contrasts and paradoxes which exemplify his position, making it concrete and convincing.

The final section of the poem, excluding the Epilogue, depends upon the speaker's initial comparison between man and beast. Having discussed the arguments of the adversary, the speaker drops that particular rhetorical stance (though we remain conscious of the adversary as part of the audience of the remaining lines). But when he no longer confronts the adversary directly, the speaker loses the immediate context against which he could develop his own specific arguments in a concrete manner, and thus it is necessary for him to resume his earlier and more extensive animal contrast. Consequently, he argues more absolutely, claiming a kind of truth for his position rather than asserting merely that his views are more satisfactory than those of the adversary. In doing so, as we shall see, the speaker takes a step that is fraught with satiric danger.

In the first stage of his final argument, the speaker proposes wisdom as the intellectual criterion by which the merit of man and beast is to be weighed. He postulates that

Those creatures are the wisest who attain,
By surest means, the ends at which they aim.

(l. 117)

But it becomes clear by example that beasts more surely attain their ends than man and therefore must be wiser. Similarly, human nature itself is less trustworthy than animal, for men lack that natural loyalty to their species found in beasts, nor does man's cruelty even satisfy the basic natural wants and self-interest of beasts. Instead, the speaker continues, dropping his specific comparison with beasts to develop his major characterization of human nature, the primary motive of human society is fear:

Look to the bottom of his vast design,
Wherein man's wisdom, power, and glory join:
The good he acts, the ill he does endure,
'Tis all from fear, to make himself secure.
Merely for safety, after fame we thirst,
For all men would be cowards if they durst.

(l. 153)

Indeed, so ubiquitous is the propensity to fear that honesty is virtually impossible: if one is honest, one will suffer in a society that has no place for honesty, and, therefore, fear leads to dishonesty (even to the dishonest pretension to bravery). Thus the only difference between knavery and cowardice lies 'not in the thing itself, but the degree' (l. 171).

It is clear that this final section of the poem is dominated not so much by the rhetorical devices of contrast used in much of the earlier part of the poem as by syllogistic reasoning and the use of logical fallacies. From the premises that wisdom equals economy of means and that man's means are less direct than beasts', the speaker concludes that beasts are wiser than men are. But the first premise begs the question of whether the ends are valuable or even comparable. Moreover, the speaker jumps from his one representative example to assuming the truth of his second premise. (Thus Jowler the hound can be wiser than Aristotle as well as than Meres. But, on the other hand, the rapacity of hounds and politicians—the real ground for their comparison—does not play a formal role in the satiric argument.)

The same satiric use of reason sustains much of the speaker's attack on human nature, where he comes much closer to dealing with the question of ends. Ironically, man's 'principles' and 'morals' are inferior to beasts'. In this instance the speaker, who was perfectly able to distinguish varieties of reason, does not distinguish between principles and nature. The argument of orthodox morality is that man's principles restrain the excesses of his fallen nature. But in the ***Satyr*** those elements that would be identified as excesses of nature (treachery, self-interest, and 'wantonness') are treated as principles.

Thus the speaker proceeds by chop logic, by syllogistic reasoning, by shifting the terms of his premises, by arguing on unexamined assumptions, and by using language that departs from accepted senses (as in his use of 'wisdom'). This logical manipulation provides much of the sharpness of language in this section. The major logical fallacy is the speaker's failure to make any essential distinction between man and beast and his placing of them in classes which defy that distinction. But he also uses that satiric overlapping of distinguishable levels as the source of verbal play, as in such adjectives as 'savage' in the following couplet:

> Birds feed on birds, beasts on each other prey,
> But savage man alone does man betray.

> (l. 129)

or in his similar contrast between what is natural and what is human:

> With teeth and claws by nature armed, they hunt
> Nature's allowance, to supply their want.
> But man, with smiles, embraces, friendships, praise,
> Inhumanly his fellow's life betrays.

> (l. 133)

As the speaker's discussion of human nature develops, he moves from his contrast of man with animals, and his concomitant logical play, to emphasizing man's 'forced disguise'—the contrast between the virtues to which he claims to aspire (honour, fame, generosity, affability, kindness, wisdom, power, and glory) and his real motive of fear. At the very end of the poem he reintroduces the clergyman as his addressee and, having moved in his attack from cowardice to knavery, proceeds to negate any essential difference between them. Yet Rochester is careful to indicate that all of this follows from the particular position assumed by the speaker which, once adopted, closes any further speculation concerning human nature:

> Thus, sir, you see what human nature craves:
> Most men are cowards, all men should be knaves.
> The difference lies, as far as I can see,
> Not in the thing itself, but the degree,
> And all the subject matter of debate
> Is only: Who's a knave of the first rate?

> (l. 168)

There are several conclusions that can be drawn from such an analysis of the argument of the last section of the poem. In the first place, despite the speaker's serious allegations about man, the tone is in part playful. At least the poem depends in part on adroit juggling of words and logical categories (e.g. 'For all men would be cowards if they durst'), and this implies more emotional distance between the speaker and the object satirized than does a straightforward diatribe. Moreover, in its intellectual play, the last section of the poem employs much the same kind of reasonable, deductive argument that the speaker had attacked in the adversary. Its major intellectual movement is syllogistic, and, like the adversary, the speaker becomes victimized by the limitations of his own premises: having postulated that men and beasts can be compared on moral grounds, his vision is limited by the terms of that

comparison. Such limitation does not mean the speaker is merely wrong, for at the other end of the satiric process his remarks gain whatever truth they possess when the implied reader (whose sympathies in the argument ought, after all, to lie with the speaker rather than the adversary) senses their approximate truth in terms of his own experience. But the speaker's use of reason implies that it is impossible for him to escape reason and its limitations, just as he cannot escape from dishonesty or from his human nature.

The last section of the poem and, indeed, the poem itself, provide an argument not merely for a hedonistic intellectual stance but for a hedonistic life. Man's goal is human happiness, which is derived from the senses; and since fear and knavery are the bases of human society, the honest and virtuous life is both unlikely and impractical—certainly not conducive to happiness. In providing this argument, the poem seems to follow the pattern more largely writ in Rochester's 'Love and Life' ('All my past life is mine no more'), which Vieth places in the same period as the *Satyr*.[8] There the poet's rather lyric meditations on time and memory become the excuse for infidelity. Here the dishonesty of life and the hypocrisy of virtue justify hedonism and, indeed, conventional immorality. Thus the speaker, like the adversary, is not merely defending an abstract position but justifying himself. In so doing he is motivated by self-interest, but from his own point of view such motivation is possible and consistent. His use of reason in making his argument, however, is not.

The speaker becomes, then, a complex vehicle for satire. While on one hand his assertions about human nature have conviction, on the other, the way in which he makes them is an exemplification of the very limits of human nature and human reason he has spoken of. Pinto, in describing the 'passionate vehemence' of the last passage, compares it to *Gulliver's Travels*. 'Its place is . . . beside the great things in Swift, and it recalls the King of Brobdingnag's denunciation of the human race.'[9] Swiftian the passage may be, but to my mind it seems closer to the angry remarks of Gulliver at the end of 'A Voyage to the Houyhnhnms'. Like Gulliver, the speaker of the *Satyr* is himself included in his denunciation of man, and his denunciation itself exemplifies that which he denounces. But in this case there is perhaps more humility than pride in the speaker's position. He does not attack, as Gulliver does, unmindful of his own involvement in the fear and knavery he attacks. Indeed, the element of personal defence in his attack requires such awareness.

Rochester's *Satyr against Mankind* is not, then, merely a reflection of seventeenth-century materialism in an early formal verse satire. It is a rich and complex work because Rochester uses a variety of argumentative stances to present his material, indeed to embody it in his work. It is this cohesion of satiric form and content and this appropriate shifting of satiric perspective that unify the work and give it depth and brilliance.

Notes

1. Vivian de Sola Pinto, in *Enthusiast in Wit* (1962), pp. 157-8 claims that the Epilogue, certainly by Rochester, is 'a sort of conditional recantation', which is 'of great biographical significance'. Pinto considers it, then, a later addition. David M. Vieth does not take up the question of dating the Epilogue in his *Attribution in Restoration Poetry* (New Haven, 1963), but his list of the *Satyr's* early manuscripts and texts (pp. 370-75) includes some with the Epilogue, some without it, some which call it an 'Addition', and some which present the Epilogue alone. C. F. Main ('The Right Vein of Rochester's "Satyr"', in *Essays in Literary History Presented to J. Milton French,* edited by Rudolf Kirk and C. F. Main (New Brunswick, 1960), p. 97) argues that the Epilogue is an important part of the poem, within the 'retraction' tradition of satire. I find the Epilogue less interesting in style and less forceful in subject than the main part of the poem, and, since there is reasonable bibliographical evidence for considering it an addition, I prefer to do so. I am not conscious, however, that inclusion of the Epilogue would contradict any of the points that I make without it.

2. 'Par où il paraît clairement que l'homme par la grâce est rendu comme semblable à Dieu et participant de sa divinité, et que, sans la grâce, il est comme semblable aux bêtes brutes' (*Pensées,* 434, renumbered 438, in *OEuvres Completes,* edited by Jacques Chevalier (1954), p. 1208).

3. *Enthusiast in Wit,* pp. 158, 186.

4. Thomas H. Fujimura, 'Rochester's "Satyr against Mankind": An Analysis', *S.P.,* 55 (1958), 576-90.

5. References are to *The Complete Poems of John Wilmot, Earl of Rochester,* edited by David M. Vieth (New Haven, 1968).

6. *Enthusiast in Wit,* p. 154; Howard Erskine-Hill, 'Rochester: Augustan or Explorer', in *Renaissance and Modern Essays Presented to Vivian de Sola Pinto in Celebration of his Seventieth Birthday,* edited by G. R. Hibbard (1966), pp. 53-4.

7. The speaker does argue syllogistically in claiming that man's goal is human happiness and that reason is subordinate to it. But his argument is little more than a general statement of his more concrete material. Certainly it is distinguishable from the more satiric use of syllogistic argument found later.

8. *Complete Poems of John Wilmot,* p. 200.

9. *Enthusiast in Wit,* p. 157.

Kristoffer F. Paulson (essay date 1971)

SOURCE: Paulson, Kristoffer F. "Pun Intended: Rochester's 'Upon Nothing.'" *English Language Notes* 9 no. 2 (December, 1971): 118-21.

[*In the following essay, Paulson charges that most critics have treated* Upon Nothing *with too great seriousness, arguing that one needs to understand the bawdy pun on "what" in the second stanza to appreciate its wit and tone of exuberant irreverence.*]

Critics of the satire *Upon Nothing,* written by John Wilmot, the Earl of Rochester, agree that it is a paradoxical and witty poem, a profound satire based on skeptical philosophy, and a parody of the creation myth found in the first chapter of Genesis.[1] It is witty and profound and it is a parody of Genesis, but most of the very perceptive commentaries on *Upon Nothing* have treated the satire with a singular solemnity, and most critics have failed to see the laughter, whether cosmic or not, co-existing with the serious skepticism.[2] None seem to have noticed the bawdy pun on "What?" in the second stanza. This pun establishes the controlling metaphor of generation and birth developed in a series of witty paradoxes in the first seven stanzas of the poem.

A clear idea of the wit of *Upon Nothing* and its tone of exuberant irreverence cannot be understood without an awareness of this pun.

> E're time, and place, were, time, and place, were not
> When *Primitive Nothing,* something strait begot,
> Then all proceeded from the great united—What?
>
> (Text: A-1680-HU)[3]

The final line of this stanza contains the elevated tone of mock-serious irony, common to a paradoxical encomium, but it also contains the startling pun on *What?,* a pun not elevated at all. When the line is spoken aloud the combination of final plosive consonants *t* and *d* in *united* cause the final *d* to be pronounced more like *t.* This effect is emphasized if a pause is demanded between the final *t* sound and *What?.* The final *t* sound in *united* becomes a part of the last word in the line producing *t—W'at?* (twat).[4] The bawdy pun may seem outrageous, but no more so than the verbal irony of Hamlet's "Do you think I meant count[-]ry matters?"

The final line of this stanza in Professor David M. Vieth's recent edition of *The Complete Poems of John Wilmot, Earl of Rochester* reads "Then all proceeded from the great united What," omitting the dash and question mark.[5] Vieth's copy-text is the Bodl. MS. Tanner 306, fol. 410[r].[6] However, this line in three early and reliable texts (the A-1680-HU, the Gyldenstolpe MS., and the Yale MS.) do contain the dashes and question mark.[7] The scribe of the Bodl. MS. probably did not recognize the pun, and certainly not its importance in the poem, and ignored the dash and question mark while transcribing. The pun on *What* exists with or without the punctuation, but the pun is already submerged, and excluding the dash submerges it even further. Excluding the question mark denies the irony of the line and the humorous eyebrow-raising question. Rochester deliberately used the dash and question mark, I think, to inform the pun and emphasize the great question, giving the query an assumed tone, or a pose of quizzically ironic, wide-eyed ignorance.

The pun on *What,* though at first surprising, continues the imagery of generation and birth begun in the second stanza, "When *Primitive Nothing,* something strait begot." This imagery is continued in the third stanza:

> Something, the gen'ral *Attribute* of all,
> Sever'd from thee, [its][8] sole *Original,*
> Into thy boundless self, must undistinguish'd fall.

Together the images form one extended metaphor. Figuratively and literally, "the great united—What?" is the vagina and womb of Nothing, from which "all proceeded." "Something" is born of Nothing and is "sever'd" from its "sole *Original*" as a child's umbilical cord is severed at birth from the womb of its mother.

Stanzas four through seven of **Upon Nothing** develop and return to the imagery of generation and birth: stanza four, "And from thy fruitful emptinesses hand, / Snatcht *Men, Beasts, Birds, Fire,* [Water,][9] *Aire,* and *Land*"; stanza five, "*Matter,* the wicked'st *Offspring* of thy *Race*"; stanza six, "With form, and *Matter,* time and place, did join, . . . / To spoil thy peaceful *Realm,* and ruin all thy *Line.*" Stanza seven completes the cycle; with the aid of Time the offspring which came from Nothing are ultimately driven back to the womb of Nothing: "And to thy hungry *Womb,* drives back thy *Slaves* again."

The logic of the first seven stanzas of **Upon Nothing** is a series of wonderfully self-evident contradictions. The wit and humor of Rochester's satire come from the juxtaposed incongruity of calmly revealing the incomprehensible and abstract absolute—Nothing—as a concrete, earthy personification. As Professor Anne Righter Barton points out, Rochester plays "with concepts of Being and non-Being in a way designed to call the structure of language itself into question."[10] Nothing is both the begetter and bearer of "something." To beget and bear postulates a union of some kind, but exactly "What" could have become joined together is the problem. Nothing is the "sole *Original,*" yet it "united" to give birth. The result of this most singular union, in a very literal sense, is the deliberately vague "something." John Harold Wilson states that **Upon Nothing** is "a grim parody on a famous theme in Genesis—the Creation" and "something" is "Rochester's ironic name for God or Spirit."[11] Rochester's parody of Creation is really exuberant rather than grim satire, and a single interpretation of the deliberately vague "something" discounts the variety of ironic possibilities such a general term can connote and with which Rochester plays throughout the satire.

The satire is certainly a devastating attack on revealed religion and the Christian dogma of Creation *ex nihilo,* but the blasphemy, if indeed it is such, is buoyant, bubbling with irreverent good humor. The author is obviously enjoying himself as he expands his skepticism within a framework of laughter at the attempts of theologians and philosophers who struggle to explain and prove that which must be left to faith—or to doubt.

Notes

1. John Harold Wilson, *The Court Wits of the Restoration* (Princeton, 1948), pp. 137-138. V. de Sola Pinto, *Enthusiast in Wit* (Lincoln, 1962), pp. 114-116. Ronald Berman, "Rochester and the Defeat of the Senses," *Kenyon Review,* XXVI (1964), 359. Howard Erskine-Hill, "Rochester: Augustan or Explorer?" *Renaissance and Modern Essays* (London, 1966), p. 56. Anne Righter [Barton], "John Wilmot, Earl of Rochester," *Proceedings of the British Academy,* LII (1967), 62.

2. The one exception is Pinto, but he confuses his point with an irrelevant comparison between Rochester's Nothing and Blake's Nobodaddy (p. 116).

3. Text: A-1680-HU. See *Rochester's Poems on Several Occasions,* ed. James Thorpe (Princeton, 1950), p. 51. All subsequent quotations from *Upon Nothing,* unless otherwise noted, are taken from this text.

4. The first time "twat" appears in written English according to the *OED* is in 1656 in R. Fletcher's translation of Martial. The *OED* also records a maxim from the *Vanity of Vanities* published in 1660: "They talk't of his having a Cardinalls Hat, They'd send him as soon as Old Nuns Twat." *Upon Nothing* was probably composed between 1675 and 1678.

5. *The Complete Poems of John Wilmot, Earl of Rochester,* ed. David M. Vieth (New Haven, 1968), p. 118.

6. *Ibid.,* p. 206.

7. See *The Gyldenstolpe Manuscript Miscellany of Poems by John Wilmot, Earl of Rochester and other Restoration Authors,* ed. Bror Danielsson and David M. Vieth (Uppsala, 1967), p. 153. Yale MS., p. 108. For a discussion of the Yale MS., see David M. Vieth, *Attribution in Restoration Poetry* (New Haven, 1963), pp. 65 ff. Whether this evidence demands a change in the choice of copy-text, or simply a departure from the chosen copy-text, is a question for an editor, but both the recognition of the pun and the textual evidence suggest the necessity of the dashes and the question mark.

8. The A-1680-HU (Thorpe, p. 51) reads "it's" which has to be a typographer's error.

9. This reading is found in Vieth's copy-text and in the Gyldenstolpe MS. See Danielsson and Vieth, p. 154.

10. Anne Righter [Barton], p. 62.

11. Wilson, p. 137.

Howard D. Weinbrot (essay date 1972)

SOURCE: Weinbrot, Howard D. "The Swelling of the Volume: The Apocalyptic Satire of Rochester's *Letter from Artemisia in the Town to Chloe in the Country.*" *Studies in the Literary Imagination* 5, no. 2 (October, 1972): 19-37.

[*In this essay, Weinbrot claims that Artemisia to Chloe demonstrates Rochester's breadth of satiric talent, especially his adept use of the most pessimistic or "apocalyptic" form of contemporary satire, as the work presents the degeneration of the chief character Artemisia from a worthy voice to an agent for the propagation of infamy.*]

Modern revaluation of Restoration and eighteenth-century literature has helped Rochester's reputation as both man and poet: many of the nastier myths of his life have been exploded, his poetry has been reliably edited, and critical and scholarly studies have illuminated aspects of his intellectual context and poetic achievement. The **Letter from Artemisia in the Town to Chloe in the Country** (1679), however, has received sparse critical comment and is excluded from the latest, weighty, anthology of contemporary literature.[1] This is unfortunate, not only because of our ignorance of the poem that is probably Rochester's masterpiece, but also because the **Letter** helps to show Rochester's broad exercise of satiric talent and, especially, his mastery of the most pessimistic form of serious contemporary satire.

Of course it is difficult to label and classify the varieties of so-called "Augustan" satires, but three broad and, sometimes, overlapping classes may be found. I call these punitive satire, formal verse satire, and apocalyptic or revelatory satire.[2] In the first the poet hopes to punish an adversary rather than correct him, as in Rochester's **"On Poet Ninny"** (1680), a lampoon upon Sir Carr Scroope. Though there are certain implicit and explicit norms—beauty is preferable to ugliness, pride is bad—the main thrust of the satire is towards abuse rather than instruction:

> Thou art a thing so wretched and so base
> Thou canst not ev'n offend, but with thy face.
>
> (ll. 6-7)[3]

In formal verse satire, normally in heroic couplets and based in part upon the examples of Horace, Persius, and Juvenal, the poet attacks one central vice and praises its opposite virtue. Such a form requires the presence, however faint, of a workable and working norm for this world. Two of Rochester's major poems fall roughly at opposite ends of a spectrum of formal verse satires. The **"Allusion to Horace"** (1680) affirms related norms—the critical perception of the sheltered aristocratic poet, and poetry which eschews mere popular acclaim. Both the speaker and the friends he mentions fulfill these positive values:

> I loathe the rabble; 'tis enough for me
> If Sedley, Shadwell, Shepherd, Wycherley,
> Godolphin, Butler, Buckhurst, Buckingham,
> And some few more, whom I omit to name,
> Approve my sense: I count their censure fame.
>
> (ll. 120-24)

But the **"Allusion"** is also punitive in its attack upon Dryden, who is the central target of Rochester's anger, and whose rhymes are "stol'n, unequal, nay dull many times" (l. 2). He wonders whether

> those gross faults his choice pen does commit
> Proceed from want of judgment, or of wit;
> Or if his lumpish fancy does refuse
> Spirit and grace to his loose, slattern muse?
>
> (ll. 89-92)[4]

Though Rochester is anchored in Horace's relatively mild *Satires,* I, 10, his poem hovers near the borders of punitive satire, just as the **Satyr against Mankind** hovers near those of revelatory satire.

That poem is often regarded as the embodiment of Rochester's "furious contempt for mankind" and his gloomy view that man is a beast.[5] The fury of Rochester's satire cannot be denied; but the force of his argument suggests that he still cares enough to want us to reform, and has hope enough to offer a clear alternative through which correction is possible. Speculative reason is "an *ignis fatuus* in the mind" (l. 12) and is the false reasoning he attacks. On the other hand,

> I own right reason, which I would obey:
> That reason which distinguished by sense
> And gives us rules of good and ill from thence,
> That bounds desires with a reforming will
> To keep 'em more in vigor, not to kill.
> . . . . .
> My reason is my friend, yours is a cheat.
>
> (ll. 99-103, 106)

The final paragraph of the poem's "epilogue" describes "a meek, humble man, of honest sense" (l. 212), an ideal clergyman who at least *may* exist.

> If upon earth there dwell such God-like men,
> I'll here recant my paradox to them.
>
> (ll.216-17)

Even at the end of this harsh formal verse satire the speaker is willing to keep the corrective norm alive. Rochester's slight expectation of change—rather than a demonstrated probability—is surely more extreme in this work than in more moderate satires like Pope's epistles to Arbuthnot or Bathurst, in which the adversarius finally embraces Pope's own values. The **Satyr** thus moves towards the revelatory or apocalyptic mode, which primarily intends to depict the terrible situation within or without us and, often, to suggest massively destructive results. This sort of satire is partially at work in *A Tale of a Tub* (1704), sometimes bursts from the genteel surface of Edward Young's *Love of Fame* (1725-28), and is particularly clear in *The Dunciad in Four Books* (1743). I believe that this is also the most illuminating way to view the **Letter from Artemisia in the Town to Chloe in the Country.** It has been discussed in terms of the conventions of the novel and of Restoration comedy,[6] but, as I hope to show, in ways the poem is grimmer than Swift's *Tale* and perhaps even the final *Dunciad.* In the **Letter** Rochester presents us with a world of interlocking sins and sinners with a collective ability to seduce the weak and reach out beyond the confines of the poem's 264 lines. Artemisia's words frame the poem and indicate its direction; as her reluctant beginning evolves into the eager promise of a volume to come, her better values collapse and a whore's triumph. Instead of the country going to the city to seek news of debauchery, the city actively communicates debauchery; Artemisia sows infamous tales which Chloe will reap; the town and the country begin to blend; and the poem takes on a quality of rapidly spreading evil. In the process the poem pictures venal and murderous women, stupid or foolishly clever men, the mere memory of what heavenly love could be, and the hellish actuality earthly love has become.

I. THE RELUCTANT CORRESPONDANT

The poem begins with the first part of Artemisia's frame, her protest against the essentially unfeminine act of writing poetry, something she does only, "Chloe, . . . by your command" (l.1). She supports her reluctance to engage in "lofty flights of dangerous poetry" (l.4) with the perils to both wit and woman in so writing. If "the men of wit" (l. 13), she argues, are so often "dashed back, and wrecked on the dull shore, / Broke of that little stock they had before!" how would a less talented woman's "tottering bark be tossed" (ll. 10-12)? Hence she "gravely" advises herself that "poetry's a snare" (ll. 15-16), that the poet will sadden the reader and be thought mad, and that as a jester or tool of pleasure for the town one is "Cursed if you fail, and scorned though you succeed!" (l. 23). Although Artemisia had responded only to a command, and had concluded "That whore is scarce a more reproachful name / Than poetess" (ll. 26-27), she quickly becomes "Pleased with the contradiction and the sin," and stands "on thorns till I begin" (ll. 30-31). She is "well convinced writing's a shame" (l. 25), but abandons her conviction in the face of her urge to do "the very worst thing" (l. 29) she can.

Such a movement is a microcosm of what happens to Artemisia and her world in the ***Letter,*** and is consistent with the important similarities between wit and woman. Like the putative wit, Artemisia will explore a "stormy, pathless world" (l. 9), and will be dashed back upon the shore. He reveals his creative deficiencies; she reveals her moral deficiencies and is broke of the little stock of virtue with which she starts the poem. He becomes the fiddle of the town—the jester, as Professor Vieth glosses it; she is also potentially a fiddle—an instrument to amuse and please whoever chooses to pick her up. The wit, we will see upon the Fine Lady's appearance, must know the truth about woman at his own cost; Artemisia also pursues the truth about woman and the world she inhabits at her own, but somewhat different, cost, as she already is pleased with sin and becomes worse than a whore in being a poetess. The two opening paragraphs, then, establish the contradictory nature of woman, the tentative virtue of Artemisia herself, and the similarities between wit and woman.

But Artemisia can not be condemned from the start. For all her obvious blemishes, hers is still the voice that presents the best values of the poem, values which, if preserved, could have preserved her society as well. We know little about Chloe, except that she orders her friend to write in unfeminine rhyme and expects "at least to hear what loves have passed / In this lewd town" (ll. 32-33) and who is currently sleeping with whom. Such matters, Artemisia tells Chloe, are "what I would fain forget" (l. 37). Poor Artemisia cannot "name that lost thing, love, without a tear, / Since so debauched by ill-bred customs here" (ll. 38-39). She is not so misguided that she cannot see the right path, and though apparently incapable of achieving love herself, she can describe its source, what it was and should be. The following affirmation serves as an ideal against which the current status of love is measured, and from which Artemisia—the only character with even a hope for change—so badly strays. Love, she says, is "This only joy for which poor we were made" (l. 50):

> Love, the most generous passion of the mind,
> The softest refuge innocence can find,
> The safe director of unguided youth,
> Fraught with kind wishes, and secured by truth;
> That cordial drop heaven in our cup has thrown
> To make the nauseous draught of life go down;
> On which one only blessing, God might raise
> In lands of atheists, subsidies of praise,
> For none did e'er so dull and stupid prove
> But felt a god, and blessed his power in love.
>
> (ll. 40-49)[7]

The piling on of positive words for the portrait of blessed, innocent, heavenly love is as clear as the pejoratives in the portrait of contemporary, earthly love that follows. What should be a joy, is "an arrant trade" (l. 51); a refuge for innocence and a director of youth becomes a refuge for rooks, cheats, and tricks (ll. 52-53); direction by Heaven is taken over by fallen women (ll. 54-58); those same women, created free by God, "Turn gypsies for a meaner liberty" (l. 57) and become slaves to distorted senses and fashion. The perfection of God's blessing and His generous passion of the mind is twisted:

> To an exact perfection they have wrought
> The action, love; the passion is forgot.
>
> (ll. 62-63)

Spiritual love surrenders to secular love, God's design to woman's. As a result of this collapse of values the senses are also out of order. Such women are "deaf to nature's rule, or love's advice" (l. 60), and so desire undesirable men, covet merely fashionable lovers, and do not even enjoy the amiably gross weaknesses of the flesh, since they "Forsake the pleasure to pursue the vice" (l. 61):

> 'Tis below wit, they tell you, to admire,
> And ev'n without approving, they desire.
> Their private wish obeys the public voice;
> 'Twixt good and bad, whimsey decides, not choice.
> Fashions grow up for taste; at forms they strike;
> They know what they would have, not what they like.
> Bovey's a beauty, if some few agree
> To call him so; the rest to that degree
> Affected are, that with their ears they see.
>
> (ll. 64-72)

Artemisia wins our approval as she is offended by these betrayals of Heaven's wishes, love's aims and end, nature's carnal desires and the senses. Indeed, she has been fulfilling one part of the similarity between wit and versifying woman—that of self-revelation. Having shown her own weakness, she re-engages at least some of our sympathy through her awareness of what love should be, and her disapproval of what it is. Hence, though she is a willing participant at the Fine Lady's place of assignation, she nevertheless disappears and allows the Lady her own words and actions.

This change of voice allows Rochester to enlarge the poem's point of view and to lend "objective" support for a scene intended to illustrate several of Artemisia's remarks regarding the action love. We had seen Artemisia's equation of herself with the exploited woman (and wit), the fiddle of the town; she is abused and hardened but nevertheless capable of preserving a vision of redeeming love. If there is any hope for the Restoration world, the opening part of her frame suggests, it is in that lingering memory. Artemisia is thus an improper vehicle for the ensuing section, in which a town-woman recently arrived from the country depicts, defends, and unconsciously debases the destructive battle of the sexes that Artemisia temporarily deplores. Like Artemisia, the Fine Lady also reveals herself, but what she reveals is so ugly that for the time being, at least, Artemisia is preserved as a tainted norm who disapproves of what she sees, whereas the Lady is an active participant and, as we will find, the "creator" of an even uglier character.

II. THE FINE LADY

The Fine Lady presents three categories of the action love: wife and husband, wife and gallant, wife and beast. The first demonstrates the sharp contrast between heavenly love's generous passion of the mind and earthly love's debasement of mind. The Lady's linguistic pyrotechnics, for example, are made clear at once. The husband had prevailed with his wife "through her own skill, / At his request, though much against his will / To come to London" (ll. 75-77). The earlier image of love as a "cordial drop" that Heaven has put in "the nauseous draught of life" (ll. 44, 45), contrasts with the Fine Lady's wish that her husband drink a brew that offers ill effects for him and ill opportunities for her.

> "Dispatch," says she, "that business you pretend,
> Your beastly visit to your drunken friend!
> A bottle ever makes you look so fine;
> Methinks I long to smell you stink of wine!
> Your country drinking breath's enough to kill:
> Sour ale corrected with a lemon peel.
> Prithee, farewell! We'll meet again anon."
> The necessary thing bows, and is gone.
>
> (ll. 85-92)

The process of dehumanizing and bestializing will become even more overt, though it is obvious enough in this passage. The relationship between husband and wife is a mat-

ter of social and economic necessity, devoid of any human emotion but disdain and, perhaps, shame on her part for needing such a booby (l. 82).

Nor is the relationship with the gallant any better. His presence may force the husband to leave, but it is without clear benefit to himself: "The gallant had been, / Though a diseased, ill-favored fool, brought in" (ll. 83-84). And that is all. Once the husband is gone she does not run into the arms of a lusty paramour, but flies upstairs to gossip with the mistress of the house and to insist upon the wisdom of having only a fool as husband or lover. The Fine Lady, then, has her country-fool husband and town-fool gallant, one a necessary the other a fashionable thing.

The only physical or quasi-sexual contact we see (the later episode between Corinna and the fool is narrated) occurs with the Lady and a pet monkey. She courts him, smiles at him, is generally seductive, and provides an obscene parody of love:

> She to the window runs, where she had spied
> Her much esteemed dear friend, the monkey, tied.
> With forty smiles, as many antic bows,
> As if 't had been the lady of the house,
> The dirty, chattering monster she embraced,
> And made it this fine, tender speech at last:
> "Kiss me, thou curious miniature of man!
> How odd thou art! how pretty! how japan!
> Oh, I could live and die with thee!" Then on
> For half an hour in compliment she run.
>
> (ll. 137-46)

Throughout much of the ***Letter*** both man and woman are reduced to subhuman levels; she is "an arrant bird of night" (l. 121) or "a fly, / In some dark hole" (ll. 205-06). The fool is "Ever most joyful when most made an ass" (l. 130), or is an "unbred puppy" (l. 240), or "an owl" (l. 250). But this unpleasant scene—and its probable pun on die—carries the poem's dehumanization of love to its fullest degree, especially since the monkey in its own right and as a near relation to the ape was commonly regarded as the embodiment of base sexuality and man's and woman's lowest drives.[8]

Rochester, I suggest, is using the embrace of the Fine Lady and the monkey as an emblem of what human sexuality and love have become—lust channelled into fashionable bestiality. All other liaisons in the poem are based upon passionless modes, misplaced revenge, a self-destructive desire for forbidden knowledge, or prostitution. Rochester is not attacking mere lust, since such a desire would almost be healthy—nature's voice—in comparison with the unfeeling world we actually see. He is attacking the absolute withdrawal of positive human emotion from human sexual embraces, so that the woman can be warm, friendly, and sexual only with the fashionable pet, a creature close to man—indecently so, Edward Topsell says (p. 4)—yet infinitely below him. In so doing she becomes more bestial than the beast she courts, both because normally the ape or monkey "courted" the lady, and because the monkey is merely acting its prescribed role, whereas she is a product of willingly demeaned reason. The fool, the Fine Lady says, is "Ever most joyful when most made an ass" (l. 130), and the Lady, Artemisia insists, becomes "an ass through choice, not want of wit" (l. 151). The woman who reduces man to an ass becomes one in the process, and she makes herself a fit mate for a monkey (transformed from miniature of the mistress to miniature of man) when she embraces one and becomes a "dirty, chattering monster" (l. 141) as well.

In short, the scene with the monkey is a logical extension of three themes in the poem. First, we recall that "Fashions grow up for taste; at forms they strike; / They know what they would have, not what they like" (ll. 68-69). Under such circumstances even the ugly Sir Ralph Bovey may be judged more than handsome and other women will agree. The Fine Lady's gallant is "a diseased, ill-favored fool" (l. 84), and must owe his fortunate position to just such sense-defying fashion as also leads her to court the monkey.

The Lady and her values, moreover, continue the substitution of the secular for the spiritually ordered world. She knows "everything," apparently with God's blessing, yet chooses to be an ass (ll. 150-51). This is fitting, since God's vision is clearly different from woman's as here portrayed. Nature is inadequate "in making a true fop" (l. 154), and God Himself "never made a coxcomb worth a groat. / We owe that name to industry and arts" (ll. 159-60). This product of civilization who insists upon her wisdom in marrying a fool has also made herself "An eminent fool" (l. 161). Along the way she alters God's design for her, and is ignorant of her true character:

> she . . . had turned o'er
> As many books as men; loved much, read more;
> Had a discerning wit; to her was known
> Everyone's fault and merit, but her own.
> All the good qualities that ever blessed
> A woman so distinguished from the rest,
> Except discretion only, she possessed.
>
> (ll. 162-68)

The play upon turning over "as many books as men" suggests the loss of love as a generous passion of the mind, and the blindness that comes when one rejects the truth and kind wishes of God and seeks faults with the aid of human wisdom. The final step in the replacement of God's design by woman's emerges at the end of the Lady's tale, in which the whore Corinna seduces and financially rapes a country fool after she herself had been abandoned by a wit. In this parody of divine purpose God, who ordains all things including the cordial drop of love, is replaced by "Nature," who provides vengeance, victims, and continued vice for whores.

> "Nature, who never made a thing in vain,
> But does each insect to some end ordain,
> Wisely contrived kind keeping fools, no doubt,
> To patch up vices men of wit wear out."
>
> (ll. 252-55)

In spite of this inversion of order, however, the reader is carried along by the remnant of moral sanity in Artemisia. From the moment of the Fine Lady's introduction she voices her partial disapproval of this gross-voiced creature (ll. 78-79) with malfunctioning taste in her husband, lovers, animals, language, manners, books, and personal perception. But Rochester does not leave us secure—as he might have in a formal verse satire—with the knowledge that as long as there is one good person who preserves the ideal of love there is yet hope. No more, indeed, than he lets us wholly disapprove of the Fine Lady or approve of the poor victimized man. Though Artemisia sees much to deplore in her, she also sees that she is a "mixed thing . . . / So very wise, yet so impertinent" (ll. 148-49), and that she has "All the good qualities that ever blessed / A woman" (ll. 166-67). Indeed it is attraction to the Fine Lady's world that ultimately breaks Artemisia's little store of virtue; and it is also Rochester's ability to communicate the "mixed thing" that prevents this poem from being merely another anti-feminist tract or a black-and-white moral allegory.[9] Specifically, let us examine the role of the man in creating the debauched world that also debauches him.

III. THE LADY AND CORINNA; THE WIT AND FOOL

Like Artemisia, the Fine Lady sees that there is a dangerous relationship between wit and woman. The wit is a threat to the Lady because he knows or seeks to know woman's true nature, and in the process of knowing may destroy his comfort and her worldly success. The Fine Lady, for instance, relates that when she was married "men of wit were then held *incommode*" (l. 104), primarily because they insisted upon clearly perceiving the difference between appearance and reality. Wits are:

> Slow of belief, and fickle in desire,
> . . . ere they'll be persuaded, must inquire
> As if they came to spy, not to admire.
> With searching wisdom, fatal to their ease,
> They still find out why what may, should not please;
> Nay, take themselves for injured when we dare
> Make 'em think better of us than we are,
> And if we hide our frailties from their sights,
> Call us deceitful jilts, and hypocrites.
> They little guess, who at our arts are grieved.
> The perfect joy of being well deceived;
> Inquisitive as jealous cuckolds grow:
> Rather than not be knowing, they will know
> What, being known, creates their certain woe.
> Women should these, of all mankind, avoid,
> For wonder by clear knowledge is destroyed.
> Woman, who is an arrant bird of night,
> Bold in the dusk before a fool's dull sight,
> Should fly when reason brings the glaring light.
>
> (ll. 105-23)

The portrait here is hardly flattering to women, and again illustrates the difference between the truth of Heaven's love—"This only joy for which poor we were made" (l. 50)—and "The perfect joy of being well deceived" (l. 115) which has replaced it. Woman represents deception of husband, lover, and reason itself where possible. But the wit is not much better (nor is the urban or rural fool): his knowledge does not bring him pleasure, destroys the illusions he might otherwise live by, and serves no broadly effective purpose of exposure, since even "though all mankind / Perceive us false, the fop concerned is blind" (ll. 131-32), and thus courts the woman nonetheless.

A brief contrast with Section IX of Swift's *A Tale of a Tub* will make clear the wit's complicity in the unhappy world of the *Letter.* In the *Tale* happiness as "a perpetual possession of being well-deceived" is pronounced by a modern madman. Yet behind him, indeed through him, we are aware of Swift's own insistence that knowledge of man's ugliness is necessary before we can move towards his potential beauty, that self-deception is bad because it inhibits self-improvement, that you shall know the truth, however unpleasant, because it shall make you free to seek something better, the ultimate truth in God. The savage satire of that work would not be possible if Swift did not strongly feel and need to communicate the dangers to a Church, state, and culture worth saving. The anger of the "real" speaker in the *Tale* grows with the aberration his persona communicates.

In the *Letter,* however, the wit is divorced from any theological or moral basis for his action. He does not urge us to see the earthly truth in order to correct it and work towards a corollary higher truth. He sees only the deception, depravity, and despair at the heart of life, and actually contributes to others' and his own unhappiness by offering an inadequate cerebral counter-vision, inadequate moral life (he debauches whomever he pleases and whoever pleases him), and inadequate emotional response. He is neither angry, nor spiritual, nor an effective source or model for change. He is merely destructive of his own and others' ease and offers a barren secular vision that is not even a distant shadow of the sort of divine love and truth Artemisia describes early in the poem. Under such circumstances the wit—unlike Swift in the *Tale*—helps to make the world he deplores. He already shares many of its values, offers no viable alternative, and worsens the situation by causing those he has jilted to seek revenge upon fools who, though sublimely subhuman and delighted when made asses, surely are punished out of proportion to their crime.

This disproportion is made clear in the Fine Lady's own story of Corinna—a tale within a tale that exemplifies the Lady's point regarding fools and wits just as the Lady herself exemplifies Artemisia's regarding the action love. Moreover, Corinna's story not only continues to show ruptured human relationships and the perversion of God's plan for His love on earth; it also moves the poem from black comedy to overt tragedy, from figurative to literal destruction of the family, and provides the final impetus to draw the tottering Artemisia into the Lady's world.

At first Corinna's adventure is sad, and well illustrates one consequence of the unstable wit's social life. She was a prosperous young whore—"Youth in her looks, and pleasure in her bed" (l. 196)—until she doted upon a man of wit,

> Who found 'twas dull to love above a day;
> Made his ill-natured jest, and went away.
> Now scorned by all, forsaken, and oppressed,
> She's a *memento mori* to the rest;
> Diseased, decayed, to take up half a crown
> Must mortgage her long scarf and manteau gown.
> Poor creature! who, unheard of as a fly,
> In some dark hole must all the winter lie,
> And want and dirt endure a whole half year
> That for one month she tawdry may appear.
>
> (ll. 199-208)

The wit has rendered Corinna outcast and sub-human, probably because he has exposed her, forced her to run from his searching reason that seeks to satisfy his own need to know, and then move on. However, her state is not irreparable, since "A woman's ne'er so ruined but she can / Be still revenged on her undoer, man" (ll. 185-86). Yet in this case the poor fool and his family must pay for the wit's crime. The newly arrived country-fool "Turns spark, learns to be lewd, and is undone" (l. 223) as he courts Corinna. The wits have "searching wisdom, fatal to their ease" (l. 108), and "Fools are still wicked at their own expense" (l. 225). Both are self-destructive, but the fool is more victimized—in part because he is paying the wit's penalty, but largely because his entire family is destroyed in the process. The wit makes Corinna a *memento mori*; Corinna makes the fool die. He

> falls in love, and then in debt;
> Mortgages all, ev'n to the ancient seat,
> To buy this mistress a new house for life;
> To give her plate and jewels, robs his wife.
> And when t' th' height of fondness he is grown,
> 'Tis time to poison him, and all's her own.
> Thus meeting in her common arms his fate,
> He leaves her bastard heir to his estate,
> And, as the race of such an owl deserves,
> His own dull lawful progeny he starves.
>
> (ll. 242-51)

The poem adopts the abandonment of conventional cause and effect that characterizes tragedy; that is, ordinary events have results vastly out of proportion to their usual expectations. A wit "seduces" and abandons a whore; several months later she revenges herself upon the wit by seducing a young country-fool, bankrupts his family, kills him, acquires his estate, neglects his children, and, in the process, becomes a paradigm of the good life of those women who deal with fools. It is now that the parodic perversion of divine order emerges (ll. 252-55), as all things do seem to be connected—each part has its reason for being, "Nature" ordains that "kind keeping fools" be provided "To patch up vices men of wit wear out." By synecdoche, woman is vice and man her tailor.

Let us sum up the world of this letter: with the exception of Artemisia early in the poem, women reveal themselves as destitute of divinely inspired love; they are contradictory, enjoyers of sin, foulers of their own nest, tasteless, passionless creatures motivated by fashion and desire for revenge, and reduce others and themselves to the sub-human. Man is either a blind, easily duped fool or a rest-less wit disturbed by the vision of harsh female reality he seeks, yet incapable of correcting it; he is also a prime cause of the revenge by women upon fools and their families. The poem portrays pleasureless adultery, a diseased and unattractive gallant, a murderous town wench, a murdered lover, a bastard child, and distortion of divine love and order. The true emblem of this world of bestial humans with a passion for the mode is the embrace of the Fine Lady and the monkey.

But this vision is not dark enough for Rochester. I sug-gested earlier that Artemisia's disapproval of the society she portrays is mixed and that the progress of her first two paragraphs—from reluctance to desire to write in verse—embodies her change in the poem at large. I do not wish to overstate the "dialectical" qualities of the poem since, after all, Artemisia's initial coyness may merely be a gos-sip's conventional desire to excuse her urge to chatter. Nevertheless, the view of Artemisia's decline is supported through her muted reaction to the tale of Corinna. After that tale Artemisia has a splendid opportunity to reject the world the Fine Lady has been describing. She might, for example, elaborate upon the dangers of the morality portrayed, as Rochester does in the *Satyr against Mankind.* Or she might briefly condemn it and dissociate herself from it, as Pope was to do at the end of his first *Dialogue* of the *Epilogue to the Satires* (1738): "Yet may this Verse (if such a Verse remain) / Show there was one who held it in disdain" (ll. 171-72). Artemisia's latent attraction to the Lady was implicit in her earlier dissection of this "distinguished" woman and her "good qualities" (ll. 167, 166); but now the several lines of reservation—her fop-pery, sexual license, folly, blindness, lack of discretion—are condensed into one tepid remark that comments on the Lady's rambling discourse—her inability to be perti-nent—at least as much as on her wisdom: during the Lady's long talk there were "some grains of sense / Still mixed with volleys of impertinence" (ll. 256-57). Perhaps Artemisia has been worn down by and drawn into the vigorous world she describes, as so many ordinary writers are in *The Dunciad.* Perhaps the Fine Lady's judgments concerning the need to avoid wits and cultivate fools have convinced her that as long as love inspired by Heaven is forgotten, she had better make her own market, forget the background of chastity and female heroism and fidelity as-sociated with her name, and live as best she can.[10] In any case, unlike the formal verse satirist, at a strategic point in the poem Rochester has her ignore an opportunity to reject the Lady's values and, instead, diminishes her earlier criti-cisms. We are more impressed with what Miss Righter calls Artemisia's amusement, delight, and exasperation than with any desire to expose or punish. And we are, I think, equally impressed with how much that world should be punished.

The final paragraph is even more important in character-izing Artemisia's inverted growth, as she concludes with a promise of awful tales swelling to a volume. Hitherto the letter's partially decent voice, she now becomes an agent for the propagation of infamy. Like the wits who reveal their meager talents for writing, she reveals her meager moral fiber and perseverance. She is "dashed back, and wrecked on the dull shore, / Broke of that little stock [she] had before" (ll. 10-11). She does not merely abdicate her own judgments; she accepts the Lady's. Instead of at-tempting to substitute the ideal of spiritual love, she warms to a new task of spreading—indeed planting—infamy:

> But now 'tis time I should some pity show
> To Chloe, since I cannot choose but know
> Readers must reap the dullness writers sow.
> By the next post such stories I will tell
> As, joined with these, shall to a volume swell,
> As true as heaven, more infamous than hell.
> But you are tired, and so am I.
>   Farewell.
>
>   (ll. 258-64)

Rochester is probably alluding to the biblical warning that as one sows so shall he reap. Here, however, the sowing comes from Artemisia in the city, the reaping will be from Chloe in the country—the locations are connected in a widening web of depravity (witness the Fine Lady's ar-rival from the country, and Corinna in town ruining the fool's family in the country). Chloe's request initially induces a reluctant reply that comes to 264 lines; Artemi-sia's promised letter is offered without invitation, and includes an ominous biblical allusion that denotes plant-ing, growth, and harvest of a volume. Heaven, which had been a touchstone for divine love, becomes a touchstone for the truth of diabolical victory. Artemisia, to repeat, is neither exposing nor condemning when she claims that the tales will be "more infamous than hell" (l. 263). By refus-ing to do so, or by doing so in mild terms in the ambigu-ous "volleys of impertinence" (l. 257), she is encouraging such hellish values to take root. Rochester as satirist is severely critical; Artemisia no longer is. He may be motivated by the Juvenalian need to satirize vice trium-phant; she is merely exhilarated, and by tolerating the morally intolerable fosters the decline of God's "one only blessing" (l. 46).

The structure of the poem not only shows Artemisia's increasing acceptance of the world she describes. Perhaps even more significantly it also shows a series of characters, one virtually "creating" the other, who fall more deeply into a self-regarding world. At the start Rochester offers us Artemisia, who responds to Chloe's command that she write, but laments the contents of her letter—"what I would fain forget" (l. 37)—and still remembers the proper sort of love. Artemisia then turns the poem over to the Fine Lady, who enjoys the contents of her tale and recalls Chloe's role for Artemisia. Just up from the country, she seeks news of how love is governed and "who are the men most worn of late" (ll. 101-02)—exactly the sort of ques-tion that Artemisia assumed rural Chloe would want answered. But where Artemisia also offers a picture of "that lost thing, love" (l. 38), the communicative Lady of-fers her own picture of a flourishing love that is mere modish and unsatisfying lust. As Artemisia created the Lady, a "mixed thing" (l. 148), so the Lady creates the abandoned Corinna; the lost, selfless love of Artemisia is turned on its end and becomes the propagated, selfish love of Corinna. Innocence surrenders to criminality, and the safe director of unguided youth becomes the wicked director of a prostitute who ruins the country-boy. The cordial drop is discarded from our cup, and life will no longer go down. What is thrown up quickens in the land of atheists, there is no praise of God's power in love, and woman helps her true joy to disappear in the face of plate, jewels, and land purchased by revenge, prostitution, and murder. The movement from the modest involvement of Artemisia, who knows and gives us the Lady, to the deeper involvement of the Lady, who knows and gives us Corinna, heightens the apocalyptic quality of the satire and mirrors the movement from dead spiritual to living diabolical love. At the start of the poem Artemisia at least has values she can set against the Lady's; in the middle the clever Lady has misguided values; at the end Corinna has no values at all—or only self-serving ones. Artemisia sees that such a society's works are "more infamous than hell" (l. 263), but instead of purging them she spreads them. One must at least suspect that Chloe will end like the Fine Lady—or worse—if she is to reap similar food. Artemisia's norm of defeated love is a mere ten lines; the Lady's norm of prostituted, triumphant love is sixty-six lines.

Moreover, the rhyme scheme of the final two couplets is different from the rest of the poem's and thus catches our attention. Rochester has used end-stopped couplets, run-on couplets, half-lines, half rhymes, masculine and feminine rhymes, and several triplets in a virtuoso display of poetic technique and colloquial dialogue. Now, however, he invites us to focus on the conclusion, as he presents the poem's only rhymed quatrain and supplies an important relation of rhyme and reason. The rhyme words are *tell, swell, hell,* and *farewell,* and offer one related comment: the poem will swell to tell of hellish stories which signify a farewell of any hope for the cordial drop of Heaven's love. City and country, man and woman, wit and fool, narrator and character are part of a world gathering momentum as it parodies and replaces "This only joy for which poor we were made" (l. 50). The beautiful twelve-line passage describing "Love, the most generous passion of the mind" (l. 40) will be obscured even more than it now is in the true stories willingly sent and received.

IV. CONCLUSION: A NOTE ON SATIRIC MODE

Next to such perceptions the so-called pessimism of the ***Satyr against Mankind*** is not very frightening, especially since the speaker of that poem preserves his anger against the vices he exposes. To polarize, in the ***Satyr*** the interlocutor succumbs to his opponent, the normative speaker in the poem; in the ***Letter*** the opponent (Artemisia) succumbs to the values of the interlocutor (the Fine Lady). In the ***Satyr*** the main voice is triumphant in affirming its values; in the ***Letter*** it is defeated, there is no working norm, the ideal of love is proclaimed lost even before we

hear it, and the narrator is too flimsy an anchor to hold on to the remnants of virtue. Her loss of control of that virtue is implied in her loss of control of the other characters in the poem. Samuel Johnson's formal verse satire *The Vanity of Human Wishes* (1749) works toward a climax that affirms the existence and acquisition of religious, spiritual wishes that are neither vain nor human. Rochester's ***Letter*** reverses that process; it quickly announces the death of the spiritual ideal and works towards a climax that affirms the existence and acquisition of devilish, selfish, and earthly love.

That is why the apocalyptic or revelatory satire of, say, Swift's *Tale* and the final version of *The Dunciad* are proper analogues for Rochester's poem, though they are obviously not congruent in many ways. The speaker in *The Dunciad* must finally beg the goddess Dullness for a few moments more to finish his poem before he, his civilization, and its values are put to sleep. Yet he will not capitulate, he must be conquered. Swift's narrator, on the side of dullness as soon as the *Tale* begins, and confident of writing more by its end, is sometimes undercut by a recognized sane person behind him. But Rochester's poem takes the path between dead hero and partially triumphant madman, and shows us, instead, the morally downward movement of a once decent woman and a once decent world. ***The Letter from Artemisia in the Town to Chloe in the Country*** is an apocalyptic satire that proclaims the triumph of Hell.[11] It is one of the best of its kind and, as Artemisia predicted, one of the saddest.

Notes

1. *Eighteenth-Century English Literature,* ed. Geoffrey Tillotson, Paul Fussell, Jr., and Marshall Waingrow (New York: Harcourt, Brace, and World, 1969).

2. I have dealt at greater length with these distinctions in *The Formal Strain: Studies in Augustan Imitation and Satire* (Chicago: Univ. of Chicago Press, 1969), pp. 86-94. I use the term apocalyptic not in the biblical sense of destruction of the evil old world and the beginning of the purged new but as prophetic revelation of darkness. Of course each mode of satire might appear in verse, prose, or the mingled Menippean kind. Since poetry is generally the medium of the best eighteenth-century satires which show a functioning norm, I have chosen to deal only with formal *verse* satire at this time. I should also reiterate that some of the conventions of the three satiric kinds discussed here may be shared with one another. Apocalyptic satire, for instance, is often punitive, but it punishes an age (or a culture, or a nation) rather than an individual.

3. *The Complete Poems of John Wilmot, Earl of Rochester,* ed. David M. Vieth (New Haven: Yale Univ. Press, 1968), p. 141. Subsequent quotations are from this edition.

4. For a fuller analysis of this poem, see my forthcoming essay in *Studies in Philology,* "The 'Allusion to Horace': Rochester's Imitative Mode."

5. Thomas H. Fujimura, "Rochester's 'Satyr against Mankind': An Analysis," *Studies in Philology,* 55 (1958), 590.

6. For the former see Anne Righter, "John Wilmot, Earl of Rochester," in *Proceedings of the British Academy,* 53 (1967), 55: "Artemesia [as in Pinto's spelling] herself, the woman composing the Letter, is a kind of seventeenth-century Elizabeth Bennett. Witty and self-aware, both amused and exasperated, delighted and saddened by the follies she describes, she is the sister of Jane Austen's heroines." For the latter see Vivian de Sola Pinto, *Enthusiast in Wit: A Portrait of John Wilmot Earl of Rochester 1647-1680* (London: Routledge & Kegan Paul, 1962), pp. 121, 124; Vieth, *Complete Poems,* pp. xl-xli; and James Sutherland, *English Literature of the Late Seventeenth Century* (Oxford: Clarendon Press, 1969), pp. 171-72. Some aspects of the dialogue, devices, and characters do have analogues in Restoration comedy, but these seem to me subsumed under the larger satiric, revelatory, intention.

7. George Williamson shrewdly observed that "For all his agnostic wit, Rochester's best love poems are haunted by ideas of religion": *The Proper Wit of Poetry* (Chicago: Univ. of Chicago Press, 1961), p. 126. The same can be said about his two major satires as well, even though such a reading does not conform to the conventional view of pre-Burnet Rochester as atheist-libertine. Rochester, we know, sought out Burnet, not Burnet Rochester.

While discussing the dialectical cast of Rochester's mind, V. de Sola Pinto quotes this tale Rochester told Robert Parsons:

> 'One day at an Atheistical Meeting, at a person of Qualities', I undertook to manage the Cause, and was the principal Disputant against God and Piety, and for my performances received the applause of the whole company; upon which my mind was terribly struck, and I immediately reply'd thus to myself. Good God! that a Man, that walks upright, that sees the wonderful works of God, and has the use of his senses and reason, should use them to the defying of his Creator!'

The rest of Rochester's discussion of his reaction to the "Atheistical Meeting" is also instructive:

> But tho' this was a good beginning towards my conversion, to find my conscience touched for my sins, yet it went off again. Nay, all my life long, I had a secret value and reverence for an honest man, and loved morality in others. But I had formed an odd scheme of religion to myself, which would solve all that God and conscience

might force upon me; yet I was not ever well reconciled to the business of Christianity, nor had that reverence for the Gospel of Christ as I ought to.

> (*A Sermon Preached at the Funeral of the Right Honourable John Earl of Rochester . . . August 9* [1680] [London, 1772], p. 26)

Pinto observes that "Rochester was always 'replying to himself'. His celebrated conversion to religion was no sudden *volte-face;* it was the culminating point of a dialectical process which had been going on in his mind for years": *Enthusiast in Wit,* pp. 185-86.

8. See Edward Topsell, *The Historie of Foure-Footed Beastes. Describing the true and lively figure of every Beast, with a Discourse of their several Names, Conditions, Vertues . . .* (London, 1607), pp. 3, 10-13. Topsell translates much of Konrad Gesner's *Historia animalium* (1551). The 1658 edition—eleven years after Rochester's birth—was "Revised, Corrected, and Inlarged" by John Rowland, and includes the same information and illustrations. Topsell, other contemporary and later naturalists, and lexicographers use the term *ape* to include a variety of monkeys as well. See, for example, the definitions in Johnson's *Dictionary* (1755) and the varied translations of "una ximia de bronze" in Part II, Book 4, ch. 39 of *Don Quixote* (Madrid, 1615), p. 149. Philips, Motteaux, Ozell, Smollett, and Jarvis translate *ximia* as "monkey," Shelton and Stevens as "ape."

For other seventeenth- and eighteenth-century references or discussions, see *II Henry IV* (1600; III.2.338-39); *Othello* (1622; III.3.402-03); Donne's *Progresse of the Soule* (1601; stanzas 46-49); Locke's *Essay concerning Human Understanding* (1690; III, 6, 23); and Edward Tyson's "A Philological Essay concerning the Satyrs of the Ancients," in *Ourang-Outang, Sive Homo Sylvestris* (1699), Eric Rothstein, *Restoration Tragedy: Form and the Process of Change* (Madison: Univ. of Wisconsin Press, 1967), p. 71. H.W. Janson's *Apes and Ape Lore in the Middle Ages and the Renaissance* (London: The Warburg Institute and the University of London, 1952), supplies an abundance of relevant information.

9. John Harold Wilson, however, regards the poem as "the longest and mildest of Rochester's satires against women," and observes that "The moral is clear; poor, weak, silly woman is capable of incredible monstrosities. Only the man of wit can escape her ravenings": *The Court Wits of the Restoration: An Introduction* (Princeton: Princeton Univ. Press, 1948), p. 131.

10. Artemis is the Greek name of Diana, the perpetually celibate goddess of the chase who presided over child-birth, was identified with the moon, and in a many-breasted statue at Ephesus, symbolized the productive forces of nature. Artemisia, the Queen of Caria and daughter of Lygdamis, had masculine cour-

age, performed heroically for Xerxes at Salamis, and later was so in love with Dardanus that, when he slighted her, she put out his eyes while he slept. Artemisia Queen of Caria, daughter of Hecatomnes and wife of Mausolus, immortalized herself by preserving her husband's memory in the magnificent mausoleum at Halicarnassus, lived two years after her husband's death, and was reported to have died of grief and melancholy. These tales of Artemisia were recorded in Moréri's and Bayle's encyclopedic dictionaries, first published, respectively, in 1674 and 1697. In Moréri, Artemisia the wife of Mausolus received the most attention, and it is possible that if Rochester has either model in mind as a norm, it is that of tender rather than brutal love. The masculine achievements of the Queen of Caria, however, may have inspired Rochester to have his Artemisia succeed in masculine poetry. Since the two earthly Artemisias were often mingled, both could easily supply background for Rochester. Bayle reports that "It would be too tedious to point out all those, who have confounded the two *Artemisia's. Ravisius Textor . . .* and the Authors of the *Thesaurus Fabri* are of this number. *Olivier,* who wrote a *Commentary* on *Valerius Maximus,* is also one of them." For fuller discussion of the classical and Renaissance and later seventeenth-century contexts of these names, see Des Maizeaux's edition of *The Dictionary Historical and Critical of Mr. Peter Bayle,* 2nd ed. (London, 1734), I, 522-25.

11.   The apocalyptic quality does not deny the comic aspects of *Artemisia,* any more than it does that of *A Tale of a Tub, Gulliver's Travels,* and *The Dunciad.* Indeed, one might argue that their ultimate effect is enhanced by the comedy, which serves as a comfortable entryway to terror. The Fine Lady's "conversation" with the monkey, for example, is amusing until one realizes that it becomes an emblem of upperclass depravity, just as the childish urinating contest in *The Dunciad* is raucous until one sees that the contestants include a gonorrheal publisher who is polluting his London audience. An intensive study of the intermingling of comic, tragic, and satiric modes and conventions would be of great value.

Ronald Paulson (essay date 1972)

SOURCE: Paulson, Ronald. "Rochester: The Body Politic and the Body Private." In *The Author in His Work: Essays on a Problem in Criticism,* edited by Louis L. Martz and Aubrey Williams, pp. 103-21. New Haven, Conn.: Yale University Press, 1978.

[*In the following essay, originally published in 1972, Paulson claims that obscenity, which is at the center of Rochester's best poems, is used as a analogy for private life.*]

A man could not write with life, unless he were heated by Revenge; for to make a Satyre *without Resentments,*

upon the cold Notions of Phylosophy, *was as if a man would in cold blood, cut men's throats who had never offended him.*[1]

In these words spoken by the Earl of Rochester to Gilbert Burnet during their conversion dialogues it is not difficult to detect the stereotype that underlies the satirist's apologia: it may take an evil man to detect evil in others, though only out of a desire to revenge himself for their greater success. "*Heated by* Revenge," however, seem to be Rochester's operative words. There is another interesting remark he dropped to Mr. Giffard, his tutor:

My Ld. had a natural Distemper upon him which was extraordinary, . . . which was that sometimes he could not have a stool for 3 Weeks or a Month together. Which Distemper his Lordship told him [Giffard] was a very great occasion of that warmth and heat he always expressed, his Brain being heated by the Fumes and Humours that ascended and evacuated themselves that way.[2]

The problem of evacuation carries over into Rochester's poems. In the persona of M.G. (Mulgrave) he writes to O.B. ("Old Bays" or Dryden) that "Perhaps ill verses ought to be confined / In mere good breeding, like unsavory wind," and concludes:

What though the excrement of my dull brain
Runs in a costive and insipid strain,
Whilst your rich head eases itself of wit:
Must none but civit cats have leave to shit?

And this is very close to the sense of his own argument (in the persona of Horace) with Dryden in **"An Allusion to Horace,"** where, for example: "Yet having this allowed, the heavy mass / That stuffs up his loose volumes must not pass. . . ." He is criticizing Dryden's "looseness" against the norm of his own costiveness, as Horace did with Lucilius. The "warmth and heat he always expressed," however, refer to both sexual and literary activity, emphasizing the naturalness of both but also the particular situation of a body for whom catharsis has a special meaning.

Horace writes satiric verses to ward off insomnia ("verum nequeo dormire") and Pope responds to a fool or a knave as "Bulls aim their horns, and Asses lift their heels." Rochester tells us he "never rhymed but for [his] pintle's sake." Unlike Pope, who was "dipp'd in ink" as his baptism into literature, Rochester says he "dip[s his] pen in flowers" (semen or menstrual discharge). The symptoms he describes are, needless to say, those of melancholy, for which the natural outlet is ordinarily sexual fulfilment. He might have served as a case history for Robert Burton.

Rochester is the difficult transitional figure, in some ways the father of the Augustan mode of satire, in others still an Elizabethan in the tradition of the melancholy satyr-satirist of Jonson and Marston. Some poems—the satires on Sir Carr Scroope come to mind—exist simply as the vivid expression of an individual's disgust, in the ancient tradition of Archilochus's iambics, rather than as the exposure of some general truth about man. It may, of course, take an excitation of the subject to elicit a truth otherwise not noticed in the object—something like the heightened awareness arrived at by a conscious disarranging of the senses. And we have here the alternative possibilities that he associates himself so thoroughly with a particular type, a melancholiac or a Mulgrave or a "hater of Scroope," that via impersonation a transference takes place; or that Rochester's hatred is a kind of attraction leading into the projection of an aspect of himself that he must exorcise or explore. Indeed, the relationship between his poems and his own actions (as distinct from the experience from which they may have emerged) involves the question: do the poems act as a self-criticism, a confession, and a penance for the actions; or are the actions meant to extend the disruptive effect of the satires? Rochester's involvement in the murder of Captain Downs argues for the former; his confrontation with the glass chronometers in the garden of Whitehall Palace, with his obscene but pertinent question followed by his shattering of the mechanism, argues for the latter.

Acknowledging that in his case there often seems to be a physical action in his life that corresponds in some way to a literary expression, we may start by enumerating the conventional aspects of his satires to see if anything remains that is not convention. The obscenity, for a start, was a facet of the low burlesque or travesty mode; the shock has the satiric function of awakening the reader and, by laying bare in the most vivid way his animal origins, making him reassess customary humanist values. Reacting politically and emotionally against the repressive years of the Commonwealth, many Englishmen—but most of all the Cavaliers—encouraged an attitude that was bent on exposing old pious frauds and treating grave subjects like love or life with disrespect. Long before Charles II's return from his travels, the discrediting of something so ostensibly upright as the Puritan led naturally to travesty as a satiric form. The Puritans presented and regarded themselves as paragons, and so allying them with greed for money or power and secret sexual proclivities was intended to expose the real man under the false appearance of saintliness. Begun by *Rump Songs,* the tradition was carried on by Samuel Butler's attacks on the Puritans in *Hudibras,* Cotton's irreverence for heroic attitudes in his *Scarronides,* and Rochester's attacks on the court and the morals of his age in both word and deed.

Elsewhere I have argued that travesty as a satiric device was as necessary for the anti-court forces as the mock-heroic was for the procourt forces.[3] The latter began with an assumption of the high position of king and court and showed the upstart's presumption in aspiring toward that unassailable position. The aim of the anti-court satire was to show the real hollowness, human weakness, and corruption beneath the rich and respectable, supposedly divine, facade of the court. The obvious corruption of Charles II's court and his personal predilections, like the worldliness of many of the most pious Puritans, made such an approach almost irresistible.

It is a revealing fact that the best of the anti-court satirists were also "court wits" who, though having gone over to the Opposition, shared Charles's libertine skepticism and had helped to give his court the bad name at which they leveled their diatribes. The belief in the efficacy of release and reliance on instinct that contributes to the libertine complex led to the cynical dictum that reality can be found only in the crudest sensuality; the close scrutiny of kings and their mistresses offered another way to this insight. Travesty then ends as a double revelation, of a gross reality masquerading under a glittering appearance, and of the only true reality. Love becomes obscene and life scatological in order to expose certain simpleminded illusions (or hypocrisies), but also because experience proves that love and life are no more than obscene and scatological, that perhaps this is all there is.

Obscenity, though at the center of Rochester's best poems, almost never appears alone; it is the private half of a basic analogy between public and private life.[4] Sexuality offered the most impressive symbol available for the private world, drawing upon an impressive tradition of satirists who wished to remind man of his unheroic, animal self. Even the "gentle" Horace had used sexual lust as a metaphor for a general lack of control in man (satire 1.2). The Puritan emphasis on sexual violation as the darkest of sins, and the court's opposite view, served as further authorities for the intensity of the symbol at this moment of history. There have been few occasions when sex as a vehicle has been closer to the tenor of the satire.

"The Scepter Lampoon" begins with a negative simile relating two kings—Charles II of England is *not* like the foolish Louis XIV of France—and then proceeds to prove that they are precisely alike. The first couplet gives us the generalization that England is famous "For breeding the best cunts in Christendom," as the second couplet parallels this fact about England with the wonderful appropriateness of its king, Charles, the "easiest King and best-bred man alive." The third couplet then contrasts the peaceful Charles with the war-loving Louis, who is characterized by his frantic, meaningless soldiering: he "wanders up and down / Starving his souldiers hazarding his Crown." Opposed to him is Charles: "Peace is his aim, his gentleness is such, / And love he loves, for he loves fucking much." The equation becomes explicit when we are told of Charles that (like Louis who "wanders up and down" fighting wars) "Restless he rolls about from whore to whore, / A merry monarch, scandalous and poor."[5] Kingship is the subject of the poem: Louis's kind of kingship is compared with Charles's, the one a game of war, the other a game of love, and the conclusion is, "All monarchs I hate, and the thrones they sit on, / From the hector of France to the cully of Britain." They share a common lack of serious purpose, abdication of the duties of kingship, and a frenzied, compulsive, and altogether pointless activity.

The initial analogy between war and lust remains implicit, but our attention is focused in the larger part of the poem on Charles and the second half of the comparison, which becomes an equation of Charles's scepter with his sexual organ (and, by implication, Louis's scepter with his sword). Since the king *is* in an important sense the state, public and private life are one, and the king's body is the body politic; and so quite appropriately for Charles, "His scepter and his prick are of a length." The vehicle of the metaphor—as befits an effective lampoon—is taken from the material of the tenor or subject: Louis did wage wars and Charles did have numerous whores. The metaphor is based on a physical resemblance and on a causality between private and public actions. The whore "may sway the one who plays with th' other," and, in effect, Charles's lust determines policy; conversely, his policy is characterized by the changeableness of his passion. And so when Rochester says that Charles's lust is now so jaded that Nell Gwynn can barely arouse it to action, he is saying the same for Charles's rule of the country.

Rochester begins the **"Scepter Lampoon"** with a contrast of war and lust, which could appear to be public as opposed to private activities (war is traditionally a public duty of kings). By equating them he not only exposes the frantic meaninglessness of Charles's lust (this is the part that adheres to Charles from the "war" half of the equation), but also reduces the idea of war to a level with whoring. The official view was that war was public and whoring private, that a king's public acts were separate from his private. Charles replied to Rochester's lines "He never said a foolish thing, / Nor ever did a wise one" that *he* was responsible for his words, his ministers for his actions. Rochester demonstrates that they are a unity.[6]

Rochester follows the same procedure in a nonpolitical poem, one of those that used to be taken as autobiographical, **"The Disabled [or Maimed] Debauchee."** Again he begins with the false praise of his subject, in this case debauchery:

> As some brave admiral, in former war
> Deprived of force, but pressed with courage still,
> . . . . .
> So, when my days of impotence approach,
> And I'm by pox and wine's unlucky chance. . . .

It takes six stanzas, however, to connect the retired admiral and the old poxed rake—six stanzas which elevate debauchery to the level of a heroic duty, war. The continuum is somewhat ambiguous to be sure: debauchery and war share such noble attributes as "courage," "daring," "boldness," "glory," and ideas of excitement and vigor, as opposed to "the dull shore of lazy temperance." And yet both are clearly dangerous, causing disabling wounds, and with the "honorable" scars of the syphilitic that are paid for by "past joys" a mock-heroic effect emerges.

Then in stanzas 9 to 11 the speaker presents a close-up of love-war, only indicated before through the admiral's rose-tinted telescope, and a different kind of soldiering emerges. It is no longer the beautiful abstraction of war but the physical reality of pillaging, reminiscent of Callot's *Mis-*

ères de la guerre: "whores attacked, . . . Bawds' quarters beaten up, and fortress won; / Windows demolished, watches overcome; . . . some ancient church [put] to fire. . . ." As these images suggest, the references are to love-making as a frenzied, destructive, pointless activity, which reaches its nadir in the link-boy episode, with the matter of whether the rake or his mistress will enjoy the link-boy's favors, a matter to be decided by whose kiss is the better (37-40).[7]

The debauchery and the love-war parallel are the same as Charles's rolling about "from whore to whore" and Louis's warring. The metaphor begins again with a clearly separated tenor and vehicle, but the two parts merge into a single image of debauching soldiers; what starts as a comparison or a contrast becomes a unity, or a mutual travesty. If the reality beneath the rake's glamor is squabbling with whores, it is much the same with the soldier. In both the public and the private parts of the comparison, a public aspect—a glamorous appearance—is reduced to a private, which is a squalid reality. The assumed but invisible term that joins the rake and the admiral is gallantry or some such attractive abstraction. The poem is composed in the stanzaic form of *Gondibert,* Davenant's heroic poem which contains all the "gallantry" of the sort Rochester is referring to, but treated grandiosely. Davenant portrays the kind of battle "Where even the vanquish'd so themselves behave, / The victors mourn for all they could notsave."[8] Rochester begins by setting up a high ideal against which to measure debauchery; but very soon both soldiering and debauchery are exposed as the ugly reality underlying the gallant *Gondibert* stanzas and the heroic talk of old poxed rakes. The whoremonger talks like an admiral; but, as the mock-heroic effect changes to travesty, the admiral behaves like a whoremonger.[9]

The metaphor of love-war is, of course, an ancient Petrarchan cliché. Rochester's use of it is still close to conventional love parlance in **"Second Prologue to the 'Empress of Morocco'"**: when he addresses the king with "your prosperous arms" he refers both to Charles's war with the Dutch and his amorous powers. The "Millions of cupids, hovering in the rear" are "like eagles following fatal troops," both awaiting "the slaughter" of the warriors in the play and the lovers of the outside world, including the audience in the theater and the king. Rochester's translation of Ovid's *Amores* 2.9 demonstrates his appropriation of the metaphor. Ovid's lines (in Humphries's translation),

> Old soldiers, their long term of service over,
> Retire to acres given by the state,
> And an old race horse kicks his heels in clover
> When he is done with breaking from the gate,

which refer to the peace an old lover desires, become in Rochester's translation:

> But the old soldier has his resting place,
> And the good battered horse is turned to grass.
> The harassed whore, who lived a wretch to please,

Has leave to be a bawd and take her ease.
For me, then, who have freely spent my blood,
Love, in thy service, and so boldly stood. . . . [etc.]

The last four lines, Rochester's addition of his own metaphor, carry the matter into "Celia's trenches" and toward another "Disabled Debauchee." In his rendering of Ovid, the love-war relationship is causally linked: "With doubtful steps the god of war does move / By thy example led, ambiguous Love." Cupid is directing Mars as Charles's sexual organ does him.

Rochester's poetry projects a situation in which the two areas of experience, public and (illustrated by sexuality) private, are for all practical purposes one. In **"Timon"** a bore's attempt to lure a gentleman to his dinner party is compared to a whore's soliciting; the meat and carrots served are arses and dildoes; the lady's question to Huff ("if love's flame he never felt") is answered, "Do you think I'm gelt"; the diners go into heroic verses about war from plays, which lead into talk about actual war (Huff and Dingboy at dinner are the equivalent of kings and generals and admirals running the war), and a squabble among the diners ends with a "peace" treaty. The correspondence appears in the most incidental imagery. In **"The Imperfect Enjoyment"** the speaker's organ would "invade, / Woman or Boy";[10] it "Breaks ev'ry stew, does each small whore invade." In *Satyr against Reason and Mankind* the distrust accorded wits is like that accorded whores by the clients who fear the consequences of their pleasure;[11] and in *Artemisia to Chloe* "whore is scarce a more reproachful name / Than poetess." In all of these "whore" is connected with a perversion of natural feeling that reflects on a similar perversion in the tenor of the comparison. By inference, friendship and not social climbing should be the occasion for dinners, as true love and not prostitution should be for sexual satisfaction.

The distinction between nature and its perversion points to the meaning of Rochester's sexual metaphor. In the example of Charles and Louis the terms would be freedom (nature) and license (perversion). Charles's behavior is to the ideal (or in his terms, the romantic illusion) of kingship as uncontrolled lust is to love. The relationship between the terms becomes somewhat more complex in **"The Disabled Debauchee."** The squabbling, the destruction, and the treatment of the link-boy might easily have been presented as praiseworthy freedom, opposed to the chains of custom; even the burning of "some Ancient Church" might have been shown to be a laudable gesture. But the poem presents such actions as mechanical parts of a rigid pattern of behavior passed down from debauched rakes (or retired admirals); their libertine function of freeing the human spirit is not operative.

Rochester makes his point by the comparison in the last stanza of the impotent debauchee to a statesman who sends out youths to battle. Both stand back and watch others killed for an abstraction that was once perhaps real to them: "And being good for nothing else, be wise." It is

wise to stay out of these actions but wisdom is actually mere impotence, since as long as one is able he does the unwise thing. Implicit is a contrast between two kinds of wisdom, natural (the instinct that drove the old debauchee to "Love and Wine" in his youth); and the so-called wisdom of counsellors and statesmen who curb the instinctive actions of others.

However meaningless the rake's actions in the past, Rochester implies a moral distinction between them and his present generalizations. The fact that the admiral is so feeble that he "crawls" up the hill is contrasted with his eyes that cannonlike emit "flashes of rage"; and, to the accompaniment of the rhymes "courage still" and "adjacent hill," he shows his courage by climbing a safe hill and watching the combat through a telescope. There was something good in the vice at the time—it was at least a self-fulfillment of some kind—which has been completely expunged now in the old impotent rake's proselytizing. He has himself become a symbol of the custom he flouted. (Even the stanza form underlines the formalized quality of the vice now that it is promulgated as a doctrine by the impotent debauchee.) To generalize from one's own experience is probably the greatest sin represented in the poem, coming close to Rochester's definition of custom (and also underlying his lines on Charles II, who never *said* a foolish thing, nor ever *did* a wise one).[12]

* * *

If to generalize from one's own experience is the greatest sin, what then is the "Rochester" in his works? His own ambivalence about the difference between saying and doing, or between public and private parameters, is expressed in the following lines:

Should hopeful youths[13] (worth being drunk) prove
nice,
  And from his fair inviter meanly shrink,
'Twill please the ghost of my departed vice
  If, at my counsel, he repent and drink.

Here "hopeful," "worth," "fair," "meanly," and "repent" are so ambiguous as to be pivotal words between the two parts of the poem. In terms of Rochester's own experience there was the heroic sea battle in which he *had* fought bravely but also witnessed the bloody death of Montagu; there were the later shadowy acts which were called (at least by some) cowardice and the fact that he was ill and prematurely aged.[14]

In **"The Imperfect Enjoyment"** the "brave Youth" who may "meanly shrink" has become the speaker's own sexual organ which "shrinks, and hides his head." He addresses it to curse it:

When vice, disease, and scandal lead the way,
With what officious haste dost thou obey!
Like a rude, roaring hector in the streets
Who scuffles, cuffs, and justles all he meets,
But if his King or country claim his aid,
The rakehell villain shrinks and hides his head.

Here is the resumé of all we have seen associated with evil in Rochester's satires. The activity of the "roaring hector" is exactly that of the debauching soldiers in **"The Disabled Debauchee";** and any old whore versus the woman he loves is the private part of a comparison with king or country, street fights, and civil chaos. But the poem is not about whores and street fights but the poet's unruly organ, which can succeed with whores but not with his true love (and, by the terms of the comparison, cannot serve his king and country as it ought). We might say that when he talks about a personal problem like his impotence he is really talking about a much larger issue, which he can feel so strongly because of the analogy to his own plight. The king's body (body politic) is also manifest in the microcosm of the body-Rochester.

In **"The Imperfect Enjoyment"** and **"A Ramble in St. James's Park"** the public half of the analogy can only be inferred; or, rather, the sexual experience has become a synecdoche for more general considerations of life. The **"Ramble"** begins with a short history of St. James's Park and a situation parallel to that of the speaker. The origin of the park, according to legend, was "an antient pict" lover who was jilted by his love. His natural object being thwarted, he resorted to masturbation, fertilizing the ground and giving birth to the sinister foliage which now conceals such lewd, unnatural behavior as the pict was forced into: "And nightly now beneath their shade / Are buggeries, rapes, and incests made." These—like the link-boy episode in **"The Disabled Debauchee"**—are the unnatural outlets for man's normal and natural passion for women. The speaker himself has been jilted by Corinna for a pair of fops, and while he admits "There's something generous in mere lust," he rails at this "abandoned jade" who mechanically copulates with any male who happens along, engaging in a meaningless activity divorced from affection or love, and his railing points ultimately toward the leather phallus of "Signior Dildo" which replaces the human agent entirely. The speaker's romantic love is an ideal behind the indictment of the restless woman, but his own reaction is as sterile and aimless as the ancient pict's: he merely loads curses on Corinna's head, and the outlet of outraged and pointless ejaculation is paralleled by this outpouring of invective.

Rochester's explanation for the perversion of love—and so of all other human relationships—develops in two divergent lines. One in purely satiric terms, as in the poems we have mentioned so far, places the blame on the opposite extremes of license and custom. The Restoration gentleman presumably follows the middle road of libertine love, hindered by neither marriage, indiscriminate lust, nor ideal love. This is part of the pose that connects Rochester's satires with the great comedies being written by Etherege and Wycherley.

The other explanation is hinted at in the implication that the speaker of the "Ramble" could not get together with Corinna because of a similar but unfortunately definitive trouble between Adam and Eve. Rochester's fable, turning St. James's Park into a version of Eden, suggests a certain hopelessness in the situation of present-day man, a hopelessness which surfaces in his letters when he remarks that there is "soe great a disproportion 'twixt our desires and what is ordained to content them" that love is impossible.[15] The various unnatural channels chronicled are all that is left: masturbation, invective or satire, and whores.

"The Imperfect Enjoyment," a pessimistic resolution to the problem of the **"Ramble,"** is an adaptation of Ovid's *Amores* 3.7. The latter celebrates the impossibility of controlling the flesh, but though it recalls the speaker's past successes with other women, it makes no distinction between them and the present one; this one is a whore, and so presumably were all the others. In Rochester's poem the whores are contrasted with the true love in whose arms he now lies, as lust with romantic love. In effect, Rochester says that even if the girl of the **"Ramble"** came to him he would be unable to achieve a consummation *because* he loves her, *because* he has an ideal image of her; not only do we have no control over our bodies, but they can satisfy only the pattern of lust, not the patternless complexity of love. This is an extreme statement, which even Swift does not approach, of a Strephon who doesn't need to get into Chloe's dressing room; under the most felicitous circumstances he simply could not bridge the gap between ideal and real.

Something is to be said about the relationship between the impotence in these poems (sexual, royal, moral) and the profligacy or license of the mistress who is merely a "passive pot to spend in" or "The joy at least of a whole Nation": "On her no Showers unwelcome fall, / Her willing womb retains 'em all." The receptivity of the woman is matched by the "looseness" of Rochester with any passing whore, of other "lovers" like Charles II, and, to extend the metaphor, of writers like Dryden (in the **"Allusion to Horace"**). For impotence / constipation is a general malady of Rochester / Charles, who say wisely but act foolishly, while the world around is full of mere "looseness." The custom of respect or "love" is the trap in which such as Rochester and the king, and many of his subjects, find themselves when confronted by "king" or "loved one" or any hallowed ideal. The organ will not respond. The only alternative to the costive, in love or art or politics, is the loose.

* * *

"Kings and Princes," Rochester wrote to Henry Savile, "are only as Incomprehensible as what they *pretend* to represent; but apparently as Frail as Those they Govern."[16] It is certainly noticeable that Rochester attacks in others (like Charles) what he comes around to attacking in himself. Their mutual impotence and inability to relate public and private life become the insight that one must be satisfied with whores and link-boys; Rochester turns this knowledge into a private version of the body politic metaphor, an image of the whole world's decline that looks forward to Swift's use of his own body in his Irish poems. We might, in fact, say that Rochester projects his plight into poems about the monarchy in the same way that Swift projects his into poems extending from political lampoons to "A Beautiful Young Nymph going to Bed." Rochester must have seen himself as a representative man (certainly so by 1676, when Dorimant appeared), fully as representative as the king: and it is at this point that he begins to project his alternative selves—versions of damnation, pride, and conversion. When he enquires of the postboy the way to hell, he is told: "The readiest way, my Lord, 's by Rochester." That is, by way of the city of Rochester, toward the sea and France; but also by *playing* the Earl of Rochester, or by his example, or by being himself.

Rochester's career comes to a climax, or a watershed, in 1675-76: his greatest poems are written around this time and he begins seriously to extend his poetry into life in various forms, looking toward his conversion and death. It is also the time when the two great comedies of the Restoration, *The Country Wife* and *The Man of Mode,* are first performed, reflecting Rochester mimetically and metaphorically. We know from contemporary evidence that he was seen as the model for Dorimant,[17] but Horner is equally Rochester, because Wycherley makes him a symbol in precisely the way that Rochester was making himself one. The most immediate analogue (whether source or allusion is not certain) is Harcourt's remark that Horner, like "an old married general, when unfit for action, is fittest for counsel" (3.2). Horner is a symbol that combines the repletion or retention with the covert release by both sexual and satiric catharsis that we have seen in Rochester's satire. The pose of impotence is a device for exposing the lust of the hypocritical women and the complaisance of their husbands, an outlet equally for his sexual and for his satiric satisfaction. The satire depends on the private-public analogy of Horner and the world, as of sex and china, which is painted, decorated, and collected to conceal its earthy origins.

But this is a masquerade which also educes a reality, an otherwise invisible aspect of the man. Horner's pose of impotence is a symbol of his own real moral impotence, and with him the moral (and social and political) impotence of English society as a whole. The sense in which Horner is really impotent is like that in which Volpone is really sick. Moreover, Rochester's masquerade as Alexander Bendo is very reminiscent of Horner, who derives in more ways than one from Volpone, another actor whose repertory included the role of mountebank, a self-disguise to expose politicians and clergymen and other more respectable mountebanks. In Rochester's (Bendo's) words, "the Politician is, & must be a Mountebank in State Affairs, and the Mountebank no doubt . . . is an errant Politician in Physick."[18] Bendo begins by distinguishing true physician and quack but then blurs them into one, together with politicians and clergymen. Rochester's impersonations transform the private man momentarily into the public; they extend from mountebank and city merchant to naval hero, peer sitting in the House of Lords, rake "some years

always drunk, and . . . ever doing some mischief,"[19] coward refusing to duel with Mulgrave, and atheist turned convert.[20] Etherege and Wycherley recorded some aspects of the impersonation, as later Gilbert Burnet and Robert Parsons recorded the drama of conversion and a "good death," mixing life and art in a way that is central to Rochester.

Parsons, Rochester's mother's chaplain, stresses Rochester's "commands to me, *to preach abroad, and to let all men know* (if they knew it not already,) *how severely God had disciplined him for his sins by his afflicting hand.*"[21] I have no doubt that Rochester's urge for publication was conscious: both Burnet and Parsons were his amanuenses, the first of the conversations leading up to conversion, the second of the funeral sermon describing the conversion, with the appropriate text from the parable of the prodigal son. The passage from Isaiah 53 which converted Rochester did so, I rather suspect, because of its transference of his own situation to the "Suffering Servant" of Jahveh who is a prophecy of the suffering Christ:

> He is despised and rejected of men, a man of sorrows, and acquainted with grief . . . he was despised, and we esteemed him not. Surely he hath borne our griefs, and carried our sorrows; yet we did esteem him stricken, smitten of God, and afflicted. But he was wounded for our transgressions, he was bruised for our iniquities: the chastisement of our peace was upon him, and with his stripes we are healed.[22]

Rochester must, at some level of consciousness, have remembered Lady Fidget's words to Horner:

> But, poor gentleman, could you be so generous, so truly a man of honour, as for the sakes of us women of honour, to cause yourself to be reported no man? No man! And to suffer yourself the greatest shame that could fall upon a man, that none might fall upon us women by your conversation?
>
> [2.1]

The portrait Rochester commissioned of Huysmann (c. 1675) shows the poet with an ape. In a reciprocal action he offers the ape his bays, and the ape (emblematic of imitation) offers the poet a page he has torn out of a book; he is aping the poet, sitting on a pile of books with another in his hand, a finger marking the place where he has stopped reading or has torn out pages. Rochester himself, however, is holding in his other hand a number of manuscript pages, aping the ape. Sir John Vanbrugh was later to put an ape holding a mirror atop his monument to Congreve at Stowe, but that ape could be Congreve's subject ("Vitae imitatio, / Consuetudinis Comoedia"). Rochester juxtaposes himself with the ape in a gesture of mutual give-and-take: the ape is his double.[23] Rochester has chosen not a satyr, in either of its aspects, but an emblem of the satirist's imitative faculty and his own apish aspect, which reaches into his poems ("like an ape's mock face, / By near resembling man do man disgrace") and into his life (he owned an ape and remarked to Savile that it is "a Fault to laugh at the Monkey we have here, when I compare his Condition with Mankind").[24]

Barely glimpsed in the upper right corner, beyond the pillar before which Rochester stands, are an arch and trees and sky—hints of another life. The reference is to Rochester in the country, his wife, and his recoveries from life in the court and city. The country, he writes to Savile, becomes the place "where, only, one can think; for, you at Court think not at all; or, at least, as if you were shut up in a drum; you can think of nothing, but the noise that is made about you."[25] Country seems to be almost outside the public-private division; or at least it serves Rochester, as it later did Pope, as a place to stand from which to look back at the riot of the city. He told Burnet that "when he was well furnished with materials [from the city], he used to retire into the country for a month or two to write libels."[26]

But *in* the country there was also the distinction between Adderbury, the retreat with his wife and children, and Woodstock, where with his wilder companions he revived the city in the country—or, perhaps, with friends like Buckingham plotted Country Party strategy against the court. Woodstock was near Ditchley, the house in which he spent his childhood and in which his mother lived, separated (as the name implies) from Woodstock by a ditch—with beyond the ditch the pious dowager Lady Rochester; and then at some distance further north, almost to Banbury, the wife and family waiting at Adderbury.[27]

We have strayed from the poetry into the conversations and letters and beyond. Since we will never know what Rochester really was, any more than what Charles II or the times were, we ought to prefer the fictions that derive from Rochester himself. His two earliest surviving poems, of 1660, associate him and Charles II as son and father. He was born into a relationship with the great world of the court, and specifically with Charles II: his father, Lord Wilmot, had saved Charles at Worcester. In that scene Wilmot was to Charles as father to son, and Rochester becomes, in his own terms at least, both son and brother (or alter ego) to Charles. Whether Rochester wrote these verses of 1660 (he would have been only thirteen), or whether they were revised or even dictated by his mentor Robert Whitehall, nonetheless the two poems express the essential relationship that emerged. The king took over the dead father's role, supervised Rochester's education at Oxford, his grand tour, his life at court thereafter (navy and pension), and chose a wife for him. But this father/brother was also a slave to his lusts, and his energies were scattered when they should have been focused on his duty/queen/kingdom/son/subjects—and so it is no surprise that Rochester wrote attacks on the king that could have been directed at himself and eventually, in his last year, went over to the Opposition—which was, of course, centered on the crisis of the Succession, the replacement of the brother York with the bastard son Monmouth.[28] The protagonist of **"A Ramble through St. James's Park"** and **"The Imperfect Enjoyment"** could have been either Rochester himself or Charles II: as the kind of projection of omnipotence in Bajazet could have been of the illusory power and real impotence of either.

The poems show Charles II, the father surrogate, transformed from a threatening figure to the other side of the poet, the harmless, impotent, castrated, uxorious man—the costive man of wise words and bungled deeds, safer in the country but always yearning for the city.[29] What we do know is that Rochester's mother's ancestral sympathies were Puritan, while his father (whom he can have met no more than once, when he was eight) was the staunchest of cavaliers, who saved and served Charles until his death, separated from his wife and son (when he returned that once he was travelling in disguise on a secret mission directing Royalist conspiracies to undermine the Puritan Commonwealth). Perhaps the father, in that one return, seemed a threat to the son's own monopoly of his mother, or a threat to his own identity. Presumably something of Rochester's association with his father and his glamor persisted in the life at court in London and at sea, but Rochester always followed it with a return to the country to be near his mother, to meditate and write (although keeping Woodstock at hand in which to live like a cavalier).

He disguised himself as the low to expose the low in everyone, even the highest; but also to destroy—or replace or atone for—his own identity as John Wilmot, Earl of Rochester, or as Dorimant or Bendo, moving toward what the Puritans would have considered a conversion and rebirth. But only the final conversion of many, if we look back at the poems and masquerades. The satirist perhaps requires (as Evelyn Waugh's diaries of the 1920s show) the pleasure of debauchery followed by deep Puritan hangovers. Certainly from his mother's letters we see that his "conversion" (which remains as ambiguous as Dorimant's retreat to the country with Harriet), the final immolation of the father, brought him home to her. There remained a ditch between Woodstock, where he died, and Ditchley and his pious childhood; but he broke, with his final gesture, the Puritan aim of private but exemplary salvation away from the cavalier's public duty to crown.

Notes

1. Gilbert Burnet, *Some Passages of the Life and Death of Rochester* (1680), in *Rochester: The Critical Heritage,* ed. David Farley-Hills (London, 1972), p. 54.

2. *The Remains of Thomas Hearne,* ed. John Bliss, rev. John Buchanan-Brown (Carbondale, 1966), p. 122. One thinks at once of Swift's "Digression on Madness" but also of Freud's Wolf-Man. The latter suggests that, like the Wolf-Man, Rochester was unable to have a bowel movement for long periods without the assistance of an enema: ". . . spontaneous evacuations did not occur for months at a time," writes Freud, "unless a sudden excitement from some particular direction intervened, as a result of which normal activity of the bowels might set in for a few days. His principal subject of complaint was that for him the world was hidden in a veil, or that he was cut off from the world by a veil. This veil was torn only at one moment—when, after an enema, the

contents of the bowel left the intestinal canal; and then he felt well and normal again" (Freud, *Standard Edition*, trans. James Strachey, vol. 17 [1955], pp. 74-75). In other details as well the two cases may be similar; but the conventionality of the metaphor, as it extends from medical treatises to Burton's *Anatomy of Melancholy* to Swift's *Tale of a Tub*, needs little documentation.

3. See my *Fictions of Satire* (Baltimore, 1967), pp. 106-07, from which the present essay takes off.

4. David Vieth has done more than anyone else to make Rochester available to us in his *Attribution in Restoration Poetry: A Study of Rochester's Poems of 1680* (New Haven, 1963) and his edition, *The Complete Poems of John Wilmot, Earl of Rochester* (New Haven, 1968). One full-length study, Dustin H. Griffin's *Satires against Man: The Poems of Rochester* (Berkeley, 1973), has appeared, as have a number of enlightening essays. Some of these will be mentioned in the notes that follow; here I shall mention only Vieth's "Toward an Anti-Aristotelian Poetic: Rochester's *Satyr against Mankind* and *Artemisia to Chloe*, with Notes on Swift's *Tale of a Tub* and *Gulliver's Travels*," *Language and Style* 5 (1972): 123-45, because Vieth has gradually changed his view from that of Rochester as proto-Augustan to something much closer to the view expressed in this essay. For two essays that are close to my own view of Rochester, see Carole Fabricant, "Rochester's World of Imperfect Enjoyment," *Journal of English and Germanic Philology* 73 (1974): 338-50, and "Rochester's *Valentinian* and the Subversion of the Augustan Hierarchy," *MLR,* forthcoming, on the demythologizing mode in Rochester.

5. My text is Vieth's *Complete Poems,* where he calls the poem "A Satyr on Charles II." For the problem of the arrangement of the lines, see p. 193 and Vieth, "Rochester's 'Scepter' Lampoon on Charles II," *Philological Quarterly* 37 (1958): 424-32.

6. Swift may have had the "Scepter Lampoon" in mind when he wrote: "The very same Principle that influences a *Bully* to break the Windows of a Whore, who has jilted him, naturally stirs up a Great Prince to raise mighty Armies, and dream nothing but Sieges, Battles, and Victories" (*Tale of a Tub,* ed. A. C. Guthkelch and D. Nichol Smith [2d ed., 1958], p. 165).

7. The link-boy may be a Rochester confessional purging or merely another way to outrage. It was not part of the rake's image, except perhaps for some innuendos in *The Country Wife,* where Marjorie dresses as a boy and is attacked by Horner, and in the character of Fidelio in *The Plain Dealer.* In general we must regard the link-boy in Rochester as we would in a satire of Juvenal, as a perversion of normal human activities.

8. Argument to Canto 5. The possibility must not be overlooked, however, that Dryden's *Annus Mirabilis,* with the same stanzaic form, intervened; and the

reference could as well be to that glorification of specifically British arms. Rymer noticed the allusion to *Gondibert* in his preface to Rochester's *Poems on Several Occasions* (London, 1691), p. A4, as did Pope in his copy of Rochester's *Poems* (1696, p. 97); noted by Griffin, *Satires against Man,* p. 48.

9. This sort of metaphor may have been a reflection of the virtual consonance felt by Dryden and many of his contemporaries among the worlds of politics, religion, art, and literature. Rochester participates in this tradition but with a conclusion far less sanguine than Dryden's—perhaps because he chooses the two parts of a travesty contrast, public and private, whereas Dryden relates science/politics or literature/politics in a *concordia discors,* or a way of showing the unity within apparently disparate areas of experience.

10. I prefer the 1680 edition's "boy" to Vieth's "Man."

11. This, the most anthologized of Rochester's poems, first attacks man's feigned and boasted reason and then exposes the personal fear which is the reality under this pose (as under the masks of knavery and all others that separate man from the beasts), and then it extends this personal, private situation to the public one of the court, statesmen, and clergymen.

12. One other sense of "private/public" for the king should be mentioned. Christopher Goodman, the Puritan apologist, wrote long before the Civil War that if rulers failed in their duty they would "be accounted no more for kings or lawful magistrates, but as private men: and to be examined, accused, condemned and punished by the law of God" (*How Superior Powers Ought to be Obeyed* [1558, reproduced Facsimile Society, New York, 1931], p. 139). With the trial and condemnation of Charles I this doctrine became real: he was judged not by his own but by a different law; and for this to happen, he had to become a private citizen, just as the private men who judged him became public.

13. "Hopeful" is my emendation, from the 1680 edition, for Vieth's "any."

14. Of the naval heroics, he told Gilbert Burnet that "He thought it necessary to begin his life with those Demonstrations of his courage in an Element and way of fighting, which is acknowledged to be the greatest trial of clear and undoubted Valour" (*Some Passages,* in *Critical Heritage,* p. 50); of his health, he wrote to Savile: "I am *almost Blind, utterly Lame,* and scarce within the reasonable hopes of ever seeing *London again*" (Oct. 1677, in John Hayward, ed., *Collected Works of John Wilmot, Earl of Rochester* [London, 1926], p. 252).

15. To his wife, in Hayward, *Collected Works,* p. 288. Cf. Fredelle Bruser, "Disproportion: A Study in the Work of John Wilmot, Earl of Rochester," *University of Toronto Quarterly* 15 (1945-46): 384-96.

16. Hayward, *Collected Works,* p. 252.

17. John Dennis, "Defence of Sir Fopling Flutter" (1722), in *The Critical Works of John Dennis,* ed. E. N. Hooker (Baltimore, 1943), 2:248.

18. *The Famous Pathologist, or the Noble Mountebank,* ed. V. de Sola Pinto (*Nottingham University Miscellany,* no. 1 [Nottingham, 1961]), p. 34.

19. Burnet, *History of his own Time* (1753), 1: 370-72.

20. The subject of Rochester's masquerades and their meaning has been well treated by Anne Righter, "John Wilmot, Earl of Rochester," *Proceedings of the British Academy* 53 (1967): 47-69; Griffin, *Satires against Man*; and Carole Fabricant, "John Wilmot, Earl of Rochester: A Study of the Artist as Role-Player" (Ph.D. diss., Johns Hopkins University, 1972), especially chap. 3, pp. 153-225.

21. Robert Parsons, *A Sermon Preached at the Funeral of the Rt. Honorable John Earl of Rochester . . .* (1680), p. 30.

22. Parsons, *A Sermon,* p. 24. Rochester stressed the passage to Burnet, "He hath no form nor comeliness and when we see him there is no beauty that we should desire him," glossing it: "The meanness of his Appearance and Person has made vain and foolish people disparage him, because he came not in such a Fool's-Coat as they delight in" (*Some Passages,* in *Critical Heritage,* p. 142).

23. Sir Thomas Killigrew, the last royal jester, with whom Rochester once exchanged identities to deceive two maids of honor, appears in *his* engraved portrait with a monkey sitting on the table imitating his pose, both heads supported by hands in the iconography of melancholy. See *British Museum Catalogue of Satiric Prints,* no. 1681; reproduced, Graham Greene, *Lord Rochester's Monkey* (London, 1974), p. 68.

24. "Epilogue to 'Love in the Dark,'" Vieth, *Complete Poems,* p. 92; to Savile, June 1678, in Hayward, *Collected Works,* p. 256.

25. Hayward, *Collected Works,* pp. 252, 258.

26. *History of his own Time,* in *Critical Heritage,* p. 93; see also *Some Passages,* in *Critical Heritage,* p. 54.

27. An old ditch ran directly by the house, which so fascinated Thomas Hearne when he visited the house in 1718 that he looked into its history. Ditchley got its name, he learned, from this ancient boundary-line ditch or dike, and he examined one "great Ditch, or Trench, of a vast Extent," a mile from Ditchley House, which "parts the two Manors of Ditchley and Woodstock" (*The Remains of Thomas Hearne,* p. 206).

28. But in a letter to Savile he relates Oates's trial for buggery to his accusations at King's Bench two days later "for the Honour of the Protestant Cause." The "Lowsiness of Affairs," he tells Savile, is such as "'tis not fit to entertain a *private* Gentleman, much less one of *a publick Character,* with the Retaile of them" (Hayward, *Collected Works,* p. 263).

29. For a much more elaborate attempt to place Rochester in a Freudian context, see Griffin, *Satires against Man,* pp. 120-29.

Howard D. Weinbrot (essay date 1972)

SOURCE: Weinbrot, Howard D. "'An Allusion to Horace': Rochester's Imitative Mode." *Studies in Philology* 69, no. 3 (July, 1972): 348-68.

[*In the essay which follows, Weinbrot contends that "An Allusion to Horace" is unsatisfying because it lacks complexity and depth of the Horatian satire to which it alludes, and states that the main reason for this lack of depth is that the creative strengths of Imitation as a genre are not yet clear in Rochester's work.*]

In recent years students of Restoration and eighteenth-century satire have learned a new respect for the variety and sophistication of the Augustan Imitation.[1] No longer do we praise the modern poet for imitating, say, Horace, closely, or blame him for imitating freely.[2] Nor are we surprised to find him both free *and* close at different moments in the same poem, or to find that he has imitated only a portion of the parent-poem or that he has, in Dryden's words, written in a manner "not to translate his [the author's] words, or to be confined to his sense, but only to set him as a pattern, and to write, as he supposes that author would have done, had he lived in our age, and in our country."[3] For Dryden, however, this is a pernicious form, since it violates the translator's demand to show his "author's thoughts" and thus is "the greatest wrong which can be done to the memory and reputation of the dead."[4] Another of Dryden's objections, however, may be taken as a central aspect of the creative power of the Imitation—a form that is not a malign species of translation, but a separate, if related, genre which, depending upon the author's intention, uses the parent-poem as an integral part or as a central backdrop for its own purposes. Dryden observes that in Imitation "'tis no longer to be called [the initial poet's] work, when neither the thoughts nor words are drawn from the original; but instead of them there is something new produced, which is almost the creation of another hand. By this way, 'tis true, somewhat that is excellent may be invented, perhaps more excellent than the first design."[5]

It is ironic that Rochester, so great a literary enemy of Dryden, should adapt this loose form of Imitation—though, of course, like Boileau, from whom he also learned a great deal, he never pretends to offer his reader a translation.[6] Rochester knew of the more literal or close form of Imitation as translation, and must have found it an inadequate vehicle for his purposes and temperament. In July of 1673

Dryden wrote to Rochester informing him of Etherege's alteration of Boileau's First Satire: Etherege, "changing the French names for English, read it so often that it came to their ears who were concern'd, and forced him to leave off the design, ere it were half finish'd."[7] During the following year, Rochester wrote his poem **"Timon,"** a free version of Boileau's Third Satire which, in turn, freely adapts Horace, *Satires,* II, 8. Sometime between 1674 and early 1676, he wrote *A Satyr Against Mankind,* and late in 1675 or early in 1676 he wrote his **"Allusion to Horace."**[8] The **"Allusion"** is closer to the original's structure and intention than the *Satyr*; but both fall under that class of Imitation which radically alters the original's meaning and offers something new from another hand.

The term "allusion" is discussed by Thomas Dilke, in the Preface to his own work, *XXV Select Allusions to Several Places of Horace, Martial, Anacreon, and Petron. Arbiter* (1698). Dilke has "familiarly adapted" his authors to the "present Circumstances of Time and Custom," so that they might easily be understood. "'Tis true," he continues, "I have taken a great deal of liberty both as to the manner of Composure, and as to the Matter itself, and may sometimes seem to be very foreign from the subject propos'd." But such freedom is inherent in this sort of Imitation: "Indeed 'tis my Opinion that Allusions properly admit of this scope, as soon as the hint is receiv'd, I think the Alluder may be allow'd to follow the Thread of his own Fancy."[9] The term has also been defined in Johnson's *Dictionary* (1775): "That which is spoken with reference to something supposed to be already known, and therefore not expressed; a hint; an implication."

Other contemporary lexicons and encyclopaedias also offer helpful definitions or illustrations. Although Edward Bysshe does not define the word in his *Art of English Poetry* (1702), he does use it to mean the pointing to, or abstracting of, parts of a poem for one's own purposes.[10] John Kersey states that allusion is "speaking a Thing in reference to another."[11] Edward Phillips borrows this definition and adds that "an Allusion is made to an History, Custom, Wise-saying, & c. when we Speak or Write any thing that has relation to it."[12] Nathan Bailey, in his turn, borrows the Kersey-Phillips definition and Phillips' amplification, but adds another meaning: "A Dalliance or Playing with Words alike in Sound, but unlike in Sense, by changing, adding or taking away a Letter or two."[13] Bailey's source for the latter definition may be Ephraim Chambers' *Cyclopaedia* (1728). "ALLUSION*," Chambers reports, is

> ALLUSIO, in rhetoric, a figure whereby something is applied to or understood of, another, by reason of some similitude of name, or sound.

> * The word is formed of the Latin *ad,* and *ludere* to play. Camden defines *allusion* as dalliance, or playing with words like in sound, but unlike in sense; by changing, adding, or subtracting a letter or two; whence words resembling one another become applicable to different subjects.

Thus the almighty, if we may use sacred authority, changed Abram, *i.e.* high father, into Abraham, *i.e.* father of many. Thus the Romans played on their tippling emperor Tiberius Nero, by calling him Biberius Mero: and thus in Quintillian the sour fellow Placidus is called Acidus.

Allusions come very near to what we popularly call puns.[14]

Johnson's definition and illustrative quotation for the noun *parody* also cast light upon the nature of allusion. *Parody* is a "kind of writing in which words of an author or his thoughts are taken, and by a slight change adapted to some new purpose." Johnson then quotes a passage from the 1729 edition of the *Dunciad* in quarto, with notes, and in the process suggests the relationship between serious parody and allusion: "The imitations of the ancients are added together with some of the *parodies* and allusions to the most excellent of the moderns."[15]

The conflated meanings of "allusion" current during—and after—the writing of Rochester's poem, then, include "speaking a thing in reference to another," "changing, adding, or taking away a letter or two," and adapting the thought of the work to the "present circumstances of Time and Custom" according to the alluder's "own Fancy." Even allusion as brief as partial reference or quasi-pun includes awareness of the original and the author's right to change it as he sees fit. Rochester extends this notion to a complete poem and practices allusion as an extremely free form of Imitation: he supposes that we already know Boileau's Eighth Satire and Horace's Tenth Satire of the First Book. Indeed, in most contemporary printed and manuscript versions of the latter poem, he (or the copyist or bookseller) offers part of Horace's first line as a reminder,[16] in others it is called an "Imitation,"[17] and in 1714 it was printed together with Horace's poem.[18]

John L. Moore has ably shown how independent from Boileau Rochester is, though one suspects that examination of the complete *Satyr,* including its "new" conclusion, would strengthen his case even more. But criticism of the **"Allusion to Horace"** has not advanced significantly beyond Johnson's remarks in his "Life of Rochester":

> His Imitation of Horace on Lucilius is not inelegant or unhappy. In the reign of Charles the second began that adaptation, which since has been very frequent, of ancient poetry to present times; and, perhaps, few will be found where the parallelism is better preserved than in this. The versification is, indeed, sometimes careless, but it is sometimes vigorous and weighty.[19]

For our immediate purposes, the question of parallelism is essential, for upon reading the two poems it becomes clear that, though they often proceed in the same direction, they often diverge as well, and that Rochester has designed that they never meet. Moreover, comparison and contrast of these satires, and a brief analysis of the varieties of "Augustan" poetic Imitation, may suggest reasons for the modest success of Rochester's poem.

I

Horace's *Satires,* I, 10, actually begins with I, 4, in which Horace had praised Lucilius's wit and satiric sharpness, but criticised his speed of writing, harsh metrics, and refusal or inability to write correctly (ll. 6-13). The contemporary partisans of Lucilius attacked Horace and rushed to the defence of their apparently maligned idol.[20] Horace thus begins the latter poem with direct reference to the former: he is defensive, troubled, forced to insist that he praised Lucilius and is not a mere scoffer attempting to lower the past in order to elevate the present and his role in it. Accordingly—in about the first half of the poem—he carefully creates the image of a modest and judicious critic, one who offers praise and blame to poets of the past or present without prejudice or self interest. He is instructive, aware of distinctions between poetic modes and styles, offers advice regarding the tone of satire as presently conceived, and makes clear that he is aware of the limitations of his own genius. Hence he insists—as he did in I, 4—that the satiric sharpness of Lucilius is admirable, but adds that this virtue hardly implies all others, just as Laberius' low scenes of mime may be splendid as *mime,* but utterly different from distinguished poetic discourse. The satiric poet should add terseness, variety of styles—whether of orator, poet, or wit—and jesting humor in addition to his harsher laughter. On the other hand, he should exclude a mixture of Greek and Latin verse. It is not only tiresome old stuff indeed, but also a disservice to the development of native Latin poetry. At this point, Horace finds two ways to bolster his character in the reader's eyes: he admits that he too was tempted to write in such a mingled form, and adds that Romulus himself appeared in a dream and warned him away from this error.

> When I, *a Latin,* once design'd to write
> *Greek* Verse, *Romulus* appear'd at night;
> 'Twas after Twelve, the time when dreams are true,
> And said: *Why* Horace, *what do'st mean to do?*
> *'Tis full as mad the* Greeks *vast heaps t' encrease,*
> As *'tis to carry* Water *to the* Seas.[21]

Horace, then, is aware of the temptation of such a hybrid mode, and could resist only through quasidivine and patriotic intervention; he thus lessens the degree to which Lucilius, presumably innocent of such help, is culpable, and also reinforces his commitment to Rome, a commitment that an attacker of the Roman literary heritage would not be likely to share.

Horace also makes clear his awareness of others' strengths within different genres. He knows that among the moderns Fundanius excels in comedy, Pollio in tragedy, Varius in epic, and Virgil in pastoral, and that there is still room for a contemporary's success in satire. Others who have attempted the form (like Varro of the Atax) are below his own achievement; yet he himself admittedly remains *inventore minor* (I.48):

> Yet than *Lucillius* less I freely own,
> I would not strive to blast his just renown,
> He wears and best deserves to wear the Crown.

> (p. 417)

Only after Horace employs effective precept and example of good and bad poets, shows awareness of his own strengths and shortcomings, and has established both the sanity of his evaluation of his peers and of himself, does he directly reintroduce what had been obliquely discussed after the first verse paragraph of the poem—his "attack" upon Lucilius' blemishes and his own stature.

> Doth not *Lucillius Accius* Rhimes accuse?
> And blame our *Ennius's* correcter Muse?
> For too much lightness oft his Rhimes deride,
> And when He talks of his own Verse, for Pride?

> (p. 417)

Having thus added Lucilius' authority to his own, Horace addresses himself to an audacious question. At this point the unbiased reader is aware that Horace has not malevolently attacked Lucilius and that he is correct regarding Lucilius' faults. The question then raised is *why* was Lucilius so deficient? Was it lack of genius or the rough nature of the satiric themes he employed? The answer is—neither. Instead, Horace argues that Lucilius' deficiencies stem from a desire to please an unpolished audience. In so doing, Horace continues to shift away from defence of himself for unjustly attacking Lucilius and towards a demonstration that he is Lucilian. Moreover, he also suggests that those to whom he is responding, the implied *adversarii* of the poem, are actually the enemies of Lucilius; they would propagate what Lucilius himself would abandon if he were living in the Augustan age of more correct literary values which insist that one improve his work:

> . . . did He now again new life Commence,
> He would correct, he would retrench his Sense,
> And pare off all that was not Excellence;
> Take pains, and often when he Verses made,
> Would bite his Nails to th' quick, and scratch his
> Head.

> (p. 418)

Significantly, Horace follows these lines with others in his own voice, reiterating the value of painful revision. As a result, such a Lucilian-Horatian author would reject the popularity of the schoolroom and its teachers, and the professional authors' guild: that is, precisely those critics who berated Horace at the beginning of the poem.[22] Since Horace and Lucilius are allied, the pedagogues' quarrel with Horace is also a mistaken quarrel with the author they presume is a model for emulation; such a bad, non-Augustan audience willing to accept Lucilius' flaws is responsible for them. Horace concludes by exemplifying those for whom he and, if it were chronologically possible, Lucilius, prefer to write—not Demetrius, a trainer for the mimes, or the bad poets Fannius and Hermogines Tigellius, but those who are clearly Augustan:

Let *Plotius, Varius,* and *Mecaenas* love,
Let *Caesar, Virgil, Valgius* all approve
What I compose; to these would I could joyn
The *Visci,* and *Messala's* Learned Line,
And *Pollio,* and some other Friends of mine.

(p. 418)

The relevant Latin of I.82 (the second line above) is *Octavius,* not *Caesar*: it is now thought to refer to Octavius Musa, a poet and historian, and not to Augustus Caesar. But Creech's error—that of many of his contemporaries—is understandable and reiterates the exalted nature of Horace's audience, which would make Lucilius even greater by insisting that he blot and amend.[23] Demetrius and Tigellius, in contrast, urge the transcendence of Lucilius in his uncorrected form and thereby reproduce the sort of audience that endangers the poet it praises. Horace has moved from apparent attack upon Lucilius to real alliance with him, and from apparent defense of himself against foolish critics to real attack upon them.

Thus for Horace, Lucilius is blemished but great; Horace is on Lucilius' side; the attackers are wrong, and the refined court of Augustus is responsible for much of the success of Horace and would be responsible for improving the quality of Lucilius' efforts. Horace shows his kinship with Lucilius by borrowing an important device from him. Eduard Fraenkel observes:

> In a section of his earliest published book (the twenty-sixth in the collection of his works), presumably a kind of proem to what was to follow, Lucilius had spoken, both in general terms and naming some individual persons, of the readers whom he did not wish to have and of those he would like to have. To that section belonged the line (593) *Persium non curo legere, Laelium Decumen volo*; the gist of a pronouncement made in the same context is preserved in Cicero's well-known paraphrase [De orat. 2. 25] *neque se ab indoctissimis neque a doctissimis legi velle, quod alteri nihil intelligerent, alteri plus fortasse quam ipse.* Horace borrows from Lucilius the idea of listing desirable and undesirable readers, but he uses it not in a proem but in the epilogue of his book. Lest such an outspoken pronouncement might seem vain or ponderous, Horace makes it arise easily and naturally from a discussion on the risks of hankering after the wrong kind of popularity.[24]

Though I have only touched upon a few of the major historical issues behind the poem, I believe that this analysis is a reasonably accurate gloss upon Horace's intention as understood in the later seventeenth century. It will immediately be clear that Rochester's position is different from Horace's in numerous respects, but especially so in his attitude towards the main satiric target—John Dryden.

II

Significant differences between the two poems begin in Rochester's second line. Horace sincerely praises Lucilius as an inventor of satire; but Rochester regards Dryden's dramatic verses as "stol'n." Similarly, Horace's genuine regard for Lucilius as a sharp satirist is replaced by Rochester's dubious praise of Dryden's "plays, embroidered up and down / With wit and learning [which] justly pleased the town" (ll. 5-6). Rochester thus dissociates himself from Dryden: we do not see a satirist defending himself for having attacked the inventor of the form and his admitted superior; instead, we see a satirist attacking a dramatist who is neither his superior nor an inventor. Moreover, the term *embroidered* suggests that what intelligence there is in Dryden's plays is ornamental and decorative rather than an intrinsic part of the drama.[25] Lines 11 and 12 confirm our suspicion regarding the praise of Dryden and his "just" pleasing of the town, since we now hear that "your false sense / Hits the false judgment of an audience." The illicitly pleased audience is not in Horace's corresponding lines (though it is assumed later in the poem): Lucilius-induced laughter is a lesser but genuine pleasure. Though Lucilius' audience is not of the best, it is surely a notch above the "clapping fools" and "the rabble" who praise Dryden. Furthermore, "the Court" (ll. 14-19) must be added to the list of those who improperly praise, and so Rochester again diverges from the parent-poem, since there Horace's friends were not only from the Court but seemed to include Caesar himself. Rochester baits his monarch; Horace flatters his. Rochester gives grudging and damning praise to Dryden, and concludes that pleasing "the rabble and the Court"—the vulgar of low or high social rank—is something, at least,

Which blundering Settle never could attain,
And puzzling Otway labors at in vain.

(ll. 18-9)

In the following section (ll. 21-40) Rochester evaluates Elizabethan and contemporary dramatists. The parallel passage in Horace contains praise for the mingled jesting and serious mode of the old comedy, advises the moderns to adapt this, and criticizes Hermogenes and his school for never reading, and thus not profiting from, these plays. But Rochester is talking about Dryden as a modern dramatist; and so when he praises other modern dramatic wits he is obliquely condemning Dryden. Horace associates himself with Lucilius and discredits those who claimed he had attacked him; Rochester dissociates himself from Dryden, amplifies his original attack, and covertly, as well as overtly, criticizes him:

Of all our modern wits, none seems to me
Once to have touched upon true comedy
But hasty Shadwell and slow Wycherley.

(ll. 41-3)

Both the subsequent praise of Shadwell as a poet of nature, and of Wycherley as a poet of art, exclude Dryden from the higher ranks of comedy. Shadwell "scorns to varnish his good touches o'er / To make the fools and women praise 'em more" (ll. 48-9); Dryden had his "false sense" please "the false judgment, of an audience / Of clapping fools" (ll. 12-4). Similarly, Wycherley "earns hard whate'er he he gains: / He wants no judgment, nor he spares no pains" (ll. 50-1), whereas Dryden's rhymes were not earned but "stol'n, unequal, nay dull many times" (l. 2), and he is a poet of primarily quantitative output (ll. 8-9, 93-7).

Rochester again departs from the original in the rest of his discussion of the genres and the poet who excells in each. At this point in his poem Horace shows that he must succeed in "correct" satire, which Lucilius had ignored. The poet remains personal and positive: Horace is not competing with Lucilius but fulfilling the form which he had so brilliantly invented. But the notion of Horace as a refined extension of Lucilius is foreign to Rochester's purpose, since—in terms of the poem, at least—Rochester has no desire to follow Dryden as a dramatist; he thus chooses Buckhurst "For pointed satyrs" (l. 59), and Sedley for amorous love-poetry (a genre not discussed by Horace) as a way of returning to qualitative evaluation of Dryden. Where Sedley is seductive and successful—"the poor vanquished maid dissolves away / In dreams all night, in sighs and tears all day" (ll. 69-70)—the amatory songs in Dryden's plays are merely gross, and may also reveal something about Dryden's limp sexuality:[26]

> Dryden in vain tried this nice way of wit,
> For he to be a tearing blade thought fit.
> But when he would be sharp, he still was blunt:
> To frisk his frolic fancy, he'd cry, "Cunt!"
>
> (ll. 71-4)

Rochester, then, ironically praises and really attacks Dryden, excludes him from the ranks of good dramatists, and shows him to be ineffectual in his dramatic "love" poems. With all this in mind, the reader again doubts the sincerity of Rochester's praise of Dryden.

> But, to be just, 'twill to his praise be found
> His excellencies more than faults abound;
> Nor dare I from his sacred temples tear
> That laurel which he best deserves to wear.
>
> (ll. 77-80)[27]

Rochester then introduces lines with an important reservation, and proceeds to tear away Dryden's laurels. These same lines also further distinguish him from Rochester at precisely the point at which Horace was cementing his relationship with Lucilius:

> But does not Dryden find ev'n Jonson dull;
> Fletcher and Beaumont uncorrect, and full
> Of lewd lines, as he calls 'em; Shakespeare's style
> Stiff and affected; to his own the while
> Allowing all the justness that his pride
> So arrogantly had to these denied?
>
> (ll. 81-6)

Dullness, pompous fullness, and lewdness are the traits which, according to Rochester, belong to Dryden himself. Of course Horace carefully avoids any such presumption in describing Lucilius' quarrels with his predecessors, and

assumes that Lucilius' accurate strictures serve as proper precedent for his own. Dryden's pride and arrogance thus contrast with the normative behavior of both Lucilius and Horace. The latter honestly praises his great master; Rochester shows a despicable contemporary berating his betters, and places Dryden in the distasteful situation that Horace's detractors attempted to place him in.

Unlike Horace, Rochester thus "impartially" (l. 87) attacks his author's pride and arrogance. Horace gains our sympathy through association with a good man of letters; Rochester through dissociation from a bad man of letters. Horace throws the burden of Lucilius' deficiencies on to the inadequate demands of his rough age, but this alternative is impossible for Rochester, since Dryden is of the present age. Hence he raises three questions regarding Dryden's lack of literary merit, and each depends solely upon Dryden's internal literary state. He wonders whether

> . . . those gross faults his choice pen does commit
> Proceed from want of judgment, or of wit;
> Or if his lumpish fancy does refuse
> Spirit and grace to his loose, slattern muse?
>
> (ll. 89-92)

The questions are not overtly answered because, unlike Horace's answer, by implication all three charges are accurate. It is, presumably, Dryden's lack of Wit, among other things, that makes him so poor an amatory poet ("Dryden in vain tried this nice way of wit" [l. 71]); his lack of judgment leads him to substitute quantity for quality (ll. 93-101); and as "a vain, mistaken thing" (l.104) he wishes to please a poor theatrical audience. It thus follows that Dryden does not refuse spirit and grace to his muse: as a man of neither wit nor judgment he has none to give.

Rochester's strategy continues to be radically different from Horace's. The latter argues that were Lucilius now alive "he would correct, he would retrench his sense." Rochester's same advice (ll. 98-101) is given to one who is alive, chooses not to follow it, and seeks to please the rabble. Rochester himself has "no ambition on that idle score" (l. 110) and prefers, instead, to be censured by a few critics and poets he respects.

> I loathe the rabble; 'tis enough for me
> If Sedley, Shadwell, Shepherd, Wycherley,
> Godolphin, Butler, Buckhurst, Buckingham,
> And some few more, whom I omit to name,
> Approve my sense: I count their censure fame.
>
> (ll. 120-4)[28]

Horace is truly pro-Lucilian; Rochester truly anti-Drydenian. The former's main intentions are to defend himself and to define the best satiric mode for a correct age; the latter's to attack Dryden and bad drama that seeks the favor of the mob, whether high or low. Horace discusses his own satiric role in the literary culture of the Court; Rochester functions as a gadfly in literary culture and attacks the Court. The throne is at the center of value in the former; the throne is associated with the playhouse and rabble in the latter. In short, when compared to Horace's *Satires,* I, 10, Rochester has in fact produced something new which is the creation of another hand; but that new creation can be seen only when set against the old, since as an allusion it is "spoken with reference to something supposed to be already known, and therefore not expressed."[29] Such an Imitation, in which some parallelism is preserved and some altered, could not have been ignored by poets who either translated or carried the Imitation as a form to its highest level of achievement. It is not only the source of much phrasing for Creech's translation of the same poem in 1684,[30] but may also have been one of Pope's main models of imitative freedom from the original.[31] And it is surely an example of what Thomas Rymer meant when he said of Rochester's method:

> Whatsoever he imitated or Translated, was Loss to him. He had a Treasure of his own, a Mine not to be exhausted. His own Oar and Thoughts were rich and fine: his own Stamp and Expression more neat and beautiful than any he cou'd borrow or fetch from abroad.[32]

III

Rochester's poem tells us much about his allusive mode of satiric Imitation; but it also provides a paradigm of that sub-species of Imitation which both hopes for the reader's awareness of the parent-poem and is largely neutral in its attitude towards it. With the exception of implied differences between the quality of Horace's Emperor and Rochester's King, there is little thematic interplay between the two poems; and even this contrast is blunted by means of Rochester's praise of noble figures—like Buckhurst—whom he hopes to please. There is no real sign that we are to judge Horace's age as better or worse than Rochester's. Though Lucilius is superior to Dryden, the intentions of Horace and Rochester are so different that, though the former clarifies the latter, we cannot draw any further inference.

"Augustan" Imitation is remarkably complex; we do not fully understand the modern poem unless we understand its attitude towards the poem imitated. In the *First Satire of the Second Book of Horace* (to Fortescue, 1733), Pope is aware that "an Answer from Horace was both more full, and of more Dignity, than any I cou'd have made in my own person."[33] There is an implicit metaphor in Pope's attitude and posture: like his illustrious forbear he too must defend his satiric role from those who would silence him in order to harm virtue. Horace was the victor and convinced Trebatius, a guardian of the law in the legal sphere, that he should continue to write; Pope's defense of himself and use of Fortescue are similar. The poem is thus essentially optimistic; it assumes an historic community of thought, problems, and rational men who exist and have some power, however grim the world might in fact appear. In *Fortescue* Pope regards his parent-poem as normative and full of dignity.

This was not the only alternative for an imitator. One thinks of Prior's *English Ballad, On the Taking of Namur* (1695), a comic parody of Boileau's *Ode sur la prise de Namur* (1692), in which Boileau's flattery of his King and glorification of a minor victory are ridiculed. Or, on a more serious level, one turns to Johnson's Imitation of Juvenal's Tenth Satire, *The Vanity of Human Wishes* (1749), in which Juvenal's pagan harshness, the philosophic laughter of Democritus, and the unpredictable quality of the goddess Fortune, are replaced by Johnson's Christian piety, the speaker's rejection of laughter at the human situation, and the safe, stable, world that "celestial wisdom" can make for mankind. In these poems—and many more like them—the original is used not as a subdued argument from authority, but as a clear argument for the superiority of the imitator and his culture—whether English as opposed to French, or Christian as opposed to pagan.

Yet another imitative mode is the mingling of acceptance and rejection of the parent-poem, as in Pope's *Epistle to Augustus* (1737). Here the literary values of Augustus and his age contrast with those of George Augustus in England, but the Roman political values are regarded as negative models all too extant in contemporary England.[34] One suspects, as well, that a poem like Johnson's *London* (1738), from Juvenal's Third Satire, also falls into this broad class. Only the worst attributes of Domitian's bad Rome can be evoked to characterize Walpole's London; yet Johnson, nevertheless, uses Juvenal's conclusion—in which Umbricius promises to listen to Juvenal's satires when he too quits Rome—as a sign that, today as yesterday, the virtuous retreat but continue to fight the vicious. Like Umbricius before him, Thales must write satire and define the good life.

Rochester's characteristic mode of Imitation provides still a fourth way—the way which I have called relatively neutral in attitude towards the parent-poem. Though there are occasional lapses, he generally follows his own path, with minimal use of the original. He may invite challenge on qualitative grounds, and comparison and contrast on thematic grounds; and he may—or may not—show his own genius thereby. But he also shows the limitations of such neutrality. Boileau and Horace, their values and culture, are not actors in Rochester's poems; they are known but static figures who provide the backdrop but not much more. Johnson's change of the pagan "Fortuna" to the Christian "celestial wisdom" functions as the culmination of two movements in the *Vanity of Human Wishes*: the acceptance of Christian values in the modern poem, and the rejection of pagan values in the Roman. Similarly, Pope's substitution of Bolingbroke for Maecenas in his Imitation of Horace, *Epistles,* I.1, immediately warns his audience that the poet is in political opposition to the English court, whereas Horace is in sympathy with his. The contrast of English discord with Roman concord structures our understanding of the relationship between the two poems and the cultures they represent.

It is clear that Rochester's poem lacks such resonance, such sustained qualitative assessment of the past and comparison with the present. The **"Allusion to Horace"** has neither the striking independence of the *Satyr Against Mankind,* nor the eloquent "dependence" of Pope's *Epistle to Augustus.* I would thus suggest that collateral analyses of the Imitation and the parent-poem, together with discussion of the role the latter poem plays in the former, can be a tool of both understanding and evaluation. Of course it is evident that Rochester is not as great a poet as Horace, and simply pales in comparison. Moreover, in the poem before us his attack on Dryden is not only personal and unjustified, but unconvincing, since the poetic "world" within which Dryden exists is not fully realized, as the world of Shadwell or Cibber in other unjustified attacks surely is. As both Pope and Johnson observed, the versification sometimes is harsh and inelegant. And, as I have implied, the character of Rochester's speaker lacks Horace's convincing tones of an essentially disinterested, patriotic, personally involved yet ethical and fair poet.

One should grant these as convincing reasons for Rochester's diminished achievement; but at least as convincing a reason is that he chose a form whose finest conventions were just evolving and just beginning to be defined. Perhaps it is unfair to judge Rochester's **"Allusion"** on the standards of the *Epistle to Augustus,* written some sixty years later, for each man is attempting a different sort of poem. Yet, I believe, one reason that Pope's poem is so complex in its attitude toward the original is that Rochester's is so simple. Though Rochester's imagination is fertilized by the poem imitated, he nevertheless, as Rymer claims, disdains help "from abroad." In so doing, however, he limits himself to his own mine or its immediate environs, and thereby limits the expanse of his poem. He normally parallels or diverges from Horace and only rarely touches him. The reader innocent of Horace can read Rochester's **"Allusion"** with relatively little loss of understanding;[35] nor is his understanding substantially enriched after reading Horace. The hint or implication that allusion implies remains precisely that; the reader is teased by a promise that is never fulfilled, whereas in the *Satyr against Mankind*—which, unlike the **"Allusion,"** was never printed next to its original—the reader is not directly referred to another text through the very title of the poem,[36] and in the *Letter from Artemisia* (1679) there is neither a specifically announced nor implied literary parent. In the **"Allusion,"** on the other hand, the reader is frustrated by a static backdrop, by suggestions of historial similitude and dissimilitude which remain inchoate. One of the central reasons why Rochester's poem is not fully satisfying is that the creative strengths of Imitation as a genre were not yet clear; these could not be fully realized until the limitations of Rochester's mode in the **"Allusion to Horace"** were absorbed. Paradoxically, Rochester's refusal to be substantially in debt has limited his wealth, and Pope grew rich by inverting his example.

Notes

1. For relevant works concerning Augustan Imitation, see William Francis Galloway, English Adaptations of Roman Satire, 1660-1800 (unpublished Ph.D. Diss., Unversity of Michigan, 1937); William K.

Wimsatt, Jr., "Rhetoric and Poems: The Example of Pope," in *English Institute Essays 1948* (Columbia Univ. Press, 1949), p. 183; Harold F. Brooks, "The 'Imitation' in English Poetry, Especially in Formal Satire Before the Age of Pope," *RES,* XXV (1949), 124-40; Ian Jack, *Augustan Satire* (Oxford, 1952), pp. 97-114, 135-45; Reuben A. Brower, *Alexander Pope: The Poetry of Allusion* (Oxford, 1959); John Butt, ed., *Alexander Pope: Imitations of Horace,* The Twickenham Edition of the Poems of Alexander Pope, IV (London, 1953), xxvi-xxx; Butt, "Johnson's Practice in the Poetical Imitation," in *New Light on Dr. Johnson,* ed. Frederick W. Hilles (Yale Univ. Press, 1959), pp. 19-34; Mary Lascelles, "Johnson and Juvenal," *Ibid.,* pp. 35-55; G.K. Hunter, "The 'Romanticism' of Pope's Horace," *ECl,* X (1960), 390-404; John M. Aden, "Pope and the Satiric Adversary," *SEL,* II (1962), 267-86; Aubrey L. Williams, "Pope and Horace; *The Second Epistle of the Second Book,"* in *Restoration and Eighteenth-Century Literature: Essays in Honor of Alan Dugald McKillop,* ed. Carroll Camden (Univ. of Chicago Press, 1963), pp. 309-21; Thomas E. Maresca, *Pope's Horatian Poems* (Ohio State Univ. Press, 1966); Jay Arnold Levine, "Pope's *Epistle to Augustus,* Lines 1-30," *SEL,* VII (1967), 427-51; M. N. Austin, "The Classical Learning of Samuel Johnson," *Studies in the Eighteenth Century,* ed. R. F. Brissenden (Univ. of Toronto Press, 1968), pp. 285-306; John Hardy, "Johnson's *London*: The Country versus the City," *ibid.,* pp. 251-68; Manuel Schonhorn, "The Audacious Contemporaneity of Pope's *Epistle to Augustus,"* *SEL,* VIII (1968) 431-44; Leonard A. Moskovit, "Pope and the Tradition of the Neoclassical Imitation," *SEL,* VIII (1968), 445-62; Howard D. Weinbrot, *The Formal Strain: Studies in Augustan Imitation and Satire* (Univ. of Chicago Press, 1969); John M. Aden, *Something Like Horace: Studies in the Art and Allusion of Pope's Horatian Satires* (Vanderbilt Univ. Press, 1969); Aden, "Bethel's Sermon and Pope's Exemplum: Towards a Critique," *SEL,* IX (1969), 463-70; Maynard Mack, *The Garden and the City: Retirement and Politics in the Later Poetry of Pope 1731-1743* (Univ. of Toronto Press, 1969); P.J. Koster, "Arbuthnot's Use of Quotation and Parody in His Account of the Sacheverell Affair," *PQ,* XLVIII (1969), 201-11; Koster, "Means and Meanings: Translation as a Polemic Weapon," *Echos du Monde Classique: Classical News and Views,* XIV (1970), 13-20; Wimsatt, "Imitation as Freedom, 1717-1798," *New Literary History,* I (1970), 215-36; Weinbrot, "Augustan Imitation: The Role of the Original," in *Proceedings of the Modern Language Association Conferences on Neo-Classicism, 1967-1968,* ed. Paul J. Korshin (New York, 1970), pp. 53-70; R. L. Selden, "Dr. Johnson: A Problem in Critical Methods," *CL,* XXII (1970), 289-302; Edward A. and Lillian D. Bloom, "Johnson's *London* and its Juuvenalian Texts," "Johnson's *London* and the Tools of Scholarship," *HLQ,* XXXIV (1970), 1-23, 115-39.

2. The conventional procedure in eighteenth-century France and England was to note the author's imitation of Horace or Juvenal and praise or blame him regarding the individual passage. This technique is particularly clear in the edition of Boileau by Charles Brosette in 1717, and M. de Saint-Marc in 1747. On July 6, 1700, Brosette wrote to Boileau regarding his projected edition of the works, "avec des notes, et surtout avec la conférence, et le parallel des endroits d'Horace et Juvénal que vous avez imités." *Correspondence entre Boileau Despreaux et Brosette,* ed. Auguste Laverdet (Paris, 1858), pp. 47-8. Warburton performs a similar task—a sort of piecemeal comparison and contrast—for Pope in 1751. This practice may probably be traced to the habit of reading commentators for particular lines and phrases, and is severely criticized by Joseph Spence in *Polymetis* (London, 1747), p. 287.

3. *Of Dramatic Poesy and Other Critical Essays,* ed. George Watson (London, 1967), I, 270.

4. *Ibid.,* 271.

5. *Idem.*

6. Bishop Gilbert Burnet relates that "*Boileau* among the *French,* and *Cowley* among the *English* Wits were those Rochester admired most." See *Some Passages of the Life and Death of . . . Rochester* (London, 1680), p. 8. I briefly discuss Rochester's free adaptation of Boileau's Third and Eighth Satires in *The Formal Strain,* pp. 46-9.

7. As quoted in Harold F. Brooks, *RES, XXV,* 132.

8. For the dating of these works, see David Vieth, *The Complete Poems of John Wilmot, Earl of Rochester* (Yale Univ. Press, 1968), pp. 194, 201-2, and 207, respectively. Quotations are from this edition.

9. London, sig. A2ᵛ. Rochester also uses the word in (apparently) the narrower sense of reference to part of a poem in "An Epistolary Essay from M. G. to O. B. upon their Mutual Poems" (1680). The dim-witted M. G. proclaims: "But why am I no poet of the times? / I have no allusions, similes, and rhymes." *Complete Poems,* p. 146.

10. In Part III of the second edition (London, 1705), Bysshe includes *A Collection of the Most Natural, Agreeable, and Sublime Thoughts, viz. Allusions, Similes, Descriptions and Characters of persons and Things that are in the Best English Poets,* and adds: "I have inserted not only Similes, Allusions, Characters, and Descriptions; but also the most Natural and Sublime Thoughts of our Modern Poets on all Subjects whatever" (sig. F4ᵛ).

11. *Dictionarium Anglo-Britannicum,* 2nd ed. (London, 1715).

12. *The New World of Words* (London, 1720).

13. *Dictionarium Britannicum* (London, 1730).

14. 6th ed. (London, 1750).

15. For the full context of Pope's remark, see *Alexander Pope: The Dunciad,* the Twickenham Edition of the Poems of Alexander Pope, V, ed. James Sutherland, 3rd ed. (London, 1963), p. 9.

16. See David Vieth, *Attribution in Restoration Poetry* (Yale Univ. Press, 1963), pp. 386-90.

17. In, for example, *The Works of the Right Honourable the Earls of Rochester and Roscommon,* 3rd ed. (London, 1709), p. 15, and *The Works of the Earls of Rochester, Roscommon, Dorset, the Duke of Devonshire, & c.* (London, 1721), p. 10.

18. See *Poems by John Wilmot, Earl of Rochester,* ed. Vivian de Sola Pinto, 2nd ed. (Harvard Univ. Press, 1964), p. 192. In spite of this and the poem's publication as a translation in *The Odes and Satyrs of Horace that Have Been Done into English by the Most Eminent Hands* (London, 1715; 1717; 1721; 1730; Dublin, 1730), I must disagree with Brooks's judgment that the poem "belongs to the English line of imitations that were also translations." *RES, XXV,* 133. The subsequent analysis should make clear the grounds of this view. See also my comment on David Vieth's observations in n. 35, below.

19. For Moore see "The Originality of Rochester's *Satyr Against Mankind,*" *PMLA, LVIII* (1943), 398-9, and for Johnson, *Lives of the English Poets,* ed. G. Birkbeck Hill (Oxford, 1905), I, 224. James Osborn believes that this remark was prompted by Johnson's knowledge of Pope's opinion: "Rochester has very bad versification sometimes. (He instanced this from his tenth satire of Horace, his full rhymes, etc.)." *Joseph Spence, Observations, Anecdotes, Characters of Books and Men,* ed. James M. Osborn (Oxford, 1966), I, 202. As I hope to show shortly, Johnson's remark is misleading, not only because of Rochester's different treatment of his main target, but also because of his barely Horatian conception of harsh satire. He told Bishop Burnet: "A man could not write with life unless he were heated by Revenge: For to make a Satyre without Resentment, upon the cold Notions of *Phylosophy,* was as if a man would in cold blood, cut mens' throats who had never offended him: And he said, the Lyes in these Libels came as often as Ornaments that could not be spared without spoiling the beauty of the Poem." *Some Passages of . . . Rochester,* p. 26.

20. Valuable discussions of the relationship between Lucilius and Horace may be found in George Converse Fiske, *Lucilius and Horace: A Study in the Classical Theory of Imitation,* Univ. of Wisconsin Studies in Lang. and Lit., no. 7 (1920), pp. 25-63, 219-368, *passim;* Eduard Fraenkel, *Horace* (Oxford, 1957), pp. 128-35; Niall Rudd, *The Satires of Horace* (Cambridge Univ. Press, 1966), pp. 61-131.

21. *The Odes, Satyrs, and Epistles of Horace,* tr. Thomas Creech (London, 1684), p. 416. Subsequent references are to this edition and are cited in the text.

22. See Rudd, *The Satires of Horace,* pp. 118-24, especially his brief summation on pp. 123-4.

23. The line represented a minor interpretive crux. Jacobus Cruquius argues: "Ego certe propter epitheton optimus [in *Octavius optimus*] potius iudiciarium hic signari Octavius Augustum, qui mansuetudine & morum facilitate mirabiliter ab omnibus commendatur, & poeta fuit non incelebris." *Q. Horatius Flaccus* (Leiden, 1597), p. 405. Ludovicius Desprez says: "Optimus nempe is poeta historias etiam scripsit. Cave, lector, ne Augustum accipias." *Quintus Horatii Flaci, Opera . . . In Usum Serenissimi Delphini* [169] (Philadelphia, 1814), p. 428 n. And thus William Baxter: "Ego plane sentio cum Jacobo Cruquio *Octavium optimum* non fuisse alium quam ipsum Augustum, etsi vir doctus Ludovicus Desprez hoc caveri jubeat." *Q. Horatii Flaci. Eclogae* (London, 1701), p. 310n. Somewhat later, both Dacier and Sanadon believe that Octavius is the poet, not the Emperor: see the *Oeuvres d'Horace* (Amsterdam, 1735) V, 428-9. The little controversy is not yet dead, as witnessed by *Oeuvres d'Horace . . . Satires publiès par Paul Lejay* ([first ed., Paris, 1911] Hildesheim, 1966), p. 280 n.

24. *Horace,* pp. 131-2.

25. Johnson defines the verb *embroider* in this way: "To border with ornaments; to decorate with figured works; to diversify with needlework; to adorn with raised figures" (1755).

26. By the later 1670's Dryden was exposed to such innuendo, as well, in the anonymous *An Exclamation against Julian, Secretary to the Muses; with the Character of a Libeller. By a Person of Quality* (London, 1697): in "Bed-rid Age" Dryden "has left his Sting upon the Stage" (p. 1).

27. These remarks are often regarded as sincere praise of Dryden: see John Harold Wilson, *The Court Wits of the Restoration* (Princeton Univ. Press, 1948), p. 188, and Vivian de Sola Pinto, *Enthusiast in Wit: A Portrait of John Wilmot Earl of Rochester, 1647-1680* (London, 1962), p. 99.

28. Ironically, the argument that Rochester adapts from Horace has been applied to Rochester himself. David Hume observes: "The very name of Rochester is offensive to modest ears; yet does his poetry discover such energy of style and such poignancy of satyre, as give grounds to imagine what so fine a genius, had he fallen in a more happy age and followed better models, was capable of producing. The adroit satyrists often used great liberty in their expressions, but their freedom no more resembles the license of Rochester than the nakedness of an Indian dress does that of a common prostitute" (*The History of Great Britain* [London, 1757], II, 453).

29. Of course this raises a troubling problem regarding analyses of specific Imitations. How can we determine whether the earlier poet has read the poem imitated in the way we suggest? In Pope's case the job is made easier through his reproduction of the classical poem, with certain key words drawn to our attention, on the facing page. Since Rochester does not do this, one's interpretation is on weaker grounds. A contemporary and conventional reading of Horace, *Satires,* I, 10, however, makes clear that much of the reading discussed above would have been known to Rochester. Lewis Crusius observes:

> "*Horace . . .* has not fail'd to censure [Lucilius] on . . . account [of his extravagance]; and excuses the liberty he took in doing so to one, who was his master in Satire, by that which *Lucilius* himself had taken to find fault with *Ennius. . . . Horace* therefore in gratifying his own good taste, by condemning this style of *Lucilius's,* pleas'd his prince's at the same time.

> "*Besides* these faults, *Lucilius* had a particular affectation of mixing Greek words with the Latin, which absurd as it was, found many admirers. This oblig'd that excellent writer to condemn him for it, and ridicule so absurd a mixture. Nevertheless, he readily grants, that he not only exceeded *Ennius,* and those that preceded him in his art, but would have been correct himself, had he lived to the *Augustan* Age"

> (*Lives of the Roman Poets,* 3rd ed. [London, 1753], I, xv-xvii; the first edition was published in 1726).

Crusius insists that his views are drawn from the authors' texts and "*the most* judicious Critics *concerning the* Roman Poets, *whose Labours I am much beholden to*" (sig. A4[r]); many of these critics wrote prior to, or contemporary with, Rochester.

30. Compare, for example, the opening of Rochester's poem with that of Creech's below:

> Well, Sir, I grant, I said *Lucilius* Muse Is uncorrect, his way of Writing loose, And who admires him so, what Friend of his So blindly doats as to deny me This? And yet in the same Page I freely own, His Wit as sharp as ever lash't the Town; But This one sort of Excellence allow'd, Doth not infer that all the rest is good: For on the same Account I might admit *Labenius* Farce for Poems and for Wit.

> (p. 415)

31. James Osborn observes that "despite Pope's disapproval of Rochester's versification, this poem . . . influenced Pope's own imitations of Horace. It is notable that this is one of Horace's satires that Pope did not choose to imitate." *Observations,* I, 202. For Pope's other praise and blame of Rochester, see *idem.*

32. *The Critical Works of Thomas Rymer,* ed. Curt A. Zimansky (Yale Univ. Press, 1956), p. 81. Rymer may have been aware of Bishop Burnet's similar remarks: "Sometimes other mens' thoughts mixed

with his Compositions, but that flowed rather from the Impressions they made on him when he read them, by which they came to return upon him as his own thoughts, then that he servilely copied from any. For few men ever had a bolder flight of fancy, more steadily governed by Judgment than he had." *Some Passages of . . . Rochester*, p. 8. The "originality" of Rochester's imitative poetry was a commonplace: see, for example, the comments of St. Evremond, Robert Wolsely, Anthony à Wood, Robert Parsons, and Bishop Burnet in *The Works of the Earls of Rochester, Roscommon, Dorset, The Duke of Devonshire, & c*, pp. xx, xxix, xxxii, xxxv, xxxviii, respectively.

33. *Imitations of Horace*, p. 3.

34. On this point, see Levine, *SEL*, VII, and Weinbrot, *Proc. MLA Neo-Classicism*, n. 1. To these should be added Ian Watt, "Two Historical Aspects of the Augustan Tradition," in Brissenden, *Studies in the Eighteenth Century* pp. 67-88; J.W. Johnson, *The Formation of English Neo-Classical Thought* (Princeton Univ. Press, 1967), pp. 16-30; Howard Eskine Hill, "Augustans on Augustanism: England 1655-1759," *Renaisssance and Modern Studies*, IX (1967) 55-83.

35. I hope that the pages above have made clear the grounds of my disagreement with Professor Vieth regarding the "Allusion." He states: "This poem is an 'imitation' in the same sense as Pope's 'Imitations of Horace' and is apparently the first such work in the English language. Based on Horace, *Satires*, I, 10, it requires a close knowledge of the Latin original so that the reader will be aware not only of clever adaptations of Roman circumstances to English ones, but of ironic discrepancies between the two." *Complete Poems of Rochester*, p. 120n.

36. None of the manuscript titles of the poem mention Boileau or offer the first line, as do comparable texts for Horace and the "Allusion." But the 1707 edition of the *Works* of Rochester and Roscommon (and subsequent reprints) says that the *Satyr* is "Imitated from Monsieur Boileau" (p. 1). See Vieth, *Attribution*, pp. 370-5. Contemporary readers were far more aware of the freedom of the *Satyr* than of the "Allusion"; see the prefatory comments on the former poem in Rochester's *Poems on Several Occasions* (London, 1680), sigs. A4ᵛ-6ʳ. I have discussed several aspects of the relationship between Imitation and translation in the *The Formal Strain*, pp. 14-30.

Reba Wilcoxon (essay date 1975)

SOURCE: Wilcoxon, Reba. "Pornography, Obscenity, and Rochester's 'The Imperfect Enjoyment.'" *Studies in English Literature* 15, No. 3 (Summer, 1975): 375-90.

[*In the following essay, Wilcoxon claims that Rochester's poem "The Imperfect Enjoyment" is not pornographic because it satisfies three aesthetic criteria: it uses complex* linguistic devices to achieve psychic distancing; it is linked to a classical traditional of "imperfect enjoyment" poems; and it explores not only sexual but emotional, psychological, and ethical relationships between human beings.]

In the right-hand drawer of his writing desk, where he normally kept his flutes and music books, Samuel Pepys concealed a book that he thought "unfit to mix with my other books."[1] It was *Poems on Several Occasions By the Right Honourable, E. of R———*, the abbreviation known to all as the notorious John Wilmot, Earl of Rochester. Writing to his clerk in November, 1680, four months after Rochester's death, Pepys advised, "pray let it remain there, for as he is past writing any more so bad in one sense, so I despair of any man surviving him to write so good in another."[2]

We cannot know exactly what Pepys meant by "so bad in one sense" and "so good in another," but we can guess that he considered Rochester's poems indecent and possibly immoral, yet by some artistic standard effective and worth preserving. This split judgment of "good" and "bad," essentially the ever-present dichotomy between the moral and the aesthetic, represents a common polarity among critics confronted with poetry or prose that is subject to the charge of pornography and obscenity. Rochester's long-standing reputation for pornography and obscenity has obscured the need to analyze his methods and the context in which he was working. Using as a test case **"The Imperfect Enjoyment,"** a poem blatantly shocking in sexual language and imagery, I shall attempt to clear Rochester of the blanket charge of pornography, to defend the obscenity in historical and aesthetic contexts, and to suggest a psychological and moral dimension in the poem that bears examining.

The appearance and disappearance of **"The Imperfect Enjoyment"** in the editions of Rochester's poems over a period of almost 300 years has been dependent on the moral persuasion of the editor (as would be expected, it was printed by Curll and omitted by Dr. Johnson) or the legal demands of the time. As late as 1964 Vivian de Sola Pinto was forced to exclude it from the collected poems "at the request of the publisher owing to the risk of prosecution in this country [Great Britain] under the existing law."[3] Currently, it appears in the David Vieth collection and elsewhere. The changing legal and moral status of **"The Imperfect Enjoyment"** makes attractive the proposition that pornography and obscenity are in the eye of the beholder; this, however, is a critical dead end. Understanding the effects of such poems requires an aesthetic context for the sexual images and foul language. For this purpose, it will be useful to attempt a differentiation between pornography and obscenity, an aesthetic distinction but not a legal one.

Etymology points to the exclusively sexual as the subject of pornography, *pornē* being the Greek for harlot. "Obscenity" is of doubtful etymology, although the Latin *obscēnus* or *obscaenus* is thought to be its derivation.

Obscaenus originally meant adverse, inauspicious or ill omened; according to the New English Dictionary, the meaning was transformed into abominable, disgusting, filthy, or indecent. Havelock Ellis's interpretation is suggestive: "By the 'obscene' we may properly mean what is *off the scene* and not openly shown on the stage of life."[4] In usage, obscenity has always been a more extensive term that can denote sexual, scatological, and grotesque depictions of the physical. Thus all pornography is obscene, but not all obscenity is pornographic. Let us deal with the more restrictive term first.

Much of the serious writing on pornography has been motivated by a passion for artistic, social, and intellectual freedom. The problem is compounded by the tendency to combine the visual and literary arts, for which aesthetic criteria are not necessarily the same. Moreover, discussions offering the most empirical evidence have concentrated on prose fiction rather than poetry. And there is little agreement on whether pornography is "art." The two fundamental positions on this final question are exemplified by Abraham Kaplan in "Obscenity as an Esthetic Category" and by Morse Peckham in *Art and Pornography.* To Kaplan pornography is not art because it does not effect the aesthetic experience, "a kind of disinterest or detachment, a 'psychic distance.'"[5] He explains: "Of course, art evokes feeling; but it is *imagined* feeling, not what is actually felt as a feeling of what we do and undergo. And art works against the translation of imagined feeling into action. It does so partly by providing us insight into feeling, and so allowing us to subject passion to the control of the understanding."[6] By contrast, pornography is "promotional." It is "not itself the *object* of an experience, esthetic or any other, but rather a stimulus to an experience not focussed on it. It serves to elicit not the imaginative contemplation of an expressive substance, but rather the release in fantasy of a compelling impulse."[7] On the other hand, Peckham holds that art and pornography are not mutually exclusive. Although he disclaims any absolute definition, Peckham gives as the single common denominator of all pornography "the presentation in verbal or visual signs of human sexual organs in a condition of stimulation."[8] This presentation can be art at a low cultural level (and usually is, he admits) or at a high cultural level. The higher the cultural level of pornographic art, according to Peckham, the greater its departure from conventionalized "perceptual fields," the farther removed from the pragmatic, and the more difficult are the problems offered by the use of language. A related contention is that pornography at the low cultural level is likely to be monotonous because it has "a well-restricted iconographic program, delimited by the character of the enterprise."[9]

What we have here, in two opposing aesthetic theories is a striking similarity in analysis of the object: the pornography that Kaplan sees and the low cultural level that Peckham sees are the same impoverished literary representation of sex. This deprivation has also been remarked by others. For example, in *Libertine Literature in England* David Foxon observes that pornography releases emotion by

"simple technical means which do not usually deepen the quality of our experience."[10] Herbert Gold has found: "Erotic writing mediates between art and sex, but pornography tries to perform the mediation without your being aware of the medium—like a deluxe product sold for prevention of impotence only."[11] To which he adds: "Pornography finally thinks of nothing more than the hand in the lap, and that is why it leaves sadness in its wake. But if the mind can deal with style, energy, complications and simplicity both, this sadness is overcome."[12] Steven Marcus, in his well-documented *The Other Victorians,* is another who concludes that pornography is like propaganda and advertising in its call to sexual action. In it, language is merely an obstruction: "At best, language is a bothersome necessity, for its function in pornography is to set going a series of nonverbal images, of fantasies, and if it could achieve this without the mediation of words it would."[13] At its "purest" the pornography in fiction that Marcus analyzes is the low level defined by Peckham: verbal signs of stimulated sexual organs without exploration of emotional responses, personality, or values. We cannot, he says, speak of "relations between human beings" in such representations; instead, "They are rather juxtapositions of human bodies, parts of bodies, limbs, and organs; they are depictions of positions and events, diagrammatic schema for sexual ballets—actually they are more like football plays than dances."[14] We are given "sets of abstractions" for a world in which no one is ever jealous, possessive, or truly angry.[15] Or, as another commentator sees it, the work is a fairy-tale existence in which erotic wishes are "lived out without punishment or unpleasant effects."[16]

Of course, most of these conclusions are based upon evidence from fiction rather than poetry. It is probably more difficult for poetry to be entirely "schematic" sexually, since part of its fabric is emotional expression and since formal devices, such as meter and rhyme, tend to call attention to language. Nevertheless, the characteristics of pornography discovered by these critics enable us to make distinctions among seventeenth-century poems without calling upon individual moral values. For example, an epigram ascribed to Rochester in some editions but now disallowed is a brief but clear example of simplistic pornography on these criteria:

Written under Nelly's Picture

She was so exquisite a Whore,
That in the Belly of her Mother,
She plac'd her ——— so right before,
Her father ——— them both together.[17]

The epigram is an example of what Marcus means by "diagrammatic schema for sexual ballets." Only the word "exquisite" provides any possibility of meaning beyond the image of bodies in conjunction.

A notch higher in quality is the song, "In the Fields of Lincoln's Inn," which is in the 1680 edition of Rochester's poems but attributed by Vieth to Sir Charles Sedley.

Mockery of the pastoral and the heroic enriches the meaning, but the principal purpose of the poem is to effect, in Marcus's terms, a blueprint for objects and not persons. "Nymph" Phillis solves the problem of simultaneous intercourse with two "shepherds," Coridon and Strephon:

> Nature had 'twixt C——t and A——se,
> Wisely plac'd firm separation;
> God knows else what desolation
> Had ensu'd from *Warring Tarse*.[18]

The use of the heroic is comic—including puns such as "fierce intestine bustle" and "They tilt, and thrust with horrid pudder"—but the pornographic interest is still paramount. The relations of the human beings end as they began, on a merely physical plane with the nymph "Ballock beaten" and the shepherds "soundly tir'd."

With these examples of, and specifications for, pornography in mind, let us consider Rochester's **"The Imperfect Enjoyment."** I shall argue that the poem fulfills three aesthetic demands that pornography does not: it effects psychic distance through complex linguistic devices; it is intellectually and emotionally enriched by a classical and a seventeenth-century literary tradition; and it explores an emotional relationship between human beings and sets up a norm for that relationship.

The poem begins in a pornographic style, with a juxtaposition of bodies: "Naked she lay, clasped in my longing arms, / I filled with love, and she all over charms."[19] Though this is clearly no *carpe diem* poem—both lovers are "equally inspired with eager fire, / Melting through kindness, flaming in desire" (3-4)—still the clichés of such love poetry, the "longing" and "kindness," are a disarming preface to the amplification of physical images that follows:

> With arms, legs, lips close clinging to embrace,
> She clips me to her breast, and sucks me to her face.
> Her nimble tongue, Love's lesser lightning, played
> Within my mouth, and to my thoughts conveyed
> Swift orders that I should prepare to throw
> The all-dissolving thunderbolt below.
>
>   (5-10)

The metaphors "Love's lesser lightning" and "the all-dissolving thunderbolt below" mitigate the explicitness of images by lending distance and a kind of elevation. The effect is mock-heroic, but the weight of the mockery is not being thrown at sex itself. The grandiose "all-dissolving thunderbolt," the mighty weapon of Jove transformed into the phallus, prepares the way for the speaker's subsequent self-mockery and his curse on the fallen weapon, delivered with a curious mixture of comic and tragic tone that is not uncommon in Rochester's poetry.

In the next couplet similar heightening occurs as the poet invokes Platonic (or Neo-Platonic) concepts: "My fluttering soul, sprung with the pointed kiss, / Hangs hovering o'er her balmy brinks of bliss" (11-12). We may recall Donne's "Extasie," in which "our soules, (which to advance their state, / Were gone out,) hung 'twixt her, and mee." The soul in that instance is clearly a non-physical entity; in Rochester's couplet the dualism of soul and body is not so definitely maintained. Though it may be read as designating an emotion (even a "spirit" of sorts), Rochester's "soul" almost certainly finds issue not in philosophically conventional outlets but in phallic transmission, and so "hangs hovering" over the "balmy brinks" of his mistress' sexuality. Rochester is redefining the interplay of body and soul, and skillfully suspending the grounds of judgment between the two. This shifting between the abstract and the concrete, or the ideal and the real, is furthered by the seemingly innocent "pointed" kiss which "sprung" the soul. "Pointed" is abstract if one thinks of the meaning "to the point," the essence of the intent; but it also suggests the concrete invitation to action conveyed by the "nimble tongue." Both the verbals, "pointed" and "sprung," carry a sly duality. The metaphor "balmy brinks" has an olfactory and visual tenor that further operates against the Platonic ideal. At the same time, however, "balmy brinks" has an application that moves it away from pornographic immediacy, since by its terms the female body becomes an emblem of external nature.

The aesthetic distancing, achieved by "balmy brinks," as well as by the lightning and the thunderbolt, can be appreciated by comparison with the crudity of a similar scene in "A Dream" ("Twas when the sable Mantle of the Night"), formerly attributed to Rochester:

> Methought I found her prostrate on her Bed,
> Only her Smock cov'ring her *Maidenhead*;
> I heav'd it up, sweet Linnen, by your Favour;
> I felt, but how my moisten'd Fingers then did savour!
> I look'd, and saw the *blind Boy's* happy Cloyster,
> Arch'd on both Sides, lye gaping like an Oyster;
> I had a Tool before me, which I put
> Up to the Quick, and strait the Oyster shut.[20]

That the male's mastery in this poem is cast in a dream sequence, where he meets no obstacles, is consistent with the judgment that pornography is wish-fulfillment unimpeded by the contingencies of reality. Events are otherwise in **"The Imperfect Enjoyment,"** where the promise of fulfillment is broken by a reality that no doubt elicited sympathy from Rochester's largely male audience:

> But whilst her busy hand would guide that part
> Which should convey my soul up to her heart,
> In liquid raptures I dissolve all o'er,
> Melt into sperm, and spend at every pore.
> A touch from any part of her had done 't:
> Her hand, her foot, her very look's a cunt.
>
>   (13-18)

"Convey my soul up to her heart" continues the parody of Platonic idealism, but then the language coarsens with the reversal of events. Still, "Her hand, her foot, her very look's a cunt" proves anything but a crudity. It is in fact a triumph of erotic definition, a metaphor for the mistress' sexual attraction, a power reaffirmed, more conventionally, by the subsequent reference to "her fair hand, which might bid heat return / To frozen age, and make cold hermits burn" (31-32). In short, the word "cunt" functions as synechdoche, with the part standing for a whole cluster of attributes (consider the similarity of effect if we substitute the word "Queen").

The entire description of the love scene, which is direct and comparatively unelaborated, is the stuff of pornography; yet the general meaning and the speaker's emotional reaction are antithetical to pornography, where every sexual fantasy ends in success and no one ever admits, as the poet does here, "Succeeding shame does more success prevent, / And rage at last confirms me impotent" (29-30).

Rochester is delineating a situation inherently embarrassing and one to which probably no lover outside of pornography has been immune; yet the contrast between the erotic foreplay and the sudden betrayal of the lovers' anticipation is a comic incongruity. There are both pathos and ridicule in the image of the desirable and desiring woman removing the "clammy joys" and exclaiming, "All this to love and rapture's due; / Must we not pay a debt to pleasure too?" (23-24). The satire broadens as the lover attempts to "show my wished obedience," only to discover that the body will not respond to the will. The subject can be seen as impotence or limitation, but not under a rubric either pornographic or merely negativistic. Rochester is striving for a seriocomic image of the human predicament.

Literary precedent itself militates against readings of Rochester that are overly solemn. To the extent that such precedent is brought into play, the poem acquires additional aesthetic distance by virtue of the reader's increased contemplative engagement. Pornography, it will be recalled, short-circuits the mind for the most direct route to sexual arousal. Once we recognize that Rochester is working in a tradition as old as Ovid and Petronius and as recent as his French and English contemporaries, we are less prone to conclusions that are too simplistic.

The situation in Ovid's *Amores* and in Petronius' *The Satyricon* differs from **"The Imperfect Enjoyment"** in that the male partners suffer impotence at the outset and not premature ejaculation. But the role of the women is much the same: they are willing, cooperative, and disappointed. With all three writers, the lover's recognition of his impotence is followed by chastisement of the phallus. Frustration leads to aggression, and aggression is vented on the offender, a seriocomic technique that trades on the primitive objectification of the phallus as a thing in itself, a power apart. The mock-encomium by Rochester is the most extensive and the most revelatory of the speaker's character.

Rochester begins his address to the male organ on a note of veneration, much as the epic hero would address his trusted spear. Although the military metaphor for the sexual

act is ancient and widespread, perhaps the images and the puns here owe something to Encolpius' rationalization in *The Satyricon,* "it was less myself than my instrument that failed. As your soldier, lady, I stand ready to die in the breach, but I am a soldier now without a spear."[21] Rochester makes the same dissociation of self and body as he contemplates the cause of his frustration:

> This dart of love, whose piercing point, oft tried,
> With virgin blood ten thousand maids have dyed;
> Which nature still directed with such art
> That it through every cunt reached every heart—
> Stiffly resolved, 'twould carelessly invade
> Woman or man, nor aught its fury stayed:
> Where'er it pierced, a cunt it found or made—
> Now languid lies in this unhappy hour,
> Shrunk up and sapless like a withered flower.
>
> (37-45)

This verse sentence, with a periodic postponement of the main verb ("lies"), is remarkable for its compression of detail. And yet, shot through as it is with sexual metaphors and puns, like "dye" (for orgasm) and "stiffly resolved," it is without prurience. Rather than issuing a call to sexual action, it reports the life of lust in masculine terms of violence and weaponry. Sex is shown ultimately as pure power, a rapine of male and female alike—even, presumably, inanimate objects—in any or all of which "a cunt it found or made." The significance of "invade / Woman or man" is not deviance, but the voracity of the sexual appetite. The result is a startling contrast between former sexual prowess and the present "withered flower," a descendant of Ovid's "hesterna languidora rosa."

In the satiric apostrophe that follows (46-61), beginning "Thou treacherous, base deserter of my flame," the blade as instrument is transformed into blade as person, who is characterized as a subject remiss in duty to a ruler. He is a "deserter" who mistakes allegiance, for he is "true to lewdness, so untrue to love." The personification of a disloyal subject is expanded:

> When vice, disease, and scandal lead the way,
> With what officious haste dost thou obey!
> Like a rude, roaring hector in the streets
> Who scuffles, cuffs, and justles all he meets,
> But if his King or country claim his aid,
> The rakehell villain shrinks and hides his head.
>
> (52-57)

Again, we see Rochester trading on conventions of sexual discourse that are found in Petronius and Ovid. Threatened with a razor by Encolpius, the cause of his shame "shrank, too scared to watch."[22]

Rochester's soldier demonstrates a misplaced heroism, bold in his attack on whores, a coward in the presence of "great Love":

> Ev'n so thy brutal valor is displayed
> Breaks every stew, does each small whore invade,

But when great Love the onset does command,
Base recreant to thy prince, thou dar'st not stand.

(58-61)

That which is recreant to the prince is also recreant to a principle, and perhaps the image was chosen to suggest the common origin of the two words. Throughout the passage (46-61) we see the ethical hedonist at work and perceive a distinction being drawn between qualities of pleasure. The soldier who is "true to lewdness, so untrue to love," who betrays the command of "great Love," has failed to distinguish between better and worse, higher and lower. The concept of love, whatever it may mean precisely for Rochester, is clearly a norm against which choices of action are measured. Without abandoning the pleasure principle, Rochester conveys the idea that sensuality *per se* is somehow inadequate.

The power of sexual impulses, of unbounded desires, is affirmed in the dark irony of the last lines (62-72), where the phallus again becomes object rather than person, as Rochester addresses the "Worst part of me," Ovid's "pars pessima nostri." The venomous comparison with hogs indicates that Rochester does not accept sexual gratification as a value in itself:

> Worst part of me, and henceforth hated most,
> Through all the town a common fucking post,
> On whom each whore relieves her tingling cunt
> As hogs on gates do rub themselves and grunt.

(62-65)

There is a hint of disclaimer in the "common fucking post," as if the speaker disclaims responsibility. It is possible to see an ambiguous attitude toward nature, a suggestion that, in sexual matters at least, one is inevitably a victim. In the active role, the dart of love is directed by nature (l. 39); in the passive, the instrument becomes a "common fucking post," toward which nature impels the swinish whores. In a world of mechanical appetite, he who has used others as objects becomes an object in turn.

The irony of the closing anathema is that the curse delivered on a part of the body affects the whole:

> Mayst thou to ravenous chancres be a prey,
> Or in consuming weepings waste away;
> May strangury and stone thy days attend;
> May'st thou ne'er piss, who didst refuse to spend
> When all my joys did on false thee depend.
>   And may ten thousand abler pricks agree
>   To do the wronged Corinna right for thee.

(66-72)

Rochester's lover does not seek restoration but emasculation. Although there is some justice in Ronald Berman's verdict that "In Rochester there is the same union between sexuality and destruction so much in evidence in De Sade,"[23] it must be remembered that De Sade never turns that destruction on himself. In "The Imperfect Enjoyment"

at least, there is more of the hair shirt, the plucking of the eye that offends, which is foreign to De Sade's pornography, or to any pornography for that matter.

On the aesthetic criteria here advanced, the complexities of **"The Imperfect Enjoyment"** acquit the poem of pornographic purpose or effect. Yet the charge of obscenity remains substantial, if we mean by obscenity not, as Judge Woolsey defined it in his famous *Ulysses* decision, "tending to stir the sex impulses or to lead to sexually impure and lustful thoughts,"[24] but the more general context of the offensive, the indecent, the normally hidden elemental activities of man and the "forbidden" words that apply to them.

Rochester himself, in the **"Allusion to Horace,"** speaks of "songs and verses mannerly obscene, / That can stir nature up by springs unseen, / And without forcing blushes, warm the Queen." The word "mannerly" is difficult to interpret, since it could designate either manners or morals. Although the context suggests some kind of polite prurience, a broader principle than social propriety is needed to encompass Rochester's use of the obscene. Of assistance are two comments, one by Rochester and another by his friend and defender, Robert Wolseley.

In a letter to Henry Savile, Rochester speaks of "The Lowsiness of Affairs in this place . . . (forgive the unmannerly Phrase! Expressions must descend to the Nature of Things express'd)."[25] From this we can infer that he distinguished between polite language and expressive language at a realistic level. In Wolseley's preface to Rochester's version of **Valentinian,** he declares that all he is "oblig'd to defend, is the *Wit* of my *Lord Rochester's* obscene Writings, not the *Manners*; for even Wit it self, as it may be sometimes unseasonable and impertinent, so at other times it may be also libertine, unjust, ungrateful, and every way immoral, yet still 'tis Wit."[26] Lashing out at the Earl of Mulgrave's condemnation of Rochester for "Bawdry barefac'd, that poor pretence to Wit," Wolseley retorts that "it never yet came into any man's Head who pretended to be a Critick, except this *Essayer's,* that the Wit of a Poet was to be measur'd by the worth of his Subject, and that when this was bad, that must be so too: the manner of treating his Subject has been hitherto thought the true Test, for as an ill Poet will depresse and disgrace the highest, so a good one will raise and dignifie the lowest."[27] Rochester holds that the language communicates the quality of the thing or experience; Wolseley, that the manner not the subject (i.e., *how* rather than *what*) determines literary worth. Both of these views are of a piece with the twentieth-century argument of Kaplan in "Obscenity as an Esthetic Category": "In short, obscenity, like art itself, is not a matter of referential, but of expressive meanings. What is relevant is not subject, but substance; not an isolable message, but an embodied content."[28] The importance of literary context was equally recognized by Judge Woolsey in the judgment of *Ulysses*: "In many places it seems to me to be disgusting, but although it contains, as I have mentioned above, many words usually considered dirty, I have not found anything that I consider to be dirt for dirt's sake. Each word of the book contributes like a bit of mosaic to the detail of the picture which Joyce is seeking to construct for his readers."[29]

Thus, if the obscenity of **"The Imperfect Enjoyment"** is set in place, it becomes a rhetoric of realism typical of satire. As Northrop Frye has observed, "genius seems to have led practically every great satirist to become what the world calls obscene."[30] The sexual words, which stay close to their referents, enforce an immediacy of experience not otherwise possible.[31] They make the capsule drama come alive as no euphemisms or circumlocutions could. In addition, if we recall Rochester's strictures against meaningless abstractions in the poems *Upon Nothing* and *A Satyr against Mankind* we can see how the language of sexuality could function as apposite symbols of the only sources of knowledge, the senses. When Mulgrave in his "An Essay Upon Poetry" criticized Rochester for "obscene words, too gross to move desire," he was in one sense right, but for the wrong reason. They fail to move desire not because they are too gross but because they are integral parts of a seriocomic mosaic and an index to the poet's own reality.

Judgment in this matter is also affected, we must remember, by versification, by the skillful use of the couplet. Although William Piper finds in Rochester's couplets a prevailing stiffness that is due to his "emphasis on point and wit,"[32] the movement of the discourse in **"The Imperfect Enjoyment"** is notable for a varied pace that corresponds with meaning. For example, in the love-play of lines 7-10, enjambement, with the first three verses ending on verbs, carries the sense quickly forward, consonant with "lightning," "swift orders," and the thunderbolt. The succeeding closed couplet is a pause, in keeping with "Hangs hovering." And the climax, which is at once an anti-climax, of verses 13-16, again picks up speed, accompanied by an alliteration of the liquid "l" to echo meaning. A second illustration is the beginning of what I have called the mock-encomium (37-45): the single sentence that proceeds hurriedly with the described violence and drags to a slow close in "Shrunk up and sapless like a withered flower," a line that defies rapid reading aloud. This pattern is typical of the poem. While the technique tends to bring obscene words into focus, it invests them at the same time with significance beyond the uses of perversity. In other words, the metrical ordering also operates against the impression of "dirt for dirt's sake."

Nor is the usually hidden subject matter of *ejaculatio praecox* without a redeeming level of literary allusion. Through the parallels with Ovid and Petronius, we have already seen that impotence and attention to the phallus are not original with Rochester. If the context is extended further to the seventeenth-century literary scene, we gain access to another measure of complexity. At least five French and five Restoration "imperfect enjoyment poems" (including Rochester's) appeared between 1577 and 1682,[33] and they represent irreverent burlesque of the artificial and over-idealized love poetry of their immediate predecessors.

Imperfect enjoyment poems were a naturalistic correction of attitudes expressed in the numerous "against fruition poems" which followed a Petrarchan, courtly-love tradition of the superiority of the ideal over the actual. Paradoxically, although imperfect enjoyment poems reject the contemplation of love for the physical act, they tend to affirm that, in fact, the actual is less than satisfactory.

Imbedded in Rochester's version, on the surface a depiction of a less-than-satisfactory libertine life, is a psychological and ethical mandate for a male-female relationship. In this connection, it is important to keep in mind that though pleasure is the *summum bonum* for Rochester, he constantly examines through his poetry the values by which pleasure is to be measured. Unlike De Sade, he does not equate it with the infliction of pain or with power. If the first element of morality, as Berman holds, can be found in Rochester's passionate self-consciousness,[34] part of that self-consciousness is an awareness of the needs of others. How the human predicament subverts the fulfillment of those needs, rather than an obsession with the failure of the senses, is the preoccupation of **"The Imperfect Enjoyment."**

The theme emerges through the two controlling logical propositions in the poem: in a situation where "great Love" is present, the lover is inadequate; in a situation where feeling or concern for the gratification of the sex object was not present, the lover experienced unlimited sexual power. With the speaker, we are impelled to consider what accounts for the difference. The answer is at once psychological and ethical.

The most apparent difference between the lover's past prowess and present impotence is his emotional involvement. The narrator tells us of his shame and rage; he is "trembling, confused, despairing." The emotional complication is not unmixed with an ego-drive for power and with male pride. As Theodor Reik has observed, many men—notably the Don Juan type—are in sex concerned only with victory, and "conquest becomes a matter of personal prestige."[35] But events in **"The Imperfect Enjoyment"** suggest a psychological experience beyond frustration at the failure of sexual power. In spite of the sensuality in the opening scene, and the coarse joke at the end, the narrator conveys affection and tenderness toward the disappointed mistress. She smiles, she chides, she has a fair hand, she is his "great Love," and she is the "wronged Corinna." That he wishes to show his "wished obedience" implies a concern beyond the satisfaction of lust.

In the account of past triumphs, debased sexual objects are dominant. The speaker's loathing for the hog-like whores is patent. And the insufficiency of sexual power alone is poetically reinforced by the insistence on unrefined language of sex-tingling cunt, oyster-cinder-beggar-common whore, fucking post; and by diminishing physical references—rub, grunt, ravenous chancres, consuming weepings, and the like. By contrast, when the fair mistress is present, the language of sex, though it still might be thought unrefined by some, is not conjoined with images that debase her.

Thus, one kind of sexual relationship is clearly attacked and another not. That which is not invokes an ideal of mutual consideration and equality, an ideal that Rochester also advances in a number of other poems, such as **"The Advice," "A Song of a Young Lady to Her Ancient Lover," "The Fall,"** and the short lyric, **"Leave this gaudy gilded stage."** In this last we find:

> To love's theater, the bed,
> Youth and beauty fly together,
> And act so well it may be said
> The laurel there was due to either.
> 'Twixt strifes of love and war, the difference lies in this:
> When neither overcomes, love's triumph greater is.[36]

However hedonistic the goal, there is a right way and a wrong way. In **"The Imperfect Enjoyment"** the implied criterion of right exceeds the mutual physical pleasures of the bed. The speaker, who has "wronged" Corinna, acknowledges an obligation beyond the mere satisfaction of self and an obligation to the needs and desires of another. Such a concern is surely an ethical statement, transcending any disagreement about sexual mores.

What Rochester seeks to express at gut-level through obscenity and at the intellectual level of wit in **"The Imperfect Enjoyment"** is his version of the shadow which falls, as T. S. Eliot writes, "Between the potency / And the existence." That shadow is brightened by what seems to me a sound depiction of human psychology and a clear ethical command for a relationship in which sex is necessary but not sufficient. This is Rochester as lover rather than rake, and poet rather than pornographer.

Notes

1. Arthur Bryant, *Samuel Pepys: The Years of Peril* (New York, 1935), p. 340.

2. Bryant, p. 340.

3. John Wilmot, *Poems by John Wilmot, Earl of Rochester,* ed. Vivian de Sola Pinto, 2nd ed. (Cambridge, Mass., 1964), p. xlix.

4. Havelock Ellis, "The Revaluation of Obscenity" in *More Essays of Love and Virtue* (Garden City, N. Y., 1931), p. 100.

5. Abraham Kaplan, "Obscenity as an Esthetic Category," *Law and Contemporary Problems,* 20 (1955), 548.

6. Kaplan, p. 548.

7. Kaplan, p. 548.

8. Morse Peckham, *Art and Pornography: An Experiment in Explanation* (New York, 1969), p. 47.

9. Peckham, pp. 60-61.

10. David Foxon, *Libertine Literature in England: 1660-1745* (New Hyde Park, N. Y., 1965), p. 46.

11. Herbert Gold, "The End of Pornography," *SR,* October 31, 1970, p. 26.

12. Gold, p. 64.

13. Steven Marcus, *The Other Victorians: A Study of Sexuality and Pornography in Mid-Nineteenth-Century England* (New York, 1966), p. 279.

14. Marcus, p. 274.

15. Marcus, pp. 277, 273.

16. Eberhard and Phyllis Kronhausen, *Pornography and the Law: The Psychology of Erotic Realism and Pornography* (New York, 1959), p. 265.

17. *The Works of the Earls of Rochester, Roscommon, Dorset, The Duke of Devonshire, Etc.* (London, 1721), I, 112. John Wardroper in *Love and Drollery* (New York, 1969) notes that the verse, applied to more than one Restoration courtesan, is a translation of an epigram found circulating in Madrid in 1622 (p. 296).

18. John Wilmot, *Rochester's "Poems on Several Occasions,"* ed. James Thorpe (Princeton, 1950), p. 56.

19. John Wilmot, *The Complete Poems of John Wilmot, Earl of Rochester,* ed. David M. Vieth (New Haven, 1968), p. 37. End punctuation here and elsewhere modified as necessary.

20. *Works of the Earls,* I, 94.

21. Petronius, *The Satyricon,* tr. William Arrowsmith (Ann Arbor, 1962), p. 159.

22. Petronius, p. 163.

23. Ronald Berman, "Rochester and the Defeat of the Senses," *Kenyon Review,* 26 (1964), 355.

24. John M. Woolsey, "The Monumental Decision of the United States District Court Rendered December 6, 1933, by Hon. John M. Woolsey Lifting the Ban on 'Ulysses.'" in James Joyce, *Ulysses* (New York, 1934), p. xiii.

25. John Harold Wilson, ed., *The Rochester-Savile Letters: 1671-1680* (Columbus, 1941), p. 73.

26. Robert Wolseley, "Preface to *Valetinian, A Tragedy, As 'Tis Alter'd by the Late Earl of Rochester (1685),"* in *Critical Essays of the Seventeenth Century,* ed. J. E. Spingarn (Oxford, 1909), III, 24.

27. Wolseley, ed. Spingarn, III, 15-16. Dustin Griffin in *Satires Against Man: The Poems of Rochester* (Berkeley, 1973) also calls attention to this defense and argues that Rochester's obscenity may have an aesthetic or moral purpose (pp. 83-86).

28. Kaplan, 551.

29. Woolsey, p. xii.

30. Northrop Frye, *Anatomy of Criticism: Four Essays* (New York, 1968), p. 235.

31. Marcus says that forbidden words "present them-selves to us as acts" because they have undergone the least evolution in speech (p. 280).

32. William Bowman Piper, *The Heroic Couplet* (Cleveland, 1969), p. 319.

33. Richard Quaintance, "French Sources of the Restoration 'Imperfect Enjoyment' Poem," *PQ*, 42 (1963), 190. The theme also appears in folk poetry. In Frederick J. Furnivall's *Loose and Humorous Songs: From Bishop Percy's Folio Manuscript* (Hatboro, Penn., 1963) the song "Walking in a Meadow gren" tells of a lover who suffers premature ejaculation (pp. 3-5), and a country swain in "A Creature for Feature" (pp. 53-54) laments:

> But woe mee, & woe mee! alas, I cold not raise!
> itt wold not, nor cold not, doe all I cold to please.
> his ink was run, his pen was done.

Percy's folio manuscript is dated around 1660.

34. Berman, 356.

35. Theodor Reik, *Psychology of Sexual Relations* (New York, 1945), p. 161.

36. Vieth, p. 85, ll. 5-10.

K. E. Robinson (essay date 1979)

SOURCE: Robinson, K. E. "Rochester's Dilemma." *Durham University Journal* 40 (June, 1979): 223–31.

[*In the essay below, Robinson discusses the oppositions in Rochester's poetry, noting, for example, that* A Satire Against Mankind *starts out advocating appetitive values and ends by espousing more traditional ideas, and that* Upon Nothing *can be seen as a struggle between reason and intuition.*]

Dr. Johnson once remarked to Topham Beauclerk (great-grandson of Charles II and Nell Gwynne): 'Thy body is all vice, and thy mind all virtue'.[1] He might equally well have been talking of that well-known associate of Beauclerk's great-grandfather, John Wilmot, Earl of Rochester, companion, yet sternly moral critic of Charles II. There is in Rochester an extraordinary opposition of venal life-style and moral capacity. The opposition is more than merely historically or psychologically compelling: if we dig down to its intellectual foundations we shall reveal an ambivalence of pressing modernity. For Rochester's mature life constitutes an attempt to cope with the metaphysical 'weightlessness' which is so much a part of the consciousness of post-Nietzschean man. It is the intention of this paper to explore something of this attempt.

It is not surprising that William Empson should have been drawn to Rochester:[2] the ambivalence we are to explore manifests itself in the sort of polar oppositions so dear to Empson's heart. We may begin with a question of values.

In the *Satyr against Mankind* Rochester is concerned with two quite different ways of valuing. On the one hand he theorizes upon nominalistic and appetitive values derived from sense (values clearly inspired by Hobbes):[3] on the other he practises more traditional and universal values in the second, pragmatic part of the poem (from line 112 onwards).[4] These traditional values, which are implicit in such terms as 'basest', 'inhumanly' and 'wantoness', are more closely related to the values of the 'formal band and beard' than to those of Hobbes or the Hobbists. We can see this antithetical juxtaposition at work when Rochester defines a framework relative to which he can judge man (a framework consonant with appetitive values),

> Those creatures are the wisest who attain,
> By surest means, the ends at which they aim.

(l.117)

only to leave it behind to judge the ends in absolute terms. Hobbes had ruled that in a commonwealth man's private appetite ought to be subserved to the interests of the state and that his actions could be judged good or bad in so far as he observed, or failed to observe, this social obligation.[5] For Hobbes, 'moral rules were rules found out by reason for avoiding social calamity'.[6] Conversely, Rochester's judgments go beyond the social to strike deep at man's ethical capacity. When Rochester condemns the man who 'Inhumanly his fellow's life betrays', it is the fact of betrayal itself, not the social significance of the betrayal, that irks him. This clash between the nominalistic and appetitive and the universal is summed up in a line from the fragment **'What vain, unnecessary things are men!'**: 'Things must go on in their lewd natural way' (l. 32), here taken slightly out of context but not so as to distort it in any essentials. It appears that Rochester accepted the materialist account of man's reaction to his world, with all its implications of appetitive action, as rationally just and therefore natural yet found that reaction reprehensible, lewd. He was heartily opposed to the *a priori* and the artificial,[7] the 'Affected rules of honor' (**'What cruel pains Corinna takes'**, l.12), and, in the absence of a motivating *telos*, he found it difficult to transmute his intuitive allegiance to traditional values into action which seemed natural, uncertain whether those intuitions pointed to indoctrination or truth. The **'Satyr'** dramatizes a profound epistemological and ethical dilemma which underlies the whole of Rochester's life and thought, a dilemma resolved only on his deathbed. He was in the paradoxical position of judging actions committed with rational integrity to be immoral, unable (except at the last) to wrench his support away from the abortive Hobbism which seems to have been close to the root of his perplexity.

Writing against the background of renewed interest in the famous Hobbes/Bramhall debate,[8] Rochester was acutely aware of the concomitant polarity of free-will and determinism. Briefly, Bramhall had objected that Hobbes's notion that 'such a liberty as is free from necessity, is not to be found in the will either of men or beasts'[9] robbed man of his birthright of free-will because it rendered all his actions *extrinsically* caused. Bramhall, in line with traditional thought, believed that in order to be free a man's actions should be *intrinsically* caused. This distinction between intrinsic and extrinsic causation is analogous to that between universal and nominalistic values: both spring out of a difference between the received and the new sense of right reason, as defined within the **'Satyr'**. Just as Rochester was split between *ad hoc* and absolute values, he was possessed by anxieties about his freedom. Cudworth held that praising or blaming a man presupposed his freedom,[10] but, as we have seen, Rochester's assault on the baseness of his world is juxtaposed with a theoretic justification of a hard determinist view of experience. Hobbes had discounted the possibility of a separate faculty called the will (demoting the will to the last stage in the process of deliberation which precedes an action), just as he had dismissed the notion that man possessed a soul or spirit—the spirit was for him none other than the vital motion.[11] At the beginning of the **'Satyr'** Rochester, too, appears to expropriate intrinsic volition, but his conception of the 'strange prodigious creature, man' entails a more complex view:

> Were I (who to my cost already am
> One of those strange, prodigious creatures, man)
> A spirit free to choose, for my own share,
> What case of flesh and blood I pleased to wear,
> I'd be a dog, a monkey, or a bear,
> Or anything but that vain animal
> Who is so proud of being rational.

These lines lament man's estate, in large part because of his lack of freedom. Traditionally his freedom had to do with his possession of a spirit, but here that notion of spirit is circumscribed with difficulties. Even if this spirit were free to choose, it ironically would not be free to remain a spirit: it would have to choose a host and that host could not be a beast, for to become a beast would involve self-destruction by and of an entity which is by its very nature indestructible. The optation is shot through with hopelessness: it must choose man. At the back of Rochester's worries about the freedom which this hypothetical spirit might be said to have lies the materialist conviction that 'nothing can change itself, or act upon itself, or determine its own action. Since the same thing cannot be both agent and patient at once'.[12] He would prefer to be a beast because the beast is at least experientially free. Relative to man the beast was traditionally conceived of as being unfree—a slave to the senses—but the force of the elevation of beasts above men here is to stress that man is not only subject to the same extrinsic causation but, unlike the beast, must live with a consciousness of his position. In other words, Rochester subverts man's vain pretensions to superiority, whether they be on the basis of spirituality, rationality, or both. Reason for Rochester, the reason of the new philosophy as much as the scholastic—he is careful not to qualify it in his opening lines—is an *ignis fatuus*: it removes man from the simple amorality and irrational felicity of animal existence into areas of metaphysical angst which it can do little to resolve.[13] The quest for meaning which it initiates in man

seems to him to be in vain. Yet despite the materialist basis of Rochester's dismay, he is careful not to deny the existence of the spirit within man: nor does he assert it. The ambiguous syntax of the opening lines preserves the possibility on man's possessing a spirit, a possibility which derives from those intuitions of freedom and absolute value which run counter to his reasoning. His angst is not simply nihilistic: alongside his consciousness of extrinsic causation works an ambition to be free. Later in the **'Satyr'** the same polarity exerts itself when Rochester dashes all man's virtues with the charge that they are extrinsically caused by 'fear, to make himself secure' (l. 156) only to posit an optimum man who is implicitly an embodiment of intrinsic volition, by reference to whom he makes his judgments.

It may seem that a solution for this dilemma is implied in the apparent marriage of the concept of will to appetitive action, but the solution is merely propositional. The **"Satyr"** itself records its irrelevance in practice:

> Thus, whilst against false reasoning I inveigh,
> I own right reason, which I would obey:
> That reason which distinguishes by sense
> And gives us rules of good and ill from thence,
> That bounds desires with a reforming will
> To keep 'em more in vigor, not to kill.
> . . . . .
> Thus I think reason righted, but for man,
> I'll ne'er recant; defend him if you can.
> For all his pride and his philosophy,
> 'Tis evident beasts are, in their degree,
> As wise at least, and better far than he.

(l. 98)

The gap between the propositional ideal and the actual is focused in the phrase 'reforming will'.[14] It seems to suggest that man can so govern his appetites with a conscious will that he will never suffer satiety, but, both traditionally and according to the Hobbesian scheme, man committed to appetitive values is in a state of subjection. The normal ethical sense of the phrase represents, in context, an impossible ideal whilst the technical reference to the forming and reforming process of deliberation (which Hobbes had substituted for the conscious will)[15] represents the actual. The disparity is one between being free to pursue a chosen course and not being thus free. Underlying the contrast between open and restrictive reactions to the appetites, designed to recommend the newly defined 'right reason' at the expense of the old, there is a recognition that on the materialist account it is only by chance that the appetites are not satiated. The mechanistic conception of man allows him no conscious part in governing, or attempting to govern, the outcome, or the last stage, of deliberation. Ironically, the man who 'kills' his appetite seems to be more free.

It is significant that both the adversary and the paradigm of virtue in the **'Satyr'** represent a belief in transcendental truth. Rochester's theoretic rejection of universal values and intrinsic choice is inseparable from a thoroughgoing doubt about the existence of any such truth. Yet it is only a doubt. Like Koestler's Rubashov he cannot prevent the 'grammatical fiction', the internal voice, from breaking through the facade of contingent logic.[16] His quite unmaterialistic judgments of himself and his fellow man lead inevitably to worries about judgment in the hereafter. His need for, and perhaps vestigially intuitive sense of, a *telos* is best seen in **'After death nothing is'**. At first glance Rochester's version of Seneca might appear to be a straightforward statement of unbelief, but its tone suggests that it is the utterance of a man deeply anxious about the nature of finite existence. The concluding lines have the ring of someone trying to convince himself as much as his addressee: they protest too much:

> For Hell and the foul fiend that rules
> God's everlasting fiery jails
> (Devised by rogues, dreaded by fools),
> With his grim, grisly dog that keeps the door,
>   Are senseless stories, idle tales,
>   Dreams, whimseys, and no more.

> (l. 13)

The passion of Rochester's outburst points to uncertainty about the rational, nihilistic tenets of the poem. The closeness of the language of dismissal to Hobbes's irritable exposé of false reasonings serves to underline the failure of the materialist philosophy to meet Rochester's intuitive needs. The uncertainty leads to an inconsistency. Rochester both heaps scorn on 'slavish souls' who by subscribing to the concept of the soul—and to the conception of man as quintessentially soul—subjugate themselves to a worrying eschatology and appears to allow the idea of the soul some meaning, although he claims it to be confounded at death. The inconsistency is closely related to the ambivalent attitude towards the spirit at the opening of the **'Satyr.'** A soul by its very nature would not be so confounded, nor could a mechanistic conception of man strictly speaking accommodate the soul. The illogicality (which Rochester leaves unresolved) is symptomatic of his profound incertitude.

There is a hint of the same puzzlement in the single word 'kept' in

> Dead, we become the lumber of the world,
> And to that mass of matter shall be swept
> Where things destroyed with things unborn are kept.

It cannot contain the simple neutrality which Rochester the materialist wishes to impose upon it; instead it looks beyond the bounds of the mechanical laws governing finite existence towards a purposive, directing force. We meet this same force in **Upon Nothing.** Beneath the passing ridicule of scholasts, statesmen and monarchs lies a more profound concern with the nature of things. Committed to the idea that life is nothing and leads to nothing after death, Rochester attempts to describe the genesis of human life only to find that his cause and effect thinking requires a first cause. 'Nothing' is personified, made an active force which begets 'something', a term which loosely describes a positive, purposive energy. The genealogy is

an inversion of the received idea of creation in which God, the positive, creates, amongst other things, the negative, nihilistic force of evil imaged in Satan. In the traditional account man battles against the negative so as to be reunited with his creator; in Rochester's version meaningful life (or intimation of it) is the rebellious force which must be suffered before reimmersion in nothingness. But it is in the nature of this sense of meaning to call into question the nihilistic conception of death. It is this 'something,' the need for a teleology, with which Rochester, a committed materialist, finds it difficult to cope. The notion that 'something' is *begotten* places Rochester's difficulties within the context of the Christian account of the incomprehensible Trinity. Whereas the Christian can make a virtue out of incomprehensibility (in much the same way that Wittgenstein can make a virtue out of nonsensicality in his *Lecture on Ethics*),[17] Rochester can only find it intensely disorienting. He tries to explain the world beyond experience in terms of the physical world so that the worryingly unknown and formally unknowable is described as *some thing,* but neither it nor its attendant values are so easily dismissed. Unlike material things 'something' does not return to nothingness: it is as everlasting as the 'Great Negative' itself. Moreover, Rochester seems to expect 'something' (at least he doesn't discount the possibility) to affect human life positively:

> But Nothing, why does Something still permit
> That sacred monarchs should in council sit
> With persons highly thought at best for nothing fit
> . . . ?

> (l. 37)

Unable to synthesize logic and intuition, Rochester can trust neither at the expense of the other.

Faced with this dichotomy Rochester cast around for a philosophy which might resolve it. It is easy to see why he should have become interested in Lucretius who held it as a fundamental principle that '*Nothing can ever be created by divine power out of nothing*'.[18] He looked carefully at the Lucretian gods whom he interpreted as being uninterested in, and beyond, human affairs:

> The gods, by right of reason must possess
> An everlasting age of perfect peace;
> Far off removed from us and our affairs;
> Neither approached by dangers, or by cares;
> Rich in themselves, to whom we cannot add;
> Not pleased by good deeds, nor provoked by bad.

> (l. 1)

but his translation, alongside these lines, of the invocation to Venus at the opening of *De Rerum Natura* presents an ambiguity essential to his interpretation. The invocation presupposes at least some hope for success. The ambiguity is similar to that generated by the clash of materialist reason and intuitive conviction in **Upon Nothing.** The Lucretian *via media* of gods whose existence did not help one iota to explain the genesis of the universe and who remained unconcerned in, or for, human life, was no solution for his metaphysical difficulties. Lucretius's uncomplicated materialism permitted him to deal easily with nothingness: '*Nature resolves everything into its component atoms and never reduces anything to nothing*'.[19] He is unperturbed by his apparent inability to explain creation. It is an index of Rochester's divergence from the Lucretian and materialist that, whilst endorsing the notion that matter is neither *created* nor *destroyed*, he should remain anxious about metaphysical nothingness and contingent problems of creation. Yet Rochester's interest in Lucretius is further testimony of the seriousness of his quest for the truth.

This nonplus, of a man cruelly split between two apparently irreconcilable ways of regarding human experience, is embodied in the less obviously philosophical poetry both directly in purposeful inconsistencies and indirectly in Rochester's doing the *beau monde* in different voices. The poems using personae do not merely employ the persona as a convenient polemic device. Certainly, they are keenly reductive, but the strategy of disguise renders them heuristic, too, not least because Rochester was aware that he was susceptible to many of the things that he attacks. Dr. Johnson ran division on a line from Pope to describe Beauclerk: 'Thy love of folly, and thy scorn of fools'; his alteration applies poignantly to Rochester. Everything he did showed the one, everything he said the other.[20] This is true even of the lampoons on Sheffield. Rochester did not, to be sure, share Sheffield's unintelligent conceit, but he was troubled by an inconstancy and self-interest (both corollaries of his materialism) which are related to the ideas of inconstancy and self-interest which Mulgrave is represented as pressing into his service. But these poems require a separate paper: for the remainder of the present essay I shall examine several poems concerned with love and/or sexual relations in the light of Rochester's general predicament.

Artemisia writes of love as 'That cordial drop heaven in our cup has thrown / To make the nauseous draught of life go down' (l. 44). Rochester longed for a stability based on human relationships, and the experience of love appears to have offered a glimpse of such stability. In '**Absent from thee I languish still**' the lady is represented as Rochester's secular heaven, and like heaven she offers the fixed and everlasting, the constant in contrast to the mutability of mortal life in general and the inconstancy which was so much a *modus vivendi* of courtly society, in particular. No matter how emotionally vibrant the stability caught sight of, it is, however, *only* glimpsed. Rochester is torn from it by his nominalistic commitment, by that rational integrity which seemed to him simultaneously necessary and fantastic, reasonable yet wrong, and, most ironically, in some way in contravention of the realities before him. The language of contemporary complaisance is here fired with fresh significance. It was customary in contemporary painting to embellish the portrait of the most licentious beauty with iconographic virtue,[21] but when Rochester writes of a 'safe bosom . . . Where love and peace and truth does flow' (l. 11) he is describing, within the context of the poem, a sincere, if fleeting, experience of permanence. Equally, the torments and languishings are far from that mixture of appeasement and courtesy with which it was customary to invest in the carnal services of a lady of whom one had for the moment tired. Rochester is the 'straying fool' (l. 3): cast adrift from the traditional teleology and the stable human relationships supposed to be based upon it, yet painfully in concert with it in certain important respects and without a substitute belief, his lot was to wander in ways which simultaneously removed him further from, yet strengthened his need for, traditional values. He came to fear that 'the readiest way to Hell' might be by Rochester.

It is in the nature of Rochester's thought that he should be committed to action according to immediate sensory impulse. The idea of inconstancy ought not, strictly speaking, to have carried any weight with him; as Strephon puts it:

> Since 'tis nature's law to change,
> Constancy alone is strange.
>
> ('A Dialogue between Strephon and Daphne', l. 31)

yet in '**Absent from thee**' he is much exercised by the fear and charge of inconstancy. In '**Love and Life**' where the materialist rejection of constancy is most explicitly stated, there is no celebration of a sensualist present but an elegiac resignation to mutability:

> Then talk not of inconstancy,
>   False hearts, and broken vows:
> If I, by miracle, can be
> This livelong minute true to thee,
>   'Tis all that heaven allows.
>
>   (l. 11)

The desire for stability here (as in '**The Mistress**') is balanced by Rochester's suggestion that all the forms of stability to which the lines reach out are either delusive, or offer no consolation. He exploits the inherent contradiction in the idea of being true for a minute; and the perfect heaven, almost smuggled into the argument as a transcendental point of stability, is shown (or at least implied) to be derived by a shaky logic from the imperfect world. Nor does he allow it to be a solution to conceive of heaven as synonymous with the Lucretian gods or as the province of a god who set the world ticking and left it to function according to its immutable mechanical laws; for such a conception only engenders resentment that the Lucretian gods are inactive or that the laws are limiting, that, in short, inconstancy is 'all that heaven allows'.

Despite his obedience to the present appetite, Rochester could enjoy little sensual consolation for his reduced moral stature. He had to live with the pressing awareness that even in the most rudimentary aspects of physical life man could lay little claim to autonomy. It was not simply that his moral self-repulsion led him to view himself as passion's slave; he was more fundamentally anxious about man's capacity for free action. Pleasure became a debt. In **'The Fall'** he focuses his worries upon sexual relations. He posits an ideal against which he can contrast the actual so as to stress the hard determinism which governs men's actions:

> Naked beneath cool shades they lay;
>   Enjoyment waited on desire;
> Each member did their wills obey,
>   Nor could a wish set pleasure higher.
>
> But we, poor slaves to hope and fear,
>   Are never of our joys secure;
> They lessen still as they draw near,
>   And none but dull delights endure.
>
> (l. 5)

The very fact that Rochester regards life as in some way *un*ideal points to aspirations to something beyond his experience, an unwillingness simply to accept life as determined by mechanical laws. It is clear that he would have liked to free pleasure as Lucretius had sought to do. As Lucretius puts it, 'nature is clamouring for two things only, a body free from pain, a mind released from worry and fear for the enjoyment of pleasurable sensations'.[22] But here again Lucretius's example provided no solace. The release was impossible for Rochester because he could neither give a mechanistic theory of behaviour unequivocal support nor dismiss his awareness of absolute values as superstitious. As much as he wished to free the passions from the unnatural restrictions and superstitions of old-fashioned rationalism, he had first to deal with his anxieties about the freedom with which man might be said to engage in pleasure. His substitution of the Hobbesian deliberation, or alternate succession of appetite and fear, for the conscious will made man seem a 'poor slave to hope and fear'; and his distress at the substitution both prejudiced his chances of simple hedonistic enjoyment and denied him the Lucretian *ataraxia*. He liberates the 'pleasures' from superstition only to find them unfree, and his yearning for their freedom inseparable from a yearning for some of the things he had regarded as superstitious. All Rochester has is the unstable, externally determined present in which the frailer part remains frail in spite of its revaluation in the sensualist outlook. The traditional view of the mind as dominant over the body offers no escape: it is, he suggests, a convenient rationalization of man's infirmities, simply dependent upon the lovers' willingness to collude:

> Then, Chloris, while I duly pay
>   The nobler tribute of my heart.
> Be not you so severe to say
>   You love me for the frailer part.
>
> (l. 13)

Rochester's adherence to a hard determinism could not, then, pressure his intimations of freedom out of existence any more than Rubashov could rid himself of 'illogical morality'.[23] The contradictory mixture of hope that he might achieve his desires and a conviction that such

achievement could only be coincidental created a burden which further exacerbated his difficulties. This compound of anxiety and self-consciousness is a major part of the subject of **'The Imperfect Enjoyment'** in which it leads to premature emission, represented by Rochester as symptomatic of a more general volitional impotence:

> But I, the most forlorn, lost man alive,
> To show my wished obedience vainly strive:
> I sigh, alas! and kiss, but cannot swive.
> Eager desires confound my first intent,
> Succeeding shame does more success prevent,
> And rage at last confirms me impotent.
>   . . . . .
> Trembling, confused, despairing, limber, dry,
> A wishing, weak, unmoving lump I lie.
>
> (l. 25)

The force of 'vainly', 'shame' and 'confirms' is to stress that in the very act of desiring the anxiety is felt as obstructive. The desirer believes that his desiring is probably in vain, becomes ashamed of his apparent inability to succeed and the result is a failure which seems to confirm both his fears of determinism and the illusion of those intuitions of freedom which led to the attempt to effect his will. Rochester has a keen eye for what is quintessentially disturbing in the mechanistic philosophy. Hobbes had argued that there could be no cause of motion except in a body contiguous and moved; transferred to the human context this meant for Rochester that no amount of desiring could initiate action (or movement) 'for the *cause* of his *will,* is not the *will* itself, but *something* else not in his own disposing'.[24] And yet he could neither help wishing nor finding himself weak in the face of inevitable failure.

In **'A Ramble in St. James's Park'** Rochester describes a release from this nagging self-consciousness, but he represents it as an escape into an irrational state, hedged round with a complex of limitations:

> When, leaning on your faithless breast,
> Wrapped in security and rest,
> Soft kindness all my powers did move,
> And reason lay dissolved in love!
>
> (l. 129)

The single word 'faithless' explodes the celebratory tone and language of the whole passage: the security and rest are deceptive, the lady's 'soft kindness' meretricious— 'kind' and cognate terms always demand caution in Rochester. The 'love', in short, is merely physical. The false security belongs to the momentary demise of reason at the climax of coition when 'In liquid raptures [the lover] dissolves all o'er' (**'The Imperfect Enjoyment'**, l. 13). It is no use leaning on Corinna in the hope of stability for she is as unable to be constant, as unable to act freely. She is 'a passive pot for fools to spend in' (l. 102) and Rochester is one of the fools.

It is important to remember that what Rochester wants is not simply sensual gratification: the opposite of the insignificance suffered in **'A Ramble'** would entail the freedom and stability which he so desired (and glimpsed in **'Absent from thee I languish still'**). Such ambition can only have deepened his unhappiness with his apparent lot, hence the physical loathing (direct and indirect) of both **'The Imperfect Enjoyment'** and **'A Ramble'**. Yet it is significant of his dubiety that the reader is left unsure about the nature of his feelings towards Corinna, despite the loathing. The materialist assumptions involve the reduction of traditional values to physical terms (as they do in Marvell's 'To his Coy Mistress'), but there remains a hankering after those values. It is in the nature of Rochester's dilemma that the something beyond the materialist should be felt rather than definable, like the something of *Upon Nothing*. Just as the *ignis fatuus* reason removes him from simple animal happiness into 'doubt's boundless sea' (**'Satyr'**, l. 19), so it denies him the natural sexual responsiveness of animals in which there seems to be 'something generous' and replaces it with both the awareness that the drives are extrinsically caused and the fear that they are lustful:

> Such natural freedoms are but just:
> There's something generous in mere lust.
>
> 　　　　　　　　　(**'A Ramble'**, l. 97)

This attempt to give some value to the sexual drives is ironically doomed to failure. The 'freedoms' of 'mere lust' are not consistent with freedom; nor is lust consistent with benevolence. Yet the conventional framework of judgement implies reponsibility in man. We must not expect to resolve the inconsistencies here (as elsewhere in Rochester's work): they *are* Rochester's puzzlement. To his cost he was rational.

This account of Rochester derives considerable support from Burnet's *Life*.[25] According to Burnet, Rochester was morally alert even in the midst of his infamous life: 'These Exercises in the course of his life were not always equally pleasant to him; he had often sad Intervals and severe Reflections on them' (pp. 14-15). Although he 'came to bend his Wit, and direct his Studies and Endeavours to support and strengthen these ill Principles both in himself and others' (pp. 15-16), he did not cease to detest his immoral behaviour. 'He would often break forth into such hard Expressions concerning himself as would be indecent for another to repeat' (p. 24). It is clear from Burnet that Rochester felt himself to be torn between antithetical modes of behaviour. Yet, although he could understand the necessity of morality 'both for the Government of the World, and for the preservation of Health, Life and Friendship: . . . he was very much ashamed of his former Practises, rather because he has made himself a Beast, and had brought pain and sickness on his Body, and had suffered such in his Reputation, than from any deep sense of a Supream being, or another State' (p. 35). It was not that he was merely an atheist: he confessed to Burnet 'That he had never known an entire *Atheist,* who fully believed there was no God' (p. 22). Further, he 'could not think the World was made by chance, and the regular Course of Nature seemed to demonstrate the Eternal Power of its

Author'. According to Burnet, his conception of the 'supream Being' was Lucretian: 'He looked on it as a vast Power that Wrought every thing by the necessity of its Nature: and thought that God had none of those Affections of Love or Hatred, which breed perturbation in us, and by consequence he could not see there was to be either reward or punishment' (p. 52). It is only here that the reading offered in this paper differs from Burnet. We have seen that Rochester certainly explored Lucretius, but the poetry seems to strike deeper into his puzzlement than Burnet's account.

This paper began with an assertion of Rochester's modernity: I should like to give a little solidity to that assertion by placing Rochester briefly against the following lines from Arbuthnot's 'Know Yourself':

> By adverse gusts of jarring instincts tossed,
> I rove to one, now to the other coast:
> To bliss unknown my lofty soul aspires,
> My lot unequal to my vast desires.
> As 'mongst the hinds a child of royal birth
> Finds his high pedigree by conscious worth,
> So man, amongst his fellow brutes exposed,
> Sees he's a king, but 'tis a king deposed.
> Pity him, beasts! you by no law confined,
> Are barred from devious paths by being blind;
> Whilst man, through opening views of various ways,
> Confounded, by the aid of knowledge strays;
> Too weak to choose, yet choosing still in haste,
> One moment gives the pleasure and distaste;
> Bilked by past minutes, while the present cloy,
> The flattering future still must give the joy.
> Not happy, but amused upon the road,
> And like you thoughtless of his last abode.
> Whether next sun his being shall restrain
> To endless nothing, happiness, or pain.[26]

This might seem to be remarkably close to Rochester, but it is far removed from him in at least one important respect. Arbuthnot shares the Augustan commitment to commonsensical reason as a tool with which to understand an objective truth. Vice, whether it be a surrender to the passions or an overweening trust in 'the wings of vain philosophy'[27] is a deviation from the reasonable norm. Mathematics provides the paradigm of certainty: 'the mathematics . . . charm the passions, restrain the impetuousity of the imagination, and purge the mind from error and prejudice. Vice is error, confusion and false reasoning; and all truth is more or less opposite to it'.[28] Arbuthnot's account of man's restlessness is, that is, limited by its peculiarly Augustan context of certainty: aberrations are institutionalized just as they are in Pope's *Essay on Man.* But for the Rochester we have been examining there was no certainty,[29] though there was a strong desire for it. He is cast back upon that puzzling about essential contradictions so much a characteristic of metaphysics,[30] and in so puzzling his work achieves a perennial modernity. Arbuthnot, by contrast, is at most historically interesting. This is one aspect of his modernity: the other has to do with a more particular resonance with important thinking closer to our own time, most notably with the Existentialists. Arbuthnot is, in Sartre's terms, in bad faith, like any man who 'unthinkingly accepts his condition, including the moral code which he lives by, as if it were inevitable'.[31] Although Rochester could not disengage himself from the joint pressures of the absolute and contingent logic sufficiently to see the world as an existentialist might, as 'a place in which each by himself has the power to choose his own life from the foundations, to choose what he is to be, because he can choose what to value',[32] he did not hide behind, or use, bad faith to protect himself from the recognition of his responsibility.

Notes

1. *Boswell's Life of Johnson.* ed. George Birkbeck Hill. rev. and enlarged by L.F. Powell, 6 vols. (Oxford, 1934-50), I, 250.

2. See *New Statesman*, 28 November, 1953, pp. 691-2, *Collected Poems* (London, 1955), pp. 54-5, *The Structure of Complex Words* (London, 1951), pp. 163 and 194, and *William Empson: The Man and His Work*, ed. Roma Gill (London, 1974), p. 156.

3. On the relationship between Hobbes and Rochester, see K.E. Robinson, 'Rochester and Hobbes and the Irony of *A Satyr against Reason and Mankind*', *Yearbook of English Studies*, III (1973), 108-19.

4. All subsequent line references and quotations from Rochester's poetry are from *The Complete Poems of John Wilmot, Earl of Rochester*, ed. David Vieth (New Haven, 1968).

5. *Leviathan*, intro. by A. D. Lindsay (London, 1965), p. 372.

6. P. Nowell-Smith, *Ethics* (Harmondsworth, 1954), p. 17.

7. Cf. Reba Wilcoxon, 'Rochester's Philosophical Premises: A Case for Consistency', *ECS*, VIII (1974/ 75), 183-201.

8. For a bibliography of the debate, see Hugh Macdonald and Mary Hargreaves, *Thomas Hobbes: A Bibliography* (London, 1952), passim; and for an account see Samuel I. Mintz, *The Hunting of Leviathan* (Cambridge, 1962), pp. 110-33.

9. *Body, Man, and Citizen*, ed. Richard S. Peters (New York, 1962), p. 161.

10. *A Treatise of Freewill*, printed in *British Moralists 1650-1800*, ed. D. D. Raphael, 2 vols. (Oxford, 1969), I, 120 (#136).

11. *Leviathan*, p. 211.

12. This is Cudworth representing his adversary's case: *op. cit.* I, 122 (#129).

13. For Rochester's radical difference from Hobbes here, see *Body, Man, and Citizen*, p. 106.

14. See Robinson, *op. cit.* p. 113.

15. *Leviathan*, pp. 28-9 and *Body, Man and Citizen*, pp. 269-71.

16. See *Darkness at Noon*, trans. Daphne Hardy (Harmondsworth, 1964), p. 92.

17. *Philosophical Review*, LXXIV (1965), 3-16.

18. *On the Nature of the Universe*, trans. R. E. Latham (Harmondsworth, 1951), p. 31.

19. *Ibid*, p. 33.

20. *Boswell's Life of Johnson*, I, 249-50.

21. See J. Douglas Stewart and Herman W. Liebert, *English Portraits of the Seventeenth and Eighteenth Centuries* (Los Angeles, 1974), pp. 3-43.

22. *On the Nature of the Universe*, p. 60.

23. *Darkness at Noon*, p. 205.

24. *Body, Man, and Citizen*. pp. 131 and 271.

25. *Some Passages of the Life and Death of John, Earl of Rochester* (London, 1680), All subsequent references are by page within the text.

26. *The Life and Works of John Arbuthnot*, ed. George A. Aitken (Oxford, 1892), pp. 437-38.

27. *Ibid*, p. 439.

28. *Ibid*, p. 412. On the dangers surrounding the mathematical paradigm in the later seventeenth century, see A. N. Whitehead, *Science and the Modern World*, Fontana edition (London, 1975), p. 73.

29. Cf. Howard Erskine-Hill. 'Rochester: Augustan or Explorer?' in *Renaissance and Modern Studies Presented to Vivian de Sola Pinto in Celebration of his Seventieth Birthday*, ed. G. R. Hibbard (London, 1966), pp. 51-64, and P. C. Davies, 'Rochester: Augustan or Explorer' *Durham University Journal*. LXI (1969), 59-64.

30. See James Smith. 'On Metaphysical Poetry', *Scrutiny*, II (1933), 222-39.

31. Mary Warnock, *Existentialism* (London, 1970), p. 21.

32. *Ibid*, p. 22.

David Sheehan (essay date 1980)

SOURCE: Sheehan, David "The Ironist in Rochester's *A Letter from Artemisia in the Town to Chloe in the Country*." *Tennessee Studies in Literature* 25 (1980): 72-83.

[*In this essay, Sheehan argues that previous interpretations of* Artemisia and Chloe *failed to pay sufficient attention to the main character's most distinguishing characteristic—her ironic outlook on the world.*]

Critics are presently unanimous in regarding *A Letter from Artemisia in the Town to Chloe in the Country* as perhaps Rochester's masterpiece, but there is no such unanimity about how to interpret the poem's central character, Artemisia herself. Some critics offer an essentially sympathetic assessment of her. Vivian de Sola Pinto describes Artemisia as "a witty lady" capable of making "the wise observation . . . that really excellent fools are produced not by nature but by civilization."[1] Anne Righter describes her as "a kind of seventeenth-century Elizabeth Bennett. Witty and self-aware, both amused and exasperated, delighted and saddened by the follies she describes, she is the sister of Jane Austen's heroines."[2] Other critics regard Artemisia's character as ambiguous. According to Dustin Griffin, "Artemisia, who at times seems to represent some sort of norm, is herself qualified and satirized by herself and the reader."[3] At the poem's conclusion, says Griffin, we are unsure of Artemisia's attitude toward men, the Fine Lady, Corinna, or herself—"Artemisia remains an ambiguous figure."[4] John Sitter also holds this view, with some reservation: Rochester has created "a highly relativistic framework" which prohibits complete acceptance or rejection of the speakers, although Artemisia is less discredited as an observer than are the other characters.[5] David M. Vieth also stresses the ambiguity of the characters in the *Letter*: "Each seems to possess some portion of the truth; yet each is seen through or otherwise qualified by one of the others."[6] Moving toward a "hard" view of Artemisia's character, Professor Vieth argues that she "lacks credibility as a norm because of her logical confusion and hypocrisy . . . [and] her admitted helplessness in competition with women whose total conformity to prevailing fashion becomes a 'mechanical operation of the spirit'"[7] The most extreme "hard" view of Artemisia has been offered by Howard D. Weinbrot, who argues that in the *Letter* Artemisia becomes an active agent of evil in an apocalyptic or revelatory satire. Artemisia begins with "a little stock of virtue," progressively reveals her moral deficiencies, increasingly accepts the base world she describes, until, by her promise at the poem's end to send more letters to Chloe, she has become "an agent for the propagation of infamy," spreading rather than purging evil.[8]

None of these views pays sufficient attention to Artemisia's most distinctive characteristic, her ironic way of viewing the world. Anne Righter has accurately observed that analysis of Rochester's poems is "made difficult by the fact that so much of what happens in Rochester is a matter of tone."[9] This is especially true in *A Letter from Artemisia in the Town to Chloe in the Country*. Artemisia's ironic tone permeates the *Letter*, beginning with her account in the first verse paragraph of the "lofty flights of dangerous poetry."[10] Poets among the men of wit are described metaphorically as "bold adventurers" daring to explore the "stormy, pathless world," only to be "dashed back, and wrecked on the dull shore" (4-10). But this heroic metaphor is in fact ironically undercut, for these "bold adventurers" are petty speculators in praise, "Proudly designing large returns of praise" (8) from "that little stock they had before" (11). Artemisia's irony, tinged with

sarcasm, continues in her mock anxiety about "woman's tottering bark" (12) in contrast to the "stoutest ships" (13) she has already ironically ridiculed. This first verse paragraph concludes with a self-aware. ironic self-evaluation: "When I reflect on this, I straight grow wise, / And my own self thus gravely I advise" (14-15). The verse paragraph that follows reveals the irony of this evaluation. Artemisia is the very opposite of gravely wise. She is perversely defiant of conventions and, "arrant woman" as she is,

> No sooner well convinced writing's a shame,
> That whore is scarce a more reproachful name
> Than poetess—
> Like men that marry, or like maids that woo,
> 'Cause 'tis the very worst thing they can do,
> Pleased with the contradiction and the sin,
> Methinks I stand on thorns till I begin.
>
> (25-31)

Artemisia is explicitly aware of the irony involved in her obeying Chloe's command to write poetry. Throughout the first two verse paragraphs Rochester has presented Artemisia as possessing a thoroughly ironic view of life. If we are to make sense of the crucial next section of the poem, we must fully appreciate the irony in Artemisia's character.

A fundamental question in any interpretation of this poem is whether or not we should take as ironic Artemisia's account of "Love, the most generous passion of the mind" (40-53). In "Rochester and the Defeat of the Senses," Ronald Berman says that the passage describes a "transcendent" love which "could lead to a full experiencing of what was only potential in the human condition. . . . it was at least an ideal."[11] Professor Weinbrot takes this passage as perfectly straightforward, as an "affirmation" of "an ideal against which the current status of love is measured, and from which Artemisia—the only character with even a hope for change—so badly strays."[12] But, again to cite Miss Righter, so much of what happens in Rochester is a matter of tone. This passage makes sense in terms of Artemisia's character and the meaning of the poem as a whole only if it is read ironically. And there are several clues that it should be so read. In *A Rhetoric of Irony*, Wayne Booth discusses five categories of clues to an author's ironic intention, three of which are especially clear in this section of the *Letter*: (1) conflicts of fact within the work, (2) clashes of style, and (3) conflicts between beliefs expressed and those we hold and suspect the author of holding.[13] Artemisia's description of love as "The safe director of unguided youth" seems on its face erroneous, but Rochester has not left the irony at that. As John Sitter points out, within the poem this characterization of love is "singularly undercut by the story of the young Corinna and especially in her later cynical use of the word itself as a lure for the naive Squire."[14] We are also alerted to the presence of irony by the sharp clashes of style within this passage, which begins in a matter-of-fact, conversational way:

> Y' expect at least to hear what loves have passed
> In this lewd town, since you and I met last;

What change has happened of intrigues, and whether
The old ones last, and who and who's together

(32-35)

The style then shifts dramatically. Love is termed "the most generous passion," "softest refuge," a "safe director," "Fraught with kind wishes," and a "cordial drop." The clash of styles is most dramatic when Artemisia, returning to the reductive metaphor of the poem's opening verse paragraph, describes love as the "one only blessing" on which "God might raise / In lands of atheists, subsidies of praise" (46-47). The pecuniary metaphor of God raising subsidies is an ironic reduction of love as the "one only blessing." A still further clue to the ironic intention of this passage is the conflict between the beliefs here expressed and those we suspect the author of holding. Nowhere else in Rochester's poetry do we find such an unequivocally idealistic description of love, and in almost every poem we find it directly contradicted.[15]

Having ironically undermined one false notion of "Love, the most generous passion of the mind," Artemisia proceeds directly to attack those of "Our silly sex" who are "chiefly" responsible for another corrupt conception of love. The problem with these modern lovers is that they "hate restraint, though but from infamy."

They call whatever is not common, nice,
And deaf to nature's rule, or love's advice,
Forsake the pleasure to pursue the vice.
To an exact perfection they have wrought
The action, love; the passion is forgot.

(59-63)

Such lovers are controlled by public fashion, not private taste. Through lack of reasonable restraint, and deafness to nature's rule, they forsake pleasure in their pursuit of vice and reduce love to mechanical action without passion. Although Reba Wilcoxon does not discuss the *Letter* in her essay on "The Rhetoric of Sex in Rochester's Burlesque," she shows that this attack on both the romantic ideal and on those who distort a more realistic attitude toward love into a mindless, excessive, indiscriminate sexual indulgence, is characteristic of Rochester's poetry.[16] Through his character Artemisia, Rochester has offered two views of love which are inadequate, and, with the appearance of the Fine Lady, proceeds to expand this analysis by introducing and ridiculing still another false conception of love.

II

The Fine Lady is perfectly clear about her conception of love. Fools are more desirable lovers than men of wit, because the latter, "with searching wisdom, fatal to their ease" (108), insist on knowing the truth. "They little guess, who at our arts are grieved, / The perfect joy of being well deceived" (114-15). The "kind, easy fool," on the other hand, vainly "doting on himself," is easily kept from knowing the truth about his mistress, and is thus a more manageable, preferable lover. In his unpublished disserta-

tion, "Passion and Reason in Restoration Love Poetry," Richard E. Quaintance, Jr. has shown that the Fine Lady's praise of fools is part of a clearly discernible anti-rationalistic tradition in seventeenth-century love poetry, extending from poems by Raleigh, Suckling, Carew, Cowley, and many others to Rochester's Fine Lady and beyond. According to Quaintance, "the disillusioned attitude that the intellect could only obstruct courtship and destroy love never . . . enjoyed such widespread and conspicuous popularity" as it did during the Restoration.[17] This attitude was part of the larger seventeenth-century distrust of reason, which found expression not only in libertine writing, but also in theological and philosophical debates about the limits of man's reason. As applied to the subject of love, this anti-rationalism took the form of morophilia, or praise of folly, neatly expressed as late as 1692 in a "Song" by Thomas Cheek:

Love's a Dream of mighty Treasure
    Which in Fancy we possess;
In the Folly lies the Pleasure,
    Wisdom ever makes it less.[18]

In the opening couplet of "Against Fruition I," Suckling put the anti-rational view of love this way: "Stay here fond youth and ask no more, be wise, / Knowing too much long since lost Paradise."[19] The attitude expressed here, and in many other anti-rational love poems cited by Quaintance, is also the Fine Lady's when she recommends "The perfect joy of being well-deceived" (115).

It has been suggested that we are left "unsure" about Artemisia's attitude toward the Fine Lady, and even that Artemisia voices only "partial disapproval" of her and is in fact tragically attracted to the Fine Lady's world.[20] On the contrary, I think Artemisia's attitude is unambiguous, and totally disapproving. In fact, Artemisia's rejection of the Fine Lady's concept of love is itself a part of the seventeenth-century tradition of anti-rationalist love poetry. Specifically, Rochester has aligned Artemisia with Edmund Waller (whose verse the Rochester-like Dorimant is so frequently quoting in *The Man of Mode*)in opposing the notion of fools as best lovers. In response to Suckling's "Against Fruition [I]," Waller wrote "In Answer of Sir John Suckling's Verses,"[21] refuting point by point the argument against fruition. Rejecting Suckling's claim that "Knowing too much long since lost Paradise," Waller says: "And by your knowledge, we should be bereft / Of all that Paradise, which yet is left." Like Waller, Artemisia rejects the anti-rationalist praise of ignorance, and she implicitly argues for a more realistic view of love in which restraint preserves pleasure, and passion accompanies the action of love.

Artemisia's opposition to the Fine Lady's anti-rationalism, part of a seventeenth-century literary tradition, is also unequivocal within the poem itself. From the outset Artemisia envelops the Fine Lady in her customary irony, beginning with the adjective "fine" to describe this grotesque, "antic" woman. Artemisia's negative judgment is clear in her account of the Fine Lady's relations with her husband and gallant, in her affected posturings and expressions upon arriving upstairs, and in her "forty smiles, as many antic bows" as she embraces "The dirty, chattering monster" and makes a "fine, tender speech" to the monkey. This is, as Professor Weinbrot has said, "an obscene parody of love." The whole dramatization of the Fine Lady's arrival and behavior which Artemisia presents to Chloe and to us as readers is unmistakably negative. And Artemisia follows this dramatization with an especially destructive ironic evaluation of the Fine Lady.

There is an apparent mildness in the way Artemisia begins her evaluation of the Fine Lady:

> I took this time to think what nature meant
> When this mixed thing into the world she sent,
> So very wise, yet so impertinent[.]
>
> (147-49)

By calling her a "mixed thing" Artemisia seems to be indicating at least partial approval and sympathy with the Fine Lady. But not at all. The passage proceeds to ridicule her as "an ass," "a true fop" who has attained the "very top / And dignity of folly," "a coxcomb," and "An eminent fool"—"such a one was she" (151-62). The apparent concession to her wisdom and sense is in fact ironically part of Artemisia's ridicule. What wit the Fine Lady has, Artemisia says, merely makes her that much more perfect a fool: "an eminent fool must be a fool of parts" (161). Her "discerning wit" is curiously blind: she knows "Everyone's fault and merit, but her own" (165). As she began this devastating ridicule of the Fine Lady with a triplet apparently mild in judgment, Artemisia concludes with another triplet also apparently generous:

> All the good qualities that ever blessed
> A woman so distinguished from the rest,
> Except discretion only, she possessed.
>
> (166-68)

But in the context of the dramatization of the Fine Lady's behavior, and the ridicule of her in Artemisia's evaluation, we should surely hear the tone of irony in the phrases "good qualities," "blessed," and "distinguished." And we should feel the full weight of Artemisia's judgment that "all" the Fine Lady lacked was "discretion," that is, the ability to discern or distinguish what is right, especially as regards her own conduct. "All" she lacks is judgment. Artemisia is certainly ironic but hardly ambiguous in her satiric attack on the Fine Lady.

III

The poem's final section is also its most straightforward. In telling her story of Corinna, the Fine Lady speaks without the irony characteristic of Artemisia. The story is a double progress piece. But unlike Hogarth's moral histories, the Fine Lady's story is no pure moral exemplum, but is intended to illustrate her contention that fools make better lovers than men of wit. The harlot does not, as in Hogarth's engravings, end in a pitiable death; rather

she merges into the modified rake's progress and through deceit, fraud, and eventually murder winds up with her "boody" lover's entire estate. The story of Corinna is a dark, perhaps even tragic view of the corrupt state of modern love, more dramatically detailed, if not more psychologically compelling than the "all-sin-sheltering grove" of **"A Ramble in St. James's Park."** And by her rationalizing acceptance of the murderous course of "wretched Corinna," the Fine Lady clearly associates herself with this viciously corrupt world.

Artemisia's response to the Fine Lady's story is succinct: "Thus she ran on two hours, some grains of sense / Still mixed with volleys of impertinence" (256-57). It has been suggested that in her response Artemisia has ignored "a splendid opportunity to reject the world the Fine Lady has been describing" and "instead diminishes her earlier criticisms," and that by promising in the final verse paragraph to write more such letters, Artemisia becomes "an agent for the propagation of infamy," and is encouraging such hellish values to take root.[22] But as we have already seen, from the very introduction of the Fine Lady into her poem, Artemisia has been presenting an ironic, unremittingly negative judgment of the woman and her values. Furthermore, the story of Corinna so directly describes a vicious world in which love is perverted beyond recognition, that it requires no gratuitous moralizing by Artemisia—nor by Rochester—to convey a negative judgment. Finally, Artemisia's two-line evaluation of the Fine Lady's story is a model of ironic understatement. As she "ran on two hours," Artemisia sarcastically observes, "some grains of sense" (which we have seen are essential in the making of a perfect fool) are "mixed with volleys of impertinence." Artemisia used the word "impertinent" to describe the Fine Lady in her first evaluation. The word is understated, but not tepid. It means irrelevant, presumptuous, inappropriate, perhaps even offensive, absurd and silly (see OED entry). It is a powerful word here, operating in the way Anne Righter observes is typical of Rochester: "Nothing is more characteristic of Rochester than the way a single word, particularly in the final stanza of a poem, will suddenly move into focus and reveal its possession of a variety of warring meanings."[23] "Impertinence" is a cool, perhaps cynical, certainly superior way of characterizing the Fine Lady. Yet it also has the variety of harshly condemning meanings which leave us in no doubt of Artemisia's rejection of the Fine Lady and her espousal of "The perfect joy of being well deceived" (115).

IV

Ultimately, as David Vieth and others have argued, *A Letter from Artemisia* apparently "affords no positive norm." On the basis of Artemisia's attacks on the three false conceptions of love, the reader may infer the notion of a realistic kind of love which uses restraint to achieve pleasure and passion, and which is based on knowledge, not deception, on personal taste, not public fashion. But such a positive view is purely inferential; nowhere in the poem does Rochester explicitly state it. Both in its absence of a positive norm, and in the themes it treats, Rochester's **Letter** is similar to Swift's "The Lady's Dressing Room." The attention given to the scatological imagery Swift uses in "The Lady's Dressing Room," "Strephon and Chloe," and "Cassinus and Peter" has obscured the fact that they are an extension of the seventeenth-century tradition of poems on the relation of knowledge to love in which **A Letter from Artemisia** holds such a prominent place. In these poems Swift (as did Rochester) ridicules the idea of love based on idealization and illusion. In each of these poems Swift describes a lover who has arrived at "the sublime and refined Point of Felicity, called, *the Possession of being well deceived,*"[24] only to be disabused of his illusions when he inadvertently discovers that his divine goddess is subject to the "Necessities of Nature."

"The Lady's Dressing Room" is the most perplexing of these three poems. The fundamental problem is determining Swift's attitude toward the speaker of the poem. In the final sixteen lines the speaker offers an evaluation of Strephon's state:

> I pity wretched *Strephon* blind
> To all the Charms of Female Kind;
> Should I the Queen of Love refuse,
> Because she rose from stinking Ooze?
> To him that looks behind the Scene,
> *Statira's* but some pocky Queen.
> When *Celia* in her Glory Shows,
> If *Strephon* would but stop his Nose;
> (Who now so impiously blasphemes
> Her Ointments, Daubs, and Paints and Creams,
> Her Washes, Slops, and every Clout,
> With which he makes so foul a Rout;)
> He soon would learn to think like me,
> And bless his ravisht Sight to see
> Such Order from Confusion sprung,
> Such gaudy Tulips rais'd from Dung.[25]

The "I" in these lines has been taken to be Swift, and the method and meaning of the passage to be "perfectly plain statements," a "straightforward advocacy of accepting things as they are."[26] But the speaker's complacent recommendation of illusion and delusion hardly seems like Swift. He was not one to accept "the Queen of Love" on any basis, least of all if he had to "stop his Nose" to avoid one reality in order to have his sight "ravisht" by "Such gaudy Tulips rais'd from Dung."[27] As A. B. England has said, "The kind of language that is used makes it clear that the advice is being given with conscious irony." But it is not altogether clear how we should interpret this irony. "Just where Swift stands in relation to the author's voice cannot be ascertained. . . . Swift makes his exposure with vigorous clarity, but he is not sure what attitude to take towards it."[28]

In a good recent note on this poem, Louise K. Barnett has suggested that we can, in fact, see where Swift stands by recognizing that "The satiric strategy of 'The Lady's Dressing Room' is an example of typically Swiftian devisioness: the subject is viewed through two personae, both

of whom are unreliable although neither is entirely so."[29] Both Strephon and the narrator have exaggerated responses to the body, Barnett argues: Strephon's one of disgust, the narrator's one of celebration. And where does Swift stand? "For Swift, the body must be accepted as a reality of the human condition, but its potential for bringing down the spirit must equally be recognized."[30] It is worth observing that Professor Barnett cites certain passages from the text to illustrate the exaggerated responses of Strephon and the narrator, but none to support her statement of Swift's positive stance. In fact, Swift, like Rochester, offers no explicit positive position. The satiric attacks are clear, but the positive norms can only be inferred. I would suggest that we can come still closer to ascertaining just where Swift stands by considering "The Lady's Dressing Room" in light of the tradition of poems dealing with the anti-rational attitude toward love, and in particular Rochester's **A Letter from Artemisia.**

Strephon shares certain characteristics with the Fine Lady's "men of wit."

> Slow of belief, and fickle in desire,
> Who, ere they'll be persuaded, must inquire
> As if they came to spy, not to admire.
> With searching wisdom, fatal to their ease,
> They still find out why what may, should not please;
> Nay, take themselves for injured when we dare
> Make 'em think better of us than we are,
> And if we hide our frailties from their sights,
> Call us deceitful jilts and hypocrites.

(105-13)

Strephon is, of course, a naive and foolish variant of the "men of wit." Unlike the more cynical and sophisticated men of wit who are "Slow of belief" and "must inquire" before "they'll be persuaded," Strephon is initially infatuated with Celia. But like the Fine Lady's "Inquisitive" (116) men of wit, who destroy "wonder by clear knowledge" (120), Strephon "Stole in" to his lady's dressing room, "and took a strict Survey, / Of all the litter as it lay" (78). And as the men of wit bring "the glaring light" (123) of reason to bear upon their love, "No Object *Strephon's* Eye escapes" (47); he is "Resolv'd to go thro' thick and thin" (80). And as knowledge brings "certain woe" to the Fine Lady's men of wit, Strephon is depicted as the "wretched" victim of his own search into "'Those Secrets of the hoary deep!'" (98). As Strephon is a naive version of the Fine Lady's men of wit, the narrator of Swift's poem shares an important opinion with the Fine Lady herself. She argues for "The perfect joy of being well-deceived"; the narrator advises Strephon to find joy in illusion, a joy perversely intensified by an awareness of how far the illusion is from reality. Swift's speaker, like Rochester's Fine Lady, is offering a praise of folly, a love based on ignorance not knowledge.

In the **Letter,** Artemisia ironically undermines the Fine Lady and her views, thus bringing at least that degree of clarity and certainty to the poem's meaning. Swift, however, has not included this larger ironic frame. He leaves the reader with the task of evaluating the narrator's recommendations. The exaggerations Professor Barnett has noted in the narrator's language and attitudes invite us to see him, as well as Strephon, as a satiric target. And considering the poem in light of other poems on the relation of knowledge and love helps us more clearly to see the satire directed specifically at the narrator's anti-rational praise of a love based on illusion. But Swift has not included the larger frame of irony, an Artemisia-like ironist whose perspective helps to clarify the satire. Compared to Swift's poem, Rochester's **Letter** is more complicated because of the greater number of interlocking frames of irony. But it is also clearer. In her role as ironist, Artemisia has clarified and intensified the satire against three false conceptions of love. In the final lines of the poem Artemisia is in perfect control of both her irony and her sense of satiric purpose:

> But now 'tis time I should some pity show
> To Chloe, since I cannot choose but know
> Readers must reap the dullness writers sow.
> By the next post such stories I will tell
> As, joined with these, shall to a volume swell,
> As true as heaven, more infamous than hell.
> But you are tired, and so am I.
> Farewell.
>
> (258-65)

Artemisia's account of impossible ideals, mechanized love, illusions, delusions, deceptions and murder can only ironically be described as "dullness." Such stories as Artemisia has told, joined with more of the same, would indeed "swell" a volume of satiric verse, "As true as heaven, more infamous than hell." This description would be an apt epigraph to set before the works of Rochester.

Notes

1. *Enthusiast in Wit* (Lincoln: Univ. of Nebraska Press, 1962), pp. 121, 124.

2. "John Wilmot, Earl of Rochester," *Proceedings of the British Academy,* 53 (1967), 355.

3. *Satires Against Mankind* (Berkeley: Univ. of California Press, 1973), p. 133.

4. Griffin, p. 152.

5. "Rochester's Reader and the Problem of Satiric Audience," *Papers on Language & Literature,* 12 (1976), 294.

6. "Toward an Anti-Aristotelian Poetic: Rochester's *Satyr Against Mankind* and *Artemisia to Chloe,* with Notes on Swift's *Tale of a Tub* and *Gulliver's Travels,*" *Language and Style,* 5 (1972), 136.

7. Vieth, pp. 137-38.

8. "The Swelling Volume: The Apocalyptic Satire of Rochester's *Letter from Artemisia in the Town to Chloe in the Country,*" *Studies in the Literary Imagination,* 5 (1972), 19-38.

9. Righter, p. 62.

10. *The Complete Poems of John Wilmot, Earl of Rochester,* ed. David M. Vieth (New Haven: Yale Univ. Press, 1968), p. 104. Subsequent quotations are from this edition.

11. *Kenyon Review,* 26 (1964), 364.

12. Weinbrot, p. 23.

13. (Chicago: Univ. of Chicago Press, 1974), pp. 61-76. See also D.C. Muecke's list of the principal techniques employed in Impersonal Irony in *The Compass of Irony* (London: Methuen, 1969), pp. 67-68, especially items XIV, XV, and XVII.

14. Sitter, p. 297.

15. Griffin suggests that the language of this passage "seems to recall the conception of love in some of the songs, where love is a soft 'refuge' for innocence, a director of youth, a haven of security, essentially a mother's arms," and cites "The Submission" as an example (p. 140). But as he himself argues in his discussion of the songs (pp. 100-14), Rochester characteristically parodies such a concept of love and explores "the pains of sex." Even in "The Submission" the libertine's assurance of the safety of love is not unequivocal.

16. *Papers on Language & Literature,* 12 (1976), 273-84.

17. (Unpubl. Ph.D. diss., Yale, 1962) As Quaintance shows, the tradition of anti-rationalism in seventeenth-century love poetry, which provides the immediate context for Rochester's *Letter,* is itself part of a larger tradition including Ovid, Chaucer, Erasmus, and Shakespeare.

18. Quoted by Quaintance, p. 4.

19. *The Works of Sir John Suckling,* ed. Thomas Clayton (Oxford: Clarendon Press, 1971), I, 37.

20. Griffin, p. 152, and Weinbrot, pp. 28-29.

21. Waller, *Poems* (1645; facsimile rpt. Menston, Engl.: Scolar Press, 1971), pp. 86-88.

22. Weinbrot, pp. 32-34.

23. Righter, p. 62.

24. *A Tale of a Tub,* ed. A. C. Guthkelch and D. Nichol Smith, 2nd ed. (Oxford: Clarendon Press, 1958), p. 174.

25. *The Poems of Jonathan Swift,* ed. Harold Williams, 2nd ed. (Oxford: Clarendon Press, 1958), II, 530. For the correction of "Satira's" to "Statira's" in line 134 see the items by W.A. Speck, *Notes & Queries,* 214 (1969), 398, and by Davd M. Vieth, *Notes & Queries,* 220 (1975), 562-63.

26. Donald Greene, "On Swift's Scatological Poems," *Sewanee Review,* 75 (1967), 679.

27. For further arguments against taking this passage as straightforward, see Thomas B. Gilmore, Jr., "The Comedy of Swift's Scatological Poems," *PMLA,* 91 (1976), 39-40.

28. "World Without Order: Some Thoughts on the Poetry of Swift," *Essays in Criticism,* 16 (1966), 36.

29. "The Mysterious Narrator: Another Look at 'The Lady's Dressing Room'," *Concerning Poetry,* 9 (1976), 29.

30. Barnett, p. 31.

Barbara Everett (essay date 1982)

SOURCE: Everett, Barbara. "The Sense of Nothing." In *Spirit of Wit: Reconsiderations of Rochester,* edited by Jeremy Treglown, pp. 1-41. Oxford: Basil Blackwell, 1982.

[*In the following essay, Everett examines Rochester's work in the context of Restoration England and the Court of King Charles II, discussing the poet's need to follow fashion and the way his poems point to a void beneath a smooth social surface.*]

Rochester's general character as a poet is evident to any reader. He is a realist, his world bounded by the limits of King Charles II's court and the London that lay immediately beyond. If this makes his field seem narrow, then so it is—compared at any rate with the greater of his contemporaries: Milton, Dryden, even Bunyan, all live and write in a wider, larger world. But if, in turn, the relative thinness of Rochester's work is noticed as little as it is by any enjoying reader, this is because of the poet's compensating skills: the casual certainty that makes the elegance of his style, the extremity with which he goes to the limits of his vision.

It is from the balance of these opposing elements that Rochester's work gets its peculiar character. On the one hand there is the accepted commonplaceness of its content and milieu, the lack of preliminary with which the poet takes his place ('Well, sir, 'tis granted I said'—this or that) among the 'merry gang' as Marvell called them, Dryden's 'men of pleasant conversation . . . ambitious to distinguish themselves from the herd of gentlemen', or Pope's more lethal 'mob of gentlemen who wrote with ease'. Precisely because he so takes his place, there remains a border area of his work where editors still argue about who wrote what; and about how much, precisely, can be thought to function ironically—irony in itself being an index of that social commitment. But, on the other hand, the best of Rochester's poems could have been written by no one else; just as it is a fact that he was clearly not just *one* of the 'mob of gentlemen' but himself a social legend in his own time and for at least a century after. The particular nature of Rochester's involvement in the social life of his time is perhaps a matter on which biography has never placed the right kind of stress, or from which it has never

drawn conclusions useful enough for the poetry. Those of the events in his life which we know something about suggest how necessary it was to Rochester not merely to be in the fashion but to excel in it, to transcend it almost—to do a thing so well that the mode itself broke under him, unrepeatable. It is impossible to draw any other conclusion from the Alexander Bendo incident, in which the poet impersonated a quack with high success. The affair is usually treated as evidence of his obsessive acting talents. What is not mentioned is that the trick had been played at least twice before: once by Buckingham, then more recently by Rochester's own friend Sedley. Acting a quack was in fact a fashion among the Wits.[1]

What distinguished Rochester was the strange intensity of his need not only to follow the fashion but to follow it to breaking point—the *extremity,* one might say, of his worldliness. That he had been (in youth) drunk for five years on end is something he was eager to tell Burnet on his repentant death-bed; and it is a fact that his final collapse followed on a sick man's ride back home to Somerset from London where he had returned with the King after insisting on attending the races at Newmarket. It is this quality of extremity that distinguishes Rochester's poems, balancing their realism and elegance. Or perhaps, in the end, bringing about the *im*balance that an original genius must consist in. For a work of art is recognized by its incapacity to be absorbed wholly by the society which produces it, and which it represents so admirably. Rochester's most social poems are very odd products indeed, but with an oddity that has nothing to do with eccentricity. This oddity—the oddity of art, not of social or psychological idiosyncrasy—is less easy to define than it is to illustrate, and I should like to illustrate it, as it were, from the life, taking an incident and using it as a kind of metaphor for Rochester's poetry; but the life I want to use is not, as it happens, Rochester's own, but his father's.

The elder Lord Wilmot, a general in Charles I's army and an adviser of the young King Charles II, is said to have been a brave man and a wit—as a companion of the King probably needed to be. He was made Earl of Rochester, the title his son inherited when he was only ten, for helping the King escape after the defeat at Worcester in 1651. At least, 'helping' is (again) what the history books say he did. Clearly the award of an earldom suggests that he did *something* for it: but the King himself almost implies, in the account of the flight which he dictated to Pepys thirty years later, in 1680, that it was *he* who helped *Wilmot* to escape after the battle, and this is a view not unsupported by contemporary witnesses. For it is clear that Wilmot complicated the flight in one particular way. Charles says: 'I could never get my Lord Wilmot to put on any disguise, he saying that he should look frightfully in it, and therefore did never put on any'.[2] This is one of the King's own footnotes to his account, as though he found it an importantly lingering memory, even if he could not entirely fathom it. And the refusal of disguise certainly did affect the flight, enforcing Wilmot's travelling separately, either in front or well behind, keeping his court silks and laces well away from the strenuously walnut-stained and ostler-coated King, whose menial state of dress the recording Pepys—describing it in immense and awed detail—nearly faints to think about. Wilmot, on the other hand, condescended to one compromise only: he carried a hawk on his fist. He must have been, one cannot help reflecting, glad to see the back of it, when after six long weeks they reached the coast and embarked for the continent: where Wilmot was to die in exile seven years later, during the Interregnum, leaving his title to his ten year old son. But Rochester may have inherited from that necessarily little-known father more than the title and the estate, quite as much as he had from his mother, a powerfully dominating and able Puritan lady: and what precisely he inherited is reflected somewhere, perhaps, in that curious event which the King recorded.

Probably Wilmot was being funny—certainly his remark *is* funny, when one considers that to look 'frightfully', or at least to look unlike one's normal courtly self, is the whole purpose of disguise, especially when one is running for one's life pursued by troopers across the boggy English woodlands. And Charles's evident happiness in all the play-acting of this marvellous adventure—which he harked back to, wistfully, for over thirty years afterwards—might well have aroused an acerbic wit in a more battle-scarred companion. But the humour remains conjectural. What shines principally in Wilmot's remark is its quality of sheer 'face', its highly independent disobliging *panache* that yet operates within a narrow social context that gives that mocking word 'frightfully' its peculiar character. ('One would not, sure, be frightful when one's dead.') It is the very impassivity of the general's remark, our difficulty in knowing what precisely Wilmot was at (though there is no difficulty in seeing that he did what he wanted, in his easy way) that suggests its special social function. This is an occurrence of that highly English social phenomenon, the use of *manners* to get away with almost anything: for heroism, folly, intelligence, guile, whimsy or sheer blankness of mind may lurk beneath that recorded turn of phrase.

A sense, perhaps unconscious, of what social tone may serve for must have come quite naturally to the Cavalier courtier. But when the same sense occurs in the far more conscious Restoration wit of the son, it forms the great originality of his verse. For it is Rochester, perhaps, who invents *vers de société* in English. The act of translation places a radically new stress, it might be said, on the mere proposition, so that the poem is now written 'about' rather than 'from' society, with a new kind of inside-outness that helps to explain why Rochester should be also perhaps the first user of pure irony in English after Chaucer. The complexities latent in writing English *vers de société* are nicely suggested in a recent poem by Philip Larkin which takes the actual phrase for its title; one of his most undermining poems, what is undermined in it is basically the '*société*', and yet it is, for all that, a brilliantly 'social' piece of verse.

Another and more explicit case of this highly ambiguous social fidelity can be observed through the letters of Henry James, from the moment at which the young American writer sends back home, in the late 1870s, his impressions of the English social scene—

> The people of this world seem to me for the most part nothing but *surface,* and sometimes—oh ye gods!—such desperately poor surface!

—to that, some twenty years later, at which James struggles patiently to explain to a correspondent less sympathetic than his family just what he had meant by the extraordinary art with which he had recently (in *The Awkward Age*) dealt in that world of 'surface':

> I had in view a certain special social (highly 'modern' and actual) London group and type and tone, which seemed to me to se prêter à merveille to an ironic—lightly and simply ironic!—treatment . . . with no going behind, no *telling about* the figures save by their own appearance and action and with explanations reduced to the explanation of everything by all the other things *in* the picture . . .[3]

Rochester himself would not have been caught making such 'explanations' at all: he was even further ensconced behind that social 'surface', that world of appearance and action which there was 'no *telling about*'. He inhabited, he half invented, that English social world where James was never much more than a wonderful lifelong tourist; which is why, perhaps, Rochester needed those compensating retreats to his country estates which were his equivalents to James's American nationality, his family background and his Puritan inheritance.

It is because of this very immersion and silence on Rochester's part that, despite all the differences of temperament and period and nationality, James's more self-conscious and detached reflections can be useful in suggesting some of the peculiarly ambiguous, confining conditions of a social art like Rochester's. There is an odd parallel, perhaps, between that famous Max Beerbohm cartoon which makes some sort of cool comment on the way in which the James of the *Sacred Fount* period did and did not 'belong', representing him as stooping to examine with horrified concern the mixed sexes of the pairs of shoes left to be cleaned overnight outside the bedroom doors of some hotel or house party—and a hostile aside on Rochester by a Victorian critic. Alluding to the anecdote of Rochester's having posted a footman in a sentinel's red coat and with a musket outside the doors of court ladies to watch the goings-on, the critic glosses it by saying that the poet 'for no earthly reason you can think of, set detectives to note him the indiscretions of the Court'.[4] Criticism ought perhaps to be better than this at thinking of earthly reasons.

For, if Rochester's verse transcends its own representativeness, this is by virtue of the way in which it goes, one might say, to the end of the road; the way in which his commitment to social forms was a manner of breaking those social forms. The story of his drunken destruction of the King's upward-pointing chronometer, and the apparent prudery of his for centuries unprintable reason for breaking it, is one of the best-known anecdotes that have survived him—and in the same way, even his most elegant verse often resounds with the crash of breaking glass; or where there is no crash, a startled reader will find himself glimpsing a void beneath the bright surface, a vacancy beneath the brilliant style.

As an example of this method of transcending the temporal mode, it is worth considering what happens to a Hobbesian idea of time in one of Rochester's best-known poems. In another of these often-repeated jottings that compose the legend of Rochester's life, Anthony à Wood remarks—thinking, perhaps, of the sensitive and well-read seventeen-year-old who first arrived at court with a tendency not only to blush but to stammer—that 'the Court . . . not only debauched him but made him a perfect *Hobbist*'.[5] Hobbes, whose *Elements of Law* include the laws that

> Continually to be outgone is misery.
> Continually to outgo the next before is felicity.
> And to forsake the course is to die . . .

was certainly the philosopher of Charles's court, as he had himself been the tutor of the King—as he was, in fact, the most popular philosopher of the age in some cultural sense: we are told that in the year after Rochester died 'the folly and nonsense of meer mechanism' had passed to the very craftsmen, even the labourers of the time, who were 'able to demonstrate out of *Leviathan* . . . that all things come to pass by an eternal Chain of natural Causes', and that human nature was a mere machine.[6]

It is hardly surprising that Rochester committed himself to this most fashionable system, which was also the most imaginatively challenging of his time, having a hard self-consistency not easy to refute. All the more striking is the transmutation of these ideas within the medium of Rochester's verse: within, for instance, his **'Love and Life'**. This incorporates the materialist and mechanistic doctrine of Hobbes that the only *real* time is time present: 'The *present* only has a being in Nature; things *past* have a being in the memory only, but things *to come* have no being at all . . .'[7] But in Rochester's lyric these ideas are *not* incorporated, but rather disembodied, attenuated, made to float lightly in the emptiness of the 'flying hours':

> All my past Life is mine no more,
>   The flying hours are gone
>
>   . . . . .
>
> The Time that is to come is not,
>   How can it then be mine?

If everything in Hobbes is material and mechanical, then everything in the poem is immaterial and organic.

In part this is a simple question of what happens to all statements within the quasi-musical discipline of poetry, which part liberates ideas and part destroys them. 'When a

thing is too stupid to be said, we sing it'; and conversely to sing a thing may be to make it sound stupid—or if not stupid, then released into a kind of radiant folly. It may be relevant that elsewhere Hobbes admits that he cannot explain music—'I confess that I know not for what reason one succession in tone and measure is more pleasant than another'—and this issue seems to be supported by Dryden's comment that the philosopher 'studied poetry as he did mathematics, when it was too late'. There appear to be conditions separating philosophy in modern periods from music and poetry, so that if they come together, in—say—the Metaphysicals, the result does not resemble Lucretius or Dante, but has a startled paradoxical self-undermining wit, as of a man who now knows that he is doing the impossible. In such verse, ideas get airborne, or at least stand on their heads. And Rochester's **'Love and Life'** does have this Metaphysical wit; its title is borrowed from Cowley, and the whole poem's movement has a quality of strong fantasy, an extravagance in self-commital to paradox, perhaps learned from Donne, whom Rochester sometimes seems to know by heart.

But the change in Hobbesian doctrine in **'Love and Life'** goes beyond the effect of what we may call either a 'musical' or a 'metaphysical' discipline. Nominally it is spoken by a libertine, a rake on principle, a man whose wholly selfish moral presuppositions followed hard upon Hobbesian cosmology and accepted the practical consequences of disbelief in past and future. But Rochester's libertine first translates philosophical maxims, words used as counters to win intellectual assent, into factors of human consciousness; and then, with a kind of sublime or idiot logic, extends that consciousness into a radical self-undercutting, an intelligence almost self-destructive. The conclusions of that intelligence might have surprised even Hobbes. For Rochester's libertine, having no past or future, has, in all honest logic, no present either: unless we give the name of a 'present' to the poem itself, which the poet, however 'courtly' or 'gentlemanly', speaks as out of an essential solitariness, in a surprise of realization rendered by the abrupt, lucid monosyllables, that seem to resonate in a void. 'All my past life is mine no more . . . How can it then be mine?'

One of the 'mob of gentlemen' here speaks with that peculiar lucidity which is the speech of the inward self, alone; and it is with a curiously chaste impersonality that the libertine watches the 'flying hours' carry his life away into a driftage as of dead leaves, of 'Dreams', 'Images', memory. When this same rakish lover turns at the end of the second stanza, in a beautifully located surprise, to hand over the poem to its audience and reader, the suddenly-invoked Phillis, his courtesy and gravity are hardly at all ironic; his 'Miracle', in fact, is one of those most undermining of word-plays, where a quiet literalism forestalls metaphor, irony grows serious and pretence turns real:

> If I, by Miracle, can be
> This live-long Minute true to thee
>   'Tis all that Heav'n allows.

The brilliance of this small poem, and what surely explains its great popularity and its anthology status both in the poet's time and in our own, is the way it converts a relatively sterile proposition from Hobbes into a potent human moment. The poem is a 'saying' that moves itself into action, becoming the fulfilment of the promise it half makes; its conclusion thus 'seals' the poem like a personal crest on a document now long crumbled away. Given that this hypothetical and contingent 'Phillis' is partly a mocking relic of past tradition, and partly some future dream, this ending makes of the lines a decisive handing over of the self to some unknown quantity, the 'present' being only a knowledge of what is unknown. And this sudden, ironic and yet generous self-offering is so circumspectly dealt with as to be able to suggest the perpetual existence of the self as in a void, created from moment to moment as a poem is from line to line. For the poet of **'Love and Life'** has, by definition, nothing at all to call his own—neither past nor future, nor any present that he knows, beyond that 'Miracle' of the poem's live-long Minute. Neither a philosopher nor a libertine but something more like an equilibrist, the poet balances in the void, sustaining himself on nothing whatever.

* * *

I have been hoping to suggest that Rochester's poems may only safely be said to be representative of the Restoration period if that period is defined very cautiously. The 1660s and 1670s through which Rochester lived and which, in literary terms at least, he helped to create, were something of a cultural no man's land, a pause in time equally out of touch with the past and future, the medieval and the modern. It was an age in which writers began to inch themselves along again, with what Emily Dickinson would describe as 'that precarious gait / Men call Experience'. Rochester's best poems, in short, were probably all written in that decade after the Plague had seemed to empty London, and the Fire to level it. They were written, moreover, for a court presided over by a penniless king back home from banishment and living carefully hand to mouth. The period which we name after its political Restoration has a reality not confined to its King and his court; but it is that court sphere which colours with an intensity beyond its apparent importance some of the best literature of the time. Similarly, though there were a number of different aspects of the world of that court, the one which features most vividly in writers of the period was that which the Marquis of Halifax (elder brother of Rochester's closest friend, and an even cleverer man, perhaps, than Rochester himself) was to call, in his well-known essay on the King, 'His Dissimulation'. In the drafts for his *History* Burnet had given this 'art of concealing' in the Restoration court a historical basis, deriving it from Charles's education at the hands of a Queen Mother determined that her sons should not display the (in the event) fatal unworldliness of their father. Whatever its source, this court dissimulation, evoked in Halifax's brilliant scattered phrases, suggests a kind of evasive darkness that we should perhaps see behind the sparkle of Rochester's court verse:

Men compared Notes, and got Evidence . . . His Face . . . would sometimes tell Tales to a good Observer . . . At last it cometh to Smile for Smile, meaning nothing of either Side; without any kind of Effect; mere Drawing-room Compliments . . . there was less Signification in those Things than at first was thought . . . He would slide from an asking Face, and could guess very well . . . It was a kind of implied bargain.[8]

It was for this world of 'Smile for Smile, meaning nothing of either Side', that Rochester's love poems were written; his Satires are 'Notes', 'Evidences', telling 'Tales to a good Observer'. To describe his verse as a construct from a world of surfaces implies that it is always close to irony; but the concept of irony can only be used cautiously of Rochester. For since its Socratic origins true irony has always served some polemic purpose—its 'lies' have always functioned to make clearer some truth. Rochester's poems often have a highly ironic sound, but something like a total lack of any provable intention (or even tone), except possibly the intention of hollowing out the surface they so finely construct. Apart from this latent sense of void, there is no form of what James called 'telling about', 'going behind': only the 'explanation' by 'all the other things *in* the picture'. Rather than by a smoothness so excessive as to make us defensive (as in Swiftian irony), Rochester's poems show intent by minute flaws in that smooth surface, by local shocks and coruscations of wit. Even where Rochester's tone seems cool, sweet and safe, his wit leaps to the surface in striking, even dangerous, disjunctions of language which locally fracture the style, like the minute cracks that beautify crackleware ceramics. An apparently 'polite' poem that addresses its subject as a 'Fair nasty nymph' (as does 'By all love's soft, yet mighty powers') is not going to leave quite where it was a socially-orientated 'fair' sex that relies on its unfair fairness of face to get away with murder; nor does a poem that goes on to advise in the name of hygiene a more 'cleanly sinning' leave either hygiene, or sinning, quite where it was before. Swift's famous letter to a young woman approaching matrimony which primarily advises her to wash often and thoroughly is possibly sensible but not funny in any human way, because some degree of animus towards the female makes itself plain in the intemperate style of a man who is for good or bad never a pure ironist; similarly all the smoothness of even the Modest Proposer only enforces what any reader instinctively knows, that eating people is wrong. Rochester's equally profane and good-taste-violating poem on the 'Fair nasty nymph' is more purely ironic than Swift's letter because it voices no animus at all against women (I think it highly unlikely that the poet had any)—it voices nothing: it merely sets out the flaw in the china in the cool crack about the 'Fair nasty nymph'. Bodies being as they are, it is the social insistence on 'fairness' that is the thoroughly 'nasty' thing.

In very much the same way, but with a more expansively indecorous decorum, the better-known outrageously-ending lines that tell us how 'Fair *Cloris* in a Pig-style lay' make it their business to flesh out the discrepancies between that

'Fair' and that 'Pig-stye'. But they do no more—they do not satirize; they leave both reader and Chloris 'Innocent and pleased', with their illusions in place even if not quite intact. Chloris ends happy with her fantasy of lust and her virginity both unviolated; the reader ends happy in the belief that pastoral tells him something true about life or love; everything in the pig-sty is lovely. The power of this poem, compared with that about the 'Fair nasty nymph', is the greater degree of poetic acceptance of the mode proposed, the triumphant, non-committal accomplishment of this vacuous, self-deceiving, dishonestly erotic pastoral. How good an actor Rochester really was is unclear— certainly he sometimes loathed whatever he meant by the image of 'this gawdy guilded Stage'; but he was perfect at assuming the pose of a certain verbal style. Thus the charm of the very popular **'Ancient Person of my Heart'** is its embodiment of the innocence of tone and terrible social polish that make the deb an evidently unchanging type over several centuries of English social life. The pronunciation of the time brings together in an assonance words as discrepant as the frigidly social 'Ancient Person' ('Parson') and the boldly intimate 'Heart': the comical insistence of this paradoxical refrain—'Ancient *Person* of my *Heart*'— embodies a social type on the page, as elegant and peremptory as a pedigree cat.

That refrain from the **'Song of a Young Lady'** makes relevant here an even more minute detail. In citing **'Ancient Person of my Heart'** (with its capital P, capital H), as in most other quotations from Rochester's poems up to this point, I have deliberately used Vivian de Sola Pinto's Muses' Library text (Routledge and Kegan Paul, 1952, second edition 1964), which is now to some degree superseded by David M. Vieth's scholarly modernized edition (Yale University Press, 1968). Vieth modernizes because, as he rightly argues, there is no bibliographical authority for any of the Restoration editions of the poet. But this is helpful proof of the simple fact that, where literature is concerned, bibliography is frequently (like patriotism) not enough. The primary need in presenting a poet is not to obscure his tone; and certain of Rochester's poems are so social in tone as to profit from the retention of that Restoration and Augustan habit of visual literacy, the capitalization of important nouns. Thus, Vieth's able but toneless text renders meditative and inward a poem like **'Upon his Leaving his Mistress',** a part of whose flagrant virtue it is to give the whole of social life the look of an open secret, a network of called passwords in a war, a surface of nods and becks which there is no 'going behind, no *telling about*':

> 'Tis not that I'm weary grown
> Of being yours, and yours alone:
> But with what Face can I incline,
> To damn you to be only mine?
> You, who some kinder Pow'r did fashion,
> By merit, and by inclination,
> The Joy at least of a whole Nation.

The first word the Muses' Library edition follows its 1680 text in capitalizing is the third-line 'Face'; the next in this stanza is 'Pow'r'. All the delicate contradictions of a lover's psychology, which the poem also manages to hint at, the ironies of a Petrarchan self-abasement in the sensitive lover's soul, are shouldered back behind and yet somehow expressed by the heightened capitalized forms of social observances, the agreement that socially it is 'Face' not feeling that matters, it is 'Pow'r' not love that governs ('continually to outgo the next before is felicity'); and in such a context to give or take fidelity is hardly a saving grace—it is to '*damn* you to be only mine'.

Rochester can write tenderer, more inward poems than this, such as justify Vieth's modernized reading of the poet. One of these more tender poems offers a stylistic detail as interesting as Rochester's use of capital letters: a rhythmic effect that speaks to the ear, as the capitals speak first or primarily to the eye. In each of the two, apparently highly conventional, stanzas of **'My dear Mistress has a Heart'**, the last foot of each of its four-footed lines is, in lines 2, 4, 6 and 8, a trochee ('gave me . . . enslave me . . . wander . . . asunder'); but lines 1, 3, 5 and 7 truncate their last foot by a syllable, so that 'My dear Mistress has a *Heart*' (not an ankle or an elbow). The result of this delicately asymmetrical scansion is that every line ends with what sounds like an unexplained falter, the odd lines because they have one syllable too few, the even because they have one too many. With a striking technical mastery, this effect of varying but inevitable falter, like a flaw in nature or an irony in the mind or what medicine calls a shadow behind the heart, is repeated conclusively in the structure of the whole; for the sense of the poem's first eight-lined stanza and then its succeeding six lines swells to a climax of feeling, of certainty, that is suddenly undercut by a kind of 'rhyme' the reader had not expected, the repetition at the end of the second verse of the last two lines of the first, a *reprise* like a stammer that turns the whole poem into an echo of its sustaining and yet faltering pairs of lines. And yet again, that falter finally does not seem to matter, because where the first time its rhyme-word 'asunder' occurred, it only half-rhymed with 'wander', here in the repetition it comes to rhyme with 'wonder', so the poem is after all strangely complete.

If **'My dear Mistress has a Heart'** is touching and troubling in a way we do not necessarily expect a conventional Restoration lyric to be (so that Victorian critics used to compare it with Burns), the cause is a quality not often found in Restoration poems: its power of latency, its character of reserve. The blank general words with their capitals—'Heart', 'Constancy', 'Joys', 'Mankind'— are a fine hard surface under which (we delusively feel) the real life of the poem goes on; but we feel that real life at the point of breakage, where the poem falters for an instant and then carries on—where we see the surface as *only* surface, with perhaps vacancy beneath. But for this there are no 'explanations', there is 'no going behind'.

In all these poems, minute technical details—what one might call flaws of the surface—speak of conditions that one cannot consider in a merely 'technical' way. All Rochester's most potent and idiosyncratic lyrics develop this sense of 'flaw' into a condition of discrepancy that almost breaks apart the convention he appears to be working within—almost, but not quite: the result is never true burlesque, only a kind of agitation below the social surface. That agitation, or submerged quality of personal apprehension, can render the actual treatment of a conventional subject quite unlike what a reader might expect it to be. It might be said, for instance, that Rochester approaches the question of the physical in love as a libertine, with a frank and cynical 'realism'. That he has realism is true, but to say so may imply a quality of apprehension quite different from what we actually find. To say that in **'The Fall'** Rochester portrays Adam and Eve as a pair of cool libertines caught between the acts is to predicate a poem that has little in common with what he actually wrote:

> Naked, beneath cool Shades, they lay,
> Enjoyment waited on Desire:
> Each Member did their Wills obey,
> Nor could a Wish set Pleasure higher.

The plangency of this comes partly from that negative, 'Nor could', a little like Milton's 'Not that fair field of Enna'. But what is even more striking is the absence of the sensuous, of which the 'puritan' Milton's Adam and Eve in Paradise have far more. When Poussin paints Adam and Eve in Paradise he gives them, over their naked bodies, a hair-style comically close to the great wigs of Louis's court, as though to his mind certain aspects of dress can't be taken off even in Paradise, but are generic to the human estate. Rochester, another court artist, seems to be driven by a comparable yet reversed impulse. It is as if, in order to undress his fallen couple, to get them back towards whatever innocence once meant, *he* has to take off their very bodies, which in this poem are dissolving towards the Platonic condition of shadowy Idea, under trees so abstract as to have grown mere generic 'Shades', dark reflections of themselves, in an experience so reversed as to be only the negative opposite of that dulled satiety which is the one happiness we know. In Rochester's Paradise, 'Enjoyment waited', in a past and future defended from the satisfactions of the horrible present.

If this seems a strained reading of that strange abstract stanza, it should be said that it is only consonant with the poet's representation of physical existence throughout his work: all Rochester's lovers are portrayed, at their most intense, like his Adam and Eve. If these first parents are abstracts, then the poet's typical lovers are simply ghosts, haunting a period of time never 'Now' but only a reflex of past and future. The manner of these poems will make a reader expect an art as of an expert social photographer catching smiling and solid persons in the bright light of the moment: but when looked at hard, these results are all negative. The speaker of **'Absent from thee'**, whose 'Fantastic Mind' desires only *not* to be a 'straying Fool', makes it his hope, not that he will be true, but that he will betray love *enough*—that he will tie a tight enough knot of

punished infidelity to hold himself steady in: as steady as the poem is held by the syntactic knot of the line which sums up the only available alternative of fidelity—

> To wish all Day, all Night to Mourn.

'An Age, in her Embraces past' starts its vagrancies by letting the reader down from the expected summer's night which its erotic context suggests, into its actual 'Winter's Day' of love: a chilly actuality as mistily indecorous to our conventions of love as are the divergencies of the poem's chief character, a Shade of Soul that wanders ghostily through the poem. Its path is indicated by a ramifying grammar—

> When absent from her Eyes;
> That feed my Love, which is my Soul,
> It languishes and dyes . . .

—that becomes a fragmented style from which even the poet dissociates himself contemptuously ('Love-sick Fancy'), thus disintegrating the medium still further. The poem at last rests for its stability on one conclusion only, that 'expiring' truth attained in 'Absent from thee'; here it takes the form of the stoical 'Pain can ne'er deceive', the belief that jealousy at least provides

> Proof 'twixt her and me,
> We love, and do not dream.

The time scheme proposed in this poem comes to rest, not on present moment, but on that shadowy past and future evoked in its last stanza's re-echoing rhymes, 'when past' and 'at last'. It would seem a mistake to write down this lack of the libertine art of present enjoyment to a mere bad mood of love, a passing depression. For this same insubstantial medium may be found in poems that cannot be written off as court lyrics of love. One of Rochester's strongest short poems, **'The Maim'd Debauchee'**, takes as surface (without quite burlesquing it) the graver heroic style of the period, and its vision extends as wide as state affairs: but it is a fact that its perspective on war and politics is identical with that of the lyrics on love. Immediately beneath the grave, powerful surface, all is a resonant dissolution:

> Shou'd some brave Youth (worth being drunk) prove nice,
>   And from his fair inviter meanly shrink,
> Twould please the Ghost of my departed Vice,
>   If, at my Counsel, He repent and drink.

That the warrior of love here becomes a Ghost of Vice fits the peculiar decorum of the poem, for its situation offers the temporal vertigo of a man who lightens the miseries of present love by toughening himself with the reminder of the prospects of future impotency—the future pleasure, that is, of remembering a then past potency. The fragile, hardly Socratic, self-knowing wisdom which its last two syllables tender ('be wise') is something like the knowledge that human beings love, or lust for power, in order to enjoy looking forward to the pleasure of looking back at the pain of having suffered. It moves in fact from

My Pains at last some respite shall afford . . .

to:

Past Joys have more than paid what I endure.

The brute strength of these factual-sounding lines has to be balanced against the shadowy non-existence they record. The poem celebrates fulfilments never more than ostensible. And its title, **'The Maim'd'**—or, as Vieth reads, **'Disabled'**—**'Debauchee'**, compacts into a phrase the theme of impotency or emptiness below the surface of an extreme worldly experience.

This theme, brilliantly embodied in the matter of the poem, is oddly reflected too in one specific detail. I am still quoting here from the Muses' Library text of the poems; but in that edition, this poem's climactic stanza will not be found in the text, only doubtfully added to the notes at the back of the book. And even there, it is to be read only in the more decent version which the 1680 text printed, and which Vieth rejects for one hardly printable until a decade or so ago. Thus, earlier versions, extending over nearly three centuries, all give the poem as it were a hole in the page, a void between the lines. The editorial problem, in fact, which begins with a matter as simple as Rochester's use of the notorious four-letter word, properly considered takes us right to the centre of the whole question of his aesthetic purpose, as expressed in the characteristic abstract violence of his style. For an art that so brilliantly and customarily brings together fact and fantasy, the surface and the void, also brings together with particular point the elegant and the obscene. For in obscenity, in the words unprintable—except in pirated editions—even in Rochester's time, the extreme of verbal and emotional nothingness is reached. Whatever the changing proprieties in an age, an obscenity is a non-word, a hole in the page—a betrayal of human sense and meaning to mere grunting phatic gesture.

It is clear, I think, that Rochester, who is sometimes misnamed a pornographic poet, wrote as a man capable of thinking of his obscenities in precisely this way—with the eye and ear of the sensitive man who once came to court not merely blushing but stammering, finding certain things unsayable. Consider the missing stanza from **'The Maim'd Debauchee'**:

> Nor shall our *Love-fits Cloris* be forgot,
>   When each the well-look'd *Link-Boy* strove t'enjoy
> And the best Kiss, was the deciding *Lot*,
>   Whether the *Boy* us'd you, or I the *Boy*.

It could hardly be said that this gets worse when Vieth reads,

> Whether the boy fucked you, or I the boy . . .

In fact a strong case could be made for feeling that the verse undoubtedly gets better in the more brutal transposition. For that specific, end of the road, last-ditch verbal

shock both embodies and in some curious way resolves the other much larger shock which the poem is about: which it is both about, and bespeaks in everything we mean when we gesture vaguely towards its 'mock heroic' or burlesque manner.

A more recent poem, one of Philip Larkin's, mentions the 'long perspectives / Open at each instant of our lives', meaning the deracinating shocks time brings to those whose element is said to be the temporal; and Rochester's 'obscene' stanza provides this among other shocks. It brings to a culmination, just before the end of the poem, everything *pastiche* in it up to that point: in an imitation of 'antiquity' whose soft delicate indelicate procedure has hardly been improved on in three hundred years of translation, imitation, pastiche and burlesque, up to and even including Pound's reversals and repetitions of a whole century of phoney classicism. Rochester's stanza aches with an almost Virgilian sense of distance, the yearning both of and for the classical, since all epic from Homer on looks back to an earlier innocence only surviving in an epic lumber of weapons, feasts, ships, the nicknames of gods and the code of poets. That loaded long-perspectived classic sense of life in time Rochester reaches back for and wraps around, not a battle or great feast but a memory of private pleasure; and that memory and that pleasure capsize the great mood, bring it down to a ground-bass of simple wordless obscenity. This last line is, in its way, perhaps tender, perhaps funny; it also shows reality dissolving, chaos and promiscuity taking over, and sheer nothingness opening all around.

The self-defeating lordly art of that 'unprintable' final line is generic to Rochester's work, which offers many parallels—though not, of course, in such older texts as the Muses' Library, in which a couplet or a whole poem will become that 'hole in the page': as where the poet, skating on the thin ice of obscenity, has fallen in. In all of them Rochester devotes his elaborate talent to capturing both phonetic and semantic nullity: as when he settles the scope of his monarch's affections with a noise as of a mud bath, in 'Love he loves, for he loves fucking much'; or, leaving his club or coffee house one evening, looks back, as it might be down to the bottom of a well, to see and hear the *Symposium* reduced to the sound of frogs—

> Much wine had passed, with grave discourse
> Of who fucks who and who does worse . . .

This reductiveness and this nullity are in fact the heart of the matter, for Rochester can when decorum demands maintain the same brutal art of monosyllables without the aid of obscenity, as when Artemisia gives us the whole Art of Love in wondering whether

> The old ones last, and who and who's together.

Similarly, the ***Satire against Mankind*** says the last word when it paraphrases the whole Hobbesian dance of human society as

Man undoes *Man,* to do himself no good

—an extraordinary complexity of sonic monotony, a concrete music of fallen nature.

To observe the peculiar artistry of Rochester's single-lined brutalities is to understand more clearly what he is doing in whole poems like the extraordinary complex of finesse and unrepeatability, *A Ramble in St James's Park,* whose *Symposium*-like opening pair of lines I have just quoted (from Vieth's edition). The poem is a vision of the social scene as a violent phantasm, with the darkness of night-time London showing through it. Its poised yet perhaps three-quarters-mad speaker has been betrayed by the 'infinitely vile, when fair' Corinna, taking turns with three young blades (a Whitehall gadabout, a Gray's Inn wit, and a Lady's Eldest Son) who may well embody the world, the flesh, and the devil in person; and what maddens the poet to near screaming-point is that this semi-goddess has sold him *for nothing,* as exercise of mere preference of change for change's sake, fashion in love; a preference which therefore brings the speaker in all logic to recognize his equal guilt in similarly loving a mere nothing, a mere love object, a figment of imagination. In self-punishment as much as revenge he curses her with the fate logic demands: she shall 'go mad for the north wind . . . and perish in a wild despair'.

The *Ramble*'s savage, dangerous, yet obscurely innocent fantasy—innocent from the sensed rectitude which its upside-down fury violates, the contained and quashed romantic idealism without which we could not (I think) laugh at that wilfully frightful ending—epitomizes much of what Rochester does in his elegant and obscene writings. If one says 'much' rather than 'all', this is because the violently sustained grossness of the *Ramble,* its comic extravagance or fantasy of wildly pained love, unbalances that poise which the poet more usually maintains. A more representative art may be found in a slighter poem, in the delicate brilliance of the translated 'Upon Drinking in a Bowl'. This poem is from Ronsard's version of the Anacreontic 'Cup' lines. But Rochester's final effect is radically unlike the almost Jonsonian directness Ronsard keeps to here. Its difference will illustrate well enough—better in fact, than the *Ramble*—that art by which Rochester will place obscenity up against a brilliant social surface.

For the poet makes two mutually opposed departures from Ronsard. Taking a hint from Cowley's version of this much translated poem, Rochester gives it a vein of controlled fantasy that Ronsard knows nothing of: he replaces the French poet's sober directions by allowing the poem to mime before us the shaping of the cup, to call forth to the imagination the 'contrivance' and 'Skill' of its 'trimming', the chaste feel of it to the mind as it is 'Damasked . . . round with gold'. Fantasy begins to build on the simpler sensuousness of 'Damask': the 'swelling Brim' holds an almost Mallarméan vision of imagined toasts swimming on the 'delicious Lake, / Like Ships at Sea'; and on this image, the poem flashes through each stanza scenes of War, of the Planets, of a Vine, each perceived only to be rejected. The poem grows and solidifies as the imagined cup, an exquisitely 'holding' structure, is turned before us in an imagined hand. With the sixth stanza, quietly, this whole beautiful structure is tossed away, like a wineglass thrown over the shoulder. Building on a mere hint offered by Ronsard, who introduces a vulgarism ('*Trogne*', 'mug' or 'phiz', for Bacchus's face), Rochester closes:

> *Cupid* and *Bacchus* my Saints are;
>   May Drink and Love still reign:
> With Wine I wash away my Cares,
>   And then to Love again.

In this last line, where the more seemly Muses' Library text reads 'Love', Vieth follows the 1680 text and prints a cruder monosyllable, mockingly alliterating with 'Cares'. This obscenity must be, I think, what Rochester wrote. He has given this exquisite but shocking small poem a wholly original structure, necessitating two opposed poles: the one creating in fantasy an extremity of imagining; the other with one casually dropped word shattering everything that has gone before. The final dynamic effect of the poem is not unlike the extraordinary structure which Milton's bad angels erect in hell: a brilliant energy of human creation, teetering over a void.

Rochester's biographers have noted that in his last years—his early thirties—his reading turned to history, philosophy and politics; and they have surmised on that basis that had he lived he might have given more time to the public affairs he had profoundly despised earlier. In something of the same spirit Robert Parsons implies that on his death-bed Rochester looked forward to the writing of sacred poetry. Both prospects seem unlikely. Both seem, moreover, to be associated with the kind of anxiety that impels even his best critics (like, for instance, David Farley-Hills in his admirable study) to overstress the 'positive' aspects of his work, either in the direction of making much of the philosophical importance of his ideas, or of underlining the exciting fictiveness of the more substantial poems—of finding in them even the three-dimensionality of the novelist. Both ventures risk distorting the real aesthetic quality of Rochester's poetry. A moment's consideration of some of the couplet poems will show how little truly 'fictive' they are, how little they rest within the play of psychological and social relationships.

Rochester's more overtly satirical writing makes it seem odd that there is still any question as to why he chose Timon as a persona. Shakespeare's character took the covers off the dishes at his banquet to show, beneath, nothing but spangles and warm water; and he looked forward to his removal from the great social scene with the words

> My long sickness
> Of health and living now begins to mend
> And nothing brings me all things.

Of *A Letter from Artemisia in the Town to Cloe in the Country* one might say that all things bring us nothing.[9] Some recent critics regard this as Rochester's best poem, and the quality most admired is its fictive density of substance, its moral relativism. This admiration is responding to something true in the poem which explains its sheer entertainingness; but it is a dangerous admiration that overlooks an essential element of structure. 'Dear *Artemisia*! Poetry's a Snare': and this poem is as reductive, as self-underminingly self-consuming as anything Rochester ever wrote, the seductive promise of whole Decamerons of future stories with which it ends as unaccomplished and unaccomplishable as those 'Promises' and 'Vows' which end **Upon Nothing**: for Rochester was not a man who wrote the same poem twice. And it is an unalterable condition of the poetic form that, unlike drama or the novel, poetry has no free-standing voice, each persona must be taken responsibility for by the poet—who was, in this case, as peculiarly well known to the audience for whom he wrote for his masculine gender as for his aristocratic standing. Rochester never, that is to say, writes like a woman, only like a man writing like a woman, and carefully selecting only such female attributes as may solidify the equation latent in the opening that women are to men as the individual man of wit is to the rest of society. For, as Rochester says elsewhere,

> *Witts* are treated just like common *Whores*,
> First they're enjoy'd, and then kickt out of *Doores*
> . . .
> *Women* and *Men* of *Wit*, are dang'rous Tools,
> And ever fatal to admiring *Fools.*
> Pleasure allures, and when the *Fopps* escape,
> 'Tis not that they're belov'd, but fortunate,
> And therefore what they fear, at last they hate.[10]

From the beginning we hear Artemisia, for all the brilliance of the impersonation, as Rochester's voice at one remove, and gain perpetual pleasure at the paradoxical comparisons that continually arise from his two-faced mask of man of wit and woman; indeed the pleasure derives from the exact measuring of the distance of that remove—'Thus, *like* an arrant Woman, as I am'. This is a game that grows more difficult, but all the more worth playing, as the resemblances stretch and grow thin but still sustain through the inset personae of fine lady and true whore. The poem is composed of women betraying each other—and the other sex, too, insofar as it comes in their way—and is thus made up of a descending series of self-scrutinies, of measurements of the treachery that detachment from the human self entails, when a writer (for instance) stops living in order to sigh, in an impossible self-denying act of self-scrutiny, a remark like

> Were I (who to my cost already am
> One of those strange prodigious Creatures *Man.*)
> A Spirit free, to choose . . .

This construct made out of creative treacheries, this descending spiral of darker and darker illusion analysed, may explain Rochester's choice of a name for his heroine. The word 'Artemisia' means the species of bitter herb that contains the plant wormwood, and the poet may have thought this 'flower of Artemis' a good name for his sharp-

tongued virginal heroine; but Rochester's impersonation of a female speaker suggests that he remembered the punchline of a story from Herodotus's account of the Persian Wars.[11] Artemisia, Queen of Halicarnassus, saved herself at the battle of Salamis by a brilliant act of treachery: hotly pursued by a Greek vessel and finding her way barred by one of her own allies, she promptly rammed and sank the allied ship. The Greek pursuer assumed that she must therefore after all be Athenian, and turned away; the observers of her own party assumed that the rammed vessel must after all be Athenian, and sang her praises. Xerxes said afterwards: 'My men have behaved like women, my women like men!'

In the circumstances this remark has complexities that resonate in the memory (though Herodotus did not think it his business to notice them); the likelihood is that they lingered in Rochester's, given the subtle and paradoxical games based on wars of the sexes that he goes in for in *Artemisia,* from the point of view of the unsexed, unsocial writer—

> Like Men that marry, or like Maids that woo,
> Because 'tis the very worst thing they can do.

For the poem traces a charming, casual course downwards from disloyalty to criminal treachery. The substance is so delightfully 'sociable', so randomly entertainingly gossipy, so thick with amusing observations of the known, that we barely notice its structure, which is hardly in fact extrusive: it may even be slightly flawed. But it has without doubt three descending stages. We open with the innocent but wilfully sentimental Artemisia's discovery of solaces for herself—from a social world that both governs and disgusts her—in the conscious follies and illusions of art, turning from a hated passionless love to a loved loneliness of letter writing. From there the poem moves by a refined malice on Artemisia's part to the inset treacheries of the 'fine lady', who is false not only to the other sex—her poor fool of a husband—but even to her own species, preferring the 'dirty, chatt'ring . . . Minature of Man', a monkey to be fondled instead of a human creature to be loved. And she herself glances down with a considering pity to the voiceless, unindividuated, merely type-treachery of Corinna, who—a kind of dark shadow behind the delicate Artemisia—also knows how to use her experience and others' for her own purposes, but who rests, 'diseas'd, decay'd', at the mortgaged bottom of society, 'looking gay', 'talking fine', her every feeling a lie and her whole life an illusion—her child a 'Bastard Heir' to existence itself, the shadow of a shadow of a shadow. The poem climbs down through one level of fashion and fantasy to another, and then another as through a 'snare'—

> (*Bedlam* has many Mansions; have a care)

—which catches us and lands us on the brilliant last line:

> But you are tir'd, and so am I.
>   Farewel.

In a letter to his friend Savile, Rochester wrote: 'The World, ever since I can remember, has been still so unsupportably the same'. It is on that 'tired' insight into some pure banality in social existence that the poem rests, as on a rock. And later he wrote to the same correspondent, casually: 'few Men here dissemble their being Rascals; and no Woman disowns being a Whore'.[12] *Artemisia* is a kind of undissembled dissembling, an owned disowning, because it is a social construct itself, and gives genuine pleasure thereby: it is a letter to a friend just like these often delightfully witty friendly letters Rochester wrote to Savile, or the usually charmingly kind and nonsensical notes he sent home to his wife. But at the same time it expresses the weary lucidity of Rochester's insight into the social self: it is a progressively more ruthless, more searching light turned towards the darkness that cannot be either 'dissembled' or 'disowned'. And it is on that darkness, the lack of anything beyond the self-cancelling illusions of the poem, that it rests: there is nothing else, and nothing is what it is. At the centre of *Artemisia* is the fine lady who defines the aesthetic which both poem and social world are content to share, with a line that clearly haunted Swift's imagination: 'The perfect joy of being well deceiv'd'. So long as the poem lasts the poet is content to stay within that 'perfect joy', to follow out to the end his own curiously elegant, undoubtedly entertaining construct of lies and illusions: one that is successful enough to make many of its readers ask (as does Rochester's best editor), 'Which of the poem's many characters represents the truth?'— when the only answer is, 'Fewer and fewer and less and less'.

This is something like the answer, at any rate, which Rochester gives in his most powerful poem, the *Satire against Mankind,* whose finality is its essential character, at whatever stage of the poet's career it happened to be written. It is here that a reader may see most clearly the achievement and the cost of Rochester's peculiar art of extremity, the intensity he gained by arriving at the point where something comes to an end:

> Then Old Age, and experience, hand in hand,
> Lead him to death, and make him understand,
> After a search so painful, and so long,
> That all his Life he has been in the wrong.

I mentioned earlier Rochester's use of capitals, and the faltering rhythm that breaks his strongest lines. The peculiar character and memorability of this climactic fourth line is the way that capital L 'Life' quietly dissolves into wavering distractedly weak negatives—Man is not, but 'has been', he is nowhere but 'in the wrong'. This 'satire' is no satire, but simply a poem, which we cannot understand unless we believe its medium, its verbal surface; and this poem, which seems to have so much public clarity, in fact works through a style like a misty secret labyrinth in which the person who reads well gets lost,

>   climbs with pain,
> *Mountains* of Whimseys, heap'd in his own *Brain*:
> Stumbling from thought to thought, falls head-long down.

Into doubts boundless Sea, where like to drown,
Books bear him up awhile . . .

It is, again, unsurprising that the best part of the poem, its harsh, undeniably conclusive opening prelude, moves from paradox ('who to my cost already am') to net us throughout in a rhetoric whose most memorable effects are all explicit intricacies of verbal surface, like that later famous obsessive passage in which the poet winds his subject, Man, in a knot of monosyllables:

> wretched *Man,* is still in Arms for fear;
> For fear he armes, and is of Armes afraid,
> By fear, to fear, successively betray'd
> Base fear . . .

Perhaps only Rochester among English poets could have got such power from the exploration of that purely negative form of imagination, fear.

* * *

It may be asked how a writer whom I have presented as so concerned with 'Nothing' could have made of his work a 'something' still appreciated after three hundred years— indeed, enjoyed and admired now as at no other time since that period of intense success during which the poet himself wrote. I want to finish by suggesting an answer to this question: and it will be one other than the supposal that nihilism as such is peculiarly the concern of the present. Rochester was not a philosophical nihilist, and there is no reason to suppose that, if he were, the modern reader would admire him for it. But the reasons are, I think, in some sense philosophical, so long as we are content to allow that the philosophical can include the highly paradoxical. For Rochester can, like any other poet, be more relevantly 'philosophical' when he is writing entirely playfully, with an appearance of casual randomness, than when he 'thinks' in prose. Rochester's arguments with Burnet, for instance, are well worth looking at: but at their most interesting they only include points that will be put far more forcibly and personally in the verse, even where we might least look for it.

Thus, a reader interested in Rochester's philosophical position could do worse than read the Epilogue he wrote for a friend's comedy, *Love in the Dark* (even the title is Rochesterian, suggestive of that 'mistaken magic' he calls love in **'The Imperfect Enjoyment'**), where he mocks the success of a rival company given to effects of flying spectacle:

> Players turn Puppets now at your Desire,
> In their Mouth's Nonsense, in their Tails a Wire,
> They fly through Clouds of Clouts, and show'rs of Fire.
> A kind of losing *Loadum* is their Game,
> Where the worst Writer has the greatest Fame.

These two brilliant images are better than they ought to be—than any casual satire can be expected to be. This is surely because Rochester was himself a kind of equilibrist, an expert in moving high over that vacuity he defines in

'Love and Life': no past, no future, no present to call his own, beyond a 'miraculous' minute high over the crowd. All his verse is, similarly, a 'losing *Loadum*', a card-game like a slow bicycle race where the loser wins, because he does the difficult thing. The French Symbolist dramatist Jarry wrote a blasphemous essay, which is genuinely funny and innocent, called 'The Crucifixion considered as an Uphill Bicycle Race', which gets us within the area where Rochester needs to be considered; remembering Eliot's remarks on the relative spirituality of certain kinds of blasphemy.

Rochester's angry antipathy to the worldly world of success, that world in which for long he was so anxious to succeed and in which he so long succeeded in succeeding, even to the point at which the perhaps comparably worldly Bishop Burnet remarked with some satisfaction after the poet's death, 'All the town is full of his great penitence'— this world-opposing side of his character was clearly far more evident to the other and probably more intelligent attendant on his death-bed, Robert Parsons, his Puritan mother's private chaplain. It was Parsons who brought to Rochester perhaps his only moment of true spiritual vision, by reading to him Isaiah's prophecy of the Suffering Servant, the Messiah who is a man of no importance at all; and it is Parsons, similarly, who in the sermon he preached at Rochester's funeral at once grasped the game of 'losing Loadum' the poet had played morally all his life:

> He seem'd to affect something Singular and paradoxical in his Impieties, as well as in his Writings, above the reach and thought of other men. . . . Nay so confirm'd was he in Sin, that he liv'd, and oftentimes almost died, a Martyr for it.[13]

It was surely this upside-down spirituality, or reversed idealism, that made Johnson among other eighteenth-century writers think that *Upon Nothing* was Rochester's best poem, for it is the single one of all his works which in its startling depth and largeness comes close to that classic standard, even to that image of Nature which Johnson demanded of his poets; for *Upon Nothing* is of course both cosmology and history, a mischievous rendering down of all those Renaissance histories that start with the Creation and end with the present day. Johnson, who had remarked casually to Boswell that 'Politics are now nothing more than means of rising in the world', would have appreciated Rochester's demonstration that *sub specie aeternitatis* they are also a means of falling in it:

> The great Man's Gratitude to his best Friend,
> Kings Promises, Whores Vows, tow'rds thee they bend,
> Flow swiftly into thee, and in thee ever end.

The liturgical cadence here, as in the music of an ancient Latin hymn gone slightly wrong in the translation, gives *Upon Nothing* something of that real largeness often lacking in Rochester's insubstantial verse—a verse that finally seems to hate substance—and makes of this poem an

object with the extension of a Rubens ceiling reversed, or a Purcell chorale reset for solo flute. Or, to make comparisons within the poet's own work, *Upon Nothing* is empowered, by its source in the paradoxical encomium, to bring into the forefront those elsewhere entirely latent Metaphysical elements in Rochester's imagination, such as he himself tended to dismiss with irritation as the 'extravagances' of 'my fantastic mind'; elements which make, for instance, *A Ramble in St James's Park,* when it is compared with the reductive and mean-minded work of Butler which it so admiringly seems to copy, an actual if finalizing perpetuation (for all its grossness) of earlier Renaissance modes of idealism, rather than a Butlerian destruction of them.

It is in this high and spacious abstraction that *Upon Nothing* contrasts so interestingly with another 'nothing' poem, the very late translation from Seneca's *Troades.* The best lines of this translation are those in which the poet picks up and adds to the essential materialism of his source:

> Dead, we become the Lumber of the World;
> And to that Mass of Matter shall be swept,
> Where things destroy'd, with things unborn are kept
> . . .

Bodies here become disturbingly indestructible, like old dressmakers' dummies stacked among the dusty attics of Chaos: the Lumber image has a humorous irritated homeliness in considering physical existence that is the other side of the coin to Rochester's idealism. Clearly, it was the very closeness and actuality of the Restoration poet's sense of the physical and material world—the inevitabilities of his 'realism', the close limits of the only vision he knew, like the small confines of the court he was ironically drawn to—that threw him back on an idealism markedly negative, abstract: such as Rochester himself found in another Roman poet, Lucretius, after whom he splendidly invoked gods who needed nothing, asked nothing, were angered by nothing. And similarly he maintained against Burnet's Christian God—a god deeply marked by that recurring pragmatism that can make English theology, as Coleridge once remarked, as insistently vulgar as it is realistic—that

> God had none of those Affections of Love or Hatred, which breed perturbation in us, and by consequence he could not see that there was to be either reward or punishment. He thought our Conceptions of God were so low, that we had better not think much of him: And to love God seemed to him a presumptuous thing, and the heat of fanciful men.[14]

It is easier to see, or rather to feel, the flaws in the theology of the time if we turn the kind of over-pragmatism that the romanticism in Rochester was struggling with into its more secular philosophical form: the Hobbesian philosophy that entered deeply into the imagination of the age, even into areas where nothing was consciously felt but angry hostility to Hobbes's premises. Hobbes's philosophy has more power than Burnet's theology simply because it relies more deeply on and speaks more frankly from its age's historical presuppositions than any true theology can honestly do. It is possibly easier to write a *Leviathan* out of mid-seventeenth-century history—out of the disillusioned consciousness of the age—than to create a work of dogmatic theology out of it. Hence the potency of a passage that says:

> The whole mass of all things that are, is corporeal, that is to say, body . . . also every part of body, is likewise body, and hath the like dimensions; and consequently every part of the universe, is body, and that which is not body, is no part of the universe: and because the universe is all, that which is no part of it, is *nothing*; and consequently *nowhere* . . .[15]

Where the religious imagination of a period becomes hopelessly comfortable, a conformist cul-de-sac, more life *may* be found latent in the world of blasphemy or heresy. Thus, even the intensely 'social' Henry James—whom I cite, as having used him elsewhere in this essay—at the end of the nineteenth century turned, like many good writers after him, to the murky world of the ghost story, to express moral and spiritual facts not easy to keep hold of otherwise within the philistine insensibility of contemporary middle-class England. The real subject of *The Turn of the Screw,* as he made clear in a letter, was the appalling exposure of children to lethal adult affections; it was to help him out in saying this, to a society of hard sentimentalists, that he called up the pot-boiling spooks, for whom he apologizes to his correspondent, jokily: 'I evoked the worst I could . . . "Excusez du peu!"'[16] Rochester, two centuries earlier, had 'evoked the worst *he* could': he evoked half-lovingly that 'Nothing' which Hobbes laid down like a Green Belt at the edge of his unimaginably material universe, whose 'body', in the light of what Rochester does with *his* 'Nothing', takes on something of that ghostly immateriality which the poet gave mockingly to *his* 'bodies'—the lovers who haunt his poems.

Such negativism deserves, I think, the highest respect: it should not be brushed aside, in anxious search for more substantial virtues—more positive philosophical values. Rochester's Nothing deserves, what is more, even more respect in that it entails for the poet something of a losing game, a 'losing Loadum'. To refuse, in all honesty, to trust the only world one has; to find oneself incapable, on the other hand, of any other music in one's poetry beyond the crash of breaking glass—this is a fate as grim as that appalling epitaph with which Johnson sums up the fate of Harley: 'Not knowing what to do, he did nothing; and, with the fate of a double dealer, at last he lost his power, but kept his enemies'. Rochester clearly possessed that extreme moral courage that is willing to leave behind a body of work fundamentally 'unlikeable'—that presents the self in it as unlikeable, for the work's sake: a moral courage which is the prime virtue, one would have thought, of all true artists. For, from inside Rochester's work, which is likely to have come from a personality both sensitive and generous as well as honest, no 'nice man' emerges. There is only an image strikingly like that image, now in the National Portrait Gallery, which we mainly know

Rochester by: a portrait surely planned and dictated to the painter by the poet himself, and so an actual picture to match those several verse 'Instructions to a Painter' which were a favourite literary exercise in this period. Half turned away from his audience, whom he regards with a sideways and wary inward amusement, the Earl of Rochester welcomes us with an open gesture of his shining silk left arm, which gesture at the same time directs our eyes to his raised right hand holding a laurel wreath high over the head of a pet monkey; a monkey who, like an image in a mirror, gives to the poet with his left hand a torn fragment from the book he grips open with his right. In aesthetic terms, the animal is the focus of the human being, while reversing his every gesture: its little black mask is raised devoutly towards the white unforthcoming stare that the tall young aristocrat directs down on us; the monkey's small chest slightly unnerving in its nakedness against the costly concealing taffetas that fall from a lace collar over the man's torso. Like his own 'fine lady', the poet is playing with a 'Minature of Man'.

In itself the portrait is a design of pure rebuttal, all dead ends and barriers. It is an impassive self-concealing refusal of disguise, a courtier's serious joke about looking 'frightfully': it takes us back, that is to say, to the elder Wilmot's remark, and summarizes what I have tried to say about an art of social surface. For all such charm as the Rochester portrait has is not a charm of 'personality', but is a matter of the subtle shadowings of the taffeta cascading down below the intelligent but rebuffing eyes of the poet, the silk's beauty sharpened by contrast with the disturbing nakedness of the small ape's chest beneath its blank dark averted mug. Underneath the taffeta there is to all intents and purposes nothing whatever: but the picture is not, for all that, empty—it is full of something, even if that something is couched in mockeries and denials.

Notes

1. See V. de Sola Pinto, *Sir Charles Sedley 1639-1701* (1927), pp. 62-3; also p. 62, note 5: 'The idea of masquerading as an itinerant quack always had a fascination for the Restoration gallants.' Dr Anne Barton suggests to me that Ben Jonson's story of his own disguise forms a possible precedent: 'he with ye consent of a friend Cousened a lady, with whom he had made ane apointment to meet ane old Astrologer jn the suburbs, which she Keeped & it was himself disguysed jn a Longe Gowne & a whyte beard at the light of < a Dimm burning Candle up jn a litle Cabjnet reached unto by a Ledder.' (*Conversations with Drummond,* in *Ben Jonson,* ed. C. H. Herford and P. and E. Simpson (1925-52), I, 141.)

2. *The Boscobel Tracts,* ed. J. Hughes (1830), p. 151. See also Richard Ollard, *The Escape of Charles II* (1966).

3. *The Letters of Henry James,* ed. Percy Lubbock (1920), I, 67, 341.

4. G.S. Street, *Miniatures and Moods* (1893), p. 27; quoted in *Rochester: The Critical Heritage,* ed. David Farley-Hills (1972), p. 254.

5. Anthony à Wood, *Athenae Oxonienses* (1691), II, 489.

6. Edward N. Hooker, 'Dryden and the Atoms of Epicurus', in *Essential Articles for the study of John Dryden*, ed. H.T. Swedenberg Jr. (1966), p. 241.

7. Thomas Hobbes, *Leviathan*, ed. Michael Oakeshott (1946), p. 16.

8. Gilbert Burnet, MS draft of *The History of His own Time*, printed as an Appendix to Ranke's *History of England principally in the Seventeenth Century* (1875), VI, 78; and Halifax, *A Character of King Charles the Second* (1750), pp. 15-46.

9. I quote the Muses' Library title and text for this poem, while changing the spelling of the name to Vieth's *Artemisia*, for reasons suggested in my discussion of the name's possible source.

10. In the last line of this passage from the *Satire against Mankind*, Pinto follows the 1680 text in reading 'And therefore what they fear, at least they hate'. John Hayward, in his Nonesuch Press edition (1926), reads 'And therefore what they fear, at heart they hate'. I have silently altered the Muses' Library text here to 'last', a reading which I propose as possibly underlying the erroneous *least*; in literary terms, the conclusive ring of 'at last they hate' is both more Rochesterian and more generally Augustan.

11. The relevant parts of Herodotus's *History*, Book VIII, chapters 87-8, here quoted in George Rawlinson's translation of 1858, had not been translated into English before Rochester's death, though there were both Latin and French versions. The story may have reached Rochester indirectly, but it is worth noting that most contemporary accounts support Parsons's description of the poet as 'thoroughly acquainted with all Classick authors, both Greek and Latin', and that Rochester seems to have had no less a taste for reading history than Lucius Cary, who a generation earlier was reading the Greek historians.

12. *The Rochester-Savile Letters*, ed. J. H. Wilson (1941), pp. 40, 73.

13. Robert Parsons, *A Sermon Preached at the Earl of Rochester's Funeral* (1680), p. 9.

14. Gilbert Burnet, *Some Passages of the Life and Death of John, Earl of Rochester* (1680), pp. 52-3, quoted in Farley-Hills, *Critical Heritage*, p. 60.

15. Hobbes, *Leviathan, ed. cit.*, p. 440.

16. Lubbock, *Letters of Henry James*, I, 308.

Pat Rogers (essay date 1982)

SOURCE: Rogers, Pat. "'An Allusion to Horace.'" In *Spirit of Wit: Reconsiderations of Rochester*, edited by Jeremy Treglown, pp. 166-76. Oxford: Basil Blackwell, 1982.

[*In this essay, Rogers provides a detailed analysis of "An Allusion to Horace" to show that Rochester's poem is written in a different cultural, linguistic, and critical context than the Horatian satire on which is depends, and argues that the work should be assessed as a seventeenth-century English poem and not compared too strictly with its first-century Latin inspiration.*]

The poem based on Horace's satire I. 10 has had its share of attention in recent years. It slithers in and out of the *Critical Heritage* volume, and it has been more extensively discussed in the past decade by Dustin H. Griffin, David Farley-Hills and others. There is also an important article by Howard Weinbrot.[1] I am in substantial agreement with the three critics named, for though they differ in some aspects of their reading they accord the poem roughly the same standing, and they have more shared assumptions than perhaps they acknowledge. All of them pay some attention to the link with the Horatian original, even if they describe this connection differently. For example, Farley-Hills argues that Rochester picks up the Dryden/Shadwell dispute 'by using Horace's poem to Dryden's disadvantage'. He goes on to suggest that the poem finally lacks conviction because the pose on Rochester's part is itself unconvincing—that is, the adoption of a 'role of Horatian arbiter of taste'. Weinbrot, like Griffin, notes some of the significant departures made in the later poem, and offers this statement of the general divergence: 'Horace gains our sympathy through association with a good man of letters; Rochester through disassociation from a bad man of letters.' He contends that there is, directly, 'little thematic interplay between the two poems', and speaks of Rochester's 'refusal to be substantially in debt'. The attitude towards Horace is finally neutral: the English satirist uses the Latin as a stalking-horse or point of departure, not (as with Pope) as a constant reference and moral gauge.

Much of this recent discussion seems to me to stand up well, and I do not wish to pick quarrels here. Nor shall I attempt anything comparable to Weinbrot's valuable consideration of the meaning of an 'imitation' in the Restoration context. These large-scale aerial views have their place in criticism, but it may now be time to proceed to the immediate features of the landscape.

The poem's very first phrase, for instance, points up an important divergence from the model. Horace has 'Nempe incomposito dixi pede currere versus / Lucili' ('To be sure, I said that the verses of Lucilius run with a halting foot'); Rochester, 'Well Sir, 'tis granted, I said *Dryden's* Rhimes, / Were stoln, unequal, nay, dull many times'.[2] Of course, Horace is referring to a producible text and a particular occasion (the fourth satire in this first book). Rochester, on the other hand, hadn't to my knowledge said anything to the purpose in any place, and certainly not in a parallel literary undertaking. So the Latin word 'nempe' is supported by an authentic history of previous discourse: the implied listener really would be able to turn up the minutes to find the reference. Rochester has to mount a greater feat of rhetoric, because there has been no real situation to which the verbal gesture corresponds. The 'ongoing dialogue' is a fabrication, and I think this shows: it sounds more like the opening of a Donne satire than one of Horace's. From the start, then, there is something contrived or factitious about Rochester's strategy; but he doesn't care about that, as the Augustans might.

There is an interesting linguistic point at line 3. Rochester has 'What foolish *Patron* . . . so blindly partial.' This goes back to 'Lucili fautor inepte' in the original. (I think it is possible to speak of an original in this sort of case, where the earlier work is not so much paraphrased or developed as worked on, bounced off, so that it is, as it were, left intact by the imitation.) Now without the adverb 'inepte', the term 'fautor' in classical Latin merely meant a promoter or patron; the construction here suggests 'favens', meaning one applauding or protecting in a mindless sort of way. Translators usually import a bad sense by using an English word such as 'partisan'. But on the surface the expression is pretty neutral, and Rochester's 'Patron' is apt because that term itself had not slid very far into outright opprobrium, which it sometimes later was to indicate. It's worth recalling the first sentence of Johnson's *Dictionary* definition, as well as the follow-up, which is all we usually remember:

> *Patron.* One who countenances, supports or protects. Commonly a wretch who supports with insolence, and is paid with flattery.

What 'commonly' asserts is that you *could* support without insolence. In the present context it is certain that Rochester does wish us to have hostile feelings towards Mulgrave. But after all the drift is that Dryden gets the patron he deserves: and it's right that 'patron' shouldn't be an unremittingly hostile expression—that might deflect too much of the criticism away from the main object, Dryden.

In the following lines, there is something perhaps a shade awkward in the management of tenses. Rochester speaks of Dryden's plays, 'embroider'd up and down' with wit, as having 'justly pleas'd the *Town*'. He then goes on to mention the 'heavy *Mass*, / That Stuffs up his loose *Volumes*'. Now plays are interesting because, even if they stay in the current repertoire, they tend to be identified with their first presentation on stage. As against Lucilius, available to Horace chiefly in terms of written works—*texts*, with their continuous present—Dryden is here first located by reference to dramas put on in the recent past. This is important, because it helps to elide one of the great differences in the subject-matter of the two poems. Lucilius is safely dead, a couple of generations back. Dryden is not merely alive, but, as we can now confirm with hindsight, not yet at his literary peak; he is still there in the argument. Horace has to face only the Lucilius party among contemporary critics; but at any moment Dryden may rise up and make his own contribution to the debate. This sense of a live opponent lends a certain menace to the **'Allusion'** which is highly characteristic of Rochester, and the sort of thing he turns to good poetic effect. One might point up the difference by saying that Horace is using a literary controversy with personal overtones, whilst Rochester is using a personal controversy with literary implications. But this

would be going a little too far. The main issue is that past and present have different relations, and Rochester's sequence of tenses is coping with that fact.

I am aware that this is to simplify the cultural situation on both sides of the comparison. For example, in the case of Horace, Fraenkel makes it clear that the poet is taking sides 'in a struggle between rival literary parties . . . His place is on the side of Virgil, Varius, Asinius Pollio . . . and of all those associated with them. Horace is proud to belong to this circle; without overreaching himself (*haec ego ludo*) he knows that he has contributed and is contributing his proper share to the common effort.'[3] Fraenkel even speaks of the poem as 'the manifesto of an advancing force'. Similarly, in respect of Dryden, we must obviously read between the lines a subtext of implication which derives from Dryden's critical pronouncements. As Vieth points out, there is extensive reference, beginning at line 81, to the essay 'On the Dramatic Poetry of the Last Age', the more pointed because that essay makes significant use of this very satire by Horace.[4] Less directly, when words such as 'wit', 'fancy', 'spirit' and 'grace' crop up we may be invited to hear echoes of Dryden's own discussions of imaginative qualities, for example in his preface to *Annus Mirabilis,* with its touchstone of 'apt, significant, and sounding words'.[5] But the simplification is not very damaging if we hold on to the central distinction, which is that Rochester has the beast in view in a very real sense.

One surprising degree of literalism occurs at line 25, when Rochester advises the poet 'Your *Rethorick* with your *Poetry* unite'. The phrasing is obviously infected by the terms used by Horace: '. . . modo rhetoris atque poetae'. Are we meant to think primarily of *oratory,* as the Latin noun would direct us? Eighty years later, Johnson would define *Rhetorick* primarily as 'the act of speaking not merely with propriety, but with art and elegance' (the instances he uses being all taken from the post-Rochester period: Dryden, Locke and Thomas Baker). Only as a secondary sense do we get 'the power of persuasion, oratory', with examples from Shakespeare, Milton and Fairfax. Up to the middle of the seventeenth century, one would expect the latter sense to be the dominant one. Is Rochester importing some of the newer overtones, by a sort of pun on Horace's terminology? The *Oxford English Dictionary*'s sense 3: 'skill in of faculty of using eloquent or persuasive language' might be the nearest, but I leave this question to better scholars of the period.

Moving on to line 32, we encounter an interesting epithet, 'refined' Etherege. Of course, 'gentle George' was a friend and ally of Rochester. But if you stick closely to the order and logic of Horace's original, you could just place Etherege *after* the equivalents to the writers of old comedy (here, Shakespeare and Jonson) and *before* the aping and tedious Flatman. That would mean that Etherege corresponds to 'pulcher Hermogenes'. The Loeb translation[6] here has 'the fop Hermogenes'; it is true that 'pulcher' could mean excellent or noble, but the overtones of the translation seem right. Could there be any kind of covert allusion to Sir Fopling Flutter, who first appeared on the stage at the very juncture when (according to Vieth) the satire was written? Could there, that is, be a suggestion, however affectionate and oblique, of 'over-refined', 'too fastidiously elegant'? There is certainly some such element in Swift's use of 'refine', 'refined', 'refinement' a generation later.

Next, we come to a bit of evidence on the 'dog that did not bark' pattern. Rochester's decision not to supply a parallel to Horace's short autobiographical excursus can be explained by the different course his argument is taking around line 40 and following. He does not seem to have tried very hard to find an equivalent to Horace's reference to the mixture of Latin and Greek in Lucilius. Pope had no trouble in using French as an updated version of Greek in the *Epistle to Augustus* (line 263 and following). It is true that Dryden had not obliged by producing macaronic verse, but Rochester could have got round this. He evidently did not want to introduce too much by way of autobiography: it might reinforce the sense of a merely personal attack. As it is, Horace's charming conceit, lines 31-5 of the original, is simply lost.

The case for Rochester's 'un-Augustan' phrasing and outlook is supported in lines 69-70:

> Till the poor vanquish't *Maid* dissolves away,
> In *Dreams* all *Night,* in *Sighs,* and *Tears* all day.

A hard-line Augustan could scarcely have resisted the yawning opportunity for a chiasmus in the second line, either by recasting the line as 'All Night in *Dreams,* in *Sighs* and *Tears* all Day', or by revamping the couplet altogether:

> The melting Maid is vanquisht quite,
> By day in Sighs and Tears, in Dreams by night.

Not as good as Rochester, but it does show how easy it is to make the Augustan architecture spring up at command, and to get the emphases more pronounced.

I pass on to the culminating passage, that directly implicating Dryden. At line 75, Vieth simply notes: 'A "dry-bob" is coition without emission.' Certainly; but we are now so used to the obscene that we may not always realize when strong poetry takes the form of turning to obscene ends an innocent phrase. The point underlying Rohester's expression 'a dry bawdy bob' is that a familiar phrase is being travestied. A 'dry bob' had a more ordinary or at least more respectable meaning in the sense of 'a taunt, bitter jest, or jibe' (*OED*)—very common right through the seventeenth and eighteenth centuries. But *OED* also gives a more literal meaning, 'A blow that does not break the skin'. This is surely much to the point. Dryden, though full of lubricity, is impotent, not just sexually but as a would-be damaging wit. To pursue the indelicate side of the phrase to the exclusion of all else is to miss an important part of the critique.

What then of the famous phrase 'Poet Squab'? I had always assumed this was a vague mode of abuse, based on the common sense of *squab* as 'short and plump'. But there seems to be more contemporary relevance in an alternative meaning, 'unfledged, raw, inexperienced'. That is how *OED* glosses the use by Shadwell in *The Medal of John Bayes,* and I think it must be applicable here too. The notion of Dryden in the middle 1670s as a callow youth may strike us as inapt, but the logic of lines 71-6 seems to rely on this idea of a green aspirant to the honours of Venus. Indeed, are not these lines very close in spirit to the famous story which Colley Cibber told of Pope—when the young man was 'slily seduced . . . to a certain House of Carnal Recreation, near the *Hay-Market* . . . [to] see what sort of Figure a Man of his Size, Sobriety, and Vigour (in Verse) would make, when the frail Fit of Love had got into him'? The 'little-tiny Manhood' of the poet is duly aroused, and Cibber righteously comes to the rescue of 'this little hasty Hero, like a terrible *Tom Tit*', when he is in danger of doing himself an irreparable injury.[7] One can surely detect in the passage by Rochester the scorn of a practised libertine for the bungling ineptitude of a piffling author attempting to turn urbane lover.

Lines 79-80 again have a lower autobiographical quotient. Rochester uses the image of a laurel distantly, dispassionately almost. Horace had said exactly the same thing in lines 48-9 of his satire, but in his case the remark follows on a small personal claim. What is in the English poet a mere gesture, a recognized figure of speech, has a real element of competitiveness in the Latin. Rochester will not wrest the laurel, as a *post facto* claim; Horace will not seek to wrest the laurel by his very practice, by writing a poem in the precise vein pioneered by Lucilius.

At line 93 Rochester loses particularity and point, in limiting himself to 'five hundred verses every morning writ': Horace is not only more elegant but more comic in dividing the work into sessions before and after dinner. The ending of this verse paragraph is noteworthy because it endorses a mode of composition which, we may think, conflicted with Rochester's own practice, as compared with the ultra-correct Waller school:

> To write what may securely pass the *Test,*
> Of being well read over *Thrice* at least;
> Compare each *Phrase,* examine ev'ry *Line,*
> Weigh ev'ry *Word* and ev'ry *Thought* refine;
> Scorn all applause the vile *Rout* can bestow,
> And be content to please the few who know.

Farley-Hills might say this is unconvincing because it rests on an urbanity Rochester seldom commands for long at a stretch. Or, put slightly differently, that the message requires a poise and certainty of tone which the medium resists. I am not sure about this. One could surely argue that the absence of high Augustan gloss gives the passage a sort of immediacy, of catching the poet with the rubber end of his pencil at the ready. There is occasionally something of a feeling of *de trop* when poets like Horace and Pope call on us to blot our lines more assiduously, because we know that some of their least-blotted lines were already better than anything we shall ever achieve. Rochester has a comforting degree not exactly of incompetence, but of baldness: his technique only frays at the very edges, but fray it does on occasion. His advice seems more *earned,* consequently. One is always more inclined to take advice from people who find it hard to obey their own injunctions, because they can have no vanity in promoting good practices to which they do not keep.

At line 111, Rochester introduces the figure of the courtesan Betty Morice. This enables him to get in a good Restoration riposte and convey something of the flavour of court life—a gain for his poem at this juncture. It is assuredly nowhere near as polished or deft as Horace's line and a half, where the resources of an inflectional language allow him to pack so much into the participle 'explosa':

ut audax,
contemptis aliis, explosa Arbuscula dixit.

('As the bold Arbuscula said, scornful of the rest [of the house], as they hissed her off.') 'Explodo' ('hoot off') was I suppose a good word in Latin, but it has become a better one in view of what has happened to the root in English. This is a supreme moment in the original satire, and whilst Rochester cannot match it he at least avoids disaster by the vivid anecdote.

One final difference, of course, is that Rochester omits the concluding farewell, and Horace's instructions to his boy to carry off his verses to add to his 'libellus'. A great deal is lost, for Horace does not merely round off his volume (something Rochester obviously couldn't do), but gets in a typical self-deprecating, yet purposeful remark. As we saw at the start, Horace is able to suggest that the present poem is a contribution to a larger whole—less, that is, of an off-the-cuff pronouncement. With Rochester, the finality has to be achieved internally, as it were, rather than externally. This is done through the powerful and resonant lines 120-4. He borrows 'I loathe the rabble' from another Horatian context in the *Odes* and makes a fine list of friends and admirers, all of whom seem to have good mouth-filling names. The concluding line lacks the brittle symmetry which an Augustan would have devised for it, but the point is made.

Now such hedge-hopping trips as this have their limitations. Yet within the existing accounts of the poem, it seems to me, there is a lot of detail to be filled in; and to study Rochester at close range is to come away with a realization that there is a great deal going on which has been overlooked in the broader controversies over his intellectual bearings and artistic identity.

In his fine book on Horace's satires, Niall Rudd observes that 'even if Lucilius and Horace had shared the same theories their temperaments would have led to different results'.[8] Yes: and their techniques, as well as their temperaments. Rochester is not merely writing in a differ-

ent age from Horace, about a different target. He is writing in a different linguistic and critical context, for the triumph of the new 'Augustan' poetics was not in 1675 yet assured. One of the great merits of **'Allusion to Horace'** is that it lives within seventeenth-century English as the original lived in the first-century Latin. What I have tried to do is show a few of the ways in which idiom bends in response to the needs of contemporary thought and feeling.

Notes

1. Howard Weinbrot, 'The *Allusion to Horace*: Rochester's Imitative Mode', *Studies in Philology,* 69 (1972), 348-68.

2. Quotations from Rochester's poetry are taken from the edition by V. de Sola Pinto, *Poems by John Wilmot, Earl of Rochester* (2nd edn revised, 1964).

3. E. Fraenkel, *Horace* (1957), pp. 132-3.

4. *The Complete Poems of John Wilmot, Earl of Rochester,* ed. David M. Vieth (1968), p. 124n.

5. Dryden, *Of Dramatic Poesy and Other Critical Essays,* ed. G. Watson (1962), I, 98.

6. *Horace: Satires, Epistles and 'Ars Poetica',* trans. H. R. Fairclough (1926, revised edn 1929), p. 117.

7. *Pope: The Critical Heritage,* ed. John Barnard (1973), p. 337.

8. N. Rudd, *The Satires of Horace* (1966), p. 117.

Helen Wilcox (essay date 1995)

SOURCE: Wilcox, Helen. "Gender and Artfulness in Rochester's 'Song of a Young Lady to Her Ancient Lover.'" In *Reading Rochester,* edited by Edward Burns, pp. 6-20. Liverpool, UK: Liverpool University Press, 1995.

[*In the essay below, Wilcox discusses the challenges of interpreting the highly sexual lyric "Song of a Young Lady to Her Ancient Lover" in a contemporary academic setting, and notes that the poem raises issues of voice, gender experience, wit, art, and compassion.*]

> As to the Work itself, the very Name of *Rochester* is a sufficient Passport wherever English is spoken or understood: And we doubt not but it will give the highest Delight to all those who have Youth, Fire, Wit and Discernment.[1]

This essay arises primarily out of the experience of discussing Rochester's work with readers who possess plenty of 'Youth, Fire, Wit and Discernment', namely, fascinated but perplexed undergraduates. How does Rochester, they ask, achieve that astonishing rational directness, that surprisingly delicate lyric grace? Why does he so regularly challenge these, and his readers, with cynicism and obscenity? Is his wit sharpened in anger or love?

Is it concerned or dispassionate? Is there a consistent perspective underlying and shaping the variety of poetic masks worn in and by the texts? More particularly, as a male author did he regard the human female with special distaste, or does the sometimes brutal attention given to her indicate attraction? How are human relations, Rochester-style, negotiated? And how are readers' relations and reactions to his texts to be understood and built upon?

This range of questions, adequate answers to which would fill a book, will be focused for the next few pages on just one lyric by Rochester, the one which has caused most impassioned disagreement and bewildered interest among my students—his **'Song of a Young Lady to her Ancient Lover'.** The lyric raises issues of voice, gender, experience, wit, art and compassion; a close look at it may help to suggest ways of responding to Rochester's work and to late-twentieth-century readers' dilemmas concerning it.

1

    Ancient Person, for whom I
    All the flattering Youth defy;
    Long be it e're thou grow Old,
    Aking, shaking, Crazy, Cold;
        But still continue as thou art,
        Ancient Person of my Heart.

2

    On thy withered Lips and dry,
    Which like barren Furrows lye,
    Brooding kisses I will pour,
    Shall thy youthful Heat restore.
    Such kind Show'rs in Autumn fall,
    And a second Spring recall:
        Nor from thee will ever part,
        Antient Person of my Heart.

3

    Thy Nobler part, which but to name
    In our Sex wou'd be counted shame,
    By Ages frozen grasp possest,
    From his Ice shall be releast,
    And, sooth'd by my reviving hand,
    In former Warmth and Vigor stand.
    All a Lover's wish can reach,
    For thy Joy my Love shall teach:
    And for thy Pleasure shall improve,
    All that Art can add to Love.
        Yet still I love thee without Art,
        Antient Person of my Heart.[2]

As we might expect of Rochester, the immediate impact of the poem is contradictory. It is clearly dramatic, with a constructed female voice addressing her male lover intimately and apparently, at times, with tenderness. Yet despite this dramatized individuality, the lyric is strangely impersonal, with unnamed participants not even honoured with pastoral labels. What distinguishes them is simply their gender and age—this is an anonymous young woman

verbally caressing an older man. It is important, though, to note that the title defines the relative social roles and status of these stereotypical characterizations. The female speaker is not immediately identified as a whore,[3] nor even as a mistress; she is independent and as a 'lady' has some propriety. And in an already teasing inversion of conventional relationships and prevailing social conditions, the man is rendered secondary, dependent upon the 'lady' for his identity, as he is 'her lover'.

How significant, however, are the differences in age and gender between the speaker and her lover? Initially it could be assumed that in these respects the speaker is identified with a number of disadvantages, at least in terms of seventeenth-century society. She is youthful and thus inexperienced, naïve; she is female, and thus liable to be a possession of either her father or her husband—a legal nonentity, a nameless subordinate absorbed into patriarchy just as a 'rivulet' is incorporated into a larger river.[4] The anonymity of 'young lady' in the title is therefore perfectly apt: 'young' gives place to old, 'lady' to man. However, this is to reckon without Rochester's vision of the world, in which to be male is to be at the mercy of devouring females or unwilling physique, and to be old is to realize this all the more vividly. Timon, for example, is confronted with this assumption in the opening of Rochester's satire of that name:

    What Timon does old Age begin t'approach
    That thus thou droop'st under a Nights debauch?

                     (ll.1-2)

And in Rochester's portrait of 'rational' human nature in **'Satyr',** the last stage of life is mercilessly characterized:

    Then Old Age, and experience, hand in hand,
    Lead him to death, and make him understand,
    After a search so painful, and so long,
    That all his Life he has been in the wrong;

                   (ll.25-28)

Perhaps, bearing in mind Rochester's undermining of the traditional wisdom and authority of old age, the youthful naïvety, pride and hope of the young lady are preferable to ancient disillusion.

Relationships between these two extremes, a young woman and an old man, were common in seventeenth-century England, when so many women died in childbirth, leaving widowers who sought a new partnership and security of inheritance with a second, and sometimes even a third, young wife. Such relationships were often seen in mercenary terms, as in Dorothy Osborne's lighthearted account of

An old rich Knight, that had promised mee this seven year's to marry mee whensoever his wife dyed, and now hee's dead before her, and has left her such a widow it makes mee mad to think on it, 1200 a yeare Joynter and 20000 in mony and personall Estate, and all this I might have had, if Mr Death had bin pleased to have taken her instead of him. Well whoe can help these things . . .[5]

These partnerships, however, frequently ceased to satisfy either party, and Robert Burton listed difference of age as one cause of melancholy between men and women:

A young Gentlewoman in *Basil,* was married . . . to an ancient man against her will, whom she could not affect; she was continually melancholy, and pined away for griefe.[6]

In Rochester's lyric, far from pining away, the autonomous young lady (who is not, it seems, married to her ancient beloved) puts all her energies into making the relationship physically and emotionally (and not necessarily financially) satisfying to them both. Yet again, Rochester is working against the grain of powerful social stereotypes.

Burton used the phrase 'ancient man' to refer simply to advancement in years, but it is worth pausing over the fact that Rochester distinguishes between 'ancient' and 'old'. The latter appears to refer to more extreme senility— 'aking, shaking, Crazy Cold'—while 'ancient' implies the slightly less terminal, though not very flattering, 'Withered Lips and Dry'. The chief meaning of the word 'ancient', as used in the refrain, 'Ancient person of my heart', is probably time-worn but long established, suggesting continuing loyalty to what we would term (again without direct reference to age) an 'old friend' (*OED* 5). The young lady's 'heart' stresses the ancientness of their love, not his maturity. Despite the poem's sometimes insulting references to the actual signs of great age in the lover's body, there are at the same time hints that 'ancient' has the sense of 'venerable' (*OED* 7), a person deserving care and respect. Some versions of the text adopt the spelling 'antient', itself an old-fashioned variant reminding us of the rarity of precious or antique objects (Walker shifts between the two). Does the continuing stress on the lover's physical state suggest that he is, in fact, being treated as such an object? This is, once more, an intriguing reversal of the obsessive itemising attention to the female body found in so much Renaissance and seventeenth-century English love poetry. But is this materialist attentiveness destructive or emboldening?

The young lady's account of her ancient lover's body given in the second stanza is dominated by metaphors of the natural world, metaphors in which gender associations are disrupted and blurred:

On thy withered lips and dry,
Which like barren Furrows lye,
Brooding kisses I will pour,
Shall thy youthful Heat restore.
Such kind Show'rs in Autumn fall,
And a second Spring recall:

(ll.7-12)

The male lover is the passive earth, the element so often regarded as the female principle; in Aristotle's binary world, the feminine is always associated with receptive-

ness and inactivity.[7] Here, it is the male lover's lips and (by association) wrinkled brow which are likened to the 'barren Furrows' of the ground, ploughed (in phallic manner) by life's hard experiences. This is in contrast to Rochester's more conventional gendering of nature in **'Upon his Leaving His Mistriss'**, in which the earth is a female 'seed-receiving' womb on whom 'no show'rs unwelcome fall' (ll.15-17, p. 37). The 'show'rs' which fall in the young lady's song are her own kisses; in her patently wishful account of the future, she herself is the active (masculine) life force whose loving rain ensures a springtime of renewed vigour in her autumnal partner. The gendered opposition, already thus inverted from traditional usage, is complicated. Although much of her activity appears to be associated with the masculine, the lady's language of concern and healing restoration has overtones of maternal care, introduced primarily by the adjective 'brooding' (l.9) and the action 'sooth'd' (l.19). And while she is thus credited with motherly reviving powers which restore her lover's 'Heat', in the third stanza, he is associated not with this giving of birth but with the ice of age[8] and the coldness of death, recalling the misery of a 'winter's day' in Rochester's **'The Mistress'**:

Where Life and Light with envious hast,
Are torn and snatch'd away.

(ll.3-4)

If the young lady's metaphors and envisaged successes are ambiguously gendered, her modest voice in stanza 3 is a deliberately feminine construction:

Thy Nobler part, which but to name
In our Sex wou'd be counted shame,

(ll.15-16)

The self-conscious reference to 'our Sex' is a reminder of the connection between the feminine and restraint, in language and action. Silence and chastity, not-naming and not-shaming, were closely interlinked in seventeenth-century expectations of womanhood, as the rhyme aptly underlines. Ironically of course, the ostentatious modesty of her carefully oblique reference to the lover's sexual organs ensures that the young lady's discussion is no longer oblique. It highlights her knowledge of male sexuality, as much as it demonstrates her awareness of what is expected of an innocent young lady's conversation. The personal and the social, though distinct, are shown to be inseparable here. The dangers of female obedience to the social code, when such coyness ran contrary to genuine female desire, were outlined bleakly by Rochester in the conclusion of **'Song'**:

Then if to make your ruin more,
You'll peevishly be coy,
Dye with the scandal of a Whore,
And never know the joy.

(ll.13-16)

However, the joyfully sensual language in the earlier stanza of the **'Song of a Young Lady'** defies the subsequent prim deference to feminine verbal modesty. The context of the final stanza eventually clarifies what the 'Nobler part' refers to, though in the circumstances one wonders how ironic this reference is, bearing in mind the 'withered', 'barren' and 'frozen' state of her ancient lover. Elsewhere in Rochester's work, the physical has in fact shown itself to be 'the frailer part', while the 'nobler' is an adjective reserved for the 'tribute of a heart', the metaphysical aspect of love (**'The Fall'**, ll. 14-16). Contemporary understandings of love often identified the honourable realm of love with the feminine ideal—chaste, noble—and the physical realm with masculine initiative; as a real 'Young Lady' wrote in 1691, 'Female our Souls, all Masculine our Love'.[9] There may well, therefore, be several layers of irony in this reference to the 'Nobler part'. In its immediate application, the stark reality is that the lover's penis is feeble and in need of revival; by ironic transfer, nobility refers to the ideal of love rather than its inadequate physical reality; and in taking this transfer of meaning, the 'nobler part' ceases to be a reference to virile masculinity at all but becomes associated instead with the feminine soul. To 'name' the genuinely 'nobler part' would, then, lead to not 'shame' but to a transformation of values.

The **'Song'** thus makes possible a number of metamorphoses within (and between) its lines: male to female, physical to spiritual, modesty to outspokenness, winter to spring. Perhaps most importantly, the progression of the poem marks a movement from the natural to the artful, as the strangely reversed cycle of seasonal growth is shown to have been brought about by 'all that art can add to love'. This is an artful lyric, as a look at its structure shows. The initial stanza is carefully framed in first and last lines by the 'ancient person' who is the focus and addressee of the poem. As the stanzas proceed they grow in length, mirroring the spring-like fertility recounted in the second stanza and the expansive revival of the third. Meanwhile, the underlying concept of constancy is expressed in the vocabulary and structure of the refrain, returning to the lover each time with terms implying continuation, notably the repeated 'still' of perpetuated loyalty. Even as the lyric speaks of improvements and additions—and the stanzas add their extra lines in mimicry—the unchanging refrain works in a contrary motion, defying the very notion of change which the young lady promises. That change, too, is knowingly artful, a conscious reversal of the conventional romance narrative in which the love of a young man transforms an old hag into a beautiful maiden; in this newly engendered tale, the loyalty of a young lady transforms an ancient person into a vigorous lover.

The word 'art' occurs three times during the lyric, and its developing meanings epitomize the progress of the poem. Its first appearance is not as a noun at all, but incidentally, as part of the verb to be: 'But still continue as thou art' (l.5). This provides both an aural anticipation of the artistry referred to later and an indication of the status quo at the beginning of the poem, a kind of naturalness, the state of being. The second and third uses of 'art' come in adjacent lines towards the end of the poem:

> All a Lover's wish can reach,
> For thy Joy my Love shall teach:
> And for thy Pleasure shall improve,
> All that Art can add to Love.
>   Yet still I love thee without Art,
>   Antient Person of my Heart.

>   (ll.21-26)

What is it that 'art' can add to love? Clearly this is a use of art as skill (*OED* 1), a reference to a lover's techniques learned, perhaps, from Ovid's *Ars Amatoria* and undoubtedly echoing its title. There is an implication that pleasure in love may be learned (and taught); that the young lady is 'mistress' of these arts is implied in the steady growth of the stanzas and their ever more hopeful sense of improvement. Similarly in Rochester's poem **'Verses Put Into a Lady's Prayer-Book'**, the speaker urges that, with the aid of love, he and his lady:

> . . . By easie steps may rise
> Through all the Joys on Earth, to those Above.

>   (ll.16-17)

In both poems the lovers' experience of joy is progressively upgraded, the 'easie steps' here echoing the idea of the lover as a pupil in the young lady's school of love. But in contrast to this practical sense of art as learned skills, the final use of the word in **'Song of a Young Lady'** introduces overtones of undesirable unnaturalness (*OED* 2), deceit and trickery, as she assures her lover that her affection for him is 'without Art'—in other words, unaffected and without guile. But if such meanings are prominent in this final usage, may they not also lurk in the earlier references to art? Can any interference of art in nature ever be trusted?

This question, one which underlay many Renaissance and seventeenth-century debates about love, is particularly pointed when we recall the artfulness of the poem itself, not just in its self-conscious lyric structuring but also as an artifact, a 'counterfeit' as Sidney would have it.[10] If this is potentially true of most poems, it is especially true here when the character of the speaker is so obviously artificial: a female voice constructed by a poet known to be male. There are, moreover, significant implications in the idea of artistry when applied to a female writing verse, suggesting extra layers of deceit and danger. As Rochester famously wrote in *A Letter From Artemiza in the Towne to Chloe in the Countrey* (p. 83), a woman speaking in poetry was hardly to be trusted:

> Whore is scarce a more reproachable name,
> Than Poetess:

>   (ll.26-27)

Nor was Rochester alone in implying this. Margaret Cavendish, who wrote prolifically at this time, knew that to be a 'writing lady' was seen as an aberration and a threat; her texts encroached upon male rights, for men

> hold books as their crown, and the sword as their sceptre, by which they rule and govern.[11]

Literary artistry and the arts of social control were not far apart in the later seventeenth-century. Even the outspoken Cavendish distinguished between her writing and that of her husband: while he 'wrote' with 'wit', she 'scribbled' with mere 'words'.[12] And as the anonymous female author of 'The Emulation' wrote in 1683, men

> let us learn to work, to dance, to sing,
> Or any such like trivial thing,
> Which to their profit may Increase or Pleasure bring.
> But they refuse to let us know
> What sacred Sciences doth impart
> Or the mysteriousness of Art.

Yet, despite being denied access to the sanctuary of high art, this female poet concluded that women can produce poetry in their own way:

> To Nature only, and our softer Muses, we
> Will owe our Charms of Wit, of Parts, and Poetry.[13]

This recalls the statement of the 'young lady' at the end of her song, that she loves 'without Art' both in her honest passion and her simple lyricism. A plain style without the counterfeits of complex rhetoric was also favoured by Dorothy Osborne, who commented that, in contrast to the frank artistry of a female writer, it was

> an admirable thing to see how some People will labour to find out term's that may obscure a plain sence, like a gentleman I knew, whoe would never say the weather grew cold, but that Winter began to salute us.[14]

So, while the artful 'young lady' risks her reputation as a woman by making so bold as to write in verse at all, her conclusion in its denial of art typifies the peculiar entanglement of the female writer, who uses art to hide it in order to retain some vestige of acceptable and apparently honest femininity.

However, within her **'Song'** the young lady makes reference to other arts than poetry. The art which 'teaches' love is a particularly brazen subject for a female speaker, and introduces ideas not only of sensual prowess but also of the art so often associated with the feminine: making the female body itself into a work of art, to attract a lover. In contrast to this female social artistry, Rochester depicts the equivalent art of the masculine in military terms, using the vocabulary of conquest in the **'Imperfect Enjoyment'**: the male approaching with 'stiffly resolv'd' penis like a 'dart of love' which violently 'pierc'd' its object (ll.41-43). Female 'arts' are rarely seen by Rochester as so direct or aggressive; even the less accomplished women in **'Upon His Leaving His Mistriss'** attempt 'by their Arts' to make '*one* happy Man' (ll.10-11). And if they are deceptive or underhand, female arts are generally shown to be manipulative rather than destructive. As another of Rochester's female voices comments in *Artemiza to Chloe*:

> They little guesse, who att Our Arts are griev'd,
> The perfect Joy of being well deceaved.

(ll.114-15)

How well, then, are we readers deceived by the arts of **'Song of a Young Lady'**? Initially we tend to connive contentedly in the fiction of a crafted female persona, a double counterfeit because of the known gender of the author. But beyond this, what are the possible deceptions operating? The young lady asserts at the beginning that she defies 'all the flattering Youth' in order to remain true to her ancient lover; but how far is her song itself an instance of superficial flattery rather than tender concern? And if such flattery has a hollow ring to it, how far can 'age' turn the tables on youth and defy its deceiving flattery? But when we pause to consider the possible reactions of the ancient person(a), we realize that, for all the female artfulness, the focus of the poem, in addition to being the current inadequacies of his physical being, is in fact his own joy, his 'pleasure'; the song holds out tempting mirages of new life and restored virility for him. Equally, there is a strong sense of the lady's delight in her powers of restoration and her proffered arts, recalling the lines in **'To a Lady in a Letter'**:

> For did you love your pleasure lesse,
> You were noe Match for mee.

(ll.27-28)

The lady and her lover, despite imbalances of weakness and power, experience and innocence, seem to be on equal terms when it comes to agreeing to the pursuit of pleasure. Or is this another of the song's riddling deceptions, making us forget temporarily the inevitable inequalities also explored in the poem?

With all its layers of irony, the **'Song'** has to be read as a wryly amusing poem; it certainly contains the ingredients of a comic scenario in its complex juxtapositions of youth and age, art and nature, loving and insulting language. But is the laughter affectionate or mocking, and does the lady laugh, or just her reader? There is undoubtedly some irony at the expense of her ancient lover, particularly focused on his 'Nobler part' and all that is signified by that phrase and its careful contextualising in the song. But it is difficult to discern how knowing the young lady is, especially with regard to her own self-ridicule. The mock-modesty of the beginning of the third stanza seems to me to be well under her control; she has assumed too many powers in stanza 2 to remain unaware of the falseness of her coy tones in the subsequent lines. But the denial of 'art' at the end of a precisely-constructed work of art in which the 'arts' of love have been so ostentatiously displayed, is a layer of irony which appears to be the poet's own rather than that of his persona. There is an implication that the male poet will not permit his 'young lady' to get away with controlling the ambivalences in a woman's role as simultaneously experienced and naive lover, as artful but required by social and literary convention to be artless. The lady, then, is mocked by her creator for thinking that she can really love 'without Art' when the very statement is an acknowledgement of her social arts. Her loyalty, too, which might be seen as her genuinely 'Nobler part', is perhaps itself the subject of mockery; why should a young lady turn down all the attentive youth to devote her time to this 'withered' ancient? It is possible, however, that this devotion is not a cause of amusement but of hope, offering reassurance to the male author (and male readers) that a powerful woman (despite all kinds of powerlessness) can be a source of restoration rather than intimidation. The poem is in some ways an answer to the obsessive male fear of dependency and impotence, expressed most forcefully by Rochester in the mock-heroic lines of the **'Imperfect Enjoyment'**:

> Eager desires, confound my first intent,
> Succeeding shame, does more success prevent,
> And Rage, at last, confirms me impotent.
> Ev'n her fair Hand, which might bid heat return,
> To frozen *Age,* and make cold *Hermits* burn,
> Apply'd to my dead *Cinder,* warms no more,
> Than Fire to *Ashes,* cou'd past Flames restore.
>
> (ll.28-34)

The **'Song'**, echoing the metaphors of passionate heat and 'frozen age' employed here, is the antidote to this fear, the assertion that a fair female 'hand' as both caresser and written art can indeed kindle new fires, even in the most ancient of men.

But no poem, especially by Rochester, is likely to be quite as simple as that in its optimism. The **'Song'** appears to be simultaneously a railing of the male ventriloquist-poet against his own sex's vulnerability to the frailness of the physical (and to the attentions of women), and a searching for an image of the youthful life force—which mingles male and female as the lady's metaphors reveal—to ensure rejuvenation. It is a reassuring assertion of the potential of loyalty and affection against the odds; yet it is also a disconcerting exploration of the power of art (particularly female arts) to conceal and trick as well as to heal. William Hazlitt said of Rochester that 'his verses cut and sparkle like diamonds',[15] and like diamonds they also have innumerable surfaces, the source of their teasingly unfathomable wit. The **'Song'** sparkles with a multiplicity of implications about women and men, about art and truth. As readers we have to learn, like Artemiza, to be 'Pleas'd with the Contradiction' (l.30) and to perceive within that the beginnings of a vision. In the case of the **'Song'**, this entails an understanding of the social and personal constraints on women and the implications of 'art' in their hands, but further, hints at the possibility of a destabilising of fixed gender roles in language and in relationships. What is perhaps most startling about the poem is the almost impudent control taken by the young lady, despite her comments on the possible 'shame' of her attitude. In Rochester's poem **'Womans Honor'** (p. 22) he establishes gendered meanings of honour, conventionally regarded in the seventeenth-century as chastity in women and public integrity in men:[16]

> Consider reall Honour then,
>   You'll find hers cannot be the same,
> 'Tis Noble confidence in Men,
>   In Women, mean mistrustful shame.
>
> (ll.21-24)

These terms are triumphantly inverted in **'Song of a Young Lady'**; her tone and approach ring with 'Noble confidence', the serenely perceived vision of a lover restored through her art and her love. 'Shame' is absent from her dealings (even ironically, banished from her language) and is transferred instead to the unspoken shame of male sexual failure. What makes it, finally and surprisingly, into a love song, is the fact that the bitterness of the often discomforting contradictions is subsumed into a refrain of overriding affection. 'Art' and 'heart' remind us of the constraining opposition of the constructed and the natural, in poetry and in gender, but these binaries are allowed, for the duration of the poem at least, the harmony of a rhyme:

> Yet still I love thee without Art,
> Antient Person of my Heart.
>
> (ll.25-26)

Notes

1. From the preface to *The Poetical Works of Rochester* (1761 p. v, in *Rochester: The Critical Heritage,* ed. David Farley-Hills (London, 1972), p. 202.

2. The text is taken from *The Poems of John Wilmot, Earl of Rochester,* ed. Keith Walker (Oxford, 1984), pp. 32-33. All subsequent references to Rochester's works are from this edition; page numbers are given in the main text.

3. See Rochester's *A Letter from Artemiza in the Town to Chloe in the Countery* (pp. 83-85) on pp. 129-34 and further discussion below.

4. See T. E., *The Lawes Resolutions of Womens Rights* (1632), pp. 124-25.

5. Dorothy Osborne, *Letters to Sir William Temple,* ed. Kenneth Parker (Harmondsworth, 1987), p. 87.

6. Robert Burton, *The Anatomy of Melancholy,* ed. Thomas C. Faulkner, Nicolas K. Kiessling and Rhonda L. Blair (Oxford, 1989), part 1. Sect.2 Memb.4. Subs. 7, Vol.I. p. 366.

7. See discussion of this and other fundamental ideas of women 'coming second' in Patricia Parker, *Literary Fat Ladies: Rhetoric, Gender, Property* (London, 1987), pp. 178-233.

8. Because of the uncertainty of seventeenth-century punctuation, some modern texts print 'ages'' instead of 'age's' in line 17, following it with 'From their ice' instead of 'From his ice' (Veith's emendation). Rochester may well have intended the initial ambiguity, implying ancientness across the ages as well as in one man's age. Walker's text respects this by printing 'Ages', though he adopts the emendation to 'his'.

9. A Young Lady, 'Maria to Henric' (1691) in *Kissing the Rod: An Anthology of Seventeenth-Century Women's Verse,* ed. Germaine Greer, Jeslyn Medoff, Melinda Sansone and Susan Hastings (London, 1988), p. 371.

10. Sir Philip Sidney, *An Apology for Poetry,* ed. Geoffrey Shepherd (Manchester, 1973), p. 101.

11. Margaret Cavendish, preface 'To All Writing Ladies', *Poems and Fancies* (1653), no pagination.

12. Cavendish, 'A True Relation of my Birth, Breeding and Life' (1656) in *Her Own Life: Autobiographical Writings by a Seventeenth-Century Englishwoman,* ed. Elspeth Graham, Hilary Hinds, Elaine Hobby and Helen Wilcox (London, 1989), p. 93.

13. 'Triumphs of Female Wit, in some Pindarick Odes. Or the Emulation' (1683), in *Kissing the Rod,* pp. 310-12.

14. Osborne, *Letters,* p. 131.

15. William Hazlitt, *Lectures on the English Poets* (1818), in *Rochester: The Critical Heritage,* p. 214.

16. For a contemporary reference to this difference of meaning according to gender, see 'The Memoirs of Ann, Lady Fanshawe' in *The Memoirs of Anne, Lady Halkett and Ann, Lady Fanshawe,* ed. John Loftis (Oxford, 1979), p. 116.

Stephen Clark (essay date 1995)

SOURCE: Clark, Stephen. "'Something Genrous in Meer Lust'?: Rochester and Misogyny." In *Reading Rochester,* edited by Edward Burns, pp. 21-41. Liverpool, UK: Liverpool University Press, 1995.

[*In the essay that follows, Clark points out that female readers and critics have been surprisingly uncritical of the misogynistic elements in Rochester's poetry, concluding there must be a quality in his poetry that elicits this response. Clark seeks to discern this quality by assessing the degree of "progressivism" in his libertinism, analyzing his plaintiveness and vulnerability, and exploring the paradoxes of the failure of the body in his poetry.*]

Given Rochester's undisputed status as 'one of the dirtiest poets in the canon',[1] one might think that any sustained consideration of his work would at some point involve detailed attention to the issue of misogyny. This has not, however, proved to be the case. It is not that feminist criticism has neglected his writing: in the last 20 years Fabricant, Wilcoxon, Wintle and Nussbaum have all provided illuminating commentaries.[2] Yet considering the attention devoted to inceties of satiric form or problems of textual attribution, this aspect of his work has suffered at least comparative neglect, the issues involved apparently being regarded as simultaneously too self-evident and too problematic. The general impression given is that Rochester has been too readily indulged by his proponents and too easily dismissed by his detractors, and that both parties have tended to rest their respective cases upon the more restricted question of obscenity.

In degree of physical specificity, lines such as 'whether the *Boy* fuck'd you, or I the Boy' (**'The Disabled Debauchee'**, l.40) look positively anodyne in comparison with Dorset's 'strange incestuous stories / Of Harvey and her long clitoris', or claims that Mulgrave 'rears a little when his feeble tarse' is presented with 'a straight well-sphincter'd arse'.[3] As Dustin Griffin observes, 'his obscenity and misogyny are mild when compared to Oldham or Robert Gould or a number of anonymous Restoration satirists'.[4] Barbara Everett finds these terms evidence of 'betrayal of human sense and meaning to mere grunting phatic gesture'.[5] Perhaps, but they may equally well be seen as part of the Royal Society ideal of purifying the dialect of the tribe.[6] Lines such as 'Her Hand, her Foot, her very look's a *Cunt*' (**'The Imperfect Enjoyment'**, l.18) content themselves with the naming of parts as a talismanic invocation. Rochester may not be quite as briskly commonsensical as Suckling ('As for her Belly, 'tis no matter, so / There be a Belly, and a Cunt, below'),[7] but there is still little sense of uneasy lingering on threatening physicality. As Farley-Hills points out,[8] a line such as 'A thing whose bliss depends upon thy will' (**'The Discovery'**, l.23) seems almost to disdain innuendo, the impulse to 'cry cunt' in order to 'friske his frollique fancy' (**'An Allusion to Horace'**, l.74). Instead there is a kind of tactile empiricism concerned to define the qualities of the object at hand. Rochester's 'And a Cunt has no sence of conscience or law' (**'Against Marriage'**, l.8) makes the same play as Shakespeare's 'Love is too young to know what conscience is' (Sonnet 151, l.5); but without an equivalent erotic charge of phonetic decomposition: 'con-science', 'consense', 'cuntsense'.[9] Rochester is equally disinclined to extend the trope in the manner of Oldham's 'Her conscience stretch'd, and open as the Stews' (**'A Satyr upon a woman'**, l.85).[10] Elusiveness within a formulaic diction is far more characteristic than lurid or surreal metaphoric extrapolation.

I take it for granted that sexual explicitness is not a regrettable occasional blemish in Rochester's poetry, but one of its chief attractions. Attempts to segregate the salacious, or if one prefers, pornographic, elements from the aesthetic are misguided and inappropriate, if not downright hypocritical. The phenomenon is, however, by no means a simple one. The powerful misogynistic elements would lead one to expect a reinforcement of authority, covert or explicit strategies of dominance: 'And therefore what they fear, at heart they hate' (**'A Satyr against Reason'**, l.45). Yet this is not supported by the history of reception. The '*Lady*' in **'Timon'** famously 'Complain'd our love was course, our *Poetry,* / Unfit for modest Eares' (ll.102-03); the 'Prologue' to **Sodom** declares, 'I do presume there are no women here / 'tis too debauch'd for their fair sex I fear'; and Robert Wolsley insisted in 1785, 'neither did my *Lord Rochester* design those Songs the *Essayer* is so offended with . . . for the Cabinets of Ladies'.[11] Nevertheless, of an admittedly sparse documentary record, female readers from Aphra Behn to Barbara Everett have proved singularly undeterred by this aspect of his work and willingly heeded the opening address of **'Signior Dildo'**: 'You Ladyes all of Merry England' (l.1).

For this response to be possible, Rochester's poetry must offer 'something Genrous in meer Lust' (**'A Ramble'**, l.98). In order to locate and define this quality, I will assess the degree of 'progressiveness' in his libertinism, in the context of recent models of homosocial bonding. I shall then analyse his distinctive plaintiveness and vulnerability, and explore some of the paradoxes of the truth of the failure of the body in his verse.

II

The perennial problem of Rochester criticism has been to link his satirical and lyric modes, and Hobbesian individualism has regularly been invoked to perform this generic unification. The only truth is that provided by the none too reliable senses: the only legitimate ethics must be founded on their possibilities and limitations. In Lockean epistemology, awareness of the 'flying Houres . . . Whose Images are kept in store / By Memory alone' (**'Love and Life'**, ll.4-5) produces an imperative to conserve, hoard and protect a finite and dwindling 'stock of ideas': in fairly simplistic terms, a bourgeois philosophy of accumulation. The libertine recuperation of Hobbes, in contrast, provokes a spendthrift pursuit of immediate and intense sensation: 'The Pleasures of a Body, Lam'd with lewdness, / A meer perpetual motion makes you happy'.[12]

It has frequently been argued that the libertine ideal of mutually reciprocated desire ('For did you love your pleasure lesse, / You were not fit for me' (**'Song'**, ll.19-20) has implications for the social and political domain: as Sarah Wintle puts it, 'pleasure through sexual variety' may 'lead to an attitude which grants rights or equal pleasure and promiscuity to women'.[13] This potentially emancipatory aspect is, however, embedded in and impeded by a matrix of reactionary attitudes. Rochester's poetry 'oscillates' between the two, providing an empirical confirmation of their continued incompatibility.

Several immediate objections may be lodged against such an approach. It divests Rochester's poetry of cognitive status by treating it as a secondary manifestation of intellectual debates that precede it, and so reduces it to a merely symptomatic status. Secondly, the ameliorative nature of an atomistic individualism may be questioned. Even celebration of female sexual desire defines the gender in terms of an innate eroticism rather than an autonomous subjectivity. It requires immediate reconstitution in terms of contract, which Hobbes simply underwrites an authoritarian status quo. It is simple enough to regard the variety of relations women have with men—sexual, familial, economic—as entered into a formal if unspecified point. Hobbes may point out that 'If there be no contract, the Dominion is in the Mother',[14] but this is surely one reason why one always seems to exist. Thirdly, the relative equality of 'In Love 'tis equal measure' (**'Song'**, l.14) relies on

a fictitious balance, disregarding the actual economic and political status underlying the 'nice allowances of Love' (**'A Ramble'**, l.110), such as those made by, for example, Rochester to his mistress, Elizabeth Barry. 'For none did e're soe dull, and stupid, / But felt a God, and blest his pow'r in Love' (*Artemiza,* l.48-49); but that 'power' manifests itself in a variety of cultural forms unavailable to a woman.

Mastery is not so much absent in Rochester as reversible: to be enslaved is quite as appealing an option as to enslave, though the question of who ultimately stages the scenario remains. In **'Fair Cloris'**, the swain, although 'Lustfull' remains a 'Slave' (l.26). The language of decorous sadomasochism abounds in the early lyrics: 'To see my Tyrant at my Feet; / Whil'st taught by her, unmov'd I sit / A Tyrant in my Turn' (**'Pastoral Dialogue'** ll.53-55). 'Kindness' itself 'guilds the Lovers Servile Chaine and makes the Slave grow pleas'd and vaine' (**'Song'**, ll.15-16). In **'Insulting *Beauty*'**, it is boasted, 'I triumph in my Chain', (l.14); and the speaker of **'The Discovery'** goes so far as to regret 'dying' only because 'I must be no more your slave' (l.44). In this context it is even possible to put a positive gloss on the power of the testicles to 'make a Man a Slave / To such a Bitch as *Willis*' (**'On Mistress Willis'**, ll.3-4).

Mutuality, equality, in Rochester, tends to be achieved in terms of stand-offs, explicit negotiation, rather than persuasion, consummation. This needs to be reduced, as Wintle does, to a 'bleak notion of contract: I use you, you use me'.[15] There is an unusual (if not unprecedented) sense of considering one's mistress worth talking to even after sleeping with her. There is no influx of power through casual disparagement, none of the animus in excess so deplored by Ricks in Donne.[16] Whatever hostility there is seems primarily self-directed, a point to which I wish to return.

Adult equals are by no means the automatic paradigms for sexual encounters. Rochester's erotic landscape is inhabited by a broad and varied cast, including Signior Dildo, the oceanic Duchess of Cleveland and a herd of grunting pigs. It is mistaken to presume condemnation of or repulsion from grotesquerie. There remains something uniquely calm, unflustered, practical, about the attitude of the 'Young Lady' towards her 'Ancient Lover', whatever the relative proportions of nature and 'Art' in the 'reviving hand' (ll.25, 19).[17]

The 'something Genrous in meer lust' permits an unmisgivingness about a wide variety of sexual scenarios that extends far beyond the point of simple amoralism: 'Things must go on in their lewd natural way' (**'Fragment'**). Where Keats's proclamation 'even now, clammy dew is beading on my brow' implies solitude and self-absorption,[18] in Rochester, the 'clammy joys' (**'The Imperfect Enjoyment'**, l.20) seem to involve actual and specific modes of conduct. The attention of the poetic voice is concentrated on the niceties of its etiquette: Everett rightly stresses 'tis power of latency, its character of reserve'.[19]

Restoration anti-feminist satire habitually denounces women for both harbouring animal lust and then pretending to restrain it: 'Poor helplesse Woman, is not favour'd more. She's a sly Hypocrite, or Publique Whore' (**'An Epistolary Essay'**, ll.95-96). In Rochester, the *grande dame* becomes a figure of urgent self-gratification: in **'Mistress Knights Advice to the Dutchess of Cleavland in Distress for a Prick'**, despite the demurral, 'Though Cunt be not Coy, reputation is Nice', the Duchess states a forthright preference for being 'Fuct by Porters and Carmen / Than thus be abus'd by Churchill and German', (ll.4, 11-12), a contest between female desire and male hypocrisy that recurs throughout Rochester.

The ethic of 'generosity' is espoused in numerous contexts: in addition to the title of this essay, 'Be generous, and wise and take our part'. (**'Second Prologue'**, l.38); be not 'Generous and grateful never' (**'Dialogue'**, l.26); seek 'true gen'rous *Love*' (**'Woman's Honor'**, l.11); praise those 'whose Principles most gen'rous are, and just' (**'A Satyr against Reason'**, l.125); 'In a generous Wench theres nothing of Trouble' (**'Against Marriage'**, l.10); and 'Love, the most gen'rous passion of the mynde' (*A Letter from Artemiza*, l.40).

From here it would seem a short step to celebration of a universal principle of fecundity: the Lucretian Venus. This, it seems, is provided in **'Upon his leaving his Mistress'**:

> Whilst mov'd by an impartial Sense,
> Favours like *Nature* you dispense,
> With Universal influence.
>
> See the kind Seed-receiving Earth,
> To Ev'ry Grain affords a *Birth*;
> On her no Show'rs unwelcome fall,
> Her willing *Womb*, regains 'em all,
> And shall my *Celia* be confin'd?
> No, live up to thy mighty *Mind*,
> And be the Mistress of *Mankind*.
>
> (ll.12-21)

'Confin'd' expands beyond possession by an individual male ('To damn you only to be mine', l.4) to a vision of unlimited universal access. However, the problem with such a celebration of impassive abundance is that the iconography cannot be kept on a solely mythological level: it must necessarily become involved in narratives of contract and estrangement. In **'Song'**, 'She's my delight, all Mankinds wonder; But my Jelous heart would break, should we live one day asunder' (ll.14-16), the speaker fears being asunder from 'Mankind' as much as from his mistress. To be included is always to be included alongside, amongst: the most forceful assertion of female autonomy is simultaneously the strongest confirmation of the social bond between men. Thus the 'Mistress of *Mankind*' (typically endowed with a 'mighty *Mind*') fuses personal with cultural libido: 'By merit, and by inclination, the joy at least of one whole *Nation*' (ll.6-7). Or, more crudely, 'Each Man had as much room, as *Porter, Blunt,* or *Harris,* had, in *Cullens, Bushel Cunt*' (**'Timon'**, ll.93-94).[20]

This communalizing function is evident in the middle section of **'A Ramble in St James's Park'**, a conjunction of satiric commentary on sexual mores, specific, empirical, concrete, with the apostrophic mode, more usually delivered from an unspecified vantage to an unidentified mistress:

> Gods! that a thing admir'd by mee
> Shou'd fall to so much Infamy.
> Had she pickt out to rub her Arse on
> Some stiff prickt Clown or well-hung Parson
> Each jobb of whose spermatique sluce
> Had fill'd her Cunt with wholesome Juice
> I the proceeding shou'd have prais'd
> In hope she had quence'd a fire I'd raised.
> Such naturall freedomes are but Just
> There's something Genrous in meer lust . . .
>
> (ll.89-98)

Corinna retains initiative, choice, the power of 'picking out': the speaker bewails his exclusion from the her 'Divine Abode', (l.39). (The initial 'Consecrate to Prick and Cunt', (l.10) and final 'dares prophane the Cunt I swive' (l.166) gives a religious framing to the whole poem.) Everett describes the poem as a 'savage, dangerous, yet obscurely innocent fantasy—innocent from the sensed rectitude which its upside down fury violates, the contained and quashed romantic idealism'; and her instinct is sound, I believe, to see the poem as 'an actual if finalizing perpetuation (for all its grossness) of earlier Renaissance modes of idealization'.[21] The sexual 'thing' is initially 'admir'd', and the note of limpid self-pity retains a sense of etiquette, humility, deference ('praised'). The 'Infamy' to which it is opposed remains indeterminate. The capacity of the narrator to make such a judgement is uncertain after his initial departure from the 'grave discourse'. Hence the oddness of the subsequent accusation, 'To bring a blott on Infamy', (l.104): not so much to exceed the bounds of shame as bring the category itself into disrepute. 'Thing' can also be read as penis (with a play on 'fall'): and it is tempting to make the psychoanalytic extrapolation, of Corinna representing the virility that the speaker lacks.

There is a querulous comic note in the feminine rhymes; and also an absence of hierarchy recalling the social as well as sexual dimensions of the 'all-sin-sheltering Grove': 'And here promiscuously they swive', (l.25, 32). The 'spermatique sluce' of 'stiff-prickt Clowns' and 'well-hung Parson' provides not corruption or disease but a 'wholesome Juice'. 'To rub her arse on' continues the 'proud bitch' image: but as with the later 'longing Arse' (l.41) has a potential homo-erotic dimension. 'Quence'd the fire' is a typical literalization of a precieux diction, dousing the 'flame' with other men's semen.[22] 'I'd raised' suggests the arousal of the 'knight errant Paramours' by the speaker himself. The 'natural freedomes' represent not liberation from but facilitation of exchange between men: 'meer lust' is not an underlying impulse, basic motivation, but an unattainable, longed-for, standard.

The relation of 'I' to 'all Mankind' initially seems antithetical, but in the course of the passage undergoes a physical assimilation. There is a typically determinist note in the severity of 'Fate'. 'Priviledge above' and 'nice allowances' attribute a certain authority to the speaker, but this is immediately compromised by the infantile dependence of 'humble fond believing me'. The 'meanest part' could be genitals of either sex or a role in 'loves Theatre the Bed' (**'Leave this gawdy guilded Stage',** l.5). 'Ungratefull' most immediately refers to the flouting of contract by Corinna, but can be extended to the speaker's own behaviour or the reader, pre-emptively rebuked for simultaneously witnessing and violating the erotic intimacy. There remains a sense of decorum, almost gentility, in the 'digestive surfiet water' served up; and an infinite poignancy in 'content', whose obvious sexual play cannot detract from the peculiar resonance of 'Grace'.

'Pleasure for excuse' seems to ascribe a libertine autonomy, 'naturall freedoms': 'abuse' refers to his own 'dram of sperm' as much as Corinna's behaviour. 'Meer lust' cannot be taken as simply an anti-inflationist view of 'pleasure': a secular pastime. (Though there is no compunction about describing Corinna as 'joyfull and pleas'd' (l.80) at her liaison.) The poem would be much simpler and more manageable if this were a clearly available standard. Yet the 'pleasure' of the speaker lies more in his relation with Corinna's other lovers than in any momentary spasm of ejaculation. Indeed, orgasm as an entity in itself is immediately redefined in term of two overlaid relations: an apostrophic address to Corinna, and an indirect communion with 'halfe the Town'. 'Spewing home' seems more appropriate to the behaviour of the narrator himself; and if one pursues this somewhat lurid transference, he receives as well as adds to the 'seed' within. The voracity of the 'devouring Cunt' seems part of its attraction rather than a cause of repulsion. 'Full gorges' would seem attached to 'Cunt', but transfers itself to the speaker in both active and passive senses: he is himself swallowed up[23] but also bloated by receiving the 'vast meal'. The 'nasty slime' is displaced from the juices of female arousal onto the male ejaculate; but the point is that the two are inseparable, and satisfaction is received from contact with both.

One might go so far as to say that the affair is only fully consummated in the moment of infidelity. The term 'betray' comes to represent both revelation and exposure. The expression that gives public significance is brought into existence by a movement inseparable from fickleness and duplicity.[24] As Everett says, the narrator of a Rochester poem is always hoping 'that he will betray love enough'.[25] Logically, Corinna cannot reveal 'secrets' until they have been confided in her, but the implication seems to be that she already has been 'faithless'. This, of course, conforms to the argument for mutable desire espoused in some of the lyrics. Nevertheless, the implication is that she is attractive precisely because of, not in spite of, her 'Treachery'. 'When leaneing' refers both backwards to the 'Paramours' engaged in love-making and forward to the narrator seeking comfort: the two are telescoped into being simultaneously present. 'And Reason lay dissolv'd in Love' is not the prelude to disaster, Samson in Delilah's lap, but the desired outcome, the culmination of the preceding accelerated pattern of inversions.

The primary tension of the passage lies in its conflation of third-person satire with second-person apostrophe: 'But mark what Creatures women are How infinitly vile when fair', (ll.41-42). The definition is not the result of taxonomy, categorization, but of the movement between vileness and fairness: the apparent stability containing progressively more estranged extremes. There is a summoning and makingpresent of physical residue, an inverted and arguably perverse idealization of a gluttonous absorption of the male body. The hostility towards the male rivals is merely an inversion of the attraction towards physical contact via the 'devouring Cunt'. I now wish to discuss the relation of this mutual accentuation to the presence of communal judgement in Rochester's verse.

III

One by-product of the foregrounding of the instance of utterance in Rochester's lyrics is the reduction of the masculine community to 'The false Judgement of an Audience / Of Clapping-Fooles' (**'An Allusion to Horace',** (ll.13-14). In Rochester there is never any sense of transmission of a received and proven wisdom. **'The Mistress',** for example, offers a series of outward addresses: 'You Wiser men despise me not'; 'Had you not been profoundly dull, You had gone mad like me'; 'Nor Censure us You who perceive My best belov'd and me' (ll.13, 19-20, 21). These are not apologies or appeals for social endorsement so much as a kind of pre-emptive debunking. Yet there is no corresponding idealization of the lovers: where Donne's 'The Good Morrow' celebrates the power which 'makes one little roome an every where',[26] the lines, 'To make the old *World,* a new withdrawing Room, Whereof another *World* she's brought to *Bed!*' provoke nothing but mockery in 'Timon' (ll.148-49).

The testimony of the isolated speaker is displaced onto an almost phenomenological emphasis on the personal body; it articulates not the authority of collective experience but an estrangement from and within it. There is no protective persona of a public self, but equally no post-romantic subjectivity conflating the two spheres. Not only Rochester, but also Sedley, Dorset and the rest seem almost devoid of political and social identities in their verse. It has often been noted how little Rochester deals with the public sphere: attempts such as Paulson's to read the obscene as 'the private half of a basic analogy between public and private life',[27] have little purchase compared to the reverse movement that transforms Charles II into an alter-ego and displaced father-figure, and his mistresses into demonic maternal presences.

It can, of course, be argued that Rochester's verse at all times presupposes a homosocial bonding. There would seem ample support for this in comments such as Pope's

'Mob of Gentlemen who wrote with Ease', Marvell's 'merry gang', and Dryden's 'men of pleasant conversation . . .' ambitious to distinguish themselves from the herd of gentlemen, by their party![28]

> Scorne all Applause the Vile Rout can bestow,
> And be content to please those few, who know . . .
> I loathe the Rabble, 'tis enough for me,
> If Sidley, Shadwell, Shepherd, Witcherley,
> Godolphin, Buttler, Buckhurst, Buckingham,
> And some few more, whom I omit to name,
> Approve my Sense, I count their Censure Fame.

('An Allusion to Horace', ll.102-03, 120-25)

There is a predictable hauteur in the roll-call perhaps, but the 'few, who know' have scarcely any significant presence in Rochester's verse. There is a peculiar solipsism, a sense of self-directedness, with little or no sense of a Rochester poem being for anyone, whether wife or mistress, specific male confidante or broader circle.

'Love a *Woman!* y'are an *Ass*' advises staying at home with a 'lewd well-natur'd *Friend*, Drinking, to engender *Wit*' (ll.11-2). Yet there is no equivalent to the cheerfully louche exchanges between Buckhurst and Etherege. Where their verse-letters celebrate a benign itinerary of collective indulgence ('Then the next morning we all hunt / To find whose fingers smell of cunt'),[29] Rochester's 'Regime d'viver' offers an irascible filofax of cyclic, solitary debauchery, whose culminating animus—'Then crop-sick, all Morning, I rail at my *Men*, And in Bed I lye Yawning, till Eleven again' (ll.13-14)—expands out from an immediate circle of servants onto a whole gender: '*Men*' in general.

Even in Sade, as has often been noted, there is an ethic of friendship[30] and a certain clubbability has accompanied most outbursts of ethical antinomianism and romantic diabolism. In contrast, Rochester's ultimate slight in **'On Poet Ninny'**, 'The worst that I cou'd write, wou'd be noe more, Than what thy very Friends have said before' (ll.27-28), reflects much more on the companions than the supposed target. No distinction is drawn between Artemiza's 'To heare, what Loves have past, In this Lewd Towne' (ll.32-33), and the 'grave discourse, Of who Fucks who and who does worse' ('A Ramble', ll.1-2). The monkey that she addresses as a 'curious Minature of Man' is a 'dirty chatt'ring Monster' (*Artemiza*, ll.143, 141) and while 'dirty' may do no more than reflect contemporary standards of hygiene, 'chatt'ring', voluble, gossipy, empty-headed, reverses the stereotype of feminine volubility.

The 'dull dining *Sot*' pursues Timon, 'but as a *Whore*, With modesty enslaves her *Spark*, the more' (ll.9-10), a comparison that both refuses to differentiate between male honour and female modesty, and gives an explicitly sexualized dimension to male social intercourse. After attributing a libel to Timon (which may or may not be the poem itself, yet to be written), 'to his dear mistake, Which he, by this, had spread o're the whole Town, And me, with an

officious Lye, undone' (ll.28-30). This vulnerability to public opinion again feminized ('undone'), is powerfully prefigured in Strephon's early dialogue with Alexis:

> As Trees are by their Barks Embrac'd,
> Love to my Soul doth cling;
> When torn by th' Herd's greedy taste,
> The injur'd Plants feel they're defac't,
> They wither in the Spring.

('Pastoral Dialogue', ll.61-65)

The arboreal 'Soul' is divided into 'Tree', 'Bark' and the 'Herd's greedy taste': 'Love' serves the function of a protective surface, but is itself 'defac't', 'torn', and 'injur'd'. In 'Timon', the congregation of 'all brave *Fellows*', the rompish camaraderie of the 'tough *Youth*', provokes a fastidious shudder (ll.37, 86):

> Their rage once over, they begin to treat,
> And six fresh *Bottles*, must the peace compleat.
> I ran down Stairs, with a Vow never more
> To drink Bear Glass, and hear the *Hectors* roar.

(ll.174-77)

The persona never dominates, seldom interjects, but rather witnesses with varying degrees of tacit fascination and contempt. There is no single *adversarius*, but rather a whole social group, and Timon hates himself for being unable to differentiate himself from them: 'No means, nor hopes, appear of a retreat' (l.42). The speaker of **'Tunbridge Wells'** responds similarly to the 'crowd':

> Endeavouring this irksome sight to Balke,
> And a more irksome noyse, their silly talke,
> I silently slunke down to th' lower walke:

('Tunbridge Wells', ll.35-37)

He repeatedly attempts to absent himself from his own poem: 'th' hearing what they said, I did myself the kindness to evade' (ll.34-35), and 'Tir'd with this dismall Stuffe, away I ran' (ll.26). Even the narrator of **'Upon His Drinking Bowl'** defines himself in terms, not of belonging to, but of separation from: 'I'm none of those that took *Mastrich*, Nor *Yarmouth Leaguer* knew': 'For I am no Sir *Sydrophell*, Nor none of his *Relations*' (ll.11-12, 15-16).

Given a masculine community as brutish and rapacious in its pleasures as one could wish (or perhaps envy), an explanation is needed of how Rochester speaks (or appears to be speaking) from a point outside this collectivity.

One tradition of feminist reading would stress the residual equality of desires: 'When neither overcomes Loves triumph greater is' (**'Leave this gawdy guilded Stage'**, l.10). There is undoubtedly a willingness to allow independent female voices into the poems. Satiric modes are directed as (if not more) frequently against men than women; and the conventions of cavalier lyric themselves become feminized, transposable, in poems such as **'Against Constancy', 'The Platonick Lady',** and **'The Song of a Young Lady to her Ancient Lover'.** There is a complex empathy with the host's wife in 'Timon' (ll.49-56).

The '*Lady*' has scarcely worn worse than Timon himself; and the passage reflects the same ambivalence towards its object as the reader feels towards its narrator. '*Age*' is the 'incurable disease of others beside '*Beauty*'; and the gap between 'desire' and 'pow'r to please' is famously commented upon by Rochester himself: 'soe great a disproportion twixt our desires and what has been ordained to content them'.[31] 'Fit to give love' is almost the finest compliment that can be paid; 'prevent despair' is a gently unrecriminative term for sexual availability. '*Cocks*' gives a momentary masculinity, force, not wholly retracted by 'old bleer *Eyes*', no less to be respected than the disabled debauchee; 'smite' has overtones of both heroic endeavour and social flirtation. There is a note of admirable defiance, 'in despight of time'; 'affection' also acquires a certain dignity as a conscious role-playing. She shares her preoccupation with love with Rochester himself; and the resulting dialogue is closer to Eliot's 'Portrait of a Lady' than to the witches' sabbath of Pope's 'Ghosts of Beauty' ('**To a Lady**', 1.241). Her tone is gently reproachful, unflustered, graceful, with a note of disdain towards the 'Hair-brain'd *Youth*', deemed 'Too rotten to consummate the Intrigue' (ll.104, 106). In perhaps the morally finest line in Rochester, and certainly the most understated epithet, she is allowed to depart undisparaged, undiminished: 'And decently my *Lady*, quits the Room' (l.110).

Wintle dismisses this persistent tactic of gender-reversal as simply offering a 'parody of a woman',[32] but this is to underestimate the slitheriness of role-playing in Rochester. The demand for 'mutual Love' ('**The Advice**', 1.16) precludes full appreciation of the instability, the solipsism, and the impassioned lyricism of sexual failure.

Sex is ethical, even conceptual, before it is erotic; and the key instances to be debated are not those of ecstasy and fulfilment but disappointment and inadequacy. There is a truth of the body to be found through its very humiliation, in the pursuit of a pleasure known to be insufficient beforehand.

In 'The Women about Town', 'a Fate which noe man can oppose; The losse of his heart and the fall of his Nose' ('**Lampoone**', ll.9-10) does not merely refer to possible infection, but extends to a whole betrayal by the body. It is not 'just' but nevertheless inevitable that 'our Tarses be burnt by our hearts taking fire' (ll.15-16). There is no specific guilt or punishment for indulgence beyond the acceleration of an inevitable decline. There is little or nothing of the *poète maudit* in Rochester, seeking transgression as an end in itself. Despite ultimate conversion, there is similarly little sense of blasphemy as an inverted mode of belief. Physical corruption is not the correlative of sin; and, as previously noted, there is no sense of the disgusting in itself arousing. Instead there is a certain stoic dignity in conscious acceptance, even pursuit, of this corporeal transformation.

The disabled debauchee boasts of the 'Honourable scars, Which my too forward valour did procure'; and in 'To the Post Boy' even the more graphic 'Sear cloaths and ulcers

from the top to toe' remain 'Heroick scars' (ll.8-9). The couplet, 'So charming Oyntments, made an Old *Witch* flie, And bear a Crippled Carcass through the Skie' ('**A Satyr against Reason**', ll.86-87) also has something of this last-standness. There is a stark pathos to 'Old', an unsparing naturalism but no disgusted recoil in 'Carcass', and an immense respect for the refusal of the '*Witch*' to capitulate to the state of 'Crippled'. The '*Oyntments*' are 'charming' because they are casting a spell, but also felicitous, because they are successful in doing so when there is no alternative but to inculcate an illusion.

> Trembling, confus'd, despairing, limber dry,
> A wishing, weak, unmoving lump I ly.
> This *Dart* of Love, whose piercing point oft try'd,
> With *Virgin blood, Ten thousand Maids* has dy'd;
> Which *Nature* still directed with such *Art*,
> That through it ev'ry *Cunt*, reacht ev'ry *Heart*.
> Stiffly resolv'd, twou'd carelessly invade,
> *Woman* or *Man*, nor ought its fury staid,
> Where e're it pierc'd, a *Cunt* it found or made.
> Now languid lies, in this unhappy hour,
> Shrunk up, and Sapless, like a wither'd *Flow'r*.
> Thou treacherous, base, deserter of my flame,
> False to my passion, fatal to my *Fame*;
> Through what mistaken *Magick* dost thou prove,
> So true to lewdness, so untrue to Love?
>
> (ll.35-49)

The '**Satire on Charles** II' is concerned with the obvious political dimension to virility in terms of the royal succession, but what is striking is his more universal masculine ungainliness: 'Yett his dull graceless Ballocks hang an arse' (1.27). There is no political respect, but a biological empathy. A displaced self-loathing and curious solicitation are directed towards the bodily imperatives of the ageing debauchee: clapped out in every sense. This extends to Mistress Willis, who, like Charles, represents a persona to be occupied. She 'Rails and Scolds when she sits down, And Curses when she Spends' (ll.15-16), terms with both a generic and psychological appositeness to Rochester and Restoration satire in general, with its close conjunction of arousal and abuse. Further points of connection are the odd poignancy of 'And yet with no man Friends'; in what might be seen as a highly apposite summation of Rochester's own style, 'Bawdy in Thoughts, precise in Words'; and even perhaps an oblique glance at the poet's constipation, the 'Belly' which is 'a Bagg of Turds' (ll.13-14, 17, 19-20).

In the rivalry between Count Cazzo and Signior Dildo, there is only one winner: the substitute clearly surpasses the original, a situation which 'Flesh and Blood cou'd not bear' (1.80). Witnessing the subsequent ambush and pursuit by 'A Rabble of Pricks' (1.83):

> The good Lady Sandys, burst into a Laughter
> To see how their Ballocks came wobbling after,
> And had not their weight retarded the Fo
> Indeed't had gone hard with Signior Dildo.
>
> (ll.89-92)

'Retarded' is delayed, but also rendered imbecilic; and 'gone hard' merely reinforces the superiority of the intruder, and the dispensability of the original. Harold Weber astutely notes how the poem demonstrates that 'from the female point of view the male body provides an essentially comic spectacle'. 'Reducing men to their pricks' makes them 'objects of derision', and there is unsparing indictment of the 'anatomical insufficiency of the male body', in particular, the ballocks as 'the male body's betrayal of itself'.[33] As Weber points out, the inadequacy of feminist models built around the unitary phallus becomes immediately apparent when confronted with the testicles, in all their queasy dangling vulnerability. But he fails to follow through this insight, instead reverting to ascribing to Rochester a 'conventional misogynous understanding of hierarchical relations between the sexes' (1992; p. 115).[34]

The poems represent, Weber claims, 'an attempt to transform the penis into the phallus, to recapture an endemic wholeness which would banish death'. It is 'their inability to effect this transformation' which 'generates the rate and anxiety that so often disfigure the verse, marking the moment when the male will discovers the limits of its own power and authority' (1992; p. 110).[35] Like Robinson, Weber is reluctant to acknowledge that 'rage and anxiety' might be what we read for. That which 'disfigures the verse' might be what produces it in the first place.

In Rochester, however, there is not a failed attempt to 'transform the penis into the phallus', but often a strikingly literal dramatization of the reverse process: what is sought is not power, but powerlessness. If, as Timon insists, he 'never Rhym'd, but for my *Pintles* sake', this may imply not self-aggrandizement but self-deprecation. **'The Imperfect Enjoyment'** offers the most complex display of what Claude Rawson called Rochester's 'machismo of sexual debility' (1985; p. 335).[36] Weber argues that 'the failure to control desire, to overcome the gap between the mind and the body, transforms a genuinely erotic moment into a bitter litany of foul complaints' (1992; p. 103).[37] A more productive way of looking at the poem is that it exposes this 'gap'. The genuinely erotic' cannot be simply opposed to the 'bitter litany': the one is implicit within and generated out of the other. The speaker's inability to respond to his mistress's desires with 'wisht Obedience', what **'The Advice'** dubs 'the Freedom to Obey' (l.12), prompts the final outburst of '*Rage*' (l.25).

The speaker appears not merely to address but actually to become his penis. The vain-glorious boast of previous exploits is delivered from the point of minimum performance, leading to the suspicion that they are purely verbal and compensatory. Yet it should be stressed that erotic failure is the condition rather than the cessation of this indiscriminate assault, which, as in **'Mock Song'**, subjects an infinitely penetrable body to a random incision that verges on the sadistic and grotesque. It is noteworthy that the previous description of ejaculation might easily be transposed into female orgasm: 'In liquid *Raptures*, I dis-

solve all o're, Melt into Sperme, and spend at ev'ry Pore' (ll.15-16). 'Stiffly resolv'd' reverses the relation of conscious purpose to sexual arousal from one of prohibition and restraint. The '*All-dissolving Thunderbolt*' (l.10) becomes a display of authority, the antithesis of the yielding assimilation of the 'wishing, weak, unmoving lump'. Yet this state is broadly continuous with the ideal of protective enclosure prevalent elsewhere. An obvious parallel may be found in the masturbatory passivity of Bloom's 'languid floating flower',[38] suggesting that the 'wither'd *Flow'r*' that 'languid lies' might be truer 'to love' than the rampaging virility with which it is contrasted.

> Worst part of me, and henceforth hated most,
> Through all the *Town*, a common *Fucking Post*:
> On whom each *Whore*, relieves her tingling *Cunt*,
> As *Hogs*, on *Gates*, do rub themselves and grunt.
> May'st thou to rav'nous *Shankers*, be a *Prey*,
> Or in consuming *Weepings* waste away.
> May *Strangury*, and *Stone*, thy *Days* attend,
> May'st thou ne're Piss, who didst refuse to spend,
> When all my joys, did on false thee depend.
> And may *Ten thousand* abler *Pricks* agree,
> To do the wrong'd *Corinna* right for thee.
>
> (ll.62-72)

Abuse of the penis seems a more than adequate substitute for utilization of it. A dismemberment of his own body is performed through a series of violently repudiatory apostrophes; a making present of that which, as it were, had been gouged out of himself.

Rancour is drained away from all other possible targets: the unqualified intimacy of the opening lines paradoxically presupposes this eventual outlet. There is, as Treglown points out (1982; p. 85),[39] a disconcerting urbanity to the pun on 'depend' and on the previous 'confirm me impotent' (l.28), ushering in a final compliment to the 'wrong'd *Corinna*'. The 'Worst part' is not so much expelled as expanded to fill the narrative present of the poem. It is then denounced for precisely what it is manifestly failing to do: provide 'a common *Fucking Post*'. The ferocity of invective is thus displaced from the state of powerlessness onto the state of potency, apparently only invoked as a negative contrast. The punishment becomes a jubilant kind of release: not from the 'drudgery' of heterosexual intercourse, but from the necessity to 'agree' with, conform to, the hallucinatory array of 'abler *Pricks*'. Belief, opinion, scandal, are all set aside in favour of a reiteration of common physical limitation, whose buoyant explicitness refuses the grotesque or macabre. The 'Consuming *Weepings*' of venereal sores might be seen as Rochester's version of 'lacrimae rerum'; and, in their more restricted fashion, as partaking of some of the grandeur of the Virgilian pathos.

Rochester may be seen as the great articulator of the malfunctioning body, a typology superimposed upon its most flagrant and ostentatious debaucheries. In the context of my original concern, misogyny, it is possible to offer a provisional conclusion. The generic continuities with antifeminist satire, and inventive, occasionally horrifying, results of generic inversion of lyric, are of little consequence compared to the foregrounding and evocation of masculinity as a cultural bond. The continual recourse to a negative testimony of the body represents a kind of obdurate refusal of a culturally endorsed mastery, and it is in this precarious movement, I believe, that we may discover and applaud the generosity of Rochester's poetry.

Notes

1. The Professional Amateur', in *Spirit of Wit: Reconsiderations of Rochester's Wit,* ed. Jeremy Treglown (Oxford, 1982), pp. 58-74.

2. Carole Fabricant, 'Rochester's World of Imperfect Enjoyment', *Journal of English and German Philology,* (1974), pp. 338-50. Reba Wilcoxon 'Rochester's Sexual Politics', *Studies in Eighteenth-Century Culture* (1979), pp. 137-49 reprinted in *John Wilmot: Earl of Rochester: Critical Essays,* ed. David M. Vieth (New York, 1988), pp. 113-26; Sarah Wintle 'Libertinism and Sexual Politics', in Treglown, pp. 133-65; and Felicity A. Nussbaum, *The Brink of All We Hate: English Satires Upon Women, 1660-1750,* (Lexington, 1984), pp. 57-60.

3. All quotations from *The Poems of John Wilmot, Earl of Rochester,* ed. Keith Walker (Oxford, 1984). The Dorset quotations are taken from 'Colon', ll.44-45 and 'A Faithful Catalogue of our most Eminent Ninnies', ll.112-13, in *The Poems of Charles Sackville Sixth Earl of Dorset,* ed. Brice Harris (New York and London, 1979), pp. 125-26, 140.

4. 'Rochester and the "Holiday Writers"', in *Rochester and Court Poetry,* ed. Alan Roper (Los Angeles, 1988), pp. 33-66.

5. 'The Sense of Nothing', in Treglown, ll.1-41.

6. 'As they conceiv'd lewdly, so they wrote in plain *English,* and took no care to cover up the worst of their thoughts in clean Linnen', Daniel Defoe, in *The Works of Sir Charles Sedley* (1722 for 1721), i ll.8-9; cited in *Rochester: The Critical Heritage,* ed. David Farley-Hills (London, 1972), p. 192.

7. 'The Deformed Mistress', in *The Works of Sir John Suckling: The Non-Dramatic Works,* ed. Thomas Clayton (Oxford, 1971), p. 34, ll.27-28.

8. Farley-Hills, *Rochester's Poetry,* (London, 1978), p. 45.

9. 'See the exhaustive commentary by Stephen Booth in *Shakespeare's Sonnets* (New Haven, 1977), pp. 525-26.

10. 'A Satyr upon a woman, who by her falshood and scorn was the death of his friend', *The Poems of John Oldham,* ed. Harold F. Brooks and Raman Selden (Oxford, 1987), p. 82. Compare also Robert Gould, 'Nor are their consciences (which can betray / Where e're they're sworn to love) less large than

they', in *Love Given O're: Or, a Satyr against the Pride, Lust and Inconstancy etc. of Women* (London, 1682). Reprinted in *Satires on Women* (Augustan Reprint Society no. 180, intro. Felicity A. Nussbaum (Los Angeles, 1977).

11. *Rochester's Sodom,* ed. L. S. A. M. von Romer (H. Welter: Paris and Amsterdam, 1904, 1905). For discussion of the problem of attribution, see J. W. Johnson, 'Did Lord Rochester write *Sodom?' Papers of the Bibliographical Society of America* (1987), pp. 119-53. Wolsey's comment comes in 'Preface to *Valentinian'* (1685), in *Rochester: the critical heritage* ed. D. Farley-Hills, p. 155.

12. '*Valentinian: a tragedy: as 'tis altered by the late Earl of Rochester* (London, 1685), 5ii, 61.

13. Sarah Wintle, 'Libertinism and Sexual Politics', in Treglown, p. 155.

14. *Leviathan,* ed. C. B. Macpherson (Harmondsworth, 1968), p. 253.

15. Sarah Wintle, 'Libertinism and Sexual Politics', in Treglown, p. 134.

16. 'Donne after Love', *Literature and the Body,* ed. Elaine Scary (Baltimore, 1988), pp. 33-69.

17. 'The Imperfect Enjoyment' also stresses the 'busie hand' and the 'fair hand, which might bid heat return / To frozen *Age'* (p. 13, ll.31-32).

18. *Endymion* III, pp. 567-68, in the *Poetical Works of John Keats,* ed. H. W. Garrod (Oxford, 1970), p. 119.

19. Everett, 'The Sense of Nothing', in Treglown, p. 17.

20. The most graphic illustration comes in Sedley's 'In the Fields of Lincoln Inn', published in *Poems on Several Occasions* (London, 1680), p. 57. Phillis, faced with two gallants, acts decisively: 'Coridon's Aspiring Tarse, she fitted / To her less frequented *Arse'* while Strephon 'into her *Cunt* she thrust: Now for Civil Wars prepare, / Rais'd by fierce intestine Bustle. / When these Heroes meeting Justle / In the Bowels of the Fair'. 'Nature had 'twixt *Cunt* and *Arse* / Wisely plac'd firm separation, / God knows else what desolation / Had insu'd from warring *Tarse'*. Compare Gloria, in *The Devil in Miss Jones,* similarly circumstanced: 'can you feel his cock against yours, can you feel it'. Cited in Anne McClintock, 'Gonad and the Barbarian and the Venus Flytrap: Portraying the female and the male orgasm', *Sex Exposed: sexuality in the pornography debate* (London, 1992), pp. 111-31.

21. Everett, 'The Sense of Nothing', in Treglown, pp. 25, 27.

22. Compare 'Dialogue' (ll.33-40): 'the Show'rs that fall / Quench the fire, and quiet all;' and 'The Advice' (ll.23-24): 'for even streams have desires, / Cool as they are, they feel Love's powerful fires'.

23. Compare *Sodom,* where Flux comments: 'Men's Pricks are eaten of the secret parts / Of Women' (l.51).

24. From a host of examples: 'To betray, and engage, and inflame my Desire' ('The Submission', l.6); 'employ that Art / Which first betray'd, to ease my heart' ('Dialogue', ll.6-7); 'my unfaithfull eyes / Betray a kinder story' ('Song', ll.7-8); and 'But Virgins Eyes their hearts betray, / And give their Tongues the lie' ('Song', ll.19-20). In 'A Satyr against Reason', 'But Savage *Man* alone, does Man Betray' (l.130), allows, by the logic of its own argument, that the primitive impulses are superior because they are closer to the spontaneous behaviour of the animal kingdom.

25. Everett, 'The Sense of Nothing', in Treglown, p. 19.

26. 'The Good Morrow', *The Elegies and the Songs and Sonnets,* ed. Helen Gardner (Oxford, 1965), p. 70.

27. 'Rochester: the Body Political and the Body Private', in *The Author in his Work: Essays on a problem in criticism,* ed. Louis L. Martz and Aubrey Williams (New Haven and London, 1978), pp. 103-21; reprinted in Vieth, 1988, pp. 45-67. See also Robert Holton 'Sexuality and Social Hierarchy in Sidney and Rochester', *Mosaic,* 24:1 (1991), pp. 47-65.

28. *The Twickenham Edition of The Poems of Alexander Pope,* ed. John Butt *et al.* (New Haven and London, 1939-1969), vol. 4, *Imitations of Horace,* ed. John Butt, III 108, 203; to Sir Edmund Harley, 1677; *The Poems and Letters of Andrew Marvell,* ed. H. M. Margoliouth, vol. 2 (Oxford, 1972; 2nd edition, 1981), p. 329; Dryden, 'Preface to "All for Love"' (1678), cited in *Rochester: The Critical Heritage,* ed. Farley-Hills, p. 32.

29. 'Mr Etherege's Answer' (to 'Another Letter by the Lord Buckhurst to Mr Etherege'), in *Poems of Dorset* (ll.34-35), p. 115.

30. Simone de Beauvoir, 'Must we burn Sade?' Introduction to Marquis de Sade, 'One Hundred and Twenty Days of Sodom' (London: Arrow, 1989), pp. 3-64; Angela Carter, *The Sadean Woman: an exercise in cultural history* (London, 1979), p. 90.

31. *The Letters of John Wilmot, Earl of Rochester,* ed. Jeremy Treglown (Oxford, 1980), pp. 241-42. Compare Dorset's 'The Antiquated Coquette': 'Desire's asleep and cannot wake / When women such advances make: / Both time and charms thus Philis Wastes, / Since each must surfeit ere he tastes. / Nothing escapes her wand'ring eyes, / No one she thinks too mean a prize' (pp. 39-45).

32. Sarah Wintle, 'Libertinism and Sexual Politics', in Treglown, p. 151.

33. Harold Weber, 'Drudging in fair Aurelia's Womb: Constructing Homosexual Economies in Rochester's Poetry', *The Eighteenth Century,* 33:2 (1992), pp. 99-117, 110, 108.

34. *Ibid.,* p. 115.

35. *Ibid.,* p. 110.

36. Claude Rawson, 'Systems of Excess', *Times Literary Supplement,* 29 March (1985), pp. 335-36.

37. 'Drudging In Fair Aurelia's Womb: Constructing Homosexual Economics in Rochester's Poetry', *op. cit.,* p. 103.

38. *Ulysses,* 3 vols, ed. Hans W. Gabler (New York, 1984), 1:175.

39. Treglown, p. 85.

Tony Barley (essay date 1995)

SOURCE: Barley, Tony. "'Upon Nothing': Rochester and the Fear of Non-entity." In *Reading Rochester,* edited by Edward Burns, pp. 98-113. Liverpool, UK: Liverpool University Press, 1995.

[*In this essay, Barley explores Rochester's treatment of "nothing" and finds that even as he appears to be advocating non-entity the poet is anxious to distance and distinguish himself from it.*]

Because of its knowing exhibitionism, because of its flair, because of its mock-solemn pride in its own achievement, Rochester's poem *Upon Nothing* brushes aside the kind of readerly interrogation invited by similarly impressive metaphysical displays. If Donne's 'Lecture on the Shadow' or 'A Nocturnall upon S. Lucie's Day' or Marvell's 'Definition of Love', provide a recent generic pedigree for *Upon Nothing,* Rochester's salient improvisation on non-entity requires of its readership qualitatively less imaginative effort to succumb to its arguments and admire its paradoxes. *Upon Nothing* asks, supposing it asks anything of its readers, for a take-it-or-leave-it sense of delightedly amused awe. The strength of its regal negligence acts to make the poem seemingly impregnable.

The conceptual game seems everything in *Upon Nothing,* which ostensibly delivers an extended descriptive definition of non-entity, but which couches the absolute with which it deals in terms of the dissolutions of a vigorously playful relativism. Knowing that his subject will of itself take the breath away, Rochester's title advertises and enacts what is to prove an unremitting sequence of dextrous disintegrations. What can be constructed upon nothing? Why, nothing, of course, and with that apodictic flourish, the poem proper begins, apostrophizing Nothing as personage, attracting Nothing's attention, engaging Nothing in one-sided dialogue, lauding Nothing with priest-like compliment, taking for granted its pre-eminent dominion over the universe.

Immediately, the absolute Nothing is conceived in terms of a relativism and a negativity which instantly destabilize much, though not all, of the sense of Nothing as a supreme idealist essence. Although Nothing can have no point of origin, Nothing is here historicized. Although Nothing necessarily lacks parentage, Nothing is here familial, fraternally related to the lesser nothing, Shade. Although Nothing extends its compass throughout an atemporal domain and is therefore 'well fixt', Nothing is here both exclusive of Time's parabola, and contradictorily, is in a contiguous relationship with Time's eternally travelling arrow:

> Nothing thou Elder Brother even to Shade
> Thou hadst a being ere the world was made
> And well fixt art alone of ending not afraid.

> (ll. 1-3)[1]

Not the father, and not the eldest, but merely the 'elder brother' to the shadow that Something implicitly casts, or to the shade which cloaks death, Nothing pre-exists the world's formation not as a total state but as a curiously indefinite condition, with 'a' being, rather than being as such. By avoiding the superlative, the poet prevents the polarization that could give the reader fixed points of reference.

Because exempt from finality, Nothing cannot fear it; because non-existent, the threat of non-existence holds no terrors, but what might have been expressed as a positive disdain for closure is given here in the unsettling negative form ('not afraid'). In eschewing a specified opposite, the poet alludes to a vaguely circumscribed 'other' realm enjoying no discrete category. With similar effect, the noun-participle 'ending', which delays conclusion infinitely, undercuts Nothing's fearlessness by an indeterminacy which is already Nothing's own attribute. This first stanza then admits no solid ground even in commencement, the certainty of its tone establishing itself in contradiction to its ambiguously provisional sense. Such a tension holds, to a greater or lesser extent, throughout the following ten stanzas of the poem, in which Rochester rehearses his heretical cosmology and dismisses all denials of Nothing's omnipotence as pretentious.

David Vieth, in his edition of Rochester's poems, summarizes and contextualizes the poem's thesis as follows:

> Orthodox Christian theology holds that God created the universe out of nothing (the usual version) or chaos (the variation adopted by Milton in *Paradise Lost*). Hence, according to a paradoxical tradition which developed as a corollary, this non-existent nothing is the source or unformed raw material of all things in the Creation, without which they could not exist.[2]

Having run the film of creation in reverse until it has spun off its reel, the poet steps back authoritatively into the absences of pre-existence, characterizing in a single disarming line the negative pre-conditions which pertained prior to substance and dimension: 'Ere Time and Place were, Time and Place were not', a statement of such necessary tautology that its bewildering resonance is offset by the persuasive force of its simple logic. The insistent combination of Time and Place, and the impossibility of imagining a time before Time and matter before Place, both governed by that seemingly artless 'Ere' (which, used quite unembarrassedly, demonstrates language's inability to convey non-existence), challengingly harks back of course to (Augustinian) theology's refusal to take interest in the absence 'before' creation, but also anticipates modern scientific myths of origin in which the problem of the ultimate anterior stubbornly remains.

It is interesting—though inevitable—that modern, popular-scientific accounts of cosmology encounter an identical incapacity to explain other than in notional abstractions the initial configurations that led to the formation of the universe. This, for example, is Stephen Hawking in his wryly titled *A Brief History of Time*:

> In order to predict how the universe should have started off, one needs laws that hold at the beginning of time. If the classical theory of general relativity was correct, the singularity theorems that Roger Penrose and I proved show that the beginning of time would have been a point of infinite density and infinite curvature of space-time. All the known laws of science would break down at such a point.[3]

> (p. 133)

> It was at the conference in the Vatican mentioned earlier that I first put forward the suggestion that maybe time and space together formed a surface that was infinite in size but did not have any boundary or edge.[4]

> (p. 136)

According to these characteristic accounts, the occurrence itself 'happens' in a zone of wordlessness; there is and was no beforehand, literally nothing preceded creation. The moment of origin moreover, is literally inconceivable: to grasp experientially what is proposed in the notions of 'a point of infinite density and curvature of space-time', or of a finite surface without boundary, is impossible. The concept of infinity here proves as teasingly elusive as Rochester's autonomous Nothing which in that one unspecified moment of 'When . . . straight begott' Something, thus initiating Time; 'Then all proceeded from the great united what'. The *gravitas* is hardly straight-faced in this second stanza where the bizarrely abrupt 'What'—an explosive capitulation to non-sense—parodies the quiet disorientations carried by that governing preposition and those conjunctional adverbs 'Ere', 'When', and 'Then'; 'the known laws of science . . . break down' in this mockery of linear progression. The poet's amusement is barely contained (with Rochester sneering at 'the Something and Nothing of logicians' and punning obscenely on 'twat', as Dustin Griffin[5] suggests).

Rochester's playfulness in this first, cosmological section of the poem depends upon the promotion of a giddying sequence of mutually exclusive, but not self-cancelling, definitions of non-existence and theories of creation which the tone of self-aware panegyric winkingly pretends to find self-consistent. So Nothing features alternately as a positive and as a negative condition. The imagination has little problem picturing a positive nothing as an absence within and in opposition to which substance exists, the model for which might be that of an inverse vacuum. Negative nothing on the other hand, demands a fraction more sleight of mind in conceiving. Carl Sagan's attempt to describe such negative nothing in relation to the 'Big Bang' hypothesis of the origin of the universe is unsatisfying, but nonetheless helpful:

> In that titanic cosmic explosion, the universe began an expansion which has never ceased. It is misleading to describe the expansion of the universe as a sort of distending bubble viewed from the outside. By definition, nothing we can ever know about *was* outside. It is better to think of it from the inside, perhaps with grid lines—imagined to adhere to the moving fabric of space—expanding uniformly in all directions . . .[6]

It is particularly in the later parts of the poem that Nothing comes increasingly to feature as pure non-entity. At the outset however, negative Nothing is as yet a shadow of that other multiple Nothing with its own 'being'—the 'primitive' presence, the 'sole original', the 'fruitful Emptiness', the begetter of a 'race' of 'offspring', the dark 'mighty power' ruling a once 'peaceful realm'.

In his reading of the poem, Griffin rightly notes that it proposes variant, mutually exclusive 'stories of creation':

> (1) Nothing begot Something, and from their incestuous union all else followed (st.2); (2) Something was severed or sundered from Nothing, as Eve was sundered from Adam's side, and subsequently severed or 'snatched' from Nothing's hand 'men, beasts', etc. (sts.3-4); (3) with terms now shifted from concrete to abstract, from 'Something' to 'Matter', Matter is born of Nothing but frustrates Nothing's desire for incestuous union, fleeing from its embrace, joining in rebellion against Nothing with Form, Light, Time, and Place (sts.5-6).[7]

p. 270

By transposing Rochester's mainly active formulations (stanza 3 excepted) into his own mainly passive account, Griffin avoids the wheeling ambiguities of, for example, stanza 4, where the possible syntactical reversal confuses subject and object, and thus upsets all sense of the respective powers of Something and Nothing:

> Yet Somthing did thy mighty power command
> And from thy fruitfull Emptinesses hand
> Snatcht, Men, Beasts, birds, fire, water, Ayre, and land.
>
> (ll. 10-12)

If a God-like Something commands Nothing's 'mighty power', equally, Nothing's 'mighty power' commands Something, which proceeds thenceforth to its hyper-Promethean mission, purloining from Nothing not only fire, but every other component of being. Nonetheless, Griffin's inventory of the poet's tales of creation illuminates what the poem pretends to obscure, and the

critic is persuasive in suspecting both that Rochester is parodying 'the double account of man's creation in Genesis' and is intentionally deploying 'discrepancies and uncertainties in order to mock the process of explaining origins'.

The jumbled, anti-linear catalogue which ends the stanza quoted above, blasphemously jibes at the divine ordering related in Genesis I, its repeated commas refuting hierarchy and suggesting a chaotic equality. Moreover stanzas 3-6 tease not only Cowley's 'Hymn to Light', but also, and more obviously, the Miltonic gospel's narrative of Satan's rebellion in *Paradise Lost*:

> Somthing, the generall Attribute of all
> Severed from thee its sole Originall,
> Into thy boundless selfe must undistinguished fall.
>
> (ll. 7-9)

> Matter, the Wickedst offspring of thy Race
> By forme assisted flew from thy Embrace
> And Rebell-Light obscured thy Reverend dusky face.

> With forme and Matter, Time and Place did joyne
> Body thy foe with these did Leagues combine
> To spoyle thy Peaceful Realme and Ruine all thy Line.
>
> (ll. 13-18)

The luck of history and social status precluded the imposition of any Protestant *fatwah* on the writer of these Satanic Verses. Something's predicted 'undistinguished fall' into a 'boundless' future oblivion (Nothing's 'self') distends and twists the Angel Satan's celebrated descent. Severed from the a-Deity Nothing, which alone had particularity (as 'sole originall'), Something is merely 'the *generall* attribute of all', hence 'undistinguished' from the outset. The mass rebellion of the alliance of the implicitly God-given abstractions, qualities, components and conditions of existence turns the world of Miltonic morality and the Biblical 'good' upside down. The revolt provides a compendium of all possible modes of immoral and unnatural challenge to rightful, established authority: the ungrateful 'Wickedst' betrayal of a loved child ('Matter'), the cowardly treachery of that 'offspring' in accepting the assistance of an outsider ('Form') and ignominiously fleeing the parental 'Embrace', the deliberate, murderous deceit of 'Rebell-Light' in obliterating Nothing's 'Reverend dusky face'. In the obscurity provided by Light, the confederacy of Form, Matter, Time, Place and Body hatch a military conspiracy, motivated it seems, by nothing more than envy: 'To spoyle thy Peaceful Realme and Ruine all thy Line' (l.18).

The fact that Nothing's 'Line' comprises none other than the aforementioned confederates makes for a very quiet irony that passes almost unnoticed. But the following stanza (7) underscores the joke as, when all seems quite lost for Nothing, Nothing finds the decisive counter-stroke:

> But Turncote-time assists the foe in vayne
> And brib'd by thee destroyes their short liv'd Reign

And to thy hungry wombe drives back thy slaves
again.

(ll.19-21)

Nothing's victory in this epic conflict is soon assured—not
only because one of the conspirators is the inevitable
'Turncote', but because utterly malleable, Nothing can
outdo its enemies in policy, bribing Time to destroy their
brief tenure on power, reenslaving this would-be independence movement in the 'hungry womb' of a new female
Nothing which begat it in the first place. Once masculine,
now feminine, the munificent womb greedily ingests and
absorbs; the once creative space becomes a place of
constriction and retention.

The two comparatively restrained stanzas which ensue
(8-9) function almost in parenthesis as a kind of unintended
ruminative digression. They show the poem beginning to
stray a little into a less ambiguous modest and serious
mode, where for once the wit serves a subordinate role,
very nearly integrated with the thought—until now suppressed—that Nothing's 'truth' is a mystery:

> Though Misteries are barr'd from Laick Eyes
> And the Divine alone with warrant pries
> Into thy Bosome, where thy truth in private lyes.
>
> Yet this of thee the wise may truly say
> Thou from the virtuous Nothing doest delay
> And to be part of thee the wicked wisely pray.

(ll.22-27)

The voice here is unassuming. The extended play on the
right of the divine to pry into Nothing's privacy to find
'the truth' which 'lies', for once does not dominate, and if
it causes a double-take on the reader's part, the result is
not more than a smile, which does not detract from the
reader's straightforward assent with the primary sense of
Nothing's inviolable mystery. Similarly with stanza 9.
Nothing takes nothing away from the virtuous, Nothing
delays the final end of the virtuous which is to become
nothing; in contrast, the wish for oblivion is the wise
prayer of the wicked.

If stanzas 8 and 9 arise unexpectedly, and in a different
key, as though another more subdued and solemn-wise
meditation might be emerging in counterpoint, they also
serve to mark the poem's place of transition from
cosmological philosophy to social satire. Stoic wisdom,
the judicious acknowledgement of the limitations of human knowledge, and of its paltry pretensions, is the
transitional theme. The wicked may be wise but the wise
are less wicked than laughably pathetic: 'Great Negative'
(the tone of ironical assurance returns):

> how vainly would the wise
> Enquire, define, distinguish, teach, devise,
> Didst Thou not stand to poynt their blind Phyloso-
> phies.

(ll.28-30)

Here the irony is engagingly obvious. Being blind, the
wise do in fact see nothing, do 'vainly . . . Enquire,
define, distinguish, teach, devise' despite Nothing's standing point, pricking all such bubbles of pretension. And
again obviously, the catalogue of the vanities of the wise
erases in dismissive self-parody the entire preceding science of Nothing which the poem has until now so
sympathetically recorded.

Why is Rochester writing **Upon Nothing**—and which of
the poem's two main perspectives interests him more: the
dazzling, all-embracing maze of cosmology we have so far
been led (by the nose) through, or the gleefully contemptuous assault against a civilization in which every element
of social dignity, social achievement and social virtue is
shown to have as much substance as the new clothes of
the fairytale Emperor? Does the poem's process enact a
diminution, as has been suggested, or is that first part an
extended, delaying prelude to a position which finds more
excitement in the real absurdities of social organization
than in mythological speculation? So well balanced is the
poem that to suggest an answer favouring either of these
alternatives might well seem inappropriate. Indeed, it
practically becomes a matter of taste as to whether or not
the pyrotechnic brilliance of the first half's epic metaphysics seems of greater moment than the second half's slow-
growing crescendo of satirical invective. Yet the very
extent of the shift of attention in the poem keeps such
questions naggingly alive.

When the metaphysics of cosmology are to all intents and
purposes done with, the substantial world of social
(mis)behaviour remains. And here experience can be
pinned down and named for what it is. Exaggerated political, national and sexual stereotypes mask their basis in the
truths such clichés typically inscribe. This grimly funny,
utterly enjoyable humour tells the world's whole story
from the perspective of the satirist so persuasively as to
gainsay all and any challenge to it, all and any detraction
or contradiction or qualification:

> Is or is not, the two great Ends of ffate
> And true or false the Subject of debate
> That perfect or destroy the vast designes of State—
>
> When they have wrackt the Politicians Brest
> Within thy Bosome most Securely rest
> And when reduc't to thee are least unsafe and best
>
> But (Nothing) why does Something still permitt
> That Sacred Monarchs should at Councell sitt
> With persons highly thought, at best for nothing fitt,
>
> Whilst weighty Somthing modestly abstaynes
> ffrom Princes Coffers and from Statesmens braines
> And nothing there like Stately nothing reignes?
>
> Nothing who dwell'st with fooles in grave disguise
> ffor whom they Reverend Shapes and formes devise
> Lawn-sleeves and ffurs and Gowns, when they like
> thee looke wise:

ffrench Truth, Dutch Prowess, Brittish policy
Hibernian Learning, Scotch Civility
Spaniards Dispatch, Danes witt, are Mainly seen in
  thee;

The Great mans Gratitude to his best freind
Kings promises, Whors vowes towards thee they bend
fflow Swiftly into thee, and in thee ever end.

                                            (ll.31-51)

Four stanzas (11-14) attend quasi-discreetly to the state and government, indicting the hollowness of political programmes and social administration in alternately objective, delicate and quizzical tones, but with an increasingly venomous off-handedness and a noticeable increase in acceleration. They are followed by three driving stanzas of uncompromisingly overt invective, one speedily ridiculing and dismissing the clergy, the next reeling off scornfully a varied handful of national inadequacies (15-16), the last, an abruptly halted coda (17), that is a chilling judgement on what is promised, owed and delivered in relationships between people: this being the only stanza of the poem to broach the subject of *personal* interaction—or rather its absence. The momentum of the second part of *Upon Nothing* suddenly brakes in this concluding stanza, and the poem stops short—and dead.

It takes only a moment of reflection to realize that Rochester is attaching precious little weight to the observations which make up his social critique, notwithstanding the validity of many of those self-same observations. The poet entertains no thought whatsoever of political or ecclesiastical reform, indulges no wish to remedy deficiencies in 'national character': any impulse towards correction would instance yet another of Nothing's gestures. At the same time, the inevitability of a state of affairs in which 'the vast designs of state' reduce to nothing, because treasuries are always empty and counsellors always empty-headed, is matter merely for perennial enjoyment. The ironical anger which underpins this whole section does not come from a stance of unheeded, malcontent worldly-wisdom, nor is it actually directed against its ostensible targets which are merely butts for the sparkling, mischievous humour overlying that anger. The bathos of stanzas 11 and 12 in which questions of Fate and Truth are the context for the 'vast designes of State' over which politicians 'wrack' their breasts (!) teases without griping, without outrage, while the puzzled-pained confusions of 13 and 14 do likewise, with the joke depending throughout on those simple-sarcastic qualifiers: 'highly thought, at best', 'weighty', 'modestly', 'stately'.

To be sure, all trace of the jovial seems instantly to vanish in the explosive scorn of stanza 15 where Nothing is found at home with clerical 'fooles in grave disguise' who flatter and mimic it, appearing 'wise' by devising and donning an amorphous array of 'reverend' paraphernalia which both expresses and cloaks their folly. But here too, the dismissive contempt acts as if in excess of its stated referent, as though it were either a gratuitous outburst, or had

been transferred from some other unnamed source. This same feeling is induced in the brilliant, and lighter, penultimate stanza which rapidly counts off and discounts 'ffrench Truth, Brittish policy, Hibernian Learning' and the rest in an apparently self-generating list. Again, the unsettling combination of show-off playfulness and antagonism jars on, as much as it excites, the reader, suggesting that the poet's game has an ulterior function, one that is actually careless of national fallibilities. One suspects that the more wide-rangingly Rochester the sportsman pursues this Nothing, the more his quarry is actually hounding him.

It is the final stanza which perhaps provides a psychological key to the discrepancy between the tone of the assumed voice of *Upon Nothing* and the oddly disturbing effect the poem intermittently produces. The suspicion that there is an individual identity present at some remove from the poetic persona periodically arises, and never more so than in this concluding stanza. The notion that the poem comprises a masterly set-piece exercise, is a demonstration of the playful possibilities inherent in the paradoxes of the conventional topos 'nothing', is one which the poet would like to have us believe yet does not ever quite believe himself: the satisfactions of closure are withheld or unattained. A sense of personal disappointment and personal hurt dominates the last stanza in those masochistically selected instances of unfulfilled expectation and betrayal. 'The great mans Gratitude to his best friend, / Kings promises, Whors vowes'. The very occlusion of the personal, the child-like transference of hurt onto blamed hurtful others who thereby represent an entire world of failed personal interaction (already defensively mediated by obstructive incompatibilities of status and role: 'great man', 'King', 'Whors'), suggests that the experience of emptiness is here Rochester's own, and that the moments of anger in the poem express the flip-side of the poet's own hurt. The indefinite nature of the poem's sudden closing thought, in which gratitude, promises and vows bend towards nothing, flow swiftly into nothing, and ever end in nothing, confirms this feeling—the on-going tendency *towards* nothingness in all such arrested interpersonal transactions inscribes a pathetic, rueful condition, despite the formal adroitness of these final lines.

What I am suggesting here is that *Upon Nothing* consists of a series of defensive strategies through which the poet tentatively touches upon his own sense of non-identity. The external nothings of the poem are projections of a feared internal non-entity. The pressure exerted by a feeling of personal non-being occasions the poem but the poem itself seeks to resist that pressure by any means that it can find at its disposal. Neither the parodic philosophical game of the first half, nor the tongue-in-cheek social satire of the second encapsulates the dominant interest since the choice of subject matter and its treatment throughout the poem are primarily functional.

To protect himself from Nothing, the poet begins by juggling with the notional components of an external (idealist, original, ultimate) Nothing, ventriloquising the languages we use in the ultimately fruitless attempt to comprehend what is (apparently) outside of experience. Rochester assumes the existence of no positive absolute, no secure ontological frame or fabric which might effectively combat the Nothing which Being impotently interrupts. The perception of non-being that seems external proves continually to threaten the real world of experience and, more than that, to invade it. Thus, even while it is affecting to speak directly to Nothing, or to be speaking on Nothing's behalf, the poetic voice is unable to maintain completely its assurance. For all that the poet-persona takes pride in, and enjoys, the easy skill of rhetorical argument, the conceptual virtuosity, the witty humour, the capriciousness, these cannot be sustained, and the assured tone is finally a posture, a temporary stand against the overwhelming sense of negation.

In the first part of the poem the moments of slippage where the mask of the speaker, Nothing's eulogist, is slyly allowed to drop while Rochester draws attention to his own ingenuity, act to confirm the poet's self-confidence. In such moments the reader is let in on the parodic in-jokes and is tantalized with a sense of shared participation, with being offered the possibility of identification with the poet. But at the same time, the poet maintains the comedian's distance by fluidly re-emerging with his persona, refusing full identification, denying the reader security, and thereby manages temporarily to bolster his own sense of stability.

In the heady world of metaphysics, such defense mechanisms can work for a time but the process of the poem cannot put off for ever the need to attend to the real world, and Nothing's presence therein. So the social, and the personal which the social implicitly forms, come to dominate the later stages, thus offering insight into the poem's private motive. The humour is deeper, more assimilated here, and the reader has no effort to make in recognizing the truth of the poet's knowing social critique. But the changes in tome during the poem's final movement are more marked, and the coy, inflated, sweeping, knowing, jibing, inventively abandoned social observations which appear with such cavalier effortlessness throughout the resolution hint at an anarchic flair symptomatic of near breakdown. The posture of careless flourish fails to withstand the unlocated anger beneath it; the stubborn residue of what seem specific past frustrations and disappointments suggest a feared loss of control on the poet's part, with potential exhausted collapse just an arm's length away.

Upon Nothing is not about Death, or the fear of death unlike Rochester's other (later) foray onto that thematic terrain—his translation of the Chorus of Act II of Seneca's *Troades*:

> After Death, nothing is, and nothing, Death,
> The utmost Limit of a gaspe of Breath;

> (ll. 1-2)

From beginning to end, Rochester's version is concerned with common-sense deflation and demystification, adopting an attitude which is level-headedly pedagogic. As noth-

ing, death should hold no terrors whatsoever, any dread of non-existence is invented, is fantasy. 'Dead, wee become the Lumber of the World', nothing more, and if 'Devouring tyme swallows us whole' we should simply accept that 'impartial' fate:

> For Hell, and the foule Fiend that Rules
> Gods everlasting fiery Jayles
> (Devis'd by Rogues, dreaded by Fooles),
> With his grim, griezly Dogg, that keepes the Doore,
> Are senselesse Storyes, idle Tales,
> Dreames, Whimseys, and noe more.

> (ll. 13-18)

The tone of the piece is completely self-consistent; no fractures or fissures interrupt it. Whether pagan or Christian, all 'devised' myths of *post mortem* retribution should be discounted *en masse*. Straightforward, unshakeable conviction is the keynote here, the assurance is real and unassailable but in no way dogmatic or strained— there is no need to insist. Rather amused by all the fuss, the speaking voice simply sets the record to rights.

The comparative complexities of **Upon Nothing** might well lead to the deduction that without Seneca's guidance, Rochester is far less sanguine about reaching 'The utmost limit' of the last 'gasp of breath'. In his *Self and Others,* the psychiatrist R. D. Laing addresses the pathology initially associated with the fear of non-entity in terms of the following:

> Tillich (1952) speaks of the possibilities of non-being in the three directions of ultimate meaninglessness, ultimate condemnation, and ultimate annihilation in death. In those three directions man as a spiritual being, as a moral being, as a biological being, faces the possibility of his own annihilation, or non-being.[8]

Yet it is not the apprehension of these three 'ultimate' possibilities which is disturbing in Rochester's poem. The future as such occupies little of the poet's attention, the awareness is not of awaiting the eventual arrival of self-*annihilation*. The anxiety expressed in **Upon Nothing** is already contained in, and centred in, the immediacies of the present.

Referring to his earlier study *The Divided Self,* Laing advances a supplementary category of disintegration experienced by the individual:

> The ontological insecurity described in The *Divided Self* is a fourth possibility. Here, man as a person, encounters non-being, in a preliminary form, as a partial loss of the synthetic unity of self, concurrently with a partial loss of relatedness with the other, and in an ultimate form, in the hypothetical state of *chaotic nonentity,* total loss of relatedness with self and other.

It is this fourth possibility which applies most nearly to Rochester's composition. The strategies employed by the poet to erect and fortify a structure of personal security in the face of what seems a total loss of relatedness with the world outside the self are compellingly desperate. The witty playfulness, the poised elusiveness, together with all the varied voices and changing perspectives displayed in *Upon Nothing,* indicate the poet at some deep level operating neurotically against that invasive chaos of non-entity which mirrors his own internal sense of imminent disintegration from within.

Perhaps it is significant that the extreme expression of contempt in the poem occurs in stanza 15, the stanza which attacks the clergy, but more important in this context, the stanza which deals most explicitly with the pretences of deception and disguise. A case of both transference and projection, one might think. Rochester feels he knows inside out what is crucially at stake in the adoption of disguises, or of personae. In his Introduction to *The Complete Poems,* Vieth makes especial note of the fact that the 'male speakers in Rochester's poems can be ranged on a spectrum of identities' (*Introduction,* xli), and he goes a step further in exploring the attendant implications by drawing attention to the poet's 'real-life' predilection for varying his own identities:

> Augmenting this multiplication of identities was the real-life Rochester's practice of disguises. As Burnet relates,
>
> He took pleasure to disguise himself, as a *Porter,* or as a *Beggar*; sometimes to follow some mean Amours, which, for the variety of them, he affected; At other times, meerly for diversion, he would go about in odd shapes, in which he acted his part so naturally, that even those who were on the secret, and saw him in these shapes, could perceive nothing by which he might be discovered.
>
> The outstanding instance, of course, was the affair of Alexander Bendo, in which 'he disguised himself, so that his nearest Friends could not have known him . . .'
>
> (*Introduction,* xlii)

Upon Nothing affects to be just such a pleasurable diversion but its dependence upon changing identities, acted so naturally, betrays anxious compulsion underlying its play. Disguised as Nothing's friendly advocate, Rochester seeks to distance and distinguish himself from non-entity; with the poem's concluding stanza this operation finally proves to fail.

Notes

1. Quotations from 'Upon Nothing' are from Keith Walker's edition: *The Poems of John Wilmot, Earl of Rochester* (Oxford, 1984), pp. 62-64.

2. David M. Vieth's edition: *The Complete Poems of John Wilmot, Earl of Rochester* (New Haven and London, 1974), p. 118.

3. Stephen W. Hawking, *A Brief History of Time: from the Big Bang to Black Holes* (London, 1988), p. 133.

4. *Ibid.,* p. 136.

5. Dustin H. Griffin, *Satires Against Man: the Poems of Rochester,* (Berkeley, 1973), p. 271.

6. Carl Sagan, *Cosmos: the story of cosmic evolution, science and civilisation* (London, 1983), p. 279.

7. Griffin, *op.cit.,* p. 270.

8. R. D. Laing, *Self and Others* (rev. edition Harmondsworth, 1971), p. 51.

David Quentin (essay date 2000)

SOURCE: Quentin, David. "The Missing Foot of *Upon Nothing* and Other Mysteries of Creation." In *That Second Bottle: Essays on John Wilmot, Earl of Rochester,* edited by Nicholas Fisher, pp. 89-100. Manchester, UK: Manchester University Press, 2000.

[*In the following essay, Quentin examines the relationship of form and content in* Upon Nothing, *considering the question of whether the missing metrical foot at the end of line 42 reveal something about the qualities of nothing discussed in the poem.*]

In John Lennard's *Poetry Handbook,* subtitled 'A Guide to Reading Poetry for Pleasure and Practical Criticism', there is a section intended to bring comfort to worried A-level students and undergraduates, and it advises them when confronted with a poem in an exam to 'make a short technical description', after which it assures them they will suffer 'an embarrassment of things to remark', top of the list being 'metrical conformity and deviation'.[1] Armed with this advice, a practical criticism examinee would be overjoyed to reach the line 42 of Rochester's *Upon Nothing,* 'And Nothing there, like stately Nothing Reigns'.[2] Unlike the hexameter one has come to expect at the end of each stanza, this line has but ten syllables. It is missing a foot on the end, a foot that is all too easy to imagine reigning at the end of the line like stately Nothing itself. Surely if any example of metrical deviation has semantic value contingent upon its context, this does. But did Rochester put it there with that purpose in mind? Is there a contemporary theory of contingent metrical semantics to justify our reading of a putative empty sixth foot? In 1690, Sir William Temple wrote that the Greek name for poets, and this would have been no news to anyone, signified 'makers or Creators, such as raise admirable Frames and Fabricks out of nothing'.[3] The purpose of this chapter is to decide whether there is anything in the qualities of Nothing generally, and Rochester's Nothing particularly, to help answer this question of the relationship between frame and fabric in his poem.

It is by no means a critical contrivance to expect of *Upon Nothing* an elucidation of an aspect of poetics. To write of Nothing that it had 'a Being e're the World was made', which Rochester does in the second line of this poem, is to alert the reader to the linguistic ontology of Nothing. The word is anomalous; the 'no' denotes absence of 'thing', but it operates like an adjective. 'Nothing . . . / Thou had'st a Being e're the World was made' is grammatically similar to 'wild thing, you make my heart sing', or any other sentence in which a qualified thing is the subject of an active verb. The word makes non-existence an accident, rather than an absence, of body. In the Rochester, the verb is the very verb 'to have being', which emphasises the spurious existence afforded Nothing by its having a name. 'This word *nothing* is a name', as Hobbes puts it in *De Corpore,* 'which yet cannot be the name of any thing'.[4] This is what led Parmenides to warn us in such strenuous terms of the dangers of the path of 'is not', for 'you could not know what is not . . . nor indicate it'.[5] To indicate Nothing is to give to Nothing a local habitation and a name, which is of course the preserve of the lunatic, the lover and the poet. A poem which indicates Nothing, then, is a sort of poem squared. Puttenham wrote that poets are makers 'such as we may say of God who . . . made all the world of nought'.[6] A poem about Nothing would therefore be a parody of the very process of poetic creation.

What then of the relationship in seventeenth-century poetics between form and content, frame and fabric? Sir William Temple's observation about poetry originating in Nothing is nicely balanced between the two, and that poetry is 'making' in these two distinct fields, what Harington described as 'the two parts of poetry',[7] is widely acknowledged by the theorists of the seventeenth century and their Elizabethan forebears. There is, however, a consensus that the frame is less important than the fabric. Hobbes writes that 'they that take for poesy whatsoever is writ in verse . . . they err', or as Sidney put it, 'it is not rhyming and versing that maketh a poet', and for Sidney, poetry seems for the most part to be roughly synonymous with fiction.[8] According to William Drummond, Jonson was occasionally prepared to maintain that 'verses stood by sense without either colours or accent',[9] and so much of the debate in the field of poetics over the course of this period appears to be about what should go on within the arbitrary prescribed limits of poetic form, rather than concerning itself with the nature of that arbitrary prescription. Bacon writes that 'poesie is a part of learning in measure of words for the most part restrained, but in all other points extreamely licensed',[10] and goes on to discuss at length the licence of fiction while barely mentioning again the restraint of measure. Ironically, this theoretical predilection for the idea of fiction was held responsible for the kind of restrictive evils we moderns associate with prescribed verse. Sir William Alexander writes that 'many would bound the boundless Liberty of a Poet, binding him only to the Birth of his own Brains', against which position Davenant replies 'how much pleasure they loose . . . who take away the liberty of a Poet, and fetter his feet in the shackles of an Historian'.[11]

The poet is nevertheless, as Jonson puts it 'tyed . . . to numbers', and there is no doubt that poets were to get them right according to what Dryden was happy to refer to by the end of the century as the 'mechanical rules' of English prosody.[12] Jonson, it will be recalled, thought that Donne deserved hanging for not keeping of accent.[13] 'The counting of the Syllables is the least part of the Poet's Work', wrote Robert Wolseley in the preface to *Valentinian,* exemplifying the overall ethos that metre is a pre-existing requirement; the actual poetry goes into the words that fulfil that requirement.[14] 'Though the Laws of Verse . . . put great constraint upon the natural course of Language', writes Hobbes, 'yet the Poet, having liberty to depart from what is obstinate, and to chuse somewhat else that is more obedient to such Laws, and no less fit for his purpose, shall not be, neither by the measure nor the necessity of Rime, excused'.[15]

Hobbes dismisses Herbert's experiments in the most primitive of formally mimetic modes; 'in a . . . Sonnet, a man may vary his measures, and seek glory from a needlesse difficulty, as he that contrived verses into the form of . . . a paire of Wings'.[16] In this he is in accord with the prevalent sense that the relationship between form and content is arbitrary. According to Samuel Daniel, form is *of necessity* an arbitrary restriction unrelated to content, 'especially seeing our passions are often without measure', as he points out.[17] When Chapman claims a semantic quality to verse in the following lines 'Our Monosyllables so kindly fall, / And meete, opposde in rhyme, as they did kisse',[18] he clearly does not mean this kissing to relate to the content of the rhymed lines; he is, after all, writing about a martial epic. Davenant alerts us to the pitfalls of trying to extract sense from the formal and metrical properties of verse when he writes to Hobbes, 'I shall say a little why I have chosen my interwoven *Stanza* of four, though I am not oblig'd to excuse the choice; for numbers in Verse must, like distinct kinds of Musick, be expos'd to the uncertain and different taste of several Eares'.[19]

As it happens, this indeterminacy is exemplified in criticism of *Upon Nothing,* the stanza form of which has been variously interpreted as assertive of the triumph of measure,[20] evocative of the chaotic,[21] and even indicative of an elegiac and ultimately finite largeness whose precision makes the heterodoxy of the poem more subversive.[22] Incidentally, the stanza occurs in Dryden's translation of the *Aeneid.* This is from the dedicatory letter to the Earl of Mulgrave: 'Spenser has also given me the boldness to make use sometimes of his alexandrine line . . . it adds a certain majesty to the verse, when 'tis used with judgment, and stops the sense from overflowing into another line'. Shortly afterwards, he writes 'I frequently make use of triplet rhymes, and for the same reason, because they bound the sense. And therefore, I generally join these two licences together, and make the last verse of the triplet a Pindaric [i.e. an Alexandrine]: for, besides the majesty which it gives, it confines the sense within the barriers of three lines, which would languish if it were lengthened into four'.[23] The business about majesty is a fiction. 'When 'tis used with judgement' means when the line is so written as not to fall apart into two trimeters, or when the content of the line is itself majestical. There is nothing majestical, for example, in the Alexandrine from *Upon*

Nothing 'And to be part of thee, the wicked wisely Pray' (line 27), with its obvious caesura in the middle, and its alliteration on the paradoxical and distinctly unmajestical topic of the wicked wisely praying for oblivion. Dryden's fictitious hexametrical majesty is intended to excuse the manifest licence he is taking in order to keep his sense within his verses, a motivation he is happy to admit. But there is another excuse in the mention of Spenser, the evocation of a prosodic convention, an arbitrary limit defined by precedent.

Puttenham insists that 'the Poet makes and contriues out of his owne braine both the verse and the matter of his poeme', not 'by any paterne or mould, as the Platonicks . . . do phantastically suppose'.[24] But anyone reading his manual, however taxonomic it might be in intention, could take one of the verse forms therein and use it as a pattern or mould for his own poem. In any case, formal prescription comes into play, at the very latest, as soon as the first stanza of a stanzaic poem is written; and certainly, if one sits down to write a sonnet, the standard sonnet forms exist already, as formal conventions, waiting to be given tangible existence by the words one writes on the page. As regards metre, does Puttenham expect us to believe what Jonson calls the observing of accent to have been re-invented anew for every poem written? If verse is made of naught then, whether Puttenham likes it or not, there is alongside that naught an empty pattern or mould such as the Platonicks do phantastically suppose. Verse form, to paraphrase Rochester, has a being ere the poem is made.

That form pre-exists substance is acknowledged by Sidney as an occasional phenomenon in bad rhymed verse: 'It will be found', he writes, 'that one verse did but beget another'.[25] It is famously celebrated, however, by Daniel: 'Ryme', he tells us, 'is no impediment to [the poet's] conceit, but rather giues him wings to mount, and carries him, not out of his course, but as it were beyond his power.'[26] Jonson's claim that he wrote all his poems first in prose and then versified them would appear to contradict this theory, but even he I think could not deny Sidney's assertion that if rhyme is to be done well it requires 'ordering at the first what should be at the last', a clear statement of the pre-existing and prescriptive nature of poetic form, rather more convincing than his earlier suggestion that verse is merely ornament to matter.[27] This aspect of poetics is modelled in terms of the creation of the cosmos. Pre-existing prescriptive form is justified as analogous to the Pythagorean, and indeed Platonic, idea that the Universe is ordered by number. Campion writes that 'the world is made by Simmetry and proportion, and is in that respect compared to Musick, and Musick to Poetry'.[28] Even Sidney, despite his insistence that 'it is not rhyming and versifying that maketh a poet', acknowledges poetry's 'planet-like music'.[29]

Nevertheless, it is to be assumed that matter as well as formal prescription pre-exists the poem; it is rare that poets fill formal requirements with unpremeditated words and see what emerges. This pre-existing matter is also understood cosmogonically, in this case as primordial chaos: 'The body of our imagination', asks Daniel, 'being as an Vnformed *Chaos* without fashion, without day, if by the diuine power of the spirit it be wrought into an Orbe of order and forme, is it not more pleasing to Nature?'[30] In the same vein, Dryden describes primordial poetic matter as 'a confused mass of thoughts, tumbling over one another in the dark'.[31] So where is Nothing in all this, the Nothing from which Puttenham, Theseus, Sir William Temple and the rest think poetry is made? There hardly seems space for it if symmetry and chaos have coexisted all along.

Clearly, the ubiquitous metaphor of God and the poet as analogous creators *ex nihilo* brings with it a complex cosmogonical problem, as indeed do most cosmogonies irrespective of their application in poetics. Genesis conflates chaos and non-existence by stating that the earth was both formless and void. It represents a point midway between the ancient Mesopotamian cosmogonies in which it originated, according to which Chaos precedes the ordering intelligence of the creator, and medieval Christian doctrine, according to which God is the sole originator of all things and creates out of nothing.[32] Substance cannot be made out of nothing, because if body came into being, there would have been a time when it was not, and this is to take the Parmenidean path of 'is not', which way error lies. But body must have come into being during the creation, because otherwise God would not be the sole originator of all things, being therefore coeval with chaos.

Though this latter position is clearly heretical, it survived the Thomist onslaught[33] and lived on into the Renaissance for two reasons. Firstly, the doctrine of creation *ex nihilo* does not fit with the Old Testament, which admits only creation from the seas of chaos, except in two verses, Genesis 1.2 and 2 Maccabees 7.28, in which creation *ex nihilo* is hardly positively endorsed. Secondly, the classical tradition in favour of the chaos narrative is strong, particularly in Plato's *Timaeus,* the only Platonic dialogue to have had a significant doctrinal influence over the medieval period,[34] and also in Ovid's *Metamorphoses,* the creation narrative of which is thoroughly rooted in the Hesiodic cosmogony of chaos.

Nevertheless, Renaissance poets by no means forgot that the world was made of nothing too, and the coexistence of nothing and chaos is imagined sequentially. When Romeo comes across what he calls a 'Misshapen chaos of well-seeming forms', he exclaims 'O brawling love, O loving hate, / O anything of nothing first create'.[35] When Donne in the 'Nocturnall upon S. Lucies day' is transformed from one of 'two Chaosses', into a quintessence of nothingness, he becomes the elixir 'of the first nothing'.[36] Romeo is presumably not a doctrinal expert, and in Donne the primacy of Nothing is both a concession to orthodoxy and an integral part of his metaphor. Spenser's solution to the problem of the coexistence of Nothing and chaos, in the Garden of Adonis passage of the *Faerie Queene,* however, engages much more directly with the actual ontological problem of creation. He writes that

in the wide wombe of the world there lyes,
In hatefull darknesse and in deep horrore,
An huge eternall Chaos, which supplyes
The substances of natures fruitfull progenyes.

All things from thence doe their first being fetch,
And borrow matter.[37]

Chaos here partakes of the origins of things; it is in the womb of the world, not the world itself. The matter from which temporal tangible things are made exists prior to the existence of those things, and, as Spenser goes on to indicate, it exists after those things to which it has given substance cease to exist:

That substance is eterne, and bideth so,
Ne when the life decayes, and forme does fade,
Doth it consume, and into nothing go.

(*Faerie Queene,* III.vi.37)

Tangible reality is clearly then not substance, but the temporary combination of substance and form; substance itself does not partake of the order of reality in which things are or are not. An absence, a 'nothing', in tangible reality before or after the existence of a thing means that its matter is in the realm of pure substance, the womb of the world.

This ontology is Platonic: it comes from the *Timaeus,* in which there are three orders of being: the realm of pure form, the realm of pure substance which is a homogeneous chaos, and the space in which the combination of form and substance is manifest. Plato helps us here with an analogy that reverses the qualities of substance and tangible reality. Eternal substance is like a sheet of gold, into which shapes are pressed. The tangible world has the ontological status of those shapes while visible as impressions in the gold. In this cosmology, 'nothing', has the status of space, the absence of impressions in the gold being equivalent to nothing in tangible reality. When Donne partakes of the first nothing he is re-begot 'of absence, darkness, death, things which are not'; things, in fact, which, like 'nothing', are merely names denoting absences.

Here, then, is a cosmogony of poetry. Poetry, like Plato's cosmos, has three orders of being: the pre-existing conventions of metre and poetic form, imagined as we have seen as the eternal numbers according to which the world was made; the pre-existing substance of the poet's thoughts, imagined as we have seen as a chaos; and the nothing that is the absence of a poem before it has been written. It is this nothing that is the backbone of my contention that the relationship between form and content in poetry written according to the theories of the Elizabethans and their successors is arbitrary, not collaborative. Nothing is what form and content have in common before they are combined in the tangible world of the poem. Their only accident in common is absence. 'Because I count it without reason', writes Sir John Harington of a Latin epigram, 'I will English it without rhyme',[38] giving rhyme and reason a mutual contingency that is ontological and nothing more.

In fact, just as the tangible world is imperfect, so the actual poem is imperfect; it will be recalled that Hobbes described how the sense is not aided but compromised by metre, and that Dryden described the licences he took with metre to contain the sense. Is there any space left for a collaborative understanding of form and content? It could be argued, and I would agree, that the imaginative links between cosmology and poetics faded over the course of the seventeenth century, and a collaborative understanding of form and content crept in. In 1674, apparently the year of composition of Rochester's poem, Thomas Rymer wrote of a verse of Virgil's: 'the *numbers* are so ratling that nothing can be more repugnant to the general repose and silence which the Poet describes'.[39] He is anticipating Pope's dictum 'The *Sound* must seem an *Eccho* to the Sense',[40] which, though it implies no semantic of metrical *deviation,* certainly implies a secondary acoustic semantic, to which metre and verse form might contribute. So what of Rochester himself? Was he heir to the Elizabethan cosmogony of poetics or was he a pioneer of formal mimeticism? Does the missing foot mean Nothing, or does it not mean anything at all?

Rochester's cosmogony in **Upon Nothing** is principally concerned with a question that does not arise in the cosmology of poetics, the old question of why nothing should become something in the first place. 'What need', asked Parmenides, 'would have driven [that which is] later rather than earlier, beginning from the nothing, to grow?'[41] If nothing had a being ere the world was made, in that before the world was made, nothing existed, then what made the world? Of course in line 6 Rochester tells us that 'What' did indeed make the world, where 'What' is the creator God shaved to infinitesimal thickness by Occam's razor. 'What' is that which existed along with primitive Nothing and caused it to become something. The problem is explored through a paradoxical chronology; the creation happened at the moment when time began, and at that moment Nothing something *straight* begot, and then, presumably a 'then' of chronological succession rather than simultaneity, 'all proceeded from the great united What!'. In this stanza, 'Something' is synonymous with the 'What'; it was begot at the very moment when time began and all, that is everything, proceeded from it. If everything proceeded from it after it itself came into being then it must be no thing, which is why Nothing begot it straight: that first something is in fact coeval with Nothing and partakes of it. This explains how the primal Nothing can be predicated by a past participle in line 3: Nothing is 'Well fixt' because it was fixed by that generative principle that is and is not nothing, that does not partake of existence, but must exist to cause existence. Nothing and the 'great united What!' begot each other at that eternity of infinitesimal duration at the beginning of time. The third and fourth stanzas restate the paradox. Line 7 points out that something is 'the General Attribute of all', and line 10 reminds us that the existence of all is contingent upon the prior existence of something. Nevertheless, this paradox having been exploited long enough, we suddenly find ourselves on familiar territory in stanzas 5 and 6.

Nothing has a kind of extended family; we saw it in Donne's 'absence, darkness, death, things which are not', and we see it here. 'Matter' is the offspring of Nothing's 'Race', and assisted by form it combines to ruin Nothing's 'Line', by producing body, Nothing's 'Foe'. Clearly body is opposed to Nothing, but it is preceded by rebellious agents that partake of Nothing. Matter has been held in Nothing's embrace since the moment of creation. This is just the kind of ontology we found in Spenser, and in line 21 Spenser's very womb image is recalled. A Lucretian version of the same ontology is explored in Rochester's eschatological Nothing poem, the translation from Seneca beginning 'After Death nothing is, and nothing Death'.[42] 'Dead', he writes, 'we become the Lumber of the World: / And to that Mass of Matter shall be swept, / Where things destroy'd, with things unborn are kept' (lines 8-10). Here is that same identity of non-entity that makes unformed matter a kind of nothing, coeval with the Nothing into which form and matter become body. When Hobbes discusses what he calls *Materia Prima* in *De Corpore,* he says of it that it is body in general, it is just a name, and it is nothing.[43] He explains this with the following analogy. If one were to invent a name for the substance that can be either water or ice, it would refer to water and ice in general, it would be just a name, and it would be nothing. Body in general, then, is primordial matter, which is no thing, and corresponds exactly to that kind of nothing that is chaos in Plato or Spenser. It goes without saying that form too is not in itself tangible body, and is therefore also no thing. Just as we found in ontology and poetics elsewhere, form and matter, prior to creation, are only linked by common familial ties with primordial absence.

This is roughly in accord with Cowley's *Davideis,* apparently one of the sources of **Upon Nothing**. Cowley's creation narrative has an unusually comprehensive cosmogony of poetics. Having just previously narrated that '*All . . . / From out the womb of fertile Nothing ris*',[44] he sets up the following analogy:

> As first a various unform'd *Hint* we find
> Rise in some god-like *Poets* fertile *Mind,*
> Till all the parts and words their places take,
> And with just marches *verse* and *musick* make;
> Such was *Gods Poem,* this *Worlds* new *Essay;*
> So wild and rude in its first draught it lay;
> Th'ungovern'd parts no *Correspondence* knew,
> An artless *war* from thwarting *Motions* grew;
> Till they to *Number* and *fixt* rules were brought
> By the *eternal Minds Poetique Thought.*
>
> (p. 253)

Cowley has already explained that God's '*spirit* contains / The well-knit *Mass,* from him each Creature gains / *Being*' (p. 251); in other words, the primordial stuff has no more tangible being than the 'fixt rules' with which it will be combined, and according to which it will be knit by the spirit of God. The 'first draught' was a '*Hint*' of being.

I do not, however, consider my anti-mimetic argument about Rochester's metre to be proved by his acknowledgment of this orthodox post-Renaissance cosmogony of

poetics. It is clearly the very act of bringing something out of nothing that interests Rochester, not the mechanical details of that act, or the different kinds of nothing that in combination produce something. If stanzas five and six are merely toeing the orthodox ontological line of his time for want of a more interesting cosmogony to explore, we cannot necessarily expect of Rochester an engagement with their implications for poetics generally, and for the ontology of the sixth foot of the 42nd line of his poem specifically. Furthermore, were I to consider my point proved, it would automatically undermine itself. My inferences pertaining to 'Well fixt' in line 3, for example, are invalid if 'Well fixt' is there to make up the Alexandrine. If form and content in poetry are indeed an unsatisfactory compromise between arbitrary numbers and matter without measure, then 'Well fixt' could so easily be an addition to an original pentameter 'And art alone of ending not afraid'. The line is much smoother as a pentameter without 'Well fixt' than it is as a hexameter with a caesura after the first syllable and a trochee for a second foot. 'Well fixt' is not even necessary for the sense. Is it just there to ratify the numbers? The same could be asked of the word 'strait' in line 5, so central to my contention that the generative principle is coeval with Nothing. Is the word in fact not there for its sense of chronological immediacy, but because it makes up the pentameter in the way that having 'did beget' instead of 'begot' would do, but without necessitating a change of rhyme? In denying the semantic properties of metrical feet, does the poetic cosmogony of the time by implication deny the semantic properties of the words required to fill them?

Such a denial would certainly explain Rochester's interest in the paradoxical nature of the creative act itself rather than the process by which that act occurs. If the correlation between cosmogony and poetics does inhere in this poem, the question, 'What quality in nothing causes it to become something?' is analogous to the question, 'What quality in the absence of a poem causes the poet to sacrifice his measureless pre-poetic chaos on the altar of arbitrary form?' It will be recalled that to write a poem upon nothing is to satirise the very process of poetical composition. If this poem argues for a pervasive semantic ambiguity in poetry as a result of poetry's compromisive nature, then it thereby shows why the very process of poetical composition is so deserving of such satire. In the field of poetics it is a great united why? Twice in the first seven stanzas Rochester reminds us that all this creation will fall back into the boundless self of Nothing, driven back into its womb, and I am reminded of the end of Daniel's *Defence of Ryme,* where having defended the arbitrary limit of form as creating an orb of order out of chaos, he tells us, the very *mise en page* tailing off into nothing, that 'we must heerein be content to submit ourselves to the law of time, which in few yeeres wil make al that for which we now contend Nothing'.[45]

Appealing to Rochester's other pronouncements on poetry is not entirely helpful. He does advocate respect for a vague kind of formal prescription in **'An Allusion to**

Horace': 'within due proportions circumscribe / What e're you write' (lines 20-1) but this is no mechanical formalism, for he mocks Dryden for finding Fletcher and Beaumont 'uncorrect' (line 82) and appears to espouse a doctrine of liberty from extremes of prescription, without positive advocacy of a semantics of metrical deviation. He makes it clear, in the Sidneyan vein of denying the definitive status of form and metre in poetry, that 'Five hundred Verses every morning writt / Proves you no more a Poet than a Witt' (lines 93-4), and in *An Epistolary Essay* asks 'Why shoud my prostituted sence be drawn / To ev'ry Rule their mustie Customes spawn?' (lines 85-6), though of course it is not clear on whose behalf. Nevertheless he appears to show tendencies towards collaborative poetics in the imitation of Boileau, when he mocks Halfwit's exclamation 'There's fine Poetry! you'd sweare 'twere Prose, / Soe little on the Sense, the Rhymes impose' (*Satyr.* ['Timon'], lines 119-20), an exclamation based on the theoretical assumption that form and content are arbitrarily linked, and the less the two impose on each other, the better both are.

The most positive theory, however, to emerge from Rochester's explicit engagements with poetics seems to advocate sheer hard work. In **'An Allusion to Horace'** he advises that the poet 'Compare each Phrase, Examine every Line, / Weigh every word, and every thought refine' (lines 100-1). But this is by no means an advocacy of formal and semantic collaboration, it argues rather for the Hobbesian considered approach to minimum compromise mocked in the figure of Halfwit. In any case, I do not believe a word of it. I am much happier believing as Rochester's own thoughts on the matter the sentiment expressed in the epistolary essay; 'But 'tis your choice whether you'l read or no. / If likewise of your smelling it were so: / I'd fart just as I write, for my own ease' (lines 34-6). It seems unlikely that Rochester, so adept at disseminating the image of himself as the readiest way to hell, would want us to extrapolate from his advice to other poets an image of him hunched over a paper cross-hatched with deletions, trying to impress us with his compared phrases, examined lines, weighted words and refined thoughts. On the contrary, it is much more likely that he would wish to be thought of as concerning himself with idle nothing, than with poetry.

I say 'idle' nothing with good reason.[46] Idleness is a primordial quality as Wycliffe shows in his 1388 *Genesis,* in which he, not inaccurately, translates the Vulgate's 'inanis' as 'idle'; 'the erthe was idel and voide'. Creation in Rochester spoils Nothing's 'Peaceful Reign' (line 18), a reign in which matter and Nothing would have lain in eternal embrace if it were not for the activities of 'the great united What!' (line 6). Nothing is, as we have seen, a womb, and according to Rochester in *Love to a Woman,* the womb is the 'dullest part of Gods Creation' (line 4). This poem shares certain concerns with *Upon Nothing*: it denounces the normal processes of procreation in the way that *Upon Nothing* satirises creation itself, on the grounds that created things are fated eventually to become nothing.

To 'Drudg in fair *Aurelias* womb' like a slave, is only to 'gett supplies for Age and Graves' (lines 7-8), the same process as turncoat Time's driving of Nothing's slaves back to her 'hungry Womb' (line 21) in *Upon Nothing.* In both cases the effort required to snatch things from the idleness of Nothing's womb serves only to return those things to it. That 'slaves' are required to sate Nothing's hunger only adds to the picture of Nothing's decadent idleness.

The idleness of Nothing, however, reflects on its encomiast. In the song *Love to a Woman* he gives the alternative to reproductive drudgery in idle parts, which is (as well as busy love with a personage of parts less idle) engendering wit. But this is clearly an idle pursuit; not choosing out for one's happiness the idlest part of God's creation gives one the leisure, that 'the Porter and the Groom' (line 5) do not have, to be idle oneself. *Upon Nothing* is certainly the result of an engendering of wit; in permitting himself to satirise creation rather than engaging in procreation, might Rochester be putting into practice the idleness that he has thereby earned himself?

In *Paradoxica Epidemica,* Rosalie Colie identifies two main kinds of writing about nothing, the one being the simple and superficial use of the linguistic and ontological paradox of nothing to produce amusing trivialities, in which category she places Rochester's poem, and the other being the use of nothing to articulate large-scale tragic themes, as in Shakespeare's tragedies. The former category is poetry with a mock subject, the latter is poetry in which the true subject is the human race. But if the former is poetry with a mock subject, then it too must have a true subject, and I think that subject is the author. This is well exemplified by another work in the category of 'entirely trivial', Fielding's essay *On Nothing,* in which he writes towards the end 'surely it becomes a wise man to regard Nothing with the utmost awe and adoration; to pursue it with all his parts and pains; and to sacrifice to it his ease . . . and his present happiness'.[47] Fielding implies that the truly wise man pursues only ease and happiness, a pursuit manifestly engaged in by the encomiast of Nothing, for whom the subject itself is nothing, and the facility and paradoxical pleasure of its praise is everything. Of course the passage explicitly states that the wise man *is* the encomiast of Nothing, a man not just characterised by his interest in the topic of Nothing, and his pursuit of ease, but also characterised as not regarding anything with awe; he is a leisured satirist, who does nothing with any great sincerity of endeavour. This is the Rochester with whom we are familiar, a man who blasphemes his God and libels kings for his own and our amusement, a man who writes great poetry about nothing at all. Is the careful weighing of syllables appropriate to such a man?

Fortunately, it does not matter to us if this self-image of the encomiast of Nothing is a fiction or not. If, bearing in mind the Davenant Metrical Indeterminacy Principle,[48] we adopt a new interpretation of the missing foot of line 42, the question of whether there is a semantically active empty foot there is solved. Let us interpret it, not as signifying stately Nothing reigning at the end of the line, but as indicative of Rochester's leisured carelessness, in which case it makes no difference if it is a genuine metrical error, or a carefully considered strategy to portray himself as too much at his ease to care about or even notice a metrical error. The effect is the same. It is in any case no great interpretative leap thus to unite the two sides of an argument which has only ever been about whether the missing foot means Nothing, or does not mean anything at all. It was perhaps overly optimistic to expect an unequivocal answer to the question, 'Is there or is there not an empty sixth foot at the end of line 42?', or an unequivocal answer to the question, 'Is there or is there not a semantics of metre?', from the poem itself, a poem which as much as anything can, or indeed as only Nothing can, blurs the distinction between those two great ends of Fate, 'Is', and 'is not'.

Notes

1. John Lennard, *The Poetry Handbook* (Oxford, 1996), p. 184.

2. All quotations are taken from the broadside version illustrated in figure 11.

3. Sir William Temple, 'Of Poetry' (1690), in *Critical Essays of the Seventeenth Century*, edited by J. E. Spingarn, 3 vols (Oxford, 1908-9), III, 73-109 (p. 74).

4. Thomas Hobbes, *De Corpore* (English version 1656), I.ii.6, in *The Complete Works of Thomas Hobbes*, edited by Sir William Molesworth, 10 vols (London, 1839), vol. I.

5. G. S. Kirk, J. E. Raven, M. Schofield, *The Presocratic Philosophers*, 2nd edition (Cambridge, 1983), p. 245.

6. George Puttenham, *The Arte of English Poesie* (1589) in *Elizabethan Critical Essays*, edited by G. Gregory Smith, 2 vols (Oxford, 1904), II, 1-193 (p. 3).

7. Sir John Harington, *A Preface, or rather a Briefe Apologie of Poetrie* (1591), in Smith, II, 194-222 (p. 204).

8. Thomas Hobbes, *Answer to Davenant's Preface to Gondibert* (1650), in Spingarn, II, 54-6 (p. 55); Sir Philip Sidney, *An Apology for Poetry* (1595), edited by Geoffrey Shepherd (Manchester, 1973), p. 103.

9. *Ben Jonson,* edited by Ian Donaldson (Oxford, 1985), p. 603.

10. Francis Bacon, *The Advancement of Learning* (1605), in Spingarn, I, 1-9 (p. 5).

11. Sir William Alexander, *Anacrisis* (1634), in Spingarn, I, 180-9 (p. 185); and Sir William Davenant, *Preface to* Gondibert (1650), in Spingarn, II, 1-53 (p. 10).

12. *Ben Jonson,* p. 587; John Dryden, *Of Dramatic Poesy, and other Critical Essays,* edited by George Watson, 2 vols (London, 1962), II, 236.

13. *Ben Jonson,* p. 596.

14. Robert Wolseley, *Preface to* Valentinian (1685), in Spingarn, III, 1-31 (p. 27).

15. Thomas Hobbes, *Preface to Homer* (1675), in Spingarn, II, 67-76 (p. 69).

16. Hobbes (1650), p. 57.

17. Samuel Daniel, *A Defence of Ryme* (1603?), in Smith, II, 356-84 (p. 366).

18. George Chapman, *Preface to Homer* (1610-16?), in Spingarn, I, 67-81 (p. 79).

19. Davenant, p. 19.

20. David Farley-Hills, *Rochester's Poetry* (London, 1978), p. 178.

21. Griffin, p. 279.

22. Paul Baines, 'From "Nothing" to "Silence": Rochester and Pope' in *Reading Rochester,* edited by Edward Burns (Liverpool, 1995), pp. 137-65 (p. 149).

23. Dryden, II, 237, 247.

24. Puttenham, p. 3.

25. Sidney, p. 133.

26. Daniel, p. 365.

27. *Ben Jonson,* p. 603; Sidney, pp. 133, 103.

28. Thomas Campion, *Observations on the Art of English Poesie* (1602), in Smith, II, 327-55 (p. 329).

29. Sidney, pp. 103, 142.

30. Daniel, p. 366.

31. Dryden, I, 2.

32. For a useful summary of this issue, see under 'Creation' in *A Dictionary of Biblical Interpretation,* edited by R. Coggins and J. Houlden (London, 1990).

33. 'It is more unthinkable that matter exist in actuality without form than an accident without a subject', St Thomas Aquinas, *Summa Theologica,* translated and edited by T. Gilby (London, 1964-80), X, 66.1.

34. See Plato, *Timaeus and Critias,* translated and edited by H. D. P. Lee (Harmondsworth, 1971), pp. 21-2.

35. *Romeo and Juliet,* I.ii.174-6.

36. *Donne: The Complete English Poems,* edited by C. Patrides, revised by R. Hamilton (London, 1994), p. 40.

37. *Spenser: Poetical Works,* edited by J. C. Smith and E. De Selincourt (Oxford, 1912): *Faerie Queene,* III.vi.36-7.

38. Harington, p. 201.

39. Thomas Rymer, *Preface to* Rapin (1674), in Spingarn, II, 163-80 (p. 175).

40. *The Twickenham Edition of the Poems of Alexander Pope,* edited by John Butt and others, 11 vols (London, 1939-69): *An Essay on Criticism,* line 365.

41. Kirk, Raven and Schofield, p. 249.

42. *Senec. Troas. Act. 2. Chor. Thus English'd by a Person of Honour.*

43. *De Corpore,* II.viii.24.

44. See *Davideis,* in *Abraham Cowley, Poems,* edited by A. R. Waller (Cambridge, 1905), p. 251.

45. Daniel, p. 384; the *mise en page,* however, is not reproduced in Gregory Smith.

46. See *Oxford English Dictionary,* where its first sense (as used by Wycliffe) is given as 'Empty, vacant', and its second sense as 'Void of any real worth, usefulness, or significance'.

47. Rosalie Colie, *Paradoxica Epidemica* (Princeton, 1966), p. 229; Henry Fielding, 'On Nothing', in *A Book of English Essays (1600-1900),* edited by S. Makower and B. Blackwell (Oxford, 1912), pp. 78-90 (p. 90).

48. See above, p. 91.

Gillian Manning (essay date 2000)

SOURCE: Manning, Gillian. "*Artemiza to Chloe*: Rochester's 'Female' Epistle." In *That Second Bottle: Essays on John Wilmot, Earl of Rochester,* edited by Nicholas Fisher, pp. 101-18. Manchester, UK: Manchester University Press, 2000.

[*In the essay below, Manning points out that in* Artemisia and Chloe *Rochester presents a favorable picture of the female condition largely because of the subtly argued point of view presented by Artemisa, which is especially effective because to the powerful use of intertextual reference.*]

In a virulent, anti-feminist satire of 1691, Robert Gould invokes Rochester, and appropriates lines 26-7 from *A Letter from Artemiza in the Towne to Chloe in the Countery*:

> Hast thou not heard what Rochester declares?
> That Man of Men . . .
> He tells thee, *Whore's the like reproachful Name,*
> *As Poetress*—the luckless Twins of Shame.[1]

Pace Gould, I should like to consider some of what (on balance) I take to be the predominantly female-friendly perspectives of Rochester's *Artemiza to Chloe.* These I suggest result largely from the controlling viewpoint of Artemiza, the poem's chief speaker and fictive composer, and the techniques and strategies employed to construct and define this view point: in particular a complex intertextual web of significance. Before discussing this, however, a few contextual details may be noted relating, firstly, to Rochester himself, and, secondly, to the poem's reception.

Despite Rochester's reputation among both contemporary and later readers as a misogynistic rake, and the perpetrator of some obscene, anti-female verse, there is evidence that he was regarded with affectionate respect, both as friend and literary mentor, by at least two women writers: his niece, Anne Wharton, and Aphra Behn. Wharton's elegy on her uncle describes generally how

> He civiliz'd the rude and taught the young,
> Made Fools grow wise; such artful magick hung
> Upon his useful kind instructing Tongue,
>
> (lines 20-2)

and more personally recalls her assisted *gradus ad Parnassum*:

> He led thee up the steep and high Ascent
> To Poetry, the Sacred Way he went.
> He taught thy Infant Muse the Art betime
> Tho' then the way was difficult to climb.[2]

Behn's own elegy for Rochester caused Wharton to reply in complimentary vein with *To Mrs. A. Behn, On what she writ of the Earl of Rochester,* a poem which in turn elicited a politely supportive response from the established writer: *To Mrs. W. On her Excellent Verses (Writ in Praise of some I had made on the Earl of Rochester) Written in a Fit of Sickness.* Here Behn describes an inspiring vision: a visitation by the 'Lovely *Phantom*' of her late fellow-poet, 'the Great, the God-like *Rochester*', whom she depicts as continuing to offer her the same gracious, if characteristically stringent, artistic advice as he had in his lifetime:

> It did advance, and with a Generous Look,
> To me Addrest, to worthless me it spoke:
> With the same wonted Grace my Muse it prais'd,
> With the same Goodness did my Faults Correct:
> And Careful of the Fame himself first rais'd
> Obligingly it School'd my loose Neglect.[3]

Interestingly, the penultimate line suggests also that Rochester had been in some way instrumental in helping to establish Behn's literary reputation.

If Rochester himself encouraged both Behn and Wharton in their writing, so *Artemiza to Chloe* may have prompted several other women writers to engage with some of its materials and techniques. I am discounting here the many eighteenth-century writers, male and female, who merely cite the poem, or who, like Gould, appropriate the occasional line or phrase for their own ends, and note only those who appear effectively to enter into creative dialogue with Rochester's poem: taking up and developing issues central to the latter work, especially women's views on love, attitudes to men and the predicament of the woman poet in a predominantly hostile or dismissive society. Given such titles as *Chloe to Sabina, An Epistle to Artemisia. On Fame,* and perhaps also *Cloe to Artimesa,* it seems arguable that these works are deliberately flagged as bearing some relation to Rochester's tour de force of ventriloquism, *Artemiza to Chloe.*[4] If so, then it might suggest that several Restoration and eighteenth-century women poets read *Artemiza to Chloe* not as a satire relating primarily to the misogynistic tradition which includes Juvenal's sixth satire, Boileau's tenth satire and Pope's *Epistle to a Lady,* but as a less biased, though still complex and rigorous, assessment of the contemporary female condition. Endorsing such an approach, I shall first canvass some possible implications of Artemiza's name, and then discuss two key related, though neglected, aspects of the poem: its allusions to specific texts, and the significance of its epistolary nature.

Artemiza hardly seems to have been a popular name, and it is unlikely that Rochester's decision to bestow it on his protagonist was simply casual, especially since he gives proper names only to Artemiza and Timon, of the main speakers in his major satires.[5] The possible implications of Artemiza's name proposed by recent readers have been diverse and numerous. As in Timon's case, however, all seem broadly compatible and relevant to Rochester's portrayal of his speaker, and some would also seem to offer significant hints as to the precise nature of Artemiza's role, character and situation.

Weinbrot is the first critic to consider the matter of Artemiza's name in any detail, though, in consequence of his somewhat sensational reading of the poem, he is moved to fancy that, as part of the process of her gradual corruption, Artemiza may have been persuaded to 'forget the background of chastity and female heroism and fidelity associated with her name'. However, he usefully outlines the stories concerning the two most famous bearers of the name, the classical queens and heroines Artemisia of Caria, and Artemisia of Halicarnassus, and he also implies a possible additional link between Rochester's Artemiza and Artemis, the 'perpetually celibate goddess of the chase'. Of the two celebrated queens, Artemisia of Caria was perhaps the better known in the seventeenth century, but writers often confounded the two figures. Jonson, for instance, in his *Masque of Queens,* rightly describes Artemisia of Caria as 'renowm'd for her chastety and love to her Husband, *Mausolus,* whose bones, (after he was dead) she preseru'd in ashes, and drunke in wine, making her selfe his tombe', but mistakenly attributes to the same lady the 'excellence of spirit' and more than manly prowess displayed by her namesake, Artemisia of Halicarnassus, who fought to such effect with Xerxes against the Greeks at Salamis. Since Rochester could hardly have been unaware, either of the famous stories concerning the two queens or of the commonly accepted derivation of the name Artemisia from that of the goddess Artemis (whose festivals were, in addition, called Artemisia), it seems probable that his intention in using the name was to suggest a range of possible implications and associations to enhance the subtlety and significance of his protagonist's persona. There may also be a slighter, more playful and contemporary reference to the high-minded Princess Artemise of La Calprenède's popular romance *La Cléopâtre.*[6]

Clearly, a good many of the characteristics noted above appear applicable in varying degrees to Rochester's Ar-

temiza, if rather more ironically, or obliquely, than some readers have suggested. For instance, it seems inappropriate in view of the poem's elusive nature, and the lack of positive evidence, that Artemiza should be seen as 'virginal', or at least that her 'apparent non-engagement in sexual relationships [should attributed to] the affinity with her namesake, Artemis'.[7] Equally unsubstantiated is Weinbrot's theory that Artemiza may have been led, in the course of the poem, to reject such an affinity. If, as seems probable, Rochester is alluding more lightly, tenuously and creatively to Artemiza's possible affinities both with Artemis and with the two heroic, classical queens, there is no more reason necessarily to suppose Artemiza herself a virgin, like Artemis, or (after Weinbrot) a hitherto principled lady who has had a recent change of lifestyle, than to suppose her, for example, a faithful and devoted widow, like Artemisia of Caria. Since Artemiza's letter appears designed to offer (albeit indirectly) both information and advice (to stimulate, not merely interest in, but thoughtful assessment of, various attitudes and patterns of conduct open to women, especially in the sphere of love and sexual relationships), it seems reasonable to hold that her name carries associations variously suggestive of Artemis's role as the patron of young girls and approver of chastity, as well, perhaps, as of her liking for a simple life in rural surroundings (Chloe's name, incidentally, bears the literal meaning, 'young plant' or 'green shoot').[8] Clearly, such allusions, like those relating to the two queens, relate only in subtle or ironic ways to Artemiza's own views, situation, and activities; Chloe may be in the country, but Artemiza herself is writing from 'this Lewd Towne' (line 33). Also, Chloe may be young and innocent, but while she is not, perhaps, 'lust[ing] for the game of gossip' in quite the manner that one critic suggests,[9] it is evident that, in Artemiza's view, Chloe is at least looking to be brought up to date with the latest gossip and news of love affairs about town, and in fact Artemiza makes this the pretext for diverting the course of her letter into rather more demanding channels. Moreover, though obviously disapproving of the 'fine Lady' (line 74) and her libertine notions, Artemiza makes no explicit attempt to define the kind of views and practice that she herself might endorse with regard to love. Even her lament for 'that lost thing (Love)' (lines 36-53) can hardly be taken as a direct, unequivocal encouragement to the practice either of a species of idealised, sublimated passion that might be acceptable to an Artemis, or of the kind of chaste, devoted love exemplified by Artemisia of Caria.[10]

In contrast to the two latter figures, Artemisia of Halicarnassus would seem to constitute a more ambiguous exemplar. Though indisputably courageous and great-hearted, according to Herodotus she escaped personal disaster at Salamis only by an action as ruthless and cunning as it was resourceful and daring.[11] In Rochester's poem, Artemiza's wary, self-mocking, but determined venture 'for the Bayes' (line 7) might seem to carry a witty allusion to her heroic namesake's exploits in the famous sea-battle; even the imagery used in these lines (7-13) is appropriately, if fortuitously, naval. Nor is the implied parallel quite of the sort to be found in **'Timon'**, where, by comparison with a classical heroic figure, a modern counterpart is diminished. Though Artemiza's poem is intimate and conversational, rather than heroic in kind, this seems appropriate, in view both of the debased and unheroic nature of the age she depicts, and of the disasters already encountered by more impetuous and hubristic male writers. Moreover, her preoccupations and, finally, her achievement are not trivial, while it is arguable that her courage and craft serve worthier ends than did those of Artemisia of Halicarnassus.

Perhaps the most important of the possible implications brought together by Rochester in naming his speaker 'Artemiza' was first touched on by Rothstein, who notes succinctly (though inaccurately) that '"Artemisia", in Latin, is wormwood', and suggests that 'the letter showers the bitter medicine of urban vice on sheltered innocence', the latter being, as we have seen, in his view somewhat less innocent than may at first sight appear. Everett makes much the same point, remarking that the 'word "Artemisia" means the species of bitter herb that contains the plant wormwood, and the poet may have though this "flower of Artemis" a good name for his sharp-tongued virginal heroine'.[12]

In fact, the nature and significance of Rochester's herbal allusion seem likely to be more extensive and complex than either of these readers suggests. *Artemisia* is the Latin name not for wormwood (the Latin for which is *absinthium*) but for mugwort, a plant which, according to Pliny, resembles wormwood in appearance, but which, up to the eighteenth century at least, does not appear to have been considered of the same species. Thus the properties which a seventeenth-century reader would have associated with *Artemisia* are those connected with the mugwort, rather than with the wormwood, plant. English herbalists of the sixteenth and seventeenth centuries leaned heavily upon Pliny, and their esteem for the many useful properties of mugwort would have rendered it a familiar plant to both professional and amateur physicians. It seems to have been quite well known, too, by its Latin name; Elisha Coles, for instance, in his popular *English Dictionary* (1676) has as his (somewhat selective) entry for 'Artemisia': 'Queen of Halicarnassus, also Mug-wort'. The general character of the species is described by Gerard as 'hot, and dry in the second degree, and somewhat astringent', and the little group of plants then considered to belong to the species is credited with diverse properties, often either of a protective or a bracing nature. Gerard notes, for example, that mugwort prevents weariness, and serves as a protection against 'poysonsome medicines', and the effects of the sun and 'wilde beast[s]', besides being 'drunke against *Opium*'. It was best known, however, for its supposed efficacy in treating women's diseases, and Pliny suggests that it may derive its Latin name from 'Artemis Ilithyia, because the plant is specific for the troubles of women', though he also notes that it may have been named after 'Artemisia, the wife of Mausolus'.[13]

In view of Rochester's well-attested interest both in 'Books of Physick' and in the more practical aspects of the subject, it seems likely that he would have been familiar with the works of such standard herbalists as John Gerard and John Parkinson, and perhaps, too, with the relevant portions of Pliny's *Natural History*.[14] Moreover, his decision to call his main speaker Artemiza, perhaps with allusion to the herb of the same name, may have been partly influenced by the example of his favourite English poet, Cowley. Cowley not only shared Rochester's interest in physick, but had also studied medicine professionally, and his friend Sprat records how, in the course of these studies, Cowley 'proceeded to the Consideration of Simples; and having furnish'd himself with Books of that Nature, he retir'd into a fruitful part of *Kent,* where every Field and Wood might show him the real Figures of those Plants of which he read'. As a result of this sojourn, he composed a Latin poem concerning plants, which was published in six books in 1668, though Books I and II had appeared already in 1662.[15] Both these books may well have engaged Rochester's interest, and the second may have given him a hint for **Artemiza to Chloe,** since it concerns only those herbs which are used specifically in the treatment of women's conditions, and which Cowley characterises as female themselves, giving a prominent role to *Artemisia.* Nahum Tate, in his introduction to the complete English translation of the *Six Books of Plants,* gives the scene of the second book as 'the Physick-Garden at *Oxford*', and the occasion, a council of those herbs which 'come under the Female Province, and are serviceable in Generation or Birth'.[16] The assembly of plants begins at twelve on an April night, and is finally abruptly adjourned by its president, *Artemisia,* when just before dawn, the gardener is seen approaching in urgent search of herbs to ease his wife's labour pains, whereupon the plants hastily retreat to their beds. Throughout the poem, *Artemisia* plays a dominant and controlling role: as president of the council, her title is '*Mat[er] herbarum*', she delivers the opening speech of the meeting, prescribes the topic for discussion and bids each herb speak in turn and given an account of its properties and duties in combating female disease.[17] Later, when the discussion has turned into impassioned altercation, she contributes an important speech in a successful move to conciliate a number of herbs who react furiously to being attacked as abortifacients by their fellows. Before steering the debate into other channels, *Artemisia* admits that she herself shares the maligned properties of the former group, and points out judiciously their usefulness in times of disease, remarking that herbs intended to prove helpful remedies can hardly be blamed if they are misused.

It seems probable that Rochester knew Cowley's *Sex Libri Plantarum,* especially since his father, Henry Wilmot, receives a respectful mention in Book VI, which, though ostensibly devoted to trees, is largely concerned with relating 'the History of the late Rebellion, the King's Affliction and Return, and the beginning of the *Dutch* Wars'. It seems equally likely that Cowley's characterisation of *Artemisia* in Book II, and his general handling there of the herbs 'under the Female Province', may have proved a contributory factor in Rochester's naming his main speaker Artemiza.[18] The implications of a possible herbal allusion in Rochester's choice of name for his female protagonist are not far to seek, and are compatible with the range of other such allusions already mooted. Several of *Artemisia*'s more diverse medicinal properties, as an astringent, as an antidote to opium and as a protection against poisons and weariness, seem metaphorically applicable to the character and function of Rochester's Artemiza. Her sharp wit and perceptive insights regarding herself and others often appear astringent, and her narrative is far from anodyne. In view of the herb's reputed capacity to prevent weariness, her final reference to her own and Chloe's tiredness may be something of a joke on Rochester's part, as well as a conventionally witty way to conclude a letter.[19] More seriously, Artemiza's obliquely presented, but powerfully pejorative, disclosures concerning the corrupt state of love in 'this lewd Towne' (line 33), may parallel mugwort's discutient properties, and its supposed efficacy against poisons. There may also be a more general allusion, of a kind similar to that in *Tunbridge Wells,* to the traditional concept of satire as a form of physick.

Mugwort's specific reputation for being helpful in the treatment of women's diseases, relates self-evidently to Rochester's Artemiza, in that she endorses at least a positive moral stance regarding the corrupt views and practices her letter describes, if not a prescriptive code of wholesome ethics by which they should be countered. Moreover, Rochester, like Cowley, gives his speaker, Artemiza, the leading, authoritative role, in a poem where the characters, view points and preoccupations are almost exclusively female. Again, while Cowley's *Artemisia* sees her true function as cleansing and health-bringing, she laments that, as one of the '*Ecbolicks*',[20] she may be wickedly misapplied to produce abortions. Equally, Artemiza fears that her poem, whatever its intrinsic merits, may be maliciously received and abused by 'th'ill-humour'd' (line 22).

In all, then, Rochester brings together a range of possible allusions—medical, literary, historical and mythological—most of them familiar, and some already often interlinked, or even confounded. All combine to enrich the poem's significance and to add depth and definition to Artemiza's complex role and character. Of the various possible allusions suggested by Artemiza's name, however, it is those relating to her herbal namesake which are central to the poem's themes and subject. Such allusions supply a unifying metaphor to the whole poem. This links together a chain of associations which extends throughout the work, and adds resonance to such details as the 'Diseas'd' state of Corinna at her nadir (line 203), her final poisoning of her duped protector and, by contrast, 'That Cordiall dropp' (line 44) which Artemiza, at the outset, suggests might once have more truly figured the nature and function of love.

Artemiza's 'Cordiall dropp' not only contributes to the medicinal and disease-linked imagery and detail which inform the poem as a whole, but is also one of many intertextual allusions to be found throughout the work. The significance of these allusions, however, and in some cases even their presence, has been largely overlooked; in consequence, some important hints as to the poem's general tone and character have been missed, and its degree of literariness underestimated. Readers have in the main been content to note the undoubted general similarities which exist between **Artemiza to Chloe** and some of the stage comedies of the period, though Vieth has pointed out more specifically that the poem shares a group of related ideas with Etherege's *The Man of Mode*.[21] In addition, however, **Artemiza to Chloe** contains a range of precise and often pointed allusions to poetic and philosophical works. While some of these references are of limited and local significance, others plays a major role in focusing the prime concerns of the poem. All combine to provide a context which is not only appropriate to the refined character and literary sensibility of the writer and true-wit, Artemiza, but which also define the pretensions of her counter-type, the 'fine Lady'.

The allusions of relatively local significance include the lines in which Artemiza describes love as 'That Cordiall dropp Heav'n in our Cup has throwne, / To make the nauseous draught of Life goe downe' (lines 44-5). This well-known couplet seems to refer to a famous passage in *De Rerum Natura,* which first appears in Book I, lines 936-47, and is later repeated verbatim in Book IV, lines 11-22.[22] Here Lucretius likens his practice of conveying in pleasing poetic form a doctrine which in itself may appear as rather harsh or unacceptable to that of physicians who persuade children to drink bitter medicines by coating the rim of their patients' cups with honey. Rochester appropriates Lucretius's thought and expression in a characteristically inventive manner. As suggested above, Lucretius's medical simile (similar in concept to Cowley's reference to his books of herbs as '*small Pills . . . gilt with a certain brightness of Style*'), is neatly absorbed into the medicinal metaphor associated with Artemiza's name, and may even touch on her epistolary strategy of promising Chloe gossip, and in fact presenting her with entertaining, but morally (if obliquely) pointed, portraits.[23] As regards its specific context, moreover, it underlines the ironic ambivalence of Artemiza's lament for 'that lost thing (Love)' (line 38). In Lucretius, the patients are described as deceived but not betrayed by the doctors' ruse, since by this means they are restored to health, and the writer expresses similar confidence in the efficacy of his bitter but intrinsically wholesome philosophic 'draught'. Artemiza, however, presents both the gift of love and heaven's action in bestowing it on humanity, in a rather more dubious light. Unlike the careful pagan physicians in Lucretius, who coat the rims of sick children's cups with honey, an ostensibly Christian 'Heav'n' is described by Artemiza as having 'throwne' a mere 'dropp' of sweetened and heartening (or perhaps only heart-affecting) liquid into 'our Cup',[24] in an effort to bribe hapless humanity into swallowing the 'draught of Life' which is not merely bitter but 'nauseous', and for which no compensatory properties are claimed.

Elsewhere in Rochester's poem, apparent allusions to works by Boileau, Sidney and Hobbes are put to similarly ironic purposes. These appropriations may be grouped together, since they all serve primarily to define various aspects of the pretensions of the 'fine Lady' (line 74). The Boileau reference occurs in this character's first speech to the assembled company when, preparatory to holding forth on why women should prefer fools as lovers, she remarks: 'When I was marry'd, Fooles were a la mode, / The Men of Witt were then held incommode' (lines 103-4). The lines to which Rochester alludes here occur in Boileau's first satire (itself loosely based on Juvenal's third satire). The speaker, a penurious poet, about to leave Paris where his talents have been despised and neglected, comments bitterly that: 'Un Poëte à la Cour fut jadis à la mode: / Mais des Fous aujourd'hui c'est le plus incommode' (lines 109-10).[25] In adapting these lines for use by his affected francophile, Rochester has followed Boileau's rhyme, but wittily varied the sense. In Boileau's satire, the honest speaker laments the time, now long since past, when true poets, rather than fools, were favoured at Court. By contrast, in Rochester's poem, the overbearing female fop recalls the time of her youth when fashionable women favoured fools as lovers above 'Men of Witt', and makes it plain that she, at least, has not changed her tastes in this respect. Having pronounced this opinion, she then proceeds to give her reasons for holding it, and her following speech contains several allusions which either ironically conflict with her viewpoint, or confirm that lack of 'discretion' later remarked on by Artemiza (lines 166-8); in the course of the strictures of the 'fine Lady' upon 'Men of Witt', she argues that such men should be avoided as less easy to deceive than fools, and advises that:

> Woman, who is an Arrant Bird of night,
> Bold in the Duske, before a Fooles dull sight,
> Should flye, when Reason brings the glaring light.
>
> (lines 121-3)

These last lines may owe something to Sidney's seventy-first sonnet in *Astrophil and Stella,* which describes:

> all vices' overthrow,
> Not by rude force, but sweetest soveraigntie
> Of reason, from whose light those night-birds flie.
>
> (lines 5-7)[26]

Rochester adjusts this sentiment to accord with the views of a speaker who fails to share even the qualified idealism regarding love expressed by Sidney's Astrophil, let alone the Platonism of the famous Petrarchan original (*Rime,* 248) to which Sidney alludes. Where, in Sidney's lines, the 'night-birds' represent man's vices, gently but inexorably put to flight by the light of Stella's virtuous reason, in the Rochester passage, by contrast, it is 'Woman' who is labelled 'an Arrant Bird of night', and

advised to fly from the harsh and oppressive glare of man's excoriating reason. By inverting the terms of Sidney's sonnet, Rochester stresses the degree to which the 'fine Lady', in cheerfully degrading the status accorded woman (and reason) in an earlier less 'ill-bred' age, conforms to the lamentable pattern of behaviour previously decried by Artemiza (lines 54-8).

The coolly rationalistic and amoral argument of the 'fine Lady' is grounded on self-interest and a desire to maintain at least a limited form of dominance over men. As such, it might appear to owe something directly to Hobbes, but any reference here to *Leviathan,* however, serves merely to pinpoint the 'fine Lady''s deficiencies. The libertine lady may have fashionable Hobbist pretensions, and she is certainly not without intelligence, but she lacks judgment, the one attribute essential not merely to a philosopher but to any person of good sense:

> All the good qualityes, that ever blest
> A Woman, soe distinguisht from the rest,
> Except discretion onely; she posset.
>
> (lines 166-8)

The term 'discretion', that is, judgment, may relate to a chapter in *Leviathan,* where Hobbes praises the importance of the 'Vertue . . . called DISCRETION', arguing that without it, even people of intelligence and imagination may run to folly:

> And in any Discourse whatsoever, if the defect of Discretion be apparent, how extravagant soever the Fancy be, the whole discourse will be taken for a signe of want of wit; and so will it never when the Discretion is manifest, though the Fancy be never so ordinary.[27]

In Hobbes's view, want of 'discretion' signifies 'want of wit' (and vice versa), wit being the very faculty upon which the 'fine Lady' prides herself, as her mock-modest disclaimer plainly reveals (lines 171-2). The lack of self-knowledge which she displays in this respect, and which Artemiza shrewdly points out (lines 164-5), merely confirms the former's essential lack of 'discretion'. Moreover, in general terms, the 'fine Lady' may be seen as exemplifying in her speech and behaviour what Hobbes in the same chapter calls 'GIDDINESSE, and *Distraction*', and which he claims results from 'hav[ing] Passions indifferently for everything'.[28] The 'fine Lady' feels no strong desire for anything, or anyone, in particular—being akin in this regard to those female libertines of whom Artemiza earlier remarks: 'To an exact perfection they have wrought / The Action *Love,* the Passion is forgott' (lines 63-6). The prime concern of the 'fine Lady' is not with her own desires, but with conforming to fashionable tastes; hence her behaviour towards her hostess's pet monkey, behaviour which, far from being 'warm, friendly, and sexual', therefore rendering her 'more bestial than the beast she courts', is essentially affected and dispassionate.[29] To the 'fine Lady', the animal (like a lover) is merely a fashionable property, to be picked up and dropped at will. Such 'indifference' convicts her, again, of lack of judgment, since, according to Hobbes, a person who is 'indifferent . . . cannot possibly have either a great Fancy, or much Judgement. For the Thoughts, are to the Desires, as Scouts, and Spies, to range abroad, and find the way to the things Desired: All Stedinesse of the minds motion, and all quicknesse of the same, proceeding from thence.'[30] The terms used by the lady in condemning the 'Men of Witt' for their wary and critical approach to women recall those employed by Hobbes in defining why 'indifferent' people (of whom she herself is one) lack judgment.

These local allusions to the works of such diverse writers as Hobbes, Sidney and Boileau indirectly confirm and substantiate Artemiza's assessment of the 'fine Lady' as 'a Foole of Parts' (line 161), one whose lack of the fundamental qualities of judgment and good sense perverts her undoubted gifts of intelligence and percipience. Thus, in a sense, the 'fine Lady' represents a more dangerous and disturbing exemplum than Corinna, whose tale she relates with a patronising scorn, and complacently insistent wit. Weinbrot complains that at the close of this narrative, 'Rochester has [Artemiza] ignore an opportunity to reject the lady's values and, instead, diminishes her earlier criticisms', adding that 'we are more impressed with . . . Artemisia's amusement, delight, and exasperation than with any desire to expose or punish'.[31] In the face of such a tale and such a teller, however, there seems little that even the most rabid moralist might add by way of further exposure. In fact, it is hard to know which is the more disturbing: the inexorable process of corruption which leads Corinna from her state of heedless and deceived innocence, to eventual triumph as cheat, whore and murderess; or the distorted lens which the loquacious narrator brings to bear upon this history. Moral condemnation features here only as a passing reference to Corinna's 'Man of Witt' (line 198), and serves merely to bear out the narrator's defined 'Rule' (line 177). In essence, the 'fine Lady' invites her audience to ignore all the obvious moral enormities exemplified in her tale, and to deprecate instead the meanness and folly of its chief characters. Thus Corinna's dupe and his family are viewed as receiving their just deserts as fools, while Corinna herself is regarded as a whore of attainments too mediocre, and too painfully acquired, to occasion any great wonder or admiration. In her own eyes, the teller is relating a common story of common and foolish people, the main purpose of which is to illustrate and confirm her own previously proclaimed views, and to enable her to display what she takes to be her own vastly superior wit, judgment and accomplishments. Lengthy or more strident criticism from Artemiza at this stage of her letter would be superfluous: she has already plainly indicated her disapproval of the 'fine Lady', comprehensively indicting, by a variety of means, the latter's character, manners and opinions. The story of Corinna, and the figure cut by its narrator are left to speak for themselves, and Artemiza pauses only to add a tersely dismissive comment, and to promise Chloe accounts of more such 'infamous' characters and events, before briskly concluding her letter.

While it is clear that Artemiza unreservedly condemns the 'fine Lady', Corinna and all their works, it is less immediately obvious what kind of positive attitudes (if any) she may endorse regarding the areas of concern uppermost in her letter. At no point does she presume to offer Chloe direct advice, let alone to dogmatise in the opinionated manner favoured by the 'fine Lady', nor does she make any explicit attempt to define the kind of views or practice she herself might approve or seek to promote with regard to love, life or literature. None the less, her letter, though often brilliantly entertaining, treats serious issues in a complex and thoughtful way that clearly distinguishes it from the familiar verse epistle that is merely trying to be witty, and is concerned with presenting gossip or trivia. As noted earlier, Artemiza (albeit with characteristic tact) fails to comply with what she assumes is Chloe's desire to hear the latest details of the love affairs about town, and, though some of her letter's basic materials are sufficiently scandalous to satisfy the most avid gossip, their handling and careful positioning within the letter's sophisticated structure ensure their subjection to oblique but powerful condemnation. The reader is left in no doubt that they are present on the grounds not of sheer sensationalism but of their relevance to the letter's essentially moral themes and focus. Though Artemiza seems wary of offering anything very direct or explicit by way of positive advice or definition, her whole approach being characterised by an ironic, tentative, oblique and even somewhat devious quality, this seems appropriate given the nature of her enterprise. Not only is it fitting to the refined and complex character of her moral and literary preoccupations, which are themselves subtly intertwined with her roles as woman, friend, correspondent and poet, but it suits also with the decorum of the literary mode which is used to encompass all these: the familiar moral epistle. It seems likely, moreover, that in *Artemiza to Chloe,* Rochester is both alluding to and seeking to emulate the practice of the greatest master of this kind, Horace.

Reference in *Artemiza to Chloe* to the famous first line of Horace's *Epistles*, I.vi, seems to be of a different kind from some of the literary allusions discussed above. Firstly, it could hardly be missed, and seems intended to be recognised, in contrast to some of the other allusions, such as that to the Sidney sonnet, or to Boileau's first satire, where recognition of the source may constitute more in the way of an additional bonus than an absolute requirement for readers.[32] Secondly, it seems to serve more than a purely local function—in fact one might argue that to an extent it informs the whole poem. Thirdly, it occurs not on one occasion but on several, each time in a slightly varied form, echoing through the poem like a musical motif. The allusion first occurs quite early in the poem, in the course of Artemiza's deprecating account of the injurious views and practices of fashionable women, who, not content with debasing both their own status, and that of love, by their libertinism, do not even take account of their personal preferences in choosing lovers but seek instead to conform to whatever is the current taste in men among their modish acquaintance. Artemiza records with some astonishment their attempts to justify this practice: ''Tis below Witt, they tell you, to admire, / And e'ne without approving they desire' (lines 64-5). Rochester is referring here to 'nil admirari', the opening words of *Epistles,* I.vi, in which Horace advises his friend Numicius that the only sure way of leading a happy and virtuous life is to cultivate a philosophic attitude of calm, moderation and independent rational judgment: to avoid violent extremes of emotion, whether of fear or desire, and to crave nothing in excess. The misuse of this axiom by the fashionable female libertines whom Artemiza decries is only one of several instances in the poem of the misapplication of this or other aphorisms. In the case related by Artemiza, the irony is clear: that the advice 'nil admirari' should be used to justify the kind of fashionable and pointless libertinism of the women in question could hardly be further removed from its intended moral and philosophic purpose. The failure of understanding revealed by this misapplication only underlines the women's grievous lack of the 'witt' to which they lay such claim.

A further allusion to 'nil admirari' occurs in the first address of the 'fine Lady' to the company (line 107), and is apparently conflated both with the glance at *Leviathan* noted above and perhaps more importantly with a reference to the second of Seneca's *Epistulae Morales.* Rochester would seem to make several references to the Seneca epistle, and the first of these occurs at the beginning of the poem, where Artemiza is warily reflecting on the risks involved in writing poetry. Hammond notes in lines 7-10 of Rochester's poem 'a variant of the traditional image of the poet as explorer', and he implies a possible connection with a phrase from Seneca, *Epistles,* II.5-6: 'non tamquam transfuga, sed tamquam explorator'.[33] In this epistle, Seneca offers his friend, Lucilius, advice on reading habits, and recommends using his own custom of selecting each day from an approved author a single thought or saying for careful consideration. He then remarks that he took his thought for today from Epicurus, adding that he is accustomed to make such forays into the rival philosophic camp, 'non tamquam transfuga, sed tamquam explorator'—not as a deserter, but as a scout or spy. Both the epistle and the cited phrase were well known in the seventeenth century, and the latter was often alluded to in connection with literary endeavour, at times apparently feeding into the more general notion of the writer as explorer.[34] Rochester's reference to Seneca's phrase is rather more oblique. Seneca's image of exploring, or scouting through, enemy territory to see what he can abstract for his own advantage is wittily martial and mercenary; in Rochester's lines, it becomes assimilated into a more inclusive and damning image of ambitious poets as explorers and exploitative merchant adventurers. The latter image may even subsume a reference to Milton's Satan.[35] Such implications lend weight to the pejorative tone of Artemiza's shrewd assessment of the failed poetic fortunes of some of her male counterparts. These so-called 'Men of Witt' evince greed, hubris and reckless daring, rather than the alert, self-critical and humorous attitude evidenced by Seneca's epistle, and exemplified by Artemiza herself.

Rochester makes what may be a further allusion to the same epistle later in the poem, where Artemiza offers a penetrating analysis of her own anti-type, that sententious would-be wit, the 'fine Lady'. In noting the latter's not inconsiderable 'Parts', Artemiza remarks sharply that 'such a One was shee, who had turn'd o're / As many Bookes, as Men, lov'd much, reade more' (lines 161-3). Seneca's epistle is largely concerned with warning Lucilius against reading too many books of different kinds, and advises him to concentrate instead on acquiring a thorough knowledge of a few select masterpieces. Moreover, Seneca anticipates that his friend might, by way of objection to this advice, indicate a preference for turning over first one book and then another, and comments that it is the sign of an over-nice appetite to pick at too many dishes. Rochester's lines may imply a parallel between the reading habits of the libertine lady and those condemned by the Stoic philosopher: Artemiza's witty linking of the lady's way with books and her way with men stresses again the latter's characteristic quality of 'GIDDINESSE and *Distraction*', as well as hinting at her incapacity to distinguish adequately between people and objects.

The most complex of Rochester's allusions to Seneca's epistle, however, occurs in line 107, and, as already mentioned, appears to be conflated with a second allusion to 'nil admirari', and with the *Leviathan* reference noted earlier. The fact that this line contains a further allusion to the Horace epistle seems to be signalled and emphasised by the triple rhyme 'desire/inquire/admire' of lines 105-7, which repeats the rhyme 'admire/desire' in lines 64-5, where the first allusion to 'nil admirari' occurs. Finally, the triple rhyme appears again with the rhyme words slightly varied in lines 124-6, where a last echo of the allusion may be caught. Such repetition is unlikely to be merely casual (despite Pope's censure of Rochester as having 'very bad versification, sometimes'[36]), and it would seem that rochester is not only stressing the 'nil admirari' allusion, but is also encouraging the reader to compare and contrast its uses in these passages.

On its first appearance the allusion is employed to endorse Artemiza's strictures on the general lack of wit and moral judgment of fashionable female libertines, since it indicates how the latter, through ignorance or perversity, misapply a famous Horatian aphorism. On its second appearance, its significance is more complex, as one might expect from the manner in which it is conflated with the allusions to Seneca and to Hobbes, and from its presence in a speech delivered by a perfect exemplar of the female type it has earlier been used to condemn. In fact, the 'fine Lady' compounds the errors of her sisters' misapplication of 'nil admirari', by using it herself, not as they did, to justify their own perverse practice by asserting their claim to wit, but as the basis for lambasting the 'Men of Witt'. Evidently her 'rules' are not only morally and intellectually dubious but are intended for selective and arbitrary application to accord with her own self-interested designs. Thus while she and women of her type pride themselves on having too much wit to 'admire' men, they are illogically outraged at those men who have the temerity to do likewise (*mutatis mutandis*) and who wilfully refuse to settle for 'The perfect Joy of being well deceaved' (line 115). As we have seen, the ironic allusion to Hobbes in lines 105-7 convicts the speaker herself of a basic lack of judgment; Rochester's central conflation in line 107 of the allusion to 'nil admirari' with that to Seneca's 'tamquam explorator' further defines and emphasises this failing. Nevertheless, the attitude of the 'Men of Witt' to women is not thereby condoned. They share the selfish and dispassionate approach to love of the 'fine Lady', though they do not (apparently) seek to justify it by misapplying moral aphorisms, and there is no evidence that they also share that quality of ineffable blindness to their own faults which so distinguishes their female counterpart. The allusions to the moral epistles of Horace and Seneca, however, testify to the fine, but clear, line to be drawn between the alert, ironic, moral-awareness which informs Artemiza's attitude, and the kind of dispassionate, self-interested prudence variously exemplified by the 'fine Lady' and her crew, by the 'Men of Witt', and belatedly, but to chilling effect, by Corinna. Throughout, then, **Artemiza to Chloe** expresses a subtly argued critique of the female condition, which draws much of its efficacy from Rochester's powerfully resonant use of intertextual reference.

Chloe to Sabina

My Deare Sabina why should you & I
Inn these soft times be foes to Poetry?
We cannot sure suspect yt ye chast Nine
Should prove as bauds to lead us into sin
Nor need we much those blasts of censure feare
With which ye men of wit so shaken are;
Wee are secure, ye low shrubs of ye plain,
Whilst they, ye tall Oakes, by the Stormes are slain.
Where can a Muse more soft retirement find
Then in a fair white womans gentle mind?
Where ye young son of Venus may indite,
And make ye dire Poetick virgin write
As her own forehead smooth, whilst her bright eye
Sends fire & flashes to her poetry.
But I too far am wander'd from the Theme
At which I chiefly in my letter aime;
My Dear Sabina since you left ye town
There is among us a strang faction grown,
A new discover'd crew call'd men of wit,
The silliest rogues yt ever aim'd at it:
So vain, so loud, so ungentily ill—
Their wit is froth, whose floods wʰere they swell
Fall like ye headlong cataracts of Nile.
Which neither cherish nor refresh the ground
But make much noise & deafen all around;
Their wickednesse appears more dull to me
Then aged country Parson's Poetry.
Some of this new society are from
That Mistresse of all follies London come
To people here like collonies from Rome.
Some from ye Scools & colledges appeare
Where natures unshapt whelps by art & care
Were lickt & form'd each into perfect Beare.
And some are country Squires new come to town
Being happily arriv'd at twenty one
These no acquir'd follies seem to adorne

But are the same rude lumps yt they were born.
Amidst ye many yt infest this place
Up started one extraordinary Asse
Who like ye rest not satisfied yt bare
Mien & behaviour should a Fop declare
Gave in a scurrilous & sencelesse Scrole
Under his own hand yt he was a fool.
Twas a lampoon & by Lord Blany writ
An Engine by which fooles sometimes do hit
Because at flocks they allways levell it.
The Oph I hear to forreigne lands is gon
To End ye fool which nature has begun:
So wild geese with ye Season disappeare
To hatch new goslings for ye Ensueing yeare.
Let him go on ye Oph to natures Schoole
But sure no care ere can redeem yt soul
Whom God predestinated to be fool.
But Dear Sabina we alas! have found
That bluntest weapons give a cruell wound
Would it not vex a saint thus damn'd to bee
And nere to tast of ye forbidden tree?
The Devil himself shew'd us less cruelty.
We should not much of our hard fate complaine
Had we been nobly in the battle slain
Or by ye hand of some fam'd warrior ta'ne
Who like true Venus son had bore his sire
And household gods safe from amidst ye fire:
But to be thus by beardlesse foes undone
Raw puny cocks whose spurs are not yet grown
Sabina for my part for ever more
I am resolv'd to shut up Eden door
Where a strict guard still flameing in their eyes
Shall stop mens passage to yt Paradise.
Mrs Jean Fox.

Copy text: Dublin MS 2093, pp. 112-16

Notes

1. *A Satyrical Epistle to the Female Author of a Poem called Sylvia's Revenge Etc.* (London, 1691), p. 19. For details of Gould's attack on the 'Female Author', see F. Nussbaum, *The Brink of All We Hate: English Satires on Women 1660-1750* (Lexington, 1984), pp. 34-7.

2. *Kissing the Rod: An Anthology of Seventeenth-century Women's Verse,* edited by G. Greer *et al.* (London, 1988), pp. 287-8. The second extract was omitted from the first published version of the elegy in 1685.

3. *Kissing the Rod,* pp. 249-50.

4. There is a copy of *Chloe to Sabina* (reproduced at the end of this paper in an appendix) in the National Library of Ireland, Dublin MS 2093, pp. 112-16, where it is attributed to Mrs Jean Fox (as yet unidentified, though perhaps the Fox attacked as an 'Irish whore' in Rochester's lampoon, 'To longe the Wise Commons have been in debate', lines 6-7). For details of Dublin MS 2093, see Peter Beal, *Index of Literary Manuscripts,* 2, pt 2 (London, 1993), p. 232. *Chloe to Sabina* follows closely after *Artemiza to Chloe* in the Dublin MS, there being only one intervening poem, also attributed to Rochester ('This

Bee alone of all his race': see Rochester 1999, pp. 282-4), which may indicate that the scribe recognised a link between the two verse epistles. However, while I have suggested that Fox's poem responds to *Artemiza to Chloe,* the reverse cannot be ruled out, given the uncertain date of *Chloe to Sabina. An Epistle to Artemisia. On Fame* is printed in Mary Leapor, *Poems Upon Several Occasions,* vol. 2 (London, 1751), pp. 43-54; *Cloe to Artimesa* is unascribed in *A New Miscellany of Original Poems Translations and Imitations By the Most Eminent Hands* (London, 1720), p. 123, though the compiler, A[nthony] H[ammond], lays claim to 'the pieces which appear without any name' ('Preface', sigs Ar-Av).

5. Other contemporary spellings of Artemiza are: Artemisia, Artemisa, Artimesa, Artemise.

6. H. D. Weinbrot, '"The Swelling Volume": the Apocalyptic Satire of Rochester's *Letter from Artemisia In the Town To Chloe In The Country'*, *Studies in the Literary Imagination* 5 (1972), 19-37 (p. 33 and n. 10); Ben Jonson, *The Works,* edited by C. H. Herford, and Percy and Evelyn Simpson (Oxford, 1941), 7, 308. Jonson also quotes what (according to Herodotus) was Xerxes' comment on Artemisia's courage at Salamis: '"Viri quidem extiterunt mihi feminae, feminae autem viri"'. *La Cléopâtre,* first published 1646-8, was translated by Robert Loveday as *Hymen's Praeludia, Or Loves Master-Piece Being That so much admired Romance entituled Cleopatra,* twelve parts (London, 1665).

7. B. Everett, 'The Sense of Nothing' in *Spirit of Wit,* p. 29; C. Fabricant, 'The Writer as Hero and Whore: Rochester's *Letter From Artemisia To Chloe'*, *Essays in Literature,* West Illinois University 3 (1976), 158.

8. E. Rothstein, *Restoration and Eighteenth-Century Poetry 1660-1780* (London, 1981), p. 33.

9. *Ibid.*

10. See Fabricant, 'The Writer as Hero and Whore', 157.

11. Noted by Everett in *Spirit of Wit,* pp. 29-30.

12. Rothstein, *Restoration and Eighteenth-century Poetry,* p. 33; Everett, *Spirit of Wit,* p. 29.

13. Pliny, *Natural History,* with an English translation in ten volumes by W. H. S. Jones, Loeb Library (Cambridge, Mass., 1956), VII, Book 25, XXXVI, 73, p. 189; John Gerard, *The Herball or General Historie of Plantes. Very Much enlarged and Amended by Thomas Johnson* (London, 1636), p. 1104.

14. See *Critical Heritage,* p. 54; *Letters,* p. 142.

15. 'An Account of the Life and Writings of Mr Abraham Cowley' in *The Works of Abraham Cowley,* 3 vols (London, 1707), 1, xxvii-xxviii; *Plantarum Libri duo* (1662); *Poemata Latina. In quibus Continentur, Sex Libri Plantarum* (London, 1668).

16. Cowley, *Poemata Latina,* p. 60, n. 1 and *The Works,* 3, sig. P7r.

17. 'Non immerito in hoc conventu praesidet Artemisia (quam honoris puto, causa quidam matrem herbarum appellant)', Cowley, *Poemata Latina,* p. 67, note to line 5.

18. Cowley, *The Works,* 3, sigs P4v-P5r, P7r.

19. Cf. Wycherley to Shadwell: 'I wou'd turn o're the Leafe, but know / My Muse has tyr'd her self and you / *And so Adieu'*, *The Works of Thomas Shadwell,* edited by Montague Summers, 5 vols (London, 1927), 5, 232. Noted also Thormählen, p. 137, n. 63.

20. '*I.e.* such Medicines as bring away dead Children, or cause Abortion', Cowley, *The Works,* 3, p. 323, note*.

21. 'Etherege's *Man of Mode* and Rochester's *Artemisia to Chloe'*, *Notes and Queries,* New Series, 5 (1958), 473-4.

22. Griffin, p. 139.

23. Cowley, *The Works,* 3, sig. Qv. Artemisia was often administered in sweet wine (see Pliny, *Natural History,* vol. 7, Book 25 LXXXI, 130, p. 229; and vol. 7, Book 26 XLIX, 81, p. 325).

24. Perhaps, also, a biblical allusion. Cf. that in line 17, noted by Walker in Rochester 1984, p. 278; and that in line 260, noted by Fabricant, 'The Writer as Hero and Whore', 162, and by Weinbrot, 'The Swelling Volume', 34.

25. First noted by P. C. Davies, 'Rochester and Boileau: a Reconsideration', *Comparative Literature,* 21 (1969), 354.

26. *The Poems of Sir Philip Sidney,* edited by William A. Ringler, Jr (Oxford, 1962), p. 201. We have no other evidence to suggest Rochester knew Sidney's works. There were twelve editions of *Astrophil and Stella* between 1599 and 1739.

27. T. Hobbes, *Leviathan,* edited by C. B. Macpherson (Harmondsworth, 1968), pp. 135 and 137. Cited by Walker in Rochester 1984, p. 280, note to line 168.

28. Hobbes, *Leviathan,* p. 139.

29. Weinbrot, 'The Swelling Volume', 27.

30. Hobbes, *Leviathan,* p. 139.

31. Weinbrot, 'The Swelling Volume', 33.

32. Only two modern scholars have noted its presence: C. Rawson, 'Rochester's Systems of Excess', *The Times Literary Supplement* (29 March 1985), 336; and Frank H. Ellis (Rochester 1994), p. 347, note to line 64. Pope's reference in his Imitation of Horace *Epistles,* I.vi to 'Wilmot' and the '"cordial drop"' (lines 126-7), suggests that he recognised Rochester's appropriation of 'nil admirari'.

33. *John Wilmot, Earl of Rochester: Selected Poems,* edited by Paul Hammond (Bristol, 1982), p. 102, note to lines 7-10.

34. The epistles were also included in summarised form in Sir Roger L'Estrange's *Seneca's Morals By Way of abstract . . .* (London, 1678), which ran to many editions, and see, for instance, the prologue to Behn's first play, *The Forc'd Marriage, or the Jealous Bridegroom* (London, 1671), where the speaker remarks of the new female playwright:

> Today one of their party ventures out,
> Not with design to conquer, but to Scout:
> Discourage but this first attempt, and then,
> They'le hardly dare to sally out again.
>
> (lines 23-6)

35. For Satan as a merchant adventurer, see *Paradise Lost,* 2, 629-43 (*The Poems of John Milton,* edited by John Carey and Alastair Fowler (London, 1968)). See, too, Book 10, where the fallen angels await the return of 'their great adventurer from the search / Of foreign worlds' (lines 440-1). Rochester evidently knew *Paradise Lost* (see *Letters,* p. 202, n.).

36. Recorded by Joseph Spence, *Observations, Anecdotes, and Characters of Books and Men,* edited by James M. Osborn, 2 vols (Oxford, 1966), I, 202, para. 471.

Brean Hammond and Paulina Kewes (essay date 2000)

SOURCE: Hammond, Brean and Kewes, Paulina. "*A Satyre Against Reason and Mankind* from Page to Stage." In *That Second Bottle: Essays on John Wilmot, Earl of Rochester,* edited by Nicholas Fisher, pp. 133-52. Manchester, UK: Manchester University Press, 2000.

[In the following essay, Hammond and Kewes examine the impact of A Satire Against Mankind *upon Restoration dramatists and claims that the poem should be understood in the context of the contemporary theater, especially considering its importance for the libertine debates of the 1670s, which were conducted through the medium of drama.]*

Rochester's *A Satyre against Reason and Mankind,* written in the earlier 1670s, is widely recognised as one of the formative poems of its decade and period.[1] By and large, interest in the poem has centred on its ideas. Editors and critics of *Against Reason and Mankind* have been concerned with establishing the philosophical, intellectual and religious contexts of the poem's inception and reception, and have situated it against native and continental, particularly French, poetic traditions.[2] Our contention is that the Restoration theatre is a context of at least equal importance for the understanding of the poem's literary influences in terms of both subject-matter and language. The broad affinity between Rochester's poetic *oeuvre* and the drama of its time has long been recognised: Dustin

Griffin's *Satires against Man,* for example, includes a chapter on 'Rochester and Restoration Drama'. However, Griffin is chiefly interested in the common settings (the park, the watering-places), characters (the rake, the railer, the coquette) and ethical assumptions which Rochester's poetry shares with contemporary plays, both heroic and comedic, and he does not see any one poem as having uniquely strong intertextual links with the drama. We believe that *Against Reason and Mankind* is such a poem. In the decade following its composition, the satire generated several vigorous responses from dramatists, notably John Crowne in *Calisto: or, The Chaste Nimph* and Thomas Shadwell in *The Libertine* and *The History of Timon of Athens, the Man-Hater.* Those reactions have gone largely unnoticed in the critical literature. It is almost as if the flamboyant stage portrayals of Rochester 'the man'—as the glamorous and suave Dorimant in Etherege's *The Man of Mode* (1676), as the viciously immoral Nemours in Lee's *The Princess of Cleve* (*c.* 1681-2), and as the contemptibly hypocritical libertine Florio (and to an extent Artall) in Crowne's *City Politiques* (1682)[3]—have prevented scholars from perceiving the more specific reprises of the ideas and vocabulary of *Against Reason and Mankind* in contemporary plays, Rochester's own adaptation of John Fletcher's *Valentinian* (*c.* 1675-6) among them.

That neglect, admittedly, is understandable. First, although remarkable for its handling of the dialogue form, and its games with the persona of the author-speaker, *Against Reason and Mankind* appears an abstract work, distant from the hustle and bustle of the theatre. In that respect it contrasts sharply with '**An Allusion to Horace**' and **Satyr.** [**'Timon'**], two poems brimming with references to plays and playwrights. Second and more important, the dramatic redactions by Crowne and Shadwell of the scandalous creed of *Against Reason and Mankind* may at times appear scarcely distinct from the quite commonplace use of Hobbesian cliches in contemporary plays. Indeed it would be fatuous to deny that the decade's libertinism was steeped in a post-Restoration reading of Hobbes's *Leviathan* (1651).[4] Hobbes's insistence on the subjectivity of judgments about good and evil, for example, has its effect on *Against Reason and Mankind* and resounds through the libertine drama of the time:

> whatsoever is the object of any mans Appetite or Desire; that is it, which for his part he calleth *Good*: And the object of his Hate, and Aversion, *Evill*; And of his Contempt, *Vile* and *Inconsiderable.* For these words of Good, Evill, and Contemptible, are ever used with relation to the person that useth them: There being nothing simply and absolutely so.[5]

What Hobbes has to say about future punishments and rewards, and in general terms his materialist account of human psychology and motivation, could be used to underpin the iconoclastic creed that stage libertines represented. And Hobbes's account of the human race's savage and self-regarding behaviour in the state of nature could be adapted to convey the ferocity of social relations in the modern world.[6] Rochester's poem, however, gave memorable formulation to a complex of ideas drawn from many sources, Montaigne and Boileau as prominent as Hobbes, that were particularly charismatic because they carried the authority of the Earl's own manner of living. As we shall see, specific verbal echoes and borrowings indicate that it was often to *Against Reason and Mankind* rather than to Hobbes that Crowne and Shadwell directly applied. If at times it does seem as if they are writing with a copy of *Leviathan* open on the desk, Rochester's poem has sent them back to the book.

That the impact of *Against Reason and Mankind*—Rochester's best-known and most widely circulated longer poem—upon the plays of the mid- to late 1670s should have been considerable need not surprise us, for in those years the Earl's involvement in theatrical affairs was at its peak; he was an eagerly sought-after patron of the drama, as many as five plays having been dedicated to him between 1672 and 1677.[7] It was his intervention that secured Crowne the commission to supply a masque—*Calisto*—for performance at Court in 1675;[8] it was also the Earl's praise and support that gained Otway's *Don Carlos* a favourable (and bounteous) reception from the king and the Duke of York in 1676.[9] He wrote prologues and epilogues for new plays by Elkanah Settle, Sir Francis Fane and Charles Davenant, and for a revival by an all-female cast of an old play, most likely Beaumont and Fletcher's *The Bloody Brother*.[10] Rochester was not only a sometime patron of a number of professional playwrights (Settle, Lee, Dryden, Crowne, Otway)—even though he ridiculed former favourites in his satires—and a friend of aristocratic amateurs and Court Wits (the Duke of Buckingham, Sir Robert Howard, Sir George Etherege, Sir Francis Fane). He himself tried his hand at playwriting and issued influential versified criticism of recent theatrical offerings (for instance in **'An Allusion to Horace'** and **Satyr.** [**'Timon'**]). Besides his revision of Fletcher's *Valentinian* (for which he invited Fane to supply a masque),[11] we have a fragment of a dramatic lament intended for a never-written tragedy, a draft of a comic scene intended for a never-written comedy, and a heroic scene he contributed to Howard's unfinished *The Conquest of China*.[12] And though the story of his coaching Elizabeth Barry to become the period's greatest tragic actress is most likely apocryphal, his long-term liaison with the rising star of the London stage would have brought him into close contact with playhouse affairs.[13]

Rochester's contribution to the Restoration theatrical enterprise in his capacity as patron, critic and amateur playwright, and the fact that several of his satiric verses were inspired by, and responded to, others' plays, ensured that any new poem of his—and especially one so substantial as *Against Reason and Mankind*—would be read with keen interest and attention by his protégés, former protégés and other aspiring dramatists. It is the dramatised polemic to which the poem gave rise that we wish to explore in this discussion. What was the impact of *Against Reason and Mankind* upon the drama in the years immediately following its composition and circulation? How were ideas voiced by Rochester in the poem, and the vocabulary in which he couched them, appropriated, countered or reformulated in the plays of the 1670s? And how did he render them in his version of Fletcher's *Valentinian*? First, however, we need to read the poem, to emphasise those parts that were most suggestive to contemporary dramatists, those ideas that could be most effectively embodied in stage character and action.

* * *

In his rage, misanthropy and condescension toward other mortals, the speaker of *Against Reason and Mankind* resembles a Thersites or an Apemantus (and in 1678 and 1679 respectively, both Apemantus and Thersites would again be on stage, in Shadwell's version of *Timon of Athens* and Dryden's of *Troilus and Cressida*). That rhetorical stance is underlined by the opening of the 'Addition' written sometime between 1675 and 1676:

> All this with Indignation have I hurl'd
> At the pretending part of the proud World,
> Who swoln with selfish Vanity, devise
> False Freedomes, Holy Cheats and formal Lyes,
> Over their fellow Slaves to tyrannize.

(lines 174-8)

The persona's excoriation of the pretentious and the vain—of those philosophers, clerics and courtier-lawyers who terrify the less able with their intellectual bugbears—seems to derive from an ongoing discussion, a continuation perhaps, of one of the 'Genial Nights' amongst the Wits that Dryden describes in his dedication to *The Assignation; or, Love in a Nunnery* (1673), 'where our discourse is neither too serious, nor too light; but always pleasant, and for the most part instructive'.[14] The poem's opening statement is a self-consciously sensational adaptation of the theriophilic tradition as expounded, for instance, in Montaigne's *Apologie de Raymond de Sebonde*. Rochester establishes his basic position—that in conjuring up the 'Ignis fatuus' of deceptive Reason rather than following their 'certain' instincts, humans are inferior to beasts—by means of an impertinent paradox: 'Were I a spirit free to choose'. What would that 'I' be that is doing the choosing, and what kind of a 'Dog, a Monky, or a Bear' would result from the exercise of this election? Would it not be to real dogs, monkeys and bears as Swift's Gulliver is to the Yahoos? Is not the act of choosing a supremely *human* one—indeed, in the Protestant tradition, the defining act of being human? Being witty in the construction of an argument that leads to the abandoning of one's wits is a pervasive feature of this period's wit, upon which John Sitter's comment is illuminating:

> The paradoxical process of asserting a bodily norm by conspicuously intellectual or 'artful' means is part of the game of parody and burlesque, which work only if an author manages to display mastery of the modes 'contained' by the representation. Is a rational argument against rationality, for instance, simply an argument for better rationality?[15]

The question whether Rochester *does* master the modes contained by his poem is certainly one that the reader will pose; and a 'better rationality' is exactly what Rochester's poem will *propose*.

Meanwhile back in the poem, the 'sixth Sense' Reason is being stacked up against the other five; and is pursuing a journey that, through a suppressed allusion to Satan's journey in *Paradise Lost,* is represented as a diabolical departure from the one true path:

> Pathless and dangerous wandring wayes it takes,
> Through Errours fenny boggs and thorny brakes:
> Whilst the misguided follower climbs with pain
> Mountains of whimseys heapt in his own brain;
> Stumbling from thought to thought, falls headlong
>   down
> Into doubts boundless Sea.
>
> (lines 14-19)

Freedom of choice, the exercise of the free will, is surely in the standard Christian account the *product* of rationality and the evidence of the Godhead in us. Here, free choice is pitted *against* rationality, and the latter is redefined as a satanic illusion, a faculty external to its possessor, leading him on schizophrenically to darkness and a disillusioned death. Book learning, strikingly rendered in the image of buoyancy bladders, can provide only temporary relief from the 'Sea' of scepticism that debilitates and deluges the rationalist. The satirist's position from line 20 onwards is almost that of a cruel, mocking deity as he looks down upon the 'reasoning Engine', once so animated—albeit by pride, wit and wisdom—now measuring out its length of earth 'hudled in dirt'. If contemporary readers did not take this sneering Olympian voice to be a badge of atheistical libertinism, they would surely hear such a creed announced in lines 33-4: 'His Wisedome did his Happiness destroy, / Ayming to know that World he should enjoy'. 'Wit' consists in the vain attempt to *know* the world rather than experiencing it directly through the pleasure to be gained from sense impressions. It is, at least at this point in the poem, allied to wisdom or knowledge of a Faustian kind. But in the very moment of defining 'wit' as a wasted, prideful attempt to gain an epistemological purchase on the created world, Rochester moves sideways into a socially defined account of *the* wit, of the kind of person who tries to possess such knowledge. This in turn sets up the comparison between wits and whores, and the dialectic between pleasure in them and hatred of them, that brings the world of Restoration comedy into focus but does little to focus the poem itself.

That such a hedonist philosophy caught the attention of Latitudinarians such as Stillingfleet, Barrow and Martin Clifford, whose *A Treatise of Humane Reason* (1674) was the first tract to respond to Rochester in print, is not surprising and is by now well-established.[16] And as Roger Lund suggestively argues, it was as much the witty form in which the argument was cast as the subversive content that drew their attention.[17] The path leading to Jeremy Col-lier starts out in the reactions of such as Barrow and Glan-vill to the Hobbesian account of ridicule and laughter. Rochester's poem inoculates itself against the Latitudinar-ian cast of mind by embodying it in a 'formal band and beard' (lines 46-71). This *adversarius* figure, who may be Isaac Barrow, is thoroughly sent up, initially by his catch-ing the fag-end of the previous passage (lines 37-44) in which something (he wots not exactly what) is said against 'men of Witt' that provokes him to a Sparkish-like self-advertisement: 'For, I profess, I can be very smart / On witt, which I abhor with all my heart' (lines 52-3). Clearly this foppish, formalistic understanding of wit as a 'gibe-ing, gingling knack' is not at all what the satirist has been discussing, and the brief alliance of the 'Rev. Formal' with the satirist against wit is rapidly succeeded by a scanda-lised reaction to the latter's misanthropy. In response to this, the 'formal band and beard' relies upon Reason to take what Pope in *The Dunciad* will call 'the high Priori road', a prideful, speculative journey into the secrets of futurity that human beings are never meant to fathom. The clerical *adversarius* is used by Rochester to line up the distinction between rationality and a better rationality that the poem goes on to draw.

The object of the next verse paragraph (lines 72-111) is to 'right reason', in the punning senses of 'to put reason to rights', to define reason properly, and to demonstrate how to reason properly (or, as one of his real-life adversaries put it, 'To reason Reason out of Countenance').[18] Here, Rochester has in his sights the activities of the group that Louis Althusser once referred to as 'the intellectually semi-retired':[19] those who are in the luxurious position of being paid to think in the abstract, 'modern Cloystred Coxcombs, who / Retire to think,'cause they have nought to do'. *Caveat lector!* Rochester champions a form of reason that we might more adequately term 'common sense', a form that co-operates with sensory information and appetite, that above all is geared to practical action in the world. What the reader is invited to consider, however, is the relationship between this form of rationality and ethical conduct:

> That Reason which distinguishes by Sense,
> And gives us Rules of Good and Ill from thence:
> That bounds Desires with a reforming Will,
> To keep them more in vigour, not to kill.
> Your Reason hinders, mine helps to enjoy,
> Renewing appetites yours would destroy.
>
> (lines 100-5)

This definition of 'Good and Ill' is prudential rather than moral, in that 'good' and 'ill' is whatever conduces towards, or compromises, the continuing health of the organism. If desires are to be restrained at all, they are to be so only to avoid cloying, not because they may be harmful to the self and others. And it was to this ambigu-ous issue, more than to any other, that several contempo-rary dramatists responded, most notably Crowne, Shadwell and Lee, and which Rochester himself took up in his adaptation of Fletcher's **Valentinian.** The second half of **Against Reason and Mankind** reprises the theriophilic arguments of the opening, and it bears upon the crucial central argument in so far as it denies that any altruistic account of human action can be given. For Rochester, any account of moral action is inevitably tinged by altruism, and the effort he makes to banish such an account leads him into the realm of behavioural psychology. Fear is the key to the human psyche: 'virtuous' conduct is simply hypocritical. Recognising this leads to paradoxical formulations worthy of Shaw and Brecht: 'all men would be Cowards if they durst' (line 158). One thinks of Mother Courage boxing her son Schweitzerkäse's ears because he was stupid enough to behave heroically in war. It is this sonorous paradox that Rochester stakes on the bet that no 'just man' can be found to contradict it. The final section describes the types of the just statesman and clergyman who, in the very unlikely event that they could be found, would force him to 'recant [his] paradox to them' and adopt the orthodox morality of the rabble. The concession made in the final couplet, that maybe such exemplars do exist, is one indication of the poem's rhetoricity—and it is partially rescinded by the sceptical inference that, if they do, they are scarcely recognisable as belonging to the human species.

The dramatic responses to *Against Reason and Mankind* fall basically into two categories. To the first category belong those plays which echo, or allude to, particular lines and ideas but which do not purport to offer either a comprehensive endorsement or a rebuttal of the poem's argument. At times a character—for example that of the stage libertine—cites or near-paraphrases a snippet from the satire the same way one would recycle a *bon mot* heard in another company as does Ramble, 'a wild young Gentleman of the Town', in Crowne's *The Countrey Wit* (1675):

> The order of Nature? the order of Coxcombs; the order of Nature is to follow my appetite: am I to eat at Noon, because it is Noon, or because I am hungry? to eat because a Clock strikes, were to feed a Clock, or the Sun, and not my self.[20]

True, Ramble is a professed libertine and uses the appropriated lines to bolster up his rakish credentials but there is little philosophical depth in his hedonist ejaculations and he is more than happy to recant, reform and embrace monogamy and matrimony at the end of the play. Other local resonances from *Against Reason and Mankind* can be found in such plays as Dryden's *Aureng-Zebe* (1676) and *Oedipus* (1678), the latter written in collaboration with Nathaniel Lee.[21] By contrast, John Crowne's masque *Calisto* and Thomas Shadwell's tragedies *The Libertine* and *Timon of Athens* provide more spirited and more sustained retorts to Rochester's *Against Reason and Mankind,* which go beyond mere verbal allusions or repetition of libertine commonplaces.

Calisto: or, The Chaste Nimph, written in the autumn of 1674 and produced at Court in the early months of 1675, was the first answer to, or comment on, Rochester's poem in dramatic form. Crowne was asked to provide the masque on the strength of Rochester's recommendation even though it was Dryden, the then Poet Laureate, who would have been the obvious choice for such a commission. As he tells us in the preface to the printed text of the masque, Crowne had little time allowed him to choose a subject for the piece, and having lighted in the second Book of Ovid's *Metamorphoses* on the story of Calisto—the Arcadian nymph raped and impregnated by Jupiter, transformed into a bear by his jealous wife Juno and later stellified by her lover—he had difficulty in fitting it for the occasion, for the chief roles were to be taken by two teenage daughters of the Duke of York, Princesses Mary and Anne. Forced drastically to alter the Ovidian narrative so as 'to write a clean, decent, and inoffensive Play, on the Story of a Rape',[22] Crowne turned the rape into would-be rape thus fortuitously saving Calisto's chastity. Yet if Jupiter's assault on the nymph's virtue fails, his rhetoric of arbitrary power and appetitive lust prevails, introducing a curious disjunction between the action of the play and its impact upon the audience.[23]

In his characterisation of the God of Gods as a tyrant and a libertine—'I will be controul'd in no amour; / My Love is arbitrary as my power' (III, p. 36)—who envies mortals their sexual felicity, and who, in order to satisfy his lust, does not shrink from adopting shapes of sundry deities (including female ones such as Diana), men and beasts, Crowne enters into a clever dialogue with his patron's recent pronouncement on the morality (and rationality) of the unrestrained gratification of the senses. He specifically takes up and modifies the Rochesterian account of the relative standing of man and beast, with its theriophilic emphasis on the superiority of animal existence, by introducing a new factor into the equation, a lustful god who easily traverses the 'vertical' scale of creation. For Jupiter, ever catholic in his tastes, both animal and human existence hold irresistible sensual attractions:

JUP.

> [I]f to Mortals I present Delight,
> I to the Feast will still my self invite.

MER.

> —Yes Yes, we know *Joves* Appetite; [*Aside.*
> E're quite abstain from Loves sweet Feasts,
> Hee'l humbly dine with Birds and Beasts.

JUP.

> —I still provide with care,
> We Gods in all Delights should share;
> Besides the loves by us embrac'd
> Would kill a poor weak Mortal, but to tast,
> We know what pleasure Love affords,
> To Heavy Beasts and Mettled Birds;
> Here and there at will we fly,
> Each step of Natures Perch we try;
> Down to the Beast, and up again
> To the more fine delights of Man:
> We every sort of pleasure try;
> So much advantage has a Deity.

M<small>ER.</small>

> Nay, if *Jove* Rents the World to Man and Beast,
> He may preserve the Royalty at least,
> And freedom take to Hunt in any Grounds;
> The Pleasures of great *Jove* should have no Bounds.

(I, pp. 3-4)

Safely sheltered from criticism of the religious who targeted the iconoclasm of *Against Reason and Mankind,* Crowne flaunts the libertine ethics and political despotism of the supreme classical deity. In an inspired parody of the rants of villains in heroic plays, he has Jupiter declare himself a fount of morality to which, however, he himself is superior:

> I cannot erre, what e're my Actions be;
> There's no such thing as good or ill to me.
> No Action is by Nature good or ill;
> All things derive their Natures from my will.
> If Vertue from my will distinct could be,
> Vertue would be a Power Supream to me.
> What no dependency on me will own,
> Makes me a Vassal, and usurps my Throne.
> If so I can revenge me in a Trice,
> Turn all the Ballance, and make Vertue Vice.

(II, pp. 15-16)

While Jupiter's doctrine of absolute sovereignty, which overrides both ethics and law, ultimately derives from Hobbes,[24] his demagogic deployment of it to rationalise his ruthless quest for sexual fulfilment has its source in Rochester's poem.

If amusing in the mouth of a Greek god played by a teen-age girl in a Court masque, such moral relativism becomes chilling when professed by a Roman tyrant in a tragedy designed for production at Whitehall by leading professionals.[25] Rochester's Valentinian considers himself above laws human and divine, as he imperiously tells his victim: 'Know I am farre above the faults I doe / And those I doe I'me able to forgive' (IV.iv.87-8). Here the rape is real, Lucina's off-stage shrieks being audible to both other characters and the audience. Yet, like Jupiter's unrelenting pursuit of Calisto, the Emperor's sexual violence is eminently reasonable: he merely seeks to satisfy his appetite in accordance with the dictates of nature:

> Tis nobler like a Lion to invade
> Where appetite directs, and seize my prey
> Than to wait tamely like a begging Dogg
> Till dull consent throws out the scraps of Love.
> I scorne those Gods who seek to cross my wishes
> And will in spite of them be happy—Force
> Of all powers is the most Generous
> For what that gives it freely does bestow
> Without the after Bribe of Gratitude.
> I'le plunge into a Sea of my desires
> And quench my Fever though I drowne my Fame
> And tear up pleasure by the roots—no matter
> Though it never grow againe—what shall ensue
> Let Gods and fates look to it; 'tis their business.

(IV.ii.197-210)

Valentinian's of course is an extreme interpretation of the dictate to follow that 'Reason which distinguishes by Sense, / And gives us Rules of Good and Ill from thence' (*Against Reason and Mankind,* lines 100-1) and we instinctively condemn him as a despot and a reprobate. Yet a powerful reinforcement of his natural creed has already been made much less controversially in III.iii, a scene which, except for the first four lines, radically departs from Fletcher's original.

Rochester rewrites Fletcher's punning and clenching exchange between Lucina's two maidservants, Marcellina and Claudia, in the process staging a contention between artificial virtue (Honour) and natural or rational propensity to fulfil one's sexual appetites (Pleasure). The virtuous Claudia is 'sway'd by Rules not naturall but affected' (III.iii.50)—that is, human-derived—and 'thinke[s] the World / A Dreadfull wildernesse of Savage Beasts' (lines 47-8)—that is, men as bad as, or worse than, beasts—thereby adopting a misanthropic posture ('I hate Mankind for feare of beeing Lov'd' (line 51)). She also launches an attack upon 'cheating witt' which, by 'false wisdome' (lines 71ff), serves to justify vice (note the habitual association of wit and moral corruption). By contrast the frail Marcellina follows the dictates of nature seconded by reason (the better rationality familiar from *Against Reason and Mankind*): 'what Nature prompts us to / And reason seconds why should wee avoyd?' (lines 54-5). Though neither as pompous nor as easily discredited as the 'formal band and beard', Claudia seems to lose the argument. Or, rather, her highly moralistic stance is undermined by the very terms she uses to defend it, for example styling herself 'Honours Martyr' (line 19) and 'the Slave of Vertue' (line 46). For should virtue and honour breed fear and misanthropy? And, if they do, are they worth adhering to?

There are no moral absolutes in the world of Rochester's *Valentinian.* Even Lucina, the victim of rape, is far less obviously 'good' than in Fletcher. And the tyrant's 'poetically just' death at the hands of his rebellious subjects hardly brings about reinstatement of a divinely ordained moral order. Though momentarily overawed by Lucina's husband Maximus who upbraids him for his innumerable sins, treacheries and transgressions—'Reason noe more, thou troublest mee with Reason' (V.v.163)—Valentinian soon repents of his near-repentance, his end being not only defiant but mischievously sadistic. 'Would the Gods raise Lucina from the grave / And fetter thee but while I might enjoy her / Before thy face', he exclaims, 'I'de ravish her againe' (V.v.240-2). Harold Love's contribution to this collection suggests that the rape scene was identifiably located in Rochester's own lodgings in Whitehall, very close to the Court Theatre where the *play itself* was designed to be performed.[26] Had it been performed, we can imagine the thrill of recognition in the audience. We can imagine, too, that the numerous architectural allusions to Charles's royal palace would have made the fate of the late Roman tyrant appear topical, if not directly applicable to the political situation in England in the mid-1670s. That topicality, as

Love points out, would have vanished by the time of the play's eventual production at Court nearly a decade later, in February 1684.

We encounter another unrepentant villain, Don John, in Thomas Shadwell's *The Libertine,* a satirical tragedy which constitutes the most substantial dramatised reply to *Against Reason and Mankind.*[27] The play was premièred in June 1675 at the Dorset Garden Theatre. Though it draws plot elements from various European sources, and in deploying the Don Juan legend is working with very old material, *The Libertine* derives its contemporary energy from an implicit debate with Rochester's stance in the satire. Rochester's poem, as we have seen, recommends a form of rationality that, eschewing recondite subjects favoured by the pseudo-intellectual, directs our practical actions in the world. What is good and what is ill are to be determined entirely by what gratifies and renews our appetites; we are to live according to the immediate dictates of our senses, not according to ethical prescriptions that false rationality abstracts from the flux of everyday living. Rochester's *Against Reason and Mankind* has argued that supposed human 'virtues' are in fact the hypocritical outcomes of a base passion, fear. Animal behaviour is determined by an instinctual need to survive. Reason merely enables humans to devise refined forms of vice beyond the ken of the animal kingdom. Shadwell's *The Libertine* deploys the Don Juan legend to imagine what might be the consequences of trying to live according to his understanding of the Rochesterian code proposed in *Against Reason and Mankind.*

What is at issue is how to define the term 'Nature' and its cognates. The action of Shadwell's play will take the form of a series of situations in which characters act 'naturally' or 'according to Nature'; and it will become apparent that a set of ethical prescriptions not derivable from 'nature' in any simple way, but derivable from religious authority, is absolutely necessary to regulate human conduct. Don John's philosophy expounded in the opening scene carries unmistakably Rochesterian echoes:

D. ANTO.

> By thee, we have got loose from Education,
> And the dull slavery of Pupillage,
> Recover'd all the liberty of Nature,
> Our own strong Reason now can go alone,
> Without the feeble props of splenatick Fools,
> Who contradict our common Mother, Nature.

D. JOHN.

> Nature gave us our Senses, which we please:
> Nor does Reason war against our Sense.
> By Natures order, Sense should guide our Reason,
> Since to the mind all objects Sense conveys.[28]

In dramatic context there are, however, immediate challenges to the complacency of this position. As the cronies recount their recent conquests, the emphasis on acts that would be widely considered 'unnatural' is hard to miss:

Don Lopez has murdered his elder brother for his estate; Don Antonio has impregnated both his sisters; and Don John has plotted the murder of his own father, has murdered Don Pedro for trying to preserve his own sister's chastity, and has ravished scores of women, nuns prominent among them. 'Nature' has therefore prompted these men to act directly contrary to what is 'natural'. All of these crimes are enumerated by Don John's valet, Jacomo, whose dramatic function throughout is to represent a conception of ordinary, unheroic humanity that operates as some kind of a touchstone for 'human nature'. In the opening scene, the jilted Leonora has come in search of Don John, and is apprised by Jacomo of his real nature: 'He owns no Deity, but his voluptuous appetite, whose satisfaction he will compass by Murders, Rapes, Treasons, or ought else' (I, pp. 29-30). Thus brusquely informed, Leonora swoons; and Jacomo considers taking advantage of her while she is unconscious. This crude fantasy is interrupted by her revival, but the point is made that Jacomo is no angel, that he would not let a decent opportunity go to waste—and perhaps many males in the audience would empathise with this. However, Jacomo is subjected to a regime of terror by his master, one of whose pleasures is to make him act *against* his natural predisposition—to fight, when he is a poltroon, and to assist in the commission of crimes that flout the conventional morality to which he subscribes. A dynamic so pronounced as to become almost obsessive in the final act, John's goading of Jacomo goes beyond the comic master-servant stereotype and all the jokes about Jacomo's 'antipathy to Hemp' (II, p. 38), just as Don John himself is well beyond the classification 'rake'.

Female characters in the play also operate to test out the limits of what is 'natural'. In Act II, Leonora's reckoning with Don John makes the point familiar from many of the 1670s sex plays, that 'nature' appears to have invested differently in the two genders. Where she speaks the language of love, vows and constancy, Don John speaks of obeying his constitution and of loving only as long as his natural desires will last. What is in the biological interest of men is not, apparently, in the interest of women. When, in Shadwell's later *Timon of Athens* (1678), Timon is taxed by the equally pathologically constant Evandra with breach of the vows he made to her, he responds that:

> [W]e cannot create our own affections;
> They're mov'd by some invisible active Pow'r,
> And we are only passive, and whatsoever
> Of imperfection follows from th' obedience
> To our desires, we suffer, not commit.

> (I, p. 212)

The pop-up appearance to Don John of six women all claiming to be his wives (a device later imitated by Gay in *The Beggar's Opera*) leads to a climax of cartoonish vice in which one of his 'wives' kills herself, an old woman is raped and a sacramental view of marriage is further burlesqued by a mock 'Epithalamium':

> *Since Liberty, Nature for all has design'd,*
> *A pox on the Fool who to one is confin'd.*

All Creatures besides,
When they please change their Brides.
All Females they get when they can,
Whilst they nothing but Nature obey,
How happy, how happy are they?
But the silly fond Animal, Man,
Makes laws 'gainst himself, which his Appetites sway;
Poor Fools, how unhappy are they?

(II, pp. 43-4)

By the end of Act II, the libertine's conception of the natural has been subjected to further pressure. Maria—a woman whose lover Octavio has been killed in Act I and impersonated by Don John—enters cross-dressed. In contrast to Don John's programmatic promiscuity, her commitment to monogamy is so extreme that it has turned her into a bloodthirsty revenger. Arguably, the audience is not much more comfortable with this than with Don John's polygamous permissiveness; and we are to see its effects again later, when Leonora continues to be in thrall to Don John no matter how much she comes to know about his nature and actions. At this point in Act II, Maria's function is further to vex the conception of human nature by introducing the country-city dichotomy, contending that 'barbarous Art' has debauched the innocent natures of all urban dwellers: 'More savage cruelty reigns in Cities, / Than ever yet in Desarts among the / Most venemous Serpents' (II, p. 48). In Act IV this thread is taken up in a pastoral masque, the point of which is to suggest that 'uncorrupted Nature' exists only in the improbable setting of nymphs and shepherds—though their intention to 'geld' Jacomo (the shepherds apprehend him after he has been forced to take part in his master's rape of the nymphs; apparently he lacks Don John's aristocratic fleetness of foot) suggests that these shepherds are not entirely idealised. They also possess some 'georgic' skills! Before Act II ends, the appearance of the Ghost of Don John's father threatening Divine vengeance upon the whole pack of them throws the conception of what is natural into the melting-pot. A legend in which, famously, a stone statue of the murdered Governor of Seville accepts an invitation to supper is one in which, at the very least, what is 'natural' cannot be taken for granted: and in Shadwell's play the supernatural is deployed to interrogate this worldly philosophies of experience.

Act III is the philosophical heart of the play, where the action responds most directly to Rochester's poem. Fleeing from a Seville that has become too hot for them, our heroes are caught in a storm at sea and later precipitated upon a seemingly strange coast—which is in fact their native land—where they meet with a religious hermit, who is horrified by their demand for whores and is provoked into this discussion:

HERM.

Oh Monsters of impiety! are you so lately scap'd the wrath of Heaven, thus to provoke it?

D. ANT.

How! by following the Dictates of Nature, who can do otherwise?

D. LOP.

All our actions are necessitated, none command their own wills.

HERM.

Oh horrid blasphemy! would you lay your dreadful and unheard of Vices upon Heaven? No, ill men, that has given you free-will to do good.

D. JOH.

I find thou retir'st here, and never read'st or think'st.
    Can that blind faculty the Will be free
    When it depends upon the Understanding?
    Which argues first before the Will can chuse;
    And the last Dictate of the Judgment sways
    The Will, as in a Balance, the last Weight
    Put in the scale, lifts up the other end,
    And with the same Necessity.

(III, p. 55)

Don John argues that the understanding is programmed by the sense impressions conveyed to it, and thus we do not have free will. So if we are evil, we are so by 'nature', acting as we must according to the sharpness with which sensory imperatives are conveyed to the understanding. To some extent, the irrational behaviour of Leonora and of two local women, Flavia and Clara, appears to bear out Don John's view. The girls are to be married the following day, but they have heard that English women have much more liberty than Spanish, that in England anything goes in sexual mores—and they desire a taste of such 'natural' freedom. The song they sing sets out to vindicate female libertinism:

Woman who is by Nature wild,
Dull bearded man incloses;
Of Nature's freedom we're beguil'd
By Laws which man imposes:
Who still himself continues free,
Yet we poor Slaves must fetter'd be.

(III, p. 60)

But their attempt to follow through on this desire for sexual liberation provokes an orgy of crime culminating in the murder of their father, the death of Maria, and the wounding of their two bridegrooms, such that they are brought to a religious recognition—''Twas our vile disobedience / Caus'd our poor Fathers death, which Heaven / Will revenge on us' (IV, pp. 73-4)—and they determine to expiate their sins in a religious sanctuary. In the event, they do not spend long enough in the cloister to achieve this because they are smoked out of it like bees in a hive by Don John's gang intent upon their rape. Significantly again in view of this play's attempt to combat vice with pastoral, it is the shepherds who foil the attempt. In what remains of the play, the supernatural machinery of the legend takes over, as Don John's gang are made by the ghost and the statue to celebrate a ritual black mass in the company of the ghosts of all those they have murdered. In the Faustian finale, Don John is haled off to hell still refusing to repent, meeting his death with all the bravado of the villain in a Jacobean tragedy.

Rochester not only recognised *The Libertine* as a reply to *Against Reason and Mankind* but effectively gave it his imprimatur: his self-mocking poetic riposte, **To the Post Boy,** figures the Earl's own imminent damnation in terms that unmistakably recall Don John's brazen end, complete with the prospect of hell, fire and brimstone.[29] Shadwell, however, was not finished yet. In *The Libertine,* he was primarily concerned with staging (and rebutting) the sexual ethics embodied in *Against Reason and Mankind*; in his adaptation of Shakespeare's *Timon of Athens,* which he claimed to have 'Made into a Play', his interest is in the corruption of human nature and the supposed inferiority of men to beasts.

Written at the suggestion of Rochester's friend and political ally, the Duke of Buckingham, to whom it was dedicated, *The History of Timon of Athens, the Man-Hater* (1678) targets the section of *Against Reason and Mankind* in which the speaker renews his onslaught on mankind in rejoinder to the *adversarius*'s vindication of 'Blest glorious Man' (lines 112-73). This is not to say that the poem's libertine creed embodied in the speaker's apology for 'right reason' (lines 72-111) has been forgotten: indeed, Shadwell's most striking alteration of the Shakespearian original is the introduction of Evandra, Timon's loyal and loving mistress, who is abandoned by him for Melissa, a mercenary coquette, but who, in spite of his faithlessness and perjured vows, is the only person to offer support and help when bankruptcy looms by returning the gifts he had bestowed upon her. (Melissa immediately gives him up for Alcibiades whose fortune is now in the ascendant.) One could even argue—perversely—that if Timon had remained true to Evandra, the effect on him of the financial disaster would not have been half so dire. As it is, this good-natured if thoughtless spendthrift and would-be libertine is shocked to discover not only that the erstwhile beneficiaries of his bounty have abandoned him but also that the only person genuinely eager to help him is the woman he had wronged and to whom he had callously expounded his rationale for male sexual freedom:

Tɪᴍ.

> Man is not master of his appetites,
> Heav'n swayes our mind to Love. (I, p. 210)
> . . . . .
> Why are not our desires within our power?
> Or why should we be punisht for obeying them?[30]

Evandra's retort to this torrent of ingenious self-justification is telling: 'Your Philosophy is too subtle' (I, p. 212). It certainly is: later on in the play Timon assures her with disarming candour: 'I can love two at once, trust me I can' (II, p. 227).

Shadwell uses Evandra to expose and castigate Timon's libertinism; he uses Apemantus and Timon himself to carry out a scorching attack on human treachery, pride and dishonesty.[31] As in Shakespeare, both Apemantus's and Timon's misanthropic diatribes are pervaded by animal imagery, but Apemantus's speeches have been adjusted to underline thematic correspondence to specific passages in *Against Reason and Mankind.* It is as if the poem's persona had an on-stage deputy:

Aᴘᴇᴍ.

> When I can find a man that's better than
> A beast, I will fall down and worship him.

> (II, p. 222)

Compare *Against Reason and Mankind*:

> If upon Earth there dwell such God-like men,
> I'le here Recant my Paradox to them;
> Adore those Shrines of Virtue, homage pay,
> And with the rabble World, their Laws obey.
>   If such there be, yet grant me this at least,
> Man differs more from Man, than Man from Beast.

> (lines 220-5)

And later,

> I fear not man no more than I can love him.
> 'Twere better for us that wild beasts possest
> The Empire of the Earth, they'd use men better,
> Than they do one another. They'd ne're prey
> On man but for necessity of Nature.
> Man undoes man in wantonness and sport,
> Bruits are much honester than he; my dog
> When he fawns on me is no Courtier,
> He is in earnest; but a man shall smile,
> And wish my throat cut.

> (III, pp. 231-2)

compared with *Against Reason and Mankind*:

> Be Judge your self, I'le bring it to the test,
> Which is the Basest Creature, Man or Beast.
> Birds feed on birds, Beasts on each other prey,
> But savage Man alone does man betray:
> Prest by necessity they kill for food,
> Man undoes Man to do himself no good.
> With teeth and claws by nature arm'd, they hunt
> Natures allowance to supply their want.
> But Man with smiles, embraces, friendship, praise,
> Inhumanly his fellows life betrayes;
> With voluntary pains works his distress,
> Not through Necessity, but Wantonness.
> For hunger or for Love they fight and teare,
> Whilst wretched man is still in arms for Feare:
> For feare he Arms, and is of arms afraid,
> By fear to fear successively betray'd.

> (lines 127-42)

Timon too denounces the 'wicked humane race' ('all such Animals' as 'walk . . . upon two legs'), for 'they are not honest, / Those Creatures that are so, walk on all four' (IV, pp. 251-2). Yet in contrast to the persona of *Against Reason and Mankind* (and to Apemantus), Timon, who claims to be as 'savage as a Satyr' (IV, p. 253), is compelled, by Evandra's unceasing solicitude, loyalty and generosity, to recant his paradox and acknowledge that among two-legged beasts 'there is / One woman honest; if they ask me more / I will not grant it' (Act IV, p. 253).

Crowne undercuts the ostensible moral idealism of *Calisto* by imbuing both the masque proper (the story of Jupiter's abortive rape of Calisto) and the pastoral intermezzi of nymphs and shepherds with elements of libertine philosophy and rhetoric extrapolated from *Against Reason and Mankind*; in *The Libertine* and *Timon,* Shadwell grafts elements of libertine comedy (again traceable to Rochester's poem) on to essentially tragic structures,[32] again with a view to literalising and demolishing the precepts put forward by the persona of *Against Reason and Mankind.* The result is a satirical masque and two satirical tragedies respectively. By engaging with its language and topics, all three plays, but especially the two of Shadwell's, strive to question and counter the libertine and misanthropic ethos of *Against Reason and Mankind.* In that attempt they are only partially successful. For although the outcomes of their plots toe the morally correct (and poetically just) line—Jupiter's assault on the nymph is prevented, Don John and his confederates are hauled off to hell, Timon dies a broken man—the imperative to create a figure (or figures) who will embody the satire's creed, and will then be exposed and duly chastised, leads, paradoxically, not to edifying catharsis but to moral ambivalence and generic corruption. To this fact the original audiences were fully alive. The mixed reception of the English Don Juan is a case in point. John Downes, the Duke's Company prompter, recalled that 'it got the Company great Reputation' and that 'The *Libertine* perform'd by Mr. *Betterton* Crown'd the Play';[33] Robert Hooke who saw a performance during the first run was outraged by this 'Atheistical wicked play';[34] Charles Gildon classed it as a 'Comedy', which, he thought, was 'diverting enough';[35] and John Dryden damned it as a 'Farce'.[36]

* * *

Our discussion confirms the importance of Rochester's *Against Reason and Mankind* for the libertine debates of the 1670s, especially as they were conducted through the medium of drama. The biographical episodes in which the Earl tried to put libertine beliefs into practice are amongst the best known in Restoration lore: those episodes were strikingly immortalised in the portrayals of Rochester in plays by Etherege, Crowne and Lee. We hope to have demonstrated that *Against Reason and Mankind* prompted Shadwell and Crowne to represent on stage forms of behaviour even more excessive than Rochester's real-life scrapes (if that is an adequate word), searching for a point at which his ethical naturalism would break down, testing it to destruction. Audiences watching representations of behaviour sanctioned by Rochester's arguments would surely reject the premises, though, as we have hinted, the generic complexities that result from such stage experiments do not make it easy to pass moral verdicts. To this extent, the poem is of its time and formative in its time.

The impact of Rochester's *Against Reason and Mankind* (and of his colourful lifestyle) upon the drama did not extend beyond the 1680s. Written as it was for a Court occasion, Crowne's masque was never performed after 1675; by contrast, Shadwell's *The Libertine* and *Timon* proved immensely popular and were regularly revived well into the eighteenth century.[37] It is unlikely, however, that by then many people would have associated the figurations of libertinism in those plays with the person of the Earl or indeed with *Against Reason and Mankind.*[38] Even so, by the eighteenth century the poem seems to have become something of a definitive, if also—paradoxically—a dangerously fluid, statement on 'Man' and 'Reason'. *Against Reason and Mankind* was not only reprinted as a matter of course in successive editions of Rochester's works,[39] but substantial excerpts from it were routinely anthologised under those headings in poetry manuals and dictionaries of quotations such as Edward Bysshe's much-reprinted *The Art of English Poetry* (1702) and his *The British Parnassus* (1714) and Charles Gildon's *The Complete Art of Poetry* (1718). *The Art of English Poetry* prints as many as seventy-two lines from *Against Reason and Mankind* under the heading 'MAN', their tenor being unequivocally misanthropic and cynical.[40] In the Preface to *The British Parnassus* Bysshe professed to 'have carefully avoided to insert any single Line, much less any whole Passage, in this Collection, that was in the former'.[41] Accordingly, under the heading 'MAN', he included twelve lines of the *adversarius*'s apology for 'Bless'd glorious Man . . .', which he had previously excluded from *The Art of English Poetry* (II, 536). But under the heading 'REASON', he now placed a further twenty-five lines from *Against Reason and Mankind,* comprising the persona's scathing debunking of the *adversarius*'s speech (II, 749-50). The impact of such a combination upon the readers of Bysshe's anthologies could hardly have been more ambivalent and contradictory.

In the eighteenth century Rochester's *Against Reason and Mankind* (and his poetic output more generally) influenced verse and prose satire, not drama. In Rochester's poetry can be found some of the most important formal blueprints for eighteenth-century satirical verse; on the level of theme and content, too, he is a model for later writers: the Pope-Swift-Gay circle in particular. The sensational opening statement of *Against Reason and Mankind,* inspired by Montaigne and Plutarch, is echoed in several Scriblerian works. In Book IV of *Gulliver's Travels,* Gulliver's Houyhnhnm 'master' observes that his ability to survive and defend himself in the wild is considerably inferior to that of the average beast. By the end of the fourth voyage the point is thoroughly made that Gulliver is not only *not* an animal, he is less than one.[42] Mortification of human pride is central to this poem's intention, as it is to Scriblerian satire generally. Other lines of *Against Reason and Mankind* bring irresistibly to mind John Gay's fable 'The Man and the Flea':

> And tis this very Reason I despise.
> This supernatural Gift, that makes a mite
> Think hee's the Image of the Infinite;

Comparing his short life, voyd of all rest,
To the Eternall, and the ever blest.

(lines 75-9)

In Gay's fable a man, wrought to a pitch of self-congratulation by observing the universe created for his pleasure, is humbled by a flea on his nose.[43] The flea, not the man, is the capstone of the creation. Gay was also drawn to Rochester's Hobbesian account of human beings as the only species who destroy others without any advantage to themselves (lines 129 onwards). An exactly similar account is given by Lockit in *The Beggar's Opera*.[44] Preeminently, however, Rochester's poem is a source of inspiration for Alexander Pope.[45] Lines 14 onwards construct a bridge from Milton to his eighteenth-century successors: to Swift's Spider in the *Battle of the Books*, spinning his house out of his own entrails; or to Pope's King of the Dunces, trying to compose in surroundings created by the detritus of his own (de)composition. 'Stumbling from thought to thought' becomes in the *Dunciad* 'Sinking from thought to thought, a vast profound', as Rochester's trip becomes a lead-weighted dive, and the sea changes from the sceptic's doubt to the poet's Sargasso of hopeless images. Joseph Spence records several instances of Pope's attention to Rochester, of his earnestness in comparing him to Oldham and Dorset and in assessing his strengths and weaknesses against those peers:

> Oldham is too rough and coarse. Rochester is the medium between him and the
> Earl of Dorset. Lord Dorset is the best of all those writers.
> 'What, better than Lord Rochester?'
> Yes; Rochester has neither so much delicacy nor exactness as Dorset.
>
> [Instance: his Satire on Man.][46]

If Pope is ambivalent in his verdict, he is no more so than contemporary playwrights were, or than modern readers of Rochester's most significant individual poem continue to be.[47] Stephen Jeffreys is the latest dramatist to put Rochester's life on the stage, in his play *The Libertine*, premièred in 1994. As the lights come up, Rochester walks front stage and, Restoration style, issues a direct challenge to the audience: 'Allow me to be frank at the commencement: you will not like me'.[48] The events of his life unfold and the play closes with Rochester again in direct address to the audience: 'Well. Do you like me now? Do you like me now?' (p. 84). Do we?

Notes

1. That formative status is enhanced if we accept recently discovered evidence suggesting that the poem was composed in 1672 rather than 1674 as was previously supposed. See Harold Love and Stephen Parks, 'A Reasonable Satyr', *Times Literary Supplement,* 1 August 1997, p. 13.

2. The most comprehensive discussions of the context of *Against Reason and Mankind* are those in Griffin (pp. 156-96) and Thormählen (pp. 162-89); neither

considers its impact upon the drama. For an account of verse responses see David M. Vieth, *Attribution in Restoration Poetry: A Study of Rochester's 'Poems' of 1680* (New Haven, 1963), pp. 178-80.

3. On Etherege's and Lee's portraits of Rochester see Robert D. Hume, 'Reading and Misreading *The Man of Mode*', *Criticism*, 14 (1972), 1-11, and his 'The Satiric Design of Nat. Lee's *The Princess of Cleve*', *Journal of English and German Philology*, 75 (1976), 117-38 respectively. Harold Weber discusses Rochester as a prototype of a Hobbesian libertine rake in the context of 1670s comedies in *The Restoration Rake-hero: Transformations in Sexual Understanding in Seventeenth-century England* (Madison, 1986), pp. 49-90.

4. For a discussion of late seventeenth-century *libertinage* in the context of both drama and poetry see Dale Underwood, *Etherege and the Seventeenth-century Comedy of Manners* (New Haven, 1957), pp. 10-40.

5. Thomas Hobbes, *Leviathan* (1651), edited by Richard Tuck (Cambridge, 1996), Part I, ch. 6, p. 39.

6. Chernaik, p. 24.

7. David Farley-Hills's contribution to the present volume reinforces the points we make in our introduction.

8. 'The Effect of this [a particular Pique to *Dryden*] was discover'd by his Lordship's setting up *Crown* in Opposition to *Dryden*; he recommended him to the King, ordering him to make a Masque for the Court, when it was the Business of the Poet Laureat': 'The Memoiers [*sic*] of the Life of *John Wilmot,* Earl of *Rochester.* Written By Monsieur *St Evremont,* in a Letter to her Grace the Dutchess of *Mazarine. Translated from the Original Manuscript*', in *The Works of the Right Honourable the Late Earls of Rochester and Roscommon. With a Collection of Original Poems, Translations, Imitations, & c. by the most Eminent Hands* (2nd edition, London, 1707), sig. b7v. To be the recipient of that commission was both a great boon and a great honour, for the production of the masque was an important cultural and political event. See Andrew R. Walkling, 'Masque and Politics at the Restoration Court: John Crowne's *Calisto*', *Early Music* (February 1996), 27-62.

9. In his preface to *Don Carlos Prince of Spain* (London, 1676), Otway writes, 'I can never enough acknowledge the unspeakable Obligations I received from the *Earl* of *R.* who far above what I am ever able to deserve from him, seem'd almost to make it his business to establish it in the good opinion of the *King,* and his *Royal Highness,* from both of which I have since received Confirmations of their good liking of it, and Encouragement to proceed; and it is to him I must in all gratitude confess I owe the greatest part of my good success in this, and on whose Indulgency I extreamly build my hopes of a next' (sig. A3v).

10. Some time between the winter of 1671-2 and the spring of 1673, he supplied the prologue for a Court performance of Settle's *The Empress of Morocco*, and in the spring of 1677 the epilogue for Charles Davenant's *Circe*. He contributed an epilogue for an all-female production of a revived play in 1672 (see Edward L. Saslow, 'A "New" Epilogue by Rochester', *Restoration*, 23.1 (1999), 1-9) and may also have written the epilogue for Fane's *Love in the Dark* which opened in the spring of 1675.

11. Fane's *A Mask. Made at the Request of the late Earl of Rochester, for the Tragedy of Valentinian* was published in *Poems by Several Hands, and on Several Occasions* (London, 1685), a poetical miscellany edited by Nahum Tate.

12. Howard thanked Rochester for 'the screen you are pleased to write' in a letter dated 7 April 1676. See *Letters*, p. 116.

13. See Robert D. Hume, 'Elizabeth Barry's First Roles and the Cast of *The Man of Mode*', *Theatre History Studies*, 5 (1985), 16-20.

14. *The Assignation or Love in a Nunnery*, in *The Works of John Dryden*, edited by Edward Niles Hooker *et al.*, 20 vols (Berkeley, 1956-), XI, 320-1. All further references to Dryden's works are to this edition and given parenthetically in the text.

15. John Sitter, *Arguments of Augustan Wit* (Cambridge, 1991), p. 95.

16. Thormählen, p. 195; David Trotter, 'Wanton Expressions' in *Spirit of Wit*, pp. 111-32.

17. Roger D. Lund, 'Irony as Subversion: Thomas Woolston and the Crime of Wit' in *The Margins of Orthodoxy: Heterodox Writing and Cultural Response, 1660-1750*, edited by Lund (Cambridge, 1995), pp. 170-94 (p. 171).

18. 'An Answer to the Satyr *against* Mankind. By the Reverend Mr. *Griffith*', in *The Works of John Earl of Rochester* (London, 1714), pp. 59-65 (p. 64). On the authority of Anthony à Wood, Vieth ascribes this poem to Griffith (though he does not altogether reject its attribution to Edward Pococke made in some contemporary transcripts (Vieth, *Attribution in Restoration Poetry*, pp. 178-9)).

19. See his 'Ideology and Ideological State Apparatuses (Notes towards an Investigation)', first published in *La pensée* (1970), reprinted in Louis Althusser, *Essays on Ideology* (London, 1984), p. 29.

20. John Crowne, *The Countrey Wit* (London, 1675), sig. A4v and II, p. 22 respectively. This echo of lines 105-9 has been noted by Love and earlier critics and editors.

21. In *Aureng-Zebe* (whose dedication to the Earl of Mulgrave contains two verbal echoes of the poem: see Paul Hammond's 'Two Echoes of Rochester's *Satire* in Dryden', *Notes and Queries*, 233 (1988), 171), the eponymous hero resists what he perceives as an unreasonable suggestion of his beloved Indamora—that they should part now that his jealousy makes him unable to trust her—in a vein reminiscent of the defence of 'right reason' by the persona of *Against Reason and Mankind* (lines 99ff):

> Must I new bars to my own joy create?
> Refuse, my self, what I had forc'd from Fate?
> What though I am not lov'd?
> Reason's nice taste does our delights destroy:
> Brutes are more bless'd, who grosly feed on joy.

(V.i.553-7)

In *Oedipus*, the blind prophet Tiresias condemns the insolence of Man's epistemological hankerings in words which recall the rebuttal of the 'formal band and beard' in *Against Reason and Mankind* (lines 76ff):

> But how can Finite measure Infinite?
> Reason! alas, it does not know it self!
> Yet Man, vain Man, wou'd with this short-lin'd Plummet,
> Fathom the vast Abysse of Heav'nly justice.

(III.i.241ff)

And Dryden's unperformed opera *The State of Innocence* (c. 1673-4) based on Milton's *Paradise Lost* rewrites Satan's seduction of Eve so as to emphasise the 'rationality' of the woman's aspirations to the godhead (IV.ii) in a way which resonates with the diabolical presentation of human pursuit of (false) reason in Rochester's poem.

22. *Calisto: or, The Chaste Nimph. The Late Masque at Court, As it was frequently Presented there, By several Persons of Great Quality. With the Prologue, and the Songs betwixt the Acts. All Written by J. Crowne* (London, 1675), 'Epistle to the Reader', sig. a1v.

23. Jupiter's ultimate victory is wittily brought home in the Epilogue: in the final scene of the masque the audience have witnessed Jupiter bestow upon Calisto (and upon her equally chaste sister Nyphe) 'the small dominion of a Star' (V, p. 79); now he revokes his decree and decides to keep the two beauties in '*this inferiour World*' (p. 82).

24. See Louis Teeter, 'The Dramatic Use of Hobbes's Political Ideas' in *John Dryden*, edited by Earl Miner (London, 1972), pp. 27-57 (p. 36).

25. A manuscript cast list preserved in two scribal copies of *Lucina's Rape* (as Rochester called his revision of *Valentinian*) suggests that the play was produced, or intended to be produced, by the King's Company *c.* 1675-6. The first recorded performance of the play took place at Court on 11 February 1684. See John Downes, *Roscius Anglicanus*, edited by Judith Milhous and Robert D. Hume (London, 1987), p. 83n.

26. Harold Love, 'Was Lucina Betrayed at Whitehall?', pp. 179-90 above.

27. Raman Selden notes that '[t]he philosophy of the play's libertines has some general similarities to the views expressed in Rochester's *A Satyr against Reason and Mankind*', though he does not explore them. We believe that those similarities are both more specific and more pervasive than Selden allows. See his 'Rochester and Shadwell' in *Spirit of Wit,* pp. 177-87 (p. 189).

28. All references are to *The Complete Works of Thomas Shadwell,* edited by Montague Summers, 5 vols (London, 1927; repr. New York, 1968), vol. III, I, 25-6.

29. The attribution of this poem to Rochester has been disputed. For a convenient summary of the debate see Rochester 1999, 367-8.

30. Compare also Timon's exclamation against human-derived rules which bound and unnecessarily restrict pleasure with the passage in *Against Reason and Mankind* (lines 105-9) appropriated by Crowne in *The Countrey Wit*:

    Alas, by Nature we are too much confin'd,
    Our Libertie's so narrow, that we need not
    Find fetters for our selves: No, we should seize
    On pleasure wheresoever we can find it,
    Lest at another time we miss it there.

    (II, pp. 215-16)

31. Shadwell apportions to Apemantus and to Evandra many of the lines of Shakespeare's steward Flavius who, renamed Demetrius, in his version proves as dishonest and hypocritical as the rest of Timon's hangers-on.

32. See Robert D. Hume, *The Development of English Drama in the Late Seventeenth Century* (Oxford, 1976), pp. 312, 327.

33. *Roscius Anglicanus,* p. 78.

34. The entry for 25 July 1675, from *The Diary of Robert Hooke,* quoted in *The London Stage, 1600-1800, Part I: 1660-1700,* edited by William Van Lennep *et al.* (Carbondale, 1965), p. 234.

35. Charles Gildon, *Lives and Characters of the English Dramatick Poets* (London, [1699]), p. 124.

36. *The Vindication of The Duke of Guise,* in Dryden's *Works,* XIV, 319.

37. The latter, Charles Gildon noted in his *Lives and Characters* of 1699, was 'for a few Years past, as often acted at the Theatre Royal, as any Tragedy I know' (p. 129). For dates of eighteenth-century revivals of both of Shadwell's plays and Rochester's *Valentinian* see *The London Stage, 1660-1800. Part II: 1700-1729,* edited by Emmett L. Avery, 2 vols (Carbondale, 1960). Rochester's own *Valentinian,* though it commanded critical respect—John Dunton's *The Athenian Mercury* (vol. 5, no. 2, Saturday 5 December 1691) confidently pronounced that '*Val-*

entinian shall outlast, as it does outweigh whole Cart-loads of theirs whose persons have survived him'—and though it was sometimes revived, was less a fixture of the repertory.

38. By contrast, the readers of Rochester's *Works* (London, 1707) were reminded, by St Evremond's 'Memoirs of the Earl of Rochester's Life', that 'Sir *George Etherege* wrote *Dorimant* in Sir *Fopling,* in Compliment to him, as drawing his Lordship's Character, and burnishing all the Foibles of it, to make them shine like Perfections' (sig. b8r).

39. Significantly, *Against Reason and Mankind* was accorded pride of place, being situated at the front of the volume, in the *Works* of 1707 published by Curll, and it was the one poem picked out for discussion in Rymer's preface to Rochester's *Works* of 1714 brought out by Tonson, which also prints Griffith's 'Answer'. Rymer's preface appeared with an edition of Rochester's poems published by Jacob Tonson in 1691 'with no editor's name and an unsigned preface', and was included in subsequent reprints of that edition in 1696, 1705, 1710, 1714 and 1732. It was only in the 1714 edition that the preface was attributed to Rymer. See *The Critical Works of Thomas Rymer,* edited by Curt A. Zimansky (New Haven, 1956), pp. 224-5.

40. See *The Art of English Poetry,* edited by Edward Bysshe, 2 vols (London, 1702), I, 223-5. Though he attributes these lines to Rochester, Bysshe does not specify the poem from which they derive. Gildon includes the very same extract from *Against Reason and Mankind* in his *The Complete Art of Poetry,* 2 vols (London, 1718), II, 227-9. Though there are minor differences of spelling and punctuation between his version and Bysshe's, it is clear that Gildon used the earlier compilation as his copy-text, for his version makes the same cuts to the original.

41. See *The British Parnassus: Or, A Compleat Common-Place-Book of English Poetry: Containing The most genuine, instructive, diverting and sublime Thoughts,* 2 vols (London, 1714), I, sig. A1v. Excerpts from *Valentinian,* too, appeared in contemporary anthologies: see Bysshe (ed.), *The Art of English Poetry* under headings 'FATE' and 'RAPE' respectively, I, 127, 296; and *Thesaurus Dramaticus. Containing all the Celebrated Passages, Soliloquies, Similies, Descriptions, and Other Poetical Beauties in the Body of English Plays, Antient and Modern, Digested under Proper Topics; with the Names of the Plays, and their Authors, referr'd to in the Margin,* 2 vols (London, 1724), I, 20, 240.

42. *Gulliver's Travels,* Book IV, chs 1-4.

43. John Gay, *Fables* (London, 1727), XLIX.

44. John Gay, *The Beggar's Opera,* III.ii.4ff: 'Lions, Wolves, and Vulturs don't live together in Herds, Droves or Flocks.—Of all Animals of Prey, Man is

the only sociable one. Every one of us preys upon his Neighbour, and yet we herd together' (*John Gay: Dramatic Works,* edited by John Fuller, 2 vols (Oxford, 1983), II, 46).

45. The influence is more pervasive than is suggested by Paul Baines in his detailed study 'From "nothing" to "silence": Rochester and Pope' in *Reading Rochester,* edited by Edward Burns (Liverpool, 1995), pp. 137-65. Julian Ferraro's contribution to the present volume is thus especially welcome in the attention it pays to the relationship between Rochester's 'An Allusion to Horace' and *Satyr.* [*Timon*] and Pope's *Epistle to Arbuthnot.*

46. Joseph Spence, *Observations, Anecdotes, and Characters of Books and Men: Collected from Conversation,* edited by James M. Osborn, 2 vols (Oxford, 1966), no. 472, I, 202.

47. The latest of these is Ferraro, who explores some of the reasons behind Pope's ambivalence, in showing how Pope the professional writer has appropriated, but must also transform, the 'holiday writer's aristocratic self-presentation'.

48. Stephen Jeffreys, *The Libertine* (London, 1994), p. 3.

FURTHER READING

Bibliography

Vieth, David. *Rochester Studies, 1925-1982: An Annotated Bibliography.* New York: Garland, 1984, 174 p.

Annotated bibliography of most important critical works on Rochester from 1925 to 1982; includes an introduction that surveys the trends in Rochester studies since 1680.

Biographies

Adlard, John, ed., *The Debt to Pleasure: John Wilmot, Earl of Rochester in the Eyes of His Contemporaries and in His Own Poetry and Prose.* Manchester, UK: Carcanet, 1974, 141 p.

Composite biography of Rochester made up of comments made by his contemporaries as well as his own poetry and prose, presented in chronological order.

Greene, Graham. *Lord Rochester's Monkey being the Life of John Wilmot, Second Earl of Rochester.* New York: Viking, 1974, 231 p.

Biography written by the noted novelist in 1934 but not published until 1974; mistakenly credits Rochester with having written poems that in the intervening years were discovered not to be his.

Murdock, Kenneth B. "'A Very Profane Wit': John Wilmot, Earl of Rochester, 1647-1680." In *The Sun at Noon: Three Biographical Sketches,* pp. 269-306. New York: Macmillan, 1939.

Describes Rochester as a man who pursued sensual pleasures but was searching for more spiritual fulfillment.

Norman, Charles. *Rake Rochester.* New York: Crown, 1954, 224 p.

Non-scholarly work relating Rochester's story from its "bright beginnings" to its "tortured end," noting that his reputation as a rake could not disguise his happiness nor his greatness as a poet.

Pinto, Vivian de Sola. *Rochester: Portrait of a Restoration Poet.* London: John Lane, Bodley Head, 1935); revised as *Enthusiast in Wit: A Portrait of John Wilmot Earl of Rochester 1647-1680.* London: Routledge & Kegan Paul, 1962, 294 p.

Considered the definitive biography of Rochester; includes analyses of his poetry and Rochester's psychological profile in the context of the intellectual and cultural climate in which he lived.

Criticism

Clark, John R. "The Satiric Singing: An Example from Rochester." *The English Record* 24 (Fall, 1973): 16-20.

Interpretation of "Song of Young Lady to her Ancient Lover" as a satire and not a romantic piece.

Edwards, A. S. G. "The Authorship of *Sodom.*" *Papers of the Bibliographical Society of America* 71 (Second Quarter 1977): 208-212.

Contends that *Sodom* was written by at least three different people.

Fabricant, Carole. "Rochester's World of Imperfect Enjoyment." *Journal of English and Germanic Philology* 73 (July, 1974): 338-50.

Claims that Rochester's bawdy poems focus on the frustration of sexuality.

Farley-Hills, David. *Rochester: The Critical Heritage.* London: Routledge & Kegan Paul, 1972, 230 p.

Anthology surveying the attitudes to Rochester's work from the seventeenth century to 1903.

———. Introduction to *Rochester's Poetry,* pp. 1-9. Totowa, NJ: Rowman and Littlefield, 1978.

Argues that Rochester's poetry reveals his knowledge of the conventions of morality and manners despite its tone of rebelliousness.

Griffin, Dustin H. *Satires Against Man: The Poems of Rochester.* Berkeley & Los Angeles: University of California Press, 1973, 317 p.

Full-length critical study of Rochester's poetry using a psychological approach, with a great deal of attention devoted to *A Satire Against Mankind.*

Johnson, J. W. "Did Lord Rochester Write *Sodom?*" *Papers of the Bibliographical Society of America* 81 (June 1987): 119-153.

Provides evidence to show that Rochester was the writer responsible for *Sodom*—or a least that nobody else was as likely to have written the short play as Rochester was.

Johnson, Ronald W. "Rhetoric and Drama in Rochester's "Satyr Against Reason and Mankind." *Studies in English Literature* 15, No. 3 (Summer, 1975): 365-73.

Contends that with *A Satire of Reason and Mankind* Rochester produces satire of the widest scope because the rhetorical and dramatic structures in the work complement one another.

Johnson, Samuel. "Rochester." In *Lives of the English Poets,* Volume 3, edited by George Birkneck Hill. Written 1779; originally published 1905 by the Clarendon Press; reprint New York: Octagon Books, 1967, pp. 219-28.

Presents a brief biographical sketch, assesses the poet's character, and evaluates its literary merits; is generally guarded in its praise of Rochester's work.

Moore, John F. "The Originality of Rochester's *Satyr Against Mankind.*" *PMLA: Publications of the Modern Language Association of America* 58, No. 3 (June, 1943): 393-401.

Maintains that although Rochester relied on several sources (including works by Boileau and Montaigne) in composing his satire, he must be credited with the same degree of originality as others who are inspired by other works and develop them into their own writing.

O'Neill, John H. "Rochester's 'Imperfect Enjoyment': 'The True Veine of Satyre in Sexual Poetry." *Tennessee Studies in Literature* 25 (1980): 57-71.

Views "Imperfect Enjoyment" as a satire of pride (specifically, the pride of the flesh) in the tradition of classical satire.

Pasch, Thomas K. "Concentricity, Christian Myth, and the Self-Incriminating Narrator in Rochester's *A Ramble in St. James's Park.*" *Essays in Literature* 6 (Spring, 1979): 21-28.

Demonstrates that "A Ramble in St. James's Park" overturns the reader's expectations because of the arrangment of its five sections, its biblical imagery, and the seemingly reliable but actually self-deluded narrator.

Patterson, John D. "Rochester's Second Bottle: Attitudes to Drink and Drinking in the Works of John Wilmot, Earl of Rochester." *Restoration: Studies in English Literary Culture, 1660-1700* 5 (Spring 1981): 6-15.

Explores the poet's attitudes to drink and women in relation to friendship, wisdom, and literary inspiration.

Pinto, Vivian de Sola. "The Poetry of John Wilmot, Earl of Rochester." *Essays by Divers Hands, Being the Transactions of the Royal Society of Literature of the United Kingdom* New Series Volume 13 (1934): 107-33.

Detailed discussion of Rochester's poems which emphasizes their intellectual complexity and seriousness.

———. "John Wilmot, Earl of Rochester and the Right Veine of Satire." In *Seventeenth-Century English Poetry: Modern Essays in Criticism,* edited by William R. Keast, pp. 359-74. New York: Oxford University Press, 1962.

Judges Rochester as the most gifted of the Restoration court poets and as the pioneer satirist of his age.

Thormählen, Marianne. *Rochester: The Poems in Context.* Cambridge: Cambridge University Press, 1993, 383 p.

Study that attempts to present Rochester as a complex and serious artists; includes lengthy analyses of individual poems, including "The Imperfect Enjoyment," "A Ramble in Saint James's Park," *Artemisia and Chloe, Upon Nothing, A Satire Against Reason and Mankind,* "Tunbridge Wells," and "Timon."

Vieth, David M. *Attribution in Restoration Poetry: A Study of Rochester's "Poems" of 1680.* New Haven & London: Yale University Press, 1963, 537 p.

Analyzes the authorship of close to a hundred of the 250 poems that have been attributed (some erroneously) to Rochester.

———. "Toward and Anti-Aristotelian Poetic: Rochester's *Satyr against Mankind* and *Artemisia to Chloe,* with Notes on Swift's *Tale of a Tub* and *Gulliver's Travels.*" *Language and Style* 5 (Spring, 1972): 123-45.

Discusses the form of *Satyr against Mankind* and *Artemisia to Chloe,*.

———. "Pleased with the Contradiction and the Sin: The Perverse Artistry of Rochester's Lyrics." *Tennessee Studies in Literature* 25 (1980): 3-36.

Detailed analysis of a number of Rochester lyrics, including "Upon Leaving His Mistress," "Absent from Thee," "The Mistress," and "Song of Young Lady to her Ancient Lover," comparing the poet's technique to that of other seventeenth-century masters.

Wilcoxon, Reba. "Rochester's Philosophical Premises: A Case for Consistency." *Eighteenth-Century Studies* 8 (Winter 1974/75): 183-201.

Focuses on the philosophical premises that shape Rochester's work and undergird his satire.

———. "The Rhetoric of Sex in Rochester's Burlesque." *Papers on Language and LIterature* 12 (Summer, 1976): 273-84.

Examines Rochester's satires on sexual behavior and finds that while they are clearly bawdy and seek to violate conventions of love poetry, they are not altogether cynical about the nature of love.

————. "Rochester's Sexual Politics." *Studies in Eighteenth-Century Culture,* edited by Roseann Runte. Madison: University of Wisconsin Press, 1979, pp. 137-149.

> Claims that Rochester satirizes male dominance, condemns the male use of women as objects, and celebrates female sexuality.

Wilson, J. Harold. "Satirical Elements in Rochester's *Valentinian.*" *Philological Quarterly* 16, No. 1 (January, 1937): 41-48.

> Provides evidence to show that the character of Valentinian was intended by Rochester as a satire of Charles II.

Additional coverage of Rochester's life and career is contained in the following source published by the Gale Group: *Dictionary of Literary Biography,* **Vol. 131.**

Georges de Scudéry
1601-1667

French playwright, novelist, poet, and critic.

INTRODUCTION

Scudéry was a popular playwright, a successful poet and novelist, and a member of the Académie Française. He was also well known for several influential works of literary criticism, particularly *Observations sur Le Cid* (1637). This critique of Pierre Corneille's play *Le Cid* started a heated literary debate on the proper definition of tragedy, known as the "Querelle du *Cid.*" Scudéry's career as a novelist has been more difficult to assess. His younger sister, Madeleine de Scudéry, was also a novelist, and it is believed that she either shared authorship or wholly wrote many of the novels published under Scudéry's name. Despite such unresolved questions, Scudéry has been regarded as a vital force in seventeenth-century French literature.

BIOGRAPHICAL INFORMATION

Scudéry was born in 1601, the son of Georges de Scudéry and Madeleine de Martel de Goustimesnil. Of the couple's five children, only Scudéry and his sister Madeleine survived past infancy. Scudéry's father was of noble extraction, served in the army as an officer and administrator, and was the captain of the port of Le Havre. Scudéry and his sister were orphaned when their parents died within months of each other in 1613. The children were reared by an uncle who, well schooled himself, gave them an excellent education. In the early 1620s Scudéry joined the military, serving in several campaigns and in a regiment of the Guards. Scudéry often bragged of his military exploits to the point of exaggeration, but most scholars believe his service was generally honorable. His time in the military coincided with the start of his literary career. In 1623 he published his first work, *Elégie sur l'arrest de Théophile,* in defense of Théophile de Viau, who had been forced into exile from Paris because his writings were declared obscene. Around 1630, about the time he left the army, Scudéry's first play, *Lygdamon et Lidias; ou, La Ressemblance,* was staged. Between that time and 1643 he wrote sixteen plays. After the failure of *Arminius* (1643), Scudéry ceased writing plays and began producing novels. Although these multi-volume works were published under Scudéry's name, critics note that many volumes were written in collaboration with his sister—some insist that most if not all were composed by Madeleine. In 1644 Scudéry left Paris, having been named the governor and *capitaine des gallères*

of Notre Dame de la Garde at Marseilles. He returned to Paris three years later, possibly having been dismissed from his post. In 1649 Scudéry published one of his several volumes of poetry, *Poésies diverses,* and was elected to the Académie Française the following year. He was forced to leave Paris in the early 1650s as a result of his support of the rebels in the Fronde, an abortive revolution. He went first to Granville, then to Normandy, where he married Marie Madeleine de Martin-Vast in 1654. About this time he became estranged from his sister. In 1661 Scudéry returned to Paris and received a pension from the king. In his last years he did some translating work and wrote *Les Femmes illustres; ou, Les Harangues héroïques.* He died on May 14, 1667.

MAJOR WORKS

Scudéry's first literary success came in the theater. Twelve of his sixteen plays were tragicomedies, including his first, *Lygdamon et Lidias,* and the one often considered his best, *L'Amour tyrannique* (1638). Scudéry was also well known for several influential works of literary criticism. *Observations sur Le Cid* was one of his most important critical works. In this essay, published in 1637, he censured Corneille's drama *Le Cid* on several fronts, including the morality of the play, the liberties Corneille took with established dramatic rules, the quality of the dialogue, and the questionable merit of the subject matter itself. Corneille's vicious response to *Observations sur Le Cid* and his other critiques of Scudéry's work began the so-called "Querelle du *Cid,*" a heated literary debate on the proper definition of tragedy. Scudéry further elaborated his views on drama in *L'Apoligie du théâtre* (1639). Scudéry's reputation as a novelist is clouded by questions of the degree to which he or his sister should be considered the author of the works published under his name. While scholars concede that Scudéry's share in *Ibrahim, Artamène, ou Le Grand Cyrus* (1649-53), *Clélie* (1654-60), and *Almahide; ou, L'Esclave reine* (1660-63) can never be definitively established, most acknowledge that he contributed in some manner to these works—possibly creating plot outlines and constructing battle scenes. Throughout his career, Scudéry also wrote verse of varied subject matter and form. Notable among his poetic works are *Le Cabinet de M. de Scudéry* (1646), a collection of poems based on paintings, both contemporary and ancient, and *Alaric, ou Rome vaincue* (1654), a twelve-volume epic poem on the king of the Visigoths that went through seven editions in Scudéry's lifetime.

CRITICAL RECEPTION

A highly regarded playwright and novelist, Scudéry was a prominent figure in his day. His theatrical pieces were admired by his contemporaries as well as by later critics; Scudéry's most famous play, *L'Amour tyrannique,* won him the respect of Honore de Balzac, who contended that Scudéry was a great poet. Scudéry's plays have continued to be studied by modern critics, such as Henry Carrington Lancaster, who has examined his last tragicomedy, *Le Prince déguisé,* and praised its unity, intrigue, and "spectacular setting." Barbara Matulka has also studied *Le Prince déguisé,* focusing on the possible sources of the play and listing the Spanish novel *Primaleón* (1512) and Juan de Flores's *Historia de Aurelio e Isabella* as primary sources for Scudéry's play. The critic noted that although Scudéry relied heavily on his sources for his plot and themes, he was able to position his play "in a new and clever disguise," thus introducing a sense of novelty to the well-worn themes of his sources. Scudéry's novels have also been the subject of many critical studies. Jerome W. Schweitzer has investigated the influence of Scudéry's works on Samuel Richardson, who is considered by many to be the father of the modern English novel, and on playwright John Dryden, who used *Almahide* as source material for his plays. The authorship question has inevitably played a role in the criticism of Scudéry's novels. Both William Roberts and Schweitzer have contended that Scudéry, not his sister, wrote *Almahide.* Schweitzer also noted the novel's value as "a document of seventeenth-century life" and contended that it is worthy of more praise than it has received. Scudéry's poetry has not been as highly esteemed as his novels and plays. Schweitzer has maintained that much of his poetry is "worthless," contending that "as a poet he was admittedly mediocre except on those rare occasions when inspired by nature or by a sense of history." Scudéry's literary criticism and theoretical works, particularly *Observations sur Le Cid* and his preface to *Ibrahim,* have also been studied by critics for their influence on his contemporaries and later writers.

PRINCIPAL WORKS

Elégie sur l'arrest de Théophile (poetry) 1623

Lygdamon et Lidias; ou, La Ressemblance (play) 1630

Le Trompeur puni; ou, L'Histoire septentrionalde (play) 1631

La Vassal généreux, poème tragi-comique (play) 1632

Orante (play) 1633

Le Temple, poème à la gloire du Roi et de M. le cardinal de Richelieu (poetry) 1633

La Comédie des comédiens, poème de nouvelle invention (play) 1634

Le Fils supposé (play) 1634

Le Prince déguisé (play) 1634

Discours de la France à Mgr le cardinal duc de Richelieu après son retour de Nancy (poetry) 1635

La Mort de César (play) 1635

Didon (play) 1635-36

L'Amant libéral (play) 1636-37

Observations sur Le Cid (criticism) 1637

L'Amour tyrannique (play) 1638

L'Apoligie du théâtre (essay) 1639

Eudoxe (play) 1639

Andromire (play) 1640

Ibrahim; ou, L'Illustre Bassa. 4 vols. [with Madeleine de Scudéry] (novel) 1641

Ibrahim; ou, L'Illustre Bassa (play) 1641-42

Axiane, tragi-comédie en prose (play) 1642-43

Arminius; ou, Les Frères ennemis (play) 1643

Epitaphe sur le Roi Louis XIII (poetry) 1643

L'Ombre du grand Armand (poetry) 1643

Le Cabinet de M. de Scudéry (poetry) 1646

Le Grand Exemple. À Mgr. le duc de Richelieu (poetry) 1647

Poésies diverses (poetry) 1649

Salomon instruisant le Roi, par de Scudéry (poetry) 1651

Artamène; ou, Le Grand Cyrus. 10 vols. [with Madeleine de Scudéry] (novel) 1653-77

Alaric; ou, Rome vaincue, poème héroïque. 12 vols. (poetry) 1653

Clélie, histoire romaine. 10 vols. [with Madeleine de Scudéry] (novel) 1654-60

Ode sur le retour de M. le Prince (poetry) 1660

Almahide; ou, L'Esclave reine. 8 vols. [with Madeleine de Scudéry; unfinished] (novel) 1660-63

Poésies nouvelles (poetry) 1661

Les Femmes illustres; ou, Les Harangues héroïques. 2 vols. (nonfiction) 1642-44

CRITICISM

Henry Carrington Lancaster (essay date 1929)

SOURCE: Lancaster, Henry Carrington. "Tragi-comedy from 1630 to 1634: Tragi-comedies by Scudéry, du Ryer, and Rotrou." In *A History of French Dramatic Literature in the Seventeenth Century. Part I: The Pre-Classical Period, 1610-1634,* Volume II, pp. 472-500. Baltimore: The Johns Hopkins Press, 1929.

[*In following excerpt, Lancaster analyzes Scudéry's tragicomedies, discussing their sources and providing original production information.*]

We come now to three authors who were well known in their century and have preserved a certain amount of celebrity even today, Georges de Scudéry, the soldier, Pierre Du Ryer, the scholar, and Jean Rotrou, the magistrate. Of these the last two had written plays before 1630, while Scudéry made his début probably in this year. His father belonged to a noble family of Provence, but had taken up his residence at Le Havre because of his career as an army officer and administrator. There he married and became in 1601 the father of Georges, of the more famous Madeleine in 1608[1]. After the death of his parents, Georges was apparently brought up by his relatives and served in the army for a number of years, taking part in the affair of the Pas de Suze (March, 1629). He left the regiment of Guards not long after this date and wrote his first play[2], which could hardly have been composed and acted before 1630. His first published work had appeared in 1629[3]. Two years later he brought out **Le Temple,** a poem in honor of Richelieu, and, the following year, published an edition of Théophile's works with a fiery introduction in which he defends this "grand et divin" author. But his literary activity during this decade is largely dramatic. He composed sixteen plays[4] and took a leading part in the attack made upon Corneille's *Cid.* Long before he retired from the stage he was one of the principal dramatists of the day, distinguishing himself in comedy and tragedy as well as in his favorite genre, tragi-comedy. His subsequent collaboration with his sister in the novels that appeared under his name, but for which the chief credit is due to her, is well known. They were both prominent figures in the upper society of their day. Georges became a member of the Academy and was for a number of years Governor of Notre Dame de la Garde at Marseilles. His epic, **Alaric,** appeared in 1654. He died in 1667.

Both by nature and by his life in the army he was fitted for the kind of tragi-comedy, depending chiefly on startling episodes and rapid action, to which he first devoted himself. He began his dramatic career by writing three tragi-comedies based upon the *Astrée.* The first of these, **Ligdamon et Lidias ou la Ressemblance,** was printed in 1631[5] with an introduction in which he defies his critics and defends his action in stooping to write plays, although he is a nobleman and an officer, by citing the example of Julius Caesar[6]!

The subject is one of the most extraordinary episodes of d'Urfé's romance. Plautus could claim for his *Menaechmi* that it was based upon the phenomenon of identical twins, but, as life offers no example of such resemblance elsewhere, d'Urfé's story and Scudéry's imitation of it are as impossible as the marvelous resemblance between brother and sister upon which Shakespeare based his *Twelfth Night.* Like Shakespeare, again, these French authors were interested in writing a romantic love story rather than a Plautine comedy[7].

In his **A qui lit** Scudéry takes the position that when you are dramatizing a fabulous subject, you have the right to change it as you please, then he goes on to excuse himself from obeying the law of the three unities:

> Ie ne suis pas si peu versé dans les regles des anciens Poëtes Grecs et Latins, et dans celles des modernes Espagnols[8] et Italiens, que ie ne sçache bien qu'elles obligent celuy qui compose vn Poëme Epique à le

reduire au terme d'vn an, et le Dramatique en vn iour naturel de vingt-quatre heures, et dans l'vnité d'action et de lieux; mais i'ay voulu me dispenser de ces bornes trop estroites, faisant changer aussi souuent de face à mon Theatre que les Acteurs y changent de lieu; chose qui selon mon sentiment a plus d'esclat que la vieille Comedie.

The freedom here described is, indeed, characteristic of the play. While the greater portion of the plot is based on the *Astrée,* Part I, Bk. XI, and the last scene on Part IV, Bk. XI, the part of the story devoted to the love of Mélandre for Lidias is entirely omitted. The interest is centered chiefly upon Ligdamon and to Silvie is given a larger rôle than she has in the *Astrée,* but the other lovers are not forgotten and appear in all of the acts except the second. Certain scenes are developed and others are added. The events connected with the siege of Marcilly are omitted and the play is brought more promptly to a close by the introduction of Lidias and Silvie into the scene in which their sweethearts are revived. Nevertheless the action remains a double one and its unity is further destroyed by the large rôle given to chance. It takes place at Rouen, in Forez, and on a battle-field in northern France. The time covered is probably several months.

Both the ridiculous and the heroic characteristics of the author are displayed in this tragi-comedy. Nothing can be more absurd than Ligdamon's monologue in which he is seeking a means of committing suicide (I, 1):

> Alons à chef baissé nous abismer dans l'onde;
> Mais la mer pour cela n'est point assez profonde,
> Car à chaque moment mes yeux font des ruisseaux,
> Et ie vy cependant au milieu de ces eaux,
> Ioint que le feu cuisant qui me force à me plaindre
> Ressemble au feu Gregeois que l'eau ne peut esteindre:
> Comme Porcie encor finit ses accidens,
> Essayons de mourir par des charbons ardens;
> Nullement, ce trespas n'a garde de me prendre,
> Car ie suis tout de flame, etc.

Again, in the description of a battle (III, 1) we learn that

> A chaque coup donné sans doute on voyait bas
> Ou la teste, ou la cuisse, ou la iambe, ou le bras;
> L'abondance du sang respandu par la plaine
> Augmenta d'vn ruisseau les ondes de la Seine,
> Et rougit tellement la riuiere en son flus,
> Qu'à l'abord l'Ocean ne la connoissoit plus.

On the other hand such lines as

> Mais vn cœur genereux est maistre de son sort

> (I, 1)

and

> Celuy meurt doublement qui vit sans se vanger

> (II, 1)

would not be out of place in a Cornelian tragedy[9]. Moreover there is a patriotic spirit about the play that is shown not only by the fact that the scene is laid in France and that a French ruler is introduced, but by the following passage with its appeal for unity under a strong king, the kind of unity that Scudéry represented in his own person by his union of Norman and Provençal blood (II, 3):

> Faites donc adorer la puissance Royale
> Des flots de Normandie à la mer Prouençale,
> Et regnant souuerain qu'vn clin d'œil, qu'vne voix
> Fasse courber chacun sous la rigueur des loix.

Scudéry has no objection to killing on the stage, but at times the limits of dramatic art oblige him to make use of *récit* rather than action. For this reason, although a duel had been witnessed by the audience in the first act, the battle is described, not acted (III, 1), and, after the hero has been placed in the lion's enclosure, the fight is related to us by the judges. According to Mahelot, the back stage represented the palace where the trial takes place. On the right is a forest, probably the one in which Silvie speaks her *stances* of lament in III, 2; on the left a temple, used for the marriage ceremony of the last act, and a prison, underneath which is a cave out of which come lions, also a "barriere garnie de ballustres". The lions must, then, have been seen, just as the lion had appeared in Théophile's *Pyrame,* but the fight must have taken place behind the scenes, as its representation before the audience would not have been convincing. This play, like the following, formed a part of the repertory of the Hôtel de Bourgogne. It was performed three times in succession before the court at Fontainebleau, according to the preface to Scudéry's **Arminius.**

Scudéry claims similar success for his second play, **Le Trompeur puny**[10], which formed part of the repertory of the Hôtel de Bourgogne and was played by Floridor's troupe "with better approbation than the other[11]" in the Cockpit Playhouse in Drury Lane, London, on April 4, 1635[12]. It was published early in 1633[13] with a dedication to Mme de Combalet[14], subsequently the Duchess of Aiguillon, a preface by his friend de Chandeville, and complimentary poems from Mairet, Boisrobert, Corneille, Du Ryer, the actor Montdory, etc. Chandeville finds in Scudéry "mieux qu'en aucun autre cet enthousiasme et cette esleuation d'esprit qui a fait appeler la Poésie diuine,[15]" declares that the subject of the play is drawn from the *Astrée* and from *Polexandre,* and mentions *le Vassal généreux* and *la Comédie des comédiens* as soon to appear[16]. The sources indicated by Chandeville have been studied in detail by Batereau, who shows that they are contained in the *Astrée,* Part III, Bk. IV, and in Gomberville's *Polexandre,* Part II, Bk. IV, pp. 770-833 (ed. of 1637). Scudéry probably began with the *Astrée*[17], but, finding the material insufficient, added to it from the other novel. The first three acts follow the *Astrée* closely enough, except for the change of names and the addition of the villain's death. Two scenes (I, 5, and III, 2) are added to prepare for the second part of the plot, which is contained chiefly in the last two acts. Here the location in Denmark, the rescue of Alcandre, and the tournament are suggested by Gomberville. Not only the names, but the incidents are considerably altered, notably in respect to the termination.

Scudéry has, in short, used Gomberville merely to complete a plot derived from another novelist.

The play lacks unity in a different way from *Ligdamon,* for its two plots are no longer parallel, but one follows the other. The scene is laid in England and in Denmark and probably represents a period of several months. The language is somewhat less rhetorical and the incidents not quite so extraordinary as in the earlier play. Batereau calls attention to a conversation in every-day language between Nérée and her aunt (I, 6) and to a comic monologue of the keeper of the inn at which the hero finds lodging in Denmark (IV, 5):

> Apres auoir traisné quatorze ans vne gaine
> Auec peu de profit, auec beaucoup de peine,
> Enfin espouuentail ie fais peur aux corbeaux . . .

He omits, however, some of the most interesting lines:

> Apres auoir passé par les degrez d'honneur,
> Goüjat, Fiffre, Tambour, Viuandier sans bon-heur . . .
> Non, non, contentons nous, nostre auenture est belle,
> Vne Table, vn Chaslit, vn Banc, vne Scabelle,
> Quatre Plats, deux Linceuls, vn muid de Vin clairet,
> Ne suffisent-ils pas à tenir Cabaret?
> Heureux celuy qui craind aussi peu qu'il espere
> Mesurant sa fortune à celle de son pere,
> Esueillé chaque iour (pour empoigner le soc)
> Par l'horloge reglé de la voix de son Cocq[18] . . .

We learn from Mahelot that on the stage he was known as Capitaine l'Ormeau. We have already seen an innkeeper's rôle made humorous by Mairet in *Chryséide.* Here there seems to be the influence of the picaresque novel and also of life, for Scudéry had doubtless seen veterans established as keepers of inns. It is unfortunate that he did not give the rôle more importance in his play.

The **Trompeur puny** contains two examples of *stances* (II, 3 and V, 1), a letter in prose (II, 5), and a sonnet (III, 6). There is a conflict between love and friendship, insufficiently developed, which makes the hero cry (V, 3):

> Riual que ie cheris
> Que ne peut vne fille espouser deux maris.

The belief in monarchy that we have seen expressed in *Ligdamon* is found here (V, 4):

> Pour iuger des Rois, il faut estre des Dieux.

But apparently this maxim does not hold if the king is not your own sovereign, for the hero promises to be so little mindful of respect for a royal presence that he will find his rival in Denmark (III, 10)

> Et là, dessus le Thrône, osant se prendre à moy,
> Ie le poignarderay dans les bras de son Roy.

The stage setting given by Mahelot helps to explain the play. In the background is seen a house with two doors side by side, where the trick is played upon the hero. Next to this, on the right, is the garden of the King of England. Evidently the villain enters one of the doors and reappears within the garden when the hero has departed. The hero's room is on the right, near the front of the stage, separated from the palace by the garden. In it are seen a table, two seats, a writing-desk with books, paper, pens, and ink. On the left, opposite this room, is the palace of the King of Denmark and next it is the inn with the sign "L'Ormeau". The sea is also represented, though it is not shown in the drawing. It must be visible in IV, 3, when Arsidor lands on the coast of Denmark, and probably was represented by a curtain or a piece of movable scenery, which replaced one of the other decorations.

Scudéry's **Vassal généreux** will be discussed under the next heading, for it is built too much round an idea to be considered a typical tragi-comedy. It was followed by his **Comédie des comédiens,** which belongs in the next chapter. After this realistic play, it is not surprising to find that his next tragi-comedy, **Orante,** is nearer than the preceding ones to ordinary life. The author notes this fact himself in the preface to his **Arminius** and attributes to it the play's success: "ie repris le ton ordinaire dans mon Orante: et par elle, ie tirai cent et cent fois des larmes, non seulement des yeux du Peuple, mais des plus beaux yeux du monde." It was probably acted as early as 1633, by Montdory's troupe, rather than by that of the Hôtel de Bourgogne, for it is not mentioned by Mahelot. It was published in 1635[19] with a dedication to the Duchess of Longueville.

It is the fourth play that Scudéry extracted from the *Astrée.* Batereau has shown that it is taken from the seventh book of the third part, which concerns the early portion of the history of Chryséide and Arimant, before the episode that Mairet had treated in 1625. Batereau finds few changes except in the last act and even notes certain close verbal resemblances. The location of the play and the names of the persons are altered. The villain becomes an old man and the author makes changes necessitated by the dramatic and poetic form the story has received[20]. Although the action is practically unified and there is a brief struggle in the hero's soul (V, 1), the play shows no conversion to classicism, for the action, which covers many days, takes place both in Naples and Pisa and there is killing on the stage. The important rôle assigned the heroine's mother is somewhat unusual at this time. There is a good deal of metrical variety, manifested by two examples of *stances* (I, 5, II, 2), a sonnet (I, 1), three letters (II, 3, 8, III, 2), and a challenge (V, 1). Batereau suggests as a source for the following verses (III, 7):

> Ordonnez-luy de mettre Osse sur Pelion.
> I'attaqueray le ciel et dans cette escalade
> Ie seray plus heureux que ne fut Encelade.
> Si ces lambris d'azur peuuent plaire à vos yeux,
> I'oseray vous placer dans le throsne des cieux,

lines 184, 197-200 from Hardy's *Gigantomachie,* which show a striking resemblance both in thought and rime:

> Or sus venez enter Osse sur Pelion . . .
> Ma dextre suffiroit, ouy le seul Encelade
> Hardy peut emporter l'Olympe d'escalade,
> Son farouche regard met en fuite les Dieux,
> Et ne pretends borner mon Empire des Cieux.

Another passage (V, 9) resembles in thought, if not in form, the *qu'il mourût* of *Horace*:

> Qu'il reuienne vainqueur, ou qu'il reste vaincu,
> Ie desire qu'il meure ainsi qu'il a vescu.

Another Cornelian line is found in I, 5:

> La mort n'est point vn mal, à qui la connoist bien.

On the other hand, less heroic sentiments, inspired by existing situations in Italy and in France are expressed by these two passages:

> La haine hereditaire (execrable folie,
> Qui semble estre fatale à toute l'Italie).
>
> (V, 3)

> O dangereux voisins, temeraires Gaulois,
> Dont les mauuaises mœurs ont peruerty nos loix,
> Que par vous mon esprit souffre vne peine amere,
> Suiuant ce point d'honneur qui n'est qu'vne chimere.
>
> (V, 1)

Scudéry's last tragi-comedy of this period possesses somewhat the same stuctural qualities as those we have just noted, but is characterized by greater unity, a more exciting intrigue, and a more spectacular setting. **The Prince Déguisé** was probably first acted in 1634. According to the author's preface to his **Arminius,** it met with extraordinary success:

> Iamais ouurage de cette sorte n'eut plus de bruit; et iamais chose violente n'eut plus de durée, tous les hommes suiuoient cette Piece, par tout où elle se representoit; toutes les Dames en sçauoient les Stances par cœur; et il se trouue mesme encor auiourd'hui [in 1643] mille honnestes gens qui soûtiennent que ie n'ay iamais rien fait de plus beau.

He had previously noted, when he published his play[21], "le superbe appareil de la Scene, la face du Theatre, qui change cinq ou six fois entierement, à la représentation de ce Poëme, la magnificence des habits, l'excellence des Comediens," as contributory causes of its popularity[22]. It has, indeed, many qualities that won for it deservedly the honor of being designated[23] with Du Ryer's *Cléomédon* as giving a typical example of a play with a "belle intrigue"[24].

Batereau was unable to discover the source of this play. M. Reynier[25] holds that it was the *Jugement d'Amour,* otherwise known as the *Histoire d'Aurelio et d'Isabelle,* a Spanish novel by Juan de Flores that appeared at the end of the fifteenth century and was often translated into French and Italian during the sixteenth. Indeed this novel does appear to have inspired the main portion of the play, the arrest of the lovers, the law that the first offender should be burned, the contest in generosity between the lovers, and the thought of suicide on the part of each, but, as the first three acts of the play and the dénouement are largely free from such influence, it is clear that Scudéry got a good deal of material from other sources, more especially, it seems to me, from his favorite source-book, the *Astrée*[26], where he could find parallels for the fact that the hero is a Gaulois, for the snoring *gouvernante* (III, 5), the bribing of the jailer, the heroine's escape from prison by the help of an attendant who takes her place, and the claiming of a reward for offering up one's self as a criminal. These episodes he might have found elsewhere, but, as his four previous tragi-comedies had been based on the *Astrée,* and as in one of these he had drawn his story partly from that novel, partly from another, it is reasonable to suppose that in the **Prince déguisé** he again used "contamination", taking his episodes partly from d'Urfé and partly from Flores[27]. In spirit, however, it is much more like the *Astrée,* for the *Jugement d'Amour* is primarily concerned with the debate as to whether, in a case of seduction, the man or the woman is more to blame, its ending is tragic, and its tone brutal, while Scudéry, like d'Urfé, is most interested in writing a good story, in emphasizing the self-sacrificing love of the chief characters, and in bringing his plot to a happy termination.

The structure possesses real rather than formal unity. The action covers ten days and takes place in several localities in the city of Palermo. The efforts of the hero's friends to rescue him have no effect upon the action, but take up so small a part of the play that they violate its unity little. The events preceding the arrival of the hero at Palermo are told in a lengthy *récit*[28], after which the action moves rapidly from that point to the dénouement. It furnishes a good example of the tendency towards a well constructed plot even among those who had not yet accepted Mairet's formulae.

The spectacular elements include the temple ceremony before a large number of people, the garden scenes in which the hero goes through a magic ceremony and digs up a cup and jewels he pretends to have discovered, the use of night and moonlight, the judicial contest between the lovers, disguised by their armor. The hero recites *stances* to the heroine[29]. Scudéry makes use of such familiar romantic devices as disguise, recognition, and overheard conversation. The self-sacrificing conflict between the two lovers must have added to the play's attractions. There is also a conflict in the mind of the gardener's wife (II, 3) and in that of the queen (IV, 7):

> Ie suis Reine, il est vray; mais pourtant ie suis mere
> Et de quelque discours que ie flatte mon dueil,
> Ie songe à son berceau pensant à son cercueil.
> Hélas! ie n'en puis plus, en vain ie m'éuertüe
> Fille, ie t'ay faict naistre, et ta faute me tuë.

The queen finds herself in another difficult situation when she discovers that the man her daughter loves is the prince she holds guilty of her husband's death. Nobody seems to have noticed that the situation is here remarkably like that of Chimène in the *Cid,* a fact that is the more striking as, only a few years later, Scudéry was to criticize Corneille because his heroine does not refuse to marry her father's slayer. Argire, it is true, seeks to kill herself, saying (V, 8):

> Vn nom me faict horreur dont i'aime la personne,

but when her mother consents to her marriage, she shows no further hesitation in the matter. Her father, too, had not been poisoned by Cléarque, but neither she nor her mother had any proof of the hero's innocence, and at any rate the king's death had been caused by the war which was begun on account of Cléarque. The queen and her daughter agree to the marriage, while Chimène merely leaves us to understand that she will marry Rodrigue a year later. Scudéry was evidently criticizing Corneille for a situation for which he had himself furnished a model, much as Mairet criticized him for imitating a Spanish play when he had himself just made an adaptation of an Italian tragedy.

Notes

1. The best account of Georges de Scudéry's life, with abundant biographical references and elaborate analyses of his plays, is found in A. Batereau's *Georges de Scudéry als Dramatiker,* Leipzig, Emil Stephan, 1902. It should be supplemented by the frequent references to this author in Lachèvre's *Bib. Rec.* and *Rec. Lib.*

2. "Ligdamon que je fis en sortant du Régiment des Gardes, et dans ma premiere jeunesse", *Au Lecteur* to his *Arminius.*

3. A *sixain* to the Archbishop of Aix in the *Ostreomyomachie,* a collection of poems by various authors published at Toulouse by S. David in 1629.

4. This is a list of them with the most probable dates of the first performance of each: *Ligdamon et Lidias* (early in 1630), *le Trompeur puny* (1631), *le Vassal généreux* (1632), *la Comédie des comédiens* (1632), *Orante* (1633), *le Fils supposé* (1634), *le Prince déguisé* (1634), *la Mort de César* (early in 1635), *Didon* (end of 1635 or early in 1636), *l'Amant libéral* (1636 or first half of 1637), *l'Amour tyrannique* (1638), *Eudoxe* (1639), *Andromire* (1640), *Ibrahim* (end of 1641 or 1642), *Arminius* (written in 1642 or 1643, but not acted before the end of 1643), *Axiane* (end of 1643). These dates are determined partly by the time of printing, partly by the following considerations: the first was composed after he left the army; the third and fourth are mentioned in the preface to the second; the *Gazette* states that the fourth was played on Nov. 28, 1634; the fifth, sixth and seventh are mentioned in the preface to the fourth; the *Mort de César* was in its third act when La Pinelière's *Parnasse* (1635) was prepared for publication and before April 3, 1635, when reference is made to it by Guez de Balzac; Scudéry was at work on *Didon* when he wrote the preface to the *Comédie des comédiens,* printed April 10, 1635; *l'Amant libéral* is mentioned

during the controversy over the *Cid. L'Amour tyrannique* probably followed the *Sentiments de l'Académie sur le Cid; Eudoxe* preceded *Andromire,* which was Scudéry's thirteenth play; *L'illustre Bassa* was not written till after *Andromire* was published; the last two plays had not been acted when the preface to *Arminius* was written. This last document is especially important, as Scudéry gives in it the names of his previous plays and the order in which he had composed them. These dates differ considerably from those given by Batereau, whose usually reliable book is marred in respect to dates of acting by his pathetic confidence in the frères Parfaict.

5. Paris, Targa, 8°; *priv.,* July 17, *achevé,* Sept. 18. It is dedicated to the duc de Montmorency and accompanied by complimentary verses from Hardy, Corneille, Du Ryer, Rotrou, Scarron, and others.

6. The absurdity of this preface did not escape Scudéry's enemies. Cf. A. Gasté, *la Querelle du Cid,* Paris, Welter, 1898, p.148: "Vous ne vous estes pas souvenu que vous avez mis un *A qui lit,* au devant de Ligdamon, ny des autres chaleurs Poëtiques et militaires, qui font rire le lecteur, presques dans tous vos livres".

7. Ligdamon et Lidias live in different parts of France and do not meet until the end of Scudéry's play. The former, unable to get from Silvie an admission of love, attempts suicide, but is persuaded to try war instead and joins the Frankish army. He kills a stranger, Nicandre, who had challenged him to a duel for killing his cousin, of whom Ligdamon had never heard. After being captured in battle, he is accused of murdering Nicandre, of fighting against his country, and of denying that he is named Lidias. For these offences he is condemned to be thrown into the *parc aux lions,* but, permitted to use a sword, he kills a lion and is rescued by a girl named Amerine on condition that she be allowed to marry him. This she is glad to do, since she takes him for her lover, Lidias, who had fled to Forez after killing a man in a duel. As Ligdamon is resolved to die rather than to be unfaithful to Silvie, he sends his attendant to a physician for poison and when he reaches the point in the ceremony where he is to drink from the holy cup, swallows what the physician has sent and, after explaining his motives, falls unconscious. Amerine also swoons. An epitaph is prepared for the couple, but Lidias and Silvie, who have met in Forez, where she mistook him for Ligdamon, enter the temple and their sorrow is turned into joy by the physician, who explains that the supposed poison is only a sleeping-potion.

8. Scudéry could have read neither Spanish plays nor Lope's *Arte nuevo de hacer comedias* when he wrote this. Even the Spanish classical critics were so free in their interpretation of the unities that he must have been ignorant of them also; cf. René Bray, *la Formation de la doctrine classique en France,* Paris, Hachette, 1927, pp. 28, 29.

9. Magendie, Maurice, *Du nouveau sur l'Astrée,* Paris, 1927, p. 444, compares two passages to lines in *Polyeucte.*

10. For its possible influence on *Isolite,* cf. my study of that play.

11. Either Corneille's *Mélite* or Du Rocher's *Mélize.*

12. Cf. J. P. Collier, *History of English Dramatic poetry,* London, 1831, II, 67.

13. Paris, Pierre Billaine, 80; *priv.,* Dec. 18, 1632, *achevé,* Jan. 4, 1633. It was reprinted by Sommaville in 1634 and 1635.

14. Richelieu's niece. Scudéry dedicated his first play to Montmorency, whom Richelieu had beheaded only a few months before the *Trompeur puny* was published. Evidently his loyalty to Théophile did not extend to the latter's protector.

15. Cf. Batereau, *op. cit.,* p. 46.

16. This means, of course, that they were soon to appear in print and shows that they had probably been played by this time, though Batereau dates the latter 1634.

17. Unable to win Nérée, Cléonte tells his rival, Arsidor, that he is to spend the night with her and that he may see him enter her house. He leads him to the door and goes in, but passes the night in the palace garden. Next, Cléonte gets Arsidor to write for him a letter thanking a woman for granting her favors to the king, but instead of giving it to the latter he shows it to Nérée. Each of the lovers is thus brought by Cléonte to believe the other faithless, but when they meet, they exculpate themselves easily, for Nérée had not been at home on the night that Cléonte entered her house and Arsidor explains how he came to write the letter. As the hero kills Cléonte in a duel, the play would end with the third act, except that the author has introduced the new element from *Polexandre,* namely, that the heroine's hand has been promised by the King of England to Alcandre, a favorite of the King of Denmark. It is to the latter country that Arsidor flees after his duel and there he saves Alcandre from three men who have attacked him. They become good friends and agree to fight each other for Nérée. Alcandre falls. Arisdor bids him rise and continue the fight, but Alcandre, touched by this generosity, gives up Nérée, who has come to Denmark and will remain there with Arsidor unless their pardon is obtained from the King of England.

A long quotation from the play is given in the *Bib. du th. fr.,* II, 116, 117.

18. Cf. with this last line the couplet cited above, p. 271, from La Morello, *Endymion,* IV, 3.

19. Paris, Courbé, 80; also 1636; *priv.,* June 30, *achevé,* Sept. 1, 1635.

20. Isimandre, son of the Governor of Naples, and Orante are in love, but the latter's mother objects to their marriage on account of the hostility that exists

between the two families and takes her daughter to the home of her relative, Ormin, Governor of Pisa, who plans to marry the girl to Florange, a wealthy old man, and then, although he is married himself, make her his mistress. Orante, however, resists, and, as she has been bled for a fever, tears off the bandage, writes a note with her blood to her lover, and falls to the ground. Ormin is so moved that he promises her she shall not marry Florange. Meanwhile Isimandre, who had thought of killing himself when he heard of her death, now learns the truth, disguises himself as a merchant, gets an interview with Orante, and persuades her to fly with him. Attacked by Florange, Isimandre wounds, but spares him, and the lovers escape to Naples. Ormin follows and challenges the hero to a duel, but when the latter reaches the appointed place, he sees Ormin attacked by two bandits and by Florange, who holds Ormin responsible for breaking off his marriage. Isimandre kills the old man and puts the ruffians to flight. In gratitude for this, Ormin allows Orante to be married to her lover, and returns to his wife.

21. Paris, Courbé, 1636, 80; *priv.,* Aug. 11, 1635, *achevé,* Sept. 1, 1635. It is dedicated to Mlle de Bourbon. Tallemant des Réaux declares this to have been the piece that Richelieu ordered to be played for his amusement by young Jacqueline Pascal, but he must have confused it with Scudéry's *Amour tyrannique,* the play designated by Mme Périer and one that was a more recent production when the performance was given in February, 1639. Cf. Tallemant, *op. cit.,* IV, 119, 122.

22. It is among the plays mentioned in Poisson's *Baron de la Crasse* as forming part of provincial repertories as late as 1662.

23. Cf. the abbé d'Aubignac, *op. cit.,* p. 67.

24. In order to win the hand of Argire, a Sicilian princess, Cléarque, son of the King of Naples, must win her affection and overcome her mother's belief that he had poisoned the late king, her father, who had died at the court of Naples after he had been captured in battle. The war had been begun in order to force this King of Sicily to give his daughter to Cléarque, but now the latter has caused the fighting to cease while he makes use of another method. In disguise he reaches the Sicilian court and is present in the temple when Argire's mother, Queen Rosemonde, swears to give her daughter's hand to anyone who will bring her Cléarque's head. Then he bribes the gardener to take him as his assistant and thus succeeds in meeting Argire and gaining her love, but he also infatuates the gardener's wife, who, to avenge herself for his cold reception of her advances, listens to his conversations with Argire and reports their love to the queen. The lovers are arrested and the law is read declaring that the one who first showed love must be burned. Each claims to be guilty and the decision is left to a judicial contest. Cléarque bribes his jailer

and goes to fight for Argire, who, leaving her *fille d'honneur* to take her place, also puts on armor and meets Cléarque in the lists. The fight leads to a double recognition. Cléarque reveals his identity and demands the hand of Argire as a reward for bringing his head to the queen. Rosemonde hesitates, but the efforts of the lovers to commit suicide move her so much that she finally consents to their union.

25. *Le Roman sentimental avant l'Astrée,* Paris, A. Colin, 1908, pp. 76-86.

26. Episodes of Chryséide and of Lidias. The queen's offer of Argire's hand may come from *la Fidelle tromperie,* or its source, the *Amadis.*

27. M. Martinenche, *la Comedia espagnole,* p. 155, notes a resemblance between the gardener scene and scenes in Lope's *No son todos ruiseñores* and his *Ramilletes de Madrid.* As the first of these was not published until 1635, it could not have influenced the *Prince déguisé.* The resemblance to the other play amounts to little more than the fact that in each the hero is disguised as a gardener. *La ley ejecutada,* attributed to Lope, descends from the novel of Juan de Flores, but gives no evidence of having been imitated by Scudéry.

28. While condemning lengthy narratives in general, the abbé d'Aubignac (*op. cit.,* p. 295) admits that they are not utterly "insupportables" at the beginning of a play, for which reason the description of the tempest in the first act of the *Prince déguisé* "a passé pour bonne, quoy qu'elle soit trop chargée de paroles". Indeed the speech that contains it occupies 6½ pages. In his edition of the *Pratique du théâtre,* M. Martino notes that Scudéry describes a naval battle, not a tempest.

29. For the text of these verses cf. *Bib. du th. fr.,* II, 122, 123.

Barbara Matulka (essay date 1931)

SOURCE: Matulka, Barbara. "The Influence of the *Grisel y Mirabella* in France: Scudéry: *Le Prince Déguisé.*" In *The Novels of Juan de Flores and Their European Diffusion: A Study in Comparative Literature,* pp. 203-11. New York: Institute of French Studies, 1931.

[*In the excerpt below, Matulka argues that while* Le Prince déguisé *is indebted to Flores's* Historia de Aurelio e Isabella, *for its principal themes, the play incorporates elements from a number of other sources as well.*]

The principal influence in France of Juan de Flores' *Historia de Aurelio e Isabella* is found in Scudéry's **Le Prince Déguisé**.[1] In a general way this connection has been noted by scholars,[2] but the exact relation of Scudéry's tragicomedy to its Spanish, as well as to its other sources, has been only lately investigated. For the purposes of the present study, we shall condense here the conclusions at which we arrived in a previous publication.[3]

Clearque, son of the King of Naples, had wandered over Europe disguised as a knight, to study statecraft. During these travels he fell in love with Argenie, the fair daughter of the King of Sicily, and asked his father's consent to marry her. His father was pleased at his choice and sent an embassy to Argenie's father. But, for some unknown reason, the King of Sicily rejected the suit. In order to avenge himself therefore, Clearque's father declared war on him, won the victory after a long and terrible battle, and took his royal enemy prisoner. The King of Sicily died heart-broken at this defeat, but a rumor spread that Clearque had poisoned him. The widowed Queen then proclaimed that she would not rest until Clearque had been killed, and promised Argenie's hand to any man who brought her the Prince's head.

Clearque could not forget the beautiful Princess. He disguised himself as a gardener's helper, calling himself Policandre, and offered to serve the Queen's gardener, telling him that he was versed in the magic arts, that he knew of some treasures hidden in the royal gardens, and would share these if he would but be allowed the leisure to unearth them. Now, the Princess, who often walked in the royal garden, met the disguised Clearque, was astonished at his courtly bearing, and learned to love him.

In the meanwhile, however, the wife of the gardener, called Melanire, fell in love with Clearque and made advances to him. But when he only spurned her, she decided to avenge her unrequited love, and spied upon him. As soon as she had learned his secret,—his amorous meetings with the Princess,—she betrayed it to the Queen. Here then, for the first time, Scudéry drew upon the Spanish novelette, but in the following scenes he imitated his model closely. The Queen was greatly perplexed, for a severe law of the Kingdom forbad the Princess to love anyone but a prince worthy of her. The law read very much like that of Juan de Flores:

> Lors qu'un Roy sera pris de la Parque meurtrière,
> S'il ne laisse en mourant qu'une fille heritière,
> Nous voulons que la vefve ait tousjours en la main,
> Le Sceptre qui luy donne, un pouvoir souverain,
> Jusqu'à tant que l'Himen achevant sa tutelle,
> Mette dedans le Throsne un Prince digne d'elle.[4]

and continued:[5]

> Des amans, qui le premier aura
> Monstré la sale ardeur qu'il nourrissoit en l'ame,
> Afin de le punir, qu'il meure dans la flame.

The lovers then engaged in a long combat of generosity, each trying to assume all the blame in order to spare the other's life, just as the faithful lovers had done in *Aurelio e Isabella*. But here Scudéry departed from his Spanish source, and rather turned to the related episode of Ginevra

in Ariosto's *Orlando Furioso*. For, instead of settling this dilemma as to which of the lovers was the more guilty by a debate on the merits and defects of women, he adopted the *dénouement* of the law theme as found in Ariosto, and settled it by a tourney,—a solution common enough in the plays of the period. The law included this provision:[6]

> S'il arrive parfois que la force d'amour,
> Oppose aux yeux de tous l'espoisseur d'une nuë,
> Et que la verité ne soit pas bien connuë,
> Qu'ils soustiennent tous deux avoir premier peché,
> Pour connoistre l'autheur de ce crime caché;
> Nous voulons en ce cas, que le combat le preuve;
> Et leur donnons huict jours, à dessein qu'il se treuve
> Suivant le cry public, et faict en chaque endroit,
> Un guerrier qui defende, et conserve leur droit;
> Afin que le vainqueur descouvrant le coupable,
> Rende par sa valeur, nostre arrest equitable.
> Que si l'un d'eux en manque, et que l'autre en ait un,
> Nous defendons de faire, un chastiment commun,
> Voulons que l'assisté s'exempte du supplice,
> Mais que n'en ayant point, l'un et l'autre perisse.

The lovers were imprisoned, but managed, without the other's knowledge, to escape. Each one came armed to champion the other's cause, for thus he found a means of saving his beloved's life. They joined in combat, but of course Clearque, who had come as the champion of Argenie, overcame his adversary, who turned out to be no other than his lady. He thus saved Argenie's life and forfeited his own. But still Agenie refused to yield, insisting that *she* was the more guilty. Clearque therefore asked the Queen to fulfill her vow of giving Argenie's hand to the man who brought her the head of her enemy. He revealed that he was that "odieux" Clearque, and added that he demanded nothing but the life of Argenie, for he was willing to die even though he was innocent of the crime imputed to him. The Queen was touched by the nobility of these two great souls and pardoned them by condemning the fictitious Policandre (the name Clearque had used while disguised) to die, and permitting the living lover to marry her daughter.

* * *

It is evident, from this brief outline of the plot of *Le Prince Déguisé,* that Scudéry drew freely upon Juan de Flores' novel for his tragi-comedy. At the same time, however, he added many episodes from other works, and resorted to the storehouse of commonplace motives upon which many seventeenth century dramatists drew, so that his work resulted very different in tonality and intent from the tragic novel which had afforded him his point of departure. From the novel of Juan de Flores he derived his principal themes, which he embellished by grafting on them other romanesque incidents. There he found the "Law" with all the provisions Juan de Flores had introduced, and reproduced it with striking similarity,[7] though modifying the *dénouement*. In the *Prince Déguisé,* it decrees, as we have already seen, that whichever of the lovers had been the first to give signs of the base passion which he harbored,—that one was to die in the flames as a punishment for his wickedness.

The Law of the Spanish text is much like it:

> Y las leyes de su reyno mandauan que qualquiere que
> en tal yerro cayesse, el que más causa fuesse al otro de
> hauer amado, que padeciesse muerte, y el otro destyerro
> para toda su vida.

THE COMBAT OF GENEROSITY

After the reading of the law, there follows in both Juan de Flores and Scudéry a combat of generosity between the two lovers, each of whom tries to assume the greater guilt in order to spare the other's life. This episode in the play is again remarkably similar to that in the novel, although Scudéry may have borrowed details from the numerous other works in which a similar combat of generosity occurs and which he in all probability knew, since this was one of the most common themes in the literature of Europe and of France.[8]

While Scudéry's debt to Juan de Flores cannot be denied, since from him he took the central situation of his romanesque play, nevertheless this was not his only borrowing. Almost every episode had been used time and again before him, while others, like the "Law" and the "Combat of Generosity", although more striking and original,— pointing rather to a single source in Juan de Flores,— nevertheless added details from other works. For example, the stock themes that Scudéry employed were numerous: the disguise of the hero and heroine, a prince who wanders incognito from land to land in order to school himself in the art of ruling and who finally falls in love with a beautiful princess, or again, and slightly more unusual, the theme of the declaration of war on the father who refuses to permit his daughter to marry the prince.

THE CID THEME

These literary commonplaces he may have borrowed from any number of sources, for they were the indispensable ingredients of fairy tales, popular stories, and even elegant fiction. But he introduced still more significant changes which transformed the bare and somber plot of Juan de Flores into a pleasing romanesque *imbroglio,* full of movement, grace and gallantry. The chief modification by which he effected this change was by weaving into the simple groundwork supplied by Juan de Flores, the Cid theme. In this tradition the knight finds himself obliged to kill the father of his beloved; upon the lady, then, falls the duty of avenging her father's death, and therefore she persecutes her enemy; he wins her love by his valor, and finally marries the lady who had sought his death. This simple theme was embellished with certain courtly motives which had already been gathered together in the *Florisel de Niquea* romance of the *Amadís.*[9] the *head-motive,* in which the heroine promises to give her hand in marriage to the champion who brings her the head of her enemy; the *love versus revenge* theme, in which the lady continually struggles between the love she bears her enemy, and her duty of revenge; the *sword-motive,* in which the hero, no longer able to suffer the enmity of his beloved, offers her

his sword, begging her to take his life rather than make him suffer longer; and finally the *living-head motive,* in which the head of the enemy is indeed brought to the heroine but not cut off as she had expected, but living, and on the shoulders of the man whose death she had sought.

In the **Prince Déguisé** the whole primary story is introduced, somewhat modified, and all the motives added by the current represented by the *Florisel de Niquea* romance except the sword-motive. Yet in using this elaborated Cid theme, Scudéry was again merely following traditional paths.[10] Indeed, Scudéry's head-motive perhaps follows the *Florisel de Niquea* more closely than any other work which makes use of this plot. In **Le Prince Déguisé,** it is the mother, Rosemonde, who offers her daughter's hand in marriage to any man who brings her the head of Clearque, just as Queen Sidonia, in the *Florisel de Niquea,* offers her daughter's hand to any knight who avenges her honor.[11]

THE CHARLATAN-NOBLEMAN THEME

The disguise of a prince into a gardener and the situations which this brought about were derived from still another source. Such a gardener or other humble laborer was certainly no novelty on the early seventeenth century stage, but when Scudéry combined Clearque's disguise with a feigned knowledge of the magic arts, he intimated that he had followed a more specific example. This theme had won great popularity through a play of Ariosto, *Il Negromante,* first staged in 1530, in which the hero is also a "Charlatan" who pretends to be initiated in black magic.[12]

But while Scudéry may have known Ariosto's comedy, his work offers a closer parallel to several episodes of the *Francion* of Sorel.[13] This novel contains two episodes which Scudéry may have welded together in order to evolve his gardener Policandre incident: the episode of a charlatan called upon to render service by means of his magic arts, and that of a nobleman who disguises himself as a lowly shepherd in order to win the favor of a lady, and does succeed, in spite of his supposedly humble station, by his courtly graces. There are several other episodes in **Le Prince Déguisé** which are duplicated in the novel. Thus the comic fright of the gullible gardener on hearing invocations of the devil, etc., is strikingly similar to the scene of the necromancer in the *Francion.* Moreover, just as Francion unwittingly inflamed the passion of his employer's wife, so Clearque aroused the love of Melanire, the wife of the Queen's gardener. Both women became suspicious when their advances were rejected, for they could not understand why their favor should not be deemed an honor by such humble servants. Scudéry combined the resulting jealousy with the rôle of the serving maid in Juan de Flores, and had her betray the Princess' secret to the Queen.[14]

THE TOURNAMENT

After the combat of generosity, Scudéry switched from Juan de Flores in order to give a different *dénouement* to the law theme. Instead of introducing a long debate on the relative merits and defects of men and women, Scudéry adopted a solution similar to that of the Ginevra episode of the *Orlando Furioso,* and settled his law by a tournament, one of the most popular literary themes of his day. A provision had been prepared, granting each of the lovers a week in which to find a champion to fight in his behalf. This law reads in the *Orlando Furioso*:

> L'aspra legge di Scozia, empia e severa,
> Vuol ch'ogni donna, e di ciascuna sorte,
> Ch'ad uom si giunga e non gli sia mogliera,
> S'accusata ne viene, abbia la morte
> Ne riparar si puo ch'ella non pera,
> Quando per lei non venga un guerrier forte
> Che tolga la difesa, e che sostegna
> Che sia innocente e di morire indegna.

Similarly in Scudéry:

> Nous voulons en ce cas, que le combat le preuve;
> Et leur donnons huict jours, a dessein qu'il se treuve
> Suivant le cry public, et faict en chaque endroit,
> Un guerrier qui defende, et conserve leur droit;
> Afin que le vainqueur descouvrant le coupable,
> Rende par sa valeur, nostre arrest equitable . . .

If only one finds a champion, he will be pardoned and the other put to death; but if neither, both will lose their lives. Here, however, Scudéry embellished still further the combat which takes place in the Ginevra story. Whereas in the epic Ariodante, the lover, comes in disguise to champion his lady's cause, he does not fight Ginevra herself, while Scudéry, on the other hand, used the tourney as a continuation of the combat of generosity, having the lovers fight each other in disguise. Each succeeded in escaping from prison without the other's knowledge, and offered to champion the other's cause, hoping thus to be able to spare the life of his beloved.[15]

The conclusion is scarcely more original than the themes already discussed. Scudéry had but to join neatly each of the threads he had left unravelled. Clearque made a last effort to save Argenie's life,—he reminded the Queen of her promise to grant Argenie's hand to the man who brought her the head of Clearque, and then confessed that he was the "hateful though innocent" prince whose death she had been seeking. He begged as a reward,—not the hand of Argenie, but her life. This motive of the living-head, as pointed out above, was an embellishment of the *Cid* tradition by the *Florisel de Niquea* romance. From the same tradition was suggested Argenie's attempt to kill herself when she heard that the man she loved was no other than the reputed murderer of her father. The Queen, touched by their nobility and faithfulness, absolved the guilty lovers with the merciful gesture so often bestowed upon sovereigns. She kept the vow she had made to her husband's shade by condemning to death the fictitious Policandre (the name Clearque had used while disguised as a gardener) and granting Clearque his lady, thus through the marriage of Argenie to the prince, uniting the two warring countries in a perpetual peace.

* * *

It is evident, therefore, that from Juan de Flores, Scudéry derived: the characters of the faithful lovers, the suggestion of their betrayal, their imprisonment, the law theme, and the combat of generosity. To these fundamental themes he added various episodes that reproduce scenes found in innumerable plays: the swift change of scene, the quick succession of incidents, the disguise of a prince and princess, a tourney between lovers, etc. Other contributions were drawn from the tradition of the *Cid* theme as embellished in the *Florisel de Niquea* romance: the offering of the lady's hand to any man who brings her the head of her enemy as vengeance; the love of the heroine for this supposed enemy, the romanesque turn by which this very man offers his own living head as a price for the displeasure he has caused his beloved, and finally the reconciliation of the steadfast lovers. The comic elements, which readily suggest the favorite farcical scenes of the Italian theatre: the credulous and avaricious gardener, the treasure-digging, humorous invocations of spirits, etc.,—are strongly reminiscent of the *Francion.* Moreover his *dénouement* switches to the Ariosto development, for the law is solved by a tournament, instead of a suicide of the lovers as in Juan de Flores.

Thus, while the *Aurelio e Isabella* was no doubt the starting point of his "belle intrigue", Scudéry combined it with so many other themes, and so modified its tragic, sombre solemnity in his efforts to make a charming playlet, that the influence of Juan de Flores recedes into the background leaving **Le Prince Déguisé** but another of those pleasing romanesque tragi-comedies that delighted the gentle ladies of the court, and taught the gallant gentlemen the rôle to play in pursuing their amatory quests.

Notes

1. This play was granted a *Privilège* on August 11, 1635, and bears an *achevé d'imprimer* of September 1st of the same year. The *Catalogue Soleinne* (V, *Suppl.,* p. 42) also refers to an edition of 1635. However, it was reissued at Paris, by Augustin Courbé, with a title page bearing the date of 1636.

2. Puibusque in his *Histoire comparée des littératures espagnole et française* (Paris, 1843, p. 420), vaguely suggested a Spanish source, while A. Batereau in his *Georges de Scudéry als Dramatiker* (Leipzig-Plagwitz, 1902, p. 74), said that he had been unable to find any source. Among those who indicated Juan de Flores as Scudéry's model are Menéndez y Pelayo, *Orígenes de la Novela,* I, pp. CCCXXXII-CCCXXXVIII; Reynier, *Le Roman Sentimental avant l'Astrée,* p. 85, etc.

3. See B. Matulka, Georges de Scudéry, *Le Prince Déguisé,* Republished with an Introduction, N.Y., Institute of French Studies, Columbia University, 1929.

4. See the republication, *op. cit.,* p. 80.

5. *Idem,* p. 81.

6. *Idem,* p. 83.

7. The betrayal of the lovers was also, quite probably, suggested by Juan de Flores' novel, although for its details Scudéry borrowed from another source, as we shall indicate further on.

8. The work which made this theme most popular in Europe is, perhaps, Tasso's *Gerusalemme Liberata,* where it occurs in Book Two. This episode was dramatized in France in 1599 by Aymard de Veins in his tragedy, *La Sophronie,* and furnished the plot of a story, *Hierusalem assiégée,* by de Nervèze first published in 1599. Moreover, several plays before Scudéry had made use of the combat of generosity: *Celinde* of Balthazar Baro (1629); *La Dorimène* by the Sieur de Comte (1632); *Pyrandre et Lisimène* by Boisrobert (1633) and others.

9. See B. Matulka, *The Cid as a Courtly Hero: From the Amadís to Corneille,* N. Y., Institute of French Studies, Columbia University, 1928.

10. The Cid theme had been used in France several times before Scudéry, as, for example in Du Perier's *La Hayne et d'Amour d'Arnoul et de Clairemonde,* published three times between 1600 and 1627. (See G. L. van Roosbroeck, *The Cid Theme in France in 1600,* Minneapolis, Pioneer Printers, 1920). Moreover, Scudéry may have read the *Florisel de Niquea* romance either in the original, or in a French translation, for it had won popularity in France. (See Hughes Vaganay, *Amadis en français,* Firenze, 1906, p. 81 ff.)

11. Moreover, Scudéry may have known some intermediate adaptations of the novel, for Gougenot had dramatized this part of the *Amadís* as early as 1633, in his *La Fidelle tromperie.*

12. This theme had been used before Ariosto in the twentieth novel of Masuccio's *Novellino.* Ariosto's play was translated into French in 1572 by Jean de la Taille under the title of *Le Négromant.*

13. *La Vraye Histoire Comique de Francion,* composée par Nicolas de Moulinet, sieur Du Parc, Gentilhomme Lorrain.

14. H. C. Lancaster, *A History of French Dramatic Literature,* II, p. 482, suggests the episodes of Chryséide and of Lidias in the *Astrée* as additional sources of certain incidents of Scudéry's play: ". . . He could find parallels [in the *Astrée*] for the fact that the hero is a Gaulois, for the snoring *gouvernante* (III, 5), the bribing of the jailer, the heroine's escape from prison by the help of an attendant who takes her place, and the claiming of a reward for offering up one's self as a criminal."

15. However, such a tourney of disguised lovers fighting each other, finally to learn each other's identity, occurs in other French plays before Scudéry, and may

have suggested details which he added to the combat. Such plays were, for example, *Agimée, ou l'Amour extravagant* (1629) and *Les Aventures Amoureuses d'Omphale* by Grandchamp (1630), etc.

Barbara Matulka (essay date 1934)

SOURCE: Matulka, Barbara. "The Main Source of Scudéry's *Le Prince Déguisé*: The *Primaleon.*" *The Romanic Review* XXV (January-March 1934): 1-14.

[*In following essay, Matulka explores in detail the possible sources that inspired Scudéry's* Le Prince déguisé *and analyzes the themes of the play.*]

The sources of Scudéry's popular **Prince déguisé** offer an intriguing problem for the genesis of the romanesque tragi-comedy at the time of Corneille's *Cid.*[1] In a previous publication,[2] I have pointed out that for his "belle intrigue" he had amalgamated motives from many sources: from Juan de Flores he took the law condemning the more guilty of two lovers, from the *Orlando Furioso* he adopted the final duel, from Sorel's *Francion* he borrowed comic scenes, and he did not disdain the commonplace literary motives disseminated in the literature of his day. Furthermore I showed,—and this is perhaps more important from the esthetic point of view,—that he elaborated a variation of the courtly *Cid* theme, which he might have known through various sources as, for instance, Feliciano de Silva's *Florisel de Niquea* of the *Amadís* series, where the theme of Love versus Hatred is already clearly developed.[3] Scudéry's heroine, the Princess Argénie, passes through the same psychological crisis as Chimène.[4] The **Prince déguisé** drew upon one of the intermediaries of the courtly *Cid* theme,—possibly upon the *Florisel de Niquea* romance,—although I made sure to state that this novel should be considered only a *link* in the evolution of the *Cid* tradition, an example of the combination of motives that led to Guillén de Castro's masterpiece, and consequently to Corneille's triumph.[5] This caution was justified: this embellished *Cid* theme of romance is already found amply elaborated in a Spanish novel of chivalry, the *Primaleón* of 1512. There we find the main theme of the **Prince déguisé,** the episode of a high-born prince disguised as a humble gardener in order to win the lady of his choice,—the central situation as well as the principal parts of the plot of Scudéry's play. He has reproduced so closely all the main and subsidiary themes and situations of this romance of chivalry, that there can be no doubt that it is the principal and direct source of the **Prince déguisé,** though for some details he borrowed color from other works within his reach.

For the sake of clarity the complicated plot of Scudéry may be analysed as follows: 1) the main plot, consisting of the disguised prince-gardener theme, based on the *Primaleón* as I shall explain further on; 2) a related episode from the *Primaleón* grafted on it,—the *Cid* theme, according to which the lady, to avenge her father's death, offers her hand in marriage to the one who brings her the head of his killer.[6] This "adored enemy" himself offers her his head, and at the same time hands her his sword, so that she might appease her wrath by beheading him;[7] and 3) the secondary sources:—the borrowings from Juan de Flores, Ariosto, the *Francion,* and several other themes of lesser importance.[8] The present study deals with the hitherto unnoticed main source of the *Prince déguisé,*— the chivalric novel *Primaleón.*

SUMMARY OF THE *PRINCE DÉGUISÉ*

To bring out the close parallel between the *Prince déguisé* and the *Primaleón,* we may briefly recall the outline of Scudéry's play, so typical of the 1629-1635 period in France: The Prince Cléarque of Naples, disguised as a gardener, attempted to win the hand of the Princess Argénie, daughter of Rosemonde, Queen of Sicily. This ambition, however, was difficult to achieve, for he was reputed to be the murderer of Argénie's father. This unfortunate king had been defeated in battle by Cléarque's father and, as a prisoner, had died of a broken heart. It was rumored, without any foundation, that he had been poisoned by Cléarque, and therefore, upon the king's death, the Queen had put a price on his head. In spite of the danger which he thus courted when he entered his enemies' land, he could not live without seeing the Princess. Instructing his followers to remain in hiding with costly jewels and arms in a near-by village, the Prince donned the humble costume of a peasant, and boldly offered his services to Rutile, the Queen's gardener. Playing upon his avarice, Cléarque (who now assumed the name of Policandre) feigned that he knew the secret of rich treasures buried in the royal garden and that, at night, he could unearth these with incantations under favorable auspices. He offered to share these jewels, and the gullible Rutile eagerly welcomed him.

Now, Cléarque had sought entrance to the royal garden because he knew that it was Argénie's favorite haunt. He soon attracted her attention for she was amazed at his bearing and at his gallant speech. Who but a courtier could tell her that "the flowers display their colors only to please the most beautiful eye in the world?" When she turned to the fountain to drink from its limpid water, Cléarque-Policandre begged her to accept a beautiful goblet encrusted with gems which he promptly brought her. Again surprised that such a lowly gardener could possess so costly a cup, she was satisfied only when she learned of its origin:—how he had won it as a prize at a poetic contest. In obedience to her wish, he recited the *Stances* which had crowned him victor, veiling in his verses his own love plaints.

In the meanwhile, the gardener had so overcome the Princess by his grace that she could no longer find rest. One night, after making sure that none of her ladies-in-waiting perceived it, she went out into the garden with a single confidante, Philise. There the gardener was waiting

to see her, pretending to be searching for treasure. So wan had she grown, so sad in mood, that her maid now begged her to reveal the cause of her malady. After many sighs and vacillations, the Princess confessed that she had fallen hopelessly in love with that "squire of low degree." Philise, though startled at the news, nevertheless approved of her mistress' choice; she was convinced that he was a prince in disguise. As Argénie debated whether to confess her love to him, Cléarque himself, who had been listening to this conversation, came forward to reveal part of his secret: she was right in believing him of high rank, for his parents were to leave him nothing less than a scepter. He continued that he had travelled there only to win her love, and that "he was hoping while fearing, and living while dying." Afraid of staying longer, Argénie promised to see him again on the following night.

In the meanwhile, however, the wife of the gardener had also fallen a victim to Cléarque's charms, but when he only spurned her, she spied upon him to learn his secret. She was thus present to overhear their conversation, and to avenge herself, reported it to the Queen. Greatly angered, she ordered the lovers to be seized at their rendez-vous the following night, and had them cast in prison to await punishment. They were to be judged according to a law which decreed that if a princess loved beneath her station, the more guilty of the two lovers in arousing that illicit passion should suffer death; if both claimed guilt, the dispute would have to be settled by a tourney. Both managed to escape from their prison by bribing the jailors, each fighting as the champion of the other without the other's knowledge. Cléarque of course overcame his adversary, and his victory thus saved Argénie.

But now Cléarque-Policandre had two death sentences on his head: the first as the murderer of the former king, and the second as the lover of the Princess, since his champion had been defeated. However, the first decree had also provided to bestow the hand of the Princess on the man who brought her the head of Cléarque. He therefore revealed that he himself was the supposed murderer, but professed his innocence, nevertheless offering his head to satisfy her vengeance. The Queen remained in a dilemma, caught in her own decree. She was honor-bound to give her daughter's hand to the very enemy she had been seeking, since he had fulfilled the terms. Touched by their constant and magnanimous love, she found a verbal solution for her difficulty: she sentenced the fictitious Policandre to death, and bestowed her daughter's hand on the valiant Cléarque.

* * *

Before comparing this plot to that of the *Primaleón,* its principal source, it may not be superfluous to point out that Scudéry must of necessity have been acquainted with this Spanish novel of chivalry. It appeared in 1512[9] as a sequel to the popular *Palmerín de Oliva,* and soon became widely diffused in France, so that the romanesque preferences of Scudéry found ample resources on which to draw from it. In 1550 the First Book was translated, and three issues appeared in Paris. The successive publication of the Second and Third Books probably preceded the reprinting of the entire work. At least twenty-five editions, either partial or complete, were issued in French between 1550 and 1618,[10] whereas at the same time at least ten Italian editions helped to popularize the work.[11] It is even remarkable that the number of French printings surpassed the number of editions in Spain itself.[12]

Towards the end of the First Book of the *Primaleón,* and running all through the Second and Third, there are interwoven the two stories that furnished Scudéry his model: 1) the disguise of the prince, Don Duardos, into a gardener for the sake of Flérida, an enemy princess, and 2) the decree by which the hand of the Duchess Gridonia is offered as a reward to the man who brings her the head of Primaleón, guilty of her father's death. Scudéry telescoped these two tales into a single plausible plot. He adopted its two heroes, focussing them into *one*: his Clérque-Policandre combines the rôles of Primaleón and Don Duardos; while similarly his heroine, Argénie, is a composite of the gentle Flérida and the vengeance-seeking, Gridonia. I shall discuss these two episodes of the *Primaleón* separately in order to show the extent of Scudéry's debt to each in their just proportion.

THE DON DUARDOS-GARDENER THEME

In the *Primaleón,* Don Duardos, son of the King of England, disguised himself as a gardener for the love of Flérida, daughter of the Emperor Palmerin de Oliva, and won her in spite of his apparently humble station by his gallantry and grace. This valiant knight had come to challenge Primaleón, but had been so struck with the beauty of his sister. Flérida, that he was glad to stop his combat for her sake. He was now unable to live without at least beholding the object of his love, and grew disconsolate, for he was in despair of ever winning so fair a lady, against whose blood he had raised his lance. While he was thus pining away, an enchantress, whom he had formerly succored, brought him aid: she gave him a golden goblet "guarnida con piedras preciosas," which had the virtue of making anyone who drank of it fall passionately in love with the giver. Heartened by this talisman, Don Duardos stationed a few of his trusted men in a neighboring village to guard his arms and jewels, while he returned to Constantinople alone, disguised as a humble toiler, to execute the plan suggested by the enchantress.

As he was walking about the city, pondering on a way to win access to the Princess, he chanced to pass by the royal garden, and through the momentarily open door he caught a glimpse of the dazzling beauty of Flérida. Overjoyed to learn of her pastime, he approached the gardener Julián, who was standing at the gate, and offered his services. He confided that he knew of certain treasures hidden in the royal park, and that through magic arts he could unearth them. When the old gardener heard that he would share these riches, he gladly took him in. In order to avoid suspicion, he pretended that he was his own son, just returned from a long journey.

In his humble disguise, Don Duardos now called himself Julián, like the gardener. As in the *Prince déguisé,* he had his faithful servitors bring him part of his treasures which he was to feign to unearth at night. With such costly gifts he won the gardener's confidence and aroused his greed for more of this buried wealth. Proud of his guest, he presented him as his son to the Princess and her ladies-in-waiting, who all marveled at his beauty and stateliness, so unsuited to his gardener's attire. They were still more astonished when they heard his courtly and gallant speech. Soon after, Don Duardos found occasion to use his magic charm. Flérida (like Scudéry's Argénie) said that she would like to drink of the clear water of the fountain, and Don Duardos quickly brought her the magic cup. The Princess and all her ladies admired its workmanship, and inquired where so humble a youth could have obtained so kingly a treasure. He replied that he had carried it off as a prize at a tourney (as in a similar way Clérque had mentioned a poetic contest). The Princess then drank, and felt a new and strange emotion; she became passionately fond of this handsome newcomer, but could not explain her feelings. Debating with herself, and ashamed of such an uncontrollable love for one so base, she absented herself from the park in order to forget him. But to no avail, for she could find no peace when she was not in his company.

Don Duardos, of course, was greatly perturbed when his lady did not visit the park any longer. But no less tortured was Flérida who, in the meanwhile, had become so pale that her favorite attendant, Artada, begged her mistress to reveal to her the cause of her sorrow. Flérida (like Scudéry's Argénie), debated between her princely duty and her base love, and finally yielded to the pleas of her confidante, disclosing her unrestrainable passion for the newly-arrived gardener. Artada (like Scudéry's Philise) was at first startled by the news, but she was convinced that he was no humble "villano," but of high station, for otherwise he would not be so bold as to aspire to the love of so mighty a princess. The day following this nocturnal confession, Flérida went out into the royal park, looking more joyous than she had been for several days. Don Duardos (like Scudéry's Clérque) entertained her with a sorrowful song, expressing his superhuman love and his despair of ever winning her, as well as his fear of being separated from her. All the ladies were astonished at this courtly lyric, filled with amorous subtleties. He amazed them still more, however, when, in reply to Flérida's question as to where he had learned it, he declared that Love itself had taught it to him. Again as in the *Prince déguisé,* Flérida noticed the beautiful hands of the pretended gardener, and because of them judged that he could not be of lowly station.

But as her affection grew deeper and deeper, so also did her shame and anxiety. To justify her passion, she asked him who he was. Gently he replied that he could not tell her without incurring her anger, but he assured her that her premonitions were well founded: that he was not of the lowly station he seemed to be, but of the highest nobility. He promised to prove this by deeds of knightly valor. He instructed his squire to bring him his arms, and engaged in a combat, defeating a boastful knight who had, until then, overcome all his adversaries. When she saw his valor and prowess, the Princess loved him still more passionately, and declared that she would always remain faithful to him, no matter whether he were base or noble.

After his encounters for her sake, during which he won fame as the bravest knight at the court, Don Duardos returned to the royal garden, and begged the Princess to grant him an interview that very night. She consented after much hesitation. Impatiently she waited until her ladies were fast asleep, and went down into the garden with only the faithful Artada, to meet her lover. Don Duardos explained how he was striving to win her through personal merit rather than by glory of rank or name. The Princess thus found her conviction that he was noble verified, and again pledged him her lasting love. The *dénouement* of this episode is a happy one: Don Duardos performed many feats of valor, wandering far and wide. He finally returned to elope with Flérida who was ashamed to remain longer at her father's court. They fled, but were brought back to the Emperor who, having learned Don Duardos' identity, pardoned the lovers and celebrated a magnificent wedding. Now, instead of employing this simple *dénouement*, Scudéry switched to the interlinked episode of Primaleón and Gridonia of the romance, as we shall see presently.

* * *

The main theme of Scudéry's ***Prince déguisé*** thus corresponds exactly and in detail to the adventures of Don Duardos: the sudden and insurmountable love with which the Princess smites an enemy Prince; his disguise as a gardener in order to be able to approach her and win her love by his real worth; the entrance into the royal garden by the subterfuge of buried treasure, by which an avaricious and gullible gardener is readily deceived. We find the same costly goblets; the same jewels supplied by faithful followers, so that the Prince might keep his promise of sharing the gems with the rustics. Moreover, both Princes meet their ladies frequently in the garden, and find occasion to recite a poem of their own composition, expressing their hidden sentiments; both ladies are encouraged in their love by a lady-in-waiting who is certain that the gardener is a prince in disguise; both heroes subtly intimate that they are not of the lowly rank they seem to be, and they win their ladies by courtly gallantry. All these episodes in the development of the love plot are practically identical, and step by step constitute a parallel in the novel and in Scudéry's play.

No doubt, there are minor differences,—largely exigencies for dramatic purposes, since in the play the possible number of incidents had to be far more sparing than in an involved, slow-moving chivalric novel, which appealed to the popular fancy largely because of its exhaustive enumeration of details. So, for example, the many meetings of the Prince and his lady in the garden at night in the *Primaleón* are limited to two in the ***Prince déguisé***; the many combats in which Don Duardos wins the crown of

victory to prove his worth to his lady, are necessarily omitted in the play; the two cup and song incidents are combined in a single garden scene in the ***Prince déguisé***, although in the *Primaleón* they occur at a week's interval. The magic and the giants are, of course, entirely suppressed by Scudéry, who in his attack on Corneille was to set up "vraisemblance" as the primary requisite of a well-constructed play.[13]

Paradoxically enough, his romanesque plot springs largely from the rationalization of the fantastic supernatural scenes of the late chivalric tradition. To give a striking example, let us take the episode of the goblet, which can be fully understood only when its source is borne in mind. In the *Primaleón* the cup had magic powers, making the Princess unwittingly fall in love with a rustic, without understanding how such a change could come about. But Scudéry, by eliminating the magic, converted the scene into a courtly one, using it to mark a contrast between the richness of the chalice and the humble state of the giver. Thus, in the ***Prince déguisé*** the episode loses much of its original effectiveness and *raison d'être*, for it becomes merely an unmotivated accident and embellishment. Scudéry has suppressed the magic, but not the scene.[14]

THE *PRIMALEÓN* EPISODE: THE *CID* THEME

After making full use of this idyllically romantic love of a great prince disguised as a gardener to win a princess' hand, Scudéry switched for his *dénouement* to the principal plot of the *Primaleón*, to one closely interwoven with the Don Duardos episode. It is the meandering story recounting the love of the high-born and invincible Primaleón for the fair Duchess Gridonia, which constitutes the earliest courtly *Cid* theme[15] in Spanish literature thus far discovered.[16] In his ***Prince déguisé*** Scudéry makes but little use of the dramatic possibilities of these embellished knightly attitudes which are worked out at considerable length in the *Primaleón*. It remained for Guillén de Castro to employ so effectively in his *Mocedades* these highly dramatic motives comprising the struggle of Love versus Hatred, the seeking of a lover's head in expiation of a father's life, the desire of the heroine to kill herself, once she had restituted the family honor, the victorious return of the unconquered hero who himself offers her his head, and fearing the unflinching severity of his beloved, hands her his sword to end his suffering.[17] All of these intense situations are so minimized by Scudéry that they only serve to yield unexpected romanesque turns, instead of being the nucleus of powerful dramatic situations. This meagre treatment is, perhaps, the most conclusive sign of the inferiority of Scudéry as a playwright, since he did not perceive the possibilities of just those themes, embodied in the love of a high-born lady for the paragon of chivalry, shattered by a rightful duel, which lead to so dramatic a climax in Guillén de Castro and Corneille.[18]

This *Primaleón* episode narrates how Nardides, the Duke of Ormedes, had been vanquished by the Emperor Palmerín de Oliva. His wife, upon the birth of a daughter, whom she called Gridonia to symbolize her sorrow, took an oath never to marry her to anyone but the man who should avenge her husband's death. At fifteen years of age, Gridonia was so beautiful that many knights came to court her. One of these suitors, her cousin Perequín de Duaces, son of the King of Poland, was determined to win the Duchess by avenging her. He decided to go to Constantinople where Primaleón, the worthy son of his noble father, was holding a tournament. He there planned to kill Primaleón, but instead he himself met with death at the hands of the hero. However, it was rumored that he had overcome Perequín by treachery, and Gridonia made a vow to avenge the death of both her father and her suitor by pursuing him relentlessly: she swore to bestow her hand on any man who should lay his head at her feet.

Now it happened that, on the mere report of her beauty, this very abhorred Prince fell in love with her. He was sorely grieved at her anger against him, and would gladly have laid at her feet not only his head, but the whole empire of Constantinople. He was especially pained at the false report to which she gave credence, that he had overcome Perequín by treachery, whereas he had slain him in honorable combat, and according to all the rules of knightly conduct. Under the assumed name of the "Caballero de la Roca Partida" (the very name of Gridonia's castle), he went to her court, where she was pining away in despair of ever being avenged, and desiring nothing so much as Primaleón's head: ". . . Muy ledo fuera mi coraçon con la cabeça de Primaleón, y esta vengança no espero yo haver segun la ventura me es esquiva."

Though realizing that he was in a land where discovery would mean his death, Primaleón nevertheless engaged in battle, and drove out the enemies who were besieging the Duchess' lands. Without revealing his identity, he was brought in triumph, after his victory, to Gridonia's castle. During their conversation, Primaleón confessed his love for her, and to his delight she responded to his affection. However, bound as she was by her oath of revenge, she immediately requested him to bring her the head of her enemy as a token that would seal their happiness.

In spite of the renewed demands of Gridonia that he fulfill his promise, Primaleón did not, of course, reveal that he was the beloved enemy whom she was pursuing with so cruel a vengeance. Finally, after ever-mounting proofs of his devotion and valor, he led her to his father's court in Constantinople. There, in the presence of all the nobility (as in the court of Argénie's mother in the *Prince déguisé*), he disclosed that he was the long-sought Primaleón, and knelt before his lady. Bowing his head, he offered it to her in fulfillment of his vow, and handed her his sword, begging her to behead him with her own hands. Like Argénie, she was torn between paroxysms of grief, love, and desire of revenge, and in despair tried to draw the sword against herself in order to end her anguish,—for she could not strike the man she loved in spite of the guilt she imputed to him. Here again love triumphed, but in the *Primaleón* it was helped by a supernatural event: a sweetly scented dew

of rain trickled over the whole gathering, washing away enmity and replacing it by love and reconciliation. Again as in Scudéry, the revengeful Queen was softened by the insurpassable constancy of the lovers, and sealed their marriage with her blessing.[19]

* * *

Even in this final climax the parallel between the *Primaleón* and the *Prince déguisé* is exact even in detail: in both the hero enters the country where a price has been set on his head, because of his love, and in both he is accused of having murdered treacherously a relative of the damsel. In Scudéry's play, Cléarque was said to have poisoned her father; in the *Primaleón* the hero was rumored to have slain her lover unawares, while at the same time he was to expiate the death of her father; in both works mother and daughter take a vow to avenge these deaths, and in both the hand of the lady is offered as a reward to the knight who would bring back the head of the accused Prince. In both, the hero swears he is innocent of the death imputed to him; he finally wins forgiveness, and is married by the mother who had been pursuing him so vengefully. Even many of the details are similar as, for example, the church ceremony during which the hero is publicly declared an enemy and responsible for the death of the ruler, or again the war between the two families, during which the lady's father is killed.

It is true that from this *Cid* episode, as from the Don Duardos story, Scudéry selected only the essential features, modifying and omitting what was irrelevant to his purpose. For instance, he made his Argénie far sweeter and less revengeful than the violent Gridonia. His heroine continued to love the brave Cléarque, and secretly hoped for his victory; she sacrificed her heart only because of filial duty. This struggle did not arise in Gridonia, because she had never set eyes on Primaleón before his arrival at her court.[20] But the main outline is identical, and the incidents succeed one another in the same order.

* * *

The *Prince déguisé* thus remains an amalgamation of several themes, though the sustaining framework is derived from the *Primaleón*,—that of the prince disguised as a gardener who wins a lady's heart by his poetry and gallant speech, and by his complicity with a rustic to whom he offers treasures supposedly unearthed by magic arts. To this he added the fundamental *Cid* motive,—that of the lady who promises her hand as a reward for the head of her father's slayer, yet marries this invincible enemy and lover. This Scudéry found in the *Primaleón* (1512), but it must also have been known to him as it had filtered through Feliciano de Silva's continuation of the *Amadís* (1532.) His indebtedness to the *Primaleón* is further confirmed by the number of details that seem accidental and unmotivated in the *Prince déguisé,* and thus betray their derivation. On the other hand Scudéry omitted much that seemed irrelevant or improbable for his plausible "intrigue." His romanesque tragi-comedy clearly indicates how the fantastic motives of the romances of chivalry had gradually become rationalized, and this very omission of the numerous supernatural elements makes this play take on a significant rôle in the development of the doctrine of the *Vraisemblable* in the early decades of the seventeenth century.

But even the complex *Primaleón* plots did not entirely satisfy Scudéry. They do not account for the secondary themes with which he abundantly diversified them: the law and the combat of generosity of the lovers, derived from Juan de Flores and Ariosto, the treachery of the gardener's wife, although this was intimated in the Don Duardos episode, nor the comic gardener-magician episode that seems largely reminiscent of Sorel's *Francion,* etc. These and other commonplace literary motives Scudéry grafted on the main branch of his "intrigue", thus lending his highly-lauded tragicomedy a semblance of novelty,—a newness of assortment of well-worn popular themes, rather than of original invention. He delighted his courtly audience by carrying it back to the romances of chivalry on which it had been nurtured, and through this retrograde appeal awakened sympathy for the well-known in a new and clever disguise.

Notes

1. Part of a paper read before the Modern Language Association at Yale University, December, 1932.

2. *Georges de Scudéry, "Le Prince déguisé," Republished with an Introduction,* N. Y., Publications of the Institute of French Studies, 1929; *The Novels of Juan de Flores and Their European Diffusion. A Study in Comparative Literature, Idem,* Comparative Literature Series, 1931, pp. 203-211.

3. The composite nature of Scudéry's sources as to detail has since been corroborated: Professor M. Schlauch has pointed out that Scudéry may well have had in mind John Barclay's novel, *Argenis,* while composing his play: "From Barclay's romance Scudéry seems to have taken the heroine's name (Argenis: Argénie) and the localization in Sicily; possibly also the hero's name (Poliarchus: Cléarque) and his appearance in disguise" (*Romanic Review,* XXII, No. 3, 1931, p. 238). This suggestion was expanded by Professor A. Steiner, who pointed out that "Policandre," the assumed name of the hero, was directly reminiscent of Barclay's novel, and that the name of the high-priest, Anthenor, was borne by a character in the *Argenis* (*Juan de Flores, Barclay, and Georges de Scudéry, Romanic Review,* XXII, No. 4, 1931, pp. 323-324). Professor H. C. Lancaster has suggested that Scudéry may have derived minor details of his plot from the *Astrée,* "where he could find parallels for the fact that the hero is a Gaulois, for the snoring *gouvernante* (III, 5), the bribing of the jailor, the heroine's escape from prison by the help of an attendant who takes her place, and the claiming of a reward for offering up one's self as a criminal" (*A*

History of French Dramatic Literature . . . , Baltimore, 1929, II, p. 482).

4. Professor R. Bray has stressed, and rightly so, that to the audience the *supposed* murder of a father and the *real* murder of a father are quite different; that the innocent supposed murderer commands sympathy, whereas Scudéry, at least, might have thought that the real killer of his beloved's father was hardly excusable in pushing his suit. Historically I agree fully with Professor Bray, for Scudéry felt himself justified to criticize the morality of Corneille's Chimène, calling her "impudique, prostituée, parricide, monstre." Nevertheless, may I not suggest that *artistically,*—a point of view which Professor Bray evidently shares,—the audience had the same sympathy for Rodrigue as for Cléarque, the "Prince déguisé"? Dramatically, the pathos of the Cid was greatly heightened by the dire expiation of the hero, who killed only out of a sense of duty and honor, and in order to feel worthy of his lady. His torments both before and after the deed, his complete abnegation of self for a social code superior to any individual, resulted in an intense human tragedy, of beings at odds with superior forces, Love and Duty, whereas Scudéry's *imbroglio* remains only a pleasing disentanglement of misunderstandings of which the audience could foresee the outcome from the start. The interest here lies rather in the superficial "inside information" of the spectators, who await with curiosity the effects of the "mystery solution" on the supposedly unwitting actors, whereas in the *Cid* it rises from the inevitable internal conflict of the protagonists. Cf. Professor Bray's review of *Georges de Scudéry, "Le Prince déguisé,"* in the *Revue d'Histoire littéraire de la France,* XXXVII, 1930, pp. 448-449; H. C. Lancaster, *A History of French Dramatic Literature . . . ,* Part II, Vol. I, p. 143, note 2; Professor Bray's review of this work in the *Revue d'Hist. lit.,* XL, 1933, pp. 126-127.

5. B. Matulka, *The Cid as a Courtly Hero: from the Amadís to Corneille,* N. Y., Publications of the Institute of French Studies, 1928.

6. In this case, the "killer" is the son of the knight who had engaged in the fatal combat, for we have here a transmission of blood guilt. See the more detailed discussion of the *Cid* theme following.

7. Cf. the Head and Sword Motives in Guillén de Castro and Corneille.

8. These secondary sources should by no means be minimized, for they are precisely the innovations in the main theme that lent the play its novelty in the estimation of Scudéry's contemporary audiences. They all contributed to the "well-constructed" plot of which the author was so proud.

9. *Libro segundo del Emperador Palmerín en que se recuentan los grandes e hazañosos fechos de Primaleón e Polendos sus hijos e otros buenos caval-*

leros estranjeros que a su corte venieron. At the end: "Fué trasladado este segundo libro de *Palmerín* llamado *Primaleón* y ansimesmo el primero llamado *Palmerín* de griego en nuestro lenguaje castellano y corregido y enmendado en la muy noble ciudad de Ciudad Rodrigo por Francisco Vázquez. Emprimido en la muy noble y leal ciudad de Salamanca a tres días del mes de Julio. MVXII años." It has been attributed to an anonymous woman writer of Burgos, who is said to have been assisted for the descriptions of battles by her son, and also to Francisco Vázquez of Ciudad Rodrigo. Cf. H. Thomas, *Spanish and Portuguese Romances of Chivalry,* London, 1920, pp. 96-100. Many Spanish editions followed the first: Salamanca, 1516, Sevilla, 1524, Toledo, 1528, Ciudad del Senado Veneciano, 1534, Sevilla, 1540, Medina del Campo, 1563, Lisboa, 1566, Bilbao, 1585, another, 1588, Lisboa, 1598. Cf. Palau; H. Vaganay, *Les Romans de Chevalerie italiens d'Inspiration espagnole,* in *La Bibliofilia* (Firenze), vol. IX, 1908, pp. 121-131; vol. X, 1909, pp. 121-134, 161-167; H. Thomas, *op. cit.*

10. The numerous French translations were apparently based on both the Spanish version and the Italian translation, as we may gather from the title of the first French translation of 1550: *L'Histoire de Primaleon de Grece continuant celle de Palmerin d'Olive Empereur de Constantinople son Pere, naguere tirée tant de l'Italien comme de l'Espagnol et mise en nostre vulgaire par François de Vernassal Quercinois.* A Paris . . . , Estienne Groulleau, 1550. In the same year the translation was issued with two other imprints: "Paris, Vincent Sertenas," and "Paris, Ian Longis." It was republished in Orléans, Paris and Lyon in 1572; Lyon, Pierre Rigaud, Lyon, Iean Beraud, Anvers, and Paris, 1577; Lyon, 1580, 1600, and 1618. The Second and Third Books, which largely contain the stories upon which Scudéry drew, were frequently issued separately. Book II was thus issued in 1576: *Second livre de l'histoire de Primaleon de Grece, traduict nouvellement d'espagnol en françois par Guillaume Landré d'Orléans,* Paris, Galliot du Pré, 1576, and reissued in Lyon, Paris and Anvers in 1577. Still another French translation was made of this volume by Gabriel Chappuis Tourengeau, Lyon, 1588 and re-issued in 1612. The same Gabriel Chappuis also translated *Le Troisième livre de Primaleon de Grece . . . ,* Lyon, 1579, reissued in Lyon, 1587. An edition "corrigé et augmenté" appeared in Paris, 1587. This Third Book also appeared in Lyon, 1597, 1600 and 1609. Following the Italian, even a Fourth Book was translated into French (1583 and 1597). To attest still further the extraordinary popularity this novel enjoyed in France, I may also mention the curious *Petit discours d'un chapitre du livre de Primaleon autrefois envoyé par le seigneur des Essars, N. de Herberay . . . a une damoiselle espagnolle, belle, et de meilleure grace,* Paris, Vincent Sertenas,

1549. A Dutch translation of Book II, by Samuel Minel, based on Gabriel Chappuis' French rendering, was published at Rotterdam, Jan van Waesberghe, 1621.

11. The first Italian translation appeared in 1548: *Primaleone nel quale si narra a pieno l'historia de' suoi valerosi fatti et di Polendo suo fratello. Nuovamente tradotto della lingua Spagnuola nella nostra buona Italiana.* In Venegia, Michael Tramezzino, 1548, 3 parts. The translation is anonymous, but has been ascribed to Mambrino Roseo. Other editions appeared in 1556, Vinegia, 1559, Venetia, 1563, 1573, 1579, 1584, 1597, 1608, and even a Fourth Part was invented: *La quarta parte del libro di Primaleone, nuovamente ritrovata & aggiunta,* 1560. In 1566 Pietro Lauro issued a supplement to the first twenty chapters of the *Primaleón* (Cf. Thomas, p. 187). Besides, Ludovico Dolce versified the novel (1562). There appeared even an English translation, based on the Italian and French renderings: Part I, attributed to Antony Munday, was issued in 1595, Book II in 1596, while in 1619 all three parts were published in London by Thomas Snodham.

12. There appeared in Spain several dramatizations of the very episodes of this novel that Scudéry employed: the early *Tragicomedia he sóbre os amores de D. Duardos, Principe de Inglaterra, com Flerida filha do Imperador Palmeirim de Constantinopla,* by Gil Vicente, (Cf. *Obras de Gil Vicente,* ed. Mendes dos Remedios, Coimbra, 1914, III, pp. 145-199). There exists, however, no reason for believing that Scudéry would have made direct use of this comparatively unknown play instead of the very well-known French translation of the *Primaleón.* This is substantiated by the lack of verbal parallels, and the fact that several episodes of the *Primaleón* are found in the *Prince déguisé,* though not in *Don Duardos.* The prince disguised as a gardener is, of course, found in other Spanish plays as, for example, in Torres Naharro's *Comedia Aquilana.* The possible relation between this work and Gil Vicente's and the *Primaleón* has been pointed out by Professor J. P. W. Crawford, *Spanish Drama Before Lope de Vega,* Philadelphia, 1922, p. 98. However, this play shows little similarity, outside of this theme, with the *Prince déguisé.* The highly fantastic and gongoristic play of Fray Hortensio Félix Paravicino, *La Gridonia o Ciclo de Amor vengado,* based on part of the *Primaleón,* apparently did not appear until 1641, after Scudéry's play. During the *Siglo de Oro,* the theme of the lover disguised as a gardener was frequently employed in the drama, though interwoven with so many other *comedia de capa y espada* motives, that its source can hardly be determined. Examples of this disguised gardener theme are found in Tirso de Molina's *La fingida Arcadia,* his *La Huerta de Juan Fernández,* Calderón's *La Selva confusa,* etc. Cf. G. T. Northup, *La Selva confusa de Don Pedro Calderón de la Barca,* in the *Revue hispanique,* XXI, 1909, p. 176.

13. *Observations sur le Cid*, in A. Gasté, *La Querelle du Cid*, Paris, 1898.

14. On the other hand, Scudéry did not only eliminate certain chivalric and magic elements so indispensable to a popular narrative of the time, but he amplified certain of its suggestions by grafting on this main theme striking scenes from other works. So, for example, he makes his gardener a comic character, gullible and superstitious, frightened by a false necromancer in a scene similar to one in the *Francion* of Sorel. Similarly, he makes the gardener's wife fall in love with the disguised prince, and his spurning of her affection makes her jealously spy upon him and betray his secret. Now, even this episode may have been suggested by the *Primaleón*, for there also the gardener's wife is curious to know why the youth remains in the garden at night, and discovers the lovers at their rendezvous. When her husband comes out on hearing his wife's cries, he thinks at first that she is unfaithful to him, and reproaches himself for his folly in taking into his house so young and gallant a helper. Scudéry thus probably derived his original inspiration for his treacherous-Melanire episode from the *Primaleón* itself, but for the details of working it out, he must have remembered similar situations in other works, such as the *Francion*, where a scene like his is developed in the same way. Moreover, he joined the rôle of vengeance-seeking for injured pride with the betrayal rôle in Juan de Flores' novel, *Grisel y Mirabella,* and thus his character of Melanire seems to be a composite one, skillfully combining several converging tendencies, which harmonized to form a plausible villain-motive for his play.

15. By the courtly *Cid* theme I mean those characteristics, attitudes and actions which differentiate the Cid of Guillén de Castro and Corneille from that of the chronicles and ballads.

16. The novel of Loubayssin de La Marque, *Les Advantures heroyques et amoureuses du conte Raymond de Thoulouze, et de don Roderic de Vivar,* Paris, 1619, and *Seconde partie des Avantures heroyques et amoureuses des braves et excellens princes, Raymond comte de Thoulouze, et de don Roderic de Vivar,* Paris, 1619, although dealing with the historical figure of the Cid, does not at all treat of the courtly Cid as he was to appear in Guillén de Castro's *Mocedades.* This mediocre Gascon author stayed entirely true to the chivalric tradition, and made but few excursions into the sentimental and courtly realm from which the Cid of Guillén de Castro and Corneille was to derive his glorification as a hero both supremely brave and incomparably gallant. Loubayssin's Cid romance is but an amalgamation of nondescript incidents from the romances of chivalry without any psychological deepening or analysis, whereas the value of the character of the Cid and Jimena as conceived by Castro and Corneille consists primarily in their psychological conflict. The entire absence of such struggles in Loubayssin de La

Marque's unfinished romance stamps his work as retrograde in comparison with his contemporaries. Cf. G. Reynier, *Le Cid en France avant "Le Cid,"* in *Mélanges Lanson,* Paris, 1922, pp. 217-221, and M. D. Lorch, *The Cid and Raymond of Toulouse, Heroes of a Novel of Chivalry, Revue de Littérature comparée,* XIII, No. 3, 1933, pp. 469-486.

17. I am not here concerned with the relation of this *Cid* theme to that occuring in Feliciano de Silva's continuation of the *Amadís,* that in the *Mocedades,* nor that in Corneille's *Cid.* I intend to work out these relationships in a forthcoming study.

18. It should be well understood that I am not here concerned with isolated *Cid* motives, such as those of head or sword, etc., since these occur very early, and are scattered all through European literature.

19. Du Perier's *La Hayne et l'Amour d'Arnoul et de Clairemonde* of 1600, is a transposition into contemporary life of this romanesque story, with the elimination of the magic. De Sallebray's play, *L'Amante ennemie,* is similarly based upon it. Cf. Professor G. L. van Roosbroeck, *The Cid Theme in France in 1600,* Minneapolis, Pioneer Printers, 1920, and his study, *The Source of De Sallebray's 'Amante ennemie',* in *Modern Language Notes,* XXXVI, No. 2, 1921, pp. 92-95.

20. Again, in order not to complicate his play unduly, he omitted the whole sub-plot of Zerfira, the lady-in-waiting of Gridonia, as well as the countless adventures of the Duchess with her malicious cousins, or the incidents of the faithful lion guarding her, gentle to Primaleón but savage to all others, etc.

Jerome W. Schweitzer (essay date 1939)

SOURCE: Schweitzer, Jerome W. "*Almahide*: Its Component Parts, Composition, and Style" and "Conclusion." In *George de Scudéry's* Almahide: *Authorship, Analysis, Sources and Structure,* pp. 105-54. Baltimore: The Johns Hopkins Press, 1939.

[*In the excerpt that follows, Schweitzer investigates a number of themes, devices, motifs, and techniques deployed in* Almahide.]

With the exception of an analysis of the plots of the several *histoires* in **Almahide,** this study has thus far been concerned primarily with an examination of the novel as it is related to its predecessors, its authorship, its place in French literature, and its relationship to its sources. It has been pointed out that it includes elements of the historical novel and the novel of chivalry, and mention has been made that it is a social study of Seventeenth Century society with its echoes from the salons of the period, the painting of word portraits, the composition of maxims, discussions of many subjects, particularly of love, and that with the *Astrée,* it is a forerunner of Diderot's *Salons.* These points were necessarily introduced earlier in this work in order to show that **Almahide** was heir to most of the elements included in the romantic novel prior to 1660. It is now proposed to discuss these points in greater detail.

CUSTOMS AND MANNERS

Almahide, like many of its contemporaries, is a study of manners and customs. Although its background is the court of Granada, the manners and customs of which Scudéry set out to study (*v.* **Au lecteur,** T. I), it is really the society of his own French milieu that he has in mind as his novel progresses. So similar were Boabdil's court as [Pérez de Hita] painted it and the courts of Louis XIII and Louis XIV that Scudéry was neither called upon to exert his imagination, nor to go further than Hita for local color. His sojourn in Marseille, the cosmopolitan city, also afforded him the opportunity of interviewing visitors from Granada who probably supplied the information necessary to fill in the lacunae in his own material. In the light of what has been said above, it at once becomes obvious that some difficulties are encountered in drawing a line of demarcation between French and Granadine manners. Where do French manners end and Moorish customs begin?

Scudéry opens his discussion of manners in the **Au lecteur** of the first volume in which he points out that the Moors lead the world in gallantry and have taught the Spaniards all they know of it. He also insists that the reader should not suppose that the Moors of Granada are black of skin since they reside on the Iberian peninsula and not in a country adjacent to the Congo. The Granadines are *claire* of complexion and their women are *lindas morenas.* In character they are by nature a joyous people, fond of diversion, but they pass easily from joy to sorrow (I, 66). They are naturally inclined to love making (I, 82) and from birth have an inclination for writing verse. The Moors are also naturally vindictive (III, 1713), and their theology teaches them to forget no insult and pardon no offense (VII, 556). In addition to his reading of Hita and possible conversations with Moors in Marseille, the *Koran,* translated into French by André Du Ryer, possibly provided Scudéry with information on matters of Mohammedan theology, law, and attitude towards women. Allusions to the *Koran* and supposed quotations therefrom are frequent, but as we shall see presently, Scudéry takes liberties with the text. With the missionary spirit of Christianity, Scudéry refutes what he terms the falsity and absurdities of the teachings of the Prophet (I, 341 f.).

The *Koran* is his source for Moorish prayers such as the Çalla (III, 1799); he asserts that it is his authority for the statement that slaves caught bearing arms must be put to death (I, 49), though I find no mention of such a law in the work cited. Statues of animate things are forbidden (I, 595) by the *Koran,* Scudéry asserts. It is the opinion of orientalists that by "statues," the *Koran* means idols, for statues are not condemned (*Koran,* XXXIV, 12). Scudéry

states that the *Koran* permits a man to have three wives (I, 342), although the *Koran* allows four. Mention is made that the Mohammedan religion permits divorces (III, 1945, 2015).

The attitude towards women is that of the Middle Ages and the days of the Knights of the Round Table. Though the ladies of Granada are set upon a pedestal and adored by the gentlemen (it is explained that their freedom is much greater than that of most Mohammedan women), they are placed under certain restrictions. According to Scudéry they are not permitted to enter a mosque (III, 1950), although Sale points out that women were not permitted to pray with men in public and were required to confine their visits to the mosque to hours when the men were absent.[1] They are not allowed to plead before a bar of justice (V, 1122); and Scudéry reiterates several times that immortality of the soul is denied them (III, 2073). Sale's attention is called to this erroneous belief and he refutes it.[2] The *Koran* states that "Dieu a promis aux croyants, hommes et femmes, les jardins arrosés par des cours d'eau; ils y demeuront éternellement" (IX, 73), and that "Les justes entreront dans les jardins d'Eden ainsi que leurs pères, leurs épouses, etc." (XIII, 23). Though the women of Granada mingle freely with men in the social functions, upon appearing on the streets, they are required to wear the traditional veil (V, 995). When they are married, the officiating churchman offers a prayer for their chastity in marriage (III, 1960). In deference to male vanity, they are permitted to appear on the balcony when they are honored by a serenade (IV, 657). Bodies are embalmed (VII, 432), and the dead are put away in burial urns (IV, 91). No death sentence can be carried out during the festival of *Bairan* (Beîram, cf. Sale, p. 107) which lasts for eight days (VI, 2442).

Local color is supplied by such details as use of the Arabic names for the months of the years: Sahaben for August and Rhamadan for September (VI, 2331); Muley's instrument of abdication is dated the sixth of Tzephar, year of the Hegira (III, 1795); allusions to Moorish costumes: the doliman (IV, 336), the albornoz (II, 795), and the turban (with its fifty ells of cloth, VIII, 40); and the *almayzar* or *antifas,* the traditional veil for women (V, 1419). Musical instruments are mentioned: the *nacaire,* the *agnafiel,* the *dulcin,* the *timbe, timbale, atabale, cornet à bouqin, guitar, saque-bute,* most of which are found in Hita. Government officials are given their Moorish titles with French equivalents: the *Emiralem* or deputy, the *visir* or connétable, the *degnis* or admiral, the *nassangi* or chancellor, the *depthtermin* or finance minister, the *tesquerigis* or secretary of state, and the *dragoman* or interpreter, etc. (III, 1767), names which Scudéry probably took from Davity. Though Scudéry builds many edifices in Granada and environs, he supplies the proper settings with descriptions of the Alhambra, the Zacatin, the Vivarambla, etc.

Dances common to the Moors and to the Spaniards are mentioned or described: the *Zambra* (IV, 341), the *Zarabanda* which, as he points out, was forbidden by the

Inquisition as licentious (IV, 347 f.),[3] the *Turque,* the *Greque,* the *Alexandrine,* the *Babilonienne,* the *Persane,* the *Tartare* (IV, 353), the Spanish Phoenix dance (IV, 380), the Spanish *Pavane* and the *Chaconne* (IV, 388-389), and the Greek *Pyrrhique* (IV, 413).

Scudéry's attention to detail is manifested in his description of a Moorish bow made "en se courbant fort bas, en portant la main gauche à son Turban, & la droite sur son coeur & apres leur auoir dit *Salamalech*: c'est à dire, ie vous saluë . . ." (I, 135 f.).

In conclusion certain odds and ends should not be omitted. Public baths are operated for men and for women, with separation of the sexes. Men entering baths designated for use by women are severely punished (V, 998). As in the *Cid,* warriors fighting under the banners of the king are required to deliver to the monarch one-fifth of the booty (IV, 549). Richelieu's edicts against duelling are recalled for such encounters are forbidden. Abindarrays' combat with a certain opponent is hushed up to save him from civil punishment (V, 1293).

As for French customs and manners, many found in *Almahide* have been indicated from time to time in this study. The salon has been mentioned and with it goes the *ruelle* (III, 2009) and the *alcove* (I, 70). Allusion is made to the *lever* of the king (III, 2006).

An idea of urban life is gained from the novel as a whole, but interesting information on the provinces is available in one of the conversations. Many of the statements made are also applicable to courtiers. Scudéry attacks the universal custom of tracing genealogies and aims a blow at those provincials "qui repassant ainsi tous leurs Deuanciers, vous font vne Histoire de Vilage, à faire mourir d'ennuy, si par bon-heur l'on ne s'y endormoit pas" (II, 1374). He also derides the insufferable provincials who talk only of their *procès,* entertaining everybody with them "comme s'ils consultoient leur affaire à vn Cadi" (*loc. cit.*). Others bore with conversation about "leur ménage, de leurs Raues; & de leurs choux." A dart is aimed at scandal mongers of the provinces who display the dirty linen of their neighbors to every stranger polite enough to listen (II, 1376); at indiscreet husbands and wives who seek to amuse by ridiculing their mates (II, 1377); and especially at provincial knights-errant who pass from house to house, abusing the hospitality of their hosts (II, 1378 f.).

ALMAHIDE AND THE THEATRE

As he had written many plays, it is not strange that Scudéry should include in the pages of his novel some discussion of the theatre. It has already been indicated that two of his plays served as source material for the novel and that the autobiographical portions allude to a purported love affair between the dramatist and the great actress Madeleine Béjart. As a dramatist, Scudéry was intimately connected with actors and actresses of his day, and it is interesting to note the indirect tribute which he tenders them in his description of the difficult life which they are forced to live. Unconsciously perhaps, he praises them for the mental effort exerted during long hours of study and rehearsals in order to be able to offer a finished production during the two or three hours of performance on the stage:

> . . . Premierement Abindarrays trouua qu'il fallait que Iebar estudiast tous les matins & tous les soirs comme vn Escolier . . . & repassast sa leçon l'apresdinée . . . trois fois la Semaine reglement, sa Maistresse deuint publique. . . .
>
> (V, 1545)

Iebar has little time for Abindarrays for when she is not diverting her audiences, the duties of her profession demand that she go from "Maison en Maison le soir, donner le mesme plaisir, & se donner la mesme fatigue" (*loc. cit.*). Reference has already been made to the plays in which she took part and to her ability as an actress.

Scudéry lifts the mask from the theatre and reveals it as a land of make-believe in his description of back-stage after the play is over and the audience has departed:

> . . . comme il (Abindarrays) a l'imagination delicate, elle se trouua choquée, lors qu'aprés auoir veu Iebar toute brillante de Pierreries, & sur vne superbe Scene d'Or & d'Azur, il vit derriere le Theatre, que ces Pierreries estoient fausses: & qu'au lieu de ces magnifiques Palais, Cleopatre estoit dans vne miserable Loge fort obscure, & auec vne Toilette & vn deshabiller peu dignes de cette Reyne d'Egypte: & dans laquelle on ne voyoit pas ces Perles dont l'Histoire a fait tant de bruit: car il n'y en auoit que de contrefaites, & mesmes encore assez mal. La delicatesse de ses yeux, se trouua encore blessée, de cinq ou six hommes à demy nuds, qu'il vit trop prés de son Heroïne: & cette familiarité peu honneste, ne fut nullement de son goust, quoy qu'elle fust de la necessité de leur Mestier.
>
> (V, 1546 f.)

In the sections of the novel dealing with his relationship with la Béjart, Scudéry describes himself as a novice who in his enthusiasm for this actress's art assumes the rôle of a claque:

> A chaque Vers que Iebar recitoit, il se pasmoit d'admiration & de joye; il se recrioit à tous les beaux endroits de son Rosle; il en auoit le corps agité comme l'esprit: & cette amour Comique luy donnoit des conuultions, comme certaines maladies en donnent, à ceux qui en sont tourmentez. Il excitoit les acclamations du Peuple par son exemple; il le faisoit crier malgré qu'il en eust, en criant luy mesme le premier; & l'on entendoit dire par tout, aprés luy, *cela est beau; cela est excellent; cela est diuin.*
>
> (V, 1541)

Fernand de Solís describes, in the history of Ponce and Almahide, Riquelme's play *Antigone,* which is staged in the apartments of the Queen of Spain. Rennert mentions one Alonso Riquelme as a favorite *autor de comedias*[4] of Lope de Vega and adds that he was a native of Seville and had a company of players as early as 1602.⁵ As there is no evidence that he was an author, Scudéry is probably alluding to the French *Antigone* he is most likely to have known, that of Rotrou.

With the arrival of the king and queen for the performance . . . "l'on entend le bruit & le tumulte" which is always a part of such occasions. The curtain is then raised, and by the splendor of a thousand lights which glittered without being seen:

> . . . on vit . . . que la face du Theatre representoit celle d'vn grand & superbe Palais, toute pleine de Niches & de Statuës, de Phrises & de Corniches, de Moulures & de Cordons, de Festons & de Cartouches, de Bazes & de Chapiteaux, de Colomnes & de Pilastres d'Ordre Corinthien: car ce magnifique Palais, estoit celuy de Creon Roy de Corinthe (*sic*) . . .
>
> (II, 1042)⁶

Music is rendered during intermission (II, 1043), but it does not interrupt the conversation of Alvare and Almahide in the audience. The former points out that "la Tragedie a esté inuentée pour instruire en diuertissant" (II, 1047) and asks Almahide if she does not wish to permit herself to be instructed by the moral of the play. Reference is also made to plays of the same title by Sophocles and Seneca (II, 1046). Alvare reproves Almahide at the end of the second act for having found it "beau que l'on n'enterre point les Morts" and for wishing in an inhuman manner that "les Corbeaux mangent les corps du mal-heureux Polynice" (II, 1051). He also refers to the number of acts in the classical Spanish *comedia*: ". . . les Poëmes Dramatiques ne soient que de trois Actes en Espagne" (II, 1053).

The novelist's reference to the *commedia dell'arte* is an anachronism for there is no evidence that Italian players visited Spain earlier than 1538, "when one Muzio, 'Italiano de la comedia,' was in Seville."⁷ Scudéry in his novel criticizes those who monopolize conversation to such an extent as to "ne laisser rien à dire aux autres; ioüer continuellement le rosle ridicule du Docteur de la Comedie Italienne; estourdir tout le monde de leur babil; faire des Muets de leurs infortunez Auditeurs; n'examiner rien; hazarder tout; bon & mauuais; plaisant et sot; le necessaire & l'inutile; l'agreable & le facheux; tourner les autres en ridicules, & l'estre eux-mesmes; blasmer mal à propos; loüer de la mesme sorte: & par vne prodigalité de parolles, pire mille fois que n'en seroit l'auarice . . ." (IV, 516 f.).

Allusions are made to "la Troupe Royalle" and to the tragicomedy and its requirements for a happy ending (VII, 48); to the legend of Alonso Guzmán which was probably inspired by Vélez de Guevara's play *Más pesa el rey que la sangre* since the title is given (VIII, 436); to Aeschylus and Aristophanes who "ne paroissoient iamais sur le Theatre que masquez"⁸ (VIII, 377), and to the Roman *comedien* Roscius (*loc. cit.*).

While Scudéry's references to the theatre offer no new information, yet they are of interest to the student of Seventeenth Century French drama, and have some importance in the study of theatrical history and of manners of the court. They are a reflection of Scudéry's fondness for the theatre, and as such share in interest with the two plays he included in the novel.

ALMAHIDE AND THE PHILOSOPHY OF LOVE

The sometimes seemingly interminable pages which Georges de Scudéry devotes to discussions of love in *Almahide* are but another reflection of its own milieu and of the tastes of authors of the contemporary heroic novel. The scores of questions on matters of love asked and discussed in *Almahide* are but a small percentage of those under discussion in the salons of the period as well as in the novel. Inane as they may seem, they are important, because, as Aragonnès points out, "toute cette dialectique amoureuse, c'est la psychologie faisant ses gammes, ce sont des préludes à la littérature d'observation morale que l'époque suivante nous donnera."⁹

That the questions debated in *Almahide* were part of a long list of those making the rounds of the salons is obvious when one reads that the Marquis de Sourdis, a frequent visitor of Mme de Sablé and Madeleine de Scudéry, gave a serious discourse on the following questionnaire:

> Si l'amour et le désir sont deux affections contraires? Si l'amour d'une fille est plus violent que celui d'une femme? Quel amour est le plus agréable ou celui d'une femme fort vertueuse ou celui d'une femme qui l'est moins?

And we learn that the dramatist Quinault undertook to answer in verse five theorems of love propounded by Mme de Brégy. It should therefore not be surprising that these questions found their way into the novels of the Scudérys. Their inclusion in these romances, however, sets no precedent, for d'Urfé gives no little attention to a consideration of discussions of love as an examination of his *Astrée* will show. In *Clélie* are found such questions as "si l'absence augmente ou refroidit l'amour, si l'amour est plus ridicule chez un vieil homme ou chez une vieille femme?" etc. In *Almahide* such questions are scattered through the central action as well as through the intercalated stories. They offer no new contribution to this element in novelesque literature. Furthermore, it is impossible to seize upon any argument and declare that this is Scudéry's attitude towards a certain question, and that contrary to his belief. Such conclusions are not to be made for he examines each question from every possible angle; his characters argue a point *pro* and *con,* and as will be indicated the conclusions are almost invariably that no solution is possible because each person is entitled to his own opinion. For example, the circle convenes and someone proposes a discussion of love. Obviously the point of departure should be a definition of love. At the beginning the premise is submitted that love "est ie ne sçay quoy, qui vient de ie ne sçay où, & qui finit ie ne sçay comment." After many pages of discussion in which the subject is dissected, the participants agree that in spite of the many definitions offered, the mystery is as great as ever, and that no better definition than the one above can be given.

What are the questions of love discussed in *Almahide*? There is no need to cite more than a few examples to give some idea as to their nature. Many of them are interesting because they demonstrate Scudéry's skill as a debater since he has prepared an answer and a rebuttal to every argument offered:

> lequel est le plus incommode, ou d'aimer sans estre aimé, ou d'estre aimé sans aimer? (I, 169); laquelle doit estre cruë la plus aimable & la plus digne d'estre aimée, ou de la beauté du corps; ou de celle de l'esprit; ou de la beauté de l'ame; ou de celle de la voix? (III, 1666); d'où vient que l'on n'aime pas tout ce que l'on trouue beau, & pourquoy tous les hommes n'aiment pas vne mesme personne? (IV, 164); lequel doit preferer vn Amant, ou d'estre aimé, & ne voir iamais sa Maistresse, ou de n'estre point aimé, & la voir toûjours? (IV, 771); Lequel vne Dame deuoit preferer, ou d'vn Braue ou d'vn Sçauant?

> (V, 1319)

And so the queries run: when a lady is impervious to love, should one not abandon her? Why do some men love blonds and others brunettes? How should one treat an indiscreet lover? How may a lover be kept when once he or she is captured? How may love be increased when it has once been sparked to life? Should one love privately or in public? Which is the more annoying, to see one's love without speaking to her or to speak to her without seeing her? Who suffers more patiently as a lover, the "homme d'esprit ou le stupide"?

Following the neo-platonic trend, Scudéry, in search of an answer to the question "What is love?" turns to Plato:

> L'Amour est vn Dieu grand, merueilleux, beau, & qui porte au bien & à l'honneste. Qui met en paix les Hommes & les Animaux, qui change la rusticité en politesse; qui apaise les discordes; qui vnit les amitiez; qui incline à la douceur. . . .

> (VIII, 507 f.)

To these observations he adds those of Euripides, Philostratus, and Plautus. The next step in unraveling the mass of information on love is to discover the Seventeenth Century conception of the perfect lover. In *Almahide* it is agreed that

> les Amans doiuent estre propres, & qu'ils ne doiuent iamais paroistre negligez deuant leurs Maistresses, si ce n'est lors qu'il leur importe de les émouuoir à pitié par ce desordre . . . (I, 130 f.); continuellement doux, ciuil, & complaisant, soigneux, assidu. . . .

> (I, 329)

For the lover, the loved one must be "l'aimant de son cœur" (I, 329); he must "viure plutost en ce qu'il aime, qu'il vive en soy-mesme" (I, 398); the "plus grand soin des Amans est toûjours de plaire" (I, 407); he must be liberal (IV, 159). Above all, the lover must be discreet, for, "comme cette passion fait des Misteres des moindres choses, vn Amant ne les peut iamais reueler sans estre prophane" (I, 415).

Having generalized, Scudéry studies different types of lovers and the effects of love. He deals with the effects of absence on a lover (II, 1242) and draws a portrait of an anxious lover awaiting news from the beloved:

> . . . il chancela deux ou trois fois, le visage pasle, le front couuert d'vne sueur froide, la veuë foible, & les yeux troublez; les genoux tremblans; le cœur palpitant; & l'ame encore plus emuë que le corps, par la crainte qu'il auoit d'aprendre quelque chose de funeste. . . .

> (II, 1337)

The work resembles in places a new *Art of Loving* with a brief treatise on love and its relationship to marriage (V, 1050); the pitfalls of wooing a very young girl (V, 1030); how to love a married woman (V, 1002); etc.

How does Scudéry handle his discussions? An example or two will give some idea of the mechanics of the love questions. The question is "lequel est le plus ancien, ou de l'Amour ou de la Beauté?" (V, 1210). One participant states that Beauty is the older, and, quoting Plato, submits that one (Beauty) is the cause and the other (Love) is the effect. A second participant argues in favor of Love "puis que toutes les Belles doiuent leur naissance à l'Amour." A third participant objects, claiming that Beauty and beautiful women have been confused, whereas they are two separate and distinct things, whereupon another speaker invites his immediate predecessor to try to separate them. A logical conclusion is reached when they agree that "puis que nous sommes tous Parties, & que nous n'auons point de Iuge, nostre Procés demeurera indecis" (V, 1213).

The thread of this discussion is continued when a new question asks "lequel est le plus puissant de l'amour ou de la beauté?" The argument proceeds along the same lines: one states that "puis que c'est de la beauté que vient la force de l'amour, il s'ensuit que l'amour est moins puissant que la beauté," to which some one answers that "la beauté ne peut rien sans l'amour, & que l'amour peut tout sans la beauté" (V, 1214).

In *Almahide,* jealousy is the hand-maiden of love. It is the attitude of all of the lovers that there can be no deep affection if the lover is not jealous. However, it is reluctantly admitted that jealousy indicates "mépris de soy-mesme, & estime de son Riual." Mustapha, however, characterizes this malady adequately when he declares that "s'il n'y a point de ialousie en Enfer, il n'y a point de supplice; les Damnez ne sont pas damnez; & toutes leurs peines sont vn jeu . . ." (VIII, 683).

And so Almahide becomes another echo of dissertations on love in the salon. This novel offers only variations of common-place conversations of the *ruelle* on the honor of men, the virtue of women, constancy and inconstancy of love, loyalty and perfidy, coquetry and simplicity, discourses on all types of lovers, the fickle, the jealous, the melancholy, the merry, the ugly, the halt, the lame, and the blind. From time to time the maxims on love are real gems (cf. VII, 730), and as Voltaire will state a century later in regard to Marivaux "l'on y pèse des œufs de mouche dans des balances de toiles d'araignées.""[10]

The presence of such questions in *Almahide* again raises the question of authorship, for Madeleine de Scudéry was famed for such discussions. Yet, as has been indicated, these arguments were so common at the time, they are so frequent in other novels of the century, that it cannot be said that Madeleine had a monopoly on them. It should be remembered that Mme de Scudéry was fully equipped to continue the tradition if the testimony of her contemporaries can be accepted at face value.

In conclusion, the words of Aragonnès should be cited as an adequate evaluation of this element in *Almahide*:

> Le tort de ces discussions était de s'agiter dans le vide; au lieu de propositions abstraites à discuter, il y avait là des cas vivants à peindre. Mettez des noms propres et des circonstances, supprimez tout l'oiseux des propos, et vous aurez le roman psychologique. C'est à quoi, un jour, réussira la comtesse de La Fayette, qui n'est pas la moins assidue, en attendant, aux soutenances de ces thèses sentimentales.[11]

THE MAXIMS

Along with a study of the philosophy of love must be included brief mention of the adages scattered through the pages of *Almahide.* The presence of such short, pithy sayings is another manifestation of the novel's milieu and also carries on the tradition of the *Astrée,* though they are not as numerous in Scudéry's novel. While most of them deal with love, there are some which make observations on other subjects, as a few examples will show:

> Le Temps . . . a toûjours esté regardé, comme l'vnique Medecin de l'Ame (III, 1420); . . . les loüanges données auec iugement, sont le meilleur biais que l'on puisse prendre pour s'insinuer insensiblement dans vn esprit . . . (V, 1231); . . . tous les excés sont vicieux, oüy mesme dans les vertus . . . (V, 1777); . . . l'esperance est le dernier bien qui abandonne les malheureux . . . (VI, 1859); la necessité fait les ingenieux . . . (*idem.*); le regret des choses passées . . . est absolument inutile, s'il ne sert à remedier au present, & à regler mieux l'auenir (VI, 1864 f.); les Femmes sont plus fines que vous ne pensez: & rien n'est difficile pour elles . . . (VI, 2000); . . . le danger ouure l'esprit des plus stupides . . . (VI, 2243); la iuste punition des menteurs, est de n'estre iamais creus, quand mesme ils seroient veritables: tout ce qui vient de leur part est suspect; toutes leurs parolles le sont; toutes leurs promesses le deuiennent: & l'ame qui se tient tousiours en garde contre eux, & qui se mefie tousiours de leur malice, ne s'en laisse plus iamais surprendre, quelque fine, quelque adroite, & quelque artificieuse qu'elle soit . . . (VI, 2249); . . . les parolles ne sont que du vent; l'abondance n'en couste rien; l'on en peut estre prodigue sans s'apauurir; le Fourbe s'en sert comme le sincere . . . (VIII, 82); . . . vn Roy ignorant, n'est qu'vn Asne couronné . . . (VIII, 303); La colere aueugle est vn mauuais Guide (IV, 125); la temerité est

moins vtile que la preuoyance (*idem.*); Qui delibere trop, ne fait rien . . . (IV, 126); qui regarde trop le Precipice, n'y passera iamais dessus . . . (*idem.*); Rien n'est si trompeur que les coniectures . . . (IV, 139); rien ne reconcilie si tost deux Ennemis genereux qu'vn malheur qui leur est commun (IV, 274); . . . tout ce qui vient d'vn Ennemy doit estre suspect . . . (*idem.*).

It is needless to point out that there is little originality in these maxims, and that some of them are with us today with slight changes in phrasing: "time heals everything"; "hope springs eternal in the human breast"; "necessity is the mother of invention"; "talk is cheap"; etc.

THE PSYCHOLOGICAL ELEMENT

Aragonnès's statement cited above regarding the psychological novel raises the important question: is *Almahide* a psychological novel? It is as psychological as any novel in France before *La Princesse de Clèves,* that is, it has a number of monologues in which the author lays bare the thoughts of the characters as love and duty, or love and something else struggle for dominance. But according to the present-day conception of what this type of novel should be, *Almahide* falls short of meeting the requirements, for, while Scudéry tells us what his characters are thinking, he does not allow them growth and development of character. Taken as a whole, the characters in *Almahide* remain static psychologically. They are stereotyped mentally as well as physically: all the men struggle between love and duty; they hesitate; they make a decision; they change it and return to the condition existing before the struggle began. The women struggle between love and virtue, but since they are under the complete domination of the wills of their parents, why struggle in the first place? Of course, it is absurd to point out that it is really the will of the novelist that retards their psychological progression. Furthermore, how can there be such progression when there is no psychological suspense for the reader? One finds all the lovers together at the very beginning of these intercalated novels and there is no doubt left by the author that their stories will end with matrimony. We know that the hero has already won the heroine and that it is a mere question of time before they will be wed. Even the central action lacks psychological suspense after page two hundred and twenty of the first volume, for here the horoscope tells us that Almahide will wed Ponce and we even know what trials she must endure before attaining this felicity. The only section of *Almahide* in which we find the prerequisites of growth and development in character is in that portion added by the English translator Phillips. Ponce reaches the true estate of vigorous manhood here; he is no longer the vacillating, procrastinating mealy-mouthed lover; too long has he been denied his love, too long has he suffered; he casts aside all values of loyalty or allegiance and throws the might of his sword on the side that can enable him to attain his ends: marriage to Almahide. But the change is too sudden, just as the decision of Alvare to withdraw his suit and yield Almahide to his rival is too sudden. It catches the reader unawares and leaves him breathless. The waters which have been backed up against the dam at the same level all through the novel suddenly surge up many feet, and with the onward rush carry everything before them, dam and all. One must, of course, take into account that Phillips realized the psychological disadvantage of presenting to the English reader an unfinished novel; he knew that many unimaginative readers would find no appeal in a romance left dangling in the air, in spite of the horoscope. The style of the last book in the English version shows that it was written hurriedly and just as hurried is the change in Ponce and Alvare: there is a sudden explosion and we have the *fait accompli*.

It can be said then that *Almahide* is a novel containing psychological elements in so far as analysis of the thoughts of the characters are concerned, but that in the original of Scudéry there is no growth and development of character.

DIDACTICISM IN *ALMAHIDE*

As Magendie's study reveals, the Seventeenth Century French novel before *Almahide* is pregnant with didacticism and moralizing. Like its predecessors, *Almahide* was not written solely for entertainment but also to instruct. Scudéry implies in his *Au lecteur* (Vol. I) that he proposes to acquaint his readers with the customs and manners of the Moors of Granada, and throughout the novel there is valuable educational information although necessarily superficial. This didactic material includes the life of the Prophet Mohammed; the discussion of painting and the extensive training and vast amount of information which a great painter must possess; Mustapha's dissertations on rhetoric, law, astrology, medicine, mathematics, architecture, painting, music, philosophy, history, poetry, agriculture, topography and cosmography, military science and tactics, the theatre, political theory, etc. In addition there is limited material treating honor and virtue, the relationship between parents and children, patriotism, and questions of morals. A character is sent on a voyage into Africa, and while following the itinerary of the trip he and the reader are broadened by the things he sees. The novelist emphasizes the fact that a knowledge of the manners, customs, and religion of a foreign people, different interests of princes, a knowledge of the nature of these countries, their expanse and limits, the differences in climates, are all quite necessary in the make-up of "vn fort honneste homme" (VII, 477 f.). Nor is the mind alone developed, for the body is important also. A healthy mind needs a healthy body, a knowledge of the liberal arts is not sufficient; physical development too must be promoted by means of horsemanship, dancing, fencing, and other exercises (I, 477 f.).

Scudéry's methods of introducing these materials are clever. Mythology is presented through the description of paintings and sculpture (I, 552), and a biography is recorded in the same manner (IV, 302 f.). A deranged person, hardly responsible for his actions, discourses at length on various edifying subjects to the amusement of his audiences who even prompt him by means of leading questions. But Scudéry is apparently in earnest, and Mustapha is more than a madman: he is the author's *porteparole.* Though Scudéry may invite his readers to pass over such materials as Mustapha's discourses, descriptions of châteaux, estates, paintings, and the like, it is obvious that he would prefer otherwise. While his descriptions are given in the greatest detail, Mustapha's discourses at times degenerate into mere lists, for example the enumeration of all the known countries of the world, oceans and rivers, mountains, animals, and principal cities (VIII, 350 f.).

It is also Mustapha's task to reintroduce George de Scudéry's long didactic poem on political theory, *Salomon instrvisant le roy,* so frequently mentioned in these pages. Within the more than two-score pages of this poem is a complete set of rules for the guidance of a king in the administration of his government.

From the lips of *personnages sympathiques* we learn of Scudéry's attitude towards monarchs. To him the king was a holy of holies whose prerogatives are derived from heaven. A character points out that:

> Ce n'est point aux Peuples à examiner les actions des Princes, c'est à eux leur obeïr: & les Souuerains, qui sont independans de leurs Vassaux, ne leur doiuent aucun compte de ce qu'ils font, & se doiuent bien empescher de leur en rendre: s'ils ne veulent commettre leur authorité; hazarder leur Estat; & perdre leur gloire.
>
> (VI, 2264)

The person of the king is inviolable, and a potential assassin dismisses his plans with the statement that "Les Testes Souueraines sont sacrées; c'est vn Sacrilege de les attaquer" (III, 1864). But in spite of his rights, the novelist reminds all kings that clemency is a great virtue and that justice is the greatest support of which a throne can boast (III, 1756). In meting out justice, a king should not restrict himself to his friends and his own citizens. To be sure, the protection of the weak against the strong is the action of a "Roy magnanime; mais celle de proteger ses Ennemis innocens, contre ses Sujets coupables" is the action of a hero, whose glory should be immortal (VII, 118).

This brings us to the poem, *Salomon instrvisant Muley Hazen.* Solomon begins his discourse with the statement that only a king can instruct kings, for a subject's position and inferiority in rank intimidate him and restrain him from speaking freely. A king must remember that his subjects' eyes are upon him: "Tu dois compte aux plus hauts, tu dois compte aux plus bas" (VIII, 547), and he must keep in mind that all equity, all strength, all goodness and wisdom come from Heaven:

> Leue les yeux au Ciel, car par luy les Roys regnent
> . . . . .
> Les Roys portent vn Sceptre, & Dieu porte la Foudre:
> Thrône, Sceptre, Couronne, & Roy, tout n'est que poudre.
>
> (VIII, 547-8)

The glory of princes depends upon a great and numerous people but to have a populous kingdom "Il faut de la douceur; il faut de la clemence" (VIII, 552). Solomon admonishes his pupil to further the welfare of his people by ever seeking peace though it be at the very hour of impending battle. He urges liberal reward for all noble acts and the careful choice of confidants for "Vne erreur, dans leur choix, ne seroit pas petite" (VIII, 553) and "C'est par les Seruiteurs que l'on iuge du Maistre" (*idem.*).

A faithful minister should be loved and cherished, but the monarch is warned not to make such a servant one's master. Let him sit at the foot of the throne and not on it; listen to his advice, Solomon says, but the king himself must make and carry out his own decisions. He must attend in person all meetings of the Privy Council; thereby he will gain the experience necessary for a happy and prosperous reign and will learn to know his state better. In only one instance does Solomon advise his pupil to heed the council of others in making decisions, that is, in considering declarations of war. A king should be slow to wage war, remembering that many of his subjects are to be affected by it. If conflict must come

> Que ta Guerre soit iuste, & de necessité;
> Ne te l'attire point; sois-y sollicité;
> Fais, pour t'en exempter, toute chose possible;
> Mets Dieu de ton Party, tu seras inuincible.
>
> (VIII, 558 f.)

When war comes, the king must know how to conduct himself, and the poem includes instruction on this subject (VIII, 559).

A king must be liberal; he must do many favors, always remembering that every favor granted will be returned manifold:

> . . . le Monarque auare est digne de mépris
> Cette bassesse d'ame est indigne des Princes:
> Elle les deshonnore aux yeux de leurs Prouinces:
> Elle les met plus bas, que leur Thrône n'est haut.
>
> (VIII, 561)

The sovereign must defend the poor against the powerful; he must detest the evil and the impious, and, acting in the rôle of shield and sword of God's honor, should exterminate them (VIII, 564). He must suppress his anger, practising self-mastery, for wrath is unworthy of a monarch, and sweetness and joy painted on his face reassure his subjects and give them peace (VIII, 566). The young king is reminded that a ruler's word is inviolable "Et tout Prince menteur, qui violle sa foy, Est indigne d'estre homme, & non seulement Roy" (VIII, 570).

Truth and mercy should be the guides of kings together with the Commandments of "le Seigneur des Seigneurs," but

> De là, descends plus bas, dans les Lettres humaines:
> Elles parẽt le Thrône, & meritẽt tes peines:

> Vn Monarque ignorant, à faute de sçauoir,
> Opprime ses Suiets, & manque à son deuoir.
>
> (VIII, 574)

All of the *beaux arts* should be mastered:

> Mais entre tous les Arts, que ton esprit s'applique,
> A sçauoir la Morale, auec la Politique:
> L'vne regle les Mœurs; l'autre regle l'Estat.
>
> (VIII, 575)

After warning him to be firm, yet not cruel, to be vigilant against deceit, striking it down as soon as discovered, to maintain secrecy in affairs of state, and to avoid excess in self-indulgence, the Wise King summarizes briefly. He warns that God sounds the hearts of all kings and that they are responsible to him. He urges them to drink deeply of the spring of wisdom, for it is wisdom that leads to the reign eternal:

> Aime cette Sagesse, auecques passion:
>   . . . . .
> Elle vient de Dieu mesme, & retourne à Dieu mesme:
> Elle seule affermit l'Authorité Supréme:
> Enfin elle rendra, si tu l'escoutes bien,
> Ton Regne pacifique, ainsi que fut le mien.
>
> (VIII, 586-587)

Elsewhere in the same volume Mustapha speaks of kings and courtiers: the type of persons with whom the king should surround himself and the attributes of the successful courtier. Philosophers and poets are especially favored. Antiochus honored the philosopher Phormion; Croesus, the philosopher Anacharsis; Dionysius, Plato; the Egyptian kings, the poet Menandre; Augustus favored Vergil; Vespasian, Salerius Bassus, etc. (VIII, 500-501).

Rules of conduct for the courtier are set down:

> . . . il faut qu'il ne die iamais tout ce qu'il sçait à son Maistre; qu'il ne face iamais voir tout son bien; qu'il ne prenne iamais tout ce qu'il peut prendre; & qu'il ne face iamais tout qu'il peut faire. . . . Qu'il ait bien soin d'empescher que son interest ne paroisse dans ses conseils. . . . Il faut, disie, que l'adroit Courtisan soit propre, courtois, liberal, ciuil auec les Dames, & obligeant enuers tout le monde . . . veritable, fidelle, & sur tout patient: car c'est proprement la vertu de la Cour. . . .
>
> (VIII, 502 f.)

The duties of ambassadors and the criteria to follow in their selection are listed: "On les doit toujours choisir les plus honnestes gens, & les plus habiles du Royaume dont ils sont: afin qu'ils soûtiennent bien parmi les Estrangers, la gloire de leur Patrie . . ." (VIII, 514). The ambassador should have the following qualifications: "vn esprit souple & penetrant . . . de la fidellité pour leur Roy: de la fermeté . . . de la richesse & de la liberalité . . . de la hardiesse . . . de la dignité . . . & de la Noblesse" (VIII, 515 f.).

I have indicated that Scudéry reproves the court for its many vices. One of the principal sins is that of *la médisance*. Scudéry quotes Seneca, Plutarch, Democritus, Socrates, and Theophrastus on the subject, and then vigorously indicts the slanderer:

> Ce sont des Assassins, qui cachent le Poignard dont ils veulent fraper: ce sont des Empoisonneurs, qui sucrent le venin qu'ils donnent; ce sont des Crocodyles, dont la voix trompeuse ne flatte que pour deuorer: & ce sont des Monstres qu'il faudroit estouffer eux-mesmes, pour l'honneur de la Nature, & pour le repos de l'Vniuers.

(VIII, 518)

Another dart is fired at the court for its lack of sincerity: speaking of a prime minister Scudéry asserts: ". . . Corchut, (qui) estoit nay à la Court, c'est à dire vn Pays où dans tous les temps, la sincerité n'a pas esté fort commune . . ." (VI, 2144).

Ambition and cupidity are scored. Lyparis warns Homar that

> ceux qui ne peuuent se contenter d'vne fortune comme la vostre, ne seront iamais contens: & l'insatiable desir de la Gloire & de la Grandeur, les rendra tousiours infortunez, mesme dans la Grandeur & dans la Gloire. Après auoir aquis vne haute Dignité, ils en voudront encore auoir vne plus haute: de Roys, ils voudront estre Monarques: & de cette sorte allant iusques à l'infiny, par leurs vastes imaginations, & par leur vanité demesurée; plus la Fortune fera pour eux, plus ils voudront qu'elle fasse: & sans donner de bornes à leurs desirs, ils seront dans vne agitation perpetuelle. La fin d'vne Entreprise est le commencement d'vne autre: ce qui les deuroit pleinement contenter, ne les contente point du tout: & méprisant tout ce qu'ils ont, ils courent aprés ce qu'ils n'ont pas, & fort souuent aprés ce qu'ils ne peuuent iamais auoir.

(VI, 2076 f.)

Virtue and good works are always rewarded in *Almahide,* and the evil likewise receive their just desserts. True it is that the virtuous have to suffer the martyrdom of a Job before the wheels of Justice begin to grind. Homar, for his misstep, is persecuted, loses position, fortune, and wife, but he lives to see his enemies punished and his reinstatement to grace. It should be mentioned that Homar is a romantic hero, and Scudéry has no patience with men who wail that fate ties their hands. Lyparis reminds Homar that in so far as the wives of such men are concerned

> dans les grands malheurs, celles qui ne font que se pleindre, cherchent plustost à soulager leur douleur, qu'à seruir ceux qui la causent: & les pleurs inutiles qu'elles répandent, sont . . . des marques de leur foiblesse. . . .

(VI, 2208)

In the Seventeenth Century obedience to parental command was something of a cult. The Duke of Medina Sidonia writes his son that he must obey his wishes "car quelque grande que soit la gloire où vous aspirez, celle de m'obeïr ne l'est pas moins" (II, 989). Elsewhere Scudéry writes that "Les Fils qui ont des Peres, ne sont pas maistres de leurs parolles" (VI, 2734).

Marriage must not be contracted without parental consent. This law is applicable to sons and daughters alike. Abindarrays rejects a proposal of marriage with this plea (V, 1053), and Rodrigue or Abdalla sees his marriage to Fatime endangered by an obdurate father (VI, 2695 f.). Yet Scudéry is fair and just in his attitude towards this question. He conveys the idea that, after all, parents should consult their daughters before taking a step which may mean life-long unhappiness:

> . . . ce n'est pas tousiours la Grandeur qui fait la felicité: il est des mal-heureux sur le Thrône; il est des infortunez dans les Palais, aussi bien que dans les Cabannes; & lors qu'il s'agit de rendre vne Fille malheureuse pour toute sa vie, ie crois qu'vn bon Pere n'y sçauroit trop long-temps songer: & que sans blesser son authorité, il peut la consulter vn peu làdessus.

(VIII, 644)

Spanish *pundonor* in its milder form is duly emphasized. The ladies of Almahide's court love well but wisely; there are no passionate scenes and the love salute does not go beyond the courtly kiss on the hand. Furthermore Almahide, Lindarache, Galiane, etc., refuse absolutely to make any move which will in any way compromise their honor. Ponce de León proposes to Almahide that she go away with him, but she retorts that not only must daughters refrain from promising themselves in marriage without parental consent, but even less is it their right "à consentir à des enleuemens honteux, qui laissent vne tache à la reputation d'vne Dame, que rien ne sçauroit effacer" (III, 1483). Later Almahide tells Ponce that the two of them have something to combat that is stronger than ambition and grandeur, something that no one ought to resist, something that she never will resist. "Et quelle est-elle, cette redoubtable Ennemie? s'écria le feint Leonce: c'est ma vertu, c'est ma gloire, luy repliqua la belle Almahide, qui me vaincra tousiours, & que vous ne vaincrez iamais" (III, 1886). Indeed, she will yield her life before her reputation (III, 1891). Miriam also would rather be dead "que de faire rien indigne de ma vertu" (III, 1922).

Again the gentlemen are no less jealous of their honor than the women. Abindarrays avenges his own honor in challenging those who seek to destroy Donique's reputation. Honor also involves gratitude to the point of self-sacrifice for favors received. Thus Zelebin is ready to forfeit his love because of the gratitude he owes Audalla (VIII, 252). It forces him to speak to his own hurt when temptation seeks to sway him.

Although suicide is generally condemned in many of the Seventeenth Century novels, mention of it from a moral point of view is restricted in *Almahide* to the statement that among the Spaniards suicide is forbidden. Were it not for that, Ponce admits, he would prefer to take his life rather than suffer the anguish which torments him during his separation from Almahide (III, 1419, 1992). There are two suicides in the novel. Alicot plunges into the waves in desperation after Orcan (or Palsi) is deaf to his plea that he be released in order to enable him to rescue Fatime (VI, 2682-2683). The perfidious Alabée, seeing herself threatened with a life of poverty, stabs herself (VI, 2550).

Finally, patriotism is strongly stressed. Scudéry transfers to the soil of Granada his deep-abiding love for country. Zarcan, Boaudilin's favorite, seeks to worm out of Fernand de Solís the secret of the identity of the unknown lovers of Almahide by promising him his freedom and return to Spain. Fernand replies that "chacun aime à mourir où il est nay" (VI, 1852). It is patriotism and love for Granada which impel Muley Hazen to relinquish his throne to Boaudilin (III, 1772 f.). Almahide tells Alvare that if she declared that she preferred Les Fontaines as a home to all the remainder of the earth, she would not do anything unjust "pourueu que i'en excepte ma Patrie" (II, 1297), and it is her sense of duty to her king and her love of her country which finally induce her to continue her false position as queen. Had she consulted her personal feelings, she would have willingly stepped down from the throne, but she is convinced that the peace of Granada and the welfare of her country are at stake:

> Il est naturel d'aimer & de chercher le repos, mais il n'est pas iuste de preferer ce repos à son deuoir, à son honneur, à son Roy, ny à sa Patrie.

> (VI, 1887 f.)

Thus Georges de Scudéry and his wife continue the tradition of Madeleine, their sister, in whose pages one may find similar expressions of lofty idealism. These ideas had been repeated before in many forms, but Scudéry deserves praise for having lent the weight of his own pen in preaching such things as the sanctity of marriage, the inviolability of the home, filial obedience of children, justice and kindness in monarchs, and love of country. In this respect, *Almahide* is universal in its appeal.

THE PASTORAL ELEMENT

One of the most obvious influences of the *Astrée* noticeable in *Almahide* is the presence of a trace of the pastoral element. The essential difference is that in the *Astrée* those characters who have pastoral rôles are supposed to be shepherds and shepherdesses, while in *Almahide* the characters who assume pastoral dress are definitely known to be disguised.

As part of the pastoral effect Almahide takes the name *Aminte*; Ponce that of *Leonce*; and Alvare that of *Ramire* (I, 449). ". . . ayant connû que l'habit galant des Bergers" was pleasing to Aminte, Leonce "ne le quitoit presques point non plus qu'elle." As an additional means of providing pleasure for his love, Leonce composes verse modeled upon the *Bucolics* of Vergil (I, 450). Even the Duke of Medina Sidonia, shrouded in gloom as the result of temporary political disaster, is afforded some measure of solace by "cette agreable galanterie" (II, 1177).

The height of artificiality is reached in an argument by Almahide upon being reproached by Ponce for accepting Boaudilin's proposal of marriage:

> Ouy, ouy . . . la Bergere Aminte estoit plus heureuse que ne le sera la Princesse Almahide: sa Houlette estoit préferable au Sceptre: sa Cabane valoit bien mieux qu'vn Palais: ses Chiens estoient plus fideles, que ne le seroient ses Gardes: & ses Moutons plus obeïssants que ne le sçauroient estre ses Subjects.

> (II, 1279)

Nor is the court of Granada immune to the pastoral influence. However, Scudéry confesses in a way that the pastoral cloak assumed is lacking in reality as will be seen in the following passage. The king, queen, and court take a promenade and find themselves

> dans vne Grand Prairie, dont le vert l'emportoit sur les Esmeraudes, & qui estoit toute bordée des plus grands & des plus beaux Arbres que le Soleil eust iamais fait naistre, & que la Nature eust iamais faits. . . . (elle) estoit alors toute couuerte de Troupeaux de Moutons, de Brebis, & d'Aigneaux: & ces Aigneaux, ces Brebis, & ces Moutons, tous couuerts de Rubans de diuerses couleurs: mais ces aimables Animaux estoient si blancs, si propres, si gras, & si potelez, qu'il estoit aisé de voir que l'on songeoit plus au plaisir qu'à l'vtilité. . . . Plusieurs Bergers & plusieurs Bergeres, parurent meslez parmy eux, la Houlette à la main, & la Panetiere au costé, proprement & galamment habillez. . . .

> (VII, 311 f.)

No further comment is necessary except to observe that certainly nothing could be less "blancs" and no one less "propres habillez" than a genuine flock of sheep with its attendants. Scudéry might have commented also on the "vtilité" of the shepherds in the above passage.

In conclusion, it should be pointed out that included in the pages of *Almahide* are numerous discussions in which the advantages and disadvantages of life at court and in the country are debated. In one curious discourse Abindarrays speaks of the provinces with their life and manners as if these districts were in another nation, separate and apart from Paris and other cities (V, 1513). Perhaps the best defense of rustic life is made by Mustapha who enumerates the pleasures it has to offer (VIII, 470 f.). But again, as is the case with most of the arguments found in *Almahide*, Scudéry does not commit himself, and the debate settles nothing.

DESCRIPTION OF CHARACTER AND SCENE

I have already indicated the fact that *Almahide* is in part a *roman à clef*, and that there are a number of anagrammatic names in the novel intended to veil thinly the identities of the living persons they represent. Scudéry presents also a number of graphic portraits of other characters whose identities it is more difficult to discern because they bear Moorish names, because, as tradition relates it, Scudéry distorts their portraits if these appeared too obvious, making blonds brunettes, brunettes blonds, and because identification through the portraits usually hinges on some brief key phrase or sentence. As an example of the last statement, it will be recalled that Livet identified Lydice by the fact that she was fourteen years older than her oldest daughter. However, literary portraits were very much *à la mode* at the time of the appearance of **Almahide**. Madeleine de Scudéry had contributed no little towards making them so since 1649 as Cousin indicates,[12] and in **Almahide** Georges de Scudéry continues to cater to the tastes of the day.

In the same manner, the portrait as handled by Scudéry in this novel continues the stereotyped manner of presentation as found in the **Cyrus** and in **Faramond**. As Koerting points out:

> Ist doch auch nicht nur die Zeichnung der Charaktere, sondern auch die Beschreibung des Äusseren der Personen eine nahezu stereotype. Insbesondere die Schilderung der Frauenschönheit hält sich fast durchgängig genau an folgendes Schema: Haltung, Gang, Teint, Augen, Mund, Zähne, Haare, Busen, Hände.[13]

This model is followed in the portrait painting of Almahide (I, 478); Ponce (I, 475); Alvare (I, 500); Abindarrays (IV, 465); Semahis (I, 295); Lydice (III, 1656); Emir (V, 1657); Myris (V, 1659); Aldoradine (V, 1669); Ebal (V, 1674); Odomar (VIII, 292); Orthobule (VIII, 295); Mechmet (VIII, 296); Therose (VIII, 423); Carralil (VIII, 277); Amouda (VIII, 282); Rapagy (VIII, 285), and Hyamene (VIII, 287). However, the portrait in **Almahide** may appear either in the form of oral narration by Fernand de Solís as is the usual case, or in the form of a letter (Almahide and Ponce, I, 475 f.) or in metrical form (Myris, ode, V, 1661, and Saluze, elegy, V, 1309). In the case of Therose (VIII, 423) Scudéry eliminates a physical description and gives only a character study. All of the portraits given are those of "des honnestes gens." In the case of the *méchants,* the author prefers to let the reader form his own opinion as in the case of Alabée (VI, 1957) and Olimane (VII, 419).

Comparing in outline some of the portraits in **Almahide** with the scheme given by Koerting, it is found that in the case of Ponce de León, Scudéry describes figure, body, bearing, hair, eyes, nose, mouth, facial features, complexion, talents, esprit, and disposition (*loc. cit.*), and for Alvare we have figure, hair, complexion, eyes, mouth, voice, gait, esprit, and character (*loc. cit.*). For female characters the procedure is virtually the same. Scudéry describes Almahide's figure, gait, body, esprit, hair, eyes, complexion, mouth, features, talents, more esprit, character, and disposition (*loc. cit.*).

There is more amplification in the presentation of Abindarrays-Scudéry's portrait. The author is careful to explain that he is describing Abindarrays in the full bloom of youth. He gives memory, esprit, intelligence, inclinations, character, voice, accomplishments (poetry, music, painting, etc.), propensity for amorous affairs, figure, bearing, gait, hair, face, eyes, eyebrows, complexion, nose, mouth, hands, and education, all of which covers ten pages (IV, 465 f.).

Let us examine this portrait more closely. Abindarrays' portrait is selected because it is a composite of the others, including all the features which may appear in some and be omitted in others. Moreover, it is exactly what one would expect of a *Capitaine Fracasse* or a *miles gloriosus* to say about himself.

Abindarrays possesses "vne memoire prodigieuse; vn esprit vif" and "toutes ses inclinations estoient nobles & eleuées . . ." (IV, 465). He is generous, magnificent, liberal, and never was a friend more true and faithful than he. He is humane and sympathetic, not only towards men but also towards animals. The tone of his voice is "doux," and "son temperament . . . un peu . . . melancholique" and "le feu lumineux" of his "esprit" makes him quick to anger, "mais ce Tonnerre ne dure point" (IV, 468). Georges describes his bravery and modesty (?), his musical, poetic, and artistic accomplishments, and his amorous inclinations (IV, 468 f.).

As for his physical appearance, he declares

> sa taille . . . mediocre, & iustement entre la trop grande & la trop petite: mais si belle, si noble. . . . Il a l'air haut, le port maiestueux, le marcher graue, & l'action vn peu fiere. . . . Ses cheueux . . . ni fort noirs ni fort blonds . . . d'vne couleur fort agreable: son visage . . . ouale . . . ses yeux . . . noirs, grands, & bien fendus . . . ses sourcils bruns & fort espais; son teint vif; le nez bien fait, quoy qu'vn peu grand pour vn Grenadin: & la bouche si extraordinairement belle . . . qu'il n'est point de si belle Dame qui n'en fust contente, si elle l'auoit ainsi. . . . Il a encore les plus belles mains du monde pour vn homme.
>
> (IV, 471 f.)

The same portrait except for variations in stature and colorations would fit most of the feminine characters.

> Lydice est de la plus riche & de plus belle taille du monde: & l'on voit quelque chose de si noble, de si grand, & de si Majestueux en son port, que l'on diroit que c'est vne Reine qui vient de descendre du Thrône . . . Elle a l'air si haut, & l'action si libre & si aisée, que mal-gré le Caractere de Grandeur qu'elle a toûjours sur le visage, les Graces ne l'abandonnent iamais . . . Comme le Soleil couchant à ses beautez, aussi bien que celuy qui se leue; dans vn âge auncé, elle a encore presques tout l'éclat & tout l'agréement de la ieunesse: & ie la compare à ces pompeux débris, & à ces precieuses ruines de Marbre, de Porphire, & de Iaspe; qui par ce qu'elles sont encore, font voir ce qu'elles ont esté: & qui mal-gré les efforts du Temps, & l'iniure des Saisons, sont tousiours belles & magnifiques. Pour ses cheueux . . . (d'vne) couleur rare. Son taint . . . tout le blanc, & tout l'incarnat des Roses: ses yeux . . . si doux, . . . si plein d'esprit . . . si perçant. . . . Sa bouche . . . le dernier effort de la Nature. . . . Son visage est d'vne figure Ouale . . . iuste en toutes ses proportions. . . . Sa gorge . . . pleine & bien taillée: & sa blancheur a tant d'éclat, qu'apres l'auoir comparée à celle de la Neige, de l'Iuoire, & de l'Albastre; l'on voit qu'il n'est point de comparaison iuste pour elle. . . .

Like Abindarrays,

> Son temperamment de feu, luy donne bien quelque panchant vers la colere: mais cette flame s'éteint en naissant, comme celle des Esclairs: & le tumulte finit presques aussi-tost qu'il commence. Naturellement elle a l'ame tendre & passionnée: & cependant la raison l'a tousiours emporté sur ce panchant naturel, qui l'incline à aimer comme elle est aimable, & comme on l'aime. . . . Elle mesle pourtant quelquefois à sa douceur, toute la fierté d'vne Amazone: & la Nature luy a donné vn cœur si grand & si ferme, que le danger le plus affreux ne la sçauroit épouuanter. Aussi luy a-t'on veû proteger des Princes exilez, sans craindre la puissance des Rois, ny la colere des Fauoris: & la vertu persecutée, a trouué retraite chez elle, & dequoy se consoler de son exile. . . .

(III, 1657-1663)

More than twenty-one hundred pages later we learn that "Lydice n'auoit que quatorze ans plus qu'Emire sa Fille aisnée" (V, 1698-1699), and this one sentence is sufficient to give Livet the clue he had been seeking. He identifies her as the Duchess of Lesdiguières.

Included among the characters whom I was unable to identify is Amouda

> vne personne extrememement aimable, fort froide, & fort melancolique, & pourtant la plus agreable du Monde, quand il luy plaist . . . bien qu'elle face profession d'vne fort grande pieté dans la Religion où elle est née; elle a neantmoins l'air galant & languissant. . . .

She is extremely fond of her husband "qui est vn homme si bien fait, qu'on luy a donné le nom d'vn Heros. . . ." For one of her friends "elle a solicité vn grand Procés, contre son propre interest . . ." If she had followed her own inclinations "elle feroit des Satyres fort plaisantes & fort ingenieuses, de ceux qui n'en ont point," but her virtue prevents her from doing so (VIII, 282).

A few of the portraits, for example that of the old and gouty lover, are of abstract types which recall those of La Bruyère. Of this type, Scudéry wrote:

> . . . vn homme qui laisse tous les soirs ses cheueux & ses dents sous la Toilette; qui n'est blondin que par de la poudre; ou qui n'est noir que par la teinture de son poil; est vne mauuaise Figure de Galant: & il auroit besoin de pouuoir faire, ce que nous a fait voir vne Deuise, où vne Aigle s'arrachoit ses vieilles plumes au Soleil, afin d'en auoir de nouuelles: auec ce mot escrit à l'entour, "Renouuelons Novs." Car quelques iolies choses que die vne Dame, vn Amant decrepit n'en oseroit rire, de peur de montrer ses dents noires en riant: c'est vn spectacle ridicule, de ne pouuoir lire sans Lunettes, les Billets doux d'vne Maistresse: & de ne luy en pouuoir escrire, que par ces yeux empruntez. Tout de mesme vn Amant gouteux, n'a garde de la diuertir au Bal: puis que bien loin de pouuoir dancer, il ne marche qu'auecques peine: puis qu'au lieu de luy donner la main, il a besoin qu'elle la luy donne: & qu'elle soit son baston de vieillesse, au lieu qu'il deuroit estre son Escuyer. . . .

(V, 1754 f.)

This portrait is followed by one of the youthful lover, and to this list of abstract portraits should be added most of the women loved by Abindarrays, since they represent all types, blonds and brunettes, tall women and small, robust and thin, melancholy and merry, etc.

DESCRIPTION OF SCENE IN *ALMAHIDE*

Description is one of the most important elements in ***Almahide*** and as such truly deserves more than passing treatment in this study.[14] Hundreds of pages are devoted by Scudéry to graphic presentations of the fanfare and pageantry which were so much a part, not only of Granada and Moorish life, but of his own Paris as well.

Pitou, in his study of *Faramond*,[15] mildly reproves La Calprenède for his failure at times to take advantage of the opportunity to depict in a descriptive passage color and detail afforded by the subject under treatment. Magendie makes a like charge against many of the Seventeenth Century novels, including ***Ibrahim***. No such indictment can be made against Scudéry in his ***Almahide***, for detail and color are his forte. All of the colors of the rainbow and their combinations pass before the eye of the reader in almost endless procession as the author describes now a religious procession,[16] now a coronation, now a Moorish wedding,[17] a bull-fight,[18] a carrousel,[19] or a series of tableaux. Nature is not neglected, and again colors are myriad in a dawn, a sunset, or in a sea storm. Possibly in imitation of Hita Scudéry offers some colors as being symbolical; elsewhere he devotes several pages to a discussion of the merits of the various colors.

As has been stated above, Scudéry gives special attention to descriptions of the various festivals, carrousels, and *courses de bague* which are so prevalent in Hita's work. He is at his best when engaged in such description, and it is not surprising since his own imagination was supplemented by similar festivities in Paris and in the provinces. When one reads of such pageants as the following in La Croix[20] or in Voltaire, one wonders who was the father of the thought, Scudéry or those who planned festivities for Louis XIV.

In 1662 Louis authorized an appropriation of one million, two hundred thousand livres to defray expenses for a magnificent spectacle which took place on June 5 and 6 of that year. The festivities included *courses en char, courses de tête,* and *courses de bague.* "Les concurrents avaient été divisés en quadrilles de nations différentes," La Croix states, and the king appeared dressed *à la romaine.* Monsieur represented the Persians, Condé, the Turks, the Duc d'Enghien, the "Indiens," and the Duc de Guise, the "sauvages." The Queen, the Queen Mother, and the Queen of England were present to distribute prizes which included "une boîte à portraits enrichie de diamants," a reward common for many of the heroes of the novel. Such spectacles, Voltaire points out, reawakened interest in devices, emblems, tourneys, magnificent costumes, superb horses, games of lance and ring, and theatrical machines, as well as in ballets, exhibitions of mythological figures, music, dancing, pantomime, and ingenious and singular mascarades.[21]

As for Paul La Croix's description given above, it finds its parallel in *Almahide* with the exception that the Sultana proposes that for the festival "chaque Dame soit habillée selon la mode des Femmes de toutes les differentes Nations, & des principales Villes où la Religion Mahometane est establie . . ." (IV, 250). Preparations are made according to the Queen's command, and Morayma appears as a Persian Queen, Galiane as the Queen of Tartary, Aldoradine as a lady of Constantinople, etc. (IV, 251).

Perhaps the most brilliant spectacle in *Almahide* and one which represents Scudéry's skill in handling detail and in blending color is the wedding of Almahide. Because Moorish women are not permitted to enter the mosques (this point has been discussed briefly above), it is necessary to hold the ceremony out of doors, midst palms, orange blossoms, myrtles, and playing fountains.

> Tous les Trompetes du Roy, tous ses Tambours, tous ses Fiffres, & tous ses Ioüeurs de Timbes, de Timbales, & d'Attabales; de Dulcines, d'Agnafiles, de Nacaires, de Musettes, de Haut-bois, & d'autres Instrumens à la Moresque, sortirent les premiers de l'Halambre. . . .

The heralds follow in their gorgeous costumes, bearing their golden maces. Following the richly dressed guards rides Boaudilin

> sur vn Char d'or, orné de Trophées en basse taille, & tiré par quatre Barbes blancs, attelez de frõt, auec des Housses en broderie. . . . Cent Esclaues marchoient à l'entour de son Char, ayant des Tuniques de Toile d'argẽt, à gros boutons d'or; & des Coliers de mesme metal.

Other members of his entourage follow equally as resplendent.

At the same time Almahide has left her father's palace, preceded by players of harps, lutes, guitars, and other Moorish instruments, and for the first time in this description colors vary from the white, silver, and gold of her bridegroom's party. Preceding the bride are

> Cinquante Esclaues fort magnifiques . . . portant . . . des Capelines d'or traict, enrichies de Pierreries; des Pianelles d'or massif, ornez de Turquoises & de Rubis; des Liures de Prieres à la Turque, couuerts de Diamans: des Brasselets; des Colliers & des Pendants d'oreilles d'Esmeraudes de la vieille Roche; vn grand Coffre de Cristal garny d'Orphevrerie, plein de Perles. . . . Vn autre grand cofre d'Agathe tout plein d'Ambre gris, de Musq, de Ciuette, & d'autres parfums. . . .

Twenty-four camels follow laden with coffers "de Vernix de la Chine, à feüillages d'or & de Nacarat, tout pleins de Chemises en broderie d'or & de Perles . . . des Bandeaux & des Voiles de mesme . . . ," followed by four chariots of slave girls, escorted by twelve black eunuchs. After them come

> Trois grands Flambeaux allumez, & tous brillans d'or & de flame, aussi hauts & aussi gros qüe les Mats des plus grands Nauires . . . traisnez sur vne Machine faite

en Candelabre d'or. . . . Vn char d'argent cizele (pour conuenir à la pureté de l'Espouse) attelé de Barbes blancs, à Housses couuertes de broderie d'argent, & le Chanfrain orné de grandes Aigrettes, suiuoit . . . & comme ce Char estoit découuert, douze Esclaues richement habillez, y soutenoient au dessus, vn double Dais de Velours rouge cramoisy, tout enrichy de broderie d'or, sous lequel l'incomparable Almahide estoit assise, au milieu de Morayzel & de Semahis.

The bride is described; she had "Vne Cimarre de Toile d'or, r'ataché d'vne Enseigne de Diamans, au derriere de la teste. On luy voyait la gorge, les mains, & les bras, dont la blancheur ébloüissante, auroit terny de la Neige . . . Quatre Esclaues" march beside the chariot, "tenant de grands Esuentails de Plumes d'Austruche de diuerses couleurs garnis d'or. . . ."

The two parties arrive at the scene designated for the wedding at the same moment; the king mounts the steps of the *estrade* on one side, while Almahide ascends another set of stairs on the opposite end of the platform, both being followed by their attendants. From the near-by mosque comes the Muphti

> vestu de l'habit des anciens Caliphes, & suiuy des Talismans, des Alfaquis, des Marabous, des Calanders, & de tous les autres Religieux Mahometans de la Ville de Grenade; chantans tous ensemble auec beaucoup de iustesse & d'harmonie, en Langue Arrabique. *Au Nom de Dieu misericordieux & propice;* qui sont des paroles tirées de l'vn des *Sorats* de l'Alcoran, . . . par lesquelles ce Clergé Mahometan souhaitoit que ce Mariage fust heureux, estant fait au nom d'ALLA, dont ils estoient comme nous, que viennent toutes les graces. Alors le Muphty monta seul sur ce Theatre, par le troisiéme Escalier: & apres auoir salüé le Roy, & la Princesse Almahide, il s'aprocha d'eux & leur dit certaines paroles Arrabes . . . & les faisant courber tous deux, il leur porta les mains sur la teste, comme par vne imposition Pontificale. . . . En suite de cela, le Muphty ayant acheué la Ceremonie Nuptiale, fit signe à ces Musiciens qu'ils changeassent de Cantique: de sorte qu'ils commencerent d'entonner ces mots, en langue Arrabique, *Deffends-la, Seigneur, s'il te plaist, du mauuais Ange.*

This ceremony is followed by the traditional "long live the queen," accompanied by the music of Moorish instruments which is mingled with the customary salute from all the cannon of the city (III, 1950).

As for the architecture, as in *Faramond*, Scudéry's descriptions usually fall into the category of interior decorating, for as Fernand de Solís explains:

> Ie ne m'arresteray pourtant pas à vous en décrire particulierement toutes les beautez exterieures, parce que vous les pouuez voir tous les iours vous mesme, du haut du Chasteau de l'Halãbre. . . .
>
> (III, 1760)

However, he does not hesitate to describe the exterior architecture of a building if it is not located in Granada, and for that reason cannot be viewed by Roderic de Navarre for whose benefit he is making the entire recital. Many of the edifices, such as the Alhambra, actually existed, but Scudéry has not failed "selon" his "coustume, de bastir en Andalouzie & à Grenade de fort belles & de fort magnifiques Maisons" (*Au lecteur,* I). Such is the magnificent mansion of Lydice at Besmeliane:

> vn grand & superbe Bastiment de figure ouale; & vn grand & superbe Donjon quarré: de qui la structure est si vieille & si massiue, que l'on voit auec quelque sorte de veneration, que ceux des vieux Siècles qui l'ont edifiée, ont basti pour l'éternité. . . . Ce vieux Chasteau est flanqué par tout de Tours & de Guerites; & bordé de Pieces de Canon; & comme la coustume des Maures, est d'orner le haut des Murailles de leurs Villes & de leurs Places fortes, des testes de leurs Ennemis, qu'ils ont tuez à la Guerre; la genereuse & pitoyable Lydice, pour conseruer le souuenir des Victoires de ses Peres, par vn moyen plus humain; a fait oster ces Cranes affreux; & bordet (*sic*) ces hauts Murs de distance en distance, de belles testes de Sculpture. . . .[22]

The mansion has its own magnificent mosque, its stables and out-houses, all surrounded by moats, and to the rear of these buildings is "vn petit Iardin solitaire auec des Grottes: mais si couuert, & si retiré, que les Murailles en estant couuertes de verdure." A description of the walls about the old château is given. They were

> basties auec vn certain Ciment, où s'est trouué vn Sel si merueilleux & si fertile, qu'elles sont toutes couuertes d'Oeillets, depuis la surface de l'eau, iusques au haut du Parapet: de sorte qu'en la Saison de ces Fleurs, ce grand & antique Bastiment paroist tout en feu.

> (V, 1634 f.)

The grounds surrounding these palaces are the traditional French parks found in so many of the novels of the Seventeenth Century. The beautiful land surrounding Besmeliane is stocked with "Cerfs, de Biches, de Daims, de Cheureüils, & de Sangliers, qui ne se font aucun mal, & qui n'en font à personne: tant on les a rendus prieuz, & tant ils sont bien accoustumez ensemble" (V, 1630). The air is sweet with the song of a thousand birds.[23] There is

> vne Pelouse d'vne Lieuë de long & de deux ou trois cens pas de large: toute vnie, toute verte; & toute couuerte de Lapins, que l'on y voit bondir & courir, sortir & rentrer dans leurs trous. . . . Cette belle Pelouse est bornée à la main gauche de la Mer, que l'on voit toute pleine de Bateaux & de Nauires, & toute bordée d'Oyzeaux Aquatiques & Maritimes . . . & à la main droite est vn Lac de mesme longueur que la Plaine, & d'vn quart de lieuë de large: dont l'eau pure & transparante, paroist de Cristal. . . .

The crowning feature of this lake is a little isle covered with rushes and flowers and populated by swans that glide majestically on the water's surface. Valleys and dales covered with trees and dotted with cabins, hamlets, and mosques, greet the eye from every direction (V, 1629 f.).

Other estates described by Scudéry are similar to this one with the exception that most are more resplendent with their statues placed at regular intervals along the many

walks and avenues, lined with stately trees of all species, and invariably there are several fountains from which jets of water play.[24]

The houses are immense, and contain innumerable rooms all of which are described to the last detail. To enter the palace of Therose (VIII, 394), one crosses a moat bordered on either side by "vne Balustrade de Marbre blanc: & l'on voit la Court formée par les trois faces du Bastiment." Two lines of busts adorn this court. The vestibule is paved with black and white marble and is ornamented with medals and trophies.

> L'Escalier spacieux et aisé, a d'vn costé vne Balustrade de Marbre blanc, & de l'autre de grands Païsages peints à fresque contre la Muraille . . . & tous ces Repos sont pauez de ces mesmes Marbres blancs & noirs. Le Dôme[25] de cét Escalier, a quatre Tableaux en Camayeu, deux jaunes & deux verds: representant des Sacrifices à l'antique; des Festõs, des Fleurs & de Fruits, colorez au naturel; & beaucoup d'autres ornemens d'Architecture. Lors que l'on est monté, l'on se trouue dans vne Sale d'vn quarré oblong, fort peinte & fort enrichie: & qui a vn Balcon à Balustrade de fer peint & doré. . . .

> (VIII, 394 f.)

From this room one passes into an ante-chamber, equally as magnificent, and then into "vne chambre d'Alcoue, à l'Italienne," with its decorations of the seven liberal arts "representez par des Femmes assises sur la Corniche, & par des Enfans, des Vazes, & des Festons, qui trompent les yeux. . . . Le Lit, la Tapisserie, le Tapis, les Chaises & les Fauteüils, y sont de Toile d'argent à Fleurs naturelles: dont la beauté & la richesse disputent le prix. . . ."

Every mansion described by Scudéry in *Almahide* has its art gallery with its busts and statues, its murals and its tapestries. Thérose's home has a private mosque with adjoining apartments for meditation. From this room one passes into "vne Terrasse balustrée" and then across a small bridge into six great "Parterres à grands Fleurons, bordez d'Arbustes rares, & fleuris, & divisez par de grandes Allées sablées" and in these gardens one finds the expected group of priceless sculptured pieces, grottoes, and treelined walks. Parallel with these walks are canals from which jets of water rise.

THE RÔLE OF PAINTING AND THE "SALONS" IN *ALMAHIDE*

The descriptions discussed above will give some idea of Scudéry's method and style in treating architecture and interior decorating. Included in the latter category are the innumerable paintings which he has described in this novel and which, as has been indicated, should be included along with d'Urfé's treatment of the same subjects as forerunners of the *Salons* of Diderot in the Eighteenth Century. As has been shown, Scudéry was intensely interested in this phase of the *beaux arts* and goes a step further than his predecessor in the *Astrée,* because to d'Urfé's descriptions, he has added discussions of the technique of painting. One cannot help but believe that Scudéry is sincere when he declares that painting is so beautiful and noble an art that it is worthy of great esteem and that those who do not care for it are worthy of much scorn. To him a great painter is much more than a mere man wielding a brush and transcribing images to a strip of canvas. An artist to be great must have a vast knowledge of all the arts:

> car outre que cette imitation trompeuse qui deçoit les yeux, & qui . . . fait croire veritable ce qui ne l'est pas, est vne chose admirable; car outre que ce merueilleux racourcy, qui dans vn petit espace, nous fait voir vn grand Païs, & fort loin ce qui est fort prés, donne de l'estonnement; car outre que la varieté du Coloris, l'opposition de la lumiere & de l'ombre, & . . . la Carnation, les Drapperies, les beaux plis, la diminution des Objets, par les diuerses teintes; l'vnion, l'ordonnance, & plusieurs autres rares parties, qui regardent l'Art & la justesse du Pinceau, meritent bien de l'estime . . . il faut necessairement qu'il sçache l'Architecture, la Geometrie, la Perspectiue, l'Optique, le Poinct de Veuë, l'Anatomie . . . qu'il n'ignore ny l'Histoire ny la Fable . . . qu'il connoisse tous les Siecles & toutes les Nations; pour donner à ceux qu'il representera, les habillemens & les Armes qui leur conuiennent; pour ne pas trauestir les Nations & les Siecles; & pour ne pas faire voir son ignorance, en pensant monstrer son sçauoir. . . . Quoy plus? il faut qu'il s'esleue jusques à la Philosophie, pour connoistre parfaitement la nature des passions, afin de les pouuoir bien representer: comme la joye & la douleur; l'amour & la haine; la colere & la pitié; celles qui resserrent le cœur, & celles qui le dilattent; celles qui doiuent estre modestes, & celles qui doiuent éclatter. . . .
>
> (VII, 655 f.)

When Abenamin attacks the aesthetic ignorance of Lindarache's visitors who praise the work of his brush without discrimination, he is making a pointed attack on "the majority of persons of quality who are hardly more versed in the art of painting." These visitors gaze at Abenamin's art and speak of it:

> comme la pluspart des jeunes Gens de la Cour . . . c'est à dire en ne s'y connoissant point du tout; en loüant ce qu'il ne faut pas loüer; en ne loüant pas ce qui merite bien de la loüange; en disant que c'est la plus belle chose du monde, sans sçauoir si elle est belle ou laide, & presques sans la regarder; en ne parlant que des belles Couleurs, & comptant pour rien toutes les autres rares parties de la Peinture; en demandant pourquoy les Figures ont du noir à costé du nez, sans comprendre que c'en est l'ombre; & voulant encore sçauoir la raison de ce qu'il y en a de si grandes & de si petites, sans conceuoir que c'est l'effet de l'esloignement, & le plus beau de la Perspectiue & de l'Optique. Et au bout de tout cela, vn pas de Sarabande; vn mot de quelque Chanson; vne Piroüette, vne Gambade; porter la main à ses cheueux; siffler vn peu à demy-bas; se tourner preste comme sur vn Piuot; & demander quel temps il fait, & quelle heure est il? n'ayant rien de meilleur à dire. . . .
>
> (VII, 614 f.)

> selon eux, il n'y a point de distinction entre le plus grand Peintre du Monde & vn Broyeur d'Ocre: ni entre ce grand Peintre, & le plus bas Artisan: & le mal est, qu'ils ne sont pas seuls dans cette honteuse ignorance: & que la pluspart des gens de qualité, ne sont gueres plus sçauants.
>
> (VII, 657 f.)

It has been indicated elsewhere that the subject of the Scudéry salon is almost always from Greek or Roman mythology. An example or two of his descriptions of paintings will suffice to demonstrate his ability. Describing a picture of dancing nymphs, he writes:

> On croyoit effectiuement les voir danser et sauter. Le vent agitoit leurs cheueux & faisoit voler leurs Robes . . . cét exercise violent sembloit leur auoir mis sur le visage, vn incarnat vif & animé. . . . Vn Berger, pressant sa Musette du bras gauche, soufflant à ioües enflées dans l'vn de ses chalumeaux, & paroissant remuër les doigts de l'vne & de l'autre main. . . .
>
> (VII, 135)

Atalanta in the race is described thus:

> Elle estoit peinte en courant de toute sa force, vn pied leué, & l'autre à terre; la jambe droite racourcie; les bras auancez; le corps à demy courbé en auant; ses cheueux & la Draperie de son habillement poussez en arriere par le Vent, qui resistoit à la vistesse de sa course; & Hypomene qui la suiuoit, auec vne legereté aprochante de la sienne. Il sembloit auoir jetté vne Pomme d'Or; cette Belle sembloit aussi tourner la teste pour la regarder; & le Peintre auoit si bien exprimé son irresolution, par l'action douteuse qu'elle faisoit, que l'on connoissoit aisément qu'elle hesitoit, qu'elle balançoit. . . .
>
> (VII, 139 f.)

The same technique is used by Scudéry in his other renditions of tableaux which have been pointed out in a preceding chapter.[26] No detail is omitted to convey life-likeness to the figures of the pictures. The mythological subjects are included primarily as exterior decorations, while others, especially the series of tableaux depicting Mohammed's life, are obviously for educational purposes and for local color.

DESCRIPTION OF NATURE

Scudéry's nature descriptions in *Almahide* suffer from the same artificiality found in so many of its contemporaries. The presentation of country estates in Granada as was shown above with their orderliness, their walks laid out symmetrically and lined with trees and statues, their fountains, and their stocks of tame animals seems drawn from a blue-print methodically followed. Even a description of a pirate abode on the island of Origny offers nothing of the wildwood which one would naturally expect it to possess. Scudéry would have the reader believe that nature has followed a plan which would be well for art to imitate, but the handiwork of civilization is detected even here:

Vne haute esleuation de terre . . . au delà de ce Marais
. . . forme vn grand demy Cercle.

This prominence is covered with pines, firs, and cypress
trees. At several points the usual fountains throw forth
their jets

> De sorte que l'on voit en ce lieu là, comme vn superbe
> Amphitheatre, dont la Scene pompeuse, & pourtant
> rustique, seroit toute preparée pour representer vne
> Pastorale: tant il est vray que la Nature est digne d'estre
> imitée par l'Art.
>
> (I, 245)

The contrast between mobility and its antithesis is interesting. Aquatic birds plunge and swim, but nearby stands a
crane on one foot, head hidden beneath a wing. In the
same picture wild geese and ducks rend the air with the
screams as they frolic in the rushes.

The descriptions of the sunrise and sunset are marked by
the same artificiality. They differ from most other descriptions of the kind found in the contemporary novel because
of the use of color. Scudéry's suns cast forth more than a
golden hue:

> l'Aurore monta sur l'Horison plus belle & plus éclat-
> tante que les Poëtes & les Peintres ne la representent;
> & fit voir en l'air parmy vne riche impression de lum-
> iere, mille couleurs differentes, & pourtant toutes rares
> en beauté: qui meslant le sombre à l'éclattant, l'incarnat
> au jaune doré & la couleur de feu au bleu pasle, & qui
> se confondant & s'effaçant en suite les vnes apres les
> autres, exposoient aux yeux le plus changeant & le plus
> magnifique objet du monde. Il en faut pourtant excepter
> celuy du grand Astre qui le suiuit: car il parut ce iour
> là auec tant de pompe & tant d'éclat, tant de rayons &
> tant de lumiere, que toute la magnificence des Rois
> eust paru pauure, en comparaison de la superbe richesse
> que le Soleil estala & répandit sur l'Hemisphere . . . Il
> communiqua mesmes ses beautez à tout le reste de la
> Nature: les Prez, les Champs, & les Bois, en parurent
> beaucoup plus verds, & beaucoup plus agreables: les
> Riuieres & les Fontaines redoublerent leur esclat, en
> seruant de Miroirs à ce bel Astre: & sa splendeur se
> meslant à celle de leur Cristal, en fit rejalir de nouueaux
> feux sur tous ces charmans Riuages. Mille & mille
> Perles liquides brilloient dessus les Buissons, & bro-
> doient toutes les Herbes: & le Zephire doux & flateur
> murmuroit comme les Ruisseaux, & temperoit l'ardeur
> du Soleil, par son haleine fraische, douce, parfumée, &
> delicieuse. Toutes les Fleurs s'ouvrant à ce beau matin,
> faisoient que la Terre disputoit au Ciel, la beauté,
> l'éclat, & la magnificence: & les Oiseaux saluant la
> clarté naissante, & meslant leur joye & leurs chants, à
> tant de choses rauissantes, firent entendre vne harmonie,
> qui charmoit l'ame comme les oreilles. . . .
>
> (VII, 120 f.)

This description is balanced by one of a sunset, and just as
the sunrise has awakened all nature, with the dropping of
the golden orb below the horizon, she drowses off to sleep
again. This description is not as lengthy, nor is the use of
colors so pronounced (cf. VII, 341 f.).

The tinge of fierceness often characteristic of nature is
given her by Scudéry in his picture of a storm at sea, but
this description differs from the classical model of Vergil's
Aeneid only in length and greater detail:

> vn bruit sourd & confus commença de se faire entendre
> confusément, & du costé de la pleine Mer, & du costé
> de la Terre; & le Vent s'eschapant d'entre les Mon-
> tagnes, s'en vint souleuer les flots; mesler les Cord-
> ages; enfler trop les Voiles; & faire gemir le Vaisseau,
> sous la violence des vagues qui le heurtoient.

The efforts of the expert pilot to control the movement of
his ship are in vain, and the roar of the wind and the
waves, the splashing of the rain, the pounding of the hail
stones, and the crash of the thunder prevent the sailors
from hearing one another or from being able to execute
the captain's orders:

> Milles fois les Vagues enflées, esleuerent nostre Nauire
> iusques dans le Ciel: & mille fois les Vagues fenduës le
> laisserent retomber auec elles iusques dans l'abisme.
> Quoy que la nuict eust vsurpé l'Empire du iour, apres
> auoir esté quelque temps sans rien voir, tout d'vn coup,
> les éclairs remplissant tout l'air obscurcy d'vn feu ser-
> pentant & prompt, faisoient voir les Montagnes de flots
> noirs, & des Montagnes blanches d'escume. . . . Et
> puis, ce feu subit s'esteignant subitement, remettoit
> tous ces horribles obiets, dans des tenebres encore plus
> noires & plus espaisses, qu'elles n'estoient auparauant:
> tant il est vray que les contraires opposez seruent à se
> faire paroistre l'vn l'autre.

The conscious effort of the author for antithesis is again
evident here. The ship is pushed by one blast of wind to
the right, by another to the left, and the vessel is caught
fore and aft at the same time by the crushing fingers of
Aeolus which cause it to spin for a quarter of an hour!

> Du fond des Rochers cauerneux, la Mer poussoit
> comme de longs gemissemens, capables de transir de
> crainte, l'ame la plus assurée: les Vents glissant entre
> les Cordages, & retentissant entre les Tillacs, où ils
> entroient & sortoient, mesloient encore à ce premier
> bruit, vn sifflement espouuentable: & tous les Mats
> esbranlez & prests à rompre, par de si rudes secousses
> sembloient encore gemir, sous l'effort de ce Demon
> inuisible qui les agitoit.

Colors again provide a striking effect for "Tout le Ciel &
toute la Mer, paroissoient comme vn meslange de feu, de
noir, de blanc, & de bleu. . . . Vn autre Vent soûterrain,
sousleuoit le sable du fond de la Mer, à gros tourbillons,
& le rouloit confusément parmy les ondes."

The ship continues to be tossed in all directions, and the
play of lightning becomes so horrific that the victims of
the storm begin to wonder whether they are to be drowned
or burned to death. Fire and water again give a powerful
contrast. A gigantic wave smashes the prow, just as a bolt
of lightning demolishes the poop. The destruction is
complete as the ship, leaking like a sieve, is cut asunder
against a rock and "l'impitoyable Mer, engloutit pesle-
mesle dans ses vastes & profonds abysmes, Cordages,
voiles, Planches brisées, Mats rompus, & gens noyez" (I,
259 f.).

This description, while an amplification of Vergil's, is perhaps the best treatment of nature in *Almahide* and is a departure from the order found in others of this subject in the novel. It is also the least artificial of them. However, it is the nature of the subject under treatment rather than Scudéry's own talent which makes it so. A storm at sea is a terrible thing, but Scudéry by force of habit exaggerates, or amplifies if you will, and at times he is amusing: picture the ship whirling like a top for fifteen minutes on the crest of a wave! Or a *subterranean sea* wind strewing sand over the surface of the waves!

The Use of Colors in *Almahide*

As even a casual examination of Scudéry's descriptions of costumes and festivals in *Almahide* will indicate, colors run riot. This point is important in the light of Magendie's criticism of the lack of color in descriptions in most Seventeenth Century French novels. Not only are colors utilized profusely in descriptive passages, but their origin and respective merits are discussed, and following many earlier novelists, there is a trace of color symbolism, although not so much as one finds in *Las Guerras Civiles*. However, Scudéry or his characters speak of colors objectively: they are discussed impersonally and in the descriptions they produce no emotional reaction on the part of the characters. In this respect, he merely amplifies the usage of Pérez de Hita, and differs from that of Saint-Pierre and of Nineteenth Century novelists, for his colors are restricted to use where they are necessary; i.e., costumes, physical traits, buildings, landscapes, etc.

In his treatment of the origin of color, he writes:

> Qui sçait si le blanc n'est point la couleur primitiue, dont le noir n'est que la priuation? comme la nuit n'est autre chose que celle du iour: & si toutes les Couleurs ne se font point des changemens de celles-cy? Qui sçait encore, s'il n'est pas vray, qu'il n'y a que trois couleurs en la Nature? le noir, le blanc, & le rouge: le premier, qui assemble les autres; le second, où elles s'élargissent & s'étendent, receuant celles qui s'y meslent: & le troisiéme, dont se compose la diuersité des couleurs, par le meslange des deux autres? Et qui sçait encore, si le noir ne vient pas de la Terre? le blanc de l'Air? & le rouge du Feu? l'Eau n'ayant point de couleur, & ne seruant qu'à nourrir & faire croistre les Plantes. Qui sçait . . . si le rouge n'est point la couleur unique, qui produit toutes les autres? le noir ny le blanc n'estans pas veritablement des couleurs; mais seulement cette premiere resserrée, ou étenduë, & qui par là, fait apres les couleurs brunes, ou les couleurs éclatantes. Nous ne sçauons . . . rien de tout cela bien precisément: mais peut-estre qu'il viendra vn iour quelqu'vn apres nous, qui éclaircira le Monde de toutes ces choses. . . .

> (I, 431 f.)

Color symbolism is employed to a certain extent. Morayzel ousts Almadan from Semahis' favor. The two cavaliers prepare to engage in a duel and take care

> de se fournir d'vn équipage, proportionné à l'estat present de leur fortune: dont . . . les couleurs, pussent bien exprimer celuy de leur ame. . . .

Morayzel, known as the *insensible,* had formerly worn a silvery white symbolical of his imperviousness to love, but now "pour exprimer la nouvelle & haute esperance qu'il auoit, sa Cotte d'armes, & la Housse de son Cheual, estoient de velours vert en broderie d'argent," and he wears a "Panache de la mesme couleur." Almadan to represent his despair dresses in garments of "feüillemorte," and has a plume of the same color (I, 193 f.). In the carrousel Zelebin wears green as the symbol of hope (II, 741). As for Abenamin, "comme la belle Lindarache estoit alors en deüil, pour la mort d'vn de ses proches Parens; & que de plus le braue Abenamin son Amant . . . estoit vn peu broüillé auec elle: l'on vit entrer" his entourage clad in black (II, 749).

Scudéry delights in shifting colors before the eye of the reader so that they become merged into a thing of beauty. Two groups of Moors, one garbed in red, the other in silvery white, meet in a tourney:

> Quelquesfois on voyoit tous les Caualiers blancs sur vne mesme ligne; & tous ceux qui portoient la couleur de feu, sur vne autre: & puis tout d'vn coup, l'vn & l'autre Party faisant la demy volte; les gens de Morayzel se retrouuoient à la place de ceux d'Almadan, & ceux d'Almadan à la place de ceux de Morayzel. Vne autre fois on voyoit ces deux couleurs meslées également par tout, auec vn art qui paroissoit estre sans art: & puis tous ces Caualiers tournans leurs cheuaux la croupe en dedans, faisoient changer l'objet de couleur, & redonnoient vne autre forme à leur Combat. . . .

> (I, 98)

The tulip was Scudéry's favorite flower because in it is found all of the colors scattered among the other flowers. The following description affords a parade of colors concentrated within a page or two:

> les vnes (tulips) sont toutes rouges; les autres toutes blanches; les autres sont toutes jaunes: quelques-vnes iaunes & rouges; quelques-autres rouges & blanches; celles-cy de couleur de Pourpre & de blanc; celles-là de blanc & d'incarnat . . . d'Amarante brun . . . blanc & de violet: & quelques autres de quatre ou cinq couleurs differentes & distinctes . . . du coulombin, du gris, de lin, & de l'Isabelle . . . de la feüille-morte, de la Laque, & de la couleur de Citron . . . du gris, cendré, du minime, & de la fiamette . . . de l'Orangé, de la couleur de Rose, & de la couleur de Brique . . . l'vne est couleur de Feu, couleur de Pensée, & de Chamois: l'autre est de couleur de cou de Pigeon, d'Aurore, & de rouge brun velouté. Celle-cy se fait voir de Fleur de Pescher, de Nacarat, & de vert: & celle-là de couleur de Souffre, & de Rose seche. L'vne est d'vn Drap d'or . . . & l'autre d'vn Drap d'Argent le plus riche que l'on puisse voir.

> (I, 428 f.)

During one of the many sessions of the king's circle, someone brings up the question: which is the most beautiful of the colors? Each color is taken up in turn as each person defends his or her own favorite in a cold, impersonal manner. The argument has a logical ending since the whole matter is a question of taste. The evidence offered in favor of the color blue will give some idea of the nature of the discussion:

> comme la Nature sçait . . . le prix de tous ses Ouurages . . . elle parle visiblement en faueur du bleu: car en ayant formé le Ciel, qui la plus grande & la plus noble partie de l'Vniuers; il semble qu'il n'est pas douteux que c'en est aussi la plus belle, puis que son choix ne sçauroit errer: & par consequent, que cette couleur peut aspirer sans iniustice & sans tyrannie, à la Royauté des autres couleurs, c'est à dire au premier rang. De plus, la Nature ne s'est pas contentée d'en orner cette merueilleuse Voute, dont tout le Monde est couuert, car elle en a encore paré la Terre: diuerses Fleurs sont peintes de son bel Azur: & les Zaphirs tiennent vn rang trop considerable entre les rares Pierreries, pour estre oubliez en cette occasion: eux de qui le bleu Celeste plaist tant à la veuë . . . Mais ce ne sont ni les Fleurs, ni les Zaphirs, ni le Ciel mesme, qui parlent le plus hautement en sa faueur: il est vn Azur plus precieux & plus brillant que le leur ne nous paroist . . . ce dangereux Azur que l'on voit dans les yeux bleus . . .
>
> (IV, 360)

In conclusion, it should be pointed out that in costume description Scudéry utilizes various precious stones quite effectively by which colors are suggested to the reader without their being actually mentioned. Mere reference to the ruby, the opal, the sapphire, the emerald, the pearl is of course synonymous with color. Costumes are resplendent especially with diamonds which render a wonderful color effect when caught properly by the rays of the sun.

POETIC AND EPISTOLARY FORMS IN *ALMAHIDE*

Like its model the *Astrée*, **Almahide** contains a large collection of verses and letters. The poetry suspends the action, often needlessly, and is characterized by excessive affectation in the best *précieuse* manner and a dearth of ideas. All of the male characters in the novel are poets if need be, and their efforts are usually prompted by the beauty of their loved one, ardent outbursts of love, or disappointment. There are two hundred and fourteen pieces of poetry distributed through the eight volumes, including fifty *stances,* forty-four sonnets, thirty-three epigrams, five elegies, two eclogues, three madrigals, three *récits,* one *prière,* two romances or ballads, three serenades, one mascarade, nine odes, twelve quatrains, nineteen chansons, two epitaphs in verse, and twenty-three pieces of unclassified verse.[27] The few poems which bear titles include **"Les Fleurs"** (I, 434); **"Les Egyptiennes"** (IV, 429); **"Pallas aux Muses"** (V, 1309); **"Les Vainqvevrs Esclaues"** (VII, 265); **"Elegie sur vne absence"** (III, 1401); **"Sur vn cœur brulé par le Soleil"** (II, 1094), etc.

As indicated above, the poetry of **Almahide** is extremely *précieuse.* An example or two will suffice to support this statement:

> Sa gorge est de la Neige, en vn tas amassée:
> Mais cette Neige brusle, eust-on l'ame glacée:

> Et sur ces deux beaux Monts, que la Nature orna,
> L'on trouue & Neige, & Feux, ainsi que sur l'Ætna.
> Son visage accomply fait voir cent belles choses:
> Des Perles, du Coral, & des Lis, & des Roses:
>
> (V, 1313)

> Par l'oreille & non par les yeux,
> Prenant le Poison qui me tuë,
> Ha! ie l'aime comme les Dieux,
> C'est à dire sans l'auoir veuë.

> Ouy, par vn Papier enchanté,
> Et de ce beau feu qui l'anime,
> L'inuisible Diuinité,
> Me brusle comme sa Victime.
>
> (V, 1590)

Rarely does Scudéry depart from the love theme, but there are two noteworthy digressions from this subject. The didactic element enters into the **Salomon instrvisant Muley Hazen,** as has been shown above, and in his ode **"Au Roy,"** he follows the tendency of many of his contemporaries in appealing to Louis XIV to patronize poets. The final stanza will give some idea as to its contents:

> Protege donc ces Grands Hommes,
> Qui font reuiure les Rois;
> Tu peux en auoir le choix,
> Dans l'heureux Siecle où nous sommes.
> C'est dans leurs diuins trauaux,
> Que sur tes Nobles Riuaux,
> L'on te verra l'auantage:
> Et que mesme apres la Paix,
> Le Genil vainera le Tage,
> Et le vainera pour iamais.
>
> (VIII, 388)

One of the stances, although dealing with love, recalls the famous verse of Juan Ruiz, Archpriest of Hita, in *El libro de buen amor,* dedicated to little women (v. *Clásicos Castellanos,* II, 252):

> Celle que i'adore est petite,
> A ne la voir que par dehors:
> Mais i'y découure vn grand merite,
> Qu'elle cache en vn petit corps.

> Ces Chefs-d'œuures de la Nature;
> Ses yeux pleins de flame & d'attraits,
> Nous font vne grande blessure,
> En nous lançant de petits Traits.

> Elle paroist peu redoutable,
> Lors qu'elle me veut escouter:
> Mais comme on la voit toute aimable,
> On la doit pourtant redouter.

> Par mille graces sans pareilles,
> Quand ie la voy sans cruauté,
> C'est vn abregé des Merueilles,
> Dont se compose la beauté.

> Enfin auant que de me taire,
> Ie veux encore dire icy,

Que c'est la Reyne de Cithere,
Peinte en vn Portrait racourcy.

(IV, 743)

Scudéry points out that the *coplas* are the Spanish equivalent of *stances* and composes in Spanish the *coplas Por la niña enferma,* the first of the five stanzas of which follows:

Niño Amor, la Niña bella,
Pierde donaire y color;
Aduierte que su dolor
Te harà (*sic*) morir con ella,
Si a mudar no vas aquella
Malina y sangrienta Estrella
D'esta Niña, Niño Amor.

(VIII, 460)

As for the metrical system employed in **Almahide,** Scudéry is consistent in following the tendencies of his contemporaries in the sonnet, the ode, and the elegy. For the ode he uses generally the ten-verse stanza of seven syllables. The rhyme is *ababccdeed.* The sonnet is written in alexandrines of two quatrains and two tercets, the rhyme being *abbaabbaccdeed.* The elegy is found in varying lengths, the longest of them being of sixty-six verses written in couplets. The verses are usually decasyllabic:

Sombre Séjour, où demeure l'effroy;
Tombeau funeste, et moins triste que moy
De quelque horreur qu'vne ame soit atteinte
Quand ta noirceur la fait paslir de crainte.

(III, 1401)

As I have indicated, the *stance* is the most frequent. The length of the stanza is quite variable: four (II, 1058); six (II, 1165); or eight (IV, 576) verses. The number of syllables in the verses within the stanza varies also. A four-syllable line alternates with one of five syllables; in another *stance* of six verses, one finds twelve syllables in the two initial lines in each stanza, which are followed by four verses of eight syllables. Some of the poems of this form are consistent with stanzas of four verses, octosyllabic. The eight-verse stanza rimes *ababcdcd;* the six-verse stanza *abbacc;* the four-verse stanza *abab.*

In one instance, obviously influenced by the many *romances* found in *Las Guerras Civiles,* Scudéry attempts this type of versification in seven-syllabic blank verse (IV, 505).[28]

The epistolary forms found in **Almahide** are like most of those found in the Seventeenth Century French novel. With their stiff formality and preciosity, they are a far cry from the delightful epistles of Mme de Sévigné or even from the conversational letters of the *Astrée.* Some are characterized by the same redundancy which typifies those of the *Astrée:* they are preceded by such captions as "le Malhevrevx Ponce de León à la crvelle Aminte" and "Aminte à l'Illvstre Ponce de León." The name of the addressee is repeated in the body of the letter, and that of the writer in the signature. No more need be said of them except to cite an example which will illustrate their balanced structure, their lack of the writer's personality, and of warmth, even in a love epistle. Ponce addresses Almahide thus:

Ie n'ay manqué de respect; mais i'ay manqué de patience: ie n'ay point songé à vous déplaire, mais i'ay cherché à me consoler: & lors que mes Riuaux possedent un bien effectif, i'en ay demandé vn en Peinture. Cependant l'ombre & le corps sont deux choses bien differentes, belle & fiere Aminte: & durant qu'ils ioüissent de la veuë de l'vn, vous ne deuiez pas me refuser l'autre. Mais puisque vous ne m'auez pas iugé digne de cét honneur, ie ne me iuge plus digne de viure, & vous deuez desia compter parmy les Morts. . . .

(II, 1082)

Structure and Style of *Almahide*

As Tallemant des Réaux has stated, the novels of the Scudérys are perhaps the best written of all the *romans de longue haleine.* Georges' **Almahide** especially deserves this compliment, for it is well-planned. Every line written by Scudéry seems to follow a preconceived outline, and though **Almahide** has all of the characteristics of the long-winded novel, i. e., *in medias res* and intercalated stories, it is superior in the fact that with the exception of one of the five intercalations, all are completed in one continuous narration instead of being divided and scattered through ten or twelve volumes. The criticism that can be made is that these stories in themselves are strung out by the insertion of descriptions of buildings, costumes, festivals, portraits, and by the inclusion of seventy-nine monologues, one hundred and twenty-four letters, two hundred and fourteen poems, seventy-one discussions of love, and eighteen harangues varying in length from one to three hundred pages. Delete these and the action is sufficiently compact.

The main action lasts only twelve days approximately. The whole structure is marked by balance. Just as there is no suspense concerning the final outcome of the various stories, there is no uncertainty as to the structure, so methodically does the author follow the blue-print. A harangue by one leader of two rival factions will be followed by a harangue by the chief of the second faction (I, 10-12; 14-15). A horoscope for the heroine is followed by one for the hero (I, 220; I, 235); an act of valor by one rival is balanced by a similar act by the second (II, 1618 f.); if Alvare writes a poem for Almahide, it is certain that Ponce will duplicate his efforts (III, 1584, 1591). Letters are always answered: if two letters are dispatched to two different people, two replies are forthcoming.

The structure of the various volumes is consistent, and the same plan is followed through each. Let us examine two typical volumes: IV and V. They are arranged in this manner:

I. Volumes IV and V.

A. Main action.
    1. Brief review of the unhappy situation of the main characters.
    2. A new diversion is announced to alleviate a tense situation (pp. 1-130).
    3. The circle meets to discuss love or to review past spectacles and to plan for a future one (pp. 130-253).
    4. The five principals, Almahide, Ponce, Alvare, Esperanza de Hita, and Fernand de Solís meet to review their affairs (pp. 253-271).
    5. The single intercalated historiette within an *histoire* is resumed by Fernand (pp. 271-298).
    6. The new festival is described, in this case a *sarrao*. The discussion includes a description of setting, costumes, discussions, and then the details of the various events in the *sarrao*, ballets, dances, etc. (pp. 299-447).
    7. Transition to an intercalated history. Roderic de Navarre becomes interested in one of the couples and insists on hearing a story.
B. An intercalated story related by Fernand de Solís.
    1. Background and qualities of the characters being treated (pp. 455-474).
    2. Adventures of the hero and heroine, in which the plan of the main action is adhered to. In this instance, Ferdinand's story begins on page 455, and continues through the next volume.

Attention should be called to the fact that, after devoting the first three volumes of the novel to the affairs of Almahide, Ponce, Alvare, and their parents, Scudéry has cleared away all unfinished business, and is prepared to pursue the stories of the subordinate characters in pairs. Though Tallemant states that Scudéry came to Paris to publish a novel of twelve volumes, it is likely that it would have reached sixteen, since at the conclusion of the original there remain eight couples whose stories had not been given. Scudéry thought probably that Abindarrays deserved two volumes since he himself is represented in this character, but, beginning with the sixth volume, he followed the plan of devoting one volume to each of the couples.

As I have stated, the structure and style of *Almahide* is characterized by perfect orderliness and precision. These traits, however, are accompanied by a certain monotony that can become deadly to one who does not have the leisure time for reading that the Seventeenth Century public must have had. All characters behave exactly the same way in similar circumstances, all go through the same trials and tribulations. If there are twenty-four contestants in a bull-fight or a carrousel, Scudéry describes their costumes one by one, and then begins over again as he gives an individual account of their actions on the field. If he describes twelve booths of a bazaar in detail, at the conclusion of the twelfth description, he returns to the first booth and relates the action taking place before it and then on through the twelfth again.

Scudéry is aware of the fact that he is too wordy, and he apologizes for it: "ie crains d'abuser de la fauorable audience que vous me faites la grace de me donner," Fernand tells Roderic (I, 210). Apparently he fears that the reader

too may become lost in detail for there are several cases in which he gives a brief summary or repetition of all preceding action. For example, the many loves of Abindarrays are summed up in a page or two (V, 1560 f.). He is also aware evidently that his narrator may appear to have too prodigious a memory, for Fernand is constantly repeating such remarks as this: "Il (Alvare) releua ces deux Papiers qu'ils auoient rompus . . . & les ayant mis dans sa poche, il me les montra depuis: ce qui m'a mis en estat de vous les pouuoir reciter" (III, 1718).

As for the language of ***Almahide*** it soon becomes apparent that Scudéry's stock of adjectives is very limited. Many of them are over-worked; the adjective *belle*, for example, appears fifty-four times within ninety-four pages (II, 1030-1124). Other words frequently encountered are *genereux*, *divine*, and *invincible*. Adjectives are an important index to the character of the various figures of the novel: *le violent Dragut, la melancholique Zelindore,* and, when one of the more despicable characters is being treated, the invectives flow. Alabée is described as "cette Furie invisible, cette Fourbe adroite, la sanguinaire Alabée, cette infernale Furie, cette Megere," etc.

Scudéry's style is also characterized by the frequent use of the metaphor, simile, and other figures of speech. Darkness during a storm at sea is described as the usurper of the day (I, 260); Almahide's tears become "de Perles liquides" (III, 1586), a resigning monarch and his successor are called "le Soleil Leuant" and "le Soleil Couchant" (III, 1754). Bold lovers are called "les Torrents qui bondissent" and timid ones "Les Riuieres qui coulent si vniment" (IV, 192). A woman is described as "vne masse informe de blanc & d'incarnat" or a "bel amas de neige" (IV, 478), and a loquacious man is "vn Torrent continuel de paroles" (IV, 515). Night is "la Mer du Silence" (IV, 522). Abindarrays' amorous heart is made of "Abeste, de Bithume, & de Naphte" (V, 1496).

A few additional examples will suffice: "des yeux où l'amour sembloit nager dans la ioye" (VI, 1993); "vn nouueau Poison dans ses beaux yeux" (II, 1287); "le lion lançant des regards enflamez" (III, 1617); "vne brulante neige" (V, 1665).

The use of similes is also frequent. Abindarrays' fickleness is "comme les Etoiles errantes" which "ne deuiennent pas Etoiles fixes" (IV, 710); Osmane's "esprit pique pour guerir, comme la Lancette du Chirurgien" (V, 1261), and Alabée appears before Homar "fiere comme vn Aspic" (VI, 2351).

As for sentence structure, the following observations can be made. The partitive is quite common and may be used singly in a series "de la rage & de la fureur . . . beaucoup de plaisir . . . de l'allegresse . . . de la confusion . . . de la honte . . ." (I, 64) or in pairs "de la tendresse & de la melancholie; de la douleur & de l'amour" (I, 668).

Often one finds a series of nouns connected by the conjunction *et*:

L'amour partageoit egalement entre ces deux nobles cœurs, toutes ses Roses & toutes ses Espines: c'est à dire, tous ses plaisirs, & toutes ses peines; toutes ses ioyes & toutes ses douleurs; tous ses rauissemens & toutes ses inquietudes.

(I, 368)

The preposition *de* and *à* may be combined in a series:

ils passerent bientost du plaisir à la douleur, de la satisfaction à l'ennuy, de la tranquilité à l'inquietude, de la joye au chagrin, & presques de l'amour à la haine.

(V, 1337)

The interjection *o* is another word performing double duty. On a single page I find "O cher Pere, ô cher Esclaue, ô chere personne, ô Dieu, ô genereux Captif" (I, 41); on two others "ô belle, & trop fiere Semahis . . . ô aimable Despine, ô charmante Algadire; ô parfaite Miriane . . . O trop malicieux Zaniel . . . ô trop adroit Machmut; ô trop fin Ismael; ô trop eloquent Zizim" (I, 172-173). Observe the use of the adverb *trop* and the adjectives in the examples just cited.

A series of nouns preceded by *ni* is frequently encountered (II, 963). Scudéry also makes effective use of a series of short sentences, perfectly balanced, all containing the same number of words: a pronoun, a verb, and an adjective: "Il fut propre, il fut magnifique, il fut liberal, il fut complaisant" (I, 174), or "Elle est douce; elle est complaisante; elle est ciuile; elle est flateuse" (I, 481). In the following examples three short balanced sentences are in turn balanced in idea: "il est ieune, il est homme, il est absent . . . mais tu es ieune, tu es fille, tu es absente . . ." (II, 965). Sometimes the sentence is balanced, but the word order is reversed: "L'Amant soupira & gemit; l'Amante gemit & soupira" (III, 1882). Another noticeable trick of Scudéry is the repetition of the verb in the semi-conclusion or conclusion (the decision of the speaker) in the monologue: "perdons le donc, perdons-le" (VI, 1846), the monologuist cries. Or "cherche . . . cherche" (VI, 2208) or "espere donc, espere" (VII, 587).

The conditional sentence is quite common. At times, three *if* clauses may have one conclusion (II, 1289). There are two pages on which there are conditional sentences only consisting of the condition and the conclusion (V, 1266-7). On another "il faut" is used exactly nine times (III, 1854). If a phrase catches the fancy of Scudéry, he will repeat it, for example, "vn discours qui *auroit pû toucher le cœur* d'vn Tigre (VI, 2024, 2210, 2339, 2859; VII, 424; V, 1231), and "vn cœur faist comme le mien" (IV, 488, 570, 752; V, 1181; VI, 1867, 1878, 2018, 2322, 2461; VIII, 707); and "noire melancholie" (II, 1302, 1336; III, 1539, 2075; VII, 474; VIII, 274, 313, 663).

In conclusion, the style of **Almahide** is marked by clearness, rhythmic flow of periods, mathematical precision of balance with a tendency to become monotonous. While *précieuse* to a certain degree, **Almahide** does not become offensive or ridiculous. The vocabulary is limited with a

consistent use of metaphors and similes. As for the treatment of content, the procedure is the same as in many other contemporary novels: monologues, discussions, and poetry. The structure is that of *in medias res* with the intercalated story.

CONCLUSION

Little remains to be said in this study that has not already been stated above. **Almahide** deserves more attention than it has received for the following reasons: 1. it is the first important Hispanic-Moorish novel in France; 2. of all the novels appearing under Georges de Scudéry's name, it appears to be the only one in which Madeleine did not have a hand, judging by a vast amount of internal evidence available together with contemporary testimony; 3. **Almahide** enjoys a peculiar position among its contemporaries because, as far as we know, it is the only one in which an author republishes within the frame of a different literary classification, works which he had already offered to the public. In **Almahide** there are three such works. 4. It is also remarkable as a *roman à clef* and for its extensive use of color.

I have stated elsewhere in this study that **Almahide** deserves a better fate. An examination of novels contemporary with **Almahide** or studies made of these novels reveal that **Almahide** possesses every element which made those novels popular. Bochet, in his evaluation of the *Astrée,* states that

Une œuvre n'est vraiment *significative* dans l'histoire littéraire que si elle réunit les trois conditions suivantes: elle doit se rattacher à une tradition intellectuelle et artistique, représenter fidèlement le goût et les idées de son époque, et contenir des éléments viables dont la génération suivante peut faire son profit. Tournée vers le passé, elle reçoit l'héritage préparé, éprouvé par le tempérament national; au présent elle demande la vie.[29]

Almahide meets every requirement mentioned by M. Bochet. In its various elements it follows every intellectual and artistic tradition set up by its forerunners, as has been shown; it certainly represents the tastes and ideas of its day; it contains many elements which could have been of value to future generations, and the present generation is not excluded. It is an admirable study of Seventeenth Century manners and customs, and has many fine lessons in morality and virtue to teach. Then why did it fail; why was there only one edition; why has it been almost completely neglected as a potential literary source by writers who followed Scudéry? There can be only one definitive answer: it appeared about ten years too late; in range of intercalated stories it was too limited; and it was left unfinished, an important factor from a psychological point of view. Otherwise, there is no reason to believe that it would not have taken a place alongside the **Cyrus** and **Clélie** in popularity. It includes the same sort of materials, the same kind of love stories, the same *péripétie* of the heroic novel; space is given to neo-platonic discussions of love, to a study of the "anatomie" of the heart; heroism, constancy, and courage in men are exalted; the virtue and beauty of womanhood are extolled. It cannot be argued that its lack of success is due to this repetition of materials and themes, for *Almahide* in its birth went through biological processes which are as natural for pieces of literature as for human beings, or animals, or flowers. If *Clélie* enjoyed such popularity though its last volumes appeared in 1660, then why the sudden change in taste which doomed *Almahide* to oblivion? Let the reader be reminded that I am not pleading that *Almahide* is a great novel, far from it. The contention is that *Almahide* is not inferior to others of its literary kind which did receive public applause. It is then to be supposed that the fact that it was left dangling without a conclusion is responsible for the reception accorded it. This alone can explain the sudden change in tastes, unless it was that the public was weary of itself, weary of watching an endless parade of its own reflection in the novels of d'Urfé, La Calprenède, and Mlle de Scudéry.

Forgetting for the moment its lack of originality and its great length and considering it apart from its contemporaries, *Almahide* is a valuable document of Seventeenth Century life, and as such should be of value to a student of sociology and history, as well as to those interested in French life and letters of the period treated.

Notes

1. George Sale, *The Koran,* London and New York, 1891, p. 77.

2. *Ibid.,* p. 73.

3. Detailed description of the Zarabanda is particularly interesting.

4. *Autor* here must mean "stage director." Rennert lists him with actors and actresses.

5. Rennert, *The Spanish Stage in the Time of Lope de Vega,* New York, 1909, pp. 63 and 573.

6. "Creon Roy de *Corinthe*" is evidently an error. It should be *Thebes.*

7. Cf. Rennert, *op. cit.,* p. 29, n.

8. Scudéry apparently means that Aeschylus and Aristophanes wore the masks.

9. Aragonnès, *Madeleine de Scudéry, reine du tendre,* Paris, 1934, p. 69.

10. Cited by Aragonnès, *op. cit.,* p. 70.

11. *Ibid.,* p. 71.

12. Koerting, *Geschichte des Französischen Romans im XVII Jahrhundert,* Leipzig, 1891, p. 172.

13. *Op. cit.,* I, 372-3.

14. For comment on Scudéry's descriptive ability v. Loret, *La muse historique,* Letter XXXVII, Book VI, September, 1655, T. I. p. 97, and Gautier's *Les Grotesques,* Paris, 1856, p. 317.

15. Pitou, *La Calprenède's Faramond,* Baltimore, 1938, p. 115.

16. V. T. I, p. 21.

17. Cf. below and Vol. III, p. 1766 f.

18. T. VI, 1913.

19. T. II, 733.

20. *XVIIme Siècle Institutions, Usages, et Costumes,* Firmin-Didot, Paris, 1880, p. 471 f.

21. Cited by La Croix, *op. cit., loc. cit.*

22. Cf. I, 300, and I, 548. These descriptions are stereotyped.

23. Cf. I, 307.

24. Cf. I, 300, 546 f.; VII, 133 f.; VII, 190 f.

25. Cf. I, 310 and I, 548.

26. V. especially his descriptions of the flood, I, 311 f.

27. The poetry is distributed as follows: I, fourteen; II, twelve; III, eighteen; IV, eighteen; V, forty-four; VI, nine; VII, thirty; VIII, sixty-nine.

28. D'Urfé had used blank verse in his *Sylvanire.*

29. Bochet, *L'Astrée, ses origines, son importance dans la formation de la littérature classique,* Geneva, 1923, p. 179.

Bibliography

Aragonnès, Claude, *Madeleine de Scudéry, reine du tendre,* Paris, 1934.

Bochet, Henry, *L'Astrée, ses origines, son importance dans la formation de la littérature classique,* Geneva, 1923.

Davity, Pierre, *Nouveau Theatre du Monde,* Paris, 1644.

Gautier, Théophile, *Les Grotesques,* Paris, 1856.

Koerting, Heinrich, *Geschichte des Französischen Romans im XVII Jahrhundert,* Leipzig, 1891.

La Croix, Paul, *XVIIe Siècle Institutions, Usages, et Costumes,* Paris, 1880.

Magendie, Maurice, *Du nouveau sur l'Astrée,* Paris, 1927.

————. *L'Astrée, analyse et extraits,* Paris, 1928.

————. *Le roman français au XVIIe siècle de l'Astrée au Grand Cyrus,* Paris, 1932.

Pérez de Hita (Ginés), *Historia de los vandos de los Zegrís y Abencerrages, cavalleros moros de Granada; de las civiles guerras que hubo en ella, y batallas que se dieron entre Christianos y moros, hasta que el rey Don Fernando V la ganó,* edit. Blanchard-Demouge, Madrid, 1913.

Pitou, Spire, Jr., *La Calprenède's Faramond,* The Johns Hopkins Studies in Romance Literatures and Languages, XXXI, Baltimore, 1938.

Rennert, Hugo, *The Spanish Stage in the Time of Lope de Vega,* New York, 1909.

Sale, George, *The Koran,* London and New York, 1891.

Scudéry, Georges de, *Almahide ou l'Esclaue Reine,* 8 vols., Paris, 1660-3.

Jerome W. Schweitzer (essay date 1968)

SOURCE: Schweitzer, Jerome W. "The Scudérys Revisited: Georges de Scudéry (1601-1667)." In *Renaissance and Other Studies in Honor of William Leon Wiley,* edited by George Bernard Daniel, Jr., pp. 203-14. Chapel Hill: The University of North Carolina Press, 1968.

[*In the essay below, Schweitzer surveys Scudéry's career and attempts to assess his place in literary history.*]

> *Un grotesque? Un fantoche? Un matamore? Sans doute . . . Mais, dans son outrance même, un type bien latin. Moustache de chat, feutre emplumé, fou comme don Quichotte, fier comme Bragance et vantard comme Tartarin, ce bohème de lettres d'autrefois a des titres à notre indulgence. On l'oublie, on l'ignore, on ne le comprend plus. Après tout, c'est peut-être dommage. . . .*[1]

May 14, 1967, marked the tercentenary of the death of Georges de Scudéry.[2] As some critics have remarked and Rathéry and Boutron intimate,[3] this so-called *matamore des lettres* had less merit than he thought but more than his adversaries attributed to him.

It is fitting, I think, that some notice be taken at this time of the life and works of this man who, despite all his foibles, his vanity, his conceit, his jealousy and pettiness at times, had in truth no little merit as a writer; he was a warm and faithful friend in the adversity of those who befriended him or had his admiration, and he was a kind and considerate husband to the lady who became his wife in 1654, just seven years prior to his death.

Born of an old family of Apt in Provence, the Scudérys claimed Italian origin. Their grandfather, Elzéar Escuyer, was a soldier of distinction and governor of La Coste under Charles IX. Georges Scudéry, père, left Apt near the end of the Sixteenth Century, adopted the spelling "Scudéry" and followed Brancas-Villars to Lyons, Rouen, and finally to Le Havre, where he served as captain of ports. In 1599 he married Madeleine de Goustimesnil, a demoiselle of good family by whom he fathered five children. Only Georges born in 1601 and Madeleine in 1607 survived infancy. Scudéry, père, was imprisoned shortly for sinking a Dutch vessel off the coast of Brazil. He died in 1613 to be followed soon after in death by his wife. Georges entered the army at age fifteen while Madeleine entered the household of an uncle who reared and educated her. In 1620 Georges was back in Apt where he encountered his first love and first poetic inspiration, Catherine de Rouyère who jilted him for another.

It should be noted here that Scudéry in *Almahide* (IV, p. 471 ff.) introduced himself as Abindarrays Abencerrage. The latter is somewhat like the Hylas of d'Urfé's *Astrée,* constant in his inconstancy, dabbling in love with a large variety of women, rich and poor, young and old, comely and homely, until he finally wed Aldoradine (Mlle de Martin-Vast, his future wife). Now Georges was a confirmed bachelor until his marriage in 1654 to a girl in her early twenties and all of the biographical material I have read indicates there were only three women in his life: Catherine de Rouyère; Angélique-Céleste de Harville-Palaiseau, seduced and abandoned by Scarron and later taken into his house as housekeeper when the convent in which she resided went bankrupt; and Mlle de Martin-Vast whom he married. The affair with la Sœur Céleste went no further than Georges for a time standing in the street watching her window as he munched on a crust of bread. Thus the only serious love affair he had appears to have been with his future wife. He may have been willing but evidently the ladies were not attracted to him.

Before picking up anew the threads of this brief biographical sketch, perhaps I should include here the portrait which he draws of himself which is a sort of parallel with that of Madeleine (Sapho) in *le Grand Cyrus.* He states that Abindarrays possessed a prodigious memory and all of his inclinations were noble and elevated (*Almahide,* IV, 465). He was generous, magnificent, liberal, and never was a friend more true and faithful than he. The last part of this self-estimate is more fact than fiction as attested to by his loyalty to the Condés in their disgrace and by his defense of Théophile de Viau, thus risking violent royal displeasure and imprisonment at the least. The tone of his voice was "doux," his temperament "un peu mélancholique" and "le feu lumineux" of his "esprit" made him quick to anger "mais ce Tonnerre ne dure point" (IV, 468). He describes his bravery of which there is no doubt and his modesty (?); his musical, poetic, and artistic accomplishments, and his amorous inclinations (IV, 468 ff.) which, as I have pointed out above, were probably highly exaggerated.

He was already 59 years old when the first volume of *Almahide* appeared in 1660; thus we may assume that the following portrait of himself is highly exaggerated also:

> sa taille . . . mediocre, & iustement entre la trop grande & la trop petite: mais si belle, si noble . . . Il a l'air haut, le port maiestueux, le marcher graue, & l'action vn peu fiere . . . Ses cheueux . . . ni fort noirs ni fort blonds . . . d'vne couleur fort agreable; son visage . . . ouale . . . ses yeux . . . noirs, grands, & bien fendus . . . ses sourcils bruns & fort espais; son teint vif; le nez bien fait, quoy qu'vn peu grand pour vn Grenadin (which Georges was not): & la bouche si extraordinairement belle . . . qu'il n'est point de si belle Dame qui n'en fust contente, si elle l'avoit ainsi . . . Il a encore les plus belles mains du monde pour vn homme.

(IV, 471 ff.)

This is the *miles gloriosus* speaking and bears little resemblance to the description given of him by Lenôtre or to reproductions of portraits published in various biographies.

Now that we have met Georges as he saw himself, let us return to his biography. Little is known of his life for the next ten years after the adventure with Catherine de Rouyère but it appears that during this period he was in the service of his king on land and sea. He speaks of his military experience in his foreword to **Ligdamon et Lidias** although some would have us believe that he commanded nothing more than the troops of the Hôtel de Bourgogne and of the Marais. In 1629 he served under Louis XIII during the Piedmontese expedition and seems to have distinguished himself in the retreat from the Pass of Suse. Substituting the pen for the sword, he began a career of letters, editing the works of his friend Théophile in 1632, and as a result of his sixteen theatrical productions won a position as one of the better second-rate dramatists. In 1637 he gained prominence as author of **Observations sur le Cid** and his **Lettre à l'Académie.** During these years he maintained with Madeleine a household on la Rue Beauce but, as we shall see, life with her does not appear to have been particularly happy and when he departed for Normandy in 1654 it was for Madeleine a relief and a liberation. Never again did he share the same roof with her: once when he appeared at her home asking for hospitality, he was told that all beds were taken.

In 1644 through the influence of his sister he was appointed governor of Notre-Dame-de-la-Garde in Marseille whence he returned in 1647. Relationships between Georges and Madeleine did not improve and her platonic friendship for Pellison did not improve matters. With the outbreak of the Wars of the Fronde he fled to Normandy where he met and married Françoise de Martin-Vast and with her encouragement and aid wrote **Almahide.** Their marriage was blessed with a gifted son who later entered the Church. When Condé and his friends were granted political amnesty in 1660, Scudéry returned to Paris with his wife, was granted a pension by the king, and spent his remaining years translating the Italian Marini's *Calloandro fedele* published posthumously in three volumes in 1668.

In 1638 or 1639 Madeleine came to Paris to establish a literary partnership that was to be broken permanently by his flight to Normandy and his marriage. Tallemant de Réaux did not have a high opinion of Madame de Scudéry but she seems to have been a beauteous and gifted young woman who was flattered by the attentions of the novelist, poet, and dramatist. Bussy-Rabutin, however, held her in the highest esteem and corresponded with her. Her correspondence shows that she had the gift of writing well and there is no doubt in my mind concerning her collaboration in composing **Almahide.** When she was widowed, she mourned Georges' passing as a true and loving wife and she wrote to friends that he was a good husband, a friend, a good man who always praised and esteemed her and treated her well. What more could a wife ask?

As for Scudéry and his sister, aside from their literary collaboration, their life together was at times stormy as has been indicated. Already seemingly headed for bachelorhood when she joined him, he was set in his ways and apparently was determined to be the master of the household. G. Lenôtre states in his preface to Clerc's biography that Georges was "si sincère dans sa suffisance, si plein d'admiration pour son propre talent, si parfaittement dédaigneux de celui des autres, si amusant—non point dans ses œuvres, mais dans sa personnalité . . ."[4] Moreover, he claimed all the credit for his sister's success despite the fact they had been separated for years during the period of her intellectual formation. "Je l'ai faite . . . ce qu'elle est", he wrote to Eléanore de Rohan-Montabazon, abbesse de Caen.

At the same time as a man of exquisite tastes who took pride in his status as an *amateur des arts,* extravagantly collecting paintings or engravings or tulips, he was at the same time disdainful of her financial assistance which he so desperately needed. He is charged with having dominated Madeleine for fifteen years and is held responsible for breaking up a possible marriage with Pellisson with whom she shared a tender friendship for about forty years. Pellisson arrived at court in 1650 and without doubt drove a wedge between brother and sister. Pellisson was noted for his homeliness and Madeleine was no raving beauty. They in our day and time would have been called the "gruesome twosome"! Georges is also accused of keeping Madeleine locked up while she completed some literary chore assigned to her by himself. His dislike for Pellisson stemmed from the fact that he had allotted Georges little space in his *Histoire de l'Académie française.* As rebuttal of the charge of breaking up the romance it is more likely that Madeleine as a *précieuse* prized *amitié* far more than marriage and there is no evidence to disprove that she could not have married Pellisson had she so willed. To the charge of keeping Madeleine a prisoner it is more likely that she needed and demanded privacy and quiet to work on her literary productions (and to be free of Georges so she could relax). As for Pellisson's *Histoire* I can find nothing to justify Scudéry's reaction to his treatment therein. As Dorothy McDougall points out[5] Pellisson allotted twice as much space to Georges as to Pierre Corneille and the author stated categorically that he could not deal as freely with living academicians as with the dead. For that reason he did not give Scudéry the eulogy the latter felt he merited.

As for the Scudéry *modus operandi,* it is so well-known that there is no need to do more than summarize. In the preface of his long heroic poem **Alaric** he took credit for the authorship of both **Ibrahim** and **le Grand Cyrus.** Tallemant wrote that for the latter novel Georges prepared only the prefaces and the *épîtres dédicatoires.* According to La Calprenède Georges touched up portraits appearing in the Scudéry novels. Victor Cousin states:

> ils faisaient ensemble le plan. Georges, qui avait de l'invention et de la fécondité, fournissait les aventures et toute la partie romanesque, et il laissait à Madeleine

le soin de jeter sur ce fond assez médiocre son élégante broderie de portraits, d'analyses sentimentales, de lettres, de conversations.[6]

But Rathery and Boutron reply:

> Peut-être ne faut-il voir là qu'une exagération en sens contraire de l'opinion primitivement reçue. Car il y eut réaction dans les jugements de littérateurs et des bibliographes, quant aux ouvrages d'imagination portant le nom Scudéry. Après avoir tout attribué au frère, on veut maintenant donner tout à la sœur. La vérité ne serait-elle pas entre ces deux extrêmes? Ainsi, lorque'on se rappelle que Scudéry avait servi, et qu'on le voit, en toute circonstance, se piquer de ses connaissances dans l'art militaire, il est difficile de croire que les épisodes de guerre, où se complaît l'auteur du *Cyrus* . . . ne soient l'ouvrage du soldat romancier dont le nom figure partout, sur le titre et dans les dédicaces de l'ouvrage.[7]

I am inclined to agree with this judgement that Georges contributed a great deal more to the common effort than contemporaries credit him. I attempted to prove in my study of *Almahide*[8] that not only did Georges have the ability and the know-how to write a long-winded novel without his sister's assistance but that he and his wife actually wrote the unfinished eight-volume effort (1660-1663). This work was in the making at a time when he and Madeleine were physically and mentally separated. His effort also became the dumping ground of several of his own works which had met with some success, including two tragi-comedies *Axiane* and *le Prince déguisé,* as well as the didactic poem *Solomon instruissant le Roy.*

What then is the place merited by this much maligned author? Lenotre wrote that "Scudéry méritait de trouver son historien, car il est une de ces figures qui résument une époque et caractérisent toute une société . . ."[9]

Le Cabinet de M. Georges de Scudéry is such in the plasticity of description of paintings (the same plasticity of description is found in *Almahide*) that these descriptions are reminiscent of Diderot's *Salons*. Two centuries later, Clerc states, the Parnassian poets would have recognized him as one of themselves because he had a sense of the plastic in what he described: he did so as a connaisseur, as an expert, and with the practiced eye of an art critic.[10]

The author of more than sixteen tragicomedies he was certainly one of the most applauded tragic poets of his time notwithstanding the fact that Théophile Gautier includes him among his *Grotesques*. Chapelain, perhaps overly enthusiastic, termed him "L'Apollon du Marais". Guez de Balzac, after referring to some emendations he would suggest in *l'Amour tyrannique,* continues "Mais le reste, à mon gré, est incomparable".

As a man of the theater he was a recognized purveyor of the Hôtel de Bourgogne and of the Marais, and his plays were staged at the royal court.[11] In his theater he was attracted by the melodramatic. He falls short of a Racine because his plays lacked simplicity and true emotion and

his *préciosité* went to the extremes which Molière took to task. His best work is to be found in his comedies noted in spots for their verve. But generally he used the tone habitual to the *Précieux,* thus becoming the victim of his own facile pen.

Yet his theater won the praise of Alexandre Hardy and of Pierre Corneille in his early years and Scudéry was idolized by apprentices in letters as a master of his craft. Rotrou, who helped to lend prestige and dignity to the stage before Corneille, received Scudéry's early plays with acclaim which may prove that Scudéry was no mean dramatist, at least no worse than those outside the great Triumvirate. Nevertheless, he is forgotten today. Like many a dramatic hero of his day he possibly has been punished more than he deserved as a dramatist.

H. Carrington Lancaster in his monumental history of French dramatic literature in the seventeenth century has studied the complete theater of Scudéry and it is to that work and to Alfred Batereau's *Georges de Scudéry als Dramatiker* that the reader is referred for details.

Lancaster points to *le Prince déguisé,* first acted in 1634 and used as an intercalated episode in Scudéry's *Almahide,* as a play with greater unity, more exciting intrigue, and a more spectacular setting than earlier plays such as *Ligdamon et Lidias, le Trompeur puny* and *Orante*. This play was designated along with Du Ryer's *Cléomédon* as a typical example of a play with a "belle intrigue". Lancaster wrote: "Nobody seems to have noticed that the situation is here remarkably like that of Chimène in the Cid." (I, p. 483). He points out that a few years later Scudéry was to criticize Corneille because Chimène did not decline to wed Rodrigue, her father's slayer. Cléarque in Scudéry's play is innocent but there was no way for others to know it. So he criticizes Corneille for a situation for which he had himself furnished the model!

La Comédie des comédiens (1632) consists of two acts in prose followed by an insipid pastoral play in verse which is in reality the rehearsal for the actors of the first two acts. This play is interesting as a study of manners and of the criticism to which plays and actors were subjected in the seventeenth century. It includes a defense of actors against charges of moral turpitude and is a forerunner of Molière's *Critique de l'Ecole des femmes.*

La mort de César (1635) was classed by Lancaster with Tristan l'Hermite's *Mariane* and Jean Mairet's *Sophonisbe*. In this play Scudéry showed his characteristic predilection for spectacle and physical action, his dislike for hampering rules, and his inability to make careful character study. Professor Lancaster wrote of this play that for the modern reader the most interesting thing about it is that Scudéry produced something of a critical edition of his own play providing elaborate marginal notes including interpretations of his own allusions. Some contemporary critics including Guérin de Bouscal termed it among the leading tragedies of 1634-1635, and Lancaster points out that some of its details were imitated by Corneille in *Cinna, Polyeucte,* and *Pompée.*

Eudoxe (1639), Lancaster shows, has details resembling Racine's *Andromaque* and *Phèdre*. The play won the praise of Richelieu.

L'Amour tyrannique (1639) was apparently written to give Corneille a lesson in the art of dramaturgy but it falls short of the mark. It was composed in accord with the unities of time and place and the *bienséances* but is melodramatic in style. However, some spectacular, animated and dramatic scenes won success for the play and it led Balzac to insist that Scudéry was a great poet, not sufficiently admired. Chapelain, while refusing to state that it surpassed the *Cid,* termed it one of Scudéry's best and it was admired by Richelieu and Sarazin. It was translated to Dutch four times between 1647 and 1746.

Andromire (1641) is an example of Scudéry's ingenuity in plot construction; it is lacking in some of the bombast and absurdities of other Scudéry plays and was in the repertory of the Hôtel de Bourgogne in 1646-1647. *Ibrahim* (1643) was also popular. It was better written than earlier plays of the author and it was republished several times. Although *Arminius* (1643), the last of his plays that have survived, was weak in motivation and structure, it was successful enough to have had a run of several years and was in the repertory of the Bourgogne in 1646-1647.

As a poet he wrote much that is worthless but in certain passages are to be found a lyrical note, a feeling for nature in all her moods which preclude treating Scudéry as negligible as a versifier. McDougall, citing Scudéry's series of sonnets *La fameuse fontaine de Vaucluse* said that when Scudéry was inspired by nature, he forgot his heroics. His second sonnet, she writes, opens in a mood in which on these real occasions he shows himself to have been a lyrical poet of no mean order.[12]

Indeed, Charles Livet in his *Précieux et Précieuses* (pp. 257-258) writes:

> Il semble que tout ait été dit sur le poème d'*Alaric,* le jour où Despréaux [Boileau] en a raillé le premier vers:
>
> Je chante le vainqueur des vainqueurs de la terre.
>
> . . . Que si l'on ne se laisse pas arrêter, dès le début, par une opinion preconçue, j'ose penser que l'on trouvera dans l'*Alaric,* comme dans les sonnets que nous avons loués plus haut (p. 247), des passages parfaitement beaux et d'une ampleur vraiment cornélienne. Je ne dis pas qu'on puisse citer partout au hasard, mais j'affirme qu'on trouve dans l'*Alaric* plus d'un morceau digne d'être conservé: tel est cet admirable tableau de Rome dans la décadence (l^{er} livre, vers 45 et suiv.)
>
> . . . le poème d'*Alaric* fut accueilli avec faveur, reçut les honneurs de plusieurs éditions fort rapprochées, et fut publié dans tous les formats.

The influence of Scudéry and his sister as novelists is evident on Samuel Richardson, father of the modern English novel. He and they were noted for the character drawing of real people though changes in taste later in the

Seventeenth Century relegated the Scudéry works to the limbo of the half-forgotten. But Madeleine and Georges de Scudéry cannot be totally forgotten.

Thomas P. Haviland has studied the vogue of the French *roman de longue haleine* in England[13] and notes that they were read in England until the second quarter of the Eighteenth Century. John Dryden used *Almahide* as source material for his own theater.

Ibrahim was translated by Henry Cogan in 1652 and another edition was published in 1674 and possibly still others in 1665 and 1723. *Le Grand Cyrus* was translated by F. G. Gent (1653-55) followed by another edition in 1691 and the first two parts of *Clélie* were published in translation in 1655 and 1656 followed by a complete edition (1656-1661), while other editions appeared in 1659 and 1678. *Almahide* was translated in 1677 by J. Phillips who also added an ending to the unfinished novel to satisfy English readers.

In conclusion, Scudéry cannot be dismissed on the grounds of his foibles. He was vain, he was bombastic, he wrote too facilely to be a careful workman: of these weaknesses he was guilty and of a lot more along with many writers of his epoch. However, his virtues must be placed in the other balance of the scales: he was a good husband; he was a faithful friend when discretion might have been the better part of valor. He was a man of integrity: witness his refusal to make certain deletions from *Alaric* in exchange for a valuable gold chain offered him by Christina of Sweden. He was a good soldier even though he boasted of his deeds like a Captain Fracasse. But he was not wholly lacking in humility as is shown in the opening remarks of his *Discours* before the French Academy on the occasion of his admission in 1650:

> Je ne sçay comment j'ai l'audace de venir mêler les défauts qui sont en moy avec les perfections qui sont en vous, et d'oser me mettre au rang des Dieux, moy qui suis parmy le commun des hommes. Il est vray que je suis d'une profession à qui la témérité est sinon permise, au moins tolérée; en un mot, je suis soldat, et par conséquent obligé d'être hardy. Et puis, Messieurs, je ne me présente pas à votre illustre corps avec la croyance d'en être digne, mais avec l'intention de tâcher de me le rendre, et de vous témoigner par mes services, à tous en général et à chacun en particulier, combien je me sens votre redevable de l'honneur que vous me faites.[14]

His plays were no masterpieces despite his exalted opinion of his own work but they were no worse than most and if his purpose was to entertain and please, then he succeeded, regardless of the opinions of more discriminating critics. As a poet he was admittedly mediocre except on those rare occasions when inspired by nature or by a sense of history. The Scudéry novels have their settings in exotic climes but they portray life in the France of their day and time and their characters are for the most part men and women who were no figments of the authors' imagination but real flesh and blood men and women who lived, loved, suffered, and died, representing both the nobility (*le grand Cyrus*) and the bourgeoisie (*Clélie*).

Charles Livet writes:

> Qui sait? Un temps viendra peut-être où des gens de goût trouveront trop timide un éloge que nous croyons presque téméraire.

The laudatory comment was applied to Scudéry's volume of poetry, one-third of which Livet says "est très remarquable".[15]

Perhaps in the not too remote future his work will find a literary historian and critic who, without being biased by Tallemant or Boileau, will make a thoroughly objective study of Georges de Scudéry's total work and demonstrate by use of internal evidence his true worth as a writer. His role in the Quarrel of the *Cid* has assured his immortality in letters if nothing else.

Notes

1. G. Lenôtre in his preface to Charles Clerc, *la Vie tragicomique de Georges de Scudéry,* Paris, 1929, p. 247.

2. Bibliographical note: Since the cut-off date in 1959 of the Cabeen and Brody critical bibliography, very little has been published on Georges de Scudéry, in fact only one article according to the *PMLA International Bibliography.* Stedman Kitchen, Jr., of North Carolina State University has in progress a dissertation which studies *Ibrahim* in detail. Other articles mentioned by *PMLA* deal with specialized subjects in the work of Madeleine.

3. *Mlle de Scudéry, sa vie et sa correspondance,* Paris, 1873, pp. 49-50.

4. Clerc, *op. cit.,* pp. 10-11.

5. *Madeleine de Scudéry, Her Romantic Life and Death,* London, 1938, p. 142.

6. *La société française au dix-septième siècle d'après "Le Grand Cyrus",* Delbos edit., Oxford University Press, London, 1909, p. 169.

7. See *supra,* note 3.

8. *Georges de Scudéry's 'Alhamide',* Baltimore, 1939.

9. Clerc, *op. cit.,* p. 12.

10. Idem., p. 121.

11. McDougall, *op. cit.,* p. 16.

12. *Op. cit.,* p. 51.

13. The *"Roman de longue haleine"* on *English Soil,* Philadelphia, 1931.

14. Quoted by Charles Livet, *Précieux et Précieuses,* Paris, 1897, p. 248.

15. *Ibid.,* p. 247.

William Roberts (essay date 1971)

SOURCE: Roberts, William. "New Light on the Authorship of *Almahide.*" *French Studies* 25, no. 2 (April 1971): 271-80.

[*In the essay below, Roberts presents evidence that Scudéry, not his sister, wrote* Almahide.]

Since its appearance in 1660-63, a long-term controversy has gone on concerning the true authorship of a rather rare eight-volume Moorish novel ***Almahide, ou l'esclave reine,*** printed by the well-known Parisian publisher Augustin Courbé. In spite of the title-page crediting its origin to 'Mr de Scudery, Gouverneur de Nostre Dame de la Garde', the privilege granted to 'le Sieur de Scudéry', and the dedicatory letters signed by him, libraries to this day continue to classify it under the name of his sister Madeleine.[1] This practice stems probably from the authority of Nicéron, Graesse and especially Brunet who considered the attribution that had earlier been made to Georges 'mal à propos'.[2] Eugène Asse in *La Grande Encyclopédie*—vol. 29 (1900-01), 834—lists ***Almahide*** with all the Scudéry novels as Madeleine's work, excepting perhaps for 'l'invention du sujet et de leurs nombreux incidents'. He does note the existence of contrary testimony by Chapelain. Lanson's *Manuel bibliographique* (1921) continues the traditional listing, as does Tchemerzine in 1933, cautioning the reader against being misled by the title-page designation.[3]

In the same year Georges Mongrédien analysed the novel's physical composition under Madeleine's name in his extensive 'Bibliographie des ouvrages de Georges et de Madeleine de Scudéry'—*RHL,* XL (1933), 551-3—but believed it a work of collaboration. He admitted the likelihood, based on a reference by Tallemant des Réaux and one by Chapelain, that Georges had had a considerable hand in its composition. Later in a 'Supplément'—*RHL,* XLII (1935), 549—he reversed his denial of the existence of an English *Almahide* (the J. Phillips translation).

The doctoral dissertation of Jerome W. Schweitzer, published in 1939, discussed in detail this confused question of authorship, noting the contemporary references to collaboration by brother and sister on earlier novels.[4] He decided, following Brunetière and A. Batereau, that 'probably' Georges aided by his wife did the entire work, without Madeleine's help. His arguments include the presence in the novel of large amounts of poetry, the abundance of events and skilful intrigue, technical descriptions of paintings, numerous classical references and autobiographical material; Georges' illness which delayed publication; Madeleine's preoccupation with ***Clélie***; the marriage which in 1654/55 separated Georges and his sister. Emile Magne, reviewing this book for the *Mercure de France*—297

(1940), 626-7—conceded that Schweitzer had established his case, posited on a very logical argumentation. Antoine Adam, in his *Histoire de la littérature française au XVIIe siècle* (Paris, 1954), IV, 171 n., pointed out Schweitzer's findings and definitively accepted them. In 1961 he reaffirmed this conviction: 'On peut considérer comme certain qu'*Almahide* est l'œuvre, non de Madeleine, mais de Georges de Scudéry aidé de sa femme'.[5] It might then seem reasonable to believe the question closed.

Nonetheless in the B.N. printed catalogue—vol. 169 (1946)—one must still look for *Almahide* under Madeleine's name, and in addition find a note specifying that she published most of her works under her brother's name. In 1954 the *Dictionnaire des lettres* (pp. 938-40) came to the same conclusion about *Almahida* (sic) and the other novels. The Cabeen *Bibliography* (1961) treats Madeleine and Georges together under the heading of 'Précieux novel', and reviews Schweitzer's 'well-documented study' in some detail.[6] Mongrédien's more recent bibliography in his *Les Précieux et les Précieuses* (Paris, 1963, pp. 24-50) simply credits *Almahide* to Madeleine without commentary and does not cite Schweitzer's book. The new B.M. printed catalogue—vol. 217 (1964), col. 833-90—lists the latter three times as 'suggesting' authorship by Georges and his wife, but for the novels it sets up an intermediate category between brother and sister: 'SCUDÉRY (GEORGE DE [sic]), *pseud.* [i.e. MADELÉNE DE SCUDÉRI (sic)]', which does not conform to standard spelling. R. W. Baldner's revised *Bibliography of Seventeenth-Century French Prose Fiction* (New York, 1967, p. 88) cites the B.M. and B.N. copies by call numbers, but credits the work to Madeleine. The just recently available Cioranescu volume lists several new titles for Georges (conscientiously including Schweitzer), but continues to classify *Almahide* among his sister's novels.[7] Schweitzer's findings obviously have not yet had their desired effect.

For some three hundred years, however, documentary evidence has made of *Almahide* an exception to the generally unquestioned tradition that Madeleine wrote all the novels published under her brother's name. Jean Chapelain in three separate personal letters to Scudéry discusses the forthcoming novel ('vostre Reyne More') as a close family friend and literary critic.[8] On 12 June 1659, after regretting Georges's illness, he takes pleasure in learning to what extent 'c'est moy qui vous ai inspiré cette belle entreprise', and assures its success 'voyant que c'est vous qui vous estes chargé de l'exécuter'. He admits having sent some time ago 'l'original espagnol', most probably the source book which recent authorities reaffirm as primordial—Pérez de Hita's *Guerras Civiles de Granada*.[9] Cordial leave is taken of Georges's wife Marie. More than a year later (25 August 1660), nearly eleven weeks after the assignment of the novel's privilege, Chapelain missed the couple on two successive visits [in Paris?]. These were undertaken for the purpose of discussing the MS. text ('Je voulois . . . Monsieur, vous entretenir de quelques endroits de vostre *Almahide*'), not as a censor but as a friend

interested in Georges's literary reputation. Along with the letter of 8 November 1660 he sends back 'les cinq cahiers qui finissent la deuxiesme partie d'Almahide', after a careful critical reading. These may well have been the author's preliminary page proofs, since the three volumes comprising Part I were then in print and completed by 30 November.[10] Responding to an invitation—'puisque vous l'ordonnés'—Chapelain prudently advises a more classical restraint ('modération . . . retranchement . . . espargne'), less repetition, a more varied style, unexpected plot developments, some comedy, and an Hylas character or two (!). Readers are mostly courtiers and women, and such matter is 'la pasture de ces sortes de personnes'. The author should avoid long laments, soliloquies and 'agitations de l'âme', and should correct two specific sections, isolated by Chapelain's folding of the paper. The latter's intimate knowledge of the plot and characters is evident, as well as his accurate appraisal of the reading public's taste, which would in effect soon reject the published *Almahide*. E. J. B. Rathery, Madeleine's biographer, concluded in 1873 that the attribution of all the imaginative works to either Georges or Madeleine was excessive, and that the letters cited above prove that Chapelain treated Georges as 'l'auteur incontesté' of *Almahide*.[11]

The fact that Scudéry charged a friend with the reading would seem a further indication of his authorship, since he himself obligatorily assumed the task of checking and editing his sister's novels, according to Tallemant.[12] This source also reports that Georges came to Paris early in 1660 to have a novel printed—'une paraphrase des guerres civiles de Granade'. His apparent error on the number of volumes (12 vs. 8) may reflect an original announcement of the (eventually unfinished) novel, and he does supply a motive for the undertaking: to contradict public opinion which had credited Georges with the composition of *Cyrus* and *Clélie*. Even the latter's wife Marie had had great difficulty in abandoning this notion. However, the *Dictionnaire des Précieuses* reports that Marie did help to write *Almahide* ('Saràide y a mis la main'), and indeed it was a compatibility of literary talents which prompted their marriage. This occasion for Tallemant elicits a typical comment: 'c'estoit mettre un rien avec un autre rien', provoking the sharp disagreement of his modern editor.[13] Without having read it, Somaize is sure in 1661 that Georges's recently printed novel 'des guerres des Mores en Hesperie' can only be magnificent. Charles Sorel, after discussing the reported collaboration of brother and sister on *Clélie* and affirming the respective merits of each, notes in 1664 that 'M. de Scudery a commencé depuis quelques années *l'Almahide ou l'Esclaue Reine*', containing 'quantité de belles auantures d'Amour & de Guerre'. His account of the authorship and composition period thus ties in with the others cited.[14]

Additional contemporary evidence exists to support the belief that Georges did write the novel. Although one may have to discount Boileau's ironic intent, it is apparent that he holds Georges responsible for the *romans-fleuves* appearing in rapid succession during the fifties and early sixties:

Bienheureux Scuderi, dont la fertile plume
Peut tous les mois sans peine enfanter un volume!

Satire II (Pléiade ed., p. 19)

A hitherto unnoticed mention, quite specific, is that of the indefatigable Michel de Marolles, whose best title to the gratitude of scholars is that his privately assembled collection of prints formed the basis for the royal (now B.N.) Cabinet des Estampes. The posthumous edition by Goujet of his *Mémoires* contains a bibliographical section entitled 'Dénombrement', probably written *c.* 1672-81, in which this fellow-collector of prints and engravings distinguishes between brother and sister and states categorically about Georges *de Scuderi* (sic) that 'son dernier Roman porte le nom d'Almaide'.[15]

In the *Poems* (written before 22 June 1664) of Katherine Philips, an English Caroline poetess better known as the 'Matchless Orinda', occurs a long verse translation from the French entitled 'A Pastoral of *Mons. de Scudery's* in the first volume of Almahide, Englished'.[16] This poem, beginning 'Slothful deceiver', is her version of the eclogue 'Paresseuse, mensongere' in *Almahide* I, 450-69. Reputedly quite knowledgeable in recent French fiction, Orinda credits the novel to Georges de Scudéry. Milton's nephew John Phillips, completing the novel in an English version (1677), does likewise. F. A. Pernauer, the German translator of *Almahide* (1682-96) who enlarged Part III and gave it a suitable ending, believed too that he was rendering 'Aus dem Herrn Scudery' who had died before having the time to finish it.[17]

But the 'matamore des lettres' himself appears to claim the work more positively. It has long been noted that several of his previous texts were incorporated into the novel. Mongrédien (op. cit., pp. 418, 552) had pointed out the reappearance of a long didactic poem from 1651— *Salomon instruisant le roy,* with a slight change of title—in *Almahide* VIII, 545-87. Schweitzer (pp. 10, 18, 76-93, 153) noted as quite unique the republication within the body of the novel of two of Scudéry's much earlier plays, *Axiane* (1644) and *Le Prince déguisé* (1636), the first of which is 'repeated practically verbatim'. He later discovered (p. 158) the re-use of Scudéry's prose *Epitaphe* to Cardinal Richelieu (1642), in *Almahide* V, 1376-9.

The early presence in *Almahide* (I, 434-39) of a poem praising the tulip could be interpreted as a signature motif: Georges is well known for his love of this flower, even if he was not allowed to represent it in the *Guirlande de Julie*.[18] This tulip poem, **'Puis que, de tant de Fleurs de qui la Terre est peinte',** was also included by Scudéry in his collected *Poésies nouvelles,* published in Amsterdam in 1661.[19] It directly precedes his original of the eclogue (Cauchie no. 467) which Katherine Philips translated, and which contains 372 verses, exactly the same length as the text in the novel. Another poem from *Almahide* (VI, 2553-4), the sonnet **'Elle s'en va mourir, cette vertu visible',** turns up in *Poésies nouvelles* and had been printed a year before as Georges's contribution to a biography of the

lady in question.[20] A parallel case of triple publication occurs with the long portrait ode **'Belles Filles de Mémoire'** (*Almahide* V, 1661-8), which closes the volume of *Poésies nouvelles,* and which was used later in an Elzevier collection of 1665 (Cauchie nos. 557, 567 bis). These would represent eight instances so far noted of texts from *Almahide* being utilized elsewhere by Scudéry. In a similar vein, Cioranescu (no. 62005) newly lists as Georges's last separate poetic publication *L'Ombre d'Almahide, reine de Granade, au Roy, sur son carrousel* (1962). This occasional piece apparently attests to the novel's being well known at Court during its printing years, and also recalls somewhat enigmatically a Scudéry title of nearly a generation before—*L'Ombre du grand Armand* (1643)![21]

The *Poésies nouvelles* volume, unmentioned by Schweitzer, turns out upon closer examination to have a very intimate connection with *Almahide*. A detailed tabular analysis demonstrates that this collection, as described by Cauchie, is nothing other than a reprinting in precisely the same order of most of the poems from *Almahide,* excepting for its own introductory (unpaginated) poem.[22] To his original titles the author has added explicative material from the context of the novel; such changes may be noted by reference to Cauchie's 'Bibliographie', which does not cite the verses in *Almahide*. The above relationship, as well as the minor spelling and punctuation changes, would suggest that the text of the novel antedates the poetry volume.

One can only speculate why Scudéry released his *Poésies nouvelles* to a Dutch publisher during the French printing of these same poems in *Almahide*. He may have planned it ahead of the Paris edition, while still confident of the novel's success. His habit of marketing the same material in various forms has been noted above; it may have helped to account for the kind of success which Balzac caustically repudiates: 'D'attendre de moy cette bienheureuse facilité qui fait produire des volumes à M. de Scudery, ce serait me connaistre mal.'[23] In this case the likelihood of a different reading public would hint at some financial consideration. The existence in England of an apparently second Amsterdam edition (1662), unknown to previous scholars, strengthens this hypothesis.[24]

The insertion into *Almahide* (VI, 2876-8) of a translated 'Privilège des Estats de Hollande' offers additional matter for conjecture. Granted to Jean Blaeu, well known for his atlas printings and associate of the novel's wealthy Parisian publisher, it is dated 13 May 1658—exactly two years before the French privilege (VI, 2872-5). If 1658 is not a misprint, accidental or otherwise (the translation is notarized), then this document would set an earlier limit on the known dates of composition. It gives the impression that Georges first intended to release the novel in Amsterdam, and finally compromised with a different format, published concurrently, for the poetry alone. The fact that no poems from the last quarter of volume VI (printed by 2 January 1661) nor from volumes VII-VIII (1663) were reproduced in the *Poésies nouvelles* brings one to believe that the poetic text of Part III of the novel had not been composed by 1661. Since both the Dutch and French privileges in volume VI specify Parts I and II only, and since a later printing of the same French document in volume VII drops this restriction, we may infer that by the French privilege date (13 May 1660) none or very little of the prose of Part III had as yet been undertaken (and never was altogether completed) by Scudéry.

Statistically, the **Poésies nouvelles** represents 13 per cent of Scudéry's known versification as listed by Cauchie, or about one-fifth of his separate poems. According to my count its contents (printed in 12°) correspond to a total of some 265 of the 6533 pages in *Almahide* (in 8°); hence the **Poésies nouvelles** 'reprinting' comprises an equivalent of 4 per cent of the entire novel. If we were to add the other texts which Scudéry integrated into the prose work (**Salomon,** 42 pp.; **Epitaphe,** 4 pp.; **Le Prince déguisé,** 116 pp.; **Axiane,** 176 pp. in 4°), the page percentage of known and universally accepted Scudéry compositions in *Almahide* might rise to a total of nearly 12 per cent. Along with this factual evaluation should be weighed the justifications made by Brunetière and Schweitzer for considering the prose generally to be of Georges's style.

Discovery of the identity relation of the poetry collection to the novel, which itself contains at least 115 separate and undisputed Scudéry texts dating back as far as 1636, should reinforce previous arguments and evidence. It should lend definitive credence, after Magne and Adam, to the Schweitzer thesis that Georges, aided by his wife and not by his sister, composed **Almahide.** Literary scholars, bibliographers and library cataloguers should take this long-standing debate more into account, at least concede a joint authorship for the novel, and list it under Georges's name also from now on, pending further clarification. This new information supplements the Mongrédien and Cauchie bibliographies and exposes Scudéry's efficiently 'modern' publication practices. It ought to lead to additional investigations of his rather substantial poetic output (30,268 lines), and perhaps to the re-discovery of other forgotten printings by this exuberant and picturesque personality, this remarkable versifier and 'authentique poète'.[25]

Notes

1. *Almahide, ou l'esclave reine* (Paris, A. Courbé, 1660-63), 8 vol. (B.M., B.N., Arsenal, Institut, Sainte-Geneviève, Versailles; considered 'assez rare' by Tchemerzine). U.S. holdings as reported in 1939 by Schweitzer (see n. 4 infra) were Cornell, Harvard, Johns Hopkins, Yale; we must now delete the latter (English and German translations only), but can add the copies at Chicago, Northwestern and Princeton. Some sets are imperfect and wanting certain pp. (B.M., Northwestern, and Johns Hopkins originally). American libraries generally follow L.C. practice in classifying Georges's name on the novels as a pseudonym.

2. J.-P. Nicéron, *Mémoires pour servir . . .* (Paris, 1731), XV, 131-41, explaining the misleading pseudonym arrangement for the first four novels; *Almahide* listed without comment. J. C. Brunet, *Manuel du libraire,* 5th ed. (Paris, 1864), V, 251 and *Supplément* (1880), II, 621; J. G. T. Graesse, *Trésor de livres rares et précieux* (Dresden, 1865), VI, 336.

3. Lanson no. 4325; A. Tchemerzine, *Bibliographie d'éditions originales et rares d'auteurs français* (Paris, 1933), X, 284.

4. J. W. Schweitzer, *Georges de Scudéry's 'Almahide': Authorship, Analysis, Sources and Structure* (Baltimore, London, Paris, 1939); also issued as thesis 'Reprinted from the Johns Hopkins Studies in Romance Literatures and Languages, v. 34' (Baltimore, 1939). See pp. 13-22.

5. In his Tallemant des Réaux, *Historiettes,* Pléiade ed. (Paris, 1961), II, 1460-61.

6. D. C. Cabeen and J. Brody, *A Critical Bibliography of French Literature,* III (N. Edelman, ed.) (Syracuse, 1961), p. 132.

7. A. Cioranescu, *Bibliographie de la littérature française du XVIIᵉ siècle* (Paris, 1966), III, 1832-7.

8. J. Chapelain, *Lettres,* P. Tamizey de Larroque, ed. (Paris, 1880-3), II, 41-2; 92 n.; 110-11.

9. Maria S. Carrasco, *El moro de Granada en la literatura (dal siglo XV al XX)* (Madrid, 1956), pp. 105-11. See also her thesis (Columbia, 1954), *The Moor of Granada in Spanish Literature of the Eighteenth and Nineteenth Centuries,* in *Dissertation Abstracts,* XV (1955), 263-4. F. L. Estrada and J. E. Keller, *Antonio de Villages' 'El Abencerraje'* (Chapel Hill, 1964), pp. 34-5. Schweitzer, op. cit., pp. 64-76.

10. *Achevé d'imprimer* at the end of vol. III.

11. In E. J. B. Rathery et Boutron, *Mademoiselle de Scudéry, sa vie et sa correspondance* (Paris, 1873), pp. 49-50 n.

12. *Historiettes* (ed. cit.), pp. 690-1.

13. A. B. de Somaize, *Le grand Dictionnaire des Prétievses, historiqve, poétiqve,* etc. (Paris, 1661), II, 131-3; *Historiettes* (ed. cit.), II, 695; 1465 (5).

14. *La Bibliothèqve Françoise* (Paris, 1664), pp. 166-7; privilege transferred 9 September 1662.

15. Paris, 1656-7, 2 vols.; C. P. Goujet, ed. (Amsterdam, 1755), I, 334; II, 221; III, 362. See also the favourable account of his accomplishments in Frits Lugt, *Les marques de collections, de dessins & d'estampes* (Amsterdam, 1921), pp. 339-40.

16. *Poems* (London, H. Herringman, 1667), pp. 184-96; repr. 1669, 1678 with same pagination.

17. J. Phillips, *Almahide; or, the Captive Queen* (London, 1677). F. A. Pernauer (sic), *Almahide oder die Leibeigne Königin* (Nürnberg, 1682-96, 1701): see

his Introduction: 'wie bekannt, M. Scuderi die Frantzösische Almahide nicht ganz verfertigkt, sondern darüber gestorben ist . . .', cited in C. Von Faber du Faur, *German Baroque Literature* (New Haven, 1958), p. 159.

18. O. Uzanne, ed., *La Guirlande de Julie* (Paris, 1875), pp. x-xi and passim. In 1655 a long introductory poem of Scudéry's was printed in *Le floriste françois, Traitant de l'origine des Tulipes* (Cauchie no. 453—see n. 19 infra).

19. *Poësies nouvelles, ou Recueil de divers ouvrages, Par Monsieur de Scudery, Gouverneur de Nostre-Dame de la Garde* (Amsterdam, Jean Nuoremberkz [sic], 1661). Considered 'rarissime' by Mongrédien ('Bibliographie', p. 418) who knows of no other copy than that of the Arsenal (B.L. 6777). Not listed in B.M., B.N., L.C., Nicéron, Brunet, Graesse, Lanson, Tchemerzine. The Union Catalog Division of L.C. has circularized for it, without finding an American location. Maurice Cauchie in his 'Bibliographie des poésies de Georges de Scudéry'—BBB (1956), 243-53—has examined this work in considerable detail, and we shall utilize his numerical classification and analysis in the discussion which follows.

20. Cauchie nos. 562 bis; 454—*La vie de demoiselle Elizabeth Ranquet* (Paris, 1660).

21. It must be noted that H. Gaston Hall has warned against dependence on Cioranescu's references in cases of attribution or early editions (*French Studies*, XXII [1968], 151-52).

22. Table. For the Cauchie numbers see note 19. Respective lengths and first lines correspond throughout.

Cauchie no.	*Almahide* (vol., pp.)	Title
456	—	
457	I, 67-8	Sonnet.
458	68-9	Sonnet.
459	148-9	Stances.
460	161-4	Stances.
461	205-8	Stances.
462	394	Epigramme.
463	396-8	Stances.
464	408-11	Stances.
465	418	Chanson.
466	434-9	Les flevrs.
467	450-69	Eglogve.
468	600-02	Stances.
469	620-2	Stances.
470	649-50	Sonnet.
471	II, 694-6	Sonnet.
472	984-6	Sonnet.

Cauchie no.	*Almahide* (vol., pp.)	Title
473	1024-5	La riviere de Genile à celle de Betis.
474	1058-61	Stances.
475	1092-3	Stances svr vn portrait.
476	1094-5	Stances svr vn coevr brvlé par le soleil.
477	1125-6	Sonnet.
478	1130-1	Sonnet.
479	1132-3	Sonnet.
480	1134-5	Sonnet.
481	1165-9	Stances svr vn retovr.
482	1183-5	Stances.
483	III, 1401-4	Elegie svr vne absence.
484	1406-8	Stances svr vn despit.
485	1516-9	Stances. L'esclave amovrevx.
486	1584-9	Ode.
487	1591-8	Ode.
488	1612-3	Stances.
489	1614-6	Stances.
490	1624-5	Madrigal.
491	1626	Epigramme.
492	1627	Epigramme.
493	1640	Epigramme.
494	1710-11	Stances.
495	1716-7	Stances.
496	1752-3	Sonnet.
497	2028-35	Epithalame.
498	2067-8	Sonnet.
499	IV, 4-5	Sonnet.
500	291-4	Stances.
501	296-8	Stances.
502	393	Recit.
503	IV, 397	Les lions. Premiere entrée.
504	397	Les singes. Seconde entrée.
505	398	Les avtrvches. Troisiesme entrée.
506	398	Les renards. Qvatriesme entrée.
507	405-6	Recit.
508	407	Qvatre astrologves. Premiere entrée.
509	407	Qvatre alchimistes. Seconde entrée.

Cauchie no.	*Almahide* (vol., pp.)	Title
510	408	Six voyagevrs. Troisiesme entrée.
511	408	Six volevrs arrabes. Qvatriesme entrée.
512	416-17	Recit.
513	418	Qvatre portevrs de cassolettes. Premiere entrée.
514	418-19	Six marchands de pierreries. Seconde entrée.
515	419	Six chassevrs. Troisiesme entrée.
516	420	Qvatre bergers et qvatre bergeres. Qvatriesme entrée.
517	429-30	Les Egiptiennes.
518	480-1	Chanson.
519	505-08	Romance.
520	512-3	Sonnet.
521	576-8	Stances.
522	636-7	Sonnet.
523	655-6	Serenade.
524	704-5	Sonnet.
525	716-19	Stances.
526	743-4	Stances.
527	V, 856-9	Ode.
528	862	Epigramme.
529	876	Stances.
530	891-2	Sonnet. Le ialovx sans rival.
531	914-6	Stances.
532	957-9	Stances. [2nd pagination]
533	988-9	Sonnet.
534	1039-40	Serenade.
535	1098-9	Sonnet.
536	1194-5	Sonnet.
537	1196-7	Stances.
538	1242-4	Stances.
539	1263-5	Stances.
540	1333-5	Elegie.
541	1399-1400	Sonnet.
542	1422-3	Stances.
543	1427-8	Stances.
544	1453-63	Eglogve maritime.
545	1492-4	Stances.
546	1508	Epigramme.

Cauchie no.	*Almahide* (vol., pp.)	Title
547	1525-7	Stances.
548	1530	Epigramme.
549	1531	Epigramme.
550	1531	Epigramme.
551	1538-40	Stances.
552	1557-8	Sonnet.
553	1590-7	L'amant [sic] extraordinaire. Stances.
554	1608-9	Sonnet.
555	1626-7	Sonnet.
556	1649-51	Epitaphe d'vn Cygne.
557	1661-8	Le portrait de Myris. Ode.
557 bis	1661-8	Le portrait de Myris. Ode.
558	1706-7	Sonnet.
559	1708-9	Sonnet.
560	1726-7	Stances.
561	V, 1731-5	Stances.
562	VI, 1910-12	Mascarade. Les Chevaliers Errans, aux Dames.
562 bis	2553-4	Sonnet. [= no. 454]
563	2555	Epigramme.
564	2610	Svr vn bovqvet, Epigramme.
565	2610-11	Svr vne gvirlande, Epigramme.
566	2612	Svr vne covronne de Lavrier. Epigramme.
567	2624-9	Le portraict d'Isa. Ode.
[567 bis]		[See no. 557]

23. Cited in Boileau, *Œuvres complètes,* Pléiade ed. (Paris, 1966), p. 883 (12).

24. In 1926 Maggs Brothers listed this same title at 12/10s, along with Scudéry's *Cabinet* and *Poésies diverses,* in 12mo calf, but published in 1662 by Jean Nnorember [sic: Mongrédien had read the publisher's name as Nnoremberkz, which is a third variant]. In Cat. no. 484 *French Books from 1470 to 1700 A.D.,* no. 636.

25. Cauchie, op. cit., p. 127.

English Showalter, Jr. (essay date 1972)

SOURCE: Showalter, English, Jr. "Techniques of Realism in Early Fiction: Serious Fiction." In *The Evolution of the*

French Novel, 1641-1782, pp. 124-93. Princeton, N.J.: Princeton University Press, 1972.

[*In following excerpt, Showalter examines Scudéry's theories of the novel, as delineated in his preface to* Ibrahim.]

Serious fiction is a great deal more nebulous a concept than the comic novel, which can be limited to a dozen or so major works. A serious novel is one in which an effort is made to reproduce reality, however it be defined. As I have pointed out, most comic novels contain examples of serious novels; furthermore, the comic novelist almost unwittingly has to reproduce reality as part of his burlesque of some serious form. I will omit these serious elements of comic fiction from the rest of the discussion, however, so as to avoid ambiguous cases, even though a mistake would only introduce some confusion, not undermine the argument. Most other fiction I take to be serious in intent. As I have already showed, novelists of this era had many different ideas about the nature of reality and the novel's proper relation to it. In principle, I am imposing no *a priori* standards of realism on the novels, as part of the definition of seriousness. *Le Diable boiteux* is a serious novel, despite its fantastic frame, and so are many less known allegories, romances, and tales. I have looked for the five elements of reality—chronology, geography, names, money, and narrator—in all the two hundred and some works I located from the years 1700 to 1720. It was quickly apparent that this standard does in fact separate realistic from non-realistic fictions; the latter deliberately violate or ignore at least one, and usually several of the systems. What remains is not by any means all Realistic fiction; but the historical romance, for example, does make an effort to keep the systems of the real world intact, and thereby sets the direction for its evolution toward Realism.

From the point of view of technique, serious novels stand in direct opposition to comic novels on the central question of realism. The comic novelist deliberately keeps his fictional forms intact, while forcing into them realities which are incongruous and therefore grotesque. The serious novelist moves in the opposite direction. He perceives reality through the filter of literary forms, or attempts to describe it in literary terms; but his intention is neither to ridicule the literary viewpoint, nor to seek out incongruity. On the contrary, he writes because he thinks there is a deeper knowledge of reality to be gained from the literary analysis of it. Thus, while the comic novel tends to move from romance to its diametric opposite, from the gallant hero to the crude peasant, or from exotic settings to the nearest gutter, the serious novel tends to move by smaller steps, from the aristocratic hero to a wealthy bourgeois hero, from the palace into the townhouse. This is less an invasion of literature by ever more plebeian characters and commonplace events than an invasion by literature of ever wider areas of reality.

As I suggested before, the serious novelist resembles Don Quixote—his education and literary formation determine the way he sees his world. Don Quixote represents an extreme case, where the education excludes any lessons of experience; but Cervantes wanted to use his hero as a comic figure. The novelist need not imitate Don Quixote's intransigence to share his outlook, although it is probably true that the more unconscious the novelist's own perspective, the more convincing the portrayal. Where the bias is too obvious, the novel seems to have a thesis, although of course the author's artistic skill may compensate for his intellectual prejudices.

In the first chapters, I have given some elements of a history of serious fiction. The whole history is much too complex to undertake. In the limited area which I want to examine, the comic novels have afforded a useful summary by indirection. Every comic novel tends to touch on all the problems of the recent past. The author satirizes everything he has found ridiculous, and goes out of his way to have a pretext to mention it. The serious novelist, on the other hand, avoids any problem not essential to his theme, and often tries to conceal those he can not escape. Each comic novel gives a static picture of the condition of the novel at that time, or slightly earlier, whereas any given serious novel probably contains no more than fragmentary indications of the general situation.

The evolution implied by the comic novels starts with all the significant problems already present to some degree. The development of the genre leads to heavier and heavier emphasis on rules, derived by and large from some other literary genre. Moreover, the work itself is extended by logical deductions into the real world. Again, this is a quixotic process; the literal truth of the novel is assumed, and the consequences deduced. As these consequences came to light, the concern of the comic novelist shifted away from style, which was Scarron's chief interest, toward the narrator, which was the dominant interest of Challe, Furetière, and Marivaux. Diderot finally attacks the narrator's domination, and restores the other elements of Realism to a position of importance.

A consideration of the serious novel will reveal that progress occurs only in a very limited sense during the eighteenth century. The novel had encountered the fundamental difficulties of realism by the early years of the century, no later; yet the solutions are never satisfactory, and seldom applicable to other works, in all the five areas I have singled out. The most durable contribution in many fields was to have exhausted most of the blind alleys, notably in the conception of the narrator.

It is generally recognized that the first flowering of French rationalism occurred in the decade of the 1630's, marked by such events as the publication of Descartes's *Discourse on Method,* the founding of the French Academy, and the quarrel over *Le Cid.* Well before the triumphant years of French classicism, scholars and critics were formulating, and popular taste was imposing, the doctrine of rules. For all its lowliness as a genre, the novel did not escape the examination of reason, and it is here that the problems begin. In 1641 Georges de Scudéry published a long theoretical preface with his novel ***Ibrahim.*** Although I have already referred to this preface several times, its date as well as its intrinsic merit make a fuller consideration worthwhile. Scudéry frequented the famous salon of the Hôtel de Rambouillet, where he would have met such literary legislators as Vaugelas, Chapelain, and Ménage; and as Henri Coulet observes: ". . . comme Chapelain, comme d'Aubignac, Scudéry croit à l'infaillibilité des règles."[1]

If one is accustomed to the common idea of the Scudérys' novels as monuments of extravagance, the theory behind them is indeed astonishingly and outstandingly rational, laying heavy emphasis on such concepts as nature and verisimilitude. The writings of the Scudérys and La Calprenède are so sound as theory, that they have been cited by Arthur Cooke as possible sources for Henry Fielding's theories. As Cooke observes, "Mlle de Scudéry and Henry Fielding enunciated principles which were in many respects almost identical; yet there is certainly little resemblance between **The Grand Cyrus** and *Tom Jones*."[2] Cooke explains this by referring to changes in the meanings of terms like probability, unity, and morality; and no doubt this semantic vagueness played a role. Another factor, however, is almost certainly the difference in approaches; the Scudérys seem to have the idea that the novel can be derived from the rules, not vice versa, whereas Fielding tries to derive a theory which will justify what he instinctively knows to be a good novel.

The apparent excellence of the Scudérys' theory is misleading; they did not invent the modern novel, any more than did Horace and Aristotle, from whom they took their theory. The main significance of the preface to **Ibrahim** is, I believe, the proof it affords of the new seriousness with which authors were treating the novel. In a short time this theory would contribute to the downfall of the genre it was written to defend—just as Descartes's method was eventually used to overthrow his physics, and just as the emulation of the ancients finally produced the moderns. The reader of the 1660's held ideas of reality and verisimilitude similar to Racine's. It was natural that they should favor a novel which incorporated similar qualities—density, psychological intensity, dramatic crises, abstraction—and prefer the short *nouvelle* to the long *roman*.

The preface to **Ibrahim** touches, sometimes indirectly, on the themes I have been discussing. Scudéry admires the epic chronology, because it enables the author to preserve a unity of time: ". . . et pour s'enfermer dans des bornes raisonnables, ils ont fait (et moy aprés eux) que l'Histoire ne dure qu'une année, et que le reste est par narration. . . ."[3] Although, as Scudéry states, he is merely copying Homer, Virgil, Tasso, and Heliodorus, it is worthwhile to note his justification for the principle of a unity of time: "Ils n'ont pas fait comme ces Peintres qui font voir en une mesme toile un Prince dans le berceau, sur le Trône, et dans le cercueil, et qui par cette confusion peu judicieuse embarassent celuy qui considere leur Ouvrage." The rationale for the unity of time lies outside the work, in the reader's perception. He must be able to embrace the work

within a clear rational framework. Similar demands of reason, all purely external to the work itself, will be made regarding the narrator and even the details of the story; and it seems probable that this rationalism, more than anything else, led to the collapse of the long *roman*. **Ibrahim** was more than three thousand pages long, **Clélie** over seven thousand, and **Le Grand Cyrus** over thirteen thousand. No factitious structure could overcome the truly embarrassing confusion of such works.

A second element of chronology is the use of historical facts. Scudéry proposes to combine historical facts with poetic beauties to create the novel. History serves primarily to lend verisimilitude, which Scudéry calls "la pierre fondamentale de ce bastiment . . . sans elle rien ne peut toucher; sans elle rien ne sçauroit plaire. . . ." (p. 46). Scudéry's method is described plainly: ". . . pour donner plus de vraysemblance aux choses, j'ay voulu que les fondemens de mon Ouvrage fussent historiques, mes principaux personnages marquez dans l'Histoire veritable comme personnes illustres, et les guerres effectives." This doctrine did not, however, extend to the chronological veracity of the events; Scudéry is explicit about that: "Or de peur qu'on ne m'objecte que j'ay rapproché quelques incidens que l'Histoire a fait voir plus éloignez, le grand Virgile sera mon garant, luy qui, dans sa divine Eneïde, a fait paroistre Didon quatre Siecles aprés le sien" (p. 48). The same application can of course be found in the classical theatre. By verisimilitude, the classicists clearly had in mind only the possible existence of a thing, or the possible occurrence of an event, and the possibility was to be judged by reason. Historical realism was a partial guarantee of verisimilitude, but the possibility of a battle, or of a heroic deed, was extra-temporal once it had occurred. In the classical spirit, the rules of art take precedence; it is better to sacrifice the chronology than the unity of time. Clearly, though, a major self-contradiction underlies the doctrine, and the arbitrary unit of time would increasingly yield before the demands of historical veracity.

Money, geography, and names are fairly technical matters, and do not receive much attention from Scudéry. Money, indeed, is not mentioned, except that any but the most general allusion to it would be banned from the novel by the following precept on style: "sans parler comme les extravagans, ny comme le peuple, j'ay essayé de parler comme les honnestes gens" (p. 49). Geography is touched on; but the epic of antiquity had had no discernible unity of place, and so the question did not much concern Scudéry. He rejects the use of mythical kingdoms, asking: "comment seray-je touché des infortunes de la Reine de Guindaye, et du Roy d'Astrobacie, puisque je sçay que leurs Royaumes mesmes ne sont point en la Carte universelle, ou pour mieux dire, en l'estre des choses?" (p. 46). The judge of plausibility once again turns out to be a pedantic form of reason, and the places, like the historical events, have an abstract existence. To name them is to make them exist in the reader's mind, which has accepted them on the authority of the historians. Passing to personal names, Scudéry remarks that "l'imposition des noms est une chose à laquelle chacun doit songer, et à laquelle neantmoins tout le monde n'a pas songé" (p. 48). Scudéry has carefully given Turkish names to Turkish characters, where in the past many authors had used Greek names. We are still in the distant exotic past, and Ibrahim, Artamène, Clélie, or Pharamond may pass for realistic names because real people once bore them. But the principle will constitute a grave problem once the novel begins to treat subjects closer to the present and closer to home. Then the reader will still want to know where and who (and perhaps even how much), and the author will be hard pressed to stay in the no-man's-land between particular realities and general possibilities.

Since Scudéry relates the novel to the epic, he accepts the epic narrator, who is a creator and who can therefore go beyond the limits of a single point of view. In the preface he appears even to advocate a fuller usage of this power by authors in saying: "Après avoir descrit une avanture, un dessein hardy, ou quelque évenement surprenant, capable de donner les plus beaux sentimens du monde, certains Autheurs se sont contentez de nous asseurer qu'un tel Heros pensa de fort belles choses, sans nous les dire, et c'est cela seulement que je desirois sçavoir" (p. 47). The main thrust of his argument is toward the matter of the novel, however, not its style of narration; Scudéry opposes the piling up of adventures and favors psychological analysis. This in itself looks to the future and shows the kinship between the long novels and the *nouvelles* which succeeded them. Scudéry comments on the adventure stories: "cette narration seche et sans art est plus d'une vieille Chronique que d'un Roman . . ." (p. 46), and therein lay the difficulty. As novelists sought more and more to take shelter under the rules of historical writing, the historical narrator became more and more dominant, and he did not have the right to explore the mind. Even Scudéry is ambiguous, for although he wants to know the thoughts and feelings of the heroes, he talks most about their speeches. For example, he writes: "Ce n'est point par les choses de dehors, ce n'est point par les caprices du destin que je veux juger de luy; c'est par les mouvemens de son ame, et par les choses qu'il dit." Or again he writes: "Or pour les faire connoistre parfaitement, il ne suffit pas de dire combien de fois ils ont fait naufrage, et combien de fois ils ont rencontré des voleurs: mais il faut faire juger par leurs discours quelles sont leurs inclinations . . . ," and he cites with approbation the sentence: "Parle afin que je te voye" (p. 47). In short, he at least leaves the way open for such devices as the overheard soliloquy and the confidant, the conventions by which the seventeenth-century novelist tried to accomplish the study of the human soul.

* * *

CHRONOLOGY: Scudéry's epic rule for the unity of time enjoyed a short prominence. It was applied in the long romances, and therefore satirized by Scarron, Furetière, and Marivaux. When the *nouvelle* came into vogue, however, this principle ceased to be relevant.[4] It does not,

in fact, have any relation to the question of realism, but is a purely formal matter. The decline of the long romance and the rise of the *nouvelle* indicate the growing dominance of the historical element over the epic.

If the rule for the unity of time had little future after 1660, the principles of historical verisimilitude were full of consequences. Scudéry, under the sheltering authority of the Ancients, argued that the historical precedent guaranteed the possibility of the event; he did not really intend to put his novels into a real historical chronology. At sufficient distance in time and space, the method works reasonably well. The average reader is likely to know that the events took place, and that the characters existed; he is not likely to know precisely when.

Notes

1. Coulet, *Anthologie,* p. 44.

2. Arthur L. Cooke, "Henry Fielding and the Writers of Heroic Romance," *PMLA,* 62 (1947), 994.

3. Coulet, *Anthologie,* p. 45.

4. René Godenne, in *Histoire de la nouvelle française,* argues that the *nouvelle* quickly adopted all the conventions of the *roman,* including the epic chronology, and preserved them intact well into the eighteenth century (pp. 108-110). I do not challenge the accuracy of his facts, but question the value of his rigid genre distinctions, for he analyzes only works designated "nouvelle" on the title page or in the preface. As I showed in chapter one, the *roman* actually absorbed all the innovations presented by the *nouvelle* around 1660, as well as later innovations associated with subgenres like the *nouvelle historique,* the *histoire véritable,* the *mémoires,* etc. The persistence of an archaic technique like the epic chronology, even in works designated *nouvelle,* does not alter the fact that around 1660 the sudden vogue of the *nouvelle* signaled a shift in interest from the epic approach to the historical.

FURTHER READING

Biography

Levi, Anthony. "Georges de Scudéry, 1601-1667." In *Guide to French Literature: Beginnings to 1789,* pp. 821-27. Detroit: St. James Press, 1994.
    Provides an overview of Scudéry's life and works.

Criticism

Boyce, Benjamin. Introduction to *Prefaces to Fiction,* pp. i-x. Augustan Reprint Society Publication Number 32. Los Angeles: William Andrews Clark Memorial Library, University of California, 1952.
    Surveys Scudéry's role in codifying early theories of the novel by examining the preface to *Ibrahim* and a conversation included in *Clélie.* The volume reprints the preface to *Ibrahim.*

John Suckling
1609-1641

English poet, playwright, essayist, and epistler.

INTRODUCTION

Suckling is commonly considered the quintessential Cavalier Poet—a soldier-poet associated with the court of Charles I. His poems, like those of his fellow Cavalier Poets Thomas Carew, Richard Lovelace, and Edmund Waller, are noted for their sophisticated wit, urbanity, and exaggerated gallantry, often tinged with cynicism and irony. Suckling was also infamous for his gambling, womanizing, and involvement in political conspiracy, and the image of him as a libertine courtier who effortlessly composed highly polished verse earned him the epithet "Natural, easy Suckling." Suckling was also an accomplished amateur playwright whose first play, the richly extravagant *Aglaura* (1638), was both a critical and a popular success.

BIOGRAPHICAL INFORMATION

Suckling was born in 1609 in Twickenham, Middlesex, the eldest son of an aristocratic and influential family. His father, John Suckling, was a prosperous landowner and member of Parliament who held various court positions; his mother, Martha Cranfield, was the daughter of a wealthy merchant and the sister of Lionel Cranfield, who became Lord Treasurer of England. Suckling entered Trinity College, Cambridge, in 1623, but left without obtaining a degree. As a student, Suckling led a dissolute life, gambling and carousing. In 1627 he was admitted to Gray's Inn, where he hoped to continue his education; however, the death of his father soon afterward put an end to his studies. After inheriting nearly the whole of his father's large estate, Suckling entered the military. He fought during the Thirty Years' War, accompanying the Duke of Buckingham to the Island of Ré in 1627, and joining Lord Wimbledon's expedition to the Low Countries in 1629. Suckling returned to his studies at the University of Leydon for a brief time in 1630, and was knighted in the same year by King Charles. He then entered the service of Sir Henry Vane, ambassador to the King of Sweden, until he returned to England in 1632. Upon his return Suckling led an extravagant life, conducting numerous affairs with women and incurring massive gambling debts, which forced him to sell off much of his inherited estate. At this time he began to pursue the heiress Anne Willoughby, probably seeking to replenish his wealth, but he ultimately failed in his effort after years of intrigue and

violent opposition from her father and rival suitors. Suckling began writing poetry in the early 1630s, but the majority of his works were not published until after his death; his first published work was *Aglaura*, a play which was produced in 1638 by the King's Company at court and at the Blackfriars Theatre. His appointment as a Gentleman of the Privy Chamber Extraordinary in 1638 may have been connected to the flattering depiction of courtly life in *Aglaura*, which was meant to catch the attention of the court. Suckling became active in the military again in 1639, during the First Bishops' War, and served as the captain of a troop of carabineers in 1640. Around this time Suckling was elected to Parliament, but his political life was cut short by his involvement in the Army Plot of 1641—an attempt to free condemned prisoner Sir Thomas Wentworth, an advisor to the King and an opponent of Parliament. After the plot failed, a writ for Suckling's arrest was issued, but he fled to France. He was subsequently convicted, in absentia, of high treason. Suckling died soon after his escape to France. Although there are conflicting accounts of his death, the most credible evidence suggests that he committed suicide by drinking poison.

MAJOR WORKS

The canon of Suckling's poems is uncertain because they were not collected during his lifetime; the first volume of his works, *Fragmenta Aurea,* (1646) was not published until five years after his death. Suckling wrote poetry in a variety of forms, including satires, songs, sonnets, verse epistles, epithalamia, and epigrams. Thematically, his poems often reflect his libertine outlook. A great many of his poems concerned with love, courtship, and the relationship between the sexes—such as his early work "Loving and Beloved"—illustrate his humor and cynicism. One of Suckling's most famous poems, "A Ballade. Upon a Wedding," parodies the typical epithalamion in honor of a bride and groom and demonstrates that even such a sacred event was not safe from his satiric wit and cynical view of romantic relationships. "Woman's Constancy" presents a similarly jaded view of love and characterizes women as untrustworthy, deceitful, and inconstant—a common stereotype of women during the Renaissance. One of Suckling's most important and often imitated poems is "The Wits," a satirical depiction of a group of poets who are competing for the crown of poetic excellence. Suckling uses the poem to ridicule his contemporaries—as well as himself—by mocking their poetry, attitudes, and physical appearance. In addition to writing poetry, Suckling also composed three plays, all of which were popular in their time. *Aglaura,* his most successful play, is a dazzling spectacle that was first staged in a lavish production apparently paid for by Suckling himself. A tale of excessive love, jealousy, and infidelity, the play centers on the title character, a Persian woman who is wanted in marriage by both a king and his son. Suckling wrote two versions of the final act—a tragic and tragicomic ending. The tragic version ends with the death of all the main characters; the tragicomic version features forgiveness and repentance. The play was evidently written to impress an aristocratic audience. Not only was the production at court opulent in its costuming and painted sets (a theatrical innovation), Suckling gave a printed folio copy of the play to each of the audience members and presented a manuscript copy to the king. The tragicomic version was probably composed to please Queen Henrietta Maria, who disliked tragic endings.

CRITICAL RECEPTION

Suckling was widely admired in his own day, and his reputation rose to great heights during the Restoration with the frequent and successful revivals of his plays. Although his literary stature has diminished since that time, modern critics still regard Suckling as an important poet of the seventeenth century, and note his influence on later poets. Critics have observed that, like most Cavalier Poets, Suckling was influenced by Ben Jonson's unadorned style and use of iambic pentameter and tetrameter. In addition, scholars such as Fletcher Orpin Henderson have explored how the works of John Donne and the *libertin* poets of France also affected Suckling's poetry. Michael P. Parker has compared Suckling's poems to those of fellow Cavalier Poet Thomas Carew, contending that while Carew's poetry looks back to earlier seventeenth-century poets, Suckling's poetry looks forward and anticipates future trends. Many twentieth-century critics have searched for deeper meaning in Suckling's poetry, beneath its surface cynicism and wit, and have discovered a more serious layer to many of his works. Frans Dirk de Soet has studied several of Suckling's songs and poems and has found that "at times he could be inspired by sublime and elevated thoughts." Like de Soet, Raymond A. Anselment has argued that Suckling was not a typical Cavalier Poet. In his examination of Suckling's love poetry Anselment found that beyond their apparent cynicism lies "a complex and even sensitive search for the wisdom in love." Other modern critical studies have focused on the establishment of a canon of Suckling's works; examinations of his letters and the short essay, *An Account of Religion by Reason* (1637); and assessments of his dramatic works. In general, modern critics have been less impressed with Suckling's plays than his poems. Many commentators have suggested that his plays do not translate well to today's readers and audiences, and some have found that their plots are absurdly convoluted. However, Charles L. Squier has defended Suckling's abilities as a playwright, maintaining that his dramatic genius may be found in his "distinctive and brilliant" dialogue.

PRINCIPAL WORKS

An Account of Religion by Reason (essay) 1637

Aglaura (play) 1638

The Goblins (play) 1641?

Brennoralt, or The Discontented Colonel (play) 1641?

A Coppy of a Letter Found in the Privy Lodgeings at Whitehall (letter) 1641

The Coppy of a Letter Written to the Lower House of Parliament Touching Divers Grievances and Inconveniences of the State & c. London (letter) 1641

Fragmenta Aurea. A Collection of all the Incomparable Peeces (collected works) 1646

The Last Remains of Sir John Suckling. Being a Full Collection of His Poems and Letters (poems and letters) 1659

The Works of Sir John Suckling: The Non-Dramatic Works (poems and letters) 1971

The Works of Sir John Suckling: The Plays (plays) 1971

*This work was republished as "To Mr. Henry German, in the beginning of Parliament, 1640," in *Fragmenta Aurea* in 1646.

CRITICISM

Frans Dirk de Soet (essay date 1932)

SOURCE: de Soet, Frans Dirk. "Chapter IV." In *Puritan and Royalist Literature in the Seventeenth Century*, pp. 117-23. Delft, Netherlands: N.V. Technische Boekhandel en Drukkerij J. Waltman Jr., 1932.

[*In the following essay, de Soet provides a brief overview of Suckling's life and praises his talents as a poet.*]

A very important place among the cavalier poets who wrote between the accession of Charles I and the Restoration must be allowed to Sir John Suckling,[1] the son of the secretary of state and comptroller of the household of James I.

He was born in his paternal house at Twickenham, in 1609. What we know of his life commences with the year 1623, when he was sent to Trinity college, Cambridge, from which he four years later removed to Gray's Inn.

The death of his father, who was one of the richest noblemen of England, made him the possessor of the family title and the greater part of the property, but put an end to his academical life. He wandered on the continent, seeking adventure, visited France and Italy, and after serving a campaign under the marquis of Hamilton, the commander of the English troops in the army of Gustavus Adolphus, he returned to Londen, in 1632. His uncle the Earl of Middlesex introduced him at court where he was received with distinction.

Suckling possessed all the advantages which a graceful person, rank, fortune and wit could give, but in morals and extravagance he proved a thorough precursor of Rochester and Buckingham.

One of his worst vices was his passionate love of gaming. That in spite of his own vows and the prayers of his sisters, who, says Aubrey, charged him with having squandered their fortunes, he often fell a victim to it, we may infer from his own words in his **"Session of the Poets"** where he says that

> "He loved not the Muses so well as his sport,
> And prized black eyes, or a lucky hit
> At bowls, above all the trophies of wit."[2]

But the pleasure loving court of Charles I thought it expedient to connive at these and other faults and as Suckling had many accomplishments and was also gallant and generous, he became a favourite with every one at Whitehall. He soon rose to considerable popularity by his light-hearted witty lyrics, which amused the cavalier gentlemen and in after years won the praise of Congreve[3].

In gaiety and ease many of them are unsurpassed but in subject and moral tone they differ considerably. Suckling was among the earliest whose love songs strike a new note. Instead of following the lead of Carew, Waller, Lovelace, and other poetic lovers of his day, whose verses are characterized by exaggerated gallantry and chivalrous devotion to the ladies, he ridicules the lover who, by his pale colour and muteness; tries to make impression on his mistress.

> "This cannot take her
> If of herself she will not love,
> Nothing can make her:
> The devil take her!"[4]

He boasts of having been faithful three days together, glories in inconstancy and with cynical outspokenness tells us that he had to raise the siege of a lady's heart because

> "Honour was there
> And did command in chief"[5]

He celebrates the attractions of the countess of Carlisle and makes her the subject of a dialogue between himself and Thomas Carew, but the tone in which he does so differs considerably from that of his friend.

The same degeneration of courtly manners we see in the famous poem in which he immortalized the marriage of Lady Margaret Howard, the daughter of the Earl of Suffolk with his friend Roger Boyle, Lord Broghill.

Contrary to the usage of his time he did not celebrate the event in a conventional nuptial song, consisting of praises of the bridegroom and bride with the usual wishes for their happiness but in a lively ballad. This famous production, which was first published in "Witts Recreations" of 1640, is among the most elegant and beautiful of all Caroline poems.

In a lively and humorous manner the author, in the character of a rustic describes to his friend Lovelace, the ceremony at Northumberland House and pictures the happy pair to him. Especially "the maid" is placed before us with a fidelity to nature and vividness of portraiture, which remind us strongly of Chaucer.

How admirable for instance is the discription of the colour of her cheeks, the shape of her mouth or the movement of her feet.

Suckling's Epithalamium says Hazlitt "is his masterpiece, and is indeed unrivalled in that class of compositions for the voluptuous delicacy of the sentiments and the luxuriant richness of the images"[6].

But with all his merits of wit, gracefulness and fancy, his verses are frequently immoral; yet it cannot be denied that in his more serious moments he had a genuine vein of poetry, that is to say of really noble feelings. His well-known song, **"When dearest, I but think of thee"**, or his lines "Upon the first sight of my Lady Seymour", show him in a different light and prove that at times he could be inspired by sublime and elevated thoughts.

A violent quarrel with Lord Digby, a rival suitor caused his withdrawal from the court and led to a closer intimacy with John Hales, D'Avenant, Chillinworth, and other scholars, poets, and divines who held their meetings at Lord Falkland's house at Great Tew in Oxfordshire and discussed there questions of theology, philisophy and literature. In 1637, he published his prose pamphlet on socinianism, and early in the same year his **"Session of the Poets"**, in which he launches his good humoured satire against the foibles of the literary celebrities of the day, among whom he espially mentions Jonson, Carew, D'Avenant, Matthew and himself.

It is written in his usual careless manner and possesses only historical value. Yet it is often quoted, for his allusions to these popular writers are very curious while many of his criticisms are just. At the period of the Scottish rebellion the poet displayed his loyalty and love of show by spending £1200 in equipping a troop of horse, who proved too fine for fighting. Without striking a blow they fled when Lesley made preparations to attack them at Dunce Law, an event which afterwards gave rise to many a satirical ballad. One of the most amusing was written by a rival wit Sir John Mennes, a military officer of high rank and author of a number of popular political songs, which in 1656 appeared in "Musarum Deliciae".

Suckling retaliated on the ridicule levelled against his finery and cowardice by an ostentatious display of defiance, but his verses are far less lively and witty than those of his anonymous antagonist. Shortly before the appearance of this poem, he turned to dramatic writing and in the course of a few years produced three tragedies and one comedy. Contrary to his other works there is a spirit of chivalry in them but they do not deserve much praise for none of these plays can be called altogether a good one. His first the drama of *Aglaura* was performed with great splendour in the presence of the court, in 1638, and had a considerable success, probably because he had provided it with scenes, dresses and an orchestre, which, before this time, had only been used in the performance of masques.

The central idea was no doubt to exhibit the fatal effect, which love, ambition, jealousy, and hatred, when not kept within proper bounds could produce on human life. There is a genuine tragic element in the interpretation of the sufferings of the poor heroine, a Persian lady, whose hand is the occasion for a strife between the king and his son. But nobody is now likely to contradict Pepys unfavourable criticism for the tragedy has many faults. The most vital is the want of unity, not merely in plot but in the leading thought. The author is often very obscure and difficult to understand. The incidents succeed each other too rapidly, while the catastrophe is brought about in a manner too unnatural and artificial. As all the principal personages, among, whom is the king of the country in which the scene is laid, either kill each other or themselves, we can easily understand that Charles's feelings were shocked. At his request Suckling altered the fifth act and by giving it a fortunate conclusion changed it into a tragi-comedy.

The campaign against the Scots drew from him his tragedy, *The Discontented Colonell* which seven years later was published under the title of *Brennoralt.* It exhibits much fancy and contains some really elevated passages, but in general it possesses nearly all the defects of its predecessor, while still more than *Aglaura* it abounds with improbable incidents and unnatural characters. The only personage who succeeds in interesting us is the hero. He has evidently been presented as an idealized portrait of the author himself. There is an undertone of sadness in him, a despondency about the country, a bitterness about the times and a cynisicm about men and women. He is concious of the shortcomings of his sovereign but noble patriot as he is, he remains loyal to the end. Suckling evidently gave vent to his own feelings when he wrote:

> "Dost think, cause I am angry with the king and state
>   sometimes,
> I am fallen out with virtue and myself?"

> "He that would think me a villain, is one; and I
> Do wear this toy to purge the world of such."[7]

His next piece, *The Goblins* is remarkable for the humour and vivacity of the dialogue but there is not the slightest attempt at cahraterization or description of manners, while it is overcharged by so much intrigue that it is difficult to follow the whole series of events. The Goblins, from whom the comedy is named, were a strong band of outlaws, who in the manner of Robin Hood and his followers formed a kind of government among themselves and often played rough practical jokes on the people. The last of his dramatic productions, a tragedy, *The sad One,* was published in the third edition of his *Fragmenta Aurea,* a collection of his works, which appeared for the first time four years after his death. The hero Clarimont, a Sicilian nobleman, whose father has fallen a victim to political inntrigue, shows an evident imitation of the character of Hamlet. Both in matter and in imagery this piece seems to have suggested much to Suckling. Yet *The sad One* is not entitled to criticism for what was afterwards printed was nothing but the outline of a play. There is no unravelling of the plot and although it has the usual number of acts, these are so short and seem to be so hastily constructed that the author no doubt gave less than he originally intended to do.

All these dramas have now sunk into obscurity. Some of the songs, however, with which they are interspersed, such as Orsame's in *Aglaura* or Grainevert's in *Brennoralt,* will always continue in high favour with the public for they are exquisitely elegant, sprightly and natural.

Besides poems, tracts and plays, the *Fragmenta Aurea* contain a number of letters, which passed between the poet and his friends. They extend from 1631 to 1642, and are very interesting from the glimpses they afford us into the writer's own life and from the opinions they express on the politics of his day. Their style is pure and they are unaffected and exhibit a pleasing view of the author, whose character appears very advantageously in his private correspondence. Two of the earliest were written on the continent in the winter of 1631, some months before the battle of Lutzen, for there is many an allusion in them to his military service under Gustavus Adolphus in Silesia. His letter addressed to Lucius Carey, who, in 1634, had withdawn from Whitehall and had buried himself in the delightful solitude of Great Tew, contains the advice to return to London and devote himself again to the king's affairs. It displays much knowledge of human nature and abounds both in wit and in observation. His epistles written during the Scottish campaign give us very little information about himself or the military operations which were then in progress. All that we can gather from them is his firm belief in the victory of the English army and his contempt of the enemy, whose strength was much undervalued by him. In the course of the same year (1639) we find him writing a letter on the treaty of Berwick for which negotiations were then carried on. Though he does not give his own opinion, it is evident from his words that he regarded it as a perfect failure. "There are here, he writes," who think that necessity, not good nature produced this treaty and that the same necessity which made them thus wise for peace, will make them as desperate for war, if it succeed not suddenly,"[8] a prophecy, which proved accurate enough.

The most important of his epistolary compositions is his letter to Henry Germyn. To this nobleman; who was the favourite or as some called him the lover of Henrietta Maria, he unbosoms himself with great freedom. Yet it is not easy to avoid thinking that when he appeared to write only for his friend, he was also casting an eye towards the king and the queen for whom his words breathe great affection.

To pacify the discontents of the people it is absolutely necessary, he writes, that the king should voluntarily concede to all their claims and that he should break with his habit of balancing one party against another. He also advises him for the sake of public peace and the safety of the royal family to dismiss the Earl of Strafford.

Whether these upright counsels ever reached the king is unknown. Forced by necessity Charles made some concessions but they came too late to lay the coming storm, One of the first steps taken by the Long Parliament was to cast the hated minister into prison. Suckling, who became involved in the political difficulties and intrigues that preceded the civil war, tried to rescue him by bringing the army to London, but the plot was detected and he was obliged to fly to France. Here he lived for some time in great poverty and in the summer of 1642, died prematurely at Paris, probably by taking poison.

Notes

1. Sir John Suckling. *The works in prose and verse.* E. H. Thompson Londen 1910

W. J. Courthope. *History of English poetry* vol III. 1903
J. H. Masterman. *The Age of Milton London.* 1919
The Cambridge History of English Literature vol VII. 1920
W. Hazlitt. *Lectures on the English Comic Writers.* 1819
Dictionary of National Biography.

2. l. 78-80.

3. *Way of the World.* Act IV, Sc 4.

4. *Aglaura* scene II.

5. "Tis now, since I sat down before." l 31, 32.

6. *Lectures on the English Comic Writers.* Lect. III.

7. Act. III sc 2

8. The works of Sir John Suckling p. 334.

Fletcher Orpin Henderson (essay date 1937)

SOURCE: Henderson, Fletcher Orpin. "Traditions of *Précieux* and *Libertin* in Suckling's Poetry." *ELH* 4, no. 4 (December 1937): 274-98.

[*In the essay below, Henderson explores how the works of John Donne and French poetic traditions influenced Suckling's works.*]

The few students of recent times who have mentioned Sir John Suckling have uniformly recognized that he was influenced by the *précieuse* cult which grew up around Henrietta Maria. Among the first to discuss his poetry was J. B. Fletcher, who, in "Précieuses at the Court of Charles I,"[1] shows that one may draw up a code book of platonic love from the letters of Suckling. The lover is constant, although he recognizes a "curious permissive exception." Finding "Aglaura" gone from town, he writes,[2]

> though you have left behind you faces whose beauties might well excuse perjury in others, yet in me they cannot, since to the making that no sin love's casuists have most rationally resolved that she for whom we forsake ought to be handsomer than the forsaken, which would be here impossible.

The lover expects no reward. He serves for the love of service, and nothing more.

> After all, the wages will not be high, for it [his heart] hath been brought up under Platonics, and knows no other way of being paid for service than by being commanded more; which truth when you doubt, you have but to send to its master and your humble servant,
>
> J. S.[3]

He will follow her will blindly, without asking the reason.

Yet, hearing you have resolved it otherwise for me, my faith shall alter without becoming more learned upon it, or once knowing why it should do so.[4]

He protests his humility, and recognizes that he has no more claim to her favour than all men have to light and beauty. Secrecy is essential, and although he is not ashamed to worship at her shrine,

> yet since the world is full of profane eyes, the best way, sure, is to keep all mysteries from them, and to let privacy be (what indeed it is) the best part of devotion.[5]

Professor Lynch dealt with *précieuse* influence on Suckling's verse.[6] She found that since he was "brought up under the Platonics," there are numerous poems by him where that influence overbalances all others.[7] "The poet has a Platonic mistress whose 'Love's philosophy' he endeavors to accept. Love's flame, he promises, shall purge him of 'the dross—desire.'" His two poems **"Against Fruition"** seem to echo the familiar arguments of *Astrée.* Professor Lynch believes that this is also true of the lines **"Against Absence."** In one poem addressed to his rival, he warns that their only reward from their mistress for past service will be the opportunity for future fidelity. In a second, he proposes that the first one to die shall leave his stock of love to the surviving lover, since,

> . . . no one stock can ever serve
> To love so much as she'll deserve.[8]

It is well known that the origins of the Caroline *précieuse* cult are to be found in France, in the *salon* of Madame de Rambouillet. But another contemporary French movement made its appearance in England. French *libertinage* crossed the Channel. *Libertinage*[9] is a word which has more than one meaning. The sixteenth century used it to describe the belief of those who were no longer able to accept the old faith. It was applied to those independent spirits who followed neither Rome nor Geneva. In the seventeenth century this meaning persisted; *libertinage* was freedom of thought. So the word was used by Garasse, Charron, Pascal, and others. But in the first decade of the seventeenth century it took on a new meaning. A *libertin* came, as was natural enough, to be a man who was irregular not only in his faith, but in his conduct as well. Morality has always been the handmaid of religion, and when a man's beliefs are attacked for being too free, his conduct is suspect as well. Probably the *libertins* were as moral as their adversaries, but the known excesses of the few brought condemnation on the whole group.

> Pour être compris aujourd'hui quand nous voulons rendre au vocable décrié sa signification primitive, nous en sommes réduits à l'expliquer, sans espoir de séparer jamais, dans le langage courant, les deux acceptions qu'il a successivement reçues: indépendance de l'esprit et dévergondage des mœurs.[10]

Montaigne was the immediate ancestor of the *libertins.* While he can hardly be said to be the originator of the skeptical notions of the *Essays,* they came with some

novelty. It is to their popularity that we may trace much of the ethical naturalism, either directly or indirectly, which we find both in England and in France in the seventeenth century.

> Montaigne began as an adherent of Stoicism, which, with Platonism, had been interwoven with Christian thought and become a part of Renaissance idealism in both personal and political ethics. But Stoicism was not long to his taste. His nature was too supple for its restraints, and too easy and tolerant to submit long to its discipline or to feel long the attractiveness of its elevation. . . . But his apostasy from Stoicism was hastened when about 1575 he became enthusiastic over Greek scepticism, as expounded in the *Hypotyposes* of Sextus Empiricus. . . .
>
> For a short period, Montaigne, under the influence of the philosophy of Sextus, regarded custom and tradition as his best guide. But such a philosophy is a worse tyranny than Stoicism, and contains in itself the acid of dissolution; Montaigne soon passed through it, to his third and mature philosophy of individualism based on "Nature." Nature then meant to him primarily his own nature, which he regarded as his own unique lawgiver. . . . Distrustful of all speculations in ethical idealism, thoroughly sceptical regarding conventions and traditions, he followed nature in everything, and in case of doubt, "nature" meant his own nature.[11]

To this "Nature" Montaigne's "libertine" followers turned, but they found there authority for thought and conduct which might not have been approved by their master. In religion, Montaigne's skepticism led him, not toward atheism or deism, but toward the authority of the Roman Church. His questioning had undermined his faith in the human reason, but this did not plunge him into intellectual anarchy. Rather, his distrust of reason strengthened his trust in what was for him the oldest, the native, and hence the strongest tradition.

> Now by the knowledge of my volubilitie, I have by accidence engendred some constancy of opinions in my self; yea have not so much altered my first and naturall ones. For, what apparance soever there be in novelty, I do not easily change, for feare I should lose by the bargaine: And since I am not capable to chuse, I take the choise from others; and keep myself in the seat, that God hath placed me in. Else could I hardly keepe my selfe from continuall rowling. Thus have I by the grace of God preserved my selfe whole (without agitation or trouble of conscience) in the ancient beliefe of our religion, in the middest of so many sects and divisions, which our age hath brought forth.[12]

Although this method of justifying faith in tradition because of a lack of faith in the human reason was to prove fruitful in later writers, it was not his fideism which attracted the *libertins* to Montaigne. Even he seems more to have accepted Catholicism than to have developed a deep and noble religious feeling, as Pascal, and, to a certain extent Dryden, did at a later date, working in this skeptical tradition. It was the appeal to nature which made the *Essays* the handbook of the libertines. But nature has many meanings; to Montaigne and his followers, it had at least two. First, as Professor Bredvold has shown, nature was the nature of each individual. Second, it was a nature uncorrupted by man. The Golden Age was the time when man was uncorrupted by custom and law, and it was to this hypothetical Golden Age that man should turn to find his way of life. The freedom of a soft primitivistic society such as this, where every man lived according to the dictates of his nature, appealed strongly to the gentle soul of Montaigne. Some of his followers, amongst whom Théophile de Viau has attracted most attention, expounded this view of nature in their verse.[13] For the most part, however, "libertine" poetry did not assume the robes of philosophy. Rather, the naturalism of Montaigne served as a source for a light and cynical justification for their verse and their conduct.

In many cases, justification was needed. Centering around taverns and *cabarets* such as the *Pomme de Pin,* the dissolute life led by the *beaux esprits* was notorious. At this time, the *cabaret* filled the place of the coffee house of the eighteenth century. There the *libertins* would gather to drink too much wine and to recite their skeptical and indecent verses.[14] It was verse of this sort which crowded the *recueils* of the first quarter of the century. *Le Cabinet Satyrique,* for example, is almost entirely composed of obscene verses. Théophile contributed to that anthology, and the inclusion of some stanzas believed to be his in the *Parnasse Satyrique* led to his condemnation. The poetic standard of these two works is on about the same level as in the drolleries of the Restoration.

One must not forget that the *libertins* were not strictly a school. At best, they were a loosely connected group, the members of which differed widely in seriousness and in poetic ability. Their common inheritance from Montaigne was a distrust and disbelief in any form of ethical idealism. They further had in common an Epicurean naturalism which coloured their life and work. The extent to which this naturalism was recognized and expressed varied with the individual poet. Few seemed to argue in verse as deliberately as did Théophile. Even he can not be called a philosopher. Like that of his fellows, most of his poetry is light in manner.

> Théophile et son disciple Des Barreaux étaient, en bonne santé, incapables de rechercher autre chose que le plaisir et la volupté; leur intelligence trop mobile n'aurait pu s'arrêter longtemps à des spéculations métaphysiques.[15]

We may look upon the *libertins* as a group because of their common appeal to nature to justify their pleasures. Because of the immortality of their verse, which only reflected their lives, we may accept M. Lachevre's definition:[16]

> Un libertin est un homme aimant le plaisir, tout les plaisirs, sacrifiant à la bonne chère, le plus souvent de mauvaises moeurs, raillant la religion, n'ayant autre Dieu que la Nature, niant l'immortalité de l'âme et dégagé des erreurs populaires.
>
> En un mot c'est un esprit fort doublé d'un débauché.

To this "libertine" tradition John Donne seems to have belonged for a time.[17] His *Songs and Sonnets,* which enjoyed a great popularity both before and after printing, are permeated with a skeptical naturalism. The restraints of society have no justification, save in custom. In olden days, plurality of loves was perfectly proper. It is in our man-made laws that we have gone astray from nature.

> How happy were our Syres in ancient times,
> Who held plurality of loves no crime!
> With them it was accounted charity
> To stirre up race of all indifferently;
> Kindreds were not exempted from the bands:
> Which with the Persians still in usage stands.
> Women were then no sooner asked than won,
> And what they did was honest and well done,
> And since this title honour hath been us'd,
> Our weake credulity hath been abus'd;
> The golden laws of nature are repeald,
> Which our first Fathers in such reverence held;
> Our liberty's revers'd, our Charter's gone,
> And we're made servants to opinion,
> A monster in no certain shape attir'd,
> And whose originall is much desir'd,
> Formelesse at first, but goeing on it fashions,
> And doth prescribe manners and laws to nations.[18]

In these early poems, Donne looked upon love as an appetite, not a spiritual relationship. But he does not condemn it for that reason. Rather, he appeals to nature not only to justify that view, but to excuse the inconstancy which he proudly flaunts. In "Confined Love"[19] he points out the freedom of other elements of nature, and compares man's position with them.

> Are Sunne, Moone, or Starres by law forbidden,
> To smile where they list, or lend away their light?
> Are birds divorc'd, or are they chidden
> If they leave their mate, or lie abroad a night?
> Beasts do no joyntures lose
> Though they new lovers choose,
> But we are made worse than those.

But Donne is set off from the main body of libertines by his passion, his learning, and the keenness of his wit. No doubt, as Professor Bredvold concludes, he was too susceptible to idealism to remain long a worshipper of the earthly Aphrodite. With his marriage, he became the devoted husband, and repented of his early life. It is to his spiritually slighter successors that we must turn to find the continuation of the "libertine" spirit in England.

Although Donne's philosophy of love underwent a great change between the composition of the *Songs and Sonnets* and the composition of his deeply sincere poems to his wife, it was the first group that made him the great influence that he was in the seventeenth century. When Carew wrote

> Here lies a king that ruled as he thought fit
> The universal monarchy of wit;[20]

he meant the Donne of the gay, youthful skepticism. These early poems served to spread widely the ideas of the "libertine" spirit. Montaigne, of course, also reached a large audience. And in England, as in France, skeptical thought can not be considered merely as a philosophical movement.[21] Minor poets who followed in Donne's footsteps echoed the ideas of their master.

Such a follower was Sir John Suckling. His indebtedness to Donne is obvious. Although he professed to be a great admirer of Shakespeare, it is the echoes of Donne which are heard most frequently. Occasionally he borrows directly from the Dean of Paul's, as in **"The Guiltless Inconstant."**[22] His wit, never so piercing nor so impassioned as Donne's, is reminiscent. Although less intellectual, he does employ the so-called metaphysical conceit in the same manner. Most striking is his flippant inconstancy; it is the same amoral inconstancy of the *Songs and Sonnets.* In his **"Farewell to Love"** he dallies with the metaphysical *frisson,* as had Donne in *The Funerall* and *The Relique.* Upon the internal evidence of his poems, Suckling could be classed with the English "libertine" successors to Donne.

Suckling was also familiar with the French *libertins.* It is known that he traveled abroad when he was young. A letter dated November 18, 1629, indicates that he was in Dunkirk at that time. Another letter dated 1632 proves that he had just returned from Germany.[23] By 1630 he seems to have visited France, Germany, and Italy. From the few known facts of his life, it appears evident that he had spent a good deal of time on the continent before he settled down at court in 1632.

Perhaps it was while he was abroad that he made his acquaintance with French literature. That he had some acquaintance may be proved from his poems. The first collected edition of his work was entitled *Fragmenta Aurea,* and was issued in 1646 by Humphrey Moseley. This volume, and the second edition of it, which came out in 1648, contain little more than a half of his poetry and letters. The fourth edition of *Fragmenta Aurea,* published in 1659,[24] adds forty-two new poems, twelve new letters, and an imperfect play. Among these new poems is a little French piece called **"Desdain."** Following it is Suckling's translation. The Reverend Alfred Inigo Suckling, in the *Life* which he appended to his edition of the **Works** in 1836 (and which Hazlitt lifted for his editions), remarks that Sir John's translation "unites much freedom and grace with very great fidelity to the original, and leaves us to regret that more of the light ballads and odes of our neighbours had not engaged his attention."[25] Except for this, little attention has been paid to the poem. As far as I can discover, no attempt has been made to identify it. In the **Last Remains,** the following version is printed:[26]

1.

A quoy servent d'artifices
Et serments aux vent iettez,
Si vos amours & vos services
Me sont des imprtunitez.

2.

L'amour a d'autres voeuz mi appelle
Entendez jamais rien de moy,
Ne pensez nous rendre infidele,
A mi tesmoignant vostre foy.

3.

L'amant qui mon amour possede
Est trop plein de perfection,
Et doublement il vous excede
De merite & d'affection.

4.

Je ne puis estre refroidie,
Ni rompre un cordage si deux,
Ni le rompre sans perfidie,
In d'estre perfidi pour vous.

5.

Vos attentes sons toutes en vain,
Le vous dire est nous obliger,
Pour vous faire espergner vos peines
Du vous & du temps mesnager.

This version is so corrupt that it is largely nonsense. The copy may have been in bad autograph,[27] and whoever saw the **Last Remains** through the press could have had very little French. Some of the lines will not scan, some words are misspelled, and there are mistakes of sense in the use of pronouns.[28]

Suckling translates fairly closely. He changes the stanza form slightly, but maintains the same rime scheme.

1.

To what end serve the promises
    And oaths lost in the air,
Since all your proffer'd services
    To me but tortures are?

2.

Another now enjoys my love,
    Set you your heart at rest:
Think not me from my faith to move
    Because you faith protest.

3.

The man that does possess my heart,
    Has twice as much perfection,
And does excel you in desert,
    As much as in affection.

4.

I cannot break so sweet a bond,
    Unless I prove untrue:
Nor can I ever be so fond,
    To prove untrue for you.

5.

Your attempts are but in vain
    (To tell you is a favour):

For things that may be, rack your brain:
    Then lose not thus your labour.[29]

While he has not deviated very much from his French original, he has changed its spirit. The English version is flippant, an effect heightened by his stanza form. It is also a good deal more matter of fact. He has missed the almost mordant tone of the French; and the fourth stanza, which has a definite cumulative effect in the original, is just a little silly in English. The last stanza in the French has a cutting effect; Suckling's last stanza is awkward with no effect. One can hardly agree with the Reverend Alfred Suckling's opinion of his ancestor's ability as a translator.

There were a number of places where Suckling could have found this poem. It first appeared in a *recueil* called *Les Muses Gaillardes.* This was first published in 1609; a second edition followed the same year, and a third edition exists which is undated. The poem may also be found in the *Satyres Regnier,* one of the most popular collections of the century.[30] A third possible source for Suckling is the *Recueil des Plus Excellans Vers Satyriques de Ce Temps,* published in 1617. There is no signature attached to the poem in either of the first two *recueils,* but it is attributed to Motin in the third.

Pierre Motin (1566?-1613?) was one of the minor *libertins.* He was a friend and disciple of Regnier, and of de Berthelot and de Sigognes. He was among the crowd of *beaux esprits* who frequented such taverns as the *Pomme de Pin,* the *Fosse aux Lions,* and the *Croix de Lorraine.* His verse has never been collected; it was published in the various *recueils* along with that of other libertine writers. In general, it is light, brisk, and markedly anti-feminist. Although it is seldom philosophical, he is typical of the group.[31]

On at least one other occasion Suckling borrowed from across the Channel, this time without acknowledgment. In **The Last Remains,** immediately preceding **"Desdain,"** is a poem called **"Profer'd Love rejected."** It has been printed in this position in subsequent editions.

It is not four years ago,
    I offered forty crowns
To lie with her a night or so:
    She answer'd me in frowns.

Not two years since, she meeting me
    Did whisper in my ear,
That she would at my service be
    If I contented were.

I told her I was cold as snow,
    And had no great desire;
But should be well content to go
    To twenty but no higher.
Some three months since or thereabouts,
    She that so coy had been,
Bethought herself and found me out,
    And was content to sin.

I smil'd at that, and told her I
    Did think it something late,
And that I'd not repentance buy
    At above half the rate.

This present morning early she
    Forsooth came to my bed,
And *gratis* there she offered me
    Her high priz'd maidenhead.

I told her that I thought it then
    Far dearer than I did,
When at first the forty crowns
    For one night's lodging bid.[32]

As in the case of **"Desdain,"** the original for this is to be sought in the French *recueils.* Its first printing, so far as I have been able to discover, was in the 1614 editions of the *Satyres Regnier.* Subsequently it turns up in three other *recueils.* These are *Les Satyres Bastardes et Autres Oeuvres Folastres du Cadet Angoulevent,* the *Recueil des Vers Satyrique,* and the *Cabinet Satyrique.* In the *Recueil des Vers Satyrique* it is attributed to Desportes.

Suckling's translation does not follow the French version very closely. As the verses are printed in the *Satyres Regnier,*[33] they read:

Il y peut auoir quatre années
Qu'à Phillis i'ay voulu conter
Deux mille pieces couronnées,
Et plus haut i'eusse peu monter,
Deuz ans apres elle me mande
Que pour mille elle condecent,
Ie trouuay la somme si grande
Ie n'en voulus donner que cent,
Au bout de six, ou sept sepmaines
A cent escus elle reuint,
Ie dis qu'elle perdoit ses peines
S'elle en pretendoit plus de vingt,
L'autre jour elle fut contente
De venir pour six duatons,
I'ay trouue trop haute la vente
S'elle passoit quatre testons:
Ce matin elle est arriuée,
Gratis voulant s'abandonner
Ou ie l'ay plus chere trouuée
Que quand i'en voulus tant donner.

There can be no question but that Suckling's verses are translated, but it is interesting to notice the changes which he has introduced. His version is almost half again as long, but it is less concentrated. Deliberately or through ignorance he has avoided the implication contained in the last lines of the French. Perhaps it is debatable, but Suckling's poem seems to be the expression of the Cavalier refusing something easy to get which he desired when it was more difficult. I do not feel that he is making the what may be called clinical observation of the French.[34] Whatever the reason, his version is more pleasant and gay. It is conversation in verse—the quality which made him the poet whom Millamant praised.

Where Suckling read these poems cannot be easily determined. As we have seen, **"Desdain"** appeared in three different *recueils,* and **"A Phyllis"** in four. It will be noticed that they are both found in two collections. These are the *Satyres Regnier* and the *Recueil des Vers Satyrique.* While it is quite possible that Suckling could have read one poem in one anthology, and the other in another, the inference is, lacking further evidence, that he read them both in the same place.

Where Suckling came across these poems is, after all, not important. That he did come across them at all is definite proof of his acquaintance with the lighter poetry of the *libertins.* All of the anthologies in question were given over to their verse. Their publication came at the first peak of the movement, and they are its chief monuments.

> . . . Denombrer les recueils libres des premières an-
> nées du XVIIe siècle c'est suivre pas à pas l'extension
> du libertinage, ils marquent en quelque sont les degrés
> de la moralité publique, plus dernière baisse, plus les
> recueils se propagent.[35]

Motin, whose career was outlined above, is typical of the *libertins.* **"A Phyllis"** is a poem of a *beau esprit,* and illustrates admirably the moral tone induced by the skeptical background. That it is by Desportes may be questioned. The manner is not his, and the poem was not attributed to him until 1617, eleven years after his death. It is questionable whether a poem would appear for the first time in an anthology eight years after its author's death. It does not seem to be in the *Michiels* edition of 1858. In any event, attribution to a poet of an older generation by the editor of a *recueil* carries slight authority.[36] But whether by Desportes or not, Suckling must have got it from some libertine anthology, and hence was familiar with other poems of the school.

Most of the verse found in these collections are light, a good many of them are indecent, and some of them are witty. It is poetry which is not unlike the poetry of Suckling. It is no wonder, then, that scholars have commented on the French-like quality of Sir John.[37] Knowing that he was familiar with this aspect of *libertinage,* an examination of his works will show that he worked this tradition independently.

In crossing the Channel ideas often lose some of their definiteness. We should hardly expect to find the same thing in England as in France. Perhaps the greatest single difference between the "libertine" spirit in the two countries lies in the respective attitudes toward religious matters. This is somewhat emphasized by the reaction of the Roman Church in one country and the Episcopal in the other. The Jesuit, Father Garasse, vigorously condemned the *beaux esprits* for many reasons. Not only did he accuse them of immorality in their life and letters, but he found evidence of what he considered heresy and atheism. Looking only to Nature for guidance, the libertins often expressed a vague pantheism. On this score Théophile was attacked by Garasse, who attempted to prove that Théophile denied the immortality of the soul. On the other hand, Théophile was accused of writing certain poems

which certainly were both immoral and sacrilegious.[38] In England, the Church was less strict. Both Catholics and extreme Protestants were granted a greater degree of freedom than in France, provided that they did not take part in political intrigue. "Libertine" arguments based on an appeal to nature did not seem to have been considered as dangerous as in France. This liberal attitude toward the poets may, perhaps, have resulted in the poets' liberal attitude toward the Church. In any event, there are fewer of the deliberately flippant epigrams on sacred topics in England than in France, and the implicit heresy of skeptical naturalism passed uncensored.

The essential element of *libertinage* is, however, to be found in England. Donne, perhaps knowing Montaigne as Professor Bredvold suggests,[39] had popularized skeptical naturalism, and had not only expressed it in his light verse, but had upon occasion argued seriously for it in some of his longer poems.[40] The combined influence of the Dean of Paul's and of Montaigne spread this complex of ideas widely. Although the history of ethical naturalism in the seventeenth century is yet to be written, enough examples have been gathered[41] to prove its currency.

Suckling was not a philosophical poet, in even the remotest sense. Hence, he does not argue in his poetry that love is an appetite, as had Donne. Rather, he accepts that as his first premise, and argues from there. His attitude toward the relations between the sexes is entirely physical. In a **"Song"**[42] he stated his view, using a figure which was a favorite of his:

> Some youth that has not made his story,
> Will think, perchance, the pain's the glory,
> And mannerly fit out love's feast;
> I shall be carving of the best,
> Rudely call for the last course 'fore the rest.

Here love is reduced to its lowest common denominator. Woman is no more than a good dinner. Frequently he expresses this idea in one way or another.[43] He attacks a lady who will not succumb to him because of her honor, and the tacit implication is that she is unnatural.[44] He scoffs at the idea that a man must love any particular woman.[45] In a poem in which he professes to be in love, he laughs at the idea of dying for love.[46]

> I visit, talk, do business, play,
> And for a need laugh out the day:
> Who does not this in Cupid's school,
> He makes not love, but plays the fool:
>   She's fair, she's wondrous fair,
>   But I care not who know it,
>   Ere I'll die for love, I'll fairly forego it.

Several poems remind one of verses in the *Satyres Regnier.* **"Perjury Excused"**[47] seems to be a reworking of the ideas expressed in **"Desdain."** The concluding lines of **"Love and Debt Alike Troublesome"**[48] resemble in spirit "De L'Amour des Chambrieres."[49] In this poem, as well as in the fourth act of ***Brennoralt*** and the fourth act of ***The***

Goblins,[50] Suckling expresses his preference for the simplicity of the country maid to her more sophisticated urban sister. Like many another renaissance poet, he rings his changes on the old theme of "Gather ye rosebuds,"[51] and here his "libertine" naturalism is explicit. The lady in question was not formed to die a maid. Not only is she beautiful, but nature has designed her beauty to be used. It would be worse than "murder, and a greater sin" to stay chaste until marriage; to remain single and chaste would be an inexpiable sin. She must follow "wise nature's" commands, for "one is no number, till that two be one."

Since love is but an appetite, with no spiritual values, his inconstancy follows naturally. He is guiltless in this, he argues,[52] and places the blame squarely on his first mistress who scorned him. She first aroused passion in him, and since then he has sought her perfection in all womankind. One he loves for her face, another for her shape; he can find a reason for loving all. But women are no less inconstant. All mankind is alike to them.[53] They are accessible to all men, and their so-called sympathy is their love for any and every man. The only chaste women are those who have never had the opportunity to be unchaste. Since he is convinced that a woman can love any man, he is further justified in his philandering.[54]

> I'll give my fancy leave to range
> Through everywhere to find out change;
> The black, the brown, the fair shall be
> But objects of variety;
> I'll court you all to serve my turn,
> But with such flames as shall not burn.

Even in Suckling's plays his naturalism intrudes itself. When Orbella, the guilty queen in *Aglaura,* wishes to justify her love for her brother-in-law, she appeals to nature:[55]

> . . . Ye're but my husband's brother:
> And what of that? do harmless birds or beasts
> Ask leave of curious Heraldry at all?
> Does not the womb of one fair spring
> Bring unto the earth many sweet rivers,
> That wantonly do one another chase,
> And in one bed kiss, mingle, and embrace?
> Man (Nature's heir) is not by her will tied,
> To shun all creatures are allied unto him.

Since Sir John's view of the relation between the sexes is so entirely a physical one, it would be surprising if he had taken much stock in the new Platonic love of the *précieuses.* That he shows the influence of the cult is no doubt true; but in his case, the influence was almost entirely in the form of reaction. Professor Lynch found[56] that in *Aglaura* all of the ladies are Platonics, and she quotes a speech of Aglaura which seems to bear this out. But Aglaura marries the prince Thersames early in the play, and two of the minor climaxes arise from his visits to her to consummate their love. The tragedy, as it first was written, is a direct result of his third visit, when under cover of night, his wife stabs him by mistake. On his second attempt, when he is in danger of his life, he tells her[57]

> Come to bed, my love!
> And we will there mock tyranny and fate.
> Those softer hours of pleasure and delight
> That, like so many single hearts, should have
> Adorn'd our thread of life, we will at once
> By love's mysterious power and this night's help,
> Contract to one, and make but one rich draught
> Of all.

AGL.

> What mean you, sir?

THER.

> To make myself incapable of misery,
> By taking strong preservatives of happiness:
> I would this night enjoy thee.

AGL.

> Do, sir, so what you will with me;
> For I am too much yours to deny the right
> However claim'd. . . .

To what extent Orbella, the queen, was a Platonic may be determined from her second-act soliloquy which I have quoted above.

In this play, the only true Platonics are the minor female members of the cast, and the fad is in general held up to ridicule. One courtier calls the new religion of love "a mere trick to enhance the price of kisses."[58] His friend replies that the "silly women," by feeding their expectations so high, are unable at last to grant their favors, for fear of not satisfying those expectations. Orithie, one of the Platonics, has one of the few sympathetic speeches. Her love for Thersames is gratified by his happy marriage, and she does not grudge his wife her fortune. On the whole, the cult does not do well in *Aglaura.*

Even in the letters, where the manners of the *précieuses* are reflected, there is proof that in Suckling's case he has passed the bounds of Platonic love. One of the letters, presumably addressed to "Aglaura,"[59] hints of something more than spiritual kinship.

> Since you can breath no one desire that was not mine before it was yours, or full as soon (for hearts united never knew divided wishes), I must chide you, dear princess, not thank you, for your present; and (if at least I knew how) be angry with you for sending him a blush, who needs must blush because you sent him one. If you are conscious of much, what am I then, who guilty am of all you can pretend to, and something more—unworthiness. But why should you at all, heart of my heart, disturb the happiness you have so newly given me, or make love feed on doubts, that never yet could thrive on such a diet? *If I have granted your request!* O, why will you say you have studied me, and give so great interest to the countrary! . . .

In several other letters, apparently addressed to the same person, he indicates by the warmth of his tone a deeper feeling than mere Platonic love. The difference between these letters and the strict attitude of the *précieuses* will easily be seen if one compares the so-called "Aglaura" letters with four of his more formal addresses.[60] The mannered style is much the same, and the same conventions are employed, but the emotional content is much altered.

Professor Lynch noted that the importance of consummation in love is one of Suckling's favorite themes.[61] In this I believe that she is quite correct, but Suckling has two approaches to this topic. One finds the question debated in the first act of *Aglaura,* where the familiar Platonic arguments are aired. Orithie, one of the Platonic ladies, would make the finer spirits different from the beast and the peasant.[62]

> Will you, then, place the happiness but there,
> Where the dull ploughman and the ploughman's horse
> Can find it out? Shall souls refin'd not know
> How to preserve alive a noble flame,
> But let it die—burn out to appetite?

Her friend Semanthe adds

> Love's a chameleon, and would live on air,
> Physic for agues; starving is his food.

But I think Suckling's arguments against fruition in his poems are something quite different.

A number of his poems treat this subject. In all of them his observations are not those of a *précieux,* but of a sophisticate. He does not suggest that there is a higher type of love than the physical; rather, he insists that the most exciting part of love comes before actual fruition, and that once past, love tends to die. So it is in his first poem **"Against Fruition."**[63]

> Fruition adds no new wealth, but destroys,
> And while it pleaseth much the palate, cloys;
> Who thinks he shall be happier for that,
> As reasonably might hope he might grow fat
> By eatining to a surfeit; . . .
> Women enjoyed (whate'er before t' have been)
> Are like romances read, or sights once seen
> Fruition's dull, and spoils the play much more,
> Than if one read or knew the plot before;

In a poem addressed to a young man who has been unlucky in love,[64] he urges him to go back to his mistress to be cured.

> Return then back, and feed thine eye,
> Feed all thy senses, and feast high.
> Spare diet is the cause love lasts,
> For surfeit sooner kills than fasts.

A second poem entitled **"Against Fruition"**[65] seems to echo a speech from Act I of *Aglaura.* The additions, however, change the force of the argument. He warns his mistress that if she would hold him, she must deny him. Only by keeping up his hope can she keep up his interest. **"Sonnet II"**[66] finds him more explicit.

> Of thee, kind boy, I ask no red and white,
> To make up my delight:
> No odd becoming graces,
> Black eyes, or little know-not-whats in faces;
> Make me but mad enough, give me good store
> Of love for her I court:
> I ask no more,
> 'Tis love in love that makes the sport. . . .
> 'Tis not the meat, but 'tis the appetite
> Makes eating a delight,

Most definite of all are his lines **"Upon A. M."**[67]

> Yield all my love; but be withal as coy,
> As if thou knew'st not how to sport and toy:
> The fort resigned with ease, men cowards prove
> And lazy grow. Let me besiege my love,
> Let me despair at least three times a day,
> And take repulses upon each essay; . . .
> Take no corruption from thy grandame Eve;
> Rather want faith to save thee, than believe
> Too soon; for credit me 'tis true,
> Men most of all enjoy, when least they do.

In these verses Suckling is not echoing the fine ideals of the Platonics. There is nothing Platonic, in any of the meanings of that much abused word, about his observations. He is restating something which had occurred to other writers on love.

Although he seems to argue against fruition, there is no question in any of the cited passages about ultimate fruition. He urges that the lover be held off as long as possible to heighten his pleasure; he does not propose that the lovers are to remain forever apart. It may be appetite which makes eating a delight, but he always has the eating in mind. Suckling plans no more than did the Cavaliers of his plays to worship a mistress with no hope of reward; he cared nothing for the struggles portrayed by his friend D'Avenant in the character of Theander.[68]

His theories on fruition in love are, in the main, the ideas of a young man who had no respect for women. They were not ideas new with him, and they are perfectly consonant with the rest of his "libertine" philosophy. Ovid had expressed almost the same notions in the *Amores*:[69] "A love fed fat and too compliant is turned to cloying, and harms us, like sweet fare that harms the stomach." Closer at hand, Montaigne, in "An Apologie of Raymond Sebond,"[70] followed the same path.

> And that there is nothing so naturally opposite to our taste, as satiety, which comes from ease and facility, nor nothing that so much sharpeneth it, as rareness and difficulty. . . . *Rareness and difficulty giveth esteem unto things.* . . . Our appetite doth contemne and passe over what he hath in his free choise and owne possession, to runne after and pursue what he hath not. . . . *To forbid us any thing, is the ready way to make us long for it.* . . . Wishing and injoying trouble us both alike. The rigor of a mistris is yrkesome, but ease and facility (to say true) much more; forasmuch as discontent and vexation proceed of the estimation we have of

the thing desired, which sharpen love, and set it afire: Whereas *Satiety begets distaste*: It is a dull, blunt, weary, and drouzy passion. . . . Whereto serves this mayden-like bashfulnesse, this wilfull quaintnesse, this severe countenance, this seeming ignorance of those things, which they know better than our selves, that goe about to instruct them, but to increase a desire, and endeare a longing in us, to vanquish, to gourmandize, and at our pleasure, to dispose all this squeamish ceremonie, and all these peevish obstacles?

No one will suggest that either Ovid or Montaigne were advocating a Platonic relationship, nor was Suckling. It is quite possible that from one of these two sources he drew his ideas, but it was not necessary. All three men were sophisticates, and the point of view of all three was naturalistic. To write against fruition by advancing "libertine" arguments at a time when the subject was being treated more or less seriously by other court poets, is part of the wit of Sir John which has not been fully appreciated.

Occasionally Suckling wrote in the *précieuse* vein, but there is generally an astringent turn at the end which changes its apparent intention. Such is **"To a Lady that Forbade to Love before Company."**[71] There the manners of courtly society are reported—the hidden glances, the sighs, the treasuring of the ribbons for favors, and the little services of the courtier. But after all are retold, he snaps out a last line which shows his real attitude. Similarly, the first of two poems addressed to his rival has been taken as an honest expression of Platonic love. In reality, he is gently ironic with the professed behavior of the courtly lover.

Very rarely was he serious in his love poetry. An exception is his **"Song,"**[72] in which, reminiscent of Donne's "Ecstacy," he describes what he thinks is truly love. He recognizes that his mistress feels that she has completely spiritualized love, and that for her, souls can meet without the bodies. As for himself, he holds

> . . . that perfect joy makes all our parts
>   As joyful as our hearts.
> Our senses tell us if we please not them,
> Our love is but a dotage or a dream . . .
> There rests but this, that whilst we sorrow here,
>   Our bodies may draw near:
> And when no more their joys they can extend,
> Then let our souls begin where they did end.

The poem lacks the intensity of Donne, to be sure, but he is repeating Donne's views. This is as near as Suckling ever comes to recognizing any spiritual element in love, except in his plays and in a few of his lesser poems.

Of these poems, perhaps the best is **"Detraction Execrated."**[73] There he is the writer of the Platonics *par excellence*. The conventions of secrecy, of complete innocence, and of lack of physical desire are accepted wholeheartedly. The flippancy which one expects in Suckling is absent. For once he seems to have taken his

tongue from his cheek; the poem opens vigorously, and although it does not maintain the level of the first few lines, it is an illustration of what he might have done had he cared to write more frequently in the purely artificial manner of the new religion of love. Amongst his other Platonic verses is **"The Invocation,"**[74] a highly conventional piece, and little more than a jingle. The song **"I prithee send me back my heart"**[75] is another stock bit of verse, although written with a good deal more grace. But by and large, it was not in the conventional *précieuse* tradition that Suckling did his best work.

An examination of the major portion of Suckling's love poetry has indicated that although he was one of the principal court poets of the reign of Charles and Henrietta, he seldom wrote in praise of the new cult of the *précieuse*, which the Queen had introduced from France. In practice, he either ridiculed it or ignored it. He was fully conscious of the ideas represented by this new Platonic movement, and in his plays are many allusions to the group. His usual expression in love poetry was guided by a "libertine" naturalism which he derived directly from Donne, whose poetic disciple he was, and from the minor *libertin* poets in France, of whom he had firsthand knowledge. Because of his popularity during the latter part of the century, his is not the least important place in the history of skeptical naturalism which may be traced throughout the Restoration.[76]

Notes

1. *Journal of Comparative Literature,* 1 (1903). 120-53.

2. *Works,* 1892, 2. 179. Unless otherwise noted all references to Suckling will be to this edition.

3. *Ibid.* 2. 180.

4. *Ibid.* 2. 182.

5. *Ibid.* 2. 198.

6. In *The Social Mode of Restoration Comedy,* New York, 1926.

7. *Ibid.,* pp. 55-6.

8. *Works* 1. 40.

9. See F. T. Perrens, *Les Libertins en France au XVIIe Siècle* (Paris, n. d.).

10. Perrens, *op. cit.,* p. 25. For further discussion, see his introduction.

11. L. I. Bredvold, "The Naturalism of Donne," *JEGP* 22 (1923), 494-5.

12. Montaigne, trans. Florio, Bk. II, chap. 12. *Works* (London, 1897) 4. 21-2.

13. See, for example, Théophile's "Satyre prémière" and the ode beginning "Hereux, tandis qu'il est vivant." *Works,* ed. Alleaume (Paris, 1856) 1. 236-41 and 190-1. These two were among the poems singled out by the Jesuit, Père Garasse, in his attack on the poet.

14. Perrens, *op. cit.,* pp. 72-4.

15. F. Lachèvre, *Le Procès du Poète Théophile de Viau* (Paris, 1909) 1. xx.

16. *Ibid.* 1. xxiii.

17. Bredvold, *op. cit.,* pp. 427-7, 498-502.

18. *The Poems of John Donne,* ed. by H. J. C. Grierson, Elegie XVII, in 1. 114-5.

19. *Ibid.* 1. 36.

20. "An elegy upon the death of Doctor Donne, Dean of Paul's."

21. "Skepticism in the seventeenth century cannot be appreciated as an historical force if it is defined narrowly as a philosophical system. It had popular as well as learned traditions, and it appealed to the most heterogeneous authorities, both ancient and modern." L. I. Bredvold, *The Intellectual Milieu of John Dryden* (Ann Arbor, 1934), p. 16.

22. Suckling's poem concludes
    And as a looking glass from the aspect
    Whilst it is whole, doth but one face reflect;
    But being crack'd or broken, there are grown
    Many less faces, where there was but one:
    So love unto my heart did first prefer
    Her image, and there placed none but her;
    But since 'twas broke and marty'd by her scorn,
    Many less faces in her place are born.

    (*Works* 1. 54)

    Donne's *The broken heart* contains the lines
    . . . but Love, alas,
    At one first blow did shiver it [his heart] as glass.
    . . .
    And now as broken glasses show
    A hundred lesser faces.

    (*Works* 1. 49)

23. *Works,* 2. 173-9. The first letter is addressed to Will, whom Hazlitt presumed to be D'Avenant. The second is probably addressed to Sir Henry Vane.

24. The main title-page to the volume bears the date 1658, but I think that this is not correct. Before the new matter, a separate title-page has been placed which states that here is *The Last Remains of Sir John Suckling.* This separate page is dated 1659. *The Last Remains* was also issued separately.

25. *Works* I. lxii.

26. Pp. 15-6.

27. Perhaps Suckling's own. "But after the several Changes of those Times, being Sequestred from the more Serene Contentments of his Native Country, he first took care to secure the Dearest and Choicest of his Papers in the several Cabinets of his Noble and Faithful Friends; and among other Testimonies of his Worth, these Elegant and Florid Pieces of his Fancy, were preserved in the Custody of his Truly Honourable and Vertuous Sister; with whose free permission they were Transcribed, and now Published exactly according to the Original." "The Stationer to the Reader," *The Last Remains,* A3.

28. Hazzlitt, who did have French, attempted to correct the text. He regularized the lines, corrected the obvious misspellings, and in general tried to make sense out of the corrupted poem. Proof that he was not familiar with the French original is found in his version of the second stanza:
    L'amour a d'autres voeux m'appelle;
    N'tendez jamais rien de moy,
    Ne pensez nous rendre infidele,
    A mi tesmoignant vostre foy.

    See *Works* 1. 60-1.

29. *Works* 1. 61-2.

30. *Les Satyres du Sr Regnier. Reueües, corrigées, & augmentées de plusieurs Satyres, des Sieurs de Sigogne, Motin, Touuant, & Bertelot, qu'autres des plus beaux Esprits de ce temps.* The first edition with the additions of Motin, Sigogne, etc. was in 1614. There were ten editions published before 1638, twenty-one by 1667.

31. F. Lachèvre, *Le Libertinage au XVIIᵉ Siècle.* 4. (Paris, 1914), 308. M. Lachèvre's bibliographical analyses are invaluable to the student wishing to locate and identify minor poems of this century.

32. *Works* 1. 59-60.

33. *Satyres Regnier* (Rouen, 1626, fol. 128). Here they are titled "A Phyllis."

34. Not so Charles Cotton, who also translated this poem.
    Some four years ago I made Phillis an offer,
    Provided she would be my wh-re,
    Of two thousand good crowns to put in her coffer,
    And I think should have given her more.

    About two years after, a message she sent me,
    She was for a thousand my own,
    But unless for a hundred she now would content me,
    I sent her word I would have none.

    She fell to my price six or seven weeks after,
    And then for a hundred would do;
    I then told her in vain she talk'd of the matter,
    Than twenty no farther I'd go.

    T'other day for six ducatoons she was willing,
    Which I thought a great deal too dear.
    And told her unless it would come for two shilling,
    She must seek a chapman elsewhere.

    This morning she's come, and would fain buckle gratis,
    But she's grown so fulsome a wh-re,
    That now methinks nothing a far dearer rate is
    Than all that I offer'd before.

Chalmers, *British Poets* (1810), 6. 722. Either the Restoration poet was more outspoken than Suckling, or else he knew French better. The latter is more probable, for Suckling has no modest restraint in such poems as "The Candle" and "The Deformed Mistress."

35. Lachèvre, *Le Libertinage devant le Parlement de Paris* 1. xxiii-xxiv.

36. See the Berthon-Katzner controversy in *MLR,* 6. (1911). 221-3. M. Berthon notes that "Profer'd Love rejected" has a French original. He then states that he got his information from M. Georges Bernard, "who, a couple of years ago, submitted to the Sorbonne a very interesting thesis on Suckling and his French sources." Of this thesis I can find no trace. M. Berthon does not mention "Desdain." It was only after I had identified the two poems, through the kind aid of Professor H. Carrington Lancaster, that I stumbled across this now forgotten controversy.

37. For instance, "His ease and flippancy are French rather than English, and it has been thought that a sojourn which he made in France before he was twenty influenced his Muse." Emile Legouis, in Legouis and Cazamian, *A History of English Literature,* One-vol. ed. (New York, 1930), p. 562. Of course all of the verse of the *recueils* is not light. In the *Satyres Regnier,* the first eighty-four fols. are devoted to his excellent satires, and there is other substantial matter in the volume.

38. *Works* 1. c-ci, cii; 2. 446.

39. *JEGP* 22 (1913). 498.

40. "Elegie III" 1. 83.

41. *JEGP* 22 (1913). 500.

42. *Works* 1. 22-23.

43. *Ibid.,* pp. 15, 19, 26, 52.

44. *Ibid.,* p. 30.

45. *Ibid.,* p. 30. Also the familiar "Why so pale and wan, fair lover?" pp. 29-30.

46. *Ibid.,* pp. 50-51.

47. *Ibid.,* p. 63.

48. *Ibid.,* p. 51.

49. Particularly the third and fourth stanzas:
    Ie n'ay soucy de l'artifice,
    Ny des parfums, ny des odeurs,
    Pourueu qu'en amour ie iouysse,
    Et passe soudain mes ardeurs.
        Quand nostre bouche est alterée,
    Et que la soif nous fait seicher,
    Faut-il one couppe dorée,
    Pour nostre chaleur estancher?

    Satyres Regnier, fol. 194ᵛ.

50. 2. 118, 46-47.

51. "Lutea Allison." *Works* 1. 62-3.

52. "The Guiltless Inconstant." *Ibid.,* p. 54.

53. *Ibid.,* pp. 19-20. "There never yet was woman made."

54. *Ibid.,* pp. 82-3 and note 1.

55. Act. 2. *Works* 1. 113.

56. *Social Mode of Restoration Comedy,* p. 70.

57. *Works* 1. 122. Act 3.

58. *Ibid.,* p. 111.

59. *Works,* 2. 190.

60. *Ibid.,* pp. 204-6.

61. *Op. cit.,* p. 74.

62. *Works* 1. 102.

63. *Ibid.* I. 18-9.

64. "Against Absence." *Ibid.,* pp. 26-7.

65. *Ibid.,* pp. 33-4.

66. *Ibid.,* p. 15.

67. *Ibid.,* p. 68.

68. In *The Platonic Lovers* (acted 1635).

69. pinguis amor nimiumque patens in taedia nobis
    vertitur et, stomacho dulcis ut esca, nocet.

    II. xix, 25-6. *Ovid's Heroides and Amores,* with an English translation by Grant Showerman (London, 1914), pp. 440-1.

70. *Ed. cit.* 4. 90-102.

71. *Works* 1. 53.

72. *Ibid.,* pp. 57-9.

73. *Ibid.,* pp. 76-7.

74. *Ibid.,* pp. 47-8.

75. *Ibid.,* pp. 52-3. It is at least possible that this song is not by Suckling. See Norman Ault's *Seventeenth Century Lyrics* (New York, 1928), p. 480.

76. Besides the examples cited by Professor Bredvold, one might mention Rochester's "Love and Life," Congreve's "A Nymph and a Swain," and Oldmixon's "Prithee, Chloe, not so fast." In these minor poems, as in Suckling, there is little philosophy. Nevertheless, the same naturalistic tradition seems to lie behind them, and to have colored the viewpoints of their respective authors.

L. A. Beaurline (essay date 1960)

SOURCE: Beaurline, L. A. "The Canon of Sir John Suckling's Poems." *Studies in Philology* 57, no. 3 (July 1960): 492-518.

[*In the following essay, Beaurline addresses authorship issues related to a number of poems ascribed to Suckling.*]

No scholar has attempted a systematic study of the authorship of Sir John Suckling's poems, and this is not surprising for the problems are very great. Modern editors frequently admit the confusion and doubt that surround the canons of most seventeenth century lyric poets. Many poets did not publish their work. Borrowing and imitating were common. Early editors and printers were sometimes not qualified to judge the attributions in their books. As many as three or four men were rival claimants for a single poem. Above all, the evidence is quite slight and insubstantial. Compared with other collections in the century, Sir John Suckling's poems are probably in the worst condition. Herrick, Waller, Lovelace, Cowley, Milton and Jonson supervised the printing of most of their work; Donne, Carew, George Herbert, Marvell and Rochester were but newly buried when their writings came out. But poor Suckling had been dead four or five years before **Fragmenta Aurea** (1646) appeared. And it was thirteen years more before the dubious collection, **The Last Remains of Sir John Suckling** (1659) was printed. Only a third of the small corpus has so far been found preserved in manuscripts, and there is good reason to doubt the authenticity of many pieces in the collections. Consequently an editor has the nearly impossible task of making bricks out of the tiniest bits of straw. Nevertheless he cannot honestly avoid the job of sifting the available facts and making the best decisions he can. Here I shall make a preliminary examination of those facts—discuss the canon with a little fuller detail than would be possible in a textual introduction, keeping in mind the practical decisions of an editor. These decisions, of course, may be altered, as new evidence is uncovered; hence it must be understood that this is merely a preliminary study of the canon based on the new evidence that I have found.[1]

Different kinds and amounts of evidence will produce several degree of proof. We shall have to accept as authentic an unchallenged and carefully printed collection of poems when the manuscripts generally unite to support the claims of the book, as Grierson did with the 1633 edition of Donne. Stylistic similarity offers the next degree of proof, better than most manuscript attributions, in spite of the many dangers and abuses of parallel passages. Frequent use of similar thoughts in identical phrases and extensive parallels must be accepted as probable proof of authorship; and conversely, when some unknown copyist says that a poem is by a certain author although it has little in common with that author's other work, we take this as quite weak proof. When stylistic evidence corroborates a seventeenth-century attribution, whether in manuscript or printed text, we have rather strong grounds for inference. When a later seventeenth-century printed text offers new poems of mixed authority, the burden of proof lies on each poem to demonstrate its claims to enter the canon. In the absence of stylistic or other internal evidence, rival claims must create doubt of authority; although sometime the dispute can be settled in favour of the stronger claim, in favour of, for instance, a printed text by a known editor over an unknown manuscript attribution, in favour of an obscure writer over a magnetic name, in favour of a regular attribution at the end of a poem over a fanciful title like "Sir Walter Raleigh on his deathbed." But a later scholar's mere guesses based on an impression of mood or style are worthless.

In his lifetime, Suckling saw published only a handful of poems: commendatory verses to Lord Leppington's translation of Malvezzi's *Tarquin and Romulus,* second edition, 1638, and to Davenant's *Madagascar and Other Poems,* 1638; and the songs in **Aglaura,** 1638, and possibly in **The Discontended Colonell** [1642]. Not until five years after the author fled to the continent did **Fragmenta Aurea,** 1646,[2] appear, *"published by a Friend to perpetuate his memory. Printed by his owne Copies."* This book stands as the must valuable source of his work, and all its contents are probably authentic.

An impressive number of facts point to the general authenticity of the poems in this book. Not one of the poems has ever been seriously challenged for its genuineness. On the other hand, many different sources confirm Humphrey Moseley, the publisher, in his assertion that the work is Suckling's: **"Why so pale and wan,"**[3] **"No, no, fair Heretick"** also appear in *Aglaura*; **"I tell thee *Dick* where I have been"** attributed to Suckling in B. M. MS. *Harl. 6917* f. 103[v]-5; commendatory verses to Lord Leppington and to Davenant attributed to him; **"My whining Lover, what needs all"** attributed to him in Bodl. MS. *Rawl. Poet. 116* f. 55[v]; **"A Session was held the other day," "Wonder not if I stay not here," "My whining Lover, what needs all," "I Prethee spare me, gentle Boy,"** and **"Stay here fond youth and ask no more"** are all found among the papers of Suckling's uncle, the first Earl of Middlesex, to whom the poet frequently wrote. (See discussion below.) There are also several extensive parallel passages between poems in **Fragmenta** and speeches in **Aglaura,** so extensive that it is highly unlikely that Suckling was borrowing from anyone but himself.

"Against Fruition" II

'Tis petty Jealousies, and little fears,
Hopes joyn'd with doubts, and joyes with *April* tears,
That crowns our Love with pleasures: these are gone
When once we come to full *Fruition.*
Like waking in a morning, when all night
Our fancy hath been fed with true delight.
     etc. . . .

Aglaura I. v. 1-7.

Thinke you it is not then
The little jealousies (my Lord) and feares,
Joy mixt with doubt, and doubt reviv'd with hope
That crownes all love with pleasure? these are lost
When once wee come to full fruition;
Like waking in the morning when all night
Our fancie has beene fed with rare delight.[4]
     etc. . . .

"My dearest Rival. . . ."

Thou shalt be ravisht at her wit;
And I, that she so governs it:

And in good language them adore:
While I want words, and do it more.
Thus will we do till paler death
Come with a warrant for our breath,
And then whose fate shall be to die
 etc. . . .

 Aglaura IV. iv. 77-83.

Thou shalt be praising of his wit while I
Admire he governes it so well:
And in good language him for these adore,
While I want words to doo't, yet doe it more.
Thus will wee doe, till death it selfe shall us
Divide, and then whose fate 'tshall be to die
 etc. . . .

Two or three other poems in *Fragmenta* have a phrase or two repeated in *Aglaura,* but we need not bother with the weaker evidence when the stronger is so obvious. Finally, it argues a single author that the poems in *Fragmenta* are remarkably uniform in style, tone, and ideas.

The only thing that makes us doubt the reliability of the bookseller, Humphrey Moseley, is that several of the poems may not have been printed from autograph papers, contrary to the advertisement on the title page. **"A Sessions of the Poets"** omits a stanza and makes numerous mistakes. A collation of this version with Bodl. MS. *Malone 13,* the MS. *Sackville (Knole)* (#46 in packet of Miscellaneous verses in the Dorset Papers), and Hunt. MS. *198* vol. II, pp. 199-201, reveals over fifteen corruptions or errors in the print.[5] In **"A Ballade. Upon a Wedding"** stanzas 14, 15, and 16 are out of order and 16 has the first three and last three lines transposed. The Dialogue, **"*Upon my Lady* Carliles *walking in* Hampton-Court garden,"** between *T. C.* and *J. S.* contains several passages that are inferior to readings in Bodl. MS. *Rawl. Poet. 199* f. 95-6. For instance, the printed version has:

In spite of masks and hoods descry
The parts deni'd unto the eye;
I was undoing all she wore,

while the MS. reads for the first line,

In spite of silkes and lawn descry [.]

But worse yet the print lacks the final stanza, which might have been omitted for reasons of delicacy.

    :S:

'Troth in her face I could descry
Noe danger, no divinity.
But since the pillars were soe good
On which the lovely fountaine stood,
Being once come soe neere, I thinke
I should have ventur'd hard to drinke.
What ever foole like me had beene
If I'd not done as well as seene?
 There to be lost why should I doubt
 Where fooles with ease goe in and out [.]

The initials at the end of MS. *Rawl. Poet. 199* are "T: C:" and there is a real possibility that Carew had something to do with the poem. One image in the first stanza of the Rawlinson MS. sounds a good deal like Carew: "Such as Arabian gumtrees beare." *Fragmenta* substitutes for it a simile much more characteristic of Suckling: "Such as bean-blossoms newly out," (used again in *Aglaura* I. v. 40). A plausible hypothesis is that Suckling and Carew wrote their speeches successively, and then Suckling touched up Carew's part with the bean-blossom image. The effect is similar to the letters that the poets may have exchanged, which were printed in *Fragmenta,* p. 68. However, there is strong evidence that Suckling wrote the whole poem, since Carew's statements seem nicely calculated for Suckling's rejoinders, and since Suckling appears to have had the last word, according to the Rawlinson MS.

On the whole, the inferiority of the texts of some poems in *Fragmenta* is not enough in itself to cause us to question their authorship. The absence of rival claims, the numerous external confirmations of authenticity and several strikingly parallel passages must outweigh the inexactness of Moseley's claim to be using the author's copy for all the poems.

Just before the Restoration Moseley rushed into print with a much more suspicious batch of verses, miscellaneous letters, and a fragment of a play purporting to be

THE LAST / REMAINS / OF S[r] *JOHN SUCKING.* / [rule] / Being a Full / COLLECTION / Of all his / POEMS and LETTERS / which have been so long expected, / and never till now Published. WITH / The *Licence* and *Approbation* of his / Noble and Dearest / FRIENDS. / [rule] / *LONDON:* / Printed for *Humphrey Moseley* at the Prince's / Arms in St. *Pauls* Churchyard. 1659.

Collation: A[8] (Al + a[4]) B—G[8] [G2 missigned F2, A3 unsigned].[6]

The Thomason copy has the MS note "June" by the date, which probably means that the book was issued separately. But in fact it is most often bound up with the third edition of *Fragmenta,* "with some New Additionals. 1658." And both volumes were the work of the same printer, Thomas Newcombe, as witnessed by the devices used in both parts of the book. So it looks as if Moseley had a third edition of *Fragmenta* done in 1658, but before he sold much of it, he decided to come out with some new material, dated 1659, although he actually didn't enter it in the Stationer's Register until June 29, 1660. He must have known that he was going to use new work in the volume when he had the general title page made, else what did he mean by "Additionals"?

The three causes of suspicion about the *Remains* are the publisher's remarks, the use of initials "*J. S.*" at the end of each poem, and the numerous rival claims for authorship. When, in 1659, people hoped for the return of Charles II, Moseley appeared to be trying to capitalize on the new political interest in Suckling, who was viewed as a kind of martyr for the Stuart cause. In "The Stationer to the Reader" Moseley speaks of the great eagerness with which these new gleanings were looked for.

> Among the highest and most refin'd Wits of the Nation, this Gentile and Princely Poet took his generous rise from the Court; where having flourish'd with splendor and reputation, he liv'd only long enough to see the Sun-set of that Majesty from whose auspicious beams he derived his lustre, and with whose declining state his own loyal Fortunes were obscured. But after the several changes of those times, being sequestred from the more serene Contentments of his native Country, He first took care to secure the dearest and choisest of his Papers in the several Cabinets of his Noble and faithful Friends; and among other Testimonies of his worth, these elegant and florid Peeces of his Fancie were preserved in the custody of his truly honorable and vertuous Sister, with whose free permission they were transcribed, and now published exactly according to the Originals.

> This might be sufficient to make you acknowledge that these are the real and genuine Works of Sir *John Suckling*. But if you can yet doubt, let any Judicious soul seriously consider the Freedom of the Fancie, Richness of the Conceipt, proper Expression, with that air and spirit diffus'd through every part, and he will find such a perfect resemblance with what hath been formerly known, that he cannot with modestie doubt them to be his.

> I could tell you further, (for I my self am the best witness of it) what a thirst and general enquiry hath been after what I here present you, by all that have either seen, or heard of them. And by that time you have read them, you will believe me, who have (now for many years) annually published the Productions of the best Wits of our own, and Forein Nations.

H. M.

The Dedication is to Lady Southcot, the "honorable and vertuous Sister" who allowed the poems to be transcribed.

> . . . Your *Ladiship* best knows, that I now bring the Last *Remains* of your Incomparable Brother. . . . And as here are all the World must ever hope for, so here are nothing else but his, not a line but what at first flow'd from him, and will soon approve it self to be too much his to be alter'd or supplied by any other hand; and sure he were a bold man had thoughts to attempt it. . . .

Of course, Moseley was quite right in feeling proud of his list of publications, and we should be grateful to him for his services to literature.[7] Nevertheless one feels that the publisher doth protest too much. The two prefaces were clearly designed to create confidence in the book; yet the impression that is conveyed, particularly by the first selection above, is less than authoritative. He seems to be saying that he got the papers from Lady Southcot, who said they were Suckling's and perhaps some came from the "Cabinets of his Noble and faithful Friends," but that the

publisher himself had his doubts about their authenticity until he read them over. Then he was convinced, on the basis of internal evidence, that they were genuine.

Moseley's self-consciousness about the authorship of *The Last Remains* is further revealed by the strange use of initials "*J. S.*" after almost every one of the poems. Only "Out Upon it," Sir Toby Matthews' reply, and **"Never believe me"** omit the initials and **"Out Upon it"** has "Sir *J. S.*" as a title. The obvious inference is that Moseley copied these poems from some manuscript miscellanies, belonging to Lady Southcot and other noble friends, where the alleged Suckling poems were signed in the fashion usual for such miscellanies—with initials only. Hence they were not autograph papers. A bit of negative evidence on the general title page corroborates the theory of non-authorial papers. Unlike the claim for *Fragmenta Aurea,* "Printed by his owne Copies," Moseley here says ". . . Published. With The *Licence* and *Approbation* of his Noble and Dearest Friends." If, indeed, the publisher or his advisors had to depend on copies of poems in manuscript miscellanies signed "*J. S.*," then the whole collection in *Last Remains* stands in doubt. The fact that a poem is here attributed to Suckling is only a little better claim for him than for such seventeenth century figures as James Smith, James Shirley, John Sadler, John Shank, Jonathon Sidman, Joseph Simons, John Speed, or John Squire. In 1659 Suckling had been dead for about seventeen years, Moseley was working with private transcripts of poems, and he had to depend on initials and internal evidence in deciding what was an authentic work. These facts do not provide a strong basis for accepting Moseley's judgment in the matter.[8]

Doubt about the book grows apace when more and more poems are found attributed to other writers. Thus far I have examined almost all of the printed miscellanies up to 1700 and have seen all the relevant manuscripts in the British Museum and Bodleian Library, and I find that seven pieces are assigned to other men; and seven is a considerable number from a collection of forty-one.

1. **"When, Dearest, I but think of thee"** was printed among Owen Felltham's *Lusoria* 1661, with the note: "This ensuing Copy the late Printer hath been pleased to honour, by mistaking it among those of the most ingenious and too early lost, *Sir John Suckling.*"[9] It is found anonymously in B. M. MSS. *Harl. 6918* f. 17 and *Add. 25,707* f. 103[v].

2. **"I Prithee send me back my heart,"** one of the best poems in the book, appears in Henry Lawes' *Ayres, and Dialogues . . . Third Book,* 1658, where it is said to have words by "Dr. Henry Hughes,"[10] a poet from whom Lawes got most of the verses in the song-book. Norman Ault, who first discovered this, still believes that internal evidence makes the poem Suckling's. It appears anonymously in Playford's *Select Musicall Ayres* 1653, *Wits Interpreter* 1655, *Musick's Delight* 1666, *Wit and Mirth* Vol. III, 1707, and *Songs Compleat,* Vol. V, 1719. And, of course, it is also found in the Lawes autograph MS belonging to the Misses Church of Beaconsfield (B. M. Loan #35, f. 129), B. M. MSS. *Harl. 3991* ff. 74ᵛ-75, *Harl. 3511* f. 2ᵛ, and *Harl. 3889* f. 27.

3. **"If you refuse me once, and think again"** was printed in a longer and better version with the *Occasional Verses,* 1665, of Lord Herbert of Cherbury, and is in B. M. MS. *Add. 37,157* f. 2ᵛ, corrected by Herbert's own hand.

4. **"Oh that I were all Soul, that I might prove,"** is run together with the previous piece, in the *Remains,* and appears in B. M. MS. *Add. 11,811* ff. 32-32ᵛ, with the note at the end, "Sr: R: E:." Sir Robert Aytoun is said to be the author in B. M. MS. *Add. 10,308* ff. 6ᵛ-7.[11] B. M. MS. *Harl. 6917* ff. 42ᵛ-43 reproduces the poem anonymously.

5. **"I know your heart cannot so guilty be,"** which stands right before the two garbled poems (number 3 and 4 above), is said to be by a certain "P. Apsley"[12] in Bodl. MS. *Malone 13* f. 101. Its title there is "To the Lady Desmond" and it contains several variants that are superior to the version in *Remains.* B. M. MS. *Add. 11,811* f. 42ᵛ has a copy of the superior version, anonymous.

6. **"I Will not love one minute more I swear"** is an attractive bit near the beginning of the **Remains.** Unfortunately this is disputed by Bodl. MS. *Rawl. Poet. 147* f. 158ᵛ, where the title reads, "Capt. Tyrell. Of Mʳˢ Winchcombe," and there follows a reply by "Mʳ Womack."[13] Without further evidence either way, this must remain a doubtful poem. B. M. MS. *Add. 4968* f. 1 contains this poem anonymously.

7. **"My first Love whom all beauties did adorn"** has been printed with Carew's *Poems,* 1640, and appears in two manuscripts attributed to "Walter Poole," B. M. MS. *Add. 33,998* f. 73ᵛ-74 and a MS once belonging to P. J. Dobell.[14] B. M. MS. *Egerton 2725* f. 62 assigns the poem to "T. C." in the title and to "W. P." at the end.

The Felltham and Lord Herbert claims appear to be *prima facie* genuine. I see no compelling internal evidence for authorship of the remaining disputed poems, except for **"My first Love whom all beauties did adorn,"** which will be discussed below. On internal evidence, any one of ten poets could have written them. The conservative rule that ought to apply to all of these remaining disputes is that the less known person is the more likely author; just as in textual criticism, the more difficult reading is probably the correct one. Of course, it is possible for a person of no talents to appropriate the verses of a dead poet and send them to Lady Desmond or Mrs. Winchcombe, but it is more probable that the verses of the imitator will cluster around a more magnetic name. Even Lord Herbert and Felltham were less notorious than Suckling, the gambler, vaunter, wit, courtier, and martyr. A parallel case is the attribution of Sir John Roe's poems to Donne.

Thus the above evidence leads us to accept Suckling's authorship of poems in *Fragmenta Aurea,* 1646, but to doubt it in **The Last Remains.** The questionable tone of

Moseley's prefaces, the unknown sources of his information and the seven rival claims cause the entire contents of the book to be in doubt. In these circumstances, each poem must present some positive evidence of genuineness before it can be admitted to the canon. The problem then becomes one of identifying the authentic pieces in the **Remains** largely by comparing their style and content with known works. This process is highly dangerous, especially for a period like Suckling's, for there were too many poets living who were capable of writing in various modes. Carew, Herrick, Randolph, Strode, Waller, Cartwright, and King— all could imitate metaphysical verse or could be sons of Ben, all could be platonic in love or libertine. They could write for or against any topic that was supplied them, as they were educated to do. The same applies to Suckling, who writes for fruition and against fruition, for absence and against absence, who makes his ladies in *Aglaura,* platonics and his men libertines; he can praise Davenant for imitating Donne, the great lord of wit, and yet censure Carew for a "hard bound" muse, for not being "easie and free," and censure Sidney Godolphin for writing "so strong." Nevertheless there are some characteristics common to most of the poems in **Fragmenta Aurea.** Suckling does generally eschew the metaphysical way, the strong lines, hyperbole, catachresis, the extended conceit and the technical vocabulary. Nor does he seem to show the mass of classical references, the craftmanship, the clarity, unity and symmetry of Jonson and Herrick. His best verse shows "Natural, easie *Suckling*"; it is a combination of colloquial language and metrical regularity; he is the polished gentleman of ease, a courtier, a virtuoso, a flamboyant lover, singer of songs and ballads. As Dryden said (*An Essay of Dramatick Poesie*) there is "nothing so courtly writ, or which expresses so much the Conversation of a Gentleman, as Sir *John Suckling.*" But one concrete fact might provide more of a test of authorship than these generalizations: that Sucking had only a small stock of words, phrases, and images, which he used repeatedly. Comparisons of love and deer hunting or eating a feast or besieging a city are frequent; hope, fear, expectation and joy are the ideas with which he builds many love poems. We have already seen that when he wrote *Aglaura,* he ransacked his lyric verse for use in witty dialogue. Hence style and content can help us to identify authentic works, and parallel passages, if they are truly parallel, are valuable evidence.

What positive evidence do we have for admitting any poem in the **Remains** to the canon?

1. **"Out Upon it"** has a good claim on the strength of its title "Sir *J. S.*" which is more explicit in the first printing of the piece in *Wit and Drollery,* 1656 (2nd ed. 1661; not in 3d ed. 1682), **"A Song by Sir John Suckling"** (superior version). In the same book the answer is, no doubt, erroneously said to be "*by the same Author*" instead of Sir Toby Matthews. Internal evidence offers slight confirmation of Suckling's authorship because of the echo of Orsames's remarks in *Aglaura* II, ii, 3-8.

this is the first she
I ever swore to heartily, and (by those eyes)
I thinke I had continued unperjur'd a whole moneth,
(And that's faire you'll say.) . . .
Had she not run mad betwixt.

2. **"Ye juster Powers of Love and Fate"** was used extensively in *Aglaura* IV, v, 63-9, and must predate the play, for rime words are carried over into the blank verse. The closest lines are:

Poem

Ye juster Powers of Love and Fate . . .
It is but just, and Love needs must
Confess it is his part,
When he doth spie
One wounded lie,
To pierce the others heart.
But yet if he so cruel be
To have one breast to hate,
If I must live
And thus survive,
How far more cruel's Fate?

Play

Yee mightie Powers of Love and Fate, where is
Your Justice here? It is thy part (fond Boy)
When thou do'st finde one wounded heart, to make
The other so, but if thy Tyranny
Be such, that thou wilt leave one breast to hate,
If we must live, and this survive,
How much more cruell's Fate?

3. **"Alas it is too late! I can no more"** has a definite connection with Aglaura's speech to the King (IV, iv, 95-99), but which is the first cannot be surely said.

Poem

I am no Monster sure, *I* cannot show
Two hearts; one *I* already ow: . . .
Oh no, 'tis equally impossible that I
Should love again, or you love Perjury.

Play

I am no monster, never had two hearts;
One is by holy vowes another now, . . .
For 'tis alike impossible for mee,
To love againe, as you love Perjurie.

4. **"If thou bee'st Ice, I do admire,"** entitled **"The Miracle,"** has a distant relation to some speeches in *Aglaura* IV, v, 25-34.

Poem

Or how thy fire could kindle me,
Thou being Ice, and not melt thee; . . .

Wonder of Love, that canst fulfill,
Inverting nature thus, thy will;

Play

Such fires as these still kindle . . .
In such a cold, and frozen place, as is
Thy breast? how should they kindle to themselves
   Semanthe?
Thou art thy selfe the greatest miracle,
. . . thy crueltie (next to thy selfe,)
Above all things on earth takes up my wonder.

I see a parallel here of the very close relation in both contexts of the words *fire, kindle, miracle,* and *wonder.*

5. **"Hast thou seen the Down in the air,"** appears twice in the *Remains,* in the poems and in the fragment *The Sad One.* They are slightly different versions, so Moseley must have found the poem attributed to Suckling in two different places.

6. **"Never believe me if I love"** has two parallels with pieces in *Fragmenta.*

Remains

When I am hungry I do eat,
And cut no fingers 'stead of meat;
Nor with much gazing on her face
Do ere rise hungry from the place:

And when tis nam'd anothers health,
I never make it hers by stealth:

"Honest Lover whosoever"

If when thy stomack calls to eat,
Thou cutt'st not fingers 'steed of meat,
And with much gazing on her face
Dost not rise hungry from the place, . . .

"A Ballade. etc . . ."

And when 'twas nam'd anothers health,
Perhaps he made it hers by stealth.

7. **"What no more favors"** is attributed to "S\u02b3 J: Suckling" *Harl. MS. 6917* f. 39-39\u1d5b.

There are five other poems in the *Remains* that have some slight evidence for their genuineness, but we cannot be sure of them. Most of the evidence is weak and circumstantial.

1. **"And is the Water come?"** may be Suckling's not only because of his close connection with the Earl of Middlesex, Lionel Cranfield, whose water-works the poem refers to; but also because it contains a proverbial line that is echoed in **"To his Rival."**

For Love will creep where well it cannot go.

Now we have taught our Love to know
That it must creep where't cannot go. . . .[15]

2. **"I Must confess, when I did part from you"** also contains a proverb-like line that is repeated in *Aglaura* III, ii, 99.[16]

> *Poem:* ". . . great griefs are always dumb"
>
> *Play:* "For great grief's deafe as well as it is dumbe"

3. **"Yeeld all, my Love; but be withall as coy"** has a general similarity in idea to the two poems **"Against Fruition"** and to the arguments of the Platonic ladies in *Aglaura*—that the difficulties and rareness of love-making enhance its value. And the expression of the idea in the form of a siege metaphor is quite reminiscent of **"Tis now since I sate down before"** and Thersames' addresses to Aglaura (I, vi, 19-25).

4. **"Wonder not much, if thus amaz'd I look"** has two verbal parallels, neither of which is very convincing. The first two words recall the opening of **"Wonder not if I stay not here,"** although Carew has a poem that begins with the same two words, "Wonder not though I am blind." Another parallel, "I have been Planet-strook" and "how now Planet strooke?" (*Aglaura* IV, iii, 58), is a less common expression.

5. **"My first Love whom all beauties did adorn,"** which we saw above was attributed to both Carew and Walter Poole, has some possible connection with Suckling. It is either Suckling's work or a very close imitation of him.

> a) "Each wanton eye can kindle my desire" is quite close to "Each wanton eye Enflam'd before" in "Farewell to Love."
> b) This for her shape I love, that for her face,
>   This for her gesture, or some other grace:
>
> "Upon Two Sisters"
> This lip, this hand, this foot, this eye, this face,
> The others body, gesture, or her grace:
> c) The loss in love compared to a merchant's loss is repeated in *Aglaura* IV, iv, 59-64.

Thus we have positive arguments of some sort for at least twelve Suckling poems in the *Remains,* seven strong ones and five weaker ones, and good reason to reject six other poems, (the seventh, **"My first Love"** may be kept as a doubtful work on the strength of the positive evidence.) That leaves twenty-four items unaccounted for.[17] In the absence of any argument, we must consider the remaining twenty-four as doubtful poems. Probably some of them are genuine and some are not. Some are, no doubt, early works. Few are of much literary value, so we need not be hasty in giving them to a dead poet who cannot defend himself.

II

Between 1659 and 1850 no generally known addition to the canon appeared. Recently A[lexander] D[yce?], W. C. Hazlitt, Norman Ault, and R. G. Howarth have set forth some new candidates. Their method has been to pick up anything in older books or manuscripts that has Suckling's name attached to it.

A[lexander] D[yce?] was the first scholar to add to the corpus of Sucking's works.[18] He said he found a poem in a little quarto manuscript of the time of Charles I, headed **Sir John Suckling's Verses.** It was the well-known poem **"I am confirm'd a woman can."** W. C. Hazlitt reprinted it in 1874 and all editors since have accepted it without question. Mr. Howarth inadvertently added, "Printed in Henry Lawes' *Musical Airs and Dialogues,* 1653." In fact it was printed a number of times in the seventeenth century, but not in Lawes' volume. Perhaps Howarth was thinking of Playford's *Select Musicall Ayres, and Dialogues,* 1652, 1653, and 1659, and in *Musick's Delight,* 1666. The first printing of the poem was in *The Academy of Complements,* 1646 (1650, 1662 and 1670).[19] *Windsor Drollery,* 1672, B. M. MS. *Harl. 3991* f. 35, and B. M. MS. *Harl. 6396* f. 14 supply substantially the same version. Another, better version is found in Playford's volumes and can be traced back to the autograph MS of Henry Lawes, B. M. MS. *Loan 35.*[20] Something very close to Lawes' text reappears in *Wits Interpreter* 1655, 1662, and 1671. None of these old texts attributes the poem to Suckling and none is exactly the same as Dyce's text, but the poorer version is closer. Fortunately the Folger Library has the very MS that Dyce must have used, a small quarto, MS. *452.4* f. 23[v]. The wording is identical, except for line 5, Dyce has *find* for *finds;* line 6, Dyce has *She's* where the MS reads *she;* and line 9, Dyce has *fairsome* for *faire-one.* The title is "S[r] John Suckling verses" in a later style of handwriting than the body of the poem. Apparently some reader thought the piece sounded like Suckling. The lines explaining the lover's taste in women,

> The black, the browne, the faire shall be
> But Objects of varietye.[21]

do have an authoritative air about them, for similar sentiments appear in **"There never yet was woman made"** and **"I Prethee spare me, gentle Boy."** The difficulty is that the majority of Suckling's contemporaries had very similar ideas. Hence, **"I am confirm'd a woman can"** is not an unquestionable addition to the canon.

W. C. Hazlitt first printed the amateurish ballad "Cantilena Politica-jocunda facta post Principis discensum in Hispanian, 1623" ("I came from England into France") among Suckling's *Poems and Plays* 1874, with the footnote

> Now printed from Harl. MS., 367, where it is anonymous, but in the handwriting of the late Sir Henry Ellis is attributed to Suckling. There is little doubt that it is his. If so, it was a very early production, even if (which is probable) it was not written quite so early as 1623. On the back is the endorsement: *Cantilena de Gallico itinere,* 1623.

In addition to seven errors in transcription, including the title, and the fact that there are better versions of the poem in B. M. MS. *Add. 10,309* ff. 101-3 and *Eg. 2725* ff. 35[v]-

37ᵛ,[22] Hazlitt made his great mistake in not asking where Sir Henry Ellis learned that this was Suckling's poem. The answer is that Ellis probably learned it form one of the printed miscellanies entitled *Wit and Mirth: or, Pills to Purge Melancholy,* 1682, 1684, 1699, and 1707-9. In the 1682 and 1684 editions the poem is headed "Dr. Corbets Journy into France." The 1699 and 1707 printings entitled it, "John Dory, *made upon his expedition into France,*" and the next page has "*A Second part of* John Dory, *to the same Tune. Upon Sir* John S————*Expedition into* Scotland, 1639." The second poem is the scurrilous "Sir John got him an ambling nag." It is very possible that Ellis saw the name of Suckling thus associated with "I came from England into France," and he then made the identification erroneously, when he saw the poem in MS. *Harl. 367. Folly in Print* (1667) also associates the name of Suckling with the old ballad in the title "*Three Merry Boyes of* Kent. *To the Tune of an old song, beginning thus I rode from* England *into* France. *Or to the Tune of Sir* John Sucklings *Ballad.*"

The truth is that as early as 1876 J. W. Ebsworth in his reprint of *Merry Drollery* 1661 cited John Aubrey's statement that Thomas Goodwyn wrote the poem (although Ebsworth believed that it belonged to Richard Corbett). And Aubrey is very positive on the point, saying,

> *The Journey into France,* crept into bishop Corbet's poems, was made by him, by the same token it made him to misse of the preferment of . . . at court, Mary the queen-mother remembering how he had abused her brother, the king of France; which made him to accept of the place at Ludlowe, out of the view of the world. . . . *The Journey into France* was made by Mr. Thomas Goodwyn of Ludlowe, . . . ; certaine.[23]

Fortunately Mr. Howarth does not include this poem in his edition of Suckling, in *Minor Poets of the Seventeenth Century,* (1931, rev. 1953).

The same book, *Wit and Mirth* 1699, is probably responsible for another blunder in assigning the much recopied doggerel that begins, "Down came grave ancient Sir John Crooke" to Suckling. It is a tiresome production often entitled "On a Fart in the Parliament-House" that appears in twelve manuscript versions in the British Museum alone, and also in *Wits Recreations* 1640, *Musarum Deliciae* 1655, the various editions of *Wit and Mirth,* and *A Cabinet of Choice Jewels,* 1688. The old Sloan MSS Catalogue gives the poem to Suckling, apparently on the weight of the heading in that same 1699 edition of *Wit and Mirth,* (p. 346), "by Sir John Sucklin"; for in none of the other transcriptions of the work is an author given.

I cannot prove who did write "On a Fart in the Parliament-House," but I can easily show that Suckling could not possibly have done the deed. He was only one year old when it was completed, for almost all of the participants in the poem sat in Parliament in 1610. It may have been composed even before 1610, for by that date it was a notorious piece.[24] In *The Alchemist* (1610) Sir Epicure Mammon, that pillar of sensibility, says that he will have as his poet

The same that writ so subtly of the *fart,*
Whom I will entertaine, still, for that subject.[25]

There is a distant possibility that Suckling's father, also named Sir John, was the author, for he coneributed a few lines to *Coryats Crudities.* But my guess is that he was just as innocent of it as his son.

"Sir John Sucklinges Answer" to **"Upon John Sucklings hundred horse"** is a more difficult problem. All editors since Hazlitt have included it among his works, without question. It appears in Bodl. MSS. *Ash. 36, 37* f. 53ᵛ-54 (where Hazlitt found it), and f. 130, *Tanner 465* f. 90, B. M. MSS. *Harl. 6383* f. 70, *Harl. 6917* f. 57-58, *Harl. 3991* f. 55-6, *Eg. 923* f. 74-5, and in *Wit and Drollery* 1656, and *Le Prince d'Amour, or The Prince of Love* 1660. Professor Ebsworth in 1876 was the first one who ever doubted the authorship, when he said that it "has a smack of Cleveland about it (it certainly is not Suckling's) . . ."[26] We wish that we could be as certain, but at least the probabilities are against Suckling's authorship. First, both the satire and the answer were obviously written before the engagement at Berwick, May 1639, because they look forward to the war, now known as the first Bishops' War. If they had been written after the rout of the English forces, they would have undoubtedly mentioned the particularly ignoble role that Suckling's horse played; they would have been more like "Sir John got him an ambling nag" (MS. *Harl. 3991* f. 44-5, *Musarum Deliciae* 1655, *The Second Book of the Pleasant Musical Companion* 1686, and *Wit and Mirth* 1699, 1707-9). At a moment before the big march northward, we would expect the poet-soldier to be too busy to bother with some silly lampoon.[27] But if we reject the poem from the canon, the rejection must be on a firmer basis; internal evidence is all that remains. It is enlightening to compare the versification of this piece with the use of the same stanza in **"A Ballade. Upon a Wedding."** The genuine Suckling poem is colloquial, flexible, full of interrupters, easy. Lines such as

> Passion oh me! how I run on!
> There's that that would be thought upon,
>   (I trow) besides the Bride.

are beyond the powers of the author of "I tell thee, Jack . . ." The crudity of

> But now I am John for the King
> You say I am but a poor Suckling . . .

is certainly more characteristic of Cleveland than Suckling. Therefore I believe that this poem belongs in the category of rejected poems.

The most recent addition to the canon are the twelve lines "On King Richard the third supposed to be buried under the bridge at Lycester," beginning "What means this watry Canopy." R. G. Howarth found them in B. M. MS. *Harl. 6917* f. 50ᵛ and MS. *Add. 11,811* ff. 2ᵛ-3; in the latter they are attributed to Suckling, by the same hand as the body of the poem. This poem hardly fits anything else we know about Suckling. He seldom uses periphrasis like "streaming vapours" for water and "scaly frye" for fish; none of the imagery reflects a thing in any other authentic work.

Norman Ault recently discovered a poem supposed to be by Suckling in *The Grove* 1721 (reissued 1732 with Theobald's name as editor), "To Celia, an Ode" beginning "Youth and beauty now are thine." It is a slight little thing that has some claim of authorship, for it might fit nicely into one of the plays by Suckling. Perhaps it is the lost song that Orsames sang in Suckling's most famous play, *Aglaura*.[28] Of course, there is no character named Celia in the play. But the most important questions are where did Theobald get these poems? Do the other poems in *The Grove* rightfully belong to the older writers to whom they have been assigned? The Donne poem is said to have been found in an old manuscript of Sir John Cotton of Stratton in Huntingdonshire. It begins "Absence, hear my Protestation," and was printed five times in the seventeenth century, 1602, 1603, 1611, and 1621, in Francis Davison's *A Poetical Rapsody,* and in *Wit Restored* 1658. Grierson notes that it appears also in several manuscripts and is probably by John Hoskins. The Cowley poem, a Latin epitaph on himself, had previously been printed in the numerous editions of his *Works* 1668. The Dryden piece "Farewell, too, little, and too lately known" had, of course, been printed before in *Remains of Mr. John Oldham* 1684. Thus Theobald's claim that he is presenting these authentic works for the first time appears to be less than the truth. And in the absence of internal evidence, we cannot accept Theobald as a reliable witness.

III

The previous discussion has shown that all of the attributions to Suckling since the **Last Remains** are either erroneous or at least questionable. Only **"I am confirm'd a woman can"** has the apparent stylistic quality of the poet; only the Richard the Third poem can present evidence of a mid-seventeenth century identification of the author. None of the additional poems has an unshakable claim to be admitted to the canon. Yet the surprising fact is that some undoubtedly genuine, unpublished verses have been kept in a large and fairly wellknown collection of manuscripts, the Sackville (Knole) MSS. They are clearly juvenilia, with a few sparks of promise, on pious subjects. They are in a rather pretty professional hand-writing, largely Italian in character, with many flourishes, and are inscribed "J. Sucklyn Esq." Thus they must date from before 1630, when he was knighted; and they could not be his father's poems, for the elder Suckling was knighted in 1616 on January 22, and an allusion in the second poem is to "smooth fac'd Buckingham, . . . *Favourite* heere." The earliest association of the name Buckingham with George Villiers was in 1617 when he became Earl of Buckingham. Buckingham died in 1628, so the pieces probably are earlier still. It is also quite easy to account for the presence of these poems among the Sackville MSS, for most of the documents of the early 17th century are those belonging to the first Earl of Middlesex, Suckling's uncle,

and father of Frances Cranfield who married Richard Sackville, the fifth Earl of Dorset. Frances was the eventual heir of her father and thus the old Earl's papers came into the Sackville family's hands. Suckling was very close to Lionel Cranfield, the first Earl of Middlesex, and seems to have been in regular correspondence with him.[29] Other known Suckling poems, published in **Fragmenta Aurea,** are extant in the *Sackville MSS.* Several of them came through Cranfield's hands too, for they have his writing on the back. Hence there would be little difficulty in juvenile pieces getting into Cranfield's hands too.

Below is a transcription of the two pieces, with abbreviations expanded, and long *s, u, ff* and *v* modernized.[30]

> [*f. 1*] That *Heaven* should visitt *Earth* and come to see
> Poore wreched *Man,* rich but in Miserie
> That *Hee* whom all the *Heavens* could not contayne
> Should in a Virgin-wombe soe long remayne,
> Is such a wonder and soe great! that heere
> Our *Faith* not *Reason* must us steere.
> But that the *God* of life, should come to dy
> And dye for us, O there's the howe, and why!
> Each *Man* is *Thomas* heere, and faine would see
> Something to helpe his Infidellitie,
> But I beleive; *Lord* helpe my faithlesse mynd
> And with sainct *Thomas* lett mee Pardon find.
>
> *J. Sucklyn Esq*

"A Dreame."

> [*f. 2*] Scarce had I slept my wonted rownd
> But that meethoughts I heard the last *Trompe* sownd:
> And in a Moment *Earth's* faire *Frame* did passe,
> The *Heav'ns* did melt, and all confus'on was.
> My thoughts straight gave mee, *Earth's* great daie
>   was come,
> And that I was nowe to receive my doome.
> 'Twixt Hope and Feare, whil'st I thus trembling stood
> Feareing the Bad, and yet expecting Good:
> Summon'd I was, to showe howe I had spent,
> That span-long tyme which *God* on earth mee lent.
> Cold Feares possest mee; for I knewe noe lyes
> (Though guilded o're) could blynd th'Eternall's Eyes.
> Besides my Bosome frend my *Conscience* mee
>   accus'd,
> That I too much this little Tyme abus'd,
> And nowe noe summes of gould, noe bribes (alasse)
> Could mee repreive, Sentence must straight waie
>   passe.
> Great Frends could nothing doe, noe lustful Peere
> Noe smooth-fac'd *Buckingham,* was *Favourite* heere.
> Theis helpes were vaine; what could I then saie more,
> I had done ill, and death lay at the dore.
> But yet meethoughts it was too much to dy
> To die a while, much lesse eternally:
> And therefore streight I did my Sinnes unmaske
> And in *Christ's* name, a *Pardon* there did aske
> Which God then granted; And god grant hee may
> Make this my dreame proove true 'ith' latter day.
>
> *J Sucklyn. Esq*

The first poem gives us an early glimpse of the skeptic who wrote **An Account of Religion by Reason** and ended with an appeal to faith in things that are beyond human understanding, the Suckling who makes a display of daring, but is really quite conventional. The second poem is a little more like the later Suckling in manner, with the usual trembling **"'Twixt Hope and Feare"** and in the more mannered couplets 11-12, and 17-18. Two of the lines are close parallels with lines in *The Sad One,* the undoubtedly authentic fragment of a play printed in the *Remains,* Act IV, sc. iii.

> Those were the *golden* times of Innocence,
> There were no Kings then, nor *no lustful Peers,*
> *No smooth-fac'd Favorites,* nor no Cuckolds sure.

(italics mine)

The existence of these two early poems makes one wonder about other early work by Suckling. Are there any pieces in *Fragmenta* or the *Remains* that can be dated with any precision, so as to distinguish between juvenile and mature poems? The only poem in *Fragmenta* that can be proved to have been written before 1630 is **"Love, Reason and Hate,"** which is found in a MS miscellany, B. M. *Add. 29,492* f. 42ᵛ, between poems dated 1625 and 1626; and all the dated poems in the volume were copied in chronological order. No poem in the book bears a date later than 1630.[31] Stylistically, the verses are less characteristic of Suckling as seen in *Fragmenta,* more like the abstract, hyperbolical, juvenile poems from the Sackville MSS.

In another way we can recognize several uncharacteristic poems in the *Remains,* for instance, the three parallel ones, **"I Am a Barber, and I'de have you know," "I am a man of war and might,"** and **"A Pedlar I am, that take great care."** They are rather crude metrically and have none of the wit or phraseology found in *Fragmenta.* If they are Suckling's, they belong to an earlier period, along with **"Love, Reason and Hate"** because an allusion in **"I Am a Barber"** refers to

> . . . great *Swedens* force,
> Of *Witel,* and the Bourse, and what 'twill cost
> To get that back which was this Summer lost.

In 1631 Suckling joined Sir Henry Vane's embassy to Gustavus Adolphus, as shown by some very interesting unpublished letters in the Sackville (Knole) MSS, and the great Swede died in 1632. In the same catagory would go the labored metaphysical piece **"Upon Sir John Laurence's bringing Water over the hills to my L. Middlesex his House at Witten,"** which must have been written about September 2-10, 1630, when the Earl installed some water works.[32]

On the other hand, the known dates of the mature poems in *Fragmenta* all fall in 1637 or later. **"A Ballade. Upon a Wedding"** is found in B. M. MS. *Harl.* 6917 f. 103ᵛ-5, with the title **"On the Marriage of the Lord Lovelace."** John, 2nd Baron Lovelace, married Lady Anne Wentworth on 11 July, 1638, at St. Giles in the Fields.[33] **"A Sessions of the Poets,"** which P. H. Gray dates in the summer of 1637,[34] is found in the Sackville (Knole) MSS, Dorset

Papers, with an endorsement by Lionel Cranfield, Suckling's uncle, "Rymes / Of som (?) Poetts / Of som (?) Wittes / About London / Septembʳ 1637." The verses to Lord Leppington's *Malvezzi* and Davenant's *Madagascar* belong to 1638. The other known dates are the 1640 New Year poem to King Charles and the dialogue **"Upon my Lord Brohalls Wedding,"** 1641. Other mature literary activity appears to fall in the years 1637-41, *The Sad One* c. 1637, *Aglaura* 1637, *Brennoralt* 1639-41, *The Goblins* 1637-41,[35] **"To Mr. Henry German, in the beginning of Parliament,** 1640," and *An Account of Religion by Reason* written in 1637, as Davenant told Aubrey.[36] Aside from letters, the only mature literary work that appears to belong to a year earlier than 1637 is **"Why so pale and wan fond Lover?,"** for when Orsames finishes the song in *Aglaura,* he says that it was a little advice that he gave a friend "foure or five yeares agoe." This may be Suckling's way of apologizing for using an older piece of his verse.[37]

In general, the facts suggest that the less characteristic verse in *Fragmenta* and the *Remains* is earlier writing, if it is Suckling's work at all. The mature verse belongs to the later 1630's and early 40's.

A more interesting poem in the Sackville collection is one that would come from Suckling's mature period. It is in the same hand on the same sheets of paper as a group of poems in *Fragmenta Aurea* 1646, sewn together in a quarto size booklet; f. 1 and 1ᵛ have **"My whineing lover! what needs all,"** f. 2 **"I pray thee spare me gentle Boy,"** ff. 2ᵛ-3 **"Stay here fond youth and aske no more,"** f. 3 **"Pedlar in love, that with the common Art,"** f. 3ᵛ blank, f. 4 **"Wonder not if I stay not here."** The new poem in the booklet is the one on f. 3.[38]

> Pedlar in love, that with the common Art
> Of traffiquers dost fly from Mart to Mart
> Thinking thy passions (false as their false ware)
> Will, if not here, vent in another fare.
> As if thy subtle threatning to remove
> From hence would raise the price of thy poore love.
> Thou know'st the deere being shot, the hunter may
> Securely trust him, though he run away.
> For fleeing with his Wound, the arrow more
> Doth gal and vexe him then it did before.
> Absence from her you love, that love being true,
> Is but a thin cloud t'wixt the Sun and you,
> Takes not the too-strong objict from your Eye
> But makes you fit and abler to descry.
> Then know (my loving smal Philosopher)
> You vainely take the Paynes to fly from her
> On whom in absence you doe ever thinke
> For thats akind of seeing when you winke.

This piece was printed among *The Works of Sir William Davenant* 1673, "Consisting of *Those which were formerly Printed,* and *Those which he design'd for the Press:* Now Published out of the Authors Originall Copies." It is in the section of new poems. The dedication of the book is signed by "Mary D'Avenant." What makes one wonder if Davenant was the author is the fact that the printed version is inferior to the MS, particularly in lines 12-15, which read:

Is a thin Cloud between the Sun and you;
It does not take the object from your Eye
But rather makes you abler to descry
Then know my wandring weake Philosopher . . .

The title in Davenant's volume is ***"To Mr, W**[at] **M.**[on-tague?] *Against Absence."* Another poem, **"Wonder not if I stay not here,"** which follows in the Sackville MS has a parallel title in *Fragmenta Aurea,* **"To Mr. Davenant *for Absense."*** The imagery of "Pedlar in love" and "Wonder not" is parallel too: note the wounded deer and the eye beams images. Either Sucking wrote the two copies of verses as an exercise, or, more likely, Davenant wrote the first poem and Suckling replied with the second. What keeps one in doubt of Davenant's authorship is the total lack of other poems of the same type in Davenant's work.

Another hitherto unnoticed lyric might be considered as a doubtful poem of Suckling's. It is found in B. M. MS. *Harl. 3991* f. 83, which contains a number of songs from plays, mostly Restoration plays or adaptations. The title says, *"In Brennoralt,"* Suckling's tragedy published c. 1642, but there is no evidence of a lost song in the printed text. However on several occasions the gay cavaliers could easily have added another song to their list. Nevertheless I believe that the piece was probably written for a revival, as we know of several performances after 1660.[39] I print the modest effort here hoping that someone will recognize the author.

> Thy Love is Chast shee tells thee so
> But how young Soldier shalt thou know
>   Doe by her
>   as by thy Sword
>   take no friends word
>   but try her
>
> t'will raise her honor one step higher
> Fame has her tryall at Love's bar
>   Deify'd Venus from a Star
>   shoots her lustre
>   she had never bin Goddess't
>   If Mars had bin modest
>   try and trust her.

IV

In summary, this paper has discussed the major problems of authorship of Suckling's poems. *Fragmenta Aurea* is the unimpeached authority, while *The Last Remains* is deeply suspect in at least six cases. Several other pieces have been recognized as relatively early works, while seven poems in *Remains* are considered authentic. All other additions to the canon are either spurious or doubtful. Two juvenile efforts are here suggested. These results lead to several significant inferences: 1) Previous work on the canon has been very casual. 2) We need a scholarly edition of the poems. 3) Many of the poorer poems hitherto attributed to Suckling are spurious or doubtful. 4) Two good poems **"When dearest, I but think on thee"** and **"I Prithee send me back my heart"** probably must be dropped from the canon. 5) A great deal more work needs to be done before we can establish the canon of the poems.

Notes

1. I am indebted to the generosity of Mr. T. S. Clayton of Yale for his suggestions and numerous corrections concerning this paper. But, of course, I accept all responsibility for any errors.

2. Reprinted 1648, 1658. Having fled in the spring of 1641, he probably never authorized *The Discontented Colonell.*

3. "Why so pale and wan" is also attributed to Suckling in B. M. MSS. *Eg. 923* f. 85[v] and *Add. 47,111* f. 37 (S[r] J. S.), but both of these appear to have been copies from one of the printed versions.

4. Line 7 is corrected by a reading from B. M. MS. *Royal 18 C xxv.*

5. The Huntington Library MS was first reported on by P. H. Gray, Suckling's *A Sessions of the Poets* as a Ballad," *SP,* XXXVI (1939) 63. Mr. Clayton reports that it is textually similar to the Malone MS.

6. *Carl H. Pforzheimer Library,* ed. W. A. Jackson (1940) and W. W. Greg, *A Bibliography of the English Printed Drama* vol. III (1957) and Mr. T. S. Clayton report a number of copies in which the "a[4]" gathering has been split up and inserted at appropriate places in the book.

7. See J. C. Reed, "Humphrey Moseley, Publisher," *Oxford Bibliographical Society,* II (1928), 57-142.

8. It might be objected that many of the undoubtedly authentic letters in *Fragmenta* and *Remains* are subscribed with only the initials *J. S.,* and therefore the initials on the poems prove nothing at all and do not suggest a selection from miscellanies. I think that my argument holds because there is a great difference between signing at the end of a letter and at the end of a poem. Such initials are not regular in the printing of seventeenth century poets, except when there are several author's poems brought together in commendatory verses or in miscellanies. They are pointless in a volume presumably by only one writer; hence their presence requires an explanation. Manuscript collections by one writer do not normally have initials, but MS miscellanies frequently do.

9. Discovered by Norman Ault, *Seventeenth Century Lyrics* (1927) note to p. 307.

10. Henry Hughes, son of Andrew Hughes of Wilsborough, Kent, matriculated at St. John's College, Oxford, 14 February, [1618?] took a B. A. 1622-3. (J. Foster, *Alumni Oxonienses*). He became a medical doctor later and ran off to Holland in 1642. (W. M. Evans, *Henry Lawes,* 1941, p. 222). B. M. MS. *Add. 29,386* f. 67[v] also attributes the song to Hughes, but it is a copy made from Lawes' "3[d] Book of Airs." Mr. Clayton informs me that Bodl. MS. *Rawl. Poet. 16* p. 16 attributes this poem to "Lady Alice Egerton."

11. Sir Robert Aytoun (Aiton, Ayton) was private secretary to Queen Henrietta Maria and wrote some verses that appear in Henry Lawes' *Treasury of Music* and in the Lawes MS. His poems have been edited by Charles Roger in 1844 (revised 1871), chiefly from MS. *Add. 10,308,* a collection made by a relative of the poet.

12. Peter Apsley, brother of Sir Allen Apsley, falconer to Charles II, matriculated at Christ Church, Oxford, in 1621, aged 15, took a B. A. in 1622-3, (Foster). He was imprisoned for challenging the Earl of Northumberland then in attendance upon the King, in 1633; petitioned for release in 1634, and was a Captain in Lord Goring's regiment in 1639, (*Cal. S. P. D.* June 9, 1633, January 31, 1633-4, July 1634, May 9, 1639).

13. A certain Captain Tyrrel (Tirrell) is mentioned as a leader of a troup of horse near Aylsbury and Abington on June 3, August 3, and December 31, 1644, (*Cal. S. P. D.*).

14. See C. L. Powell, "New Material on Thomas Carew," *MLR,* XI (1916), 288.

15. "Children (Knowledge, Love) must creep where they cannot go" is a common proverb, according to Morris Tilley, *A Dictionary of the Proverbs in England,* 1950.

16. Although this does not appear in the proverb collections.

17. "A Pedlar of small wares" and "Love and Debt alike toublesome," ascribed to "J. S.", are listed in the *Third Report of the Historical Manuscripts Commission,* (1872) p. 296, among the MSS of Matthew Wilson Esq. Mr. Clayton reports that the MSS at Eshton were sold in 1916 to G. D. Smith of New York, but their present whereabouts is unknown. "It is quite possible, of course, that the poems were copied from the printed texts, since they have exactly the same titles. More improbably, they could have been 1659's source."

18. *Notes and Queries,* ser. 1, I (1849), 72.

19. Mr. Clayton reports that the poem is also in 1646 (Bodl.), 1662. I have seen 1650 and 1670.

20. E. F. Hart, "Caroline Lyrics and Comtemporary Song-Books," *Library,* 5th ser., VIII (1953), 105, was the first to reprint this version.

21. Transcribed from the Lawes MS.

22. Other MSS where the poem appears are: B. M. MSS. *Add. 30,892* ff. 152-3, *Eg. 923* f. 77ᵛ (attributed to Goodwyn), Bodl. MSS. *Ash. 36-7* ff. 44ᵛ-6, *Rawl. D 398* f. 188ᵛ-9, *Rawl. Poet. 62* ff. 29ᵛ-32, and *Rawl. Poet. 26* f. 58-59ᵛ (attributed to R. Goodwin).

23. *Brief Lives,* Clark, ed., (1898) I, 270.

24. The same Parliament met 1604-1610.

25. *Ben Jonson,* ed. Herford and Simpson (1925-53) vol II, *The Alchemist* II.ii.63-64. B. M. MS. *Harl. 5191* f. 17 dates the poem 1607.

26. *Choice Drollery 1656,* (1876) p. 393.

27. It is important to observe that "Upon Sir John Sucklin's Hundred Horse" is written in the same stanza form as "A Ballade. Upon a Wedding" and begins with the same words, "I tell thee Jack . . ." parodying "I tell thee *Dick*. . . ." We know that "I tell thee Jack . . ." was written before May 1639, hence "I tell thee *Dick* . . ." must have been written even earlier than the spring of 1639.

28. B. M. MS. *Royal 18 C xxv,* a scribal transcription of the play, has a stage direction "*sings*" next to Orsames speech at I.v.12, but no song is extant that would fit there.

29. See Herbert Berry's unpublished "Life of Sir John Suckling," (Ph. D. dissertation, University of Nebraska, 1953). Mr. Berry also observed several of the above parallel passages which I found independently.

30. Printed with the kind permission of Major-General Lord Sackville.

31. At the end of the poem is the note, "dedit Francis Kneuett," which is presumed to mean that the copyist was given the poem by Knevett, not that Knevett was the author.

32. Herbert Berry, "Life of Sir John Suckling."

33. Of course, the title could have been given on the strength of the reference to "Dick" in the first line; thus this date is not entirely reliable.

34. *Op. cit.,* pp. 67-69.

35. G. E. Bentley, *The Jacobean and Caroline Stage,* (1941-56) V, 1201-1214.

36. Aubrey, II, 242-244.

37. First pointed out by W. M. Evans, *Henry Lawes,* p. 146.

38. Printed with the kind permission of Major-General Lord Sackville.

39. The song also appears anonymously in *The New Academy of Complements,* 1671, along with the same Restoration songs, where it has no title and one word differs from the MS.

John Freehufer (essay date 1968)

SOURCE: Freehufer, John. "*The Italian Night Piece* and Suckling's *Aglaura.*" *Journal of English and Germanic Philology* 67, no. 2 (April 1968): 249-65.

[*In the following excerpt, Freehufer discusses a 1638 staging of Suckling's* Aglaura, *arguing that this piece was likely the* Italian Night Masque *mentioned by contemporary critic Henry Wotton.*]

Of the plays known to have been acted with scenery by the Caroline King's men, all but one can be shown to differ from *The Italian Night Masque* as Robinson described it. Fletcher's *Faithful Shepherdess* was by no means "new" in 1633/4. Cartwright's *Royal Slave* was withheld from public performance by the King. Habington's *Queen of Aragon* was not performed until after Wotton's death. Henry Killigrew's *Conspiracy* may have been performed with scenery on 8 January 1634/5, but that performance, at York House, was private, and the Lord Chamberlain, who presented the play, probably had it performed by his "servants out of his own family," as he did when he later staged a play by another kinsman,[1] not by the King's players. Carlell's *Passionate Lovers* is a two-part play; known scenery for it exists; and it shows no connection with *Luminalia*. Only one other Caroline play that the King's players are known to have acted with scenery remains; but fortunately that play—Sir John Suckling's *Aglaura*—is indeed likely to have been called "the rarest thing . . . that hath ever been seen on a stage." Aubrey tells us that when Suckling's "*Aglaura* was put on, he bought all the Cloathes himselfe, which were very rich; no tinsell, all the lace pure gold and silver. . . . He had some scaenes to it, which in those dayes were only used at Masques."[2] The reference to masque scenes is significant. Furthermore, Aubrey's statement implies public use of such scenes, since scenes had been used in quite a few private productions of Caroline plays, including seven or eight associated with the King's players, and at least five others— *L'Artenice, The Shepheard's Paradise, The Queen's Masque, Florimene,* and *The Floating Island.* Hence, a mere private performance of a play with scenes would scarcely have justified either Aubrey's statement or Robinson's.[3] The private use of scenes in a play was, indeed, not even new in the days of Charles I, for Jones had mounted movable play scenes in Christ Church hall, Oxford, in 1605.[4]

Several contemporary sources suggest that *Aglaura* made unusual (that is, public) use of scenes. S. Hall, in his commendatory verses before Samuel Harding's tragedy *Sicily and Naples* (1640), declares of Harding's muse:

> She'le out-blaze bright *Aglaura*'s shining robe:
> Her *scene* shall never change, the world's her *Globe*

—and suggests the place of *Aglaura*'s changing scenes by a reference to "*Blacke-Fryers*"; the Globe was then the summer theater of the same company. Richard Brome, in the prologue to his *Antipodes,* which is stated on the title page to have been produced in 1638, jibes at *Aglaura* in a reference to plays

>   that carry state
> In Scene-magnificent and language high;
> And Cloathes worth all the rest, except the Action
>   . . .
> See, yet, those glorious *Playes*; and let their sight
> Your Admiration moove; these [Brome's plays] your
>   Delight.

Again, in the prologue to his *Court Begger* (produced in 1640), a play in which Brome savagely attacks Suckling,

he scoffs at *Aglaura*'s "*gaudy Sceane.*" Newcastle (or his ghost writer) evidently refers to the same production in the prologue to *The Country Captain*:

> Gallants, I'le tell you what we doe not meane
> To shew you here, a glorious painted Scene,
> With various doores, to stand in stead of wit,
> Or richer cloathes with lace, for lines well writ;
> Taylors and Paynters thus, your deare delight,
> May prove your Poets onely for your sight.

W. J. Lawrence's assertion that the competing play with scenery to which Newcastle refers was "undoubtedly" Habington's *Queen of Aragon*[5] has little to recommend it. Newcastle's play appears to have been acted only at Blackfriars, whereas Habington's play was acted with scenery at Court. Since Habington was his kinsman, Herbert (p. 58) gives an unusually explicit account of the performances with scenery. Both of them took place "in the hall at Whitehall," and they were presented by the Lord Chamberlain, not by the "Poet." Furthermore, *The Queen of Aragon* was performed at Court not by the King's players, but by the Lord Chamberlain's "servants out of his own family." Newcastle's lines therefore correspond with the known details of the performances of *Aglaura,* but not with those of *The Queen of Aragon.* Furthermore, Newcastle's charge that the rival poet has substituted fancy scenery and lavish costumes for wit is just what Brome charged Suckling with. In addition, since Newcastle refers (I, i) to "the league at Berwick," which was signed on 18 June 1639, his play may well have preceded *The Queen of Aragon,* which was not acted until 9 April 1640. Therefore, Newcastle too was probably jibing at *Aglaura,* a production so expensive that even the wealthiest of courtiers was loath to follow its precedent. As Lawrence suggests, but in connection with the wrong play (pp. 124-25), Newcastle's reference to "various doores" may give a clue to the staging of *Aglaura.* It is therefore worth noting that the stage direction "*Goes to the mouth of the Cave*" in the original fifth act of *Aglaura* is replaced in the revised fifth act by "ZORANNES *goes to the Doore.*" The possible significance of this equation of a cave mouth with a door is enhanced by the fact that the revised fifth act was surely printed hastily, from prompt copy. A striking evidence that prompt copy was used is provided in Act V, scene iv, where the prompt direction, "*Be ready,* COURTIERS, *and* GUARD, *with their swords drawne, at the brests of the Prisoners,*" precedes the stage entrance of the courtiers, guard, and prisoners by about twenty-five lines.

According to the second "Prologue to the Court," which is printed before the alternate fifth act, the original tragic version of *Aglaura* was first presented "At Christmas" 1637-38, and the tragicomic version followed "at Easter" 1638; the reference to "last Sizes" in the corresponding public prologue suggests that the public premières of the two versions occurred about the same time. Since "Christmas" here designates a season ending at Shrove Tuesday, 6 February 1637/8, and the earliest description of the first production of *Aglaura* comes from a letter of February 7, *Aglaura* may have been the play acted at

Court on February 3,[6] when Sir Humphrey Mildmay went in the evening "To White hall . . . & Came home durty & weary the playe being full," which suggests that the play may have been new, as does the fact that two days later, in the afternoon and hence at a public theater, Mildmay "Wente & sawe the fooleishe Newe play."[7] The play of these two performances may have been *Aglaura,* or perhaps William Berkeley's *Lost Lady.* Bentley's suggestion (v, 1106) that *Aglaura* "was attracting attention at Blackfriars in February 1637/8" is plausible, but his statement that "probably the King's men tried out the play at Blackfriars in the autumn before the Christmas production" (v, 1206) is not warranted. By 1637 most courtier dramatists did not offer the royal family secondhand goods, but arranged to have their plays acted first (or even exclusively) at Court. This practice was begun by Carlell, who, in the dedication to his *Deserving Favourite* (1629), declares that it was written for the Court and "at first was not design'd to trauell so farre as the common Stage." The court plays of Cartwright and Montagu were indeed withheld from performance on the public Caroline stage, and such other courtiers as Rutter, Henry Killigrew, Berkeley, Marmion, Glapthorne, Mayne, and Habington arranged to have some, or all, of their plays acted first before the royal family. Suckling surely did not deviate from this precedent in the case of *Aglaura.*

Aglaura contains several striking references to the preparation and staging of masques, which combine with the fact that Suckling probably wrote a masque to show his interest in such staging; his incomplete play, **The Sad One,** was to have ended with a masque like that which ends the anonymous *Revenger's Tragedy.* "Two young Lords make love," we are told in *Aglaura* (II, ii), "as Embroyderers worke against a Maske, night and day." The Prince "made no more of the Guard, than they would of a Taylor on a Maske night, that has refus'd trusting before" (IV, i). Finally, Ariaspes says of a pliable courtier:

> Hee is as lights in Scenes at Masques,
> What glorious shew so ere hee makes without,
> I that set him there, know why, and how.

> (IV, iii)

These references further suggest the possibility that Suckling was influenced by the months of laborious preparation for the two great court masques of 1637/8. They were the first court masques in three years, since Charles I, a great lover of the graphic arts, had decided that no more masques might be presented in the Banqueting House after the presentations of *The Temple of Love* in February 1634/5, for fear that smoke from the candles and lamps used to light the masques would damage the ceiling paintings, which had been recently supplied by the great Rubens. On 29 September 1637, however, the King authorized the building of a temporary wooden structure in which masques might be performed.[8] During the following four months, the work of building the masquing house and mounting the King's and Queen's masques kept from one to two hundred artisans busy.[9] This unprecedented

activity at Court may well have influenced the writing of Suckling's *Aglaura,* as well as the subsequent staging of it; perhaps Suckling's play was not completed until after the presentation of the King's masque, *Britannia Triumphans,* on 7 January 1637/8. There is good evidence to show that Suckling had written at least part of a play by July 1637, but it does not support Bentley's suggestion that "a manuscript of *Aglaura* was in existence by the end of" that month (v, 1206). The play in question may have been **The Sad One,** parts of which were reused in *Aglaura*; even **The Goblins** is, like *Aglaura,* a possibility.

On 7 February 1637/8, two days after Mildmay saw "the fooleishe Newe play," George Garrard reported that "Two of the King's Servants, Privy-Chamber Men both, have writ each of them a Play, Sir *John Sutlin* and *Will. Barclay,* which have been acted in Court, and at the *Black Friars,* with much Applause. *Sutlin's* Play cost three or four hundred Pounds setting out, eight or ten Suits of new Cloaths he gave the Players; an unheard of Prodigality."[10] It should be noted that Garrard says nothing of scenery, which, especially if used at Blackfriars, would have been much more remarkable than Persian costumes like those recently used in *The Temple of Love* and *The Royal Slave.* Nor is it likely that Jones could have supplied scenery for *Aglaura* at a time when he was occupied not only in mounting two masques, but in building a masquing house as well. Jones speaks with excusable pride of the fact that his mounting of *Luminalia* was "with all celerity performed in shorter time, than any thing here hath beene done in this kind." The Persian costumes, on the other hand, could have been made up by others from designs Jones already had on hand, several of which still exist (Nos. 225, 226, 445). Since the earliest reference to scenes in *Aglaura* comes from the prologue to Brome's *Antipodes,* which was produced in 1638, it may well be that no scenes were used in the original production of the tragic version of *Aglaura.* In any case, scenery from *Luminalia* could not have been used, for *Luminalia* was the final production of the Christmas season, and therefore followed the tragic version of *Aglaura*; nor can it be supposed that the Queen would have allowed Suckling to use the scenes from her masque prior to the presentation of the masque itself. Nor could Sir Henry Wotton have accepted an invitation to visit the actor Robinson at the time of the first performance of *Aglaura* in the tragic version. In a letter to Sir Edmund Bacon, written on the very day that Garrard reported the first performances of *Aglaura,* Wotton lamented that Sir Edmund was in London "at a time when I cannot fly thither," and explained that he had been ill for nearly a year.[11] About the same time, Wotton wrote to his friend Izaak Walton that his illness had confined him to his chamber at Eton; and it caused him to draw up his will, which was dated 1 October 1637.[12] Hence, Wotton could scarcely have accepted Robinson's invitation during the year ending 7 February 1637/8, a period within which the first performance of *Aglaura* surely took place.

Thus, the lack of reference to scenes in Garrard's letter, the preoccupation of Jones with other stage productions, the illness of Wotton, and the date of *Luminalia* all combine to indicate that scenes may not have been introduced in *Aglaura* until the tragicomic version of the play was produced "at Easter" 1638. The court premiere of that version, at the Cockpit in Whitehall on Tuesday evening, 3 April 1638,[13] may have been the one for which the King's players prepared in their special afternoon rehearsal, which may well have occurred on a Tuesday afternoon, since it preceded the public performance on a Wednesday afternoon of which Wotton speaks. Such a rehearsal for a court performance was exceptional, but not unprecedented. In 1632/3 the King's men had received "20[li] for the rehersall of" a play at Court, "by which meanes they lost their afternoone at the House,"[14] and in 1636/7 they had received a similar extra payment "for their paynes in studying . . . The Royall Slaue" for a special performance at Court.[15] The King, of course, paid for these two rehearsals; but he did not pay for such a rehearsal in the 1638-39 season.[16] It is significant, therefore, that Suckling is the only other person of the time whom we have grounds to suspect of having paid for such a special rehearsal, since Brome, in the prologue and final prose speech of his *Court Begger,* not only accuses Suckling of having paid the actors to perform his play, but treats that action as not merely unusual, but scandalous. Suckling indeed showed exceptional skill and insight as a briber of the actors. The Persian costumes he gave them replaced those that they had been forced to relinquish after their court performance of *The Royal Slave* a year before, which must have mortified the actors, because the critics of the time compared their acting unfavorably with that of the Oxford students who had originally acted Cartwright's "Persian" play. Thus, Suckling not only replenished the wardrobes and the purses of the actors, but he enabled them to repair this damage to their reputations by acting a successful "Persian" play that was all their own; and he did so at a time when they were still recovering from the effects of a plague closing that had prevented them from acting in public for nearly seventeen months. It is small wonder, then, that Robinson the actor should have felt obliged to honor a peremptory order to appear in a Suckling play, or that John Phillips should say, "Lest the Players should grow poor, / Send them Aglauras more and more."[17]

Evidently Suckling presented an elegant manuscript copy of the original tragic version of *Aglaura* to the King,[18] and he may have chosen the title of his play to please the Queen, who apparently favored plays named after sentimental heroines. James Shirley, explaining the fact that he called one of his plays *Rosania,* remarked on the vogue of such titles in his prologue:

> others that have seen,
> And fashionably observ'd the English Scene,
> Say, (but with lesse hope to be understood)
> Such titles unto Playes are now the mood,
> *Aglaura, Claricilla,* names that may
> (Being Ladies) grace, and bring guests to the Play.

Inigo Jones, who knew and catered to the Queen's taste in such matters, refers to *The Queen of Aragon* as "*Cleodora*"

(designs 362 and 363) and describes *The Temple of Love* as "*y[e] Quens masq of Indamora*" (design 229), after the character personated by the Queen herself. How far the Queen identified herself with that character, who is a royal priestess of Platonic love, may be judged by the fact that she presented this masque three or four times within one week—an indulgence which may well have led to the King's order forbidding future performances of masques in the Banqueting House. Even if Indamora had not appeared in a masque that also featured "noble Persian youths," her kinship with Aglaura would seem as evident as their close relationship to such other title heroines as Florimene, Claricilla, Rosania, and Cleodora.

Nevertheless, *Aglaura* is not likely to have been altogether pleasing to the Queen, for she did not care for plays with tragic endings, and the acceptability of Suckling's heroine may have been offset by his characteristic digs at the Queen's cult of Platonic love, in the person of the "Antiplatonique" Orsames, in his famous song "Why so pale and wan, fond Lover?" and in the "Platonic" love-making of his sensual Queen and her incestuous lover. A hint that Suckling may have prepared the alternate happy ending of *Aglaura* to please the Queen, the scenery for whose masque he evidently wished to use, is contained in the public prologue to the tragicomic version, which Suckling expressly commends to the

> Ladies you, who never lik'd a plot,
> But where the Servant had his Mistresse got,
> And whom to see a Lover dye it grieves.

The term "Servant" was, of course, a well recognized part of the cant of the Queen's "Platonic" coterie.

Re-use of court scenery, such as evidently occurred in the production of *Aglaura,* was nothing new. As design 227 shows, Jones modified the proscenium of *Coelum Britannicum* for use in *The Temple of Love,* and Herbert's account of the performance of Fletcher's *Faithful Shepherdess* at Court (pp. 53-54) is generally taken as proof that the scenery for that performance was re-used. In any case Ben Jonson, who knew his former collaborator's ways well, asks, in "An Expostulation with Inigo Jones,"

> But wisest Inigo; who can reflect
> On the new priming of thy old sign-posts,
> Reviving with fresh colours the pale ghosts
> Of thy dead standards; or with marvel see
> Thy twice conceived, thrice paid for imagery;
> And not fall down before it, and confess
> Almighty Architecture? . . .

Since *Luminalia* is a "night piece," it is noteworthy that most of *Aglaura* takes place at night, and that two of the night scenes are exteriors. In Act III, scene i, the "sceane of night" from *Luminalia* may have been used. In both versions of *Aglaura,* Act V begins with Iolas' exclamation, "A Glorious night!" and the "sceane of night" may have been shown again. Later the "City of Sleepe" may have been shown when the Prince begins a long soliloquy with

The Dog-star's got up high, it should be late:
And sure by this time everie waking eare,
And watchfull eye is charm'd. . . .

In the staging of *Luminalia,* "the lights were . . . carefully
trained on the performers, and in the night scene wonderfully subdued by means of oiled papers."[19] Suckling, who
refers in his play to "lights in Scenes at Masques" (IV, iii),
may have wished to reproduce these striking scenes and
lighting effects in a play well suited to employ them.

In addition to the two extant night scenes, furthermore, the
third existing scene from *Luminalia* also gives evidence of
having been used in *Aglaura.* Of this two-part design,
Simpson and Bell say,

> This is one of the most perplexing sheets in the collec-
> tion. It is made up, like some others already described,
> of several pieces of paper joined together. The period
> when this operation was effected remains uncertain; but
> if it was (and this seems unlikely) later than Inigo's
> time, the artificer has proceeded to the length of
> completing, in the brown ink used for the upper subject,
> the top of the canopy and surrounding clouds of the
> lower. . . . Several discrepancies between the lower
> design and the text of the masque are so serious that
> they almost raise a suspicion that it is not connected
> with *Luminalia.* The masquers are of both sexes and
> fall short by no less than ten of the complement of
> fifteen, all ladies, specified in the book. Inigo was, as
> we have already noted, inexact in such details of his
> designs; but it is inconceivable that the machine shown
> could have held many more than the number of persons
> represented in it.[20]

Since both Francis Lenton,[21] "the Queenes Poet," and the
Venetian ambassador report that in *Luminalia* the Queen
"herself danced with fourteen of the most beautiful Court
ladies,"[22] in exact accordance with the book, the redrawn
lower part of this sheet apparently is not an original design
for *Luminalia,* but an alteration of such a design, with
which it agrees in "the details of the seat itself." The
altered design, which seems to show a queen enthroned in
an alcove covered by palm branches, with two female and
two male attendants,[23] corresponds with Act IV, scene ii, of
Aglaura, which features the Queen, two ladies (Semanthe
and Orithie), and two lords (Philan and Orsames).

Another design that was evidently used for *Aglaura* is a
large hunting scene that must have been built, since it is
"squared . . . for enlargement, and splashed with scene-
painters' distemper."[24] Professor Beaurline has aptly suggested that it "may have been done for Suckling's play."[25]
This design includes a proscenium, on each side-pilaster
of which appears an evident representation of a scene
from *Aglaura.* The scene on the left, including a fallen
huntsman, can be related, along with the hunting scene
itself, to Act I, scene iv, of *Aglaura*; and the scene on the
right pilaster may represent the latter part of Act IV, scene
iv, in which Aglaura supplicates the King and Zorannes.
As Beaurline has pointed out, the hunting scene can be
linked to several other designs (394, 395 and 395 *verso*),

which appear to be sketches for it, and hence related to
Aglaura. It would appear, therefore, that besides re-using
scenery from *Luminalia,* Jones prepared this hunting scene
and proscenium expressly for *Aglaura.* Although Brome,
in his sarcastic poem "*Vpon* Aglaura in Folio," remarks on
"She that in *Persian* habits, made great brags," there is no
evidence that the scenery was "Persian," and the text of
the play fails to support such a notion. Although Beaurline
has shown that the main plot and other details of the play
derive from Plutarch's *Life of Artaxerxes,*[26] the play shows
little respect for either the religious reforms of Artaxerxes
II or the geography of his realm. As references to Osiris,
Chaos, Elysium, and Diana indicate, the religion of *Aglaura* is a mixture of Egyptian, Grecian, Latin, and ancient
Italian; and the geography of the piece is similarly
confused. Alongside admissible references to Cadusia and
Carimania, Suckling includes not only Delphos, "*Diana's*
Grove" and "Diana's Nunnerie," but even "the Towne"—
that is, London. The author of "You poor sonnes of the
Muses Nyne," who may have been Thomas May, and
hence a better classicist than Suckling, says of *Aglaura,*
not without reason, "sure thie sceane / was London, thou
greate *Persian Queene.*"[27] Therefore, the pseudo-Egyptian
"sceane of night" and the palm branches over the Queen's
throne may have provided as much local color as was
expected in Suckling's "Persian" play. Suckling's reference to "Diana's Nunnerie" suggests that his imitation of
Shakespeare may have included borrowing from North's
Plutarch, a translation notorious for its remoteness from
the Greek original—"a Nunrie of Diana"[28] is North's Latinized approximation of Plutarch's reference to a shrine of
Artemis.

Although Wotton could not be in London at the time that
the tragic version of *Aglaura* was first performed, his
health improved in the spring of 1638. It was then that
Wotton met John Milton and wrote his celebrated and
prescient letter praising the as yet unknown author of *Co-
mus.* From two of Wotton's letters, furthermore, it appears
that Wotton was in London, probably at Easter,[29] and also
at the time of the creation of Prince Charles as Prince of
Wales, in May.[30] Hence it is not merely possible, but likely,
that Wotton could have accepted an invitation from the actor Robinson at the time of the first performance of the
tragicomic version of *Aglaura.* Bentley's suggestion (II,
552) that the player who informed Wotton of *The Italian
Night Masque* was Richard Robinson needs to be re-
examined. It seems more likely that he was William Robbins, a prominent member of the King's men after 1637,
who was commonly known as "Robinson." Since the Robinson to whom Wotton referred had a "rare" collection of
pictures, it is arresting to learn that Robbins died while
defending the home of a nobleman with artistic tastes,
who then had among his guests some of the most
celebrated artists in England. The Marquis of Winchester's
lieutenant general in the defense of Basing House was Sir
Robert Peake, a painter and seller of pictures.[31] Winchester's guests also included not only the celebrated engravers
Hollar[32] and Faithorne, but also "the famous Surveyor . . .
Innico Jones," who "was carried away in a blanket, having

lost his clothes."[33] At least five sources report the death of "Robinson the Player" in this engagement,[34] and William Robbins is surely meant, since Bentley (II, 553) has discovered that "Richard Robinson a Player" was buried several years later. There may also have been other ties between Robbins and Winchester and his other guests for, like them, Robbins was both a reputed Romanist[35] and a former servant of the Queen, to whose company of actors he had belonged from 1625 to 1636. Therefore, William Robbins was probably the "Robinson" of Wotton's letter; and an actor who collected "rare" pictures and was perhaps personally acquainted with Inigo Jones could have played a key part in the staging of *Aglaura* with scenery.

As the foregoing discussion indicates, a production of *Aglaura* in April 1638 with scenery borrowed from *Luminalia* agrees at every point with the production described in Wotton's letter. It was "new"; it was a "play"; it was acted both publicly and privately; it was presented by the King's players; it evidently was hastily mounted, and specially rehearsed at the author's expense; it was called *The Italian Night Masque* through confusion with the production from which most of its scenery was borrowed; it occurred at a time when Wotton, Jones, and "Robinson" were all free to give it their attention; and it merited the description of "the rarest thing . . . that hath ever been seen on a stage" because, as I hope to demonstrate in another article, it was not only the first English play to be publicly acted by professional players with changeable scenery, but the only one to be so presented prior to the Restoration.

Notes

1. Sir Henry Herbert, *Dramatic Records,* ed. Joseph Q. Adams (New Haven, 1917), p. 58.

2. John Aubrey, *Brief Lives,* ed. Oliver L. Dick (London, 1950), p. 290.

3. As I hope to show elsewhere, the notion that a play by Nabbes may have been publicly acted with scenery prior to *Aglaura* is unwarranted.

4. E. K. Chambers, *The Elizabethan Stage* (Oxford, 1923), 1, 130.

5. W. J. Lawrence, *The Elizabethan Playhouse,* 2nd ser. (Philadelphia, 1913), p. 124.

6. A royal warrant reproduced in *Malone Society Collections* (London, 1907-62), II, 387, shows that this was the last court performance of the winter season by the King's men, and disproves the assertion of Irwin Smith (*Shakespeare's Blackfriars Playhouse* [New York, 1964], p. 271) that "on February 7, 1637/38, the King's Men acted Sir John Suckling's *Aglaura* at Court." It is not to be supposed, in any case, that the King's men might have acted at the Caroline Court on Ash Wednesday.

7. Gerald E. Bentley, *Jacobean and Caroline Stage* (Oxford, 1941-56), II, 678.

8. *Malone Society Collections,* II, 385.

9. Allardyce Nicoll, *Stuart Masques* (London, 1937), p. 38; *Designs by Inigo Jones,* ed. Percy Simpson and C. F. Bell (Oxford, 1924) pp. 109-10.

10. *The Earl of Strafforde's Letters and Dispatches,* ed. William Knowler (London, 1739), II, 150.

11. Logan P. Smith, *Life and Letters of Sir Henry Wotton* (Oxford, 1907), II, 374.

12. Logan P. Smith, II, 376; I, 219.

13. Herbert, p. 76.

14. *Malone Society Collections,* II, 360.

15. Peter Cunningham, *Extracts from the Accounts of the Revels* (London, 1842), p. xxiv.

16. *Malone Society Collections,* II, 388-89.

17. In *Sportive Wit,* by C. J. and others (London, 1656), p. 40.

18. W. W. Greg, *Dramatic Documents* (Oxford, 1931), I, 332-33.

19. James Lees-Milne, *The Age of Inigo Jones* (London, 1953), p. 43.

20. *Designs,* p. 116.

21. *Great Britains Beauties* (London, 1638), which is given over to praising "*the Queenes most gracious Majestie, and the Gallant Lady-Masquers in her Graces glorious Grand-Masque. Presented at White-Hall on Shrove Tuesday at Night . . . being in number fifteene.*"

22. *CSP, Venetian,* 19 Feb. 1638.

23. Nicoll, p. 119, reproduces the design.

24. *Designs,* p. 141. Nicoll, p. 52, reproduces the design.

25. Lester A. Beaurline, "*Aglaura* by Sir John Suckling: A Critical Edition" (unpub. diss., University of Chicago, 1960), p. 71.

26. Beaurline, pp. 35-41.

27. Bodleian MS Eng. poet. c. 53. Mr. T. S. Clayton has suggested May as a possible author of these lines.

28. Plutarch, *Lives,* trans. Sir Thomas North (London, 1896), VI, 123.

29. Logan P. Smith, II, 378, 378 n.

30. Logan P. Smith, II, 387.

31. Horace Walpole, *Anecdotes of Painting in England,* ed. James Dallaway (London, 1826/28), II, 23-25.

32. Hollar's view of Basing House, drawn during the siege, is reproduced in *The Victoria History of Hampshire and the Isle of Wight,* ed. William Page (London, 1900-14), opposite IV, 128.

33. J. Alfred Gotch, *Inigo Jones* (London, 1928), p. 215; *DNB*, s.v. "Faithorne, William, the Elder"; "Hollar, Wenceslaus"; and "Paulet, John."

34. Bentley, II, 549.

35. Lees-Milne, p. 51.

Thomas Clayton (essay date 1971)

SOURCE: Clayton, Thomas. "General Introduction." In *The Works of Sir John Suckling: the Non-Dramatic Works*, edited by Thomas Clayton, pp. xxvii-lxxv. Oxford: At the Clarendon Press, 1971.

[*In the excerpt below, Clayton surveys Suckling's critical reception from the seventeenth century through the nineteenth century.*]

II. SUCKLING'S REPUTATION

Suckling's literary reputation was established by 1638, when he was twenty-nine years old. **"The Wits"** had been sung to the King the year before,[1] and *Aglaura,* also completed in 1637, was 'acted in the Court, and at the *Black Friars,* with much Applause', during the Christmas season of 1637/8. Immediately after its first production, it was eulogized by an anonymous admirer:

> If learning will beseem a Courtier well,
> If honour waite on those who dare excell,
> Then let not Poets envy but admire,
> The eager flames of thy poetique fire;
> For whilst the world loves wit, *Aglaura* shall,
> Phœnix-like live after her funerall.[2]

Again, after the second production in April 1638, an anonymous encomium was addressed to Suckling,[3] and by 1640 one of the highest compliments that could be paid to a play, so it would seem, was that it would 'out-blaze bright *Aglaura's* shining robe'.[4]

Although in literary matters he was primarily famous as a poet and playwright, Suckling was apparently also well known as a discerning critic and as a patron of other writers. In the winter of 1638/9 Dudley Lord North sent him some verses to correct,[5] and on 21 January 1638/9 a Mrs. Anne Merricke wrote in a letter that she wished she could see the 'newe playe a ffreind of mine sent to S[r] Iohn Sucklyn, and Tom: Carew (the best witts of the time) to correct'.[6] Wye Saltonstall dedicated his *Ovid de Ponto* to Suckling in 1638 or 1639, expressing to Suckling the hope that, 'since you have honoured the Muses with a famous Poeme, you would express your noble mind in defending [Ovid's 'youngest daughter'] from the censure of the world'.[7] And Thomas Nabbes, in dedicating his *Covent Garden* (1638) to Suckling, compared Suckling's muse to Pindar and his own to Bacchylides, praising Suckling for both his writing of *Aglaura* and his literary patronage: 'As you are a *Patron* to all good endeavours, you merit to be

the subject of many *Encomiums*: But your selfe by your selfe in making the world (which can never be sufficiently gratefull for it) happy in the publication of your late worthy labour, have prevented the intentions of many to dignifie that in you which is so farr above them.'[8]

Suckling gave most of his time to the extravagant social life of the Court, and his reputation for conversational brilliance probably outshone that he had won by his writings. He 'grew famous at court for his readie sparkling witt which was envyed, and he was (Sir William [Davenant] sayd) the bull that was bayted. He was incomparably readie at repartyng, and his witt most sparkling when most sett-upon and provoked' (Aubrey, ii. 240). It is regrettable that social repartee not only loses in translation but is frequently lost altogether except by reputation. Aubrey's remarks constitute the best testimonial to Suckling's wit, and his own works offer the best evidence of it. What little other testimony there is is confined to such scattered anecdotal squibs as 'Jack Suckling comeing into a house with a great fair pair of Stairs and little rascally chambers said that the Chambers might come hand in hand down stayres',[9] which does, however, suggest a gift for the easy, unreflecting leaps of imagination that illuminate ordinary talk with the flash of wit.

As flagrant as Suckling's public behaviour was, most of his contemporaries were unable to see his works in isolation from his life. Until his involvement in the army plot he doubtless remained for many, as Aubrey described him, 'the greatest gallant of his time, and the greatest gamester'. And immediately after his flight to France in May 1641, which inevitably followed the exposure of his plot, he became one of the chief objects of vilification for the Roundhead pamphleteers. With his literary accomplishments either denigrated or completely ignored, he is referred to in 1641 alone in at least sixteen anti-Royalist tracts, some devoted exclusively to him.[10] To the Puritans he was a gambler, a rake-hell, a writer of licentious verses, a coward, a traitor, and—in a grand and characteristic hyperbole—'a scum of ungodliness from the seething pot of inquity'.[11] But to the Royalists, in proportional reaction, he became an even greater gallant, wit, and writer of brilliance, and was—to David Lloyd, as to many—a martyr in the King's cause. His poems appeared regularly in printed miscellanies and song-books until long after the Restoration,[12] and his literary reputation, far from fading, increased rapidly.

Perhaps not long after his death, since the manuscript collection appears to date from the early and mid 1640s, one of the longest eulogies, an 'Epitaph upon Sir John Suckling', was written by James Paulin, who praised Suckling both as poet and as man, and concluded that 'if man could bee, | Or ere was perfect, this was hee: | Twas Suckling, hee who, though his ashes have, | His honoured name shall never find a grave'. . . . And in 1646 the publisher Humphrey Moseley was at pains to keep Suckling's name alive (and doubtless his own business flourishing) by publishing a collection. For the first edition of *Fragmenta Aurea,* Thomas Stanley specially wrote a poem to accompany the engraved frontispiece:

> *SUCKLIN* whose numbers could invite
> Alike to wonder and delight
> And with new spirit did inspire
> The *Thespian* Scene and *Delphick* Lyre;
> Is thus exprest in either part
> Above the humble reach of art;
> Drawne by the Pencill here you find
> His Forme, by his owne Pen his mind.[13]

The book evidently proved very popular, for it was followed two years later, in 1648, by a second edition.

The beheading of Charles I provided George Daniel an occasion to unite the Martyr-King and the Martyr-Poet in an elegy on Charles in which he laments his own inability to treat so tragic a subject but concludes Suckling equal to the task:

>   but what Stile
> Carries a Buskin deep enough to Sing
> Royal Distresses and lament a King?
> Call *Suckling* from his Ashes, reinspir'd
> With an Elizian Trance; soe fitly fir'd
> To sing a Royall orgie. There Soules move
> Without their Passions, how to feare or Love;
> Enraptur'd with divine Beatitude,
> Beyond our Earth. Hee, while he liv'd, pursu'd
> Those noble flights, as might become the name
> Of Maiestye; made greater in his flame.
> Now, might he rise, earth-freed! His only Quill
> May write of this. . . .[14]

And sometime before 1650, when he completed *The Faerie King* (though he went on revising for another four years), Samuel Sheppard paid homage to Suckling in his writers' 'Hall of Fame' (Book v, Canto vi):

> SUCLIN the next, who (like that silver Swan
> but now I mentiond) lost the earth in's prime
> and yet hee dy'de, a very old, old man
> such is the power of wit, & force of Rime,
> "though Death's uncertaine, life bee but a span
> "wise men command the Starres, & vanquish Time,
> were his AGLAURA, only, extant hee
> might claime the height of Immortallitie.[15]

And in his *Epigrams, Theological, Philosophical, and Romantick,* 1651, he extended his praise in the 'Third Pastoral' of the *Mausolean Monument* that concludes the book. Making Suckling the rival of Fletcher, Beaumont, Jonson, and Shakespeare, he continues:

> SUCKLIN, whose neat superior phrase
> At once delights, and doth amaze,
> Serene, sententious, of such worth,
> I want fit words to set it forth,
> Exactly excellent, I think,
> He us'd *Nepenthe* stead of Inke,
> In this he all else doth out-do,
> At once hee's grave and sportive too.[16]

At about the same time Robert Baron was at work in Suckling's praise in 'Doubts and Feares', a title that Suckling might have used himself:

> Yet may I ere on Earth I quit my room
> Bespeak a better in Elizium.
>   Sweet *Suckling* then, the glory of the Bower
> Wherein I've wanton'd many a geniall hower,
> Fair Plant! whom I have seen *Minerva* wear
> An ornament to her well-plaited hair
> On highest daies, remove a little from
> Thy excellent *Carew,* and thou dearest *Tom,*
> Loves Oracle, lay thee a little off
> Thy flourishing *Suckling,* that between you both
> I may find room: then, strike when will my fate,
> I'l proudly hast to such a Princely seat.

In another poem on Suckling alone Baron's enthusiasm is further vitiated by the excesses of his horticultural imagery:

> "On Sir John Suckling"

> The Rose (the Splendor of *Flora's* Treasurie)
>   *Smells sweeter* when tis *pluckt* than on the *Tree.*
> So odorous *Suckling* (when he liv'd a *Flower*
>   Able alone to make the Nine a *Bower*)
> Is held since he by Times *Sith mow'd* has been
>   The *Sweetest Plant* in the *Pierian green.*
> Nor envious *Fate,* nor *Northern blasts* together,
>   Though he was *nipt i'th'bud* can make him *wither.*[17]

Suckling is praised in three of the commendatory poems before William Cartwright's *Comedies, Tragi-Comedies, with Other Poems,* 1651,[18] and three years later he and Carew together were placed in the company of Petrarch and Sidney among the shades:

> There (purged of the folly of disdayning)
> *Laura* walk'd hand in hand with *Petrarch* joind.
> No more of Tyrant Goblin *Honour* plaining.
> There *Sidney* in rich *Stella's* arms lay twind,
> *Carew* and *Suckling* there mine eye did find,
> And thousands who my *song* with silence covers
> 'Privacy pleaseth best enjoying Lovers.'[19]

And in a play written in 1655 Suckling is placed alone in the ultimate company, when Mrs. Love-wit says to Crisis: 'Sometimes to your wife you may read a piece of *Shakspeare, Suckling,* and *Ben. Johnson* too, if you can understand him.[20]

Certainly these encomia, despite their frequent extravagance, establish Suckling's high contemporary reputation, but it must be noted at the same time that there is little direct evidence that Suckling was so highly admired by all, including the most prominent, poets of his time: Jonson, Herrick, King, Milton, and surprisingly even Carew, have nothing to say about him, and Waller's approval can only be inferred from his having written an answer to a poem by Suckling. On the other hand, there is evidence that some of his contemporaries held him in appreciably lower regard than his encomiasts (envy probably being part of the cause), as Brome's contemptuous 'Upon Aglaura in Folio' and other lampoons on Suckling show. . . .

With the Restoration and the reopening of the playhouses, Suckling came into the full glory to be expected for one who had not only suffered in the Royalist cause but also fortuitously anticipated the tastes of the Court wits of Charles II's reign. His three completed plays were frequently revived with success, as many entries in Pepys's diary show—though Pepys himself did not always think well of them (he consistently thought *Aglaura* 'a mean play; nothing of design in it', but liked *Brennoralt* more often than not).[21] The references to Suckling in Congreve's *Way of the World* (IV. i) suggest that admiration for his poetry was far more widespread than it had been in his own day, and it is, of course, there that Millamant conferred upon him that most durable character of 'natural, easy Suckling'. He had become enshrined as a lyric poet—the last age could 'produce nothing so courtly writ, or which expresses so much the Conversation of a Gentleman, as Sir John Suckling', according to Eugenius, in the *Essay of Dramatick Poesie*—and Dryden further saw him, as a dramatist, as one who had followed Shakespeare, Fletcher, and Jonson, and 'refin'd upon them'.[22]

Since Suckling was now firmly established on Parnassus by informed opinion, it is not surprising that his poems were widely imitated, as they had, of course, begun to be much earlier. In an introductory stanza to one of many imitations of **"A Ballade. Upon a Wedding"**, the author apologizes for his presumption:

> As an attendant on Sir *John*
> I wait without comparison,
> Great difference is in our pen
> And something in the Maids and Men,
> I do not write to get a name
> At best, this is but Ballad-fame,
> And *Suckling* hath shut up that door,
> To all hereafter as before.[23]

Beginning his imitation, 'Now *Tom* if *Suckling* were alive, | And knew who *Harry* were to wive, | He'd shift his scæne I trow', he further apologizes in the second stanza: 'But since his wit hath left no heir | Ile sing my song of such a pair.'

In a rather startling parallel, the Hon. Edward Howard, author of the anonymously printed *Poems and Essays . . . by a Gentleman of Quality,* shows how highly Suckling was thought of in 1674 (pp. 48-9):

> Of all the Pens of the Ancients, I judge that of *Petronius Arbiter* to be in all kindes the most polite and ingenious, it being so familiarly applicable to the Natures and converse of men, as is not to be parallel'd in Antiquity: wherefore I cannot raise his commendation higher, than to allow him their best general Writer, or Essayist. And with us, I know of none so near his parallel as the late Sir *John Suckling,* whose wit was every way at his command, proper and useful in Verse and Prose, equally gentile and pleasant: And I believe he has not too partial an esteem and memory, if allow'd the *Petronius* of his Age.

Only two years later Edward Phillips wrote that Suckling's poems 'have a pretty touch of a gentile Spirit, and seem to savour more of the Grape then Lamp, and still keep up their reputation equal with any Writ so long ago; his Plays also still bring audience to the Theater'.[24]

In 1685 Suckling was ranked among poets of enduring fame—Chaucer, Sidney, Cowley, Dryden, Jonson, Shakespeare, Spenser, and, less happily, Lee and Creech—by an anonymous judge whose enthusiasm for him is clear:

> From East to West *Sucklings* soft Muse shall run,
> Swift as the Light, and glorious as the Sun;
> Each Pole shall eccho his Eternal Fame,
> And the bright Mistress, he vouchsafes to name.[25]

To William Winstanley Suckling was 'one so filled with *Phœbean* fire, as for excellency of his wit, was worthy to be Crowned with a Wreath of Stars', who made poetry 'his Recreation, not his Study, and did not so much seek fame as it was put upon him'. The best character of Suckling, he thought, was that given by the poet himself in **"The Wits"** (ll. 79-86).[26] Gerard Langbaine, writing in 1691, subscribed to Lloyd's character of Suckling's works, '*viz.* That his Poems are Clean, Sprightly, and Natural; his Discourses Full and Convincing; his Plays well humor'd and Taking; his Letters Fragrant and Sparking: only his Thoughts were not so loose as his Expression, witness his excellent Discourse to my Lord *Dorset,* about Religion'.[27]

By the end of the seventeenth century, Cowley had far eclipsed most of the poets of Suckling's period in critical esteem. In the preface to *Letters and Poems Amourous and Gallant,* for example, the author asserts that there is 'nothing more gay or sprightly than those [poems] of Sir *John Suckling*', but he reserves his highest praise: 'we must allow Dr. *Donne* to have been a very great Wit; Mr. *Waller* a very gallant Writer; Sir *John Suckling* a very gay one, and Mr. *Cowley* a great genius'.[28] At about the same time John Dennis wrote in a letter to Dryden that 'Suckling, Cowley and Denham, who formerly Ravish'd me in ev'ry part of them, now appear tastless to me in most',[29] implicitly discrediting the whole group.

But if Suckling was in the process of being embalmed by the critics and literary historians, his works seem still to have had a popular following, which was probably due to the musical settings of many of his poems that continued to be printed, and his continuing influence on later poets. **"The Wits"** had introduced to English poetry one genre, and **"A Ballade. Upon a Wedding"** another, that many imitators found irresistible.[30] Although no musical setting survives for the **"Ballade"**, its melody, whether specially composed or of earlier origin, was so closely associated with it and so widely known that even songs that were not imitations were specified to be sung to the tune of 'I tell thee *Dick*'.[31]

In three articles Arthur H. Nethercot has surveyed the changing reputations of the Metaphysical poets: in the seventeenth century, during the age of Pope, and during the age of Johnson and the 'Romantic Revival'.[32] He does not specifically include Suckling, but the vicissitudes of

Suckling's reputation followed with fewer extremes the pattern of the others', as one would except. In *The Tatler*, in 1709 and 1710, Steele three times appreciatively refers to and quotes from Suckling, but Addison, in characterizing a 'male coquet' through the description of an imaginary visit to his bedroom, unflatteringly speaks of 'Suckling's Poems, with a little heap of black patches on it', on a bedside table.[33] Doubtless to many of Addison's contemporaries Suckling's works were merely part of the impedimenta of successors to the Sir Fopling Flutters of the Restoration, but the author of *A Miscellaneous Poem, Inscribed to the Earl of Oxford* (1712, p. 86) places Suckling in a clearer perspective than we should perhaps expect in the age of Pope:

> What *Suckling* writes, the Gentleman displays,
> And gay *Ideas* gives of former Days.
> Derives the Poets, and the Pleasures past,
> And unconstrain'd like him, his wit we taste.
> And whilst we there no intricasies find,
> 'I'll tell thee, *Dick*' revives th'enliven'd mind.
> Let then familiar Lines of hasty Birth,
> Produc'd by Accidents of wine or mirth,
> Uncensur'd pass; nor Pedants there pretend
> To find those Faults which they want wit to mend.

Although he did not explicitly do so, one supposes that Pope would have classed Suckling with 'the mob of gentlemen who wrote with ease'; but his opinion was only once implied, in a somewhat inscrutable remark made to the Rev. Joseph Spence: 'Carew (a bad Waller), Waller himself, and Lord Lansdowne, are all of one school, as Sir John Suckling, Sir John Mennes, and Prior are of another.'[34] There is rather less ambiguity in Spence's anecdote of Lockier, who remarked that, 'considering the manner of writing then in fashion, the purity of Sir John Suckling is quite surprising' (No. 663, 1730), which 'may be compared with Spence's statement in his little History of English Poetry, written in French: "Mais le Chevalier *Suckling* fut le seul Genie tout pur; & qui par sa pureté ne se laissa pas infecter de la contagion generale"' (*Anecdotes*, i. 274 n.).

John Oldmixon's judgement on Cowley indicates to what low Donne's reputation had sunk, and at the same time shows that neither Suckling nor Waller had fallen far from critical grace in his day: 'it seems strange to me, that after *Suckling* and *Waller* had written, whose Genius's were so fine and just, Mr. *Cowley* should imitate Dr. *Donne*; in whom there's hardly anything that's agreeable, or any Stroke which has any Likeness to Nature'.[35] As for Samuel Johnson's opinion of the Cavalier poets, 'Suckling he knew first and liked best; he quotes from Suckling, not very frequently, but steadily throughout the first edition of the *Dictionary*, and of the whole group it is only on Suckling that he ever passes any critical judgement.'[36] Johnson's judgement, however, that 'Suckling neither improved versification nor abounded in conceits' and could not reach the 'fashionable style [that] remained chiefly with Cowley',[37] does not favour Suckling, even as the best of his group.

If Suckling's reputation was destined to fade in the eighteenth century, he nevertheless remained more popular than the other two important poets of the 'Cavalier' group, Herrick and Carew. While there was no edition of Herrick's poems and only one of Carew's (except for his poems in *A Complete Edition of the Poets of Great Britain*, 1792-5) in the eighteenth century, Suckling's complete works were printed four times, in 1709, 1719, 1766, and 1770, and his poems also appeared in *A Complete Edition*.[38] In the nineteenth century there was little vacillation in Suckling's reputation as a sportive and wittily amorous Court poet. Although in 1798 Nathan Drake, in reprinting a table evaluating earlier poets, dismissed all others except Shakespeare and Milton as 'unable to support the contest even with the poets of the last forty or fifty years', he had clearly changed his mind six years later, for he mentions Suckling specifically as one of the beneficiaries of a 'new partiality for the whole body of our elder poetry'.[39] Two more complete editions and a comprehensive selection of his works were published in 1836, 1874, and 1892.

In the 1850s David Masson remarked that 'For one who now reads anything of Carew there are twenty who know by heart some verses of his friend and brother-courtier, Sir John Suckling'.[40] Since that time, while Carew's stock has risen along with that of the Metaphysical poets whose work some of his own best poetry resembles, Suckling's has remained comparatively steady. He has never ranked so high in popular estimation as he did in his own time and during the Restoration, but, while his position is now far humbler than it once was, it is likely to remain fixed as that of one of the more interesting as well as influential lyric poets of his century.[41] He is perhaps not least interesting in eluding the kind of stereotypy to which even Lovelace, who deserves and often receives better, lends himself as the prototype of the Cavalier poets. Arthur H. Nethercot did not include Suckling among the Metaphysical poets in his extensive study of their reputation, A. C. Partridge has not included him in *The Tribe of Ben* at least as a writer of—as his sub-title clarifies—*Pre-Augustan Classical Verse in English* (1966), he is clearly no 'post-Spenserian', Pope plainly misclassified him in his opaque remark, and such terms as 'Baroque' could do little to define his characteristic manner. In relation to the 'Schools' of Donne, Johnson, and Spenser, Suckling cannot be placed more accurately than in a *schola*—or *ludus*—*sui generis*: at its best, his work is of uncommon fluency, graceful force, and witty lucidity, and his is a rare *sprezzatura*.

Notes

1. See the 'Life' above, p. xliv.

2. *Witts Recreations,* 1640, sig. B3^v. The poem must have been written after the first production, for in the second—made a tragi-comedy by the alternative fifth act—Aglaura lived.

3. 'To Sir *John Sutlin* upon his *Aglaura*: First a bloody Tragædy, then by the said Sir *John*, turn'd to a *COMEDIE*' (q.v. in Appendix A.ii, No. 2).

4. See the commendatory verses by S. Hall before S[amuel] H[arding], *Sicily and Naples,* 1640, sig. A4ʳ.

5. See North's letter in Appendix A.iii, No. 3.

6. P.R.O., S.P. 16/409, No. 167. In *CSPD 1638-9,* p. 342, where this letter is catalogued, it is said to be 'probably a presumed letter from a fashionable lady', to which Rhodes Dunlap adds that it is 'apparently a literary exercise' (*Poems of Thomas Carew,* 1949, p. xxxviii, n. 3).

7. The dedications are printed in full in Appendix A.iii, Nos. 1-2. It is not certain when the dedication was written. *Ovid de Ponto* was licensed on 13 February 1638 (*Stationers' Registers,* iv. 382) but not printed until 1639.

8. See the full dedication in Appendix A.iii, No. 2). *Covent Garden* was licensed on 28 May 1638 (*Stationers' Registers,* iv. 385), shortly after the publication of *Aglaura.*

9. Folger MS. V. a. 180, f. 81ᵛ, the commonplace-book of Mildmay Fane, second Earl of Westmorland, compiled, on the evidence of the opening and closing letters, between 1655 and 1663; it contains, in addition to anecdotal Characters of various countries, transcripts of letters written in 1628-31 by Mary, Countess of Westmorland, to her son, Sir Francis Fane, whose travels during that time closely paralleled Suckling's, with whom he may have been in company.

10. *A Conspiracy Discovered, A Letter Sent by Sir John Suckling from France, A Bloody Masacre Plotted by the Papists, Four Fugitives Meeting, A Coppy of General Lesley's Letter to Sir John Suckling, The Liar, Newes from Rome, A Mappe of Mischiefe, The Stage-Players Complaint, Time's Alteration, Old Newes Newly Revived, The Sucklington Faction, A Letter from Rhoan in France, The Country-Mans Care, The Copie of a Letter Sent from the Roaring Boys in Elyzium,* and *Newes from Sir John Sucklin.* There are undoubtedly others.

11. *A Mappe of Mischiefe,* 1641, p. 5.

12. Poems by Suckling appear in the following collections: *The Academy of Complements,* 1646, 1650, etc.; *A Musicall Banquet,* 1651; *Catch that Catch Can,* 1652, 1658, 1663; *Select Musicall Ayres, and Dialogues,* 1652; *Select Musicall Ayres and Dialogues, in Three Bookes,* 1653; *Wits Interpreter,* 1655, 1662, and 1671; *Sportive Wit,* 1656; *Wit and Drollery,* 1656, 1661, 1682; Henry Lawes, *Ayres and Dialogues,* 1658; *Select Ayres and Dialogues,* 1659; *Select Ayres and Dialogues for One, Two, and Three Voices,* 1659, 1669; *An Antidote Against Melancholy,* 1661; *Merry Drollery* [1661], 1670, 1691; *Recreations for Ingenious Head-Peeces,* 1663 (also issued with the title *Wits Recreations Refin'd*); *Musick's Delight on the Cithren,* 1666; *Catch that Catch Can,* 1667; *The New Academy of Complements,* 1669; *Oxford Drollery,* 1671; *Windsor Drollery,* 1671; *The Musical Companion,* 1673; *Synopsis of Vocal Musick,* 1680; *Wit and Mirth,* 1682, 1684; *The Academy of Complements,* 1684 (later edition of *Windsor Drollery*); Henry Bold, *Latine Songs,* 1685; *Catch that Catch Can: Or, the Second Part of the Musical Companion,* 1685; *The Second Book of the Pleasant Musical Companion,* 1686; *Wit and Mirth: Or, Pills to Purge Melancholy,* 1706, 1707, 1709, 1720.

13. The poem is printed anonymously in *Fragmenta Aurea* but appears in Stanley's *Poems and Translations* ('Printed for the Author, and his Friends'), 1647, sig. ²A3ʳ, and *Poems,* 1651, p. 77. See also Lord Brooke's related allusion to Suckling (1641) cited in ii. 267.

14. 'An Eclogue: Spoken by Hilas and Strephon', in *Poems of George Daniel Esq. of Beswick,* ed. A. B. Grosart, 1878, ii. 195-6 (the manuscript of Daniel's poems was first printed by Grosart).

15. *The Faerie King* is described and quoted from extensively in Hyder E. Rollins, 'Samuel Sheppard and his Praise of Poets', *SP,* 1927, xxiv. 509-55 (esp. 538-55). The text is here quoted from the manuscript (Bodleian Library, MS. Rawl. Poet. 28, f. 67ʳ).

16. Quoted from Rollins, ibid. p. 533.

17. R[obert] B[aron], *Pocula Castalia,* 1650, pp. 102, 126-7. In his 'Bᴀʟʟᴀᴅᴇ Vpon the Wedding', pp. 66-72, which parallels Suckling's 'Ballade' stanza for stanza, Baron implicitly pays further homage.

18. By William Barker, sig. b7ʳ; John Leigh, sig. *1ʳ; and William Bell, sig. ***2ᵛ.

19. *Stipendariæ Lacrymæ, or, A Tribute of Teares,* The Hague, 1654, p. 15.

20. [Edmund Prestwich], *The Hectors, or the False Challenge* (III. iii), 1656, p. 50 (according to the title-page the play was written in the preceding year).

21. The relevant entries are given in G. E. Bentley, *The Jacobean and Caroline Stage,* v 1956), 1204-5, 1208, and 1210-11.

22. *Defense of the Epilogue,* following *The Conquest of Granada,* 1672, p. 169.

23. 'A Ballad on a Friends wedding, to the Tune of Sir John Sucklings *Ballad*', in [John Raymund], *Folly in Print, or A Book of Rhymes,* 1667, p. 116.

24. *Theatrum Poetarum,* 1675, p. ²116.

25. *Miscellany Poems and Translations by Oxford Hands,* 1685, p. 157.

26. *Lives of the Most Famous English Poets,* 1687, p. 154.

27. *An Account of the English Dramatick Poets,* 1691, ii. 498-9.

28. [By William Walsh], 1692, sig. A4ᵛ. It was also the author's view that among all these poets 'that Softness, Tenderness, and Violence of Passion, which the Ancients thought most proper for Love-Verses, is wanting', and that none of them would have been a 'very great Lover'.

29. 3 March 1693, *Letters upon Several Occasions,* 1696, p. 50 (reprinted in *Letters of John Dryden,* ed. Charles E. Ward, Durham, N.C.: Duke University Press, 1942, p. 68).

30. Dr. Johnson once mentions 'some stanzas . . . on the choice of a laureat; a mode of satire by which, since it was first introduced by Suckling, perhaps every generation of poets has been teazed' (*Lives of the English Poets,* ed. George Birkbeck Hill, 1905, i. 15).

31. e.g. see N[athaniel] T[hompson], *A Choice Collection of 120 Loyal Songs,* 1684, p. 243.

32. *JEGP,* 1924, xxiii. 173-98; *SP,* 1925, iv. 161-79; and *PQ,* 1925, xxii. 81-132.

33. *The Tatler,* ed. George A. Aitkin, 1898-9, i. 329; ii. 69, 256; and iv. 240.

34. *Anecdotes,* No. 455; i. 196.

35. *The Art of Logick and Rhetorick,* 1728, p. xviii.

36. W. B. C. Watkins, *Johnson and English Poetry before 1660,* Princeton, N.J., 1936, p. 83. The author notes that there are sixteen quotations from Suckling in the *Dictionary* under A, B, and C alone.

37. 'Life of Cowley', *Lives,* ed. Hill, i. 22.

38. For the editions of Herrick and Carew see *Poetical Works of Robert Herrick,* ed. L. C. Martin, 1956, pp. xix, xxxiv-xxxv, and *Poems of Thomas Carew,* ed. Rhodes Dunlap, 1949, pp. lxxvi-lxxviii.

39. *Literary Hours, or Sketches Critical and Narrative,* 1798, p. 446; cf. 3rd ed., 1804, iii. 25.

40. *Life of John Milton,* 1881-94, i. 503 (the first edition was printed in 1859-80).

41. Perhaps the extra-academic references to a poet are as much a measure of his currency as the amount of space devoted to him in scholarly publications. It is in any case interesting to note, among recent mentions of Suckling, a light poem about him by Ogden Nash ('Brief Lives in not so Brief—III', *The New Yorker,* 2 January 1960, p. 50).

References and Abbreviations

CSPD Calendar of State Papers, Domestic Series.

PQ Philological Quarterly.

P.R.O. The Public Record Office.

S.P. State Papers.

Raymond A. Anselment (essay date 1972)

SOURCE: Anselment, Raymond A. "'Men Most of All Enjoy, When Least They Do': The Love Poetry of John Suckling." *Texas Studies in Literature and Language* 14, no. 1 (spring 1972): 17-32.

[*In the essay that follows, Anselment considers both the idealism and cynicism evident in Suckling's love poetry, and argues that Suckling is not a typical Cavalier Poet.*]

Among the group of poets conveniently labeled "Cavalier," John Suckling has in particular been stereotyped. Largely because of the set anthology pieces and the limited critical studies, "Natural, easy Suckling" is commonly seen as an unabashed rakehell and a dilettante writer whose amateur love poetry is synonymous with libertine cynicism.[1] This characterization, like the more inclusive designation "Cavalier," neatly places Suckling's poetry in a literary and a philosophical tradition; but the depiction is misleading. While some of his more famous poems apparently endorse a cynical vision of love, the entire canon reveals this is only one response in a complex and even sensitive search for the wisdom in love forbidden to the "fond lover."

The short lyric **"Out Upon It,"** often cited as a typical Suckling poem, epitomizes both the traditional manner and the essential crux of his love poetry. Unlike John Donne's intensely personal immediacy, the dramatic opening stanzas establish a public, somewhat detached mode. The speaker, highly conscious of more traditional poetic attitudes, casually affects a deliberate pose:

> Out upon it! I have lov'd
> Three whole days together;
> And am like to love three more,
> If it prove fair weather.
>
> Time shall moult away his wings,
> Ere he shall discover
> In the whole wide world again
> Such a constant lover.[2]

Rather than ignore the extraneous world for a universe newly discovered in the eyes of a beloved, this poem plays to its audience. The avowedly confessional declaration with its obviously inflated diction reverses conventional expectations, and the self-dramatizing speaker displaces the lady as the object of praise. The disparity between his boasting assertion and the reality that this millenial love will perhaps last three more days if all goes well is, of course, egregiously ironic. The conscious posture, dismissing a sacrosanct tenet of Renaissance love poetry, is calculated to be amusingly outrageous; but the concluding stanzas complicate this effect. Turning momentarily to the ostensible object of his love, the speaker admits with apparent reluctance,

> But the spite on 't is, no praise
> Is due at all to me:

Love with me had made no stays,
Had it any been but she.

Had it any been but she,
And that very face,
There had been at least ere this
A dozen dozen in her place.

(ll. 9-16)

The persona's hyperbolic claim in the closing lines, although conceding the lady's great beauty, in fact questions the speaker's sincerity and seriousness. With sophisticated aplomb he lightly adds still another variation to the Petrarchan preoccupation with the constant lover, yet the levity also contains a qualified seriousness. Suckling's ironic rendition tacitly implies that the art of loving, whether Petrarchan or Cavalier, depends to some extent upon role-playing and exaggeration. While the Petrarchan lover ultimately realizes self-fulfillment through a ritualistic subjugation, in this version the male ego remains intact while it compliments the woman. The praise differs in kind, but the extremeness and improbability are consonant with the more traditional poetic expressions. The ironic perspective, however, is radically different.

Irony, as Aristotle recognizes in his discussion of the *eiron,* is a mode of decorous behavior;[3] it is for Suckling also a sign of sophisticated complexity. The speaker's urbane insouciance embodies the natural easiness or the "conversation of a gentleman" admired by the Restoration, and it seems to imitate Quintilian's strictures on "elegant facetiousness" or to anticipate Shaftesbury's on "the Freedom of Wit & Humour";[4] in any case this ethos is an integral part of Suckling's poetic vision. The poet can be wittily amusing without becoming overly serious or tediously involved, and he establishes with his audience a form of mutual compliment and admiration. **"Upon My Lady Carlisle's Walking in Hampton Court Garden,"** for example, assumes an intimate and well-defined world of peers; and the bantering exchanges and unforced raillery between Carew and Suckling are designed to amuse an audience familiar with the real natures of both the participants and the object of the ironic compliment.[5] This rapport insures the success of the coterie joke, but here and in most of Suckling's poems it is posturing that creates a detachment necessary for the success of the poem.

While the poems effortlessly sustain a desirable colloquial ease and naturalness, they often consciously affect a sense of noninvolvement. Thus the first of the three poems grouped as sonnets carefully establishes an initial indifference:

Dost see how unregarded now
That piece of beauty passes?
There was a time when I did vow
To that alone;
But mark the fate of faces;
The red and white works now no more on me,
Than if it could not charm, or I not see.

(ll. 1-7)

Ordinarily the tradition of the sonnet would demand a passionate declaration of unrequited love or an emotional denunciation of love; the speaker in this sonnet, it seems, strikes a calculated pose for the benefit of his auditor. Cool and unperplexed, the speaker musingly considers why the lady's beauty no longer attracts him; but the question is only briefly entertained. His air of studied flippancy suggests that greater concern might make him a bore; besides, he has taken the occasion to reaffirm "She every day her man does kill, / And I as often die," and the nonchalance further enhances his sophisticated image. To create an impression on his audience Suckling may, as the next sonnet in the group clearly reveals, change casual indifference to deliberate iconoclasm. In his address to Cupid conventional expectations are reversed, and instead of asking for a beautiful woman he pleads,

Make me but mad enough, give me good store
Of love for her I court:
I ask no more,
'Tis love in love that makes the sport.

(ll. 5-8)

The strikingly paradoxical "love in love" unromantically reduces love to a madness that animates a series of conventional gestures; the game and not the love is valued. Although the subsequent stanza offers a justification premised upon the fickleness of fancy, the poet is interested less in the argument and more in its impact on the audience. To insure its vividness Suckling concludes,

'Tis not the meat, but 'tis the appetite
Makes eating a delight,
And if I like one dish
More than another, that a pheasant is;
What in our watches, that in us is found;
So to the height and nick
We up be wound,
No matter by what hand or trick.

(ll. 17-24)

The debasingly antiromantic description of appetite and the explicitly phallic connotations of the final metaphor assault the reader's sensibilities; and the poem's ultimate success depends upon an exhibitionistic wit similar to **"If, When Don Cupid's Dart."**[6] Here too Suckling's final stanza, which culminates in a familiar dilemma found also in Donne's "The Triple Fool," asserts that if love's pains must discomfort both the afflicted and all who must listen to his woe,

Then thus think I:
Love is the fart
Of every heart;
It pains a man when 'tis kept close,
And others doth offend when 'tis let loose.

(ll. 14-18)

Even more outrageous than the terminal metaphor of the previous poem, this controlling image is nevertheless wittily appropriate. In both instances the humorously epigrammatic aptness opposes any offensiveness, and the audience reaction becomes even more important than the vision of love. The speaker, who assumes various degrees of emotional detachment, is the central focus in these and a number of other poems, and his carefully affected poses are the key to Suckling's poetry.

Because the expression of a cynical libertinism is particularly congenial to the poseur, Suckling could have been drawn as a matter of course to this fashionable point of view. Donne, who provides the inspiration for several of his poems, had already demonstrated its poetic potential, and the libertine philosophy was currently influential on the continent. For the modish court of Henrietta Maria with its continental ties, *libertinage* combined a mode of manners with a philosophical respectability to appeal quite naturally to a sophisticated class. Outside of the mainstream of both established morality and traditional views of love, libertine cynicism provided the court poet with an opportunity to be wittily original and emotionally composed. But Suckling's characteristic use of the persona at least questions the conclusion that he whole-heartedly endorsed this position. Tone more reliably establishes the nature and extent of Suckling's cynicism.

Although any tonal reading assumes that the sheer number of poems espousing cynicism is not as important as the attitudes developed within the poems, this fact is easily overlooked in critical analyses. Even the standard study, Fletcher Orpin Henderson's "Traditions of *Précieux* and *Libertin* in Suckling's Poetry," too readily concludes that Suckling's "attitude toward the relations between the sexes is entirely physical." Indeed the first poem he cites, appropriately the natural, easy song Millamant admires in *The Way of the World,* provides the basis for the assumption:

> In a "Song" he stated his view, using a figure which was a favorite of his: "Some youth that has not made his story, / Will think, perchance the pain's the glory / And mannerly sit out love's feast: / I shall be carving of the best, / Rudely call for the last course 'fore the rest." Here love is reduced to its lowest common denominator. Woman is no more than a good dinner. Frequently he expresses this idea in one way or another.[7]

A catalogue of other poems indicates that Suckling does explore this idea in his poetry,[8] but it is dangerous to conclude that the poet uncritically accepts the position expressed in the stanza and, for that matter, that it is "his attitude." The speaker in the poem, the first stanzas establish, is an older man—or if he is not physically aged, his self-characterization as an old hawk defines a man of experience who through "long custom" has become "sullen and wise." This worldly figure, who lacks the flippancy or lightness commonly found in Suckling's personae, also no longer has any interest in either the manners or sport of love. As his candid, almost weary disclosure reveals, love has become for him a crude physical appetite. Satiety rudely demands "the last course 'fore the rest," but the speaker presents more than an unsentimental

assessment of love. Although the knowledge gained through experience has shaped his all-mannered conduct, in the last stanza the speaker also admits a poignant dissatisfaction:

> And, oh, when once that course is past,
> How short a time the feast doth last!
> Men rise away, and scarce say grace,
> Or civilly once thank the face
> That did invite, but seek another place.
>
> (ll. 16-20)

True to his unwavering perspective, he accepts the inevitable nature of his fate; yet the sense of resignation cannot conceal the pathos and disillusionment in the final lines. Paradoxically the emotional containment accentuates the tension, and it would be difficult to neatly categorize this poem as either cynical or libertine.

The tonal ambiguity also occurs in more obviously cynical poems such as **"There Never Yet Was Woman Made"**; its cause, while more clearly discernible, is quite similar. Again the speaker has considerable experience in the ways of love and he willingly shares his knowledge:

> There never yet was woman made,
> Nor shall, but to be curs'd;
> And oh, that I, fond I, should first,
> Of any lover,
> This truth at my own charge to other fools discover!
>
> (ll. 1-5)

The arresting assertion and the theatrical self-designation as a "fond" lover are rhetorically motivated, and they challenge the audience of "other fools" to ignore a knowledgeable person who views life without illusions. Women, the speaker seems to argue, deserve to be cursed because the feminine heart is fickle and indiscriminate. Yet the poem is neither bitter nor misogynous, for the dramatic tone of the opening shifts from the matter-of-fact pronouncement to betray a sensitive concern. If women are by nature promiscuous, the poem concludes there is always a gallant who eagerly "loads his thigh":

> For still the flowers ready stand:
> One buzzes round about,
> One lights, and tastes, gets in, gets out;
> All all ways use them,
> Till all their sweets are gone, and all again refuse
> them.
>
> (ll. 21-25)

The final emphasis in the repeated use of "all" unexpectedly gives new dimension to the opening declaration that women are only made "but to be curs'd." Within the sexually charged metaphor, the gallant who "all ways" uses all women does so variously and "always." Women are then inevitably destined or cursed to a postlapsarian existence; and their lot, captured in the final image of the faded and neglected flower, evokes compassionate sympathy. This tender, quiet melancholy at first may seem out of place in a poem notable for its numerous sexual puns and suppressed allusions, but the apparent incongruity, like the tonal tension in the previous poem, stems from the poet's comprehensive perspective. The awareness that women make men fools is imparted to "You that have promis'd to yourselves / Propriety in love"; hence the lover who is conscious of his social image will curse women in both of the poem's senses just as the sensualist must offend the hostess of "love's feast" to glut his own appetite. The male ego will remain intact, and the social image will be reaffirmed, but this selfishness has its price. In short, Suckling is too sensitive to ignore the dilemma.

Yet his concern with public image and poetic originality necessarily precludes the more traditional or "honest" lover; indeed in a song that parodies this conventional lover, **"Honest Lover Whosoever,"** it leads to the conflation of honesty and fondness. The poem describes a series of extreme attitudes, and after each the refrain tauntingly reminds the would-be lover that any lapse proves "Thou lov'st amiss; / And to love true, / Thou must begin again, and love anew." The list of witty impossibilities demanding that the honest lover must always "quake" and be "struck dumb" in his lady's presence, unfailingly find great wit in her most trivial utterance, and totally ignore all else chides the most commonplace romantic beliefs; in their place the satire tacitly insists upon a social decorum that renders the behavior of the honest lover ridiculous.

The demand for an impossible constancy is a rhetorical ploy implicitly recognized in the use of parody, and like the dismissal of the "honest lover's ghost" in **"Sonnet III,"** witty ingenuity is the primary concern; however the preoccupation with absoluteness has more serious implications. The honest lover Suckling describes was, of course, quite dated in the court of Charles I; despite some currency in the précieux poetry, its Petrarchan conventions were already dead, and both the prevailing poetics and the hypersensitivity about sophisticated, decorous behavior discouraged excessive emotionalism. More important, many seventeenth-century poets could no longer unquestioningly accept the belief that love was either a unifying force or a metaphysical reality.[9] Although the change involves a number of complicated cross currents, Suckling's poetry often posits one explanation. The basis for his reassessment is a form of skeptical realism, or as Donne had earlier written, "Love's not so pure and abstract as they use / To say, which have no Mistresse but their Muse."[10] Experience, the touchstone in Suckling's poetry, suggests that love has no quintessential nature; it is, as the imagery of painting, fiction, and dreaming reminds the reader, often illusory. In reality, Suckling's poems suggest, lovers are not passively overwhelmed by love; they actively determine the existence of love through their own fancy and appetite. While the power and validity of love are not automatically denied, this psychological viewpoint introduces a disconcerting relativity; pushed far enough it could easily lead to solipsism.[11] Concomitantly, the experience of love must also be reevaluated, for "Pure love," Suckling notes, "alone no hurt would do; / But love is love and magic too."

In the absence of "pure love," the honest lover is an impossible ideal. As **"Loving and Beloved"** asserts,

> There never yet was honest man
> That ever drove the trade of love;
> It is impossible, nor can
> Integrity our ends promove;
> For kings and lovers are alike in this,
> That their chief art in reign dissembling is.
>
> (ll. 1-6)

The poem's fundamental opposition between "good nature" and "passion" recalls the Renaissance debates involving reason and passion, but the moral issue is significantly altered. No longer concerned about the threat passion poses to both the reason and the will, the speaker is fully resolved that passion must be willfully controlled if the game of love is to be successfully played. In this poem, "weary" of the state he is in and reluctant to make the necessary compromise, he chooses to retain his honesty by withdrawing, "Since (if the very best should now befall) / Love's triumph must be Honour's funeral."

Only the "wise" lover who is willing to compromise can successfully play the game of love, but even then his solution involves another eitheror. In several poems the speaker bluntly argues "T' have lov'd alone will not suffice, / Unless we also have been wise, / And have our loves enjoy'd" (**"Sonnet III,"** ll. 12-14);[12] his justification is usually little more than physical appetite. On other occasions, however, Suckling takes a quite different position; rather than seize the moment, the lover in **"Against Fruition"** is advised,

> Stay here, fond youth, and ask no more; be wise:
> Knowing too much long since lost paradise.
> The virtuous joys thou hast, thou wouldst should still
> Last in their pride; and wouldst not take it ill,
> If rudely from sweet dreams (and for a toy)
> Thou wert wak'd? he wakes himself, that does enjoy.
>
> (ll. 1-6)

Physical consummation, in this view, is like the Garden of Eden's forbidden fruit: it promises unlimited gratification yet it leaves nothing but emptiness. The wise lover who still has expectation and cannot "tell his store," the conclusion puns, is truly rich; and conscious delusion is therefore preferable to harsh reality. The two kinds of values, one focusing upon the physical and the other upon the imaginative, counsel inherently contradictory courses; thus his canon includes poems that demand "Give me the woman here" and those that include "love in love."[13]

Each of the uncompromising courses questions the traditional evaluation of love, but even the most extreme poems allow a degree of playful and witty ambiguity. **"Against Fruition,"** a succinct and pessimistic assessment of love, concludes that men blindly hope for "strange things to see, / That never were, nor are, nor e're shall be"; its arguments, however, are not *a fortiori* proof of Suckling's bitter cynicism. As the opening lines illustrate, the poem's dramatic quality is tonally suspect:

Fie upon hearts that burn with mutual fire!
I hate two minds that breathe but one desire.
Were I to curse th' unhallow'd sort of men,
I'd wish them to love, and be lov'd again.

(ll. 1-4)

While unmitigated disillusionment could conceivably prompt this outburst, its violence at least raises the possibility that the author is more concerned with the audience effect. Equally iconoclastic statements characterize the arguments which then totally reverse the normal attitude toward love; and if the speaker is serious in his denunciation, he is not too involved to miss the pun "sure I should die, / Should I but hear my mistress once say ay." But the most disquieting feature is the poem's context, for the last lines reveal that the speaker has been addressing his mistress and all along has been building to the request that she deny him her sexual favors. The unique and effective reversal of the conventional seduction poem therefore determines the reasons the speaker advances and the vision of love he develops, and wit is more important than cynicism. The same is also true of the other apparently very cynical poem **"Farewell to Love."** Although Suckling asserts at length that love is illusory, the conventional nature of this poem immediately questions his sincerity. Medieval and Renaissance poets had already established the rejection of love as a set piece, and Suckling seems to accept the challenge in his opening stanza:

Well-shadow'd landskip, fare ye well:
How I have lov'd you none can tell,
At least, so well
As he that now hates more
Than e'er he lov'd before.

(ll. 1-5)

The speaker, who underlines his self-discovery in the following stanza, has realized the deceptive nature of women, but there is some doubt whether he is more concerned with the betrayal or with his ability to articulate his discovery. When he must later again remind the reader, "Oh, how I glory now, that I / Have made this new discovery," his exclamation is suspiciously excessive; and any emotional involvement is still further dissipated in the distracting manner with which he elaborately describes his perception. In detailing the reality he has found concealed behind an illusory beauty, the speaker insists that all women will now be for him only a *memento mori*; yet the macabre imagery becomes curiously sexual as he dismisses locks that "like two masterworms" curled over each ear "Have tasted to the rest / Two holes, where they like 't best." This possible ambiguity at least questions his assurance that henceforth all women will provide a source of moral edification, and his real attitude is confirmed in the final pronouncement,

They mortify, not heighten me;
These of my sins the glasses be:
And here I see
How I have lov'd before.
And so I love no more.

(ll. 46-50)

If Suckling were serious, he would not allow the sexual pun "heighten me" to detract from the emphasis on mortification; by italicizing the last line the poet further undercuts his sincerity.[14] Irony, not embittered rancor, is his design; and the entire poem is largely a clever and logical artistic game.

A completely cynical position would be as extreme as the distasteful "whining lover"; and Suckling, unable to find a middle ground, is sometimes forced to abandon the search to ensure the emotional self-possession which complements his mannered wit. The Petrarchan imitation **"'Tis Now, Since I Sate Down Before"** reveals the damaging consequences of this compromise. At the outset of the poem the speaker raises an interesting question:

'Tis now, since I sate down before
That foolish fort, a heart,
(Time strangely spent) a year and more,
And still I did my part. . . .

(ll. 1-4)

While this introduction is primarily a pretense for the extended conceit that follows, the speaker is at odds with himself. The heart he tried to conquer was, he emphasizes, "foolish"; and still he parenthetically concedes that through this "strangely spent" experience he did his part. The ill-fated siege, moreover, is not unlike that of many Petrarchan lovers; outside of a possible pun in the decision "to lie at length, / As if no siege had been," his actions are not unusual. The speaker willingly goes through the required gestures, and he lifts his attack only when he realizes "Honour" commands the metaphoric fortress. His refusal to parley with this giant is a distinct departure from the poetic norm, and the poem might end at this point with a cynical turn. Suckling, however, cannot resist an additional twist: in retreat the speaker concludes,

To such a place our camp remove,
As will no siege abide:
I hate a fool that starves her love,
Only to feed her pride.

(ll. 37-40)

The refusal to find anything but foolish pride in the lady's conduct compounds the note of cynicism, but the conclusion also introduces an unanticipated irony. The speaker, in a situation he cannot entirely control, is the real victim of pride; and his disdainful scorn is an obvious attempt to salvage his ego. Suckling himself is also guilty of a facile poetic maneuver. Although there is a hint of uncertainty on the part of the speaker in the opening stanza, the poem's dominant intention is the straightforward development of a traditional conceit. Thus the pretended new psychological insight at the end is tonally false and structurally disjointed. Like his speaker, Suckling beats a hasty retreat; the cynical pose affords a convenient refuge.

The contrived ending, which also occurs in poems not concerned with love,[15] often results after the wit has been expended in a set piece; in the love poetry, however, it may also indicate the desire to maintain detachment. When the ironic perspective is absent, as it is in much of the previous poem, Suckling must abruptly draw back; he also has difficulty when the subject threatens to be overly serious. **"Love's World,"** for example, would be an even finer poem if the poet were less concerned about sustaining the absolute distinction between the "wise" and "honest" lovers. The poem, a highly artificial and ingenious exercise, defines the world of love in terms of the familiar relationship between the microcosm-macrocosm; Suckling, however, is very conscious of the elaborate conceit, and he calls attention to his own artifice. He also makes certain that his attitude toward love is apparent; the realm of love that he defines, as the first stanza has demonstrated, is the world "found / When first my passion reason drown'd." Despite this negative view and the subsequent vein of realism, the poem does not cynically dismiss love. Fancy, hope, and "fond credulity" are a part of this experience, and the speaker does conceal his passion and is not totally preoccupied with the thought of his beloved; yet the love has a validity. The speaker reveals the extent of its attractiveness when he admits his hopes "Sometimes would be full, and then / Oh, too too soon decrease again." Although this emotional involvement is only momentary, it obscures, perhaps unintentionally, the poem's conclusion. When the wit has run its course and the conceit is exhausted, Suckling abruptly stops:

> But soft, my Muse, the world is wide,
> And all at once was not descri'd:
> It may fall out some honest lover
> The rest hereafter will discover.

(ll. 67-70)

The ending, which achieves a somewhat sudden closure, reaffirms the speaker's image as a "wise" lover; although the conclusion entertains the possibility of a more enduring love unknown to his experience, it is also conceivable that the final stanza intends to dismiss ironically the "honest" lover. The tone is ambiguous, for Suckling's own position in the poem is not firmly resolved.

When he can distance himself, as he does in **"A Ballad. Upon a Wedding,"** the need to conceal his own ambiguous attitude is less immediate; as a result the tonal complexity is more effective. With the persona of the rustic, Suckling creates a speaker completely outside his own identity; and the fictional context, the most complete development of the conscious posture, ensures a completely controlled freedom. Through the speaker, who with wide-eyed wonder narrates "things without compare," Suckling presents his own version of the epithalamium; paradoxically his ironic acceptance of this venerable poetic form produces unique emotional immediacy. The yokel's eye-witness account, which appropriately begins with the traditional processional, ignores the ceremonial or ritualistic and realistically captures the little details. The groom, who appears to the speaker

> one pest'lent fine
> (His beard no bigger though than thine)

> Walk'd on before the rest:
> Our landlord looks like nothing to him;
> The King (God bless him!), 'twould undo him,
> Should he go still so dress'd.

> At course-a-park, without all doubt,
> He should have first been taken out
> By all the maids i' the town,
> Though lusty Roger there had been,
> Or little George upon the Green,
> Or Vincent of the Crown.

(ll. 13-24)

This humanized account counters the conventional exaggeration of the epithalamium with a distinctly unpoetic hyperbole, yet the praise succeeds. Obviously the king's treasure would scarcely miss the funds needed for this wedding, and a country landlord or a lusty Roger is a rather limited epitome of masculinity; in their very naiveté, however, these evaluations have a ring of sincerity. While the reader condescendingly smiles at the narrator's provincialism, he also realizes his unjaded innocence. Suckling, conscious of the limitations of any praise, imparts a ring of truth without seeming patronizing. Similarly the speaker's experience provides a refreshingly effective view of the bride; in his enthusiastic description,

> No grape that's kindly ripe could be
> So round, so plump, so soft as she,
> Nor half so full of juice.

> Her finger was so small, the ring
> Would not stay on which they did bring,
> It was too wide a peck;

> And to say truth (for out it must)
> It look'd like the great collar (just)
> About our young colt's neck.

(ll. 34-42)

Truth may have been stretched a bit to impress his friend Dick, but the rural world invoked in the comparisons has a satisfying decorum; its apt originality successfully establishes both the lady's sensuousness and her daintiness. The grace and beauty developed in the blazon are also realized in the same manner, and the compliment culminates naturally in the speaker's declaration,

> If wishing should be any sin,
> The parson himself had guilty bin,
> She look'd that day so purely;
> And did the youth so oft the feat
> At night, as some did in conceit,
> It would have spoil'd him surely.

(ll. 73-78)

The poem juxtaposes the physical description and these sexual witticisms partly to avoid any possibility of cloying and insincere sentimentalism; but beauty and sexuality are also in accord with the spirit of the epithalamium. After the marriage is celebrated and as the consummation approaches, the sexuality implied in the first part of the poem becomes more overt. Activity now replaces the more static description in the poem's first half, and the tempo begins to gather momentum with the progressive accounts of the feasting, drinking, and dancing. The activity of the carousing people accentuates the wedding couple's desire to be finally alone, and their frustrated anticipation is vicariously experienced by all who help them celebrate. With masterful timing Suckling builds and prolongs this yearning; then he suddenly collapses the urgency in his final stanza:

> At length the candle 's out, and now
> All that they had not done they do:
> What that is, who can tell?
> But I believe it was no more
> Than thou and I have done before
> With Bridget and with Nell.

(ll. 127-132)

Unlike the coarseness found in **"Upon My Lord Broghill's Wedding"** or the innuendo in **"That None Beguiled Be,"** the sexuality is candidly and humorously accepted. The naturalness with which Suckling universalizes the sexual impulse is a characteristic of the epithalamium; and the witty turn, although his unique hallmark, also capitalizes upon the form's humorous potentiality. The final touch of realism, in keeping with the poem's tenor, modifies the grandeur found in much epithalamic poetry; but the romantic idealism is not dispelled. The real and the ideal are integral and complementary facets of the poem's vision of love.

In writing one of the great poems of the seventeenth century, Suckling momentarily found the form and vision that most nearly suited his poetic disposition. The orthodoxy of the epithalamium, like the other established kinds of poetry Suckling parodies, allows the bright court wit to display both his sophistication and his virtuosity. At the same time his entertaining and original performance maintains a detached, comprehensive perspective because the author can totally distance himself from the fictional narrator of this dramatic monologue. Freed from the self-consciousness of the other postures and encouraged by the nature of the epithalamium, Suckling is not constrained to compartmentalize love into the opposition of "wise" and "honest" attitudes. Although this poem may not in its synthesis represent Suckling's final vision of love, it is closer to his attitude than the popularized impression of the embittered cynic. Perhaps Suckling implied this in the poem **"Upon A. M."** when he advises a lady,

> Rather want faith to save thee, than believe
> Too soon; for, credit me 'tis true,
> Men most of all enjoy, when least they do.

(ll. 14-16)

In the context of the poem the paradox concludes an argument for a relationship based upon coy moderation, but the final line may also be a pun. The best gloss of this line and also of Suckling's love poetry is a statement by C. S.

Lewis in *The Allegory of Love*: "cynicism and idealism about women are twin fruits on the same branch—are the positive and negative poles of a single thing."[16]

Notes

1. Douglas Bush observes in *English Literature in the Early Seventeenth Century, 1600-1660* (New York, 1962), "It is chiefly the cynical strain of the young Donne that Suckling carries on . . ." (p. 122); and Fletcher Orpin Henderson extensively develops Suckling's libertine cynicism in "Traditions of *Précieux* and *Libertin* in Suckling's Poetry," *ELH*, 4 (1937), 274-298. A more extreme characterization by C. V. Wedgewood in "Poets and Politics in Baroque England," *Penguin New Writing*, 21 (1944), 123-136, suggests, "From his brilliantly accomplished verse, indeed, a savage, go-getting, tomorrow-we-die materialism emerges almost naked" (p. 135); in *The Poetry of Limitation* (New Haven, Conn., 1968) Warren L. Chernaik also concludes, "The sexual act has seldom been made to look less attractive" (p. 64). More qualified and comprehensive analyses by Robin Skelton in *Cavalier Poets, Writers and Their Work No. 117* (London, 1960), pp. 18-26, and L. A. Beaurline in "'Why So Pale and Wan': An Essay in Critical Method," *Texas Studies in Literature and Language*, 4 (1962), 553-563, perceptively suggest the complexity of Suckling's poetry; the natures of each approach, however, necessarily limit the analysis.

2. "Out Upon It," ll. 1-8. Although Suckling is credited with the authorship of the posthumous publications *Fragmenta Aurea*, 1646, and *The Last Remains of Sir John Suckling*, 1659, the extent of his contribution has been disputed (see L. A. Beaurline's "The Canon of Sir John Suckling's Poems," *Studies in Philology*, 57 [1960], 492-518). In the absence of a standard edition, which is being edited by T. S. Clayton, Beaurline's suggestions have been largely followed; R. G. Howarth's *Minor Poets of the Seventeenth Century* (New York, 1966) will be hereafter cited in the text.

3. See Ian Watt's discussion of irony in "The Ironic Tradition in Augustan Prose from Swift to Johnson," pp. 21 ff. in *Restoration & Augustan Prose* (Los Angeles, 1956).

4. John Dryden's famous characterization occurs in "An Essay of Dramatic Poesy," in *Essays of John Dryden*, ed. W. P. Ker (New York, 1961), I, 35; Beaurline suggests the link with Quintilian in "'Why So Pale and Wan': An Essay in Critical Method," pp. 556 ff.; Shaftesbury's observations in "An Essay on the Freedom of Wit and Humour" in *Characteristicks of Men, Manners, Opinions, Times* (London, 1714), I, 62 ff., are also relevant.

5. Part of the game is, of course, the playfully deliberate redefinition of Carew into an excessively poetic romanticist, but the ultimate intention is the mock encomium. Lady Carlisle, the Stuart court well knew,

hardly warranted Carew's effusive praise; and the final stanza, omitted from the first and subsequent editions but discovered by L. A. Beaurline and reproduced in "The Canon of Sir John Suckling's Poems," *Studies in Philology,* 57 (1960), 495-496, bluntly climaxes the ironic ruse. In ending the game Suckling simultaneously asserts the superiority of his posture:

> 'Troth in her face I could descry
> Noe danger, no divinity.
> But since the pillars were soe good
> On which the lovely fountaine stood,
> Being once come soe neere, I thinke
> I should have ventur'd hard to drinke.
> What ever foole like me had beene
> If I'd not done as well as seene?
> There to be lost why should I doubt
> Where fooles with ease goe in and out.

6. The last stanza of "Upon my Lady Carlisle's Walking in Hampton Court Garden" is in a similar vein.

7. "Traditions of *Précieux* and *Libertin* in Suckling's Poetry," *ELH,* 4 (1937), 289-290.

8. In a footnote Henderson cites Sonnet II, "There Never Yet Was Woman Made," "Against Absence," and "I Prithee Send Me Back My Heart."

9. See A. J. Smith's "The Failure of Love: Love Lyrics after Donne" in *Metaphysical Poetry,* eds. Malcolm Bradbury and David Palmer, *Stratford-Upon-Avon Studies 11* (New York, 1970), pp. 41-71. Smith's observations about Suckling should also be considered (see pp. 58 ff).

10. John Donne, "Loves Growth," ll. 11-12, in *The Elegies and The Songs and Sonnets,* ed. Helen Gardner (Oxford, 1965).

11. Chernaik argues that unlike the idealistic position of Lovelace, "Suckling's attitude is simpler: these ideals are frauds, and so are all others. Beauty is entirely in the eyes of the beholder, and honor and loyalty are equally products of self-delusion. . . . We are left with an impotent solipsism, where even choice (for whose priority Suckling is presumably arguing) is essentially meaningless" (pp. 63-64).

12. See also, for example, "Against Absence."

13. Suckling's "Song" (p. 198) should be compared with his two poems "Against Fruition" (p. 194, p. 206).

14. This is Suckling's only use of italics. Although it ostensibly accentuates a firmness of resolution, the ploy is both poetically weak and unimaginative. Accepted at face value the conclusion is uncharacteristic of Suckling's wit; in the context of the poem, however, the italics are the final example of a disconcertingly obvious extremeness. Suckling, like another famous performer, "doth protest too much."

15. See, for example, "A Sessions of the Poets."

16. *The Allegory of Love* (New York, 1958), p. 145.

Charles L. Squier (essay date 1978)

SOURCE: Squier, Charles L. "The Prose: A Bright and Elegant Surface" and "The Plays: *The Goblins* and *Brennoralt.*" In *Sir John Suckling,* pp. 33-56; 76-95. Boston: Twayne Publishers, 1978.

[*In the first of the two following essays, Squier analyzes Suckling's prose output, including letters and nonfiction, and focuses on what insights these pieces reveal about Suckling's other works. In the second essay, Squier examines Suckling's plays, and praises his skills as a playwright.*]

I. Letters and the Hidden Self

Suckling's prose is limited in quantity, consisting of fifty-four or fifty-five letters, depending on one's view of a doubtful one,[1] and *An Account of Religion by Reason,* a short essay. From so small a sample of his prose one might be hesitant to conclude with Tucker Brooke, "There is hardly a purer English style in the seventeenth century than Suckling's, and there are few better personal letters of the period than [those] of his that have been preserved."[2] But it would be impossible not to agree that the style is indeed notable and the letters of considerable interest. Moreover, the prose, apart from its intrinsic merits, can be used to provide insights into Suckling not to be found in the poetry or plays. In addition, and more importantly, through the art of the letters one can more clearly perceive the art of the poetry and certain literary values and assumptions of the period.

The letters can be divided into four main groups: (1) letters of a personal nature, including both kinds of courtship—that is, love and manners; (2) witty letters and letters belonging to epistolary genres; (3) serious letters concerning politics and war; and finally, (4) family letters. The seventeen identified correspondents, including his sister, Lady Southcot; his uncle, the Earl of Middlesex; Mary Bulkeley, the probable Aglaura; his friend Thomas Carew; his enemy Sir Kenelm Digby, give us some sense of Suckling's social world. However, it is difficult to discover in the letters what might be called his private world or something of the actual self, the "real" John Suckling.

Of course, one letter-writer can present a variety of "selves" in a number of letters. Moods, purposes, and recipients will all affect the tone and pose of a letter. The problem is compounded in the seventeenth century by the development of the familiar letter as a genre itself. On the continent and in English translation as well the *Lettres* of Jean Louis Guez de Balzac, published in 1624 and translated into English in 1634 and 1638, enjoyed wide popularity and supplied Suckling with a phrase or idea now and then. In England the most famous example of the familiar letter was James Howell's *Epistolae Ho-Elianae,* which appeared after Suckling's death, but an earlier and popular exemplar, one which Suckling knew and used, was Nicholas Breton's *Post With a Mad Packet of Letters,* first published in 1602. In these works the letter becomes a branch of the essay. The relationship of the writer to the letter is as personal or impersonal as it is to the essay, which is simply to say that it is as erroneous to expect personal revelation from some seventeenth-century letters as it is to expect it from poems of the period. The letter can be as crafted, artificial, and uninhabited as any song to Delia, Celia, or Aglaura.

Oddly enough the most personal of Suckling's letters are those having to do with serious matters, letters which can almost be called business letters. These letters, half of them written to the Earl of Middlesex, were not published in either *Fragmenta Aurea* or *The Last Remains* and are more distinctly private than the published letters. In the letters concerning serious business, at any rate, one finds less concern with craftsmanship and less posing. If the subject matter demands a degree of impersonality, these letters plus *An Account of Religion by Reason* at the very least provide us with a glimpse of another, the least familiar, facet of Suckling's character and work.

II. War, Politics, and the Serious World

This group includes eighteen letters, addressed to five identified persons: his uncle the Earl of Middlesex, Viscount Conway, the Earl of Newcastle, Sir Henry Vane, and Henry Jermyn. The letter to Jermyn, a favorite of Queen Henrietta Maria, is a political tract, as are three other letters addressed to unknown or imaginary correspondents. Half of the letters are to Suckling's uncle. The letters fall into two periods, those written in 1630-32 when Suckling was in Europe, part of the time in the party of Sir Henry Vane, ambassador to King Gustavus Adolphus of Sweden; the other group begins six years later, and the letters concern the developing civil war in Britain.

It is in the first group of letters in particular that one sees the serious and ambitious side of Suckling not apparent in his poetry. The letters to his uncle are straightforward, businesslike reports on the military situation in Germany. Occasionally a vivid detail will charge a letter with immediacy, ". . . the Castle by assault he took the seventh of *October,* where the Souldier found such pillage, that it is ordinary for the lower ranke of them now to loose 300 Duckets upon a drums head" (120). But the reader is less struck by felicities of style than by the sense of the writer as a potentially serious and ambitious young man, caught up in the excitement of great events and anxious to play a significant part in the world of affairs.

In the letter just cited, written to the Earl of Middlesex from Würzburg on November 9, 1631, he mentions dining with James, third Marquis and first Duke of Hamilton, who was serving with the army of the Swedish King Gustavus Adolphus:

> Last night I went to supp with my Lord Marquis and wishing that some occasion might present it self wherein I might serve him, he was pleasd to tell me,

that he was now going to beseidge *Magdeburg,* and that his army would be there before him. He is between 7 and 8000 strong but they are most of them *Duch* and given him by the king, for his owne are al dead of the plage to 1200. The king esteems much of him, and the Souldier honors him, and he himself takes al the ways to become a brave souldier, and to doe some act worthy of himselfe.

(120)

If the reader fails to catch the young Suckling's excitement and his attraction here to the values Hamilton represents, one can't miss these feelings in the next sentence; for the description of Hamilton becomes the occasion for an appeal to Middlesex, in retirement since his impeachment in 1624, to return to active public life: "While all the world is thus in action, pardon me (my Lord) if I must hope your Lordshipp will not long be idle. . . . The Christian world never more needing able men then at this present" (120).

Suckling's late father had been, after all, a member of the Privy Council and Comptroller of the King's Household, with all the avenues for advancing a son such a post possessed. His uncle had been, until his impeachment, Lord Treasurer of England. How exasperating it must have been for so lively a young man to have so potentially influential a relative inactive. The intensity of Suckling's hope that his uncle might reenter political life is seen again in letter 15. The letter is uncertain both as to date and addressee, but the subject matter and relation to other letters make the argument that it was written in November 1631 and addressed to the Earl of Middlesex most convincing.[3]

The letter is an epistolary "Character" urging, like the earlier letter, a return to active involvement in affairs: "When I consider you look (to me) like—I cannot but think it as odd a thing, as if I should see *Van Dike* with all his fine colours and Pensills about him, his Frame, and right Light, and everything in order, and yet his hands tyed behind him: and your Lordship must excuse me if upon it I be as bold" (121). The comparison of Middlesex with the brilliant painter is deftly done and effectively removes any suggestion of impertinence in the proposal. Suckling goes on to argue that both honor and wealth urge active engagement in the political world. The most interesting portion of the letter, however, is found in the high-flown praise of the court of King Charles:

> The little word behind the back, the undoing whisper, which like pulling of a sheatrope at Sea, slackens the sail, and makes the gallantest ship stand still; that that heretofore made the faulty and innocent alike guilty, is a thing, I beleeve, now so forgot, or at least so unpractiz'd, that those that are the worst, have leisure to grow good, before any will take notice they have been otherwise, or at least divulge it. . . . The very women have suffered reformation, and wear through the whole Court their faces as little disguised now, as an honest mans actions should be, and if there be any have suffer'd themselves to be gained by their servants, their ignorance of what they granted may well excuse

them for the shame of what they did. So that it is more then possible to be great and good. . . .

(122-23)

On May 2, 1632, on the other hand, Suckling was writing to Sir Henry Vane, in a letter discussed in the first chapter, a report of the reception he received when he brought Vane's dispatches from Germany to court, "The pacquett to my Lord Treasurer I presented first and the takinge of *Donawart,* who both to the bearer and the news seemd alike indifferent! Somethinge coole if not cold! Perchance his garb" (126). The letter then details the intricacies of court suspicions and rivalries, including "The disposall of the Coferers place [which] makes the world thinke, that there is some staggering in the friendship betwixt my Lord Treasurer and you . . ." (127) and the maneuverings necessary to get a hearing for Vane's reports. The realism of this account contrasts sharply with the idealistic (despite the inevitable gibe in passing at court ladies) picture of the "reformed" court presented to the Earl of Middlesex. The contrast underlines the distinctly literary aspect of even some of the "business letters" and the ease with which the Caroline writer is able to move from an idealistic, imaginary, artistically created vision of the court to a perfectly realistic, straightforward description of it. The astounding facility and rapidity of this shift from the crafted, artificial world of idealized court to a real, conniving, infighting, everyday court is symptomatic of the period, and a theme which will be amplified later. For the moment one may simply note that the shift of worlds forms the basis of the delightful poem **"Upon my Lady Carliles walking in Hampton-Court garden."** Before leaving the letter to Vane it should be stated that it reinforces the view of Suckling as a competent and perceptive political operative. The letter is well constructed, lively, and acute. One comes from a reading of it impressed by Suckling's ability and by his competent service to Vane—surely exactly the impression the writer strove to create.

After this letter there is a six-year jump in the public-affairs letters. The subject matter moves from European wars to the growing civil strife in England and Scotland. The author is no longer a youth with a career to make, but a mature man of thirty, for better or worse established, as much as he ever would be, in life.

This second group opens with a pair of letters purporting to be an exchange between a "London alderman" and a "Scottish Lord." Both are political pieces written for propagandistic purposes. Neither letter is especially noteworthy, but both are mildly amusing. The tone of the pair can be seen in the concluding thrust at the London citizen in the London alderman's letter, "I therefore desire your Lordship to send me word in what state things stand there, that I may know of which side to be . . ." (141). The irony increases in the answering letter from the Scottish Lord, who professes great surprise that he and his fellows should be called "Rebels, when none are more his Majesties most humble Subjects than we, as in the front of our Petitions and Messages most plainly appears . . ."

(141). Suckling's technique in this pair of letters is to attack both the rebellious Scots and their London sympathizers through the creation of two unattractive spokesmen. Both are hypocrites, and differences dividing the kingdom are the consequence of the self-seeking unruliness of such rogues as these. Suckling can hardly have hoped to persuade anyone to the king's side by this method, but persuasion is not much found in his political writing.

The epistolary tract of April 1639, **"An Answer to a Gentleman in Norfolk that sent to enquire after the Scotish business,"** exemplifies Suckling's basic intransigence. It is worth examining in some detail simply for its polemical skill. The letter may have been written to Suckling's uncle, Charles Suckling of Woodton, Norfolk, but it is very likely that the Gentleman in Norfolk is a convenient fiction. The letter, an exercise in loyalist propaganda, was probably written from York when Suckling was on his way to Scotland and the First Bishops' War.

It begins with a statement of purpose which declares his annoyance with timid and ambiguous positions: "That you may receive an account of the Scotish businesse, and why there hath been such irresolution and alteration about the Levies lately; it is fit you know that this Northern storm (like a new Disease) hath so far pos'd the Doctors of State, that as yet they have not given it a name; though perchance they all firmly believe it to be Rebellion: . . ." (142). The complexity of the Scottish situation, he continues, developing a vivid image, leads people to think of it much as they do the moon, "the simpler think it no bigger then a Bushel, and some (too wise) imagine it a vast World, with strange things undiscovered in it . . ." (143). The comparison then leads to a central assertion: "I confess I know not how to meet it in the middle, or set it right, nor do I think you have: since I should believe the question to be rather *A King or no King,* then *A Bishop or no Bishop*" (143). The attitude, then, is one of irreconcilable opposites. Given that view, the letter moves with its own logic in a series of increasingly strong attacks. There is no argument here; for Suckling there was nothing to argue.

The religious issue he considers totally spurious, a mask for rebellion, "for Rebellion it self is so ugly, that did it not put on the vizard of Religion, it would fright rather then draw people to it . . ." (143). Nor can they claim freedom of thought as a cause Suckling airily declares: "If it be Liberty of Conscience they ask, 'tis a foolish request, since they have it already, and must have it in despight of power . . ." (143). This can only be called a very cavalier dismissal. The next step is *ad hominem* with a brilliant and nasty thrust at the Scots' military leader, Sir Alexander Leslie, who had served with the armies of the King of Sweden for thirty years: "*Lesly* himself (if his story were search'd) would certainly be found one, who because he could not live well here, took up a trade of killing men abroad, and now is return'd for Christ's sake to kill men at home" (143-44). It would be cheap enough if it weren't so well sneered a sneer. The famous general is reduced to a mere mercenary, a military tradesman and a religious hypocrite. Suckling ends the letter with a final slur, that the Scots simply want more attention from the king and that Scotland (as Dr. Samuel Johnson held a century later) is a wilderness in contrast to the English Eden, "The great and wise Husbandman hath placed the Beasts in the Outfields, and they would break hedges to come into the Garden" (144). It is all supremely superior; the challenge to the royal authority, the questions of church governance do not even deserve argument. Again, one can't help but be impressed by the totality of the pose, by the creation of the languidly superior Cavalier who can so easily and with such artful contempt dismiss the major political-religious questions of the day. Against the cavalier pose may be set the bitter reality of the ignominious nonbattle at Kelso described in a letter to the Earl of Middlesex on June 6, 1639: "And now the word was given to Charg; but by this Time wee discovered dust, and out of that dust grew a greater bodie then all the right and left hand forces were together. It was now time to think of Retreat. . . . Our horse are much harast by Continuall Alarums and hard marches, and our men, many sick of Loosnesses and Plurisies . . ." (145-46).

The last major political letter to be considered here is that **"To Mr. Henry German, In the Beginning of Parliament, 1640."** This tract marks the beginning of Suckling's active participation in the debates and plot that ended with his escape to France. However, the letter to Jermyn, is measured, temperate, and to a large degree a statesmanlike document. In the opening Suckling urges that the king must now act: "That it is fitt for the Kinge to doe somethinge extraordinary att this present, is not only the opinion of the wise, but their expectation. . . . To lie still now would att the best shewe but a calmnes of minde, not a magnanimitie . . ." (163). The balanced stateliness and the forcefulness of the lines just quoted are characteristic of the whole letter. The question of action leads naturally to the specific course of action and to the nature of advice given the king. Suckling's perception here is sound and wittily and gracefully expressed: "Then in the Court they give much Counsell, as they beleive the King inclyn'd, determine of his good by his desires, which is a kinde of Settinge the Sun by the Diall, Interest that cannot erre, by Passions which may" (163).

The interest of the king, he goes on to argue, is "union with his people," while the two main concerns of the people are religion and justice. The logic of the argument is that the king must respond in a real way to his own interests and to those of his people. The striking aspect of Suckling's thought here is that he has reduced the great questions of the period to pragmatic basics. He is not concerned with the details of religion and justice, but with the fact that the king, needing the loyal support of the people, must respond to their concerns, and indeed must do more than respond: "It will not bee enough for the King to doe what they desire, but hee must doe something more. I meane by doing more, doing something of his owne: as throwing away things they call not for, or giving

things they expected not" (165). It is rather surprising to hear a man one thinks of as a kind of arch-Cavalier arguing so pragmatically and arguing for what would be in modern terms a calculated appeal to the electorate.

The attitude might be described as cynical by some, but others would see it as something more than practical, as a natural outcome of a bent of mind inclined to look beyond the abstractions to the essences. At any rate, the position here described is not at odds with the thinking that prompted *An Account of Religion by Reason,* as shall be seen later. The following assertion shows more of Suckling's practical, realistic outlook: "For the People are naturally not valiant, and not much Cavaleir. Nowe it is the nature of Cowards to hurt, when they can receive none: They will not bee content (while they feare, and have the upper hand) to fetter onely royaltie, but perchance (as timorous Spirritts use) will not thinke themselves safe, whiles that is att all, and possibly this may bee the present state of things" (165).

If one objects to the superior attitude toward the "people," Cromwell's men gave adequate refutation to the view; more importantly, it is evident Suckling was prophetically correct as to the consequences of a royal attitude which ignored the popular will. His practicality here contrasts interestingly with traditional ideality or court artificiality in the next paragraph. The queen, he says, must be involved in any action and must support it. Indeed, the direction of the letter to Jermyn indicates that Suckling's concern is in great measure with the queen and the extremist position of Henrietta Maria and her party. The queen must join so that the royal cause be totally united; then Suckling turns from the day to day argument and language to court argument and the language of courtship:

> And to invite her, shee is to consider with herselfe, whether such great vertues and eminent Excellencies (though they bee highly admir'd and valued by those that know her and are about her) ought to rest satisfied with so narrowe a payment, as the estimation of a few: and whether it bee not more proper for a great Queen to arrive att universall honor, and love, than private esteeme and value. Then how becomeing a worke for the sweetnesse and softnesse of her Sex is composing differences, and uniting hearts; and how proper for a Queene, reconciling King and people.
>
> (165-66)

The language of this indirect appeal to Henrietta Maria takes us back to the graceful artifices of the court, the world of

> Awake (great Sir) the Sun shines heer,
> Gives all Your Subjects a New-year,
> Onely we stay till You appear,
> For thus by us Your Power is understood:
> He may make fair days, You must make them good.
>
> (84, 1-5)

But the context for the artifice is a hardheaded political tract.

This hardheaded expediency is even more tellingly revealed in Suckling's advice concerning the king's loyal ministers who incurred the displeasure of his opponents. Although he says "I shall rather propound something about it, than resolve it" (166), his position is clearly that the ministers must be abandoned because the smaller must be sacrificed to the greater good. If the ministers could be saved, they would be ineffective because of their unpopularity; the king really can't save them until he has the power to do so; to attempt to save them may result in the loss of that power, that is, the fight might result in the king's downfall. Again, Suckling's advice is sound and undogmatic. The essay concludes with a prayer which underlines the basic pragmatism of his position:

> That the King bee neither too insensible, of what is without him, nor too resolv'd from what is within him. To bee sicke in a dangerous sicknesse, and finde noe paine, cannot bee but with losse of understanding. 'Tis an Aphorisme of *Hippocrates*: And on the other side, *Opiniastrie* is a sullen Porter and (as it was wittily said of *Constancie*) shuts out oftentymes better things, than it letts in.

(167)

> I could not love thee, dear, so much,
>   Lov'd I not Honour more.

And we can understand more readily the dryness, the unlyrical edge, the just barely hidden melancholy that lurks beneath the bright surface of much of his poetry. He is not a man for doctrinaire abstractions. The silken courtier with his glamorous hundred horse, the pensive and dreamy gentleman of the Van Dyck portrait, leaning against a rock, holding his folio of Shakespeare open to *Hamlet,* remains, whatever the pose, the gambler who sees the options as win or lose. The keenness of mind, the clarity and brilliance of style in these letters concerning practical matters lead one to conclude that Suckling's Hamlet was not a dreamy, indecisive prince, but the man of action, the soldier and administrator perceived by Horatio and Fortinbras. At all events, the least one can conclude is that Suckling presents a variety of surfaces and more complexity than might be expected. That complexity is underscored by the last prose work we have to be considered in this group of letters and tracts related to serious affairs, *An Account of Religion by Reason.*

III. A LADY'S COLD SWEAT: *AN ACCOUNT OF RELIGION BY REASON*

Aubrey's story of the writing of *An Account of Religion by Reason* has been given above. Whatever the truth of its creation, *An Account* is an undeniably curious and rather charming document. Once again the reader is struck by the clarity and grace of Suckling's prose and by the direct and orderly organization of his ideas. *An Account* was directed to Edward Sackville, the fourth Earl of Dorset, the father-in-law of Suckling's first cousin, Frances Cranfield, Lady Dorset. In the epistle to Dorset (September 2, 1637) accompanying the essay Suckling declares:

> I send you here (my Lord) that Discourse enlarged, which frighted the Lady into a cold sweat, and which had like to have made me an *Atheist* at Court, and your Lordship no very good Christian. I am not ignorant that the fear of *Socinianisme* at this time, renders every man that offers to give an account of Religion by Reason, suspected to have none at all: yet I have made no scruple to run that hazard, not knowing why a man should not use the best weapon his Creator hath given him in his defence. . . . That man is deceivable, is true; but what part within him is not likelyer to deceive him then his Reason?

(169)

From this one might well expect a far more radical and rationalistic document than is actually found. What brought the lady to a sweat remains a mystery, at least for modern readers. The court discussion of the essay is supported by evidence of its circulation not long after it was written, and in his notes to *An Account* Mr. Clayton mentions that it was among the papers of a certain Mr. Vassall seized by government officials.

Perhaps modern difficulties with Suckling's *Account* are essentially responses to "Socinianism" itself. Very briefly Socinianism, which got its name from Fausto Paolo Sozzini (Latinized to Socinus), who advanced its major ideas in sixteenth-century Italy, was characterized primarily by its acceptance of the validity of the Scriptures and by its stress on the importance of reason in religion. Suckling's association with Socinianism, apart from the essay itself, is seen in the inclusion of John Hales, Lucius Cary, and William Chillingworth among the wits in **"The Wits."** All three were a part of the intellectual circle at Oxford which is associated with the foundation of the latitudinarian movement in the Church of England. "They were," one historian of religion has written, "true Broadchurchmen and apostles of tolerance."[4]

The passage already quoted from the epistle to the Earl of Dorset, is, it need hardly be argued, clearly and effectively expressed. If the style has not yet achieved the limpidity of, say, Dryden, or other prose stylists of the latter part of the century, it is clearly moving in that direction. Such a style suggests a matching clarity, openness, and logical neatness of thought. To a twentieth-century reader, however, the contents of the *Account* often seem at odds with the style; for the *Account* is in some measure quirky and eccentric. The quirkiness and eccentricity, nevertheless, belong more to the age than to Suckling in particular. Suckling's friend Sir William Davenant remembered being sent to the apothecary for powdered unicorn's horn when he was a young page and empirically testing the old tale that a spider could not get out of a circle made of powdered unicorn's horn (the spider could).[5] It helps to recall this early venture into experimental science when reading *An Account of Religion by Reason.*

The thesis of Suckling's essay is that belief in Christianity can be justified by reason. Although the argument takes some strange bends, the opening of the essay is relatively straightforward; the argument is that of uniform beliefs. Men in all times have believed in a deity. From the argument for a Superior Being Suckling moves to that of the Deity as Creator. If the argument for the existence of God because all men have believed in one suggests the uniformitarian rationalism of a later era, this argument for God as Creator surely suggests earlier philosophies: "For *if man made man, Why died not I when my Father died?* Since according to that great *Maxime* of the Philosophers, *the cause taken away, the effect does not remain*" (170). This is a fairly typical example of the methods found in *An Account of Religion by Reason.* In a brief survey of beliefs shared by three ages, the Unknown, the Fabulous, and the Historical, which has been cited "as an early attempt at a comparative study of religions,"[6] Suckling concludes that "a great part of our Religion, either directly or indirectly hath been professed by Heathens . . ." (172). Perhaps it is at this point that the lady mentioned in the dedicatory epistle begins to break into her cold sweat.

That sweat might develop more with the assertion, "They concluded to be vices which we do; nor was there much difference in their vertues; onely Christians have made ready beleef the highest, which they would hardly allow to be any" (172). The apparent glance at the easy credulity of Christians and elevation of faith above reason is swift and almost unnoticeable, but the wry, skeptical note is unmistakable. Nonetheless, Suckling does go on to argue for the superiority of Christian to pagan beliefs, centering his arguments on the absence of human and animal sacrifice, the Christian view of the afterlife, and the nature of Christian ceremonies. As to the truth of Christianity in general he argues from the source, that is, the Apostles, finding them simple, true men. From general truths he turns to the specifics of Incarnation, Passion, Resurrection, and Trinity.

The details of these arguments don't need to be repeated here. The opening argument for the Incarnation is representative: ". . . That man should be made without man, why should we wonder more in that time of the world, then in the beginning? much easier, certainly, it was here, because neerer the natural way; Woman being a more prepared matter then earth" (176). Much the same is his view concerning the Resurrection: ". . . I conceive the difficulty to lie not so much upon our Lord, as us; it being with easie Reason imagined, that he which can make a body, can lay it down, and take it up again" (178). The juxtaposition of reason and imagination is paramount here. Reasonable for Suckling is what one can believe without too great a strain. In all of this there is a hint of "self-evident truths." ". . . *Nature, Substance, Essence, Hypostasis, Suppositum,* and *Persona,* have caused sharp disputes amongst the Doctors" (179), but clearly can be dismissed, and are, with an airy wave. "But in these high mysteries, similitudes (it may be) will be the best Arguments" (179). If the parenthesis is an apology (and it is hard to believe it really is), it is the only one in the *Account.* "Now, though I know this is so far from demonstration, that it is but imperfect instance (perfect being impossible of infinite by finite things) yet there is a resemblance great enough to let us see the possibility" (180). Quite far enough for a gentleman to go, at any rate, one must feel. And that, perhaps, is the outstanding quality of the *Account of Religion by Reason.* It is a gentleman's essay written for gentlemen. One really did not need to fuss quite so much with these questions once the obvious points have been made. There are pedants with ink-stained fingers for that sort of thing.

The modernity in the *Account* is in the feeling for the *consensus gentium* that will dominate the thinking of the age to come. The antirational skepticism of the essay also looks forward to positions of men like Dryden later in the century: ". . . it were stranger for me to conclude that God did not work *ad extra,* thus one and distinct within himself, because I cannot conceive how begotten, how proceeding; then if a Clown should say the hand of a Watch did not move, because he could not give an account of the wheels within. So far it is from being unreasonable, because I do not understand it, that it would be unreasonable I should . . ." (180). For all its oddities, then, the *Account* is a gentleman's essay and the witty turn at the end is distinctly that of Sir John Suckling, the court wit: "Thus much of Christian Profession compared with others: I should not shew which (compar'd within it self) ought to be preferred: but this is the work of every pen, perchance to the prejudice of Religion it self. This excuse (though) it has, that (like the chief Empire) having nothing to conquer, no other Religion to oppose or dispute against it, It hath been forced to admit of Civil wars, and suffer under its owne excellency" (180). One could no more justifiably complain that in straining for wit Suckling has violated truth here than one could make the same complaint of any poetic conceit.

An Account of Religion by Reason is certainly not exceptional or original theology or philosophy. The position Suckling takes is in its essentials that espoused by William Chillingworth in *The Religion of Protestants a Safeway of Salvation* (1637) who believed, as Earl Morse Wilbur has described, that "Only truths necessary to salvation need be sought for, and they are so plainly taught in Scripture, and so few in number, that any open mind that will look for them may see them."[7] The *Account* places Suckling within a clear current of contemporary religious thought and with a group of loyal Royalists who espoused a moderate religious position. At first glance it might seem very surprising to find such an essay in the papers of the rakehell gambler, courtier poet. But another look and one recalls that Suckling was, after all, a Renaissance gentleman. His ideal Hamlet was Ophelia's: "The courtier's, soldier's, scholar's, eye, tongue, sword, / Th' expectancy and rose of the fair state, / The glass of fashion and the mould of form . . ." (III, i, 150-52). The range of abilities and interests demonstrated by *An Account of Religion by Reason* and by the letters is that of a gentleman. It is no more surprising that Sir John wrote an essay on religion than that he rode a horse, gambled, wenched, and wrote letters on family affairs.

IV. The Family Man: Advice and Sympathy

It is unfortunate that only three of Suckling's letters directly related to familial affairs have survived. The letters to Middlesex might be considered family letters, but their subjects are not family matters. The letter **"To a Cosin (who still loved young Girles, and when they came to be mariageable, quitted them, and fell in love with fresh) at his fathers request, who desired he might be perswaded out of the humour, and marry"** might be thought of as a family letter, but it belongs to a distinct episotlary genre and can best be considered elsewhere. The three letters are just enough to give a tantalizing hint of this side of Suckling's character and to suggest that he was a useful member of his family to whom one could turn for help.

In one letter Suckling writes to his first cousin, Martha, Lady Carey, reporting on the marriage negotiations for her daughter in which he has been engaged. A letter of Lady Carey's to her father, the Earl of Middlesex, has been preserved in which she asks her father to "thanke Sir John for the care and paines he has taken in it for me, in the treaty he put me in minde of" (199). Suckling's letter has to do with a normal enough, prosaic family matter. It is clear from it that the marriage negotiations have been complex and the bargaining tight. What makes the letter striking is the consummate grace with which Suckling manages to move from business matters to romance, to clothe the whole with wit and style. The opening sentence must serve to illustrate the point: "It is none of the least discourtesies money hath done us Mortals, the making of things easie in themselves, and natural, difficult: Young and handsome people would have come together without half this trouble, if it had never been . . ." (130). It is an elegant introduction to a business letter of this sort.

The other two family letters are one to his brother-in-law, Sir George Southcot, and the other to his sister Martha when Southcot ended their marriage by committing suicide. Both letters are marked with their own particular elegance. Martha Suckling married Sir George Southcot in July 1635; he was sixty years old and four times a widower. The chances for an unhappy marriage because of the disparity of ages were increased by Sir George's miserly nature. Suckling wrote Southcot on this subject on September 9, 1635, urging him to give up covetousness and reminding him that he had "entred into one of those neer conjunctions of which death is the onely honourable divorce . . ." (131).

The letter is graceful, elegant, and stylish but marked by an underlying mockery. The essence of the letter is the civil sneer. He reminds Southcot of his duty but cannot help jeering at the married man: "It faring with married men for the most part, as with those that at great charges wall in grounds and plant, who cheaper might have eaten Mellons elsewhere then in their owne Gardens Cucumbers" (131). Cold comfort for the miser to be told "that thing a husband is but Tenant for life in what he holds, and is bound to leave the place Tenantable to the next shall take it" (132). The fine barbs follow, one after the other; the expression is so polished we almost miss the venom: "The lure to which all stoop in this world, is either garnisht with pleasure or profit, and when you cannot throw her the one, you must be content to shew out the other" (132). If we met the passage out of context and unidentified, we should not hesitate to attribute it to some Jonsonian Truewit. A whole scene writes itself, the aging miserly gentleman, married to the lively extravagant lady, the urbane brother-in-law drawling his sardonic advice. But here, of course, it is life and not art. A gibe that must have particularly annoyed Sir George Southcot was Suckling's assertion that "Money in your hands is like the Conjurers Divel, which while you think you have that, has you" (133). At any rate, Sir George found the remark worth mentioning in a letter of complaint to the Earl of Middlesex. At moments Suckling sounds like a divine, hitting delightfully sanctimonious notes: ". . . for while you have catcht at the shadow, uncertain riches, you have lost the substance, true content" (133). How infuriated Sir George must have been at such pieties from his rakehell brother-in-law. It is a shame that there are no more letters of advice to Southcot.

Fortunately the letter of "consolation" to Martha Lady Southcot after her husband's suicide in 1639 remains and is almost a masterpiece of its kind. At any rate, it is an exceedingly witty bit of irreverence. Suckling wastes no time on hypocritical pieties over Southcot's suicide:

> It is so far from me to imagine this accident should surprize you, that in my opinion it should not make you wonder; it being not strange at all that a man who hath lived ill all his time in a house, should break a Window, or steal away in the night through an unusual Postern: you are now free, and what matter is it to a Prisoner whether the fetters be taken off the ordinary way or not.

> (149)

The similitudes reduce any possibility of actual sympathy, but the witty toughness itself so firmly establishes the context of wit that the irreverence passes as appropriate. Put more simply, the letter is more concerned with artful wittiness than with the actuality of the occasion. The occasion becomes the excuse for the demonstration of wit on a set theme.

"I would not have you so much enquire whether it were with his garters or his Cloak-bag strings" (149), the proverbial twang here, the comic baseness of garters and cloak-bag strings insure the continued toughness of tone and the blocking of emotion. An ensuing reference to "the Spanish Princesse *Leonina*" derived from the *New Epistles of Monsieur de Balzack* provides a further reminder of the literary nature of the letter. The outrageousness of the observation, "Of ill things the lesse we know, the better. Curiosity would here be as vain, as if a Cuckold should enquire whether it were upon the Couch or a Bed, and whether the Cavalier pull'd off his Spurrs first or not"

(150) is tempered by the literary, crafted character of the letter. Necessarily to see character here, to ascribe the whole to an unfeeling, sneering rake is to miss the point of the wit of the seventeenth century.

Nevertheless, one can conclude pretty easily that neither Suckling nor his sister were much saddened by the suicide. Suckling does provide a pro forma admission that "I must confesse it is a just subject for our sorrow to hear of any that does quit his station without his leave that placed him there . . ." (150), but he goes on to cite Shakespeare and suicide as a "Roman's part" (*Julius Caesar,* V, iii, 89). (Witty, irreverent, and artful as the letter is, it is still difficult to avoid thinking of Southcot's suicide and this letter in relation to Suckling's own suicide just a few years later.) In tone and to a large degree in intent this letter could be placed with letters best classified as those of wit. It is the fact of the actuality of the occasion that makes it a "family" letter, but the wit, the freedom from cant, the implied sympathy, do, in fact, serve as appropriate consolation. The letter is above all that of an artist. Its consolation is deliberately irreverent; it aims at a sort of shocked laughter. In some sense it could have been written to an abstract, supposed addressee: "To a Lady Whose Miserly Husband Committed Suicide," but in this case, of course, the lady, the husband, and the suicide were real.

V. Wit, Love, Manners, and Courtship

Inevitably classification of these letters becomes somewhat muddled. Perhaps it would be more precise to make a distinction between uninhabited and inhabited letters, for many letters here could have been written by anyone to anyone; these are letters of pure wit, duty letters, even some of the love letters. Others of the letters grouped here are more clearly personal, but all are marked by the push toward wit and artifice. Furthermore, a number of the letters in this group belong to a distinct epistolary genre and are depersonalized by that fact.

Two early letters, both to William Wallis, one dated November 18, 1629, and the other May 5, 1630, illustrate the uninhabited letters. Each presents a series of witticisms. The effect is rather like that of a stand-up comedian delivering a series of one-liners. Neither letter has any particular pattern, neither really says anything either in terms of specific content or about the feelings of the writer. The subject of the first letter is the cross-Channel trip and the nature of the Dutch: "And sure their auncestors when they begott them thought on nothing but Munkeys, and Bores, and Asses, and such like ill favor'd creatures; for their Phisnomyes are soe wide from the rules of proportion, that I should spoyle my prose to let in the description of them. In a word, they are almost as bad as those of *Leicestershire*" (113). The level of craft is not very high, and the joke is dull enough, but it is as carefully put together and as unspontaneous as any music-hall or nightclub routine, even to the turn at the end, "as bad as those of *Leicestershire*." We fleetingly think, as we read the letter, that Suckling might have been carrying a dog-

eared joke book with him to idle away his shipboard hours. What else can be said of such ancient wheezes? "The plague is here constantly, I mean Excise; and in soe greate a manner, that the whole Cuntry is sick on't. Our very Farts stand us in I know not how much Excise to the States, before we let them" (113).

The other letter to Wallis represents no great advance in humor and style, but at least develops an ingenious paradox that the inhabitants of the Netherlands have achieved a certain virtue because of their poverty, "for being there is no money, there is no usury, Nor no Corruption" (116, 117). In a passage quoted earlier Suckling also finds the opportunity for mock praise of Catholicism: ". . . as far as I conceive of it, it would suit well enough with us young men. If a man be drunke overnight, it is but Confessing it next morning or when he is sober, and the matter proves not Mortal. To the liing with ones Sister, there is no more required than the telling the truth of it to a ghostly father. And you may jumble as many wenches as you please upon bedds, provided you wil but mumble as many *Avemaries* upon beads" (117). The terminal pun is inevitable enough; and these two letters to Wallis are perhaps most interesting when set against the sober and businesslike accounts written at the same time to the Earl of Middlesex, for they point to the various personalities Suckling adopts in his letters. One must admit as well that these two letters represent a lower order of wit and not Suckling at his best. Nor are the more clearly genre letters representative of Suckling at his most polished. However, they are worth brief consideration as exemplars of the variety found in the letters and of Suckling's use of available literary types.

Letter 48, addressed to some unknown *Ladies,* apparently responds to a letter written either in a joking cryptograph or perhaps just a very illegible hand. It gives us a brief glimpse of fashionable joking, of the world of young court ladies giggling behind their fans and composing a letter to the dashing and wicked Sir John, who replies in part: "The Coronet believes there are noble things in it; but what *Beaumont* said of worth wrapt up in rivelled skin, he saith of this, Who would go in to fetch it out? . . . For Mistresse T. there are in that, certaine *je ne scay quoys,* which none but those who have studied it can discover, and Sir *Anthony* shall hold his hand till Mr. *H.* comes to Town" (153). This suggests *L'Astrée,* maps of the court of love, and a whole range of precious foolery; at the same time, it is quite like the cryptic notes still to be found in high-school annuals suggesting romances in various states of repair.

"The Wine-drinkers to the Water-drinkers, greeting" gives us the Suckling not of the salon, but of the masculine world of the tavern, promising to send from the Bear "one of our Cabinet-Councel, Colonel *Young,* with some slight Forces of Canary, and some few of Sherry . . ." (154). It is directed to friends at Bath or some other watering place and is heavily facetious. The device of the letter is of formal diplomatic or military correspondence: "Whereas by Your Ambassador two dais since sent unto us, we understand that you have lately had a plot to surprize or (to speak more properly) to take the waters . . ." (153). The pun is typical of the whole. The "*Bear* at the *Bridge-foot*" was a tavern in Southwark at the end of London Bridge, popular with court wits. The letter is no more than a *jeu d'espirit*, but through it one can glimpse a bit of that tavern world inhabited by idle young gentlemen, wits, and poets. Inevitably the letter is clubbish and clannish.

That same quality is seen in the letter (No. 50) presumably to Thomas Carew with its little punning poem and rebus and a gloss following the verse: "In honest Prose thus: We would carry our selves first, and then our Friends, manage all the little Loves at Court, make more *Tower* work, and be the Duke of *B.* of our Age, which without it, we shall never be. Think on't therefore, and be assured, That if thou joyn'st me in the Patent with thee, in the height of all my greatness I will be thine, all but what belongs to *Desdemona*, which is just, as I mean to venture at thy Horse-race *Saturday* come seven-night" (155). The prose is not exactly "honest," rather it is that of the coterie and the private joke. But beyond this it is marked by a distinct exuberance. In these trivial letters to ladies, drinking companions, and cronies there is something of the bounce, verve, and bustle of a Mercutio.

The more clearly genre letters are almost as high spirited. **"A Letter to a Friend to diswade him from marrying a Widow which he formerly had been in Love with, and quitted"** (No. 51(a)) and the matching answer to it (No. 51 (b)), **"A disswasion from Love"** (No. 52), and **"To a Cosin (who still loved young Girles, and when they came to be mariageable, quitted them, and fell in love with fresh) at his fathers request, who disired he might be perswaded out of the humour, and marry"** (No. 53) belong to distinct epistolary types, examples of which can be found in Nicholas Breton's *Post with a Mad Packet of Letters.* In addition to the epistolary tradition the letters belong as well to the tradition of the paradox and the problem, such things as Donne's "That Women Ought to Paint" and "Why Hath the Common Opinion Afforded Women Soules?" immediately come to mind. These letters, then, are essays on set topics, the object being to explore the given topic in as ingenious, outrageous, and witty a fashion as possible.

The pair of letters on the pros and cons of marrying widows couples ingenuity with a mild sort of bawdry, presenting a kind of contest in *double entendre* and naturalistic cynicism: "After all this, to marry a *Widow*, a kind of *chew'd-meat!* What a fantastical stomach hast thou, that canst not eat of a dish til another man hath cut of it? Who would wash after another, when he might have fresh water for the asking?" (156). Against which is set the response to the problem in the answering letter: ". . . I'le marry a *Widow*, who is rather the *chewer*, then *thing chewed.* . . . *Wine* when *first broacht*, drinks not half so well as after a while *drawing*. Would you not think him a mad man who whilst he might fair and easily ride on the *beaten road-way*, should trouble himself with *breaking up*

of *gaps?* . . . 'Tis *Prince*-like to marry a *Widow*, for 'tis to have a *Taster*" (157, 158). The witty similitudes are the point of the letters. Ingenuity is everything; the purported subject really doesn't matter. Instead, what counts is the play with the subject, the ingenious variations upon it. The manner is everything.

"A disswasion from Love" is directed to *Jack,* who may or may not be Jack Barry. The last paragraph mentions Mistress Howard and the Earl of Dorset, suggesting that the letter was more than just an epistolary exercise. But the preceding seven paragraphs are written in a standard genre again found in Nicholas Breton's *Post with a Mad Packet of Letters.* At any rate, the letter, with its advice on how to stay out or get out of love, is hardly serious advice. Once more the subject is of slight importance; the demonstration of wit is what counts. The usual advice to travel is rejected in favor of frequent visits to the loved one, in hopes of catching her at her worst. He is advised to see as many other beautiful girls as possible, moreover:

> I would not have you deny your self the little things (for these Agues are easier cured with Surfets than abstinence;) rather (if you can) tast all: for that (as an old Author saith) will let you see

> *That the thing for which we wooe,*
> *Is not worth so much ado.*

(158, 159)

The tired cynicism is part of the comic pose and is a note frequently struck by Suckling.

The letter **"To a Cosin (who still loved young Girles . . .) . . ."** belongs to the opposite genre type from the preceding, that is, a persuasion to marriage rather than a dissuasion. However, Suckling varies the pattern by adding a dry postscript: "I should have persuaded you to marriage, but to deal ingenuously, I am a little out of arguments that way at this present: 'Tis honourable, there's no question on't; but what more, in good faith I cannot readily tell" (161). Suckling's cousin, Charles Suckling of Bracondale, may be the "Honest Charles" addressed in the letter; he appears to have married somewhat late and may have suffered from the Lolita syndrome attacked in the letter. "Honest Charles," however, is as likely to be a fictional addressee.

The comedy of the letter comes in large measure from the situation, but from the tone of cross, avuncular irritation as well: "Were there not fooles enow before in the Common-Wealth of Lovers, but that thou must bring up a new Sect? . . . Why the divel such yong things? before these understand what thou wouldst have, others would have granted. Thou dost not marry them neither, nor any thing else. 'Sfoot it is the story of the Jack-an-apes and the Partridges: thou starest after a beauty till it is lost to thee, and then let'st out another, and starest after that till it is gone too . . ." (160).

Throughout the whole runs a fashionable mix of libertine antifeminism: "Women are like Melons: too green, or too ripe, are worth nothing; you must try till you find the right one" (160). If one is about ready to cry with Millamant, "truce with your similitudes," one can still appreciate the ease of all this, its high spirits and complete control of a particular manner. Something like "voice" is difficult to locate and to describe in anything other than impressionistic and subjective terms. But the letters, however one puts it, do read very well aloud. There is a spoken quality to them in the patterns of the sentences, in the timing of the jokes. Chunks of them could be transferred to stage dialogue with little difficulty; this spoken quality is certainly a part of Suckling's "ease."

The two groups of love letters are so marked by this quality of ease coupled with craftsmanship—put another way, are so artificed—that a problem in dealing with them is in determining the extent to which they represent real feelings and are indeed love letters rather than exercises in the genre of the love letter. One letter is to Anne Willoughby, and there is no doubt that Suckling's attachment to her was financial rather than amatory. The letters fall into two groups. The earlier group is directed to Suckling's first cousin, Mary Cranfield; the later group to Mary Bulkeley, his "Dear Princesse" and presumably his Aglaura. Suckling's actual feelings for Mary Cranfield aren't known, and the letters really don't reveal much. The florid declaration in the first letter, dated October 30, 1629, "Let it suffice, that those countryes which I am now to visit, are but soe many faire roomes in a prison, The whole world it self, not yealding halfe that pleasure which your blest company can give!" (107) sets the tone for ensuing letters, and one is more inclined to read it as mere compliment than heartfelt emotion. The claim that his heart "hath been brought up under Platonicks, and knows no other way of being paid for service, then by being commanded more" (108) in the next letter is such palpable court flummery that one is tempted to think of all of the letters in that fashion. Yet in another letter (No. 3) there is enough sense of real discourse that the debate remains open. The letter is apparently written in response to a rebuke over gambling, something Suckling "hitherto beleeved . . . to be . . . in it self as meerly indifferent as Religion to a States-man . . ." and is acidic enough to be real: "And now, since I know your Ladyship is too wise to suppose to your self impossibilities, and therefore cannot think of such a thing, as of making me absolutely good; it will not be without some impatience that I shall attend to know what sin you will be pleased to assigne me in the room of this: something that has less danger about it (I conceive it would be) and therefore if you please (Madam) let it not be Women . . ." (109). There is not much of "Platonicks" here.

Little enough of the actuality of the relationship, then, can be drawn from the eight letters to Mary Cranfield, and after all what really matters is paramountey of style and manner above content and feeling. A very short letter (No. 6) apologizing for not writing demonstrates the skill with which Suckling is able to make the most empty of social notes into an artistic event, and, out of nothing, invent an airy something. He has not written, he says, because he

has nothing to say. This commonplace leads to the first witticism, a witticism set within the context of logical argument: "So, like Women that grow proud, because they are chaste; I thought I might be negligent, because I was not troublesom" (111). The finely balanced sentence has the effect of closure of a couplet in verse. If I could not rely on your goodness to forgive my neglect, I knew I could rely on your judgment, he goes on to argue. The compliment is effective precisely because it has the appearance of argument first and compliment second. Her judgment, he continues, will lead her to conclude that such trifles are of little worth and are not "necessary to the right honouring my Lady."

With this assertion he then moves to the concluding paragraph and the development of a witty paradoxical compliment that finishes the argument: "Your Ladyship I make no doubt, will take into consideration, that superstition hath ever been fuller of Ceremony then the true worship." The tightness of the prose, the careful design, the argumentative pattern, and the wit of it all bring the letter very close to verse. That is to say, its design, its compaction, its artifice belong to verse as much as to prose; all it lacks is rhyme and meter.

It is difficult to argue that the letters to Mary Bulkeley (if the letters assumed written to her actually were to her) are really much different from those to Mary Cranfield. If passion somehow equates with disorganization, these are not very passionate letters. In them one finds the same careful design, the crafting, and the feeling of distance that frequently comes with artifice. On the other hand, the affectionate epithet "Dear Princesse" and the assertions of the letters all point to a real feeling: "And oh! Why should I write then? Why should I not come my self? Those Tyrants, businesse, honour, and necessity, what have they to do with you and I? Why should we not do Loves commands before theirs whose Soveraignty is but usurped upon us? Shall we not smell to Roses 'cause others do look on? or gather them, 'cause there are prickles, and something that would hinder us?" (138). But finally to conclude much of Suckling's real feelings from passages such as this is a risky if not impossible task.

Letters to divers Eminent Personages reads in part the title page of the letters in the first edition of ***Fragmenta Aurea,*** and in ***The Last Remains of Sir John Suckling*** the title is ***Letters to Several Persons of Honor.*** Both titles suggest the social and even public character of the letters. They may imply, or at least one should recognize, as well the sort of expectation Suckling's contemporaries would have in reading such letters. They would not be reading for biographical reasons and certainly not for psychological reasons. They would hardly expect personal revelations, nor, as should be clear, would they find any. Instead, they would read the letters, quite simply, for the style. They would look for—and find—in the letters the same elegance, wit, and control they found in the poetry. Generally speaking, those letters in which something of a personal voice can be detected, for the most part those letters relating to serious military and political affairs, were not published in either *Fragmenta Aurea* or *The Last Remains.* The letters published in those works were those displaying their author at his public best. One doesn't look at Van Dyck portraits for revelation of character, but for brilliant portrayal of surfaces and for the creation of a particular world through his art. So too with Suckling's prose.

* * *

I. Romance: "a Pretty Plot . . . the Devils . . . and the Fighting"

The date of Suckling's romance comedy, *The Goblins,* is not exactly established. A reference in the play to Suckling's own poem **"A Sessions of the Poets"** fixes the composition as not before the autumn of 1637, while its appearance in a list of plays belonging to the King's Men in 1641 supplies the outer date by which it clearly was in existence.[8] Although it was revived a number of times after the Restoration, knowledge of its stage history is slight. Mrs. Knipp, an actress much admired by Samuel Pepys, danced in it; and he saw the last two acts of the play, reporting that it was "a play I could not make anything of by these two last. . . ."[9]

It is not very likely he would have made much more of it had he seen the play in its entirely. *The Goblins* is a confusing and chaotic play; the characters hardly slow down enough to be identified, and a goodly number of them are in disguise anyway. Like *Aglaura* it is written so that individual scenes are more important than the whole, but its action is less coherent and more episodic. Sir A. W. Ward, writing in 1899, found it "a production which defies—and as a drama hardly deserves analysis" and thought "the action . . . perfectly bewildering."[10] More recently Ruth Wallerstein, in an essay pointing out Suckling's use of Shakespearean dramatic techniques in *The Goblins,* concurred with this view, calling the play "almost chaotically disunified in tone and method."[11] The undoubted chaos of the play, however, may in large measure be attributed to its type. If it is also a silly play, it is not much sillier than a Broadway musical. Its silliness, moreover, is somewhat mitigated by a measure of wit and considerable stage liveliness.

No matter what is said in the play's defense, however, the action is undeniably confusing. The setting is Francelia at the end of a civil war. The Prince is in love with Sabrina, who is also loved by Samorat. Sabrina's brothers, however, unattractive young men called Philatell and Torcular, are opposed to Samorat's marital aspirations, preferring, for obvious political reasons, the Prince's candidacy. Their opposition is expressed dramatically as the play opens by their attempt to kill Samorat. Samorat is at a disadvantage until a stranger arrives on the scene, joins the fights, and evens the odds. It is later learned that the stranger, Orsabrin (his true identity unknown even to himself) is none other than the Prince's lost brother, who had been sent to safety at a dangerous point in the civil war between the Orsabrins and the Tamorens.

After some very busy fighting in which Samorat is slightly wounded and Torcular is presumed to have been killed by Orsabrin, the stage is cleared by the sudden appearance of a band of "*Theeves in Devils habits*" who chase off Samorat and Orsabrin and bind and carry away the wounded Torcular. A bit later Samorat informs Orsabrin that the thieves first appeared in the forest after the great battle between the Orsabrins and the Tamorens. They have patterned themselves somewhat after Robin Hood's band and entertain themselves by blindfolding their prisoners, carrying them off to their underground hideaway, forcing them to tell their life stories, and punishing or rewarding them according to their prisoners' merits. Given such occupations, it hardly comes as a surprise to find that the "Thieves" are, in fact, the remnants of old Tamoren's followers and are led by his younger brother, also called Tamoren. Moreover, the heir of the Tamorens, Reginella, an innocent girl modeled on Shakespeare's Miranda, lives with them, and, just as Tamoren intended her to do, falls in love with Orsabrin as soon as he is captured.

Such are the main outlines of the plot. The action involves the tying and untying of a series of narrative knots. Orsabrin and Samorat are taken prisoner, escape, and are taken prisoner again with astonishing rapidity. At last the proper recognition signs of romance are produced—"our Commission" and "the Diamond Elephant" (V, v, 166-67)—and the essential discoveries are made. The play ends with reconciliation and reunion. The marriage of Reginella and Orsabrin will unite the Tamorens and the Orsabrins; the civil war will be resolved. Sabrina will give the Prince another day to woo her, allowing Samorat and the Prince to stand as equal rivals. Orsabrin has the last joyous word:

> A Life! a Friend! a Brother! and a Mistress!
> Oh! what a day was here: Gently my Joyes distill,
> Least you should breake the Vessell you should fill.
>
> (V, v, 285-87)

The space between the agonized beginning and triumphant conclusion has been filled with escapes, disguises, duels, mistaken identities, social satire, witty chatter, love-talk, a few songs, and a bit of dance; in sum, a good deal of excitement and very little substance.

Both Prologue and Epilogue to *The Goblins* self-consciously relate it to the work of earlier playwrights. They both claim for the audience a modernity and sophistication unknown to the past. Today's audience, the Prologue declares, is superrefined and demanding:

> When *Shakespeare, Beaumont, Fletcher* rul'd the
>   Stage,
> There scarce were ten good pallats in the age,
> More curious Cooks then guests; for men would eat
> Most hartily of any kind of meat;
>
> (123, 3-6)

and goes on to complain of the new demand placed on playwrights for prologues and epilogues at a time when dramatic genius has flagged:

The richnesse of the ground is gone and spent,
Mens braines grow barren, and you raise the Rent.

(26-27)

The Epilogue claims "a pretty plot" for *The Goblins* and asserts that if a fool had been added to the devils and the fighting, it all would have been perfectly acceptable "and 't had bin just old writing." But now, the Epilogue concludes, even the slightest and least ambitious of plays will be critically torn apart by the supercensorious audience:

The ill is only here, that 't may fall out
In Plaies as Faces; and who goes about
To take asunder oft destroyes (we know)
What altogether made a pretty show.

(176, 21-24)

All this defensiveness may appear excessive and unwarranted; probably, however, it should just be seen as thoroughly conventional. The sense of the play's worth is nonetheless correct.

II. SHAKESPEARE AT A DISTANCE

"A pretty show" is finally just what *The Goblins* really is. Tamoren and his exiles vaguely suggest the Duke and his foresters in *As You Like It*. Sabrina mistakes Orsabrin for Samorat, a mistake highly pleasing to Orsabrin:

Shees warme, and soft as lovers language:
Shee spoke too, pretilie;
Now I have forgot all the danger I was in.

(II, i, 3-5)

The device is certainly not exclusively Shakespearean, but one is reminded of Sebastian happily mistaken by Olivia in *Twelfth Night*. Of course the most obvious Shakespearean parallel is to *The Tempest;* Reginella and Orsabrin are Suckling's version of Miranda and Ferdinand. Reginella asks at their first meeting:

Tell me what thou art first:
For such a creature
Mine eyes did never yet behold.

(III, vii, 79-81)

She is not even sure if she is a woman.

I know not what I am,
For like my selfe I never yet saw any.

(III, vii, 90-91)

In such a play as this credulity cannot be strained, but Reginella's innocence frequently shades over into undeniable simplemindedness.

In fact Reginella reminds one perhaps less of Miranda than of Sir William Davenant's masculine parody of Miranda, Gridonell, a great booby in *The Platonic Lovers* who has been raised totally apart from women by a fool-ishly cautious father. This careful upbringing by no means induces the chastity for which the father had hoped, but the reverse. Reginella is perfectly well behaved, but that she suggests Gridonell at all underscores the distance from Shakespeare in *The Goblins*. Nonetheless the Shakespearean echoes from *The Tempest* and other plays are clear and unmistakable. "I'le ticke you for old ends of Plaies" (III, ii, 52), the wit Pellegrin cries, and it is easy to see the game of literary allusion as part of the fabric of the play. An outrageous exemplar is Orsabrin's parody of Hamlet's most famous soliloquy:

To die! yea what's that?
For yet I never thought on't seriously;
It may be 'tis.—hum.—It may be 'tis not too.—

(III, iii, 1-3)

Orsabrin is in prison, his fortunes are at the ebb; the dramatic mood has been that of romantic melodrama, not comedy, but it is hard to imagine such lines not producing a roar of laughter from the sophisticated audience. Suckling admired Shakespeare, but his admiration did not preclude parody; nor did his attitude toward the materials of the play prevent him from deliberately shattering a mood for the sake of a joke.

All this is not to say that *The Goblins* is essentially and consciously a parody of Shakespearean romance, but rather that the relation of the play to Shakespeare is shifting and uncertain. Orsabrin breaks into lyric celebration after meeting Reginella:

But I'de carry thee where there is a glorious light,
Where all above is spread a Canopie,
Studded with twinckling Gems,
Beauteous as Lovers eies;
And underneath Carpets of flowry Meads
To tread on.

(III, vii, 98-103)

But Reginella cannot answer "O brave new world"; the world is too palpably the same. The proposed marriage of Reginella and Orsabrin will settle the civil division of Tamorens and Orsabrins but mechanically, with no larger overtones. The great Shakespearean themes of reconciliation and rebirth are absent. Ultimately *The Goblins* is no more Shakespearean romance than is John Fletcher's version of *The Tempest, The Sea Voyage*. The imitation of Shakespeare is finally limited to scenes, ideas, character types, in sum to bits and pieces, not to the broader informing Shakespearean spirit. When Samorat is arrested Philatell's response is to echo Othello:

I'st ee'n so? Why then,
Farewell the plumed Troops, and the big Wars,
Which made ambition vertue.

(IV, iii, 49-51)

The effect of the lines is to underline the distance of the dramatic world of *The Goblins* from Shakespeare.

Indeed, if one is to see the play as "something of what Shakespearean drama looked like to at least one intelligent courtier and gifted writer just before the closing of the theatres,"[12] the conclusion, then, must be that the surfaces were observed and not much more. The sensational and showy is caught, but there is no attempt to create the larger Shakespearean vision. Prospero's island and the whole world of Shakespearean romance supersedes reality because the metaphors are real and valid. The inadequacy of *The Goblins* as imitation of Shakespeare is the lack of overall metaphoric intent. The characters, the scenes, the action simply don't exist beyond their stage presence. Yeats's remark that "We should not attribute a very high degree of reality to the Great War"[13] might have puzzled Suckling, but it points to a fundamental difference between a minor artist like Suckling and a major artist like Shakespeare and to the limitations of *The Goblins.*

The Goblins is about the reconciliation of a postwar world. Francelia has suffered a civil war; the action of the play shows the resolution of the differences of the war. But it does so in an escapist fashion. It provides a momentary respite from the realities of the growing divisions in Charles I's kingdom and a facile vision of a happy ending. But the approaching war is always real, *The Goblins* only entertainment. The dream of *The Goblins* extends only to the immediate wish of the Caroline courtier for peace in his immediate political and social world. Prospero's island, on the other hand, is finally more real than the court to which he will return. *The Goblins* is "a pretty show," no more, no less. If its limits are recognized, its particular strengths can be more easily located.

III. Scene, Satire, and Song

As with *Aglaura,* then, the strengths of *The Goblins* are with individual dramatic moments rather than with the design of the whole. The play opens with a duel; and sword fighting, wounds, and chases are never long absent. *"Flyes into the woods severall wayes pursued by Theeves in Devils habits"* (I, i) is a typical stage direction. Ardelan and Piramont are courtiers to whom young Orsabrin was entrusted in exile. When they are taken by Tamoren and the "thieves" in I, iii, a major bit of exposition is accomplished. The audience learns that young Orsabrin is alive, that he has been living (in proper romance fashion) with pirates, and that he is unaware of his true identity. But the exposition, important as it is, is clearly subordinate to the stage action. The "thieves" enter with Torcular to the sound of a horn. Torcular is taken off to a surgeon to have his wounds treated, and with more noise and bustle another entrance brings more thieves with more prisoners.

Tamoren welcomes them by singing:

> *Bring them, bring them, bring them in,*
> *See if they have mortall Sin,*
> *Pinch them, as you dance about,*
> *Pinch them till the truth come out.*

(I, iii, 7-10)

The song provides a stage direction for the ensuing stage business; and when Peridor hesitates, the direction is explicit, "Pinch him." The exposition is accomplished in some thirty lines and is followed by a second entrance of more of Tamoren's band, this time with a drunken poet in tow. The poet has no functional part in the play. In this scene he provides the opportunity for a drunken song with which to end the scene. He appears again in IV, v for some satirical treatment; it is likely that the poet is meant to be Ben Jonson and was so recognized by the court audience, but the direction of the satire is uncertain. The character exists in the play solely for his own independent possibilities for laughter and not for an integral dramatic purpose. In similar fashion in the scene just described the noise, the pinching, and the horseplay are finally more important than exposition.

The poet has just staggered off the stage when Orsabrin reappears, befuddled from having mistaken a bawdy house for a tavern. He is immediately set upon by a tailor and two sergeants who try to arrest him for debt. He drives them off, but is forced to flee himself when the constable and others arrive. He is chased from the stage and immediately reenters, this time in the garden of "a handsome house." The house is Sabrina's, and he is mistaken now for Samorat. When Orsabrin kisses Sabrina, she responds with Platonic delicacy, rebuking him for his "saucy heat." "S'foot!" he responds, "'tis a *Platonique:* / Now cannot I so much as talke that way neither" (II, i, 15-16). This little topicality is really the center of the scene. It is no more than a light satiric touch, but it serves as a reminder that Francelia and the court of Charles I are not so distant; from time to time the wishful never-never land is converted into the more immediately recognizable. The central concerns of the play, however, are not with anti-Platonism or other court satire, but simply with entertainment.

"Oh you fill a place about his Grace, and keep out men of parts, d'you not?" (III, i, 19-20) surely expresses Suckling's own sour view of the court in which he was always outside the inner circle of power and influence. When Philatell urges the Prince to pretend that he will spare Samorat and then to execute him, he does so in terms that may reflect Sir John's continued bitterness over the disgrace of his uncle, the Earl of Middlesex:

> 'Tis but now owning of the fact,
> Disgracing for a time a Secretarie
> Or so—the thing's not new—

(V, ii, 15-17)

The remark is a sharp critique of statescraft, but it, like the other satirical elements in the play, is essentially an aside. As was true with *Aglaura,* portions of *The Goblins* are essentially free-standing comic or satiric turns, doing nothing to advance plot or theme, but providing moments of fine language, wit, or topical commentary.

Nashorat and Pellegrin, the witty courtiers, discuss the virtues of country versus city women, a theme which will much engage the dramatists of the Restoration, and they do so in a fashion which forecasts the wit of Wycherly and of Congreve.

NASHORAT.

> 'Tis a rare wench, she 'ith blew stockings: what a complexion she had when she was warme—'Tis a hard question of these Country wenches, which are simpler, their beauties or themselves. There's as much difference betwixt a Towne-Lady, and one of these, as there is betwixt a wilde Pheasant and a tame.

PELLEGRIN.

> Right:—There goes such essensing, washing, perfuming, dawbing, to th' other that they are the least part of themselves. Indeed there's so much sauce, a man cannot taste the meat.

NASHORAT.

> Let me kisse thee for that; by this light I hate a woman drest up to her height, worse that I do Sugar with Muskadine: It leaves no roome for me to imagine: I could improve her if she were mine: It looks like a Jade with his tayle tied up with ribbons, going to a Fayre to be sold.

> (IV, iii, 1-14)

The dramatic prose skillfully conveys the sense of gentlemen talking. Their talk is on a set theme, a cynical variation on the praise of simplicity and artlessness. Herrick comes quickly to mind, but the artificial and the natural are skillfully combined to create the illusion of the "conversation of gentlemen" that Dryden so admired in Suckling. Passages such as this represent what is perhaps the most outstanding aspect of *The Goblins* and of Suckling's dramatic achievement in general—that is, the creation of a truly effective dramatic language capable of conveying the illusion of witty, genteel conversation.

The songs of *The Goblins* are undistinguished—two for pinching and four for drinking—but they too, along with the dance in Act IV, iii, are still another reminder of Suckling's sense of the play as a series of sometimes discrete scenes and stage events. Nashorat's "A health to the Nut browne Lasse," concluding:

> *She that has good Eyes,*
> *Has good Thighs,*
> *And it may be a better knack.*

> (III, ii, 87-89)

is the best in the play, a lively drinking song with a dash of bawdry.

The Goblins, finally, does not show Suckling to advantage as a serious writer of comedy. That is, *The Goblins* really has no enlarging thematic concerns. It is an entertainment and pretends to nothing more. It is an escapist comedy wishfully looking to a romantic world in which civil wars are resolved by forgiveness, marriage, and returned

princes. Behind it can be sensed a hard edge of satiric feeling which unfortunately never emerges save in bits and pieces. The reading of Shakespeare reduces him to moments of parody and the broadest sort of imitation. *The Goblins,* considered as sustained romantic and comic vision, is a failure, but its surfaces are bright and shiny. Individual scenes are clearly the work of a craftsman of no little skill and sometimes of real genius. Considered on its own terms as "a pretty show," a mélange of stage excitement, song, and witty dialogue, *The Goblins* is a successful entertainment. Moreover, the closer *The Goblins* pushes to witty, quasi-realistic comedy, to the comedy of cynical, bright, conversational courtiers, in short to the sort of comedy to be most fully developed after the Restoration, the better it is. *The Goblins* does show that Suckling could turn out a perfectly competent and playable bit of stage entertainment, a claim that can't be made in all honesty for some other court playwrights and which indicates Sir John's healthy recognition of the demands of public stagecraft.

IV. THE TRAGIC VOICE: *BRENNORALT*

Brennoralt, Suckling's last play, shows his stagecraft even more to advantage. Admittedly *Brennoralt* is hardly a pleasing play by modern standards, but it reasonably well constructed, is filled with considerable action, and makes at least some attempt at distinctive characterization. It seems most likely that he wrote the play after nis return from Scotland and the First Bishops' War. The political and military allusions in it provide the play with additional historical interest. It is first mentioned under its alternate title, *The Discontented Colonel,* in a list of plays belonging to the King's Men, which were not to be published without permission.[14] On April 5, 1642, however, the publisher Francis Egglesfield entered *The Discontented Colonel* in the Stationer's Register and a quarto edition was published. Undoubtedly Egglesfield was anxious to capitalize on the play's topicality.

Although the substance of the plot is borrowed from Jean Pierre Camus's French romance *L'Iphigene,* published in Paris in 1625, and is set in Poland, Suckling clearly picked the story because of its application to the English scene; the rebellion of the Lithuanians against their Polish king obviously parallels the rebellion of the Scottish Presbyterians against their English king. Brennoralt, the discontented colonel of the title, is a conventional heroic soldierlover in the tradition of Shakespeare's Antony and Chapman's Bussy d'Ambois. However, his topicality and even his rank, not nearly so elevated as that of his prototypes, suggest that he most probably represents a recognizable contemporary figure, perhaps Colonel George Goring, the daring, ambitious, and reckless cavalry officer, favorite of the queen, and governor of Portsmouth, who eventually betrayed the Army Plot to Parliament; or, even more likely, Brennoralt may represent Suckling himself.[15] Whatever the identification of the discontented colonel, the play moves between extremes of realistic topicality and the fantasies of romantic tragedy.

V. The Plot: "Breasts! / By All That's Good, a Woman!"

The world of **Brennoralt** divides its attention, as does so much Caroline drama, between love and war. Brennoralt, the discontented loyalist colonel, is in love with Francelia, the daughter of the Pallatine of Mensecke, one of the leading rebels. Unfortunately for Brennoralt, Francelia is betrothed to a gallant rebel officer, Almerin. This rather standard romantic situation is complicated by the presence of Almerin's friend, Iphigene, Pallatine of Plocence. Not only is Iphigene on the loyalist side, but she is a girl disguised as a man and has been so disguised all her life. She, of course, is in love with Almerin; and given such a design, it is hardly surprising that when she is taken prisoner by the rebels Francelia falls in love with her. Although in Camus much is made of the possibilities for smirking over transvestitism, Suckling ignores the opportunity and handles Iphigene's peculiar circumstances decorously.

The play opens with a rebel attack on the royalists in which the rebel Almerin is taken. Iphigene visits him in prison and laments in pastoral fashion:

> O *Almerin*; would we had never knowne
> The ruffle of the world! but were againe
> By golden banks, in happy solitude;
> When thou and I, Shepheard and Shepheardesse,
> So oft by turnes, as often still have wisht,
> That we as eas'ly could have chang'd our sex,
> As clothes; . . .
>
> (I, iv, 1-7)

This speech underlines one of the major peculiarities of the play. Almerin is unaware that Iphigene is a woman, knowing him/her simply as a dear friend, their friendship being of that sort exalted by so much Renaissance literature. No one, in fact, save Iphigene, knows the truth of her identity. Her sex is revealed only in the last act. Until that point there is nothing in the dialogue that would indicate to the characters or to the audience that Iphigene was a woman in disguise unless the remarks of Almerin's lieutenant colonel, Morat, and one of his soldiers are intended as a hint:

Morat.

> Doest thinke he will fight?

Soldier.

> Troth it may be not:
> Nature, in those fine peeces, does as Painters;
> Hangs out a pleasant Excellence
> That takes the eye, which is indeed,
> But a course canvas in the naked truth,
> Or some slight stuffe.

Morat.

> I have a great minde to taste him.
>
> (III, iii, 22-29)

This would, as would many other moments in the play, supply substantial dramatic irony, but that irony can exist only at the expense of surprise at the final revelation of Iphigene's true identity. Suckling's audience may have been sufficiently aware of Iphigene's story that they could chortle at appropriate moments, but the ironies are not established by action or text. Consequently one can't give Suckling overmuch credit for not making jokes about transvestitism when the audience really doesn't have sufficient information to understand them.

When Almerin escapes and Iphigene is taken prisoner by the rebels, the scene moves to the rebel fortress where Francelia immediately falls in love with Iphigene: "Would I had ne're seen this shape, 't has poyson in't. / Yet where dwells good, if ill inhabits there?" (II, iii, 27-28). When Brennoralt learns that Francelia is to marry Almerin, his love drives him to the rebel citadel—"Enough, / I am a storme within till I am there" (II, iv, 91-92)—where he manages to interview Francelia in her bed. Brennoralt waxes eloquent and surprisingly reflective at the sight of her sleeping beauty:

> So Misers looke upon their gold,
> Which while they joy to see, they feare to loose:
> The pleasure of the sight scarse equalling
> The jealousie of being dispossest by others;
> Her face is like the milky way i' th' skie,
> A meeting of gentle lights without name.
> Heavens! shall this fresh ornament
> Of the world; this precious lovelines
> Passe with other common things
> Amongst the wasts of time, what pity 'twere.
>
> (III, iv, 19-28)

All his eloquence wins him, however, is Francelia's declaration that she respects Brennoralt and does not love Almerin.

Brennoralt manages to get back to the royalist camp, and an assault is launched on the rebel fortress. In the midst of the royalist attack Almerin encounters Francelia and Iphigene together in a compromising situation. Francelia has just given Iphigene that popular love token of the Renaissance, a bracelet of her hair. In his jealous rage Almerin stabs Iphigene and Francelia. Iphigene, knowing she must die and believing that the truth should be told, confesses her sex. Almerin is understandably incredulous and with a furious "Ha, ha, ha, brave and bold!" (V, iii, 51) he charges at her again. Iphigene, however, is able to gasp out the sad truth that her father had threatened to abandon her mother unless she produced a male heir. After a succession of failures the desperate stratagem was adopted. The last girl, Iphigene, would be raised as a boy. Poor Iphigene concludes her pathetic tale and adds a further confession before she faints:

> If now thou findst that, which
> Thou thoughtst a friendship in me, Love, forget it.
> It was my joy,—and—death.
>
> (V, iii, 67-69)

Almerin goes to her aid and discovers conclusive proof of the truth of Iphigene's story:

> —Breasts!
> By all that's good, a woman!—*Iphigene*.

(V, iii, 72-73)

Iphigene recovers from her faint to add a footnote to her story, explaining that she courted Francelia to keep Almerin from her. Almerin then confesses that throughout their long friendship he had often wished Iphigene were a girl and declares he would have loved her truly had she been a girl, instead of a boy, friend:

> Canst thou doubt that?
> That hast so often seen me extasi'd,
> When thou wert drest like woman,
> Unwilling ever to beleeve thee man?

(V, iii, 87-90)

At last Almerin goes for a physician, but it is too late; Francelia dies. Brennoralt and the royalist troops break into the room. He dismisses the soldiers and discovers the dead Francelia. He then kills Iphigene straightaway, assuming him/her to have been Francelia's murderer. Almerin returns and the two begin to fight, pausing only to kiss their dead loves:

ALMERIN.

> Even so have two faint Pilgrims scorch't with heat
> Unto some neighbour fountaine stept aside,
> Kneel'd first, then laid their warm lips to the Nymph
> And from her coldnesse took fresh life againe
> As we do now.

BRENNORALT.

> Lets on our journey if thou art refresht.

(V, iii, 224-29)

After this pretty and bizarre sentiment the heroes resume their combat until Almerin falls wounded. The king enters, and Almerin manages to explain the situation once more before he dies. The king, after appropriate acknowledgment of the peculiar and unhappy situation, turns to political matters to offer the victorious Brennoralt the forfeited possessions and titles of the leading rebels, but no note of happiness is allowed to intrude. Brennoralt refuses in terms that the audience would understand as referring to Charles I's own inept handling of rewards:

> A Princely gift! But Sir it comes too late.
> Like Sun-beames on the blasted blossomes, doe
> Your favours fall: you should have giv'n me this
> When't might have rais'd me in men's thoughts, and made
> Me equall to *Francelia's* love: I have
> No end, since shee is not—
> Back to my private life I will returne.
> Cattell, though weary, can trudge homewards, after.

(V, iii, 277-84)

A final melancholy word from the King and the play ends:

> . . . we have got
> The day; but bought it at so deare a rate,
> That victory it selfe's unfortunate.

(V, iii, 289-91)

VI. CHARACTER, POLITICS, AND ENTERTAINMENT: "REAL" WORLDS

Brennoralt certainly doesn't improve with the telling of it, but the same can be said of many plays. Dramatic representation can transform the silliest stuff. **Brennoralt,** we should recall, was successfully revived at the Restoration. Samuel Pepys saw it four times, once calling it "a good tragedy that I liked well."[16] Recognition that Suckling's plays were acceptable and more to his contemporaries may not help a modern reader to like them more, but it should at least cause the reader to ask what they found to admire and what Suckling was attempting in a play like **Brennoralt.**

Alfred Harbage's comment concerning **Brennoralt** that ". . . its political allusions are purely incidental; its heroic-romantic unreality makes it kin with typical Cavalier drama"[17] isolates two main factors which account for the play's success in its own time. The unreality which can seem too absurd to a modern reader was, after all, precisely what the Caroline audience wanted. One thinks of Van Dyck's equestrian paintings of King Charles—noble, elegant horses with monumental heads, necks, chests, and graceful, dainty legs that could never carry the weight of such a beast, and the king himself, handsome, refined, royal beyond all monarchal dreams. On the stage as in painting and in poetry, what mattered was not the realism of portrayal but its idealism and elaboration.

Brennoralt is nominally a tragedy, but the ending is contrived and not very well contrived. It depends totally on chance and circumstance. It has nothing to do with character; and finally, it evokes no particular response associated with tragedy. Indeed, the last major speech is given to Brennoralt, and it shifts the focus of the play from the deaths of Iphigene, Francelia, and Almerin to a contemporary political question, that is, the use and timing of royal rewards and favors.

Obviously the ending is no accident. Instead of concentrating on the deaths and reaction to the deaths, the high point of the play's ending has been in the duel of the two lovers and their tender first and last kisses. The tragic content has not mattered; the point is in the pose, the decoration, the elaboration of love found and lost—not on the emotion and meaning of the tragic finale, but on the manner. Brennoralt exits still discontented, still melancholy, his last words unequivocally returning the audience to the unheroic, unromantic realities of the court and the troubled politics of the day.

At this point one may ask to what extent the political allusions in **Brennoralt** are really "incidental." Suckling was attracted to Camus's *L'Iphigene* because of the potentials in the parallelism of the Lithuanian-Polish rebellion to the Scottish-English rebellion. The girl disguised as a boy is a device that is standard Renaissance fare, but Suckling does not seem much interested in the situation itself. It is a paradox upon which one may embroider and little more. There is no attempt to understand in any serious fashion the consequences of such a fate as Iphigene's. The possibilities for treatment of the major themes of appearance and reality are not exploited. Politics, then, may be incidental to the love story, but not to the play as a whole and not to Sir John's concerns. One might almost claim that the political allusions are the real heart of the play, the telling of the love story becoming merely the vehicle for political observations.

At any rate, it is not the plot per se that matters, but how the plot, traditional and familiar (in Caroline terms) as it is, is treated—how, in other words, it is ornamented. Iphigene and Francelia meet in the garden of the rebel fortress. Iphigene enters first, alone, and weeps, lamenting her fate and establishing the tone of the scene:

> Tempests of wind thus (as my stormes of griefe
> Carry my teares, which should relieve my heart)
> Have hurried to the thankelesse Ocean clouds
> And showers, that neetled not at all the curtesie,
> When the poore plaines have languish't for the want,
> And almost burst asunder.—
> I'le have this Statues place, and undertake
> At my own charge to keepe the water full.
>
> (III, i, 10-17)

The concluding figure is a baroque commonplace, as Professor Beaurline points out, and can be found in poems by Donne, Jonson, and Marvell;[18] it is not too much to say that the scene almost exists in order to develop the figure. The passage emphasizes the formal, nearly emblematic quality, of the whole scene. Neither Iphigene nor Francelia is possessed of any qualities that might be identified as individual characteristics; so the scene cannot be and should not be viewed from the point of view of character. What remains is embellished language and a stylized presentation of incident.

The formal characteristics of the love story serve to set off and heighten the political commentary and certain realistic scenes. Brennoralt is a hard-liner, advocating stern measures against the Lithuanian rebels:

> If when great *Polands* honour, safety too,
> Hangs in dispute, we should not draw our Swords,
> Why were we ever taught to weare 'em Sir?
>
> (III, ii, 66-68)

The application to the Scottish rebels is clear enough. Miesla, one of the King's counselors, adopts the same contemptuous tone toward the issues of the war found in Suckling's letters:

> . . . Religion
> And Liberty, most specious names, they urge,

> Which like the Bils of subtle Mountebankes,
> Fill'd with great promises of curing all,
> —Though by the wise,
> Pass'd by unread as common cosenage,
> Yet, By th' unknowing multitude they're still
> Admir'd and flock't unto.
>
> (III, ii, 74-81)

Clearly, Suckling, always outside the real center of power in Charles's court, saw **Brennoralt** as a way of publicly stating his political views. Any fair reading of **Brennoralt** must admit its propagandistic function. All of the political allusions are greatly emphasized because they are set in an atmosphere of heroic and romantic ideality.

Similarly emphasized is the sparkling conversation of the witty and cynical Cavaliers under Brennoralt. These officers provide a genuine glimpse of the camp life of the Cavalier and offer a sharp contrast to the romantic fantasy of the heroic-love plot. In one of the liveliest, most brilliantly conceived scenes in the play, the Cavaliers engage in a drinking and extempore poetry contest.

GRAINEVERT.

> Trouble not thy selfe, childe of discontent: 'twill take no hurt I warrant thee; the State is but a little drunke, and when 'tas spued up that that made it so, 'twill be well agen, there's my opinion in short.

MARINELL.

> Th' art i' th' right. The State's a pretty forehanded State, and will doe reason hereafter. Let's drinke and talke no more on't.
>
> (II, ii, 1-6)

The great issues are casually dismissed; there is no point in worrying; they are soldiers, not thinkers. All one can do is drink and, as Grainevert does, sing:

> *Shee's pretty to walke with:*
> *And witty to talke with:*
> *And pleasant too to thinke on.*
> *But the best use of all,*
> *Is her health is a stale*
> *And helps us to make us drinke on.*
>
> (II, ii, 13-18)

The scene moves in sprightly rapidity with tags of Shakespeare, witty repartee, and song following song.

It is fine, lively theater, essentially the stuff of musical comedy, but above all it provides a sharp and welcome relief from the high-flown language and sentiment of the romantic-heroic plot. This is not to say that these insouciant Cavaliers are literally realistic portraits of Suckling's fellow royalists, but that this scene and others like it belong generically to realistic comedy. The carefree gaiety, the *sprezzatura* of the Cavaliers, moreover, establishes something of the court tone, if not the actuality, at least the kind of behavior and talk to which one might aspire.

The two-sidedness of **Brennoralt** reflects the division of Cavalier society. The easy vacillation from witty, graceful cynicism and urbane disengagement to ornate, inflated heroic romanticism defines an inescapable aspect of the court of Charles I.

Still another opposition to the idealized romance of the main plot is found in the libidinous conversation of the Cavaliers. Their lubricity, however, avoids downright ribaldry and is transformed into high comic art, as when Grainevert eloquently embroiders on the theme of a beautiful young girl to his appreciative and increasingly randy companions:

GRAINEVERT.

> Ah—a sprightly girle about fifteen
> That melts when a man but takes her by the hand!
> Eyes full, and quick; with breath
> Sweet as double violets,
> And wholesome as dying leaves of Strawberries.
> Thick silken eye-browes, high upon the fore-head;
> And cheeks mingled with pale streaks of red,
> Such as the blushing morning never wore—

VILLANOR.

> Oh my chops; my chops.

(IV, vi, 10-18)

The scene is pure interlude, an opportunity for elegant variations on themes of beauty and sex. It ends with news of approaching combat and a song by Grainevert in which he complains (again advancing one of Suckling's own views) of the disadvantages of a limited war and asks for unlimited and unrestricted warfare:

> *This moiety Warre,*
> *Twilight,*
> *Neither night nor day,*
> *Pox upon it:*
> *A storm is worth a thousand*
> *Of your calme;*
> *There's more variety in it.*

(IV, vi, 48-54)

With a song on their lips, then, the Cavaliers move off to battle, all pure pose, but political propaganda as well. The romantic idealism of the stance of the dashing Cavalier is oddly mixed with the serious political-military position Suckling advances in **Brennoralt**. Beyond all this, however, one can't help but admire the bright surface of the scene and its skillfully contrived illusion of reality.

VII. PLAYWRIGHT-COURTIER: CONCLUSION

The three completed plays are, when all is said and done, a fairly substantial achievement when one considers that Sir John was an amateur playwright whose time was also occupied in military expeditions, court politics, and certainly gambling, drinking, and wenching. His talents were such that the professional playwright Richard Brome found it worth his while to satirize Suckling and Suckling's friend, Sir William Davenant, in *The Court Beggar.*[19] Both Suckling and Davenant were fair game for satirists for a variety of reasons, but Brome specifically includes Suckling's dramatic activities along with his gambling and abortive soldiering. That the professional should be sufficiently exercised over the playwriting of this elegant amateur to attack it is testimony to Suckling's skill and the threat he posed.

Aglaura is best seen as essentially spectacle, as a sort of overgrown masque, court entertainment. As such it made its splash and served the taste of the times. Both *The Goblins* and **Brennoralt** show a similar ability to meet the tastes of the day; Suckling knew how to write a play in the fashionable court manner. The manner is foreign and may be difficult for the modern reader to appreciate. The plays are written within a set of conventions, and modern theatrical conventions are at a considerable distance from those of the court of King Charles I. Artificiality, after all, is usually pejorative in the twentieth century, a connotative shift the seventeenth century would find surprising and almost incomprehensible. Suckling mastered the dramatic conventions of the day. He was able to create worlds of extravagant adventure, high romance, noble poses, and polished rhetoric. Within the conventions of Cavalier drama Suckling created the desired world of artifice to which one could retreat from the realities of increasing political and religious strife and from the daily commonplaces.

Beyond the mastery of the conventions of his day, he achieved something more that the modern reader can more directly and more sympathetically admire. He had a strong sense for the individual dramatic scene, for the theatrical moment, in particular for the comic turn, for the development of a joke, and for the setting of a song. This sense of the dramatic moment is closely linked with Suckling's distinct abilities for comic realism. When he writes heroic-romantic sentiment and bombast, Suckling sounds like a dozen other Caroline playwrights. On the other hand, when his Cavaliers chatter unbuttoned in tavern and camp, their dialogue is distinctive and brilliant. In those scenes, filled with song and witty conversation, Suckling's dramatic genius is found. His voice is the authentic voice of imagined gentlemen, urbane, artfully artless, wry, and humorous. Fine of itself, the realistic comic dialogue plays wryly against the heroic and romantic conventions. The aspects of Suckling's theater retained and admired by the Restoration were, of course, just that creation of the ideal conversation of gentlemen and the sureness of his comic touch. It is useless to speculate on his development as a playwright if he had not fled to France and died, if the war had not arrived, and if the theaters hadn't been closed, but at least one must recognize a substantial potential as a writer of social comedy. But **Brennoralt** was written in about 1640, and Sir John Suckling was dead a year later. As it is, in his three completed plays Suckling met his own standards of entertaining spectacle, wrote some brilliant comic scenes, and demonstrated a growing dramatic potential.

Notes

1. Letter No. 55, Clayton, p. cxiv, says the letter is "worth printing as possibly though not very probably by Suckling." It is stylistically very unlike Suckling.

2. *A Literary History of England,* ed. Albert C. Baugh (New York, 1948), p. 659.

3. For the detailed argument see Clayton, pp. 314-16. The reference to Van Dyck in the passage quoted from the letter might be construed as supporting a later date. Van Dyck painted Suckling probably between 1636 and 1639. However, the reference does not necessarily imply being painted by Van Dyck, and Suckling might have visited the artist's studio when he was in Europe.

4. Earl Morse Wilbur, *A History of Unitarianism in Transylvania, England, and America* (Cambridge, Massachusetts, 1952), p. 180. Clayton, p. 337, has a full and useful note on Socinianism.

5. Aubrey, p. 85.

6. H. John McLachlan, *Socinianism in Seventeenth-Century England,* p. 65, n. 2, quoted by Clayton, p. 337.

7. Morse, p. 183.

8. Beaurline, p. 274

9. *Diary,* May 22, 1667, quoted by Bentley, V, 1211.

10. *History of Dramatic Literature to the Death of Queen Anne* (London, 1899) II, 349.

11. "Suckling's Imitation of Shakespeare," *Review of English Studies,* XIX (1943), p.290.

12. *Ibid.*

13. Quoted in Richard Ellman, *Yeats, The Man and the Masks* (New York, 1958), p. 278.

14. The history of the play's publication and production comes from Beaurline, pp. 288-94, and Bentley, V, 1207-1209.

15. Beaurline, p. 289, states that Herbert Berry, Suckling's biographer, believes so.

16. *Diary,* March 5, 1667/8, quoted by Bentley, V, 1208.

17. Harbage, p. 113.

18. Beaurline, p. 299.

19. R. J. Kaufman, *Richard Brome, Caroline Playwright,* "Suckling's New Strain of Wit" (New York and London, 1961), 151-68.

Selected Bibliography

Primary Sources

Aglaura. London: Thomas Walkley, 1638.

The Discontented Colonell. London: Francis Eaglesfield, n. d.

Fragmenta Aurea. London: Humphrey Moseley, 1646.

The Last Remains of Sir John Suckling. London: Humphrey Moseley, 1659.

Sir John Suckling's Poems and Letters from Manuscript. Ed. Herbert Berry. London, Ontario: *University of Western Ontario Studies in the Humanities,* 1960.

Aglaura. London: Thomas Walkley, 1638; facsimile reprint, London: Scolar Press, 1970.

The Works of Sir John Suckling, The Non-Dramatic Works. Ed. Thomas Clayton. Oxford: Oxford University Press, 1971.

The Works of Sir John Suckling, The Plays. Ed. L. A. Beaurline. Oxford: Oxford University Press, 1971.

Secondary Sources

Anselment, Raymond A. "'Men Most of all Enjoy, When Least They Do': The Love Poetry of Sir John Suckling." *University of Texas Studies in Literature and Language,* XIV (1972), 17-32. A useful and perceptive study which puts Suckling's "cynicism" in perspective.

Beaurline, L. A. "'Why So Pale and Wan': An Essay in Critical Method." *University of Texas Studies in Literature and Language,* IV (1963), 553-63. A stimulating approach to the critical problems raised by simple as opposed to complex poetry.

Bentley, Gerald Eades. *The Jacobean and Caroline Stage.* Oxford: Oxford University Press, 7 vols., 1940-1968. A monumental work, basic to the study of Jacobean and Caroline drama.

Berry, Herbert. "A Life of Sir John Suckling." Unpublished Ph.D. thesis. Lincoln, Nebraska: University of Nebraska, 1953. A most valuable study, to be supplemented by the life in *The Non-Dramatic Works.*

Fletcher, J. B. "*Précieuses* at the Court of Charles I." *Journal of Comparative Literature,* I (1903), 120-53. An early background study of literary fashions at court.

Flosdorf, James William. "The Poetry of Sir John Suckling: A Study of His Versification, Rhetoric, and Themes." Unpublished Ph.D. thesis. Rochester, New York: University of Rochester, 1960. Especially informative regarding technical aspects of Suckling's poetry.

Freehafer, John. "*The Italian Night Piece* and Suckling's *Aglaura.*" *Journal of English and Germanic Philology,* LXVII (1968), 249-65. *Aglaura's* role in the history of changeable stage scenery.

Harbage, Alfred. *Cavalier Drama.* New York: Modern Language Association of America, 1936. Highly useful historical and critical discussion of the drama and dramatic milieu of the period.

Henderson, F. O. "Traditions of *Précieux* and *Libertin* in Suckling's Poetry." *English Literary History,* IV (1937), 274-96. A helpful background commentary on literary fashions, asserting Suckling's libertine position.

Lynch, Kathleen. *The Social Mode of Restoration Comedy.* New York: Macmillan, 1927. Especially valuable in its delineation of the social and intellectual background of the drama.

Martz, Louis L. *The Wit of Love.* Notre Dame, Indiana: University of Notre Dame Press, 1969. Four essays on Donne, Crashaw, Carew, and Marvell. The essay on Carew is useful for a reading of Suckling. Handsomely illustrated.

Miner, Earl. *The Cavalier Mode from Jonson to Cotton.* Princeton: Princeton University Press, 1971. A very helpful analysis of the major themes and attitudes defining the Cavalier mode. The chapters on "The Social Mode" and "Love" are especially pertinent to Suckling.

Richmond, Hugh M. *The School of Love: The Evolution of the Stuart Love Lyric.* Princeton: Princeton University Press, 1964. A scholarly analysis of the background and development of the love lyric.

Skelton, Robin. *The Cavalier Poets.* "Writers and Their Work," No. 117. London: Longmans, Green, 1960. Critical appreciations of Suckling and his fellows.

Smith, A. J. "The Failure of Love: Love Lyrics after Donne." *Metaphysical Poetry, Stratford-Upon-Avon Studies,* 11 (1970), 41-71. A perceptive discussion of changing attitudes toward love as seen in the lyrics after Donne.

Summers, Joseph H. *The Heirs of Donne and Jonson.* London: Chatto and Windus, 1970. Examines the poetic heritage of Donne and Jonson and devotes part of a chapter to Suckling's relationship to them.

Wallerstein, Ruth. "Suckling's Imitation of Shakespeare," *Review of English Studies,* XIX (1943), 290-95. *The Goblins* as exemplifying a Caroline view of Shakespeare's dramatic art.

Walton, Geoffrey. "The Cavalier Poets." *From Donne to Marvell.* Ed. Boris Ford. London: Penguin Books, 1956. Brief survey of the Cavaliers, with a negative glance at Suckling.

Warnke, Frank J. *Versions of Baroque, European Literature in the Seventeenth Century.* New Haven and London: Yale University Press, 1972. A scholarly analysis of the elements of the baroque style which provides a useful perspective for Suckling and the Cavalier poets.

Wedgwood, C. V. "Cavalier Poetry and Cavalier Politics." *Velvet Studies.* London: J. Cape, 1946. Valuable social and critical commentary on the Cavalier world.

Thomas Clayton (essay date 1982)

SOURCE: Clayton, Thomas. "'At Bottom a Criticism of Life': Suckling and the Poetry of Low Seriousness." In *Classic and Cavalier: Essays on Jonson and the Sons of Ben,* edited by Claude R. Summers and Ted-Larry Penworth, pp. 217-41. Pittsburgh: The University of Pittsburgh Press, 1982.

[In the essay that follows, Clayton examines four of Suckling's lesser known poems in order to illustrate his argument that the standard critical image of Suckling as a minor poet is shortsighted and limited.]

"Natural, easy Suckling"—with two lines of "Our upon it, I have loved / Three whole days together" and two of "Why so pale and wan, fond lover? / Prithee why so pale?"—is so apt and usual an opening for a discussion of Suckling that I have now used it myself, naturally. But the phrase is not my focus, though it is tempting. In fact, it is remarkable and somewhat disquieting how much functional—and often reductive—literary history and criticism can be effected by orotund phrases and obiter dicta. T. S. Eliot cramped Grierson's "metaphysical poets" into the planisphere of "the massive music of Donne" and "the faint pleasing tinkle of Aurelian Townshend," and F. R. Leavis had at Milton with such élan that his opening thrust has been serving in paraphrase for epitaphs and otherwise ever since: "Milton's dislodgement, in the past decade, after his two centuries of predominance, was effected with *remarkably little fuss*"—but Leavis's (and Eliot's) reports of Milton's demise were greatly exaggerated.[1] As for Suckling, Millamant's formula is ubiquitous, and so telling, as far as it goes, that it seems to tell all, and seeming often leads to misbelieving. But the spirit of the phrase, and Congreve's words for that spirit, are very meet and right, and they are welcome.

In identifying and placing any poet, the received contexts of literary history and interpretation include among others the primarily diachronic ones of sources and influences, the poet's place in the tradition or traditions, and "originality"; the synchronic ones of the poet's friendships and enmities, literary affinities and disaffinities, and relations generally with social and intellectual contemporaries at home and abroad; and the achronic or rather polychronic ones within the poems—matters of idea, scope, genre, form, style, and the like—and between poems and the other arts, and their audiences, contemporary and succeeding. All of these and other contexts have their claims upon the attention of serious students of literature. But in the real world, where practical exigency and individual psychology compete with ideals and theoretical commitments, it is usual for these same students to cultivate plots—or undertake "projects"—of expediency or preference within the gardens of the whole, and cover their seeds and tracks with whatever soil they can muster. The plot I am primarily concerned with here is one in which many kinds of study begin and some end, within the poems and in the field of their interrelationships, where the primary engagement is between the poem and its readership, however delimited.

In particular, I want to say a few things that have not been said before, or said in this way, in favor of a poet usually treated condescendingly or with moralizing disapproval when addressed at all, and to comment on theoretical considerations as occasion arises. Rare indeed today is the temerity and spirit of Tucker Brooke, who wrote in 1948 that "of all the 'Cavalier' group Suckling had the most interesting mind and the largest potentialities for poetry."[2] I tend to agree with him, but invidious comparison of poets serves all ill, and I confine myself here to commenting on aspects of Suckling's art as a beginning of the end of extending appreciation of his range, not to try to make a major poet of a minor poet, but to let the minor be a poet in an age of such virtuosity that "minor" unfairly belittles achievements of some magnitude: the earlier seventeenth century was a peerless period for the lyric. This is a fact commonly lost sight of in the circumstances, almost exclusively academic, in which "we" today read—or, rather, often do not read—poets like Suckling, unless, eventually, as academic period-specialists, by which time some have become sufficiently accustomed to the mill that Suckling and others are only so much more grist to grin and bear. More's the pity, for reasons T. S. Eliot gives in "What Is Minor Poetry?" For "there are a great many casements in poetry which are not magic, and which do not open on the foam of perilous seas, but are perfectly good windows for all that"—and better than magic casements for some purposes, eminently close to home and ranging, too.[3]

In 1880, in "The Study of Poetry," Matthew Arnold characterized a poet as "a real classic, if his work belongs to the class of the very best," and "poetry" as "a criticism of life." He was surely right about "poetry" as "a criticism of life," and this formulation distinctly improved upon the one he had given in 1879 in his study of Wordsworth, where poetry was "at bottom a criticism of life."[4] "At bottom" is idiomatic and innocuous, of course, but there is a hint of obliviousness in his failing to notice this potential double entendre, though it is as nothing to that in a recent exposition of sociobiology, where the author asks, "What is the essence of maleness? What, at bottom, defines a female?"[5] Still, the habitual heights of Arnold's later vision inclined him to presbyopia: he made "true classic" status depend entirely upon "high seriousness" and "absolute sincerity," and he denied the first rank to Chaucer and Burns. Burns's poetry, he wrote, has "truth of matter and truth of manner, but not the accent of poetic virtue of the highest masters. His genuine criticism of life, when the sheer poet in him speaks, is ironic." Arnold was a circumspect critic, and one can even concede secondary rank to Chaucer and Burns, in the context of his reasons; but both Chaucer and Burns are too good, taken all in all, to stand in the second rank, so there must be some weakness in the reasons: the depreciation of irony, perhaps, and still more the earnest insistence on "high seriousness" and its supposed source in "absolute sincerity," which can never be known but by appearances and God.

If Arnold had an attenuated appreciation of irony, his Victorian antitype, Oscar Wilde, did not. In "The Critic as Artist," Wilde declared that "the primary aim of the critic is to see the object in itself as it really is *not*." Furthermore, Arnold's annunciation of poetry's advent as the agency to succeed Christianity in the office of salvation was answered in effect in "The Decay of Lying," where Wilde prophesied the second coming of the archliar: "some change will take place before this century has drawn to its close. . . . Bored by the tedious and improving conversation of those who have neither the wit to exaggerate nor the genius to romance, tired of the intelligent person whose reminis-

cences are always based upon memory, whose statements are invariably limited by probability, and who is at any time liable to be corroborated by the merest Philistine who happens to be present, society sooner or later must return to its lost leader, the cultured and fascinating liar. . . . Whatever was his name or race he certainly was the true founder of social intercourse. For the aim of the liar is simply to charm, to delight, to give pleasure. He is the very basis of civilized society."[6]

Wilde was no less serious than Arnold, but their ways of seriousness are different, whether we prefer Arnold's lofty lectern or Wilde's playful Socratism. What *ever* would the mature Arnold have replied to the suggestion of Wilde's Cyril that we "go and lie on the grass, and smoke cigarettes, and enjoy nature"? Certainly something printable. Wilde noted that "in Falstaff there is something of Hamlet, in Hamlet there is not a little of Falstaff." He himself played Falstaff to Arnold's Hamlet, and Suckling played something of both to his court, his age, and his posterity. It is appropriate as well as variously significant that in the great Van Dyck portrait Suckling is holding a Shakespeare Folio open to *Hamlet*.

Suckling's art has seldom been denied, but his seriousness or sincerity is often in question, I think because it is rarely direct or obvious, never solemn or portentous, seldom conspicuous or high. If not to be high is to be low, if not to be Theseus is to be Bottom, then Suckling's seriousness is low; and, though not invariably, it is typically skeptical and ironic. Northrop Frye's low mimetic or ironic modes do not usefully accommodate him, but there is aptness in Frye's insistence that "'high' and 'low' have no connotations of comparative value."[7] Suckling readily accepts—requires—ceremony, convention, decorum, circumstance, and sometimes even pomp. At the same time, he deplores—burlesques and ironizes—presumptuousness, affectation, vanity, and hypocrisy, violations of ethical and societal norms hardly confined to monarchies and aristocracies, or even "bourgeois democracies." The irony of manners of Suckling's muse is sui generis, and, if that phrase is audibly reminiscent of hog-calling, I cannot think his flexible wit would find it offensive or even impertinent, not least because country matters are among his proper business.

As a denizen of anthologies and literary histories, Suckling is customarily accorded the magisterial generalizations that put him in his place, and fleeting quotation of the odd couplet, quatrain, or stanza that keeps him there. The wages of restricted experience is a stereotype, one consequence of an anthology-tour of English literature without side trips or in-depth exploration: this is Tuesday, so it must be Herrick, Carew, Suckling, and Lovelace.[8] It seems to me both regrettable and a fact, especially recently, that premodern—even pre-"postmodern"—poems and poets have come to be little read and more overstood than understood, often for the worse part of "overstanding," a term recently used by Wayne Booth in defense of "Alien Modes" of criticism.[9] A corollary is a collective short shrift that is depriving even the major poets of their due—the seventeenth century's Donne, Herbert, Milton, Marvell, and Dryden, if one accepts the canon of twenty major English poets given by A. E. Dyson.[10] So much, or rather so rather so little, for Ben Jonson *and* the Cavalier poets. Here, instead of offering a survey in little or a general, guided tour of Suckling,[11] I shall attend in some detail to four differently representative poems, each inviting a distinct critical perspective and treatment. It seems appropriate, too, to comment briefly on Suckling's two relatively "major" poems.

"A Ballad upon a Wedding" was probably written in 1637, the same year in which Suckling completed **"The Wits"** and *An Account of Religion,* when he was twenty-eight. **"A Ballad"** has been much praised and is among the most often discussed of his poems. Admired and often imitated in the seventeenth century, it belongs to a genre of Suckling's own invention that I have called the "rusticated epithalamion," a marriage poem that satirically rejects the received conventions of High Pastoral in favor of a (West Country) rural vision of nuptial events which concludes with a salty, invigorating, down-home emphasis on the mighty leveler, physical love:

> At length the candle's out, and now
> All that they had not done they do:
> What that is, who can tell?
> But I believe it was no more
> Than thou and I have done before
> With Bridget and with Nell.

A jocular dramatizing of a theme Herrick epigrammatizes as "Night makes no difference 'twixt the priest and clerk; / Joan as my lady is as good i' th' dark." "Rusticated" is useful also as the quasitechnical term for temporary banishment either from the city or, particularly, from university: to be rusticated is to be "sent down," and sending down is Suckling's characteristic mode of irony in sending up serious subjects, not to dismiss them but to reflect and refract them in comic and ironic perspectives.

"The Wits" is likely always to be better known as **"A Sessions of the Poets,"** its almost certainly editorial title in *Fragmenta Aurea* (1646), published five years after Suckling's death. It has been appreciated and depreciated by turns, depending mainly on the *kind* of poem it is supposed to be. And it has been still more often quoted, especially by literary historians and biographers adopting Suckling's characters in little. Thanks to Suckling's gift for telling miniature caricatures, we have Carew's hard-bound muse, Davenant's lack of qualification for the laureateship in wanting a nose, the little Cid-ship of strong-lined Sidney Godolphin, and, best of all, Suckling himself, so finely sketched in consonance with the character—the *ethos*—of his fictions and with some of the facts of his life that the caricature is often taken for the whole historical person as well as the poet. If, as "all that were present there did agree, / A laureate's muse should be easy and free" (37-38), then in **"The Wits"** Suckling demonstrates his qualifications even as he declines to stake his claims,

an artfully self-effacing gesture that identifies the wit as *poeta generosus*: Cavalier noblesse oblige and an instance of graceful presence in absentia.

Suckling's supple conjunction of "fixed" form and ostensibly spontaneous expression is found in these two "major" poems as in most others. In **"A Ballad,"** a hearty rustic effortlessly expresses himself with the aid of the constraints of the *rime couée* supplied him. In **"The Wits,"** bob-and-wheel stanzas fuse the looseness of four-stress lines with an epigrammatic with that is at once acerbic and congenial, deflating and constructive: a graceful group-monumentalizing of a convocation of competing wits given narrative life with a master craftsman's articulation of individual figures, including his own (73-78):

> Suckling next was called, but did not appear,
> And straight one whispered Apollo in's ear,
> That of all men living he cared not for 't,
> He loved not the Muses so well as his sport;
>   And
> Prized black eyes, or a lucky hit
> At bowls, above all the trophies of wit.

It often goes unnoticed that Suckling is present in absence—he "did not appear," but here he is indeed—and also that his character is supplied by a whisperer in Apollo's ear, a telltale, a gossip. Nevertheless, one cannot resist the testimony, because it fits so well the identity or the stereotype we seek and find, conveying bonhomie and sprezzatura to some, and other qualities to others, often changing with the times—from "a gambler, wencher, and general reprobate in the court of Charles I" in the first edition (1962) of the *Norton Anthology* to "the prototype of the Cavalier playboy" in the fourth (1979), for example. The stereotype itself invites discrimination in assessing what Suckling rejects here, especially "all the *trophies* of wit," the tokens and memorials of vanity or vulgarity, or both. Suckling "loved not the Muses so well as his sport"—process, action, living, society, and play. He "*prized* black eyes," with the flash of vital attraction, and "a lucky hit at bowls," not the victory or the winnings, but the very moment of happy chance. There is no profundity in these synecdoches of sociable pleasure, engagement, and joie de vivre, but they have their charms, and the harm in them is slight enough.

Suckling is thrice-judicious in his absence from the sessions—the formal trial—of the wits, first because he has "better things to do," but also because, on a different plane, he can the easier *be* present in his absence. The narrator retails a whisperer's report, which gives credit even with detraction, not surprisingly, since Suckling the poet is characterizing Suckling the delinquent; the wink in the characterization invites a special recognition from the eye of the beholder. Finally, Suckling was right to absent himself on any account: an alderman ultimately wins the laurel, because Apollo—of all deities to sell out!—declared that "'twas the best sign / Of good store of wit to have good store of coin" (107-08). So much for wisdom, wit, and art in the world's ways, a view not very welcome but abundantly in evidence throughout recorded history, as well as in literary reflections on lived experience. Suckling is often a keener observer of society and values than he is given credit for by persons more favorably disposed to Malvolio's garb than Feste's.

The first two of my four representative poems are scarcely given short shrift, let alone riddling shrift, by critics: **"Upon St. Thomas's Unbelief"** and **"An Answer to Some Verses Made in His Praise."** The first, a juvenile sestain (written c. 1626, when Suckling was sixteen or seventeen), is the first poem in the Oxford English Text; the second is #75 of the seventy-eight canonical poems.[12] One would readily associate neither poem with such standard anthology-pieces as **"A Ballad upon a Wedding," "Out upon it,"** and **"Why so pale and wan,"** by which Suckling is best or only known. But these two poems are equally though differently representative, perhaps especially so in being evidently lesser poems.

"Upon St. Thomas's Unbelief"

Faith comes by hearsay, love by sight: then he
May well believe, and love whom he doth see.
But since men leave both hope and charity,
And faith is made the greatest of the three,
All doctrine goes for truth; then say I thus,
"More goes to heaven with Thomas Didymus."

Suckling's abiding concern with religious belief is evident especially in eleven juvenile poems (about an eighth of the canon) and *An Account of Religion by Reason,* which he wrote four years before his death at thirty-two, in 1641. Engaging and characteristic aspects of **"Upon St. Thomas's Unbelief"**—aside from the expression of a will to faith, which modern readers will take or leave as such— are its energy and ingenuity, its muted paradox and irony, its apparent sincerity and earnestness, and Suckling's self-identification with Doubting Thomas, implicit here and explicit in another poem, **"Faith and Doubt,"** where it is said that

Our faith, not reason, must us steer. . . .
Each man is Thomas here, and fain would see
Something to help his infidelity,
but I believe; Lord, help my faithless mind
and with St. Thomas let me pardon find.

From a modern perspective, the suggestions of existential angst are more evident and for most more compelling than the theological issues in the poem, but those issues are there, in the implied distinctions between "the faith believed in" (*fides quae creditur*) and "the faith whereby belief is reached" (*fides qua creditur*), which figures prominently in **"Faith and Doubt";** and between "unformed faith" (*fides informata*) and "faith formed by love" (*fides formata caritate*).

The address of **"Upon St. Thomas's Unbelief"** is closely related to the account of Thomas's doubting, seeing, and believing in John 20:24-29: Suckling's **"Faith comes by hearsay"** in part interprets the Gospel, where "the other disciples said unto" Thomas, "we have seen the Lord. But he said unto them, Except I shall see . . . I will not believe." And Suckling's "love [comes] by sight" reflects Thomas's response when the Lord reveals himself and says, in clear and present "hearsay," "be not faithless, but believing. And Thomas answered and said unto him, my Lord and my God," thus becoming the first explicitly to confess Christ's divinity. Suckling emphasizes the "eloquence" of sight, the primary sense proverbially associated both with truth and conviction and with love, for who ever loved that loved not at first sight? thomas saw, believed, loved. But "since" the Ascension, willful men neglect two of the theological virtues, hope and charity; and make faith "the greatest of the three," like Lutheran believers in justification by "faith only" (the eleventh of the Thirty-Nine Articles without the twelfth, **"Of Good Works"**). By that reasoning, "All doctrine goes"—or passes current—"for truth," leading the young Suckling to the conclusion that "More goes"—that is, more go—"to heaven with Thomas Didymus" than with heterogeneous believers, many of whom must believe in vain, because those who differ in belief cannot all be right.

In fact, the poem seems to reach the same conclusion simultaneously by two different routes, using a striking duality of expression to make the case that they also deserve who only stand and wait in faithful doubt. One argument, that already paraphrased, concludes that faithful doubt is superior to dubious credence. The other has it that, if "All doctrine goes for truth" indeed, and "faith only" is acceptable to God as truth, then Thomas "More goes to heaven with Thomas Didymus"—the More who was no martyr for Suckling and his Anglican contemporaries, much less for the "true" believers in "faith only."[13] St. Thomas almost displaces St. Paul as guide and model here, and if any was patron saint to Suckling's skepticism it was Thomas Didymus the Doubter.

Second, **"An Answer to Some Verses Made in His Praise."**

The ancient poets and their learned rhymes
We still admire in these our later times
And celebrate their fames; thus though they die,
Their names can never taste mortality:
Blind Homer's muse and Virgil's stately verse,
While any live, shall never need a hearse.
Since then to these such praise was justly due
For what they did, what shall be said to you?
These had their helps: they writ of gods and kings,
Of temples, battles, and such gallant things,
But you of nothing; how could you have writ
Had you but chose a subject to your wit?
To praise Achilles or the Trojan crew
Showed little art, for praise was but their due.
To say she's fair that's fair, this is no pains:
He shows himself most poet that most feigns.
To find out virtues strangely hid in me,
Ay, there's the art and learned poetry.
To make one striding of a barbed steed
Prancing a stately round (I use indeed
To ride Bat Jewel's jade), this is the skill,

> This shows the poet wants not wit at will.
> I must admire aloof, and for my part
> Be well contented, since you do't with art.

"An Answer" is a pleasing disavowal of self-importance, with a skeptical eye on current celebrity by contrast with posthumous renown, whose evergreen laurels are secure. Suckling offers one solution to "the problem of nothing,"[14] too, celebrating the poet as both maker and liar, and reconciling Aristotle and Plato in effect, though this is not an explicitly philosophical, much less weighty, poem—a modest kind one can appreciate in our own age, over-stocked as it sometimes is with theory and Sir Oracles ("when I ope my lips, let no dog bark").

Homer and Virgil live by their own celebrations of "Achilles or the Trojan crew" and by encomiums extolling them; yet they showed "little art," because they "had their helps" in "gods and kings" and "gallant things," whose "praise was but their due." By contrast, Suckling's encomiast has made something of nothing and shown himself the greater poet, because "he shows himself most poet that most feigns," a tautological truism that resolves a problem of great antiquity with a flourish of paradox and ambiguity—or, if one likes, duplicity and polysemy. Sidney had written that the poet "nothing affirms, and therefore never lieth," as a poet. So Suckling's encomiast does, since he "writ . . . of nothing," thus affirming it. Again according to Sidney, "it is that feigning notable images of virtues, vices, or what else . . . which must be the right describing note to know a poet by," a Renaissance redaction of mimesis notably Aristotelian in identifying poetry not with verse but with mimesis and poesis. In *As You Like It* Touchstone favors Audrey with the tidings that "the truest poetry is the most feigning, and lovers are given to poetry; and what they swear in poetry may be said as lovers they do feign" (3.3.19-22).

Unlike Sidney's, Suckling's formal purpose is not to argue in defense of poetry, but to contribute a witty poetical instance in the apothegm applied: "To find out virtues strangely hid in me, / Ay, there's the art and learned poetry." And "to *make* one striding of a barbed steed / Prancing a stately round (I use indeed / To ride Bat Jewel's jade), this is the skill, / This shows the poet wants not wit at will." It is hard to imagine when or where Suckling's customary mount would have been "Bat Jewel's jade," with its amusing rustication of the Cavalier, nor do I know who, if anyone out of this fiction, that worthy, Bat Jewel, was: perhaps an otherwise unsung competitor of Thomas Hobson, the Cambridge carrier, offering choices even worse than Hobson's. The point is that the poet has *made* a noble equestrian figure of Suckling on a draft horse. LeSueur's statue of Charles I on horseback (1633) now at the top of Whitehall and Van Dyck's painting in the National Gallery (c. 1635) come to mind, whether they came to Suckling's or not; the nobility of horsemanship had its antiquity long before Suckling's day. The genial last couplet wittily and gracefully asserts Suckling's prescribed role as admiring spectator—"I must admire aloof, and for my part / Be well contented"—together with the accomplished fact of performance in his own artful expression of "artless" appreciation: he is audience articulate; the last word is his *and* his encomiast's, "since you do't with art," the art of the poet's showing through Suckling's telling, text and performance two in one.

"An Answer" merges aesthetic and philosophical concerns with colloquial familiarity through the intermedium of a social genre tinged with shades of Great Tew, where John Earles "would frequently profess that he had got more useful learning from his conversation . . . than he had at Oxford."[15] It is a formal mimesis of a spontaneous conversational expression of gratitude and admiration; refined into graceful informality, it complements the praised work of translating rustic equitation into Cavalier urbanity, giving to airy nothing a knightly bearing and a place.

Not surprisingly, **"Why so pale and wan, fond lover?"** has received its meed of analysis and praise, most substantially in L. A. Beaurline's well-known essay, "'Why So Pale and Wan': An Essay in Critical Method."[16] Beaurline's study differs considerably from the other two major studies of Suckling of the past two decades, though all three belong to critical analogues of seventeenth-century analytical and poetical modes. Raymond Anselment's essay on "The Love Poetry of John Suckling" is an instance of what could be called "promenade" criticism, an appreciative survey of sundry flowers—about seventeen, to be specific.[17] Charles L. Squier's volume, by contrast, is an example of the "topographical" survey, which is naturally more extensive and aims at summary comprehensiveness.[18] Beaurline's analogues would be found rather in the sphere of natural philosophy and scientific investigation, and the scrutiny of telling detail, as "Critical Method" in part suggests. The essay is—happily, I think—less methodological than critical, an invaluable study that is the only detailed close reading of a poem by Suckling I know of. Does anyone *not* know the **"Song,"**

> Why so pale and wan, fond lover?
>   Prithee why so pale?
> Will, when looking well can't move her,
>   Looking ill prevail?
>   Prithee why so pale?
>
> Why so dull and mute, young sinner?
>   Prithee why so mute?
> Will, when speaking well can't win her,
>   Say nothing do't?
>   Prithee why so mute?
>
> Quit, quit, for shame, this will not move,
>   This cannot take her;
> If of herself she will not love,
>   Nothing can make her:
>   The Devil take her.

Beaurline's central "contention is that the term *elegant facetiousness* ['defined historically,' after Quintilian's *facetus*] best illuminates this poem, for it fits the peculiar tone of the song, the air of the speaker, the quality of the language, and the color of our emotional reaction." He goes on to argue that the poem's meanings and effects depend prominently on its identity and place as a song sung within a play, *Aglaura,* where it has special dramatic significance. There the song has a "double audience":

> it is sung in Act IV . . . by a gallant named Orsames, a young "anti-platonic" lord . . . who . . . does not sing the song to a fond lover; rather he sings it to the platonic ladies, Semanthe and Orithie. . . . After he sings, he says that this was a bit of advice given ["foure or five yeares agoe," 4.2.32] to a friend fallen into a consumption, and Orithie says that she could have guessed it was the product of Orsames' brain. . . . To be sure, most Elizabethan plays use songs strictly for ornament, but in this play Suckling explicitly connects the song with the dialogue; the rhetorical situation, therefore, presupposes the presence of the ladies. . . . The doubleness of the rhetorical situation is one of the reasons why this poem is so charming and playful. It gives us, the general readers or *third audience,* a special detachment, and it probably contributes to the conventional character of the speaker. The whole of the reader's relation to the poem is like a window-peeper watching an eavesdropper hearing a conversation—

a witty way of characterizing the regresses that would lead eventually to "we are such stuff as dreams are made on."

One would like to see left *in* what Orsames says in full in 4.2.31-32, that this song was "a little foolish counsell (Madam) I gave a friend of mine *foure or five yeares agoe,* when he was falling into a Consumption" (italics mine).[19] Willa McClung Evans interpreted Orsames's lines to mean that "the musical setting . . . would appear to have been written several years previous to the performance of the play and was already familiar to the audience,"[20] and Beaurline himself had earlier referred to Orsames's lines as perhaps being "Suckling's way of apologizing for using an older piece of his verse."[21] What is in question is the literary identity—or identities—of the **"Song,"** and its history bears on its poetical, dramatic, and critical status. It is reasonable for Beaurline to emphasize "the whole of the reader's relation to the poem" as it is apprehended in and through the play, but it is somewhat misleading to imply that the poem takes its primary if not sole identity from this relation. "Suckling explicitly connects the song with the dialogue," or rather the reverse, but the connection identifies the poem as a "dramatic lyric" only when it occurs *within* the play. Suckling could have provided the contextualizing dialogue long after he wrote the poem, and there is nothing *in* the poem that spells *Aglaura.*

Whenever **"Why so pale and wan"** was written, it appears in *Fragmenta Aurea* as a poem (and **"Song"**) in its own right, and it *is* an autonomous poem when so presented and received. Set to music, sung, and heard, it becomes an art-song. And it acquires—and may have first acquired—its identity and place as part in a dramatic nest of spheres within spheres when written into a play and sung to an audience within the play that is beheld by an audience witnessing the play. This state of artistic affairs it shares in part with Jonson's poem—and "Volpone's"— "Song to Celia" ("Come my Celia, let us prove"), a case still more complicated by its intimate relationship with Catullus 5, "Vivamus, mea Lesbia." In his edition, William B. Hunter, Jr., implicitly emphasizes the treble identity by giving Ferrabosco's music together with the poem and noting that "this song appears in *Volpone* III.vii. 155-83, where *Volpone uses it*" (italics mine).[22] Ian Donaldson notes in his edition: "Sung to Celia by Volpone . . . ; *in dramatic context,* a more sinister invitation than its Catullan model" (italics mine).[23]

Both editors suggest the distinction that needs to be made between the poem as poem, as art-song, and as song within a play. Suckling's song and Jonson's are made to be "dramatic lyrics" by their incorporation in a special context: neither poem in itself implies an ontologically distinct world beyond the rhetorical situation, or "heterocosm," of the poem-in-itself, *except* by the wisdom of hindsight, which purports to find "in" the poem external referents due not to its content but to its location. As Claude J. Summers and Ted-Larry Pebworth have noted, "even without knowledge of its original dramatic context in *Volpone,* readers cannot fail to grasp Jonson's satiric mode here."[24] Jonson's poem may *seem* more explicitly related to Volpone's than to an anonymous speaker's situation, but details within the poem take on particular reference in relation to the surrounding context that they do not have—or need—without it. For example, "Or his easier ears beguile" requires no antecedent for "his" because it is obvious from the poem's other details that "he" is "the husband"; the lyric monodrama makes its own necessary and sufficient sense.

The "root level" is the poem itself—within reason "the object as in itself it really is," subject to understanding, "overstanding," and misunderstanding by readers, *sine quibus non.* The other elements entering into combination with the poem are external and theoretically incidental, however different a poem's meanings and effects may be when it ceases to be the "whole" of a reader's experience and becomes a *part* of another whole, combining with music to make a song, or with a variety of elements to make a dramatic lyric *in* Suckling's *Aglaura.* In relation to song, a type of such combinations of elements, the issues have been treated in depth in Elise Bickford Jorgens's essay "On Matters of Manner and Music in Jacobean and Caroline Song": "at every level—meter and rhythm, versification and syntax, and formal and thematic structure—when there is a conflict between the formal and the semantic organization, a musical setting directs the listener's perception toward one or the other and lessens his awareness of the artful interplay between them designed by the poet. . . . The 'song-like' state for a poem, then, is one in which a single line of development serves both matter and manner and can be formalized in music."[25]

This is the case, she says, with Jonson's "Still to be neat" (*Epicoene*), which is "clearly song-like," and with Shakespeare's "Sigh no more, ladies, sigh no more" (*Much Ado*):

"if Sidney, or Jonson, or Donne" or Suckling "calls a poem **'Song,'** whether it was designed for or ever appeared in a musical setting or not, we expect it to conform in some identifiable way with the conventions of the musical lyric." This generalization is no doubt sound enough even if many poems' titles were not supplied by the poets themselves, as seems to have been the case. By contrast, Jonson's poem in *Cynthia's Revels,* "Thou more than most sweet glove," is not songlike. "Although Jonson calls it 'Song,' that title must surely be taken as a conceit"; it "could of course be sung. But it breaks as many of the conventions as it embodies." Likewise, Carew's "Parting, Celia Weeps" is "simply not a suitable poem for musical setting. A through-composed setting could make rational sense of it, but only at the expense of its formal poetic structure. And since the poetic conventions of the period dictate that those features of formal structure remain as a visible and audible frame, as Carew obviously intended that they should, a setting that cannot do both is missing a significant feature of the poem"; Henry Lawes's "musical setting has virtually destroyed the poet's tenuous but altogether appropriate balance between versification and syntax." In short, the qualities of a *poem,* whether "song-like" or not, begin—and end—in the poetic art of the poem as "creation through words of orders of meaning and sound."[26]

In his "Essay on Critical Method," Beaurline gives a detailed exposition of the dialectic of the poem as an expressive mimesis centering on "the strategy of the speaker," whom he characterizes as a worldly-wise, formally "libertine" exponent of "playful cynicism," whose counsel in the third stanza he describes thus: "At that point where force is needed, Suckling's" poem "has force. When speaking well will not 'take' (i.e. charm) a lover or a friend, a man must change and speak bluntly. The gallant [speaker] not only recommends 'speaking well,' but his own words are a model of how to speak well and a demonstration of when to be blunt. Both his words and his actions show the value of ease, brevity, urbanity, agreeableness, elegant facetiousness, and all the other ornaments of wit." Beaurline gives an admirable exposition of the qualities of the poem in itself and its modes of operation in *Aglaura,* but he leaves the force and wit of the conclusion to interpret as well as speak for themselves, as indeed they do. But they also invite comment, first to the effect that the speaker does *not* say that "a man must change and speak bluntly"; it would be odd if he did, since doing so would almost certainly prove as inefficacious as ungracious. This seems to rest on a misunderstanding of the last line of the second stanza—"Prithee why so mute?"—which is concerned not with a need to speak out but with the futility of silence (like *pale*ness in the first stanza) as a gambit; in fact, in the third stanza the would-be lover is urged to give up, move on, and leave her—not, with Gertrude, to heaven, but—to hell.

The argument of the master of experience to his novice is this: when neither the "fond lover" 's "looking well" *or* "ill" and "pale" can "move her" (stanza 1), nor the "young

sinner" 's "speaking well" *or* "saying nothing" and staying "mute" can "win her" (stanza 2), then he should

> Quit, quit, for shame, this will not move,
>   This cannot take her;
> If of herself she will not love,
>   Nothing can make her,
>   The Devil take her.

The redoubled "quit," each "quit" for an antecedent stanza and inquiry, as it were, is rhetorically felicitous as well as forcefully imperative, and the final three lines epitomize the whole poem. If **"Why so pale and wan"** were a freshman essay, one might admonish Suckling for a vague use of "This," but it refers, plainly enough, to the entire game of courtship epitomized by typical moves in the first and second stanzas. "When" (3 and 8) and "If" (13) hold the identical "linear" as well as dialectical position within stanzas, as temporally and conditionally emphatic expressions of the cause. The conclusion is certain: "Nothing can make her," an elliptical locution frequently *mis*understood in recent years through the application of current colloquial usage, but perhaps an occasion for "overstanding" that both William Empson and Wayne Booth might countenance, though one would hope not.

"The Devil take her" is the poem's pièce de résistance. If "nothing can make her" love, may she go to the devil: let "the Devil take her"—bear her away to have her as the subject of his nether reign and to hold as the object of his rude affection, *le droit sinistre du seigneur.* Or simply and keenly as Suckling has it: may "the Devil take her" to hell and "take her" himself, enjoying the love she selfishly withholds from the persistent but unsuccessful suitor addressed by the speaker in and of the poem.

There are many ways of interpreting and evaluating the ethics, politics, and sociology, as well as the aesthetics, of the relationships and situation, but most would agree that the fictionalized sentiment is consistent with "normal" and "natural" frustration in analogous circumstances: if one can't have her, him, it, whatever—to hell with the same; the perennial case of the fox's grapes, Aesopically speaking.

"Sonnet 2" is also a standard anthology-piece, but one that often draws fire for its supposed cynicism, ugliness, brutality, licentiousness, and crudity—bad enough qualities, but not so bad as Suckling fares in a Puritan assault upon him as "a scum of ungodliness from the seething pot of iniquity."[27] The poem is frequently compared invidiously with its partial source, Donne's "Community," which Charles L. Squier finds "hardly any less brutal" in concluding, "Changed loves are but changed sorts of meat, / And when he hath the kernel eat, / Who doth not fling away the shell?" Here is Suckling's poem:

> Of thee, kind boy, I ask no red and white
>   To make up my delight,
>   No odd becoming graces,
> Black eyes, or little know-not-whats, in faces;

Make me but mad enough, give me good store
Of love, for her I court,
                    I ask no more:
'Tis love in love that makes the sport.

There's no such thing as that we beauty call,
    It is mere cozenage all;
      For though some long ago
Liked certain colors mingled so and so,
That doth not tie me now from choosing new;
If I a fancy take
              To black and blue,
That fancy doth it beauty make.

'Tis not the meat, but 'tis the appetite
    Makes eating a delight,
      And if I like one dish
More than another, that a pheasant is;
What in our watches, that in us is found,
So to the height and nick
            We up be wound,
No matter by what hand or trick.

If a poem like this is to be given a fair hearing, it helps to recall that it *is* a fiction and to make due adjustments in perspective: it is neither a hymn for the sons of Belial nor a versified slice of autobiography. David Hume supplied appropriate guidance, mutatis mutandis, over two centuries ago in "Of the Standard of Taste": "every work of art, in order to produce its due effect upon the mind, must be surveyed in a certain point of view, and cannot be fully relished by persons, whose situation, real or imaginary, is not conformable to that which is required by the performance. . . . A critic of a different age or nation . . . must place himself in the same situation as the audience, in order to form a true judgment," and should place "himself in that point of view, which the performance presupposes." Dr. Johnson wrote to much the same purpose in his *Preface to Shakespeare*: "Every man's performance, to be rightly estimated, must be compared with the state of the age in which he lived, and with his own particular opportunities." With respect to the ethics of art and the politics of sin in real life and history, I am content to invoke Elizabeth Burton, who notes in *The Jacobeans at Home* that "the pleasures of whoring, wantonness, and drink, contrary to popular belief, do not cause nations to fall."[28]

"Sonnet 2" was addressed initially to a coterie of literate and literary wits well acquainted with libertinage in poetry and life, whether as practicing libertines, philosophizing platonics, or otherwise: an audience of variously behaved sophisticates—who were arguably much less "decadent," especially in relation to their Jacobethan predecessors and Restoration successors, than literary historians have often made them out to be. A. J. Smith has written, for example, "that in mid-seventeenth-century England sexual love had become categorically distinct from the love that holds the universe in sway, and that a choice compelled itself between a fashionable amorousness and the imperative search for truth"—a view that sounds rather like an extrapolation from poetry read under the influence of *The Elizabethan World Picture* and Eliot's notion of the "dis-

sociation of sensibility."[29] According to Lawrence Stone, by contrast, "after about 1590 . . . there developed general promiscuity among both sexes at Court," though "the real break-through into promiscuity at Court . . . occurred under James. The popular reaction was that of Simonds D'Ewes, who spoke of 'the holy state of matrimony perfidiously broken and amongst many made but a May game . . . and even great personages prostituting their bodies to the intent to satisfy and consume their substance in lascivious appetites of all sorts'. As early as 1603 Lady Anne Clifford said that 'all the ladies about the court had gotten such ill names that it was grown a scandalous place.'"[30] Indeed, "it was not until the reign of Charles I and Henrietta Maria that a serious effort was made to sublimate this sensual promiscuity in the ideal of neoplatonic love, which rose above both animal lusts and the turbulent passions of love, to enter the calm arena of a spiritual union of souls"![31]

The disparity between received and recent revisionary views of the Caroline social ethos—together with extraordinarily diverse estimates of our own—points up more than one shortcoming of negative critical judgments made prominently on moral grounds—the Moral Majority's or which Other's, for example? The evidence also leads to the reasonable inference that Charles I's courtiers were not exceptionally vicious—and perhaps that "we," taken all in all, are not preeminently virtuous, however sparing of cakes and ale. All "absolutes" as well as relativities include the beholder as well as the object beheld, perhaps *especially* the former, as subject, as hermeneutic theorists are wont to emphasize. And all critical observation has need not only of historical, ethical, aesthetic, and, I should say, sociobiological circumspectness, but for due allowance to be made for such significant variables as time past, time present, the poet and his medium, the idiosyncrasies of readership, and the nature of human nature, whatever it is or might be.[32] It seems quite possible that such "brutality" as there is in **"Sonnet 2,"** which is first of all fictional and otherwise relative, is in part the subjective product of anachronistic attitudes and unsuspended disbeliefs, credible and even creditable in themselves but variously applicable to the case.

As I read it, **"Sonnet 2"** wittily blends ethology, philosophy, technology, insouciance, and joviality in a "natural, easy" fictional address every bit as "courtly writ" and reflective of "the conversation of a gentleman" as Dryden's Eugenius found Suckling's lyrics when he pronounced them superior to those of the "last age." And it is not easy to find "ugliness" in a witty monodramatizing of the truism that affectional beauty is in the eye of the beholder. This, I take it, is what Suckling is talking about "at bottom," not as a jaded sexual gourmet but as a robust culinary realist: a case of *haute cuisine vis-à-vis cuisine bourgeoise*; or, one person's McDonald's is another's Tour d'Argent; or, as Suckling (or someone else) puts it in a poem not certainly by him, "this each wise man knows: / As good stuff under flannel lies as under silken clothes" (**"Love and Debt Alike Troublesome"**). The principle is of course not gender-bound.

"Sonnet 2" is likely to be distorted by overlaid resonances of late-twentieth-century usage, semitechnical, colloquial, and vulgar, in respect especially of "meat," "appetite," "dish," "watches," and "trick." But what might most offend some modern sensibilities must have afforded Suckling's audience a mild shock of recognition tempered with amusement and delight. Because instinctual human responses are spontaneously reflexive, they can be aptly expressed in terms of mechanism; thus the clock or watch is a fitting figure, even a pleasing one, for, "in the seventeenth century, when the Scientific Revolution exploded in all its exuberance and vigour, the champions of the new science manifested an avid interest in horological matters," and "in their eyes the clock was the machine *par excellence* and it fascinated them."[33] Indeed, "in the course of the sixteenth and seventeenth centuries the clock as a machine exerted deep influence on the speculations of philosophers and scientists. Kepler asserted that 'The universe is not similar to a divine living being, but is similar to a clock,'" and God Himself was spoken of as a master clockmaker.[34] "Portable" clocks, or watches, were relatively new, fashionable, costly, and intriguing.

It is this ambience that informed Suckling's poem in its origins, not that of *A Clockwork Orange,* Jan Kott's Grand Mechanism, or even that cybernetic Adam and Eve of the media, the Six Million Dollar Man and the Bionic Woman.[35] The effect was to convey provocative empirical observations on instinctual drives and behavior through the vehicle of a would-be precision instrument of certain design but—in Suckling's day—still variable working and performance. It is not farfetched to say that the essential analogy of the watch, not as used but as analogy, is the technologically attuned Caroline counterpart of "what a piece of work is a man" in *Hamlet,* where the Prince says he is Ophelia's "evermore, whilst this machine is to him" (2.2.123-24), and whose pulse "doth temperately keep time" (3.4.140). In this connection, "trick" itself is a quasitechnical term for "the mode of working a piece of mechanism, etc., the system upon which a thing is constructed" (*OED, sb.* 1.8c), with specific application to clockworks. A clockwork popperin pear is perhaps how Suckling thought of his amorous watch-man, quite without depreciation or depreciability.

In the round, **"Sonnet 2"** is an urbane wit's dramatic monologue about nature, art, attraction, appetite, pursuit, and play. It opens dramatically in mid-conversation, as it were, and the "kind boy" so familiarly and genially addressed is a compound of confidant, Eros, quartermaster, huntsman, apothecary, and procurer, of whom the speaker seeks nothing special, least of all affected, in the *object* of his love—no fashionable cosmetic arts and coquettish mannerisms, but only "good store / Of love," a simple, homely, but generous provision, "for her I court, I ask no more: / 'Tis *love* in love that *makes* the sport." This is a psychologically astute observation expressed appropriately in terms of the dual sports of venery: amour and the hunt. All the attractions the speaker rejects either are or involve fashionable artificialities, the first reducing the traditional

"rose and lily" of the conventionally attractive complexion to the mere colors of makeup, "red and white." The commonplace of love as madness figures, too, but the emphasis of sense and meter falls on love as maker of the sport: the primary agency is the will to courtship, not the arty-crafty movements and appearance of the courted.

The second stanza deprives beauty of objective existence by dividing the *verbum* from the *res* in good Baconian form: "There's no such *thing* as that we beauty *call*" briskly dismisses an ancient and vermiculate question. "Cozenage" sums up the kindred tricks of the trade, and the claims of custom and precedent are next denied, making a bridge from the currently fashionable "red and white" of the first stanza to the blank "so and so" of any age's arbitrary fashion, by contrast with the exercise of individual preference given primacy here. "Black and blue" has an emblematic force more dramatically vital than that of "red and white," because it is natural, whereas the latter is merely abstract and conventional. It is a whimsically apt paradox for expressing the subjectivity of beauty that one *might* prefer the natural "black and blue" of bruises to an artfully "perfect" complexion. (There could be shades of "S& M" in "black and blue," but I doubt it.) The stanza's last line parallels its fellow in the first stanza, and "That *fancy* doth it beauty *make*" intensifies the creative force of the wit and will by repeating "make" and placing it here as the emphatic last word: beauty is the creature of the fancy.

The first quatrain of the last stanza realizes the field side of "sport," and the second abruptly technologizes the poem with the unexpected image of the lover as timepiece, an image we may see as darkened by our own spectacles, anachronistically, as I have already suggested.[36] Within the poem, however, the controls are such that emphasis falls not on the tenor or the negative aspects of the vehicles but on the speaker and the positive aspects: the "appetite" here is the counterpart of "love" in the first stanza and "fancy" in the second. It, too, "*makes*"—"makes eating a delight"; and "if I like one dish / More than another" reinforces, in the gustatory sphere, "if I a fancy take / To black and blue" in the visual. Taste expressed as a function of the imagination, "that we beauty call," materializes here as a source of true delight in a gustatory delicacy: "If I *like* . . . , *that* a pheasant *is.*" This is the art of the heart's desire. Suckling was probably not thinking of Sir Edward Dyer's famous poem "My mind to me a kingdom is" when he wrote this line, but thematic similarities suggest the appropriate paraphrase: "My bird to me a pheasant is, however fowl."

The concluding quatrain is a miniature masterpiece of combined analogy, anatomy, physiology, phenomenology, horology, technology—*and* apt and harmless ribaldry. The first twenty lines of the poem have conversationally explained the facts of human attraction and the conclusions to be drawn from the. These four now explain *why* they are as they are, with focus on the phenomenon of desire aroused. The fusion of tenor and vehicle in itself validates the analogy of man and watch, and the terms apply almost equally to both, without alternation or transference: "height" and "nick" as "point, stage, degree"; "wind up," meaning in part "to excite" (*OED, sb.* 1.22f)—the effect of which is conveyed also by the idiomatically strenuous inversion, "up be wound"; the technically horological along with the amatory senses of "trick," read even without resort to its current cottage-industrial association with the piecework of the oldest profession. The poem ends with a variation on the theme of the whole of Suckling's poem, **"Love's Clock":** "What in our watches, that in us is found" is the technological *fons et origo,* the *mainspring,* of course, a term applied also to the spring that drives the hammer in a gunlock, a sense used with cheerful grossness by Massinger ("né" Beaumont) and Fletcher in *The Custom of the Country,*[37] and akin to the force that through the green fuse drives the flower and drove Dylan Thomas's green age. Thus Sonnet 2 concludes as it began, on a strikingly upbeat note.

A speculative point just possibly worth adding about the last stanza is that there may be an implicit unifying allusion to the "jack" as a *Jack-of-the-clock,* "the figure of a man which strikes the bell on the outside of a clock" (*OED, sb.* 1.6), itself said to be "wound up," and "a machine for turning the spit in roasting meat" that was "wound up like a clock" (*OED, sb.* 1.7). That there should be a subliminal poet's signature for Jack Suckling, Norfolk Londoner and man of parts, in a poem also concerned with every manjack and woman-jill is appropriate enough, but this may be to consider too curiously. If there are no such Sucklingjacks in the poem, a couple of them could nevertheless have been at the back of the poet's mind, prompting him by mechanical association when he moved from the image of a meal's meat to the temporal measure of amorous man and woman.

Remember the words of Henry Vaughan, how he said, "How brave a prospect is a bright backside."[38] The seriousness and sincerity in Suckling require surgical removal from their vital and engaging poetic incorporation if they are to be seen as such, but they are there with the manifest criticism of life, and they are fundamental, keeping a low profile in an art the brighter and the better for its irony and wit. All work and no play would make Sir Jack not only a dull boy but never an inch of Suckling: that he is Sir John Suckling, let him a little show it, even in this. In fine, one may well be reminded of Duke Theseus's terminal directive to the hempen-homespun players, "let your epilogue alone," and be glad of twenty words in conclusion from one of James Howell's Epistles: "Be pleased to dispense with the prolixity of this discourse, for I could not wind it up closer, nor on a lesser bottom."[39]

Notes

1. Eliot, "The Metaphysical Poets" (1921), in *Selected Essays* (New York: Harcourt, [1951]), p. 250. Leavis, "Milton's Verse," first published in *Scrutiny* 2, no. 2 (1933-34); quoted here from *Revaluation* (1947; rpt. New York: Norton, 1963), p. 42.

2. Tucker Brooke and Matthias A. Shaaber, *The Renaissance (1500-1660),* 2nd ed. (New York: Appleton-Century-Crofts, 1967), p. 658.

3. *On Poetry and Poets* (New York: Farrar, [1957]), p. 47; the essay was first published in 1944. If Eliot has lost the authority he was accorded until a decade or so ago, he has his moments still; Brian Lee notes the positive side of "the conditions of self and society which co-operated to make Eliot a critic of high classical standing, a possessor of the intuition of genius, . . . exactly those which at the same time disable him from the *consistency* which would raise his criticism even higher in future estimation" (italics mine), in *Theory and Personality: The Significance of T. S. Eliot's Criticism* (London: Athlone, 1979), p. 103.

4. *Poetry and Criticism of Matthew Arnold,* ed. A. Dwight Culler (Boston: Houghton, 1961), "Study," pp. 307, 309, and "Wordsworth," p. 339.

5. Richard Dawkins, *The Selfish Gene* (New York: Oxford University Press, 1976), p. 151.

6. *The Artist as Critic: The Critical Writings of Oscar Wilde,* ed. Richard Ellmann (New York: Random House, 1968), p. 305. Comes the revolution, of course, there will be no "civilized society," no Wilde, *and* no Arnold—"sans Wine, sans Song, sans Singer and—sans End."

7. *Anatomy of Criticism* (Princeton: Princeton University Press, 1957), p. 34. All positions beget their opposites (and others) terminologically as well as dialectically, and I am hardly the first to write of "low seriousness." In 1975, for example, Dona F. Munker wrote of "That Paltry Burlesque Style: Seventeenth-Century Poetry and Augustan 'Low Seriousness'" in *SCN* 33, 14-22, using the phrase in a generic application that inevitably overlaps with my own use of it.

8. Whether nodding acquaintance en passant is better than none is a serious question in the literary curriculum and elsewhere; in many cases I think it is, despite the real disadvantages implied by the analogy.

9. See *Critical Understanding* (Chicago: University of Chicago Press, 1979); responding to a review by Jonathan Culler, Booth stresses that "the book in fact defends critical 'improprieties'" (*TLS,* April 25, 1980, p. 468), quoting his own page 335: "Neither the nature of art works nor our own legitimate interests will allow us to reject whatever improper questions promise to lead us to new territory." I am not wholly in sympathy with the note of cheery neofrontiersmanship here.

10. *English Poetry: Select Bibliographical Guides* (New York: Oxford University Press, 1971).

11. Charles L. Squier helpfully provides this service in *Sir John Suckling* (Boston: Twayne, 1978).

12. All citations follow *The Non-Dramatic Works of Sir John Suckling,* ed. Thomas Clayton (Oxford: The Clarendon Press, 1971), pp. 9, 78-79.

13. I have my own doubts about these converging lines of coalescent meaning, but the syntactical and semantic ambiguities work together too well to seem fortuitous, including "since," whether taken as "from then till now," as in my paraphrase, or as "because." In the manuscript (Cranfield Papers MS.U.269.F.36, no. 37), which provides the sole text of this poem, there are no handwriting distinctions, of the type italics allow in print, to set off proper names; worse, "More" is the first word in the line, so the capital, too, is ambiguous. It is at least interesting that *The Mirrour of Vertue in Worldly Greatnes, or The Life of Syr Thomas More Knight* (written in 1556) was printed (in "Paris") for the first time in the same year, 1626, in which the poem was quite probably written; from the scaffold on Tower Hill More "desired . . . all the people about him to pray for him, & to beare witnesse, that he should now there suffer death in, & for the fayth of the Holy Catholique Church" (facsimile rpt. Menston, Yorkshire: Scolar Press, 1970), p. 167.

14. See Rosalie L. Colie, *Paradoxia Epidemica: The Renaissance Tradition of Paradox* (Princeton: Princeton University Press, 1966), chap. 7.

15. *The Life of Clarendon by Himself* (1759), quoted from *Clarendon: Selections from "The History of the Rebellion and Civil Wars" and "The Life by Himself,"* ed. G. Huehns, The World's Classics (London: Oxford University Press, 1955), p. 38.

16. First printed in *Texas Studies in Literature and Language* 4 (1962-63), 553-63; rpt. in W. R. Keast, *Seventeenth-Century English Poetry: Modern Essays in Criticism,* rev. ed. (New York: Oxford University Press, 1971), pp. 300-11, the source of quotation here.

17. "'Men Most of All Enjoy, When Least They Do': The Love Poetry of John Suckling," *Texas Studies in Literature and Language* 14 (1972), 17-32.

18. Nothing definitive can be inferred from elementary statistics, but it is not without interest that the ratio of discussion to poems is quite similar for Anselment and Squier, as it is, I suspect, for many treatments of many poets. In 53 pages Squier discusses 49 poems (according to the index) of the canonical 78 (63%, 1.08 pp. per poem). Anselment discusses 17 poems in 16 pages (22%, .94 p. per poem), which would have been 18 pages on Squier's scale.

19. Text from *The Works of Sir John Suckling: The Plays,* ed. L. A. Beaurline (Oxford: The Clarendon Press, 1971), p. 72.

20. *Henry Lawes, Musician and Friend of Poets* (London: Oxford University Press; New York: MLA, 1941), p. 260.

21. "The Canon of Sir John Suckling's Poems," *Studies in Philology* 57 (1960), 515.

22. *The Complete Poetry of Ben Jonson* (Garden City, N.Y.: Doubleday, 1963), p. 86.

23. *Ben Jonson: Poems* (London: Oxford University Press, 1975), p. 97.

24. *Ben Jonson* (Boston: Twayne, 1979), p. 162.

25. *ELR* 10 (1980), 239-64 (quotation, 258). For following quotations, see 239-40 and 262-64. Also see her book, *The Well-Tun'd Word: Musical Interpretations of English Poetry, 1597-1651* (Minneapolis: University of Minnesota Press, 1981).

26. "A typical contemporary definition of poetic art might run" thus, Reuben Brower wrote in 1952. The title, "The Heresy of Plot," identifies this as a piece of New Critical polemic, in one aspect, but it remains a thoughtful and provocative essay, nevertheless. The "definition" is hardly adequate for "poetic art"—as Johnson wrote in his life of Pope, "to circumscribe poetry by a definition will only show the narrowness of the definer"—but it has the right emphasis for the distinctions concerned here. The essay was first published in *English Institute Essays, 1952* (New York: Columbia University Press, 1952), pp. 44-69; rpt. in Elder Olson, ed., *Aristotle's Poetics and English Literature* (Chicago: University of Chicago Press, 1965), pp. 157-74 (quotation, p. 172).

27. *A Mappe of Mischiefe* (1641), p. 5.

28. London: Secker and Warburg, 1962, p. 286.

29. "The Failure of Love: Love Lyrics after Donne," in *Metaphysical Poetry,* ed. Malcolm Bradbury and David Palmer (1970; rpt. Bloomington: Indiana University Press, 1971), p. 52.

30. *The Crisis of the Aristocracy, 1558-1641* (Oxford: The Clarendon Press, 1965; corr. rpt., 1966), pp. 664, 665.

31. Lawrence Stone, *The Family, Sex and Marriage in England, 1500-1800* (New York: Harper, 1977), p. 504.

32. Marxist theorists tend to dismiss any reference to "(human) nature" as a specious bourgeois universalizing of the historically contingent, but there are psychobiological laws and facts of life and transcultural continuities of community to which Marxists, too, are subject.

33. Carlo M. Cipolla, *Clocks and Culture, 1300-1700* (London: Collins, 1967), p. 57. In "The Apotheosis of Faust: Poetry and New Philosophy in the Seventeenth Century," in Bradbury and Palmer, *Metaphysical Poetry,* pp. 149-79, Robert B. Hinman remarks acutely that "the notorious opposition between poets and new philosophers appears to be a largely modern construct projected backwards from a sense of

separate cultures," whereas "the same ordering, synthesizing, all-encompassing imaginative surge towards 'reality', towards as much truth as man can express, seems evident in such achievements as *The Temple* and *Principia Mathematica*" (p. 156), and many a lesser work. "Science" was not a four-letter word in the seventeenth century.

34. Cipolla, *Clocks and Culture,* p. 105.

35. Suckling dramatically updated it, but he did not invent this eminently eligible analogy. Over two centuries earlier, for example, *Li Orloges amoureuses* of Jean Froissart the chronicler (1337-c. 1404) devoted 1174 verses to the clockwork movements of the lover's heart. Later, there is a particularly choice use in *Tristram Shandy* (1.1): "*Pray, my dear,* quoth my mother, *have you not forgot to wind up the clock?——Good G-!* cried my father, making an exclamation, but taking care to moderate his voice at the same time,—*Did ever woman, since the creation of the world, interrupt a man with such a silly question?*" This "was a very unseasonable question at least," Tristram observed—with unfortunate consequences, according to Walter Shandy, who thought that "Tristram's misfortunes began nine months before he ever came into the world" (Professor Judith Herz of Concordia University, Montreal, reminded me of this at the Classic and Cavalier conference).

36. The theme of the "decadence"—quite aside from the hazards—of "smoking, drinking, and the like" is persistent. If the line between decorum and debauchery is drawn so near, there is not much breathing room for sociable indulgences *or* the licenses of fiction, even in its wish-fulfilling capacity. The appropriate lapel-button legend would seem to be "Thank you for ceasing to exist," perhaps adding in fine print, "Join me—at a distance. Whoever can tell which side of the grave is whose wins a custom-written epitaph by the immortal Saint Ben."

37. 3.3.8-10 in *Custom,* ed. R. Warwick Bond, in *The Works of Beaumont and Fletcher: Variorum Edition,* ed. A. H. Bullen (London: Bell, 1904-13), vol. 1, p. 532.

38. "Looking Back" (15), in "Pious Thoughts and Ejaculations," *Thalia Rediviva* (1678). French Fogle's edition retains the capital in "*Back-side,*" Alan Rudrum's does not. See *The Complete Poetry of Henry Vaughan,* ed. Fogle (Garden City, N.Y.: Doubleday, 1964), p. 415; *Henry Vaughan: The Complete Poems,* ed. Rudrum (Harmondsworth, Middlesex: Penguin, 1976), p. 367.

39. Howell to the Earl R[ivers] from Hamburg, October 20, 1632, 1.6.3 in *Epistolae Ho-Elianae, The Familiar Letters of James Howell (1737),* ed. Joseph Jacobs (London: D. Nutt, 1890-92), vol. 1, p. 300.

Kees van Strien (essay date 1995)

SOURCE: van Strien, Kees. "Sir John Suckling in Holland." *English Studies* 76, no. 5 (September 1995): 443-54.

[*In the following essay, van Strien examines Suckling's letters in an attempt to piece together Suckling's time in Holland as a young man in his early twenties.*]

Sir John Suckling (1609-1642) is one of the numerous British tourists who travelled in the Low Countries in the first half of the seventeenth century.[1] Unlike Sir William Brereton (1634), Peter Mundy (1640) and John Evelyn (1641) Suckling has left no extensive account of his journeys. Only one letter seems to reflect his impressions of Holland and the Dutch.[2] Suckling appears to have been one of the numerous soldiers and scholars who specifically set out for the United Provinces, where in 'the Cockpit of Christendome, the Schoole of Armes, and Rendezvous of all adventurous Spirits, and Cadets',[3] experience in warfare could be gained. Moreover there were excellent educational opportunities at Leiden 'honored with an universitie, and that of the greatest fame of all those of the reformed religion, except those of England'.[4] Suckling's letter written at Leiden on 18 November 1629, together with a certain amount of additional material has enabled us to piece together a picture of this little-known period of his life as a twenty-one-year-old gentleman-soldier, student and author.

SUCKLING AT DEN BOSCH AND LEIDEN

Suckling, who probably saw military action in France in 1627, went to Holland in 1629 to witness the siege of Den Bosch ('s-Hertogenbosch; Bois-le-Duc), a city which had remained loyal to the King of Spain since the beginning of the Dutch wars. In May 1629, stadholder Frederick Henry, Prince of Orange, began the siege which lasted until September, during which time large numbers of visitors came to watch. Suckling's name appears in a list of roughly two hundred officers and gentlemen-volunteers serving with the English regiments; he was in Sir Edward Cecil's company.[5] No other record of his presence here appears to be extant, but the atmosphere may be conveyed by the notes of another volunteer: William Bagot. After visiting the Queen of Bohemia at her country house at Rhenen in the province of Utrecht, he wrote:

> I came to a large bridge of boates over the Rhine [sic for Meuse], where I entered into Brabant. This passage is secured by a stronge fort of the States called St Andrewes sconce. I passed on to Gravicure [Crèvecoeur], another stronge fort of the States and so entered into the trenches of the renowned siege of Shertogenbosh, being the greatest wonder that ever myne eyes beheld. The outworks were of that heith that a man on a high horse could not looke over them, and in compass about thirtie three english miles. I went on to the Princes quarter where I had the honor to kiss the Kinge of Bohemias hand. I passed on into our English trenches, bateries and approaches where most clearely did ap-

peare the valor and industrie of our nation, now being put upon the most desperate attempt; but to see the most excellent order and discipline in every particular was admirable and beyond expression.[6]

Suckling must have returned to England before 22 October 1629 for on that date a pass was issued to him to proceed to the Low Countries to join Lord Wimbledon's (=Sir Edward Cecil) regiment in the States' service. However, in November when he arrived, all military activity for that year had come to a standstill and the four English regiments that had been hired for the duration of the siege, were being paid off.[7] It was in these conditions that Suckling must have decided to go to Leiden, where, on 26 February 1630, he registered as a student of mathematics. Clayton's assertion that Suckling applied himself to astrology here is rather puzzling. It is true that the arabist-mathematician Jacobus Golius taught astronomy from 1629 onwards,[8] but it is far more likely that Suckling and his friend Nicholas Selwyn, possibly a fellow-volunteer in Wimbledon's regiment at Den Bosch,[9] and like Suckling an ardent Royalist during the civil war, came to Leiden for private tuition with Frans van Schooten, who apart from mathematics also taught the art of constructing fortifications.[10] In the summer Van Schooten, as a military engineer, accompanied the army on its campaigns and during the winter he taught 'Duitsche Mathematicque', a university course set up on the initiative of Prince Maurice. Another soldier who came to study with him was René Descartes (enrolled 27 June 1630), who may have arrived at Leiden before Suckling's departure at the end of April, since many students failed to register immediately on arrival.[11]

Since the matriculation album also records students' addresses we can discuss some aspects of Suckling's social life. His lodgings were on the Rapenburg, the most fashionable street in Leiden, shaded by two rows of fine elms on each side of a canal, and only a two or three minutes' walk from the Academy building in the same street.[12] His landlord was Jean Gillot, a fervent Huguenot, whose son, later a distinguished engineer, was then a student of mathematics as well. Between 1623 and 1649 more than a hundred students stayed with Gillot, most of them foreigners. At the beginning of 1630 Suckling shared his lodgings with some Frenchmen and Germans and at least four Britons. They were Nicholas Crisp and Nicholas Selwyn, both mathematicians, and also seventeen-year-old Sir Francis Fane K.B. and his governor Thomas Ball, who enrolled on 23 April 1629 and who were still at Leiden in September 1630.[13] Possibly also Nathaniel Fiennes (9 July 1629), later a colonel in the parliamentarian army.[14] Other English students stayed with Gillot's neighbour at Rapenburg 23, André Rivet, professor of theology (1620-1632)[15] and with the French minister, Mr Maurice Agache, who had two English lodgers in the years 1628-29. One of Rivet's guests, Thomas Coppin (inscr. 24 August 1627) wrote to his uncle: 'I have good content here in all things, but I find it extraordinarye chargeable for one who would live in good fashions (you told me so much before I came)'. At this time there were relatively few English students in Leiden: in 1628-1631, years with over four hundred enrolments each, there was an annual average of only ten.[16]

Being a wealthy gentleman, with a decent education behind him (Cambridge and briefly in 1627 at Gray's Inn with its court connections), Suckling must have devoted only part of his time to study at Leiden, where in Bagot's words the 'cheife thinges of note' were 'the Annatomie schole and the Garden of Simples [. . .] hardly to be paraleled in Christendome'. French lessons, fencing and riding will have cost him far more than his professor and his books. There were also the right people to mix with, principally in The Hague, 'the prime place of Holland for pleasure', only three hours distant.[17] During the academic holidays but possibly on other occasions as well, he may have been friendly with other British noblemen looking for commissions in the next year's campaign, as for instance Lucius Cary, second Viscount Falkland.[18] Here Suckling had ample opportunity for his favourite pastime, gambling, and may well have known young Charles Killigrew, another volunteer at Den Bosch, who according to Constantijn Huygens, the very virtuous secretary to Frederick Henry, frequented 'the vilest and most infame company The Haghe affords, as players, lackeys, and the like with whom he ran headlong after all kinds of debauching'.[19] Many Britons of Suckling's social rank in The Hague were in one way or another connected with the court of Elizabeth Stuart (1596-1662), the eldest daughter of James I, who together with her husband Frederick, Elector Palatine and titular King of Bohemia, lived in exile in The Hague and Rhenen. Numerous visitors, among them James Harrington, Sir William Brereton and William Lithgow, came to pay their respects.[20] In fact Suckling's lodgings in Leiden were just opposite the 'Prince's Court', the residence of the Queen of Bohemia's children, three of whom enrolled as students at the university on 16 March 1628 (Charles Louis, b. 1617, Rupert b. 1619, and Maurice, b. 1620). Bagot wrote: 'Here I had the honor to kisse the hands of Kinge of Bohemias children, who are here educated in arts and sciences worthy of their birth and dignitie.' Several of the princes' attendants also matriculated at Leiden, among them the Queen's chaplain, Griffin Higgs, whose name appears at 6 February 1630, only three weeks before Suckling's.[21]

There is nothing to suggest that the royalist Suckling had more than superficial contacts with British dissidents[22] or members of the Established English church at Leiden, whose minister, from 1617 to 1661 was the staunch Puritan Hugh Goodyear. Suckling, who must have spoken French with his Dutch and Huguenot friends at Leiden and The Hague, may well have preferred to accompany his landlord to the more fashionable French church instead.[23] Here he may occasionally have listened to his neighbour professor Rivet, 'pasteur extraordinaire', a good friend of Constantijn Huygens, and later governor to Prince William II (1632-1646). It is not known whether Suckling did any extensive touring in the United Provinces, but it is difficult to imagine that he omitted visits to Amsterdam (an eight-hour journey from Leiden) and other major towns. When he travelled to Brussels in April or May 1630, he may have sailed direct from Rotterdam to Antwerp or made the more costly and uncomfortable journey by land via Breda, where there was the additional danger of being held up for ransom by badly paid Spanish soldiers.

SUCKLING ON HOLLAND AND THE DUTCH

As we have seen Suckling wrote the letter to his friend William Wallis just after his arrival in Leiden, following his short career as a gentleman-soldier at Den Bosch. Although on the face of it the letter deals with Suckling's crossing to Holland and his subsequent impressions of the country and its inhabitants, it hardly looks like a factual account of what happened to him or a description of what he actually saw. On the contrary, it is an almost completely facetious piece consisting of a long succession of jokes. Suckling writes:

> It is reported here a Shipboard, that the winde is as weomen are, for the most parte bad! That it altogether takes parte with the water, for it crosses him continually that crosses the Seas. [. . .] That soe much Rope is a needeles thinge in a Ship, for they drowne here altogether, not hange. That if a Wench at Land, or a Ship at Sea, spring a leake, tis fit and necessary they should be pumpt. That Dunkirke is the Papists Purgatorie, for men are faine to pay money to be free'd out of it! [. . .] That lying foure nights a shipboard, is almost as bad as sitting up, to loose money at threepenny Gleeke, and soe pray tell Mr. Brett; and thus much for Sea newes.

A less animated version of this could have been: Dear Will, after a four-day crossing in stormy weather, always in danger of attacks by privateers, I have safely arrived in Holland. Yours, as witty as ever, John Suckling.

The letter goes on in the same vein, discussing the country that many Britons knew from personal experience, its inhabitants and some of their customs. It is not unlike a picture postcard showing a caricature of a Dutchman and his wife in their national costumes with in the background their flat boggy country, in continual danger of being flooded or being taken by the Spaniards:

> Since my coming a shoare, I finde, that the people of this Cuntry, are a kinde of Infidells, not beleiving in the Scripture for though it be there promist, there shall never be another Deluge; yet they doe feare it daily, and fortifie against it. [. . .] Their auncestors when they begott them thought on nothing but Munkeys, and Bores, and Asses, and such like ill favor'd creatures; for their Phisnomyes are soe wide from the rules of proportion, that I should spoyle my prose to let in the discription of them [. . .] Their habits are as monstrous as themselves, to all strangers . . .

Clearly this has little to do with the reality as Suckling may have seen it; it is pure stereotype, a stylistic device typical of the 'character' literature of this period, in which representatives of all social classes, trades and nationalities are briefly, wittily and critically described.[24] Two other characters by Suckling are his letter from Brussels (5 May 1630), also addressed to William Wallis and one he sent to the Earl of Middlesex. These literary exercises may have been a welcome change for Suckling, who in long prosaic letters also kept his patron informed of political news.[25] Although, like most writers of literary characters Suckling did not slavishly copy his models,[26] it would appear from the letter that he did remember some of the jokes he had come across in his reading. In fact the first part of the letter is reminiscent of 'Newes from Sea' in the Overbury collection of characters (1614[1]), where we can read: 'That it's nothing so intricate and infinite to rigge a ship, as a woman, and the more either is fraught, the apter to leake. That to pumpe the one, and shreeve the other, is alike noysome'.[27] Other echoes may come from Sir Anthony Weldon's *A Perfect Description of the People and Country of Scotland* (written 1617; publ. 1647), the earliest known character of nations, which was easily available in manuscript. Weldon remarked on the Scottish climate that 'The air might be wholesome but for the stinking people that inhabit it'. This comment possibly sparked off Suckling's jibe on Holland: 'The Ayre what with their breathing in it and its owne naturall Corruption, is soe unwholesome, that a man must resolve to be at the Charge of an ague once a Moneth'. Suckling's observation that the country is 'too good for the inhabitants' looks like a standard remark in texts of this nature. Weldon wrote about Scotland: 'First, for the country I must confess it is too good for those that possess it, and too bad for others to be at the charge to conquer it'.[28]

Although there may be borrowings from other texts as well, it is perhaps more relevant, for a fuller appreciation of the letter, to try and locate the sources that provided Suckling with material for his more specific remarks on Holland and the Dutch. Two kinds of publications on the subject seem to qualify, each yielding a different picture. Firstly there were the scholarly compilations like Sir Thomas Overbury's *Observations upon the State of the Seventeen Provinces as they stood A.D. 1609,* published in 1626 but available in manuscript long before that time, and the equally popular *The Politia of the United Provinces* (c. 1620), which only circulated in manuscript. Both were used by James Howell for his remarks on Holland in his *Familiar Letters* (1645).[29] A third text is the section on Holland in John Barclay's *Icon Animorum* (1614), which provided the tourist Sir John Reresby in 1657 with much material for his 'Description of the Low Countries, Commonwealth, and its People'.[30] A fourth text is Fynes Moryson's *Itinerary,* a large encyclopedic work dealing with most countries of Europe (1617). The picture that an educated British reader might have gathered from texts like these is that Holland is a low-lying country, protected by banks against the sea just as their cities are surrounded by fortifications, a reminder of the Spaniards they have chased away. The people, who have become rich by trade, are diligent and pay high taxes to the States. The rich as well as the poor live soberly, except perhaps for an occasional drinking bout. They love their freedom and tolerate all religions. A very popular political tract which did much to reinforce this picture was *The Belgicke Pismire* (1622), written by the Rev. Thomas Scott (1580-1626), English minister at Utrecht and an indefatigable pamphleteer in the Puritan cause, who presented the Dutch as models of 'labour, providence, and prevention'.[31]

However, many travelling British gentlemen belonging to the Established Church perceived the republican Dutch very differently and emphasized the reverse side of the coin. The ordinary people did not always treat them with respect, and consequently were seen as boorish. Then there were the dull skippers and waggoners unable to understand English, Latin or French, and even well-to-do people went about in plain black clothes! The way the Dutch were lax in keeping the sabbath, together with their excessive toleration of all sorts of religions was looked upon as indifference, and their diligence was proof of the fact that they were only interested in making money.[32] Such people could of course not live in an ordinary country, so all sorts of jokes were made about that too. Something must have gone wrong at the creation, for it was neither water nor land. The Low Countries were a sort of underworld, a Hades or Hell, a fitting place for irreligious people.[33] This is also the picture of the Dutch that emerges from English character literature, in which the Dutch are invariably an object of scorn.[34]

Two texts seem to be immediately relevant here, since Suckling may well have known them. The first is Richard Verstegan's *Observations concerning the present Affayres of Holland and the United Provinces* (St Omer, 1621; 1622²),[35] an anti-Dutch pamphlet which begins with a satirical 'character' of Holland. This text was mentioned in the House of Commons on 27 November 1621 as 'a book [. . .] by an Englishman (as himselfe saith, Hispanised) . . . dishonorable to us and the old Queen and our nation'.[36] Thomas Scott also referred to it,[37] and additional echoes can be found in other contemporary references to Holland or the Dutch, such as Ben Jonson's *The Masque of Augurs* (1622)[38] and James Howell's *A Character of Itelia* [=Holland] (1640) as well as his *Familiar Letters* (publ. 1645).[39] Verstegan (c.1550-1640), who was born as Richard Rowlands in London and who later in Antwerp became the first author of 'characters' in the Dutch language (1619),[40] states that the inhabitants of the Republic would be a lot better off under the King of Spain. He blames them for breaking away from the Catholic church but more particularly for their endless toleration of all other religions. In point of fact they are so selfish that they neither care about God nor their fellow creatures: 'They had rather heare blasphemy uttered against God, then any word of the abridging of any of their priviledges.'[41]

A second text which may have influenced Suckling when writing his letter was itself heavily indebted to Verstegan and Scott, and possibly even better known. From around 1623 *Three Months/Weeks Observations of the Low-Countries Especially Holland* by Owen Felltham (c. 1604-

1668) circulated widely in manuscript, and its first edition of 1648 was followed by at least sixteen more in the course of the century.[42] Felltham did not only criticize, but writing in the tradition of Joseph Hall's *Characters of Virtues and Vices* (1608),[43] he presented two sides of the coin, trying to strike a balance between derision and praise, especially of the diligence so characteristic of the Dutch, which was held up as a mirror to the English readers.

Unlike Felltham Suckling took the usual approach of English character writers, and chose only to criticize. The passage on Holland is divided into three sections each containing four statements, after which the text is neatly concluded. The people are dealt with first; we have already been told that they live in fear of another deluge and why they look so ugly. Now we learn what made them stupid:

> They are Nature's youngest Children, and soe consequently have the least portion of Witt, and Mannors or rather that they are her Bastards and soe inherite none at all.

A similar passage in Felltham reads: 'For their conditions, they are churlish, and (without doubt) very ancient: for they were bred before manners were in fashion'. The antiquary Verstegan also uses the ancient past for a better understanding of the present, although he refers to it in connection with the country: 'Holland at the creation of the world was no Land at all, and therefore not at the first intended by God or Nature for a dwelling place of men.[44]

The country is Suckling's second subject: 'The water and the King of France [sic for: Spain], beleagre it round; sometimes the Hollander getts ground upon them, sometymes they upon him; it is soe even a Level, that a man must have more then the quantity of a graine of Mustard-seede in faith, to remove a Mountaine here, for there is none in the Cuntry'. After this second biblical joke (cf. deluge), Suckling comes up with a remark also found in Verstegan and Felltham: 'their owne Turfe is their fyring altogether, and it is to be feared, that they will burne up their Cuntry before Doomesday'. Verstegan wrote: '[they] are faigne to make use of that little [dry land] they have for their fuell, and so begin to burne up their Countery before the day of Iudgment'. This is Felltham's version: 'they burn Turffs [. . .] As if [. . .] they would prove against Philosophy the Worlds Conflagration to be natural, even shewing thereby that the very Element of Earth is Combustible'.[45]

The final section deals with a variety of subjects: taxes, learning, religion and trade (wealth). Following a mention of the ague, a disease due to the humid climate, the first item is metaphorically introduced as the plague. In 1629 there was an outbreak of the plague at Amsterdam and Gouda and in 1624-25 the disease claimed about ten thousand victims in Leiden alone.

> The plague is here constantly, I mean Excise; and in soe great a manner, that the whole Cuntry is sick on't. Our very Farts stands us in I know not how much Excise to the States, before we let them.

Learning, of course, is something impossible in the given context: 'To be learnd here is Capitall Treason of them, beleiving that Fortuna favet fatuis; and therefore that they may have the better successe in their Warrs, they chuse Burgomasters, and Burgers, as we doe our Maiors, and Aldermen, by their greate Bellyes, little witts, and full Purses'. Aldermen were proverbial dunces in character literature, for instance in John Earle and Samuel Butler. Owen Felltham wrote in connection with those in authority in Holland: 'They are all chosen, as we chuse Aldermen, more for their wealth than their wit'.[46]

Finally Suckling brings up the sensitive issue of which comes first with the Dutch, religion or their love of money. Felltham wrote: 'Marry with a Silver hook you shall catch these Gudgeons presently. The love of gain being to them as naturall as water to a Goose, or Carrion to any Kite that flies. [. . .] They place their Republick in higher esteem than Heaven it self: and had rather cross upon God than it. For whosoever disturbs the Civil Government is lyable to punishment; But the Decrees of Heaven, and Sanctions of the Deity, any one may break uncheck'd, by professing what false Religion he please'.[47] This is Suckling's version:

> Religion they use as a stuff Cloake in summer, more for shew then any thing else; their summum bonum being altogether wealth. They wholly busie themselves about it, not a man here but would doe that which Judas did, for halfe the money.[48]

After this very scornful remark, which in another context might almost be taken seriously, Suckling suddenly seems to remember that Sir Anthony Weldon was removed from court for having been too critical of the King's native country. He briefly concludes by stating that Holland is not really a country at all, an idea which by Verstegan was presented in a complicated cluster: 'Had it been meant for a habitation of men [. . .] the foure elements would not have conspired togeather to be there all naught, and by being naught unto men, to shew their dislike of usurpers that deprive fishs [sic] of their due dwelling places'.[49] Suckling prefers to use unambiguous language and brings the flow of his disparaging wit to a halt in a phrase combining the country, the people and his own prospects:

> To be short the Cuntry is stark nought, and yet too good for the inhabitants; but being our Allyes, I will forbeare their Character, and rest, Your humble servant J. Suckling.

CONCLUSION

When in November 1629 Suckling found himself studying mathematics in Leiden in pursuance of his career as a soldier and courtier, one of his occupations was to entertain a friend with a humorous description of Holland and the Dutch. The contents were determined by common stereotypes and by the conventions of the literary character; by Suckling's sense of humour and not necessarily his personal experiences. The French-speaking Dutch upper classes with whom Suckling mixed never become the target of his satire, but he made fun of the picturesque-looking, uncouth boors who were depicted in prints made after the genre scenes by Van de Venne and Pieter Brueghel.[50] His immediate literary models appear to have been Richard Verstegan and Owen Felltham, from whom he borrowed some material in a context of his own making. In England copies of the letter were presumably passed around in literary circles,[51] but its modest scope and the popularity of Owen Felltham's *Brief Character* probably prevented it from becoming very well-known. However, it is thanks to one of those copies that we are still able to enjoy Suckling's critical, witty and very brief character of Holland.

Notes

1. C. D. van Strien, *British Travellers in Holland during the Stuart Period, Edward Browne and John Locke as Tourists in the United Provinces* (Leiden/New York/Köln, 1993).

2. *The Works of Sir John Suckling,* ed. Th. Clayton (Oxford, 1971), I, pp. xxxi-xxxiii; letter, pp. 112-14. Clayton does not discuss Aubrey's assertion that Suckling made a Grand Tour before he was eighteen years old, cf. *Aubrey's Brief Lives,* ed. O. L. Dick (Harmondsworth, 1962), 343.

3. James Howell, *Instructions for Forreine Travell* (London, 1642, repr. E. Arber, London, 1869), p. 60.

4. William Bagot, Journal of a Tour in the Low Countries and France, Stafford, Staffordshire Record Office, MS D 3259/10, 2 (1629).

5. Henry Hexham, *A Historical Relation of the Famous Siege of the Busse* (Delft, 1630); in an Amsterdam edition (1630) the name is spelled 'Stuckling'.

6. Bagot, fols. 6-7. He was possibly Mr 'Bagshot', one of the 'gentlemen of qualitie' in colonel Harwood's company.

7. Cf. F. G. J. ten Raa and F. de Bas, *Het Staatsche Leger, 1568-1795,* 8 vols. (Breda, 1911-56), IV, pp. 28, 241ff. and 280.

8. University Library Leiden, MS ASF 8: 26 February 1630: Johannes Suckling, Nobilis Anglus, studiosus matheseos, annorum XXI, by Jean Gillot. The published *Album* does not indicate the address. Cf. *The Works,* I, pp. xxvii-xxxv. G. van Herk et al., *De Leidse sterrewacht,* [Leiden, 1983], pp. 12-14; Golius (1596-1667; *Nieuw Nederlands Biografisch Woordenboek* (Leiden, 1911-1937)) was also responsible for the first observatory, constructed in 1633.

9. Nicholas Selwyn, Leiden, 28 February 1630 (aged 22, Math.). Since the ages found in university registers are not always correct (cf. n. 13 under Crispe), he may possibly have been Sir Nicholas Selwyn, Oxford, 1621 (aged 17; B.A., 1625), a known royalist (cf. B. D. Henning, *The House of*

Commons 1660-1690, 3 vols., London 1983, under Edward Selwyn MP for Seaford); I am grateful to Mr Roger Davey of the East Sussex Record Office for information on the Selwyn family. Hexham mentions a 'Mr Solwin', who together with Suckling served in Cecil's company.

10. Frans van Scho[o]ten (c.1581-1645; *NNBW;* also *Leids Jaarboekje,* 1969, pp. 55-56 and P.J. van Winter, *Hoger beroepsonderwijs avant-la-lettre* (Amsterdam, 1988), *Verhandelingen der Koninklijke Nederlandse Akademie van Wetenschappen, Afd. Letterkunde,* N.R., vol. 137, pp. 21-27). Van Schooten then lived at Rapenburg 38, cf. Th. H. Lunsingh Scheurleer et al., *Het Rapenburg, geschiedenis van een Leidse gracht,* 6 vols. (Leiden, 1986-1992), V, p. 251 ff. The other professor of mathematics at that time was the arabist, who was appointed in 1629.

11. Cf. F. Alquié, *Descartes, l'homme et l'oeuvre* (Paris, 1956), pp. 37-38. Descartes had been at Franeker university (inscr. 16 April 1629) and at Amsterdam in 1629. Registration, cf. C. D. van Strien and H. H. Meier, 'John Berry: A Leiden Student as a Tourist in the Low Countries, 1649-50', *LIAS,* 18 (1991) 2, pp. 173-220.

12. Gillot lived at Rapenburg 21, which he bought in 1629, from 1627 till his death in 1650 (*Het Rapenburg,* I, pp. 359-61). For his son, cf. H. J. Witkam, 'Jean Gillot (Een Leids ingenieur)', in: *Leids Jaarboekje,* 59 (1967), pp. 29-54 (list of lodgers, pp. 43-44) and *Leids Jaarboekje,* 61 (1969), pp. 39-70.

13. Sir Nicholas Crispe (c.1608-c.1657) of the Isle of Thanet, Kent, matr. Oxford, 23 June 1626 (aged 18), Leiden, 5 March 1630 (aged 20, Math.), knighted 1 Jan. 1640. Sir Francis Fane (d.1680, *DNB*), younger son of the first Earl of Westmorland, Leiden 23 April 1629 ('eques Balnei, Anglus, annorum xvii'), M.A. Cambridge 1631. Thomas Ball (aged 28; possibly Th. Ball 1590-1659, *DNB,* M.A. Cambridge 1625, rector of St George, Northampton, 1629). A letter was addressed to Fane at Leiden by his mother on 15 September 1630 (*The Works,* I, p. 296).

14. Nathaniel Fiennes (1608-1669; *DNB*), son of the first Viscount Say and Sele, matr. Oxford 19 Nov. 1624, Leiden, 9 July 1629 (aged 21, Jur.), Franeker, 24 May 1630 (with his brothers, cf. S. J. Fockema Andreae and Th.J. Meyer, *Album Studiosorum Academiae Franekerensis* (Franeker, 1968), back in Leiden, 20 May 1631 (aged 23, Phil.) together with his brothers Joseph (20) and John (14), once again staying with Gillot.

15. André Rivet (1572-1651; *NNBW*), at no. 23, cf. *Het Rapenburg,* I, pp. 390-91 and 401-02. French church, cf. *Leids Jaarboekje,* 47 (1955), p. 128. Among his numerous correspondents were the English theologians Griffin Higgs, the high Anglican Stephen Goff (chaplain to Sir Horace Vere 1632-34) and John Forbes, minister at Delft, whose sympathies were

with the Puritans, cf. P. Dibon, *Inventaire de la correspondance d'André Rivet* (La Haye, 1971). Relatively few English students stayed with him. Coppin, cf. *The Oxinden Letters,* ed. D. Gardiner (London, 1933), p. 32.

16. Number of English students enrolled at Leiden according to the *Album,* total number of inscriptions between brackets: 1628: 7 (441); 1629: 17 (430); 1630: 5 (438); 1631: 11 (422).

17. Cf. W. R. Prest, *The Inns of Court under Elizabeth I and the Early Stuarts, 1590-1640* (London 1972), pp. 53, 140, 156. Riding etc., cf. K. van Strien and M. Ashmann, 'Scottish Law Students in Leiden at the End of the Seventeenth Century, The Correspondence of John Clerk, 1694-1697', *LIAS,* 19 (1992) 2, p. 301; also M. F. Moore, 'The Education of a Scottish Nobleman's Sons in the Seventeenth Century', in *The Scottish Historical Review,* 31 (1952), p. 1-15 (on the studies at Leiden of the Earl of Lothian's sons, 1651-53). Quotations, Bagot, fols. 1-2.

18. Falkland (1610?-1643) failed to find service in the States' army, c. 1629-30 (DNB).

19. Cf. *De Briefwisseling van Constantijn Huygens (1608-1687),* ed. J. A. Worp, 6 vols. ('s-Gravenhage, 1911-17), I, pp. 280-83, letter in English (30 March 1630), to Sir Robert Killigrew. Charles served in Harwood's company (Hexham).

20. James Har[r]ington (1611-77), joined her court c. 1630-31 (cf. *DNB*). Bagot 'kissed her hands' at Rhenen. Lithgow 'presented the Majesty of Bohemia with some of my former workes' (William Lithgow, *A True and Experimentall Discourse upon . . . this Last Siege of Breda* (London, 1637), p. 53). Brereton saw the Queen at supper and had a long conversation with her (Sir W. Brereton, *Travels in Holland, the United Provinces, England, Scotland and Ireland,* ed. E. Hawkins (Chetham Society, 1844), pp. 33-34.

21. Prinsenhof, at present nos. 4-10, cf. *Het Rapenburg,* I, pp. 26-27; II, p. 203 ff. Brereton visited them in June 1634, when there were seven boys ('Gustavus so little as not able to sit at table') and four girls (*Travels,* p. 39). Cf. P. S. Morrish, 'Dr. Griffin Higgs, 1589-1659', *Oxoniensia* 31 (1966), pp. 117-138.

22. Thomas Raymond (in Holland in 1632-33) wrote in his memoirs: 'This mynds me of the trouble we then had with the Brownists of Amsterdam, amongst whom and our other countrymen, the Presbyterians (as most of the English Church were) were ever some pestilent rayling bookes printed and writed against the Church of England and the Bishops.' cf. *Autobiography of Thomas Raymond and Memoirs of the Family of Guise,* ed. G. Davies, Camden 3rd ser., vol. 28 (London, 1917), pp. 32-33.

23. On the English church in Leiden, cf. K. L. Sprunger, *Dutch Puritanism, A History of English and Scottish Churches of the Netherlands in the Sixteenth and Seventeenth Centuries* (Leiden, 1982), pp. 123-34.

24. Cf. J. W. Smeed, *The Theophrastan 'Character'* (Oxford/New York, 1985).

25. *The Works,* vol. I, pp. 116-118. In the letter from Brussels Suckling emphasizes the poverty of the inhabitants and makes many jokes in connection with the Catholic religion (I have not identified the literary sources). Ibid., pp. 121-23 (date uncertain). For a factual report to the Earl of Middlesex, 3 May 1630, cf. pp. 114-16.

26. Cf. Smeed, p. 10.

27. Cf. *The Miscellaneous Works of Sir Thomas Overbury,* ed. E. F. Rimbault (London, 1890), 181 (first complete edn. 1622). Cf. also his 'Newes from Venice', 'From Germanie', 'From the Low-Countries' (pp. 186-87).

28. References to the reprint in J. Nichols, *The Progresses of James I* (London, 1828; repr. New York, 1973), III, pp. 338-43; quotations p. 338. For a discussion of characters of nations, cf. B. Boyce, *The Polemic Character 1640-1661* (Lincoln, Nebraska, 1955), pp. 44-46, and T.-L. Pebworth, *Owen Felltham* (Boston, 1976), pp. 71-73.

29. Sir Thomas Overbury's *Observations upon the State of the Seventeen Provinces as they stood A.D. 1609,* reprinted in the *Harleian Miscellany* (London, 1810), III, pp. 97-100. *The Politia of the United Provinces* (c.1620?), in: J. Somers, *A Collection of Scarce and Valuable Tracts* (London, 1809-1815), III, pp. 630-35. *Epistolae Ho-Elianae: the Familiar Letters of James Howell,* ed. J. Jacobs, 2 vols. (London, 1891-92), I, pp. 25-129. For these and other contemporary works on Holland, cf. Van Strien, *British Travellers,* pp. 41-49.

30. English edition: J. Barclay, *The Mirror of Minds* (London, 1631), 175 ff.: on 'Belgia' (also in later editions of his *Satyricon*). *Memoirs and Travels by Sir John Reresby, Bart.,* ed. A. Ivatt (London, 1904), pp. 130-37.

31. On Scott, cf. Sprunger, pp. 214-16 and 294-96. Letter to J. Mead, 7 February 1622 O.S., cf. T. Birch, *Court and Times of James I* (London, 1848), II, p. 361. In the library of Robert Burton, no. 1451, cf. N. K. Kiessling, *The Library of Robert Burton* (*Oxford Bibliographical Society Publications* (1988), N.S., xxii).

32. Cf. Reresby, *Memoirs and Travels,* p. 136: 'Gentlemen have there the least respect in any place, especially strangers, they paying treble rates for everything they have occasion for as they travel, and being pursued and pointed at by the rabble, until they refuge themselves in their inn'. John Ray, *Observations Made in a Journey Through Parts of the Low-Countries,* London 1673, p. 43: 'The common people of Holland, especially inn-keepers, waggoners [. . .], boatmen and porters are surly and uncivil'.

33. Cf. *Observations,* p. 3: 'I do not know any benefits peculiar to themselves wherof they may boast, except

[. . .] that by reason of the great lownes of their dwelling, they are the neerest neighbours to the Divell'.

34. Smeed, p. 39.

35. Reprinted in *English Recusant Literature, 1558-1640,* vol. 7, ed. D. M. Rogers (Menston, 1970). The text is a translation of his *Spieghel der Nederlandsche Elenden* [Mirror of the Low Countries' Woes] (1621).

36. Cf. *Commons Debates 1621,* ed. W. Notestein et al. (New Haven, 1935), III, p. 465.

37. *The Belgicke Pismire,* p. 70: '. . . whereas one saith wittily but not well, How all the elements conspire there together to be naught, to shew their dislike of the naughty people, I may truly say, All the naughty Elements are forced there to do good, to shew the vertue and diligence of the good people, who conspire together in honest labor and artificiall industrie'. Cf. text preceding n. 49.

38. Cf. *Ben Jonson,* eds. C. H. Herford, P. and E. Simpson (Oxford, 1925-1952), VII, pp. 632-33, lines 100-08, spoken by a character Vangoose: 'Dey have noting, noting van deir own, but vat they take from the eard, or de zea, or de heaven, or de hell, or the rest van de veir elementen, de place all dat be so common as de vench in the bordello'. Cf. *Observations,* pp. 1-2, quoted in the text before n. 49.

39. James Howell, *A Character of Itelia* in: *Dodona's Grove, or the Vocall Forrest* (London, 1640); Howell (p. 26) quotes from a 'Satyre [. . .] out of Elaiana' [=Spain], which has many of Verstegan's jokes. *Familiar Letters,* I, pp. 25-27, a letter to his brother, dated Amsterdam, 1 April 1617 [sic for 1619]. Many of its witticisms were probably only inserted when the *Familiar Letters* were prepared for publication. The following seems to come from Verstegan: 'the Ground here [. . .] lies not only level but [. . .] far lower than the Sea; which made the Duke of Alva say, That the Inhabitants of this Country were the nearest Neighbours to Hell (the greatest Abyss) of any People upon Earth, because they dwell lowest'. (cf. n. 33).

40. Cf. E. Rombauts, *Richard Verstegen, een polemist der contra-reformatie* (Brussel, 1933).

41. Verstegan, p. 6. Cf. also: 'Hell is nothing so odious unto this people, as is the Spanish Inquisition, albeit they live in more danger of hell then of it. [. . .] almost every Cobler is a Dutch-Doctour of Divinity, and by inward illumination of spirit understandeth the Scripture as well as they that wrote it'. (pp. 4-5).

42. Its best known title is *A Brief Character of the Low-Countries.* Thirty manuscript copies have been traced, cf. Kees van Strien, 'Owen Felltham's *A Brief Character of the Low Countries.* A Survey of the Texts', to be published in *English Manuscript Studies 1100-1700,* ed. J. Griffiths and P. Beal (London,

1995), VI. References are to the 1648 (William Ley) and the 1652 (Henry Seile) edition. A critical edition is in preparation by the author. Cf. also Pebworth.

43. Cf. Smeed, pp. 19-24.

44. Felltham, 1652, par. 40. Verstegan, p. 1.

45. Verstegan, p. 3. Felltham, 1652, par. 15.

46. Plague, cf. L. Noordegraaf and G. Valk, *De Gave Gods. De pest in Holland vanaf de late middeleeuwen* (Bergen 1988), pp. 230-31. Alderman, the joke also occurs in John Earle's 'A Mere Alderman', cf. *Microcosmography* (1628), ed. H. Osborne (London, n.d.), p. 18, and Samuel Butler's 'Alderman', cf. *Characters* (1759), ed. C. W. Daves (Cleveland/London, 1970), pp. 159-60. Felltham, 1648, par. 60.

47. Felltham, 1652, par. 41 and 65. Cf. par. 46: 'Nothing can quiet them but money and liberty, yet when they have them they abuse both.'

48. Cf. Weldon's *Scotland,* p. 339: 'had Christ been betrayed in this country [. . .], Judas had sooner found a tree of repentance than a tree to hang himself on'.

49. Verstegan, pp. 1-2. Cf. notes 37 and 38.

50. Cf. L. J. Bol, *Adriaen Pietersz. van de Venne Painter and Draughtsman* (Doornspijk, 1989), p. 112 ff. He illustrated the very popular works of Jacob Cats and Johan de Brune.

51. Clayton has located one copy; the original has not been found.

FURTHER READING

Biography

Clayton, Thomas. "An Historical Study of the Portraits of Sir John Suckling." *Journal of the Warburg and Courtauld Institute* 23 (1960): 105-26.
    Examines the many portraits of Suckling, and provides biographical and works-related information.

Criticism

Beaurline, L. A. "New Poems by Sir John Suckling." *Studies in Philology* 59, no. 4 (October 1962): 651-57.
    Considers the authenticity of the newly discovered poems of Suckling.

Benham, Allen R. "Sir John Suckling, 'A Sessions of the Poets': Some Notes and Queries." *Modern Language Quarterly* 6 (March 1945): 21-27.
    Offers analysis of Suckling's "A Sessions of the Poets."

Parker, Michael P. "'All are not born (Sir) to the Bay': 'Jack' Suckling, 'Tom' Carew, and the Making of a Poet." *English Literary Renaissance* 12, no. 3 (autumn 1982): 341-68.
    Compares Suckling's poems to those of fellow Cavalier Poet Thomas Carew.

Wallerstein, Ruth. "Suckling's Imitation of Shakespeare." *The Review of English Studies* XIX, no. 75 (July 1943): 290-95.
    Explores the relationship between Suckling's *The Goblins* and Shakespeare's *The Tempest.*

Additional coverage of Suckling's life and works can be found in the following sources published by the Gale Group: *British Writers,* **Vol. 2;** *Dictionary of Literary Biography,* **Vols. 58, 126;** *DISCovering Authors Modules: Poets; Exploring Poetry; Literature Resource Center; Poetry Criticism,* **Vol. 30;** *Poets: American and British; Reference Guide to English Literature.*

How to Use This Index

The main references

> **Calvino, Italo**
> 1923-1985 .... CLC 5, 8, 11, 22, 33, 39,
> 73; SSC 3

list all author entries in the following Gale Literary Criticism series:

BLC = *Black Literature Criticism*
CLC = *Contemporary Literary Criticism*
CLR = *Children's Literature Review*
CMLC = *Classical and Medieval Literature Criticism*
DA = *DISCovering Authors*
DAB = *DISCovering Authors: British*
DAC = *DISCovering Authors: Canadian*
DAM = *DISCovering Authors: Modules*
    DRAM: Dramatists Module; MST: Most-Studied Authors Module;
    MULT: Multicultural Authors Module; NOV: Novelists Module;
    POET: Poets Module; POP: Popular Fiction and Genre Authors Module
DC = *Drama Criticism*
HLC = *Hispanic Literature Criticism*
LC = *Literature Criticism from 1400 to 1800*
NCLC = *Nineteenth-Century Literature Criticism*
NNAL = *Native North American Literature*
PC = *Poetry Criticism*
SSC = *Short Story Criticism*
TCLC = *Twentieth-Century Literary Criticism*
WLC = *World Literature Criticism, 1500 to the Present*

The cross-references

> See also CANR 23; CA 85-88;
> obituary CA116

list all author entries in the following Gale biographical and literary sources:

AAYA = *Authors & Artists for Young Adults*
AITN = *Authors in the News*
BEST = *Bestsellers*
BW = *Black Writers*
CA = *Contemporary Authors*
CAAS = *Contemporary Authors Autobiography Series*
CABS = *Contemporary Authors Bibliographical Series*
CANR = *Contemporary Authors New Revision Series*
CAP = *Contemporary Authors Permanent Series*
CDALB = *Concise Dictionary of American Literary Biography*
CDBLB = *Concise Dictionary of British Literary Biography*
DLB = *Dictionary of Literary Biography*
DLBD = *Dictionary of Literary Biography Documentary Series*
DLBY = *Dictionary of Literary Biography Yearbook*
HW = *Hispanic Writers*
JRDA = *Junior DISCovering Authors*
MAICYA = *Major Authors and Illustrators for Children and Young Adults*
MTCW = *Major 20th-Century Writers*
SAAS = *Something about the Author Autobiography Series*
SATA = *Something about the Author*
YABC = *Yesterday's Authors of Books for Children*

Literary Criticism Series
Cumulative Author Index

5, 10, 52; DAM NOV, POET; PC 26;
SSC 9
See also AMW; CA 5-8R; 45-48; CANR 4,
60; CDALB 1929-1941; DLB 9, 45, 102;
EXPS; HGG; MTCW 1, 2; RGAL; RGSF;
SATA 3, 30; SSFS 8

Aiken, Joan (Delano) 1924- **CLC 35**
See also AAYA 1, 25; CA 9-12R, 182;
CAAE 182; CANR 4, 23, 34, 64; CLR 1,
19; DLB 161; FANT; HGG; JRDA; MAI-
CYA; MTCW 1; RHW; SAAS 1; SATA
2, 30, 73; SATA-Essay 109; WYA; YAW

Ainsworth, William Harrison 1805-1882
NCLC 13
See also DLB 21; HGG; RGEL; SATA 24;
SUFW

Aitmatov, Chingiz (Torekulovich) 1928- **CLC
71**
See also CA 103; CANR 38; MTCW 1;
RGSF; SATA 56

Akers, Floyd
See Baum, L(yman) Frank

Akhmadulina, Bella Akhatovna 1937- **CLC
53; DAM POET**
See also CA 65-68; CWP; CWW 2

Akhmatova, Anna 1888-1966 **CLC 11, 25, 64,
126; DAM POET; PC 2**
See also CA 19-20; 25-28R; CANR 35;
CAP 1; DA3; EW 10; MTCW 1, 2;
RGWL

Aksakov, Sergei Timofeyvich 1791-1859
NCLC 2
See also DLB 198

Aksenov, Vassily
See Aksyonov, Vassily (Pavlovich)

Akst, Daniel 1956- **CLC 109**
See also CA 161

Aksyonov, Vassily (Pavlovich) 1932- **CLC 22,
37, 101**
See also CA 53-56; CANR 12, 48, 77;
CWW 2

Akutagawa Ryunosuke 1892-1927 **TCLC 16;
SSC 44**
See also CA 117; 154; DLB 180; MJW;
RGSF; RGWL

Alain 1868-1951 **TCLC 41**
See also CA 163; GFL 1789 to the Present

Alain-Fournier TCLC 6
See also Fournier, Henri Alban
See also DLB 65; GFL 1789 to the Present;
RGWL

Alarcon, Pedro Antonio de 1833-1891 **NCLC
1**

Alas (y Urena), Leopoldo (Enrique Garcia)
1852-1901 **TCLC 29**
See also CA 113; 131; HW 1; RGSF

Albee, Edward (Franklin III) 1928- **CLC 1,
2, 3, 5, 9, 11, 13, 25, 53, 86, 113; DA;
DAB; DAC; DAM DRAM, MST; DC
11; WLC**
See also AITN 1; AMW; CA 5-8R; CABS
3; CAD; CANR 8, 54, 74; CD; CDALB
1941-1968; DA3; DFS 2, 3, 8, 10, 13;
DLB 7; INT CANR-8; LAIT 4; MTCW
1, 2; RGAL; TUS

Alberti, Rafael 1902-1999 **CLC 7**
See also CA 85-88; 185; CANR 81; DLB
108; HW 2; RGWL

Albert the Great 1193(?)-1280 **CMLC 16**
See also DLB 115

Alcala-Galiano, Juan Valera y
See Valera y Alcala-Galiano, Juan

Alcayaga, Lucila Godoy
See Godoy Alcayaga, Lucila

Alcott, Amos Bronson 1799-1888 **NCLC 1**
See also DLB 1, 223

Alcott, Louisa May 1832-1888 **NCLC 6, 58,**

83; DA; DAB; DAC; DAM MST, NOV;
SSC 27; WLC
See also AAYA 20; AMWS 1; BPFB 1;
BYA 2; CDALB 1865-1917; CLR 1, 38;
DA3; DLB 1, 42, 79, 223, 239, 242;
DLBD 14; FW; JRDA; LAIT 2; MAI-
CYA; NFS 12; RGAL; SATA 100; WCH;
WYA; YABC 1; YAW

Aldanov, M. A.
See Aldanov, Mark (Alexandrovich)

Aldanov, Mark (Alexandrovich)
1886(?)-1957 **TCLC 23**
See also CA 118; 181

Aldington, Richard 1892-1962 **CLC 49**
See also CA 85-88; CANR 45; DLB 20, 36,
100, 149; RGEL

Aldiss, Brian W(ilson) 1925- **CLC 5, 14, 40;
DAM NOV; SSC 36**
See also AAYA 42; CA 5-8R; CAAE 190;
CAAS 2; CANR 5, 28, 64; CN; DLB 14;
MTCW 1, 2; SATA 34; SFW

Alegria, Claribel 1924- **CLC 75; DAM
MULT; HLCS 1; PC 26**
See also CA 131; CAAS 15; CANR 66, 94;
CWW 2; DLB 145; HW 1; MTCW 1

Alegria, Fernando 1918- **CLC 57**
See also CA 9-12R; CANR 5, 32, 72; HW
1, 2

Aleichem, Sholom TCLC 1, 35; SSC 33
See also Rabinovitch, Sholem

Aleixandre, Vicente 1898-1984 **TCLC 113;
HLCS 1**
See also CANR 81; DLB 108; HW 2;
RGWL

Alencon, Marguerite d'
See de Navarre, Marguerite

Alepoudelis, Odysseus
See Elytis, Odysseus
See also CWW 2

Aleshkovsky, Joseph 1929-
See Aleshkovsky, Yuz
See also CA 121; 128

Aleshkovsky, Yuz CLC 44
See also Aleshkovsky, Joseph

Alexander, Lloyd (Chudley) 1924- **CLC 35**
See also AAYA 1, 27; BPFB 1; BYA 5, 6,
7, 9, 10, 11; CA 1-4R; CANR 1, 24, 38,
55; CLR 1, 5, 48; CWRI; DLB 52; FANT;
JRDA; MAICYA; MAICYAS; MTCW 1;
SAAS 19; SATA 3, 49, 81; SUFW; WYA;
YAW

Alexander, Meena 1951- **CLC 121**
See also CA 115; CANR 38, 70; CP; CWP;
FW

Alexander, Samuel 1859-1938 **TCLC 77**

Alexie, Sherman (Joseph, Jr.) 1966- **CLC 96,
154; DAM MULT**
See also AAYA 28; CA 138; CANR 95;
DA3; DLB 175, 206; MTCW 1; NNAL

Alfau, Felipe 1902-1999 **CLC 66**
See also CA 137

Alfieri, Vittorio 1749-1803 **NCLC 101**
See also EW 4; RGWL

Alfred, Jean Gaston
See Ponge, Francis

Alger, Horatio, Jr. 1832-1899 **NCLC 8, 83**
See also DLB 42; LAIT 2; RGAL; SATA
16; TUS

Al-Ghazali, Muhammad ibn Muhammad
1058-1111 **CMLC 50**
See also DLB 115

Algren, Nelson 1909-1981 **CLC 4, 10, 33;
SSC 33**
See also AMWS 9; BPFB 1; CA 13-16R;
103; CANR 20, 61; CDALB 1941-1968;
DLB 9; DLBY 81, 82, 00; MTCW 1, 2;
RGAL; RGSF

Ali, Ahmed 1908-1998 **CLC 69**
See also CA 25-28R; CANR 15, 34

Alighieri, Dante
See Dante

Allan, John B.
See Westlake, Donald E(dwin)

Allan, Sidney
See Hartmann, Sadakichi

Allan, Sydney
See Hartmann, Sadakichi

Allard, Janet CLC 59

Allen, Edward 1948- **CLC 59**

Allen, Fred 1894-1956 **TCLC 87**

Allen, Paula Gunn 1939- **CLC 84; DAM
MULT**
See also AMWS 4; CA 112; 143; CANR
63; CWP; DA3; DLB 175; FW; MTCW
1; NNAL; RGAL

Allen, Roland
See Ayckbourn, Alan

Allen, Sarah A.
See Hopkins, Pauline Elizabeth

Allen, Sidney H.
See Hartmann, Sadakichi

Allen, Woody 1935- **CLC 16, 52; DAM POP**
See also AAYA 10; CA 33-36R; CANR 27,
38, 63; DLB 44; MTCW 1

Allende, Isabel 1942- **CLC 39, 57, 97; DAM
MULT, NOV; HLC 1; WLCS**
See also AAYA 18; CA 125; 130; CANR
51, 74; CWW 2; DA3; DLB 145; DNFS;
FW; HW 1, 2; INT CA-130; LAIT 5;
LAWS 1; MTCW 1, 2; NCFS 1; NFS 6;
RGSF; SSFS 11; WLIT 1

Alleyn, Ellen
See Rossetti, Christina (Georgina)

Alleyne, Carla D. CLC 65

Allingham, Margery (Louise) 1904-1966 **CLC
19**
See also CA 5-8R; 25-28R; CANR 4, 58;
CMW; DLB 77; MSW; MTCW 1, 2

Allingham, William 1824-1889 **NCLC 25**
See also DLB 35; RGEL

Allison, Dorothy E. 1949- **CLC 78, 153**
See also CA 140; CANR 66; CSW; DA3;
FW; MTCW 1; NFS 11; RGAL

Alloula, Malek CLC 65

Allston, Washington 1779-1843 **NCLC 2**
See also DLB 1, 235

Almedingen, E. M. CLC 12
See also Almedingen, Martha Edith von
See also SATA 3

Almedingen, Martha Edith von 1898-1971
See Almedingen, E. M.
See also CA 1-4R; CANR 1

Almodovar, Pedro 1949(?)- **CLC 114; HLCS
1**
See also CA 133; CANR 72; HW 2

Almqvist, Carl Jonas Love 1793-1866 **NCLC
42**

Alonso, Damaso 1898-1990 **CLC 14**
See also CA 110; 131; 130; CANR 72; DLB
108; HW 1, 2

Alov
See Gogol, Nikolai (Vasilyevich)

Alta 1942- **CLC 19**
See also CA 57-60

Alter, Robert B(ernard) 1935- **CLC 34**
See also CA 49-52; CANR 1, 47, 100

Alther, Lisa 1944- **CLC 7, 41**
See also BPFB 1; CA 65-68; CAAS 30;
CANR 12, 30, 51; CN; CSW; GLL 2;
MTCW 1

Althusser, L.
See Althusser, Louis

Althusser, Louis 1918-1990 **CLC 106**
See also CA 131; 132; CANR 102; DLB
242

Altman, Robert 1925- **CLC 16, 116**
See also CA 73-76; CANR 43

Alurista
    See Urista, Alberto H.
    See also DLB 82; HLCS 1
Alvarez, A(lfred) 1929- **CLC 5, 13**
    See also CA 1-4R; CANR 3, 33, 63, 101;
    CN; CP; DLB 14, 40
Alvarez, Alejandro Rodriguez 1903-1965
    See Casona, Alejandro
    See also CA 131; 93-96; HW 1
Alvarez, Julia 1950- **CLC 93; HLCS 1**
    See also AAYA 25; AMWS 7; CA 147;
    CANR 69, 101; DA3; MTCW 1; NFS 5,
    9; WLIT 1
Alvaro, Corrado 1896-1956 **TCLC 60**
    See also CA 163
Amado, Jorge 1912-2001 **CLC 13, 40, 106;**
    DAM MULT, NOV; HLC 1
    See also CA 77-80; CANR 35, 74; DLB
    113; HW 2; LAW; LAWS 1; MTCW 1, 2;
    RGWL; WLIT 1
Ambler, Eric 1909-1998 **CLC 4, 6, 9**
    See also BRWS 4; CA 9-12R; 171; CANR
    7, 38, 74; CMW; CN; DLB 77; MSW;
    MTCW 1, 2
Ambrose, Stephen E(dward) 1936- **CLC 145**
    See also CA 1-4R; CANR 3, 43, 57, 83,
    105; NCFS 2; SATA 40
Amichai, Yehuda 1924-2000 **CLC 9, 22, 57,**
    116; PC 38
    See also CA 85-88; 189; CANR 46, 60, 99;
    CWW 2; MTCW 1
Amichai, Yehudah
    See Amichai, Yehuda
Amiel, Henri Frederic 1821-1881 **NCLC 4**
    See also DLB 217
Amis, Kingsley (William) 1922-1995 **CLC 1,**
    2, 3, 5, 8, 13, 40, 44, 129; DA; DAB;
    DAC; DAM MST, NOV
    See also AITN 2; BPFB 1; BRWS 2; CA
    9-12R; 150; CANR 8, 28, 54; CDBLB
    1945-1960; CN; CP; DA3; DLB 15, 27,
    100, 139; DLBY 96; HGG; INT CANR-8;
    MTCW 1, 2; RGEL; RGSF; SFW
Amis, Martin (Louis) 1949- **CLC 4, 9, 38, 62,**
    101
    See also BEST 90:3; BRWS 4; CA 65-68;
    CANR 8, 27, 54, 73, 95; CN; DA3; DLB
    14, 194; INT CANR-27; MTCW 1
Ammons, A(rchie) R(andolph) 1926-2001
    CLC 2, 3, 5, 8, 9, 25, 57, 108; DAM
    POET; PC 16
    See also AITN 1; AMWS 7; CA 9-12R;
    193; CANR 6, 36, 51, 73; CP; CSW; DLB
    5, 165; MTCW 1, 2; RGAL
Amo, Tauraatua i
    See Adams, Henry (Brooks)
Amory, Thomas 1691(?)-1788 **LC 48**
    See also DLB 39
Anand, Mulk Raj 1905- **CLC 23, 93; DAM**
    NOV
    See also CA 65-68; CANR 32, 64; CN;
    MTCW 1, 2; RGSF
Anatol
    See Schnitzler, Arthur
Anaximander c. 611B.C.-c. 546B.C. **CMLC 22**
Anaya, Rudolfo A(lfonso) 1937- **CLC 23, 148;**
    DAM MULT, NOV; HLC 1
    See also AAYA 20; BYA 13; CA 45-48;
    CAAS 4; CANR 1, 32, 51; CN; DLB 82,
    206; HW 1; LAIT 4; MTCW 1, 2; NFS
    12; RGAL; RGSF; WLIT 1
Andersen, Hans Christian 1805-1875 **NCLC**
    7, 79; DA; DAB; DAC; DAM MST,
    POP; SSC 6; WLC
    See also CLR 6; DA3; EW 6; MAICYA;
    RGSF; RGWL; SATA 100; WCH; YABC
    1

Anderson, C. Farley
    See Mencken, H(enry) L(ouis); Nathan,
    George Jean
Anderson, Jessica (Margaret) Queale 1916-
    CLC 37
    See also CA 9-12R; CANR 4, 62; CN
Anderson, Jon (Victor) 1940- **CLC 9; DAM**
    POET
    See also CA 25-28R; CANR 20
Anderson, Lindsay (Gordon) 1923-1994 **CLC**
    20
    See also CA 125; 128; 146; CANR 77
Anderson, Maxwell 1888-1959 **TCLC 2;**
    DAM DRAM
    See also CA 105; 152; DLB 7, 228; MTCW
    2; RGAL
Anderson, Poul (William) 1926-2001 **CLC 15**
    See also AAYA 5, 34; BPFB 1; BYA 6, 8,
    9; CA 1-4R, 181; CAAE 181; CAAS 2;
    CANR 2, 15, 34, 64; CLR 58; DLB 8;
    FANT; INT CANR-15; MTCW 1, 2;
    SATA 90; SATA-Brief 39; SATA-Essay
    106; SCFW 2; SFW; SUFW
Anderson, Robert (Woodruff) 1917- **CLC 23;**
    DAM DRAM
    See also AITN 1; CA 21-24R; CANR 32;
    DLB 7; LAIT 5
Anderson, Roberta Joan
    See Mitchell, Joni
Anderson, Sherwood 1876-1941 **TCLC 1, 10,**
    24; DA; DAB; DAC; DAM MST, NOV;
    SSC 1, 46; WLC
    See also AAYA 30; AMW; BPFB 1; CA
    104; 121; CANR 61; CDALB 1917-1929;
    DA3; DLB 4, 9, 86; DLBD 1; EXPS;
    GLL 2; MTCW 1, 2; NFS 4; RGAL;
    RGSF; SSFS 4, 10, 11
Andier, Pierre
    See Desnos, Robert
Andouard
    See Giraudoux, Jean(-Hippolyte)
Andrade, Carlos Drummond de **CLC 18**
    See also Drummond de Andrade, Carlos
    See also RGWL
Andrade, Mario de **TCLC 43**
    See also de Andrade, Mario
    See also LAW; RGWL; WLIT 1
Andreae, Johann V(alentin) 1586-1654 **LC**
    32
    See also DLB 164
Andreas Capellanus fl. c. 1185- **CMLC 45**
    See also DLB 208
Andreas-Salome, Lou 1861-1937 **TCLC 56**
    See also CA 178; DLB 66
Andress, Lesley
    See Sanders, Lawrence
Andrewes, Lancelot 1555-1626 **LC 5**
    See also DLB 151, 172
Andrews, Cicily Fairfield
    See West, Rebecca
Andrews, Elton V.
    See Pohl, Frederik
Andreyev, Leonid (Nikolaevich) 1871-1919
    TCLC 3
    See also CA 104; 185
Andric, Ivo 1892-1975 **CLC 8; SSC 36**
    See also CA 81-84; 57-60; CANR 43, 60;
    DLB 147; EW 11; MTCW 1; RGSF;
    RGWL
Androvar
    See Prado (Calvo), Pedro
Angelique, Pierre
    See Bataille, Georges
Angell, Roger 1920- **CLC 26**
    See also CA 57-60; CANR 13, 44, 70; DLB
    171, 185
Angelou, Maya 1928- **CLC 12, 35, 64, 77,**
    155; BLC 1; DA; DAB; DAC; DAM

MST, MULT, POET, POP; PC 32;
WLCS
    See also AAYA 7, 20; AMWS 4; BPFB 1;
    BW 2, 3; BYA 2; CA 65-68; CANR 19,
    42, 65; CDALBS; CLR 53; CP; CPW;
    CSW; CWP; DA3; DLB 38; EXPN;
    EXPP; LAIT 4; MAICYAS; MAWW;
    MTCW 1, 2; NCFS 2; NFS 2; PFS 2, 3;
    RGAL; SATA 49; WYA; YAW
Angouleme, Marguerite d'
    See de Navarre, Marguerite
Anna Comnena 1083-1153 **CMLC 25**
Annensky, Innokenty (Fyodorovich)
    1856-1909 **TCLC 14**
    See also CA 110; 155
Annunzio, Gabriele d'
    See D'Annunzio, Gabriele
Anodos
    See Coleridge, Mary E(lizabeth)
Anon, Charles Robert
    See Pessoa, Fernando (Antonio Nogueira)
Anouilh, Jean (Marie Lucien Pierre)
    1910-1987 **CLC 1, 3, 8, 13, 40, 50; DAM**
    DRAM; DC 8
    See also CA 17-20R; 123; CANR 32; DFS
    9, 10; EW 13; GFL 1789 to the Present;
    MTCW 1, 2; RGWL
Anthony, Florence
    See Ai
Anthony, John
    See Ciardi, John (Anthony)
Anthony, Peter
    See Shaffer, Anthony (Joshua); Shaffer,
    Peter (Levin)
Anthony, Piers 1934- **CLC 35; DAM POP**
    See also AAYA 11; BYA 7; CA 21-24R;
    CANR 28, 56, 73, 102; CPW; DLB 8;
    FANT; MAICYAS; MTCW 1, 2; SAAS
    22; SATA 84; SFW; SUFW; YAW
Anthony, Susan B(rownell) 1820-1906 **TCLC**
    84
    See also FW
Antoine, Marc
    See Proust, (Valentin-Louis-George-Eugene-
)Marcel
Antoninus, Brother
    See Everson, William (Oliver)
Antonioni, Michelangelo 1912- **CLC 20, 144**
    See also CA 73-76; CANR 45, 77
Antschel, Paul 1920-1970
    See Celan, Paul
    See also CA 85-88; CANR 33, 61; MTCW
    1
Anwar, Chairil 1922-1949 **TCLC 22**
    See also CA 121
Anzaldua, Gloria (Evanjelina) 1942-
    See also CA 175; CSW; CWP; DLB 122;
    FW; HLCS 1; RGAL
Apess, William 1798-1839(?) **NCLC 73; DAM**
    MULT
    See also DLB 175, 243; NNAL
Apollinaire, Guillaume 1880-1918 **TCLC 3,**
    8, 51; DAM POET; PC 7
    See also CA 152; EW 9; GFL 1789 to the
    Present; MTCW 1; RGWL; WP
Apollonius of Rhodes
    See Apollonius Rhodius
    See also AW 1; RGWL
Apollonius Rhodius c. 300B.C.-c. 220B.C.
    CMLC 28
    See also Apollonius of Rhodes
    See also DLB 176
Appelfeld, Aharon 1932- **CLC 23, 47; SSC**
    42
    See also CA 112; 133; CANR 86; CWW 2;
    RGSF
Apple, Max (Isaac) 1941- **CLC 9, 33; SSC 50**
    See also CA 81-84; CANR 19, 54; DLB
    130

Appleman, Philip (Dean) 1926- **CLC 51**
See also CA 13-16R; CAAS 18; CANR 6, 29, 56

Appleton, Lawrence
See Lovecraft, H(oward) P(hillips)

Apteryx
See Eliot, T(homas) S(tearns)

Apuleius, (Lucius Madaurensis) 125(?)-175(?) **CMLC 1**
See also AW 2; DLB 211; RGWL; SUFW

Aquin, Hubert 1929-1977 **CLC 15**
See also CA 105; DLB 53

Aquinas, Thomas 1224(?)-1274 **CMLC 33**
See also DLB 115; EW 1

Aragon, Louis 1897-1982 **CLC 3, 22; DAM NOV, POET**
See also CA 69-72; 108; CANR 28, 71; DLB 72; EW 11; GFL 1789 to the Present; GLL 2; MTCW 1, 2; RGWL

Arany, Janos 1817-1882 **NCLC 34**

Aranyos, Kakay 1847-1910
See Mikszath, Kalman

Arbuthnot, John 1667-1735 **LC 1**
See also DLB 101

Archer, Herbert Winslow
See Mencken, H(enry) L(ouis)

Archer, Jeffrey (Howard) 1940- **CLC 28; DAM POP**
See also AAYA 16; BEST 89:3; BPFB 1; CA 77-80; CANR 22, 52, 95; CPW; DA3; INT CANR-22

Archer, Jules 1915- **CLC 12**
See also CA 9-12R; CANR 6, 69; SAAS 5; SATA 4, 85

Archer, Lee
See Ellison, Harlan (Jay)

Archilochus c. 7th cent. B.C.- **CMLC 44**
See also DLB 176

Arden, John 1930- **CLC 6, 13, 15; DAM DRAM**
See also BRWS 2; CA 13-16R; CAAS 4; CANR 31, 65, 67; CBD; CD; DFS 9; DLB 13, 245; MTCW 1

Arenas, Reinaldo 1943-1990 **CLC 41; DAM MULT; HLC 1**
See also CA 124; 128; 133; CANR 73, 106; DLB 145; GLL 2; HW 1; LAW; LAWS 1; MTCW 1; RGSF; WLIT 1

Arendt, Hannah 1906-1975 **CLC 66, 98**
See also CA 17-20R; 61-64; CANR 26, 60; DLB 242; MTCW 1, 2

Aretino, Pietro 1492-1556 **LC 12**
See also RGWL

Arghezi, Tudor CLC 80
See also Theodorescu, Ion N.
See also CA 167; DLB 220

Arguedas, Jose Maria 1911-1969 **CLC 10, 18; HLCS 1**
See also CA 89-92; CANR 73; DLB 113; HW 1; LAW; RGWL; WLIT 1

Argueta, Manlio 1936- **CLC 31**
See also CA 131; CANR 73; CWW 2; DLB 145; HW 1

Arias, Ron(ald Francis) 1941-
See also CA 131; CANR 81; DAM MULT; DLB 82; HLC 1; HW 1, 2; MTCW 2

Ariosto, Ludovico 1474-1533 **LC 6**
See also EW 2; RGWL

Aristides
See Epstein, Joseph

Aristophanes 450B.C.-385B.C. **CMLC 4; DA; DAB; DAC; DAM DRAM, MST; DC 2; WLCS**
See also AW 1; DA3; DFS 10; DLB 176; RGWL

Aristotle 384B.C.-322B.C. **CMLC 31; DA; DAB; DAC; DAM MST; WLCS**
See also AW 1; DA3; DLB 176; RGEL

Arlt, Roberto (Godofredo Christophersen) 1900-1942 **TCLC 29; DAM MULT; HLC 1**
See also CA 123; 131; CANR 67; HW 1, 2; LAW

Armah, Ayi Kwei 1939- **CLC 5, 33, 136; BLC 1; DAM MULT, POET**
See also AFW; BW 1; CA 61-64; CANR 21, 64; CN; DLB 117; MTCW 1; WLIT 2

Armatrading, Joan 1950- **CLC 17**
See also CA 114; 186

Arnette, Robert
See Silverberg, Robert

Arnim, Achim von (Ludwig Joachim von Arnim) 1781-1831 **NCLC 5; SSC 29**
See also DLB 90

Arnim, Bettina von 1785-1859 **NCLC 38**
See also DLB 90; RGWL

Arnold, Matthew 1822-1888 **NCLC 6, 29, 89; DA; DAB; DAC; DAM MST, POET; PC 5; WLC**
See also BRW 5; CDBLB 1832-1890; DLB 32, 57; EXPP; PAB; PFS 2; WP

Arnold, Thomas 1795-1842 **NCLC 18**
See also DLB 55

Arnow, Harriette (Louisa) Simpson 1908-1986 **CLC 2, 7, 18**
See also BPFB 1; CA 9-12R; 118; CANR 14; DLB 6; FW; MTCW 1, 2; RHW; SATA 42; SATA-Obit 47

Arouet, Francois-Marie
See Voltaire

Arp, Hans
See Arp, Jean

Arp, Jean 1887-1966 **CLC 5**
See also CA 81-84; 25-28R; CANR 42, 77; EW 10; TCLC 115

Arrabal
See Arrabal, Fernando

Arrabal, Fernando 1932- **CLC 2, 9, 18, 58**
See also CA 9-12R; CANR 15

Arreola, Juan Jose 1918- **CLC 147; DAM MULT; HLC 1; SSC 38**
See also CA 113; 131; CANR 81; DLB 113; DNFS; HW 1, 2; LAW; RGSF

Arrian c. 89(?)-c. 155(?) **CMLC 43**
See also DLB 176

Arrick, Fran CLC 30
See also Gaberman, Judie Angell
See also BYA 6

Artaud, Antonin (Marie Joseph) 1896-1948 **TCLC 3, 36; DAM DRAM; DC 14**
See also CA 104; 149; DA3; EW 11; GFL 1789 to the Present; MTCW 1; RGWL

Arthur, Ruth M(abel) 1905-1979 **CLC 12**
See also CA 9-12R; 85-88; CANR 4; CWRI; SATA 7, 26

Artsybashev, Mikhail (Petrovich) 1878-1927 **TCLC 31**
See also CA 170

Arundel, Honor (Morfydd) 1919-1973 **CLC 17**
See also CA 21-22; 41-44R; CAP 2; CLR 35; CWRI; SATA 4; SATA-Obit 24

Arzner, Dorothy 1900-1979 **CLC 98**

Asch, Sholem 1880-1957 **TCLC 3**
See also CA 105; GLL 2

Ash, Shalom
See Asch, Sholem

Ashbery, John (Lawrence) 1927- **CLC 2, 3, 4, 6, 9, 13, 15, 25, 41, 77, 125; DAM POET; PC 26**
See Berry, Jonas
See also AMWS 3; CA 5-8R; CANR 9, 37, 66, 102; CP; DA3; DLB 5, 165; DLBY 81; INT CANR-9; MTCW 1, 2; PAB; PFS 11; RGAL; WP

Ashdown, Clifford
See Freeman, R(ichard) Austin

Ashe, Gordon
See Creasey, John

Ashton-Warner, Sylvia (Constance) 1908-1984 **CLC 19**
See also CA 69-72; 112; CANR 29; MTCW 1, 2

Asimov, Isaac 1920-1992 **CLC 1, 3, 9, 19, 26, 76, 92; DAM POP**
See also AAYA 13; BEST 90:2; BPFB 1; BYA 4, 6, 7, 9; CA 1-4R; 137; CANR 2, 19, 36, 60; CLR 12; CMW; CPW; DA3; DLB 8; DLBY 92; INT CANR-19; JRDA; LAIT 5; MAICYA; MTCW 1, 2; RGAL; SATA 1, 26, 74; SCFW 2; SFW; YAW

Assis, Joaquim Maria Machado de
See Machado de Assis, Joaquim Maria

Astell, Mary 1666-1731 **LC 68**
See also DLB 252; FW

Astley, Thea (Beatrice May) 1925- **CLC 41**
See also CA 65-68; CANR 11, 43, 78; CN

Astley, William 1855-1911
See Warung, Price

Aston, James
See White, T(erence) H(anbury)

Asturias, Miguel Angel 1899-1974 **CLC 3, 8, 13; DAM MULT, NOV; HLC 1**
See also CA 25-28; 49-52; CANR 32; CAP 2; DA3; DLB 113; HW 1; LAW; MTCW 1, 2; RGWL; WLIT 1

Atares, Carlos Saura
See Saura (Atares), Carlos

Athanasius c. 295-c. 373 **CMLC 48**

Atheling, William
See Pound, Ezra (Weston Loomis)

Atheling, William, Jr.
See Blish, James (Benjamin)

Atherton, Gertrude (Franklin Horn) 1857-1948 **TCLC 2**
See also CA 104; 155; DLB 9, 78, 186; HGG; RGAL; SUFW; TCWW 2

Atherton, Lucius
See Masters, Edgar Lee

Atkins, Jack
See Harris, Mark

Atkinson, Kate CLC 99
See also CA 166; CANR 101

Attaway, William (Alexander) 1911-1986 **CLC 92; BLC 1; DAM MULT**
See also BW 2, 3; CA 143; CANR 82; DLB 76

Atticus
See Fleming, Ian (Lancaster); Wilson, (Thomas) Woodrow

Atwood, Margaret (Eleanor) 1939- **CLC 2, 3, 4, 8, 13, 15, 25, 44, 84, 135; DA; DAB; DAC; DAM MST, NOV, POET; PC 8; SSC 2, 46; WLC**
See also AAYA 12; BEST 89:2; BPFB 1; CA 49-52; CANR 3, 24, 33, 59, 95; CN; CP; CPW; CWP; DA3; DLB 53, 251; EXPN; FW; INT CANR-24; LAIT 5; MTCW 1, 2; NFS 4, 12, 13; PFS 7; RGSF; SATA 50; SSFS 3, 13; YAW

Aubigny, Pierre d'
See Mencken, H(enry) L(ouis)

Aubin, Penelope 1685-1731(?) **LC 9**
See also DLB 39

Auchincloss, Louis (Stanton) 1917- **CLC 4, 6, 9, 18, 45; DAM NOV; SSC 22**
See also AMWS 4; CA 1-4R; CANR 6, 29, 55, 87; CN; DLB 2, 244; DLBY 80; INT CANR-29; MTCW 1; RGAL

Auden, W(ystan) H(ugh) 1907-1973 **CLC 1, 2, 3, 4, 6, 9, 11, 14, 43, 123; DA; DAB; DAC; DAM DRAM, MST, POET; PC 1; WLC**
See also AAYA 18; AMWS 2; BRW 7; BRWR 1; CA 9-12R; 45-48; CANR 5, 61,

105; CDBLB 1914-1945; DA3; DLB 10, 20; EXPP; MTCW 1, 2; PAB; PFS 1, 3, 4, 10; WP

Audiberti, Jacques 1900-1965 **CLC 38; DAM DRAM**
See also CA 25-28R

Audubon, John James 1785-1851 **NCLC 47**
See also ANW; DLB 248

Auel, Jean M(arie) 1936- **CLC 31, 107; DAM POP**
See also AAYA 7; BEST 90:4; BPFB 1; CA 103; CANR 21, 64; CPW; DA3; INT CANR-21; NFS 11; RHW; SATA 91

Auerbach, Erich 1892-1957 **TCLC 43**
See also CA 118; 155

Augier, Emile 1820-1889 **NCLC 31**
See also DLB 192; GFL 1789 to the Present

August, John
See De Voto, Bernard (Augustine)

Augustine, St. 354-430 **CMLC 6; DA; DAB; DAC; DAM MST; WLCS**
See also DA3; DLB 115; EW 1; RGWL

Aunt Belinda
See Braddon, Mary Elizabeth

Aurelius
See Bourne, Randolph S(illiman)

Aurelius, Marcus 121-180 **CMLC 45**
See also Marcus Aurelius
See also RGWL

Aurobindo, Sri
See Ghose, Aurabinda

Austen, Jane 1775-1817 **NCLC 1, 13, 19, 33, 51, 81, 95; DA; DAB; DAC; DAM MST, NOV; WLC**
See also AAYA 19; BRW 4; BRWR 2; BYA 3; CDBLB 1789-1832; DA3; DLB 116; EXPN; LAIT 2; NFS 1; WLIT 3; WYAS 1

Auster, Paul 1947- **CLC 47, 131**
See also CA 69-72; CANR 23, 52, 75; CMW; CN; DA3; DLB 227; MTCW 1

Austin, Frank
See Faust, Frederick (Schiller)
See also TCWW 2

Austin, Mary (Hunter) 1868-1934 **TCLC 25**
See also Stairs, Gordon
See also ANW; CA 109; 178; DLB 9, 78, 206, 221; FW; TCWW 2

Averroes 1126-1198 **CMLC 7**
See also DLB 115

Avicenna 980-1037 **CMLC 16**
See also DLB 115

Avison, Margaret 1918- **CLC 2, 4, 97; DAC; DAM POET**
See also CA 17-20R; CP; DLB 53; MTCW 1

Axton, David
See Koontz, Dean R(ay)

Ayckbourn, Alan 1939- **CLC 5, 8, 18, 33, 74; DAB; DAM DRAM; DC 13**
See also BRWS 5; CA 21-24R; CANR 31, 59; CBD; CD; DFS 7; DLB 13, 245; MTCW 1, 2

Aydy, Catherine
See Tennant, Emma (Christina)

Ayme, Marcel (Andre) 1902-1967 **CLC 11; SSC 41**
See also CA 89-92; CANR 67; CLR 25; DLB 72; EW 12; GFL 1789 to the Present; RGSF; RGWL; SATA 91

Ayrton, Michael 1921-1975 **CLC 7**
See also CA 5-8R; 61-64; CANR 9, 21

Azorin CLC 11
See also Martinez Ruiz, Jose
See also EW 9

Azuela, Mariano 1873-1952 **TCLC 3; DAM MULT; HLC 1**
See also CA 104; 131; CANR 81; HW 1, 2; LAW; MTCW 1, 2

Baastad, Babbis Friis
See Friis-Baastad, Babbis Ellinor

Bab
See Gilbert, W(illiam) S(chwenck)

Babbis, Eleanor
See Friis-Baastad, Babbis Ellinor

Babel, Isaac
See Babel, Isaak (Emmanuilovich)
See also EW 11; SSFS 10

Babel, Isaak (Emmanuilovich) 1894-1941(?) **TCLC 2, 13; SSC 16**
See also Babel, Isaac
See also CA 104; 155; MTCW 1; RGSF; RGWL

Babits, Mihaly 1883-1941 **TCLC 14**
See also CA 114; DLB 215

Babur 1483-1530 **LC 18**

Babylas 1898-1962
See Ghelderode, Michel de

Baca, Jimmy Santiago 1952-
See also CA 131; CANR 81, 90; CP; DAM MULT; DLB 122; HLC 1; HW 1, 2

Bacchelli, Riccardo 1891-1985 **CLC 19**
See also CA 29-32R; 117

Bach, Richard (David) 1936- **CLC 14; DAM NOV, POP**
See also AITN 1; BEST 89:2; BPFB 1; BYA 5; CA 9-12R; CANR 18, 93; CPW; FANT; MTCW 1; SATA 13

Bache, Benjamin Franklin 1769-1798 **LC 74**
See also DLB 43

Bachman, Richard
See King, Stephen (Edwin)

Bachmann, Ingeborg 1926-1973 **CLC 69**
See also CA 93-96; 45-48; CANR 69; DLB 85; RGWL

Bacon, Francis 1561-1626 **LC 18, 32**
See also BRW 1; CDBLB Before 1660; DLB 151, 236, 252; RGEL

Bacon, Roger 1214(?)-1294 **CMLC 14**
See also DLB 115

Bacovia, George 1881-1957 **TCLC 24**
See also Vasiliu, Gheorghe
See also DLB 220

Badanes, Jerome 1937- **CLC 59**

Bagehot, Walter 1826-1877 **NCLC 10**
See also DLB 55

Bagnold, Enid 1889-1981 **CLC 25; DAM DRAM**
See also BYA 2; CA 5-8R; 103; CANR 5, 40; CBD; CWD; CWRI; DLB 13, 160, 191, 245; FW; MAICYA; RGEL; SATA 1, 25

Bagritsky, Eduard 1895-1934 **TCLC 60**

Bagrjana, Elisaveta
See Belcheva, Elisaveta

Bagryana, Elisaveta CLC 10
See also Belcheva, Elisaveta
See also CA 178; DLB 147

Bailey, Paul 1937- **CLC 45**
See also CA 21-24R; CANR 16, 62; CN; DLB 14; GLL 2

Baillie, Joanna 1762-1851 **NCLC 71**
See also DLB 93; RGEL

Bainbridge, Beryl (Margaret) 1934- **CLC 4, 5, 8, 10, 14, 18, 22, 62, 130; DAM NOV**
See also BRWS 6; CA 21-24R; CANR 24, 55, 75, 88; CN; DLB 14, 231; MTCW 1, 2

Baker, Carlos (Heard) TCLC 119
See also CA 5-8R; 122; CANR 3, 63; DLB 103

Baker, Elliott 1922- **CLC 8**
See also CA 45-48; CANR 2, 63; CN

Baker, Jean H. TCLC 3, 10
See also Russell, George William

Baker, Nicholson 1957- **CLC 61; DAM POP**
See also CA 135; CANR 63; CN; CPW; DA3; DLB 227

Baker, Ray Stannard 1870-1946 **TCLC 47**
See also CA 118

Baker, Russell (Wayne) 1925- **CLC 31**
See also BEST 89:4; CA 57-60; CANR 11, 41, 59; MTCW 1, 2

Bakhtin, M.
See Bakhtin, Mikhail Mikhailovich

Bakhtin, M. M.
See Bakhtin, Mikhail Mikhailovich

Bakhtin, Mikhail
See Bakhtin, Mikhail Mikhailovich

Bakhtin, Mikhail Mikhailovich 1895-1975 **CLC 83**
See also CA 128; 113; DLB 242

Bakshi, Ralph 1938(?)- **CLC 26**
See also CA 112; 138; IDFW 3

Bakunin, Mikhail (Alexandrovich) 1814-1876 **NCLC 25, 58**

Baldwin, James (Arthur) 1924-1987 **CLC 1, 2, 3, 4, 5, 8, 13, 15, 17, 42, 50, 67, 90, 127; BLC 1; DA; DAB; DAC; DAM MST, MULT, NOV, POP; DC 1; SSC 10, 33; WLC**
See also AAYA 4, 34; AFAW 1, 2; AMWS 1; BW 1; CA 1-4R; 124; CABS 1; CAD; CANR 3, 24; CDALB 1941-1968; CPW; DA3; DFS 11; DLB 2, 7, 33, 249; DLBY 87; EXPS; LAIT 5; MTCW 1, 2; NFS 4; RGAL; RGSF; SATA 9; SATA-Obit 54; SSFS 2

Bale, John 1495-1563 **LC 62**
See also DLB 132; RGEL

Ball, Hugo 1886-1927 **TCLC 104**

Ballard, J(ames) G(raham) 1930- **CLC 3, 6, 14, 36, 137; DAM NOV, POP; SSC 1**
See also AAYA 3; BRWS 5; CA 5-8R; CANR 15, 39, 65; CN; DA3; DLB 14, 207; HGG; MTCW 1, 2; NFS 8; RGEL; RGSF; SATA 93; SFW

Balmont, Konstantin (Dmitriyevich) 1867-1943 **TCLC 11**
See also CA 109; 155

Baltausis, Vincas 1847-1910
See Mikszath, Kalman

Balzac, Honore de 1799-1850 **NCLC 5, 35, 53; DA; DAB; DAC; DAM MST, NOV; SSC 5; WLC**
See also DA3; DLB 119; EW 5; GFL 1789 to the Present; RGSF; RGWL; SSFS 10; SUFW

Bambara, Toni Cade 1939-1995 **CLC 19, 88; BLC 1; DA; DAC; DAM MST, MULT; SSC 35; WLCS**
See also AAYA 5; AFAW 2; BW 2, 3; BYA 12, 14; CA 29-32R; 150; CANR 24, 49, 81; CDALBS; DA3; DLB 38, 218; EXPS; MTCW 1, 2; RGAL; RGSF; SATA 112; SSFS 4, 7, 12; TCLC 116

Bamdad, A.
See Shamlu, Ahmad

Banat, D. R.
See Bradbury, Ray (Douglas)

Bancroft, Laura
See Baum, L(yman) Frank

Banim, John 1798-1842 **NCLC 13**
See also DLB 116, 158, 159; RGEL

Banim, Michael 1796-1874 **NCLC 13**
See also DLB 158, 159

Banjo, The
See Paterson, A(ndrew) B(arton)

Banks, Iain
See Banks, Iain M(enzies)

Banks, Iain M(enzies) 1954- **CLC 34**
See also CA 123; 128; CANR 61, 106; DLB 194; HGG; INT 128; SFW

Banks, Lynne Reid CLC 23
See also Reid Banks, Lynne
See also AAYA 6; BYA 7
Banks, Russell 1940- CLC 37, 72; SSC 42
See also AMWS 5; CA 65-68; CAAS 15;
CANR 19, 52, 73; CN; DLB 130; NFS 13
Banville, John 1945- CLC 46, 118
See also CA 117; 128; CANR 104; CN;
DLB 14; INT 128
**Banville, Theodore (Faullain) de 1832-1891
NCLC 9**
See also DLB 217; GFL 1789 to the Present
**Baraka, Amiri 1934- CLC 1, 2, 3, 5, 10, 14,
33, 115; BLC 1; DA; DAC; DAM MST,
MULT, POET, POP; DC 6; PC 4;
WLCS**
See also Jones, LeRoi
See also AFAW 1, 2; AMWS 2; BW 2, 3;
CA 21-24R; CABS 3; CAD; CANR 27,
38, 61; CD; CDALB 1941-1968; CP;
CPW; DA3; DFS 3, 11; DLB 5, 7, 16, 38;
DLBD 8; MTCW 1, 2; PFS 9; RGAL; WP
**Baratynsky, Evgenii Abramovich 1800-1844
NCLC 103**
See also DLB 205
**Barbauld, Anna Laetitia 1743-1825 NCLC
50**
See also DLB 107, 109, 142, 158; RGEL
Barbellion, W. N. P. TCLC 24
See also Cummings, Bruce F(rederick)
Barber, Benjamin R. 1939- CLC 141
See also CA 29-32R; CANR 12, 32, 64
Barbera, Jack (Vincent) 1945- CLC 44
See also CA 110; CANR 45
**Barbey d'Aurevilly, Jules-Amedee 1808-1889
NCLC 1; SSC 17**
See also DLB 119; GFL 1789 to the Present
Barbour, John c. 1316-1395 CMLC 33
See also DLB 146
Barbusse, Henri 1873-1935 TCLC 5
See also CA 105; 154; DLB 65; RGWL
Barclay, Bill
See Moorcock, Michael (John)
Barclay, William Ewert
See Moorcock, Michael (John)
Barea, Arturo 1897-1957 TCLC 14
See also CA 111
Barfoot, Joan 1946- CLC 18
See also CA 105
**Barham, Richard Harris 1788-1845 NCLC
77**
See also DLB 159
Baring, Maurice 1874-1945 TCLC 8
See also CA 105; 168; DLB 34; HGG
Baring-Gould, Sabine 1834-1924 TCLC 88
See also DLB 156, 190
Barker, Clive 1952- CLC 52; DAM POP
See also AAYA 10; BEST 90:3; BPFB 1;
CA 121; 129; CANR 71; CPW; DA3;
HGG; INT 129; MTCW 1, 2
**Barker, George Granville 1913-1991 CLC 8,
48; DAM POET**
See also CA 9-12R; 135; CANR 7, 38; DLB
20; MTCW 1
Barker, Harley Granville
See Granville-Barker, Harley
See also DLB 10
Barker, Howard 1946- CLC 37
See also CA 102; CBD; CD; DLB 13, 233
Barker, Jane 1652-1732 LC 42
See also DLB 39, 131
Barker, Pat(ricia) 1943- CLC 32, 94, 146
See also BRWS 4; CA 117; 122; CANR 50,
101; CN; INT 122
**Barlach, Ernst (Heinrich) 1870-1938 TCLC
84**
See also CA 178; DLB 56, 118
Barlow, Joel 1754-1812 NCLC 23
See also AMWS 2; DLB 37; RGAL

Barnard, Mary (Ethel) 1909- CLC 48
See also CA 21-22; CAP 2
**Barnes, Djuna 1892-1982 CLC 3, 4, 8, 11, 29,
127; SSC 3**
See also Steptoe, Lydia
See also AMWS 3; CA 9-12R; 107; CAD;
CANR 16, 55; CWD; DLB 4, 9, 45; GLL
1; MTCW 1, 2; RGAL
**Barnes, Julian (Patrick) 1946- CLC 42, 141;
DAB**
See also BRWS 4; CA 102; CANR 19, 54;
CN; DLB 194; DLBY 93; MTCW 1
Barnes, Peter 1931- CLC 5, 56
See also CA 65-68; CAAS 12; CANR 33,
34, 64; CBD; CD; DFS 6; DLB 13, 233;
MTCW 1
Barnes, William 1801-1886 NCLC 75
See also DLB 32
**Baroja (y Nessi), Pio 1872-1956 TCLC 8;
HLC 1**
See also CA 104; EW 9
Baron, David
See Pinter, Harold
Baron Corvo
See Rolfe, Frederick (William Serafino
Austin Lewis Mary)
Barondess, Sue K(aufman) 1926-1977 CLC 8
See also Kaufman, Sue
See also CA 1-4R; 69-72; CANR 1
Baron de Teive
See Pessoa, Fernando (Antonio Nogueira)
Baroness Von S.
See Zangwill, Israel
**Barres, (Auguste-)Maurice 1862-1923 TCLC
47**
See also CA 164; DLB 123; GFL 1789 to
the Present
Barreto, Afonso Henrique de Lima
See Lima Barreto, Afonso Henrique de
Barrett, Andrea 1954- CLC 150
See also CA 156; CANR 92
Barrett, Michele CLC 65
Barrett, (Roger) Syd 1946- CLC 35
**Barrett, William (Christopher) 1913-1992
CLC 27**
See also CA 13-16R; 139; CANR 11, 67;
INT CANR-11
**Barrie, J(ames) M(atthew) 1860-1937 TCLC
2; DAB; DAM DRAM**
See also BRWS 3; BYA 4, 5; CA 104; 136;
CANR 77; CDBLB 1890-1914; CLR 16;
CWRI; DA3; DFS 7; DLB 10, 141, 156;
FANT; MAICYA; MTCW 1; SATA 100;
SUFW; WCH; WLIT 4; YABC 1
Barrington, Michael
See Moorcock, Michael (John)
Barrol, Grady
See Bograd, Larry
Barry, Mike
See Malzberg, Barry N(athaniel)
Barry, Philip 1896-1949 TCLC 11
See also CA 109; DFS 9; DLB 7, 228;
RGAL
Bart, Andre Schwarz
See Schwarz-Bart, Andre
**Barth, John (Simmons) 1930- CLC 1, 2, 3, 5,
7, 9, 10, 14, 27, 51, 89; DAM NOV; SSC
10**
See also AITN 1, 2; AMW; BPFB 1; CA
1-4R; CABS 1; CANR 5, 23, 49, 64; CN;
DLB 2, 227; FANT; MTCW 1; RGAL;
RGSF; RHW; SSFS 6
**Barthelme, Donald 1931-1989 CLC 1, 2, 3, 5,
6, 8, 13, 23, 46, 59, 115; DAM NOV;
SSC 2**
See also AMWS 4; BPFB 1; CA 21-24R;
129; CANR 20, 58; DA3; DLB 2, 234;
DLBY 80, 89; FANT; MTCW 1, 2;
RGAL; RGSF; SATA 7; SATA-Obit 62;
SSFS 3

Barthelme, Frederick 1943- CLC 36, 117
See also CA 114; 122; CANR 77; CN;
CSW; DLB 244; DLBY 85; INT CA-122
**Barthes, Roland (Gerard) 1915-1980 CLC
24, 83**
See also CA 130; 97-100; CANR 66; EW
13; GFL 1789 to the Present; MTCW 1, 2
Barzun, Jacques (Martin) 1907- CLC 51, 145
See also CA 61-64; CANR 22, 95
Bashevis, Isaac
See Singer, Isaac Bashevis
Bashkirtseff, Marie 1859-1884 NCLC 27
Basho, Matsuo
See Matsuo Basho
See also RGWL; WP
Basil of Caesaria c. 330-379 CMLC 35
Bass, Kingsley B., Jr.
See Bullins, Ed
Bass, Rick 1958- CLC 79, 143
See also ANW; CA 126; CANR 53, 93;
CSW; DLB 212
Bassani, Giorgio 1916-2000 CLC 9
See also CA 65-68; 190; CANR 33; CWW
2; DLB 128, 177; MTCW 1; RGWL
Bastian, Ann CLC 70
Bastos, Augusto (Antonio) Roa
See Roa Bastos, Augusto (Antonio)
Bataille, Georges 1897-1962 CLC 29
See also CA 101; 89-92
**Bates, H(erbert) E(rnest) 1905-1974 CLC 46;
DAB; DAM POP; SSC 10**
See also Gawsworth, John
See also CA 93-96; 45-48; CANR 34; DA3;
DLB 162, 191; EXPS; MTCW 1, 2;
RGSF; SSFS 7
Bauchart
See Camus, Albert
**Baudelaire, Charles 1821-1867 NCLC 6, 29,
55; DA; DAB; DAC; DAM MST,
POET; PC 1; SSC 18; WLC**
See also DA3; DLB 217; EW 7; GFL 1789
to the Present; RGWL
Baudouin, Marcel
See Peguy, Charles (Pierre)
Baudouin, Pierre
See Peguy, Charles (Pierre)
Baudrillard, Jean 1929- CLC 60
Baum, L(yman) Frank 1856-1919 TCLC 7
See also CA 108; 133; CLR 15; CWRI;
DLB 22; FANT; JRDA; MAICYA;
MTCW 1, 2; NFS 13; RGAL; SATA 18,
100; WCH
Baum, Louis F.
See Baum, L(yman) Frank
Baumbach, Jonathan 1933- CLC 6, 23
See also CA 13-16R; CAAS 5; CANR 12,
66; CN; DLBY 80; INT CANR-12;
MTCW 1
Bausch, Richard (Carl) 1945- CLC 51
See also AMWS 7; CA 101; CAAS 14;
CANR 43, 61, 87; CSW; DLB 130
**Baxter, Charles (Morley) 1947- CLC 45, 78;
DAM POP**
See also CA 57-60; CANR 40, 64, 104;
CPW; DLB 130; MTCW 2
Baxter, George Owen
See Faust, Frederick (Schiller)
Baxter, James K(eir) 1926-1972 CLC 14
See also CA 77-80
Baxter, John
See Hunt, E(verette) Howard, (Jr.)
Bayer, Sylvia
See Glassco, John
Baynton, Barbara 1857-1929 TCLC 57
See also DLB 230; RGSF

Beagle, Peter S(oyer) 1939- **CLC 7, 104**
See also BPFB 1; BYA 9, 10; CA 9-12R; CANR 4, 51, 73; DA3; DLBY 80; FANT; INT CANR-4; MTCW 1; SATA 60; SUFW; YAW

Bean, Normal
See Burroughs, Edgar Rice

Beard, Charles A(ustin) 1874-1948 **TCLC 15**
See also CA 115; 189; DLB 17; SATA 18

Beardsley, Aubrey 1872-1898 **NCLC 6**

Beattie, Ann 1947- **CLC 8, 13, 18, 40, 63, 146; DAM NOV, POP; SSC 11**
See also AMWS 5; BEST 90:2; BPFB 1; CA 81-84; CANR 53, 73; CN; CPW; DA3; DLB 218; DLBY 82; MTCW 1, 2; RGAL; RGSF; SSFS 9

Beattie, James 1735-1803 **NCLC 25**
See also DLB 109

Beauchamp, Kathleen Mansfield 1888-1923
See Mansfield, Katherine
See also CA 104; 134; DA; DA3; DAC; DAM MST; MTCW 2

Beaumarchais, Pierre-Augustin Caron de 1732-1799 **LC 61; DAM DRAM; DC 4**
See also EW 4; GFL Beginnings to 1789; RGWL

Beaumont, Francis 1584(?)-1616 **LC 33; DC 6**
See also BRW 2; CDBLB Before 1660; DLB 58

Beauvoir, Simone (Lucie Ernestine Marie Bertrand) de 1908-1986 **CLC 1, 2, 4, 8, 14, 31, 44, 50, 71, 124; DA; DAB; DAC; DAM MST, NOV; SSC 35; WLC**
See also BPFB 1; CA 9-12R; 118; CANR 28, 61; DA3; DLB 72; DLBY 86; EW 12; FW; GFL 1789 to the Present; MTCW 1, 2; RGSF; RGWL

Becker, Carl (Lotus) 1873-1945 **TCLC 63**
See also CA 157; DLB 17

Becker, Jurek 1937-1997 **CLC 7, 19**
See also CA 85-88; 157; CANR 60; CWW 2; DLB 75

Becker, Walter 1950- **CLC 26**

Beckett, Samuel (Barclay) 1906-1989 **CLC 1, 2, 3, 4, 6, 9, 10, 11, 14, 18, 29, 57, 59, 83; DA; DAB; DAC; DAM DRAM, MST, NOV; SSC 16; WLC**
See also BRWR 1; BRWS 1; CA 5-8R; 130; CANR 33, 61; CBD; CDBLB 1945-1960; DA3; DFS 2, 7; DLB 13, 15, 233; DLBY 90; GFL 1789 to the Present; MTCW 1, 2; RGSF; RGWL; WLIT 4

Beckford, William 1760-1844 **NCLC 16**
See also BRW 3; DLB 39, 213; HGG; SUFW

Beckman, Gunnel 1910- **CLC 26**
See also CA 33-36R; CANR 15; CLR 25; MAICYA; SAAS 9; SATA 6

Becque, Henri 1837-1899 **NCLC 3**
See also DLB 192; GFL 1789 to the Present

Becquer, Gustavo Adolfo 1836-1870 **NCLC 106; DAM MULT; HLCS 1**

Beddoes, Thomas Lovell 1803-1849 **NCLC 3; DC 15**
See also DLB 96

Bede c. 673-735 **CMLC 20**
See also DLB 146

Bedford, Donald F.
See Fearing, Kenneth (Flexner)

Beecher, Catharine Esther 1800-1878 **NCLC 30**
See also DLB 1, 243

Beecher, John 1904-1980 **CLC 6**
See also AITN 1; CA 5-8R; 105; CANR 8

Beer, Johann 1655-1700 **LC 5**
See also DLB 168

Beer, Patricia 1924- **CLC 58**
See also CA 61-64; 183; CANR 13, 46; CP; CWP; DLB 40; FW

Beerbohm, Max
See Beerbohm, (Henry) Max(imilian)

Beerbohm, (Henry) Max(imilian) 1872-1956 **TCLC 1, 24**
See also BRWS 2; CA 104; 154; CANR 79; DLB 34, 100; FANT

Beer-Hofmann, Richard 1866-1945 **TCLC 60**
See also CA 160; DLB 81

Beg, Shemus
See Stephens, James

Begiebing, Robert J(ohn) 1946- **CLC 70**
See also CA 122; CANR 40, 88

Behan, Brendan 1923-1964 **CLC 1, 8, 11, 15, 79; DAM DRAM**
See also BRWS 2; CA 73-76; CANR 33; CBD; CDBLB 1945-1960; DFS 7; DLB 13, 233; MTCW 1, 2

Behn, Aphra 1640(?)-1689 **LC 1, 30, 42; DA; DAB; DAC; DAM DRAM, MST, NOV, POET; DC 4; PC 13; WLC**
See also BRWS 3; DA3; DLB 39, 80, 131; FW; WLIT 3

Behrman, S(amuel) N(athaniel) 1893-1973 **CLC 40**
See also CA 13-16; 45-48; CAD; CAP 1; DLB 7, 44; IDFW 3; RGAL

Belasco, David 1853-1931 **TCLC 3**
See also CA 104; 168; DLB 7; RGAL

Belcheva, Elisaveta 1893-1991 **CLC 10**
See also Bagryana, Elisaveta

Beldone, Phil "Cheech"
See Ellison, Harlan (Jay)

Beleno
See Azuela, Mariano

Belinski, Vissarion Grigoryevich 1811-1848 **NCLC 5**
See also DLB 198

Belitt, Ben 1911- **CLC 22**
See also CA 13-16R; CAAS 4; CANR 7, 77; CP; DLB 5

Bell, Gertrude (Margaret Lowthian) 1868-1926 **TCLC 67**
See also CA 167; DLB 174

Bell, J. Freeman
See Zangwill, Israel

Bell, James Madison 1826-1902 **TCLC 43; BLC 1; DAM MULT**
See also BW 1; CA 122; 124; DLB 50

Bell, Madison Smartt 1957- **CLC 41, 102**
See also AMWS 10; BPFB 1; CA 111, 183; CAAE 183; CANR 28, 54, 73; CN; CSW; DLB 218; MTCW 1

Bell, Marvin (Hartley) 1937- **CLC 8, 31; DAM POET**
See also CA 21-24R; CAAS 14; CANR 59, 102; CP; DLB 5; MTCW 1

Bell, W. L. D.
See Mencken, H(enry) L(ouis)

Bellamy, Atwood C.
See Mencken, H(enry) L(ouis)

Bellamy, Edward 1850-1898 **NCLC 4, 86**
See also DLB 12; RGAL; SFW

Belli, Gioconda 1949-
See also CA 152; CWW 2; HLCS 1

Bellin, Edward J.
See Kuttner, Henry

Belloc, (Joseph) Hilaire (Pierre Sebastien Rene Swanton) 1870-1953 **TCLC 7, 18; DAM POET; PC 24**
See also CA 106; 152; CWRI; DLB 19, 100, 141, 174; MTCW 1; SATA 112; WCH; YABC 1

Belloc, Joseph Peter Rene Hilaire
See Belloc, (Joseph) Hilaire (Pierre Sebastien Rene Swanton)

Belloc, Joseph Pierre Hilaire
See Belloc, (Joseph) Hilaire (Pierre Sebastien Rene Swanton)

Belloc, M. A.
See Lowndes, Marie Adelaide (Belloc)

Bellow, Saul 1915- **CLC 1, 2, 3, 6, 8, 10, 13, 15, 25, 33, 34, 63, 79; DA; DAB; DAC; DAM MST, NOV, POP; SSC 14; WLC**
See also AITN 2; AMW; BEST 89:3; BPFB 1; CA 5-8R; CABS 1; CANR 29, 53, 95; CDALB 1941-1968; CN; DA3; DLB 2, 28; DLBD 3; DLBY 82; MTCW 1, 2; NFS 4; RGAL; RGSF; SSFS 12

Belser, Reimond Karel Maria de 1929-
See Ruyslinck, Ward
See also CA 152

Bely, Andrey **TCLC 7; PC 11**
See Bugayev, Boris Nikolayevich
See also EW 9; MTCW 1

Belyi, Andrei
See Bugayev, Boris Nikolayevich
See also RGWL

Benary, Margot
See Benary-Isbert, Margot

Benary-Isbert, Margot 1889-1979 **CLC 12**
See also CA 5-8R; 89-92; CANR 4, 72; CLR 12; MAICYA; SATA 2; SATA-Obit 21

Benavente (y Martinez), Jacinto 1866-1954 **TCLC 3; DAM DRAM, MULT; HLCS 1**
See also CA 106; 131; CANR 81; GLL 2; HW 1, 2; MTCW 1, 2

Benchley, Peter (Bradford) 1940- **CLC 4, 8; DAM NOV, POP**
See also AAYA 14; AITN 2; BPFB 1; CA 17-20R; CANR 12, 35, 66; CPW; HGG; MTCW 1, 2; SATA 3, 89

Benchley, Robert (Charles) 1889-1945 **TCLC 1, 55**
See also CA 105; 153; DLB 11; RGAL

Benda, Julien 1867-1956 **TCLC 60**
See also CA 120; 154; GFL 1789 to the Present

Benedict, Ruth (Fulton) 1887-1948 **TCLC 60**
See also CA 158; DLB 246

Benedikt, Michael 1935- **CLC 4, 14**
See also CA 13-16R; CANR 7; CP; DLB 5

Benet, Juan 1927-1993 **CLC 28**
See also CA 143

Benet, Stephen Vincent 1898-1943 **TCLC 7; DAM POET; SSC 10**
See also CA 104; 152; DA3; DLB 4, 48, 102, 249; DLBY 97; HGG; MTCW 1; RGAL; RGSF; SUFW; WP; YABC 1

Benet, William Rose 1886-1950 **TCLC 28; DAM POET**
See also CA 118; 152; DLB 45; RGAL

Benford, Gregory (Albert) 1941- **CLC 52**
See also BPFB 1; CA 69-72, 175; CAAE 175; CAAS 27; CANR 12, 24, 49, 95; CSW; DLBY 82; SCFW 2; SFW

Bengtsson, Frans (Gunnar) 1894-1954 **TCLC 48**
See also CA 170

Benjamin, David
See Slavitt, David R(ytman)

Benjamin, Lois
See Gould, Lois

Benjamin, Walter 1892-1940 **TCLC 39**
See also CA 164; DLB 242; EW 11

Benn, Gottfried 1886-1956 **TCLC 3; PC 35**
See also CA 106; 153; DLB 56; RGWL

Bennett, Alan 1934- **CLC 45, 77; DAB; DAM MST**
See also CA 103; CANR 35, 55, 106; CBD; CD; MTCW 1, 2

15, 32; DA; DAC; DAM MST, POET;
PC 3, 34
See also AMWS 1; CA 5-8R; 89-92; CABS
2; CANR 26, 61; CDALB 1968-1988;
DA3; DLB 5, 169; GLL 2; MAWW;
MTCW 1, 2; PAB; PFS 6, 12; RGAL;
SATA-Obit 24; WP

Bishop, John 1935- **CLC 10**
See also CA 105

Bishop, John Peale 1892-1944 **TCLC 103**
See also CA 107; 155; DLB 4, 9, 45; RGAL

Bissett, Bill 1939- **CLC 18; PC 14**
See also CA 69-72; CAAS 19; CANR 15;
CCA 1; CP; DLB 53; MTCW 1

Bissoondath, Neil (Devindra) 1955- **CLC 120;
DAC**
See also CA 136; CN

Bitov, Andrei (Georgievich) 1937- **CLC 57**
See also CA 142

Biyidi, Alexandre 1932-
See Beti, Mongo
See also BW 1, 3; CA 114; 124; CANR 81;
DA3; MTCW 1, 2

Bjarme, Brynjolf
See Ibsen, Henrik (Johan)

Bjoernson, Bjoernstjerne (Martinius)
1832-1910 **TCLC 7, 37**
See also CA 104

Black, Robert
See Holdstock, Robert P.

Blackburn, Paul 1926-1971 **CLC 9, 43**
See also CA 81-84; 33-36R; CANR 34;
DLB 16; DLBY 81

Black Elk 1863-1950 **TCLC 33; DAM MULT**
See also CA 144; MTCW 1; NNAL; WP

Black Hobart
See Sanders, (James) Ed(ward)

Blacklin, Malcolm
See Chambers, Aidan

Blackmore, R(ichard) D(oddridge)
1825-1900 **TCLC 27**
See also CA 120; DLB 18; RGEL

Blackmur, R(ichard) P(almer) 1904-1965
CLC 2, 24
See also AMWS 2; CA 11-12; 25-28R;
CANR 71; CAP 1; DLB 63

Black Tarantula
See Acker, Kathy

Blackwood, Algernon (Henry) 1869-1951
TCLC 5
See also CA 105; 150; DLB 153, 156, 178;
HGG; SUFW

Blackwood, Caroline 1931-1996 **CLC 6, 9,
100**
See also CA 85-88; 151; CANR 32, 61, 65;
CN; DLB 14, 207; HGG; MTCW 1

Blade, Alexander
See Hamilton, Edmond; Silverberg, Robert

Blaga, Lucian 1895-1961 **CLC 75**
See also CA 157; DLB 220

Blair, Eric (Arthur) 1903-1950
See Orwell, George
See also CA 104; 132; DA; DA3; DAB;
DAC; DAM MST, NOV; MTCW 1, 2;
SATA 29

Blair, Hugh 1718-1800 **NCLC 75**

Blais, Marie-Claire 1939- **CLC 2, 4, 6, 13,
22; DAC; DAM MST**
See also CA 21-24R; CAAS 4; CANR 38,
75, 93; DLB 53; FW; MTCW 1, 2

Blaise, Clark 1940- **CLC 29**
See also AITN 2; CA 53-56; CAAS 3;
CANR 5, 66, 106; CN; DLB 53; RGSF

Blake, Fairley
See De Voto, Bernard (Augustine)

Blake, Nicholas
See Day Lewis, C(ecil)
See also DLB 77; MSW

Blake, William 1757-1827 **NCLC 13, 37, 57;**

DA; DAB; DAC; DAM MST, POET;
PC 12; WLC
See also BRW 3; BRWR 1; CDBLB 1789-
1832; CLR 52; DA3; DLB 93, 163; EXPP;
MAICYA; PAB; PFS 2, 12; SATA 30;
WCH; WLIT 3; WP

Blanchot, Maurice 1907- **CLC 135**
See also CA 117; 144; DLB 72

Blasco Ibanez, Vicente 1867-1928 **TCLC 12;
DAM NOV**
See also BPFB 1; CA 110; 131; CANR 81;
DA3; EW 8; HW 1, 2; MTCW 1

Blatty, William Peter 1928- **CLC 2; DAM
POP**
See also CA 5-8R; CANR 9; HGG

Bleeck, Oliver
See Thomas, Ross (Elmore)

Blessing, Lee 1949- **CLC 54**
See also CAD; CD

Blight, Rose
See Greer, Germaine

Blish, James (Benjamin) 1921-1975 **CLC 14**
See also BPFB 1; CA 1-4R; 57-60; CANR
3; DLB 8; MTCW 1; SATA 66; SCFW 2;
SFW

Bliss, Reginald
See Wells, H(erbert) G(eorge)

Blixen, Karen (Christentze Dinesen)
1885-1962
See Dinesen, Isak
See also CA 25-28; CANR 22, 50; CAP 2;
DA3; DLB 214; MTCW 1, 2; SATA 44

Bloch, Robert (Albert) 1917-1994 **CLC 33**
See also AAYA 29; CA 5-8R; 179; 146;
CAAE 179; CAAS 20; CANR 5, 78;
DA3; DLB 44; HGG; INT CANR-5;
MTCW 1; SATA 12; SATA-Obit 82; SFW;
SUFW

Blok, Alexander (Alexandrovich) 1880-1921
TCLC 5; PC 21
See also CA 104; 183; EW 9; RGWL

Blom, Jan
See Breytenbach, Breyten

Bloom, Harold 1930- **CLC 24, 103**
See also CA 13-16R; CANR 39, 75, 92;
DLB 67; MTCW 1; RGAL

Bloomfield, Aurelius
See Bourne, Randolph S(illiman)

Blount, Roy (Alton), Jr. 1941- **CLC 38**
See also CA 53-56; CANR 10, 28, 61;
CSW; INT CANR-28; MTCW 1, 2

Bloy, Leon 1846-1917 **TCLC 22**
See also CA 121; 183; DLB 123; GFL 1789
to the Present

Blume, Judy (Sussman) 1938- **CLC 12, 30;
DAM NOV, POP**
See also AAYA 3, 26; BYA 1, 8, 12; CA 29-
32R; CANR 13, 37, 66; CLR 2, 15, 69;
CPW; DA3; DLB 52; JRDA; MAICYA;
MAICYAS; MTCW 1, 2; SATA 2, 31, 79;
WYA; YAW

Blunden, Edmund (Charles) 1896-1974 **CLC
2, 56**
See also BRW 6; CA 17-18; 45-48; CANR
54; CAP 2; DLB 20, 100, 155; MTCW 1;
PAB

Bly, Robert (Elwood) 1926- **CLC 1, 2, 5, 10,
15, 38, 128; DAM POET; PC 39**
See also AMWS 4; CA 5-8R; CANR 41,
73; CP; DA3; DLB 5; MTCW 1, 2; RGAL

Boas, Franz 1858-1942 **TCLC 56**
See also CA 115; 181

Bobette
See Simenon, Georges (Jacques Christian)

Boccaccio, Giovanni 1313-1375 **CMLC 13;
SSC 10**
See also EW 2; RGSF; RGWL

Bochco, Steven 1943- **CLC 35**
See also AAYA 11; CA 124; 138

Bodel, Jean 1167(?)-1210 **CMLC 28**

Bodenheim, Maxwell 1892-1954 **TCLC 44**
See also CA 110; 187; DLB 9, 45; RGAL

Bodker, Cecil 1927- **CLC 21**
See also CA 73-76; CANR 13, 44; CLR 23;
MAICYA; SATA 14

Boell, Heinrich (Theodor) 1917-1985 **CLC 2,
3, 6, 9, 11, 15, 27, 32, 72; DA; DAB;
DAC; DAM MST, NOV; SSC 23; WLC**
See also Boll, Heinrich
See also CA 21-24R; 116; CANR 24; DA3;
DLB 69; DLBY 85; MTCW 1, 2

Boerne, Alfred
See Doeblin, Alfred

Boethius c. 480-c. 524 **CMLC 15**
See also DLB 115; RGWL

Boff, Leonardo (Genezio Darci) 1938- **CLC
70; DAM MULT; HLC 1**
See also CA 150; HW 2

Bogan, Louise 1897-1970 **CLC 4, 39, 46, 93;
DAM POET; PC 12**
See also AMWS 3; CA 73-76; 25-28R;
CANR 33, 82; DLB 45, 169; MAWW;
MTCW 1, 2; RGAL

Bogarde, Dirk
See Van Den Bogarde, Derek Jules Gaspard
Ulric Niven
See also DLB 14

Bogosian, Eric 1953- **CLC 45, 141**
See also CA 138; CAD; CANR 102; CD

Bograd, Larry 1953- **CLC 35**
See also CA 93-96; CANR 57; SAAS 21;
SATA 33, 89; WYA

Boiardo, Matteo Maria 1441-1494 **LC 6**

Boileau-Despreaux, Nicolas 1636-1711 **LC 3**
See also EW 3; GFL Beginnings to 1789;
RGWL

Bojer, Johan 1872-1959 **TCLC 64**
See also CA 189

Bok, Edward W. 1863-1930 **TCLC 101**
See also DLB 91; DLBD 16

Boland, Eavan (Aisling) 1944- **CLC 40, 67,
113; DAM POET**
See also BRWS 5; CA 143; CANR 61; CP;
CWP; DLB 40; FW; MTCW 2; PFS 12

Boll, Heinrich
See Boell, Heinrich (Theodor)
See also BPFB 1; EW 13; RGSF; RGWL

Bolt, Lee
See Faust, Frederick (Schiller)

Bolt, Robert (Oxton) 1924-1995 **CLC 14;
DAM DRAM**
See also CA 17-20R; 147; CANR 35, 67;
CBD; DFS 2; DLB 13, 233; LAIT 1;
MTCW 1

Bombal, Maria Luisa 1910-1980 **SSC 37;
HLCS 1**
See also CA 127; CANR 72; HW 1; LAW;
RGSF

Bombet, Louis-Alexandre-Cesar
See Stendhal

Bomkauf
See Kaufman, Bob (Garnell)

Bonaventura NCLC 35
See also DLB 90

Bond, Edward 1934- **CLC 4, 6, 13, 23; DAM
DRAM**
See also BRWS 1; CA 25-28R; CANR 38,
67, 106; CBD; CD; DFS 3,8; DLB 13;
MTCW 1

Bonham, Frank 1914-1989 **CLC 12**
See also AAYA 1; BYA 1, 3; CA 9-12R;
CANR 4, 36; JRDA; MAICYA; SAAS 3;
SATA 1, 49; SATA-Obit 62; TCWW 2;
YAW

Brave Bird, Mary
See Crow Dog, Mary (Ellen)
See also NNAL

Braverman, Kate 1950- **CLC 67**
See also CA 89-92

Brecht, (Eugen) Bertolt (Friedrich)
1898-1956 **TCLC 1, 6, 13, 35; DA;**
DAB; DAC; DAM DRAM, MST; DC 3;
WLC
See also CA 104; 133; CANR 62; DA3;
DFS 4, 5, 9; DLB 56, 124; EW 11; IDTP;
MTCW 1, 2; RGWL

Brecht, Eugen Berthold Friedrich
See Brecht, (Eugen) Bertolt (Friedrich)

Bremer, Fredrika 1801-1865 **NCLC 11**
See also DLB 254

Brennan, Christopher John 1870-1932 **TCLC 17**
See also CA 117; 188; DLB 230

Brennan, Maeve 1917-1993 **CLC 5**
See also CA 81-84; CANR 72, 100

Brent, Linda
See Jacobs, Harriet A(nn)

Brentano, Clemens (Maria) 1778-1842 **NCLC 1**
See also DLB 90; RGWL

Brent of Bin Bin
See Franklin, (Stella Maria Sarah) Miles
(Lampe)

Brenton, Howard 1942- **CLC 31**
See also CA 69-72; CANR 33, 67; CBD;
CD; DLB 13; MTCW 1

Breslin, James 1929-
See Breslin, Jimmy
See also CA 73-76; CANR 31, 75; DAM
NOV; MTCW 1, 2

Breslin, Jimmy CLC 4, 43
See also Breslin, James
See also AITN 1; DLB 185; MTCW 2

Bresson, Robert 1901(?)-1999 **CLC 16**
See also CA 110; 187; CANR 49

Breton, Andre 1896-1966 **CLC 2, 9, 15, 54;**
PC 15
See also CA 19-20; 25-28R; CANR 40, 60;
CAP 2; DLB 65; EW 11; GFL 1789 to
the Present; MTCW 1, 2; RGWL; WP

Breytenbach, Breyten 1939(?)- **CLC 23, 37,**
126; DAM POET
See also CA 113; 129; CANR 61; CWW 2;
DLB 225

Bridgers, Sue Ellen 1942- **CLC 26**
See also AAYA 8; BYA 7, 8; CA 65-68;
CANR 11, 36; CLR 18; DLB 52; JRDA;
MAICYA; SAAS 1; SATA 22, 90; SATA-
Essay 109; WYA; YAW

Bridges, Robert (Seymour) 1844-1930 **TCLC**
1; DAM POET; PC 28
See also BRW 6; CA 104; 152; CDBLB
1890-1914; DLB 19, 98

Bridie, James TCLC 3
See also Mavor, Osborne Henry
See also DLB 10

Brin, David 1950- **CLC 34**
See also AAYA 21; CA 102; CANR 24, 70;
INT CANR-24; SATA 65; SCFW 2; SFW

Brink, Andre (Philippus) 1935- **CLC 18, 36,**
106
See also AFW; BRWS 6; CA 104; CANR
39, 62; CN; DLB 225; INT CA-103;
MTCW 1, 2; WLIT 2

Brinsmead, H(esba) F(ay) 1922- **CLC 21**
See also CA 21-24R; CANR 10; CLR 47;
CWRI; MAICYA; SAAS 5; SATA 18, 78

Brittain, Vera (Mary) 1893(?)-1970 **CLC 23**
See also CA 13-16; 25-28R; CANR 58;
CAP 1; DLB 191; FW; MTCW 1, 2

Broch, Hermann 1886-1951 **TCLC 20**
See also CA 117; DLB 85, 124; EW 10;
RGWL

Brock, Rose
See Hansen, Joseph
See also GLL 1

Brod, Max 1884-1968 **TCLC 115**
See also CA 5-8R; 25-28R; CANR 7; DLB
81

Brodkey, Harold (Roy) 1930-1996 **CLC 56**
See also CA 111; 151; CANR 71; CN; DLB
130

Brodskii, Iosif
See Brodsky, Joseph
See also RGWL

Brodsky, Iosif Alexandrovich 1940-1996
See Brodsky, Joseph
See also AITN 1; CA 41-44R; 151; CANR
37, 106; DA3; DAM POET; MTCW 1, 2

Brodsky, Joseph CLC 4, 6, 13, 36, 100; PC 9
See also Brodsky, Iosif Alexandrovich
See also AMWS 8; CWW 2; MTCW 1

Brodsky, Michael (Mark) 1948- **CLC 19**
See also CA 102; CANR 18, 41, 58; DLB
244

Brodzki, Bella ed. CLC 65

Brome, Richard 1590(?)-1652 **LC 61**
See also DLB 58

Bromell, Henry 1947- **CLC 5**
See also CA 53-56; CANR 9

Bromfield, Louis (Brucker) 1896-1956 **TCLC 11**
See also CA 107; 155; DLB 4, 9, 86;
RGAL; RHW

Broner, E(sther) M(asserman) 1930- **CLC 19**
See also CA 17-20R; CANR 8, 25, 72; CN;
DLB 28

Bronk, William (M.) 1918-1999 **CLC 10**
See also CA 89-92; 177; CANR 23; CP;
DLB 165

Bronstein, Lev Davidovich
See Trotsky, Leon

Bronte, Anne 1820-1849 **NCLC 4, 71, 102**
See also BRW 5; BRWR 1; DA3; DLB 21,
199

Bronte, (Patrick) Branwell 1817-1848 **NCLC 109**

Bronte, Charlotte 1816-1855 **NCLC 3, 8, 33,**
58, 105; DA; DAB; DAC; DAM MST,
NOV; WLC
See also AAYA 17; BRW 5; BRWR 1; BYA
2; CDBLB 1832-1890; DA3; DLB 21,
159, 199; EXPN; LAIT 2; NFS 4; WLIT
4

Bronte, Emily (Jane) 1818-1848 **NCLC 16,**
35; DA; DAB; DAC; DAM MST, NOV,
POET; PC 8; WLC
See also AAYA 17; BPFB 1; BRW 5;
BRWR 1; BYA 3; CDBLB 1832-1890;
DA3; DLB 21, 32, 199; EXPN; LAIT 1;
WLIT 3

Brontes
See Bronte, Anne; Bronte, Charlotte; Bronte,
Emily (Jane)

Brooke, Frances 1724-1789 **LC 6, 48**
See also DLB 39, 99

Brooke, Henry 1703(?)-1783 **LC 1**
See also DLB 39

Brooke, Rupert (Chawner) 1887-1915 **TCLC**
2, 7; DA; DAB; DAC; DAM MST,
POET; PC 24; WLC
See also BRWS 3; CA 104; 132; CANR 61;
CDBLB 1914-1945; DLB 19, 216; EXPP;
GLL 2; MTCW 1, 2; PFS 7

Brooke-Haven, P.
See Wodehouse, P(elham) G(renville)

Brooke-Rose, Christine 1926(?)- **CLC 40**
See also BRWS 4; CA 13-16R; CANR 58;
CN; DLB 14, 231; SFW

Brookner, Anita 1928- **CLC 32, 34, 51, 136;**
DAB; DAM POP
See also BRWS 4; CA 114; 120; CANR 37,
56, 87; CN; CPW; DA3; DLB 194; DLBY
87; MTCW 1, 2

Brooks, Cleanth 1906-1994 **CLC 24, 86, 110**
See also CA 17-20R; 145; CANR 33, 35;
CSW; DLB 63; DLBY 94; INT CANR-
35; MTCW 1, 2

Brooks, George
See Baum, L(yman) Frank

Brooks, Gwendolyn (Elizabeth) 1917-2000
CLC 1, 2, 4, 5, 15, 49, 125; BLC 1; DA;
DAC; DAM MST, MULT, POET; PC
7; WLC
See also AAYA 20; AFAW 1, 2; AITN 1;
AMWS 3; BW 2, 3; CA 1-4R; 190; CANR
1, 27, 52, 75; CDALB 1941-1968; CLR
27; CP; CWP; DA3; DLB 5, 76, 165;
EXPP; MAWW; MTCW 1, 2; PFS 1, 2,
4, 6; RGAL; SATA 6; SATA-Obit 123;
WP

Brooks, Mel CLC 12
See also Kaminsky, Melvin
See also AAYA 13; DLB 26

Brooks, Peter 1938- **CLC 34**
See also CA 45-48; CANR 1

Brooks, Van Wyck 1886-1963 **CLC 29**
See also AMW; CA 1-4R; CANR 6; DLB
45, 63, 103

Brophy, Brigid (Antonia) 1929-1995 **CLC 6,**
11, 29, 105
See also CA 5-8R; 149; CAAS 4; CANR
25, 53; CBD; CN; CWD; DA3; DLB 14;
MTCW 1, 2

Brosman, Catharine Savage 1934- **CLC 9**
See also CA 61-64; CANR 21, 46

Brossard, Nicole 1943- **CLC 115**
See also CA 122; CAAS 16; CCA 1; CWP;
CWW 2; DLB 53; FW; GLL 2

Brother Antoninus
See Everson, William (Oliver)

The Brothers Quay
See Quay, Stephen; Quay, Timothy

Broughton, T(homas) Alan 1936- **CLC 19**
See also CA 45-48; CANR 2, 23, 48

Broumas, Olga 1949- **CLC 10, 73**
See also CA 85-88; CANR 20, 69; CP;
CWP; GLL 2

Broun, Heywood 1888-1939 **TCLC 104**
See also DLB 29, 171

Brown, Alan 1950- **CLC 99**
See also CA 156

Brown, Charles Brockden 1771-1810 **NCLC 22, 74**
See also AMWS 1; CDALB 1640-1865;
DLB 37, 59, 73; FW; HGG; RGAL

Brown, Christy 1932-1981 **CLC 63**
See also BYA 13; CA 105; 104; CANR 72;
DLB 14

Brown, Claude 1937-2002 **CLC 30; BLC 1;**
DAM MULT
See also AAYA 7; BW 1, 3; CA 73-76;
CANR 81

Brown, Dee (Alexander) 1908- **CLC 18, 47;**
DAM POP
See also AAYA 30; CA 13-16R; CAAS 6;
CANR 11, 45, 60; CPW; CSW; DA3;
DLBY 80; LAIT 2; MTCW 1, 2; SATA 5,
110; TCWW 2

Brown, George
See Wertmueller, Lina

Brown, George Douglas 1869-1902 **TCLC 28**
See also Douglas, George
See also CA 162

Brown, George Mackay 1921-1996 **CLC 5,**
48, 100
See also BRWS 6; CA 21-24R; 151; CAAS
6; CANR 12, 37, 67; CN; CP; DLB 14,
27, 139; MTCW 1; RGSF; SATA 35

Brown, (William) Larry 1951- **CLC 73**
See also CA 130; 134; CSW; DLB 234; INT 133

Brown, Moses
See Barrett, William (Christopher)

Brown, Rita Mae 1944- **CLC 18, 43, 79; DAM NOV, POP**
See also BPFB 1; CA 45-48; CANR 2, 11, 35, 62, 95; CN; CPW; CSW; DA3; FW; INT CANR-11; MTCW 1, 2; NFS 9; RGAL

Brown, Roderick (Langmere) Haig-
See Haig-Brown, Roderick (Langmere)

Brown, Rosellen 1939- **CLC 32**
See also CA 77-80; CAAS 10; CANR 14, 44, 98; CN

Brown, Sterling Allen 1901-1989 **CLC 1, 23, 59; BLC 1; DAM MULT, POET**
See also AFAW 1, 2; BW 1, 3; CA 85-88; 127; CANR 26; DA3; DLB 48, 51, 63; MTCW 1, 2; RGAL; WP

Brown, Will
See Ainsworth, William Harrison

Brown, William Wells 1815-1884 **NCLC 2, 89; BLC 1; DAM MULT; DC 1**
See also DLB 3, 50, 183, 248; RGAL

Browne, (Clyde) Jackson 1948(?)- **CLC 21**
See also CA 120

Browning, Elizabeth Barrett 1806-1861 **NCLC 1, 16, 61, 66; DA; DAB; DAC; DAM MST, POET; PC 6; WLC**
See also BRW 4; CDBLB 1832-1890; DA3; DLB 32, 199; EXPP; PAB; PFS 2; WLIT 4; WP

Browning, Robert 1812-1889 **NCLC 19, 79; DA; DAB; DAC; DAM MST, POET; PC 2; WLCS**
See also BRW 4; BRWR 2; CDBLB 1832-1890; DA3; DLB 32, 163; EXPP; PAB; PFS 1; RGEL; TEA; WLIT 4; WP; YABC 1

Browning, Tod 1882-1962 **CLC 16**
See also CA 141; 117

Brownson, Orestes Augustus 1803-1876 **NCLC 50**
See also DLB 1, 59, 73, 243

Bruccoli, Matthew J(oseph) 1931- **CLC 34**
See also CA 9-12R; CANR 7, 87; DLB 103

Bruce, Lenny CLC 21
See also Schneider, Leonard Alfred

Bruin, John
See Brutus, Dennis

Brulard, Henri
See Stendhal

Brulls, Christian
See Simenon, Georges (Jacques Christian)

Brunner, John (Kilian Houston) 1934-1995 **CLC 8, 10; DAM POP**
See also CA 1-4R; 149; CAAS 8; CANR 2, 37; CPW; MTCW 1, 2; SCFW 2; SFW

Bruno, Giordano 1548-1600 **LC 27**
See also RGWL

Brutus, Dennis 1924- **CLC 43; BLC 1; DAM MULT, POET; PC 24**
See also AFW; BW 2, 3; CA 49-52; CAAS 14; CANR 2, 27, 42, 81; CP; DLB 117, 225

Bryan, C(ourtlandt) D(ixon) B(arnes) 1936- **CLC 29**
See also CA 73-76; CANR 13, 68; DLB 185; INT CANR-13

Bryan, Michael
See Moore, Brian
See also CCA 1

Bryan, William Jennings 1860-1925 **TCLC 99**

Bryant, William Cullen 1794-1878 **NCLC 6,** 46; DA; DAB; DAC; DAM MST, POET; PC 20
See also AMWS 1; CDALB 1640-1865; DLB 3, 43, 59, 189, 250; EXPP; PAB; RGAL

Bryusov, Valery Yakovlevich 1873-1924 **TCLC 10**
See also CA 107; 155; SFW

Buchan, John 1875-1940 **TCLC 41; DAB; DAM POP**
See also CA 108; 145; CMW; DLB 34, 70, 156; HGG; MSW; MTCW 1; RGEL; RHW; YABC 2

Buchanan, George 1506-1582 **LC 4**
See also DLB 132

Buchanan, Robert 1841-1901 **TCLC 107**
See also CA 179; DLB 18, 35

Buchheim, Lothar-Guenther 1918- **CLC 6**
See also CA 85-88

Buchner, (Karl) Georg 1813-1837 **NCLC 26**
See also DLB 133; EW 6; RGSF; RGWL

Buchwald, Art(hur) 1925- **CLC 33**
See also AITN 1; CA 5-8R; CANR 21, 67; MTCW 1, 2; SATA 10

Buck, Pearl S(ydenstricker) 1892-1973 **CLC 7, 11, 18, 127; DA; DAB; DAC; DAM MST, NOV**
See also AAYA 42; AITN 1; AMWS 2; BPFB 1; CA 1-4R; 41-44R; CANR 1, 34; CDALBS; DA3; DLB 9, 102; LAIT 3; MTCW 1, 2; RGAL; RHW; SATA 1, 25

Buckler, Ernest 1908-1984 **CLC 13; DAC; DAM MST**
See also CA 11-12; 114; CAP 1; CCA 1; DLB 68; SATA 47

Buckley, Vincent (Thomas) 1925-1988 **CLC 57**
See also CA 101

Buckley, William F(rank), Jr. 1925- **CLC 7, 18, 37; DAM POP**
See also AITN 1; BPFB 1; CA 1-4R; CANR 1, 24, 53, 93; CMW; CPW; DA3; DLB 137; DLBY 80; INT CANR-24; MTCW 1, 2; TUS

Buechner, (Carl) Frederick 1926- **CLC 2, 4, 6, 9; DAM NOV**
See also BPFB 1; CA 13-16R; CANR 11, 39, 64; CN; DLBY 80; INT CANR-11; MTCW 1, 2

Buell, John (Edward) 1927- **CLC 10**
See also CA 1-4R; CANR 71; DLB 53

Buero Vallejo, Antonio 1916-2000 **CLC 15, 46, 139**
See also CA 106; 189; CANR 24, 49, 75; DFS 11; HW 1; MTCW 1, 2

Bufalino, Gesualdo 1920(?)-1990 **CLC 74**
See also CWW 2; DLB 196

Bugayev, Boris Nikolayevich 1880-1934 **TCLC 7; PC 11**
See also Bely, Andrey; Belyi, Andrei
See also CA 104; 165; MTCW 1

Bukowski, Charles 1920-1994 **CLC 2, 5, 9, 41, 82, 108; DAM NOV, POET; PC 18; SSC 45**
See also CA 17-20R; 144; CANR 40, 62, 105; CPW; DA3; DLB 5, 130, 169; MTCW 1, 2

Bulgakov, Mikhail (Afanas'evich) 1891-1940 **TCLC 2, 16; DAM DRAM, NOV; SSC 18**
See also BPFB 1; CA 105; 152; NFS 8; RGSF; RGWL; SFW

Bulgya, Alexander Alexandrovich 1901-1956 **TCLC 53**
See also Fadeyev, Alexander
See also CA 117; 181

Bullins, Ed 1935- **CLC 1, 5, 7; BLC 1; DAM** DRAM, MULT; DC 6
See also BW 2, 3; CA 49-52; CAAS 16; CAD; CANR 24, 46, 73; CD; DLB 7, 38, 249; MTCW 1, 2; RGAL

Bulwer-Lytton, Edward (George Earle Lytton) 1803-1873 **NCLC 1, 45**
See also DLB 21; RGEL; SFW; SUFW

Bunin, Ivan Alexeyevich 1870-1953 **TCLC 6; SSC 5**
See also CA 104; RGSF; RGWL

Bunting, Basil 1900-1985 **CLC 10, 39, 47; DAM POET**
See also BRWS 7; CA 53-56; 115; CANR 7; DLB 20; RGEL

Bunuel, Luis 1900-1983 **CLC 16, 80; DAM MULT; HLC 1**
See also CA 101; 110; CANR 32, 77; HW 1

Bunyan, John 1628-1688 **LC 4, 69; DA; DAB; DAC; DAM MST; WLC**
See also BRW 2; BYA 5; CDBLB 1660-1789; DLB 39; RGEL; WCH; WLIT 3

Buravsky, Alexandr CLC 59

Burckhardt, Jacob (Christoph) 1818-1897 **NCLC 49**
See also EW 6

Burford, Eleanor
See Hibbert, Eleanor Alice Burford

Burgess, Anthony CLC 1, 2, 4, 5, 8, 10, 13, 15, 22, 40, 62, 81, 94; DAB
See also Wilson, John (Anthony) Burgess
See also AAYA 25; AITN 1; BRWS 1; CD-BLB 1960 to Present; DLB 14, 194; DLBY 98; MTCW 1; RGEL; RHW; SFW; YAW

Burke, Edmund 1729(?)-1797 **LC 7, 36; DA; DAB; DAC; DAM MST; WLC**
See also BRW 3; DA3; DLB 104, 252; RGEL

Burke, Kenneth (Duva) 1897-1993 **CLC 2, 24**
See also AMW; CA 5-8R; 143; CANR 39, 74; DLB 45, 63; MTCW 1, 2; RGAL

Burke, Leda
See Garnett, David

Burke, Ralph
See Silverberg, Robert

Burke, Thomas 1886-1945 **TCLC 63**
See also CA 113; 155; CMW; DLB 197

Burney, Fanny 1752-1840 **NCLC 12, 54, 107**
See also BRWS 3; DLB 39; RGEL

Burney, Frances
See Burney, Fanny

Burns, Robert 1759-1796 **LC 3, 29, 40; DA; DAB; DAC; DAM MST, POET; PC 6; WLC**
See also BRW 3; CDBLB 1789-1832; DA3; DLB 109; EXPP; PAB; RGEL; WP

Burns, Tex
See L'Amour, Louis (Dearborn)
See also TCWW 2

Burnshaw, Stanley 1906- **CLC 3, 13, 44**
See also CA 9-12R; CP; DLB 48; DLBY 97

Burr, Anne 1937- **CLC 6**
See also CA 25-28R

Burroughs, Edgar Rice 1875-1950 **TCLC 2, 32; DAM NOV**
See also AAYA 11; BPFB 1; BYA 4, 9; CA 104; 132; DA3; DLB 8; FANT; MTCW 1, 2; RGAL; SATA 41; SCFW 2; SFW; YAW

Burroughs, William S(eward) 1914-1997 **CLC 1, 2, 5, 15, 22, 42, 75, 109; DA; DAB; DAC; DAM MST, NOV, POP; WLC**
See also Lee, William; Lee, Willy
See also AITN 2; AMWS 3; BPFB 1; CA 9-12R; 160; CANR 20, 52, 104; CN;

CPW; DA3; DLB 2, 8, 16, 152, 237; DLBY 81, 97; HGG; MTCW 1, 2; RGAL; SFW

Burton, Sir Richard F(rancis) 1821-1890 **NCLC 42**
See also DLB 55, 166, 184

Burton, Robert 1577-1640 **LC 74**
See also DLB 151; RGEL

Busch, Frederick 1941- **CLC 7, 10, 18, 47**
See also CA 33-36R; CAAS 1; CANR 45, 73, 92; CN; DLB 6, 218

Bush, Ronald 1946- **CLC 34**
See also CA 136

Bustos, F(rancisco)
See Borges, Jorge Luis

Bustos Domecq, H(onorio)
See Bioy Casares, Adolfo; Borges, Jorge Luis

Butler, Octavia E(stelle) 1947- **CLC 38, 121; BLCS; DAM MULT, POP**
See also AAYA 18; AFAW 2; BPFB 1; BW 2, 3; CA 73-76; CANR 12, 24, 38, 73; CLR 65; CPW; DA3; DLB 33; MTCW 1, 2; NFS 8; SATA 84; SCFW 2; SFW; SSFS 6; YAW

Butler, Robert Olen, (Jr.) 1945- **CLC 81; DAM POP**
See also BPFB 1; CA 112; CANR 66; CSW; DLB 173; INT CA-112; MTCW 1; SSFS 11

Butler, Samuel 1612-1680 **LC 16, 43**
See also DLB 101, 126; RGEL

Butler, Samuel 1835-1902 **TCLC 1, 33; DA; DAB; DAC; DAM MST, NOV; WLC**
See also BRWS 2; CA 143; CDBLB 1890-1914; DA3; DLB 18, 57, 174; RGEL; SFW; TEA

Butler, Walter C.
See Faust, Frederick (Schiller)

Butor, Michel (Marie Francois) 1926- **CLC 1, 3, 8, 11, 15**
See also CA 9-12R; CANR 33, 66; DLB 83; EW 13; GFL 1789 to the Present; MTCW 1, 2

Butts, Mary 1890(?)-1937 **TCLC 77**
See also CA 148; DLB 240

Buxton, Ralph
See Silverstein, Alvin; Silverstein, Virginia B(arbara Opshelor)

Buzo, Alexander (John) 1944- **CLC 61**
See also CA 97-100; CANR 17, 39, 69; CD

Buzzati, Dino 1906-1972 **CLC 36**
See also CA 160; 33-36R; DLB 177; RGWL; SFW

Byars, Betsy (Cromer) 1928- **CLC 35**
See also AAYA 19; BYA 3; CA 33-36R, 183; CAAE 183; CANR 18, 36, 57, 102; CLR 1, 16, 72; DLB 52; INT CANR-18; JRDA; MAICYA; MAICYAS; MTCW 1; SAAS 1; SATA 4, 46, 80; SATA-Essay 108; WYA; YAW

Byatt, A(ntonia) S(usan Drabble) 1936- **CLC 19, 65, 136; DAM NOV, POP**
See also BPFB 1; BRWS 4; CA 13-16R; CANR 13, 33, 50, 75, 96; DA3; DLB 14, 194; MTCW 1, 2; RGSF; RHW

Byrne, David 1952- **CLC 26**
See also CA 127

Byrne, John Keyes 1926-
See Leonard, Hugh
See also CA 102; CANR 78; INT CA-102

Byron, George Gordon (Noel) 1788-1824 **NCLC 2, 12, 109; DA; DAB; DAC; DAM MST, POET; PC 16; WLC**
See also BRW 4; CDBLB 1789-1832; DA3; DLB 96, 110; EXPP; PAB; PFS 1, 14; RGEL; WLIT 3; WP

Byron, Robert 1905-1941 **TCLC 67**
See also CA 160; DLB 195

C. 3. 3.
See Wilde, Oscar (Fingal O'Flahertie Wills)

Caballero, Fernan 1796-1877 **NCLC 10**

Cabell, Branch
See Cabell, James Branch

Cabell, James Branch 1879-1958 **TCLC 6**
See also CA 105; 152; DLB 9, 78; FANT; MTCW 1; RGAL; SUFW

Cabeza de Vaca, Alvar Nunez 1490-1557(?) **LC 61**

Cable, George Washington 1844-1925 **TCLC 4; SSC 4**
See also CA 104; 155; DLB 12, 74; DLBD 13; RGAL

Cabral de Melo Neto, Joao 1920-1999 **CLC 76; DAM MULT**
See also CA 151; LAW; LAWS 1

Cabrera Infante, G(uillermo) 1929- **CLC 5, 25, 45, 120; DAM MULT; HLC 1; SSC 39**
See also CA 85-88; CANR 29, 65; DA3; DLB 113; HW 1, 2; LAW; LAWS 1; MTCW 1, 2; RGSF; WLIT 1

Cade, Toni
See Bambara, Toni Cade

Cadmus and Harmonia
See Buchan, John

Caedmon fl. 658-680 **CMLC 7**
See also DLB 146

Caeiro, Alberto
See Pessoa, Fernando (Antonio Nogueira)

Caesar, Julius CMLC 47
See also Julius Caesar
See also AW 1; RGWL

Cage, John (Milton, Jr.) 1912-1992 **CLC 41**
See also CA 13-16R; 169; CANR 9, 78; DLB 193; INT CANR-9

Cahan, Abraham 1860-1951 **TCLC 71**
See also CA 108; 154; DLB 9, 25, 28; RGAL

Cain, G.
See Cabrera Infante, G(uillermo)

Cain, Guillermo
See Cabrera Infante, G(uillermo)

Cain, James M(allahan) 1892-1977 **CLC 3, 11, 28**
See also AITN 1; BPFB 1; CA 17-20R; 73-76; CANR 8, 34, 61; CMW; DLB 226; MSW; MTCW 1; RGAL

Caine, Hall 1853-1931 **TCLC 97**
See also RHW

Caine, Mark
See Raphael, Frederic (Michael)

Calasso, Roberto 1941- **CLC 81**
See also CA 143; CANR 89

Calderon de la Barca, Pedro 1600-1681 **LC 23; DC 3; HLCS 1**
See also EW 2; RGWL

Caldwell, Erskine (Preston) 1903-1987 **CLC 1, 8, 14, 50, 60; DAM NOV; SSC 19**
See also AITN 1; AMW; BPFB 1; CA 1-4R; 121; CAAS 1; CANR 2, 33; DA3; DLB 9, 86; MTCW 1, 2; RGAL; RGSF; TCLC 117

Caldwell, (Janet Miriam) Taylor (Holland) 1900-1985 **CLC 2, 28, 39; DAM NOV, POP**
See also BPFB 1; CA 5-8R; 116; CANR 5; DA3; DLBD 17; RHW

Calhoun, John Caldwell 1782-1850 **NCLC 15**
See also DLB 3, 248

Calisher, Hortense 1911- **CLC 2, 4, 8, 38, 134; DAM NOV; SSC 15**
See also CA 1-4R; CANR 1, 22, 67; CN; DA3; DLB 2, 218; INT CANR-22; MTCW 1, 2; RGAL; RGSF

Callaghan, Morley Edward 1903-1990 **CLC 3, 14, 41, 65; DAC; DAM MST**
See also CA 9-12R; 132; CANR 33, 73; DLB 68; MTCW 1, 2; RGAL; RGSF

Callimachus c. 305B.C.-c. 240B.C. **CMLC 18**
See also AW 1; DLB 176; RGWL

Calvin, Jean
See Calvin, John
See also GFL Beginnings to 1789

Calvin, John 1509-1564 **LC 37**
See also Calvin, Jean

Calvino, Italo 1923-1985 **CLC 5, 8, 11, 22, 33, 39, 73; DAM NOV; SSC 3, 48**
See also CA 85-88; 116; CANR 23, 61; DLB 196; EW 13; MTCW 1, 2; RGSF; RGWL; SFW; SSFS 12

Cameron, Carey 1952- **CLC 59**
See also CA 135

Cameron, Peter 1959- **CLC 44**
See also CA 125; CANR 50; DLB 234; GLL 2

Camoens, Luis Vaz de 1524(?)-1580
See also EW 2; HLCS 1

Camoes, Luis de 1524(?)-1580 **LC 62; HLCS 1; PC 31**
See also RGWL

Campana, Dino 1885-1932 **TCLC 20**
See also CA 117; DLB 114

Campanella, Tommaso 1568-1639 **LC 32**
See also RGWL

Campbell, John W(ood, Jr.) 1910-1971 **CLC 32**
See also CA 21-22; 29-32R; CANR 34; CAP 2; DLB 8; MTCW 1; SFW

Campbell, Joseph 1904-1987 **CLC 69**
See also AAYA 3; BEST 89:2; CA 1-4R; 124; CANR 3, 28, 61; DA3; MTCW 1, 2

Campbell, Maria 1940- **CLC 85; DAC**
See also CA 102; CANR 54; CCA 1; NNAL

Campbell, (John) Ramsey 1946- **CLC 42; SSC 19**
See also CA 57-60; CANR 7, 102; HGG; INT CANR-7; SUFW

Campbell, (Ignatius) Roy (Dunnachie) 1901-1957 **TCLC 5**
See also AFW; CA 104; 155; DLB 20, 225; MTCW 2; RGEL

Campbell, Thomas 1777-1844 **NCLC 19**
See also DLB 93, 144; RGEL

Campbell, Wilfred TCLC 9
See also Campbell, William

Campbell, William 1858(?)-1918
See Campbell, Wilfred
See also CA 106; DLB 92

Campion, Jane CLC 95
See also AAYA 33; CA 138; CANR 87

Camus, Albert 1913-1960 **CLC 1, 2, 4, 9, 11, 14, 32, 63, 69, 124; DA; DAB; DAC; DAM DRAM, MST, NOV; DC 2; SSC 9; WLC**
See also AAYA 36; AFW; BPFB 1; CA 89-92; DA3; DLB 72; EW 13; EXPN; EXPS; GFL 1789 to the Present; MTCW 1, 2; NFS 6; RGSF; RGWL; SSFS 4

Canby, Vincent 1924-2000 **CLC 13**
See also CA 81-84; 191

Cancale
See Desnos, Robert

Canetti, Elias 1905-1994 **CLC 3, 14, 25, 75, 86**
See also CA 21-24R; 146; CANR 23, 61, 79; CWW 2; DA3; DLB 85, 124; EW 12; MTCW 1, 2; RGWL

Canfield, Dorothea F.
See Fisher, Dorothy (Frances) Canfield

Canfield, Dorothea Frances
See Fisher, Dorothy (Frances) Canfield

Canfield, Dorothy
See Fisher, Dorothy (Frances) Canfield
Canin, Ethan 1960- **CLC 55**
See also CA 131; 135
Cankar, Ivan 1876-1918 **TCLC 105**
See also DLB 147
Cannon, Curt
See Hunter, Evan
Cao, Lan 1961- **CLC 109**
See also CA 165
Cape, Judith
See Page, P(atricia) K(athleen)
See also CCA 1
Capek, Karel 1890-1938 **TCLC 6, 37; DA; DAB; DAC; DAM DRAM, MST, NOV; DC 1; SSC 36; WLC**
See also CA 104; 140; CDWLB 4; DA3; DFS 7, 11 !**; DLB 215; EW 10; MTCW 1; RGSF; RGWL; SCFW 2; SFW
Capote, Truman 1924-1984 **CLC 1, 3, 8, 13, 19, 34, 38, 58; DA; DAB; DAC; DAM MST, NOV, POP; SSC 2, 47; WLC**
See also AMWS 3; BPFB 1; CA 5-8R; 113; CANR 18, 62; CDALB 1941-1968; CPW; DA3; DLB 2, 185, 227; DLBY 80, 84; EXPS; GLL 1; LAIT 3; MTCW 1, 2; NCFS 2; RGAL; RGSF; SATA 91; SSFS 2
Capra, Frank 1897-1991 **CLC 16**
See also CA 61-64; 135
Caputo, Philip 1941- **CLC 32**
See also CA 73-76; CANR 40; YAW
Caragiale, Ion Luca 1852-1912 **TCLC 76**
See also CA 157
Card, Orson Scott 1951- **CLC 44, 47, 50; DAM POP**
See also AAYA 11, 42; BPFB 1; BYA 5, 8; CA 102; CANR 27, 47, 73, 102, 106; CPW; DA3; FANT; INT CANR-27; MTCW 1, 2; NFS 5; SATA 83, 127; SCFW 2; SFW; YAW
Cardenal, Ernesto 1925- **CLC 31; DAM MULT, POET; HLC 1; PC 22**
See also CA 49-52; CANR 2, 32, 66; CWW 2; HW 1, 2; LAWS 1; MTCW 1, 2; RGWL
Cardozo, Benjamin N(athan) 1870-1938 **TCLC 65**
See also CA 117; 164
Carducci, Giosue (Alessandro Giuseppe) 1835-1907 **TCLC 32**
See also CA 163; EW 7; RGWL
Carew, Thomas 1595(?)-1640 **CLC 13; PC 29**
See also BRW 2; DLB 126; PAB; RGEL
Carey, Ernestine Gilbreth 1908- **CLC 17**
See also CA 5-8R; CANR 71; SATA 2
Carey, Peter 1943- **CLC 40, 55, 96**
See also CA 123; 127; CANR 53, 76; CN; INT CA-127; MTCW 1, 2; RGSF; SATA 94
Carleton, William 1794-1869 **NCLC 3**
See also DLB 159; RGEL; RGSF
Carlisle, Henry (Coffin) 1926- **CLC 33**
See also CA 13-16R; CANR 15, 85
Carlsen, Chris
See Holdstock, Robert P.
Carlson, Ron(ald F.) 1947- **CLC 54**
See also CA 105; CAAE 189; CANR 27; DLB 244
Carlyle, Thomas 1795-1881 **NCLC 22, 70; DA; DAB; DAC; DAM MST**
See also BRW 4; CDBLB 1789-1832; DLB 55, 144, 254; RGEL
Carman, (William) Bliss 1861-1929 **TCLC 7; DAC; PC 34**
See also CA 104; 152; DLB 92; RGEL
Carnegie, Dale 1888-1955 **TCLC 53**
Carossa, Hans 1878-1956 **TCLC 48**
See also CA 170; DLB 66

Carpenter, Don(ald Richard) 1931-1995 **CLC 41**
See also CA 45-48; 149; CANR 1, 71
Carpenter, Edward 1844-1929 **TCLC 88**
See also CA 163; GLL 1
Carpentier (y Valmont), Alejo 1904-1980 **CLC 8, 11, 38, 110; DAM MULT; HLC 1; SSC 35**
See also CA 65-68; 97-100; CANR 11, 70; DLB 113; HW 1, 2; LAW; RGSF; RGWL; WLIT 1
Carr, Caleb 1955(?)- **CLC 86**
See also CA 147; CANR 73; DA3
Carr, Emily 1871-1945 **TCLC 32**
See also CA 159; DLB 68; FW; GLL 2
Carr, John Dickson 1906-1977 **CLC 3**
See also Fairbairn, Roger
See also CA 49-52; 69-72; CANR 3, 33, 60; CMW; MSW; MTCW 1, 2
Carr, Philippa
See Hibbert, Eleanor Alice Burford
Carr, Virginia Spencer 1929- **CLC 34**
See also CA 61-64; DLB 111
Carrere, Emmanuel 1957- **CLC 89**
Carrier, Roch 1937- **CLC 13, 78; DAC; DAM MST**
See also CA 130; CANR 61; CCA 1; DLB 53; SATA 105
Carroll, James P. 1943(?)- **CLC 38**
See also CA 81-84; CANR 73; MTCW 1
Carroll, Jim 1951- **CLC 35, 143**
See also AAYA 17; CA 45-48; CANR 42
Carroll, Lewis NCLC 2, 53; PC 18; WLC
See also Dodgson, Charles Lutwidge
See also AAYA 39; BRW 5; BYA 5, 13; CD-BLB 1832-1890; CLR 2, 18; DLB 18, 163, 178; DLBY 98; EXPN; EXPP; FANT; JRDA; LAIT 1; NFS 7; PFS 11; RGEL; SUFW; WCH
Carroll, Paul Vincent 1900-1968 **CLC 10**
See also CA 9-12R; 25-28R; DLB 10; RGEL
Carruth, Hayden 1921- **CLC 4, 7, 10, 18, 84; PC 10**
See also CA 9-12R; CANR 4, 38, 59; CP; DLB 5, 165; INT CANR-4; MTCW 1, 2; SATA 47
Carson, Rachel Louise 1907-1964 **CLC 71; DAM POP**
See also AMWS 9; ANW; CA 77-80; CANR 35; DA3; FW; LAIT 4; MTCW 1, 2; NCFS 1; SATA 23
Carter, Angela (Olive) 1940-1992 **CLC 5, 41, 76; SSC 13**
See also BRWS 3; CA 53-56; 136; CANR 12, 36, 61, 106; DA3; DLB 14, 207; EXPS; FANT; FW; MTCW 1, 2; RGSF; SATA 66; SATA-Obit 70; SFW; SSFS 4, 12; WLIT 4
Carter, Nick
See Smith, Martin Cruz
Carver, Raymond 1938-1988 **CLC 22, 36, 53, 55, 126; DAM NOV; SSC 8, 51**
See also AMWS 3; BPFB 1; CA 33-36R; 126; CANR 17, 34, 61, 103; CPW; DA3; DLB 130; DLBY 84, 88; MTCW 1, 2; RGAL; RGSF; SSFS 3, 6, 12, 13; TCWW 2
Cary, Elizabeth, Lady Falkland 1585-1639 **LC 30**
Cary, (Arthur) Joyce (Lunel) 1888-1957 **TCLC 1, 29**
See also BRW 7; CA 104; 164; CDBLB 1914-1945; DLB 15, 100; MTCW 2; RGEL
Casanova de Seingalt, Giovanni Jacopo 1725-1798 **LC 13**

Casares, Adolfo Bioy
See Bioy Casares, Adolfo
See also RGSF
Casas, Bartolome de las 1474-1566
See Las Casas, Bartolome de
See also WLIT 1
Casely-Hayford, J(oseph) E(phraim) 1866-1903 **TCLC 24; BLC 1; DAM MULT**
See also BW 2; CA 123; 152
Casey, John (Dudley) 1939- **CLC 59**
See also BEST 90:2; CA 69-72; CANR 23, 100
Casey, Michael 1947- **CLC 2**
See also CA 65-68; DLB 5
Casey, Patrick
See Thurman, Wallace (Henry)
Casey, Warren (Peter) 1935-1988 **CLC 12**
See also CA 101; 127; INT 101
Casona, Alejandro CLC 49
See also Alvarez, Alejandro Rodriguez
Cassavetes, John 1929-1989 **CLC 20**
See also CA 85-88; 127; CANR 82
Cassian, Nina 1924- **PC 17**
See also CWP; CWW 2
Cassill, R(onald) V(erlin) 1919- **CLC 4, 23**
See also CA 9-12R; CAAS 1; CANR 7, 45; CN; DLB 6, 218
Cassiodorus, Flavius Magnus c. 490(?)-c. 583(?) **CMLC 43**
Cassirer, Ernst 1874-1945 **TCLC 61**
See also CA 157
Cassity, (Allen) Turner 1929- **CLC 6, 42**
See also CA 17-20R; CAAS 8; CANR 11; CSW; DLB 105
Castaneda, Carlos (Cesar Aranha) 1931(?)-1998 **CLC 12, 119**
See also CA 25-28R; CANR 32, 66, 105; HW 1; MTCW 1
Castedo, Elena 1937- **CLC 65**
See also CA 132
Castedo-Ellerman, Elena
See Castedo, Elena
Castellanos, Rosario 1925-1974 **CLC 66; DAM MULT; HLC 1; SSC 39**
See also CA 131; 53-56; CANR 58; DLB 113; FW; HW 1; LAW; MTCW 1; RGSF; RGWL
Castelvetro, Lodovico 1505-1571 **LC 12**
Castiglione, Baldassare 1478-1529 **LC 12**
See also Castiglione, Baldesar
See also RGWL
Castiglione, Baldesar
See Castiglione, Baldassare
See also EW 2
Castillo, Ana (Hernandez Del) 1953- **CLC 151**
See also AAYA 42; CA 131; CANR 51, 86; CWP; DLB 122, 227; DNFS; FW; HW 1
Castle, Robert
See Hamilton, Edmond
Castro (Ruz), Fidel 1926(?)-
See also CA 110; 129; CANR 81; DAM MULT; HLC 1; HW 2
Castro, Guillen de 1569-1631 **LC 19**
Castro, Rosalia de 1837-1885 **NCLC 3, 78; DAM MULT**
Cather, Willa (Sibert) 1873-1947 **TCLC 1, 11, 31, 99; DA; DAB; DAC; DAM MST, NOV; SSC 2, 50; WLC**
See also AAYA 24; AMW; AMWR 1; BPFB 1; CA 104; 128; CDALB 1865-1917; DA3; DLB 9, 54, 78, 256; DLBD 1; EXPN; EXPS; LAIT 3; MAWW; MTCW 1, 2; NFS 2; RGAL; RGSF; RHW; SATA 30; SSFS 2, 7; TCWW 2
Catherine II
See Catherine the Great
See also DLB 150

Catherine the Great 1729-1796 LC 69
  See also Catherine II
Cato, Marcus Porcius234B.C.-149B.C.
  CMLC 21
  See also Cato the Elder
Catton, (Charles) Bruce 1899-1978 CLC 35
  See also AITN 1; CA 5-8R; 81-84; CANR
  7, 74; DLB 17; SATA 2; SATA-Obit 24
Catullusc. 84B.C.-54B.C. CMLC 18
  See also AW 2; DLB 211; RGWL
Cauldwell, Frank
  See King, Francis (Henry)
Caunitz, William J. 1933-1996 CLC 34
  See also BEST 89:3; CA 125; 130; 152;
  CANR 73; INT 130
Causley, Charles (Stanley) 1917- CLC 7
  See also CA 9-12R; CANR 5, 35, 94; CLR
  30; CWRI; DLB 27; MTCW 1; SATA 3,
  66
Caute, (John) David 1936- CLC 29; DAM
  NOV
  See also CA 1-4R; CAAS 4; CANR 1, 33,
  64; CBD; CD; CN; DLB 14, 231
Cavafy, C(onstantine) P(eter) TCLC 2, 7;
  DAM POET; PC 36
  See also Kavafis, Konstantinos Petrou
  See also CA 148; DA3; EW 8; MTCW 1;
  RGWL; WP
Cavallo, Evelyn
  See Spark, Muriel (Sarah)
Cavanna, Betty CLC 12
  See also Harrison, Elizabeth (Allen) Ca-
  vanna
  See also JRDA; MAICYA; SAAS 4; SATA
  1, 30
Cavendish, Margaret Lucas 1623-1673 LC
  30
  See also DLB 131, 252; RGEL
Caxton, William 1421(?)-1491(?) LC 17
  See also DLB 170
Cayer, D. M.
  See Duffy, Maureen
Cayrol, Jean 1911- CLC 11
  See also CA 89-92; DLB 83
Cela, Camilo Jose 1916-2002 CLC 4, 13, 59,
  122; DAM MULT; HLC 1
  See also BEST 90:2; CA 21-24R; CAAS
  10; CANR 21, 32, 76; DLBY 89; EW 13;
  HW 1; MTCW 1, 2; RGSF; RGWL
Celan, Paul CLC 10, 19, 53, 82; PC 10
  See also Antschel, Paul
  See also DLB 69; RGWL
Celine, Louis-Ferdinand CLC 1, 3, 4, 7, 9,
  15, 47, 124
  See also Destouches, Louis-Ferdinand
  See also DLB 72; EW 11; GFL 1789 to the
  Present; RGWL
Cellini, Benvenuto 1500-1571 LC 7
Cendrars, Blaise CLC 18, 106
  See also Sauser-Hall, Frederic
  See also GFL 1789 to the Present; RGWL;
  WP
Centlivre, Susanna 1669(?)-1723 LC 65
  See also DLB 84; RGEL
Cernuda (y Bidon), Luis 1902-1963 CLC 54;
  DAM POET
  See also CA 131; 89-92; DLB 134; GLL 1;
  HW 1; RGWL
Cervantes, Lorna Dee 1954- PC 35
  See also CA 131; CANR 80; CWP; DLB
  82; EXPP; HLCS 1; HW 1
Cervantes (Saavedra), Miguel de 1547-1616
  LC 6, 23; DA; DAB; DAC; DAM MST,
  NOV; HLCS; SSC 12; WLC
  See also BYA 1, 14; EW 2; LAIT 1; NFS 8;
  RGSF; RGWL
Cesaire, Aime (Fernand) 1913- CLC 19, 32,
  112; BLC 1; DAM MULT, POET; PC
  25
  See also BW 2, 3; CA 65-68; CANR 24,
  43, 81; DA3; GFL 1789 to the Present;
  MTCW 1, 2; WP
Chabon, Michael 1963- CLC 55, 149
  See also CA 139; CANR 57, 96
Chabrol, Claude 1930- CLC 16
  See also CA 110
Challans, Mary 1905-1983
  See Renault, Mary
  See also CA 81-84; 111; CANR 74; DA3;
  MTCW 2; SATA 23; SATA-Obit 36
Challis, George
  See Faust, Frederick (Schiller)
  See also TCWW 2
Chambers, Aidan 1934- CLC 35
  See also AAYA 27; CA 25-28R; CANR 12,
  31, 58; JRDA; MAICYA; SAAS 12;
  SATA 1, 69, 108; WYA; YAW
Chambers, James 1948-
  See Cliff, Jimmy
  See also CA 124
Chambers, Jessie
  See Lawrence, D(avid) H(erbert Richards)
  See also GLL 1
Chambers, Robert W(illiam) 1865-1933
  TCLC 41
  See also CA 165; DLB 202; HGG; SATA
  107; SUFW
Chamisso, Adelbert von 1781-1838 NCLC 82
  See also DLB 90; RGWL; SUFW
Chandler, Raymond (Thornton) 1888-1959
  TCLC 1, 7; SSC 23
  See also AAYA 25; AMWS 4; BPFB 1; CA
  104; 129; CANR 60; CDALB 1929-1941;
  CMW; DA3; DLB 226, 253; DLBD 6;
  MSW; MTCW 1, 2; RGAL
Chang, Eileen 1921-1995 SSC 28
  See also CA 166; CWW 2
Chang, Jung 1952- CLC 71
  See also CA 142
Chang Ai-Ling
  See Chang, Eileen
Channing, William Ellery 1780-1842 NCLC
  17
  See also DLB 1, 59, 235; RGAL
Chao, Patricia 1955- CLC 119
  See also CA 163
Chaplin, Charles Spencer 1889-1977 CLC 16
  See also Chaplin, Charlie
  See also CA 81-84; 73-76
Chaplin, Charlie
  See Chaplin, Charles Spencer
  See also DLB 44
Chapman, George 1559(?)-1634 LC 22; DAM
  DRAM
  See also BRW 1; DLB 62, 121; RGEL
Chapman, Graham 1941-1989 CLC 21
  See also Monty Python
  See also CA 116; 129; CANR 35, 95
Chapman, John Jay 1862-1933 TCLC 7
  See also CA 104; 191
Chapman, Lee
  See Bradley, Marion Zimmer
  See also GLL 1
Chapman, Walker
  See Silverberg, Robert
Chappell, Fred (Davis) 1936- CLC 40, 78
  See also CA 5-8R; CAAS 4; CANR 8, 33,
  67; CN; CP; CSW; DLB 6, 105; HGG
Char, Rene(-Emile) 1907-1988 CLC 9, 11, 14,
  55; DAM POET
  See also CA 13-16R; 124; CANR 32; GFL
  1789 to the Present; MTCW 1, 2; RGWL
Charby, Jay
  See Ellison, Harlan (Jay)

Chardin, Pierre Teilhard de
  See Teilhard de Chardin, (Marie Joseph)
  Pierre
Charitonfl. 1st cent. (?)- CMLC 49
Charlemagne742-814 CMLC 37
Charles I 1600-1649 LC 13
Charriere, Isabelle de 1740-1805 NCLC 66
Chartier, Emile-Auguste
  See Alain
Charyn, Jerome 1937- CLC 5, 8, 18
  See also CA 5-8R; CAAS 1; CANR 7, 61,
  101; CMW; CN; DLBY 83; MTCW 1
Chase, Adam
  See Marlowe, Stephen
Chase, Mary (Coyle) 1907-1981 DC 1
  See also CA 77-80; 105; CAD; CWD; DFS
  11; DLB 228; SATA 17; SATA-Obit 29
Chase, Mary Ellen 1887-1973 CLC 2
  See also CA 13-16; 41-44R; CAP 1; SATA
  10
Chase, Nicholas
  See Hyde, Anthony
  See also CCA 1
Chateaubriand, Francois Rene de 1768-1848
  NCLC 3
  See also DLB 119; EW 5; GFL 1789 to the
  Present; RGWL
Chatterje, Sarat Chandra 1876-1936(?)
  See Chatterji, Saratchandra
  See also CA 109
Chatterji, Bankim Chandra 1838-1894
  NCLC 19
Chatterji, Saratchandra TCLC 13
  See also Chatterje, Sarat Chandra
  See also CA 186
Chatterton, Thomas 1752-1770 LC 3, 54;
  DAM POET
  See also DLB 109; RGEL
Chatwin, (Charles) Bruce 1940-1989 CLC
  28, 57, 59; DAM POP
  See also AAYA 4; BEST 90:1; BRWS 4;
  CA 85-88; 127; CPW; DLB 194, 204
Chaucer, Daniel
  See Ford, Ford Madox
  See also RHW
Chaucer, Geoffrey 1340(?)-1400 LC 17, 56;
  DA; DAB; DAC; DAM MST, POET;
  PC 19; WLCS
  See also BRW 1; BRWR 2; CDBLB Before
  1660; DA3; DLB 146; LAIT 1; PAB; PFS
  14; RGEL; WLIT 3; WP
Chavez, Denise (Elia) 1948-
  See also CA 131; CANR 56, 81; DAM
  MULT; DLB 122; FW; HLC 1; HW 1, 2;
  MTCW 2
Chaviaras, Strates 1935-
  See Haviaras, Stratis
  See also CA 105
Chayefsky, Paddy CLC 23
  See also Chayefsky, Sidney
  See also CAD; DLB 7, 44; DLBY 81;
  RGAL
Chayefsky, Sidney 1923-1981
  See Chayefsky, Paddy
  See also CA 9-12R; 104; CANR 18; DAM
  DRAM
Chedid, Andree 1920- CLC 47
  See also CA 145; CANR 95
Cheever, John 1912-1982 CLC 3, 7, 8, 11, 15,
  25, 64; DA; DAB; DAC; DAM MST,
  NOV, POP; SSC 1, 38; WLC
  See also AMWS 1; BPFB 1; CA 5-8R; 106;
  CABS 1; CANR 5, 27, 76; CDALB 1941-
  1968; CPW; DA3; DLB 2, 102, 227;
  DLBY 80, 82; EXPS; INT CANR-5;
  MTCW 1, 2; RGAL; RGSF; SSFS 2
Cheever, Susan 1943- CLC 18, 48
  See also CA 103; CANR 27, 51, 92; DLBY
  82; INT CANR-27

Chekhonte, Antosha
See Chekhov, Anton (Pavlovich)
Chekhov, Anton (Pavlovich) 1860-1904
**TCLC 3, 10, 31, 55, 96; DA; DAB;
DAC; DAM DRAM, MST; DC 9; SSC
2, 28, 41, 51; WLC**
See also BYA 14; CA 104; 124; DA3; DFS
1, 5, 10, 12; EW 7; EXPS; LAIT 3;
RGSF; RGWL; SATA 90; SSFS 5, 13
Cheney, Lynne V. 1941- **CLC 70**
See also CA 89-92; CANR 58
Chernyshevsky, Nikolai Gavrilovich
See Chernyshevsky, Nikolay Gavrilovich
See also DLB 238
Chernyshevsky, Nikolay Gavrilovich
1828-1889 **NCLC 1**
See also Chernyshevsky, Nikolai Gavrilov-
ich
Cherry, Carolyn Janice 1942-
See Cherryh, C. J.
See also CA 65-68; CANR 10; FANT; SFW;
YAW
Cherryh, C. J. CLC 35
See also Cherry, Carolyn Janice
See also AAYA 24; BPFB 1; DLBY 80;
SATA 93; SCFW 2
Chesnutt, Charles W(addell) 1858-1932
**TCLC 5, 39; BLC 1; DAM MULT; SSC
7**
See also AFAW 1, 2; BW 1, 3; CA 106;
125; CANR 76; DLB 12, 50, 78; MTCW
1, 2; RGAL; RGSF; SSFS 11
Chester, Alfred 1929(?)-1971 **CLC 49**
See also CA 196; 33-36R; DLB 130
Chesterton, G(ilbert) K(eith) 1874-1936
**TCLC 1, 6, 64; DAM NOV, POET; PC
28; SSC 1, 46**
See also BRW 6; CA 104; 132; CANR 73;
CDBLB 1914-1945; CMW; DLB 10, 19,
34, 70, 98, 149, 178; FANT; MSW;
MTCW 1, 2; RGEL; RGSF; SATA 27;
SUFW
Chiang, Pin-chin 1904-1986
See Ding Ling
See also CA 118
Ch'ien Chung-shu 1910- **CLC 22**
See also CA 130; CANR 73; MTCW 1, 2
Chikamatsu Monzaemon 1653-1724 **LC 66**
See also RGWL
Child, L. Maria
See Child, Lydia Maria
Child, Lydia Maria 1802-1880 **NCLC 6, 73**
See also DLB 1, 74, 243; RGAL; SATA 67
Child, Mrs.
See Child, Lydia Maria
Child, Philip 1898-1978 **CLC 19, 68**
See also CA 13-14; CAP 1; DLB 68; RHW;
SATA 47
Childers, (Robert) Erskine 1870-1922 **TCLC
65**
See also CA 113; 153; DLB 70
Childress, Alice 1920-1994 **CLC 12, 15, 86,
96; BLC 1; DAM DRAM, MULT, NOV;
DC 4**
See also AAYA 8; BW 2, 3; BYA 2; CA 45-
48; 146; CAD; CANR 3, 27, 50, 74; CLR
14; CWD; DA3; DFS 2, 8; DLB 7, 38,
249; JRDA; LAIT 5; MAICYA; MAIC-
YAS; MTCW 1, 2; RGAL; SATA 7, 48,
81; TCLC 116; WYA; YAW
Chin, Frank (Chew, Jr.) 1940- **CLC 135;
DAM MULT; DC 7**
See also CA 33-36R; CANR 71; CD; DLB
206; LAIT 5; RGAL
Chislett, (Margaret) Anne 1943- **CLC 34**
See also CA 151
Chitty, Thomas Willes 1926- **CLC 11**
See also Hinde, Thomas
See also CA 5-8R; CN

Chivers, Thomas Holley 1809-1858 **NCLC 49**
See also DLB 3, 248; RGAL
Choi, Susan CLC 119
Chomette, Rene Lucien 1898-1981
See Clair, Rene
See also CA 103
Chomsky, (Avram) Noam 1928- **CLC 132**
See also CA 17-20R; CANR 28, 62; DA3;
DLB 246; MTCW 1, 2
**Chopin, Kate TCLC 5, 14; DA; DAB; SSC
8; WLCS**
See also Chopin, Katherine
See also AAYA 33; AMWS 1; CDALB
1865-1917; DLB 12, 78; EXPN; EXPS;
FW; LAIT 3; MAWW; NFS 3; RGAL;
RGSF; SSFS 2, 13
Chopin, Katherine 1851-1904
See Chopin, Kate
See also CA 104; 122; DA3; DAC; DAM
MST, NOV
Chretien de Troyesc. 12th cent. - **CMLC 10**
See also DLB 208; EW 1; RGWL
Christie
See Ichikawa, Kon
Christie, Agatha (Mary Clarissa) 1890-1976
**CLC 1, 6, 8, 12, 39, 48, 110; DAB; DAC;
DAM NOV**
See also AAYA 9; AITN 1, 2; BPFB 1;
BRWS 2; CA 17-20R; 61-64; CANR 10,
37; CBD; CDBLB 1914-1945; CMW;
CPW; CWD; DA3; DFS 2; DLB 13, 77,
245; MSW; MTCW 1, 2; NFS 8; RGEL;
RHW; SATA 36; YAW
Christie, (Ann) Philippa
See Pearce, Philippa
See also CA 5-8R; CANR 4; CWRI; FANT
Christine de Pizan 1365(?)-1431(?) **LC 9**
See also DLB 208; RGWL
Chubb, Elmer
See Masters, Edgar Lee
Chulkov, Mikhail Dmitrievich 1743-1792 **LC
2**
See also DLB 150
Churchill, Caryl 1938- **CLC 31, 55; DC 5**
See also BRWS 4; CA 102; CANR 22, 46;
CBD; CWD; DFS 12; DLB 13; FW;
MTCW 1; RGEL
Churchill, Charles 1731-1764 **LC 3**
See also DLB 109; RGEL
Churchill, Sir Winston (Leonard Spencer)
1874-1965 **TCLC 113**
See also BRW 6; CA 97-100; CDBLB
1890-1914; DA3; DLB 100; DLBD 16;
LAIT 4; MTCW 1, 2
Chute, Carolyn 1947- **CLC 39**
See also CA 123
Ciardi, John (Anthony) 1916-1986 **CLC 10,
40, 44, 129; DAM POET**
See also CA 5-8R; 118; CAAS 2; CANR 5,
33; CLR 19; CWRI; DLB 5; DLBY 86;
INT CANR-5; MAICYA; MTCW 1, 2;
RGAL; SAAS 26; SATA 1, 65; SATA-
Obit 46
Cibber, Colley 1671-1757 **LC 66**
See also DLB 84; RGEL
Cicero, Marcus Tullius 106B.C.-43B.C.
CMLC 3
See also AW 1; DLB 211; RGWL
Cimino, Michael 1943- **CLC 16**
See also CA 105
Cioran, E(mil) M. 1911-1995 **CLC 64**
See also CA 25-28R; 149; CANR 91; DLB
220
Cisneros, Sandra 1954- **CLC 69, 118; DAM
MULT; HLC 1; SSC 32**
See also AAYA 9; AMWS 7; CA 131;
CANR 64; CWP; DA3; DLB 122, 152;
EXPN; FW; HW 1, 2; LAIT 5; MTCW 2;
NFS 2; RGAL; RGSF; SSFS 3, 13; WLIT
1; YAW

Cixous, Helene 1937- **CLC 92**
See also CA 126; CANR 55; CWW 2; DLB
83, 242; FW; MTCW 1, 2
Clair, Rene CLC 20
See also Chomette, Rene Lucien
Clampitt, Amy 1920-1994 **CLC 32; PC 19**
See also AMWS 9; CA 110; 146; CANR
29, 79; DLB 105
Clancy, Thomas L., Jr. 1947-
See Clancy, Tom
See also CA 125; 131; CANR 62, 105;
CPW; DA3; DLB 227; INT 131; MTCW
1, 2
Clancy, Tom CLC 45, 112; DAM NOV, POP
See also Clancy, Thomas L., Jr.
See also AAYA 9; BEST 89:1, 90:1; BPFB
1; BYA 10, 11; CMW; MTCW 2
Clare, John 1793-1864 **NCLC 9, 86; DAB;
DAM POET; PC 23**
See also DLB 55, 96; RGEL
Clarin
See Alas (y Urena), Leopoldo (Enrique
Garcia)
Clark, Al C.
See Goines, Donald
Clark, (Robert) Brian 1932- **CLC 29**
See also CA 41-44R; CANR 67; CBD; CD
Clark, Curt
See Westlake, Donald E(dwin)
Clark, Eleanor 1913-1996 **CLC 5, 19**
See also CA 9-12R; 151; CANR 41; CN;
DLB 6
Clark, J. P.
See Clark Bekedermo, J(ohnson) P(epper)
See also DLB 117
Clark, John Pepper
See Clark Bekedermo, J(ohnson) P(epper)
See also AFW; CD; CP; RGEL
Clark, M. R.
See Clark, Mavis Thorpe
Clark, Mavis Thorpe 1909- **CLC 12**
See also CA 57-60; CANR 8, 37; CLR 30;
CWRI; MAICYA; SAAS 5; SATA 8, 74
Clark, Walter Van Tilburg 1909-1971 **CLC
28**
See also CA 9-12R; 33-36R; CANR 63;
DLB 9, 206; LAIT 2; RGAL; SATA 8
Clark Bekedermo, J(ohnson) P(epper) 1935-
**CLC 38; BLC 1; DAM DRAM, MULT;
DC 5**
See also Clark, J. P.; Clark, John Pepper
See also BW 1; CA 65-68; CANR 16, 72;
DFS 13; MTCW 1
Clarke, Arthur C(harles) 1917- **CLC 1, 4, 13,
18, 35, 136; DAM POP; SSC 3**
See also AAYA 4, 33; BPFB 1; BYA 13;
CA 1-4R; CANR 2, 28, 55, 74; CN; CPW;
DA3; JRDA; LAIT 5; MAICYA; MTCW
1, 2; SATA 13, 70, 115; SCFW; SFW;
SSFS 4; YAW
Clarke, Austin 1896-1974 **CLC 6, 9; DAM
POET**
See also CA 29-32; 49-52; CAP 2; DLB 10,
20; RGEL
Clarke, Austin C(hesterfield) 1934- **CLC 8,
53; BLC 1; DAC; DAM MULT; SSC 45**
See also BW 1; CA 25-28R; CAAS 16;
CANR 14, 32, 68; CN; DLB 53, 125;
DNFS; RGSF
Clarke, Gillian 1937- **CLC 61**
See also CA 106; CP; CWP; DLB 40
Clarke, Marcus (Andrew Hislop) 1846-1881
NCLC 19
See also DLB 230; RGEL; RGSF
Clarke, Shirley 1925-1997 **CLC 16**
See also CA 189
Clash, The
See Headon, (Nicky) Topper; Jones, Mick;
Simonon, Paul; Strummer, Joe

Claudel, Paul (Louis Charles Marie) 1868-1955 **TCLC 2, 10**
See also CA 104; 165; DLB 192; EW 8; GFL 1789 to the Present; RGWL

Claudian370(?)-404(?) **CMLC 46**
See also RGWL

Claudius, Matthias 1740-1815 **NCLC 75**
See also DLB 97

Clavell, James (duMaresq) 1925-1994 **CLC 6, 25, 87; DAM NOV, POP**
See also BPFB 1; CA 25-28R; 146; CANR 26, 48; CPW; DA3; MTCW 1, 2; NFS 10; RHW

Clayman, Gregory **CLC 65**

Cleaver, (Leroy) Eldridge 1935-1998 **CLC 30, 119; BLC 1; DAM MULT**
See also BW 1, 3; CA 21-24R; 167; CANR 16, 75; DA3; MTCW 2; YAW

Cleese, John (Marwood) 1939- **CLC 21**
See also Monty Python
See also CA 112; 116; CANR 35; MTCW 1

Cleishbotham, Jebediah
See Scott, Sir Walter

Cleland, John 1710-1789 **LC 2, 48**
See also DLB 39; RGEL

Clemens, Samuel Langhorne 1835-1910
See Twain, Mark
See also CA 104; 135; CDALB 1865-1917; DA; DA3; DAB; DAC; DAM MST, NOV; DLB 12, 23, 64, 74, 186, 189; JRDA; MAICYA; SATA 100; YABC 2

Clement of Alexandria 150(?)-215(?) **CMLC 41**

Cleophil
See Congreve, William

Clerihew, E.
See Bentley, E(dmund) C(lerihew)

Clerk, N. W.
See Lewis, C(live) S(taples)

Cliff, Jimmy **CLC 21**
See also Chambers, James
See also CA 193

Cliff, Michelle 1946- **CLC 120; BLCS**
See also BW 2; CA 116; CANR 39, 72; DLB 157; FW; GLL 2

Clifton, (Thelma) Lucille 1936- **CLC 19, 66; BLC 1; DAM MULT, POET; PC 17**
See also AFAW 2; BW 2, 3; CA 49-52; CANR 2, 24, 42, 76, 97; CLR 5; CP; CSW; CWP; CWRI; DA3; DLB 5, 41; EXPP; MAICYA; MTCW 1, 2; PFS 1, 14; SATA 20, 69; WP

Clinton, Dirk
See Silverberg, Robert

Clough, Arthur Hugh 1819-1861 **NCLC 27**
See also BRW 5; DLB 32; RGEL

Clutha, Janet Paterson Frame 1924-
See Frame, Janet
See also CA 1-4R; CANR 2, 36, 76; MTCW 1, 2; SATA 119

Clyne, Terence
See Blatty, William Peter

Cobalt, Martin
See Mayne, William (James Carter)

Cobb, Irvin S(hrewsbury) 1876-1944 **TCLC 77**
See also CA 175; DLB 11, 25, 86

Cobbett, William 1763-1835 **NCLC 49**
See also DLB 43, 107, 158; RGEL

Coburn, D(onald) L(ee) 1938- **CLC 10**
See also CA 89-92

Cocteau, Jean (Maurice Eugene Clement) 1889-1963 **CLC 1, 8, 15, 16, 43; DA; DAB; DAC; DAM DRAM, MST, NOV; TCLC 119; WLC**
See also CA 25-28; CANR 40; CAP 2; DA3; DLB 65; EW 10; GFL 1789 to the Present; MTCW 1, 2; RGWL

Codrescu, Andrei 1946- **CLC 46, 121; DAM POET**
See also CA 33-36R; CAAS 19; CANR 13, 34, 53, 76; DA3; MTCW 2

Coe, Max
See Bourne, Randolph S(illiman)

Coe, Tucker
See Westlake, Donald E(dwin)

Coen, Ethan 1958- **CLC 108**
See also CA 126; CANR 85

Coen, Joel 1955- **CLC 108**
See also CA 126

The Coen Brothers
See Coen, Ethan; Coen, Joel

Coetzee, J(ohn) M(ichael) 1940- **CLC 23, 33, 66, 117; DAM NOV**
See also AAYA 37; AFW; BRWS 6; CA 77-80; CANR 41, 54, 74; CN; DA3; DLB 225; MTCW 1, 2; WLIT 2

Coffey, Brian
See Koontz, Dean R(ay)

Coffin, Robert P(eter) Tristram 1892-1955 **TCLC 95**
See also CA 123; 169; DLB 45

Cohan, George M(ichael) 1878-1942 **TCLC 60**
See also CA 157; DLB 249; RGAL

Cohen, Arthur A(llen) 1928-1986 **CLC 7, 31**
See also CA 1-4R; 120; CANR 1, 17, 42; DLB 28

Cohen, Leonard (Norman) 1934- **CLC 3, 38; DAC; DAM MST**
See also CA 21-24R; CANR 14, 69; CN; CP; DLB 53; MTCW 1

Cohen, Matt(hew) 1942-1999 **CLC 19; DAC**
See also CA 61-64; 187; CAAS 18; CANR 40; CN; DLB 53

Cohen-Solal, Annie 19(?)- **CLC 50**

Colegate, Isabel 1931- **CLC 36**
See also CA 17-20R; CANR 8, 22, 74; CN; DLB 14, 231; INT CANR-22; MTCW 1

Coleman, Emmett
See Reed, Ishmael

Coleridge, Hartley 1796-1849 **NCLC 90**
See also DLB 96

Coleridge, M. E.
See Coleridge, Mary E(lizabeth)

Coleridge, Mary E(lizabeth) 1861-1907 **TCLC 73**
See also CA 116; 166; DLB 19, 98

Coleridge, Samuel Taylor 1772-1834 **NCLC 9, 54, 99; DA; DAB; DAC; DAM MST, POET; PC 11, 39; WLC**
See also BRW 4; BRWR 2; BYA 4; CD-BLB 1789-1832; DA3; DLB 93, 107; EXPP; PAB; PFS 4, 5; RGEL; WLIT 3; WP

Coleridge, Sara 1802-1852 **NCLC 31**
See also DLB 199

Coles, Don 1928- **CLC 46**
See also CA 115; CANR 38; CP

Coles, Robert (Martin) 1929- **CLC 108**
See also CA 45-48; CANR 3, 32, 66, 70; INT CANR-32; SATA 23

Colette, (Sidonie-Gabrielle) 1873-1954 **TCLC 1, 5, 16; DAM NOV; SSC 10**
See also Willy, Colette
See also CA 104; 131; DA3; DLB 65; EW 9; GFL 1789 to the Present; MTCW 1, 2; RGWL

Collett, (Jacobine) Camilla (Wergeland) 1813-1895 **NCLC 22**

Collier, Christopher 1930- **CLC 30**
See also AAYA 13; BYA 2; CA 33-36R; CANR 13, 33, 102; JRDA; MAICYA; SATA 16, 70; WYA; YAW 1

Collier, James Lincoln 1928- **CLC 30; DAM POP**
See also Williams, Charles
See also AAYA 13; BYA 2; CA 9-12R; CANR 4, 33, 60, 102; CLR 3; JRDA; MAICYA; SAAS 21; SATA 8, 70; WYA; YAW 1

Collier, Jeremy 1650-1726 **LC 6**

Collier, John 1901-1980 **SSC 19**
See also CA 65-68; 97-100; CANR 10; DLB 77, 255; FANT; SUFW

Collingwood, R(obin) G(eorge) 1889(?)-1943 **TCLC 67**
See also CA 117; 155

Collins, Hunt
See Hunter, Evan

Collins, Linda 1931- **CLC 44**
See also CA 125

Collins, (William) Wilkie 1824-1889 **NCLC 1, 18, 93**
See also BRWS 6; CDBLB 1832-1890; CMW; DLB 18, 70, 159; MSW; RGEL; RGSF; SUFW; WLIT 4

Collins, William 1721-1759 **LC 4, 40; DAM POET**
See also BRW 3; DLB 109; RGEL

Collodi, Carlo **NCLC 54**
See also Lorenzini, Carlo
See also CLR 5; WCH

Colman, George
See Glassco, John

Colonna, Vittoria 1492-1547 **LC 71**
See also RGWL

Colt, Winchester Remington
See Hubbard, L(afayette) Ron(ald)

Colter, Cyrus 1910- **CLC 58**
See also BW 1; CA 65-68; CANR 10, 66; CN; DLB 33

Colton, James
See Hansen, Joseph
See also GLL 1

Colum, Padraic 1881-1972 **CLC 28**
See also BYA 4; CA 73-76; 33-36R; CANR 35; CLR 36; CWRI; DLB 19; MAICYA; MTCW 1; RGEL; SATA 15; WCH

Colvin, James
See Moorcock, Michael (John)

Colwin, Laurie (E.) 1944-1992 **CLC 5, 13, 23, 84**
See also CA 89-92; 139; CANR 20, 46; DLB 218; DLBY 80; MTCW 1

Comfort, Alex(ander) 1920-2000 **CLC 7; DAM POP**
See also CA 1-4R; 190; CANR 1, 45; CP; MTCW 1

Comfort, Montgomery
See Campbell, (John) Ramsey

Compton-Burnett, I(vy) 1892(?)-1969 **CLC 1, 3, 10, 15, 34; DAM NOV**
See also BRW 7; CA 1-4R; 25-28R; CANR 4; DLB 36; MTCW 1; RGEL

Comstock, Anthony 1844-1915 **TCLC 13**
See also CA 110; 169

Comte, Auguste 1798-1857 **NCLC 54**

Conan Doyle, Arthur
See Doyle, Sir Arthur Conan
See also BPFB 1; BYA 4, 5, 11

Conde (Abellan), Carmen 1901-1996
See also CA 177; DLB 108; HLCS 1; HW 2

Conde, Maryse 1937- **CLC 52, 92; BLCS; DAM MULT**
See also BW 2, 3; CA 110; CAAE 190; CANR 30, 53, 76; CWW 2; MTCW 1

Condillac, Etienne Bonnot de 1714-1780 **LC 26**

Condon, Richard (Thomas) 1915-1996 **CLC**

4, 6, 8, 10, 45, 100; DAM NOV
See also BEST 90:3; BPFB 1; CA 1-4R;
151; CAAS 1; CANR 2, 23; CMW; CN;
INT CANR-23; MTCW 1, 2

Confucius 551B.C.-479B.C. CMLC 19; DA;
DAB; DAC; DAM MST; WLCS
See also DA3

Congreve, William 1670-1729 LC 5, 21; DA;
DAB; DAC; DAM DRAM, MST,
POET; DC 2; WLC
See also BRW 2; CDBLB 1660-1789; DLB
39, 84; RGEL; WLIT 3

Connell, Evan S(helby), Jr. 1924- CLC 4, 6,
45; DAM NOV
See also AAYA 7; CA 1-4R; CAAS 2;
CANR 2, 39, 76, 97; CN; DLB 2; DLBY
81; MTCW 1, 2

Connelly, Marc(us Cook) 1890-1980 CLC 7
See also CA 85-88; 102; CANR 30; DFS
12; DLB 7; DLBY 80; RGAL; SATA-Obit
25

Connor, Ralph TCLC 31
See also Gordon, Charles William
See also DLB 92; TCWW 2

Conrad, Joseph 1857-1924 TCLC 1, 6, 13,
25, 43, 57; DA; DAB; DAC; DAM MST,
NOV; SSC 9; WLC
See also AAYA 26; BPFB 1; BRW 6;
BRWR 2; BYA 2; CA 104; 131; CANR
60; CDBLB 1890-1914; DA3; DLB 10,
34, 98, 156; EXPN; EXPS; LAIT 2;
MTCW 1, 2; NFS 2; RGEL; RGSF; SATA
27; SSFS 1, 12; WLIT 4

Conrad, Robert Arnold
See Hart, Moss

Conroy, Pat
See Conroy, (Donald) Pat(rick)
See also BPFB 1; LAIT 5; MTCW 2

Conroy, (Donald) Pat(rick) 1945- CLC 30,
74; DAM NOV, POP
See also Conroy, Pat
See also AAYA 8; AITN 1; CA 85-88;
CANR 24, 53; CPW; CSW; DA3; DLB 6;
MTCW 1

Constant (de Rebecque), (Henri) Benjamin
1767-1830 NCLC 6
See also DLB 119; EW 4; GFL 1789 to the
Present

Conway, Jill K(er) 1934- CLC 152
See also CA 130; CANR 94

Conybeare, Charles Augustus
See Eliot, T(homas) S(tearns)

Cook, Michael 1933-1994 CLC 58
See also CA 93-96; CANR 68; DLB 53

Cook, Robin 1940- CLC 14; DAM POP
See also AAYA 32; BEST 90:2; BPFB 1;
CA 108; 111; CANR 41, 90; CPW; DA3;
HGG; INT CA-111

Cook, Roy
See Silverberg, Robert

Cooke, Elizabeth 1948- CLC 55
See also CA 129

Cooke, John Esten 1830-1886 NCLC 5
See also DLB 3, 248; RGAL

Cooke, John Estes
See Baum, L(yman) Frank

Cooke, M. E.
See Creasey, John

Cooke, Margaret
See Creasey, John

Cooke, Rose Terry 1827-1892 NCLC 110
See also DLB 12, 74

Cook-Lynn, Elizabeth 1930- CLC 93; DAM
MULT
See also CA 133; DLB 175; NNAL

Cooney, Ray CLC 62
See also CBD

Cooper, Douglas 1960- CLC 86

Cooper, Henry St. John
See Creasey, John

Cooper, J(oan) California(?)- CLC 56; DAM
MULT
See also AAYA 12; BW 1; CA 125; CANR
55; DLB 212

Cooper, James Fenimore 1789-1851 NCLC 1,
27, 54
See also AAYA 22; AMW; BPFB 1;
CDALB 1640-1865; DA3; DLB 3, 183,
250, 254; LAIT 1; NFS 9; RGAL; SATA
19; WCH

Coover, Robert (Lowell) 1932- CLC 3, 7, 15,
32, 46, 87; DAM NOV; SSC 15
See also AMWS 5; BPFB 1; CA 45-48;
CANR 3, 37, 58; CN; DLB 2, 227; DLBY
81; MTCW 1, 2; RGAL; RGSF

Copeland, Stewart (Armstrong) 1952- CLC
26

Copernicus, Nicolaus 1473-1543 LC 45

Coppard, A(lfred) E(dgar) 1878-1957 TCLC
5; SSC 21
See also CA 114; 167; DLB 162; HGG;
RGEL; RGSF; SUFW; YABC 1

Coppee, Francois 1842-1908 TCLC 25
See also CA 170; DLB 217

Coppola, Francis Ford 1939- CLC 16, 126
See also AAYA 39; CA 77-80; CANR 40,
78; DLB 44

Corbiere, Tristan 1845-1875 NCLC 43
See also DLB 217; GFL 1789 to the Present

Corcoran, Barbara (Asenath) 1911- CLC 17
See also AAYA 14; CA 21-24R; CAAE 191;
CAAS 2; CANR 11, 28, 48; CLR 50;
DLB 52; JRDA; RHW; SAAS 20; SATA
3, 77, 125

Cordelier, Maurice
See Giraudoux, Jean(-Hippolyte)

Corelli, Marie TCLC 51
See also Mackay, Mary
See also DLB 34, 156; RGEL; SUFW

Corman, Cid CLC 9
See also Corman, Sidney
See also CAAS 2; DLB 5, 193

Corman, Sidney 1924-
See Corman, Cid
See also CA 85-88; CANR 44; CP; DAM
POET

Cormier, Robert (Edmund) 1925-2000 CLC
12, 30; DA; DAB; DAC; DAM MST,
NOV
See also AAYA 3, 19; BYA 1, 2, 6, 8, 9;
CA 1-4R; CANR 5, 23, 76, 93; CDALB
1968-1988; CLR 12, 55; DLB 52; EXPN;
INT CANR-23; JRDA; LAIT 5; MAI-
CYA; MTCW 1, 2; NFS 2; SATA 10, 45,
83; SATA-Obit 122; WYA; YAW

Corn, Alfred (DeWitt III) 1943- CLC 33
See also CA 179; CAAE 179; CAAS 25;
CANR 44; CP; CSW; DLB 120; DLBY
80

Corneille, Pierre 1606-1684 LC 28; DAB;
DAM MST
See also EW 3; GFL Beginnings to 1789;
RGWL

Cornwell, David (John Moore) 1931- CLC 9,
15; DAM POP
See also le Carre, John
See also CA 5-8R; CANR 13, 33, 59; DA3;
MTCW 1, 2

Cornwell, Patricia (Daniels) 1956- CLC 155;
DAM POP
See also AAYA 16; BPFB 1; CA 134;
CANR 53; CMW; CPW; CSW; MSW;
MTCW 1

Corso, (Nunzio) Gregory 1930-2001 CLC 1,
11; PC 33
See also CA 5-8R; 193; CANR 41, 76; CP;
DA3; DLB 5, 16, 237; MTCW 1, 2; WP

Cortazar, Julio 1914-1984 CLC 2, 3, 5, 10,
13, 15, 33, 34, 92; DAM MULT, NOV;
HLC 1; SSC 7
See also BPFB 1; CA 21-24R; CANR 12,
32, 81; DA3; DLB 113; EXPS; HW 1, 2;
LAW; MTCW 1, 2; RGSF; RGWL; SSFS
3; WLIT 1

Cortes, Hernan 1485-1547 LC 31

Corvinus, Jakob
See Raabe, Wilhelm (Karl)

Corvo, Baron
See Rolfe, Frederick (William Serafino
Austin Lewis Mary)
See also GLL 1; RGEL

Corwin, Cecil
See Kornbluth, C(yril) M.

Cosic, Dobrica 1921- CLC 14
See also CA 122; 138; CWW 2; DLB 181

Costain, Thomas B(ertram) 1885-1965 CLC
30
See also BYA 3; CA 5-8R; 25-28R; DLB 9;
RHW

Costantini, Humberto 1924(?)-1987 CLC 49
See also CA 131; 122; HW 1

Costello, Elvis 1955- CLC 21

Costenoble, Philostene 1898-1962
See Ghelderode, Michel de

Costenoble, Philostene 1898-1962
See Ghelderode, Michel de

Cotes, Cecil V.
See Duncan, Sara Jeannette

Cotter, Joseph Seamon Sr. 1861-1949 TCLC
28; BLC 1; DAM MULT
See also BW 1; CA 124; DLB 50

Couch, Arthur Thomas Quiller
See Quiller-Couch, Sir Arthur (Thomas)

Coulton, James
See Hansen, Joseph

Couperus, Louis (Marie Anne) 1863-1923
TCLC 15
See also CA 115; RGWL

Coupland, Douglas 1961- CLC 85, 133;
DAC; DAM POP
See also AAYA 34; CA 142; CANR 57, 90;
CCA 1; CPW

Court, Wesli
See Turco, Lewis (Putnam)

Courtenay, Bryce 1933- CLC 59
See also CA 138; CPW

Courtney, Robert
See Ellison, Harlan (Jay)

Cousteau, Jacques-Yves 1910-1997 CLC 30
See also CA 65-68; 159; CANR 15, 67;
MTCW 1; SATA 38, 98

Coventry, Francis 1725-1754 LC 46

Cowan, Peter (Walkinshaw) 1914- SSC 28
See also CA 21-24R; CANR 9, 25, 50, 83;
CN; RGSF

Coward, Noel (Peirce) 1899-1973 CLC 1, 9,
29, 51; DAM DRAM
See also AITN 1; BRWS 2; CA 17-18; 41-
44R; CANR 35; CAP 2; CDBLB 1914-
1945; DA3; DFS 3, 6; DLB 10, 245;
IDFW 3, 4; MTCW 1, 2; RGEL

Cowley, Abraham 1618-1667 LC 43
See also BRW 2; DLB 131, 151; PAB;
RGEL

Cowley, Malcolm 1898-1989 CLC 39
See also AMWS 2; CA 5-8R; 128; CANR
3, 55; DLB 4, 48; DLBY 81, 89; MTCW
1, 2

Cowper, William 1731-1800 NCLC 8, 94;
DAM POET
See also BRW 3; DA3; DLB 104, 109;
RGEL

Cox, William Trevor 1928-
See Trevor, William
See also CA 9-12R; CANR 4, 37, 55, 76, 102; DAM NOV; INT CANR-37; MTCW 1, 2

Coyne, P. J.
See Masters, Hilary

Cozzens, James Gould 1903-1978 **CLC 1, 4, 11, 92**
See also AMW; BPFB 1; CA 9-12R; 81-84; CANR 19; CDALB 1941-1968; DLB 9; DLBD 2; DLBY 84, 97; MTCW 1, 2; RGAL

Crabbe, George 1754-1832 **NCLC 26**
See also BRW 3; DLB 93; RGEL

Craddock, Charles Egbert
See Murfree, Mary Noailles

Craig, A. A.
See Anderson, Poul (William)

Craik, Mrs.
See Craik, Dinah Maria (Mulock)
See also RGEL

Craik, Dinah Maria (Mulock) 1826-1887 **NCLC 38**
See also Craik, Mrs.; Mulock, Dinah Maria
See also DLB 35, 163; MAICYA; SATA 34

Cram, Ralph Adams 1863-1942 **TCLC 45**
See also CA 160

Crane, (Harold) Hart 1899-1932 **TCLC 2, 5, 80; DA; DAB; DAC; DAM MST, POET; PC 3; WLC**
See also AMW; CA 104; 127; CDALB 1917-1929; DA3; DLB 4, 48; MTCW 1, 2; RGAL

Crane, R(onald) S(almon) 1886-1967 **CLC 27**
See also CA 85-88; DLB 63

Crane, Stephen (Townley) 1871-1900 **TCLC 11, 17, 32; DA; DAB; DAC; DAM MST, NOV, POET; SSC 7; WLC**
See also AAYA 21; AMW; BPFB 1; BYA 3; CA 109; 140; CANR 84; CDALB 1865-1917; DA3; DLB 12, 54, 78; EXPN; EXPS; LAIT 2; NFS 4; PFS 9; RGAL; RGSF; SSFS 4; WYA; YABC 2

Cranshaw, Stanley
See Fisher, Dorothy (Frances) Canfield

Crase, Douglas 1944- **CLC 58**
See also CA 106

Crashaw, Richard 1612(?)-1649 **LC 24**
See also BRW 2; DLB 126; PAB; RGEL

Craven, Margaret 1901-1980 **CLC 17; DAC**
See also BYA 2; CA 103; CCA 1; LAIT 5

Crawford, F(rancis) Marion 1854-1909 **TCLC 10**
See also CA 107; 168; DLB 71; HGG; RGAL; SUFW

Crawford, Isabella Valancy 1850-1887 **NCLC 12**
See also DLB 92; RGEL

Crayon, Geoffrey
See Irving, Washington

Creasey, John 1908-1973 **CLC 11**
See also Marric, J. J.
See also CA 5-8R; 41-44R; CANR 8, 59; CMW; DLB 77; MTCW 1

Crebillon, Claude Prosper Jolyot de (fils) 1707-1777 **LC 1, 28**
See also GFL Beginnings to 1789

Credo
See Creasey, John

Credo, Alvaro J. de
See Prado (Calvo), Pedro

Creeley, Robert (White) 1926- **CLC 1, 2, 4, 8, 11, 15, 36, 78; DAM POET**
See also AMWS 4; CA 1-4R; CAAS 10; CANR 23, 43, 89; CP; DA3; DLB 5, 16, 169; DLBD 17; MTCW 1, 2; RGAL; WP

Crevecoeur, Hector St. John de
See Crevecoeur, Michel Guillaume Jean de
See also ANW

Crevecoeur, Michel Guillaume Jean de 1735-1813 **NCLC 105**
See also Crevecoeur, Hector St. John de
See also AMWS 1; DLB 37

Crevel, Rene 1900-1935 **TCLC 112**
See also GLL 2

Crews, Harry (Eugene) 1935- **CLC 6, 23, 49**
See also AITN 1; BPFB 1; CA 25-28R; CANR 20, 57; CN; CSW; DA3; DLB 6, 143, 185; MTCW 1, 2; RGAL

Crichton, (John) Michael 1942- **CLC 2, 6, 54, 90; DAM NOV, POP**
See also AAYA 10; AITN 2; BPFB 1; CA 25-28R; CANR 13, 40, 54, 76; CMW; CN; CPW; DA3; DLBY 81; INT CANR-13; JRDA; MTCW 1, 2; SATA 9, 88; SFW; YAW

Crispin, Edmund CLC 22
See also Montgomery, (Robert) Bruce
See also DLB 87; MSW

Cristofer, Michael 1945(?)- **CLC 28; DAM DRAM**
See also CA 110; 152; CAD; CD; DLB 7

Croce, Benedetto 1866-1952 **TCLC 37**
See also CA 120; 155; EW 8

Crockett, David 1786-1836 **NCLC 8**
See also DLB 3, 11, 183, 248

Crockett, Davy
See Crockett, David

Crofts, Freeman Wills 1879-1957 **TCLC 55**
See also CA 115; 195; CMW; DLB 77; MSW

Croker, John Wilson 1780-1857 **NCLC 10**
See also DLB 110

Crommelynck, Fernand 1885-1970 **CLC 75**
See also CA 189; 89-92

Cromwell, Oliver 1599-1658 **LC 43**

Cronenberg, David 1943- **CLC 143**
See also CA 138; CCA 1

Cronin, A(rchibald) J(oseph) 1896-1981 **CLC 32**
See also BPFB 1; CA 1-4R; 102; CANR 5; DLB 191; SATA 47; SATA-Obit 25

Cross, Amanda
See Heilbrun, Carolyn G(old)
See also BPFB 1; MSW

Crothers, Rachel 1878-1958 **TCLC 19**
See also CA 113; 194; CAD; CWD; DLB 7; RGAL

Croves, Hal
See Traven, B.

Crow Dog, Mary (Ellen)(?)- **CLC 93**
See also Brave Bird, Mary
See also CA 154

Crowfield, Christopher
See Stowe, Harriet (Elizabeth) Beecher

Crowley, Aleister TCLC 7
See also Crowley, Edward Alexander
See also GLL 1

Crowley, Edward Alexander 1875-1947
See Crowley, Aleister
See also CA 104; HGG

Crowley, John 1942- **CLC 57**
See also BPFB 1; CA 61-64; CANR 43, 98; DLBY 82; SATA 65; SFW

Crud
See Crumb, R(obert)

Crumarums
See Crumb, R(obert)

Crumb, R(obert) 1943- **CLC 17**
See also CA 106

Crumbum
See Crumb, R(obert)

Crumski
See Crumb, R(obert)

Crum the Bum
See Crumb, R(obert)

Crunk
See Crumb, R(obert)

Crustt
See Crumb, R(obert)

Crutchfield, Les
See Trumbo, Dalton

Cruz, Victor Hernandez 1949- **PC 37**
See also BW 2; CA 65-68; CAAS 17; CANR 14, 32, 74; CP; DAM MULT, POET; DLB 41; DNFS; EXPP; HLC 1; HW 1, 2; MTCW 1; WP

Cryer, Gretchen (Kiger) 1935- **CLC 21**
See also CA 114; 123

Csath, Geza 1887-1919 **TCLC 13**
See also CA 111

Cudlip, David R(ockwell) 1933- **CLC 34**
See also CA 177

Cullen, Countee 1903-1946 **TCLC 4, 37; BLC 1; DA; DAC; DAM MST, MULT, POET; PC 20; WLCS**
See also AFAW 2; AMWS 4; BW 1; CA 108; 124; CDALB 1917-1929; DA3; DLB 4, 48, 51; EXPP; MTCW 1, 2; PFS 3; RGAL; SATA 18; WP

Cum, R.
See Crumb, R(obert)

Cummings, Bruce F(rederick) 1889-1919
See Barbellion, W. N. P.
See also CA 123

Cummings, E(dward) E(stlin) 1894-1962 **CLC 1, 3, 8, 12, 15, 68; DA; DAB; DAC; DAM MST, POET; PC 5; WLC**
See also AAYA 41; AMW; CA 73-76; CANR 31; CDALB 1929-1941; DA3; DLB 4, 48; EXPP; MTCW 1, 2; PAB; PFS 1, 3, 12, 13; RGAL; WP

Cunha, Euclides (Rodrigues Pimenta) da 1866-1909 **TCLC 24**
See also CA 123; LAW; WLIT 1

Cunningham, E. V.
See Fast, Howard (Melvin)

Cunningham, J(ames) V(incent) 1911-1985 **CLC 3, 31**
See also CA 1-4R; 115; CANR 1, 72; DLB 5

Cunningham, Julia (Woolfolk) 1916- **CLC 12**
See also CA 9-12R; CANR 4, 19, 36; CWRI; JRDA; MAICYA; SAAS 2; SATA 1, 26

Cunningham, Michael 1952- **CLC 34**
See also CA 136; CANR 96; GLL 2

Cunninghame Graham, R. B.
See Cunninghame Graham, Robert (Gallnigad) Bontine

Cunninghame Graham, Robert (Gallnigad) Bontine 1852-1936 **TCLC 19**
See also Graham, R(obert) B(ontine) Cunninghame
See also CA 119; 184

Currie, Ellen 19(?)- **CLC 44**

Curtin, Philip
See Lowndes, Marie Adelaide (Belloc)

Curtis, Price
See Ellison, Harlan (Jay)

Cutrate, Joe
See Spiegelman, Art

Cynewulf c. 770- **CMLC 23**
See also DLB 146; RGEL

Cyrano de Bergerac, Savinien de 1619-1655 **LC 65**
See also GFL Beginnings to 1789; RGWL

Czaczkes, Shmuel Yosef Halevi
See Agnon, S(hmuel) Y(osef Halevi)

Dabrowska, Maria (Szumska) 1889-1965 **CLC 15**
See also CA 106; DLB 215

Dabydeen, David 1955- **CLC 34**
See also BW 1; CA 125; CANR 56, 92; CN;
CP

Dacey, Philip 1939- **CLC 51**
See also CA 37-40R; CAAS 17; CANR 14,
32, 64; CP; DLB 105

Dagerman, Stig (Halvard) 1923-1954 **TCLC 17**
See also CA 117; 155

D'Aguiar, Fred 1960- **CLC 145**
See also CA 148; CANR 83, 101; CP; DLB 157

Dahl, Roald 1916-1990 **CLC 1, 6, 18, 79;
DAB; DAC; DAM MST, NOV, POP**
See also AAYA 15; BPFB 1; BRWS 4; BYA
5; CA 1-4R; 133; CANR 6, 32, 37, 62;
CLR 1, 7, 41; CPW; DA3; DLB 139, 255;
HGG; JRDA; MAICYA; MTCW 1, 2;
RGSF; SATA 1, 26, 73; SATA-Obit 65;
SSFS 4; YAW

Dahlberg, Edward 1900-1977 **CLC 1, 7, 14**
See also CA 9-12R; 69-72; CANR 31, 62;
DLB 48; MTCW 1; RGAL

Daitch, Susan 1954- **CLC 103**
See also CA 161

Dale, Colin **TCLC 18**
See also Lawrence, T(homas) E(dward)

Dale, George E.
See Asimov, Isaac

Dalton, Roque 1935-1975(?) **PC 36**
See also CA 176; HLCS 1; HW 2

Daly, Elizabeth 1878-1967 **CLC 52**
See also CA 23-24; 25-28R; CANR 60;
CAP 2; CMW

Daly, Maureen 1921- **CLC 17**
See also AAYA 5; BYA 6; CANR 37, 83;
JRDA; MAICYA; SAAS 1; SATA 2;
WYA; YAW

Damas, Leon-Gontran 1912-1978 **CLC 84**
See also BW 1; CA 125; 73-76

Dana, Richard Henry Sr. 1787-1879 **NCLC 53**

Daniel, Samuel 1562(?)-1619 **LC 24**
See also DLB 62; RGEL

Daniels, Brett
See Adler, Renata

Dannay, Frederic 1905-1982 **CLC 11; DAM POP**
See also Queen, Ellery
See also CA 1-4R; 107; CANR 1, 39;
CMW; DLB 137; MTCW 1

D'Annunzio, Gabriele 1863-1938 **TCLC 6, 40**
See also CA 104; 155; EW 8; RGWL

Danois, N. le
See Gourmont, Remy(-Marie-Charles) de

Dante 1265-1321 **CMLC 3, 18, 39; DA; DAB;
DAC; DAM MST, POET; PC 21;
WLCS**
See also DA3; EFS 1; EW 1; LAIT 1;
RGWL; WP

d'Antibes, Germain
See Simenon, Georges (Jacques Christian)

Danticat, Edwidge 1969- **CLC 94, 139**
See also AAYA 29; CA 152; CAAE 192;
CANR 73; DNFS; EXPS; MTCW 1;
SSFS 1; YAW

Danvers, Dennis 1947- **CLC 70**

Danziger, Paula 1944- **CLC 21**
See also AAYA 4, 36; BYA 6, 7, 14; CA
112; 115; CANR 37; CLR 20; JRDA;
MAICYA; SATA 36, 63, 102; SATA-Brief
30; WYA; YAW

Da Ponte, Lorenzo 1749-1838 **NCLC 50**

Dario, Ruben 1867-1916 **TCLC 4; DAM
MULT; HLC 1; PC 15**
See also CA 131; CANR 81; HW 1, 2;
LAW; MTCW 1, 2; RGWL

Darley, George 1795-1846 **NCLC 2**
See also DLB 96; RGEL

Darrow, Clarence (Seward) 1857-1938 **TCLC 81**
See also CA 164

Darwin, Charles 1809-1882 **NCLC 57**
See also BRWS 7; DLB 57, 166; RGEL;
WLIT 4

Darwin, Erasmus 1731-1802 **NCLC 106**
See also DLB 93; RGEL

Daryush, Elizabeth 1887-1977 **CLC 6, 19**
See also CA 49-52; CANR 3, 81; DLB 20

Dasgupta, Surendranath 1887-1952 **TCLC 81**
See also CA 157

**Dashwood, Edmee Elizabeth Monica de la
Pasture** 1890-1943
See Delafield, E. M.
See also CA 119; 154

Daudet, (Louis Marie) Alphonse 1840-1897 **NCLC 1**
See also DLB 123; GFL 1789 to the Present;
RGSF

Daumal, Rene 1908-1944 **TCLC 14**
See also CA 114

Davenant, William 1606-1668 **LC 13**
See also DLB 58, 126; RGEL

Davenport, Guy (Mattison, Jr.) 1927- **CLC 6,
14, 38; SSC 16**
See also CA 33-36R; CANR 23, 73; CN;
CSW; DLB 130

David, Robert
See Nezval, Vitezslav

Davidson, Avram (James) 1923-1993
See Queen, Ellery
See also CA 101; 171; CANR 26; DLB 8;
FANT; SFW; SUFW

Davidson, Donald (Grady) 1893-1968 **CLC 2,
13, 19**
See also CA 5-8R; 25-28R; CANR 4, 84;
DLB 45

Davidson, Hugh
See Hamilton, Edmond

Davidson, John 1857-1909 **TCLC 24**
See also CA 118; DLB 19; RGEL

Davidson, Sara 1943- **CLC 9**
See also CA 81-84; CANR 44, 68; DLB 185

Davie, Donald (Alfred) 1922-1995 **CLC 5, 8,
10, 31; PC 29**
See also BRWS 6; CA 1-4R; 149; CAAS 3;
CANR 1, 44; CP; DLB 27; MTCW 1;
RGEL

Davies, Ray(mond Douglas) 1944- **CLC 21**
See also CA 116; 146; CANR 92

Davies, Rhys 1901-1978 **CLC 23**
See also CA 9-12R; 81-84; CANR 4; DLB
139, 191

Davies, (William) Robertson 1913-1995 **CLC
2, 7, 13, 25, 42, 75, 91; DA; DAB; DAC;
DAM MST, NOV, POP; WLC**
See also Marchbanks, Samuel
See also BEST 89:2; BPFB 1; CA 33-36R;
150; CANR 17, 42, 103; CN; CPW; DA3;
DLB 68; HGG; INT CANR-17; MTCW
1, 2; RGEL

Davies, Walter C.
See Kornbluth, C(yril) M.

Davies, William Henry 1871-1940 **TCLC 5**
See also CA 104; 179; DLB 19, 174; RGEL

Da Vinci, Leonardo 1452-1519 **LC 12, 57, 60**
See also AAYA 40

Davis, Angela (Yvonne) 1944- **CLC 77; DAM
MULT**
See also BW 2, 3; CA 57-60; CANR 10,
81; CSW; DA3; FW

Davis, B. Lynch
See Bioy Casares, Adolfo; Borges, Jorge
Luis

Davis, B. Lynch
See Bioy Casares, Adolfo

Davis, Gordon
See Hunt, E(verette) Howard, (Jr.)

Davis, H(arold) L(enoir) 1896-1960 **CLC 49**
See also ANW; CA 178; 89-92; DLB 9,
206; SATA 114

Davis, Rebecca (Blaine) Harding 1831-1910
TCLC 6; SSC 38
See also CA 104; 179; DLB 74, 239; FW;
RGAL

Davis, Richard Harding 1864-1916 **TCLC 24**
See also CA 114; 179; DLB 12, 23, 78, 79,
189; DLBD 13; RGAL

Davison, Frank Dalby 1893-1970 **CLC 15**
See also CA 116

Davison, Lawrence H.
See Lawrence, D(avid) H(erbert Richards)

Davison, Peter (Hubert) 1928- **CLC 28**
See also CA 9-12R; CAAS 4; CANR 3, 43,
84; CP; DLB 5

Davys, Mary 1674-1732 **LC 1, 46**
See also DLB 39

Dawson, Fielding 1930- **CLC 6**
See also CA 85-88; DLB 130

Dawson, Peter
See Faust, Frederick (Schiller)
See also TCWW 2, 2

Day, Clarence (Shepard, Jr.) 1874-1935
TCLC 25
See also CA 108; DLB 11

Day, John 1574(?)-1640(?) **LC 70**
See also DLB 62, 170; RGEL

Day, Thomas 1748-1789 **LC 1**
See also DLB 39; YABC 1

Day Lewis, C(ecil) 1904-1972 **CLC 1, 6, 10;
DAM POET; PC 11**
See also Blake, Nicholas
See also BRWS 3; CA 13-16; 33-36R;
CANR 34; CAP 1; CWRI; DLB 15, 20;
MTCW 1, 2; RGEL

Dazai Osamu **TCLC 11; SSC 41**
See also Tsushima, Shuji
See also CA 164; DLB 182; MJW; RGSF;
RGWL

de Andrade, Carlos Drummond
See Drummond de Andrade, Carlos

de Andrade, Mario 1892-1945
See Andrade, Mario de
See also CA 178; HW 2

Deane, Norman
See Creasey, John

Deane, Seamus (Francis) 1940- **CLC 122**
See also CA 118; CANR 42

**de Beauvoir, Simone (Lucie Ernestine Marie
Bertrand)**
See Beauvoir, Simone (Lucie Ernestine
Marie Bertrand) de

de Beer, P.
See Bosman, Herman Charles

de Brissac, Malcolm
See Dickinson, Peter (Malcolm)

de Campos, Alvaro
See Pessoa, Fernando (Antonio Nogueira)

de Chardin, Pierre Teilhard
See Teilhard de Chardin, (Marie Joseph)
Pierre

Dee, John 1527-1608 **LC 20**
See also DLB 136, 213

Deer, Sandra 1940- **CLC 45**
See also CA 186

De Ferrari, Gabriella 1941- **CLC 65**
See also CA 146

Defoe, Daniel 1660(?)-1731 **LC 1, 42; DA;**

Duncan, Dora Angela
See Duncan, Isadora
Duncan, Isadora 1877(?)-1927 **TCLC 68**
See also CA 118; 149
Duncan, Lois 1934- **CLC 26**
See also AAYA 4, 34; BYA 6, 8; CA 1-4R;
CANR 2, 23, 36; CLR 29; JRDA; MAI-
CYA; MAICYAS; SAAS 2; SATA 1, 36,
75; WYA; YAW
Duncan, Robert (Edward) 1919-1988 **CLC 1,
2, 4, 7, 15, 41, 55; DAM POET; PC 2**
See also CA 9-12R; 124; CANR 28, 62;
DLB 5, 16, 193; MTCW 1, 2; PFS 13;
RGAL; WP
Duncan, Sara Jeannette 1861-1922 **TCLC 60**
See also CA 157; DLB 92
Dunlap, William 1766-1839 **NCLC 2**
See also DLB 30, 37, 59; RGAL
Dunn, Douglas (Eaglesham) 1942- **CLC 6, 40**
See also CA 45-48; CANR 2, 33; CP; DLB
40; MTCW 1
Dunn, Katherine (Karen) 1945- **CLC 71**
See also CA 33-36R; CANR 72; HGG;
MTCW 1
Dunn, Stephen (Elliott) 1939- **CLC 36**
See also CA 33-36R; CANR 12, 48, 53,
105; CP; DLB 105
Dunne, Finley Peter 1867-1936 **TCLC 28**
See also CA 108; 178; DLB 11, 23; RGAL
Dunne, John Gregory 1932- **CLC 28**
See also CA 25-28R; CANR 14, 50; CN;
DLBY 80
Dunsany, Lord TCLC 2, 59
See also Dunsany, Edward John Moreton
Drax Plunkett
See also DLB 77, 153, 156, 255; FANT;
IDTP; RGEL; SFW; SUFW
**Dunsany, Edward John Moreton Drax
Plunkett** 1878-1957
See Dunsany, Lord
See also CA 104; 148; DLB 10; MTCW 1
du Perry, Jean
See Simenon, Georges (Jacques Christian)
Durang, Christopher (Ferdinand) 1949- **CLC
27, 38**
See also CA 105; CAD; CANR 50, 76; CD;
MTCW 1
Duras, Marguerite 1914-1996 **CLC 3, 6, 11,
20, 34, 40, 68, 100; SSC 40**
See also BPFB 1; CA 25-28R; 151; CANR
50; CWW 2; DLB 83; GFL 1789 to the
Present; IDFW 4; MTCW 1, 2; RGWL
Durban, (Rosa) Pam 1947- **CLC 39**
See also CA 123; CANR 98; CSW
Durcan, Paul 1944- **CLC 43, 70; DAM POET**
See also CA 134; CP
Durkheim, Emile 1858-1917 **TCLC 55**
Durrell, Lawrence (George) 1912-1990 **CLC
1, 4, 6, 8, 13, 27, 41; DAM NOV**
See also BPFB 1; BRWS 1; CA 9-12R; 132;
CANR 40, 77; CDBLB 1945-1960; DLB
15, 27, 204; DLBY 90; MTCW 1, 2;
RGEL; SFW
Durrenmatt, Friedrich
See Duerrenmatt, Friedrich
See also EW 13; RGWL
Dutt, Toru 1856-1877 **NCLC 29**
See also DLB 240
Dwight, Timothy 1752-1817 **NCLC 13**
See also DLB 37; RGAL
Dworkin, Andrea 1946- **CLC 43, 123**
See also CA 77-80; CAAS 21; CANR 16,
39, 76, 96; FW; GLL 1; INT CANR-16;
MTCW 1, 2
Dwyer, Deanna
See Koontz, Dean R(ay)

Dwyer, K. R.
See Koontz, Dean R(ay)
Dwyer, Thomas A. 1923- **CLC 114**
See also CA 115
Dybek, Stuart 1942- **CLC 114**
See also CA 97-100; CANR 39; DLB 130
Dye, Richard
See De Voto, Bernard (Augustine)
Dyer, Geoff 1958- **CLC 149**
See also CA 125; CANR 88
Dylan, Bob 1941- **CLC 3, 4, 6, 12, 77; PC 37**
See also CA 41-44R; CP; DLB 16
Dyson, John 1943- **CLC 70**
See also CA 144
E. V. L.
See Lucas, E(dward) V(errall)
Eagleton, Terence (Francis) 1943- **CLC 63,
132**
See also CA 57-60; CANR 7, 23, 68; DLB
242; MTCW 1, 2
Eagleton, Terry
See Eagleton, Terence (Francis)
Early, Jack
See Scoppettone, Sandra
See also GLL 1
East, Michael
See West, Morris L(anglo)
Eastaway, Edward
See Thomas, (Philip) Edward
Eastlake, William (Derry) 1917-1997 **CLC 8**
See also CA 5-8R; 158; CAAS 1; CANR 5,
63; CN; DLB 6, 206; INT CANR-5;
TCWW 2
Eastman, Charles A(lexander) 1858-1939
TCLC 55; DAM MULT
See also CA 179; CANR 91; DLB 175;
NNAL; YABC 1
Eberhart, Richard (Ghormley) 1904- **CLC 3,
11, 19, 56; DAM POET**
See also AMW; CA 1-4R; CANR 2;
CDALB 1941-1968; CP; DLB 48; MTCW
1; RGAL
Eberstadt, Fernanda 1960- **CLC 39**
See also CA 136; CANR 69
**Echegaray (y Eizaguirre), Jose (Maria
Waldo)** 1832-1916 **TCLC 4; HLCS 1**
See also CA 104; CANR 32; HW 1; MTCW
1
Echeverria, (Jose) Esteban (Antonino)
1805-1851 **NCLC 18**
See also LAW
Echo
See Proust, (Valentin-Louis-George-Eugene-
)Marcel
Eckert, Allan W. 1931- **CLC 17**
See also AAYA 18; BYA 2; CA 13-16R;
CANR 14, 45; INT CANR-14; SAAS 21;
SATA 29, 91; SATA-Brief 27
Eckhart, Meister 1260(?)-1327(?) **CMLC 9**
See also DLB 115
Eckmar, F. R.
See de Hartog, Jan
Eco, Umberto 1932- **CLC 28, 60, 142; DAM
NOV, POP**
See also BEST 90:1; BPFB 1; CA 77-80;
CANR 12, 33, 55; CPW; CWW 2; DA3;
DLB 196, 242; MSW; MTCW 1, 2
Eddison, E(ric) R(ucker) 1882-1945 **TCLC
15**
See also CA 109; 156; DLB 255; FANT;
SFW; SUFW
Eddy, Mary (Ann Morse) Baker 1821-1910
TCLC 71
See also CA 113; 174
Edel, (Joseph) Leon 1907-1997 **CLC 29, 34**
See also CA 1-4R; 161; CANR 1, 22; DLB
103; INT CANR-22
Eden, Emily 1797-1869 **NCLC 10**

Edgar, David 1948- **CLC 42; DAM DRAM**
See also CA 57-60; CANR 12, 61; CBD;
CD; DLB 13, 233; MTCW 1
Edgerton, Clyde (Carlyle) 1944- **CLC 39**
See also AAYA 17; CA 118; 134; CANR
64; CSW; INT 134; YAW
Edgeworth, Maria 1768-1849 **NCLC 1, 51**
See also BRWS 3; DLB 116, 159, 163; FW;
RGEL; SATA 21; WLIT 3
Edmonds, Paul
See Kuttner, Henry
Edmonds, Walter D(umaux) 1903-1998 **CLC
35**
See also BYA 2; CA 5-8R; CANR 2; CWRI;
DLB 9; LAIT 1; MAICYA; RHW; SAAS
4; SATA 1, 27; SATA-Obit 99
Edmondson, Wallace
See Ellison, Harlan (Jay)
Edson, Russell 1935- **CLC 13**
See also CA 33-36R; DLB 244; WP
Edwards, Bronwen Elizabeth
See Rose, Wendy
Edwards, G(erald) B(asil) 1899-1976 **CLC 25**
See also CA 110
Edwards, Gus 1939- **CLC 43**
See also CA 108; INT 108
Edwards, Jonathan 1703-1758 **LC 7, 54; DA;
DAC; DAM MST**
See also AMW; DLB 24; RGAL
Efron, Marina Ivanovna Tsvetaeva
See Tsvetaeva (Efron), Marina (Ivanovna)
Egoyan, Atom 1960- **CLC 151**
See also CA 157
Ehle, John (Marsden, Jr.) 1925- **CLC 27**
See also CA 9-12R; CSW
Ehrenbourg, Ilya (Grigoryevich)
See Ehrenburg, Ilya (Grigoryevich)
Ehrenburg, Ilya (Grigoryevich) 1891-1967
CLC 18, 34, 62
See also CA 102; 25-28R
Ehrenburg, Ilyo (Grigoryevich)
See Ehrenburg, Ilya (Grigoryevich)
Ehrenreich, Barbara 1941- **CLC 110**
See also BEST 90:4; CA 73-76; CANR 16,
37, 62; DLB 246; FW; MTCW 1, 2
Eich, Guenter 1907-1972 **CLC 15**
See also Eich, Gunter
See also CA 111; 93-96; DLB 69, 124
Eich, Gunter
See Eich, Guenter
See also RGWL
Eichendorff, Joseph 1788-1857 **NCLC 8**
See also DLB 90; RGWL
Eigner, Larry CLC 9
See also Eigner, Laurence (Joel)
See also CAAS 23; DLB 5; WP
Eigner, Laurence (Joel) 1927-1996
See Eigner, Larry
See also CA 9-12R; 151; CANR 6, 84; CP;
DLB 193
Einhard c. 770-840 **CMLC 50**
See also DLB 148
Einstein, Albert 1879-1955 **TCLC 65**
See also CA 121; 133; MTCW 1, 2
Eiseley, Loren Corey 1907-1977 **CLC 7**
See also AAYA 5; ANW; CA 1-4R; 73-76;
CANR 6; DLBD 17
Eisenstadt, Jill 1963- **CLC 50**
See also CA 140
Eisenstein, Sergei (Mikhailovich) 1898-1948
TCLC 57
See also CA 114; 149
Eisner, Simon
See Kornbluth, C(yril) M.
Ekeloef, (Bengt) Gunnar 1907-1968 **CLC 27;
DAM POET; PC 23**
See also Ekelof, (Bengt) Gunnar
See also CA 123; 25-28R

Ekelof, (Bengt) Gunnar
　See Ekeloef, (Bengt) Gunnar
　See also EW 12
Ekelund, Vilhelm 1880-1949 **TCLC 75**
　See also CA 189
Ekwensi, C. O. D.
　See Ekwensi, Cyprian (Odiatu Duaka)
Ekwensi, Cyprian (Odiatu Duaka) 1921-
　CLC 4; BLC 1; DAM MULT
　See also AFW; BW 2, 3; CA 29-32R;
　CANR 18, 42, 74; CN; CWRI; DLB 117;
　MTCW 1, 2; RGEL; SATA 66; WLIT 2
Elaine TCLC 18
　See also Leverson, Ada
El Crummo
　See Crumb, R(obert)
Elder, Lonne III 1931-1996 **DC 8**
　See also BLC 1; BW 1, 3; CA 81-84; 152;
　CAD; CANR 25; DAM MULT; DLB 7,
　38, 44
Eleanor of Aquitaine 1122-1204 **CMLC 39**
Elia
　See Lamb, Charles
Eliade, Mircea 1907-1986 **CLC 19**
　See also CA 65-68; 119; CANR 30, 62;
　DLB 220; MTCW 1; SFW
Eliot, A. D.
　See Jewett, (Theodora) Sarah Orne
Eliot, Alice
　See Jewett, (Theodora) Sarah Orne
Eliot, Dan
　See Silverberg, Robert
Eliot, George 1819-1880 **NCLC 4, 13, 23, 41,
　49, 89; DA; DAB; DAC; DAM MST,
　NOV; PC 20; WLC**
　See also BRW 5; BRWR 2; CDBLB 1832-
　1890; CN; CPW; DA3; DLB 21, 35, 55;
　RGEL; RGSF; SSFS 8; WLIT 3
Eliot, John 1604-1690 **LC 5**
　See also DLB 24
Eliot, T(homas) S(tearns) 1888-1965 **CLC 1,
　2, 3, 6, 9, 10, 13, 15, 24, 34, 41, 55, 57,
　113; DA; DAB; DAC; DAM DRAM,
　MST, POET; PC 5, 31; WLC**
　See also AAYA 28; AMW; AMWR 1; BRW
　7; BRWR 2; CA 5-8R; 25-28R; CANR
　41; CDALB 1929-1941; DA3; DFS 4, 13;
　DLB 7, 10, 45, 63, 245; DLBY 88; EXPP;
　LAIT 3; MTCW 1, 2; PAB; PFS 1, 7;
　RGAL; RGEL; WLIT 4; WP
Elizabeth 1866-1941 **TCLC 41**
Elkin, Stanley L(awrence) 1930-1995 **CLC 4,
　6, 9, 14, 27, 51, 91; DAM NOV, POP;
　SSC 12**
　See also AMWS 6; BPFB 1; CA 9-12R;
　148; CANR 8, 46; CN; CPW; DLB 2, 28,
　218; DLBY 80; INT CANR-8; MTCW 1,
　2; RGAL
Elledge, Scott CLC 34
Elliot, Don
　See Silverberg, Robert
Elliott, Don
　See Silverberg, Robert
Elliott, George P(aul) 1918-1980 **CLC 2**
　See also CA 1-4R; 97-100; CANR 2; DLB
　244
Elliott, Janice 1931-1995 **CLC 47**
　See also CA 13-16R; CANR 8, 29, 84; CN;
　DLB 14; SATA 119
Elliott, Sumner Locke 1917-1991 **CLC 38**
　See also CA 5-8R; 134; CANR 2, 21
Elliott, William
　See Bradbury, Ray (Douglas)
Ellis, A. E. CLC 7
Ellis, Alice Thomas CLC 40
　See also Haycraft, Anna (Margaret)
　See also DLB 194; MTCW 1

Ellis, Bret Easton 1964- **CLC 39, 71, 117;
　DAM POP**
　See also AAYA 2, 43; CA 118; 123; CANR
　51, 74; CN; CPW; DA3; HGG; INT 123;
　MTCW 1; NFS 11
Ellis, (Henry) Havelock 1859-1939 **TCLC 14**
　See also CA 109; 169; DLB 190
Ellis, Landon
　See Ellison, Harlan (Jay)
Ellis, Trey 1962- **CLC 55**
　See also CA 146; CANR 92
Ellison, Harlan (Jay) 1934- **CLC 1, 13, 42,
　139; DAM POP; SSC 14**
　See also AAYA 29; BPFB 1; BYA 14; CA
　5-8R; CANR 5, 46; CPW; DLB 8; HGG;
　INT CANR-5; MTCW 1, 2; SCFW 2;
　SFW; SSFS 13; SUFW
Ellison, Ralph (Waldo) 1914-1994 **CLC 1, 3,
　11, 54, 86, 114; BLC 1; DA; DAB; DAC;
　DAM MST, MULT, NOV; SSC 26;
　WLC**
　See also AAYA 19; AFAW 1, 2; AMWS 2;
　BPFB 1; BW 1, 3; BYA 2; CA 9-12R;
　145; CANR 24, 53; CDALB 1941-1968;
　CSW; DA3; DLB 2, 76, 227; DLBY 94;
　EXPN; EXPS; LAIT 4; MTCW 1, 2; NFS
　2; RGAL; RGSF; SSFS 1, 11; YAW
Ellmann, Lucy (Elizabeth) 1956- **CLC 61**
　See also CA 128
Ellmann, Richard (David) 1918-1987 **CLC
　50**
　See also BEST 89:2; CA 1-4R; 122; CANR
　2, 28, 61; DLB 103; DLBY 87; MTCW
　1, 2
Elman, Richard (Martin) 1934-1997 **CLC 19**
　See also CA 17-20R; 163; CAAS 3; CANR
　47
Elron
　See Hubbard, L(afayette) Ron(ald)
Eluard, Paul TCLC 7, 41; PC 38
　See also Grindel, Eugene
　See also GFL 1789 to the Present; RGWL
Elyot, Thomas 1490(?)-1546 **LC 11**
　See also DLB 136; RGEL
Elytis, Odysseus 1911-1996 **CLC 15, 49, 100;
　DAM POET; PC 21**
　See also Alepoudelis, Odysseus
　See also CA 102; 151; CANR 94; CWW 2;
　EW 13; MTCW 1, 2; RGWL
Emecheta, (Florence Onye) Buchi 1944- **CLC
　14, 48, 128; BLC 2; DAM MULT**
　See also AFW; BW 2, 3; CA 81-84; CANR
　27, 81; CN; CWRI; DA3; DLB 117; FW;
　MTCW 1, 2; NFS 12; SATA 66; WLIT 2
Emerson, Mary Moody 1774-1863 **NCLC 66**
Emerson, Ralph Waldo 1803-1882 **NCLC 1,
　38, 98; DA; DAB; DAC; DAM MST,
　POET; PC 18; WLC**
　See also AMW; ANW; CDALB 1640-1865;
　DA3; DLB 1, 59, 73, 183, 223; EXPP;
　LAIT 2; PFS 4; RGAL; WP
Eminescu, Mihail 1850-1889 **NCLC 33**
Empedocles 5th cent. B.C.- **CMLC 50**
　See also DLB 176
Empson, William 1906-1984 **CLC 3, 8, 19,
　33, 34**
　See also BRWS 2; CA 17-20R; 112; CANR
　31, 61; DLB 20; MTCW 1, 2; RGEL
Enchi, Fumiko (Ueda) 1905-1986 **CLC 31**
　See also CA 129; 121; DLB 182; FW; MJW
Ende, Michael (Andreas Helmuth)
　1929-1995 **CLC 31**
　See also BYA 5; CA 118; 124; 149; CANR
　36; CLR 14; DLB 75; MAICYA; MAIC-
　YAS; SATA 61; SATA-Brief 42; SATA-
　Obit 86
Endo, Shusaku 1923-1996 **CLC 7, 14, 19, 54,**

99; DAM NOV; SSC 48
　See also Endo Shusaku
　See also CA 29-32R; 153; CANR 21, 54;
　DA3; MTCW 1, 2; RGSF; RGWL
Endo Shusaku
　See Endo, Shusaku
　See also DLB 182
Engel, Marian 1933-1985 **CLC 36**
　See also CA 25-28R; CANR 12; DLB 53;
　FW; INT CANR-12
Engelhardt, Frederick
　See Hubbard, L(afayette) Ron(ald)
Engels, Friedrich 1820-1895 **NCLC 85**
　See also DLB 129
Enright, D(ennis) J(oseph) 1920- **CLC 4, 8,
　31**
　See also CA 1-4R; CANR 1, 42, 83; CP;
　DLB 27; SATA 25
Enzensberger, Hans Magnus 1929- **CLC 43;
　PC 28**
　See also CA 116; 119; CANR 103
Ephron, Nora 1941- **CLC 17, 31**
　See also AAYA 35; AITN 2; CA 65-68;
　CANR 12, 39, 83
Epicurus 341B.C.-270B.C. **CMLC 21**
　See also DLB 176
Epsilon
　See Betjeman, John
Epstein, Daniel Mark 1948- **CLC 7**
　See also CA 49-52; CANR 2, 53, 90
Epstein, Jacob 1956- **CLC 19**
　See also CA 114
Epstein, Jean 1897-1953 **TCLC 92**
Epstein, Joseph 1937- **CLC 39**
　See also CA 112; 119; CANR 50, 65
Epstein, Leslie 1938- **CLC 27**
　See also CA 73-76; CAAS 12; CANR 23,
　69
Equiano, Olaudah 1745(?)-1797 **LC 16; BLC
　2; DAM MULT**
　See also AFAW 1, 2; DLB 37, 50; WLIT 2
Erasmus, Desiderius 1469(?)-1536 **LC 16**
　See also DLB 136; EW 2; RGWL
Erdman, Paul E(mil) 1932- **CLC 25**
　See also AITN 1; CA 61-64; CANR 13, 43,
　84
Erdrich, Louise 1954- **CLC 39, 54, 120; DAM
　MULT, NOV, POP**
　See also AAYA 10; AMWS 4; BEST 89:1;
　BPFB 1; CA 114; CANR 41, 62;
　CDALBS; CN; CP; CPW; CWP; DA3;
　DLB 152, 175, 206; EXPP; LAIT 5;
　MTCW 1; NFS 5; NNAL; PFS 14; RGAL;
　SATA 94; TCWW 2
Erenburg, Ilya (Grigoryevich)
　See Ehrenburg, Ilya (Grigoryevich)
Erickson, Stephen Michael 1950-
　See Erickson, Steve
　See also CA 129; SFW
Erickson, Steve CLC 64
　See also Erickson, Stephen Michael
　See also CANR 60, 68
Ericson, Walter
　See Fast, Howard (Melvin)
Eriksson, Buntel
　See Bergman, (Ernst) Ingmar
Ernaux, Annie 1940- **CLC 88**
　See also CA 147; CANR 93
Erskine, John 1879-1951 **TCLC 84**
　See also CA 112; 159; DLB 9, 102; FANT
Eschenbach, Wolfram von
　See Wolfram von Eschenbach
Eseki, Bruno
　See Mphahlele, Ezekiel
Esenin, Sergei (Alexandrovich) 1895-1925
　TCLC 4
　See also CA 104; RGWL

Eshleman, Clayton 1935- **CLC 7**
See also CA 33-36R; CAAS 6; CANR 93; CP; DLB 5
Espriella, Don Manuel Alvarez
See Southey, Robert
Espriu, Salvador 1913-1985 **CLC 9**
See also CA 154; 115; DLB 134
Espronceda, Jose de 1808-1842 **NCLC 39**
Esquivel, Laura 1951(?)- **CLC 141; HLCS 1**
See also AAYA 29; CA 143; CANR 68; DA3; DNFS; LAIT 3; MTCW 1; NFS 5; WLIT 1
Esse, James
See Stephens, James
Esterbrook, Tom
See Hubbard, L(afayette) Ron(ald)
Estleman, Loren D. 1952- **CLC 48; DAM NOV, POP**
See also AAYA 27; CA 85-88; CANR 27, 74; CMW; CPW; DA3; DLB 226; INT CANR-27; MTCW 1, 2
Euclid 306B.C.-283B.C. **CMLC 25**
Eugenides, Jeffrey 1960(?)- **CLC 81**
See also CA 144
Euripides c. 484B.C.-406B.C. **CMLC 23; DA; DAB; DAC; DAM DRAM, MST; DC 4; WLCS**
See also AW 1; DA3; DFS 1, 4, 6; DLB 176; LAIT 1; RGWL
Evan, Evin
See Faust, Frederick (Schiller)
Evans, Caradoc 1878-1945 **TCLC 85; SSC 43**
See also DLB 162
Evans, Evan
See Faust, Frederick (Schiller)
See also TCWW 2
Evans, Marian
See Eliot, George
Evans, Mary Ann
See Eliot, George
Evarts, Esther
See Benson, Sally
Everett, Percival
See Everett, Percival L.
See also CSW
Everett, Percival L. 1956- **CLC 57**
See also Everett, Percival
See also BW 2; CA 129; CANR 94
Everson, R(onald) G(ilmour) 1903-1992 **CLC 27**
See also CA 17-20R; DLB 88
Everson, William (Oliver) 1912-1994 **CLC 1, 5, 14**
See also CA 9-12R; 145; CANR 20; DLB 5, 16, 212; MTCW 1
Evtushenko, Evgenii Aleksandrovich
See Yevtushenko, Yevgeny (Alexandrovich)
See also RGWL
Ewart, Gavin (Buchanan) 1916-1995 **CLC 13, 46**
See also BRWS 7; CA 89-92; 150; CANR 17, 46; CP; DLB 40; MTCW 1
Ewers, Hanns Heinz 1871-1943 **TCLC 12**
See also CA 109; 149
Ewing, Frederick R.
See Sturgeon, Theodore (Hamilton)
Exley, Frederick (Earl) 1929-1992 **CLC 6, 11**
See also AITN 2; BPFB 1; CA 81-84; 138; DLB 143; DLBY 81
Eynhardt, Guillermo
See Quiroga, Horacio (Sylvestre)
Ezekiel, Nissim 1924- **CLC 61**
See also CA 61-64; CP
Ezekiel, Tish O'Dowd 1943- **CLC 34**
See also CA 129

Fadeyev, A.
See Bulgya, Alexander Alexandrovich
Fadeyev, Alexander TCLC 53
See also Bulgya, Alexander Alexandrovich
Fagen, Donald 1948- **CLC 26**
Fainzilberg, Ilya Arnoldovich 1897-1937
See Ilf, Ilya
See also CA 120; 165
Fair, Ronald L. 1932- **CLC 18**
See also BW 1; CA 69-72; CANR 25; DLB 33
Fairbairn, Roger
See Carr, John Dickson
Fairbairns, Zoe (Ann) 1948- **CLC 32**
See also CA 103; CANR 21, 85; CN
Fairman, Paul W. 1916-1977
See Queen, Ellery
See also CA 114; SFW
Falco, Gian
See Papini, Giovanni
Falconer, James
See Kirkup, James
Falconer, Kenneth
See Kornbluth, C(yril) M.
Falkland, Samuel
See Heijermans, Herman
Fallaci, Oriana 1930- **CLC 11, 110**
See also CA 77-80; CANR 15, 58; FW; MTCW 1
Faludi, Susan 1959- **CLC 140**
See also CA 138; FW; MTCW 1
Faludy, George 1913- **CLC 42**
See also CA 21-24R
Faludy, Gyoergy
See Faludy, George
Fanon, Frantz 1925-1961 **CLC 74; BLC 2; DAM MULT**
See also BW 1; CA 116; 89-92; WLIT 2
Fanshawe, Ann 1625-1680 **LC 11**
Fante, John (Thomas) 1911-1983 **CLC 60**
See also CA 69-72; 109; CANR 23, 104; DLB 130; DLBY 83
Farah, Nuruddin 1945- **CLC 53, 137; BLC 2; DAM MULT**
See also AFW; BW 2, 3; CA 106; CANR 81; CN; DLB 125; WLIT 2
Fargue, Leon-Paul 1876(?)-1947 **TCLC 11**
See also CA 109
Farigoule, Louis
See Romains, Jules
Farina, Richard 1936(?)-1966 **CLC 9**
See also CA 81-84; 25-28R
Farley, Walter (Lorimer) 1915-1989 **CLC 17**
See also BYA 14; CA 17-20R; CANR 8, 29, 84; DLB 22; JRDA; MAICYA; SATA 2, 43; YAW
Farmer, Philip Jose 1918- **CLC 1, 19**
See also AAYA 28; BPFB 1; CA 1-4R; CANR 4, 35; DLB 8; MTCW 1; SATA 93; SCFW 2; SFW
Farquhar, George 1677-1707 **LC 21; DAM DRAM**
See also BRW 2; DLB 84; RGEL
Farrell, J(ames) G(ordon) 1935-1979 **CLC 6**
See also CA 73-76; 89-92; CANR 36; DLB 14; MTCW 1; RGEL; RHW; WLIT 4
Farrell, James T(homas) 1904-1979 **CLC 1, 4, 8, 11, 66; SSC 28**
See also AMW; BPFB 1; CA 5-8R; 89-92; CANR 9, 61; DLB 4, 9, 86; DLBD 2; MTCW 1, 2; RGAL
Farrell, Warren (Thomas) 1943- **CLC 70**
See also CA 146
Farren, Richard J.
See Betjeman, John

Farren, Richard M.
See Betjeman, John
Fassbinder, Rainer Werner 1946-1982 **CLC 20**
See also CA 93-96; 106; CANR 31
Fast, Howard (Melvin) 1914- **CLC 23, 131; DAM NOV**
See also AAYA 16; BPFB 1; CA 1-4R, 181; CAAE 181; CAAS 18; CANR 1, 33, 54, 75, 98; CMW; CN; CPW; DLB 9; INT CANR-33; MTCW 1; RHW; SATA 7; SATA-Essay 107; TCWW 2; YAW
Faulcon, Robert
See Holdstock, Robert P.
Faulkner, William (Cuthbert) 1897-1962 **CLC 1, 3, 6, 8, 9, 11, 14, 18, 28, 52, 68; DA; DAB; DAC; DAM MST, NOV; SSC 1, 35, 42; WLC**
See also AAYA 7; AMW; AMWR 1; BPFB 1; BYA 5; CA 81-84; CANR 33; CDALB 1929-1941; DA3; DLB 9, 11, 44, 102; DLBD 2; DLBY 86, 97; EXPN; EXPS; LAIT 2; MTCW 1, 2; NFS 4, 8, 13; RGAL; RGSF; SSFS 2, 5, 6, 12
Fauset, Jessie Redmon 1882(?)-1961 **CLC 19, 54; BLC 2; DAM MULT**
See also AFAW 2; BW 1; CA 109; CANR 83; DLB 51; FW; MAWW
Faust, Frederick (Schiller) 1892-1944(?) **TCLC 49; DAM POP**
See also Austin, Frank; Brand, Max; Challis, George; Dawson, Peter; Dexter, Martin; Evans, Evan; Frederick, John; Frost, Frederick; Manning, David; Silver, Nicholas
See also CA 108; 152; DLB 256
Faust, Irvin 1924- **CLC 8**
See also CA 33-36R; CANR 28, 67; CN; DLB 2, 28, 218; DLBY 80
Fawkes, Guy
See Benchley, Robert (Charles)
Fearing, Kenneth (Flexner) 1902-1961 **CLC 51**
See also CA 93-96; CANR 59; CMW; DLB 9; RGAL
Fecamps, Elise
See Creasey, John
Federman, Raymond 1928- **CLC 6, 47**
See also CA 17-20R; CAAS 8; CANR 10, 43, 83; CN; DLBY 80
Federspiel, J(uerg) F. 1931- **CLC 42**
See also CA 146
Feiffer, Jules (Ralph) 1929- **CLC 2, 8, 64; DAM DRAM**
See also AAYA 3; CA 17-20R; CAD; CANR 30, 59; CD; DLB 7, 44; INT CANR-30; MTCW 1; SATA 8, 61, 111
Feige, Hermann Albert Otto Maximilian
See Traven, B.
Feinberg, David B. 1956-1994 **CLC 59**
See also CA 135; 147
Feinstein, Elaine 1930- **CLC 36**
See also CA 69-72; CAAS 1; CANR 31, 68; CN; CP; CWP; DLB 14, 40; MTCW 1
Feke, Gilbert David CLC 65
Feldman, Irving (Mordecai) 1928- **CLC 7**
See also CA 1-4R; CANR 1; CP; DLB 169
Felix-Tchicaya, Gerald
See Tchicaya, Gerald Felix
Fellini, Federico 1920-1993 **CLC 16, 85**
See also CA 65-68; 143; CANR 33
Felsen, Henry Gregor 1916-1995 **CLC 17**
See also CA 1-4R; 180; CANR 1; SAAS 2; SATA 1
Felski, Rita CLC 65
Fenno, Jack
See Calisher, Hortense

Fenollosa, Ernest (Francisco) 1853-1908
TCLC 91

Fenton, James Martin 1949- CLC 32
See also CA 102; CP; DLB 40; PFS 11

Ferber, Edna 1887-1968 CLC 18, 93
See also AITN 1; CA 5-8R; 25-28R; CANR
68, 105; DLB 9, 28, 86; MTCW 1, 2;
RGAL; RHW; SATA 7; TCWW 2

Ferdowsi, Abu'l Qasem 940-1020 CMLC 43
See also RGWL

Ferguson, Helen
See Kavan, Anna

Ferguson, Niall 1964- CLC 134
See also CA 190

Ferguson, Samuel 1810-1886 NCLC 33
See also DLB 32; RGEL

Fergusson, Robert 1750-1774 LC 29
See also DLB 109; RGEL

Ferling, Lawrence
See Ferlinghetti, Lawrence (Monsanto)

Ferlinghetti, Lawrence (Monsanto) 1919(?)-
CLC 2, 6, 10, 27, 111; DAM POET; PC
1
See also CA 5-8R; CANR 3, 41, 73;
CDALB 1941-1968; CP; DA3; DLB 5,
16; MTCW 1, 2; RGAL; WP

Fern, Fanny
See Parton, Sara Payson Willis

Fernandez, Vicente Garcia Huidobro
See Huidobro Fernandez, Vicente Garcia

Fernandez-Armesto, Felipe CLC 70

Fernandez de Lizardi, Jose Joaquin
See Lizardi, Jose Joaquin Fernandez de

Ferre, Rosario 1942- CLC 139; HLCS 1; SSC
36
See also CA 131; CANR 55, 81; CWW 2;
DLB 145; HW 1, 2; LAWS 1; MTCW 1;
WLIT 1

Ferrer, Gabriel (Francisco Victor) Miro
See Miro (Ferrer), Gabriel (Francisco
Victor)

Ferrier, Susan (Edmonstone) 1782-1854
NCLC 8
See also DLB 116; RGEL

Ferrigno, Robert 1948(?)- CLC 65
See also CA 140

Ferron, Jacques 1921-1985 CLC 94; DAC
See also CA 117; 129; CCA 1; DLB 60

Feuchtwanger, Lion 1884-1958 TCLC 3
See also CA 104; 187; DLB 66

Feuillet, Octave 1821-1890 NCLC 45
See also DLB 192

Feydeau, Georges (Leon Jules Marie)
1862-1921 TCLC 22; DAM DRAM
See also CA 113; 152; CANR 84; DLB 192;
GFL 1789 to the Present; RGWL

Fichte, Johann Gottlieb 1762-1814 NCLC 62
See also DLB 90

Ficino, Marsilio 1433-1499 LC 12

Fiedeler, Hans
See Doeblin, Alfred

Fiedler, Leslie A(aron) 1917- CLC 4, 13, 24
See also CA 9-12R; CANR 7, 63; CN; DLB
28, 67; MTCW 1, 2; RGAL

Field, Andrew 1938- CLC 44
See also CA 97-100; CANR 25

Field, Eugene 1850-1895 NCLC 3
See also DLB 23, 42, 140; DLBD 13; MAI-
CYA; RGAL; SATA 16

Field, Gans T.
See Wellman, Manly Wade

Field, Michael 1915-1971 TCLC 43
See also CA 29-32R

Field, Peter
See Hobson, Laura Z(ametkin)
See also TCWW 2

Fielding, Helen 1959(?)- CLC 146
See also CA 172; DLB 231

Fielding, Henry 1707-1754 LC 1, 46; DA;
DAB; DAC; DAM DRAM, MST, NOV;
WLC
See also BRW 3; BRWR 1; CDBLB 1660-
1789; DA3; DLB 39, 84, 101; RGEL;
WLIT 3

Fielding, Sarah 1710-1768 LC 1, 44
See also DLB 39; RGEL

Fields, W. C. 1880-1946 TCLC 80
See also DLB 44

Fierstein, Harvey (Forbes) 1954- CLC 33;
DAM DRAM, POP
See also CA 123; 129; CAD; CD; CPW;
DA3; DFS 6; GLL

Figes, Eva 1932- CLC 31
See also CA 53-56; CANR 4, 44, 83; CN;
DLB 14; FW

Finch, Anne 1661-1720 LC 3; PC 21
See also DLB 95

Finch, Robert (Duer Claydon) 1900-1995
CLC 18
See also CA 57-60; CANR 9, 24, 49; CP;
DLB 88

Findley, Timothy 1930- CLC 27, 102; DAC;
DAM MST
See also CA 25-28R; CANR 12, 42, 69;
CCA 1; CN; DLB 53; FANT; RHW

Fink, William
See Mencken, H(enry) L(ouis)

Firbank, Louis 1942-
See Reed, Lou
See also CA 117

Firbank, (Arthur Annesley) Ronald
1886-1926 TCLC 1
See also BRWS 2; CA 104; 177; DLB 36;
RGEL

Fish, Stanley
See Fish, Stanley Eugene

Fish, Stanley E.
See Fish, Stanley Eugene

Fish, Stanley Eugene 1938- CLC 142
See also CA 112; 132; CANR 90; DLB 67

Fisher, Dorothy (Frances) Canfield
1879-1958 TCLC 87
See also CA 114; 136; CANR 80; CLR 71,;
CWRI; DLB 9, 102; MAICYA; YABC 1

Fisher, M(ary) F(rances) K(ennedy)
1908-1992 CLC 76, 87
See also CA 77-80; 138; CANR 44; MTCW
1

Fisher, Roy 1930- CLC 25
See also CA 81-84; CAAS 10; CANR 16;
CP; DLB 40

Fisher, Rudolph 1897-1934 TCLC 11; BLC
2; DAM MULT; SSC 25
See also BW 1, 3; CA 107; 124; CANR 80;
DLB 51, 102

Fisher, Vardis (Alvero) 1895-1968 CLC 7
See also CA 5-8R; 25-28R; CANR 68; DLB
9, 206; RGAL; TCWW 2

Fiske, Tarleton
See Bloch, Robert (Albert)

Fitch, Clarke
See Sinclair, Upton (Beall)

Fitch, John IV
See Cormier, Robert (Edmund)

Fitzgerald, Captain Hugh
See Baum, L(yman) Frank

FitzGerald, Edward 1809-1883 NCLC 9
See also BRW 4; DLB 32; RGEL

Fitzgerald, F(rancis) Scott (Key) 1896-1940
TCLC 1, 6, 14, 28, 55; DA; DAB; DAC;
DAM MST, NOV; SSC 6, 31; WLC
See also AAYA 24; AITN 1; AMW; AMWR
1; BPFB 1; CA 110; 123; CDALB 1917-
1929; DA3; DLB 4, 9, 86, 219; DLBD 1,
15, 16; DLBY 81, 96; EXPN; EXPS;
LAIT 3; MTCW 1, 2; NFS 2; RGAL;
RGSF; SSFS 4

Fitzgerald, Penelope 1916-2000 CLC 19, 51,
61, 143
See also BRWS 5; CA 85-88; 190; CAAS
10; CANR 56, 86; CN; DLB 14, 194;
MTCW 2

Fitzgerald, Robert (Stuart) 1910-1985 CLC
39
See also CA 1-4R; 114; CANR 1; DLBY
80

FitzGerald, Robert D(avid) 1902-1987 CLC
19
See also CA 17-20R; RGEL

Fitzgerald, Zelda (Sayre) 1900-1948 TCLC
52
See also AMWS 9; CA 117; 126; DLBY 84

Flanagan, Thomas (James Bonner) 1923-
CLC 25, 52
See also CA 108; CANR 55; CN; DLBY
80; INT 108; MTCW 1; RHW

Flaubert, Gustave 1821-1880 NCLC 2, 10,
19, 62, 66; DA; DAB; DAC; DAM MST,
NOV; SSC 11; WLC
See also DA3; DLB 119; EW 7; EXPS;
GFL 1789 to the Present; LAIT 2; RGSF;
RGWL; SSFS 6

Flavius Josephus
See Josephus, Flavius

Flecker, Herman Elroy
See Flecker, (Herman) James Elroy

Flecker, (Herman) James Elroy 1884-1915
TCLC 43
See also CA 109; 150; DLB 10, 19; RGEL

Fleming, Ian (Lancaster) 1908-1964 CLC 3,
30; DAM POP
See also AAYA 26; BPFB 1; CA 5-8R;
CANR 59; CDBLB 1945-1960; CMW;
CPW; DA3; DLB 87, 201; MSW; MTCW
1, 2; RGEL; SATA 9; YAW

Fleming, Thomas (James) 1927- CLC 37
See also CA 5-8R; CANR 10, 102; INT
CANR-10; SATA 8

Fletcher, John 1579-1625 LC 33; DC 6
See also BRW 2; CDBLB Before 1660;
DLB 58; RGEL

Fletcher, John Gould 1886-1950 TCLC 35
See also CA 107; 167; DLB 4, 45; RGAL

Fleur, Paul
See Pohl, Frederik

Flooglebuckle, Al
See Spiegelman, Art

Flora, Fletcher 1914-1969
See Queen, Ellery
See also CA 1-4R; CANR 3, 85

Flying Officer X
See Bates, H(erbert) E(rnest)

Fo, Dario 1926- CLC 32, 109; DAM DRAM;
DC 10
See also CA 116; 128; CANR 68; CWW 2;
DA3; DLBY 97; MTCW 1, 2

Fogarty, Jonathan Titulescu Esq.
See Farrell, James T(homas)

Follett, Ken(neth Martin) 1949- CLC 18;
DAM NOV, POP
See also AAYA 6; BEST 89:4; BPFB 1; CA
81-84; CANR 13, 33, 54, 102; CMW;
CPW; DA3; DLB 87; DLBY 81; INT
CANR-33; MTCW 1

Fontane, Theodor 1819-1898 NCLC 26
See also DLB 129; EW 6; RGWL

Fontenot, Chester CLC 65

Foote, Horton 1916- CLC 51, 91; DAM
DRAM
See also CA 73-76; CAD; CANR 34, 51;
CD; CSW; DA3; DLB 26; INT CANR-34

Foote, Mary Hallock 1847-1938 TCLC 108
See also DLB 186, 188, 202, 221

Foote, Shelby 1916- **CLC 75; DAM NOV, POP**
See also AAYA 40; CA 5-8R; CANR 3, 45, 74; CN; CPW; CSW; DA3; DLB 2, 17; MTCW 2; RHW

Forbes, Esther 1891-1967 **CLC 12**
See also AAYA 17; BYA 2; CA 13-14; 25-28R; CAP 1; CLR 27; DLB 22; JRDA; MAICYA; RHW; SATA 2, 100; YAW

Forche, Carolyn (Louise) 1950- **CLC 25, 83, 86; DAM POET; PC 10**
See also CA 109; 117; CANR 50, 74; CP; CWP; DA3; DLB 5, 193; INT CA-117; MTCW 1; RGAL

Ford, Elbur
See Hibbert, Eleanor Alice Burford

Ford, Ford Madox 1873-1939 **TCLC 1, 15, 39, 57; DAM NOV**
See also Chaucer, Daniel
See also BRW 6; CA 104; 132; CANR 74; CDBLB 1914-1945; DA3; DLB 34, 98, 162; MTCW 1, 2; RGEL

Ford, Henry 1863-1947 **TCLC 73**
See also CA 115; 148

Ford, John 1586-1639 **LC 68; DAM DRAM; DC 8**
See also BRW 2; CDBLB Before 1660; DA3; DFS 7; DLB 58; IDTP; RGEL

Ford, John 1895-1973 **CLC 16**
See also CA 187; 45-48

Ford, Richard 1944- **CLC 46, 99**
See also AMWS 5; CA 69-72; CANR 11, 47, 86; CN; CSW; DLB 227; MTCW 1; RGAL; RGSF

Ford, Webster
See Masters, Edgar Lee

Foreman, Richard 1937- **CLC 50**
See also CA 65-68; CAD; CANR 32, 63; CD

Forester, C(ecil) S(cott) 1899-1966 **CLC 35**
See also CA 73-76; 25-28R; CANR 83; DLB 191; RGEL; RHW; SATA 13

Forez
See Mauriac, Francois (Charles)

Forman, James Douglas 1932- **CLC 21**
See also AAYA 17; CA 9-12R; CANR 4, 19, 42; JRDA; MAICYA; SATA 8, 70; YAW

Fornes, Maria Irene 1930- **CLC 39, 61; DC 10; HLCS 1**
See also CA 25-28R; CAD; CANR 28, 81; CD; CWD; DLB 7; HW 1, 2; INT CANR-28; MTCW 1; RGAL

Forrest, Leon (Richard) 1937-1997 **CLC 4; BLCS**
See also AFAW 2; BW 2; CA 89-92; 162; CAAS 7; CANR 25, 52, 87; CN; DLB 33

Forster, E(dward) M(organ) 1879-1970 **CLC 1, 2, 3, 4, 9, 10, 13, 15, 22, 45, 77; DA; DAB; DAC; DAM MST, NOV; SSC 27; WLC**
See also AAYA 2, 37; BRW 6; BRWR 2; CA 13-14; 25-28R; CANR 45; CAP 1; CDBLB 1914-1945; DA3; DLB 34, 98, 162, 178, 195; DLBD 10; EXPN; LAIT 3; MTCW 1, 2; NCFS 1; NFS 3, 10, 11; RGEL; RGSF; SATA 57; SUFW; WLIT 4

Forster, John 1812-1876 **NCLC 11**
See also DLB 144, 184

Forster, Margaret 1938- **CLC 149**
See also CA 133; CANR 62; CN; DLB 155

Forsyth, Frederick 1938- **CLC 2, 5, 36; DAM NOV, POP**
See also BEST 89:4; CA 85-88; CANR 38, 62; CMW; CN; CPW; DLB 87; MTCW 1, 2

Forten, Charlotte L. 1837-1914 **TCLC 16; BLC 2**
See also Grimke, Charlotte L(ottie) Forten
See also DLB 50, 239

Foscolo, Ugo 1778-1827 **NCLC 8, 97**
See also EW 5

Fosse, Bob CLC 20
See also Fosse, Robert Louis

Fosse, Robert Louis 1927-1987
See Fosse, Bob
See also CA 110; 123

Foster, Hannah Webster 1758-1840 **NCLC 99**
See also DLB 37, 200; RGAL

Foster, Stephen Collins 1826-1864 **NCLC 26**
See also RGAL

Foucault, Michel 1926-1984 **CLC 31, 34, 69**
See also CA 105; 113; CANR 34; DLB 242; EW 13; GFL 1789 to the Present; GLL 1; MTCW 1, 2

Fouque, Friedrich (Heinrich Karl) de la Motte 1777-1843 **NCLC 2**
See also DLB 90; RGWL; SUFW

Fourier, Charles 1772-1837 **NCLC 51**

Fournier, Henri Alban 1886-1914
See Alain-Fournier
See also CA 104; 179

Fournier, Pierre 1916- **CLC 11**
See also Gascar, Pierre
See also CA 89-92; CANR 16, 40

Fowles, John (Robert) 1926- **CLC 1, 2, 3, 4, 6, 9, 10, 15, 33, 87; DAB; DAC; DAM MST; SSC 33**
See also BPFB 1; BRWS 1; CA 5-8R; CANR 25, 71, 103; CDBLB 1960 to Present; CN; DA3; DLB 14, 139, 207; HGG; MTCW 1, 2; RGEL; RHW; SATA 22; WLIT 4

Fox, Paula 1923- **CLC 2, 8, 121**
See also AAYA 3, 37; BYA 3, 8; CA 73-76; CANR 20, 36, 62, 105; CLR 1, 44; DLB 52; JRDA; MAICYA; MTCW 1; NFS 12; SATA 17, 60, 120; WYA; YAW

Fox, William Price (Jr.) 1926- **CLC 22**
See also CA 17-20R; CAAS 19; CANR 11; CSW; DLB 2; DLBY 81

Foxe, John 1517(?)-1587 **LC 14**
See also DLB 132

Frame, Janet CLC 2, 3, 6, 22, 66, 96; SSC 29
See also Clutha, Janet Paterson Frame
See also CN; CWP; RGEL; RGSF

France, Anatole TCLC 9
See also Thibault, Jacques Anatole Francois
See also DLB 123; GFL 1789 to the Present; MTCW 1; RGWL; SUFW

Francis, Claude CLC 50
See also CA 192

Francis, Dick 1920- **CLC 2, 22, 42, 102; DAM POP**
See also AAYA 5, 21; BEST 89:3; BPFB 1; CA 5-8R; CANR 9, 42, 68, 100; CDBLB 1960 to Present; CMW; CN; DA3; DLB 87; INT CANR-9; MSW; MTCW 1, 2

Francis, Robert (Churchill) 1901-1987 **CLC 15; PC 34**
See also AMWS 9; CA 1-4R; 123; CANR 1; EXPP; PFS 12

Francis, Lord Jeffrey
See Jeffrey, Francis
See also DLB 107

Frank, Anne(lies Marie) 1929-1945 **TCLC 17; DA; DAB; DAC; DAM MST; WLC**
See also AAYA 12; BYA 1; CA 113; 133; CANR 68; DA3; LAIT 4; MAICYAS; MTCW 1, 2; NCFS 2; SATA 87; SATA-Brief 42; WYA; YAW

Frank, Bruno 1887-1945 **TCLC 81**
See also CA 189; DLB 118

Frank, Elizabeth 1945- **CLC 39**
See also CA 121; 126; CANR 78; INT 126

Frankl, Viktor E(mil) 1905-1997 **CLC 93**
See also CA 65-68; 161

Franklin, Benjamin
See Hasek, Jaroslav (Matej Frantisek)

Franklin, Benjamin 1706-1790 **LC 25; DA; DAB; DAC; DAM MST; WLCS**
See also AMW; CDALB 1640-1865; DA3; DLB 24, 43, 73, 183; LAIT 1; RGAL; TUS

Franklin, (Stella Maria Sarah) Miles (Lampe) 1879-1954 **TCLC 7**
See also CA 104; 164; DLB 230; FW; MTCW 2; RGEL; TWA

Fraser, George MacDonald 1925- **CLC 7**
See also CA 45-48; 180; CAAE 180; CANR 2, 48, 74; MTCW 1; RHW

Fraser, Sylvia 1935- **CLC 64**
See also CA 45-48; CANR 1, 16, 60; CCA 1

Frayn, Michael 1933- **CLC 3, 7, 31, 47; DAM DRAM, NOV**
See also BRWS 7; CA 5-8R; CANR 30, 69; CBD; CD; CN; DLB 13, 14, 194, 245; FANT; MTCW 1, 2; SFW

Fraze, Candida (Merrill) 1945- **CLC 50**
See also CA 126

Frazer, Andrew
See Marlowe, Stephen

Frazer, J(ames) G(eorge) 1854-1941 **TCLC 32**
See also BRWS 3; CA 118

Frazer, Robert Caine
See Creasey, John

Frazer, Sir James George
See Frazer, J(ames) G(eorge)

Frazier, Charles 1950- **CLC 109**
See also AAYA 34; CA 161; CSW

Frazier, Ian 1951- **CLC 46**
See also CA 130; CANR 54, 93

Frederic, Harold 1856-1898 **NCLC 10**
See also AMW; DLB 12, 23; DLBD 13; RGAL

Frederick, John
See Faust, Frederick (Schiller)
See also TCWW 2

Frederick the Great 1712-1786 **LC 14**

Fredro, Aleksander 1793-1876 **NCLC 8**

Freeling, Nicolas 1927- **CLC 38**
See also CA 49-52; CAAS 12; CANR 1, 17, 50, 84; CMW; CN; DLB 87

Freeman, Douglas Southall 1886-1953 **TCLC 11**
See also CA 109; 195; DLB 17; DLBD 17

Freeman, Judith 1946- **CLC 55**
See also CA 148; DLB 256

Freeman, Mary E(leanor) Wilkins 1852-1930 **TCLC 9; SSC 1, 47**
See also CA 106; 177; DLB 12, 78, 221; EXPS; FW; HGG; MAWW; RGAL; RGSF; SSFS 4, 8; SUFW; TUS

Freeman, R(ichard) Austin 1862-1943 **TCLC 21**
See also CA 113; CANR 84; CMW; DLB 70

French, Albert 1943- **CLC 86**
See also BW 3; CA 167

French, Marilyn 1929- **CLC 10, 18, 60; DAM DRAM, NOV, POP**
See also BPFB 1; CA 69-72; CANR 3, 31; CN; CPW; FW; INT CANR-31; MTCW 1, 2

French, Paul
See Asimov, Isaac

Freneau, Philip Morin 1752-1832 **NCLC 1**
See also AMWS 2; DLB 37, 43; RGAL

Freud, Sigmund 1856-1939 **TCLC 52**
See also CA 115; 133; CANR 69; EW 8; MTCW 1, 2

Freytag, Gustav 1816-1895 **NCLC 109**
See also DLB 129

Friedan, Betty (Naomi) 1921- **CLC 74**
    See also CA 65-68; CANR 18, 45, 74; DLB 246; FW; MTCW 1, 2

Friedlander, Saul 1932- **CLC 90**
    See also CA 117; 130; CANR 72

Friedman, B(ernard) H(arper) 1926- **CLC 7**
    See also CA 1-4R; CANR 3, 48

Friedman, Bruce Jay 1930- **CLC 3, 5, 56**
    See also CA 9-12R; CAD; CANR 25, 52, 101; CD; CN; DLB 2, 28, 244; INT CANR-25

Friel, Brian 1929- **CLC 5, 42, 59, 115; DC 8**
    See also BRWS 5; CA 21-24R; CANR 33, 69; CBD; CD; DFS 11; DLB 13; MTCW 1; RGEL

Friis-Baastad, Babbis Ellinor 1921-1970 **CLC 12**
    See also CA 17-20R; 134; SATA 7

Frisch, Max (Rudolf) 1911-1991 **CLC 3, 9, 14, 18, 32, 44; DAM DRAM, NOV**
    See also CA 85-88; 134; CANR 32, 74; DLB 69, 124; EW 13; MTCW 1, 2; RGWL

Fromentin, Eugene (Samuel Auguste) 1820-1876 **NCLC 10**
    See also DLB 123; GFL 1789 to the Present

Frost, Frederick
    See Faust, Frederick (Schiller)
    See also TCWW 2

Frost, Robert (Lee) 1874-1963 **CLC 1, 3, 4, 9, 10, 13, 15, 26, 34, 44; DA; DAB; DAC; DAM MST, POET; PC 1, 39; WLC**
    See also AAYA 21; AMW; AMWR 1; CA 89-92; CANR 33; CDALB 1917-1929; CLR 67; DA3; DLB 54; DLBD 7; EXPP; MTCW 1, 2; PAB; PFS 1, 2, 3, 4, 5, 6, 7, 10, 13; RGAL; SATA 14; WP; WYA

Froude, James Anthony 1818-1894 **NCLC 43**
    See also DLB 18, 57, 144

Froy, Herald
    See Waterhouse, Keith (Spencer)

Fry, Christopher 1907- **CLC 2, 10, 14; DAM DRAM**
    See also BRWS 3; CA 17-20R; CAAS 23; CANR 9, 30, 74; CBD; CD; CP; DLB 13; MTCW 1, 2; RGEL; SATA 66

Frye, (Herman) Northrop 1912-1991 **CLC 24, 70**
    See also CA 5-8R; 133; CANR 8, 37; DLB 67, 68, 246; MTCW 1, 2; RGAL

Fuchs, Daniel 1909-1993 **CLC 8, 22**
    See also CA 81-84; 142; CAAS 5; CANR 40; DLB 9, 26, 28; DLBY 93

Fuchs, Daniel 1934- **CLC 34**
    See also CA 37-40R; CANR 14, 48

Fuentes, Carlos 1928- **CLC 3, 8, 10, 13, 22, 41, 60, 113; DA; DAB; DAC; DAM MST, MULT, NOV; HLC 1; SSC 24; WLC**
    See also AAYA 4; AITN 2; BPFB 1; CA 69-72; CANR 10, 32, 68, 104; CWW 2; DA3; DLB 113; DNFS; HW 1, 2; LAIT 3; LAW; LAWS 1; MTCW 1, 2; NFS 8; RGSF; RGWL; WLIT 1

Fuentes, Gregorio Lopez y
    See Lopez y Fuentes, Gregorio

Fuertes, Gloria 1918-1998 **PC 27**
    See also CA 178, 180; DLB 108; HW 2; SATA 115

Fugard, (Harold) Athol 1932- **CLC 5, 9, 14, 25, 40, 80; DAM DRAM; DC 3**
    See also AAYA 17; AFW; CA 85-88; CANR 32, 54; CD; DFS 3, 6, 10; DLB 225; DNFS; MTCW 1; RGEL; WLIT 2

Fugard, Sheila 1932- **CLC 48**
    See also CA 125

Fukuyama, Francis 1952- **CLC 131**
    See also CA 140; CANR 72

Fuller, Charles (H., Jr.) 1939- **CLC 25; BLC 2; DAM DRAM, MULT; DC 1**
    See also BW 2; CA 108; 112; CAD; CANR 87; CD; DFS 8; DLB 38; INT CA-112; MTCW 1

Fuller, Henry Blake 1857-1929 **TCLC 103**
    See also CA 108; 177; DLB 12; RGAL

Fuller, John (Leopold) 1937- **CLC 62**
    See also CA 21-24R; CANR 9, 44; CP; DLB 40

Fuller, Margaret
    See Ossoli, Sarah Margaret (Fuller)
    See also AMWS 2; DLB 183, 223, 239

Fuller, Roy (Broadbent) 1912-1991 **CLC 4, 28**
    See also BRWS 7; CA 5-8R; 135; CAAS 10; CANR 53, 83; CWRI; DLB 15, 20; RGEL; SATA 87

Fuller, Sarah Margaret
    See Ossoli, Sarah Margaret (Fuller)

Fuller, Sarah Margaret
    See Ossoli, Sarah Margaret (Fuller)
    See also DLB 1, 59, 73

Fulton, Alice 1952- **CLC 52**
    See also CA 116; CANR 57, 88; CP; CWP; DLB 193

Furphy, Joseph 1843-1912 **TCLC 25**
    See also CA 163; DLB 230; RGEL

Fuson, Robert H(enderson) 1927- **CLC 70**
    See also CA 89-92; CANR 103

Fussell, Paul 1924- **CLC 74**
    See also BEST 90:1; CA 17-20R; CANR 8, 21, 35, 69; INT CANR-21; MTCW 1, 2

Futabatei, Shimei 1864-1909 **TCLC 44**
    See also CA 162; DLB 180; MJW

Futrelle, Jacques 1875-1912 **TCLC 19**
    See also CA 113; 155; CMW

Gaboriau, Emile 1835-1873 **NCLC 14**
    See also CMW; MSW

Gadda, Carlo Emilio 1893-1973 **CLC 11**
    See also CA 89-92; DLB 177

Gaddis, William 1922-1998 **CLC 1, 3, 6, 8, 10, 19, 43, 86**
    See also AMWS 4; BPFB 1; CA 17-20R; 172; CANR 21, 48; CN; DLB 2; MTCW 1, 2; RGAL

Gaelique, Moruen le
    See Jacob, (Cyprien-)Max

Gage, Walter
    See Inge, William (Motter)

Gaines, Ernest J(ames) 1933- **CLC 3, 11, 18, 86; BLC 2; DAM MULT**
    See also AAYA 18; AFAW 1, 2; AITN 1; BPFB 2; BW 2, 3; BYA 6; CA 9-12R; CANR 6, 24, 42, 75; CDALB 1968-1988; CLR 62; CN; CSW; DA3; DLB 2, 33, 152; DLBY 80; EXPN; LAIT 5; MTCW 1, 2; NFS 5, 7; RGAL; RGSF; RHW; SATA 86; SSFS 5; YAW

Gaitskill, Mary 1954- **CLC 69**
    See also CA 128; CANR 61; DLB 244

Galdos, Benito Perez
    See Perez Galdos, Benito
    See also EW 7

Gale, Zona 1874-1938 **TCLC 7; DAM DRAM**
    See also CA 105; 153; CANR 84; DLB 9, 78, 228; RGAL

Galeano, Eduardo (Hughes) 1940- **CLC 72; HLCS 1**
    See also CA 29-32R; CANR 13, 32, 100; HW 1

Galiano, Juan Valera y Alcala
    See Valera y Alcala-Galiano, Juan

Galilei, Galileo 1564-1642 **LC 45**

Gallagher, Tess 1943- **CLC 18, 63; DAM POET; PC 9**
    See also CA 106; CP; CWP; DLB 120, 212, 244

Gallant, Mavis 1922- **CLC 7, 18, 38; DAC; DAM MST; SSC 5**
    See also CA 69-72; CANR 29, 69; CCA 1; CN; DLB 53; MTCW 1, 2; RGEL; RGSF

Gallant, Roy A(rthur) 1924- **CLC 17**
    See also CA 5-8R; CANR 4, 29, 54; CLR 30; MAICYA; SATA 4, 68, 110

Gallico, Paul (William) 1897-1976 **CLC 2**
    See also AITN 1; CA 5-8R; 69-72; CANR 23; DLB 9, 171; FANT; MAICYA; SATA 13

Gallo, Max Louis 1932- **CLC 95**
    See also CA 85-88

Gallois, Lucien
    See Desnos, Robert

Gallup, Ralph
    See Whitemore, Hugh (John)

Galsworthy, John 1867-1933 **TCLC 1, 45; DA; DAB; DAC; DAM DRAM, MST, NOV; SSC 22; WLC**
    See also BRW 6; CA 104; 141; CANR 75; CDBLB 1890-1914; DA3; DLB 10, 34, 98, 162; DLBD 16; MTCW 1; RGEL; SSFS 3

Galt, John 1779-1839 **NCLC 1, 110**
    See also DLB 99, 116, 159; RGEL; RGSF

Galvin, James 1951- **CLC 38**
    See also CA 108; CANR 26

Gamboa, Federico 1864-1939 **TCLC 36**
    See also CA 167; HW 2; LAW

Gandhi, M. K.
    See Gandhi, Mohandas Karamchand

Gandhi, Mahatma
    See Gandhi, Mohandas Karamchand

Gandhi, Mohandas Karamchand 1869-1948 **TCLC 59; DAM MULT**
    See also CA 121; 132; DA3; MTCW 1, 2

Gann, Ernest Kellogg 1910-1991 **CLC 23**
    See also AITN 1; BPFB 2; CA 1-4R; 136; CANR 1, 83; RHW

Garber, Eric 1943(?)-
    See Holleran, Andrew
    See also CANR 89

Garcia, Cristina 1958- **CLC 76**
    See also CA 141; CANR 73; DNFS; HW 2

Garcia Lorca, Federico 1898-1936 **TCLC 1, 7, 49; DA; DAB; DAC; DAM DRAM, MST, MULT, POET; DC 2; HLC 2; PC 3; WLC**
    See also Lorca, Federico Garcia
    See also CA 104; 131; CANR 81; DA3; DFS 10; DLB 108; HW 1, 2; MTCW 1, 2

Garcia Marquez, Gabriel (Jose) 1928- **CLC 2, 3, 8, 10, 15, 27, 47, 55, 68; DA; DAB; DAC; DAM MST, MULT, NOV, POP; HLC 1; SSC 8; WLC**
    See also AAYA 3, 33; BEST 89:1, 90:4; BPFB 2; BYA 12; CA 33-36R; CANR 10, 28, 50, 75, 82; CPW; DA3; DLB 113; DNFS; EXPN; EXPS; HW 1, 2; LAIT 2; LAW; LAWS 1; MTCW 1, 2; NFS 1, 5, 10; RGSF; RGWL; SSFS 1, 6; WLIT 1

Garcilaso de la Vega, El Inca 1503-1536
    See also HLCS 1; LAW

Gard, Janice
    See Latham, Jean Lee

Gard, Roger Martin du
    See Martin du Gard, Roger

Gardam, Jane (Mary) 1928- **CLC 43**
    See also CA 49-52; CANR 2, 18, 33, 54, 106; CLR 12; DLB 14, 161, 231; MAICYA; MTCW 1; SAAS 9; SATA 39, 76; SATA-Brief 28; YAW

Gardner, Herb(ert) 1934- **CLC 44**
    See also CA 149; CAD; CD

Gardner, John (Champlin), Jr. 1933-1982 **CLC 2, 3, 5, 7, 8, 10, 18, 28, 34; DAM NOV, POP; SSC 7**
    See also AITN 1; AMWS 6; BPFB 2; CA 65-68; 107; CANR 33, 73; CDALBS;

CPW; DA3; DLB 2; DLBY 82; FANT; MTCW 1; NFS 3; RGAL; RGSF; SATA 40; SATA-Obit 31; SSFS 8

Gardner, John (Edmund) 1926- **CLC 30; DAM POP**
See also CA 103; CANR 15, 69; CMW; CPW; MTCW 1

Gardner, Miriam
See Bradley, Marion Zimmer
See also GLL 1

Gardner, Noel
See Kuttner, Henry

Gardons, S. S.
See Snodgrass, W(illiam) D(e Witt)

Garfield, Leon 1921-1996 **CLC 12**
See also AAYA 8; BYA 1, 3; CA 17-20R; 152; CANR 38, 41, 78; CLR 21; DLB 161; JRDA; MAICYA; MAICYAS; SATA 1, 32, 76; SATA-Obit 90; WYA; YAW

Garland, (Hannibal) Hamlin 1860-1940 **TCLC 3; SSC 18**
See also CA 104; DLB 12, 71, 78, 186; RGAL; RGSF; TCWW 2

Garneau, (Hector de) Saint-Denys 1912-1943 **TCLC 13**
See also CA 111; DLB 88

Garner, Alan 1934- **CLC 17; DAB; DAM POP**
See also AAYA 18; BYA 3, 5; CA 73-76; 178; CAAE 178; CANR 15, 64; CLR 20; CPW; DLB 161; FANT; MAICYA; MTCW 1, 2; SATA 18, 69; SATA-Essay 108; SUFW; YAW

Garner, Hugh 1913-1979 **CLC 13**
See also Warwick, Jarvis
See also CA 69-72; CANR 31; CCA 1; DLB 68

Garnett, David 1892-1981 **CLC 3**
See also CA 5-8R; 103; CANR 17, 79; DLB 34; FANT; MTCW 2; RGEL; SFW; SUFW

Garos, Stephanie
See Katz, Steve

Garrett, George (Palmer) 1929- **CLC 3, 11, 51; SSC 30**
See also AMWS 7; BPFB 2; CA 1-4R; CAAS 5; CANR 1, 42, 67; CN; CP; CSW; DLB 2, 5, 130, 152; DLBY 83

Garrick, David 1717-1779 **LC 15; DAM DRAM**
See also DLB 84, 213; RGEL

Garrigue, Jean 1914-1972 **CLC 2, 8**
See also CA 5-8R; 37-40R; CANR 20

Garrison, Frederick
See Sinclair, Upton (Beall)

Garro, Elena 1920(?)-1998
See also CA 131; 169; CWW 2; DLB 145; HLCS 1; HW 1; LAWS 1; WLIT 1

Garth, Will
See Hamilton, Edmond; Kuttner, Henry

Garvey, Marcus (Moziah, Jr.) 1887-1940 **TCLC 41; BLC 2; DAM MULT**
See also BW 1; CA 120; 124; CANR 79

Gary, Romain CLC 25
See also Kacew, Romain
See also DLB 83

Gascar, Pierre CLC 11
See also Fournier, Pierre

Gascoyne, David (Emery) 1916- **CLC 45**
See also CA 65-68; CANR 10, 28, 54; CP; DLB 20; MTCW 1; RGEL

Gaskell, Elizabeth Cleghorn 1810-1865 **NCLC 5, 70, 97; DAB; DAM MST; SSC 25**
See also BRW 5; CDBLB 1832-1890; DLB 21, 144, 159; RGEL; RGSF

Gass, William H(oward) 1924- **CLC 1, 2, 8,** 11, 15, 39, 132; SSC 12
See also AMWS 6; CA 17-20R; CANR 30, 71, 100; CN; DLB 2, 227; MTCW 1, 2; RGAL

Gassendi, Pierre 1592-1655 **LC 54**
See also GFL Beginnings to 1789

Gasset, Jose Ortega y
See Ortega y Gasset, Jose

Gates, Henry Louis, Jr. 1950- **CLC 65; BLCS; DAM MULT**
See also BW 2, 3; CA 109; CANR 25, 53, 75; CSW; DA3; DLB 67; MTCW 1; RGAL

Gautier, Theophile 1811-1872 **NCLC 1, 59; DAM POET; PC 18; SSC 20**
See also DLB 119; EW 6; GFL 1789 to the Present; RGWL; SUFW

Gawsworth, John
See Bates, H(erbert) E(rnest)
See also DLB 255

Gay, John 1685-1732 **LC 49; DAM DRAM**
See also BRW 3; DLB 84, 95; RGEL; WLIT 3

Gay, Oliver
See Gogarty, Oliver St. John

Gaye, Marvin (Pentz, Jr.) 1939-1984 **CLC 26**
See also CA 195; 112

Gebler, Carlo (Ernest) 1954- **CLC 39**
See also CA 119; 133; CANR 96

Gee, Maggie (Mary) 1948- **CLC 57**
See also CA 130; CN; DLB 207

Gee, Maurice (Gough) 1931- **CLC 29**
See also AAYA 42; CA 97-100; CANR 67; CLR 56; CN; CWRI; RGSF; SATA 46, 101

Gelbart, Larry (Simon) 1928- **CLC 21, 61**
See also Gelbart, Larry
See also CA 73-76; CANR 45, 94

Gelbart, Larry 1928-
See Gelbart, Larry (Simon)
See also CAD; CD

Gelber, Jack 1932- **CLC 1, 6, 14, 79**
See also CA 1-4R; CAD; CANR 2; DLB 7, 228

Gellhorn, Martha (Ellis) 1908-1998 **CLC 14, 60**
See also CA 77-80; 164; CANR 44; CN; DLBY 82, 98

Genet, Jean 1910-1986 **CLC 1, 2, 5, 10, 14, 44, 46; DAM DRAM**
See also CA 13-16R; CANR 18; DA3; DFS 10; DLB 72; DLBY 86; EW 13; GFL 1789 to the Present; GLL 1; MTCW 1, 2; RGWL

Gent, Peter 1942- **CLC 29**
See also AITN 1; CA 89-92; DLBY 82

Gentile, Giovanni 1875-1944 **TCLC 96**
See also CA 119

Gentlewoman in New England, A
See Bradstreet, Anne

Gentlewoman in Those Parts, A
See Bradstreet, Anne

Geoffrey of Monmouth c. 1100-1155 **CMLC 44**
See also DLB 146

George, Jean
See George, Jean Craighead

George, Jean Craighead 1919- **CLC 35**
See also AAYA 8; BYA 2, 4; CA 5-8R; CANR 25; CLR 1; DLB 52; JRDA; MAICYA; SATA 2, 68, 124; WYA; YAW

George, Stefan (Anton) 1868-1933 **TCLC 2, 14**
See also CA 104; 193; EW 8

Georges, Georges Martin
See Simenon, Georges (Jacques Christian)

Gerhardi, William Alexander
See Gerhardie, William Alexander

Gerhardie, William Alexander 1895-1977 **CLC 5**
See also CA 25-28R; 73-76; CANR 18; DLB 36; RGEL

Gersonides 1288-1344 **CMLC 49**
See also DLB 115

Gerstler, Amy 1956- **CLC 70**
See also CA 146; CANR 99

Gertler, T. CLC 134
See also CA 116; 121

Ghalib NCLC 39, 78
See also Ghalib, Asadullah Khan

Ghalib, Asadullah Khan 1797-1869
See Ghalib
See also DAM POET; RGWL

Ghelderode, Michel de 1898-1962 **CLC 6, 11; DAM DRAM; DC 15**
See also CA 85-88; CANR 40, 77; EW 11

Ghiselin, Brewster 1903-2001 **CLC 23**
See also CA 13-16R; CAAS 10; CANR 13; CP

Ghose, Aurabinda 1872-1950 **TCLC 63**
See also CA 163

Ghose, Zulfikar 1935- **CLC 42**
See also CA 65-68; CANR 67; CN; CP

Ghosh, Amitav 1956- **CLC 44, 153**
See also CA 147; CANR 80; CN

Giacosa, Giuseppe 1847-1906 **TCLC 7**
See also CA 104

Gibb, Lee
See Waterhouse, Keith (Spencer)

Gibbon, Lewis Grassic TCLC 4
See also Mitchell, James Leslie
See also RGEL

Gibbons, Kaye 1960- **CLC 50, 88, 145; DAM POP**
See also AAYA 34; AMWS 10; CA 151; CANR 75; CSW; DA3; MTCW 1; NFS 3; RGAL; SATA 117

Gibran, Kahlil 1883-1931 **TCLC 1, 9; DAM POET, POP; PC 9**
See also CA 104; 150; DA3; MTCW 2

Gibran, Khalil
See Gibran, Kahlil

Gibson, William 1914- **CLC 23; DA; DAB; DAC; DAM DRAM, MST**
See also CA 9-12R; CAD 2; CANR 9, 42, 75; CD; DFS 2; DLB 7; LAIT 2; MTCW 2; SATA 66; YAW

Gibson, William (Ford) 1948- **CLC 39, 63; DAM POP**
See also AAYA 12; BPFB 2; CA 126; 133; CANR 52, 90, 106; CN; CPW; DA3; DLB 251; MTCW 2; SCFW 2; SFW

Gide, Andre (Paul Guillaume) 1869-1951 **TCLC 5, 12, 36; DA; DAB; DAC; DAM MST, NOV; SSC 13; WLC**
See also CA 104; 124; DA3; DLB 65; EW 8; GFL 1789 to the Present; MTCW 1, 2; RGSF; RGWL

Gifford, Barry (Colby) 1946- **CLC 34**
See also CA 65-68; CANR 9, 30, 40, 90

Gilbert, Frank
See De Voto, Bernard (Augustine)

Gilbert, W(illiam) S(chwenck) 1836-1911 **TCLC 3; DAM DRAM, POET**
See also CA 104; 173; RGEL; SATA 36

Gilbreth, Frank B(unker), Jr. 1911-2001 **CLC 17**
See also CA 9-12R; SATA 2

Gilchrist, Ellen (Louise) 1935- **CLC 34, 48, 143; DAM POP; SSC 14**
See also BPFB 2; CA 113; 116; CANR 41, 61, 104; CN; CPW; CSW; DLB 130; EXPS; MTCW 1, 2; RGAL; RGSF; SSFS 9

Giles, Molly 1942- **CLC 39**
See also CA 126; CANR 98

Gill, Eric 1882-1940 **TCLC 85**

Gill, Patrick
  See Creasey, John
Gillette, Douglas CLC 70
Gilliam, Terry (Vance) 1940- **CLC 21, 141**
  See also Monty Python
  See also AAYA 19; CA 108; 113; CANR
  35; INT 113
Gillian, Jerry
  See Gilliam, Terry (Vance)
Gilliatt, Penelope (Ann Douglass) 1932-1993
  CLC 2, 10, 13, 53
  See also AITN 2; CA 13-16R; 141; CANR
  49; DLB 14
Gilman, Charlotte (Anna) Perkins (Stetson)
  1860-1935 **TCLC 9, 37, 117; SSC 13**
  See also BYA 11; CA 106; 150; DLB 221;
  EXPS; FW; HGG; LAIT 2; MAWW;
  MTCW 1; RGAL; RGSF; SFW; SSFS 1
Gilmour, David 1949- **CLC 35**
  See also CA 138, 147
Gilpin, William 1724-1804 **NCLC 30**
Gilray, J. D.
  See Mencken, H(enry) L(ouis)
Gilroy, Frank D(aniel) 1925- **CLC 2**
  See also CA 81-84; CAD; CANR 32, 64,
  86; CD; DLB 7
Gilstrap, John 1957(?)- **CLC 99**
  See also CA 160; CANR 101
Ginsberg, Allen 1926-1997 **CLC 1, 2, 3, 4, 6,
  13, 36, 69, 109; DA; DAB; DAC; DAM
  MST, POET; PC 4; WLC**
  See also AAYA 33; AITN 1; AMWS 2; CA
  1-4R; 157; CANR 2, 41, 63, 95; CDALB
  1941-1968; CP; DA3; DLB 5, 16, 169,
  237; GLL 1; MTCW 1, 2; PAB; PFS 5;
  RGAL; WP
Ginzburg, Eugenia CLC 59
Ginzburg, Natalia 1916-1991 **CLC 5, 11, 54,
  70**
  See also CA 85-88; 135; CANR 33; DLB
  177; EW 13; MTCW 1, 2; RGWL
Giono, Jean 1895-1970 **CLC 4, 11**
  See also CA 45-48; 29-32R; CANR 2, 35;
  DLB 72; GFL 1789 to the Present; MTCW
  1; RGWL
Giovanni, Nikki 1943- **CLC 2, 4, 19, 64, 117;
  BLC 2; DA; DAB; DAC; DAM MST,
  MULT, POET; PC 19; WLCS**
  See also AAYA 22; AITN 1; BW 2, 3; CA
  29-32R; CAAS 6; CANR 18, 41, 60, 91;
  CDALBS; CLR 6, 73; CP; CSW; CWP;
  CWRI; DA3; DLB 5, 41; EXPP; INT
  CANR-18; MAICYA; MTCW 1, 2;
  RGAL; SATA 24, 107; YAW
Giovene, Andrea 1904-1998 **CLC 7**
  See also CA 85-88
Gippius, Zinaida (Nikolayevna) 1869-1945
  See Hippius, Zinaida
  See also CA 106
Giraudoux, Jean(-Hippolyte) 1882-1944
  TCLC 2, 7; DAM DRAM
  See also CA 104; 196; DLB 65; EW 9; GFL
  1789 to the Present; RGWL
Gironella, Jose Maria 1917-1991 **CLC 11**
  See also CA 101; RGWL
Gissing, George (Robert) 1857-1903 **TCLC
  3, 24, 47; SSC 37**
  See also BRW 5; CA 105; 167; DLB 18,
  135, 184; RGEL
Giurlani, Aldo
  See Palazzeschi, Aldo
Gladkov, Fyodor (Vasilyevich) 1883-1958
  TCLC 27
  See also CA 170
Glanville, Brian (Lester) 1931- **CLC 6**
  See also CA 5-8R; CAAS 9; CANR 3, 70;
  CN; DLB 15, 139; SATA 42

Glasgow, Ellen (Anderson Gholson)
  1873-1945 **TCLC 2, 7; SSC 34**
  See also AMW; CA 104; 164; DLB 9, 12;
  MAWW; MTCW 2; RGAL; RHW; SSFS
  9
Glaspell, Susan 1882(?)-1948 **TCLC 55; DC
  10; SSC 41**
  See also AMWS 3; CA 110; 154; DFS 8;
  DLB 7, 9, 78, 228; MAWW; RGAL;
  SSFS 3; TCWW 2; YABC 2
Glassco, John 1909-1981 **CLC 9**
  See also CA 13-16R; 102; CANR 15; DLB
  68
Glasscock, Amnesia
  See Steinbeck, John (Ernst)
Glasser, Ronald J. 1940(?)- **CLC 37**
Glassman, Joyce
  See Johnson, Joyce
Gleick, James (W.) 1954- **CLC 147**
  See also CA 131; 137; CANR 97; INT CA-
  137
Glendinning, Victoria 1937- **CLC 50**
  See also CA 120; 127; CANR 59, 89; DLB
  155
Glissant, Edouard 1928- **CLC 10, 68; DAM
  MULT**
  See also CA 153; CWW 2
Gloag, Julian 1930- **CLC 40**
  See also AITN 1; CA 65-68; CANR 10, 70;
  CN
Glowacki, Aleksander
  See Prus, Boleslaw
Gluck, Louise (Elisabeth) 1943- **CLC 7, 22,
  44, 81; DAM POET; PC 16**
  See also AMWS 5; CA 33-36R; CANR 40,
  69; CP; CWP; DA3; DLB 5; MTCW 2;
  PFS 5; RGAL
Glyn, Elinor 1864-1943 **TCLC 72**
  See also DLB 153; RHW
Gobineau, Joseph-Arthur 1816-1882 **NCLC
  17**
  See also DLB 123; GFL 1789 to the Present
Godard, Jean-Luc 1930- **CLC 20**
  See also CA 93-96
Godden, (Margaret) Rumer 1907-1998 **CLC
  53**
  See also AAYA 6; BPFB 2; BYA 2, 5; CA
  5-8R; 172; CANR 4, 27, 36, 55, 80; CLR
  20; CN; CWRI; DLB 161; MAICYA;
  RHW; SAAS 12; SATA 3, 36; SATA-Obit
  109
Godoy Alcayaga, Lucila 1899-1957 **TCLC 2;
  DAM MULT; HLC 2; PC 32**
  See also Mistral, Gabriela
  See also BW 2; CA 104; 131; CANR 81;
  DNFS; HW 1, 2; MTCW 1, 2
Godwin, Gail (Kathleen) 1937- **CLC 5, 8, 22,
  31, 69, 125; DAM POP**
  See also BPFB 2; CA 29-32R; CANR 15,
  43, 69; CN; CPW; CSW; DA3; DLB 6,
  234; INT CANR-15; MTCW 1, 2
Godwin, William 1756-1836 **NCLC 14**
  See also CDBLB 1789-1832; CMW; DLB
  39, 104, 142, 158, 163; HGG; RGEL
Goebbels, Josef
  See Goebbels, (Paul) Joseph
Goebbels, (Paul) Joseph 1897-1945 **TCLC 68**
  See also CA 115; 148
Goebbels, Joseph Paul
  See Goebbels, (Paul) Joseph
Goethe, Johann Wolfgang von 1749-1832
  **NCLC 4, 22, 34, 90; DA; DAB; DAC;
  DAM DRAM, MST, POET; PC 5; SSC
  38; WLC**
  See also DA3; DLB 94; EW 5; RGWL
Gogarty, Oliver St. John 1878-1957 **TCLC
  15**
  See also CA 109; 150; DLB 15, 19; RGEL

Gogol, Nikolai (Vasilyevich) 1809-1852
  **NCLC 5, 15, 31; DA; DAB; DAC; DAM
  DRAM, MST; DC 1; SSC 4, 29; WLC**
  See also DFS 12; DLB 198; EW 6; EXPS;
  RGSF; RGWL; SSFS 7
Goines, Donald 1937(?)-1974 **CLC 80; BLC
  2; DAM MULT, POP**
  See also AITN 1; BW 1, 3; CA 124; 114;
  CANR 82; CMW; DA3; DLB 33
Gold, Herbert 1924- **CLC 4, 7, 14, 42, 152**
  See also CA 9-12R; CANR 17, 45; CN;
  DLB 2; DLBY 81
Goldbarth, Albert 1948- **CLC 5, 38**
  See also CA 53-56; CANR 6, 40; CP; DLB
  120
Goldberg, Anatol 1910-1982 **CLC 34**
  See also CA 131; 117
Goldemberg, Isaac 1945- **CLC 52**
  See also CA 69-72; CAAS 12; CANR 11,
  32; HW 1; WLIT 1
Golding, William (Gerald) 1911-1993 **CLC 1,
  2, 3, 8, 10, 17, 27, 58, 81; DA; DAB;
  DAC; DAM MST, NOV; WLC**
  See also AAYA 5; BPFB 2; BRWR 1;
  BRWS 1; BYA 2; CA 5-8R; 141; CANR
  13, 33, 54; CDBLB 1945-1960; DA3;
  DLB 15, 100, 255; EXPN; HGG; LAIT 4;
  MTCW 1, 2; NFS 2; RGEL; RHW; SFW;
  WLIT 4; YAW
Goldman, Emma 1869-1940 **TCLC 13**
  See also CA 110; 150; DLB 221; FW;
  RGAL
Goldman, Francisco 1954- **CLC 76**
  See also CA 162
Goldman, William (W.) 1931- **CLC 1, 48**
  See also BPFB 2; CA 9-12R; CANR 29,
  69, 106; CN; DLB 44; FANT; IDFW 3, 4
Goldmann, Lucien 1913-1970 **CLC 24**
  See also CA 25-28; CAP 2
Goldoni, Carlo 1707-1793 **LC 4; DAM
  DRAM**
  See also EW 4; RGWL
Goldsberry, Steven 1949- **CLC 34**
  See also CA 131
Goldsmith, Oliver 1730-1774 **LC 2, 48; DA;
  DAB; DAC; DAM DRAM, MST, NOV,
  POET; DC 8; WLC**
  See also BRW 3; CDBLB 1660-1789; DFS
  1; DLB 39, 89, 104, 109, 142; IDTP;
  RGEL; SATA 26; TEA; WLIT 3
Goldsmith, Peter
  See Priestley, J(ohn) B(oynton)
Gombrowicz, Witold 1904-1969 **CLC 4, 7,
  11, 49; DAM DRAM**
  See also CA 19-20; 25-28R; CANR 105;
  CAP 2; DLB 215; EW 12; RGWL
Gomez de la Serna, Ramon 1888-1963 **CLC
  9**
  See also CA 153; 116; CANR 79; HW 1, 2
Goncharov, Ivan Alexandrovich 1812-1891
  NCLC 1, 63
  See also DLB 238; EW 6; RGWL
Goncourt, Edmond (Louis Antoine Huot) de
  1822-1896 **NCLC 7**
  See also DLB 123; EW 7; GFL 1789 to the
  Present; RGWL
Goncourt, Jules (Alfred Huot) de 1830-1870
  NCLC 7
  See also DLB 123; EW 7; GFL 1789 to the
  Present; RGWL
Gongora (y Argote), Luis de 1561-1627 **LC
  72**
  See also RGWL
Gontier, Fernande 19(?)- **CLC 50**
Gonzalez Martinez, Enrique 1871-1952
  TCLC 72
  See also CA 166; CANR 81; HW 1, 2

Goodison, Lorna 1947- **PC 36**
See also CA 142; CANR 88; CP; CWP;
DLB 157

Goodman, Paul 1911-1972 **CLC 1, 2, 4, 7**
See also CA 19-20; 37-40R; CAD; CANR
34; CAP 2; DLB 130, 246; MTCW 1;
RGAL

Gordimer, Nadine 1923- **CLC 3, 5, 7, 10, 18,
33, 51, 70, 123; DA; DAB; DAC; DAM
MST, NOV; SSC 17; WLCS**
See also AAYA 39; AFW; BRWS 2; CA
5-8R; CANR 3, 28, 56, 88; CN; DA3;
DLB 225; EXPS; INT CANR-28; MTCW
1, 2; NFS 4; RGEL; RGSF; SSFS 2;
WLIT 2; YAW

Gordon, Adam Lindsay 1833-1870 **NCLC 21**
See also DLB 230

Gordon, Caroline 1895-1981 **CLC 6, 13, 29,
83; SSC 15**
See also AMW; CA 11-12; 103; CANR 36;
CAP 1; DLB 4, 9, 102; DLBD 17; DLBY
81; MTCW 1, 2; RGAL; RGSF

Gordon, Charles William 1860-1937
See Connor, Ralph
See also CA 109

Gordon, Mary (Catherine) 1949- **CLC 13,
22, 128**
See also AMWS 4; BPFB 2; CA 102;
CANR 44, 92; CN; DLB 6; DLBY 81;
FW; INT CA-102; MTCW 1

Gordon, N. J.
See Bosman, Herman Charles

Gordon, Sol 1923- **CLC 26**
See also CA 53-56; CANR 4; SATA 11

Gordone, Charles 1925-1995 **CLC 1, 4; DAM
DRAM; DC 8**
See also BW 1, 3; CA 93-96, 180; 150;
CAAE 180; CAD; CANR 55; DLB 7; INT
93-96; MTCW 1

Gore, Catherine 1800-1861 **NCLC 65**
See also DLB 116; RGEL

Gorenko, Anna Andreevna
See Akhmatova, Anna

Gorky, Maxim **TCLC 8; DAB; SSC 28; WLC**
See also Peshkov, Alexei Maximovich
See also DFS 9; EW 8; MTCW 2

Goryan, Sirak
See Saroyan, William

Gosse, Edmund (William) 1849-1928 **TCLC
28**
See also CA 117; DLB 57, 144, 184; RGEL

Gotlieb, Phyllis Fay (Bloom) 1926- **CLC 18**
See also CA 13-16R; CANR 7; DLB 88,
251; SFW

Gottesman, S. D.
See Kornbluth, C(yril) M.; Pohl, Frederik

Gottfried von Strassburg fl. c. 1170-1215
CMLC 10
See also DLB 138; EW 1; RGWL

Gould, Lois **CLC 4, 10**
See also CA 77-80; CANR 29; MTCW 1

Gourmont, Remy(-Marie-Charles) de
1858-1915 **TCLC 17**
See also CA 109; 150; GFL 1789 to the
Present; MTCW 2

Govier, Katherine 1948- **CLC 51**
See also CA 101; CANR 18, 40; CCA 1

Goyen, (Charles) William 1915-1983 **CLC 5,
8, 14, 40**
See also AITN 2; CA 5-8R; 110; CANR 6,
71; DLB 2, 218; DLBY 83; INT CANR-6

Goytisolo, Juan 1931- **CLC 5, 10, 23, 133;
DAM MULT; HLC 1**
See also CA 85-88; CANR 32, 61; CWW
2; GLL 2; HW 1, 2; MTCW 1, 2

Gozzano, Guido 1883-1916 **PC 10**
See also CA 154; DLB 114

Gozzi, (Conte) Carlo 1720-1806 **NCLC 23**

Grabbe, Christian Dietrich 1801-1836 **NCLC
2**
See also DLB 133; RGWL

Grace, Patricia Frances 1937- **CLC 56**
See also CA 176; CN; RGSF

Gracian y Morales, Baltasar 1601-1658 **LC
15**

Gracq, Julien **CLC 11, 48**
See also Poirier, Louis
See also CWW 2; DLB 83; GFL 1789 to
the Present

Grade, Chaim 1910-1982 **CLC 10**
See also CA 93-96; 107

Graduate of Oxford, A
See Ruskin, John

Grafton, Garth
See Duncan, Sara Jeannette

Graham, John
See Phillips, David Graham

Graham, Jorie 1951- **CLC 48, 118**
See also CA 111; CANR 63; CP; CWP;
DLB 120; PFS 10

Graham, R(obert) B(ontine) Cunninghame
See Cunninghame Graham, Robert
(Gallnigad) Bontine
See also DLB 98, 135, 174; RGEL; RGSF

Graham, Robert
See Haldeman, Joe (William)

Graham, Tom
See Lewis, (Harry) Sinclair

Graham, W(illiam) S(idney) 1918-1986 **CLC
29**
See also BRWS 7; CA 73-76; 118; DLB 20;
RGEL

Graham, Winston (Mawdsley) 1910- **CLC 23**
See also CA 49-52; CANR 2, 22, 45, 66;
CMW; CN; DLB 77; RHW

Grahame, Kenneth 1859-1932 **TCLC 64;
DAB**
See also BYA 5; CA 108; 136; CANR 80;
CLR 5; CWRI; DA3; DLB 34, 141, 178;
FANT; MAICYA; MTCW 2; RGEL;
SATA 100; WCH; YABC 1

Granger, Darius John
See Marlowe, Stephen

Granin, Daniil **CLC 59**

Granovsky, Timofei Nikolaevich 1813-1855
NCLC 75
See also DLB 198

Grant, Skeeter
See Spiegelman, Art

Granville-Barker, Harley 1877-1946 **TCLC
2; DAM DRAM**
See also Barker, Harley Granville
See also CA 104; RGEL

Granzotto, Gianni
See Granzotto, Giovanni Battista

Granzotto, Giovanni Battista 1914-1985 **CLC
70**
See also CA 166

Grass, Guenter (Wilhelm) 1927- **CLC 1, 2, 4,
6, 11, 15, 22, 32, 49, 88; DA; DAB;
DAC; DAM MST, NOV; WLC**
See also BPFB 2; CA 13-16R; CANR 20,
75, 93; DA3; DLB 75, 124; EW 13;
MTCW 1, 2; RGWL

Gratton, Thomas
See Hulme, T(homas) E(rnest)

Grau, Shirley Ann 1929- **CLC 4, 9, 146; SSC
15**
See also CA 89-92; CANR 22, 69; CN;
CSW; DLB 2, 218; INT CANR-22;
MTCW 1

Gravel, Fern
See Hall, James Norman

Graver, Elizabeth 1964- **CLC 70**
See also CA 135; CANR 71

Graves, Richard Perceval 1895-1985 **CLC 44**
See also CA 65-68; CANR 9, 26, 51

Graves, Robert (von Ranke) 1895-1985 **CLC
1, 2, 6, 11, 39, 44, 45; DAB; DAC; DAM
MST, POET; PC 6**
See also BPFB 2; BRW 7; BYA 4; CA 5-8R;
117; CANR 5, 36; CDBLB 1914-1945;
DA3; DLB 20, 100, 191; DLBD 18;
DLBY 85; MTCW 1, 2; NCFS 2; RGEL;
RHW; SATA 45

Graves, Valerie
See Bradley, Marion Zimmer

Gray, Alasdair (James) 1934- **CLC 41**
See also CA 126; CANR 47, 69, 106; CN;
DLB 194; HGG; INT CA-126; MTCW 1,
2; RGSF

Gray, Amlin 1946- **CLC 29**
See also CA 138

Gray, Francine du Plessix 1930- **CLC 22,
153; DAM NOV**
See also BEST 90:3; CA 61-64; CAAS 2;
CANR 11, 33, 75, 81; INT CANR-11;
MTCW 1, 2

Gray, John (Henry) 1866-1934 **TCLC 19**
See also CA 119; 162; RGEL

Gray, Simon (James Holliday) 1936- **CLC 9,
14, 36**
See also AITN 1; CA 21-24R; CAAS 3;
CANR 32, 69; CD; DLB 13; MTCW 1;
RGEL

Gray, Spalding 1941- **CLC 49, 112; DAM
POP; DC 7**
See also CA 128; CAD; CANR 74; CD;
CPW; MTCW 2

Gray, Thomas 1716-1771 **LC 4, 40; DA;
DAB; DAC; DAM MST; PC 2; WLC**
See also BRW 3; CDBLB 1660-1789; DA3;
DLB 109; EXPP; PAB; PFS 9; RGEL;
WP

Grayson, David
See Baker, Ray Stannard

Grayson, Richard (A.) 1951- **CLC 38**
See also CA 85-88; CANR 14, 31, 57; DLB
234

Greeley, Andrew M(oran) 1928- **CLC 28;
DAM POP**
See also BPFB 2; CA 5-8R; CAAS 7;
CANR 7, 43, 69, 104; CMW; CPW; DA3;
MTCW 1, 2

Green, Anna Katharine 1846-1935 **TCLC 63**
See also CA 112; 159; CMW; DLB 202,
221; MSW

Green, Brian
See Card, Orson Scott

Green, Hannah
See Greenberg, Joanne (Goldenberg)

Green, Hannah 1927(?)-1996 **CLC 3**
See also CA 73-76; CANR 59, 93; NFS 10

Green, Henry **CLC 2, 13, 97**
See also Yorke, Henry Vincent
See also BRWS 2; CA 175; DLB 15; RGEL

Green, Julian (Hartridge) 1900-1998
See Green, Julien
See also CA 21-24R; 169; CANR 33, 87;
DLB 4, 72; MTCW 1

Green, Julien **CLC 3, 11, 77**
See also Green, Julian (Hartridge)
See also GFL 1789 to the Present; MTCW
2

Green, Paul (Eliot) 1894-1981 **CLC 25; DAM
DRAM**
See also AITN 1; CA 5-8R; 103; CANR 3;
DLB 7, 9, 249; DLBY 81; RGAL

Greenberg, Ivan 1908-1973
See Rahv, Philip
See also CA 85-88

Greenberg, Joanne (Goldenberg) 1932- **CLC
7, 30**
See also AAYA 12; CA 5-8R; CANR 14,
32, 69; CN; SATA 25; YAW

Greenberg, Richard 1959(?)- **CLC 57**
    See also CA 138; CAD; CD
Greenblatt, Stephen J(ay) 1943- **CLC 70**
    See also CA 49-52
Greene, Bette 1934- **CLC 30**
    See also AAYA 7; BYA 3; CA 53-56; CANR 4; CLR 2; CWRI; JRDA; LAIT 4; MAICYA; NFS 10; SAAS 16; SATA 8, 102; WYA; YAW
Greene, Gael **CLC 8**
    See also CA 13-16R; CANR 10
Greene, Graham (Henry) 1904-1991 **CLC 1, 3, 6, 9, 14, 18, 27, 37, 70, 72, 125; DA; DAB; DAC; DAM MST, NOV; SSC 29; WLC**
    See also AITN 2; BPFB 2; BRWR 2; BRWS 1; BYA 3; CA 13-16R; 133; CANR 35, 61; CBD; CDBLB 1945-1960; CMW; DA3; DLB 13, 15, 77, 100, 162, 201, 204; DLBY 91; MSW; MTCW 1, 2; RGEL; SATA 20; WLIT 4
Greene, Robert 1558-1592 **LC 41**
    See also DLB 62, 167; IDTP; RGEL; TEA
Greer, Germaine 1939- **CLC 131**
    See also AITN 1; CA 81-84; CANR 33, 70; FW; MTCW 1, 2
Greer, Richard
    See Silverberg, Robert
Gregor, Arthur 1923- **CLC 9**
    See also CA 25-28R; CAAS 10; CANR 11; CP; SATA 36
Gregor, Lee
    See Pohl, Frederik
Gregory, Lady Isabella Augusta (Persse) 1852-1932 **TCLC 1**
    See also BRW 6; CA 104; 184; DLB 10; IDTP; RGEL
Gregory, J. Dennis
    See Williams, John A(lfred)
Grekova, I. **CLC 59**
Grendon, Stephen
    See Derleth, August (William)
Grenville, Kate 1950- **CLC 61**
    See also CA 118; CANR 53, 93
Grenville, Pelham
    See Wodehouse, P(elham) G(renville)
Greve, Felix Paul (Berthold Friedrich) 1879-1948
    See Grove, Frederick Philip
    See also CA 104; 141, 175; CANR 79; DAC; DAM MST
Grey, Zane 1872-1939 **TCLC 6; DAM POP**
    See also BPFB 2; CA 104; 132; DA3; DLB 9, 212; MTCW 1, 2; RGAL; TCWW 2
Grieg, (Johan) Nordahl (Brun) 1902-1943 **TCLC 10**
    See also CA 107; 189
Grieve, C(hristopher) M(urray) 1892-1978 **CLC 11, 19; DAM POET**
    See MacDiarmid, Hugh; Pteleon
    See also CA 5-8R; 85-88; CANR 33; MTCW 1; RGEL
Griffin, Gerald 1803-1840 **NCLC 7**
    See also DLB 159; RGEL
Griffin, John Howard 1920-1980 **CLC 68**
    See also AITN 1; CA 1-4R; 101; CANR 2
Griffin, Peter 1942- **CLC 39**
    See also CA 136
Griffith, D(avid Lewelyn) W(ark) 1875(?)-1948 **TCLC 68**
    See also CA 119; 150; CANR 80
Griffith, Lawrence
    See Griffith, D(avid Lewelyn) W(ark)
Griffiths, Trevor 1935- **CLC 13, 52**
    See also CA 97-100; CANR 45; CBD; CD; DLB 13, 245
Griggs, Sutton (Elbert) 1872-1930 **TCLC 77**
    See also CA 123; 186; DLB 50

Grigson, Geoffrey (Edward Harvey) 1905-1985 **CLC 7, 39**
    See also CA 25-28R; 118; CANR 20, 33; DLB 27; MTCW 1, 2
Grillparzer, Franz 1791-1872 **NCLC 1, 102; DC 14; SSC 37**
    See also DLB 133; EW 5; RGWL
Grimble, Reverend Charles James
    See Eliot, T(homas) S(tearns)
Grimke, Charlotte L(ottie) Forten 1837(?)-1914
    See Forten, Charlotte L.
    See also BW 1; CA 117; 124; DAM MULT, POET
Grimm, Jacob Ludwig Karl 1785-1863 **NCLC 3, 77; SSC 36**
    See also DLB 90; MAICYA; RGSF; RGWL; SATA 22; WCH
Grimm, Wilhelm Karl 1786-1859 **NCLC 3, 77; SSC 36**
    See also DLB 90; MAICYA; RGSF; RGWL; SATA 22; WCH
Grimmelshausen, Hans Jakob Christoffel von
    See Grimmelshausen, Johann Jakob Christoffel von
    See also RGWL
Grimmelshausen, Johann Jakob Christoffel von 1621-1676 **LC 6**
    See also Grimmelshausen, Hans Jakob Christoffel von
    See also DLB 168
Grindel, Eugene 1895-1952
    See Eluard, Paul
    See also CA 104; 193
Grisham, John 1955- **CLC 84; DAM POP**
    See also AAYA 14; BPFB 2; CA 138; CANR 47, 69; CMW; CN; CPW; CSW; DA3; MSW; MTCW 2
Grossman, David 1954- **CLC 67**
    See also CA 138; CWW 2
Grossman, Vasily (Semenovich) 1905-1964 **CLC 41**
    See also CA 124; 130; MTCW 1
Grove, Frederick Philip **TCLC 4**
    See also Greve, Felix Paul (Berthold Friedrich)
    See also DLB 92; RGEL
Grubb
    See Crumb, R(obert)
Grumbach, Doris (Isaac) 1918- **CLC 13, 22, 64**
    See also CA 5-8R; CAAS 2; CANR 9, 42, 70; CN; INT CANR-9; MTCW 2
Grundtvig, Nicolai Frederik Severin 1783-1872 **NCLC 1**
Grunge
    See Crumb, R(obert)
Grunwald, Lisa 1959- **CLC 44**
    See also CA 120
Guare, John 1938- **CLC 8, 14, 29, 67; DAM DRAM**
    See also CA 73-76; CAD; CANR 21, 69; CD; DFS 8, 13; DLB 7, 249; MTCW 1, 2; RGAL
Gubar, Susan (David) 1944- **CLC 145**
    See also CA 108; CANR 45, 70; FW; MTCW 1; RGAL
Gudjonsson, Halldor Kiljan 1902-1998
    See Laxness, Halldor
    See also CA 103; 164; CWW 2
Guenter, Erich
    See Eich, Guenter
Guest, Barbara 1920- **CLC 34**
    See also CA 25-28R; CANR 11, 44, 84; CP; CWP; DLB 5, 193
Guest, Edgar A(lbert) 1881-1959 **TCLC 95**
    See also CA 112; 168

Guest, Judith (Ann) 1936- **CLC 8, 30; DAM NOV, POP**
    See also AAYA 7; CA 77-80; CANR 15, 75; DA3; EXPN; INT CANR-15; LAIT 5; MTCW 1, 2; NFS 1
Guevara, Che **CLC 87; HLC 1**
    See also Guevara (Serna), Ernesto
Guevara (Serna), Ernesto 1928-1967 **CLC 87; DAM MULT; HLC 1**
    See also Guevara, Che
    See also CA 127; 111; CANR 56; HW 1
Guicciardini, Francesco 1483-1540 **LC 49**
Guild, Nicholas M. 1944- **CLC 33**
    See also CA 93-96
Guillemin, Jacques
    See Sartre, Jean-Paul
Guillen, Jorge 1893-1984 **CLC 11; DAM MULT, POET; HLCS 1; PC 35**
    See also CA 89-92; 112; DLB 108; HW 1; RGWL
Guillen, Nicolas (Cristobal) 1902-1989 **CLC 48, 79; BLC 2; DAM MST, MULT, POET; HLC 1; PC 23**
    See also BW 2; CA 116; 125; 129; CANR 84; HW 1; LAW; RGWL; WP
Guillevic, (Eugene) 1907-1997 **CLC 33**
    See also CA 93-96; CWW 2
Guillois
    See Desnos, Robert
Guillois, Valentin
    See Desnos, Robert
Guimaraes Rosa, Joao
    See Rosa, Joao Guimaraes
    See also LAW
Guimaraes Rosa, Joao 1908-1967
    See also CA 175; HLCS 2; LAW; RGSF; RGWL
Guiney, Louise Imogen 1861-1920 **TCLC 41**
    See also CA 160; DLB 54; RGAL
Guinizelli, Guido c. 1230-1276 **CMLC 49**
Guiraldes, Ricardo (Guillermo) 1886-1927 **TCLC 39**
    See also CA 131; HW 1; LAW; MTCW 1
Gumilev, Nikolai (Stepanovich) 1886-1921 **TCLC 60**
    See also CA 165
Gunesekera, Romesh 1954- **CLC 91**
    See also CA 159; CN
Gunn, Bill **CLC 5**
    See also Gunn, William Harrison
    See also DLB 38
Gunn, Thom(son William) 1929- **CLC 3, 6, 18, 32, 81; DAM POET; PC 26**
    See also BRWS 4; CA 17-20R; CANR 9, 33; CDBLB 1960 to Present; CP; DLB 27; INT CANR-33; MTCW 1; PFS 9; RGEL
Gunn, William Harrison 1934(?)-1989
    See Gunn, Bill
    See also AITN 1; BW 1, 3; CA 13-16R; 128; CANR 12, 25, 76
Gunn Allen, Paula
    See Allen, Paula Gunn
Gunnars, Kristjana 1948- **CLC 69**
    See also CA 113; CCA 1; CP; CWP; DLB 60
Gurdjieff, G(eorgei) I(vanovich) 1877(?)-1949 **TCLC 71**
    See also CA 157
Gurganus, Allan 1947- **CLC 70; DAM POP**
    See also BEST 90:1; CA 135; CN; CPW; CSW; GLL 1
Gurney, A(lbert) R(amsdell), Jr. 1930- **CLC 32, 50, 54; DAM DRAM**
    See also AMWS 5; CA 77-80; CAD; CANR 32, 64; CD
Gurney, Ivor (Bertie) 1890-1937 **TCLC 33**
    See also BRW 6; CA 167; PAB; RGEL

Gurney, Peter
See Gurney, A(lbert) R(amsdell), Jr.

Guro, Elena 1877-1913 **TCLC 56**

Gustafson, James M(oody) 1925- **CLC 100**
See also CA 25-28R; CANR 37

Gustafson, Ralph (Barker) 1909-1995 **CLC 36**
See also CA 21-24R; CANR 8, 45, 84; CP; DLB 88; RGEL

Gut, Gom
See Simenon, Georges (Jacques Christian)

Guterson, David 1956- **CLC 91**
See also CA 132; CANR 73; MTCW 2; NFS 13

Guthrie, A(lfred) B(ertram), Jr. 1901-1991 **CLC 23**
See also CA 57-60; 134; CANR 24; DLB 6, 212; SATA 62; SATA-Obit 67

Guthrie, Isobel
See Grieve, C(hristopher) M(urray)

Guthrie, Woodrow Wilson 1912-1967
See Guthrie, Woody
See also CA 113; 93-96

Guthrie, Woody CLC 35
See also Guthrie, Woodrow Wilson
See also LAIT 3

Gutierrez Najera, Manuel 1859-1895
See also HLCS 2; LAW

Guy, Rosa (Cuthbert) 1928- **CLC 26**
See also AAYA 4, 37; BW 2; CA 17-20R; CANR 14, 34, 83; CLR 13; DLB 33; JRDA; MAICYA; SATA 14, 62, 122; YAW

Gwendolyn
See Bennett, (Enoch) Arnold

H. D. CLC 3, 8, 14, 31, 34, 73; PC 5
See also Doolittle, Hilda

H. de V.
See Buchan, John

Haavikko, Paavo Juhani 1931- **CLC 18, 34**
See also CA 106

Habbema, Koos
See Heijermans, Herman

Habermas, Juergen 1929- **CLC 104**
See also CA 109; CANR 85; DLB 242

Habermas, Jurgen
See Habermas, Juergen

Hacker, Marilyn 1942- **CLC 5, 9, 23, 72, 91; DAM POET**
See also CA 77-80; CANR 68; CP; CWP; DLB 120; FW; GLL 2

Haeckel, Ernst Heinrich (Philipp August) 1834-1919 **TCLC 83**
See also CA 157

Hafiz c. 1326-1389(?) **CMLC 34**
See also RGWL

Haggard, H(enry) Rider 1856-1925 **TCLC 11**
See also BRWS 3; BYA 4, 5; CA 108; 148; DLB 70, 156, 174, 178; FANT; MTCW 2; RGEL; RHW; SATA 16; SCFW; SFW; SUFW; WLIT 4

Hagiosy, L.
See Larbaud, Valery (Nicolas)

Hagiwara, Sakutaro 1886-1942 **TCLC 60; PC 18**
See also CA 154

Haig, Fenil
See Ford, Ford Madox

Haig-Brown, Roderick (Langmere) 1908-1976 **CLC 21**
See also CA 5-8R; 69-72; CANR 4, 38, 83; CLR 31; CWRI; DLB 88; MAICYA; SATA 12

Hailey, Arthur 1920- **CLC 5; DAM NOV, POP**
See also AITN 2; BEST 90:3; BPFB 2; CA 1-4R; CANR 2, 36, 75; CCA 1; CN; CPW; DLB 88; DLBY 82; MTCW 1, 2

Hailey, Elizabeth Forsythe 1938- **CLC 40**
See also CA 93-96; CAAE 188; CAAS 1; CANR 15, 48; INT CANR-15

Haines, John (Meade) 1924- **CLC 58**
See also CA 17-20R; CANR 13, 34; CSW; DLB 5, 212

Hakluyt, Richard 1552-1616 **LC 31**
See also DLB 136; RGEL

Haldeman, Joe (William) 1943- **CLC 61**
See also Graham, Robert
See also AAYA 38; CA 53-56, 179; CAAE 179; CAAS 25; CANR 6, 70, 72; DLB 8; INT CANR-6; SCFW 2; SFW

Hale, Sarah Josepha (Buell) 1788-1879 **NCLC 75**
See also DLB 1, 42, 73, 243

Halevy, Elie 1870-1937 **TCLC 104**

Haley, Alex(ander Murray Palmer) 1921-1992 **CLC 8, 12, 76; BLC 2; DA; DAB; DAC; DAM MST, MULT, POP**
See also AAYA 26; BPFB 2; BW 2, 3; CA 77-80; 136; CANR 61; CDALBS; CPW; CSW; DA3; DLB 38; LAIT 5; MTCW 1, 2; NFS 9

Haliburton, Thomas Chandler 1796-1865 **NCLC 15**
See also DLB 11, 99; RGEL; RGSF

Hall, Donald (Andrew, Jr.) 1928- **CLC 1, 13, 37, 59, 151; DAM POET**
See also CA 5-8R; CAAS 7; CANR 2, 44, 64, 106; CP; DLB 5; MTCW 1; RGAL; SATA 23, 97

Hall, Frederic Sauser
See Sauser-Hall, Frederic

Hall, James
See Kuttner, Henry

Hall, James Norman 1887-1951 **TCLC 23**
See also CA 123; 173; LAIT 1; RHW 1; SATA 21

Hall, (Marguerite) Radclyffe 1880-1943 **TCLC 12**
See also BRWS 6; CA 110; 150; CANR 83; DLB 191; MTCW 2; RGEL; RHW

Hall, Rodney 1935- **CLC 51**
See also CA 109; CANR 69; CN; CP

Hallam, Arthur Henry 1811-1833 **NCLC 110**
See also DLB 32

Halleck, Fitz-Greene 1790-1867 **NCLC 47**
See also DLB 3, 250; RGAL

Halliday, Michael
See Creasey, John

Halpern, Daniel 1945- **CLC 14**
See also CA 33-36R; CANR 93; CP

Hamburger, Michael (Peter Leopold) 1924- **CLC 5, 14**
See also CA 5-8R; CAAE 196; CAAS 4; CANR 2, 47; CP; DLB 27

Hamill, Pete 1935- **CLC 10**
See also CA 25-28R; CANR 18, 71

Hamilton, Alexander 1755(?)-1804 **NCLC 49**
See also DLB 37

Hamilton, Clive
See Lewis, C(live) S(taples)

Hamilton, Edmond 1904-1977 **CLC 1**
See also CA 1-4R; CANR 3, 84; DLB 8; SATA 118; SFW

Hamilton, Eugene (Jacob) Lee
See Lee-Hamilton, Eugene (Jacob)

Hamilton, Franklin
See Silverberg, Robert

Hamilton, Gail
See Corcoran, Barbara (Asenath)

Hamilton, Mollie
See Kaye, M(ary) M(argaret)

Hamilton, (Anthony Walter) Patrick 1904-1962 **CLC 51**
See also CA 176; 113; DLB 10, 191

Hamilton, Virginia (Esther) 1936-2002 **CLC 26; DAM MULT**
See also AAYA 2, 21; BW 2, 3; BYA 1, 2, 8; CA 25-28R; CANR 20, 37, 73; CLR 1, 11, 40; DLB 33, 52; DLBY 01; INT CANR-20; JRDA; LAIT 5; MAICYA; MAICYAS; MTCW 1, 2; SATA 4, 56, 79, 123; WYA; YAW

Hammett, (Samuel) Dashiell 1894-1961 **CLC 3, 5, 10, 19, 47; SSC 17**
See also AITN 1; AMWS 4; BPFB 2; CA 81-84; CANR 42; CDALB 1929-1941; CMW; DA3; DLB 226; DLBD 6; DLBY 96; LAIT 3; MSW; MTCW 1, 2; RGAL; RGSF

Hammon, Jupiter 1720(?)-1800(?) **NCLC 5; BLC 2; DAM MULT, POET; PC 16**
See also DLB 31, 50

Hammond, Keith
See Kuttner, Henry

Hamner, Earl (Henry), Jr. 1923- **CLC 12**
See also AITN 2; CA 73-76; DLB 6

Hampton, Christopher (James) 1946- **CLC 4**
See also CA 25-28R; CD; DLB 13; MTCW 1

Hamsun, Knut TCLC 2, 14, 49
See also Pedersen, Knut
See also EW 8; RGWL

Handke, Peter 1942- **CLC 5, 8, 10, 15, 38, 134; DAM DRAM, NOV**
See also CA 77-80; CANR 33, 75, 104; CWW 2; DLB 85, 124; MTCW 1, 2

Handy, W(illiam) C(hristopher) 1873-1958 **TCLC 97**
See also BW 3; CA 121; 167

Hanley, James 1901-1985 **CLC 3, 5, 8, 13**
See also CA 73-76; 117; CANR 36; CBD; DLB 191; MTCW 1; RGEL

Hannah, Barry 1942- **CLC 23, 38, 90**
See also BPFB 2; CA 108; 110; CANR 43, 68; CN; CSW; DLB 6, 234; INT CA-110; MTCW 1; RGSF

Hannon, Ezra
See Hunter, Evan

Hansberry, Lorraine (Vivian) 1930-1965 **CLC 17, 62; BLC 2; DA; DAB; DAC; DAM DRAM, MST, MULT; DC 2**
See also AAYA 25; AFAW 1, 2; AMWS 4; BW 1, 3; CA 109; 25-28R; CABS 3; CANR 58; CDALB 1941-1968; DA3; DFS 2; DLB 7, 38; FW; LAIT 4; MTCW 1, 2; RGAL

Hansen, Joseph 1923- **CLC 38**
See also Brock, Rose; Colton, James
See also BPFB 2; CA 29-32R; CAAS 17; CANR 16, 44, 66; CMW; DLB 226; GLL 1; INT CANR-16

Hansen, Martin A(lfred) 1909-1955 **TCLC 32**
See also CA 167; DLB 214

Hansen and Philipson eds. CLC 65

Hanson, Kenneth O(stlin) 1922- **CLC 13**
See also CA 53-56; CANR 7

Hardwick, Elizabeth (Bruce) 1916- **CLC 13; DAM NOV**
See also AMWS 3; CA 5-8R; CANR 3, 32, 70, 100; CN; CSW; DA3; DLB 6; MAWW; MTCW 1, 2

Hardy, Thomas 1840-1928 **TCLC 4, 10, 18, 32, 48, 53, 72; DA; DAB; DAC; DAM MST, NOV, POET; PC 8; SSC 2; WLC**
See also BRW 6; BRWR 1; CA 104; 123; CDBLB 1890-1914; DA3; DLB 18, 135; EXPN; EXPP; LAIT 2; MTCW 1, 2; NFS 3, 11; PFS 3, 4; RGEL; RGSF; WLIT 4

Hare, David 1947- **CLC 29, 58, 136**
See also BRWS 4; CA 97-100; CANR 39, 91; CBD; CD; DFS 4, 7; DLB 13; MTCW 1

Harewood, John
    See Van Druten, John (William)
Harford, Henry
    See Hudson, W(illiam) H(enry)
Hargrave, Leonie
    See Disch, Thomas M(ichael)
Harjo, Joy 1951- **CLC 83; DAM MULT; PC 27**
    See also CA 114; CANR 35, 67, 91; CP; CWP; DLB 120, 175; MTCW 2; NNAL; RGAL
Harlan, Louis R(udolph) 1922- **CLC 34**
    See also CA 21-24R; CANR 25, 55, 80
Harling, Robert 1951(?)- **CLC 53**
    See also CA 147
Harmon, William (Ruth) 1938- **CLC 38**
    See also CA 33-36R; CANR 14, 32, 35; SATA 65
Harper, F. E. W.
    See Harper, Frances Ellen Watkins
Harper, Frances E. W.
    See Harper, Frances Ellen Watkins
Harper, Frances E. Watkins
    See Harper, Frances Ellen Watkins
Harper, Frances Ellen
    See Harper, Frances Ellen Watkins
Harper, Frances Ellen Watkins 1825-1911 **TCLC 14; BLC 2; DAM MULT, POET; PC 21**
    See also AFAW 1, 2; BW 1, 3; CA 111; 125; CANR 79; DLB 50, 221; MAWW; RGAL
Harper, Michael S(teven) 1938- **CLC 7, 22**
    See also AFAW 2; BW 1; CA 33-36R; CANR 24; CP; DLB 41; RGAL
Harper, Mrs. F. E. W.
    See Harper, Frances Ellen Watkins
Harris, Christie (Lucy) Irwin 1907- **CLC 12**
    See also CA 5-8R; CANR 6, 83; CLR 47; DLB 88; JRDA; MAICYA; SAAS 10; SATA 6, 74; SATA-Essay 116
Harris, Frank 1856-1931 **TCLC 24**
    See also CA 109; 150; CANR 80; DLB 156, 197; RGEL
Harris, George Washington 1814-1869 **NCLC 23**
    See also DLB 3, 11, 248; RGAL
Harris, Joel Chandler 1848-1908 **TCLC 2; SSC 19**
    See also CA 104; 137; CANR 80; CLR 49; DLB 11, 23, 42, 78, 91; LAIT 2; MAICYA; RGSF; SATA 100; WCH; YABC 1
Harris, John (Wyndham Parkes Lucas) Beynon 1903-1969
    See Wyndham, John
    See also CA 102; 89-92; CANR 84; SATA 118; SFW
Harris, MacDonald CLC 9
    See also Heiney, Donald (William)
Harris, Mark 1922- **CLC 19**
    See also CA 5-8R; CAAS 3; CANR 2, 55, 83; CN; DLB 2; DLBY 80
Harris, Norman CLC 65
Harris, (Theodore) Wilson 1921- **CLC 25**
    See also BRWS 5; BW 2, 3; CA 65-68; CAAS 16; CANR 11, 27, 69; CN; CP; DLB 117; MTCW 1; RGEL
Harrison, Barbara Grizzuti 1934- **CLC 144**
    See also CA 77-80; CANR 15, 48; INT CANR-15
Harrison, Elizabeth (Allen) Cavanna 1909-2001
    See Cavanna, Betty
    See also CA 9-12R; CANR 6, 27, 85, 104; YAW
Harrison, Harry (Max) 1925- **CLC 42**
    See also CA 1-4R; CANR 5, 21, 84; DLB 8; SATA 4; SCFW 2; SFW

Harrison, James (Thomas) 1937- **CLC 6, 14, 33, 66, 143; SSC 19**
    See also Harrison, Jim
    See also CA 13-16R; CANR 8, 51, 79; CN; CP; DLBY 82; INT CANR-8
Harrison, Jim
    See Harrison, James (Thomas)
    See also AMWS 8; RGAL; TCWW 2
Harrison, Kathryn 1961- **CLC 70, 151**
    See also CA 144; CANR 68
Harrison, Tony 1937- **CLC 43, 129**
    See also BRWS 5; CA 65-68; CANR 44, 98; CBD; CD; CP; DLB 40, 245; MTCW 1; RGEL
Harriss, Will(ard Irvin) 1922- **CLC 34**
    See also CA 111
Harson, Sley
    See Ellison, Harlan (Jay)
Hart, Ellis
    See Ellison, Harlan (Jay)
Hart, Josephine 1942(?)- **CLC 70; DAM POP**
    See also CA 138; CANR 70; CPW
Hart, Moss 1904-1961 **CLC 66; DAM DRAM**
    See also CA 109; 89-92; CANR 84; DFS 1; DLB 7; RGAL
Harte, (Francis) Bret(t) 1836(?)-1902 **TCLC 1, 25; DA; DAC; DAM MST; SSC 8; WLC**
    See also AMWS 2; CA 104; 140; CANR 80; CDALB 1865-1917; DA3; DLB 12, 64, 74, 79, 186; EXPS; LAIT 2; RGAL; RGSF; SATA 26; SSFS 3
Hartley, L(eslie) P(oles) 1895-1972 **CLC 2, 22**
    See also BRWS 7; CA 45-48; 37-40R; CANR 33; DLB 15, 139; HGG; MTCW 1, 2; RGEL; RGSF; SUFW
Hartman, Geoffrey H. 1929- **CLC 27**
    See also CA 117; 125; CANR 79; DLB 67
Hartmann, Sadakichi 1869-1944 **TCLC 73**
    See also CA 157; DLB 54
Hartmann von Aue c. 1170-c. 1210 **CMLC 15**
    See also DLB 138; RGWL
Haruf, Kent 1943- **CLC 34**
    See also CA 149; CANR 91
Harwood, Ronald 1934- **CLC 32; DAM DRAM, MST**
    See also CA 1-4R; CANR 4, 55; CBD; CD; DLB 13
Hasegawa Tatsunosuke
    See Futabatei, Shimei
Hasek, Jaroslav (Matej Frantisek) 1883-1923 **TCLC 4**
    See also CA 104; 129; DLB 215; EW 9; MTCW 1, 2; RGSF; RGWL
Hass, Robert 1941- **CLC 18, 39, 99; PC 16**
    See also AMWS 6; CA 111; CANR 30, 50, 71; CP; DLB 105, 206; RGAL; SATA 94
Hastings, Hudson
    See Kuttner, Henry
Hastings, Selina CLC 44
Hathorne, John 1641-1717 **LC 38**
Hatteras, Amelia
    See Mencken, H(enry) L(ouis)
Hatteras, Owen TCLC 18
    See also Mencken, H(enry) L(ouis); Nathan, George Jean
Hauptmann, Gerhart (Johann Robert) 1862-1946 **TCLC 4; DAM DRAM; SSC 37**
    See also CA 104; 153; DLB 66, 118; EW 8; RGSF; RGWL
Havel, Vaclav 1936- **CLC 25, 58, 65, 123; DAM DRAM; DC 6**
    See also CA 104; CANR 36, 63; CWW 2; DA3; DFS 10; DLB 232; MTCW 1, 2
Haviaras, Stratis CLC 33
    See also Chaviaras, Strates

Hawes, Stephen 1475(?)-1529(?) **LC 17**
    See also DLB 132; RGEL
Hawkes, John (Clendennin Burne, Jr.) 1925-1998 **CLC 1, 2, 3, 4, 7, 9, 14, 15, 27, 49**
    See also BPFB 2; CA 1-4R; 167; CANR 2, 47, 64; CN; DLB 2, 7, 227; DLBY 80, 98; MTCW 1, 2; RGAL
Hawking, S. W.
    See Hawking, Stephen W(illiam)
Hawking, Stephen W(illiam) 1942- **CLC 63, 105**
    See also AAYA 13; BEST 89:1; CA 126; 129; CANR 48; CPW; DA3; MTCW 2
Hawkins, Anthony Hope
    See Hope, Anthony
Hawthorne, Julian 1846-1934 **TCLC 25**
    See also CA 165; HGG
Hawthorne, Nathaniel 1804-1864 **NCLC 2, 10, 17, 23, 39, 79, 95; DA; DAB; DAC; DAM MST, NOV; SSC 3, 29, 39; WLC**
    See also AAYA 18; AMW; AMWR 1; BPFB 2; BYA 3; CDALB 1640-1865; DA3; DLB 1, 74, 183, 223; EXPN; EXPS; HGG; LAIT 1; NFS 1; RGAL; RGSF; SSFS 1, 7, 11; SUFW; WCH; YABC 2
Haxton, Josephine Ayres 1921-
    See Douglas, Ellen
    See also CA 115; CANR 41, 83
Hayaseca y Eizaguirre, Jorge
    See Echegaray (y Eizaguirre), Jose (Maria Waldo)
Hayashi, Fumiko 1904-1951 **TCLC 27**
    See also CA 161; DLB 180
Haycraft, Anna (Margaret) 1932-
    See Ellis, Alice Thomas
    See also CA 122; CANR 85, 90; MTCW 2
Hayden, Robert E(arl) 1913-1980 **CLC 5, 9, 14, 37; BLC 2; DA; DAC; DAM MST, MULT, POET; PC 6**
    See also AFAW 1, 2; AMWS 2; BW 1, 3; CA 69-72; 97-100; CABS 2; CANR 24, 75, 82; CDALB 1941-1968; DLB 5, 76; EXPP; MTCW 1, 2; PFS 1; RGAL; SATA 19; SATA-Obit 26; WP
Hayek, F(riedrich) A(ugust von) 1899-1992 **TCLC 109**
    See also CA 93-96; 137; CANR 20; MTCW 1, 2
Hayford, J(oseph) E(phraim) Casely
    See Casely-Hayford, J(oseph) E(phraim)
Hayman, Ronald 1932- **CLC 44**
    See also CA 25-28R; CANR 18, 50, 88; CD; DLB 155
Hayne, Paul Hamilton 1830-1886 **NCLC 94**
    See also DLB 3, 64, 79, 248; RGAL
Haywood, Eliza (Fowler) 1693(?)-1756 **LC 1, 44**
    See also DLB 39; RGEL
Hazlitt, William 1778-1830 **NCLC 29, 82**
    See also BRW 4; DLB 110, 158; RGEL
Hazzard, Shirley 1931- **CLC 18**
    See also CA 9-12R; CANR 4, 70; CN; DLBY 82; MTCW 1
Head, Bessie 1937-1986 **CLC 25, 67; BLC 2; DAM MULT**
    See also AFW; BW 2, 3; CA 29-32R; 119; CANR 25, 82; DA3; DLB 117, 225; EXPS; FW; MTCW 1, 2; RGSF; SSFS 5, 13; WLIT 2
Headon, (Nicky) Topper 1956(?)- **CLC 30**
Heaney, Seamus (Justin) 1939- **CLC 5, 7, 14, 25, 37, 74, 91; DAB; DAM POET; PC 18; WLCS**
    See also BRWR 1; BRWS 2; CA 85-88; CANR 25, 48, 75, 91; CDBLB 1960 to Present; CP; DA3; DLB 40; DLBY 95; EXPP; MTCW 1, 2; PAB; PFS 2, 5, 8; RGEL; WLIT 4

Hearn, (Patricio) Lafcadio (Tessima Carlos)
1850-1904 **TCLC 9**
See also CA 105; 166; DLB 12, 78, 189;
HGG; RGAL

Hearne, Vicki 1946- **CLC 56**
See also CA 139

Hearon, Shelby 1931- **CLC 63**
See also AITN 2; AMWS 8; CA 25-28R;
CANR 18, 48, 103; CSW

Heat-Moon, William Least CLC 29
See also Trogdon, William (Lewis)
See also AAYA 9

Hebbel, Friedrich 1813-1863 **NCLC 43;**
DAM DRAM
See also DLB 129; EW 6; RGWL

Hebert, Anne 1916-2000 **CLC 4, 13, 29;**
DAC; DAM MST, POET
See also CA 85-88; 187; CANR 69; CCA
1; CWP; CWW 2; DA3; DLB 68; GFL
1789 to the Present; MTCW 1, 2

Hecht, Anthony (Evan) 1923- **CLC 8, 13, 19;**
DAM POET
See also AMWS 10; CA 9-12R; CANR 6;
CP; DLB 5, 169; PFS 6; WP

Hecht, Ben 1894-1964 **CLC 8**
See also CA 85-88; DFS 9; DLB 7, 9, 25,
26, 28, 86; FANT; IDFW 3, 4; RGAL;
TCLC 101

Hedayat, Sadeq 1903-1951 **TCLC 21**
See also CA 120; RGSF

Hegel, Georg Wilhelm Friedrich 1770-1831
NCLC 46
See also DLB 90

Heidegger, Martin 1889-1976 **CLC 24**
See also CA 81-84; 65-68; CANR 34;
MTCW 1, 2

Heidenstam, (Carl Gustaf) Verner von
1859-1940 **TCLC 5**
See also CA 104

Heifner, Jack 1946- **CLC 11**
See also CA 105; CANR 47

Heijermans, Herman 1864-1924 **TCLC 24**
See also CA 123

Heilbrun, Carolyn G(old) 1926- **CLC 25**
See also Cross, Amanda
See also CA 45-48; CANR 1, 28, 58, 94;
CMW; CPW; FW

Hein, Christoph 1944- **CLC 154**
See also CA 158; CWW 2; DLB 124

Heine, Heinrich 1797-1856 **NCLC 4, 54; PC**
25
See also DLB 90; EW 5; RGWL

Heinemann, Larry (Curtiss) 1944- **CLC 50**
See also CA 110; CAAS 21; CANR 31, 81;
DLBD 9; INT CANR-31

Heiney, Donald (William) 1921-1993
See Harris, MacDonald
See also CA 1-4R; 142; CANR 3, 58; FANT

Heinlein, Robert A(nson) 1907-1988 **CLC 1,**
3, 8, 14, 26, 55; DAM POP
See also AAYA 17; BPFB 2; BYA 4, 13;
CA 1-4R; 125; CANR 1, 20, 53; CLR 75;
CPW; DA3; DLB 8; EXPS; JRDA; LAIT
5; MAICYA; MTCW 1, 2; RGAL; SATA
9, 69; SATA-Obit 56; SCFW; SFW; SSFS
7; YAW

Helforth, John
See Doolittle, Hilda

Hellenhofferu, Vojtech Kapristian z
See Hasek, Jaroslav (Matej Frantisek)

Heller, Joseph 1923-1999 **CLC 1, 3, 5, 8, 11,**
36, 63; DA; DAB; DAC; DAM MST,
NOV, POP; WLC
See also AAYA 24; AITN 1; AMWS 4;
BPFB 2; BYA 1; CA 5-8R; 187; CABS 1;
CANR 8, 42, 66; CN; CPW; DA3; DLB
2, 28, 227; DLBY 80; EXPN; INT
CANR-8; LAIT 4; MTCW 1, 2; NFS 1;
RGAL; YAW

Hellman, Lillian (Florence) 1906-1984 **CLC**
2, 4, 8, 14, 18, 34, 44, 52; DAM DRAM;
DC 1; TCLC 119
See also AITN 1, 2; AMWS 1; CA 13-16R;
112; CAD; CANR 33; CWD; DA3; DFS
1, 3; DLB 7, 228; DLBY 84; FW; LAIT
3; MAWW; MTCW 1, 2; RGAL

Helprin, Mark 1947- **CLC 7, 10, 22, 32;**
DAM NOV, POP
See also CA 81-84; CANR 47, 64;
CDALBS; CPW; DA3; DLBY 85; FANT;
MTCW 1, 2

Helvetius, Claude-Adrien 1715-1771 **LC 26**

Helyar, Jane Penelope Josephine 1933-
See Poole, Josephine
See also CA 21-24R; CANR 10, 26; SATA
82

Hemans, Felicia 1793-1835 **NCLC 29, 71**
See also DLB 96; RGEL

Hemingway, Ernest (Miller) 1899-1961 **CLC**
1, 3, 6, 8, 10, 13, 19, 30, 34, 39, 41, 44,
50, 61, 80; DA; DAB; DAC; DAM MST,
NOV; SSC 1, 25, 36, 40; WLC
See also AAYA 19; AMW; AMWR 1; BPFB
2; BYA 2, 3, 13; CA 77-80; CANR 34;
CDALB 1917-1929; DA3; DLB 4, 9, 102,
210; DLBD 1, 15, 16; DLBY 81, 87, 96,
98; EXPN; EXPS; LAIT 3, 4; MTCW 1,
2; NFS 1, 5, 6; RGAL; RGSF; SSFS 1, 6,
8, 9, 11; TCLC 115; WYA

Hempel, Amy 1951- **CLC 39**
See also CA 118; 137; CANR 70; DA3;
DLB 218; EXPS; MTCW 2; SSFS 2

Henderson, F. C.
See Mencken, H(enry) L(ouis)

Henderson, Sylvia
See Ashton-Warner, Sylvia (Constance)

Henderson, Zenna (Chlarson) 1917-1983 **SSC**
29
See also CA 1-4R; 133; CANR 1, 84; DLB
8; SATA 5; SFW

Henkin, Joshua CLC 119
See also CA 161

Henley, Beth CLC 23; DC 6, 14
See also Henley, Elizabeth Becker
See also CABS 3; CAD; CD; CSW; CWD;
DFS 2; DLBY 86; FW

Henley, Elizabeth Becker 1952-
See Henley, Beth
See also CA 107; CANR 32, 73; DA3;
DAM DRAM, MST; MTCW 1, 2

Henley, William Ernest 1849-1903 **TCLC 8**
See also CA 105; DLB 19; RGEL

Hennissart, Martha
See Lathen, Emma
See also CA 85-88; CANR 64

Henry VIII 1491-1547 **LC 10**
See also DLB 132

Henry, O. TCLC 1, 19; SSC 5, 49; WLC
See also Porter, William Sydney
See also AAYA 41; AMWS 2; EXPS;
RGAL; RGSF; SSFS 2

Henry, Patrick 1736-1799 **LC 25**
See also LAIT 1

Henryson, Robert 1430(?)-1506(?) **LC 20**
See also BRWS 7; DLB 146; RGEL

Henschke, Alfred
See Klabund

Hentoff, Nat(han Irving) 1925- **CLC 26**
See also AAYA 4, 42; BYA 6; CA 1-4R;
CAAS 6; CANR 5, 25, 77; CLR 1, 52;
INT CANR-25; JRDA; MAICYA; SATA
42, 69; SATA-Brief 27; WYA; YAW

Heppenstall, (John) Rayner 1911-1981 **CLC**
10
See also CA 1-4R; 103; CANR 29

Heraclitusc. 540B.C.-c. 450B.C. **CMLC 22**
See also DLB 176

Herbert, Frank (Patrick) 1920-1986 **CLC 12,**
23, 35, 44, 85; **DAM POP**
See also AAYA 21; BPFB 2; BYA 4, 14;
CA 53-56; 118; CANR 5, 43; CDALBS;
CPW; DLB 8; INT CANR-5; LAIT 5;
MTCW 1, 2; SATA 9, 37; SATA-Obit 47;
SCFW 2; SFW; YAW

Herbert, George 1593-1633 **LC 24; DAB;**
DAM POET; PC 4
See also BRW 2; BRWR 2; CDBLB Before
1660; DLB 126; EXPP; RGEL; WP

Herbert, Zbigniew 1924-1998 **CLC 9, 43;**
DAM POET
See also CA 89-92; 169; CANR 36, 74;
CWW 2; DLB 232; MTCW 1

Herbst, Josephine (Frey) 1897-1969 **CLC 34**
See also CA 5-8R; 25-28R; DLB 9

Herder, Johann Gottfried von 1744-1803
NCLC 8
See also DLB 97; EW 4

Heredia, Jose Maria 1803-1839
See also HLCS 2; LAW

Hergesheimer, Joseph 1880-1954 **TCLC 11**
See also CA 109; 194; DLB 102, 9; RGAL

Herlihy, James Leo 1927-1993 **CLC 6**
See also CA 1-4R; 143; CAD; CANR 2

Hermogenesfl. c. 175- **CMLC 6**

Hernandez, Jose 1834-1886 **NCLC 17**
See also LAW; RGWL; WLIT 1

Herodotusc. 484B.C.-c. 420B.C. **CMLC 17**
See also AW 1; DLB 176; RGWL

Herrick, Robert 1591-1674 **LC 13; DA;**
DAB; DAC; DAM MST, POP; PC 9
See also BRW 2; DLB 126; EXPP; PFS 13;
RGAL; RGEL; WP

Herring, Guilles
See Somerville, Edith Oenone

Herriot, James CLC 12; DAM POP
See also Wight, James Alfred
See also AAYA 1; BPFB 2; CA 148; CANR
40; LAIT 3; MAICYAS; MTCW 2; SATA
86

Herris, Violet
See Hunt, Violet

Herrmann, Dorothy 1941- **CLC 44**
See also CA 107

Herrmann, Taffy
See Herrmann, Dorothy

Hersey, John (Richard) 1914-1993 **CLC 1, 2,**
7, 9, 40, 81, 97; DAM POP
See also AAYA 29; BPFB 2; CA 17-20R;
140; CANR 33; CDALBS; CPW; DLB 6,
185; MTCW 1, 2; SATA 25; SATA-Obit
76

Herzen, Aleksandr Ivanovich 1812-1870
NCLC 10, 61

Herzl, Theodor 1860-1904 **TCLC 36**
See also CA 168

Herzog, Werner 1942- **CLC 16**
See also CA 89-92

Hesiodc. 8th cent. B.C.- **CMLC 5**
See also AW 1; DLB 176; RGWL

Hesse, Hermann 1877-1962 **CLC 1, 2, 3, 6,**
11, 17, 25, 69; DA; DAB; DAC; DAM
MST, NOV; SSC 9, 49; WLC
See also AAYA 43; BPFB 2; CA 17-18;
CAP 2; DA3; DLB 66; EW 9; EXPN;
LAIT 1; MTCW 1, 2; NFS 6; RGWL;
SATA 50

Hewes, Cady
See De Voto, Bernard (Augustine)

Heyen, William 1940- **CLC 13, 18**
See also CA 33-36R; CAAS 9; CANR 98;
CP; DLB 5

Heyerdahl, Thor 1914- **CLC 26**
See also CA 5-8R; CANR 5, 22, 66, 73;
LAIT 4; MTCW 1, 2; SATA 2, 52

Heym, Georg (Theodor Franz Arthur)
1887-1912 **TCLC 9**
See also CA 106; 181

Heym, Stefan 1913- **CLC 41**
See also CA 9-12R; CANR 4; CWW 2;
DLB 69

Heyse, Paul (Johann Ludwig von) 1830-1914
TCLC 8
See also CA 104; DLB 129

Heyward, (Edwin) DuBose 1885-1940 **TCLC 59**
See also CA 108; 157; DLB 7, 9, 45, 249;
SATA 21

Heywood, John 1497(?)-1580(?) **LC 65**
See also DLB 136; RGEL

Hibbert, Eleanor Alice Burford 1906-1993
CLC 7; DAM POP
See also Holt, Victoria
See also BEST 90:4; CA 17-20R; 140;
CANR 9, 28, 59; CMW; CPW; MTCW 2;
RHW; SATA 2; SATA-Obit 74

Hichens, Robert (Smythe) 1864-1950 **TCLC 64**
See also CA 162; DLB 153; HGG; RHW;
SUFW

Higgins, George V(incent) 1939-1999 **CLC 4, 7, 10, 18**
See also BPFB 2; CA 77-80; 186; CAAS 5;
CANR 17, 51, 89, 96; CMW; CN; DLB
2; DLBY 81, 98; INT CANR-17; MSW;
MTCW 1

Higginson, Thomas Wentworth 1823-1911
TCLC 36
See also CA 162; DLB 1, 64, 243

Higgonet, Margaret ed. CLC 65

Highet, Helen
See MacInnes, Helen (Clark)

Highsmith, (Mary) Patricia 1921-1995 **CLC 2, 4, 14, 42, 102; DAM NOV, POP**
See also Morgan, Claire
See also BRWS 5; CA 1-4R; 147; CANR 1,
20, 48, 62; CMW; CPW; DA3; MSW;
MTCW 1, 2

Highwater, Jamake (Mamake) 1942(?)-2001
CLC 12
See also AAYA 7; BPFB 2; BYA 4; CA 65-
68; CAAS 7; CANR 10, 34, 84; CLR 17;
CWRI; DLB 52; DLBY 85; JRDA; MAI-
CYA; SATA 32, 69; SATA-Brief 30

Highway, Tomson 1951- **CLC 92; DAC; DAM MULT**
See also CA 151; CANR 75; CCA 1; CD;
DFS 2; MTCW 2; NNAL

Hijuelos, Oscar 1951- **CLC 65; DAM MULT, POP; HLC 1**
See also AAYA 25; AMWS 8; BEST 90:1;
CA 123; CANR 50, 75; CPW; DA3; DLB
145; HW 1, 2; MTCW 2; RGAL; WLIT 1

Hikmet, Nazim 1902(?)-1963 **CLC 40**
See also CA 141; 93-96

Hildegard von Bingen 1098-1179 **CMLC 20**
See also DLB 148

Hildesheimer, Wolfgang 1916-1991 **CLC 49**
See also CA 101; 135; DLB 69, 124

Hill, Geoffrey (William) 1932- **CLC 5, 8, 18, 45; DAM POET**
See also BRWS 5; CA 81-84; CANR 21,
89; CDBLB 1960 to Present; CP; DLB
40; MTCW 1; RGEL

Hill, George Roy 1921- **CLC 26**
See also CA 110; 122

Hill, John
See Koontz, Dean R(ay)

Hill, Susan (Elizabeth) 1942- **CLC 4, 113; DAB; DAM MST, NOV**
See also CA 33-36R; CANR 29, 69; CN;
DLB 14, 139; HGG; MTCW 1; RHW

Hillard, Asa G. III CLC 70

Hillerman, Tony 1925- **CLC 62; DAM POP**
See also AAYA 40; BEST 89:1; BPFB 2;
CA 29-32R; CANR 21, 42, 65, 97; CMW;
CPW; DA3; DLB 206; MSW; RGAL;
SATA 6; TCWW 2; YAW

Hillesum, Etty 1914-1943 **TCLC 49**
See also CA 137

Hilliard, Noel (Harvey) 1929-1996 **CLC 15**
See also CA 9-12R; CANR 7, 69; CN

Hillis, Rick 1956- **CLC 66**
See also CA 134

Hilton, James 1900-1954 **TCLC 21**
See also CA 108; 169; DLB 34, 77; FANT;
SATA 34

Himes, Chester (Bomar) 1909-1984 **CLC 2, 4, 7, 18, 58, 108; BLC 2; DAM MULT**
See also AFAW 2; BPFB 2; BW 2; CA 25-
28R; 114; CANR 22, 89; CMW; DLB 2,
76, 143, 226; MSW; MTCW 1, 2; RGAL

Hinde, Thomas CLC 6, 11
See also Chitty, Thomas Willes

Hine, (William) Daryl 1936- **CLC 15**
See also CA 1-4R; CAAS 15; CANR 1, 20;
CP; DLB 60

Hinkson, Katharine Tynan
See Tynan, Katharine

Hinojosa(-Smith), Rolando (R.) 1929-
See also CA 131; CAAS 16; CANR 62;
DAM MULT; DLB 82; HLC 1; HW 1, 2;
MTCW 2; RGAL

Hinton, S(usan) E(loise) 1950- **CLC 30, 111; DA; DAB; DAC; DAM MST, NOV**
See also AAYA 2, 33; BPFB 2; BYA 2, 3;
CA 81-84; CANR 32, 62, 92; CDALBS;
CLR 3, 23; CPW; DA3; JRDA; LAIT 5;
MAICYA; MTCW 1, 2; NFS 5, 9; SATA
19, 58, 115; WYA; YAW

Hippius, Zinaida TCLC 9
See also Gippius, Zinaida (Nikolayevna)

Hiraoka, Kimitake 1925-1970
See Mishima, Yukio
See also CA 97-100; 29-32R; DA3; DAM
DRAM; MTCW 1, 2

Hirsch, E(ric) D(onald), Jr. 1928- **CLC 79**
See also CA 25-28R; CANR 27, 51; DLB
67; INT CANR-27; MTCW 1

Hirsch, Edward 1950- **CLC 31, 50**
See also CA 104; CANR 20, 42, 102; CP;
DLB 120

Hitchcock, Alfred (Joseph) 1899-1980 **CLC 16**
See also AAYA 22; CA 159; 97-100; SATA
27; SATA-Obit 24

Hitler, Adolf 1889-1945 **TCLC 53**
See also CA 117; 147

Hoagland, Edward 1932- **CLC 28**
See also ANW; CA 1-4R; CANR 2, 31, 57;
CN; DLB 6; SATA 51; TCWW 2

Hoban, Russell (Conwell) 1925- **CLC 7, 25; DAM NOV**
See also BPFB 2; CA 5-8R; CANR 23, 37,
66; CLR 3, 69; CN; CWRI; DLB 52;
FANT; MAICYA; MTCW 1, 2; SATA 1,
40, 78; SFW

Hobbes, Thomas 1588-1679 **LC 36**
See also DLB 151, 252; RGEL

Hobbs, Perry
See Blackmur, R(ichard) P(almer)

Hobson, Laura Z(ametkin) 1900-1986 **CLC 7, 25**
See also Field, Peter
See also BPFB 2; CA 17-20R; 118; CANR
55; DLB 28; SATA 52

Hoccleve, Thomasc. 1368-c. 1437 **LC 75**
See also DLB 146; RGEL

Hoch, Edward D(entinger) 1930-
See Queen, Ellery
See also CA 29-32R; CANR 11, 27, 51, 97;
CMW; SFW

Hochhuth, Rolf 1931- **CLC 4, 11, 18; DAM DRAM**
See also CA 5-8R; CANR 33, 75; CWW 2;
DLB 124; MTCW 1, 2

Hochman, Sandra 1936- **CLC 3, 8**
See also CA 5-8R; DLB 5

Hochwaelder, Fritz 1911-1986 **CLC 36; DAM DRAM**
See also Hochwalder, Fritz
See also CA 29-32R; 120; CANR 42;
MTCW 1

Hochwalder, Fritz
See Hochwaelder, Fritz
See also RGWL

Hocking, Mary (Eunice) 1921- **CLC 13**
See also CA 101; CANR 18, 40

Hodgins, Jack 1938- **CLC 23**
See also CA 93-96; CN; DLB 60

Hodgson, William Hope 1877(?)-1918 **TCLC 13**
See also CA 111; 164; CMW; DLB 70, 153,
156, 178; HGG; MTCW 2; SFW; SUFW

Hoeg, Peter 1957- **CLC 95, 156**
See also CA 151; CANR 75; CMW; DA3;
DLB 214; MTCW 2

Hoffman, Alice 1952- **CLC 51; DAM NOV**
See also AAYA 37; AMWS 10; CA 77-80;
CANR 34, 66, 100; CN; CPW; MTCW 1,
2

Hoffman, Daniel (Gerard) 1923- **CLC 6, 13, 23**
See also CA 1-4R; CANR 4; CP; DLB 5

Hoffman, Stanley 1944- **CLC 5**
See also CA 77-80

Hoffman, William 1925- **CLC 141**
See also CA 21-24R; CANR 9, 103; CSW;
DLB 234

Hoffman, William M(oses) 1939- **CLC 40**
See also CA 57-60; CANR 11, 71

Hoffmann, E(rnst) T(heodor) A(madeus) 1776-1822 **NCLC 2; SSC 13**
See also DLB 90; EW 5; RGSF; RGWL;
SATA 27; SUFW; WCH

Hofmann, Gert 1931- **CLC 54**
See also CA 128

Hofmannsthal, Hugo von 1874-1929 **TCLC 11; DAM DRAM; DC 4**
See also CA 106; 153; DFS 12; DLB 81,
118; EW 9; RGWL

Hogan, Linda 1947- **CLC 73; DAM MULT; PC 35**
See also AMWS 4; ANW; BYA 12; CA 120;
CANR 45, 73; CWP; DLB 175; NNAL;
TCWW 2

Hogarth, Charles
See Creasey, John

Hogarth, Emmett
See Polonsky, Abraham (Lincoln)

Hogg, James 1770-1835 **NCLC 4, 109**
See also DLB 93, 116, 159; HGG; RGEL;
SUFW

Holbach, Paul Henri Thiry Baron 1723-1789
LC 14

Holberg, Ludvig 1684-1754 **LC 6**
See also RGWL

Holcroft, Thomas 1745-1809 **NCLC 85**
See also DLB 39, 89, 158; RGEL

Holden, Ursula 1921- **CLC 18**
See also CA 101; CAAS 8; CANR 22

Holderlin, (Johann Christian) Friedrich 1770-1843 **NCLC 16; PC 4**
See also DLB 90; EW 5; RGWL

Holdstock, Robert
See Holdstock, Robert P.

Holdstock, Robert P. 1948- **CLC 39**
See also CA 131; CANR 81; FANT; HGG;
SFW

Holinshed, Raphaelfl. 1580- **LC 69**
See also DLB 167; RGEL

Kirk, Russell (Amos) 1918-1994 **TCLC 119**
See also AITN 1; CA 1-4R; 145; CAAS 9;
CANR 1, 20, 60; HGG; INT CANR-20;
MTCW 1, 2

Kirkland, Caroline M. 1801-1864 **NCLC 85**
See also DLB 3, 73, 74, 250, 254; DLBD
13

Kirkup, James 1918- **CLC 1**
See also CA 1-4R; CAAS 4; CANR 2; DLB
27; SATA 12

Kirkwood, James 1930(?)-1989 **CLC 9**
See also AITN 2; CA 1-4R; 128; CANR 6,
40; GLL 2

Kirshner, Sidney
See Kingsley, Sidney

Kis, Danilo 1935-1989 **CLC 57**
See also CA 109; 118; 129; CANR 61; DLB
181; MTCW 1; RGSF; RGWL

Kissinger, Henry A(lfred) 1923- **CLC 137**
See also CA 1-4R; CANR 2, 33, 66; MTCW
1

Kivi, Aleksis 1834-1872 **NCLC 30**

Kizer, Carolyn (Ashley) 1925- **CLC 15, 39,
80; DAM POET**
See also CA 65-68; CAAS 5; CANR 24,
70; CP; CWP; DLB 5, 169; MTCW 2

Klabund 1890-1928 **TCLC 44**
See also CA 162; DLB 66

Klappert, Peter 1942- **CLC 57**
See also CA 33-36R; CSW; DLB 5

Klein, A(braham) M(oses) 1909-1972 **CLC
19; DAB; DAC; DAM MST**
See also CA 101; 37-40R; DLB 68; RGEL

Klein, Joe CLC 154
See also Klein, Joseph

Klein, Joseph 1946-
See Klein, Joe
See also CA 85-88; CANR 55

Klein, Norma 1938-1989 **CLC 30**
See also AAYA 2, 35; BPFB 2; BYA 6, 7,
8; CA 41-44R; 128; CANR 15, 37; CLR
2, 19; INT CANR-15; JRDA; MAICYA;
SAAS 1; SATA 7, 57; WYA; YAW

Klein, T(heodore) E(ibon) D(onald) 1947-
CLC 34
See also CA 119; CANR 44, 75; HGG

Kleist, Heinrich von 1777-1811 **NCLC 2, 37;
DAM DRAM; SSC 22**
See also DLB 90; EW 5; RGSF; RGWL

Klima, Ivan 1931- **CLC 56; DAM NOV**
See also CA 25-28R; CANR 17, 50, 91;
CWW 2; DLB 232

Klimentov, Andrei Platonovich 1899-1951
TCLC 14; SSC 42
See also CA 108

Klinger, Friedrich Maximilian von
1752-1831 **NCLC 1**
See also DLB 94

Klingsor the Magician
See Hartmann, Sadakichi

Klopstock, Friedrich Gottlieb 1724-1803
NCLC 11
See also DLB 97; EW 4; RGWL

Knapp, Caroline 1959- **CLC 99**
See also CA 154

Knebel, Fletcher 1911-1993 **CLC 14**
See also AITN 1; CA 1-4R; 140; CAAS 3;
CANR 1, 36; SATA 36; SATA-Obit 75

Knickerbocker, Diedrich
See Irving, Washington

Knight, Etheridge 1931-1991 **CLC 40; BLC
2; DAM POET; PC 14**
See also BW 1, 3; CA 21-24R; 133; CANR
23, 82; DLB 41; MTCW 1; RGAL

Knight, Sarah Kemble 1666-1727 **LC 7**
See also DLB 24, 200

Knister, Raymond 1899-1932 **TCLC 56**
See also CA 186; DLB 68; RGEL

Knowles, John 1926-2001 **CLC 1, 4, 10, 26;**
DA; DAC; DAM MST, NOV
See also AAYA 10; BPFB 2; BYA 3; CA
17-20R; CANR 40, 74, 76; CDALB 1968-
1988; CN; DLB 6; EXPN; MTCW 1, 2;
NFS 2; RGAL; SATA 8, 89; YAW

Knox, Calvin M.
See Silverberg, Robert

Knox, John c. 1505-1572 **LC 37**
See also DLB 132

Knye, Cassandra
See Disch, Thomas M(ichael)

Koch, C(hristopher) J(ohn) 1932- **CLC 42**
See also CA 127; CANR 84; CN

Koch, Christopher
See Koch, C(hristopher) J(ohn)

Koch, Kenneth 1925- **CLC 5, 8, 44; DAM
POET**
See also CA 1-4R; CAD; CANR 6, 36, 57,
97; CD; CP; DLB 5; INT CANR-36;
MTCW 2; SATA 65; WP

Kochanowski, Jan 1530-1584 **LC 10**
See also RGWL

Kock, Charles Paul de 1794-1871 **NCLC 16**

Koda Rohan
See Koda Shigeyuki

Koda Shigeyuki 1867-1947 **TCLC 22**
See also CA 121; 183; DLB 180

Koestler, Arthur 1905-1983 **CLC 1, 3, 6, 8,
15, 33**
See also BRWS 1; CA 1-4R; 109; CANR 1,
33; CDBLB 1945-1960; DLBY 83;
MTCW 1, 2; RGEL

Kogawa, Joy Nozomi 1935- **CLC 78, 129;
DAC; DAM MST, MULT**
See also CA 101; CANR 19, 62; CN; CWP;
FW; MTCW 2; NFS 3; SATA 99

Kohout, Pavel 1928- **CLC 13**
See also CA 45-48; CANR 3

Koizumi, Yakumo
See Hearn, (Patricio) Lafcadio (Tessima
Carlos)

Kolmar, Gertrud 1894-1943 **TCLC 40**
See also CA 167

Komunyakaa, Yusef 1947- **CLC 86, 94;
BLCS**
See also AFAW 2; CA 147; CANR 83; CP;
CSW; DLB 120; PFS 5; RGAL

Konrad, George
See Konrad, Gyorgy
See also CWW 2

Konrad, Gyorgy 1933- **CLC 4, 10, 73**
See also Konrad, George
See also CA 85-88; CANR 97; CWW 2;
DLB 232

Konwicki, Tadeusz 1926- **CLC 8, 28, 54, 117**
See also CA 101; CAAS 9; CANR 39, 59;
CWW 2; DLB 232; IDFW 3; MTCW 1

Koontz, Dean R(ay) 1945- **CLC 78; DAM
NOV, POP**
See also AAYA 9, 31; BEST 89:3, 90:2; CA
108; CANR 19, 36, 52, 95; CMW; CPW;
DA3; HGG; MTCW 1; SATA 92; SFW;
YAW

Kopernik, Mikolaj
See Copernicus, Nicolaus

Kopit, Arthur (Lee) 1937- **CLC 1, 18, 33;
DAM DRAM**
See also AITN 1; CA 81-84; CABS 3; CD;
DFS 7; DLB 7; MTCW 1; RGAL

Kops, Bernard 1926- **CLC 4**
See also CA 5-8R; CANR 84; CBD; CN;
CP; DLB 13

Kornbluth, C(yril) M. 1923-1958 **TCLC 8**
See also CA 105; 160; DLB 8; SFW

Korolenko, V. G.
See Korolenko, Vladimir Galaktionovich

Korolenko, Vladimir
See Korolenko, Vladimir Galaktionovich

Korolenko, Vladimir G.
See Korolenko, Vladimir Galaktionovich

Korolenko, Vladimir Galaktionovich
1853-1921 **TCLC 22**
See also CA 121

Korzybski, Alfred (Habdank Skarbek)
1879-1950 **TCLC 61**
See also CA 123; 160

Kosinski, Jerzy (Nikodem) 1933-1991 **CLC
1, 2, 3, 6, 10, 15, 53, 70; DAM NOV**
See also AMWS 7; BPFB 2; CA 17-20R;
134; CANR 9, 46; DA3; DLB 2; DLBY
82; HGG; MTCW 1, 2; NFS 12; RGAL

Kostelanetz, Richard (Cory) 1940- **CLC 28**
See also CA 13-16R; CAAS 8; CANR 38,
77; CN; CP

Kotlowitz, Robert 1924- **CLC 4**
See also CA 33-36R; CANR 36

Kotzebue, August (Friedrich Ferdinand) von
1761-1819 **NCLC 25**
See also DLB 94

Kotzwinkle, William 1938- **CLC 5, 14, 35**
See also BPFB 2; CA 45-48; CANR 3, 44,
84; CLR 6; DLB 173; FANT; MAICYA;
SATA 24, 70; SFW; YAW

Kowna, Stancy
See Szymborska, Wislawa

Kozol, Jonathan 1936- **CLC 17**
See also CA 61-64; CANR 16, 45, 96

Kozoll, Michael 1940(?)- **CLC 35**

Kramer, Kathryn 19(?)- **CLC 34**

Kramer, Larry 1935- **CLC 42; DAM POP;
DC 8**
See also CA 124; 126; CANR 60; DLB 249;
GLL 1

Krasicki, Ignacy 1735-1801 **NCLC 8**

Krasinski, Zygmunt 1812-1859 **NCLC 4**
See also RGWL

Kraus, Karl 1874-1936 **TCLC 5**
See also CA 104; DLB 118

Kreve (Mickevicius), Vincas 1882-1954
TCLC 27
See also CA 170; DLB 220

Kristeva, Julia 1941- **CLC 77, 140**
See also CA 154; CANR 99; DLB 242; FW

Kristofferson, Kris 1936- **CLC 26**
See also CA 104

Krizanc, John 1956- **CLC 57**
See also CA 187

Krleza, Miroslav 1893-1981 **CLC 8, 114**
See also CA 97-100; 105; CANR 50; DLB
147; EW 11; RGWL

Kroetsch, Robert 1927- **CLC 5, 23, 57, 132;
DAC; DAM POET**
See also CA 17-20R; CANR 8, 38; CCA 1;
CN; CP; DLB 53; MTCW 1

Kroetz, Franz
See Kroetz, Franz Xaver

Kroetz, Franz Xaver 1946- **CLC 41**
See also CA 130

Kroker, Arthur (W.) 1945- **CLC 77**
See also CA 161

Kropotkin, Peter (Aleksieevich) 1842-1921
TCLC 36
See also CA 119

Krotkov, Yuri 1917-1981 **CLC 19**
See also CA 102

Krumb
See Crumb, R(obert)

Krumgold, Joseph (Quincy) 1908-1980 **CLC
12**
See also BYA 1, 2; CA 9-12R; 101; CANR
7; MAICYA; SATA 1, 48; SATA-Obit 23;
YAW

Krumwitz
See Crumb, R(obert)

Krutch, Joseph Wood 1893-1970 **CLC 24**
See also ANW; CA 1-4R; 25-28R; CANR
4; DLB 63, 206

Krutzch, Gus
See Eliot, T(homas) S(tearns)
Krylov, Ivan Andreevich 1768(?)-1844 **NCLC 1**
See also DLB 150
Kubin, Alfred (Leopold Isidor) 1877-1959 **TCLC 23**
See also CA 112; 149; CANR 104; DLB 81
Kubrick, Stanley 1928-1999 **CLC 16**
See also AAYA 30; CA 81-84; 177; CANR 33; DLB 26; TCLC 112
Kueng, Hans 1928-
See Kung, Hans
See also CA 53-56; CANR 66; MTCW 1, 2
Kumin, Maxine (Winokur) 1925- **CLC 5, 13, 28; DAM POET; PC 15**
See also AITN 2; AMWS 4; ANW; CA 1-4R; CAAS 8; CANR 1, 21, 69; CP; CWP; DA3; DLB 5; EXPP; MTCW 1, 2; PAB; SATA 12
Kundera, Milan 1929- **CLC 4, 9, 19, 32, 68, 115, 135; DAM NOV; SSC 24**
See also AAYA 2; BPFB 2; CA 85-88; CANR 19, 52, 74; CWW 2; DA3; DLB 232; EW 13; MTCW 1, 2; RGSF; SSFS 10
Kunene, Mazisi (Raymond) 1930- **CLC 85**
See also BW 1, 3; CA 125; CANR 81; CP 7; DLB 117
Kung, Hans CLC 130
See also Kueng, Hans
Kunikida Doppo 1869(?)-1908
See Doppo, Kunikida
See also DLB 180
Kunitz, Stanley (Jasspon) 1905- **CLC 6, 11, 14, 148; PC 19**
See also AMWS 3; CA 41-44R; CANR 26, 57, 98; CP; DA3; DLB 48; INT CANR-26; MTCW 1, 2; PFS 11; RGAL
Kunze, Reiner 1933- **CLC 10**
See also CA 93-96; CWW 2; DLB 75
Kuprin, Aleksander Ivanovich 1870-1938 **TCLC 5**
See also CA 104; 182
Kureishi, Hanif 1954(?)- **CLC 64, 135**
See also CA 139; CBD; CD; CN; DLB 194, 245; GLL 2; IDFW 4; WLIT 4
Kurosawa, Akira 1910-1998 **CLC 16, 119; DAM MULT**
See also AAYA 11; CA 101; 170; CANR 46
Kushner, Tony 1957(?)- **CLC 81; DAM DRAM; DC 10**
See also AMWS 9; CA 144; CAD; CANR 74; CD; DA3; DFS 5; DLB 228; GLL 1; LAIT 5; MTCW 2; RGAL
Kuttner, Henry 1915-1958 **TCLC 10**
See also CA 107; 157; DLB 8; FANT; SCFW 2; SFW
Kuzma, Greg 1944- **CLC 7**
See also CA 33-36R; CANR 70
Kuzmin, Mikhail 1872(?)-1936 **TCLC 40**
See also CA 170
Kyd, Thomas 1558-1594 **LC 22; DAM DRAM; DC 3**
See also BRW 1; DLB 62; IDTP; RGEL; TEA; WLIT 3
Kyprianos, Iossif
See Samarakis, Antonis
Labrunie, Gerard
See Nerval, Gerard de
La Bruyere, Jean de 1645-1696 **LC 17**
See also EW 3; GFL Beginnings to 1789
Lacan, Jacques (Marie Emile) 1901-1981 **CLC 75**
See also CA 121; 104
Laclos, Pierre Ambroise Francois 1741-1803 **NCLC 4, 87**
See also EW 4; GFL Beginnings to 1789; RGWL

Lacolere, Francois
See Aragon, Louis
La Colere, Francois
See Aragon, Louis
La Deshabilleuse
See Simenon, Georges (Jacques Christian)
Lady Gregory
See Gregory, Lady Isabella Augusta (Persse)
Lady of Quality, A
See Bagnold, Enid
La Fayette, Marie-(Madelaine Pioche de la Vergne) 1634-1693 **LC 2**
See also GFL Beginnings to 1789; RGWL
Lafayette, Rene
See Hubbard, L(afayette) Ron(ald)
La Fontaine, Jean de 1621-1695 **LC 50**
See also EW 3; GFL Beginnings to 1789; MAICYA; RGWL; SATA 18
Laforgue, Jules 1860-1887 **NCLC 5, 53; PC 14; SSC 20**
See also DLB 217; EW 7; GFL 1789 to the Present; RGWL
Layamon
See Layamon
See also DLB 146
Lagerkvist, Paer (Fabian) 1891-1974 **CLC 7, 10, 13, 54; DAM DRAM, NOV**
See also Lagerkvist, Par
See also CA 85-88; 49-52; DA3; MTCW 1, 2
Lagerkvist, Par SSC 12
See also Lagerkvist, Paer (Fabian)
See also EW 10; MTCW 2; RGSF; RGWL
Lagerloef, Selma (Ottiliana Lovisa) 1858-1940 **TCLC 4, 36**
See also Lagerlof, Selma (Ottiliana Lovisa)
See also CA 108; MTCW 2; SATA 15
Lagerlof, Selma (Ottiliana Lovisa)
See Lagerloef, Selma (Ottiliana Lovisa)
See also CLR 7; SATA 15
La Guma, (Justin) Alex(ander) 1925-1985 **CLC 19; BLCS; DAM NOV**
See also AFW; BW 1, 3; CA 49-52; 118; CANR 25, 81; DLB 117, 225; MTCW 1, 2; WLIT 2
Laidlaw, A. K.
See Grieve, C(hristopher) M(urray)
Lainez, Manuel Mujica
See Mujica Lainez, Manuel
See also HW 1
Laing, R(onald) D(avid) 1927-1989 **CLC 95**
See also CA 107; 129; CANR 34; MTCW 1
Lamartine, Alphonse (Marie Louis Prat) de 1790-1869 **NCLC 11; DAM POET; PC 16**
See also DLB 217; GFL 1789 to the Present; RGWL
Lamb, Charles 1775-1834 **NCLC 10; DA; DAB; DAC; DAM MST; WLC**
See also BRW 4; CDBLB 1789-1832; DLB 93, 107, 163; RGEL; SATA 17
Lamb, Lady Caroline 1785-1828 **NCLC 38**
See also DLB 116
Lamming, George (William) 1927- **CLC 2, 4, 66, 144; BLC 2; DAM MULT**
See also BW 2, 3; CA 85-88; CANR 26, 76; DLB 125; MTCW 1, 2
L'Amour, Louis (Dearborn) 1908-1988 **CLC 25, 55; DAM NOV, POP**
See also Burns, Tex; Mayo, Jim
See also AAYA 16; AITN 2; BEST 89:2; BPFB 2; CA 1-4R; 125; CANR 3, 25, 40; CPW; DA3; DLB 206; DLBY 80; MTCW 1, 2; RGAL
Lampedusa, Giuseppe (Tomasi) di TCLC 13
See also Tomasi di Lampedusa, Giuseppe
See also CA 164; EW 11; MTCW 2; RGWL
Lampman, Archibald 1861-1899 **NCLC 25**
See also DLB 92; RGEL

Lancaster, Bruce 1896-1963 **CLC 36**
See also CA 9-10; CANR 70; CAP 1; SATA 9
Lanchester, John CLC 99
See also CA 194
Landau, Mark Alexandrovich
See Aldanov, Mark (Alexandrovich)
Landau-Aldanov, Mark Alexandrovich
See Aldanov, Mark (Alexandrovich)
Landis, Jerry
See Simon, Paul (Frederick)
Landis, John 1950- **CLC 26**
See also CA 112; 122
Landolfi, Tommaso 1908-1979 **CLC 11, 49**
See also CA 127; 117; DLB 177
Landon, Letitia Elizabeth 1802-1838 **NCLC 15**
See also DLB 96
Landor, Walter Savage 1775-1864 **NCLC 14**
See also BRW 4; DLB 93, 107; RGEL
Landwirth, Heinz 1927-
See Lind, Jakov
See also CA 9-12R; CANR 7
Lane, Patrick 1939- **CLC 25; DAM POET**
See also CA 97-100; CANR 54; CP; DLB 53; INT 97-100
Lang, Andrew 1844-1912 **TCLC 16**
See also CA 114; 137; CANR 85; DLB 98, 141, 184; FANT; MAICYA; RGEL; SATA 16; WCH
Lang, Fritz 1890-1976 **CLC 20, 103**
See also CA 77-80; 69-72; CANR 30
Lange, John
See Crichton, (John) Michael
Langer, Elinor 1939- **CLC 34**
See also CA 121
Langland, William 1332(?)-1400(?) **LC 19; DA; DAB; DAC; DAM MST, POET**
See also BRW 1; DLB 146; RGEL; WLIT 3
Langstaff, Launcelot
See Irving, Washington
Lanier, Sidney 1842-1881 **NCLC 6; DAM POET**
See also AMWS 1; DLB 64; DLBD 13; EXPP; MAICYA; PFS 14; RGAL; SATA 18
Lanyer, Aemilia 1569-1645 **LC 10, 30**
See also DLB 121
Lao-Tzu
See Lao Tzu
Lao Tzu c. 6th cent. B.C.-3rd cent. B.C. **CMLC 7**
Lapine, James (Elliot) 1949- **CLC 39**
See also CA 123; 130; CANR 54; INT 130
Larbaud, Valery (Nicolas) 1881-1957 **TCLC 9**
See also CA 106; 152; GFL 1789 to the Present
Lardner, Ring
See Lardner, Ring(gold) W(ilmer)
See also BPFB 2; CDALB 1917-1929; DLB 11, 25, 86, 171; DLBD 16; RGAL; RGSF
Lardner, Ring W., Jr.
See Lardner, Ring(gold) W(ilmer)
Lardner, Ring(gold) W(ilmer) 1885-1933 **TCLC 2, 14; SSC 32**
See also Lardner, Ring
See also AMW; CA 104; 131; MTCW 1, 2
Laredo, Betty
See Codrescu, Andrei
Larkin, Maia
See Wojciechowska, Maia (Teresa)
Larkin, Philip (Arthur) 1922-1985 **CLC 3, 5, 8, 9, 13, 18, 33, 39, 64; DAB; DAM**

MST, POET; PC 21
See also BRWS 1; CA 5-8R; 117; CANR 24, 62; CDBLB 1960 to Present; DA3; DLB 27; MTCW 1, 2; PFS 3, 4, 12; RGEL

Larra (y Sanchez de Castro), Mariano Jose de 1809-1837 NCLC 17

Larsen, Eric 1941- CLC 55
See also CA 132

Larsen, Nella 1893-1963 CLC 37; BLC 2; DAM MULT
See also AFAW 1, 2; BW 1; CA 125; CANR 83; DLB 51; FW

Larson, Charles R(aymond) 1938- CLC 31
See also CA 53-56; CANR 4

Larson, Jonathan 1961-1996 CLC 99
See also AAYA 28; CA 156

Las Casas, Bartolome de 1474-1566 LC 31; HLCS
See also Casas, Bartolome de las
See also LAW

Lasch, Christopher 1932-1994 CLC 102
See also CA 73-76; 144; CANR 25; DLB 246; MTCW 1, 2

Lasker-Schueler, Else 1869-1945 TCLC 57
See also CA 183; DLB 66, 124

Laski, Harold J(oseph) 1893-1950 TCLC 79
See also CA 188

Latham, Jean Lee 1902-1995 CLC 12
See also AITN 1; BYA 1; CA 5-8R; CANR 7, 84; CLR 50; MAICYA; SATA 2, 68; YAW

Latham, Mavis
See Clark, Mavis Thorpe

Lathen, Emma CLC 2
See also Hennissart, Martha; Latsis, Mary J(ane)
See also BPFB 2; CMW

Lathrop, Francis
See Leiber, Fritz (Reuter, Jr.)

Latsis, Mary J(ane) 1927(?)-1997
See Lathen, Emma
See also CA 85-88; 162; CMW

Lattimore, Richmond (Alexander) 1906-1984 CLC 3
See also CA 1-4R; 112; CANR 1

Laughlin, James 1914-1997 CLC 49
See also CA 21-24R; 162; CAAS 22; CANR 9, 47; CP; DLB 48; DLBY 96, 97

Laurence, (Jean) Margaret (Wemyss) 1926-1987 CLC 3, 6, 13, 50, 62; DAC; DAM MST; SSC 7
See also BYA 13; CA 5-8R; 121; CANR 33; DLB 53; FW; MTCW 1, 2; NFS 11; RGEL; RGSF; SATA-Obit 50; TCWW 2

Laurent, Antoine 1952- CLC 50

Lauscher, Hermann
See Hesse, Hermann

Lautreamont 1846-1870 NCLC 12; SSC 14
See also Lautreamont, Isidore Lucien Ducasse
See also GFL 1789 to the Present; RGWL

Lautreamont, Isidore Lucien Ducasse
See Lautreamont
See also DLB 217

Laverty, Donald
See Blish, James (Benjamin)

Lavin, Mary 1912-1996 CLC 4, 18, 99; SSC 4
See also CA 9-12R; 151; CANR 33; CN; DLB 15; FW; MTCW 1; RGEL; RGSF

Lavond, Paul Dennis
See Kornbluth, C(yril) M.; Pohl, Frederik

Lawler, Raymond Evenor 1922- CLC 58
See also CA 103; CD; RGEL

Lawrence, D(avid) H(erbert Richards) 1885-1930 TCLC 2, 9, 16, 33, 48, 61, 93; DA; DAB; DAC; DAM MST, NOV,

POET; SSC 4, 19; WLC
See also Chambers, Jessie
See also BPFB 2; BRW 7; BRWR 2; CA 104; 121; CDBLB 1914-1945; DA3; DLB 10, 19, 36, 98, 162, 195; EXPP; EXPS; LAIT 2, 3; MTCW 1, 2; PFS 6; RGEL; RGSF; SSFS 2, 6; WLIT 4; WP

Lawrence, T(homas) E(dward) 1888-1935 TCLC 18
See also Dale, Colin
See also BRWS 2; CA 115; 167; DLB 195

Lawrence of Arabia
See Lawrence, T(homas) E(dward)

Lawson, Henry (Archibald Hertzberg) 1867-1922 TCLC 27; SSC 18
See also CA 120; 181; DLB 230; RGEL; RGSF

Lawton, Dennis
See Faust, Frederick (Schiller)

Laxness, Halldor CLC 25
See also Gudjonsson, Halldor Kiljan
See also EW 12; RGWL

Layamonfl. c. 1200- CMLC 10
See also Layamon
See also RGEL

Laye, Camara 1928-1980 CLC 4, 38; BLC 2; DAM MULT
See also AFW; BW 1; CA 85-88; 97-100; CANR 25; MTCW 1, 2; WLIT 2

Layton, Irving (Peter) 1912- CLC 2, 15; DAC; DAM MST, POET
See also CA 1-4R; CANR 2, 33, 43, 66; CP; DLB 88; MTCW 1, 2; PFS 12; RGEL

Lazarus, Emma 1849-1887 NCLC 8, 109

Lazarus, Felix
See Cable, George Washington

Lazarus, Henry
See Slavitt, David R(ytman)

Lea, Joan
See Neufeld, John (Arthur)

Leacock, Stephen (Butler) 1869-1944 TCLC 2; DAC; DAM MST; SSC 39
See also CA 104; 141; CANR 80; DLB 92; MTCW 2; RGEL; RGSF

Lead, Jane Ward 1623-1704 LC 72
See also DLB 131

Lear, Edward 1812-1888 NCLC 3
See also BRW 5; CLR 1, 75; DLB 32, 163, 166; MAICYA; RGEL; SATA 18, 100; WCH; WP

Lear, Norman (Milton) 1922- CLC 12
See also CA 73-76

Leautaud, Paul 1872-1956 TCLC 83
See also DLB 65; GFL 1789 to the Present

Leavis, F(rank) R(aymond) 1895-1978 CLC 24
See also BRW 7; CA 21-24R; 77-80; CANR 44; DLB 242; MTCW 1, 2; RGEL

Leavitt, David 1961- CLC 34; DAM POP
See also CA 116; 122; CANR 50, 62, 101; CPW; DA3; DLB 130; GLL 1; INT 122; MTCW 2

Leblanc, Maurice (Marie Emile) 1864-1941 TCLC 49
See also CA 110; CMW

Lebowitz, Fran(ces Ann) 1951(?)- CLC 11, 36
See also CA 81-84; CANR 14, 60, 70; INT CANR-14; MTCW 1

Lebrecht, Peter
See Tieck, (Johann) Ludwig

le Carre, John CLC 3, 5, 9, 15, 28
See also Cornwell, David (John Moore)
See also AAYA 42; BEST 89:4; BPFB 2; BRWS 2; CDBLB 1960 to Present; CMW; CN; CPW; DLB 87; MSW; MTCW 2; RGEL

Le Clezio, J(ean) M(arie) G(ustave) 1940- CLC 31, 155
See also CA 116; 128; DLB 83; GFL 1789 to the Present; RGSF

Leconte de Lisle, Charles-Marie-Rene 1818-1894 NCLC 29
See also DLB 217; EW 6; GFL 1789 to the Present

Le Coq, Monsieur
See Simenon, Georges (Jacques Christian)

Leduc, Violette 1907-1972 CLC 22
See also CA 13-14; 33-36R; CANR 69; CAP 1; GFL 1789 to the Present; GLL 1

Ledwidge, Francis 1887(?)-1917 TCLC 23
See also CA 123; DLB 20

Lee, Andrea 1953- CLC 36; BLC 2; DAM MULT
See also BW 1, 3; CA 125; CANR 82

Lee, Andrew
See Auchincloss, Louis (Stanton)

Lee, Chang-rae 1965- CLC 91
See also CA 148; CANR 89

Lee, Don L. CLC 2
See also Madhubuti, Haki R.

Lee, George W(ashington) 1894-1976 CLC 52; BLC 2; DAM MULT
See also BW 1; CA 125; CANR 83; DLB 51

Lee, (Nelle) Harper 1926- CLC 12, 60; DA; DAB; DAC; DAM MST, NOV; WLC
See also AAYA 13; AMWS 8; BPFB 2; BYA 3; CA 13-16R; CANR 51; CDALB 1941-1968; CSW; DA3; DLB 6; EXPN; LAIT 3; MTCW 1, 2; NFS 2; SATA 11; WYA; YAW

Lee, Helen Elaine 1959(?)- CLC 86
See also CA 148

Lee, John CLC 70

Lee, Julian
See Latham, Jean Lee

Lee, Larry
See Lee, Lawrence

Lee, Laurie 1914-1997 CLC 90; DAB; DAM POP
See also CA 77-80; 158; CANR 33, 73; CP; CPW; DLB 27; MTCW 1; RGEL

Lee, Lawrence 1941-1990 CLC 34
See also CA 131; CANR 43

Lee, Li-Young 1957- PC 24
See also CA 153; CP; DLB 165; PFS 11

Lee, Manfred B(ennington) 1905-1971 CLC 11
See also Queen, Ellery
See also CA 1-4R; 29-32R; CANR 2; CMW; DLB 137

Lee, Shelton Jackson 1957(?)- CLC 105; BLCS; DAM MULT
See also Lee, Spike
See also BW 2, 3; CA 125; CANR 42

Lee, Spike
See Lee, Shelton Jackson
See also AAYA 4, 29

Lee, Stan 1922- CLC 17
See also AAYA 5; CA 108; 111; INT 111

Lee, Tanith 1947- CLC 46
See also AAYA 15; CA 37-40R; CANR 53, 102; FANT; SATA 8, 88; SFW; SUFW; YAW

Lee, Vernon TCLC 5; SSC 33
See also Paget, Violet
See also DLB 57, 153, 156, 174, 178; GLL 1; SUFW

Lee, William
See Burroughs, William S(eward)
See also GLL 1

Lee, Willy
See Burroughs, William S(eward)
See also GLL 1

Lee-Hamilton, Eugene (Jacob) 1845-1907
TCLC 22
See also CA 117

Leet, Judith 1935- **CLC 11**
See also CA 187

Le Fanu, Joseph Sheridan 1814-1873 **NCLC
9, 58; DAM POP; SSC 14**
See also CMW; DA3; DLB 21, 70, 159,
178; HGG; RGEL; RGSF; SUFW

Leffland, Ella 1931- **CLC 19**
See also CA 29-32R; CANR 35, 78, 82;
DLBY 84; INT CANR-35; SATA 65

Leger, Alexis
See Leger, (Marie-Rene Auguste) Alexis
Saint-Leger

**Leger, (Marie-Rene Auguste) Alexis
Saint-Leger** 1887-1975 **CLC 4, 11, 46;
DAM POET; PC 23**
See also Saint-John Perse
See also CA 13-16R; 61-64; CANR 43;
MTCW 1

Leger, Saintleger
See Leger, (Marie-Rene Auguste) Alexis
Saint-Leger

Le Guin, Ursula K(roeber) 1929- **CLC 8, 13,
22, 45, 71, 136; DAB; DAC; DAM MST,
POP; SSC 12**
See also AAYA 9, 27; AITN 1; BPFB 2;
BYA 5, 8, 11, 14; CA 21-24R; CANR 9,
32, 52, 74; CDALB 1968-1988; CLR 3,
28; CN; CPW; DA3; DLB 8, 52, 256;
EXPS; FANT; FW; INT CANR-32;
JRDA; LAIT 5; MAICYA; MTCW 1, 2;
NFS 6, 9; SATA 4, 52, 99; SCFW; SFW;
SSFS 2; SUFW; WYA; YAW

Lehmann, Rosamond (Nina) 1901-1990 **CLC
5**
See also CA 77-80; 131; CANR 8, 73; DLB
15; MTCW 2; RGEL; RHW

Leiber, Fritz (Reuter, Jr.) 1910-1992 **CLC 25**
See also BPFB 2; CA 45-48; 139; CANR 2,
40, 86; DLB 8; FANT; HGG; MTCW 1,
2; SATA 45; SATA-Obit 73; SCFW 2;
SFW; SUFW

Leibniz, Gottfried Wilhelm von 1646-1716
LC 35
See also DLB 168

Leimbach, Martha 1963-
See Leimbach, Marti
See also CA 130

Leimbach, Marti CLC 65
See also Leimbach, Martha

Leino, Eino TCLC 24
See also Loennbohm, Armas Eino Leopold

Leiris, Michel (Julien) 1901-1990 **CLC 61**
See also CA 119; 128; 132; GFL 1789 to
the Present

Leithauser, Brad 1953- **CLC 27**
See also CA 107; CANR 27, 81; CP; DLB
120

Lelchuk, Alan 1938- **CLC 5**
See also CA 45-48; CAAS 20; CANR 1,
70; CN

Lem, Stanislaw 1921- **CLC 8, 15, 40, 149**
See also CA 105; CAAS 1; CANR 32;
CWW 2; MTCW 1; SCFW 2; SFW

Lemann, Nancy 1956- **CLC 39**
See also CA 118; 136

Lemonnier, (Antoine Louis) Camille
1844-1913 **TCLC 22**
See also CA 121

Lenau, Nikolaus 1802-1850 **NCLC 16**

L'Engle, Madeleine (Camp Franklin) 1918-
CLC 12; DAM POP
See also AAYA 28; AITN 2; BPFB 2; BYA
2, 4, 5, 7; CA 1-4R; CANR 3, 21, 39, 66;
CLR 1, 14, 57; CPW; CWRI; DA3; DLB
52; JRDA; MAICYA; MTCW 1, 2; SAAS
15; SATA 1, 27, 75; SFW; WYA; YAW

Lengyel, Jozsef 1896-1975 **CLC 7**
See also CA 85-88; 57-60; CANR 71;
RGSF

Lenin 1870-1924
See Lenin, V. I.
See also CA 121; 168

Lenin, V. I. TCLC 67
See also Lenin

Lennon, John (Ono) 1940-1980 **CLC 12, 35**
See also CA 102; SATA 114

Lennox, Charlotte Ramsay 1729(?)-1804
NCLC 23
See also DLB 39; RGEL

Lentricchia, Frank, (Jr.) 1940- **CLC 34**
See also CA 25-28R; CANR 19, 106; DLB
246

Lenz, Gunter CLC 65

Lenz, Siegfried 1926- **CLC 27; SSC 33**
See also CA 89-92; CANR 80; CWW 2;
DLB 75; RGSF; RGWL

Leon, David
See Jacob, (Cyprien-)Max

Leonard, Elmore (John, Jr.) 1925- **CLC 28,
34, 71, 120; DAM POP**
See also AAYA 22; AITN 1; BEST 89:1,
90:4; BPFB 2; CA 81-84; CANR 12, 28,
53, 76, 96; CMW; CN; CPW; DA3; DLB
173, 226; INT CANR-28; MSW; MTCW
1, 2; RGAL; TCWW 2

Leonard, Hugh CLC 19
See also Byrne, John Keyes
See also CBD; CD; DFS 13; DLB 13

Leonov, Leonid (Maximovich) 1899-1994
CLC 92; DAM NOV
See also CA 129; CANR 74, 76; MTCW 1,
2

Leopardi, Giacomo 1798-1837 **NCLC 22; PC
37**
See also EW 5; RGWL; WP

Le Reveler
See Artaud, Antonin (Marie Joseph)

Lerman, Eleanor 1952- **CLC 9**
See also CA 85-88; CANR 69

Lerman, Rhoda 1936- **CLC 56**
See also CA 49-52; CANR 70

Lermontov, Mikhail Iur'evich
See Lermontov, Mikhail Yuryevich
See also DLB 205

Lermontov, Mikhail Yuryevich 1814-1841
NCLC 5, 47; PC 18
See also Lermontov, Mikhail Iur'evich
See also EW 6; RGWL

Leroux, Gaston 1868-1927 **TCLC 25**
See also CA 108; 136; CANR 69; CMW;
SATA 65

Lesage, Alain-Rene 1668-1747 **LC 2, 28**
See also EW 3; GFL Beginnings to 1789;
RGWL

Leskov, N(ikolai) S(emenovich) 1831-1895
See Leskov, Nikolai (Semyonovich)

Leskov, Nikolai (Semyonovich) 1831-1895
NCLC 25; SSC 34
See also Leskov, Nikolai Semenovich

Leskov, Nikolai Semenovich
See Leskov, Nikolai (Semyonovich)
See also DLB 238

Lesser, Milton
See Marlowe, Stephen

Lessing, Doris (May) 1919- **CLC 1, 2, 3, 6,
10, 15, 22, 40, 94; DA; DAB; DAC;
DAM MST, NOV; SSC 6; WLCS**
See also AFW; BRWS 1; CA 9-12R; CAAS
14; CANR 33, 54, 76; CD; CDBLB 1960
to Present; CN; DA3; DLB 15, 139;
DLBY 85; EXPS; FW; LAIT 4; MTCW
1, 2; RGEL; RGSF; SFW; SSFS 1, 12;
WLIT 2

Lessing, Gotthold Ephraim 1729-1781 **LC 8**
See also DLB 97; EW 4; RGWL

Lester, Richard 1932- **CLC 20**

Levenson, Jay CLC 70

Lever, Charles (James) 1806-1872 **NCLC 23**
See also DLB 21; RGEL

Leverson, Ada 1865(?)-1936(?) **TCLC 18**
See also Elaine
See also CA 117; DLB 153; RGEL

Levertov, Denise 1923-1997 **CLC 1, 2, 3, 5, 8,
15, 28, 66; DAM POET; PC 11**
See also AMWS 3; CA 1-4R, 178; 163;
CAAE 178; CAAS 19; CANR 3, 29, 50;
CDALBS; CP; CWP; DLB 5, 165; EXPP;
FW; INT CANR-29; MTCW 1, 2; PAB;
PFS 7; RGAL; WP

Levi, Jonathan CLC 76
See also CA 197

Levi, Peter (Chad Tigar) 1931-2000 **CLC 41**
See also CA 5-8R; 187; CANR 34, 80; CP;
DLB 40

Levi, Primo 1919-1987 **CLC 37, 50; SSC 12**
See also CA 13-16R; 122; CANR 12, 33,
61, 70; DLB 177; MTCW 1, 2; RGWL;
TCLC 109

Levin, Ira 1929- **CLC 3, 6; DAM POP**
See also CA 21-24R; CANR 17, 44, 74;
CMW; CN; CPW; DA3; HGG; MTCW 1,
2; SATA 66; SFW

Levin, Meyer 1905-1981 **CLC 7; DAM POP**
See also AITN 1; CA 9-12R; 104; CANR
15; DLB 9, 28; DLBY 81; SATA 21;
SATA-Obit 27

Levine, Norman 1924- **CLC 54**
See also CA 73-76; CAAS 23; CANR 14,
70; DLB 88

Levine, Philip 1928- **CLC 2, 4, 5, 9, 14, 33,
118; DAM POET; PC 22**
See also AMWS 5; CA 9-12R; CANR 9,
37, 52; CP; DLB 5; PFS 8

Levinson, Deirdre 1931- **CLC 49**
See also CA 73-76; CANR 70

Levi-Strauss, Claude 1908- **CLC 38**
See also CA 1-4R; CANR 6, 32, 57; DLB
242; GFL 1789 to the Present; MTCW 1,
2

Levitin, Sonia (Wolff) 1934- **CLC 17**
See also AAYA 13; CA 29-32R; CANR 14,
32, 79; CLR 53; JRDA; MAICYA; SAAS
2; SATA 4, 68, 119; YAW

Levon, O. U.
See Kesey, Ken (Elton)

Levy, Amy 1861-1889 **NCLC 59**
See also DLB 156, 240

Lewes, George Henry 1817-1878 **NCLC 25**
See also DLB 55, 144

Lewis, Alun 1915-1944 **TCLC 3; SSC 40**
See also BRW 7; CA 104; 188; DLB 20,
162; PAB; RGEL

Lewis, C. Day
See Day Lewis, C(ecil)

Lewis, C(live) S(taples) 1898-1963 **CLC 1, 3,
6, 14, 27, 124; DA; DAB; DAC; DAM
MST, NOV, POP; WLC**
See also AAYA 3, 39; BPFB 2; BRWS 3;
CA 81-84; CANR 33, 71; CDBLB 1945-
1960; CLR 3, 27; CWRI; DA3; DLB 15,
100, 160, 255; FANT; JRDA; MAICYA;
MTCW 1, 2; RGEL; SATA 13, 100;
SCFW; SFW; SUFW; WCH; WYA; YAW

Lewis, Cecil Day
See Day Lewis, C(ecil)

Lewis, Janet 1899-1998 **CLC 41**
See also Winters, Janet Lewis
See also CA 9-12R; 172; CANR 29, 63;
CAP 1; CN; DLBY 87; RHW; TCWW 2

Lewis, Matthew Gregory 1775-1818 **NCLC
11, 62**
See also DLB 39, 158, 178; HGG; RGEL;
SUFW

Lewis, (Harry) Sinclair 1885-1951 **TCLC 4,**

Lopez, Barry (Holstun) 1945- **CLC 70**
　　See also AAYA 9; ANW; CA 65-68; CANR
　　7, 23, 47, 68, 92; DLB 256; INT CANR-7,
　　-23; MTCW 1; RGAL; SATA 67
Lopez Portillo (y Pacheco), Jose 1920- **CLC 46**
　　See also CA 129; HW 1
Lopez y Fuentes, Gregorio 1897(?)-1966 **CLC 32**
　　See also CA 131; HW 1
Lorca, Federico Garcia
　　See Garcia Lorca, Federico
　　See also DFS 4; EW 11; RGWL; WP
Lord, Bette Bao 1938- **CLC 23; AAL**
　　See also BEST 90:3; BPFB 2; CA 107;
　　CANR 41, 79; INT CA-107; SATA 58
Lord Auch
　　See Bataille, Georges
Lord Byron
　　See Byron, George Gordon (Noel)
Lorde, Audre (Geraldine) 1934-1992 **CLC 18, 71; BLC 2; DAM MULT, POET; PC 12**
　　See also Domini, Rey
　　See also AFAW 1, 2; BW 1, 3; CA 25-28R;
　　142; CANR 16, 26, 46, 82; DA3; DLB
　　41; FW; MTCW 1, 2; RGAL
Lord Houghton
　　See Milnes, Richard Monckton
Lord Jeffrey
　　See Jeffrey, Francis
Loreaux, Nichol CLC 65
Lorenzini, Carlo 1826-1890
　　See Collodi, Carlo
　　See also MAICYA; SATA 29, 100
Lorenzo, Heberto Padilla
　　See Padilla (Lorenzo), Heberto
Loris
　　See Hofmannsthal, Hugo von
Loti, Pierre TCLC 11
　　See also Viaud, (Louis Marie) Julien
　　See also DLB 123; GFL 1789 to the Present
Lou, Henri
　　See Andreas-Salome, Lou
Louie, David Wong 1954- **CLC 70**
　　See also CA 139
Louis, Father M.
　　See Merton, Thomas
Lovecraft, H(oward) P(hillips) 1890-1937 **TCLC 4, 22; DAM POP; SSC 3**
　　See also AAYA 14; BPFB 2; CA 104; 133;
　　CANR 106; DA3; HGG; MTCW 1, 2;
　　RGAL; SCFW; SFW; SUFW
Lovelace, Earl 1935- **CLC 51**
　　See also BW 2; CA 77-80; CANR 41, 72;
　　CD; CN; DLB 125; MTCW 1
Lovelace, Richard 1618-1657 **LC 24**
　　See also BRW 2; DLB 131; EXPP; PAB;
　　RGEL
Lowell, Amy 1874-1925 **TCLC 1, 8; DAM POET; PC 13**
　　See also AMW; CA 104; 151; DLB 54, 140;
　　EXPP; MAWW; MTCW 2; RGAL
Lowell, James Russell 1819-1891 **NCLC 2, 90**
　　See also AMWS 1; CDALB 1640-1865;
　　DLB 1, 11, 64, 79, 189, 235; RGAL
Lowell, Robert (Traill Spence, Jr.)
　　1917-1977 **CLC 1, 2, 3, 4, 5, 8, 9, 11, 15, 37, 124; DA; DAB; DAC; DAM MST, NOV; PC 3; WLC**
　　See also AMW; CA 9-12R; 73-76; CABS
　　2; CANR 26, 60; CDALBS; DA3; DLB
　　5, 169; MTCW 1, 2; PAB; PFS 6, 7;
　　RGAL; WP
Lowenthal, Michael (Francis) 1969- **CLC 119**
　　See also CA 150

Lowndes, Marie Adelaide (Belloc) 1868-1947 **TCLC 12**
　　See also CA 107; CMW; DLB 70; RHW
Lowry, (Clarence) Malcolm 1909-1957 **TCLC 6, 40; SSC 31**
　　See also BPFB 2; BRWS 3; CA 105; 131;
　　CANR 62, 105; CDBLB 1945-1960; DLB
　　15; MTCW 1, 2; RGEL
Lowry, Mina Gertrude 1882-1966
　　See Loy, Mina
　　See also CA 113
Loxsmith, John
　　See Brunner, John (Kilian Houston)
Loy, Mina CLC 28; DAM POET; PC 16
　　See also Lowry, Mina Gertrude
　　See also DLB 4, 54
Loyson-Bridet
　　See Schwob, Marcel (Mayer Andre)
Lucan 39-65 **CMLC 33**
　　See also AW 2; DLB 211; EFS 2; RGWL
Lucas, Craig 1951- **CLC 64**
　　See also CA 137; CAD; CANR 71; CD;
　　GLL 2
Lucas, E(dward) V(errall) 1868-1938 **TCLC 73**
　　See also CA 176; DLB 98, 149, 153; SATA 20
Lucas, George 1944- **CLC 16**
　　See also AAYA 1, 23; CA 77-80; CANR
　　30; SATA 56
Lucas, Hans
　　See Godard, Jean-Luc
Lucas, Victoria
　　See Plath, Sylvia
Lucian c. 125-c. 180 **CMLC 32**
　　See also AW 2; DLB 176; RGWL
Lucretius c. 94B.C.-c. 49B.C. **CMLC 48**
　　See also AW 2; DLB 211; EFS 2; RGWL
Ludlam, Charles 1943-1987 **CLC 46, 50**
　　See also CA 85-88; 122; CAD; CANR 72, 86
Ludlum, Robert 1927-2001 **CLC 22, 43; DAM NOV, POP**
　　See also AAYA 10; BEST 89:1, 90:3; BPFB
　　2; CA 33-36R; 195; CANR 25, 41, 68,
　　105; CMW; CPW; DA3; DLBY 82; MSW;
　　MTCW 1, 2
Ludwig, Ken CLC 60
　　See also CA 195; CAD
Ludwig, Otto 1813-1865 **NCLC 4**
　　See also DLB 129
Lugones, Leopoldo 1874-1938 **TCLC 15; HLCS 2**
　　See also CA 116; 131; CANR 104; HW 1;
　　LAW
Lu Hsun TCLC 3; SSC 20
　　See also Shu-Jen, Chou
Lukacs, George CLC 24
　　See Lukacs, Gyorgy (Szegeny von)
Lukacs, Gyorgy (Szegeny von) 1885-1971
　　See Lukacs, George
　　See also CA 101; 29-32R; CANR 62; CD-
　　WLB 4; DLB 215, 242; EW 10; MTCW
　　2
Luke, Peter (Ambrose Cyprian) 1919-1995 **CLC 38**
　　See also CA 81-84; 147; CANR 72; CBD;
　　CD; DLB 13
Lunar, Dennis
　　See Mungo, Raymond
Lurie, Alison 1926- **CLC 4, 5, 18, 39**
　　See also BPFB 2; CA 1-4R; CANR 2, 17,
　　50, 88; CN; DLB 2; MTCW 1; SATA 46,
　　112
Lustig, Arnost 1926- **CLC 56**
　　See also AAYA 3; CA 69-72; CANR 47,
　　102; CWW 2; DLB 232; SATA 56
Luther, Martin 1483-1546 **LC 9, 37**
　　See also DLB 179; EW 2; RGWL

Luxemburg, Rosa 1870(?)-1919 **TCLC 63**
　　See also CA 118
Luzi, Mario 1914- **CLC 13**
　　See also CA 61-64; CANR 9, 70; CWW 2;
　　DLB 128
L'vov, Arkady CLC 59
Lyly, John 1554(?)-1606 **LC 41; DAM DRAM; DC 7**
　　See also BRW 1; DLB 62, 167; RGEL
L'Ymagier
　　See Gourmont, Remy(-Marie-Charles) de
Lynch, B. Suarez
　　See Borges, Jorge Luis
Lynch, David (K.) 1946- **CLC 66**
　　See also CA 124; 129
Lynch, James
　　See Andreyev, Leonid (Nikolaevich)
Lyndsay, Sir David 1485-1555 **LC 20**
　　See also RGEL
Lynn, Kenneth S(chuyler) 1923-2001 **CLC 50**
　　See also CA 1-4R; 196; CANR 3, 27, 65
Lynx
　　See West, Rebecca
Lyons, Marcus
　　See Blish, James (Benjamin)
Lyotard, Jean-Francois 1924-1998 **TCLC 103**
　　See also DLB 242
Lyre, Pinchbeck
　　See Sassoon, Siegfried (Lorraine)
Lytle, Andrew (Nelson) 1902-1995 **CLC 22**
　　See also CA 9-12R; 150; CANR 70; CN;
　　CSW; DLB 6; DLBY 95; RGAL; RHW
Lyttelton, George 1709-1773 **LC 10**
　　See also RGEL
Lytton of Knebworth
　　See Bulwer-Lytton, Edward (George Earle
　　Lytton)
Maas, Peter 1929-2001 **CLC 29**
　　See also CA 93-96; INT CA-93-96; MTCW
　　2
Macaulay, Catherine 1731-1791 **LC 64**
　　See also DLB 104
Macaulay, (Emilie) Rose 1881(?)-1958 **TCLC 7, 44**
　　See also CA 104; DLB 36; RGEL; RHW
Macaulay, Thomas Babington 1800-1859 **NCLC 42**
　　See also BRW 4; CDBLB 1832-1890; DLB
　　32, 55; RGEL
MacBeth, George (Mann) 1932-1992 **CLC 2, 5, 9**
　　See also CA 25-28R; 136; CANR 61, 66;
　　DLB 40; MTCW 1; PFS 8; SATA 4;
　　SATA-Obit 70
MacCaig, Norman (Alexander) 1910-1996 **CLC 36; DAB; DAM POET**
　　See also BRWS 6; CA 9-12R; CANR 3, 34;
　　CP; DLB 27; RGEL
MacCarthy, Sir (Charles Otto) Desmond 1877-1952 **TCLC 36**
　　See also CA 167
MacDiarmid, Hugh CLC 2, 4, 11, 19, 63; PC 9
　　See also Grieve, C(hristopher) M(urray)
　　See also CDBLB 1945-1960; DLB 20;
　　RGEL
MacDonald, Anson
　　See Heinlein, Robert A(nson)
Macdonald, Cynthia 1928- **CLC 13, 19**
　　See also CA 49-52; CANR 4, 44; DLB 105
MacDonald, George 1824-1905 **TCLC 9, 113**
　　See also BYA 5; CA 106; 137; CANR 80;
　　CLR 67; DLB 18, 163, 178; FANT; MAI-
　　CYA; RGEL; SATA 33, 100; SFW;
　　SUFW; WCH

Macdonald, John
  See Millar, Kenneth
MacDonald, John D(ann) 1916-1986 CLC 3, 27, 44; DAM NOV, POP
  See also BPFB 2; CA 1-4R; 121; CANR 1, 19, 60; CMW; CPW; DLB 8; DLBY 86; MSW; MTCW 1, 2; SFW
Macdonald, John Ross
  See Millar, Kenneth
Macdonald, Ross CLC 1, 2, 3, 14, 34, 41
  See also Millar, Kenneth
  See also AMWS 4; BPFB 2; DLBD 6; MSW; RGAL
MacDougal, John
  See Blish, James (Benjamin)
MacDougal, John
  See Blish, James (Benjamin)
MacDowell, John
  See Parks, Tim(othy Harold)
MacEwen, Gwendolyn (Margaret) 1941-1987 CLC 13, 55
  See also CA 9-12R; 124; CANR 7, 22; DLB 53, 251; SATA 50; SATA-Obit 55
Macha, Karel Hynek 1810-1846 NCLC 46
Machado (y Ruiz), Antonio 1875-1939 TCLC 3
  See also CA 104; 174; DLB 108; EW 9; HW 2; RGWL
Machado de Assis, Joaquim Maria 1839-1908 TCLC 10; BLC 2; HLCS 2; SSC 24
  See also CA 107; 153; CANR 91; LAW; RGSF; RGWL; WLIT 1
Machen, Arthur TCLC 4; SSC 20
  See also Jones, Arthur Llewellyn
  See also CA 179; DLB 156, 178; RGEL; SUFW
Machiavelli, Niccolo 1469-1527 LC 8, 36; DA; DAB; DAC; DAM MST; DC 16; WLCS
  See also EW 2; LAIT 1; NFS 9; RGWL
MacInnes, Colin 1914-1976 CLC 4, 23
  See also CA 69-72; 65-68; CANR 21; DLB 14; MTCW 1, 2; RGEL; RHW
MacInnes, Helen (Clark) 1907-1985 CLC 27, 39; DAM POP
  See also BPFB 2; CA 1-4R; 117; CANR 1, 28, 58; CMW; CPW; DLB 87; MSW; MTCW 1, 2; SATA 22; SATA-Obit 44
Mackay, Mary 1855-1924
  See Corelli, Marie
  See also CA 118; 177; FANT; RHW
Mackenzie, Compton (Edward Montague) 1883-1972 CLC 18
  See also CA 21-22; 37-40R; CAP 2; DLB 34, 100; RGEL; TCLC 116
Mackenzie, Henry 1745-1831 NCLC 41
  See also DLB 39; RGEL
Mackintosh, Elizabeth 1896(?)-1952
  See Tey, Josephine
  See also CA 110; CMW
MacLaren, James
  See Grieve, C(hristopher) M(urray)
Mac Laverty, Bernard 1942- CLC 31
  See also CA 116; 118; CANR 43, 88; CN; INT CA-118; RGSF
MacLean, Alistair (Stuart) 1922(?)-1987 CLC 3, 13, 50, 63; DAM POP
  See also CA 57-60; 121; CANR 28, 61; CMW; CPW; MTCW 1; SATA 23; SATA-Obit 50; TCWW 2
Maclean, Norman (Fitzroy) 1902-1990 CLC 78; DAM POP; SSC 13
  See also CA 102; 132; CANR 49; CPW; DLB 206; TCWW 2
MacLeish, Archibald 1892-1982 CLC 3, 8,

14, 68; DAM POET
  See also AMW; CA 9-12R; 106; CAD; CANR 33, 63; CDALBS; DLB 4, 7, 45; DLBY 82; EXPP; MTCW 1, 2; PAB; PFS 5; RGAL
MacLennan, (John) Hugh 1907-1990 CLC 2, 14, 92; DAC; DAM MST
  See also CA 5-8R; 142; CANR 33; DLB 68; MTCW 1, 2; RGEL
MacLeod, Alistair 1936- CLC 56; DAC; DAM MST
  See also CA 123; CCA 1; DLB 60; MTCW 2; RGSF
Macleod, Fiona
  See Sharp, William
  See also RGEL; SUFW
MacNeice, (Frederick) Louis 1907-1963 CLC 1, 4, 10, 53; DAB; DAM POET
  See also BRW 7; CA 85-88; CANR 61; DLB 10, 20; MTCW 1, 2; RGEL
MacNeill, Dand
  See Fraser, George MacDonald
Macpherson, James 1736-1796 LC 29
  See also Ossian
  See also DLB 109; RGEL
Macpherson, (Jean) Jay 1931- CLC 14
  See also CA 5-8R; CANR 90; CP; CWP; DLB 53
Macrobius fl. 430- CMLC 48
MacShane, Frank 1927-1999 CLC 39
  See also CA 9-12R; 186; CANR 3, 33; DLB 111
Macumber, Mari
  See Sandoz, Mari(e Susette)
Madach, Imre 1823-1864 NCLC 19
Madden, (Jerry) David 1933- CLC 5, 15
  See also CA 1-4R; CAAS 3; CANR 4, 45; CN; CSW; DLB 6; MTCW 1
Maddern, Al(an)
  See Ellison, Harlan (Jay)
Madhubuti, Haki R. 1942- CLC 6, 73; BLC 2; DAM MULT, POET; PC 5
  See also Lee, Don L.
  See also BW 2, 3; CA 73-76; CANR 24, 51, 73; CP; CSW; DLB 5, 41; DLBD 8; MTCW 2; RGAL
Maepenn, Hugh
  See Kuttner, Henry
Maepenn, K. H.
  See Kuttner, Henry
Maeterlinck, Maurice 1862-1949 TCLC 3; DAM DRAM
  See also CA 104; 136; CANR 80; DLB 192; EW 8; GFL 1789 to the Present; RGWL; SATA 66
Maginn, William 1794-1842 NCLC 8
  See also DLB 110, 159
Mahapatra, Jayanta 1928- CLC 33; DAM MULT
  See also CA 73-76; CAAS 9; CANR 15, 33, 66, 87; CP
Mahfouz, Naguib (Abdel Aziz Al-Sabilgi) 1911(?)- CLC 153; DAM NOV
  See also Mahfuz, Najib (Abdel Aziz al-Sabilgi)
  See also BEST 89:2; CA 128; CANR 55, 101; CWW 2; DA3; MTCW 1, 2; RGWL; SSFS 9
Mahfuz, Najib (Abdel Aziz al-Sabilgi) CLC 52, 55
  See also Mahfouz, Naguib (Abdel Aziz Al-Sabilgi)
  See also AFW; DLBY 88; RGSF; WLIT 2
Mahon, Derek 1941- CLC 27
  See also BRWS 6; CA 113; 128; CANR 88; CP; DLB 40
Maiakovskii, Vladimir
  See Mayakovski, Vladimir (Vladimirovich)
  See also IDTP; RGWL

Mailer, Norman 1923- CLC 1, 2, 3, 4, 5, 8, 11, 14, 28, 39, 74, 111; DA; DAB; DAC; DAM MST, NOV, POP
  See also AAYA 31; AITN 2; AMW; BPFB 2; CA 9-12R; CABS 1; CANR 28, 74, 77; CDALB 1968-1988; CN; CPW; DA3; DLB 2, 16, 28, 185; DLBD 3; DLBY 80, 83; MTCW 1, 2; NFS 10; RGAL
Maillet, Antonine 1929- CLC 54, 118; DAC
  See also CA 115; 120; CANR 46, 74, 77; CCA 1; CWW 2; DLB 60; INT 120; MTCW 2
Mais, Roger 1905-1955 TCLC 8
  See also BW 1, 3; CA 105; 124; CANR 82; DLB 125; MTCW 1; RGEL
Maistre, Joseph 1753-1821 NCLC 37
  See also GFL 1789 to the Present
Maitland, Frederic William 1850-1906 TCLC 65
Maitland, Sara (Louise) 1950- CLC 49
  See also CA 69-72; CANR 13, 59; FW
Major, Clarence 1936- CLC 3, 19, 48; BLC 2; DAM MULT
  See also AFAW 2; BW 2, 3; CA 21-24R; CAAS 6; CANR 13, 25, 53, 82; CN; CP; CSW; DLB 33; MSW
Major, Kevin (Gerald) 1949- CLC 26; DAC
  See also AAYA 16; CA 97-100; CANR 21, 38; CLR 11; DLB 60; INT CANR-21; JRDA; MAICYA; SATA 32, 82; WYA; YAW
Maki, James
  See Ozu, Yasujiro
Malabaila, Damiano
  See Levi, Primo
Malamud, Bernard 1914-1986 CLC 1, 2, 3, 5, 8, 9, 11, 18, 27, 44, 78, 85; DA; DAB; DAC; DAM MST, NOV, POP; SSC 15; WLC
  See also AAYA 16; AMWS 1; BPFB 2; CA 5-8R; 118; CABS 1; CANR 28, 62; CDALB 1941-1968; CPW; DA3; DLB 2, 28, 152; DLBY 80, 86; EXPS; LAIT 4; MTCW 1, 2; NFS 4, 9; RGAL; RGSF; SSFS 8, 13
Malan, Herman
  See Bosman, Herman Charles; Bosman, Herman Charles
Malaparte, Curzio 1898-1957 TCLC 52
Malcolm, Dan
  See Silverberg, Robert
Malcolm X CLC 82, 117; BLC 2; WLCS
  See also Little, Malcolm
  See also LAIT 5
Malherbe, Francois de 1555-1628 LC 5
  See also GFL Beginnings to 1789
Mallarme, Stephane 1842-1898 NCLC 4, 41; DAM POET; PC 4
  See also DLB 217; EW 7; GFL 1789 to the Present; RGWL
Mallet-Joris, Francoise 1930- CLC 11
  See also CA 65-68; CANR 17; DLB 83; GFL 1789 to the Present
Malley, Ern
  See McAuley, James Phillip
Mallowan, Agatha Christie
  See Christie, Agatha (Mary Clarissa)
Maloff, Saul 1922- CLC 5
  See also CA 33-36R
Malone, Louis
  See MacNeice, (Frederick) Louis
Malone, Michael (Christopher) 1942- CLC 43
  See also CA 77-80; CANR 14, 32, 57
Malory, Sir Thomas 1410(?)-1471(?) LC 11; DA; DAB; DAC; DAM MST; WLCS
  See also BRW 1; BRWR 2; CDBLB Before 1660; DLB 146; EFS 2; RGEL; SATA 59; SATA-Brief 33; WLIT 3

Malouf, (George Joseph) David 1934- **CLC 28, 86**
See also CA 124; CANR 50, 76; CN; CP; MTCW 2

Malraux, (Georges-)Andre 1901-1976 **CLC 1, 4, 9, 13, 15, 57; DAM NOV**
See also BPFB 2; CA 21-22; 69-72; CANR 34, 58; CAP 2; DA3; DLB 72; EW 12; GFL 1789 to the Present; MTCW 1, 2; RGWL

Malzberg, Barry N(athaniel) 1939- **CLC 7**
See also CA 61-64; CAAS 4; CANR 16; CMW; DLB 8; SFW

Mamet, David (Alan) 1947- **CLC 9, 15, 34, 46, 91; DAM DRAM; DC 4**
See also AAYA 3; CA 81-84; CABS 3; CANR 15, 41, 67, 72; CD; DA3; DFS 2, 3, 6, 12; DLB 7; IDFW 4; MTCW 1, 2; RGAL

Mamoulian, Rouben (Zachary) 1897-1987 **CLC 16**
See also CA 25-28R; 124; CANR 85

Mandelshtam, Osip
See Mandelstam, Osip (Emilievich)
See also EW 10; RGWL

Mandelstam, Osip (Emilievich) 1891(?)-1943(?) **TCLC 2, 6; PC 14**
See also Mandelstam, Osip
See also CA 104; 150; MTCW 2

Mander, (Mary) Jane 1877-1949 **TCLC 31**
See also CA 162; RGEL

Mandeville, John fl. 1350- **CMLC 19**
See also DLB 146

Mandiargues, Andre Pieyre de CLC 41
See also Pieyre de Mandiargues, Andre
See also DLB 83

Mandrake, Ethel Belle
See Thurman, Wallace (Henry)

Mangan, James Clarence 1803-1849 **NCLC 27**
See also RGEL

Maniere, J.-E.
See Giraudoux, Jean(-Hippolyte)

Mankiewicz, Herman (Jacob) 1897-1953 **TCLC 85**
See also CA 120; 169; DLB 26; IDFW 3, 4

Manley, (Mary) Delariviere 1672(?)-1724 **LC 1, 42**
See also DLB 39, 80; RGEL

Mann, Abel
See Creasey, John

Mann, Emily 1952- **DC 7**
See also CA 130; CAD; CANR 55; CD; CWD

Mann, (Luiz) Heinrich 1871-1950 **TCLC 9**
See also CA 106; 164, 181; DLB 66, 118; EW 8; RGWL

Mann, (Paul) Thomas 1875-1955 **TCLC 2, 8, 14, 21, 35, 44, 60; DA; DAB; DAC; DAM MST, NOV; SSC 5; WLC**
See also BPFB 2; CA 104; 128; DA3; DLB 66; EW 9; GLL 1; MTCW 1, 2; RGSF; RGWL; SSFS 4, 9

Mannheim, Karl 1893-1947 **TCLC 65**

Manning, David
See Faust, Frederick (Schiller)
See also TCWW 2

Manning, Frederic 1887(?)-1935 **TCLC 25**
See also CA 124

Manning, Olivia 1915-1980 **CLC 5, 19**
See also CA 5-8R; 101; CANR 29; FW; MTCW 1; RGEL

Mano, D. Keith 1942- **CLC 2, 10**
See also CA 25-28R; CAAS 6; CANR 26, 57; DLB 6

Mansfield, Katherine TCLC 2, 8, 39; DAB; SSC 9, 23, 38; WLC
See also Beauchamp, Kathleen Mansfield
See also BPFB 2; BRW 7; DLB 162; EXPS; FW; GLL 1; RGEL; RGSF; SSFS 2, 8, 10, 11

Manso, Peter 1940- **CLC 39**
See also CA 29-32R; CANR 44

Mantecon, Juan Jimenez
See Jimenez (Mantecon), Juan Ramon

Mantel, Hilary (Mary) 1952- **CLC 144**
See also CA 125; CANR 54, 101; CN; RHW

Manton, Peter
See Creasey, John

Man Without a Spleen, A
See Chekhov, Anton (Pavlovich)

Manzoni, Alessandro 1785-1873 **NCLC 29, 98**
See also EW 5; RGWL

Map, Walter 1140-1209 **CMLC 32**

Mapu, Abraham (ben Jekutiel) 1808-1867 **NCLC 18**

Mara, Sally
See Queneau, Raymond

Marat, Jean Paul 1743-1793 **LC 10**

Marcel, Gabriel Honore 1889-1973 **CLC 15**
See also CA 102; 45-48; MTCW 1, 2

March, William 1893-1954 **TCLC 96**

Marchbanks, Samuel
See Davies, (William) Robertson
See also CCA 1

Marchi, Giacomo
See Bassani, Giorgio

Marcus Aurelius
See Aurelius, Marcus
See also AW 2

Marguerite
See de Navarre, Marguerite

Marguerite d'Angouleme
See de Navarre, Marguerite
See also GFL Beginnings to 1789

Marguerite de Navarre
See de Navarre, Marguerite
See also RGWL

Margulies, Donald 1954- **CLC 76**
See also DFS 13; DLB 228

Marie de France c. 12th cent. - **CMLC 8; PC 22**
See also DLB 208; FW; RGWL

Marie de l'Incarnation 1599-1672 **LC 10**

Marier, Captain Victor
See Griffith, D(avid Lewelyn) W(ark)

Mariner, Scott
See Pohl, Frederik

Marinetti, Filippo Tommaso 1876-1944 **TCLC 10**
See also CA 107; DLB 114; EW 9

Marivaux, Pierre Carlet de Chamblain de 1688-1763 **LC 4; DC 7**
See also GFL Beginnings to 1789; RGWL

Markandaya, Kamala CLC 8, 38
See also Taylor, Kamala (Purnaiya)
See also BYA 13; CN

Markfield, Wallace 1926- **CLC 8**
See also CA 69-72; CAAS 3; CN; DLB 2, 28

Markham, Edwin 1852-1940 **TCLC 47**
See also CA 160; DLB 54, 186; RGAL

Markham, Robert
See Amis, Kingsley (William)

Marks, J
See Highwater, Jamake (Mamake)

Marks-Highwater, J
See Highwater, Jamake (Mamake)

Markson, David M(errill) 1927- **CLC 67**
See also CA 49-52; CANR 1, 91; CN

Marley, Bob CLC 17
See also Marley, Robert Nesta

Marley, Robert Nesta 1945-1981
See Marley, Bob
See also CA 107; 103

Marlowe, Christopher 1564-1593 **LC 22, 47; DA; DAB; DAC; DAM DRAM, MST; DC 1; WLC**
See also BRW 1; BRWR 1; CDBLB Before 1660; DA3; DFS 1, 5, 13; DLB 62; EXPP; RGEL; WLIT 3

Marlowe, Stephen 1928- **CLC 70**
See also Queen, Ellery
See also CA 13-16R; CANR 6, 55; CMW; SFW

Marmontel, Jean-Francois 1723-1799 **LC 2**

Marquand, John P(hillips) 1893-1960 **CLC 2, 10**
See also AMW; BPFB 2; CA 85-88; CANR 73; CMW; DLB 9, 102; MTCW 2; RGAL

Marques, Rene 1919-1979 **CLC 96; DAM MULT; HLC 2**
See also CA 97-100; 85-88; CANR 78; DLB 113; HW 1, 2; LAW; RGSF

Marquez, Gabriel (Jose) Garcia
See Garcia Marquez, Gabriel (Jose)

Marquis, Don(ald Robert Perry) 1878-1937 **TCLC 7**
See also CA 104; 166; DLB 11, 25; RGAL

Marric, J. J.
See Creasey, John
See also MSW

Marryat, Frederick 1792-1848 **NCLC 3**
See also DLB 21, 163; RGEL; WCH

Marsden, James
See Creasey, John

Marsh, Edward 1872-1953 **TCLC 99**

Marsh, (Edith) Ngaio 1899-1982 **CLC 7, 53; DAM POP**
See also CA 9-12R; CANR 6, 58; CMW; CPW; DLB 77; MSW; MTCW 1, 2; RGEL

Marshall, Garry 1934- **CLC 17**
See also AAYA 3; CA 111; SATA 60

Marshall, Paule 1929- **CLC 27, 72; BLC 3; DAM MULT; SSC 3**
See also AFAW 1, 2; BPFB 2; BW 2, 3; CA 77-80; CANR 25, 73; CN; DA3; DLB 33, 157, 227; MTCW 1, 2; RGAL

Marshallik
See Zangwill, Israel

Marsten, Richard
See Hunter, Evan

Marston, John 1576-1634 **LC 33; DAM DRAM**
See also BRW 2; DLB 58, 172; RGEL

Martha, Henry
See Harris, Mark

Marti (y Perez), Jose (Julian) 1853-1895 **NCLC 63; DAM MULT; HLC 2**
See also HW 2; LAW; RGWL; WLIT 1

Martial c. 40-c. 104 **CMLC 35; PC 10**
See also AW 2; DLB 211; RGWL

Martin, Ken
See Hubbard, L(afayette) Ron(ald)

Martin, Richard
See Creasey, John

Martin, Steve 1945- **CLC 30**
See also CA 97-100; CANR 30, 100; MTCW 1

Martin, Valerie 1948- **CLC 89**
See also BEST 90:2; CA 85-88; CANR 49, 89

Martin, Violet Florence 1862-1915 **TCLC 51**

Martin, Webber
See Silverberg, Robert

Martindale, Patrick Victor
See White, Patrick (Victor Martindale)

Martin du Gard, Roger 1881-1958 **TCLC 24**
See also CA 118; CANR 94; DLB 65; GFL 1789 to the Present; RGWL

Martineau, Harriet 1802-1876 **NCLC 26**
See also DLB 21, 55, 159, 163, 166, 190;
FW; RGEL; YABC 2

Martines, Julia
See O'Faolain, Julia

Martinez, Enrique Gonzalez
See Gonzalez Martinez, Enrique

Martinez, Jacinto Benavente y
See Benavente (y Martinez), Jacinto

Martinez de la Rosa, Francisco de Paula
1787-1862 **NCLC 102**

Martinez Ruiz, Jose 1873-1967
See Azorin; Ruiz, Jose Martinez
See also CA 93-96; HW 1

Martinez Sierra, Gregorio 1881-1947 **TCLC 6**
See also CA 115

Martinez Sierra, Maria (de la O'LeJarraga)
1874-1974 **TCLC 6**
See also CA 115

Martinsen, Martin
See Follett, Ken(neth Martin)

Martinson, Harry (Edmund) 1904-1978 **CLC 14**
See also CA 77-80; CANR 34

Marut, Ret
See Traven, B.

Marut, Robert
See Traven, B.

Marvell, Andrew 1621-1678 **LC 4, 43; DA; DAB; DAC; DAM MST, POET; PC 10; WLC**
See also BRW 2; BRWR 2; CDBLB 1660-1789; DLB 131; EXPP; PFS 5; RGEL; WP

Marx, Karl (Heinrich) 1818-1883 **NCLC 17**
See also DLB 129

Masaoka, Shiki TCLC 18
See also Masaoka, Tsunenori

Masaoka, Tsunenori 1867-1902
See Masaoka, Shiki
See also CA 117; 191

Masefield, John (Edward) 1878-1967 **CLC 11, 47; DAM POET**
See also CA 19-20; 25-28R; CANR 33; CAP 2; CDBLB 1890-1914; DLB 10, 19, 153, 160; EXPP; FANT; MTCW 1, 2; PFS 5; RGEL; SATA 19

Maso, Carole 19(?)- **CLC 44**
See also CA 170; GLL 2; RGAL

Mason, Bobbie Ann 1940- **CLC 28, 43, 82, 154; SSC 4**
See also AAYA 5, 42; AMWS 8; BPFB 2; CA 53-56; CANR 11, 31, 58, 83; CDALBS; CN; CSW; DA3; DLB 173; DLBY 87; EXPS; INT CANR-31; MTCW 1, 2; NFS 4; RGAL; RGSF; SSFS 3,8; YAW

Mason, Ernst
See Pohl, Frederik

Mason, Hunni B.
See Sternheim, (William Adolf) Carl

Mason, Lee W.
See Malzberg, Barry N(athaniel)

Mason, Nick 1945- **CLC 35**

Mason, Tally
See Derleth, August (William)

Mass, Anna CLC 59

Mass, William
See Gibson, William

Massinger, Philip 1583-1640 **LC 70**
See also DLB 58; RGEL

Master Lao
See Lao Tzu

Masters, Edgar Lee 1868-1950 **TCLC 2, 25;**

DA; DAC; DAM MST, POET; PC 1, 36; WLCS
See also AMWS 1; CA 104; 133; CDALB 1865-1917; DLB 54; EXPP; MTCW 1, 2; RGAL; WP

Masters, Hilary 1928- **CLC 48**
See also CA 25-28R; CANR 13, 47, 97; CN; DLB 244

Mastrosimone, William 19(?)- **CLC 36**
See also CA 186; CAD; CD

Mathe, Albert
See Camus, Albert

Mather, Cotton 1663-1728 **LC 38**
See also AMWS 2; CDALB 1640-1865; DLB 24, 30, 140; RGAL

Mather, Increase 1639-1723 **LC 38**
See also DLB 24

Matheson, Richard (Burton) 1926- **CLC 37**
See also AAYA 31; CA 97-100; CANR 88, 99; DLB 8, 44; HGG; INT 97-100; SCFW 2; SFW

Mathews, Harry 1930- **CLC 6, 52**
See also CA 21-24R; CAAS 6; CANR 18, 40, 98; CN

Mathews, John Joseph 1894-1979 **CLC 84; DAM MULT**
See also CA 19-20; 142; CANR 45; CAP 2; DLB 175; NNAL

Mathias, Roland (Glyn) 1915- **CLC 45**
See also CA 97-100; CANR 19, 41; CP; DLB 27

Matsuo Basho 1644-1694 **LC 62; DAM POET; PC 3**
See also Basho, Matsuo
See also PFS 2, 7

Mattheson, Rodney
See Creasey, John

Matthews, (James) Brander 1852-1929 **TCLC 95**
See also DLB 71, 78; DLBD 13

Matthews, Greg 1949- **CLC 45**
See also CA 135

Matthews, William (Procter III) 1942-1997 **CLC 40**
See also AMWS 9; CA 29-32R; 162; CAAS 18; CANR 12, 57; CP; DLB 5

Matthias, John (Edward) 1941- **CLC 9**
See also CA 33-36R; CANR 56; CP

Matthiessen, F(rancis) O(tto) 1902-1950 **TCLC 100**
See also CA 185; DLB 63

Matthiessen, Peter 1927- **CLC 5, 7, 11, 32, 64; DAM NOV**
See also AAYA 6, 40; AMWS 5; ANW; BEST 90:4; BPFB 2; CA 9-12R; CANR 21, 50, 73, 100; CN; DA3; DLB 6, 173; MTCW 1, 2; SATA 27

Maturin, Charles Robert 1780(?)-1824 **NCLC 6**
See also DLB 178; HGG; RGEL; SUFW

Matute (Ausejo), Ana Maria 1925- **CLC 11**
See also CA 89-92; MTCW 1; RGSF

Maugham, W. S.
See Maugham, W(illiam) Somerset

Maugham, W(illiam) Somerset 1874-1965
CLC 1, 11, 15, 67, 93; DA; DAB; DAC; DAM DRAM, MST, NOV; SSC 8; WLC
See also BPFB 2; BRW 6; CA 5-8R; 25-28R; CANR 40; CDBLB 1914-1945; CMW; DA3; DLB 10, 36, 77, 100, 162, 195; LAIT 3; MTCW 1, 2; RGEL; RGSF; SATA 54

Maugham, William Somerset
See Maugham, W(illiam) Somerset

Maupassant, (Henri Rene Albert) Guy de 1850-1893 **NCLC 1, 42, 83; DA; DAB;**

DAC; DAM MST; SSC 1; WLC
See also BYA 14; DA3; DLB 123; EW 7; EXPS; GFL 1789 to the Present; LAIT 2; RGSF; RGWL; SSFS 4; SUFW; TWA

Maupin, Armistead (Jones, Jr.) 1944- **CLC 95; DAM POP**
See also CA 125; 130; CANR 58, 101; CPW; DA3; GLL 1; INT 130; MTCW 2

Maurhut, Richard
See Traven, B.

Mauriac, Claude 1914-1996 **CLC 9**
See also CA 89-92; 152; CWW 2; DLB 83; GFL 1789 to the Present

Mauriac, Francois (Charles) 1885-1970 **CLC 4, 9, 56; SSC 24**
See also CA 25-28; CAP 2; DLB 65; EW 10; GFL 1789 to the Present; MTCW 1, 2; RGWL

Mavor, Osborne Henry 1888-1951
See Bridie, James
See also CA 104

Maxwell, William (Keepers, Jr.) 1908-2000 **CLC 19**
See also AMWS 8; CA 93-96; 189; CANR 54, 95; CN; DLB 218; DLBY 80; INT CA-93-96

May, Elaine 1932- **CLC 16**
See also CA 124; 142; CAD; CWD; DLB 44

Mayakovski, Vladimir (Vladimirovich) 1893-1930 **TCLC 4, 18**
See also Maiakovskii, Vladimir; Mayakovsky, Vladimir
See also CA 104; 158; MTCW 2; SFW

Mayakovsky, Vladimir
See Mayakovski, Vladimir (Vladimirovich)
See also EW 11; WP

Mayhew, Henry 1812-1887 **NCLC 31**
See also DLB 18, 55, 190

Mayle, Peter 1939(?)- **CLC 89**
See also CA 139; CANR 64

Maynard, Joyce 1953- **CLC 23**
See also CA 111; 129; CANR 64

Mayne, William (James Carter) 1928- **CLC 12**
See also AAYA 20; CA 9-12R; CANR 37, 80, 100; CLR 25; FANT; JRDA; MAICYA; SAAS 11; SATA 6, 68, 122; YAW

Mayo, Jim
See L'Amour, Louis (Dearborn)
See also TCWW 2

Maysles, Albert 1926- **CLC 16**
See also CA 29-32R

Maysles, David 1932-1987 **CLC 16**
See also CA 191

Mazer, Norma Fox 1931- **CLC 26**
See also AAYA 5, 36; BYA 1, 8; CA 69-72; CANR 12, 32, 66; CLR 23; JRDA; MAICYA; SAAS 1; SATA 24, 67, 105; WYA; YAW

Mazzini, Guiseppe 1805-1872 **NCLC 34**

McAlmon, Robert (Menzies) 1895-1956 **TCLC 97**
See also CA 107; 168; DLB 4, 45; DLBD 15; GLL 1

McAuley, James Phillip 1917-1976 **CLC 45**
See also CA 97-100; RGEL

McBain, Ed
See Hunter, Evan
See also MSW

McBrien, William (Augustine) 1930- **CLC 44**
See also CA 107; CANR 90

McCabe, Patrick 1955- **CLC 133**
See also CA 130; CANR 50, 90; CN; DLB 194

McCaffrey, Anne (Inez) 1926- **CLC 17; DAM NOV, POP**
See also AAYA 6, 34; AITN 2; BEST 89:2; BPFB 2; BYA 5; CA 25-28R; CANR 15,

Membreno, Alejandro CLC 59

Menander c. 342B.C.-c. 293B.C. **CMLC 9; DAM DRAM; DC 3**
See also AW 1; DLB 176; RGWL

Menchu, Rigoberta 1959-
See also CA 175; DNFS; HLCS 2; WLIT 1

Mencken, H(enry) L(ouis) 1880-1956 **TCLC 13**
See also AMW; CA 105; 125; CDALB 1917-1929; DLB 11, 29, 63, 137, 222; MTCW 1, 2; RGAL

Mendelsohn, Jane 1965- **CLC 99**
See also CA 154; CANR 94

Mercer, David 1928-1980 **CLC 5; DAM DRAM**
See also CA 9-12R; 102; CANR 23; CBD; DLB 13; MTCW 1; RGEL

Merchant, Paul
See Ellison, Harlan (Jay)

Meredith, George 1828-1909 **TCLC 17, 43; DAM POET**
See also CA 117; 153; CANR 80; CDBLB 1832-1890; DLB 18, 35, 57, 159; RGEL

Meredith, William (Morris) 1919- **CLC 4, 13, 22, 55; DAM POET; PC 28**
See also CA 9-12R; CAAS 14; CANR 6, 40; CP; DLB 5

Merezhkovsky, Dmitry Sergeyevich 1865-1941 **TCLC 29**
See also CA 169

Merimee, Prosper 1803-1870 **NCLC 6, 65; SSC 7**
See also DLB 119, 192; EW 6; EXPS; GFL 1789 to the Present; RGSF; RGWL; SSFS 8; SUFW

Merkin, Daphne 1954- **CLC 44**
See also CA 123

Merlin, Arthur
See Blish, James (Benjamin)

Merrill, James (Ingram) 1926-1995 **CLC 2, 3, 6, 8, 13, 18, 34, 91; DAM POET; PC 28**
See also AMWS 3; CA 13-16R; 147; CANR 10, 49, 63; DA3; DLB 5, 165; DLBY 85; INT CANR-10; MTCW 1, 2; PAB; RGAL

Merriman, Alex
See Silverberg, Robert

Merriman, Brian 1747-1805 **NCLC 70**

Merritt, E. B.
See Waddington, Miriam

Merton, Thomas 1915-1968 **CLC 1, 3, 11, 34, 83; PC 10**
See also AMWS 8; CA 5-8R; 25-28R; CANR 22, 53; DA3; DLB 48; DLBY 81; MTCW 1, 2

Merwin, W(illiam) S(tanley) 1927- **CLC 1, 2, 3, 5, 8, 13, 18, 45, 88; DAM POET**
See also AMWS 3; CA 13-16R; CANR 15, 51; CP; DA3; DLB 5, 169; INT CANR-15; MTCW 1, 2; PAB; PFS 5; RGAL

Metcalf, John 1938- **CLC 37; SSC 43**
See also CA 113; CN; DLB 60; RGSF

Metcalf, Suzanne
See Baum, L(yman) Frank

Mew, Charlotte (Mary) 1870-1928 **TCLC 8**
See also CA 105; 189; DLB 19, 135; RGEL

Mewshaw, Michael 1943- **CLC 9**
See also CA 53-56; CANR 7, 47; DLBY 80

Meyer, Conrad Ferdinand 1825-1905 **NCLC 81**
See also DLB 129; EW; RGWL

Meyer, Gustav 1868-1932
See Meyrink, Gustav
See also CA 117; 190

Meyer, June
See Jordan, June
See also GLL 2

Meyer, Lynn
See Slavitt, David R(ytman)

Meyers, Jeffrey 1939- **CLC 39**
See also CA 73-76; CAAE 186; CANR 54, 102; DLB 111

Meynell, Alice (Christina Gertrude Thompson) 1847-1922 **TCLC 6**
See also CA 104; 177; DLB 19, 98; RGEL

Meyrink, Gustav TCLC 21
See also Meyer, Gustav
See also DLB 81

Michaels, Leonard 1933- **CLC 6, 25; SSC 16**
See also CA 61-64; CANR 21, 62; CN; DLB 130; MTCW 1

Michaux, Henri 1899-1984 **CLC 8, 19**
See also CA 85-88; 114; GFL 1789 to the Present; RGWL

Micheaux, Oscar (Devereaux) 1884-1951 **TCLC 76**
See also BW 3; CA 174; DLB 50; TCWW 2

Michelangelo 1475-1564 **LC 12**
See also AAYA 43

Michelet, Jules 1798-1874 **NCLC 31**
See also EW 5; GFL 1789 to the Present

Michels, Robert 1876-1936 **TCLC 88**

Michener, James A(lbert) 1907(?)-1997 **CLC 1, 5, 11, 29, 60, 109; DAM NOV, POP**
See also AAYA 27; AITN 1; BEST 90:1; BPFB 2; CA 5-8R; 161; CANR 21, 45, 68; CN; CPW; DA3; DLB 6; MTCW 1, 2; RHW

Mickiewicz, Adam 1798-1855 **NCLC 3, 101; PC 38**
See also EW 5; RGWL

Middleton, Christopher 1926- **CLC 13**
See also CA 13-16R; CANR 29, 54; CP 7; DLB 40

Middleton, Richard (Barham) 1882-1911 **TCLC 56**
See also CA 187; DLB 156; HGG

Middleton, Stanley 1919- **CLC 7, 38**
See also CA 25-28R; CAAS 23; CANR 21, 46, 81; CN; DLB 14

Middleton, Thomas 1580-1627 **LC 33; DAM DRAM, MST; DC 5**
See also BRW 2; DLB 58; RGEL

Migueis, Jose Rodrigues 1901- **CLC 10**

Mikszath, Kalman 1847-1910 **TCLC 31**
See also CA 170

Miles, Jack CLC 100

Miles, Josephine (Louise) 1911-1985 **CLC 1, 2, 14, 34, 39; DAM POET**
See also CA 1-4R; 116; CANR 2, 55; DLB 48

Militant
See Sandburg, Carl (August)

Mill, Harriet (Hardy) Taylor 1807-1858 **NCLC 102**
See also FW

Mill, John Stuart 1806-1873 **NCLC 11, 58**
See also CDBLB 1832-1890; DLB 55, 190; FW 1; RGEL

Millar, Kenneth 1915-1983 **CLC 14; DAM POP**
See also Macdonald, Ross
See also CA 9-12R; 110; CANR 16, 63; CMW; CPW; DA3; DLB 2, 226; DLBD 6; DLBY 83; MTCW 1, 2

Millay, E. Vincent
See Millay, Edna St. Vincent

Millay, Edna St. Vincent 1892-1950 **TCLC 4, 49; DA; DAB; DAC; DAM MST, POET; PC 6; WLCS**
See also Boyd, Nancy
See also AMW; CA 104; 130; CDALB 1917-1929; DA3; DLB 45, 249; EXPP; MAWW; MTCW 1, 2; PAB; PFS 3; RGAL; WP

Miller, Arthur 1915- **CLC 1, 2, 6, 10, 15, 26, 47, 78; DA; DAB; DAC; DAM DRAM, MST; DC 1; WLC**
See also AAYA 15; AITN 1; AMW; CA 1-4R; CABS 3; CAD; CANR 2, 30, 54, 76; CD; CDALB 1941-1968; DA3; DFS 1, 3; DLB 7; LAIT 4; MTCW 1, 2; RGAL; WYAS 1

Miller, Henry (Valentine) 1891-1980 **CLC 1, 2, 4, 9, 14, 43, 84; DA; DAB; DAC; DAM MST, NOV; WLC**
See also AMW; BPFB 2; CA 9-12R; 97-100; CANR 33, 64; CDALB 1929-1941; DA3; DLB 4, 9; DLBY 80; MTCW 1, 2; RGAL

Miller, Jason 1939(?)-2001 **CLC 2**
See also AITN 1; CA 73-76; 197; CAD; DFS 12; DLB 7

Miller, Sue 1943- **CLC 44; DAM POP**
See also BEST 90:3; CA 139; CANR 59, 91; DA3; DLB 143

Miller, Walter M(ichael, Jr.) 1923-1996 **CLC 4, 30**
See also BPFB 2; CA 85-88; DLB 8; SCFW; SFW

Millett, Kate 1934- **CLC 67**
See also AITN 1; CA 73-76; CANR 32, 53, 76; DA3; DLB 246; FW; GLL 1; MTCW 1, 2

Millhauser, Steven (Lewis) 1943- **CLC 21, 54, 109**
See also CA 110; 111; CANR 63; CN; DA3; DLB 2; FANT; INT CA-111; MTCW 2

Millin, Sarah Gertrude 1889-1968 **CLC 49**
See also CA 102; 93-96; DLB 225

Milne, A(lan) A(lexander) 1882-1956 **TCLC 6, 88; DAB; DAC; DAM MST**
See also BRWS 5; CA 104; 133; CLR 1, 26; CMW; CWRI; DA3; DLB 10, 77, 100, 160; FANT; MAICYA; MTCW 1, 2; RGEL; SATA 100; WCH; YABC 1

Milner, Ron(ald) 1938- **CLC 56; BLC 3; DAM MULT**
See also AITN 1; BW 1; CA 73-76; CAD; CANR 24, 81; CD; DLB 38; MTCW 1

Milnes, Richard Monckton 1809-1885 **NCLC 61**
See also DLB 32, 184

Milosz, Czeslaw 1911- **CLC 5, 11, 22, 31, 56, 82; DAM MST, POET; PC 8; WLCS**
See also CA 81-84; CANR 23, 51, 91; CWW 2; DA3; DLB 215; EW 13; MTCW 1, 2; RGWL

Milton, John 1608-1674 **LC 9, 43; DA; DAB; DAC; DAM MST, POET; PC 19, 29; WLC**
See also BRW 2; BRWR 2; CDBLB 1660-1789; DA3; DLB 131, 151; EFS 1; EXPP; LAIT 1; PAB; PFS 3; RGEL; WLIT 3; WP

Min, Anchee 1957- **CLC 86**
See also CA 146; CANR 94

Minehaha, Cornelius
See Wedekind, (Benjamin) Frank(lin)

Miner, Valerie 1947- **CLC 40**
See also CA 97-100; CANR 59; FW; GLL 2

Minimo, Duca
See D'Annunzio, Gabriele

Minot, Susan 1956- **CLC 44**
See also AMWS 6; CA 134; CN

Minus, Ed 1938- **CLC 39**
See also CA 185

Miranda, Javier
See Bioy Casares, Adolfo
See also CWW 2

Miranda, Javier
See Bioy Casares, Adolfo

Mirbeau, Octave 1848-1917 **TCLC 55**
See also DLB 123, 192; GFL 1789 to the Present
Miro (Ferrer), Gabriel (Francisco Victor) 1879-1930 **TCLC 5**
See also CA 104; 185
Misharin, Alexandr CLC 59
Mishima, Yukio CLC 2, 4, 6, 9, 27; DC 1; SSC 4
See also Hiraoka, Kimitake
See also BPFB 2; DLB 182; GLL 1; MJW; MTCW 2; RGSF; RGWL; SSFS 5, 12
Mistral, Frederic 1830-1914 **TCLC 51**
See also CA 122; GFL 1789 to the Present
Mistral, Gabriela
See Godoy Alcayaga, Lucila
See also LAW; RGWL; WP
Mistry, Rohinton 1952- **CLC 71; DAC**
See also CA 141; CANR 86; CCA 1; CN; SSFS 6
Mitchell, Clyde
See Ellison, Harlan (Jay); Silverberg, Robert
Mitchell, James Leslie 1901-1935
See Gibbon, Lewis Grassic
See also CA 104; 188; DLB 15
Mitchell, Joni 1943- **CLC 12**
See also CA 112; CCA 1
Mitchell, Joseph (Quincy) 1908-1996 **CLC 98**
See also CA 77-80; 152; CANR 69; CN; CSW; DLB 185; DLBY 96
Mitchell, Margaret (Munnerlyn) 1900-1949 **TCLC 11; DAM NOV, POP**
See also AAYA 23; BPFB 2; BYA 1; CA 109; 125; CANR 55, 94; CDALBS; DA3; DLB 9; LAIT 2; MTCW 1, 2; NFS 9; RGAL; RHW; WYAS 1; YAW
Mitchell, Peggy
See Mitchell, Margaret (Munnerlyn)
Mitchell, S(ilas) Weir 1829-1914 **TCLC 36**
See also CA 165; DLB 202; RGAL
Mitchell, W(illiam) O(rmond) 1914-1998 **CLC 25; DAC; DAM MST**
See also CA 77-80; 165; CANR 15, 43; CN; DLB 88
Mitchell, William 1879-1936 **TCLC 81**
Mitford, Mary Russell 1787-1855 **NCLC 4**
See also DLB 110, 116; RGEL
Mitford, Nancy 1904-1973 **CLC 44**
See also CA 9-12R; DLB 191; RGEL
Miyamoto, (Chujo) Yuriko 1899-1951 **TCLC 37**
See also CA 170, 174; DLB 180
Miyazawa, Kenji 1896-1933 **TCLC 76**
See also CA 157
Mizoguchi, Kenji 1898-1956 **TCLC 72**
See also CA 167
Mo, Timothy (Peter) 1950(?)- **CLC 46, 134**
See also CA 117; CN; DLB 194; MTCW 1; WLIT 4
Modarressi, Taghi (M.) 1931-1997 **CLC 44**
See also CA 121; 134; INT 134
Modiano, Patrick (Jean) 1945- **CLC 18**
See also CA 85-88; CANR 17, 40; CWW 2; DLB 83
Mofolo, Thomas (Mokopu) 1875(?)-1948 **TCLC 22; BLC 3; DAM MULT**
See also AFW; CA 121; 153; CANR 83; DLB 225; MTCW 2; WLIT 2
Mohr, Nicholasa 1938- **CLC 12; DAM MULT; HLC 2**
See also AAYA 8; CA 49-52; CANR 1, 32, 64; CLR 22; DLB 145; HW 1, 2; JRDA; LAIT 5; MAICYAS; RGAL; SAAS 8; SATA 8, 97; SATA-Essay 113; WYA; YAW
Mojtabai, A(nn) G(race) 1938- **CLC 5, 9, 15, 29**
See also CA 85-88; CANR 88
Moliere 1622-1673 **LC 10, 28, 64; DA; DAB; DAC; DAM DRAM, MST; DC 13; WLC**
See also DA3; DFS 13; EW 3; GFL Beginnings to 1789; RGWL
Molin, Charles
See Mayne, William (James Carter)
Molnar, Ferenc 1878-1952 **TCLC 20; DAM DRAM**
See also CA 109; 153; CANR 83; DLB 215; RGWL
Momaday, N(avarre) Scott 1934- **CLC 2, 19, 85, 95; DA; DAB; DAC; DAM MST, MULT, NOV, POP; PC 25; WLCS**
See also AAYA 11; AMWS 4; ANW; BPFB 2; CA 25-28R; CANR 14, 34, 68; CDALBS; CN; CPW; DA3; DLB 143, 175, 256; EXPP; INT CANR-14; LAIT 4; MTCW 1, 2; NFS 10; NNAL; PFS 2, 11; RGAL; SATA 48; SATA-Brief 30; WP; YAW
Monette, Paul 1945-1995 **CLC 82**
See also AMWS 10; CA 139; 147; CN; GLL 1
Monroe, Harriet 1860-1936 **TCLC 12**
See also CA 109; DLB 54, 91
Monroe, Lyle
See Heinlein, Robert A(nson)
Montagu, Elizabeth 1720-1800 **NCLC 7**
See also FW
Montagu, Mary (Pierrepont) Wortley 1689-1762 **LC 9, 57; PC 16**
See also DLB 95, 101; RGEL
Montagu, W. H.
See Coleridge, Samuel Taylor
Montague, John (Patrick) 1929- **CLC 13, 46**
See also CA 9-12R; CANR 9, 69; CP; DLB 40; MTCW 1; PFS 12; RGEL
Montaigne, Michel (Eyquem) de 1533-1592 **LC 8; DA; DAB; DAC; DAM MST; WLC**
See also EW 2; GFL Beginnings to 1789; RGWL
Montale, Eugenio 1896-1981 **CLC 7, 9, 18; PC 13**
See also CA 17-20R; 104; CANR 30; DLB 114; EW 11; MTCW 1; RGWL
Montesquieu, Charles-Louis de Secondat 1689-1755 **LC 7, 69**
See also EW 3; GFL Beginnings to 1789
Montessori, Maria 1870-1952 **TCLC 103**
See also CA 115; 147
Montgomery, (Robert) Bruce 1921(?)-1978
See Crispin, Edmund
See also CA 179; 104; CMW
Montgomery, L(ucy) M(aud) 1874-1942 **TCLC 51; DAC; DAM MST**
See also AAYA 12; BYA 1; CA 108; 137; CLR 8; DA3; DLB 92; DLBD 14; JRDA; MAICYA; MTCW 2; RGEL; SATA 100; WCH; WYA; YABC 1
Montgomery, Marion H., Jr. 1925- **CLC 7**
See also AITN 1; CA 1-4R; CANR 3, 48; CSW; DLB 6
Montgomery, Max
See Davenport, Guy (Mattison, Jr.)
Montherlant, Henry (Milon) de 1896-1972 **CLC 8, 19; DAM DRAM**
See also CA 85-88; 37-40R; DLB 72; EW 11; GFL 1789 to the Present; MTCW 1
Monty Python
See Chapman, Graham; Cleese, John (Marwood); Gilliam, Terry (Vance); Idle, Eric; Jones, Terence Graham Parry; Palin, Michael (Edward)
See also AAYA 7
Moodie, Susanna (Strickland) 1803-1885 **NCLC 14**
See also DLB 99

Moody, Hiram F. III 1961-
See Moody, Rick
See also CA 138; CANR 64
Moody, Rick CLC 147
See also Moody, Hiram F. III
Moody, William Vaughan 1869-1910 **TCLC 105**
See also CA 110; 178; DLB 7, 54; RGAL
Mooney, Edward 1951-
See Mooney, Ted
See also CA 130
Mooney, Ted CLC 25
See also Mooney, Edward
Moorcock, Michael (John) 1939- **CLC 5, 27, 58**
See also Bradbury, Edward P.
See also AAYA 26; CA 45-48; CAAS 5; CANR 2, 17, 38, 64; CN; DLB 14, 231; FANT; MTCW 1, 2; SATA 93; SFW; SUFW
Moore, Brian 1921-1999 **CLC 1, 3, 5, 7, 8, 19, 32, 90; DAB; DAC; DAM MST**
See also Bryan, Michael
See also CA 1-4R; 174; CANR 1, 25, 42, 63; CCA 1; CN; DLB 251; FANT; MTCW 1, 2; RGEL
Moore, Edward
See Muir, Edwin
See also RGEL
Moore, G. E. 1873-1958 **TCLC 89**
Moore, George Augustus 1852-1933 **TCLC 7; SSC 19**
See also BRW 6; CA 104; 177; DLB 10, 18, 57, 135; RGEL; RGSF
Moore, Lorrie CLC 39, 45, 68
See also Moore, Marie Lorena
See also AMWS 10; DLB 234
Moore, Marianne (Craig) 1887-1972 **CLC 1, 2, 4, 8, 10, 13, 19, 47; DA; DAB; DAC; DAM MST, POET; PC 4; WLCS**
See also AMW; CA 1-4R; 33-36R; CANR 3, 61; CDALB 1929-1941; DA3; DLB 45; DLBD 7; EXPP; MAWW; MTCW 1, 2; PAB; PFS 14; RGAL; SATA 20; WP
Moore, Marie Lorena 1957-
See Moore, Lorrie
See also CA 116; CANR 39, 83; CN; DLB 234
Moore, Thomas 1779-1852 **NCLC 6, 110**
See also DLB 96, 144; RGEL
Moorhouse, Frank 1938- **SSC 40**
See also CA 118; CANR 92; CN; RGSF
Mora, Pat(ricia) 1942-
See also CA 129; CANR 57, 81; CLR 58; DAM MULT; DLB 209; HLC 2; HW 1, 2; SATA 92
Moraga, Cherrie 1952- **CLC 126; DAM MULT**
See also CA 131; CANR 66; DLB 82, 249; FW; GLL 1; HW 1, 2
Morand, Paul 1888-1976 **CLC 41; SSC 22**
See also CA 184; 69-72; DLB 65
Morante, Elsa 1918-1985 **CLC 8, 47**
See also CA 85-88; 117; CANR 35; DLB 177; MTCW 1, 2; RGWL
Moravia, Alberto CLC 2, 7, 11, 27, 46; SSC 26
See also Pincherle, Alberto
See also DLB 177; EW 12; MTCW 2; RGSF; RGWL
More, Hannah 1745-1833 **NCLC 27**
See also DLB 107, 109, 116, 158; RGEL
More, Henry 1614-1687 **LC 9**
See also DLB 126, 252
More, Sir Thomas 1478(?)-1535 **LC 10, 32**
See also BRWS 7; DLB 136; RGEL
Moreas, Jean TCLC 18
See also Papadiamantopoulos, Johannes
See also GFL 1789 to the Present

Murray, Albert L. 1916- **CLC 73**
See also BW 2; CA 49-52; CANR 26, 52, 78; CSW; DLB 38
Murray, James Augustus Henry 1837-1915 **TCLC 117**
Murray, Judith Sargent 1751-1820 **NCLC 63**
See also DLB 37, 200
Murray, Les(lie Allan) 1938- **CLC 40; DAM POET**
See also BRWS 7; CA 21-24R; CANR 11, 27, 56, 103; CP; DLBY 01; RGEL
Murry, J. Middleton
See Murry, John Middleton
Murry, John Middleton 1889-1957 **TCLC 16**
See also CA 118; DLB 149
Musgrave, Susan 1951- **CLC 13, 54**
See also CA 69-72; CANR 45, 84; CCA 1; CP; CWP
Musil, Robert (Edler von) 1880-1942 **TCLC 12, 68; SSC 18**
See also CA 109; CANR 55, 84; DLB 81, 124; EW 9; MTCW 2; RGSF; RGWL
Muske, Carol **CLC 90**
See also Muske-Dukes, Carol (Anne)
Muske-Dukes, Carol (Anne) 1945-
See Muske, Carol
See also CA 65-68; CANR 32, 70; CWP
Musset, (Louis Charles) Alfred de 1810-1857 **NCLC 7**
See also DLB 192, 217; EW 6; GFL 1789 to the Present; RGWL; TWA
Mussolini, Benito (Amilcare Andrea) 1883-1945 **TCLC 96**
See also CA 116
My Brother's Brother
See Chekhov, Anton (Pavlovich)
Myers, L(eopold) H(amilton) 1881-1944 **TCLC 59**
See also CA 157; DLB 15; RGEL
Myers, Walter Dean 1937- **CLC 35; BLC 3; DAM MULT, NOV**
See also AAYA 4, 23; BW 2; BYA 6, 8, 11; CA 33-36R; CANR 20, 42, 67; CLR 4, 16; DLB 33; INT CANR-20; JRDA; LAIT 5; MAICYA; MAICYAS; MTCW 2; SAAS 2; SATA 41, 71, 109; SATA-Brief 27; WYA; YAW
Myers, Walter M.
See Myers, Walter Dean
Myles, Symon
See Follett, Ken(neth Martin)
Nabokov, Vladimir (Vladimirovich) 1899-1977 **CLC 1, 2, 3, 6, 8, 11, 15, 23, 44, 46, 64; DA; DAB; DAC; DAM MST, NOV; SSC 11; WLC**
See also AMW; AMWR 1; BPFB 2; CA 5-8R; 69-72; CANR 20, 102; CDALB 1941-1968; DA3; DLB 2, 244; DLBD 3; DLBY 80, 91; EXPS; MTCW 1, 2; NFS 9; RGAL; RGSF; SSFS 6; TCLC 108
Naevius c. 265B.C.-201B.C. **CMLC 37**
See also DLB 211
Nagai, Kafu **TCLC 51**
See also Nagai, Sokichi
See also DLB 180
Nagai, Sokichi 1879-1959
See Nagai, Kafu
See also CA 117
Nagy, Laszlo 1925-1978 **CLC 7**
See also CA 129; 112
Naidu, Sarojini 1879-1949 **TCLC 80**
See also RGEL
Naipaul, Shiva(dhar Srinivasa) 1945-1985 **CLC 32, 39; DAM NOV**
See also CA 110; 112; 116; CANR 33; DA3; DLB 157; DLBY 85; MTCW 1, 2
Naipaul, V(idiadhar) S(urajprasad) 1932- **CLC 4, 7, 9, 13, 18, 37, 105; DAB;**

DAC; DAM MST, NOV; SSC 38
See also BPFB 2; BRWS 1; CA 1-4R; CANR 1, 33, 51, 91; CDBLB 1960 to Present; CN; DA3; DLB 125, 204, 207; DLBY 85, 01; MTCW 1, 2; RGEL; RGSF; WLIT 4
Nakos, Lilika 1899(?)- **CLC 29**
Narayan, R(asipuram) K(rishnaswami) 1906-2001 **CLC 7, 28, 47, 121; DAM NOV; SSC 25**
See also BPFB 2; CA 81-84; 196; CANR 33, 61; CN; DA3; DNFS; MTCW 1, 2; RGEL; RGSF; SATA 62; SSFS 5
Nash, (Frediric) Ogden 1902-1971 **CLC 23; DAM POET; PC 21**
See also CA 13-14; 29-32R; CANR 34, 61; CAP 1; DLB 11; MAICYA; MTCW 1, 2; RGAL; SATA 2, 46; TCLC 109; WP
Nashe, Thomas 1567-1601(?) **LC 41**
See also DLB 167; RGEL
Nathan, Daniel
See Dannay, Frederic
Nathan, George Jean 1882-1958 **TCLC 18**
See Hatteras, Owen
See also CA 114; 169; DLB 137
Natsume, Kinnosuke
See Natsume, Soseki
Natsume, Soseki 1867-1916 **TCLC 2, 10**
See also Soseki
See also CA 104; 195; DLB 180; RGWL
Natti, (Mary) Lee 1919-
See Kingman, Lee
See also CA 5-8R; CANR 2
Navarre, Marguerite de
See de Navarre, Marguerite
Naylor, Gloria 1950- **CLC 28, 52, 156; BLC 3; DA; DAC; DAM MST, MULT, NOV, POP; WLCS**
See also AAYA 6, 39; AFAW 1, 2; AMWS 8; BW 2, 3; CA 107; CANR 27, 51, 74; CN; CPW; DA3; DLB 173; FW; MTCW 1, 2; NFS 4, 7; RGAL
Neff, Debra **CLC 59**
Neihardt, John Gneisenau 1881-1973 **CLC 32**
See also CA 13-14; CANR 65; CAP 1; DLB 9, 54, 256; LAIT 2
Nekrasov, Nikolai Alekseevich 1821-1878 **NCLC 11**
Nelligan, Emile 1879-1941 **TCLC 14**
See also CA 114; DLB 92
Nelson, Willie 1933- **CLC 17**
See also CA 107
Nemerov, Howard (Stanley) 1920-1991 **CLC 2, 6, 9, 36; DAM POET; PC 24**
See also AMW; CA 1-4R; 134; CABS 2; CANR 1, 27, 53; DLB 5, 6; DLBY 83; INT CANR-27; MTCW 1, 2; PFS 10, 14; RGAL
Neruda, Pablo 1904-1973 **CLC 1, 2, 5, 7, 9, 28, 62; DA; DAB; DAC; DAM MST, MULT, POET; HLC 2; PC 4; WLC**
See also CA 19-20; 45-48; CAP 2; DA3; DNFS; HW 1; LAW; MTCW 1, 2; PFS 11; RGWL; WLIT 1; WP
Nerval, Gerard de 1808-1855 **NCLC 1, 67; PC 13; SSC 18**
See also DLB 217; EW 6; GFL 1789 to the Present; RGSF; RGWL
Nervo, (Jose) Amado (Ruiz de) 1870-1919 **TCLC 11; HLCS 2**
See also CA 109; 131; HW 1; LAW
Nesbit, Malcolm
See Chester, Alfred
Nessi, Pio Baroja y
See Baroja (y Nessi), Pio
Nestroy, Johann 1801-1862 **NCLC 42**
See also DLB 133; RGWL

Netterville, Luke
See O'Grady, Standish (James)
Neufeld, John (Arthur) 1938- **CLC 17**
See also AAYA 11; CA 25-28R; CANR 11, 37, 56; CLR 52; MAICYA; SAAS 3; SATA 6, 81; YAW
Neumann, Alfred 1895-1952 **TCLC 100**
See also CA 183; DLB 56
Neumann, Ferenc
See Molnar, Ferenc
Neville, Emily Cheney 1919- **CLC 12**
See also BYA 2; CA 5-8R; CANR 3, 37, 85; JRDA; MAICYA; SAAS 2; SATA 1; YAW
Newbound, Bernard Slade 1930-
See Slade, Bernard
See also CA 81-84; CANR 49; CD; DAM DRAM
Newby, P(ercy) H(oward) 1918-1997 **CLC 2, 13; DAM NOV**
See also CA 5-8R; 161; CANR 32, 67; CN; DLB 15; MTCW 1; RGEL
Newcastle
See Cavendish, Margaret Lucas
Newlove, Donald 1928- **CLC 6**
See also CA 29-32R; CANR 25
Newlove, John (Herbert) 1938- **CLC 14**
See also CA 21-24R; CANR 9, 25; CP
Newman, Charles 1938- **CLC 2, 8**
See also CA 21-24R; CANR 84; CN
Newman, Edwin (Harold) 1919- **CLC 14**
See also AITN 1; CA 69-72; CANR 5
Newman, John Henry 1801-1890 **NCLC 38, 99**
See also BRWS 7; DLB 18, 32, 55; RGEL
Newton, (Sir) Isaac 1642-1727 **LC 35, 53**
See also DLB 252
Newton, Suzanne 1936- **CLC 35**
See also BYA 7; CA 41-44R; CANR 14; JRDA; SATA 5, 77
New York Dept. of Ed. **CLC 70**
Nexo, Martin Andersen 1869-1954 **TCLC 43**
See also DLB 214
Nezval, Vitezslav 1900-1958 **TCLC 44**
See also CA 123; DLB 215
Ng, Fae Myenne 1957(?)- **CLC 81**
See also CA 146
Ngema, Mbongeni 1955- **CLC 57**
See also BW 2; CA 143; CANR 84; CD
Ngugi, James T(hiong'o) **CLC 3, 7, 13**
See also Ngugi wa Thiong'o
Ngugi wa Thiong'o 1938- **CLC 36; BLC 3; DAM MULT, NOV**
See also Ngugi, James T(hiong'o)
See also AFW; BW 2; CA 81-84; CANR 27, 58; DLB 125; DNFS; MTCW 1, 2; RGEL
Nichol, B(arrie) P(hillip) 1944-1988 **CLC 18**
See also CA 53-56; DLB 53; SATA 66
Nichols, John (Treadwell) 1940- **CLC 38**
See also CA 9-12R; CAAE 190; CAAS 2; CANR 6, 70; DLBY 82; TCWW 2
Nichols, Leigh
See Koontz, Dean R(ay)
Nichols, Peter (Richard) 1927- **CLC 5, 36, 65**
See also CA 104; CANR 33, 86; CBD; CD; DLB 13, 245; MTCW 1
Nicholson, Linda ed. **CLC 65**
Ni Chuilleanain, Eilean 1942- **PC 34**
See also CA 126; CANR 53, 83; CP; CWP; DLB 40
Nicolas, F. R. E.
See Freeling, Nicolas
Niedecker, Lorine 1903-1970 **CLC 10, 42; DAM POET**
See also CA 25-28; CAP 2; DLB 48

Nietzsche, Friedrich (Wilhelm) 1844-1900
TCLC 10, 18, 55
See also CA 107; 121; DLB 129; EW 7;
RGWL

Nievo, Ippolito 1831-1861 **NCLC 22**

Nightingale, Anne Redmon 1943-
See Redmon, Anne
See also CA 103

Nightingale, Florence 1820-1910 **TCLC 85**
See also CA 188; DLB 166

Nijo Yoshimoto 1320-1388 **CMLC 49**
See also DLB 203

Nik. T. O.
See Annensky, Innokenty (Fyodorovich)

Nin, Anais 1903-1977 **CLC 1, 4, 8, 11, 14, 60,
127; DAM NOV, POP; SSC 10**
See also AITN 2; AMWS 10; BPFB 2; CA
13-16R; 69-72; CANR 22, 53; DLB 2, 4,
152; GLL 2; MAWW; MTCW 1, 2;
RGAL; RGSF

Nisbet, Robert A(lexander) 1913-1996 **TCLC
117**
See also CA 25-28R; 153; CANR 17; INT
CANR-17

Nishida, Kitaro 1870-1945 **TCLC 83**

Nishiwaki, Junzaburo 1894-1982 **PC 15**
See also Nishiwaki, Junzaburo
See also CA 194; 107; MJW

Nishiwaki, Junzaburo 1894-1982
See Nishiwaki, Junzaburo
See also CA 194

Nissenson, Hugh 1933- **CLC 4, 9**
See also CA 17-20R; CANR 27; CN; DLB
28

Niven, Larry CLC 8
See also Niven, Laurence Van Cott
See also AAYA 27; BPFB 2; BYA 10; DLB
8; SCFW 2

Niven, Laurence Van Cott 1938-
See Niven, Larry
See also CA 21-24R; CAAS 12; CANR 14,
44, 66; CPW; DAM POP; MTCW 1, 2;
SATA 95; SFW

Nixon, Agnes Eckhardt 1927- **CLC 21**
See also CA 110

Nizan, Paul 1905-1940 **TCLC 40**
See also CA 161; DLB 72; GFL 1789 to the
Present

Nkosi, Lewis 1936- **CLC 45; BLC 3; DAM
MULT**
See also BW 1, 3; CA 65-68; CANR 27,
81; CBD; CD; DLB 157, 225

Nodier, (Jean) Charles (Emmanuel)
1780-1844 **NCLC 19**
See also DLB 119; GFL 1789 to the Present

Noguchi, Yone 1875-1947 **TCLC 80**

Nolan, Christopher 1965- **CLC 58**
See also CA 111; CANR 88

Noon, Jeff 1957- **CLC 91**
See also CA 148; CANR 83; SFW

Norden, Charles
See Durrell, Lawrence (George)

Nordhoff, Charles (Bernard) 1887-1947
TCLC 23
See also CA 108; DLB 9; LAIT 1; RHW 1;
SATA 23

Norfolk, Lawrence 1963- **CLC 76**
See also CA 144; CANR 85; CN

Norman, Marsha 1947- **CLC 28; DAM
DRAM; DC 8**
See also CA 105; CABS 3; CAD; CANR
41; CD; CSW; CWD; DFS 2; DLBY 84;
FW

Normyx
See Douglas, (George) Norman

Norris, (Benjamin) Frank(lin, Jr.) 1870-1902
TCLC 24; SSC 28
See also AMW; BPFB 2; CA 110; 160;
CDALB 1865-1917; DLB 12, 71, 186;
NFS 12; RGAL; TCWW 2; TUS

Norris, Leslie 1921- **CLC 14**
See also CA 11-12; CANR 14; CAP 1; CP;
DLB 27, 256

North, Andrew
See Norton, Andre

North, Anthony
See Koontz, Dean R(ay)

North, Captain George
See Stevenson, Robert Louis (Balfour)

North, Milou
See Erdrich, Louise

Northrup, B. A.
See Hubbard, L(afayette) Ron(ald)

North Staffs
See Hulme, T(homas) E(rnest)

Northup, Solomon 1808-1863 **NCLC 105**

Norton, Alice Mary
See Norton, Andre
See also MAICYA; SATA 1, 43

Norton, Andre 1912- **CLC 12**
See also Norton, Alice Mary
See also AAYA 14; BPFB 2; BYA 4, 10,
12; CA 1-4R; CANR 68; CLR 50; DLB
8, 52; JRDA; MTCW 1; SATA 91; SUFW;
YAW

Norton, Caroline 1808-1877 **NCLC 47**
See also DLB 21, 159, 199

Norway, Nevil Shute 1899-1960
See Shute, Nevil
See also CA 102; 93-96; CANR 85; MTCW
2

Norwid, Cyprian Kamil 1821-1883 **NCLC 17**

Nosille, Nabrah
See Ellison, Harlan (Jay)

Nossack, Hans Erich 1901-1978 **CLC 6**
See also CA 93-96; 85-88; DLB 69

Nostradamus 1503-1566 **LC 27**

Nosu, Chuji
See Ozu, Yasujiro

Notenburg, Eleanora (Genrikhovna) von
See Guro, Elena

Nova, Craig 1945- **CLC 7, 31**
See also CA 45-48; CANR 2, 53

Novak, Joseph
See Kosinski, Jerzy (Nikodem)

Novalis 1772-1801 **NCLC 13**
See also DLB 90; EW 5; RGWL

Novis, Emile
See Weil, Simone (Adolphine)

Nowlan, Alden (Albert) 1933-1983 **CLC 15;
DAC; DAM MST**
See also CA 9-12R; CANR 5; DLB 53; PFS
12

Noyes, Alfred 1880-1958 **TCLC 7; PC 27**
See also CA 104; 188; DLB 20; EXPP;
FANT; PFS 4; RGEL

Nunn, Kem CLC 34
See also CA 159

Nwapa, Flora 1931-1993 **CLC 133; BLCS**
See also BW 2; CA 143; CANR 83; CWRI;
DLB 125; WLIT 2

Nye, Robert 1939- **CLC 13, 42; DAM NOV**
See also CA 33-36R; CANR 29, 67; CN;
CP; CWRI; DLB 14; FANT; HGG;
MTCW 1; RHW; SATA 6

Nyro, Laura 1947-1997 **CLC 17**
See also CA 194

Oates, Joyce Carol 1938- **CLC 1, 2, 3, 6, 9,
11, 15, 19, 33, 52, 108, 134; DA; DAB;**
DAC; DAM MST, NOV, POP; SSC 6;
WLC
See also AAYA 15; AITN 1; AMWS 2;
BEST 89:2; BPFB 2; BYA 11; CA 5-8R;
CANR 25, 45, 74; CDALB 1968-1988;
CN; CP; CPW; CWP; DA3; DLB 2, 5,
130; DLBY 81; EXPS; FW; HGG; INT
CANR-25; LAIT 4; MAWW; MTCW 1,
2; NFS 8; RGAL; RGSF; SSFS 1, 8

O'Brian, Patrick 1914-2000 **CLC 152**
See also CA 144; 187; CANR 74; CPW;
MTCW 2; RHW

O'Brien, Darcy 1939-1998 **CLC 11**
See also CA 21-24R; 167; CANR 8, 59

O'Brien, E. G.
See Clarke, Arthur C(harles)

O'Brien, Edna 1936- **CLC 3, 5, 8, 13, 36, 65,
116; DAM NOV; SSC 10**
See also BRWS 5; CA 1-4R; CANR 6, 41,
65, 102; CDBLB 1960 to Present; CN;
DA3; DLB 14, 231; FW; MTCW 1, 2;
RGSF; WLIT 4

O'Brien, Fitz-James 1828-1862 **NCLC 21**
See also DLB 74; RGAL; SUFW

O'Brien, Flann CLC 1, 4, 5, 7, 10, 47
See also O Nuallain, Brian
See also BRWS 2; DLB 231; RGEL

O'Brien, Richard 1942- **CLC 17**
See also CA 124

O'Brien, (William) Tim(othy) 1946- **CLC 7,
19, 40, 103; DAM POP**
See also AAYA 16; AMWS 5; CA 85-88;
CANR 40, 58; CDALBS; CN; CPW;
DA3; DLB 152; DLBD 9; DLBY 80;
MTCW 2; RGAL; SSFS 5

Obstfelder, Sigbjoern 1866-1900 **TCLC 23**
See also CA 123

O'Casey, Sean 1880-1964 **CLC 1, 5, 9, 11, 15,
88; DAB; DAC; DAM DRAM, MST;
DC 12; WLCS**
See also BRW 7; CA 89-92; CANR 62;
CBD; CDBLB 1914-1945; DA3; DLB 10;
MTCW 1, 2; RGEL; WLIT 4

O'Cathasaigh, Sean
See O'Casey, Sean

Occom, Samson 1723-1792 **LC 60**
See also DLB 175; NNAL

Ochs, Phil(ip David) 1940-1976 **CLC 17**
See also CA 185; 65-68

O'Connor, Edwin (Greene) 1918-1968 **CLC
14**
See also CA 93-96; 25-28R

O'Connor, (Mary) Flannery 1925-1964 **CLC
1, 2, 3, 6, 10, 13, 15, 21, 66, 104; DA;
DAB; DAC; DAM MST, NOV; SSC 1,
23; WLC**
See also AAYA 7; AMW; BPFB 3; CA
1-4R; CANR 3, 41; CDALB 1941-1968;
DA3; DLB 2, 152; DLBD 12; DLBY 80;
EXPS; LAIT 5; MAWW; MTCW 1, 2;
NFS 3; RGAL; RGSF; SSFS 2, 7, 10

O'Connor, Frank CLC 23; SSC 5
See also O'Donovan, Michael John
See also DLB 162; RGSF; SSFS 5

O'Dell, Scott 1898-1989 **CLC 30**
See also AAYA 3; BPFB 3; BYA 1, 2, 3, 5;
CA 61-64; 129; CANR 12, 30; CLR 1,
16; DLB 52; JRDA; MAICYA; SATA 12,
60; WYA; YAW

Odets, Clifford 1906-1963 **CLC 2, 28, 98;
DAM DRAM; DC 6**
See also AMWS 2; CA 85-88; CAD; CANR
62; DFS 3; DLB 7, 26; MTCW 1, 2;
RGAL

O'Doherty, Brian 1934- **CLC 76**
See also CA 105

O'Donnell, K. M.
See Malzberg, Barry N(athaniel)

O'Donnell, Lawrence
    See Kuttner, Henry
O'Donovan, Michael John 1903-1966 CLC
    14
    See also O'Connor, Frank
    See also CA 93-96; CANR 84
Oe, Kenzaburo 1935- CLC 10, 36, 86; DAM
    NOV; SSC 20
    See also CA 97-100; CANR 36, 50, 74;
    DA3; DLB 182; DLBY 94; MTCW 1, 2
Oe Kenzaburo
    See Oe, Kenzaburo
    See also CWW; EWL; MJW; RGSF; RGWL
O'Faolain, Julia 1932- CLC 6, 19, 47, 108
    See also CA 81-84; CAAS 2; CANR 12,
    61; CN; DLB 14, 231; FW; MTCW 1;
    RHW
O'Faolain, Sean 1900-1991 CLC 1, 7, 14, 32,
    70; SSC 13
    See also CA 61-64; 134; CANR 12, 66;
    DLB 15, 162; MTCW 1, 2; RGEL; RGSF
O'Flaherty, Liam 1896-1984 CLC 5, 34; SSC
    6
    See also CA 101; 113; CANR 35; DLB 36,
    162; DLBY 84; MTCW 1, 2; RGEL;
    RGSF; SSFS 5
Ogai
    See Mori Ogai
    See also MJW
Ogilvy, Gavin
    See Barrie, J(ames) M(atthew)
O'Grady, Standish (James) 1846-1928 TCLC
    5
    See also CA 104; 157
O'Grady, Timothy 1951- CLC 59
    See also CA 138
O'Hara, Frank 1926-1966 CLC 2, 5, 13, 78;
    DAM POET
    See also CA 9-12R; 25-28R; CANR 33;
    DA3; DLB 5, 16, 193; MTCW 1, 2; PFS
    8; 12; RGAL; WP
O'Hara, John (Henry) 1905-1970 CLC 1, 2,
    3, 6, 11, 42; DAM NOV; SSC 15
    See also AMW; BPFB 3; CA 5-8R; 25-28R;
    CANR 31, 60; CDALB 1929-1941; DLB
    9, 86; DLBD 2; MTCW 1, 2; NFS 11;
    RGAL; RGSF
O Hehir, Diana 1922- CLC 41
    See also CA 93-96
Ohiyesa 1858-1939
    See Eastman, Charles A(lexander)
Okigbo, Christopher (Ifenayichukwu)
    1932-1967 CLC 25, 84; BLC 3; DAM
    MULT, POET; PC 7
    See also AFW; BW 1, 3; CA 77-80; CANR
    74; DLB 125; MTCW 1, 2; RGEL
Okri, Ben 1959- CLC 87
    See also AFW; BRWS 5; BW 2, 3; CA 130;
    138; CANR 65; CN; DLB 157, 231; INT
    CA-138; MTCW 2; RGSF; WLIT 2
Olds, Sharon 1942- CLC 32, 39, 85; DAM
    POET; PC 22
    See also AMWS 10; CA 101; CANR 18,
    41, 66, 98; CP; CPW; CWP; DLB 120;
    MTCW 2
Oldstyle, Jonathan
    See Irving, Washington
Olesha, Iurii
    See Olesha, Yuri (Karlovich)
    See also RGWL
Olesha, Yuri (Karlovich) 1899-1960 CLC 8
    See also Olesha, Iurii
    See also CA 85-88; EW 11
Oliphant
    See Oliphant, Margaret (Oliphant Wilson)
    See also SUFW
Oliphant, Laurence 1829(?)-1888 NCLC 47
    See also DLB 18, 166

Oliphant, Margaret (Oliphant Wilson)
    1828-1897 NCLC 11, 61; SSC 25
    See also Oliphant
    See also DLB 18, 159, 190; HGG; RGEL;
    RGSF
Oliver, Mary 1935- CLC 19, 34, 98
    See also AMWS 7; CA 21-24R; CANR 9,
    43, 84, 92; CP; CWP; DLB 5, 193
Olivier, Laurence (Kerr) 1907-1989 CLC 20
    See also CA 111; 150; 129
Olsen, Tillie 1912- CLC 4, 13, 114; DA; DAB;
    DAC; DAM MST; SSC 11
    See also BYA 11; CA 1-4R; CANR 1, 43,
    74; CDALBS; CN; DA3; DLB 28, 206;
    DLBY 80; EXPS; FW; MTCW 1, 2;
    RGAL; RGSF; SSFS 1
Olson, Charles (John) 1910-1970 CLC 1, 2,
    5, 6, 9, 11, 29; DAM POET; PC 19
    See also AMWS 2; CA 13-16; 25-28R;
    CABS 2; CANR 35, 61; CAP 1; DLB 5,
    16, 193; MTCW 1, 2; RGAL; WP
Olson, Toby 1937- CLC 28
    See also CA 65-68; CANR 9, 31, 84; CP
Olyesha, Yuri
    See Olesha, Yuri (Karlovich)
Omar Khayyam
    See Khayyam, Omar
    See also RGWL
Ondaatje, (Philip) Michael 1943- CLC 14,
    29, 51, 76; DAB; DAC; DAM MST; PC
    28
    See also CA 77-80; CANR 42, 74; CN; CP;
    DA3; DLB 60; MTCW 2; PFS 8
Oneal, Elizabeth 1934-
    See Oneal, Zibby
    See also CA 106; CANR 28, 84; MAICYA;
    SATA 30, 82; YAW
Oneal, Zibby CLC 30
    See also Oneal, Elizabeth
    See also AAYA 5, 41; BYA 13; CLR 13;
    JRDA; WYA
O'Neill, Eugene (Gladstone) 1888-1953
    TCLC 1, 6, 27, 49; DA; DAB; DAC;
    DAM DRAM, MST; WLC
    See also AITN 1; AMW; CA 110; 132;
    CAD; CDALB 1929-1941; DA3; DFS 9,
    11, 12; DLB 7; LAIT 3; MTCW 1, 2;
    RGAL
Onetti, Juan Carlos 1909-1994 CLC 7, 10;
    DAM MULT, NOV; HLCS 2; SSC 23
    See also CA 85-88; 145; CANR 32, 63;
    DLB 113; HW 1, 2; LAW; MTCW 1, 2;
    RGSF
O Nuallain, Brian 1911-1966
    See O'Brien, Flann
    See also CA 21-22; 25-28R; CAP 2; DLB
    231; FANT
Ophuls, Max 1902-1957 TCLC 79
    See also CA 113
Opie, Amelia 1769-1853 NCLC 65
    See also DLB 116, 159; RGEL
Oppen, George 1908-1984 CLC 7, 13, 34; PC
    35
    See also CA 13-16R; 113; CANR 8, 82;
    DLB 5, 165; TCLC 107
Oppenheim, E(dward) Phillips 1866-1946
    TCLC 45
    See also CA 111; CMW; DLB 70
Opuls, Max
    See Ophuls, Max
Origen c. 185-c. 254 CMLC 19
Orlovitz, Gil 1918-1973 CLC 22
    See also CA 77-80; 45-48; DLB 2, 5
Orris
    See Ingelow, Jean
Ortega y Gasset, Jose 1883-1955 TCLC 9;
    DAM MULT; HLC 2
    See also CA 106; 130; EW 9; HW 1, 2;
    MTCW 1, 2

Ortese, Anna Maria 1914- CLC 89
    See also DLB 177
Ortiz, Simon J(oseph) 1941- CLC 45; DAM
    MULT, POET; PC 17
    See also AMWS 4; CA 134; CANR 69; CP;
    DLB 120, 175, 256; EXPP; NNAL; PFS
    4; RGAL
Orton, Joe CLC 4, 13, 43; DC 3
    See also Orton, John Kingsley
    See also BRWS 5; CBD; CDBLB 1960 to
    Present; DFS 3, 6; DLB 13; GLL 1;
    MTCW 2; RGEL; WLIT 4
Orton, John Kingsley 1933-1967
    See Orton, Joe
    See also CA 85-88; CANR 35, 66; DAM
    DRAM; MTCW 1, 2
Orwell, George TCLC 2, 6, 15, 31, 51; DAB;
    WLC
    See also Blair, Eric (Arthur)
    See also BPFB 3; BRW 7; BYA 5; CDBLB
    1945-1960; CLR 68; DLB 15, 98, 195,
    255; EXPN; LAIT 4, 5; NFS 3, 7; RGEL;
    SCFW 2; SFW; SSFS 4; WLIT 4; YAW
Osborne, David
    See Silverberg, Robert
Osborne, George
    See Silverberg, Robert
Osborne, John (James) 1929-1994 CLC 1, 2,
    5, 11, 45; DA; DAB; DAC; DAM
    DRAM, MST; WLC
    See also BRWS 1; CA 13-16R; 147; CANR
    21, 56; CDBLB 1945-1960; DFS 4; DLB
    13; MTCW 1, 2; RGEL
Osborne, Lawrence 1958- CLC 50
    See also CA 189
Osbourne, Lloyd 1868-1947 TCLC 93
Oshima, Nagisa 1932- CLC 20
    See also CA 116; 121; CANR 78
Oskison, John Milton 1874-1947 TCLC 35;
    DAM MULT
    See also CA 144; CANR 84; DLB 175;
    NNAL
Ossian c. 3rd cent. - CMLC 28
    See also Macpherson, James
Ossoli, Sarah Margaret (Fuller) 1810-1850
    NCLC 5, 50
    See also Fuller, Margaret; Fuller, Sarah
    Margaret
    See also CDALB 1640-1865; FW; SATA 25
Ostriker, Alicia (Suskin) 1937- CLC 132
    See also CA 25-28R; CAAS 24; CANR 10,
    30, 62, 99; CWP; DLB 120; EXPP
Ostrovsky, Alexander 1823-1886 NCLC 30,
    57
Otero, Blas de 1916-1979 CLC 11
    See also CA 89-92; DLB 134
Otto, Rudolf 1869-1937 TCLC 85
Otto, Whitney 1955- CLC 70
    See also CA 140
Ouida TCLC 43
    See also De La Ramee, (Marie) Louise
    See also DLB 18, 156; RGEL
Ouologuem, Yambo 1940- CLC 146
    See also CA 111; 176
Ousmane, Sembene 1923- CLC 66; BLC 3
    See also Sembene, Ousmane
    See also BW 1, 3; CA 117; 125; CANR 81;
    CWW 2; MTCW 1
Ovid 43B.C.-17 CMLC 7; DAM POET; PC 2
    See also AW 2; DA3; DLB 211; RGWL;
    WP
Owen, Hugh
    See Faust, Frederick (Schiller)
Owen, Wilfred (Edward Salter) 1893-1918
    TCLC 5, 27; DA; DAB; DAC; DAM
    MST, POET; PC 19; WLC
    See also BRW 6; CA 104; 141; CDBLB
    1914-1945; DLB 20; EXPP; MTCW 2;
    PFS 10; RGEL; WLIT 4

DAM MST, NOV; SSC 4, 31, 43
See also AAYA 42; AITN 2; AMW; BPFB
3; CA 1-4R; 101; CANR 1, 65; CDALBS;
DA3; DLB 4, 9, 102; DLBD 12; DLBY
80; EXPS; LAIT 3; MAWW; MTCW 1,
2; RGAL; RGSF; SATA 39; SATA-Obit
23; SSFS 1, 8, 11

Porter, Peter (Neville Frederick) 1929- **CLC
5, 13, 33**
See also CA 85-88; CP; DLB 40

Porter, William Sydney 1862-1910
See Henry, O.
See also CA 104; 131; CDALB 1865-1917;
DA; DA3; DAB; DAC; DAM MST; DLB
12, 78, 79; MTCW 1, 2; YABC 2

Portillo (y Pacheco), Jose Lopez
See Lopez Portillo (y Pacheco), Jose

Portillo Trambley, Estela 1927-1998
See Trambley, Estela Portillo
See also CANR 32; DAM MULT; DLB
209; HLC 2; HW 1

Posse, Abel CLC 70

Post, Melville Davisson 1869-1930 **TCLC 39**
See also CA 110; CMW

Potok, Chaim 1929- **CLC 2, 7, 14, 26, 112;
DAM NOV**
See also AAYA 15; AITN 1, 2; BPFB 3;
BYA 1; CA 17-20R; CANR 19, 35, 64,
98; CN; DA3; DLB 28, 152; EXPN; INT
CANR-19; LAIT 4; MTCW 1, 2; NFS 4;
SATA 33, 106; YAW

Potter, Dennis (Christopher George)
1935-1994 **CLC 58, 86, 123**
See also CA 107; 145; CANR 33, 61; CBD;
DLB 233; MTCW 1

Pound, Ezra (Weston Loomis) 1885-1972
**CLC 1, 2, 3, 4, 5, 7, 10, 13, 18, 34, 48,
50, 112; DA; DAB; DAC; DAM MST,
POET; PC 4; WLC**
See also AMW; AMWR 1; CA 5-8R; 37-
40R; CANR 40; CDALB 1917-1929;
DA3; DLB 4, 45, 63; DLBD 15; EFS 2;
EXPP; MTCW 1, 2; PAB; PFS 2, 8;
RGAL; WP

Povod, Reinaldo 1959-1994 **CLC 44**
See also CA 136; 146; CANR 83

Powell, Adam Clayton, Jr. 1908-1972 **CLC
89; BLC 3; DAM MULT**
See also BW 1, 3; CA 102; 33-36R; CANR
86

Powell, Anthony (Dymoke) 1905-2000 **CLC
1, 3, 7, 9, 10, 31**
See also BRW 7; CA 1-4R; 189; CANR 1,
32, 62; CDBLB 1945-1960; CN; DLB 15;
MTCW 1, 2; RGEL

Powell, Dawn 1897-1965 **CLC 66**
See also CA 5-8R; DLBY 97

Powell, Padgett 1952- **CLC 34**
See also CA 126; CANR 63, 101; CSW;
DLB 234; DLBY 01

Powell, (Oval) Talmage 1920-2000
See Queen, Ellery
See also CA 5-8R; CANR 2, 80

Power, Susan 1961- **CLC 91**
See also BYA 14; CA 160; NFS 11

Powers, J(ames) F(arl) 1917-1999 **CLC 1, 4,
8, 57; SSC 4**
See also CA 1-4R; 181; CANR 2, 61; CN;
DLB 130; MTCW 1; RGAL; RGSF

Powers, John J(ames) 1945-
See Powers, John R.
See also CA 69-72

Powers, John R. CLC 66
See also Powers, John J(ames)

Powers, Richard (S.) 1957- **CLC 93**
See also AMWS 9; BPFB 3; CA 148;
CANR 80; CN

Pownall, David 1938- **CLC 10**
See also CA 89-92, 180; CAAS 18; CANR
49, 101; CBD; CD; CN; DLB 14

Powys, John Cowper 1872-1963 **CLC 7, 9,
15, 46, 125**
See also CA 85-88; CANR 106; DLB 15,
255; FANT; MTCW 1, 2; RGEL; SUFW

Powys, T(heodore) F(rancis) 1875-1953
TCLC 9
See also CA 106; 189; DLB 36, 162; FANT;
RGEL; SUFW

Prado (Calvo), Pedro 1886-1952 **TCLC 75**
See also CA 131; HW 1; LAW

Prager, Emily 1952- **CLC 56**

Pratt, E(dwin) J(ohn) 1883(?)-1964 **CLC 19;
DAC; DAM POET**
See also CA 141; 93-96; CANR 77; DLB
92; RGEL

Premchand TCLC 21
See also Srivastava, Dhanpat Rai

Preussler, Otfried 1923- **CLC 17**
See also CA 77-80; SATA 24

Prevert, Jacques (Henri Marie) 1900-1977
CLC 15
See also CA 77-80; 69-72; CANR 29, 61;
GFL 1789 to the Present; IDFW 3, 4;
MTCW 1; RGWL; SATA-Obit 30

Prevost, (Antoine Francois) 1697-1763 **LC 1**
See also EW 4; GFL Beginnings to 1789;
RGWL

Price, (Edward) Reynolds 1933- **CLC 3, 6,
13, 43, 50, 63; DAM NOV; SSC 22**
See also AMWS 6; CA 1-4R; CANR 1, 37,
57, 87; CN; CSW; DLB 2, 218; INT
CANR-37

Price, Richard 1949- **CLC 6, 12**
See also CA 49-52; CANR 3; DLBY 81

Prichard, Katharine Susannah 1883-1969
CLC 46
See also CA 11-12; CANR 33; CAP 1;
MTCW 1; RGEL; RGSF; SATA 66

Priestley, J(ohn) B(oynton) 1894-1984 **CLC
2, 5, 9, 34; DAM DRAM, NOV**
See also BRW 7; CA 9-12R; 113; CANR
33; CDBLB 1914-1945; DA3; DLB 10,
34, 77, 100, 139; DLBY 84; MTCW 1, 2;
RGEL; SFW

Prince 1958(?)- **CLC 35**

Prince, F(rank) T(empleton) 1912- **CLC 22**
See also CA 101; CANR 43, 79; CP; DLB
20

Prince Kropotkin
See Kropotkin, Peter (Aleksieevich)

Prior, Matthew 1664-1721 **LC 4**
See also DLB 95; RGEL

Prishvin, Mikhail 1873-1954 **TCLC 75**

Pritchard, William H(arrison) 1932- **CLC 34**
See also CA 65-68; CANR 23, 95; DLB
111

Pritchett, V(ictor) S(awdon) 1900-1997 **CLC
5, 13, 15, 41; DAM NOV; SSC 14**
See also BPFB 3; BRWS 3; CA 61-64; 157;
CANR 31, 63; CN; DA3; DLB 15, 139;
MTCW 1, 2; RGEL; RGSF

Private 19022
See Manning, Frederic

Probst, Mark 1925- **CLC 59**
See also CA 130

Prokosch, Frederic 1908-1989 **CLC 4, 48**
See also CA 73-76; 128; CANR 82; DLB
48; MTCW 2

Propertius, Sextus c. 50B.C.-c. 16B.C. **CMLC
32**
See also AW 2; DLB 211; RGWL

Prophet, The
See Dreiser, Theodore (Herman Albert)

Prose, Francine 1947- **CLC 45**
See also CA 109; 112; CANR 46, 95; DLB
234; SATA 101

Proudhon
See Cunha, Euclides (Rodrigues Pimenta)
da

Proulx, Annie
See Proulx, E(dna) Annie

Proulx, E(dna) Annie 1935- **CLC 81; DAM
POP**
See also AMWS 7; BPFB 3; CA 145;
CANR 65; CN; CPW 1; DA3; MTCW 2

**Proust,
(Valentin-Louis-George-Eugene-)Marcel**
1871-1922 **TCLC 7, 13, 33; DA; DAB;
DAC; DAM MST, NOV; WLC**
See also BPFB 3; CA 104; 120; DA3; DLB
65; EW 8; GFL 1789 to the Present;
MTCW 1, 2; RGWL

Prowler, Harley
See Masters, Edgar Lee

Prus, Boleslaw 1845-1912 **TCLC 48**
See also RGWL

Pryor, Richard (Franklin Lenox Thomas)
1940- **CLC 26**
See also CA 122; 152

Przybyszewski, Stanislaw 1868-1927 **TCLC
36**
See also CA 160; DLB 66

Pteleon
See Grieve, C(hristopher) M(urray)
See also DAM POET

Puckett, Lute
See Masters, Edgar Lee

Puig, Manuel 1932-1990 **CLC 3, 5, 10, 28,
65, 133; DAM MULT; HLC 2**
See also BPFB 3; CA 45-48; CANR 2, 32,
63; DA3; DLB 113; DNFS; GLL 1; HW
1, 2; LAW; MTCW 1, 2; RGWL; WLIT 1

Pulitzer, Joseph 1847-1911 **TCLC 76**
See also CA 114; DLB 23

Purchas, Samuel 1577(?)-1626 **LC 70**
See also DLB 151

Purdy, A(lfred) W(ellington) 1918-2000 **CLC
3, 6, 14, 50; DAC; DAM MST, POET**
See also CA 81-84; 189; CAAS 17; CANR
42, 66; CP; DLB 88; PFS 5; RGEL

Purdy, James (Amos) 1923- **CLC 2, 4, 10, 28,
52**
See also AMWS 7; CA 33-36R; CAAS 1;
CANR 19, 51; CN; DLB 2, 218; INT
CANR-19; MTCW 1; RGAL

Pure, Simon
See Swinnerton, Frank Arthur

Pushkin, Aleksandr Sergeevich
See Pushkin, Alexander (Sergeyevich)
See also DLB 205

Pushkin, Alexander (Sergeyevich) 1799-1837
**NCLC 3, 27, 83; DA; DAB; DAC; DAM
DRAM, MST, POET; PC 10; SSC 27;
WLC**
See also DA3; EW 5; EXPS; RGSF;
RGWL; SATA 61; SSFS 9

P'u Sung-ling 1640-1715 **LC 49; SSC 31**

Putnam, Arthur Lee
See Alger, Horatio, Jr.

Puzo, Mario 1920-1999 **CLC 1, 2, 6, 36, 107;
DAM NOV, POP**
See also BPFB 3; CA 65-68; 185; CANR 4,
42, 65, 99; CN; CPW; DA3; DLB 6;
MTCW 1, 2; RGAL

Pygge, Edward
See Barnes, Julian (Patrick)

Pyle, Ernest Taylor 1900-1945
See Pyle, Ernie
See also CA 115; 160

Pyle, Ernie TCLC 75
See also Pyle, Ernest Taylor
See also DLB 29; MTCW 2

Reade, Charles 1814-1884 **NCLC 2, 74**
　See also DLB 21; RGEL

Reade, Hamish
　See Gray, Simon (James Holliday)

Reading, Peter 1946- **CLC 47**
　See also CA 103; CANR 46, 96; CP; DLB 40

Reaney, James 1926- **CLC 13; DAC; DAM MST**
　See also CA 41-44R; CAAS 15; CANR 42; CD; CP; DLB 68; RGEL; SATA 43

Rebreanu, Liviu 1885-1944 **TCLC 28**
　See also CA 165; DLB 220

Rechy, John (Francisco) 1934- **CLC 1, 7, 14, 18, 107; DAM MULT; HLC 2**
　See also CA 5-8R; CAAE 195; CAAS 4; CANR 6, 32, 64; CN; DLB 122; DLBY 82; HW 1, 2; INT CANR-6; RGAL

Redcam, Tom 1870-1933 **TCLC 25**

Reddin, Keith CLC 67
　See also CAD

Redgrove, Peter (William) 1932- **CLC 6, 41**
　See also BRWS 6; CA 1-4R; CANR 3, 39, 77; CP; DLB 40

Redmon, Anne CLC 22
　See also Nightingale, Anne Redmon
　See also DLBY 86

Reed, Eliot
　See Ambler, Eric

Reed, Ishmael 1938- **CLC 2, 3, 5, 6, 13, 32, 60; BLC 3; DAM MULT**
　See also AFAW 1, 2; AMWS 10; BPFB 3; BW 2, 3; CA 21-24R; CANR 25, 48, 74; CN; CP; CSW; DA3; DLB 2, 5, 33, 169, 227; DLBD 8; MSW; MTCW 1, 2; PFS 6; RGAL; TCWW 2

Reed, John (Silas) 1887-1920 **TCLC 9**
　See also CA 106; 195

Reed, Lou CLC 21
　See also Firbank, Louis

Reese, Lizette Woodworth 1856-1935 **PC 29**
　See also CA 180; DLB 54

Reeve, Clara 1729-1807 **NCLC 19**
　See also DLB 39; RGEL

Reich, Wilhelm 1897-1957 **TCLC 57**

Reid, Christopher (John) 1949- **CLC 33**
　See also CA 140; CANR 89; CP; DLB 40

Reid, Desmond
　See Moorcock, Michael (John)

Reid Banks, Lynne 1929-
　See Banks, Lynne Reid
　See also CA 1-4R; CANR 6, 22, 38, 87; CLR 24; CN; JRDA; MAICYA; SATA 22, 75, 111; YAW

Reilly, William K.
　See Creasey, John

Reiner, Max
　See Caldwell, (Janet Miriam) Taylor (Holland)

Reis, Ricardo
　See Pessoa, Fernando (Antonio Nogueira)

Remarque, Erich Maria 1898-1970 **CLC 21; DA; DAB; DAC; DAM MST, NOV**
　See also AAYA 27; BPFB 3; CA 77-80; 29-32R; DA3; DLB 56; EXPN; LAIT 3; MTCW 1, 2; NFS 4; RGWL

Remington, Frederic 1861-1909 **TCLC 89**
　See also CA 108; 169; DLB 12, 186, 188; SATA 41

Remizov, A.
　See Remizov, Aleksei (Mikhailovich)

Remizov, A. M.
　See Remizov, Aleksei (Mikhailovich)

Remizov, Aleksei (Mikhailovich) 1877-1957 **TCLC 27**
　See also CA 125; 133

Renan, Joseph Ernest 1823-1892 **NCLC 26**
　See also GFL 1789 to the Present

Renard, Jules 1864-1910 **TCLC 17**
　See also CA 117; GFL 1789 to the Present

Renault, Mary CLC 3, 11, 17
　See also Challans, Mary
　See also BPFB 3; BYA 2; DLBY 83; GLL 1; LAIT 1; MTCW 2; RGEL; RHW

Rendell, Ruth (Barbara) 1930- **CLC 28, 48; DAM POP**
　See also Vine, Barbara
　See also BPFB 3; CA 109; CANR 32, 52, 74; CN; CPW; DLB 87; INT CANR-32; MSW; MTCW 1, 2

Renoir, Jean 1894-1979 **CLC 20**
　See also CA 129; 85-88

Resnais, Alain 1922- **CLC 16**

Reverdy, Pierre 1889-1960 **CLC 53**
　See also CA 97-100; 89-92; GFL 1789 to the Present

Rexroth, Kenneth 1905-1982 **CLC 1, 2, 6, 11, 22, 49, 112; DAM POET; PC 20**
　See also CA 5-8R; 107; CANR 14, 34, 63; CDALB 1941-1968; DLB 16, 48, 165, 212; DLBY 82; INT CANR-14; MTCW 1, 2; RGAL

Reyes, Alfonso 1889-1959 **TCLC 33; HLCS 2**
　See also CA 131; HW 1; LAW

Reyes y Basoalto, Ricardo Eliecer Neftali
　See Neruda, Pablo

Reymont, Wladyslaw (Stanislaw) 1868(?)-1925 **TCLC 5**
　See also CA 104

Reynolds, Jonathan 1942- **CLC 6, 38**
　See also CA 65-68; CANR 28

Reynolds, Joshua 1723-1792 **LC 15**
　See also DLB 104

Reynolds, Michael S(hane) 1937-2000 **CLC 44**
　See also CA 65-68; 189; CANR 9, 89, 97

Reznikoff, Charles 1894-1976 **CLC 9**
　See also CA 33-36; 61-64; CAP 2; DLB 28, 45; WP

Rezzori (d'Arezzo), Gregor von 1914-1998 **CLC 25**
　See also CA 122; 136; 167

Rhine, Richard
　See Silverstein, Alvin; Silverstein, Virginia B(arbara Opshelor)

Rhodes, Eugene Manlove 1869-1934 **TCLC 53**
　See also DLB 256

R'hoone
　See Balzac, Honore de

Rhys, Jean 1894(?)-1979 **CLC 2, 4, 6, 14, 19, 51, 124; DAM NOV; SSC 21**
　See also BRWS 2; CA 25-28R; 85-88; CANR 35, 62; CDBLB 1945-1960; DA3; DLB 36, 117, 162; DNFS; MTCW 1, 2; RGEL; RGSF; RHW

Ribeiro, Darcy 1922-1997 **CLC 34**
　See also CA 33-36R; 156

Ribeiro, Joao Ubaldo (Osorio Pimentel) 1941- **CLC 10, 67**
　See also CA 81-84

Ribman, Ronald (Burt) 1932- **CLC 7**
　See also CA 21-24R; CAD; CANR 46, 80; CD

Ricci, Nino 1959- **CLC 70**
　See also CA 137; CCA 1

Rice, Anne 1941- **CLC 41, 128; DAM POP**
　See also Rampling, Anne
　See also AAYA 9; AMWS 7; BEST 89:2; BPFB 3; CA 65-68; CANR 12, 36, 53, 74, 100; CN; CPW; CSW; DA3; GLL 2; HGG; MTCW 2; YAW

Rice, Elmer (Leopold) 1892-1967 **CLC 7, 49; DAM DRAM**
　See also CA 21-22; 25-28R; CAP 2; DFS 12; DLB 4, 7; MTCW 1, 2; RGAL

Rice, Tim(othy Miles Bindon) 1944- **CLC 21**
　See also CA 103; CANR 46; DFS 7

Rich, Adrienne (Cecile) 1929- **CLC 3, 6, 7, 11, 18, 36, 73, 76, 125; DAM POET; PC 5**
　See also AMWS 1; CA 9-12R; CANR 20, 53, 74; CDALBS; CP; CWP; DA3; DLB 5, 67; EXPP; FW; MAWW; MTCW 1, 2; PAB; RGAL; WP

Rich, Barbara
　See Graves, Robert (von Ranke)

Rich, Robert
　See Trumbo, Dalton

Richard, Keith CLC 17
　See also Richards, Keith

Richards, David Adams 1950- **CLC 59; DAC**
　See also CA 93-96; CANR 60; DLB 53

Richards, I(vor) A(rmstrong) 1893-1979 **CLC 14, 24**
　See also BRWS 2; CA 41-44R; 89-92; CANR 34, 74; DLB 27; MTCW 2; RGEL

Richards, Keith 1943-
　See Richard, Keith
　See also CA 107; CANR 77

Richardson, Anne
　See Roiphe, Anne (Richardson)

Richardson, Dorothy Miller 1873-1957 **TCLC 3**
　See also CA 104; 192; DLB 36; FW; RGEL

Richardson (Robertson), Ethel Florence Lindesay 1870-1946
　See Richardson, Henry Handel
　See also CA 105; 190; DLB 230; RHW

Richardson, Henry Handel TCLC 4
　See also Richardson (Robertson), Ethel Florence Lindesay
　See also DLB 197; RGEL; RGSF

Richardson, John 1796-1852 **NCLC 55; DAC**
　See also CCA 1; DLB 99

Richardson, Samuel 1689-1761 **LC 1, 44; DA; DAB; DAC; DAM MST, NOV; WLC**
　See also BRW 3; CDBLB 1660-1789; DLB 39; RGEL; WLIT 3

Richler, Mordecai 1931-2001 **CLC 3, 5, 9, 13, 18, 46, 70; DAC; DAM MST, NOV**
　See also AITN 1; CA 65-68; CANR 31, 62; CCA 1; CLR 17; CWRI; DLB 53; MAICYA; MTCW 1, 2; RGEL; SATA 44, 98; SATA-Brief 27

Richter, Conrad (Michael) 1890-1968 **CLC 30**
　See also AAYA 21; BYA 2; CA 5-8R; 25-28R; CANR 23; DLB 9, 212; LAIT 1; MTCW 1, 2; RGAL; SATA 3; TCWW 2; YAW

Ricostranza, Tom
　See Ellis, Trey

Riddell, Charlotte 1832-1906 **TCLC 40**
　See also Riddell, Mrs. J. H.
　See also CA 165; DLB 156

Riddell, Mrs. J. H.
　See Riddell, Charlotte
　See also HGG; SUFW

Ridge, John Rollin 1827-1867 **NCLC 82; DAM MULT**
　See also CA 144; DLB 175; NNAL

Ridgeway, Jason
　See Marlowe, Stephen

Ridgway, Keith 1965- **CLC 119**
　See also CA 172

Riding, Laura CLC 3, 7
　See also Jackson, Laura (Riding)
　See also RGAL

Riefenstahl, Berta Helene Amalia 1902-
　See Riefenstahl, Leni
　See also CA 108

Riefenstahl, Leni CLC 16
　See also Riefenstahl, Berta Helene Amalia

Riffe, Ernest
See Bergman, (Ernst) Ingmar
Riggs, (Rolla) Lynn 1899-1954 **TCLC 56;
DAM MULT**
See also CA 144; DLB 175; NNAL
Riis, Jacob A(ugust) 1849-1914 **TCLC 80**
See also CA 113; 168; DLB 23
Riley, James Whitcomb 1849-1916 **TCLC 51;
DAM POET**
See also CA 118; 137; MAICYA; RGAL;
SATA 17
Riley, Tex
See Creasey, John
Rilke, Rainer Maria 1875-1926 **TCLC 1, 6,
19; DAM POET; PC 2**
See also CA 104; 132; CANR 62, 99; DA3;
DLB 81; EW 9; MTCW 1, 2; RGWL; WP
Rimbaud, (Jean Nicolas) Arthur 1854-1891
**NCLC 4, 35, 82; DA; DAB; DAC; DAM
MST, POET; PC 3; WLC**
See also DA3; DLB 217; EW 7; GFL 1789
to the Present; RGWL; TWA; WP
Rinehart, Mary Roberts 1876-1958 **TCLC 52**
See also BPFB 3; CA 108; 166; RGAL;
RHW
Ringmaster, The
See Mencken, H(enry) L(ouis)
Ringwood, Gwen(dolyn Margaret) Pharis
1910-1984 **CLC 48**
See also CA 148; 112; DLB 88
Rio, Michel 19(?)- **CLC 43**
Ritsos, Giannes
See Ritsos, Yannis
Ritsos, Yannis 1909-1990 **CLC 6, 13, 31**
See also CA 77-80; 133; CANR 39, 61; EW
12; MTCW 1; RGWL
Ritter, Erika 1948(?)- **CLC 52**
See also CD; CWD
Rivera, Jose Eustasio 1889-1928 **TCLC 35**
See also CA 162; HW 1, 2; LAW
Rivera, Tomas 1935-1984
See also CA 49-52; CANR 32; DLB 82;
HLCS 2; HW 1; RGAL; TCWW 2; WLIT
1
Rivers, Conrad Kent 1933-1968 **CLC 1**
See also BW 1; CA 85-88; DLB 41
Rivers, Elfrida
See Bradley, Marion Zimmer
See also GLL 1
Riverside, John
See Heinlein, Robert A(nson)
Rizal, Jose 1861-1896 **NCLC 27**
Roa Bastos, Augusto (Antonio) 1917- **CLC
45; DAM MULT; HLC 2**
See also CA 131; DLB 113; HW 1; LAW;
RGSF; WLIT 1
Robbe-Grillet, Alain 1922- **CLC 1, 2, 4, 6, 8,
10, 14, 43, 128**
See also BPFB 3; CA 9-12R; CANR 33,
65; DLB 83; EW 13; GFL 1789 to the
Present; IDFW 3, 4; MTCW 1, 2; RGWL
Robbins, Harold 1916-1997 **CLC 5; DAM
NOV**
See also BPFB 3; CA 73-76; 162; CANR
26, 54; DA3; MTCW 1, 2
Robbins, Thomas Eugene 1936-
See Robbins, Tom
See also CA 81-84; CANR 29, 59, 95; CN;
CPW; CSW; DA3; DAM NOV, POP;
MTCW 1, 2
Robbins, Tom **CLC 9, 32, 64**
See also Robbins, Thomas Eugene
See also AAYA 32; AMWS 10; BEST 90:3;
BPFB 3; DLBY 80; MTCW 2
Robbins, Trina 1938- **CLC 21**
See also CA 128

Roberts, Charles G(eorge) D(ouglas)
1860-1943 **TCLC 8**
See also CA 105; 188; CLR 33; CWRI;
DLB 92; RGEL; RGSF; SATA 88; SATA-
Brief 29
Roberts, Elizabeth Madox 1886-1941 **TCLC
68**
See also CA 111; 166; CWRI; DLB 9, 54,
102; RGAL; RHW; SATA 33; SATA-Brief
27; WCH
Roberts, Kate 1891-1985 **CLC 15**
See also CA 107; 116
Roberts, Keith (John Kingston) 1935-2000
CLC 14
See also CA 25-28R; CANR 46; SFW
Roberts, Kenneth (Lewis) 1885-1957 **TCLC
23**
See also CA 109; DLB 9; RGAL; RHW
Roberts, Michele (Brigitte) 1949- **CLC 48**
See also CA 115; CANR 58; CN; DLB 231;
FW
Robertson, Ellis
See Ellison, Harlan (Jay); Silverberg, Robert
Robertson, Thomas William 1829-1871
NCLC 35; DAM DRAM
See also Robertson, Tom
Robertson, Tom
See Robertson, Thomas William
See also RGEL
Robeson, Kenneth
See Dent, Lester
Robinson, Edwin Arlington 1869-1935 **TCLC
5, 101; DA; DAC; DAM MST, POET;
PC 1, 35**
See also AMW; CA 104; 133; CDALB
1865-1917; DLB 54; EXPP; MTCW 1, 2;
PAB; PFS 4; RGAL; WP
Robinson, Henry Crabb 1775-1867 **NCLC 15**
See also DLB 107
Robinson, Jill 1936- **CLC 10**
See also CA 102; INT 102
Robinson, Kim Stanley 1952- **CLC 34**
See also AAYA 26; CA 126; CN; SATA 109;
SCFW 2; SFW
Robinson, Lloyd
See Silverberg, Robert
Robinson, Marilynne 1944- **CLC 25**
See also CA 116; CANR 80; CN; DLB 206
Robinson, Smokey **CLC 21**
See also Robinson, William, Jr.
Robinson, William, Jr. 1940-
See Robinson, Smokey
See also CA 116
Robison, Mary 1949- **CLC 42, 98**
See also CA 113; 116; CANR 87; CN; DLB
130; INT 116; RGSF
Rochester, John Wilmot, Earl of 1647-1680
LC 75
See also Wilmot, John
See also RGEL
Rod, Edouard 1857-1910 **TCLC 52**
Roddenberry, Eugene Wesley 1921-1991
See Roddenberry, Gene
See also CA 110; 135; CANR 37; SATA 45;
SATA-Obit 69
Roddenberry, Gene **CLC 17**
See also Roddenberry, Eugene Wesley
See also AAYA 5; SATA-Obit 69
Rodgers, Mary 1931- **CLC 12**
See also BYA 5; CA 49-52; CANR 8, 55,
90; CLR 20; CWRI; INT CANR-8; JRDA;
MAICYA; SATA 8
Rodgers, W(illiam) R(obert) 1909-1969 **CLC
7**
See also CA 85-88; DLB 20; RGEL
Rodman, Eric
See Silverberg, Robert
Rodman, Howard 1920(?)-1985 **CLC 65**
See also CA 118

Rodman, Maia
See Wojciechowska, Maia (Teresa)
Rodo, Jose Enrique 1871(?)-1917
See also CA 178; HLCS 2; HW 2; LAW
Rodolph, Utto
See Ouologuem, Yambo
Rodriguez, Claudio 1934-1999 **CLC 10**
See also CA 188; DLB 134
Rodriguez, Richard 1944- **CLC 155; DAM
MULT; HLC 2**
See also CA 110; CANR 66; DLB 82, 256;
HW 1, 2; LAIT 5; WLIT 1
Roelvaag, O(le) E(dvart) 1876-1931
See Rolvaag, O(le) E(dvart)
See also CA 117; 171
Roethke, Theodore (Huebner) 1908-1963
**CLC 1, 3, 8, 11, 19, 46, 101; DAM
POET; PC 15**
See also AMW; CA 81-84; CABS 2;
CDALB 1941-1968; DA3; DLB 5, 206;
EXPP; MTCW 1, 2; PAB; PFS 3; RGAL;
WP
Rogers, Samuel 1763-1855 **NCLC 69**
See also DLB 93; RGEL
Rogers, Thomas Hunton 1927- **CLC 57**
See also CA 89-92; INT 89-92
Rogers, Will(iam Penn Adair) 1879-1935
TCLC 8, 71; DAM MULT
See also CA 105; 144; DA3; DLB 11;
MTCW 2; NNAL
Rogin, Gilbert 1929- **CLC 18**
See also CA 65-68; CANR 15
Rohan, Koda
See Koda Shigeyuki
Rohlfs, Anna Katharine Green
See Green, Anna Katharine
Rohmer, Eric **CLC 16**
See also Scherer, Jean-Marie Maurice
Rohmer, Sax **TCLC 28**
See also Ward, Arthur Henry Sarsfield
See also DLB 70; MSW; SUFW
Roiphe, Anne (Richardson) 1935- **CLC 3, 9**
See also CA 89-92; CANR 45, 73; DLBY
80; INT 89-92
Rojas, Fernando de 1475-1541 **LC 23; HLCS
1**
See also RGWL
Rojas, Gonzalo 1917-
See also CA 178; HLCS 2; HW 2; LAWS 1
**Rolfe, Frederick (William Serafino Austin
Lewis Mary)** 1860-1913 **TCLC 12**
See also Corvo, Baron
See also CA 107; DLB 34, 156; RGEL
Rolland, Romain 1866-1944 **TCLC 23**
See also CA 118; 197; DLB 65; GFL 1789
to the Present; RGWL
Rolle, Richard c. 1300-c. 1349 **CMLC 21**
See also DLB 146; RGEL
Rolvaag, O(le) E(dvart) **TCLC 17**
See also Roelvaag, O(le) E(dvart)
See also DLB 9, 212; NFS 5; RGAL
Romain Arnaud, Saint
See Aragon, Louis
Romains, Jules 1885-1972 **CLC 7**
See also CA 85-88; CANR 34; DLB 65;
GFL 1789 to the Present; MTCW 1
Romero, Jose Ruben 1890-1952 **TCLC 14**
See also CA 114; 131; HW 1; LAW
Ronsard, Pierre de 1524-1585 **LC 6, 54; PC
11**
See also EW 2; GFL Beginnings to 1789;
RGWL
Rooke, Leon 1934- **CLC 25, 34; DAM POP**
See also CA 25-28R; CANR 23, 53; CCA
1; CPW
Roosevelt, Franklin Delano 1882-1945 **TCLC
93**
See also CA 116; 173; LAIT 3

Roosevelt, Theodore 1858-1919 **TCLC 69**
See also CA 115; 170; DLB 47, 186
Roper, William 1498-1578 **LC 10**
Roquelaure, A. N.
See Rice, Anne
Rosa, Joao Guimaraes 1908-1967 **CLC 23;
HLCS 1**
See also Guimaraes Rosa, Joao
See also CA 89-92; DLB 113; WLIT 1
Rose, Wendy 1948- **CLC 85; DAM MULT;
PC 13**
See also CA 53-56; CANR 5, 51; CWP;
DLB 175; NNAL; PFS 13; RGAL; SATA
12
Rosen, R. D.
See Rosen, Richard (Dean)
Rosen, Richard (Dean) 1949- **CLC 39**
See also CA 77-80; CANR 62; CMW; INT
CANR-30
Rosenberg, Isaac 1890-1918 **TCLC 12**
See also BRW 6; CA 107; 188; DLB 20,
216; PAB; RGEL
Rosenblatt, Joe CLC 15
See also Rosenblatt, Joseph
Rosenblatt, Joseph 1933-
See Rosenblatt, Joe
See also CA 89-92; CP; INT 89-92
Rosenfeld, Samuel
See Tzara, Tristan
Rosenstock, Sami
See Tzara, Tristan
Rosenstock, Samuel
See Tzara, Tristan
Rosenthal, M(acha) L(ouis) 1917-1996 **CLC
28**
See also CA 1-4R; 152; CAAS 6; CANR 4,
51; CP; DLB 5; SATA 59
Ross, Barnaby
See Dannay, Frederic
Ross, Bernard L.
See Follett, Ken(neth Martin)
Ross, J. H.
See Lawrence, T(homas) E(dward)
Ross, John Hume
See Lawrence, T(homas) E(dward)
Ross, Martin 1862-1915
See Martin, Violet Florence
See also DLB 135; GLL 2; RGEL; RGSF
Ross, (James) Sinclair 1908-1996 **CLC 13;
DAC; DAM MST; SSC 24**
See also CA 73-76; CANR 81; CN; DLB
88; RGEL; RGSF; TCWW 2
Rossetti, Christina (Georgina) 1830-1894
**NCLC 2, 50, 66; DA; DAB; DAC; DAM
MST, POET; PC 7; WLC**
See also BRW 5; BYA 4; DA3; DLB 35,
163, 240; EXPP; MAICYA; PFS 10, 14;
RGEL; SATA 20; WCH
Rossetti, Dante Gabriel 1828-1882 **NCLC 4,
77; DA; DAB; DAC; DAM MST,
POET; WLC**
See also BRW 5; CDBLB 1832-1890; DLB
35; EXPP; RGEL
Rossi, Cristina Peri
See Peri Rossi, Cristina
Rossner, Judith (Perelman) 1935- **CLC 6, 9,
29**
See also AITN 2; BEST 90:3; BPFB 3; CA
17-20R; CANR 18, 51, 73; CN; DLB 6;
INT CANR-18; MTCW 1, 2
Rostand, Edmond (Eugene Alexis)
1868-1918 **TCLC 6, 37; DA; DAB;
DAC; DAM DRAM, MST; DC 10**
See also CA 104; 126; DA3; DFS 1; DLB
192; LAIT 1; MTCW 1; RGWL
Roth, Henry 1906-1995 **CLC 2, 6, 11, 104**
See also AMWS 9; CA 11-12; 149; CANR
38, 63; CAP 1; CN; DA3; DLB 28;
MTCW 1, 2; RGAL

Roth, (Moses) Joseph 1894-1939 **TCLC 33**
See also CA 160; DLB 85; RGWL
Roth, Philip (Milton) 1933- **CLC 1, 2, 3, 4, 6,
9, 15, 22, 31, 47, 66, 86, 119; DA; DAB;
DAC; DAM MST, NOV, POP; SSC 26;
WLC**
See also AMWS 3; BEST 90:3; BPFB 3;
CA 1-4R; CANR 1, 22, 36, 55, 89;
CDALB 1968-1988; CN; CPW 1; DA3;
DLB 2, 28, 173; DLBY 82; MTCW 1, 2;
RGAL; RGSF; SSFS 12
Rothenberg, Jerome 1931- **CLC 6, 57**
See also CA 45-48; CANR 1, 106; CP; DLB
5, 193
Rotter, Pat ed. CLC 65
Roumain, Jacques (Jean Baptiste) 1907-1944
TCLC 19; BLC 3; DAM MULT
See also BW 1; CA 117; 125
Rourke, Constance (Mayfield) 1885-1941
TCLC 12
See also CA 107; YABC 1
Rousseau, Jean-Baptiste 1671-1741 **LC 9**
Rousseau, Jean-Jacques 1712-1778 **LC 14,
36; DA; DAB; DAC; DAM MST; WLC**
See also DA3; EW 4; GFL Beginnings to
1789; RGWL
Roussel, Raymond 1877-1933 **TCLC 20**
See also CA 117; GFL 1789 to the Present
Rovit, Earl (Herbert) 1927- **CLC 7**
See also CA 5-8R; CANR 12
Rowe, Elizabeth Singer 1674-1737 **LC 44**
See also DLB 39, 95
Rowe, Nicholas 1674-1718 **LC 8**
See also DLB 84; RGEL
Rowlandson, Mary 1637(?)-1678 **LC 66**
See also DLB 24, 200; RGAL
Rowley, Ames Dorrance
See Lovecraft, H(oward) P(hillips)
Rowling, J(oanne) K(athleen) 1966(?)- **CLC
137**
See also AAYA 34; BYA 13, 14; CA 173;
CLR 66; SATA 109
Rowson, Susanna Haswell 1762(?)-1824
NCLC 5, 69
See also DLB 37, 200; RGAL
Roy, Arundhati 1960(?)- **CLC 109**
See also CA 163; CANR 90; DLBY 97
Roy, Gabrielle 1909-1983 **CLC 10, 14; DAB;
DAC; DAM MST**
See also CA 53-56; 110; CANR 5, 61; CCA
1; DLB 68; MTCW 1; RGWL; SATA 104
Royko, Mike 1932-1997 **CLC 109**
See also CA 89-92; 157; CANR 26; CPW
Rozanov, Vassili 1856-1919 **TCLC 104**
Rozewicz, Tadeusz 1921- **CLC 9, 23, 139;
DAM POET**
See also CA 108; CANR 36, 66; CWW 2;
DA3; DLB 232; MTCW 1, 2
Ruark, Gibbons 1941- **CLC 3**
See also CA 33-36R; CAAS 23; CANR 14,
31, 57; DLB 120
Rubens, Bernice (Ruth) 1923- **CLC 19, 31**
See also CA 25-28R; CANR 33, 65; CN;
DLB 14, 207; MTCW 1
Rubin, Harold
See Robbins, Harold
Rudkin, (James) David 1936- **CLC 14**
See also CA 89-92; CBD; CD; DLB 13
Rudnik, Raphael 1933- **CLC 7**
See also CA 29-32R
Ruffian, M.
See Hasek, Jaroslav (Matej Frantisek)
Ruiz, Jose Martinez CLC 11
See also Martinez Ruiz, Jose
Rukeyser, Muriel 1913-1980 **CLC 6, 10, 15,**

27; **DAM POET; PC 12**
See also AMWS 6; CA 5-8R; 93-96; CANR
26, 60; DA3; DLB 48; FW; GLL 2;
MTCW 1, 2; PFS 10; RGAL; SATA-Obit
22
Rule, Jane (Vance) 1931- **CLC 27**
See also CA 25-28R; CAAS 18; CANR 12,
87; CN; DLB 60; FW
Rulfo, Juan 1918-1986 **CLC 8, 80; DAM
MULT; HLC 2; SSC 25**
See also CA 85-88; 118; CANR 26; DLB
113; HW 1, 2; LAW; MTCW 1, 2; RGSF;
RGWL; WLIT 1
Rumi, Jalal al-Din 1207-1273 **CMLC 20**
See also RGWL; WP
Runeberg, Johan 1804-1877 **NCLC 41**
Runyon, (Alfred) Damon 1884(?)-1946 **TCLC
10**
See also CA 107; 165; DLB 11, 86, 171;
MTCW 2; RGAL
Rush, Norman 1933- **CLC 44**
See also CA 121; 126; INT 126
Rushdie, (Ahmed) Salman 1947- **CLC 23, 31,
55, 100; DAB; DAC; DAM MST, NOV,
POP; WLCS**
See also BEST 89:3; BPFB 3; BRWS 4;
CA 108; 111; CANR 33, 56; CN; CPW 1;
DA3; DLB 194; FANT; INT CA-111;
MTCW 1, 2; RGEL; RGSF; WLIT 4
Rushforth, Peter (Scott) 1945- **CLC 19**
See also CA 101
Ruskin, John 1819-1900 **TCLC 63**
See also BRW 5; BYA 5; CA 114; 129; CD-
BLB 1832-1890; DLB 55, 163, 190;
RGEL; SATA 24; WCH
Russ, Joanna 1937- **CLC 15**
See also BPFB 3; CA 5-28R; CANR 11,
31, 65; CN; DLB 8; FW; GLL 1; MTCW
1; SCFW 2; SFW
Russell, George William 1867-1935
See A.E.; Baker, Jean H.
See also CA 104; 153; CDBLB 1890-1914;
DAM POET; RGEL
Russell, Jeffrey Burton 1934- **CLC 70**
See also CA 25-28R; CANR 11, 28, 52
Russell, (Henry) Ken(neth Alfred) 1927- **CLC
16**
See also CA 105
Russell, William Martin 1947- **CLC 60**
See also CA 164; DLB 233
Rutherford, Mark TCLC 25
See also White, William Hale
See also DLB 18; RGEL
Ruyslinck, Ward CLC 14
See also Belser, Reimond Karel Maria de
Ryan, Cornelius (John) 1920-1974 **CLC 7**
See also CA 69-72; 53-56; CANR 38
Ryan, Michael 1946- **CLC 65**
See also CA 49-52; DLBY 82
Ryan, Tim
See Dent, Lester
Rybakov, Anatoli (Naumovich) 1911-1998
CLC 23, 53
See also CA 126; 135; 172; SATA 79;
SATA-Obit 108
Ryder, Jonathan
See Ludlum, Robert
Ryga, George 1932-1987 **CLC 14; DAC;
DAM MST**
See also CA 101; 124; CANR 43, 90; CCA
1; DLB 60
S. H.
See Hartmann, Sadakichi
S. S.
See Sassoon, Siegfried (Lorraine)
Saba, Umberto 1883-1957 **TCLC 33**
See also CA 144; CANR 79; DLB 114;
RGWL

Sabatini, Rafael 1875-1950 **TCLC 47**
See also BPFB 3; CA 162; RHW
Sabato, Ernesto (R.) 1911- **CLC 10, 23; DAM MULT; HLC 2**
See also CA 97-100; CANR 32, 65; DLB 145; HW 1, 2; LAW; MTCW 1, 2
Sa-Carneiro, Mario de 1890-1916 **TCLC 83**
Sacastru, Martin
See Bioy Casares, Adolfo
See also CWW 2
Sacastru, Martin
See Bioy Casares, Adolfo
Sacher-Masoch, Leopold von 1836(?)-1895 **NCLC 31**
Sachs, Marilyn (Stickle) 1927- **CLC 35**
See also AAYA 2; BYA 6; CA 17-20R; CANR 13, 47; CLR 2; JRDA; MAICYA; SAAS 2; SATA 3, 68; SATA-Essay 110; WYA; YAW
Sachs, Nelly 1891-1970 **CLC 14, 98**
See also CA 17-18; 25-28R; CANR 87; CAP 2; MTCW 2; RGWL
Sackler, Howard (Oliver) 1929-1982 **CLC 14**
See also CA 61-64; 108; CAD; CANR 30; DLB 7
Sacks, Oliver (Wolf) 1933- **CLC 67**
See also CA 53-56; CANR 28, 50, 76; CPW; DA3; INT CANR-28; MTCW 1, 2
Sadakichi
See Hartmann, Sadakichi
Sade, Donatien Alphonse Francois 1740-1814 **NCLC 3, 47**
See also EW 4; GFL Beginnings to 1789; RGWL
Sadoff, Ira 1945- **CLC 9**
See also CA 53-56; CANR 5, 21; DLB 120
Saetone
See Camus, Albert
Safire, William 1929- **CLC 10**
See also CA 17-20R; CANR 31, 54, 91
Sagan, Carl (Edward) 1934-1996 **CLC 30, 112**
See also AAYA 2; CA 25-28R; 155; CANR 11, 36, 74; CPW; DA3; MTCW 1, 2; SATA 58; SATA-Obit 94
Sagan, Francoise CLC 3, 6, 9, 17, 36
See also Quoirez, Francoise
See also CWW 2; DLB 83; GFL 1789 to the Present; MTCW 2
Sahgal, Nayantara (Pandit) 1927- **CLC 41**
See also CA 9-12R; CANR 11, 88; CN
Said, Edward W. 1935- **CLC 123**
See also CA 21-24R; CANR 45, 74; DLB 67; MTCW 2
Saint, H(arry) F. 1941- **CLC 50**
See also CA 127
St. Aubin de Teran, Lisa 1953-
See Teran, Lisa St. Aubin de
See also CA 118; 126; CN; INT 126
Saint Birgitta of Swedenc. 1303-1373 **CMLC 24**
Sainte-Beuve, Charles Augustin 1804-1869 **NCLC 5**
See also DLB 217; EW 6; GFL 1789 to the Present
Saint-Exupery, Antoine (Jean Baptiste Marie Roger) de 1900-1944 **TCLC 2, 56; DAM NOV; WLC**
See also BPFB 3; BYA 3; CA 108; 132; CLR 10; DA3; DLB 72; EW 12; GFL 1789 to the Present; LAIT 3; MAICYA; MTCW 1, 2; RGWL; SATA 20
St. John, David
See Hunt, E(verette) Howard, (Jr.)
St. John, J. Hector
See Crevecoeur, Michel Guillaume Jean de

Saint-John Perse
See Leger, (Marie-Rene Auguste) Alexis Saint-Leger
See also EW 10; GFL 1789 to the Present; RGWL
Saintsbury, George (Edward Bateman) 1845-1933 **TCLC 31**
See also CA 160; DLB 57, 149
Sait Faik TCLC 23
See also Abasiyanik, Sait Faik
Saki TCLC 3; SSC 12
See also Munro, H(ector) H(ugh)
See also BRWS 6; LAIT 2; MTCW 2; RGEL; SSFS 1; SUFW
Sakutaro, Hagiwara
See Hagiwara, Sakutaro
Sala, George Augustus 1828-1895 **NCLC 46**
Saladin 1138-1193 **CMLC 38**
Salama, Hannu 1936- **CLC 18**
Salamanca, J(ack) R(ichard) 1922- **CLC 4, 15**
See also CA 25-28R; CAAE 193
Salas, Floyd Francis 1931-
See also CA 119; CAAS 27; CANR 44, 75, 93; DAM MULT; DLB 82; HLC 2; HW 1, 2; MTCW 2
Sale, J. Kirkpatrick
See Sale, Kirkpatrick
Sale, Kirkpatrick 1937- **CLC 68**
See also CA 13-16R; CANR 10
Salinas, Luis Omar 1937- **CLC 90; DAM MULT; HLC 2**
See also CA 131; CANR 81; DLB 82; HW 1, 2
Salinas (y Serrano), Pedro 1891(?)-1951 **TCLC 17**
See also CA 117; DLB 134
Salinger, J(erome) D(avid) 1919- **CLC 1, 3, 8, 12, 55, 56, 138; DA; DAB; DAC; DAM MST, NOV, POP; SSC 2, 28; WLC**
See also AAYA 2, 36; AMW; BPFB 3; CA 5-8R; CANR 39; CDALB 1941-1968; CLR 18; CN; CPW 1; DA3; DLB 2, 102, 173; EXPN; LAIT 4; MAICYA; MTCW 1, 2; NFS 1; RGAL; RGSF; SATA 67; WYA; YAW
Salisbury, John
See Caute, (John) David
Salter, James 1925- **CLC 7, 52, 59**
See also AMWS 9; CA 73-76; DLB 130
Saltus, Edgar (Everton) 1855-1921 **TCLC 8**
See also CA 105; DLB 202; RGAL
Saltykov, Mikhail Evgrafovich 1826-1889 **NCLC 16**
See also DLB 238:
Saltykov-Shchedrin, N.
See Saltykov, Mikhail Evgrafovich
Samarakis, Antonis 1919- **CLC 5**
See also CA 25-28R; CAAS 16; CANR 36
Sanchez, Florencio 1875-1910 **TCLC 37**
See also CA 153; HW 1; LAW
Sanchez, Luis Rafael 1936- **CLC 23**
See also CA 128; DLB 145; HW 1; WLIT 1
Sanchez, Sonia 1934- **CLC 5, 116; BLC 3; DAM MULT; PC 9**
See also BW 2, 3; CA 33-36R; CANR 24, 49, 74; CLR 18; CP; CSW; CWP; DA3; DLB 41; DLBD 8; MAICYA; MTCW 1, 2; SATA 22; WP
Sand, George 1804-1876 **NCLC 2, 42, 57; DA; DAB; DAC; DAM MST, NOV; WLC**
See also DA3; DLB 119, 192; EW 6; FW; GFL 1789 to the Present; RGWL
Sandburg, Carl (August) 1878-1967 **CLC 1, 4, 10, 15, 35; DA; DAB; DAC; DAM**

MST, POET; PC 2; WLC
See also AAYA 24; AMW; BYA 1, 3; CA 5-8R; 25-28R; CANR 35; CDALB 1865-1917; CLR 67; DA3; DLB 17, 54; EXPP; LAIT 2; MAICYA; MTCW 1, 2; PAB; PFS 3, 6, 12; RGAL; SATA 8; WCH; WP; WYA
Sandburg, Charles
See Sandburg, Carl (August)
Sandburg, Charles A.
See Sandburg, Carl (August)
Sanders, (James) Ed(ward) 1939- **CLC 53; DAM POET**
See also Sanders, Edward
See also CA 13-16R; CAAS 21; CANR 13, 44, 78; CP; DLB 16
Sanders, Edward
See Sanders, (James) Ed(ward)
See also DLB 244
Sanders, Lawrence 1920-1998 **CLC 41; DAM POP**
See also BEST 89:4; BPFB 3; CA 81-84; 165; CANR 33, 62; CMW; CPW; DA3; MTCW 1
Sanders, Noah
See Blount, Roy (Alton), Jr.
Sanders, Winston P.
See Anderson, Poul (William)
Sandoz, Mari(e Susette) 1900-1966 **CLC 28**
See also CA 1-4R; 25-28R; CANR 17, 64; DLB 9, 212; LAIT 2; MTCW 1, 2; SATA 5; TCWW 2
Saner, Reg(inald Anthony) 1931- **CLC 9**
See also CA 65-68; CP
Sankara788-820 **CMLC 32**
Sannazaro, Jacopo 1456(?)-1530 **LC 8**
See also RGWL
Sansom, William 1912-1976 **CLC 2, 6; DAM NOV; SSC 21**
See also CA 5-8R; 65-68; CANR 42; DLB 139; MTCW 1; RGEL; RGSF
Santayana, George 1863-1952 **TCLC 40**
See also AMW; CA 115; 194; DLB 54, 71, 246; DLBD 13; RGAL
Santiago, Danny CLC 33
See also James, Daniel (Lewis)
See also DLB 122
Santmyer, Helen Hooven 1895-1986 **CLC 33**
See also CA 1-4R; 118; CANR 15, 33; DLBY 84; MTCW 1; RHW
Santoka, Taneda 1882-1940 **TCLC 72**
Santos, Bienvenido N(uqui) 1911-1996 **CLC 22; DAM MULT**
See also CA 101; 151; CANR 19, 46; RGAL
Sapir, Edward 1884-1939 **TCLC 108**
See also DLB 92
Sapper TCLC 44
See also McNeile, Herman Cyril
Sapphire
See Sapphire, Brenda
Sapphire, Brenda 1950- **CLC 99**
Sapphofl. 6256th cent. B.C.- **CMLC 3; DAM POET; PC 5**
See also DA3; DLB 176; RGWL; WP
Saramago, Jose 1922- **CLC 119; HLCS 1**
See also CA 153; CANR 96
Sarduy, Severo 1937-1993 **CLC 6, 97; HLCS 2**
See also CA 89-92; 142; CANR 58, 81; CWW 2; DLB 113; HW 1, 2; LAW
Sargeson, Frank 1903-1982 **CLC 31**
See also CA 25-28R; 106; CANR 38, 79; GLL 2; RGEL; RGSF
Sarmiento, Domingo Faustino 1811-1888
See also HLCS 2; LAW; WLIT 1

Sarmiento, Felix Ruben Garcia
See Dario, Ruben

Saro-Wiwa, Ken(ule Beeson) 1941-1995 **CLC 114**
See also BW 2; CA 142; 150; CANR 60; DLB 157

Saroyan, William 1908-1981 **CLC 1, 8, 10, 29, 34, 56; DA; DAB; DAC; DAM DRAM, MST, NOV; SSC 21; WLC**
See also CA 5-8R; 103; CAD; CANR 30; CDALBS; DA3; DLB 7, 9, 86; DLBY 81; LAIT 4; MTCW 1, 2; RGAL; RGSF; SATA 23; SATA-Obit 24

Sarraute, Nathalie 1900-1999 **CLC 1, 2, 4, 8, 10, 31, 80**
See also BPFB 3; CA 9-12R; 187; CANR 23, 66; CWW 2; DLB 83; EW 12; GFL 1789 to the Present; MTCW 1, 2; RGWL

Sarton, (Eleanor) May 1912-1995 **CLC 4, 14, 49, 91; DAM POET; PC 39**
See also AMWS 8; CA 1-4R; 149; CANR 1, 34, 55; CN; CP; DLB 48; DLBY 81; FW; INT CANR-34; MTCW 1, 2; RGAL; SATA 36; SATA-Obit 86

Sartre, Jean-Paul 1905-1980 **CLC 1, 4, 7, 9, 13, 18, 24, 44, 50, 52; DA; DAB; DAC; DAM DRAM, MST, NOV; DC 3; SSC 32; WLC**
See also CA 9-12R; 97-100; CANR 21; DA3; DFS 5; DLB 72; EW 12; GFL 1789 to the Present; MTCW 1, 2; RGSF; RGWL; SSFS 9

Sassoon, Siegfried (Lorraine) 1886-1967 **CLC 36, 130; DAB; DAM MST, NOV, POET; PC 12**
See also BRW 6; CA 104; 25-28R; CANR 36; DLB 20, 191; DLBD 18; MTCW 1, 2; PAB; RGEL

Satterfield, Charles
See Pohl, Frederik

Satyremont
See Peret, Benjamin

Saul, John (W. III) 1942- **CLC 46; DAM NOV, POP**
See also AAYA 10; BEST 90:4; CA 81-84; CANR 16, 40, 81; CPW; HGG; SATA 98

Saunders, Caleb
See Heinlein, Robert A(nson)

Saura (Atares), Carlos 1932-1998 **CLC 20**
See also CA 114; 131; CANR 79; HW 1

Sauser-Hall, Frederic 1887-1961 **CLC 18**
See also Cendrars, Blaise
See also CA 102; 93-96; CANR 36, 62; MTCW 1

Saussure, Ferdinand de 1857-1913 **TCLC 49**
See also DLB 242

Savage, Catharine
See Brosman, Catharine Savage

Savage, Thomas 1915- **CLC 40**
See also CA 126; 132; CAAS 15; CN; INT 132; TCWW 2

Savan, Glenn(?)- **CLC 50**

Sayers, Dorothy L(eigh) 1893-1957 **TCLC 2, 15; DAM POP**
See also BPFB 3; BRWS 3; CA 104; 119; CANR 60; CDBLB 1914-1945; CMW; DLB 10, 36, 77, 100; MSW; MTCW 1, 2; RGEL; SSFS 12

Sayers, Valerie 1952- **CLC 50, 122**
See also CA 134; CANR 61; CSW

Sayles, John (Thomas) 1950- **CLC 7, 10, 14**
See also CA 57-60; CANR 41, 84; DLB 44

Scammell, Michael 1935- **CLC 34**
See also CA 156

Scannell, Vernon 1922- **CLC 49**
See also CA 5-8R; CANR 8, 24, 57; CP; CWRI; DLB 27; SATA 59

Scarlett, Susan
See Streatfeild, (Mary) Noel

Scarron 1847-1910
See Mikszath, Kalman

Schaeffer, Susan Fromberg 1941- **CLC 6, 11, 22**
See also CA 49-52; CANR 18, 65; CN; DLB 28; MTCW 1, 2; SATA 22

Schama, Simon (Michael) 1945- **CLC 150**
See also BEST 89:4; CA 105; CANR 39, 91

Schary, Jill
See Robinson, Jill

Schell, Jonathan 1943- **CLC 35**
See also CA 73-76; CANR 12

Schelling, Friedrich Wilhelm Joseph von 1775-1854 **NCLC 30**
See also DLB 90

Scherer, Jean-Marie Maurice 1920-
See Rohmer, Eric
See also CA 110

Schevill, James (Erwin) 1920- **CLC 7**
See also CA 5-8R; CAAS 12; CAD; CD

Schiller, Friedrich von 1759-1805 **NCLC 39, 69; DAM DRAM; DC 12**
See also DLB 94; EW 5; RGWL

Schisgal, Murray (Joseph) 1926- **CLC 6**
See also CA 21-24R; CAD; CANR 48, 86; CD

Schlee, Ann 1934- **CLC 35**
See also CA 101; CANR 29, 88; SATA 44; SATA-Brief 36

Schlegel, August Wilhelm von 1767-1845 **NCLC 15**
See also DLB 94; RGWL

Schlegel, Friedrich 1772-1829 **NCLC 45**
See also DLB 90; EW 5; RGWL

Schlegel, Johann Elias (von) 1719(?)-1749 **LC 5**

Schleiermacher, Friedrich 1768-1834 **NCLC 107**
See also DLB 90

Schlesinger, Arthur M(eier), Jr. 1917- **CLC 84**
See also AITN 1; CA 1-4R; CANR 1, 28, 58, 105; DLB 17; INT CANR-28; MTCW 1, 2; SATA 61

Schmidt, Arno (Otto) 1914-1979 **CLC 56**
See also CA 128; 109; DLB 69

Schmitz, Aron Hector 1861-1928
See Svevo, Italo
See also CA 104; 122; MTCW 1

Schnackenberg, Gjertrud (Cecelia) 1953- **CLC 40**
See also CA 116; CANR 100; CP; CWP; DLB 120; PFS 13

Schneider, Leonard Alfred 1925-1966
See Bruce, Lenny
See also CA 89-92

Schnitzler, Arthur 1862-1931 **TCLC 4; SSC 15**
See also CA 104; DLB 81, 118; EW 8; RGSF; RGWL

Schoenberg, Arnold Franz Walter 1874-1951 **TCLC 75**
See also CA 109; 188

Schonberg, Arnold
See Schoenberg, Arnold Franz Walter

Schopenhauer, Arthur 1788-1860 **NCLC 51**
See also DLB 90; EW 5

Schor, Sandra (M.) 1932(?)-1990 **CLC 65**
See also CA 132

Schorer, Mark 1908-1977 **CLC 9**
See also CA 5-8R; 73-76; CANR 7; DLB 103

Schrader, Paul (Joseph) 1946- **CLC 26**
See also CA 37-40R; CANR 41; DLB 44

Schreiner, Olive (Emilie Albertina) 1855-1920 **TCLC 9**
See also AFW; BRWS 2; CA 105; 154; DLB 18, 156, 190, 225; FW; RGEL; WLIT 2

Schulberg, Budd (Wilson) 1914- **CLC 7, 48**
See also BPFB 3; CA 25-28R; CANR 19, 87; CN; DLB 6, 26, 28; DLBY 81, 01

Schulman, Arnold
See Trumbo, Dalton

Schulz, Bruno 1892-1942 **TCLC 5, 51; SSC 13**
See also CA 115; 123; CANR 86; DLB 215; MTCW 2; RGSF; RGWL

Schulz, Charles M(onroe) 1922-2000 **CLC 12**
See also AAYA 39; CA 9-12R; 187; CANR 6; INT CANR-6; SATA 10; SATA-Obit 118

Schumacher, E(rnst) F(riedrich) 1911-1977 **CLC 80**
See also CA 81-84; 73-76; CANR 34, 85

Schuyler, James Marcus 1923-1991 **CLC 5, 23; DAM POET**
See also CA 101; 134; DLB 5, 169; INT 101; WP

Schwartz, Delmore (David) 1913-1966 **CLC 2, 4, 10, 45, 87; PC 8**
See also AMWS 2; CA 17-18; 25-28R; CANR 35; CAP 2; DLB 28, 48; MTCW 1, 2; PAB; RGAL

Schwartz, Ernst
See Ozu, Yasujiro

Schwartz, John Burnham 1965- **CLC 59**
See also CA 132

Schwartz, Lynne Sharon 1939- **CLC 31**
See also CA 103; CANR 44, 89; DLB 218; MTCW 2

Schwartz, Muriel A.
See Eliot, T(homas) S(tearns)

Schwarz-Bart, Andre 1928- **CLC 2, 4**
See also CA 89-92

Schwarz-Bart, Simone 1938- **CLC 7; BLCS**
See also BW 2; CA 97-100

Schwitters, Kurt (Hermann Edward Karl Julius) 1887-1948 **TCLC 95**
See also CA 158

Schwob, Marcel (Mayer Andre) 1867-1905 **TCLC 20**
See also CA 117; 168; DLB 123; GFL 1789 to the Present

Sciascia, Leonardo 1921-1989 **CLC 8, 9, 41**
See also CA 85-88; 130; CANR 35; DLB 177; MTCW 1; RGWL

Scoppettone, Sandra 1936- **CLC 26**
See also Early, Jack
See also AAYA 11; BYA 8; CA 5-8R; CANR 41, 73; GLL 1; MAICYAS; SATA 9, 92; WYA; YAW

Scorsese, Martin 1942- **CLC 20, 89**
See also AAYA 38; CA 110; 114; CANR 46, 85

Scotland, Jay
See Jakes, John (William)

Scott, Duncan Campbell 1862-1947 **TCLC 6; DAC**
See also CA 104; 153; DLB 92; RGEL

Scott, Evelyn 1893-1963 **CLC 43**
See also CA 104; 112; CANR 64; DLB 9, 48; RHW

Scott, F(rancis) R(eginald) 1899-1985 **CLC 22**
See also CA 101; 114; CANR 87; DLB 88; INT CA-101; RGEL

Scott, Frank
See Scott, F(rancis) R(eginald)

Scott, Joan CLC 65

Scott, Joanna 1960- **CLC 50**
See also CA 126; CANR 53, 92

Scott, Paul (Mark) 1920-1978 **CLC 9, 60**
See also BRWS 1; CA 81-84; 77-80; CANR 33; DLB 14, 207; MTCW 1; RGEL; RHW

Scott, Sarah 1723-1795 **LC 44**
See also DLB 39

Scott, Sir Walter 1771-1832 **NCLC 15, 69, 110; DA; DAB; DAC; DAM MST, NOV, POET; PC 13; SSC 32; WLC**
See also AAYA 22; BRW 4; BYA 2; CD-BLB 1789-1832; DLB 93, 107, 116, 144, 159; HGG; LAIT 1; RGEL; RGSF; SSFS 10; SUFW; WLIT 3; YABC 2

Scribe, (Augustin) Eugene 1791-1861 **NCLC 16; DAM DRAM; DC 5**
See also DLB 192; GFL 1789 to the Present; RGWL

Scrum, R.
See Crumb, R(obert)

Scudery, Georges de 1601-1667 **LC 75**
See also GFL Beginnings to 1789

Scudery, Madeleine de 1607-1701 **LC 2, 58**
See also GFL Beginnings to 1789

Scum
See Crumb, R(obert)

Scumbag, Little Bobby
See Crumb, R(obert)

Seabrook, John
See Hubbard, L(afayette) Ron(ald)

Sealy, I(rwin) Allan 1951- **CLC 55**
See also CA 136; CN

Search, Alexander
See Pessoa, Fernando (Antonio Nogueira)

Sebastian, Lee
See Silverberg, Robert

Sebastian Owl
See Thompson, Hunter S(tockton)

Sebestyen, Ouida 1924- **CLC 30**
See also AAYA 8; BYA 7; CA 107; CANR 40; CLR 17; JRDA; MAICYA; SAAS 10; SATA 39; WYA; YAW

Secundus, H. Scriblerus
See Fielding, Henry

Sedges, John
See Buck, Pearl S(ydenstricker)

Sedgwick, Catharine Maria 1789-1867 **NCLC 19, 98**
See also DLB 1, 74, 183, 239, 243, 254; RGAL

Seelye, John (Douglas) 1931- **CLC 7**
See also CA 97-100; CANR 70; INT 97-100; TCWW 2

Seferiades, Giorgos Stylianou 1900-1971
See Seferis, George
See also CA 5-8R; 33-36R; CANR 5, 36; MTCW 1

Seferis, George CLC 5, 11
See also Seferiades, Giorgos Stylianou
See also EW 12; RGWL

Segal, Erich (Wolf) 1937- **CLC 3, 10; DAM POP**
See also BEST 89:1; BPFB 3; CA 25-28R; CANR 20, 36, 65; CPW; DLBY 86; INT CANR-20; MTCW 1

Seger, Bob 1945- **CLC 35**

Seghers, Anna CLC 7
See also Radvanyi, Netty
See also DLB 69

Seidel, Frederick (Lewis) 1936- **CLC 18**
See also CA 13-16R; CANR 8, 99; CP; DLBY 84

Seifert, Jaroslav 1901-1986 **CLC 34, 44, 93**
See also CA 127; DLB 215; MTCW 1, 2

Sei Shonagon c. 966-1017(?) **CMLC 6**

Sejour, Victor 1817-1874 **DC 10**
See also DLB 50

Sejour Marcou et Ferrand, Juan Victor
See Sejour, Victor

Selby, Hubert, Jr. 1928- **CLC 1, 2, 4, 8; SSC 20**
See also CA 13-16R; CANR 33, 85; CN; DLB 2, 227

Selzer, Richard 1928- **CLC 74**
See also CA 65-68; CANR 14, 106

Sembene, Ousmane
See Ousmane, Sembene
See also AFW; CWW 2; WLIT 2

Senancour, Etienne Pivert de 1770-1846 **NCLC 16**
See also DLB 119; GFL 1789 to the Present

Sender, Ramon (Jose) 1902-1982 **CLC 8; DAM MULT; HLC 2**
See also CA 5-8R; 105; CANR 8; HW 1; MTCW 1; RGWL

Seneca, Lucius Annaeus c. 4B.C.-c. 65 **CMLC 6; DAM DRAM; DC 5**
See also AW 2; DLB 211; RGWL

Senghor, Leopold Sedar 1906-2001 **CLC 54, 130; BLC 3; DAM MULT, POET; PC 25**
See also AFW; BW 2; CA 116; 125; CANR 47, 74; DNFS; GFL 1789 to the Present; MTCW 1, 2

Senna, Danzy 1970- **CLC 119**
See also CA 169

Serling, (Edward) Rod(man) 1924-1975 **CLC 30**
See also AAYA 14; AITN 1; CA 162; 57-60; DLB 26; SFW

Serna, Ramon Gomez de la
See Gomez de la Serna, Ramon

Serpieres
See Guillevic, (Eugene)

Service, Robert
See Service, Robert W(illiam)
See also BYA 4; DAB; DLB 92

Service, Robert W(illiam) 1874(?)-1958 **TCLC 15; DA; DAC; DAM MST, POET; WLC**
See also Service, Robert
See also CA 115; 140; CANR 84; PFS 10; RGEL; SATA 20

Seth, Vikram 1952- **CLC 43, 90; DAM MULT**
See also CA 121; 127; CANR 50, 74; CN; CP; DA3; DLB 120; INT 127; MTCW 2

Seton, Cynthia Propper 1926-1982 **CLC 27**
See also CA 5-8R; 108; CANR 7

Seton, Ernest (Evan) Thompson 1860-1946 **TCLC 31**
See also ANW; BYA 3; CA 109; CLR 59; DLB 92; DLBD 13; JRDA; SATA 18

Seton-Thompson, Ernest
See Seton, Ernest (Evan) Thompson

Settle, Mary Lee 1918- **CLC 19, 61**
See also BPFB 3; CA 89-92; CAAS 1; CANR 44, 87; CN; CSW; DLB 6; INT 89-92

Seuphor, Michel
See Arp, Jean

Sevigne, Marie (de Rabutin-Chantal) 1626-1696 **LC 11**
See also GFL Beginnings to 1789

Sewall, Samuel 1652-1730 **LC 38**
See also DLB 24; RGAL

Sexton, Anne (Harvey) 1928-1974 **CLC 2, 4, 6, 8, 10, 15, 53, 123; DA; DAB; DAC; DAM MST, POET; PC 2; WLC**
See also AMWS 2; CA 1-4R; 53-56; CABS 2; CANR 3, 36; CDALB 1941-1968; DA3; DLB 5, 169; EXPP; FW; MAWW; MTCW 1, 2; PAB; PFS 4, 14; RGAL; SATA 10

Shaara, Jeff 1952- **CLC 119**
See also CA 163

Shaara, Michael (Joseph, Jr.) 1929-1988 **CLC 15; DAM POP**
See also AITN 1; BPFB 3; CA 102; 125; CANR 52, 85; DLBY 83

Shackleton, C. C.
See Aldiss, Brian W(ilson)

Shacochis, Bob CLC 39
See also Shacochis, Robert G.

Shacochis, Robert G. 1951-
See Shacochis, Bob
See also CA 119; 124; CANR 100; INT 124

Shaffer, Anthony (Joshua) 1926- **CLC 19; DAM DRAM**
See also CA 110; 116; CBD; CD; DFS 13; DLB 13

Shaffer, Peter (Levin) 1926- **CLC 5, 14, 18, 37, 60; DAB; DAM DRAM, MST; DC 7**
See also BRWS 1; CA 25-28R; CANR 25, 47, 74; CBD; CD; CDBLB 1960 to Present; DA3; DFS 5, 13; DLB 13, 233; MTCW 1, 2; RGEL

Shakey, Bernard
See Young, Neil

Shalamov, Varlam (Tikhonovich) 1907(?)-1982 **CLC 18**
See also CA 129; 105; RGSF

Shamlu, Ahmad 1925-2000 **CLC 10**
See also CWW 2

Shammas, Anton 1951- **CLC 55**

Shandling, Arline
See Berriault, Gina

Shange, Ntozake 1948- **CLC 8, 25, 38, 74, 126; BLC 3; DAM DRAM, MULT; DC 3**
See also AAYA 9; AFAW 1, 2; BW 2; CA 85-88; CABS 3; CAD; CANR 27, 48, 74; CD; CP; CWD; CWP; DA3; DFS 2, 11; DLB 38, 249; FW; LAIT 5; MTCW 1, 2; NFS 11; RGAL; YAW

Shanley, John Patrick 1950- **CLC 75**
See also CA 128; 133; CAD; CANR 83; CD

Shapcott, Thomas W(illiam) 1935- **CLC 38**
See also CA 69-72; CANR 49, 83, 103; CP

Shapiro, Jane 1942- **CLC 76**
See also CA 196

Shapiro, Karl (Jay) 1913-2000 **CLC 4, 8, 15, 53; PC 25**
See also AMWS 2; CA 1-4R; 188; CAAS 6; CANR 1, 36, 66; CP; DLB 48; EXPP; MTCW 1, 2; PFS 3; RGAL

Sharp, William 1855-1905 **TCLC 39**
See also Macleod, Fiona
See also CA 160; DLB 156; RGEL

Sharpe, Thomas Ridley 1928-
See Sharpe, Tom
See also CA 114; 122; CANR 85; CN; INT 122

Sharpe, Tom CLC 36
See also Sharpe, Thomas Ridley
See also DLB 14, 231

Shatrov, Mikhail CLC 59

Shaw, Bernard
See Shaw, George Bernard
See also DLB 190

Shaw, G. Bernard
See Shaw, George Bernard

Shaw, George Bernard 1856-1950 **TCLC 3, 9, 21, 45; DA; DAB; DAC; DAM DRAM, MST; WLC**
See also Shaw, Bernard
See also BRW 6; BRWR 2; CA 104; 128; CDBLB 1914-1945; DA3; DFS 1, 3, 6, 11; DLB 10, 57; LAIT 3; MTCW 1, 2; RGEL; WLIT 4

Shaw, Henry Wheeler 1818-1885 **NCLC 15**
See also DLB 11; RGAL

Smith, Sheila Kaye
See Kaye-Smith, Sheila
Smith, Stevie CLC 3, 8, 25, 44; PC 12
See also Smith, Florence Margaret
See also BRWS 2; DLB 20; MTCW 2; PAB; PFS 3; RGEL
Smith, Wilbur (Addison) 1933- CLC 33
See also CA 13-16R; CANR 7, 46, 66; CPW; MTCW 1, 2
Smith, William Jay 1918- CLC 6
See also CA 5-8R; CANR 44, 106; CP; CSW; CWRI; DLB 5; MAICYA; SAAS 22; SATA 2, 68
Smith, Woodrow Wilson
See Kuttner, Henry
Smolenskin, Peretz 1842-1885 NCLC 30
Smollett, Tobias (George) 1721-1771 LC 2, 46
See also BRW 3; CDBLB 1660-1789; DLB 39, 104; RGEL
Snodgrass, W(illiam) D(e Witt) 1926- CLC 2, 6, 10, 18, 68; DAM POET
See also AMWS 6; CA 1-4R; CANR 6, 36, 65, 85; CP; DLB 5; MTCW 1, 2; RGAL
Snow, C(harles) P(ercy) 1905-1980 CLC 1, 4, 6, 9, 13, 19; DAM NOV
See also BRW 7; CA 5-8R; 101; CANR 28; CDBLB 1945-1960; DLB 15, 77; DLBD 17; MTCW 1, 2; RGEL
Snow, Frances Compton
See Adams, Henry (Brooks)
Snyder, Gary (Sherman) 1930- CLC 1, 2, 5, 9, 32, 120; DAM POET; PC 21
See also AMWS 8; ANW; CA 17-20R; CANR 30, 60; CP; DA3; DLB 5, 16, 165, 212, 237; MTCW 2; PFS 9; RGAL; WP
Snyder, Zilpha Keatley 1927- CLC 17
See also AAYA 15; BYA 1; CA 9-12R; CANR 38; CLR 31; JRDA; MAICYA; SAAS 2; SATA 1, 28, 75, 110; SATA-Essay 112; YAW
Soares, Bernardo
See Pessoa, Fernando (Antonio Nogueira)
Sobh, A.
See Shamlu, Ahmad
Sobol, Joshua CLC 60
See also CWW 2
Socrates470B.C.-399B.C. CMLC 27
Soderberg, Hjalmar 1869-1941 TCLC 39
See also RGSF
SODERBERGH, STEVEN 1963- CLC 154
Sodergran, Edith (Irene)
See Soedergran, Edith (Irene)
See also EW 11; RGWL
Soedergran, Edith (Irene) 1892-1923 TCLC 31
See also Sodergran, Edith (Irene)
Softly, Edgar
See Lovecraft, H(oward) P(hillips)
Softly, Edward
See Lovecraft, H(oward) P(hillips)
Sokolov, Raymond 1941- CLC 7
See also CA 85-88
Sokolov, Sasha CLC 59
Solo, Jay
See Ellison, Harlan (Jay)
Sologub, Fyodor TCLC 9
See also Teternikov, Fyodor Kuzmich
Solomons, Ikey Esquir
See Thackeray, William Makepeace
Solomos, Dionysios 1798-1857 NCLC 15
Solwoska, Mara
See French, Marilyn
Solzhenitsyn, Aleksandr I(sayevich) 1918-
CLC 1, 2, 4, 7, 9, 10, 18, 26, 34, 78, 134;

DA; DAB; DAC; DAM MST, NOV; SSC 32; WLC
See also AITN 1; BPFB 3; CA 69-72; CANR 40, 65; DA3; EW 13; EXPS; LAIT 4; MTCW 1, 2; NFS 6; RGSF; RGWL; SSFS 9
Somers, Jane
See Lessing, Doris (May)
Somerville, Edith Oenone 1858-1949 TCLC 51
See also CA 196; DLB 135; RGEL; RGSF
Somerville & Ross
See Martin, Violet Florence; Somerville, Edith Oenone
Sommer, Scott 1951- CLC 25
See also CA 106
Sondheim, Stephen (Joshua) 1930- CLC 30, 39, 147; DAM DRAM
See also AAYA 11; CA 103; CANR 47, 67; LAIT 4
Song, Cathy 1955- PC 21
See also AAL; CA 154; CWP; DLB 169; EXPP; FW; PFS 5
Sontag, Susan 1933- CLC 1, 2, 10, 13, 31, 105; DAM POP
See also AMWS 3; CA 17-20R; CANR 25, 51, 74, 97; CN; CPW; DA3; DLB 2, 67; MAWW; MTCW 1, 2; RGAL; RHW; SSFS 10
Sophocles496(?)B.C.-406(?)B.C. CMLC 2, 47; DA; DAB; DAC; DAM DRAM, MST; DC 1; WLCS
See also AW 1; DA3; DFS 1, 4, 8; DLB 176; LAIT 1; RGWL
Sordello 1189-1269 CMLC 15
Sorel, Georges 1847-1922 TCLC 91
See also CA 118; 188
Sorel, Julia
See Drexler, Rosalyn
Sorokin, Vladimir CLC 59
Sorrentino, Gilbert 1929- CLC 3, 7, 14, 22, 40
See also CA 77-80; CANR 14, 33; CN; CP; DLB 5, 173; DLBY 80; INT CANR-14
Soseki
See Natsume, Soseki
See also MJW
Soto, Gary 1952- CLC 32, 80; DAM MULT; HLC 2; PC 28
See also AAYA 10, 37; BYA 11; CA 119; 125; CANR 50, 74; CLR 38; CP; DLB 82; EXPP; HW 1, 2; INT CA-125; JRDA; MAICYAS; MTCW 2; PFS 7; RGAL; SATA 80, 120; WYA; YAW
Soupault, Philippe 1897-1990 CLC 68
See also CA 116; 147; 131; GFL 1789 to the Present
Souster, (Holmes) Raymond 1921- CLC 5, 14; DAC; DAM POET
See also CA 13-16R; CAAS 14; CANR 13, 29, 53; CP; DA3; DLB 88; RGEL; SATA 63
Southern, Terry 1924(?)-1995 CLC 7
See also BPFB 3; CA 1-4R; 150; CANR 1, 55; CN; DLB 2; IDFW 3, 4
Southey, Robert 1774-1843 NCLC 8, 97
See also BRW 4; DLB 93, 107, 142; RGEL; SATA 54
Southworth, Emma Dorothy Eliza Nevitte 1819-1899 NCLC 26
See also DLB 239
Souza, Ernest
See Scott, Evelyn
Soyinka, Wole 1934- CLC 3, 5, 14, 36, 44; BLC 3; DA; DAB; DAC; DAM DRAM, MST, MULT; DC 2; WLC
See also AFW; BW 2, 3; CA 13-16R; CANR 27, 39, 82; CD; CN; CP; DA3; DFS 10; DLB 125; MTCW 1, 2; RGEL; WLIT 2

Spackman, W(illiam) M(ode) 1905-1990 CLC 46
See also CA 81-84; 132
Spacks, Barry (Bernard) 1931- CLC 14
See also CA 154; CANR 33; CP; DLB 105
Spanidou, Irini 1946- CLC 44
See also CA 185
Spark, Muriel (Sarah) 1918- CLC 2, 3, 5, 8, 13, 18, 40, 94; DAB; DAC; DAM MST, NOV; SSC 10
See also BRWS 1; CA 5-8R; CANR 12, 36, 76, 89; CDBLB 1945-1960; CN; CP; DA3; DLB 15, 139; FW; INT CANR-12; LAIT 4; MTCW 1, 2; RGEL; WLIT 4; YAW
Spaulding, Douglas
See Bradbury, Ray (Douglas)
Spaulding, Leonard
See Bradbury, Ray (Douglas)
Spelman, Elizabeth CLC 65
Spence, J. A. D.
See Eliot, T(homas) S(tearns)
Spencer, Elizabeth 1921- CLC 22
See also CA 13-16R; CANR 32, 65, 87; CN; CSW; DLB 6, 218; MTCW 1; RGAL; SATA 14
Spencer, Leonard G.
See Silverberg, Robert
Spencer, Scott 1945- CLC 30
See also CA 113; CANR 51; DLBY 86
Spender, Stephen (Harold) 1909-1995 CLC 1, 2, 5, 10, 41, 91; DAM POET
See also BRWS 2; CA 9-12R; 149; CANR 31, 54; CDBLB 1945-1960; CP; DA3; DLB 20; MTCW 1, 2; PAB; RGEL
Spengler, Oswald (Arnold Gottfried) 1880-1936 TCLC 25
See also CA 118; 189
Spenser, Edmund 1552(?)-1599 LC 5, 39; DA; DAB; DAC; DAM MST, POET; PC 8; WLC
See also BRW 1; CDBLB Before 1660; DA3; DLB 167; EFS 2; EXPP; PAB; RGEL; WLIT 3; WP
Spicer, Jack 1925-1965 CLC 8, 18, 72; DAM POET
See also CA 85-88; DLB 5, 16, 193; GLL 1; WP
Spiegelman, Art 1948- CLC 76
See also AAYA 10; CA 125; CANR 41, 55, 74; MTCW 2; SATA 109; YAW
Spielberg, Peter 1929- CLC 6
See also CA 5-8R; CANR 4, 48; DLBY 81
Spielberg, Steven 1947- CLC 20
See also AAYA 8, 24; CA 77-80; CANR 32; SATA 32
Spillane, Frank Morrison 1918-
See Spillane, Mickey
See also CA 25-28R; CANR 28, 63; DA3; DLB 226; MTCW 1, 2; SATA 66
Spillane, Mickey CLC 3, 13
See also Spillane, Frank Morrison
See also BPFB 3; CMW; DLB 226; MSW; MTCW 2
Spinoza, Benedictus de 1632-1677 LC 9, 58
Spinrad, Norman (Richard) 1940- CLC 46
See also BPFB 3; CA 37-40R; CAAS 19; CANR 20, 91; DLB 8; INT CANR-20; SFW
Spitteler, Carl (Friedrich Georg) 1845-1924 TCLC 12
See also CA 109; DLB 129
Spivack, Kathleen (Romola Drucker) 1938- CLC 6
See also CA 49-52
Spoto, Donald 1941- CLC 39
See also CA 65-68; CANR 11, 57, 93
Springsteen, Bruce (F.) 1949- CLC 17
See also CA 111

Spurling, Hilary 1940- **CLC 34**
 See also CA 104; CANR 25, 52, 94
Spyker, John Howland
 See Elman, Richard (Martin)
Squires, (James) Radcliffe 1917-1993 **CLC 51**
 See also CA 1-4R; 140; CANR 6, 21
Srivastava, Dhanpat Rai 1880(?)-1936
 See Premchand
 See also CA 118; 197
Stacy, Donald
 See Pohl, Frederik
Stael
 See Stael-Holstein, Anne Louise Germaine Necker
 See also EW 5; RGWL
Stael, Germaine de
 See Stael-Holstein, Anne Louise Germaine Necker
 See also DLB 119, 192; FW; GFL 1789 to the Present; TWA
Stael-Holstein, Anne Louise Germaine Necker 1766-1817 **NCLC 3, 91**
 See also Stael; Stael, Germaine de
Stafford, Jean 1915-1979 **CLC 4, 7, 19, 68; SSC 26**
 See also CA 1-4R; 85-88; CANR 3, 65; DLB 2, 173; MTCW 1, 2; RGAL; RGSF; SATA-Obit 22; TCWW 2
Stafford, William (Edgar) 1914-1993 **CLC 4, 7, 29; DAM POET**
 See also CA 5-8R; 142; CAAS 3; CANR 5, 22; DLB 5, 206; EXPP; INT CANR-22; PFS 2, 8; RGAL; WP
Stagnelius, Eric Johan 1793-1823 **NCLC 61**
Staines, Trevor
 See Brunner, John (Kilian Houston)
Stairs, Gordon
 See Austin, Mary (Hunter)
 See also TCWW 2
Stairs, Gordon 1868-1934
 See Austin, Mary (Hunter)
Stalin, Joseph 1879-1953 **TCLC 92**
Stancykowna
 See Szymborska, Wislawa
Stannard, Martin 1947- **CLC 44**
 See also CA 142; DLB 155
Stanton, Elizabeth Cady 1815-1902 **TCLC 73**
 See also CA 171; DLB 79; FW
Stanton, Maura 1946- **CLC 9**
 See also CA 89-92; CANR 15; DLB 120
Stanton, Schuyler
 See Baum, L(yman) Frank
Stapledon, (William) Olaf 1886-1950 **TCLC 22**
 See also CA 111; 162; DLB 15, 255; SFW
Starbuck, George (Edwin) 1931-1996 **CLC 53; DAM POET**
 See also CA 21-24R; 153; CANR 23
Stark, Richard
 See Westlake, Donald E(dwin)
Staunton, Schuyler
 See Baum, L(yman) Frank
Stead, Christina (Ellen) 1902-1983 **CLC 2, 5, 8, 32, 80**
 See also BRWS 4; CA 13-16R; 109; CANR 33, 40; FW; MTCW 1, 2; RGEL; RGSF
Stead, William Thomas 1849-1912 **TCLC 48**
 See also CA 167
Stebnitsky, M.
 See Leskov, Nikolai (Semyonovich)
Steele, Sir Richard 1672-1729 **LC 18**
 See also BRW 3; CDBLB 1660-1789; DLB 84, 101; RGEL; WLIT 3
Steele, Timothy (Reid) 1948- **CLC 45**
 See also CA 93-96; CANR 16, 50, 92; CP; DLB 120

Steffens, (Joseph) Lincoln 1866-1936 **TCLC 20**
 See also CA 117
Stegner, Wallace (Earle) 1909-1993 **CLC 9, 49, 81; DAM NOV; SSC 27**
 See also AITN 1; AMWS 4; ANW; BEST 90:3; BPFB 3; CA 1-4R; 141; CAAS 9; CANR 1, 21, 46; DLB 9, 206; DLBY 93; MTCW 1, 2; RGAL; TCWW 2
Stein, Gertrude 1874-1946 **TCLC 1, 6, 28, 48; DA; DAB; DAC; DAM MST, NOV, POET; PC 18; SSC 42; WLC**
 See also AMW; CA 104; 132; CDALB 1917-1929; DA3; DLB 4, 54, 86, 228; DLBD 15; EXPS; GLL 1; MAWW; MTCW 1, 2; RGAL; RGSF; SSFS 5; WP
Steinbeck, John (Ernst) 1902-1968 **CLC 1, 5, 9, 13, 21, 34, 45, 75, 124; DA; DAB; DAC; DAM DRAM, MST, NOV; SSC 11, 37; WLC**
 See also AAYA 12; AMW; BPFB 3; BYA 2, 3, 13; CA 1-4R; 25-28R; CANR 1, 35; CDALB 1929-1941; DA3; DLB 7, 9, 212; DLBD 2; EXPS; LAIT 3; MTCW 1, 2; NFS 1, 5, 7; RGAL; RGSF; RHW; SATA 9; SSFS 3, 6; TCWW 2; WYA; YAW
Steinem, Gloria 1934- **CLC 63**
 See also CA 53-56; CANR 28, 51; DLB 246; FW; MTCW 1, 2
Steiner, George 1929- **CLC 24; DAM NOV**
 See also CA 73-76; CANR 31, 67; DLB 67; MTCW 1, 2; SATA 62
Steiner, K. Leslie
 See Delany, Samuel R(ay), Jr.
Steiner, Rudolf 1861-1925 **TCLC 13**
 See also CA 107
Stendhal 1783-1842 **NCLC 23, 46; DA; DAB; DAC; DAM MST, NOV; SSC 27; WLC**
 See also DA3; DLB 119; EW 5; GFL 1789 to the Present; RGWL
Stephen, Adeline Virginia
 See Woolf, (Adeline) Virginia
Stephen, Sir Leslie 1832-1904 **TCLC 23**
 See also BRW 5; CA 123; DLB 57, 144, 190
Stephen, Sir Leslie
 See Stephen, Sir Leslie
Stephen, Virginia
 See Woolf, (Adeline) Virginia
Stephens, James 1882(?)-1950 **TCLC 4; SSC 50**
 See also CA 104; 192; DLB 19, 153, 162; FANT; RGEL; SUFW
Stephens, Reed
 See Donaldson, Stephen R(eeder)
Steptoe, Lydia
 See Barnes, Djuna
 See also GLL 1
Sterchi, Beat 1949- **CLC 65**
Sterling, Brett
 See Bradbury, Ray (Douglas); Hamilton, Edmond
Sterling, Bruce 1954- **CLC 72**
 See also CA 119; CANR 44; SCFW 2; SFW
Sterling, George 1869-1926 **TCLC 20**
 See also CA 117; 165; DLB 54
Stern, Gerald 1925- **CLC 40, 100**
 See also AMWS 9; CA 81-84; CANR 28, 94; CP; DLB 105; RGAL
Stern, Richard (Gustave) 1928- **CLC 4, 39**
 See also CA 1-4R; CANR 1, 25, 52; CN; DLB 218; DLBY 87; INT CANR-25
Sternberg, Josef von 1894-1969 **CLC 20**
 See also CA 81-84
Sterne, Laurence 1713-1768 **LC 2, 48; DA; DAB; DAC; DAM MST, NOV; WLC**
 See also BRW 3; CDBLB 1660-1789; DLB 39; RGEL

Sternheim, (William Adolf) Carl 1878-1942 **TCLC 8**
 See also CA 105; 193; DLB 56, 118; RGWL
Stevens, Mark 1951- **CLC 34**
 See also CA 122
Stevens, Wallace 1879-1955 **TCLC 3, 12, 45; DA; DAB; DAC; DAM MST, POET; PC 6; WLC**
 See also AMW; AMWR 1; CA 104; 124; CDALB 1929-1941; DA3; DLB 54; EXPP; MTCW 1, 2; PAB; PFS 13; RGAL; WP
Stevenson, Anne (Katharine) 1933- **CLC 7, 33**
 See also BRWS 6; CA 17-20R; CAAS 9; CANR 9, 33; CP; CWP; DLB 40; MTCW 1; RHW
Stevenson, Robert Louis (Balfour) 1850-1894 **NCLC 5, 14, 63; DA; DAB; DAC; DAM MST, NOV; SSC 11, 51; WLC**
 See also AAYA 24; BPFB 3; BRW 5; BRWR 1; BYA 1, 2, 4, 13; CDBLB 1890-1914; CLR 10, 11; DA3; DLB 18, 57, 141, 156, 174; DLBD 13; HGG; JRDA; LAIT 1, 3; MAICYA; NFS 11; RGEL; RGSF; SATA 100; SUFW; WCH; WLIT 4; WYA; YABC 2; YAW
Stewart, J(ohn) I(nnes) M(ackintosh) 1906-1994 **CLC 7, 14, 32**
 See Innes, Michael
 See also CA 85-88; 147; CAAS 3; CANR 47; CMW; MTCW 1, 2
Stewart, Mary (Florence Elinor) 1916- **CLC 7, 35, 117; DAB**
 See also AAYA 29; BPFB 3; CA 1-4R; CANR 1, 59; CMW; CPW; FANT; RHW; SATA 12; YAW
Stewart, Mary Rainbow
 See Stewart, Mary (Florence Elinor)
Stifle, June
 See Campbell, Maria
Stifter, Adalbert 1805-1868 **NCLC 41; SSC 28**
 See also DLB 133; RGSF; RGWL
Still, James 1906-2001 **CLC 49**
 See also CA 65-68; 195; CAAS 17; CANR 10, 26; CSW; DLB 9; DLBY 01; SATA 29; SATA-Obit 127
Sting 1951-
 See Sumner, Gordon Matthew
 See also CA 167
Stirling, Arthur
 See Sinclair, Upton (Beall)
Stitt, Milan 1941- **CLC 29**
 See also CA 69-72
Stockton, Francis Richard 1834-1902
 See Stockton, Frank R.
 See also CA 108; 137; MAICYA; SATA 44; SFW
Stockton, Frank R. TCLC 47
 See also Stockton, Francis Richard
 See also BYA 4, 13; DLB 42, 74; DLBD 13; EXPS; SATA-Brief 32; SSFS 3; SUFW; WCH
Stoddard, Charles
 See Kuttner, Henry
Stoker, Abraham 1847-1912
 See Stoker, Bram
 See also CA 105; 150; DA; DA3; DAC; DAM MST, NOV; HGG; SATA 29
Stoker, Bram TCLC 8; DAB; WLC
 See also Stoker, Abraham
 See also AAYA 23; BPFB 3; BRWS 3; BYA 5; CDBLB 1890-1914; DLB 36, 70, 178; RGEL; SUFW; WLIT 4
Stolz, Mary (Slattery) 1920- **CLC 12**
 See also AAYA 8; AITN 1; CA 5-8R; CANR 13, 41; JRDA; MAICYA; SAAS 3; SATA 10, 71; YAW

Stone, Irving 1903-1989 **CLC 7; DAM POP**
See also AITN 1; BPFB 3; CA 1-4R; 129; CAAS 3; CANR 1, 23; CPW; DA3; INT CANR-23; MTCW 1, 2; RHW; SATA 3; SATA-Obit 64

Stone, Oliver (William) 1946- **CLC 73**
See also AAYA 15; CA 110; CANR 55

Stone, Robert (Anthony) 1937- **CLC 5, 23, 42**
See also AMWS 5; BPFB 3; CA 85-88; CANR 23, 66, 95; CN; DLB 152; INT CANR-23; MTCW 1

Stone, Zachary
See Follett, Ken(neth Martin)

Stoppard, Tom 1937- **CLC 1, 3, 4, 5, 8, 15, 29, 34, 63, 91; DA; DAB; DAC; DAM DRAM, MST; DC 6; WLC**
See also BRWR 2; BRWS 1; CA 81-84; CANR 39, 67; CBD; CD; CDBLB 1960 to Present; DA3; DFS 2, 5, 8, 11, 13; DLB 13, 233; DLBY 85; MTCW 1, 2; RGEL; WLIT 4

Storey, David (Malcolm) 1933- **CLC 2, 4, 5, 8; DAM DRAM**
See also BRWS 1; CA 81-84; CANR 36; CBD; CD; CN; DLB 13, 14, 207, 245; MTCW 1; RGEL

Storm, Hyemeyohsts 1935- **CLC 3; DAM MULT**
See also CA 81-84; CANR 45; NNAL

Storm, Theodor 1817-1888 **SSC 27**
See also RGSF; RGWL

Storm, (Hans) Theodor (Woldsen) 1817-1888 **NCLC 1; SSC 27**
See also DLB 129; EW

Storni, Alfonsina 1892-1938 **TCLC 5; DAM MULT; HLC 2; PC 33**
See also CA 104; 131; HW 1; LAW

Stoughton, William 1631-1701 **LC 38**
See also DLB 24

Stout, Rex (Todhunter) 1886-1975 **CLC 3**
See also AITN 2; BPFB 3; CA 61-64; CANR 71; CMW; MSW; RGAL

Stow, (Julian) Randolph 1935- **CLC 23, 48**
See also CA 13-16R; CANR 33; CN; MTCW 1; RGEL

Stowe, Harriet (Elizabeth) Beecher 1811-1896 **NCLC 3, 50; DA; DAB; DAC; DAM MST, NOV; WLC**
See also AMWS 1; CDALB 1865-1917; DA3; DLB 1, 12, 42, 74, 189, 239, 243; EXPN; JRDA; LAIT 2; MAICYA; NFS 6; RGAL; YABC 1

Straboc. 64B.C.-c. 25 **CMLC 37**
See also DLB 176

Strachey, (Giles) Lytton 1880-1932 **TCLC 12**
See also BRWS 2; CA 110; 178; DLB 149; DLBD 10; MTCW 2

Strand, Mark 1934- **CLC 6, 18, 41, 71; DAM POET**
See also AMWS 4; CA 21-24R; CANR 40, 65, 100; CP; DLB 5; PAB; PFS 9; RGAL; SATA 41

Stratton-Porter, Gene(va Grace) 1863-1924
See Porter, Gene(va Grace) Stratton
See also ANW; CA 137; DLB 221; DLBD 14; MAICYA; SATA 15

Straub, Peter (Francis) 1943- **CLC 28, 107; DAM POP**
See also BEST 89:1; BPFB 3; CA 85-88; CANR 28, 65; CPW; DLBY 84; HGG; MTCW 1, 2

Strauss, Botho 1944- **CLC 22**
See also CA 157; CWW 2; DLB 124

Streatfeild, (Mary) Noel 1897(?)-1986 **CLC 21**
See also CA 81-84; 120; CANR 31; CLR 17; CWRI; DLB 160; MAICYA; SATA 20; SATA-Obit 48

Stribling, T(homas) S(igismund) 1881-1965 **CLC 23**
See also CA 189; 107; CMW; DLB 9; RGAL

Strindberg, (Johan) August 1849-1912 **TCLC 1, 8, 21, 47; DA; DAB; DAC; DAM DRAM, MST; WLC**
See also CA 104; 135; DA3; DFS 4, 9; EW 7; IDTP; MTCW 2; RGWL

Stringer, Arthur 1874-1950 **TCLC 37**
See also CA 161; DLB 92

Stringer, David
See Roberts, Keith (John Kingston)

Stroheim, Erich von 1885-1957 **TCLC 71**

Strugatskii, Arkadii (Natanovich) 1925-1991 **CLC 27**
See also CA 106; 135; SFW

Strugatskii, Boris (Natanovich) 1933- **CLC 27**
See also CA 106; SFW

Strummer, Joe 1953(?)- **CLC 30**

Strunk, William, Jr. 1869-1946 **TCLC 92**
See also CA 118; 164

Stryk, Lucien 1924- **PC 27**
See also CA 13-16R; CANR 10, 28, 55; CP

Stuart, Don A.
See Campbell, John W(ood, Jr.)

Stuart, Ian
See MacLean, Alistair (Stuart)

Stuart, Jesse (Hilton) 1906-1984 **CLC 1, 8, 11, 14, 34; SSC 31**
See also CA 5-8R; 112; CANR 31; DLB 9, 48, 102; DLBY 84; SATA 2; SATA-Obit 36

Stubblefield, Sally
See Trumbo, Dalton

Sturgeon, Theodore (Hamilton) 1918-1985 **CLC 22, 39**
See Queen, Ellery
See also BPFB 3; BYA 9, 10; CA 81-84; 116; CANR 32, 103; DLB 8; DLBY 85; HGG; MTCW 1, 2; SCFW; SFW; SUFW

Sturges, Preston 1898-1959 **TCLC 48**
See also CA 114; 149; DLB 26

Styron, William 1925- **CLC 1, 3, 5, 11, 15, 60; DAM NOV, POP; SSC 25**
See also AMW; BEST 90:4; BPFB 3; CA 5-8R; CANR 6, 33, 74; CDALB 1968-1988; CN; CPW; CSW; DA3; DLB 2, 143; DLBY 80; INT CANR-6; LAIT 2; MTCW 1, 2; NCFS 1; RGAL; RHW

Su, Chien 1884-1918
See Su Man-shu
See also CA 123

Suarez Lynch, B.
See Bioy Casares, Adolfo; Borges, Jorge Luis

Suassuna, Ariano Vilar 1927-
See also CA 178; HLCS 1; HW 2; LAW

Suckling, Sir John 1609-1642 **LC 75; DAM POET; PC 30**
See also BRW 2; DLB 58, 126; EXPP; PAB; RGEL

Suckow, Ruth 1892-1960 **SSC 18**
See also CA 193; 113; DLB 9, 102; RGAL; TCWW 2

Sudermann, Hermann 1857-1928 **TCLC 15**
See also CA 107; DLB 118

Sue, Eugene 1804-1857 **NCLC 1**
See also DLB 119

Sueskind, Patrick 1949- **CLC 44**
See also Suskind, Patrick

Sukenick, Ronald 1932- **CLC 3, 4, 6, 48**
See also CA 25-28R; CAAS 8; CANR 32, 89; CN; DLB 173; DLBY 81

Suknaski, Andrew 1942- **CLC 19**
See also CA 101; CP; DLB 53

Sullivan, Vernon
See Vian, Boris

Sully Prudhomme, Rene-Francois-Armand 1839-1907 **TCLC 31**
See also GFL 1789 to the Present

Su Man-shu TCLC 24
See also Su, Chien

Summerforest, Ivy B.
See Kirkup, James

Summers, Andrew James 1942- **CLC 26**

Summers, Andy
See Summers, Andrew James

Summers, Hollis (Spurgeon, Jr.) 1916- **CLC 10**
See also CA 5-8R; CANR 3; DLB 6

Summers, (Alphonsus Joseph-Mary Augustus) Montague 1880-1948 **TCLC 16**
See also CA 118; 163

Sumner, Gordon Matthew CLC 26
See also Police, The; Sting

Surtees, Robert Smith 1805-1864 **NCLC 14**
See also DLB 21; RGEL

Susann, Jacqueline 1921-1974 **CLC 3**
See also AITN 1; BPFB 3; CA 65-68; 53-56; MTCW 1, 2

Su Shi
See Su Shih
See also RGWL

Su Shih 1036-1101 **CMLC 15**
See also Su Shi

Suskind, Patrick
See Sueskind, Patrick
See also BPFB 3; CA 145; CWW 2

Sutcliff, Rosemary 1920-1992 **CLC 26; DAB; DAC; DAM MST, POP**
See also AAYA 10; BYA 1, 4; CA 5-8R; 139; CANR 37; CLR 1, 37; CPW; JRDA; MAICYA; MAICYAS; RHW; SATA 6, 44, 78; SATA-Obit 73; WYA; YAW

Sutro, Alfred 1863-1933 **TCLC 6**
See also CA 105; 185; DLB 10; RGEL

Sutton, Henry
See Slavitt, David R(ytman)

Suzuki, D. T.
See Suzuki, Daisetz Teitaro

Suzuki, Daisetz T.
See Suzuki, Daisetz Teitaro

Suzuki, Daisetz Teitaro 1870-1966 **TCLC 109**
See also CA 121; 111; MTCW 1, 2

Suzuki, Teitaro
See Suzuki, Daisetz Teitaro

Svevo, Italo TCLC 2, 35; SSC 25
See also Schmitz, Aron Hector
See also EW 8; RGWL

Swados, Elizabeth (A.) 1951- **CLC 12**
See also CA 97-100; CANR 49; INT 97-100

Swados, Harvey 1920-1972 **CLC 5**
See also CA 5-8R; 37-40R; CANR 6; DLB 2

Swan, Gladys 1934- **CLC 69**
See also CA 101; CANR 17, 39

Swanson, Logan
See Matheson, Richard (Burton)

Swarthout, Glendon (Fred) 1918-1992 **CLC 35**
See also CA 1-4R; 139; CANR 1, 47; LAIT 5; SATA 26; TCWW 2; YAW

Sweet, Sarah C.
See Jewett, (Theodora) Sarah Orne

Swenson, May 1919-1989 **CLC 4, 14, 61, 106; DA; DAB; DAC; DAM MST, POET; PC 14**
See also AMWS 4; CA 5-8R; 130; CANR 36, 61; DLB 5; EXPP; GLL 2; MTCW 1, 2; SATA 15; WP

Toomer, Eugene
See Toomer, Jean
Toomer, Eugene Pinchback
See Toomer, Jean
Toomer, Jean 1892-1967 **CLC 1, 4, 13, 22;**
BLC 3; DAM MULT; PC 7; SSC 1, 45;
WLCS
See also AFAW 1, 2; AMWS 3, 9; BW 1;
CA 85-88; CDALB 1917-1929; DA3;
DLB 45, 51; EXPP; EXPS; MTCW 1, 2;
NFS 11; RGAL; RGSF; SSFS 5
Toomer, Nathan Jean
See Toomer, Jean
Toomer, Nathan Pinchback
See Toomer, Jean
Torley, Luke
See Blish, James (Benjamin)
Tornimparte, Alessandra
See Ginzburg, Natalia
Torre, Raoul della
See Mencken, H(enry) L(ouis)
Torrence, Ridgely 1874-1950 **TCLC 97**
See also DLB 54, 249
Torrey, E(dwin) Fuller 1937- **CLC 34**
See also CA 119; CANR 71
Torsvan, Ben Traven
See Traven, B.
Torsvan, Benno Traven
See Traven, B.
Torsvan, Berick Traven
See Traven, B.
Torsvan, Berwick Traven
See Traven, B.
Torsvan, Bruno Traven
See Traven, B.
Torsvan, Traven
See Traven, B.
Tourneur, Cyril 1575(?)-1626 **LC 66; DAM**
DRAM
See also BRW 2; DLB 58; RGEL
Tournier, Michel (Edouard) 1924- **CLC 6,**
23, 36, 95
See also CA 49-52; CANR 3, 36, 74; DLB
83; GFL 1789 to the Present; MTCW 1,
2; SATA 23
Tournimparte, Alessandra
See Ginzburg, Natalia
Towers, Ivar
See Kornbluth, C(yril) M.
Towne, Robert (Burton) 1936(?)- **CLC 87**
See also CA 108; DLB 44; IDFW 3, 4
Townsend, Sue CLC 61
See also Townsend, Susan Elaine
See also AAYA 28; CBD; CWD; SATA 55,
93; SATA-Brief 48
Townsend, Susan Elaine 1946-
See Townsend, Sue
See also CA 119; 127; CANR 65; CD;
CPW; DAB; DAC; DAM MST; INT 127;
YAW
Townshend, Peter (Dennis Blandford) 1945-
CLC 17, 42
See also CA 107
Tozzi, Federigo 1883-1920 **TCLC 31**
See also CA 160
Tracy, Don(ald Fiske) 1905-1970(?)
See Queen, Ellery
See also CA 1-4R; 176; CANR 2
Trafford, F. G.
See Riddell, Charlotte
Traill, Catharine Parr 1802-1899 **NCLC 31**
See also DLB 99
Trakl, Georg 1887-1914 **TCLC 5; PC 20**
See also CA 104; 165; EW 10; MTCW 2;
RGWL
Transtroemer, Tomas (Goesta) 1931- **CLC**

52, 65; DAM POET
See also Transtromer, Tomas
See also CA 117; 129; CAAS 17
Transtromer, Tomas Gosta
See Transtroemer, Tomas (Goesta)
Traven, B. 1882(?)-1969 **CLC 8, 11**
See also CA 19-20; 25-28R; CAP 2; DLB
9, 56; MTCW 1; RGAL
Trediakovsky, Vasilii Kirillovich 1703-1769
LC 68
See also DLB 150
Treitel, Jonathan 1959- **CLC 70**
Trelawny, Edward John 1792-1881 **NCLC 85**
See also DLB 110, 116, 144
Tremain, Rose 1943- **CLC 42**
See also CA 97-100; CANR 44, 95; CN;
DLB 14; RGSF; RHW
Tremblay, Michel 1942- **CLC 29, 102; DAC;**
DAM MST
See also CA 116; 128; CCA 1; CWW 2;
DLB 60; GLL 1; MTCW 1, 2
Trevanian CLC 29
See also Whitaker, Rod(ney)
Trevor, Glen
See Hilton, James
Trevor, William CLC 7, 9, 14, 25, 71, 116;
SSC 21
See also Cox, William Trevor
See also BRWS 4; CBD; CD; CN; DLB 14,
139; MTCW 2; RGEL; RGSF; SSFS 10
Trifonov, Iurii (Valentinovich)
See Trifonov, Yuri (Valentinovich)
See also RGWL
Trifonov, Yuri (Valentinovich) 1925-1981
CLC 45
See also Trifonov, Iurii (Valentinovich)
See also CA 126; 103; MTCW 1
Trilling, Diana (Rubin) 1905-1996 **CLC 129**
See also CA 5-8R; 154; CANR 10, 46; INT
CANR-10; MTCW 1, 2
Trilling, Lionel 1905-1975 **CLC 9, 11, 24**
See also AMWS 3; CA 9-12R; 61-64;
CANR 10, 105; DLB 28, 63; INT CANR-
10; MTCW 1, 2; RGAL
Trimball, W. H.
See Mencken, H(enry) L(ouis)
Tristan
See Gomez de la Serna, Ramon
Tristram
See Housman, A(lfred) E(dward)
Trogdon, William (Lewis) 1939-
See Heat-Moon, William Least
See also CA 115; 119; CANR 47, 89; CPW;
INT CA-119
Trollope, Anthony 1815-1882 **NCLC 6, 33,**
101; DA; DAB; DAC; DAM MST, NOV;
SSC 28; WLC
See also BRW 5; CDBLB 1832-1890; DA3;
DLB 21, 57, 159; RGEL; RGSF; SATA
22
Trollope, Frances 1779-1863 **NCLC 30**
See also DLB 21, 166
Trotsky, Leon 1879-1940 **TCLC 22**
See also CA 118; 167
Trotter (Cockburn), Catharine 1679-1749 **LC**
8
See also DLB 84, 252
Trotter, Wilfred 1872-1939 **TCLC 97**
Trout, Kilgore
See Farmer, Philip Jose
Trow, George W. S. 1943- **CLC 52**
See also CA 126; CANR 91
Troyat, Henri 1911- **CLC 23**
See also CA 45-48; CANR 2, 33, 67; GFL
1789 to the Present; MTCW 1
Trudeau, G(arretson) B(eekman) 1948-
See Trudeau, Garry B.
See also CA 81-84; CANR 31; SATA 35

Trudeau, Garry B. CLC 12
See also Trudeau, G(arretson) B(eekman)
See also AAYA 10; AITN 2
Truffaut, Francois 1932-1984 **CLC 20, 101**
See also CA 81-84; 113; CANR 34
Trumbo, Dalton 1905-1976 **CLC 19**
See also CA 21-24R; 69-72; CANR 10;
DLB 26; IDFW 3, 4; YAW
Trumbull, John 1750-1831 **NCLC 30**
See also DLB 31; RGAL
Trundlett, Helen B.
See Eliot, T(homas) S(tearns)
Truth, Sojourner 1797(?)-1883 **NCLC 94**
See also DLB 239; FW; LAIT 2
Tryon, Thomas 1926-1991 **CLC 3, 11; DAM**
POP
See also AITN 1; BPFB 3; CA 29-32R; 135;
CANR 32, 77; CPW; DA3; HGG; MTCW
1
Tryon, Tom
See Tryon, Thomas
Ts'ao Hsueh-ch'in 1715(?)-1763 **LC 1**
Tsushima, Shuji 1909-1948
See Dazai Osamu
See also CA 107
Tsvetaeva (Efron), Marina (Ivanovna)
1892-1941 **TCLC 7, 35; PC 14**
See also CA 104; 128; CANR 73; EW 11;
MTCW 1, 2; RGWL
Tuck, Lily 1938- **CLC 70**
See also CA 139; CANR 90
Tu Fu 712-770 **PC 9**
See also Du Fu
See also DAM MULT; WP
Tunis, John R(oberts) 1889-1975 **CLC 12**
See also BYA 1; CA 61-64; CANR 62; DLB
22, 171; JRDA; MAICYA; SATA 37;
SATA-Brief 30; YAW
Tuohy, Frank CLC 37
See also Tuohy, John Francis
See also DLB 14, 139
Tuohy, John Francis 1925-
See Tuohy, Frank
See also CA 5-8R; 178; CANR 3, 47; CN
Turco, Lewis (Putnam) 1934- **CLC 11, 63**
See also CA 13-16R; CAAS 22; CANR 24,
51; CP; DLBY 84
Turgenev, Ivan (Sergeevich) 1818-1883
NCLC 21, 37; DA; DAB; DAC; DAM
MST, NOV; DC 7; SSC 7; WLC
See also DFS 6; DLB 238; EW 6; RGSF;
RGWL
Turgot, Anne-Robert-Jacques 1727-1781 **LC**
26
Turner, Frederick 1943- **CLC 48**
See also CA 73-76; CAAS 10; CANR 12,
30, 56; DLB 40
Tutu, Desmond M(pilo) 1931- **CLC 80; BLC**
3; DAM MULT
See also BW 1, 3; CA 125; CANR 67, 81
Tutuola, Amos 1920-1997 **CLC 5, 14, 29;**
BLC 3; DAM MULT
See also AFW; BW 2, 3; CA 9-12R; 159;
CANR 27, 66; CN; DA3; DLB 125;
DNFS; MTCW 1, 2; RGEL; WLIT 2
Twain, Mark TCLC 6, 12, 19, 36, 48, 59; SSC
34; WLC
See also Clemens, Samuel Langhorne
See also AAYA 20; AMW; BPFB 3; BYA 2,
3, 11, 14; CLR 58, 60, 66; DLB 11;
EXPN; EXPS; FANT; LAIT 2; NFS 1, 6;
RGAL; RGSF; SFW; SSFS 1, 7; SUFW;
WCH; WYA; YAW
Tyler, Anne 1941- **CLC 7, 11, 18, 28, 44, 59,**
103; DAM NOV, POP
See also AAYA 18; AMWS 4; BEST 89:1;
BPFB 3; BYA 12; CA 9-12R; CANR 11,
33, 53; CDALBS; CN; CPW; CSW; DLB

6, 143; DLBY 82; EXPN; MAWW;
MTCW 1, 2; NFS 2, 7, 10; RGAL; SATA
7, 90; YAW

Tyler, Royall 1757-1826 **NCLC 3**
See also DLB 37; RGAL

Tynan, Katharine 1861-1931 **TCLC 3**
See also CA 104; 167; DLB 153, 240; FW

Tyutchev, Fyodor 1803-1873 **NCLC 34**

Tzara, Tristan 1896-1963 **CLC 47; DAM POET; PC 27**
See also CA 153; 89-92; MTCW 2

Uhry, Alfred 1936- **CLC 55; DAM DRAM, POP**
See also CA 127; 133; CAD; CD; CSW;
DA3; DFS 11; INT CA-133

Ulf, Haerved
See Strindberg, (Johan) August

Ulf, Harved
See Strindberg, (Johan) August

Ulibarri, Sabine R(eyes) 1919- **CLC 83; DAM MULT; HLCS 2**
See also CA 131; CANR 81; DLB 82; HW
1, 2; RGSF

Unamuno (y Jugo), Miguel de 1864-1936
TCLC 2, 9; DAM MULT, NOV; HLC 2; SSC 11
See also CA 104; 131; CANR 81; DLB 108;
EW 8; HW 1, 2; MTCW 1, 2; RGSF;
RGWL

Undercliffe, Errol
See Campbell, (John) Ramsey

Underwood, Miles
See Glassco, John

Undset, Sigrid 1882-1949 **TCLC 3; DA; DAB; DAC; DAM MST, NOV; WLC**
See also CA 104; 129; DA3; EW 9; FW;
MTCW 1, 2; RGWL

Ungaretti, Giuseppe 1888-1970 **CLC 7, 11, 15**
See also CA 19-20; 25-28R; CAP 2; DLB
114; EW 10; RGWL

Unger, Douglas 1952- **CLC 34**
See also CA 130; CANR 94

Unsworth, Barry (Forster) 1930- **CLC 76, 127**
See also BRWS 7; CA 25-28R; CANR 30,
54; CN; DLB 194

Updike, John (Hoyer) 1932- **CLC 1, 2, 3, 5, 7, 9, 13, 15, 23, 34, 43, 70, 139; DA; DAB; DAC; DAM MST, NOV, POET, POP; SSC 13, 27; WLC**
See also AAYA 36; AMW; AMWR 1; BPFB
3; BYA 12; CA 1-4R; CABS 1; CANR 4,
33, 51, 94; CDALB 1968-1988; CN; CP;
CPW 1; DA3; DLB 2, 5, 143, 218, 227;
DLBD 3; DLBY 80, 82, 97; EXPP; HGG;
MTCW 1, 2; NFS 12; RGAL; RGSF;
SSFS 3

Upshaw, Margaret Mitchell
See Mitchell, Margaret (Munnerlyn)

Upton, Mark
See Sanders, Lawrence

Upward, Allen 1863-1926 **TCLC 85**
See also CA 117; 187; DLB 36

Urdang, Constance (Henriette) 1922-1996
CLC 47
See also CA 21-24R; CANR 9, 24; CP;
CWP

Uriel, Henry
See Faust, Frederick (Schiller)

Uris, Leon (Marcus) 1924- **CLC 7, 32; DAM NOV, POP**
See also AITN 1, 2; BEST 89:2; BPFB 3;
CA 1-4R; CANR 1, 40, 65; CN; CPW 1;
DA3; MTCW 1, 2; SATA 49

Urista, Alberto H. 1947- **PC 34**
See Alurista
See also CA 45-48, 182; CANR 2, 32;
HLCS 1; HW 1

Urmuz
See Codrescu, Andrei

Urquhart, Guy
See McAlmon, Robert (Menzies)

Urquhart, Jane 1949- **CLC 90; DAC**
See also CA 113; CANR 32, 68; CCA 1

Usigli, Rodolfo 1905-1979
See also CA 131; HLCS 1; HW 1; LAW

Ustinov, Peter (Alexander) 1921- **CLC 1**
See also AITN 1; CA 13-16R; CANR 25,
51; CBD; CD; DLB 13; MTCW 2

U Tam'si, Gerald Felix Tchicaya
See Tchicaya, Gerald Felix

U Tam'si, Tchicaya
See Tchicaya, Gerald Felix

Vachss, Andrew (Henry) 1942- **CLC 106**
See also CA 118; CANR 44, 95; CMW

Vachss, Andrew H.
See Vachss, Andrew (Henry)

Vaculik, Ludvik 1926- **CLC 7**
See also CA 53-56; CANR 72; CWW 2;
DLB 232

Vaihinger, Hans 1852-1933 **TCLC 71**
See also CA 116; 166

Valdez, Luis (Miguel) 1940- **CLC 84; DAM MULT; DC 10; HLC 2**
See also CA 101; CAD; CANR 32, 81; CD;
DFS 5; DLB 122; HW 1; LAIT 4

Valenzuela, Luisa 1938- **CLC 31, 104; DAM MULT; HLCS 2; SSC 14**
See also CA 101; CANR 32, 65; CWW 2;
DLB 113; FW; HW 1, 2; LAW; RGSF

Valera y Alcala-Galiano, Juan 1824-1905
TCLC 10
See also CA 106

Valery, (Ambroise) Paul (Toussaint Jules)
1871-1945 **TCLC 4, 15; DAM POET; PC 9**
See also CA 104; 122; DA3; EW 8; GFL
1789 to the Present; MTCW 1, 2; RGWL

Valle-Inclan, Ramon (Maria) del 1866-1936
TCLC 5; DAM MULT; HLC 2
See also CA 106; 153; CANR 80; DLB 134;
EW 8; HW 2; RGSF; RGWL

Vallejo, Antonio Buero
See Buero Vallejo, Antonio

Vallejo, Cesar (Abraham) 1892-1938 **TCLC 3, 56; DAM MULT; HLC 2**
See also CA 105; 153; HW 1; LAW; RGWL

Valles, Jules 1832-1885 **NCLC 71**
See also DLB 123; GFL 1789 to the Present

Vallette, Marguerite Eymery 1860-1953
TCLC 67
See also CA 182; DLB 123, 192

Valle Y Pena, Ramon del
See Valle-Inclan, Ramon (Maria) del

Van Ash, Cay 1918- **CLC 34**

Vanbrugh, Sir John 1664-1726 **LC 21; DAM DRAM**
See also BRW 2; DLB 80; IDTP; RGEL

Van Campen, Karl
See Campbell, John W(ood, Jr.)

Vance, Gerald
See Silverberg, Robert

Vance, Jack CLC 35
See also Vance, John Holbrook
See also DLB 8; FANT; SCFW 2; SFW;
SUFW

Vance, John Holbrook 1916-
See Queen, Ellery; Vance, Jack
See also CA 29-32R; CANR 17, 65; CMW;
MTCW 1

Van Den Bogarde, Derek Jules Gaspard Ulric Niven 1921-1999 **CLC 14**
See also Bogarde, Dirk
See also CA 77-80; 179

Vandenburgh, Jane CLC 59
See also CA 168

Vanderhaeghe, Guy 1951- **CLC 41**
See also BPFB 3; CA 113; CANR 72

van der Post, Laurens (Jan) 1906-1996 **CLC 5**
See also AFW; CA 5-8R; 155; CANR 35;
CN; DLB 204; RGEL

van de Wetering, Janwillem 1931- **CLC 47**
See also CA 49-52; CANR 4, 62, 90; CMW

Van Dine, S. S. TCLC 23
See also Wright, Willard Huntington
See also MSW

Van Doren, Carl (Clinton) 1885-1950 **TCLC 18**
See also CA 111; 168

Van Doren, Mark 1894-1972 **CLC 6, 10**
See also CA 1-4R; 37-40R; CANR 3; DLB
45; MTCW 1, 2; RGAL

Van Druten, John (William) 1901-1957
TCLC 2
See also CA 104; 161; DLB 10; RGAL

Van Duyn, Mona (Jane) 1921- **CLC 3, 7, 63, 116; DAM POET**
See also CA 9-12R; CANR 7, 38, 60; CP;
CWP; DLB 5

Van Dyne, Edith
See Baum, L(yman) Frank

van Itallie, Jean-Claude 1936- **CLC 3**
See also CA 45-48; CAAS 2; CAD; CANR
1, 48; CD; DLB 7

van Ostaijen, Paul 1896-1928 **TCLC 33**
See also CA 163

Van Peebles, Melvin 1932- **CLC 2, 20; DAM MULT**
See also BW 2, 3; CA 85-88; CANR 27,
67, 82

van Schendel, Arthur(-Francois-Emile)
1874-1946 **TCLC 56**

Vansittart, Peter 1920- **CLC 42**
See also CA 1-4R; CANR 3, 49, 90; CN;
RHW

Van Vechten, Carl 1880-1964 **CLC 33**
See also AMWS 2; CA 183; 89-92; DLB 4,
9; RGAL

van Vogt, A(lfred) E(lton) 1912-2000 **CLC 1**
See also BPFB 3; BYA 13, 14; CA 21-24R;
190; CANR 28; DLB 8, 251; SATA 14;
SATA-Obit 124; SCFW; SFW

Varda, Agnes 1928- **CLC 16**
See also CA 116; 122

Vargas Llosa, (Jorge) Mario (Pedro) 1936-
CLC 3, 6, 9, 10, 15, 31, 42, 85; DA; DAB; DAC; DAM MST, MULT, NOV; HLC 2
See also Llosa, (Jorge) Mario (Pedro) Vargas
See also BPFB 3; CA 73-76; CANR 18, 32,
42, 67; DA3; DLB 145; DNFS; HW 1, 2;
LAW; LAWS 1; MTCW 1, 2; RGWL;
WLIT 1

Vasiliu, George
See Bacovia, George

Vasiliu, Gheorghe
See Bacovia, George
See also CA 123; 189

Vassa, Gustavus
See Equiano, Olaudah

Vassilikos, Vassilis 1933- **CLC 4, 8**
See also CA 81-84; CANR 75

Vaughan, Henry 1621-1695 **LC 27**
See also BRW 2; DLB 131; PAB; RGEL

Vaughn, Stephanie CLC 62

Vazov, Ivan (Minchov) 1850-1921 **TCLC 25**
See also CA 121; 167; DLB 147

Veblen, Thorstein B(unde) 1857-1929 **TCLC 31**
See also AMWS 1; CA 115; 165; DLB 246

Vega, Lope de 1562-1635 **LC 23; HLCS 2**
See also EW 2; RGWL

Wakoski-Sherbell, Diane
See Wakoski, Diane
Walcott, Derek (Alton) 1930- **CLC 2, 4, 9, 14, 25, 42, 67, 76; BLC 3; DAB; DAC; DAM MST, MULT, POET; DC 7**
See also BW 2; CA 89-92; CANR 26, 47, 75, 80; CBD; CD; CP; DA3; DLB 117; DLBY 81; DNFS; EFS 1; MTCW 1, 2; PFS 6; RGEL
Waldman, Anne (Lesley) 1945- **CLC 7**
See also CA 37-40R; CAAS 17; CANR 34, 69; CP; CWP; DLB 16
Waldo, E. Hunter
See Sturgeon, Theodore (Hamilton)
Waldo, Edward Hamilton
See Sturgeon, Theodore (Hamilton)
Walker, Alice (Malsenior) 1944- **CLC 5, 6, 9, 19, 27, 46, 58, 103; BLC 3; DA; DAB; DAC; DAM MST, MULT, NOV, POET, POP; PC 30; SSC 5; WLCS**
See also AAYA 3, 33; AFAW 1, 2; AMWS 3; BEST 89:4; BPFB 3; BW 2, 3; CA 37-40R; CANR 9, 27, 49, 66, 82; CDALB 1968-1988; CN; CPW; CSW; DA3; DLB 6, 33, 143; EXPN; EXPS; FW; INT CANR-27; LAIT 3; MAWW; MTCW 1, 2; NFS 5; RGAL; RGSF; SATA 31; SSFS 2, 11; YAW
Walker, David Harry 1911-1992 **CLC 14**
See also CA 1-4R; 137; CANR 1; CWRI; SATA 8; SATA-Obit 71
Walker, Edward Joseph 1934-
See Walker, Ted
See also CA 21-24R; CANR 12, 28, 53; CP
Walker, George F. 1947- **CLC 44, 61; DAB; DAC; DAM MST**
See also CA 103; CANR 21, 43, 59; CD; DLB 60
Walker, Joseph A. 1935- **CLC 19; DAM DRAM, MST**
See also BW 1, 3; CA 89-92; CAD; CANR 26; CD; DFS 12; DLB 38
Walker, Margaret (Abigail) 1915-1998 **CLC 1, 6; BLC; DAM MULT; PC 20**
See also AFAW 1, 2; BW 2; CA 73-76; 172; CANR 26, 54, 76; CN; CP; CSW; DLB 76, 152; EXPP; FW; MTCW 1, 2; RGAL; RHW
Walker, Ted CLC 13
See also Walker, Edward Joseph
See also DLB 40
Wallace, David Foster 1962- **CLC 50, 114**
See also AMWS 10; CA 132; CANR 59; DA3; MTCW 2
Wallace, Dexter
See Masters, Edgar Lee
Wallace, (Richard Horatio) Edgar 1875-1932 **TCLC 57**
See also CA 115; CMW; DLB 70; MSW; RGEL
Wallace, Irving 1916-1990 **CLC 7, 13; DAM NOV, POP**
See also AITN 1; BPFB 3; CA 1-4R; 132; CAAS 1; CANR 1, 27; CPW; INT CANR-27; MTCW 1, 2
Wallant, Edward Lewis 1926-1962 **CLC 5, 10**
See also CA 1-4R; CANR 22; DLB 2, 28, 143; MTCW 1, 2; RGAL
Wallas, Graham 1858-1932 **TCLC 91**
Walley, Byron
See Card, Orson Scott
Walpole, Horace 1717-1797 **LC 2, 49**
See also BRW 3; DLB 39, 104, 213; HGG; RGEL; SUFW
Walpole, Hugh (Seymour) 1884-1941 **TCLC 5**
See also CA 104; 165; DLB 34; HGG; MTCW 2; RGEL; RHW

Walser, Martin 1927- **CLC 27**
See also CA 57-60; CANR 8, 46; CWW 2; DLB 75, 124
Walser, Robert 1878-1956 **TCLC 18; SSC 20**
See also CA 118; 165; CANR 100; DLB 66
Walsh, Gillian Paton
See Paton Walsh, Gillian
Walsh, Jill Paton CLC 35
See also Paton Walsh, Gillian
See also CLR 2, 65; WYA
Walter, Villiam Christian
See Andersen, Hans Christian
Walton, Izaak 1593-1683 **LC 72**
See also BRW 2; CDBLB Before 1660; DLB 151, 213; RGEL
Wambaugh, Joseph (Aloysius, Jr.) 1937- **CLC 3, 18; DAM NOV, POP**
See also AITN 1; BEST 89:3; BPFB 3; CA 33-36R; CANR 42, 65; CMW; CPW 1; DA3; DLB 6; DLBY 83; MSW; MTCW 1, 2
Wang Wei699(?)-761(?) **PC 18**
Ward, Arthur Henry Sarsfield 1883-1959
See Rohmer, Sax
See also CA 108; 173; CMW; HGG
Ward, Douglas Turner 1930- **CLC 19**
See also BW 1; CA 81-84; CAD; CANR 27; CD; DLB 7, 38
Ward, E. D.
See Lucas, E(dward) V(errall)
Ward, Mrs. Humphry 1851-1920
See Ward, Mary Augusta
See also RGEL
Ward, Mary Augusta 1851-1920 **TCLC 55**
See also Ward, Mrs. Humphry
See also DLB 18
Ward, Peter
See Faust, Frederick (Schiller)
Warhol, Andy 1928(?)-1987 **CLC 20**
See also AAYA 12; BEST 89:4; CA 89-92; 121; CANR 34
Warner, Francis (Robert le Plastrier) 1937- **CLC 14**
See also CA 53-56; CANR 11
Warner, Marina 1946- **CLC 59**
See also CA 65-68; CANR 21, 55; CN; DLB 194
Warner, Rex (Ernest) 1905-1986 **CLC 45**
See also CA 89-92; 119; DLB 15; RGEL; RHW
Warner, Susan (Bogert) 1819-1885 **NCLC 31**
See also DLB 3, 42, 239, 250, 254
Warner, Sylvia (Constance) Ashton
See Ashton-Warner, Sylvia (Constance)
Warner, Sylvia Townsend 1893-1978 **CLC 7, 19; SSC 23**
See also BRWS 7; CA 61-64; 77-80; CANR 16, 60, 104; DLB 34, 139; FANT; FW; MTCW 1, 2; RGEL; RGSF; RHW
Warren, Mercy Otis 1728-1814 **NCLC 13**
See also DLB 31, 200; RGAL
Warren, Robert Penn 1905-1989 **CLC 1, 4, 6, 8, 10, 13, 18, 39, 53, 59; DA; DAB; DAC; DAM MST, NOV, POET; PC 37; SSC 4; WLC**
See also AITN 1; AMW; BPFB 3; BYA 1; CA 13-16R; 129; CANR 10, 47; CDALB 1968-1988; DA3; DLB 2, 48, 152; DLBY 80, 89; INT CANR-10; MTCW 1, 2; NFS 13; RGAL; RGSF; RHW; SATA 46; SATA-Obit 63; SSFS 8
Warshofsky, Isaac
See Singer, Isaac Bashevis
Warton, Thomas 1728-1790 **LC 15; DAM POET**
See also DLB 104, 109; RGEL

Waruk, Kona
See Harris, (Theodore) Wilson
Warung, Price TCLC 45
See also Astley, William
See also DLB 230; RGEL
Warwick, Jarvis
See Garner, Hugh
See also CCA 1
Washington, Alex
See Harris, Mark
Washington, Booker T(aliaferro) 1856-1915 **TCLC 10; BLC 3; DAM MULT**
See also BW 1; CA 114; 125; DA3; LAIT 2; RGAL; SATA 28
Washington, George 1732-1799 **LC 25**
See also DLB 31
Wassermann, (Karl) Jakob 1873-1934 **TCLC 6**
See also CA 104; 163; DLB 66
Wasserstein, Wendy 1950- **CLC 32, 59, 90; DAM DRAM; DC 4**
See also CA 121; 129; CABS 3; CAD; CANR 53, 75; CD; CWD; DA3; DFS 5; DLB 228; FW; INT CA-129; MTCW 2; SATA 94
Waterhouse, Keith (Spencer) 1929- **CLC 47**
See also CA 5-8R; CANR 38, 67; CBD; CN; DLB 13, 15; MTCW 1, 2
Waters, Frank (Joseph) 1902-1995 **CLC 88**
See also CA 5-8R; 149; CAAS 13; CANR 3, 18, 63; DLB 212; DLBY 86; RGAL; TCWW 2
Waters, Mary C. CLC 70
Waters, Roger 1944- **CLC 35**
Watkins, Frances Ellen
See Harper, Frances Ellen Watkins
Watkins, Gerrold
See Malzberg, Barry N(athaniel)
Watkins, Paul 1964- **CLC 55**
See also CA 132; CANR 62, 98
Watkins, Vernon Phillips 1906-1967 **CLC 43**
See also CA 9-10; 25-28R; CAP 1; DLB 20; RGEL
Watson, Irving S.
See Mencken, H(enry) L(ouis)
Watson, John H.
See Farmer, Philip Jose
Watson, Richard F.
See Silverberg, Robert
Waugh, Auberon (Alexander) 1939-2001 **CLC 7**
See also CA 45-48; 192; CANR 6, 22, 92; DLB 14, 194
Waugh, Evelyn (Arthur St. John) 1903-1966 **CLC 1, 3, 8, 13, 19, 27, 44, 107; DA; DAB; DAC; DAM MST, NOV, POP; SSC 41; WLC**
See also BPFB 3; BRW 7; CA 85-88; 25-28R; CANR 22; CDBLB 1914-1945; DA3; DLB 15, 162, 195; MTCW 1, 2; NFS 13; RGEL; RGSF; WLIT 4
Waugh, Harriet 1944- **CLC 6**
See also CA 85-88; CANR 22
Ways, C. R.
See Blount, Roy (Alton), Jr.
Waystaff, Simon
See Swift, Jonathan
Webb, Beatrice (Martha Potter) 1858-1943 **TCLC 22**
See also CA 117; 162; DLB 190; FW
Webb, Charles (Richard) 1939- **CLC 7**
See also CA 25-28R
Webb, James H(enry), Jr. 1946- **CLC 22**
See also CA 81-84
Webb, Mary Gladys (Meredith) 1881-1927 **TCLC 24**
See also CA 182; 123; DLB 34; FW

Webb, Mrs. Sidney
See Webb, Beatrice (Martha Potter)

Webb, Phyllis 1927- **CLC 18**
See also CA 104; CANR 23; CCA 1; CP; CWP; DLB 53

Webb, Sidney (James) 1859-1947 **TCLC 22**
See also CA 117; 163; DLB 190

Webber, Andrew Lloyd CLC 21
See also Lloyd Webber, Andrew
See also DFS 7

Weber, Lenora Mattingly 1895-1971 **CLC 12**
See also CA 19-20; 29-32R; CAP 1; SATA 2; SATA-Obit 26

Weber, Max 1864-1920 **TCLC 69**
See also CA 109; 189

Webster, John 1580(?)-1634(?) **LC 33; DA; DAB; DAC; DAM DRAM, MST; DC 2; WLC**
See also BRW 2; CDBLB Before 1660; DLB 58; IDTP; RGEL; WLIT 3

Webster, Noah 1758-1843 **NCLC 30**
See also DLB 1, 37, 42, 43, 73, 243

Wedekind, (Benjamin) Frank(lin) 1864-1918 **TCLC 7; DAM DRAM**
See also CA 104; 153; DLB 118; EW 8; RGWL

Wehr, Demaris CLC 65

Weidman, Jerome 1913-1998 **CLC 7**
See also AITN 2; CA 1-4R; 171; CAD; CANR 1; DLB 28

Weil, Simone (Adolphine) 1909-1943 **TCLC 23**
See also CA 117; 159; EW 12; FW; GFL 1789 to the Present; MTCW 2

Weininger, Otto 1880-1903 **TCLC 84**

Weinstein, Nathan
See West, Nathanael

Weinstein, Nathan von Wallenstein
See West, Nathanael

Weir, Peter (Lindsay) 1944- **CLC 20**
See also CA 113; 123

Weiss, Peter (Ulrich) 1916-1982 **CLC 3, 15, 51; DAM DRAM**
See also CA 45-48; 106; CANR 3; DFS 3; DLB 69, 124; RGWL

Weiss, Theodore (Russell) 1916- **CLC 3, 8, 14**
See also CA 9-12R; CAAE 189; CAAS 2; CANR 46, 94; CP; DLB 5

Welch, (Maurice) Denton 1915-1948 **TCLC 22**
See also CA 121; 148; RGEL

Welch, James 1940- **CLC 6, 14, 52; DAM MULT, POP**
See also CA 85-88; CANR 42, 66; CN; CP; CPW; DLB 175, 256; NNAL; RGAL; TCWW 2

Weldon, Fay 1931- **CLC 6, 9, 11, 19, 36, 59, 122; DAM POP**
See also BRWS 4; CA 21-24R; CANR 16, 46, 63, 97; CDBLB 1960 to Present; CN; CPW; DLB 14, 194; FW; HGG; INT CANR-16; MTCW 1, 2; RGEL; RGSF

Wellek, Rene 1903-1995 **CLC 28**
See also CA 5-8R; 150; CAAS 7; CANR 8; DLB 63; INT CANR-8

Weller, Michael 1942- **CLC 10, 53**
See also CA 85-88; CAD; CD

Weller, Paul 1958- **CLC 26**

Wellershoff, Dieter 1925- **CLC 46**
See also CA 89-92; CANR 16, 37

Welles, (George) Orson 1915-1985 **CLC 20, 80**
See also AAYA 40; CA 93-96; 117

Wellman, John McDowell 1945-
See Wellman, Mac
See also CA 166; CD

Wellman, Mac CLC 65
See also Wellman, John McDowell; Wellman, John McDowell
See also CAD; RGAL

Wellman, Manly Wade 1903-1986 **CLC 49**
See also CA 1-4R; 118; CANR 6, 16, 44; FANT; SATA 6; SATA-Obit 47; SFW; SUFW

Wells, Carolyn 1869(?)-1942 **TCLC 35**
See also CA 113; 185; CMW; DLB 11

Wells, H(erbert) G(eorge) 1866-1946 **TCLC 6, 12, 19; DA; DAB; DAC; DAM MST, NOV; SSC 6; WLC**
See also AAYA 18; BPFB 3; BRW 6; CA 110; 121; CDBLB 1914-1945; CLR 64; DA3; DLB 34, 70, 156, 178; EXPS; HGG; LAIT 3; MTCW 1, 2; RGEL; RGSF; SATA 20; SCFW; SFW; SSFS 3; SUFW; WCH; WLIT 4; YAW

Wells, Rosemary 1943- **CLC 12**
See also AAYA 13; BYA 7, 8; CA 85-88; CANR 48; CLR 16, 69; CWRI; MAICYA; SAAS 1; SATA 18, 69, 114; YAW

Welsh, Irvine 1958- **CLC 144**
See also CA 173

Welty, Eudora 1909-2001 **CLC 1, 2, 5, 14, 22, 33, 105; DA; DAB; DAC; DAM MST, NOV; SSC 1, 27, 51; WLC**
See also AMW; AMWR 1; BPFB 3; CA 9-12R; CABS 1; CANR 32, 65; CDALB 1941-1968; CN; CSW; DA3; DLB 2, 102, 143; DLBD 12; DLBY 87, 01; EXPS; HGG; LAIT 3; MAWW; MTCW 1, 2; NFS 13; RGAL; RGSF; RHW; SSFS 2, 10

Wen I-to 1899-1946 **TCLC 28**

Wentworth, Robert
See Hamilton, Edmond

Werfel, Franz (Viktor) 1890-1945 **TCLC 8**
See also CA 104; 161; DLB 81, 124; RGWL

Wergeland, Henrik Arnold 1808-1845 **NCLC 5**

Wersba, Barbara 1932- **CLC 30**
See also AAYA 2, 30; BYA 6, 12, 13; CA 29-32R, 182; CAAE 182; CANR 16, 38; CLR 3; DLB 52; JRDA; MAICYA; SAAS 2; SATA 1, 58; SATA-Essay 103; WYA; YAW

Wertmueller, Lina 1928- **CLC 16**
See also CA 97-100; CANR 39, 78

Wescott, Glenway 1901-1987 **CLC 13; SSC 35**
See also CA 13-16R; 121; CANR 23, 70; DLB 4, 9, 102; RGAL

Wesker, Arnold 1932- **CLC 3, 5, 42; DAB; DAM DRAM**
See also CA 1-4R; CAAS 7; CANR 1, 33; CBD; CD; CDBLB 1960 to Present; DLB 13; MTCW 1; RGEL

Wesley, Richard (Errol) 1945- **CLC 7**
See also BW 1; CA 57-60; CAD; CANR 27; CD; DLB 38

Wessel, Johan Herman 1742-1785 **LC 7**

West, Anthony (Panther) 1914-1987 **CLC 50**
See also CA 45-48; 124; CANR 3, 19; DLB 15

West, C. P.
See Wodehouse, P(elham) G(renville)

West, Cornel (Ronald) 1953- **CLC 134; BLCS**
See also CA 144; CANR 91; DLB 246

West, Delno C(loyde), Jr. 1936- **CLC 70**
See also CA 57-60

West, Dorothy 1907-1998 **TCLC 108**
See also BW 2; CA 143; 169; DLB 76

West, (Mary) Jessamyn 1902-1984 **CLC 7, 17**
See also CA 9-12R; 112; CANR 27; DLB 6; DLBY 84; MTCW 1, 2; RHW; SATA-Obit 37; YAW

West, Morris L(anglo) 1916-1999 **CLC 6, 33**
See also BPFB 3; CA 5-8R; 187; CANR 24, 49, 64; CN; CPW; MTCW 1, 2

West, Nathanael 1903-1940 **TCLC 1, 14, 44; SSC 16**
See also AMW; BPFB 3; CA 104; 125; CDALB 1929-1941; DA3; DLB 4, 9, 28; MTCW 1, 2; RGAL

West, Owen
See Koontz, Dean R(ay)

West, Paul 1930- **CLC 7, 14, 96**
See also CA 13-16R; CAAS 7; CANR 22, 53, 76, 89; CN; DLB 14; INT CANR-22; MTCW 2

West, Rebecca 1892-1983 **CLC 7, 9, 31, 50**
See also BPFB 3; BRWS 3; CA 5-8R; 109; CANR 19; DLB 36; DLBY 83; FW; MTCW 1, 2; RGEL

Westall, Robert (Atkinson) 1929-1993 **CLC 17**
See also AAYA 12; BYA 2, 6, 7, 8, 9; CA 69-72; 141; CANR 18, 68; CLR 13; FANT; JRDA; MAICYA; MAICYAS; SAAS 2; SATA 23, 69; SATA-Obit 75; WYA; YAW

Westermarck, Edward 1862-1939 **TCLC 87**

Westlake, Donald E(dwin) 1933- **CLC 7, 33; DAM POP**
See also BPFB 3; CA 17-20R; CAAS 13; CANR 16, 44, 65, 94; CMW; CPW; INT CANR-16; MSW; MTCW 2

Westmacott, Mary
See Christie, Agatha (Mary Clarissa)

Weston, Allen
See Norton, Andre

Wetcheek, J. L.
See Feuchtwanger, Lion

Wetering, Janwillem van de
See van de Wetering, Janwillem

Wetherald, Agnes Ethelwyn 1857-1940 **TCLC 81**
See also DLB 99

Wetherell, Elizabeth
See Warner, Susan (Bogert)

Whale, James 1889-1957 **TCLC 63**

Whalen, Philip 1923- **CLC 6, 29**
See also CA 9-12R; CANR 5, 39; CP; DLB 16; WP

Wharton, Edith (Newbold Jones) 1862-1937 **TCLC 3, 9, 27, 53; DA; DAB; DAC; DAM MST, NOV; SSC 6; WLC**
See also AAYA 25; AMW; AMWR 1; BPFB 3; CA 104; 132; CDALB 1865-1917; DA3; DLB 4, 9, 12, 78, 189; DLBD 13; EXPS; HGG; LAIT 2, 3; MAWW; MTCW 1, 2; NFS 5, 11; RGAL; RGSF; RHW; SSFS 6, 7; SUFW

Wharton, James
See Mencken, H(enry) L(ouis)

Wharton, William (a pseudonym) CLC 18, 37
See also CA 93-96; DLBY 80; INT 93-96

Wheatley (Peters), Phillis 1753(?)-1784 **LC 3, 50; BLC 3; DA; DAC; DAM MST, MULT, POET; PC 3; WLC**
See also AFAW 1, 2; CDALB 1640-1865; DA3; DLB 31, 50; EXPP; PFS 13; RGAL

Wheelock, John Hall 1886-1978 **CLC 14**
See also CA 13-16R; 77-80; CANR 14; DLB 45

White, Babington
See Braddon, Mary Elizabeth

White, E(lwyn) B(rooks) 1899-1985 **CLC 10, 34, 39; DAM POP**
See also AITN 2; AMWS 1; CA 13-16R; 116; CANR 16, 37; CDALBS; CLR 1, 21; CPW; DA3; DLB 11, 22; FANT; MAICYA; MTCW 1, 2; RGAL; SATA 2, 29, 100; SATA-Obit 44

White, Edmund (Valentine III) 1940- **CLC 27, 110; DAM POP**
See also AAYA 7; CA 45-48; CANR 3, 19, 36, 62; CN; DA3; DLB 227; MTCW 1, 2

White, Hayden V. 1928- **CLC 148**
See also CA 128; DLB 246

White, Patrick (Victor Martindale) 1912-1990 **CLC 3, 4, 5, 7, 9, 18, 65, 69; SSC 39**
See also BRWS 1; CA 81-84; 132; CANR 43; MTCW 1; RGEL; RGSF; RHW

White, Phyllis Dorothy James 1920-
See James, P. D.
See also CA 21-24R; CANR 17, 43, 65; CMW; CN; CPW; DA3; DAM POP; MTCW 1, 2

White, T(erence) H(anbury) 1906-1964 **CLC 30**
See also AAYA 22; BPFB 3; BYA 4, 5; CA 73-76; CANR 37; DLB 160; FANT; JRDA; LAIT 1; MAICYA; RGEL; SATA 12; SUFW; YAW

White, Terence de Vere 1912-1994 **CLC 49**
See also CA 49-52; 145; CANR 3

White, Walter
See White, Walter F(rancis)

White, Walter F(rancis) 1893-1955 **TCLC 15; BLC 3; DAM MULT**
See also BW 1; CA 115; 124; DLB 51

White, William Hale 1831-1913
See Rutherford, Mark
See also CA 121; 189

Whitehead, Alfred North 1861-1947 **TCLC 97**
See also CA 117; 165; DLB 100

Whitehead, E(dward) A(nthony) 1933- **CLC 5**
See also CA 65-68; CANR 58; CD

Whitemore, Hugh (John) 1936- **CLC 37**
See also CA 132; CANR 77; CBD; CD; INT CA-132

Whitman, Sarah Helen (Power) 1803-1878 **NCLC 19**
See also DLB 1, 243

Whitman, Walt(er) 1819-1892 **NCLC 4, 31, 81; DA; DAB; DAC; DAM MST, POET; PC 3; WLC**
See also AAYA 42; AMW; AMWR 1; CDALB 1640-1865; DA3; DLB 3, 64, 224, 250; EXPP; LAIT 2; PAB; PFS 2, 3, 13; RGAL; SATA 20; WP; WYAS 1

Whitney, Phyllis A(yame) 1903- **CLC 42; DAM POP**
See also AAYA 36; AITN 2; BEST 90:3; CA 1-4R; CANR 3, 25, 38, 60; CLR 59; CMW; CPW; DA3; JRDA; MAICYA; MTCW 2; RHW; SATA 1, 30; YAW

Whittemore, (Edward) Reed (Jr.) 1919- **CLC 4**
See also CA 9-12R; CAAS 8; CANR 4; CP; DLB 5

Whittier, John Greenleaf 1807-1892 **NCLC 8, 59**
See also AMWS 1; DLB 1, 243; RGAL

Whittlebot, Hernia
See Coward, Noel (Peirce)

Wicker, Thomas Grey 1926-
See Wicker, Tom
See also CA 65-68; CANR 21, 46

Wicker, Tom **CLC 7**
See also Wicker, Thomas Grey

Wideman, John Edgar 1941- **CLC 5, 34, 36,**
67, 122; BLC 3; DAM MULT
See also AFAW 1, 2; AMWS 10; BPFB 4; BW 2, 3; CA 85-88; CANR 14, 42, 67; CN; DLB 33, 143; MTCW 2; RGAL; RGSF; SSFS 6, 12

Wiebe, Rudy (Henry) 1934- **CLC 6, 11, 14, 138; DAC; DAM MST**
See also CA 37-40R; CANR 42, 67; CN; DLB 60; RHW

Wieland, Christoph Martin 1733-1813 **NCLC 17**
See also DLB 97; EW 4; RGWL

Wiene, Robert 1881-1938 **TCLC 56**

Wieners, John 1934- **CLC 7**
See also CA 13-16R; CP; DLB 16; WP

Wiesel, Elie(zer) 1928- **CLC 3, 5, 11, 37; DA; DAB; DAC; DAM MST, NOV; WLCS**
See also AAYA 7; AITN 1; CA 5-8R; CAAS 4; CANR 8, 40, 65; CDALBS; DA3; DLB 83; DLBY 87; INT CANR-8; LAIT 4; MTCW 1, 2; NFS 4; SATA 56; YAW

Wiggins, Marianne 1947- **CLC 57**
See also BEST 89:3; CA 130; CANR 60

Wiggs, Susan **CLC 70**

Wight, James Alfred 1916-1995
See Herriot, James
See also CA 77-80; CPW; SATA 55; SATA-Brief 44; YAW

Wilbur, Richard (Purdy) 1921- **CLC 3, 6, 9, 14, 53, 110; DA; DAB; DAC; DAM MST, POET**
See also AMWS 3; CA 1-4R; CABS 2; CANR 2, 29, 76, 93; CDALBS; CP; DLB 5, 169; EXPP; INT CANR-29; MTCW 1, 2; PAB; PFS 11, 12; RGAL; SATA 9, 108; WP

Wild, Peter 1940- **CLC 14**
See also CA 37-40R; CP; DLB 5

Wilde, Oscar (Fingal O'Flahertie Wills) 1854(?)-1900 **TCLC 1, 8, 23, 41; DA; DAB; DAC; DAM DRAM, MST, NOV; SSC 11; WLC**
See also BRW 5; BRWR 2; CA 104; 119; CDBLB 1890-1914; DA3; DFS 4, 8, 9; DLB 10, 19, 34, 57, 141, 156, 190; EXPS; FANT; RGEL; RGSF; SATA 24; SSFS 7; SUFW; TEA; WCH; WLIT 4

Wilder, Billy **CLC 20**
See also Wilder, Samuel
See also DLB 26

Wilder, Samuel 1906-
See Wilder, Billy
See also CA 89-92

Wilder, Stephen
See Marlowe, Stephen

Wilder, Thornton (Niven) 1897-1975 **CLC 1, 5, 6, 10, 15, 35, 82; DA; DAB; DAC; DAM DRAM, MST, NOV; DC 1; WLC**
See also AAYA 29; AITN 2; AMW; CA 13-16R; 61-64; CAD; CANR 40; CDALBS; DA3; DFS 1, 4; DLB 4, 7, 9, 228; DLBY 97; LAIT 3; MTCW 1, 2; RGAL; RHW; WYAS 1

Wilding, Michael 1942- **CLC 73; SSC 50**
See also CA 104; CANR 24, 49, 106; CN; RGSF

Wiley, Richard 1944- **CLC 44**
See also CA 121; 129; CANR 71

Wilhelm, Kate **CLC 7**
See also Wilhelm, Katie (Gertrude)
See also AAYA 20; CAAS 5; DLB 8; INT CANR-17; SCFW 2

Wilhelm, Katie (Gertrude) 1928-
See Wilhelm, Kate
See also CA 37-40R; CANR 17, 36, 60, 94; MTCW 1; SFW

Wilkins, Mary
See Freeman, Mary E(leanor) Wilkins

Willard, Nancy 1936- **CLC 7, 37**
See also BYA 5; CA 89-92; CANR 10, 39, 68; CLR 5; CWP; CWRI; DLB 5, 52; FANT; MAICYA; MTCW 1; SATA 37, 71, 127; SATA-Brief 30

William of Ockham 1290-1349 **CMLC 32**

Williams, Ben Ames 1889-1953 **TCLC 89**
See also CA 183; DLB 102

Williams, C(harles) K(enneth) 1936- **CLC 33, 56, 148; DAM POET**
See also CA 37-40R; CAAS 26; CANR 57, 106; CP; DLB 5

Williams, Charles
See Collier, James Lincoln

Williams, Charles (Walter Stansby) 1886-1945 **TCLC 1, 11**
See also CA 104; 163; DLB 100, 153, 255; FANT; RGEL; SUFW

Williams, (George) Emlyn 1905-1987 **CLC 15; DAM DRAM**
See also CA 104; 123; CANR 36; DLB 10, 77; MTCW 1

Williams, Hank 1923-1953 **TCLC 81**

Williams, Hugo 1942- **CLC 42**
See also CA 17-20R; CANR 45; CP; DLB 40

Williams, J. Walker
See Wodehouse, P(elham) G(renville)

Williams, John A(lfred) 1925- **CLC 5, 13; BLC 3; DAM MULT**
See also AFAW 2; BW 2, 3; CA 53-56; CAAE 195; CAAS 3; CANR 6, 26, 51; CN; CSW; DLB 2, 33; INT CANR-6; RGAL; SFW

Williams, Jonathan (Chamberlain) 1929- **CLC 13**
See also CA 9-12R; CAAS 12; CANR 8; CP; DLB 5

Williams, Joy 1944- **CLC 31**
See also CA 41-44R; CANR 22, 48, 97

Williams, Norman 1952- **CLC 39**
See also CA 118

Williams, Sherley Anne 1944-1999 **CLC 89; BLC 3; DAM MULT, POET**
See also AFAW 2; BW 2, 3; CA 73-76; 185; CANR 25, 82; DLB 41; INT CANR-25; SATA 78; SATA-Obit 116

Williams, Shirley
See Williams, Sherley Anne

Williams, Tennessee 1914-1983 **CLC 1, 2, 5, 7, 8, 11, 15, 19, 30, 39, 45, 71, 111; DA; DAB; DAC; DAM DRAM, MST; DC 4; WLC**
See also AAYA 31; AITN 1, 2; AMW; CA 5-8R; 108; CABS 3; CAD; CANR 31; CDALB 1941-1968; DA3; DFS 1, 3, 7, 12; DLB 7; DLBD 4; DLBY 83; GLL 1; LAIT 4; MTCW 1, 2; RGAL

Williams, Thomas (Alonzo) 1926-1990 **CLC 14**
See also CA 1-4R; 132; CANR 2

Williams, William C.
See Williams, William Carlos

Williams, William Carlos 1883-1963 **CLC 1, 2, 5, 9, 13, 22, 42, 67; DA; DAB; DAC; DAM MST, POET; PC 7; SSC 31**
See also AMW; AMWR 1; CA 89-92; CANR 34; CDALB 1917-1929; DA3; DLB 4, 16, 54, 86; EXPP; MTCW 1, 2; PAB; PFS 1, 6, 11; RGAL; RGSF; WP

Williamson, David (Keith) 1942- **CLC 56**
See also CA 103; CANR 41; CD

Williamson, Ellen Douglas 1905-1984
See Douglas, Ellen
See also CA 17-20R; 114; CANR 39

Williamson, Jack **CLC 29**
See also Williamson, John Stewart
See also CAAS 8; DLB 8; SCFW 2

Williamson, John Stewart 1908-
See Williamson, Jack
See also CA 17-20R; CANR 23, 70; SFW

Willie, Frederick
See Lovecraft, H(oward) P(hillips)

Willingham, Calder (Baynard, Jr.)
1922-1995 **CLC 5, 51**
See also CA 5-8R; 147; CANR 3; CSW;
DLB 2, 44; IDFW 3, 4; MTCW 1

Willis, Charles
See Clarke, Arthur C(harles)

Willy
See Colette, (Sidonie-Gabrielle)

Willy, Colette
See Colette, (Sidonie-Gabrielle)
See also GLL 1

Wilmot, John
See Rochester, John Wilmot, Earl of
See also BRW 2; DLB 131; PAB

Wilson, A(ndrew) N(orman) 1950- **CLC 33**
See also BRWS 6; CA 112; 122; CN; DLB
14, 155, 194; MTCW 2

Wilson, Angus (Frank Johnstone) 1913-1991
CLC 2, 3, 5, 25, 34; SSC 21
See also BRWS 1; CA 5-8R; 134; CANR
21; DLB 15, 139, 155; MTCW 1, 2;
RGEL; RGSF

Wilson, August 1945- **CLC 39, 50, 63, 118;**
BLC 3; DA; DAB; DAC; DAM DRAM,
MST, MULT; DC 2; WLCS
See also AAYA 16; AFAW 2; AMWS 8; BW
2, 3; CA 115; 122; CAD; CANR 42, 54,
76; CD; DA3; DFS 3, 7; DLB 228; LAIT
4; MTCW 1, 2; RGAL

Wilson, Brian 1942- **CLC 12**

Wilson, Colin 1931- **CLC 3, 14**
See also CA 1-4R; CAAS 5; CANR 1, 22,
33, 77; CMW; CN; DLB 14, 194; HGG;
MTCW 1; SFW

Wilson, Dirk
See Pohl, Frederik

Wilson, Edmund 1895-1972 **CLC 1, 2, 3, 8,**
24
See also AMW; CA 1-4R; 37-40R; CANR
1, 46; DLB 63; MTCW 1, 2; RGAL

Wilson, Ethel Davis (Bryant) 1888(?)-1980
CLC 13; DAC; DAM POET
See also CA 102; DLB 68; MTCW 1;
RGEL

Wilson, Harriet
See Wilson, Harriet E. Adams
See also DLB 239

Wilson, Harriet E. Adams 1827(?)-1863(?)
NCLC 78; BLC 3; DAM MULT
See also Wilson, Harriet
See also DLB 50, 243

Wilson, John 1785-1854 **NCLC 5**

Wilson, John (Anthony) Burgess 1917-1993
See Burgess, Anthony
See also CA 1-4R; 143; CANR 2, 46; DA3;
DAC; DAM NOV; MTCW 1, 2

Wilson, Lanford 1937- **CLC 7, 14, 36; DAM**
DRAM
See also CA 17-20R; CABS 3; CAD; CANR
45, 96; CD; DFS 4, 9, 12; DLB 7

Wilson, Robert M. 1944- **CLC 7, 9**
See also CA 49-52; CAD; CANR 2, 41; CD;
MTCW 1

Wilson, Robert McLiam 1964- **CLC 59**
See also CA 132

Wilson, Sloan 1920- **CLC 32**
See also CA 1-4R; CANR 1, 44; CN

Wilson, Snoo 1948- **CLC 33**
See also CA 69-72; CBD; CD

Wilson, William S(mith) 1932- **CLC 49**
See also CA 81-84

Wilson, (Thomas) Woodrow 1856-1924
TCLC 79
See also CA 166; DLB 47

Wilson and Warnke eds. CLC 65

Winchilsea, Anne (Kingsmill) Finch
1661-1720
See Finch, Anne
See also RGEL

Windham, Basil
See Wodehouse, P(elham) G(renville)

Wingrove, David (John) 1954- **CLC 68**
See also CA 133; SFW

Winnemucca, Sarah 1844-1891 **NCLC 79;**
DAM MULT
See also DLB 175; NNAL; RGAL

Winstanley, Gerrard 1609-1676 **LC 52**

Wintergreen, Jane
See Duncan, Sara Jeannette

Winters, Janet Lewis CLC 41
See also Lewis, Janet
See also DLBY 87

Winters, (Arthur) Yvor 1900-1968 **CLC 4, 8,**
32
See also AMWS 2; CA 11-12; 25-28R; CAP
1; DLB 48; MTCW 1; RGAL

Winterson, Jeanette 1959- **CLC 64; DAM**
POP
See also BRWS 4; CA 136; CANR 58; CN;
CPW; DA3; DLB 207; FANT; FW; GLL
1; MTCW 2; RHW

Winthrop, John 1588-1649 **LC 31**
See also DLB 24, 30

Wirth, Louis 1897-1952 **TCLC 92**

Wiseman, Frederick 1930- **CLC 20**
See also CA 159

Wister, Owen 1860-1938 **TCLC 21**
See also BPFB 3; CA 108; 162; DLB 9, 78,
186; RGAL; SATA 62; TCWW 2

Witkacy
See Witkiewicz, Stanislaw Ignacy

Witkiewicz, Stanislaw Ignacy 1885-1939
TCLC 8
See also CA 105; 162; DLB 215; EW 10;
RGWL; SFW

Wittgenstein, Ludwig (Josef Johann)
1889-1951 **TCLC 59**
See also CA 113; 164; MTCW 2

Wittig, Monique 1935(?)- **CLC 22**
See also CA 116; 135; CWW 2; DLB 83;
FW; GLL 1

Wittlin, Jozef 1896-1976 **CLC 25**
See also CA 49-52; 65-68; CANR 3

Wodehouse, P(elham) G(renville) 1881-1975
CLC 1, 2, 5, 10, 22; DAB; DAC; DAM
NOV; SSC 2
See also AITN 2; BRWS 3; CA 45-48; 57-
60; CANR 3, 33; CDBLB 1914-1945;
CPW 1; DA3; DLB 34, 162; MTCW 1, 2;
RGEL; RGSF; SATA 22; SSFS 10; TCLC
108

Woiwode, L.
See Woiwode, Larry (Alfred)

Woiwode, Larry (Alfred) 1941- **CLC 6, 10**
See also CA 73-76; CANR 16, 94; CN;
DLB 6; INT CANR-16

Wojciechowska, Maia (Teresa) 1927- **CLC 26**
See also AAYA 8; BYA 3; CA 9-12R, 183;
CAAE 183; CANR 4, 41; CLR 1; JRDA;
MAICYA; SAAS 1; SATA 1, 28, 83;
SATA-Essay 104; YAW

Wojtyla, Karol
See John Paul II, Pope

Wolf, Christa 1929- **CLC 14, 29, 58, 150**
See also CA 85-88; CANR 45; CWW 2;
DLB 75; FW; MTCW 1; RGWL

Wolfe, Gene (Rodman) 1931- **CLC 25; DAM**
POP
See also AAYA 35; CA 57-60; CAAS 9;
CANR 6, 32, 60; CPW; DLB 8; FANT;
MTCW 2; SATA 118; SCFW 2; SFW

Wolfe, George C. 1954- **CLC 49; BLCS**
See also CA 149; CAD; CD

Wolfe, Thomas (Clayton) 1900-1938 **TCLC**
4, 13, 29, 61; DA; DAB; DAC; DAM
MST, NOV; SSC 33; WLC
See also AMW; BPFB 3; CA 104; 132;
CANR 102; CDALB 1929-1941; DA3;
DLB 9, 102, 229; DLBD 2, 16; DLBY
85, 97; MTCW 1, 2; RGAL

Wolfe, Thomas Kennerly, Jr. 1930- **CLC 147;**
DAM POP
See also Wolfe, Tom
See also CA 13-16R; CANR 9, 33, 70, 104;
DA3; DLB 185; INT CANR-9; MTCW 1,
2; TUS

Wolfe, Tom CLC 1, 2, 9, 15, 35, 51
See also Wolfe, Thomas Kennerly, Jr.
See also AAYA 8; AITN 2; AMWS 3; BEST
89:1; BPFB 3; CN; CPW; CSW; DLB
152; LAIT 5; RGAL

Wolff, Geoffrey (Ansell) 1937- **CLC 41**
See also CA 29-32R; CANR 29, 43, 78

Wolff, Sonia
See Levitin, Sonia (Wolff)

Wolff, Tobias (Jonathan Ansell) 1945- **CLC**
39, 64
See also AAYA 16; AMWS 7; BEST 90:2;
BYA 12; CA 114; 117; CAAS 22; CANR
54, 76, 96; CN; CSW; DA3; DLB 130;
INT CA-117; MTCW 2; RGAL; RGSF;
SSFS 4, 11

Wolfram von Eschenbach c. 1170-c. 1220
CMLC 5
See also DLB 138; EW 1; RGWL

Wolitzer, Hilma 1930- **CLC 17**
See also CA 65-68; CANR 18, 40; INT
CANR-18; SATA 31; YAW

Wollstonecraft, Mary 1759-1797 **LC 5, 50**
See also BRWS 3; CDBLB 1789-1832;
DLB 39, 104, 158, 252; FW; LAIT 1;
RGEL; WLIT 3

Wonder, Stevie CLC 12
See also Morris, Steveland Judkins

Wong, Jade Snow 1922- **CLC 17**
See also CA 109; CANR 91; SATA 112

Woodberry, George Edward 1855-1930
TCLC 73
See also CA 165; DLB 71, 103

Woodcott, Keith
See Brunner, John (Kilian Houston)

Woodruff, Robert W.
See Mencken, H(enry) L(ouis)

Woolf, (Adeline) Virginia 1882-1941 **TCLC**
1, 5, 20, 43, 56, 101; DA; DAB; DAC;
DAM MST, NOV; SSC 7; WLC
See also BPFB 3; BRW 7; BRWR 1; CA
104; 130; CANR 64; CDBLB 1914-1945;
DA3; DLB 36, 100, 162; DLBD 10;
EXPS; FW; LAIT 3; MTCW 1, 2; NCFS
2; NFS 8, 12; RGEL; RGSF; SSFS 4, 12;
WLIT 4

Woollcott, Alexander (Humphreys)
1887-1943 **TCLC 5**
See also CA 105; 161; DLB 29

Woolrich, Cornell CLC 77
See also Hopley-Woolrich, Cornell George
See also MSW

Woolson, Constance Fenimore 1840-1894
NCLC 82
See also DLB 12, 74, 189, 221; RGAL

Wordsworth, Dorothy 1771-1855 **NCLC 25**
See also DLB 107

Wordsworth, William 1770-1850 **NCLC 12,**
38; DA; DAB; DAC; DAM MST,
POET; PC 4; WLC
See also BRW 4; CDBLB 1789-1832; DA3;
DLB 93, 107; EXPP; PAB; PFS 2; RGEL;
WLIT 3; WP

Wotton, Sir Henry 1568-1639 **LC 68**
See also DLB 121; RGEL

Wouk, Herman 1915- **CLC 1, 9, 38; DAM NOV, POP**
See also BPFB 2, 3; CA 5-8R; CANR 6, 33, 67; CDALBS; CN; CPW; DA3; DLBY 82; INT CANR-6; LAIT 4; MTCW 1, 2; NFS 7

Wright, Charles (Penzel, Jr.) 1935- **CLC 6, 13, 28, 119, 146**
See also AMWS 5; CA 29-32R; CAAS 7; CANR 23, 36, 62, 88; CP; DLB 165; DLBY 82; MTCW 1, 2; PFS 10

Wright, Charles Stevenson 1932- **CLC 49; BLC 3; DAM MULT, POET**
See also BW 1; CA 9-12R; CANR 26; CN; DLB 33

Wright, Frances 1795-1852 **NCLC 74**
See also DLB 73

Wright, Frank Lloyd 1867-1959 **TCLC 95**
See also AAYA 33; CA 174

Wright, Jack R.
See Harris, Mark

Wright, James (Arlington) 1927-1980 **CLC 3, 5, 10, 28; DAM POET; PC 36**
See also AITN 2; AMWS 3; CA 49-52; 97-100; CANR 4, 34, 64; CDALBS; DLB 5, 169; EXPP; MTCW 1, 2; PFS 7, 8; RGAL; WP

Wright, Judith (Arundell) 1915-2000 **CLC 11, 53; PC 14**
See also CA 13-16R; 188; CANR 31, 76, 93; CP; CWP; MTCW 1, 2; PFS 8; RGEL; SATA 14; SATA-Obit 121

Wright, L(aurali) R. 1939- **CLC 44**
See also CA 138; CMW

Wright, Richard (Nathaniel) 1908-1960 **CLC 1, 3, 4, 9, 14, 21, 48, 74; BLC 3; DA; DAB; DAC; DAM MST, MULT, NOV; SSC 2; WLC**
See also AAYA 5, 42; AFAW 1, 2; AMW; BPFB 3; BW 1; BYA 2; CA 108; CANR 64; CDALB 1929-1941; DA3; DLB 76, 102; DLBD 2; EXPN; LAIT 3, 4; MTCW 1, 2; NCFS 1; NFS 1, 7; RGAL; RGSF; SSFS 3, 9; YAW

Wright, Richard B(ruce) 1937- **CLC 6**
See also CA 85-88; DLB 53

Wright, Rick 1945- **CLC 35**

Wright, Rowland
See Wells, Carolyn

Wright, Stephen 1946- **CLC 33**

Wright, Willard Huntington 1888-1939
See Van Dine, S. S.
See also CA 115; 189; CMW; DLBD 16

Wright, William 1930- **CLC 44**
See also CA 53-56; CANR 7, 23

Wroth, Lady Mary 1587-1653(?) **LC 30; PC 38**
See also DLB 121

Wu Ch'eng-en 1500(?)-1582(?) **LC 7**

Wu Ching-tzu 1701-1754 **LC 2**

Wurlitzer, Rudolph 1938(?)- **CLC 2, 4, 15**
See also CA 85-88; CN; DLB 173

Wyatt, Sir Thomasc. 1503-1542 **LC 70; PC 27**
See also BRW 1; DLB 132; EXPP; RGEL; TEA

Wycherley, William 1640-1716 **LC 8, 21; DAM DRAM**
See also BRW 2; CDBLB 1660-1789; DLB 80; RGEL

Wylie, Elinor (Morton Hoyt) 1885-1928 **TCLC 8; PC 23**
See also AMWS 1; CA 105; 162; DLB 9, 45; EXPP; RGAL

Wylie, Philip (Gordon) 1902-1971 **CLC 43**
See also CA 21-22; 33-36R; CAP 2; DLB 9; SFW

Wyndham, John CLC 19
See also Harris, John (Wyndham Parkes Lucas) Beynon
See also DLB 255; SCFW 2

Wyss, Johann David Von 1743-1818 **NCLC 10**
See also JRDA; MAICYA; SATA 29; SATA-Brief 27

Xenophonc. 430B.C.-c. 354B.C. **CMLC 17**
See also AW 1; DLB 176; RGWL

Yakumo Koizumi
See Hearn, (Patricio) Lafcadio (Tessima Carlos)

Yamamoto, Hisaye 1921- **SSC 34; AAL; DAM MULT**
See also LAIT 4

Yanez, Jose Donoso
See Donoso (Yanez), Jose

Yanovsky, Basile S.
See Yanovsky, V(assily) S(emenovich)

Yanovsky, V(assily) S(emenovich) 1906-1989 **CLC 2, 18**
See also CA 97-100; 129

Yates, Richard 1926-1992 **CLC 7, 8, 23**
See also CA 5-8R; 139; CANR 10, 43; DLB 2, 234; DLBY 81, 92; INT CANR-10

Yeats, W. B.
See Yeats, William Butler

Yeats, William Butler 1865-1939 **TCLC 1, 11, 18, 31, 93, 116; DA; DAB; DAC; DAM DRAM, MST, POET; PC 20; WLC**
See also BRW 6; BRWR 1; CA 104; 127; CANR 45; CDBLB 1890-1914; DA3; DLB 10, 19, 98, 156; EXPP; MTCW 1, 2; PAB; PFS 1, 2, 5, 7, 13; RGEL; WLIT 4; WP

Yehoshua, A(braham) B. 1936- **CLC 13, 31**
See also CA 33-36R; CANR 43, 90; RGSF

Yellow Bird
See Ridge, John Rollin

Yep, Laurence Michael 1948- **CLC 35**
See also AAYA 5, 31; BYA 7; CA 49-52; CANR 1, 46, 92; CLR 3, 17, 54; DLB 52; FANT; JRDA; MAICYA; MAICYAS; SATA 7, 69, 123; WYA; YAW

Yerby, Frank G(arvin) 1916-1991 **CLC 1, 7, 22; BLC 3; DAM MULT**
See also BPFB 3; BW 1, 3; CA 9-12R; 136; CANR 16, 52; DLB 76; INT CANR-16; MTCW 1; RGAL; RHW

Yesenin, Sergei Alexandrovich
See Esenin, Sergei (Alexandrovich)

Yevtushenko, Yevgeny (Alexandrovich) 1933- **CLC 1, 3, 13, 26, 51, 126; DAM POET**
See also Evtushenko, Evgenii Aleksandrovich
See also CA 81-84; CANR 33, 54; CWW 2; MTCW 1

Yezierska, Anzia 1885(?)-1970 **CLC 46**
See also CA 126; 89-92; DLB 28, 221; FW; MTCW 1; RGAL

Yglesias, Helen 1915- **CLC 7, 22**
See also CA 37-40R; CAAS 20; CANR 15, 65, 95; CN; INT CANR-15; MTCW 1

Yokomitsu, Riichi 1898-1947 **TCLC 47**
See also CA 170

Yonge, Charlotte (Mary) 1823-1901 **TCLC 48**
See also CA 109; 163; DLB 18, 163; RGEL; SATA 17; WCH

York, Jeremy
See Creasey, John

York, Simon
See Heinlein, Robert A(nson)

Yorke, Henry Vincent 1905-1974 **CLC 13**
See also Green, Henry
See also CA 85-88; 49-52

Yosano Akiko 1878-1942 **TCLC 59; PC 11**
See also CA 161

Yoshimoto, Banana CLC 84
See also Yoshimoto, Mahoko
See also NFS 7

Yoshimoto, Mahoko 1964-
See Yoshimoto, Banana
See also CA 144; CANR 98

Young, Al(bert James) 1939- **CLC 19; BLC 3; DAM MULT**
See also BW 2, 3; CA 29-32R; CANR 26, 65; CN; CP; DLB 33

Young, Andrew (John) 1885-1971 **CLC 5**
See also CA 5-8R; CANR 7, 29; RGEL

Young, Collier
See Bloch, Robert (Albert)

Young, Edward 1683-1765 **LC 3, 40**
See also DLB 95; RGEL

Young, Marguerite (Vivian) 1909-1995 **CLC 82**
See also CA 13-16; 150; CAP 1; CN

Young, Neil 1945- **CLC 17**
See also CA 110; CCA 1

Young Bear, Ray A. 1950- **CLC 94; DAM MULT**
See also CA 146; DLB 175; NNAL

Yourcenar, Marguerite 1903-1987 **CLC 19, 38, 50, 87; DAM NOV**
See also BPFB 3; CA 69-72; CANR 23, 60, 93; DLB 72; DLBY 88; EW 12; GFL 1789 to the Present; GLL 1; MTCW 1, 2; RGWL

Yuan, Chu340(?)B.C.-278(?)B.C. **CMLC 36**

Yurick, Sol 1925- **CLC 6**
See also CA 13-16R; CANR 25; CN

Zabolotsky, Nikolai Alekseevich 1903-1958 **TCLC 52**
See also CA 116; 164

Zagajewski, Adam 1945- **PC 27**
See also CA 186; DLB 232

Zalygin, Sergei-2000 **CLC 59**

Zamiatin, Evgenii
See Zamyatin, Evgeny Ivanovich
See also RGSF; RGWL

Zamiatin, Yevgenii
See Zamyatin, Evgeny Ivanovich

Zamora, Bernice (B. Ortiz) 1938- **CLC 89; DAM MULT; HLC 2**
See also CA 151; CANR 80; DLB 82; HW 1, 2

Zamyatin, Evgeny Ivanovich 1884-1937 **TCLC 8, 37**
See also Zamiatin, Evgenii
See also CA 105; 166; EW 10; SFW

Zangwill, Israel 1864-1926 **TCLC 16; SSC 44**
See also CA 109; 167; CMW; DLB 10, 135, 197; RGEL

Zappa, Francis Vincent, Jr. 1940-1993
See Zappa, Frank
See also CA 108; 143; CANR 57

Zappa, Frank CLC 17
See also Zappa, Francis Vincent, Jr.

Zaturenska, Marya 1902-1982 **CLC 6, 11**
See also CA 13-16R; 105; CANR 22

Zeami 1363-1443 **DC 7**
See also DLB 203; RGWL

Zelazny, Roger (Joseph) 1937-1995 **CLC 21**
See also AAYA 7; BPFB 3; CA 21-24R; 148; CANR 26, 60; CN; DLB 8; FANT; MTCW 1, 2; SATA 57; SATA-Brief 39; SCFW; SFW; SUFW

Zhdanov, Andrei Alexandrovich 1896-1948 **TCLC 18**
See also CA 117; 167

Zhukovsky, Vasilii Andreevich
See Zhukovsky, Vasily (Andreevich)
See also DLB 205

Zhukovsky, Vasily (Andreevich) 1783-1852 **NCLC 35**
See also Zhukovsky, Vasilii Andreevich

Literary Criticism Series
Cumulative Topic Index

This index lists all topic entries in Gale's *Classical and Medieval Literature Criticism, Contemporary Literary Criticism, Drama Criticism, Literature Criticism from 1400 to 1800, Nineteenth-Century Literature Criticism,* and *Twentieth-Century Literary Criticism.*

Topic Index

LC Cumulative Nationality Index

LC-75 Title Index

Title Index

ISBN 0-7876-5812-X